ACCOUNTING
TEXT AND CASES

The Willard J. Graham Series in Accounting

ACCOUNTING
TEXT AND CASES

ROBERT N. ANTHONY, D.B.A.

Professor Emeritus
Graduate School of
Business Administration
Harvard University

JAMES S. REECE, D.B.A., C.M.A.

Professor
Graduate School of
Business Administration
The University of Michigan

SEVENTH EDITION

RICHARD D. IRWIN, INC.
Homewood, Illinois 60430

Case material of the Harvard Graduate School of
Business Administration is made possible by the
cooperation of business firms who may wish to remain
anonymous by having names, quantities, and other
identifying details disguised while basic relationships
are maintained. Cases are prepared as the basis for
class discussion rather than to illustrate either effective
or ineffective handling of administrative situations.

ISBN 0-256-02787-0

Library of Congress Catalog Card No. 82–83417

Printed in the United States of America

1 2 3 4 5 6 7 8 9 0 D 0 9 8 7 6 5 4 3

Preface

An accounting text can be written with an emphasis on either of two viewpoints: (1) what the user of accounting information needs to know about accounting or (2) what the preparer of accounting reports needs to know about accounting. This book has as its focus the user of accounting information. Of course, such a person needs to know enough about the preparation of accounting reports to be an intelligent user of them, and this text includes the technical material needed for this purpose. The text is aimed primarily, however, at the person who wants to understand accounting so that he or she can be a knowledgeable user of accounting information.

The focus of the book makes it particularly appropriate for required "core" courses in accounting, where many of the students in the course are not planning to take further elective accounting courses. First, we believe that if a core course stresses the more analytical uses of accounting information by managers and outside analysts rather than the procedural details that the practicing accountant needs to know, then those students who do not take further accounting courses will be left with a positive view of the importance of accounting, rather than with the negative "bean counter" stereotype. Second, we feel that a user orientation in the core course is actually likely to generate a greater number of accounting majors from the class than if the course is oriented more toward the person who has already decided to major in accounting. Similarly, in our experience, the required accounting module in a management development program will generate little participant interest unless the module is oriented toward the nonaccountant user of accounting information. In sum, we think the book conveys the fact that accounting is *interesting* and *fun*, not dull and tedious.

More specifically, this book is used in at least the following four ways:

1. An introductory course where most (if not all) of the students have no prior training in accounting. In many schools, this introduction comprises two separate courses, one dealing with financial accounting and the other with management accounting. Many schools use this book for both such courses, whereas some use it only for financial accounting (Chapter 1 and Chapters 2–14) or for management accounting (Chapter 1 and Chapters 15–27). This book is used in such introductory courses at both the upper undergraduate level and in graduate programs. In addition to its widespread use in schools of business and management, it is also used in introductory accounting courses in some law schools, education schools, and schools of public health.

2. An elective course that builds on a required introductory course in accounting—particularly where the introductory course has more of a procedural orientation, whereas the elective is intended to be more conceptual, analytical, and user-oriented.

3. The accounting module in a management development program, where the participants represent a variety of functional and technical backgrounds.

4. As a nontechnical accounting reference book for nonaccountants in business and other organizations.

Although designed for beginning students, the book does not contain enough "pencil-pushing" material to meet the needs of many instructors of beginning courses. Such instructors may wish to use the companion volume, *Accounting Principles Workbook*,[1] which, in addition to key terms and discussion questions, has much problem material (10–15 problems per chapter), a short practice set, and some cases that are not in this volume.

Many instructors also assign or recommend the programmed text, *Essentials of Accounting*,[2] either as preliminary to study of the subject (it is often sent in advance to participants in MBA and management development programs) or as a review device. This book is a self-study introductory treatment of financial accounting, geared to Part 1 of this text.

---

[1] James S. Reece and Robert N. Anthony, *Accounting Principles Workbook*, 6th ed. (Homewood, Ill.: Richard D. Irwin, 1983).

[2] Robert N. Anthony, *Essentials of Accounting*, 3d ed. (Reading, Mass.: Addison-Wesley, 1983).

The Cases   As in previous editions, the cases have been selected because of their interest and educational value as a basis for class discussion. They are not necessarily intended to illustrate either correct or incorrect handling of management problems. Skill in the management use of accounting information can be acquired, we believe, only through experience. Thinking about a case, and discussing it in the classroom and in informal discussion groups, can help to provide such experience. In preparing to discuss a case in class, the student is required to *do* something—to analyze a problem, to weigh various factors involved in it, to make some calculations, to take a position, and so on. In class, the student is required to explain his or her point of view, to defend it, to understand and appraise the arguments of colleagues, and to decide what arguments are the strongest. Practice in doing these things helps to increase skill and understanding; in fact, many educators believe that the really important parts of a subject can be learned only by experience of some sort, as opposed to merely hearing or reading about them. Thus, although the case material comprises less than half the pages in this book, the discussion of these cases is by far the more important part of the educational process.

The Seventh Edition has a total of 121 cases, 10 more than the previous edition. Many of the cases are new, and the great majority of the cases that were carried over from the Sixth Edition have been updated (in some instances, with a change in case name).

Occasionally a student or instructor questions our use of small business settings for many of the cases. Such cases often avoid certain complexities at a point when the student is not yet prepared to deal with them. We also were interested to note a recent study which reported that small businesses (those employing fewer than 500 people): (1) represent 99.8 percent of all U.S. businesses, (2) produce 38 percent of the nation's GNP, (3) employ 47 percent of the nongovernment labor force, (4) contribute two out of three new jobs, and (5) produce twice as many innovations per employee as larger firms. We therefore feel that exposure to some small-business cases is beneficial to students, many of whom will eventually work in such firms or work with them as auditors or consultants.

Changes in the Seventh Edition   Developments in accounting, particularly financial accounting, have continued to be rapid in the last four years. These have resulted in many changes in the text and an overall expansion of Part 1, Financial Accounting. (Part 1 reflects FASB pronouncements through January 1983, as well as the 1981 and 1982 tax acts.) We have also modified Part 2, with particular emphasis on improving the sequencing of topics and reorganizing the longer chapters of the previous edition into shorter ones. The net result is that this edition totals 27 chapters—one introductory and 13 each on financial reporting and management accounting—compared with the 23 chapters of the previous edition.

More specifically, some of the management accounting overview has been moved forward to Chapter 1, so that this chapter is more introductory to the entire book rather than just to Part 1. Chapters 2–7 reflect evolutionary and updating changes, including introduction of the debit-credit matrix in Chapter 4's discussion of computer-based recordkeeping systems; however, the basic thrust of these chapters remains the same. The former chapter, Other Expenses and Net Income, has been reorganized into two chapters: Chapter 8, Liabilities and Interest Expense, has expanded coverage of leases and contains an appendix explaining the concept of present value and its role in liability accounting; Chapter 9, Other Expenses, Net Income, and Owners' Equity, completes the more detailed discussion of the income and balance sheet. The funds flow chapter now follows, expanded to include the net monetary asset concept of funds and new materials (including ratios) on how to analyze funds flow statement information. After the Acquisitions and Consolidated Statements chapter, a new Chapter 12, Accounting and Changing Prices, deals with inflation accounting concepts, FASB–33 requirements, and foreign currency transaction and translation problems. The final two chapters of Part 1 have been modified slightly, including a brief discussion of the role of the efficient markets hypothesis in choosing among accounting principle alternatives. In these later chapters of Part 1, where students can cope better with the complexities of the statements of real companies, we have made greater use of materials taken from actual company annual reports, as opposed to hypothetical financial statement data.

Part 2, on management accounting, begins with Chapter 15's expanded description of the contrast between financial reporting and management accounting. All discussion of cost behavior, formerly split between two chapters, is now consolidated in Chapter 16, prior to any detailed discussion of full costs, differential costs, or responsibility costs. The previous edition's two long chapters on costing concepts and systems have been rearranged into three shorter chapters (17–19), the first of which emphasizes the uses made of full cost information in various kinds of organizations. Discussion of production cost variances (Chapter 20) still immediately follows the standard costing chapter, because most instructors seem to prefer this sequence; however, Chapter 20 can also be taught as a responsibility accounting chapter, just prior to Chapter 26, Analyzing and Reporting Performance. The consolidation of cost behavior materials in Chapter 16 also enabled us to present differential accounting concepts and techniques in two chapters (rather than three): Chapter 21 looks at short-run decisions, and Chapter 22 at longer-run (capital budgeting) decisions. The previous edition's lengthy chapter on responsibility accounting has been divided into two chapters, one dealing with the management control structure (23) and the other with management control processes (24). The previous edition's final two chapters on programming, budgeting, and the reporting and analysis of performance have been retained with no substantial changes but are now followed by a new concluding chapter called Management Accounting System Design, which summarizes the concepts discussed in Part 2 of the book.

Acknowledgments   We are grateful to the many people who have made suggestions for improving this book. Included among those people are our colleagues at Harvard Business School and the Graduate School of Business Administration at The University of Michigan, particularly Robert H. Colson (Michigan). We also appreciate the comments of Brandt R. Allen, University of Virginia; Eduardo Ballarin, IESE (Barcelona); Bernard L. Beatty, Wake Forest University; F. Virgil Boyd, Loyola University of Chicago; David M. Buehlmann, University of Nebraska at Omaha; John C. Dawson, Grinnell College; Jesse F. Dillard, The Ohio State University; H. Peter Holzer and Rene P. Manes, University of Illinois at Urbana-Champaign; Wiley S. Mitchell, The University of Kansas; Frank Rose, Stanford University; William J. Ruckstuhl, The American College; and Donald R. Simons, Boston University.

Special thanks go to Pat Lougee for her excellent typing of the manuscript. Jackie Bolgos also provided valuable typing services, and Connie Kinnear did an outstanding job of revising the cases for this edition.

                                                      Robert N. Anthony
                                                      James S. Reece

Contents

3   Basic Accounting Concepts: The Income Statement   55

The Nature of Income. The Time Period Concept: *Relation between Income and Owners' Equity. Income Not the Same as Cash Receipts.* Recognition. The Conservatism Concept: *Application to Revenue Recognition.* The Realization Concept. Recognition of Expenses: *Terminology. The Matching Concept. Criteria for Expense Recognition. Expenses and Expenditures. Dividends. Summary of Expense Measurement. Gains and Losses.* The Consistency Concept. The Materiality Concept. The Income Statement: *Revenues. Cost of Sales. Gross Margin. Expenses. Net Income. Retained Earnings. Relation between Balance Sheet and Income Statement. Income Statement Percentages.* Other Concepts of Income: *Cash-Basis Accounting. Income Tax Accounting. Economic Income.*

4   Accounting Records and Systems   93

Recordkeeping Fundamentals: *The Account. Debit and Credit. The Ledger. The Chart of Accounts. The Journal. The Trial Balance.* The Adjusting and Closing Process: *Need for Adjusting Entries. Types of Adjusting Entries. Closing Entries. Ruling and Balancing Accounts. The Worksheet. Summary of the Accounting Process.* Accounting Systems: *Special Journals. Control Accounts and Subsidiary Ledgers. Imprest Funds. Internal Accounting Controls. Significant Recordkeeping Ideas.* Computer-Based Accounting Systems: *Relationship to Manual Accounting. The Matrix Concept. Two Important Differences. Extent of Computerization.* Appendix: *Locating Errors Revealed by the Trial Balance.*

5   Revenue and Monetary Assets   131

Timing of Revenue Recognition: *Basic Recognition Criteria. Delivery Method. Percentage-of-Completion Method. Production Method.*

Installment Method. Amount of Revenue Recognized: Bad Debts. Sales Discounts. Credit Card Sales. Sales Returns and Allowances. Revenue Adjustment versus Expense. Warranty Costs. Interest Revenue. Monetary Assets: Difference in Reporting Monetary and Nonmonetary Assets. Cash. Receivables. Marketable Securities. Analysis of Monetary Assets: Current Ratio. Acid-Test Ratio. Days' Cash. Days' Receivables.

Cases

6   Cost of Sales and Inventories

Types of Companies. Supplies. Merchandising Companies: Acquisition Cost. The Basic Measurement Problem. Periodic Inventory Method. Perpetual Inventory Method. Comparison of Periodic and Perpetual Methods. Retail Method. Manufacturing Companies: Inventory Accounts. Materials Used. Cost of Goods Manufactured. Cost of Goods Sold. Cost Accounting Systems. Product Costs and Period Costs. Service Companies. Inventory Costing Methods: Specific Identification Method. Average Cost Method. First-In, First-Out (FIFO) Method. Last-In, First-Out (LIFO) Method. Comparison of Methods. Lower of Cost or Market. Analysis of Inventory: Inventory Turnover.

Cases

7   Long-Lived Assets and Their Amortization

Nature of Long-Lived Assets: Types of Long-Lived Assets. Plant and Equipment: Acquisition: Distinction between Asset and Expense. Capital Leases. Items Included in Cost. Acquisitions Recorded at Other than Cost. Basket Purchases. Plant and Equipment: Depreciation: Judgments Required. Service Life. Depreciation Methods. Income Tax Considerations: Income Tax Depreciation. Investment Tax Credit. Choice of a Method. Accounting for Depreciation. Plant and Equipment: Disposal: Exchanges and Trade-Ins. Group Depreciation. Significance of Depreciation: Concluding Comment. Natural Resources: Depletion. Accretion and Appreciation. Intangible Assets: Goodwill. Patents, Copyrights. Leasehold Improvements. Deferred Charges. Research and Development Costs.

Cases

8 Liabilities and Interest Expense 255

Nature of Liabilities: *Contingencies. Liabilities as a Source of Funds. Debt Capital: Term Loans. Bonds. Recording a Bond Issue. Balance Sheet Presentation. Bond Interest. Retirement of Bonds. Refunding a Bond Issue.* Other Liabilities: *Capital Leases: Lessee Accounting. Capital Leases: Lessor Accounting. Operating Leases.* Analysis of Capital Relationships: *Debt/Equity Ratios. Times Interest Earned.* Appendix: Present Value: *The Concept of Present Value. Finding Present Values. Present Value of a Series of Payments. Present Values and Liabilities. Present Values and Assets. Calculating Bond Yields.*

Cases

9 Other Expenses, Net Income, and Owners' Equity 287

Personnel Costs: *Fringe Benefits.* Income Taxes: *Permanent Differences and Timing Differences. Accounting for Timing Differences. Accounting Entries. Nature of Deferred Income Taxes Liability. Deferred Income Taxes Asset.* Nonoperating Items: *Extraordinary Items. Discontinued Operations. Change in Accounting Principles. Correction of Errors.* Net Income. Forms of Business Organization: *Single Proprietorship. Partnership. Corporations.* Accounting for Owners' Equity: *Proprietorship Equity. Partnership Equity. Ownership in a Corporation. Preferred Stock. Common Stock. Recording a Common Stock Issue. Treasury Stock. Reserves. Retained Earnings. Dividends. Warrants and Stock Options. Balance Sheet Presentation. Earnings per Share.*

Cases

10 Funds Flow Statements 329

The Concept of Flow Statements: *Purpose of the Funds Flow Statement. Concepts of Funds.* Funds Concepts Illustrations: *Cash Flow Statement. Working Capital Flow Statements. Comparison of Cash and Working Capital Flow Statements.* Misconceptions about Depreciation: *Depreciation Fallacies.* Preparation of the Funds Flow

Statement: *Funds Flow Worksheet. Worksheet Entries. T-Account Method. Preparing the Funds Flow Statement. Summary of Preparation Procedures.* Analysis of the Funds Flow Statement: *Ratios. Funds Flow Projections.*

Cases

11 Acquisitions and Consolidated Statements

Cost and Equity Methods: *Cost Method. Equity Method.* Business Combinations: *Purchase versus Pooling. Accounting as a Pooling. Accounting as a Purchase. Balance Sheet Impact. Earnings Impact.* Consolidated Statements: *Basis for Consolidation. Consolidation Procedure. Asset Valuation. Minority Interest. Consolidation of Foreign Subsidiaries.*

Cases

12 Accounting and Changing Prices

Nature of the Problem: *Conventional Accounting and Comparisons. Two Types of Price Changes.* FASB Statement No. 33: *Constant Dollar Accounting. Current Cost Accounting. Inflation-Adjusted Current Costs. Summary of Inflation Accounting.* Foreign Currency Accounting Problems: *Foreign Currency Transactions. Foreign Currency Translation.*

Cases

13 Financial Statement Analysis

Business Objectives: *Return on Investment. Sound Financial Position. Structure of the Analysis.* Overall Measures: *Price/Earnings Ratio. Return on Investment. Investment Turnover and Profit Margin.* Tests of Profitability: *Profit Margin.* Tests of Investment Utilization: *Investment Turnover. Capital Intensity. Working Capital Measures.* Tests of Financial Condition: *Dividend Policy.* Growth Measures. Making Comparisons: *Difficulties. Possible Bases for Comparison. Use of Comparisons.*

Cases

14   Understanding Financial Statements   445

Additional Information in Annual Reports: *The Auditors' Opinion. Notes to Financial Statements. Segment Reporting. Full Disclosure. Comparative Statements. Securities and Exchange Commission Reports.* Review of Criteria and Concepts: *Criteria. Concepts.* Accounting Alternatives: *Regulatory Requirements. Income Tax Principles. Latitude in Methods. Controversies over Principles. Judgment in the Application of Principles. Implications of These Differences. Inherent Limitations.* Meaning of the Financial Statements: *The Income Statement. Statement of Changes in Financial Position. The Balance Sheet.*

Cases

PART 2
MANAGEMENT ACCOUNTING

15   Basic Management Accounting Concepts   489

Management Accounting as One Type of Information: *Information. Management Accounting.* Types of Management Accounting Information and Their Uses: *Full Cost Accounting. Differential Accounting. Responsibility Accounting. Relation to Planning and Control.* Contrast between Management Accounting and Financial Reporting: *Differences. Similarities. Source Disciplines.* Some General Observations: *Different Numbers for Different Purposes. Accounting Numbers Are Approximations. Working with Incomplete Data. Accounting Evidence Is Only Partial Evidence. People, Not Numbers, Get Things Done.*

Cases

16   The Behavior of Costs   507

Relation of Costs to Volume: *Variable and Fixed Costs. Cost-Volume Diagrams. Relation to Unit Costs. Cost Assumptions. Estimating the Cost-Volume Relationship. Measures of Volume.* The Profitgraph: *Break-Even Volume. Contribution. Contribution Profitgraphs. Cash versus Accrual Profitgraphs. Improving Profit Performance. Several Products. Other Influences on Costs.* Appendix: Learning Curves.

Cases

17 Full Costs and Their Uses 549

Cost Concepts: *General Definition. Cost Objective. Full Cost. Direct and Indirect Costs. Applicable Accounting Principles. Elements of Product Cost.* Systems for Cost Accumulation: *The Account Flowchart.* Nonmanufacturing Costs: *Merchandising Companies. Service Organizations. Nonprofit Organizations.* Uses of Full Cost: *Financial Reporting. Analysis of Profitability. What Did it Cost? Setting Regulated Prices. Normal Pricing.*

Cases

18 Additional Aspects of Product Costing Systems 579

Job-Order Costing and Process Costing: *Production Processes. Job-Order Costing. Process Costing. Choice of a System. Variations in Practice.* Measurement of Direct Costs: *Direct Labor Cost. Direct Material Cost. Direct Cost versus Variable Cost.* Allocation of Indirect Costs: *Distinction between Direct and Indirect Costs. Nature of Allocation. Cost Centers. Calculating Overhead Rates. Predetermined Overhead Rates. Procedure for Establishing Predetermined Rates. Unabsorbed and Overabsorbed Overhead.*

Cases

19 Standard Costs, Joint Costs, and Variable Costing Systems 619

Standard Costs: *Variance Accounts. Variations in the Standard Cost Idea. Terminology Ambiguities. Uses of Standard Costs.* Joint Products and By-Products: *Joint Products. By-Products.* Validity of Full Costs: *Tendencies toward Uniformity.* Variable Costing Systems: *Comparison of Absorption and Variable Costing. Why Use Full Costing?* Cost System Design Choices. Appendix A: *Standard Costing Illustration: Black Meter Company.* Appendix B: *Absorption versus Variable Costing: Income Impact.*

Cases

23 Responsibility Accounting: The Management Control Structure 791

Characteristics of Organizations: *Management. Organization Hierarchy. Management Control: Strategic Planning and Task Control. Responsibility Centers: Inputs and Outputs. Responsibility Accounting. Effectiveness and Efficiency.* Types of Responsibility Centers: *Expense Centers. Revenue Centers. Profit Centers. Transfer Prices. Investment Centers. Nonmonetary Measures.*

Cases

24 Responsibility Accounting: The Management Control Process 821

Phases of Management Control: *Programming. Budget Preparation. Operating and Reporting. Evaluation.* Accounting Information Used in Management Control: *Controllable Costs. Engineered, Discretionary, and Committed Costs.* Behavioral Aspects of Management Control: *Behavior of Participants. Motivation. Incentives. Goal Congruence. An Example: The Data Processing Department. Cooperation and Conflict. Other Types of Control.*

Cases

25 Programming and Budgeting 861

Programming: *Ongoing Programs. Proposed New Programs. Formal Programming Systems.* Budgeting: *Uses of the Budget. The Master Budget.* The Operating Budget: *Program Budgets and Responsibility Budgets. Variable or Flexible Budgets. Management by Objectives.* Preparing the Operating Budget: *Organization for Preparation of Budgets. Budget Timetable. Setting Planning Guidelines. Preparing the Sales Budget. Initial Preparation of Other Budget Components. Negotiation. Coordination and Review. Final Approval and Distribution. Revisions. Variations in Practice. The Cash Budget. The Capital Expenditure Budget: Authorization.*

Cases

Index and Source of Cases

The 121 cases included in this book are listed below in alphabetical order, together with their authors' names. Cases with no author's name shown were written by, or under the supervision of, Robert N. Anthony or James S. Reece. Unless otherwise indicated, the copyright on all cases is held by Osceola Institute. No case herein may be reproduced in any form or by any means without the permission of the copyright holder.

Permission to reproduce Osceola Institute cases should be sought through Professor Reece at the Graduate School of Business Administration, The University of Michigan, Ann Arbor, MI 48109. Comments on the text, cases, or teacher's guide, or new ideas for teaching the cases, would be welcomed and should be sent to Professor Reece.

PART 1

FINANCIAL ACCOUNTING

1

The Nature and Purpose
of Accounting

Most of the world's work is done through organizations—groups of people who work together to accomplish one or more objectives. In doing its work, an organization uses resources—material, labor, and various services. To work effectively, the people in an organization need information about these resources and the results achieved through using them. Parties outside the organization need similar information to make judgments about the organization. An important system that provides such information is called *accounting*.

Organizations can be classified broadly as either profit oriented or nonprofit. As these names suggest, a dominant purpose of organizations in the former category is to earn a profit, while organizations in the latter category have other objectives, such as governing, providing health care, providing education, and so on. Of the employed persons in the United States, approximately two thirds work in profit-oriented organizations and one third in government and other nonprofit organizations. Accounting is basically similar in both types of organizations.

THE NEED FOR INFORMATION

In its details, information differs greatly among organizations of various types. But viewed broadly, the information needs of most organizations are similar. We shall outline and illustrate these general information needs by referring to Morgan Ford Company, an automobile dealership.

Morgan Ford Company seeks to earn a profit by selling new and used automobiles and parts and accessories, and by providing repair service. It is an organization of 52 people headed by Lee Carroll, its president. It owns a building in which are located the showroom, service shop, a storeroom for spare parts and accessories, and office space. It also owns a number of new and used automobiles, which it offers for sale; a stock of spare parts, accessories, and supplies; and cash in the bank. These are examples of the resources the company needs to have to conduct its business.

Illustration 1–1 depicts the different types of information that might be useful to people interested in the Morgan Ford Company. As shown in the illustration, information can be either quantitative or nonquantitative. Visual impressions, conversations, television programs, and newspaper stories are examples of nonquantitative information. However, accounting is primarily concerned with quantitative information.

Of the many types of quantitative information, accounting is one. Accounting information is distinguished from the other types in that it usu-

ILLUSTRATION 1–1
TYPES OF INFORMATION

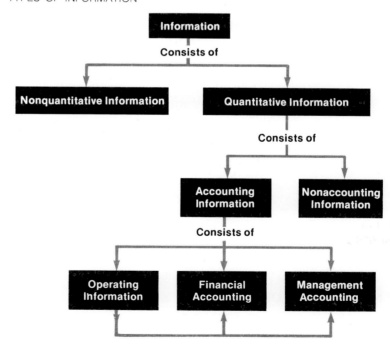

ally is expressed in *monetary* amounts. Data on the age, experience level, and other characteristics of an employee are quantitative, but they are not usually designated as accounting information. The line here is not sharply drawn, however; nonmonetary information is often included in accounting reports when it assists the reader in understanding the report. For example, an accounting sales report for Morgan Ford would show in addition to the monetary amount of sales revenue, the number of automobiles sold, which is nonmonetary information.

What information is needed about the resources used in Morgan Ford and the results achieved by the use of these resources? This information can be classified into three categories: (1) operating information, (2) financial accounting information, and (3) management accounting information. Each is shown in the bottom section of Illustration 1–1.

Operating Information

A considerable amount of *operating information* is required to conduct day-to-day activities. Employees must be paid exactly the amounts owed them, and the government requires that payroll records be maintained for each employee showing amounts earned and paid, as well as various deductions. The sales force needs to know what automobiles are available for sale and each one's cost and selling price. When an automobile is sold, a record must be made of that fact. The person in the stockroom needs to know what parts and accessories are on hand; and if the stock of a certain part becomes depleted, this fact needs to be known so that an additional quantity can be ordered. Amounts owed by the company's customers need to be known; and if a customer does not pay a bill on time, this fact needs to be known so that appropriate action can be taken. The company needs to know the amounts it owes to others, when these amounts should be paid, and how much money it has in the bank.

By far the largest quantity of accounting information consists of operating information. As suggested by the arrows at the bottom of Illustration 1–1, this operating information provides the raw data for management accounting and financial accounting.

Financial Accounting

Financial accounting information is intended both for managers and also for the use of parties external to the business, including shareholders, bankers and other creditors, government agencies, and the general public. Shareholders who have furnished capital to Morgan Ford Company want information on how well the company is doing. If they should decide to sell their shares, they need information that helps them judge how much their investment is worth. Prospective buyers of these shares need similar information. If the company wants to borrow money, the bank or other lender wants information that will show that the company is sound and that there is a high probability that the loan will be repaid when it falls due.

Only in rare instances can outside parties insist that an organization furnish information that is tailor-made to their specifications. In most cases, they must accept the information that the organization chooses to supply. They could not conceivably understand this information without knowing the ground rules that governed its preparation. Moreover, they cannot be expected to learn a new set of ground rules for each organization in which they are interested, nor can they compare the information for one organization with that of another unless both are prepared according to common ground rules. These ground rules are the subject matter of financial accounting (also called *financial reporting*).

> **Example.** When readers familiar with accounting see on an accounting report the item "Inventory at FIFO cost or market, $1,435,655," they understand that this refers to a certain category of property, and that the amount of this property has been measured according to certain prescribed ground rules. They can rely on this understanding even though they have no personal contact with the accountant who reported the information.

Management Accounting

The president, the vice president in charge of automobile sales, the service shop supervisor, and other managers of Morgan Ford Company do not have the time to examine the details of the operating information. Instead, they rely on summaries of this information. They use these summaries, together with other information, to carry out their management responsibilities. The accounting information specifically intended for this purpose is called *management accounting*. Management accounting information is used in three management functions: (1) control, (2) coordination, and (3) planning.

Control. In Morgan Ford Company, most automobile sales are made by salespersons and most service work is done by mechanics. It is not the responsibility of Lee Carroll and the other managers to do this work themselves. Rather, it is their responsibility to see that it is done, and done properly, by the employees of the organization. The process they use for this purpose is called *control*. Accounting information is used in the control process as a means of communication, of motivation, of attention-getting, and of appraisal.

As a means of *communication*, accounting reports can assist in informing employees about management's plans and policies and in general the types of action management wishes the organization to take. As a means of *motivation*, accounting reports can induce members of the organization to act in a way that is consistent with the organization's overall goals and objectives. As a means of *attention-getting*, accounting information signals that problems exist that require investigation and possibly action. As a means of *appraisal*, accounting helps show how well members of the organization have performed, and thus provides a basis for a salary increase, promotion, reassignment, corrective action of various kinds, or, in extreme cases, dismissal.

Coordination. The several parts of the organization must work together to achieve its objectives, and this requires that the activities of each unit must be coordinated with activities of other units. The stockroom must have the parts needed to service automobiles. The new car manager cannot order more automobiles than the company has resources to finance. Accounting aids in this coordination process.

Planning. Planning is the process of deciding what action should be taken in the future. The area covered by one plan may be a tiny segment of the organization or it may be the whole organization. Thus, a decision as to whether the price of one product should be increased $50 tomorrow is a plan, and so is a decision to merge the company with another company.

Some businesses have planning staffs whose full-time job is to assist in making plans. The planning function, however, is much broader than the work done by these staffs. It is performed at all levels in the organization and in all organizations, whether or not they have separate planning staffs. When the service shop supervisor decides the order in which automobiles will be repaired and which mechanic will work on each of them, the supervisor is engaged in planning in the same sense as, but on a smaller scale than, the president when the latter decides to build a new showroom.

One important form of planning is called *budgeting*. Budgeting is the process of planning the overall activity of the organization for a specified period of time, usually a year. An important objective of this process is to fit together the separate plans made for various segments of the organization so as to assure that these plans harmonize with one another. For example, the budgeting process might reveal that the automobile sales manager has planned a considerable increase in sales and that the service department supervisor has planned for a corresponding increase in service work, but that the parts manager has not planned to order the additional parts that will be needed. In a very small business, top management may have a sufficient personal awareness of overall plans so that formal budgets are unnecessary. But an organization of any considerable size is likely to be so complex that some systematic process of formulating and balancing the plans for the separate parts is essential.

Planning involves making decisions. Decisions are arrived at essentially by recognizing that a problem exists, identifying alternative ways of solving the problem, analyzing the consequences of each alternative, and comparing these consequences so as to decide which is best. Accounting information is useful especially in the analysis step of the decision-making process.

Chapter 15 will further introduce management accounting and contrast it with financial reporting.

Definition of Accounting

All of the activities described above are related to accounting, and in all of them the emphasis is on using accounting information in the process of making decisions. Investors and creditors in profit-oriented companies use accounting information in making decisions about where to invest their funds. The governing board of a hospital, university, or other nonprofit organization uses accounting information to judge how well the organization is managed, to decide how much can be spent on various programs, and whether to expand or contract the scale of activities. Thus, of the several available definitions of accounting, the one developed by an American Accounting Association committee is perhaps the best because of its focus on accounting as an aid to decision making. This committee defined accounting as *"the process of identifying, measuring, and communicating economic information to permit informed judgments and decisions by users of the information."*[1]

THE PROFESSION OF ACCOUNTING

In most organizations, the accounting group is the largest staff unit, that is, the largest group other than the "line" activities of production and marketing. The accounting group consists essentially of two types of people: (1) bookkeepers and other clerical employees who maintain the detailed operating records; and (2) professional accountants who decide how items should be reported, prepare the reports, interpret these reports, prepare special analyses, design and operate the systems through which information flows, and ensure that the information is accurate. In 1980, there were 1,904,000 bookkeepers and 1,047,000 accountants in the United States.[2]

All publicly owned companies and many other organizations have their accounting reports audited by a public accounting firm. These firms also perform other services for clients. Some of these firms are large: the eight largest (colloquially called the *Big Eight*) each have several thousand employees and hundreds of offices around the world.[3] They are far larger than any law firm, medical group practice, or other professional

---

[1]American Accounting Association, *A Statement of Basic Accounting Theory* (Evanston, Ill., 1966), p. 1.

[2]U.S. Bureau of the Census. *Statistical Abstract of the United States: 1981,* 102d ed. (Washington, D.C., 1981).

[3]Price Waterhouse, one of the Big Eight, in 1981 had 23,577 personnel, 1,613 of them partners, in over 300 offices in 89 countries. Total 1981 fees (including nonaudit services) were $850 million. (Source: *Price Waterhouse Reports,* 1981.)

firm. At the other extreme, thousands of public accountants practice as individuals.

Most public accountants are licensed by their state and are designated as Certified Public Accountants (CPAs). Many CPAs are employed by companies and other organizations. Accountants may also hold a Certificate in Management Accounting (CMA) or be Certified Internal Auditors.

Although accounting is a staff function performed by accounting professionals within an organization, the ultimate responsibility for the generation of accounting information—whether financial or managerial—rests with *management*. Management's responsibility for accounting is the reason that one of the top officers of many businesses is the *controller*. Within the division of top management's duties, the controller is the person responsible for satisfying other managers' demands for management accounting information and for complying with the regulatory demands of financial reporting. To these ends, the controller's office employs accounting professionals in both management and financial accounting. These accountants design, install, and operate the information systems required to generate financial and managerial reports.

FOCUS OF THE BOOK

Accounting can be approached from either of two directions: from the viewpoint of the accountant, or from the viewpoint of the user of accounting information. One approach emphasizes the concepts and techniques that are involved in collecting, summarizing, and reporting accounting information; the other emphasizes what the user needs to know about accounting. The difference between these two approaches is only one of emphasis. Accountants need to know how information is to be used because they should collect and report information in a form that is most helpful to those who make use of it. Users need to know what the accountant does; otherwise they are unlikely to understand the real meaning of the information that is provided.

This book focuses on accounting from the viewpoint of the user. We shall not, however, discuss the uses of accounting information to any great extent until after we have described carefully what accounting information is.

Preconceptions about Accounting

Readers have already been exposed to a great deal of accounting information. The cash register receipt at the stores where they trade, the checks that they write or (hopefully) that they receive, their bank statements, the bills which they are expected to pay—all these are parts of accounting systems. One reads in the newspaper about the profit of a company or an industry, about dividends, or about money being spent to build new buildings; this information comes from accounting systems. Even before beginning a formal study of the subject, therefore, the reader has accumulated a number of ideas about accounting.

The trouble is that some of these ideas probably are incorrect. For example, it seems intuitively sensible that accounting should report what a business is "worth." But accounting does not in fact do this, or even attempt to do it. As another example, there is a general notion that the word *asset* refers to valuable things, good things to have. But the skills and abilities of an organization's employees are not an asset in the accounting sense, even though they may be a key determinant of the organization's success.

Thus, as with many other subjects, students of accounting must be wary of preconceptions. They will discover that accounting "as it really is" may be different in important respects from what they had surmised it to be, or from what common sense tells them it should be. They will find that there are sound reasons for these differences, and it is important that they understand these reasons. In order to achieve such an understanding, they need to know enough about accounting concepts and techniques to understand the nature and limitations of the accounting information. They do not, however, need the detailed knowledge that the accountant must have.

Approach to Accounting

The approach to accounting taken here is something like that used by an airplane pilot in learning to use flight instruments. The pilot needs to know the meaning of the message conveyed by each of the instruments—such things as the fact that a clockwise movement of a certain arrow probably means one thing and that a counterclockwise movement probably means another thing, that the flashing of a red light probably means that a certain component is not functioning, and so on. The word *probably* is used because, for one reason or another, an instrument may not always give the reading that it is supposed to give. The pilot must realize this and must also understand something of the likelihood of, and the reason for, these abnormalities. On the other hand, the pilot does not need to know how to design airplane instruments, how to construct them, how to calibrate them, or how to maintain or repair them. Specialists are available for these important functions.

Similarly, those who use accounting information must understand what a given accounting figure probably means, what its limitations are, and the circumstances in which it may mean something different from the apparent "signal" that it gives. They do not, however, need to know how to design, construct, operate, or check on the accuracy of an accounting system. They can rely on accountants for these important functions.

Plan of the Book

We described above three types of accounting information: operating information, management accounting information, and financial accounting information. Since our viewpoint is that of the user, and particularly the management user, we shall not describe operating information in any great detail. The book is therefore divided into two approximately equal parts, one on financial accounting and the other on management acounting.

The discussion of financial accounting comes first because the structure of financial accounting underlies *all* accounting. This structure consists of a few basic principles and concepts, a set of relationships among the elements comprising the accounting system, a terminology, and a number of rules and guides for the application of the principles and concepts to specific situations. We shall describe the complete financial accounting structure, in a general way, in Chapters 2, 3, and 4; and we shall then go over the same ground again in more detail in Chapters 5 through 14.

The second half of the book discusses the nature and use of management accounting information. The management of an organization can establish whatever ground rules it wishes for the accounting information collected for its own use. Thus, although the principles of financial accounting are applicable to all organizations, the rules of management accounting are tailor-made to meet the needs of the management of a specific organization.

There is nevertheless a similarity in both financial accounting practices and management accounting practices in most organizations. There are obvious economies in using financial accounting information wherever possible for management accounting purposes, rather than devising two completely different systems for the two purposes.

The terms *financial accounting* and *management accounting* are not precise descriptions of the activities they comprise. All accounting is *financial* in the sense that all accounting systems are in monetary terms; and *management* is responsible for the content of financial accounting reports. (This is the first of many problems in terminology that will be noted throughout this book. You are cautioned against drawing inferences from the labels alone; you must learn the concepts that the labels represent.)

THE FINANCIAL ACCOUNTING FRAMEWORK

Suppose you were asked to keep track of what was going on in an organization so as to provide useful information for management. One way of carrying out this assignment would be to write down a narrative of important events in a log similar to that kept by the captain of a ship. After some experience with your log, you would gradually develop a set of rules to guide your efforts. For example, since it would be impossible to write down every action of every person in the organization, you would frame rules to guide you in choosing between those events that were important enough to record and those that should be omitted. Thus, if your organization were an automobile dealership, you certainly would want a record of each car sold, but you might well decide not to make a record of every person who came into the showroom.

You would also find that your log would be more valuable if you standardized certain terminology. People who studied it would then have a clearer understanding of what you meant. Furthermore, if you standardized terms and definitions of these terms, you could turn the job of keeping the log over to someone else and have some assurance that this person's report of events would convey the same information that you would have conveyed had you been keeping the log yourself.

In devising these rules of keeping a log, you would necessarily be somewhat arbitrary. There might be several ways of describing a certain event, all equally good. But in order to have a common basis of understanding, you would select just one of these for use in your recordkeeping system. Thus, since the products handled by your automobile dealership could be called vehicles, autos, cars, or trucks, some of which are synonyms and others not, it would clearly be desirable to agree on a standard nomenclature.

All the foregoing considerations were actually involved in the development of the accounting process. Accounting has evolved over a period of several hundred years, and during this time certain terminology, rules, and conventions have come to be accepted as useful. If you are to understand accounting reports—the end products of an accounting system—you must be familiar with the rules and conventions lying behind these reports.

Accounting as a Language

Accounting is aptly called the *language of business*. The task of learning accounting is essentially the same as the task of learning a new language.

This task is complicated by the fact that many words used in accounting mean almost, but not quite, the same thing as the identical words mean in everyday, nonaccounting usage. Americans learning French realize from the beginning that the words and the grammar in French are completely new to them and must therefore be learned carefully. The problem of learning accounting, however, is more like that of Americans learning to speak English as it is spoken in Great Britain. Unless they are careful, Americans will fail to recognize that words are used in Great Britain in a different sense from that used in America.

> **Example.** The grain that Americans call wheat is called corn by the British, and the British use the word *maize* for the grain that Americans call corn. To complicate the matter further, a grain grown in certain parts

of America is called maize; and it is almost, but not quite, like American corn. Unless they understand these differences in terminology, Americans and Britons will not communicate what they intend when talking with each other.

Moreover, certain terms used in accounting have different meanings in different circumstances, and the context must be understood in order to comprehend the meaning. The problem is similar to that of the word *ton*. A ton is most commonly thought of as a measure of weight, 2,000 pounds. But a ton in certain circumstances may mean 2,240 pounds, which is called a long ton. A *six-ton truck* to some people means a truck that weights 12,000 pounds fully loaded; to others it means the weight of the load alone. A *measurement ton* is not even a measure of weight; it is a measure of volume, 40 cubic feet.

Perhaps the greatest difficulty that beginning students of accounting encounter is that of distinguishing between the accounting meaning of certain terms and the meaning that they have attached to these terms in their nonaccounting, everyday usage. For example, an amount labeled *net worth* appears on many accounting reports. The commonsense interpretation is that this amount refers to what something is "worth"—what its value is; but such an interpretation is incorrect. (The correct meaning will be given in Chapter 2.)

Accounting also resembles a language in that some of its rules are definite, whereas others are not. There are differences of opinion among accountants as to how a given event should be reported, just as there are differences of opinion among grammarians as to many matters of sentence structure, punctuation, and choice of words. Nevertheless, there are many practices that are clearly "poor English," and there are also many practices that are definitely "poor accounting." In these chapters, therefore, an attempt is made to describe the elements of "good accounting" and to indicate areas in which there are differences of opinion as to what constitutes good practice.

Finally, languages evolve and change in response to the changing needs of society, and so does accounting. The rules described here are currently in use, but some of them will probably be modified to meet the changing needs of organizations and their constituencies.

Nature of Principles   The rules and conventions of accounting are commonly referred to as "principles." The word *principle* is here used to mean "a general law or rule adopted or professed as a guide to action; a settled ground or basis of conduct or practice."[4] Note that this definition describes a principle as a *general* law or rule that is to be used as a *guide* to action. This

---

[4]Committee on Terminology, American Institute of Certified Public Accountants, "Review and Résumé," *Accounting Terminology* Bulletin No. 1 (New York, 1953), p. 9.

means that accounting principles do not prescribe exactly how each event occurring in an organization should be recorded. Consequently, there are many matters in accounting practice that differ from one organization to another. In part, these differences are inevitable because a single detailed set of rules could not conceivably apply to every organization. In part, the differences reflect the fact that accountants have considerable latitude within "generally accepted accounting principles" in which to express their own ideas as to the best way of recording and reporting a specific event.

Readers should realize, therefore, that they cannot know the precise meaning of many of the items on an accounting report unless they know which of several equally acceptable possibilities has been selected by the person who prepared the report. The meaning intended in a specific situation requires knowledge of the context.

Criteria

Accounting principles are man-made. Unlike the principles of physics, chemistry, and the other natural sciences, accounting principles were not deduced from basic axioms, nor is their validity verifiable by observation and experiment. Instead, they have evolved. This evolutionary process is going on constantly; accounting principles are not "eternal truths."

The general acceptance of an accounting principle or practice usually depends on how well it meets three criteria: relevance, objectivity, and feasibility. A principle is *relevant* to the extent that it results in information that is meaningful and useful to those who need to know something about a certain organization. A principle is *objective* to the extent that the information is not influenced by the personal bias or judgment of those who furnish it. Objectivity connotes reliability, trustworthiness. It also connotes verifiability, which means that there is some way of ascertaining the correctness of the information reported. A principle is *feasible* to the extent that it can be implemented without undue complexity or cost.

We shall illustrate and expand on the significance of these criteria in connection with the discussion of the principles themselves. At this point it is sufficient to point out that these criteria often conflict with one another. The most relevant solution is likely to be the least objective and the least feasible.

Example. The development of a new product may have a significant effect on a company's real value—personal computers and Polaroid cameras being spectacular examples. Information about the value of new products is most useful to the investor. It is indeed relevant. But the best estimate of the value of a new product is likely to be that made by management, and this is a highly subjective estimate. Accounting therefore does not attempt to record such values. It sacrifices relevance in the interests of objectivity.

The measure of the value of the owners' interest in Apple Computer, Inc., obtained from the stock market quotations (i.e., multiplying the price per share of stock times the number of shares outstanding) is a much more accurate reflection of the true value than the amount at which this item appears in the corporation's accounting records. As of September 24, 1982, the marketplace gave this value as $1.04 billion; the accounting records gave it as $257 million. The difference does not indicate that there is an error in the accounting records. It merely illustrates the fact that accounting does not attempt to report market values.

In developing new principles, the essential problem is to strike the right balance between relevance, on the one hand, and objectivity and feasibility, on the other. Failure to appreciate this problem often leads to unwarranted criticism of accounting principles. It is easy to critize accounting on the grounds that accounting information is not as relevant as it might be; but the critic often overlooks the fact that proposals to increase relevance almost always involve a sacrifice of objectivity and feasibility. On balance, such a sacrifice may not be worthwhile.

Source of Accounting Principles

The foundation of accounting consists of a set of what are called *generally accepted accounting principles*, or *GAAP*, for short. Currently, these principles are established by the Financial Accounting Standards Board (FASB), which was created in 1973. The FASB consists of seven leading accountants from diverse backgrounds who work full time on developing new or modified principles. The Board is supported by a professional staff that does research and prepares a discussion memorandum on each problem that the Board addresses. The Board acts only after interested parties have been given an opportunity to suggest solutions to problems and to comment on proposed pronouncements. The FASB is a nongovernmental organization financed by contributions from business firms and the accounting profession.

The FASB superseded the Accounting Principles Board (APB) of the American Institute of Certified Public Accountants (AICPA). The APB had the same functions as the FASB, but its members did not devote full time to Board activities. In one of its first actions, the FASB adopted the principles that had been developed by the Accounting Principles Board and published as its *Opinions*. Thus, in this description of accounting we shall refer to *Opinions* of the APB as being authoritative.[5]

---

[5]Because these earlier statements have not yet been codified in a publication of the Financial Accounting Standards Board, we must cite the pronouncements of the earlier bodies. They are referred to here as *Accounting Terminology Bulletins, Accounting Research Bulletins, APB Opinions,* and *APB Statements.* (*APB Statements* are in the nature of recommendations, rather than mandates.) All of these documents are brought together in the book *Accounting Standards,* published annually by the FASB.

Each of the *Standards* of the FASB and *Opinions* of the APB deals with a specific topic. Collectively, they do not by any means cover all the important topics in accounting. If an authoritative pronouncement has not been made on a given topic, accountants can treat that topic in the way they believe most fairly presents the situation.

Companies are not legally required to adhere to GAAP as established by the FASB. As a practical matter, however, there are strong pressures for them to do so. This is because the accounting reports of companies of any substantial size are audited by certified public accountants who are members of the AICPA. Although the AICPA does not require its members to force companies to adhere to FASB Standards, it does require that if the CPA finds that the company has used a different principle, the difference must be called to public attention. Since companies usually do not like to go counter to the FASB—even though they may feel strongly that the FASB principle is not appropriate in their particular situation—they almost always conform to the FASB pronouncements.

Another source of pressure to conform to GAAP is the U.S. Securities and Exchange Commission (SEC). This agency exists to protect the interests of investors and has jurisdiction over nearly all corporations whose securities are traded in interstate commerce. It requires these companies to file accounting reports, and these reports must be prepared in accordance with GAAP. In its *Regulation S-X* and its *Accounting Series Releases*,[6] the SEC spells out acceptable accounting principles in more detail than, but generally consistent with, the pronouncements of the FASB. Legally, the Securities Exchange Act of 1934 gave the SEC the authority to promulgate GAAP; but over the years, for the most part the SEC has relied on the FASB and its predecessors for carrying out the standard-setting process.

Various regulatory bodies also prescribe accounting rules for the companies they regulate. Among those subjected to such rules are banks and other financial institutions, insurance companies, railroads, airlines, pipelines, radio and television companies, and electric and gas companies. These rules are not necessarily consistent with the principles of the FASB, although there has been a tendency in recent years to change the accounting rules of regulatory agencies so that they do conform.

Principles for nonprofit organizations come from a variety of sources. The AICPA has issued Audit Guides for hospitals, colleges and universities, welfare organizations, and state and municipal governments, and a similar document (called a Statement of Position) for other nonprofit organizations. Although these are not quite as binding as FASB Standards, many organizations follow them. Accounting standards for the

---

[6]Beginning in 1982, *Accounting Series Releases* were to be replaced by two new series: *Financial Reporting Releases* and *Accounting and Auditing Enforcement Releases.*

federal government are set by the Comptroller General of the United States. As this is written, a new body to set standards for state and municipal governments is being established.

The authority of the FASB and other agencies exists, of course, only in the United States of America. Accounting principles in other countries differ in some respects from American GAAP, but there is a basic similarity throughout the world. In 1973, efforts were begun to codify a set of accounting principles that would apply internationally, and a few statements have been published since then by the International Accounting Standards Committee (IASC). They are generally consistent with the principles described in this book.

The most convenient data about the various accounting practices used by American companies is *Accounting Trends & Techniques*, published annually by the AICPA. It summarizes the practices of 600 companies. Since these are relatively large companies, the summaries do not necessarily reflect the practices of all companies. This qualification should be kept in mind when data from this report are given in this text.

FINANCIAL STATEMENTS

The end product of the financial accounting process is a set of reports that are called financial statements. GAAP require that three such reports be prepared: (1) a balance sheet, (2) an income statement, and (3) a funds flow statement (formally called a statement of changes in financial position). As we examine the details of the financial accounting process, it is important that the reader keep in mind the objective toward which the process is aimed, namely, the preparation of these three financial statements.

Most reports, in any field, can be classified into one of two categories called, respectively, (1) reports of *stocks* or *status* and (2) reports of *flows*. The amount of water in a reservoir at a given moment of time is a measure of stock, whereas the amount of water that moves through the reservoir in a day is a measure of flow. Reports of stocks are always as of a specified *instant* in time; reports of flow always cover a specified *period* of time. Reports of stocks are like snapshots; reports of flows are more like motion pictures. One of the accounting reports, the balance sheet, is a report of stocks. It shows information about the resources of an organization at a specified moment of time. The other two reports, the income statement and the funds flow statement, are reports of flow. They report activities of the business for a period of time, such as a quarter or a year.

The next eight chapters describe the balance sheet and income statement. We shall defer a description of the funds flow statement until Chapter 10. Because this report is derived by rearranging data that were originally collected for the other two reports, it is inappropriate to discuss the funds flow statement until the balance sheet and income statement have been thoroughly explained.

Financial Statement Objectives

We indicated earlier that financial accounting statements, while also of use to management, are intended primarily to provide relevant information to parties external to the business. In 1978, the FASB issued a formal statement of financial reporting objectives.[7] The entire statement contains 63 paragraphs, and thus is too lengthy to describe here in detail. We will simply highlight the key objectives (the numbering is ours, not the FASB's):

Financial reporting should provide information:

[handwritten: not intended for lay persons]

1. That is useful to present and potential investors and creditors in making rational investment and credit decisions.
2. That is comprehensible to those who have a reasonable understanding of business and economic activities, and are willing to study the information with reasonable diligence.

[handwritten: relates to the balance sheet]

3. About the economic resources of an enterprise, the claims to those resources, and the effects of transactions and events that change resources and claims to those resources.

[handwritten: relate to income statement]

4. About an enterprise's financial performance during a period.
5. To help users assess the amounts, timing, and uncertainty of prospective cash receipts from dividends or interest and the proceeds from the sale or redemption of securities or loans.

[handwritten: funds flow statement changes in financial position]

Objectives 1 and 2 apply to all financial accounting information. Note that the intended users are expected to have attained a reasonable level of sophistication in using the statements; the statements are not prepared for laypersons. Objective 3 is related to the balance sheet; objective 4, to the income statement; and objective 5, to the funds flow statement. As the five objectives collectively suggest, financial statements provide information about the *past* to aid users in making predictions and decisions related to the *future* financial status and flows of the business.

Income Tax Reporting

The Internal Revenue Service (IRS) has certain legal powers given by Congress to regulate the ways in which taxable income is calculated for the purpose of assessing income taxes. Since the tax laws' purposes differ from those associated with GAAP, the IRS has developed regulations that taxpayers must follow for income tax purposes that differ in some

---

[7]Financial Accounting Standards Board, "Objectives of Financial Reporting by Business Enterprises," *Statement of Financial Accounting Concepts No. 1* (Stamford, Conn., November 1978).

respects from GAAP. These differences mean that the amount of pretax profit or loss shown on the taxpayer's income statement prepared according to GAAP will probably not be equal to the profit or loss shown on the taxpayer's income tax return.

Thus, in the United States, financial accounting, management accounting, and income tax accounting are essentially *separate* processes. GAAP provides the principles for financial accounting; top management, for management accounting; and the IRS and Congress, for tax accounting. The underlying operating information that is the raw data for all three processes is, of course, the same. The pieces or "building blocks" of operating information simply are put together in different ways for these three different processes. Thus, companies do not in any literal (or cynical) sense "keep three different sets of books," as is sometimes asserted. Also, while differences among the three processes do exist, in practice the similarities are more apparent than the differences.

Ratios

Throughout this book we shall discuss not only the preparation of financial statements but also their use in decision making. For the latter purpose, it is often helpful to express the accounting numbers as ratios or percentages. A *ratio* is one number expressed in terms of another; that is, it is the quotient of two numbers. For example, if the market price of stock in a company is $40 per share and if the earnings of that company are $4 per share, the price/earnings ratio is $40 ÷ $4 = 10.

A percentage is one kind of ratio in which the base is taken as equaling 100 and the quotient is expressed as "per hundred" of the base; that is, the base is divided into 100 parts. For example, with sales of $100,000 used as a base, if earnings are $5,000, earnings are 5 percent of sales.

SUMMARY

A business has three types of accounting information: (1) operating information, which has to do with the details of operations; (2) management accounting information, which is used internally for control, coordination, and planning; and (3) financial accounting information, which is used both by management and by external accounting parties.

Financial accounting is governed by ground rules that are referred to as generally accepted accounting principles (GAAP). These ground rules may be different than the student believes them to be, based on previous exposure to accounting information. They are prescribed by the Financial Accounting Standards Board. They attempt to strike the optimum balance between the criterion of relevance, on the one hand, and the criteria of objectivity and feasibility, on the other hand.

The end products of the financial accounting process are three financial statements: the balance sheet, the income statement, and the funds flow statement. The balance sheet is a report of status or stocks as of a moment of time, whereas the other two statements summarize flows over a period of time. The FASB has developed broad objectives for these statements.

In the United States, calculating taxable income for income tax purposes is not the same process as calculating pretax profit for the financial accounting income statement.

Cases

CASE 1–1 David Robinson

In the early fall of 1979, David Robinson was employed as a district sales engineer for a large chemical firm. He learned during one of his periodic discussions with plant chemists that the company had developed a use for the material, in pulverized form, of which plastic soda-pop bottles are made. Since Robinson lived in a state with mandatory deposits on all beverage bottles, he realized that a ready supply of this material was available. All that was needed was an organization to tap that bottle supply, grind the bottles, and deliver the pulverized plastic to his company. It was an opportunity Robinson had long waited for, a chance to get into business for himself.

In November 1979, Robinson began checking into the costs involved in setting up his grinding business. He found a used truck and three trailers to pick up the empty bottles. He purchased one

used grinding machine but had to buy a second one new. He also purchased necessary supplies and parts for the machines. These items used most of the $50,000 Robinson had saved from an inheritance and from his salary. He had found a warehouse well located for his business, at a cost of $108,000. Robinson was able to interest members of his family enough in his project so that three of them, two sisters and a brother, invested $20,000 each.

These funds gave Robinson more than enough money to put a down payment on the warehouse. He was able to get a mortgage for the balance on the building. In granting the mortgage, however, the bank official suggested that Robinson start from the beginning with proper accounting records. He said these records would help not only with future bank dealings but also with tax returns and general management of the company. He suggested Robinson find a good accountant to assist him from the start, to get things going on the right foot.

Robinson sat down a few days later with his neighbor, Robert Neff, an accountant with a local firm. Robinson explained that he knew little about keeping proper records. Neff suggested that Robinson start by listing all of the items purchased for the business and all the debts incurred. He also pointed out that Robinson should start a daybook of transactions. Neff said he would find an accountant who would be willing to take Robinson on as a client and who would build a set of accounts for him as soon as regular business was under way.

Confident now that he was starting his venture on solid ground, David Robinson opened his warehouse. He signed contracts with two local bottling companies and hired two grinding machine workers and a truck driver. By February 1980, he

was making regular deliveries to his former employer.

Questions

1. Why did Robinson need any records? What did he need?

2. See what you can do to draw up a list of Robinson's assets and liabilities, as the accountant suggested, making any assumptions you consider useful. How should Robinson go about putting a value on his assets?

3. Now that Robinson has started to make sales, what information should he keep to determine his "profit and loss"? What should be the general construction of a profit and loss analysis for Robinson's business? How frequently would he wish to provide himself with such an analysis?

4. What other kinds of changes in assets, liabilities, and proprietary claims will need careful recording and reporting if Robinson is to keep in control of his business?

CASE 1–2   Baron Coburg

Once upon a time many, many years ago, there lived a feudal landlord in a small province of Western Europe. The landlord, Baron Coburg, lived in a castle high on a hill. He was responsible for the well-being of many peasants who occupied the lands surrounding his castle. Each spring, as the snow began to melt and thoughts of other, less influential men turned to matters other than business, the Baron would decide how to provide for all his peasants during the coming year.

One spring, the Baron was thinking about the wheat crop of the coming growing season. "I believe that 30 acres of my

land, being worth five bushels of wheat per acre, will produce enough wheat for next winter," he mused, "but who should do the farming? I believe I'll give Ivan and Frederick the responsibility of growing the wheat." Whereupon Ivan and Frederick were summoned for an audience with Baron Coburg.

"Ivan, you will farm on the 20-acre plot of ground and Frederick will farm the 10-acre plot," the Baron began. "I will give Ivan 20 bushels of wheat for seed and 20 pounds of fertilizer. (Twenty pounds of fertilizer are worth two bushels of wheat.) Frederick will get 10 bushels of wheat for seed and 10 pounds of fertilizer. I will give each of you an ox to pull a plow, but you will have to make arrangements with Feyador, the Plow-maker, for a plow. The oxen, incidentally, are only three years old and have never been used for farming, so they should have a good 10 years of farming ahead of them. Take good care of them, because an ox is worth 40 bushels of wheat. Come back next fall and return the oxen and the plows along with your harvest."

Ivan and Frederick genuflected and withdrew from the Great Hall, taking with them the things provided by the Baron.

The summer came and went, and after the harvest Ivan and Frederick returned to the Great Hall to account to their master for the things given them in the spring. Ivan said, "My Lord, I present you with a slightly used ox, a plow, broken beyond repair, and 223 bushels of wheat. I, unfortunately, owe Feyador, the Plow-maker, three bushels of wheat for the plow I got from him last spring. And, as you might expect, I used all the fertilizer and seed you gave me last spring. You will also remember, my Lord, that you

took 20 bushels of my harvest for your own personal use."

Frederick spoke next. "Here, my Lord, is a partially used-up ox, the plow for which I gave Feyador, the Plowmaker, 3 bushels of wheat from my harvest, and 105 bushels of wheat. I, too, used all my seed and fertilizer last spring. Also, my Lord, you took 30 bushels of wheat several days ago for your own table. I believe the plow is good for two more seasons."

"You did well," said the Baron. Blessed with this benediction the two peasants departed.

After they had taken their leave, the Baron began to contemplate what had happened. "Yes," he thought, "they did well, but I wonder which one did better?"

Questions

1. For each farm, prepare balance sheets as of the beginning and end of the growing season, and an income statement for the season. (Do not be concerned that you do not have much understanding of what a balance sheet and income statement are; just use your intuition as best you can.)

2. Which peasant was the better farmer?

2

Basic Accounting Concepts:
The Balance Sheet

This chapter describes five of the basic concepts from which principles of accounting are derived. Also described, in a preliminary way, are the nature of the balance sheet and the principal categories of items that appear on it. Finally, the chapter shows how amounts that appear on the balance sheet are changed to reflect events that affect an organization's resources.

The material presented here should be regarded as an overview. Each of the topics introduced will be discussed in more depth in later chapters.

BASIC CONCEPTS

Accounting principles are built on a foundation of a few basic concepts. These concepts are so basic that most accountants do not consciously think of them; they are regarded as being self-evident, obvious, to be taken for granted. Nonaccountants will not find these concepts to be self-evident, however. Accounting could be constructed on a foundation of quite different concepts; indeed, some accounting theorists argue that certain of the present concepts are wrong and should be changed. Nevertheless, in order to understand accounting as it now exists, one must understand what the underlying concepts currently are.

Several years after beginning its "Conceptual Framework" project, the

FASB began issuing a series of *Statements of Financial Accounting Concepts*. As of late 1982, four such statements had been issued.[1] These statements are intended to provide the FASB with explicit conceptual criteria to help resolve future accounting issues, rather than trying to deal with each issue on an ad hoc basis. The concept statements themselves do not establish generally accepted accounting principles (GAAP).

Prior to the current FASB effort, other groups had addressed the task of identifying basic accounting concepts. These earlier efforts resulted in specific lists of basic concepts.[2] To date, no similar succinct but comprehensive list has emerged from the FASB project, which deals at length with accounting objectives and definitions, as well as basic concepts.

The concepts we shall use in this book, while not identical to those listed by other authors or groups, nevertheless reflect concepts that are widely accepted and applied in practice by accountants in North America. These 11 concepts are:

1. Money measurement.	7. Conservatism.
2. Entity.	8. Realization.
3. Going concern.	9. Matching.
4. Cost.	10. Consistency.
5. Dual aspect.	11. Materiality.
6. Time period.	

The first five are discussed below, and the other six are discussed in Chapter 3.

1. The Money Measurement Concept

In financial accounting, a record is made only of information that can be expressed in monetary terms. The advantage of doing this is that money provides a common denominator by means of which heterogeneous facts about an entity can be expressed as numbers that can be added and subtracted.

Example. Although it may be a fact that a business owns $30,000 of cash, 6,000 pounds of raw material, six trucks, 10,000 square feet of building space, and so on, these amounts cannot be added together to produce a meaningful total of what the business owns. Expressing these items in monetary terms—$30,000 of cash, $8,000 of raw material, $90,000 of trucks, and $700,000 of buildings—makes such an addition possible.

---

[1]*No. 1*, "Objectives of Financial Reporting by Business Enterprises" (November 1978); *No. 2*, "Qualitative Characteristics of Accounting Information" (May 1980); *No. 3*, "Elements of Financial Statements of Business Enterprises" (December 1980); and *No. 4*, "Objectives of Financial Reporting by Nonbusiness Organizations" (December 1980).

[2]AAA, *A Statement of Basic Accounting Theory* (Evanston, Ill., 1966), lists four "basic standards" and five "guidelines." AICPA, "Basic Concepts and Accounting Principles Underlying Financial Statements of Business Enterprises," *APB Statement No. 4* (New York, October 1970), lists 13 "basic features."

Thus, despite the old cliché about not adding apples and oranges, it *is* easy to add them if all of them are expressed in terms of their respective monetary values.

Despite its advantage, this concept imposes a severe limitation on the scope of an accounting report. Accounting does not report the state of the president's health, that the sales manager is not on speaking terms with the production manager, that a strike is beginning, or that a competitor has placed a better product on the market. Accounting therefore does not give a complete account of the happenings in an organization or a full picture of its condition. It follows, then, that the reader of an accounting report should not expect to find therein all, or perhaps even the most important, facts about an organization.

Money is expressed in terms of its value at the time an event is recorded in the accounts. Subsequent changes in the purchasing power of money do not affect this amount. Thus, a machine purchased in 1983 for $200,000 and land purchased in 1976 for $200,000 are both listed in the 1983 accounting records at $200,000, although the purchasing power of the dollar in 1983 was only about half of what it was in 1976. It is sometimes said that accounting assumes that money is an unvarying yardstick of value, but this statement is inaccurate. Accountants know full well that the purchasing power of the dollar changes. They do not, however, attempt to reflect such changes in the accounts.[3]

2. The Entity Concept

Accounts are kept for entities, as distinguished from the persons who are associated with these entities. In recording events in accounting, the important question is: "How do these events affect the entity?" How they affect the persons who own, operate, or otherwise are associated with the entity is irrelevant. For example, suppose that $100 is removed from a clothing store's cash register by the store's owner for his or her personal use. The real effect of this event on the owner as a person may be negligible: although the cash has been taken out of the business' "pocket" and put into the owner's "pocket," in either "pocket" the cash belongs to the owner. Nevertheless, because of the entity concept, the accounting records show that the business has less cash than previously.

It is sometimes difficult to define with precision the entity for which a set of accounts is kept. Consider the case of a married couple who own and operate an unincorporated retail store. In *law*, there is no distinction between the financial affairs of the store and those of its owners. A creditor of the store can sue and, if successful, collect from the owners'

---

[3]Recent requirements for large corporations to disclose certain accounting data restated in dollars of constant purchasing power are described in Chapter 12. It should be noted here that these disclosures are *supplemental* data; the money measurement concept still applies in the basic financial statements.

personal resources as well as from the resources of the business. In *accounting*, by contrast, a set of accounts is kept for the store as a separate business entity, and the events reflected in these accounts must be those of the store. The nonbusiness events that affect the couple must not be included in these accounts. In accounting, the *business* owns the resources of the store, even though the resources are legally owned by the couple. In accounting, debts owned by the *business* are kept separate from personal debts owed by the couple. The expenses of operating the store are kept separate from the couple's personal expenses for food, clothing, shelter, and the like.

The necessity for making such a distinction between the entity and its owners can create problems. Suppose, for example, that the couple lives on the business premises. How much of the rent, electric bill, and property taxes of these premises is properly an expense of the business, and how much is personal expense of the family? Answers to questions like these often are difficult to arrive at, and indeed are somewhat arbitrary.

For a corporation, the distinction is often quite easily made. A corporation is a legal entity, separate from the persons who own it, and the accounts of many corporations correspond exactly to the scope of the legal entity. There may be complications, however. In the case of a group of legally separate corporations that are related to one another by shareholdings, the whole group may be treated as a single entity for financial reporting purposes, giving rise to what are called *consolidated* accounting statements. Conversely, within a single corporation, a separate set of accounts may be maintained for each of its principal operating units. For example, General Electric Company maintains separate accounts for each of its over 200 business units.

An entity is any organization or activity for which accounting reports are prepared. Although our examples tend to be drawn from business companies, accounting entities include governments, churches, universities, and other nonbusiness organizations.

One entity may be part of a larger entity. Thus, a set of accounts may be maintained for an individual elementary school, another set for the whole school district, and still another set for all the schools in a state. There even exists a set of accounts, called the national income accounts, for the entire economic activity of the United States. In general, detailed accounting records are maintained for entities at the lowest level in the hierarchy, and reports for higher levels are prepared by summarizing the detailed data of these low-level entities.

**3. The Going-
Concern Concept**

Unless there is good evidence to the contrary, accounting assumes that an entity will continue to operate for an indefinitely long period in the future. The significance of this assumption can be indicated by contrasting it with a possible alternative, namely, that the entity is about to be liquidated. Under the latter assumption, accounting would attempt to measure at all times what the entity's resources are currently worth to potential buyers. Under the going-concern concept, by contrast, there is no need to do this, and in fact it is not done. Instead, it is assumed that the resources currently available to the entity will be used in its future operations. In a manufacturing company, for example, resources will be used to create goods that will eventually be sold to customers. At the time such a sale takes place, accounting recognizes the value of the goods as evidenced by their selling price. The current resale values of the individual machines, supplies, and other resources used in the manufacturing process are irrelevant because there is no intention of selling them individually; rather, they will be used as part of the manufacturing process, and it is the resulting goods that will be sold.

> **Example.** At any given moment (say, December 31, 1982), a blue jean manufacturer has jeans in various stages of the production process. If the business were liquidated at that moment, these partially completed jeans would have little if any value. Accounting does not attempt to value these jeans at what they are currently worth. Instead, accounting assumes that the manufacturing process will be carried through to completion, and therefore that the amount for which the partially completed jeans could be sold if the company were liquidated at that moment is irrelevant.

If, however, the accountant has good reason to believe that an entity *is* going to be liquidated, then its resources would be reported at their liquidation value. Such circumstances are uncommon.

4. The Cost Concept   The economic resources of an entity are called its *assets*. They consist of money, land, buildings, machinery, and other property and property rights, as will be described in a subsequent section. A fundamental concept of accounting, closely related to the going-concern concept, is that an asset is ordinarily entered in the accounting records at the price paid to acquire it—that is, at its cost. This cost is the basis for all subsequent accounting for the asset.

Since, for a variety of reasons, the real worth of an asset may change with the passage of time, the accounting measurement of assets does not necessarily—indeed, does not ordinarily—reflect what assets are worth, except at the moment they are acquired. There is therefore a considerable difference between the way in which assets are measured in accounting and the everyday, nonaccounting notion that assets are measured at what they are worth. In accounting, assets are initially recorded at the exchange price paid to acquire them, that is, at their cost. (For emphasis, this is also referred to as an asset's *historical* cost.) This amount is ordinarily unaffected by subsequent changes in the value of the asset. By contrast, in ordinary usage the "value" of an asset usually means the amount for which it currently could be sold.

Example. If a business buys a plot of land, paying $50,000 for it, this asset would be recorded in the accounts of the business at the amount of $50,000. If a year later the land could be sold for $70,000, or if it could be sold for only $40,000, no change would ordinarily be made in the accounting records to reflect this fact.

Thus, the amounts at which assets are shown in an entity's accounts do *not* indicate sales values of the assets. One of the most common mistakes made by uninformed persons reading accounting reports is that of believing there is a close correspondence between the amount at which an asset appears on these reports and the actual value of the asset.

The amount reported as cash *is*, of course, the value of the cash the entity owns. However, the amounts reported for land, buildings, equipment, and similar assets have no necessary relationship to what these items are currently worth. In general, it is safe to say that the longer an asset has been owned by an entity, the less likely it is that the amount at which it appears on the accounting records corresponds to its current market value.

The cost concept does not mean that all assets remain on the accounting records at their original purchase price for as long as the entity owns them. The cost of an asset that has a long, but nevertheless limited, life is systematically reduced over that life by the process called *depreciation,* as discussed in Chapter 7. The purpose of the depreciation process is systematically to remove the *cost* of the asset from the accounts and to show it as a cost of operations; depreciation has no necessary relationship to changes in market value or in the real worth of the asset.

Goodwill. It follows from the cost concept that if an entity pays *nothing* for an item it acquires, this item will usually *not* appear on the accounting records as an asset. Thus, the knowledge and skill that is built up as a business operates, the teamwork that grows up within the organization, a favorable location that becomes of increasing importance as time goes on, a good reputation with its customers, trade names developed by the company—none of these appears as an asset in the accounts of the company.

On some accounting reports the term *goodwill* appears. Reasoning from everyday definition of this word, one might conclude that it represents the accountant's appraisal of what the company's name and reputation are worth. This is not so. Goodwill appears in the accounts of a company only when the company has *purchased* some intangible and valuable economic resouce. A common case is when one company buys another company and pays more than the fair value of its tangible assets. The amount by which the purchase price exceeds the value of the tangible assets may be called goodwill, representing the value of the name, reputation, location, or other intangible resources of the purchased company. Unless a business has actually purchased such intangibles, however, no item for "goodwill" is shown in its accounts. If the item does appear, the amount shown initially is the purchase price, even though the management may believe that its real value is considerably higher.

> **Example.** A few years ago, Philip Morris Inc. purchased the Seven-Up Company for $520 million, of which $398 million was for the value of the Seven-Up name and organization. This $398 million was recorded in the Philip Morris accounts as goodwill.

To emphasize the distinction between the accounting concept and the ordinary meaning of value, the term *book value* is used for the historical cost amounts as shown in the accounting records and the term *market value* for the actual value of the asset as reflected in the marketplace.

Rationale for the Cost Concept. The cost concept provides an excellent illustration of the problem of applying the three basic criteria discussed in Chapter 1: relevance, objectivity, and feasibility. If the only criterion were *relevance*, then the cost concept would not be defensible. Clearly, investors and others are more interested in what the business is actually worth today rather than what the assets cost originally.

But who knows what a business is worth today? Any estimate of current value is just that—an estimate—and informed people will disagree on what the estimate should be. For example, on the same day, some people will say that the stock of a given company is overpriced and others will say that it is underpriced. Furthermore, accounting reports are prepared by an organization's management; if these reports contained estimates of what the entity is actually worth, these would be management's estimates. It is quite possible that such estimates would be biased.

The cost concept, by contrast, provides a relatively *objective* foundation for accounting. It is not *purely* objective, for, as we shall see, judgments are necessary in applying it. It is much more objective, however, than the alternative of attempting to estimate current values. Essentially, readers of an accounting report must recognize that it is based on the cost concept, and they must arrive at their own estimate of current value, partly by analyzing the information in the report and partly by using nonaccounting information.

Furthermore, a "market value" or "current worth" concept would be difficult to apply because it would require that the accountant attempt to keep track of the ups and downs of market prices. The cost concept leads to a system that is much more *feasible*.

In summary, adherence to the cost concept indicates a willingness on the part of the accounting profession to sacrifice some degree of relevance in exchange for greater objectivity and greater feasibility.

5. The Dual-Aspect Concept

As stated above, the economic resources of an entity are called assets. The claims of various parties against these assets are called *equities*. There are two types of equities: (1) *liabilities,* which are the claims of creditors, that is, everyone other than the owners of the business; and (2) *owners' equity*, which are the claims of the owners of the business. Since all of the assets of a business are claimed by someone (either by the owners or by creditors), and since the total of these claims cannot exceed the amount of assets to be claimed, it follows that

$$\text{ASSETS} = \text{EQUITIES}$$

This is the fundamental accounting equation, and as we shall see, all accounting procedures are derived from it.

Accounting systems are set up in such a way that a record is made of *two aspects* of each event that affects these records, and in essence these aspects are changes in assets and changes in equities. Because of the two different types of equities, the equation is also often expressed as

$$\text{ASSETS} = \text{LIABILITIES} + \text{OWNERS' EQUITY}$$

Suppose that Ms. Jones starts a business and that her first act is to open a bank account in which she deposits $40,000 of her own money. The dual aspect of this action is that the business now has an asset, cash, of $40,000, and Ms. Jones, the owner,[4] has a claim against this asset, also of $40,000, or

$$\text{Assets (cash), \$40,000} = \text{Equities (owner's), \$40,000}$$

If the business borrowed $15,000 from a bank, the accounting records would show an increase in cash, making the amount $55,000, and a new claim against the assets by the bank in the amount of $15,000. At this point, the accounting records of the business would show the following:

Cash	$55,000	Owed to bank	$15,000
		Owner's equity	40,000
Total assets	$55,000	Total equities	$55,000

Every event recorded in the accounts affects at least two items; there is no conceivable way of making only a single change in the accounts. Accounting is thus properly called a *double-entry system*.

THE BALANCE SHEET

A balance sheet shows the financial position of an accounting entity as of a specified moment of time; in fact, it is sometimes called a *state-*

---

[4]Recall from the entity concept that the accounts of the business are kept separate from those of Ms. Jones as an individual.

ment of financial position.[5] It is therefore a status report, rather than a flow report.

A simplified balance sheet for a corporation is shown in Illustration 2–1. Let us first examine this balance sheet in terms of the basic concepts listed above. The amounts are *expressed in money* and reflect only those matters that can be measured in monetary terms. The *entity* involved is the Garsden Corporation, and the balance sheet pertains to that entity rather than to any of the individuals associated with it. The statement assumes that Garsden Corporation is a *going concern*. The asset amounts stated are governed by the *cost concept*. The *dual-aspect* concept is evident from the fact that the assets listed on the left-hand side of this balance sheet are equal in total to the equities (liabilities and shareholders' equity) listed on the right-hand side.

The two sides *necessarily* add up to the same total because of the dual-aspect concept. This equality does not tell anything about the company's financial health. The label *balance sheet* can give the impression that there is something significant about the fact that the two sides balance. This is not so; the two sides always balance.

In the Garsden Corporation balance sheet, assets are listed on the left and equities on the right. An alternative practice is to list assets at the top of the page and to list equities beneath them. The former format is called the *account* form, and the latter is called the *report* form of balance sheet.

An Overall View   The balance sheet is the fundamental accounting statement in the sense that *every* accounting transaction can be analyzed in terms of its effect on the balance sheet. In order to understand the information a balance sheet conveys and how economic events affect the balance sheet, it is essential that the reader be absolutely clear as to the meaning of its two sides. They can be interpreted in either of two ways, both of which are correct.

Resources and Claims View.   One way has already been indicated. The items listed on the asset side are the economic resources of the entity as of the date of the balance sheet. The amounts stated for each asset are recorded consistent with the basic concepts described above. Equities are claims against the entity as of the balance sheet date. Liabilities are the claims of outside parties—amounts that the entity owes to banks,

---

[5]A balance sheet dated "December 31" is implicitly understood to mean "at the close of business on December 31." Sometimes the identical balance sheet may be dated "January 1," meaning "at the beginning of business on January 1," which from the standpoint of accounting is the same moment of time. Ordinarily, the "close of business" connotation is the correct one because the balance sheet is ordinarily dated as of the end of the year or other period for which accounting reports are prepared.

ILLUSTRATION 2–1

GARSDEN CORPORATION ← | Name of Entity |

Balance Sheet ← | Name of Statement |

As of December 31, 1982 ← | Moment of Time |

Assets

Current assets:		
Cash	$ 3,448,891	
Marketable securities (market value, $248,420)	246,221	
Accounts receivable	5,954,588	
Inventories	12,623,412	
Prepaid expenses	388,960	
Total current assets		$22,651,072
Property, plant, and equipment:		
Land		642,367
Buildings and equipment, at cost	26,303,481	
Less: Accumulated depreciation	13,534,069	
Net property, plant, and equipment		12,769,412
Other assets:		
Investments	110,000	
Intangible assets	63,214	173,214
Total assets		$36,236,065

Liabilities and Shareholders' Equity

Current liabilities:		
Accounts payable	$ 6,301,442	
Taxes payable	1,672,000	
Accrued expenses	640,407	
Deferred revenues	205,240	
Current portion of long-term debt	300,000	
Total current liabilities		$ 9,119,089
Long-term debt		3,000,000
Total liabilities		12,119,089
Shareholders' equity:		
Paid-in capital	5,000,000	
Retained earnings	19,116,976	
Total shareholders' equity		24,116,976
Total liabilities and shareholders equity		$36,236,065

vendors, its employees, and other creditors. The owners' equity shows the claim of the owners.

The fact is, however, that the owners do not have a claim in the same sense that the creditors do. In the Garsden Corporation illustration, it can be said with assurance that the suppliers of Garsden's long-term debt funds had a claim of $3,300,000 as of December 31, 1982—that the corporation owed them $3,300,000, neither more nor less. The amount of $24,116,976 shown as shareholders' equity is more difficult to interpret as a claim, however. If the corporation were liquidated as of December 31, 1982, if the assets were sold for their book value, and if the creditors were paid the $12,119,089 owed them, the shareholders would get what was left, which would be $24,116,976. These conditions are obviously unrealistic. According to the going-concern concept, the corporation is not going to be liquidated; and according to the cost concept, the assets are not shown at their liquidation values. The shareholders' equity might actually be worth considerably more or less than $24,116,976.

The shareholders' equity of a healthy, growing company may be sold for considerably more than the amount shown on the balance sheet; but if a company is liquidated and the assets sold piecemeal, the owners' proceeds often are only a small fraction of stated shareholders' equity. If a bankrupt company's assets are liquidated, it is not unusual for the proceeds to be inadequate to satisfy 100 percent of the creditors' claims, in which case the owners receive nothing.

Sources and Uses of Funds View. Because of the difficulty of understanding the meaning of shareholders' equity as a claim, the second way of interpreting the balance sheet has considerable appeal. In this view the left-hand side of the balance sheet is said to show the forms in which the funds provided to the entity have been invested, or "locked up," as of the date of the balance sheet. On the right-hand side the several liability items describe how much of those funds was obtained from trade creditors (accounts payable), from lenders (long-term debt), and from other creditors. The owners' equity section shows the funds supplied by the owners. If the business is a corporation, the owners are shareholders and their contribution consists of two principal parts: funds directly supplied (paid-in capital) and funds that the shareholders provided by permitting earnings to remain in the business (retained earnings). Both liabilities (especially long-term debt) and owners' equity are often referred to as the business' sources of "capital."

Capital obtained from various sources has been invested according to the management's best judgment of the optimum mix, or combination, of assets for the business. A certain fraction is invested in buildings, another fraction in inventories, another fraction is in the form of cash, and so on. The asset side of the balance sheet therefore shows the result of these management judgments as of the date of the balance sheet.

It should be emphasized that both of these views of the balance sheet are correct. In certain circumstances, the former is easier to understand, and in other circumstances, the latter is easier.

Note, incidentally, that the amounts in Illustration 2–1 are rounded to the nearest dollar. Pennies are rarely shown; and in a large company, the amounts are usually rounded to thousands or even millions of dollars.

Account Categories

Although each individual asset or equity—each building, each piece of equipment, bank loan, and so on—could conceivably be listed separately on the balance sheet, it is more practicable and more informative to summarize and group related items into categories or *account classifications*. There is no fixed pattern as to the number of such categories or the amount of detail reported. Rather, the format is governed by management's opinion as to the most useful way of presenting significant information about the status of the entity.

As in any classification scheme, the categories are defined so that (1) the individual items included in a category resemble one another in essential and significant respects, and (2) the items in one category are essentially different from those in all other categories. Although the items included in a category are similar to one another, they are not identical.

> **Example.** The category labeled *cash* usually includes money on deposit at savings banks as well as money on deposit in checking accounts. These two types of money are *similar* in that they both are in highly liquid form, but they are not *identical* because certain restrictions may apply to withdrawals from savings banks that do not apply to checking accounts. Some companies report cash and marketable securities as a single category, thus combining all of their highly liquid assets into one amount.

The balance sheet in Illustration 2–1 gives a minimum amount of detail. The terms used on this balance sheet are common ones, and they are described briefly below. More detailed descriptions are given in Chapters 5 through 9.

Assets

We shall now supersede the short definition of asset given in the preceding section by the following more exact statement: *Assets are economic resources controlled by an entity whose cost at the time of acquisition can be objectively measured.* The three key points in this definition are the following: (1) an asset must be an economic resource, (2) the resource must be controlled by the entity, and (3) its cost at the time of acquisition must be objectively measurable.

A resource is an *economic* resource if it provides future benefits to the entity. Resources provide future benefits under any of three conditions: (1) they are cash or can be converted to cash, (2) they are goods that are expected to be sold, or (3) they are expected to be used in future activities of the entity. Thus, economic resources either are cash or will eventually result in cash inflows to the entity.

> **Examples.** Garsden Corporation is a manufacturing company. The cash that it has on deposit in banks is an asset because it is money that can be used to acquire other resources. Amounts owned by customers are assets that when collected will generate cash. The goods Garsden has manufactured and still has on hand are assets because it is expected that they will be sold. The equipment and other manufacturing facilities it owns are assets because it is expected that they will be used to produce additional goods. However, merchandise that because of damage or obsolescence cannot be sold is not an asset, even though it is owned by the business, because it will not generate cash.

Control is an accounting concept that is similar to but not quite the same as the legal concept of ownership. When a business buys an automobile on the installment plan, the business may not own the car in the legal sense because title to the car does not pass to the buyer until the last installment has been paid. Nevertheless, if the business is responsible for maintaining and insuring the car, the automobile is regarded as being fully controlled by the business and is an asset. Possession or temporary control is not enough to qualify the item as an asset, however.

> **Examples.** Office space leased on an annual basis is not an asset, nor is an automobile or other piece of equipment that is leased for a relatively short time. In both cases, the entity's control over the use of the item is only temporary. However, if a business leases a building or an item of equipment for a period of time that equals or almost equals its useful life, such an item is an asset, even though the entity does not own it. Goods on consignment are assets of the consignor who owns them, not of the consignee who has possession of them.

The *objective measurability* test is usually clear-cut, but in some instances it is difficult to apply. If the resource was purchased for cash or for the promise to pay cash, it is an asset. If the resource was manufactured by the business, then money was paid for the costs of manufacture, and it is an asset. If the resource was acquired by trading in some other asset or by issuing shares of capital stock, it is an asset. On the other hand, as already pointed out, a valuable reputation is not an asset if it arose gradually over a period of time, rather than being acquired at a specifically measurable cost.

Assets are recorded at their total cost, not the entity's "equity" in them. If a business buys land for $100,000, pays $30,000 cash, and borrows the remaining $70,000, the asset is recorded at $100,000, not $30,000.

On most business balance sheets, assets are listed in decreasing order of their liquidity, that is, in order of the promptness with which they are expected to be converted into cash. On some balance sheets, notably those of public utilities, the order is reversed, and the least liquid assets are listed first.

Assets are customarily grouped into categories. Current assets are almost always reported in a separate category. All noncurrent assets may be grouped together, or various groupings may be used, such as "Property, plant, and equipment" and "Other assets" as shown on the Garsden Corporation balance sheet.

Current Assets.   *Current assets* include cash and other assets that are reasonably expected to be realized in cash or sold or consumed during the normal operating cycle of the entity or within one year, whichever is longer.

The distinction between current assets and noncurrent assets is important since much attention is given by lenders and others to the total of current assets. The essence of the distinction is *time.* Current assets are those resources that are held only for a short period of time. Although the usual time limit is one year, exceptions occur in companies whose normal operating cycle is longer than one year. Tobacco companies and distilleries, for example, include their inventories as current assets even though tobacco and liquor remain in inventory for an aging process that lasts two years or more.

Cash consists of funds that are readily available for disbursement. Most of these funds are on deposit in checking accounts in banks, and the remainder are in cash registers or petty cash boxes on the entity's premises.

Marketable securities are investments that are both readily marketable and are expected to be converted into cash within a year. They are investments made so as to earn some return on cash that otherwise would be temporarily idle.

Accounts receivable are amounts owed to the entity by its customers. Accounts receivable are reported on the balance sheet at the amount owed less an allowance for that portion that probably will not be collected. Methods of estimating this "allowance for doubtful accounts" are described in Chapter 5. An amount owed the entity by someone other than a customer would appear under the heading *other receivables*, rather than accounts receivable. If the amounts owed are evidenced by written promises to pay, they are listed as *notes receivable.*

Inventory means the aggregate of those items of tangible personal property that (1) are held for sale in the ordinary course of business, (2) are in process of production for such sale, or (3) are to be currently consumed in the production of goods or services to be available for sale. Note that inventory relates to goods that will be sold in the ordinary course of business. A truck offered for sale by a truck dealer is inventory. A truck used by the dealer to make service calls is not inventory; it is an item of equipment, which is a noncurrent asset.

The item *prepaid expenses* represents certain assets, usually of an intangible nature, whose usefulness will expire in the near future. An example is an insurance policy. A business pays for insurance protection in advance. Its right to this protection is an asset—a valuable economic resource. Since this right will expire within a fairly short period of time, it is a current asset. The amount on the balance sheet is the future amount of the benefit.

> **Example.** If on January 1, 1983, Garsden Corporation paid $50,000 for insurance protection for two years, the amount of prepaid insurance expense on the December 31, 1983, balance sheet would be $25,000, representing the one year of protection then remaining.

Property, Plant, and Equipment. The category *Property, plant, and equipment* consists of assets that are tangible and relatively long-lived. (The term *fixed assets* is also used for this category.) The organization has acquired these assets, ordinarily, in order to use them to produce goods and services. If the assets are held for resale, they are classified as inventory, even though they are long-lived assets.

In the balance sheet shown in Illustration 2–1, the first item of property, plant, and equipment is land, which is reported at its cost, $642,367. It is shown separately because it is not depreciated, as are buildings and equipment. The first amount shown for buildings and equipment, $26,303,481, is the *original cost* of all the items of tangible long-lived property other than land, that is, the amounts paid to acquire these items. The next item, accumulated depreciation, means that a portion of the original cost of the buildings and equipment, amounting to $13,534,069, has already been allocated as a cost of doing business. Depreciation will be discussed in detail in Chapter 7.

Other Assets. *Investments* are securities of one company owned by another in order either to control the other company or in anticipation of earning a return from the investment. They are therefore to be distinguished from marketable securities, which are a current asset reflecting the temporary use of excess cash.

Intangible assets include goodwill (briefly described earlier in this chapter), patents, copyrights, trademarks, licenses, franchises, and similar valuable but nonphysical things controlled by the business. They are distinguished from prepaid expenses (which are intangible *current* assets) in that they have a longer life span than prepaid expenses.

Liabilities

In general, liabilities are the entity's present obligations to pay money or to provide goods or services in the future. (A few items that may appear in the liabilities section of the balance sheet do not fit this definition. These more complicated items will be discussed in later chapters.) Liability obligations exist as a result of *past* transactions or events.

Thus, on December 31, wages not yet paid to an employee who worked from December 27 to December 31 are a liability; but that person's wages for next week (the first week in January) are not a liability as of December 31.

Liabilities are claims against the entity's assets. Unless otherwise noted, the individual liabilities shown on the balance sheet are not claims against any *specific* asset or group of assets. Thus, although accounts payable typically arise through the purchase of items for inventory, accounts payable are claims against the assets in general, not specifically against inventories. Even if a liability is a claim against a specific asset, as is a mortgage note, it is shown separately on the right-hand side of the balance sheet, rather than as a deduction from the asset amount to which it relates.

Liabilities are reported at the amount owed as of the balance sheet date, including interest accumulated to that date. (Often the accumulated or "accrued" interest is shown separately from the "principal" owed.) Note that it is the total amount owed that is reported, not the portion of that total that is due and payable as of the balance sheet date. A loan is a liability even though there may be no payment due for another 10 years.

Current Liabilities. *Current liabilities* are obligations that are expected to be satisfied either by the use of current assets or by the creation of other current liabilities. The one-year time interval or current operating cycle criterion applies to classifying current liabilities as well as current assets.

Accounts payable represent the claims of suppliers related to goods or services they have furnished to the entity for which they have not yet been paid. Usually these claims are unsecured. Amounts owned to financial institutions (which are suppliers of funds, rather than of goods or services) are called *notes payable, short-term loans,* or some other name that describes the nature of the debt instrument, rather than accounts payable.

Taxes payable is the amount owed government agencies for taxes. It is shown separately from other obligations both because of its size and because the amount owed may not be precisely known as of the date of the balance sheet. Often, the liability for federal and state income taxes is shown separately from other tax liabilities, such as property taxes.

Accrued expenses are the converse of prepaid expenses. They represent valid obligations, but they are not evidenced by an invoice or other document submitted by the person to whom the money is owed. An example is the wages and salaries owed to employees for work they have performed but for which they have not yet been paid.

Deferred revenues represent the liability that arises because the entity has received advance payment for a service it has agreed to render in the future. An example is unearned subscription revenues, which represent magazine subscription payments received in advance, for which the publishing company agrees to deliver issues of its magazine during some future period.

Current portion of long-term debt represents that part of a long-term loan that is due within the next year.

Other Liabilities.   *Other liabilities* are simply those obligations that do not meet the criteria for being classified as current liabilities. They are sometimes therefore called *noncurrent liabilities* or *long-term debt.*

Garsden Corporation has a $3,300,000 loan outstanding. Of this amount, $300,000 is due within the next year and is therefore a current liability. The remaining $3,000,000 is due in some future period beyond the next year (i.e., after December 31, 1983), and is thus shown as long-term debt.

Owners' Equity

The owners' equity section of the balance sheet shows the amount the owners have invested in the entity. The terminology used in this section varies with different forms of organization. In a corporation, the ownership interest is evidenced by shares of stock, and the owners' equity section of its balance sheet is therefore usually labeled *shareholders' equity* or *stockholders' equity.*

Paid-In Capital.   The shareholders' equity is divided into two main categories. The first category, called *paid-in capital* or *contributed capital,* is the amount the owners have invested directly in the business. Paid-in capital in most corporations is further subdivided into *capital stock* and *other* (or *additional*) *paid-in capital.* Each share of stock has a stated or "par" value; capital stock shows this value per share times the number of shares. If investors actually paid more into the corporation than the stated value, the excess is shown separately as other paid-in capital.

> **Example.**   Garsden Corporation has outstanding one million shares of common stock with a stated value of $1 per share. Investors actually paid into the corporation $5 million for these shares. The balance sheet in Illustration 2–1 could be modified to show:

```
Paid-in capital:
   Common stock.....................................  $1,000,000
   Other paid-in capital.............................   4,000,000
      Total paid-in capital.........................               $5,000,000
```

Retained Earnings.   The second category of shareholders' equity is labeled *retained earnings.* The owners' equity increases through *earnings* (i.e., the results of profitable operations) and decreases when earnings are paid out in the form of dividends. The difference between the total earnings to date and the total amount of dividends paid out to the shareholders to date is *retained earnings.* That is, the difference represents that part of the total earnings that have been retained for use in the business.[6] If the difference is negative, the item is labeled *deficit*.

Note that the amount of retained earnings on a given date is the *cumulative* amount that has been retained in the business from the beginning of the corporation's existence up to that date. The amount shown for Garsden Corporation means that since the company began operations, the total amount it has paid out in dividends is $19,116,976 less than the total amount of its earnings.

Note also that the amount of retained earnings does not indicate the *form* in which the earnings were retained. They may be invested in *any* of the resources that appear on the assets side of the balance sheet. (This is true of all equities, not just retained earnings.) We emphasize this fact because there is a common misconception that there is some connection between the amount of retained earnings and the amount of cash. That no such connection exists should be apparent from the fact that the Garsden Corporation balance sheet shows over $19 million of retained earnings but only $3.4 million of cash.

> **Example.** In a magazine article,[7] Philip Moore wrote: "It [General Motors Corporation] has $8 billion of cash surplus on deposit in some 380 banks around the world." When a reader pointed out that the GM balance sheet showed only $550 million of cash as an asset, Moore replied, "The $8 billion figure refers to what I understand to be General Motors' current capital surplus, which I assumed to be either in cash or highly liquid form such as treasury bills, most of which would be on deposit either in cash or as nominee in the 380 banks."[8] If Mr. Moore had taken a course in accounting, he would have realized that "earned surplus" on the equities side of the balance sheet [which was GM's terminology for retained earnings] has no relationship whatsoever to any specific asset, such as cash, or "highly liquid assets."

Other Terms. Instead of "retained earnings," the term *earned surplus* or simply *surplus* was formerly used, and is still used by some companies. The term is misleading, since it connotes something tangible, something "left over." There is, in fact, nothing tangible about retained earnings. All the tangible things owned by the business appear as assets on the balance sheet. It is because of this misleading connotation (illustrated above) that the use of "surplus" is no longer recommended. The word *surplus* is also sometimes used with other modifiers (capital surplus, paid-in surplus) to label the item that is more appropriately called *other paid-in capital*.

---

[6]Shareholders' equity is also affected by events other than the accumulation of earnings and the withdrawal of these earnings. Examples are donations of capital, revaluation of stock, and the creation of special reserves. Some of these events will be discussed in Chapter 9.

[7]"What's Good for the Country Is Good for GM," *Washington Monthly*, December 1970, pp. 10–18.

[8]*Washington Monthly*, March 1971, p. 4.

Net *worth* is another term whose use in financial statements is frowned upon. It is a synonym for "owners' equity," but can be misleading because it implies that the amount indicates what the owners' interest is "worth," which, as has been emphasized above, is erroneous. Nevertheless, the term *net worth* is frequently used in articles and conversation.

Owners' equity is also sometimes called *net assets*, since the amount shown for owners' equity is always equal to assets net of (i.e., minus) liabilities. Similarly, the FASB defines owners' equity simply as "the residual interest in the assets of an entity that remains after deducting its liabilities."[9] The use of the word *residual* reflects the fact that in law, owners' claims rank below creditors' claims. For the same reason, common stock is sometimes referred to as a "residual security."

Unincorporated Businesses. In unincorporated businesses, different terminology is used in the owners' equity section. In a *proprietorship*, a business owned by one person, the owner's equity is customarily shown as a single number with a title such as "John Jones, capital," rather than making a distinction between the owner's initial investment and the accumulated earnings retained in the business.

In a *partnership*, which is an unincorporated business owned jointly by several persons, there is a capital account for each partner, thus:

Jane Davis, capital	$15,432
John Smith, capital	15,432
Total partners' equity	$30,864

A proprietorship or partnership balance sheet also may show a reconciliation of the beginning and ending balance in each owner's capital account. An owner's capital is increased by his or her share of the entity's earnings during the period, and is decreased by the owner's *drawings*. For example, a proprietorship's 1982 year-end balance sheet might show the following:

John Jones, capital, as of January 1, 1982	$80,000
Add: 1982 earnings	35,000
Deduct: 1982 drawings	(24,000)
John Jones, capital, as of December 31, 1982	$91,000

The reader may have heard of the terms *partnership accounting* and *corporation accounting*, and may have formed the impression that different accounting systems are used for different forms of business organizations. This is not so. The treatment of assets and liabilities is generally the same in all forms of business organizations; differences occur principally in the owners' equity section, as noted above. Nonbusiness

[9]FASB, *Statement of Financial Accounting Concepts No. 3*, par. 43.

organizations do treat certain items differently than businesses, but these differences are beyond the scope of this book.

CURRENT RATIO

In using financial statement information, it often is helpful to express certain important relationships as ratios or percentages. Some of these ratios will be introduced at appropriate places throughout the book, and they will be summarized in Chapter 13. A *ratio* is simply one number expressed in terms of another. It is found by dividing one number, the base, into the other. Since Garsden Corporation (Illustration 2–1) had current assets of $22,651,072 and current liabilities of $9,119,089, the ratio of its current assets to its current liabilities was $22,651,072 ÷ $9,119,089, or 2.5 to 1.

The ratio of current assets to current liabilities is called the *current ratio*. It is an important indication of an entity's ability to meet its current obligations, for if current assets do not exceed current liabilities by a comfortable margin, the entity may be unable to pay its current bills. This is because most current assets are expected to be converted into cash within a year or less, whereas most current liabilities are obligations expected to use cash within a year or less. As a very rough rule of thumb, a current ratio of at least 2 to 1 is believed to be desirable in a typical manufacturing company.

BALANCE SHEET CHANGES

At the moment an entity begins, its financial status can be recorded on a balance sheet. From that time on, events occur that change the numbers on this first balance sheet, and the accountant records these changes in accordance with the concepts given earlier in this chapter. Accounting systems accumulate and summarize these changes as a basis for preparing new balance sheets at prescribed intervals, such as the end of a quarter or a year. Each balance sheet shows the financial condition of the entity as of the date it was prepared, after giving effect to all of these changes.

Although in practice a balance sheet is prepared only at prescribed intervals, in learning the accounting process it is useful to consider the changes one by one. This makes it possible to study the effect of individual events without getting entangled with the mechanisms used to record these events. The technical name given to an event that affects an accounting number is *transaction*. Examples of the effects of a few transactions on the balance sheet will now be given. For simplicity, they are assumed to occur on successive days.

Original Capital Contribution

Jan. 1   John Smith starts a record and tape store, called Music Mart, by depositing $25,000 of his own funds in a bank account that he has opened in the name of the business entity. The balance sheet of Music Mart will then be as follows:

MUSIC MART
Balance Sheet
As of January 1

Assets		Equities	
Cash	$25,000	John Smith, capital	$25,000

Bank Loan

Jan. 2.   Music Mart borrows $12,500 from a bank, giving a note therefor. This transaction increases the asset cash, and the business incurs a liability to the bank called notes payable. The balance sheet after this transaction will appear thus:

MUSIC MART
Balance Sheet
As of January 2

Assets		Equities	
Cash	$37,500	Notes payable	$12,500
		John Smith, capital	25,000
Total	$37,500	Total	$37,500

Purchase of Merchandise

Jan. 3.   The business buys inventory (merchandise it intends to sell) in the amount of $5,000, paying cash. The balance sheet is as follows:

MUSIC MART
Balance Sheet
As of January 3

Assets		Equities	
Cash	$32,500	Notes payable	$12,500
Inventory	5,000	John Smith, capital	25,000
Total	$37,500	Total	$37,500

Sale of Merchandise

Jan. 4.   The store sells for $750 cash, merchandise that cost $500. The effect of this transaction is to decrease inventory by $500, increase cash by $750, and increase John Smith's own equity by the difference, or $250. The $250 is the profit on this sale. The balance sheet will then look like this:

MUSIC MART
Balance Sheet
As of January 4

Assets		Equities	
Cash	$33,250	Notes payable	$12,500
Inventory	4,500	John Smith, capital	25,250
Total	$37,750	Total	$37,750

This was an *earnings* transaction. In contrast with the transactions on January 2 and 3, which resulted in changes in asset and liability amounts but not in the owner's equity, this transaction resulted in changes in both asset amounts and owner's equity. As the balance sheet shows, the sale increased John Smith's capital by $250. The balance sheet does not explain how this change came about. Such an explanation is provided by the *income statement*, which will be described in Chapter 3.

Concluding Comment

In subsequent chapters we shall expand considerably on the concepts and terms introduced here. We shall describe modifications and qualifications to certain of the basic concepts, and we shall introduce many additional terms that are used on balance sheets. We shall not, however, discard the basic structure that was introduced in this chapter. Furthermore, it is important to remember that *every* accounting transaction can be recorded in terms of its effect on the balance sheet. The reader should be able to relate all the new material to this basic structure.

SUMMARY

The basic concepts discussed in this chapter may be briefly summarized as follows:

1. *Money measurement.* Accounting records only those facts that can be expressed in monetary terms.
2. *Entity.* Accounts are kept for entities as distinguished from the persons associated with those entities.
3. *Going concern.* Accounting assumes that an entity will continue to exist indefinitely and that it is not about to be liquidated.
4. *Cost.* An asset is ordinarily entered in the accounts at the amount paid to acquire it; and this cost, rather than current market value, is the basis for subsequent accounting for the asset.
5. *Dual aspect.* The total amount of assets equals the total amount of equities. Equities include liabilities and owners' equity.

The balance sheet shows the financial condition of an entity as of a specified moment in time. It consists of two sides. The assets side shows the economic resources that are expected to provide future benefits to the business and that were acquired at objectively measureable amounts. The equities side shows the liabilities, which are obligations of the business, and the owners' equity, which are amounts invested by the owners. Equities are claims against the business as a whole, not against specified assets.

Each transaction can be recorded in terms of its balance sheet effect in such a way that the basic equation, Assets = Equities, is always maintained.

SUGGESTIONS FOR FURTHER READING ON ACCOUNTING PRINCIPLES
(For Chapters 2–14)

There are several excellent textbooks, any of which may be useful either for additional information or to obtain a different viewpoint on topics discussed here. In addition, the following are useful:

Burton, John C., et al. *Handbook of Accounting and Auditing.* Boston: Warren, Gorham & Lamont, 1981.

Kohler, Eric L. *A Dictionary for Accountants.* 5th ed. Englewood Cliffs, N.J.: Prentice-Hall, 1975. Much more than a dictionary, it contains a good discussion of many terms and concepts, and because of its dictionary format provides a quick way of locating desired information.

Seidler, Lee J., and D. R. Carmichael, eds. *Accountants' Handbook.* 6th ed. New York: Ronald Press, 1981.

Publications of the **Financial Accounting Standards Board** and the **U.S. Securities and Exchange Commission** referred to in Chapter 1 are important sources of the latest information on what constitutes "generally accepted accounting principles." Several publishers offer comprehensive volumes that include summaries of FASB pronouncements, together with helpful indexes and cross-references. Some of these volumes are in loose-leaf form, with the publisher providing a monthly updating service; others are revised annually.

Cases

CASE 2–1   Saunders Company (A)

Helen Saunders made the following request of a friend:

> My bookkeeper has quit, and I need to see the balance sheets of my company. She has left behind a book with the numbers already entered in it. Would you be willing to prepare balance sheets for me? Also, any comments you care to make about the numbers would be appreciated. The Cash account is healthy, which is a good sign, and she has told me that the net income in May was $5,030.

The book contained a detailed record of transactions, and from it the friend was able to copy off the balances at the beginning of the month and at the end of the month as shown in Exhibit 1. Helen Saunders owned all the stock of Saunders Company.

Questions

1. Prepare balance sheets as of May 1 and as of May 31, in proper format.
2. Make such comments as you can about how the financial condition as of the end of May compared with that at the beginning of May.
3. Why does retained earnings not increase by the amount of May net income?
4. How much do you feel Saunders Company is worth as of May 31?

EXHIBIT 1

Account Balances

	May 1	May 31
Accounts payable	$ 1,684	$ 5,465
Accounts receivable	5,589	6,681
Accrued wages payable	256	449
Accumulated depreciation on building	40,000	40,500
Accumulated depreciation on equipment	1,360	1,520
Bank notes payable	2,000	7,500
Building	150,000	150,000
Capital stock	100,000	100,000
Cash	7,470	16,749
Equipment (at cost)	3,400	9,400
Land	23,000	23,000
Merchandise inventory	7,650	6,800
Note receivable, Helen Saunders	3,000	0
Other assets	1,245	1,350
Other liabilities	128	128
Prepaid insurance	600	550
Retained earnings	56,786	58,816
Supplies on hand	1,300	1,700
Taxes payable	1,040	1,852

CASE 2–2   Music Mart

On a sheet of paper, set up in pencil the balance sheet of Music Mart as it appears after the last transaction described in the text (January 4), leaving considerable space between each item. Record the effect, if any, of the following events on the balance sheet, either by revising existing figures (cross out, rather than erase) or by adding new items as necessary. At least one of these events does not affect the balance sheet. The basic equation, Assets = Equities, must be preserved at all times. Errors will be minimized if you make a separate list of the balance sheet items affected by each transaction and the amount (+ or −) by which each is to be changed.

After you have recorded these events, prepare a balance sheet in proper form. Assume that all these transactions occurred in January and that there were no other transactions in January.

1. The store purchased and received merchandise for inventory for $4,000, agreeing to pay within 30 days.
2. Merchandise costing $1,200 was sold for $1,900, which was received in cash.
3. Merchandise costing $1,500 was sold for $2,250, the customers agreeing to pay $2,250 within 30 days.
4. The store purchased a three-year fire insurance policy for $600, paying cash.
5. The store purchased two lots of land of equal size for a total of $20,000. It paid $4,000 in cash and gave a 10-year mortgage for $16,000.

6. The store sold one of the two lots of land for $10,000. It received $2,000 cash, and in addition, the buyer assumed $8,000 of the mortgage; that is, Music Mart became no longer responsible for this half.

7. Smith received a bona fide offer of $35,000 for the business; and although his equity was then only $26,700, he rejected the offer. It was evident that the store had already acquired goodwill of $8,300.

8. Smith withdrew $1,200 cash from the store's bank account for his personal use.

9. Smith took merchandise costing $500 from the store's inventory for his personal use.

10. Smith learned that the man who purchased the land (No. 6 above) subsequently sold it for $12,000. The lot still owned by Music Mart was identical in value with this other plot.

11. The store paid off $5,000 of its note payable (disregard interest).

12. Music Mart was changed to a corporation, Music Mart, Inc. Smith received common stock with a par value of $25,000 in exchange for his equity in the store. (Disregard costs of organizing the corporation. Note that this event creates a new entity.)

13. Smith sold one fourth of the stock he owned in Music Mart, Inc., for $7,800 cash.

14. Merchandise costing $750 was sold for $1,150, which was received in cash.

CASE 2–3   Cascade Cafe (A)*

On March 31, 1983, the partnership that had been organized to operate the Cascade Cafe was dissolved under unusual circumstances; and in connection with its dissolution, preparation of a balance sheet became necessary.

The partnership was formed by Mr. and Mrs. Frank Rayburn and Mrs. Grace Harris, who had become acquainted while working in a Portland, Oregon, restaurant. On November 1, 1982, each of the three partners contributed $9,000 cash to the partnership. The Rayburns' contribution represented practically all of their savings. Mrs. Harris' payment was the proceeds of her late husband's insurance policy.

On that day also the partnership signed a one-year lease to the Cascade Cafe, located in a nearby recreational area. The monthly rent on the cafe was $1,100. This facility attracted the partners in part because there were living accommodations on the floor above the restaurant. One room was occupied by the Rayburns and another by Mrs. Harris.

The partners borrowed $11,000 from a local bank and used this plus $21,400 of partnership funds to buy out the previous operator of the cafe. Of this amount, $30,600 was for equipment and $1,800 was for the food and beverages then on hand. The partnership paid $430 for local operating licenses, good for one year be-

*Based on a case decided by the Supreme Court of the State of Oregon (216 P2d 1005).

ginning November 1, and paid $900 for a new cash register. The remainder of the $38,000 was deposited in a checking account.

Shortly after November 1, the partners opened the restaurant. Mr. Rayburn was the cook, and Mrs. Rayburn and Mrs. Harris waited on customers. Mrs. Rayburn also ordered the food, beverages, and supplies, operated the cash register, and was responsible for the checking account.

The restaurant operated throughout the winter season of 1982–83. It was not very successful. On the morning of March 31, 1983, Mrs. Rayburn discovered that Mr. Rayburn and Mrs. Harris had disappeared. Mrs. Harris had taken all her possessions, but Mr. Rayburn had left behind most of his clothing, presumably because he could not remove it without warning Mrs. Rayburn. The new cash register and its contents were also missing. Mrs. Rayburn concluded that the partnership was dissolved. (The court subsequently affirmed that the partnership was dissolved as of March 30.)

Mrs. Rayburn decided to continue operating the Cascade Cafe. She realized that an accounting would have to be made as of March 30 and called in Frank Whittaker, an acquaintance who was knowledgeable about accounting.

In response to Mr. Whittaker's questions, Mrs. Rayburn said that the cash register had contained $198 and that the checking account balance was $662. Ski instructors who were permitted to charge their meals had run up accounts totaling $517. (These accounts subsequently were paid in full.) Cascade Cafe owed suppliers amounts totaling $943. Mr. Whittaker estimated that depreciation on the assets amounted to $1,440.

Food and beverages on hand were estimated to be worth $1,450. During the period of its operation, the partners drew salaries at agreed-upon amounts, and these payments were up to date. The clothing that Mr. Rayburn left behind was estimated to be worth $540. The partnership had also repaid $900 of the bank loan.

Mr. Whittaker explained that in order to account for the partners' equity, he would prepare a balance sheet. He would list the items that the partnership owned as of March 30, subtract the amounts that it owed to outside parties, and the balance would be the equity of the three partners. Each partner would be entitled to one third of this amount.

Questions

1. Prepare a balance sheet for the Cascade Cafe as of November 2, 1982.
2. Prepare a balance sheet as of March 30, 1983.
3. Disregarding the marital complications, do you suppose that the partners received the equity determined in Question 2? Why?

CASE 2–4   Early Years Day Care Center

After six months of operations, Mrs. Frances Nissen wanted to analyze the performance of Early Years Day Care Center. She wanted to know where the company stood as of December 31, 1982, and what its future prospects were.

Early Years Day Care Center was a company organized by Mrs. Nissen early in 1982 to provide supervised care, preschool education, a snack, and a noonday meal primarily for children of working mothers. For its initial capital, Mrs. Nissen took out a $24,000 mortgage on her own house. She invested $21,000 of this in common stock of the center. Friends of hers invested $11,000 in cash, receiving stock in return. A government agency made a one-year loan of $6,500 to the center.

With these funds, the center purchased property for $40,000, of which $8,000 was for land and $32,000 was for a building on the land. The purchase was financed in part with a $27,000 mortgage, the remainder being paid in cash. Interest on the mortgage was to be paid quarterly, but no principal repayment was required until the company had become established. The center also purchased $13,200 of furniture and equipment for cash.

During the first six months of operations, which ended December 31, 1982, the center paid out the following additional amounts in cash:

Salary* to Mrs. Nissen	$ 8,000
Salaries* of part-time employees	5,120
Insurance (one-year policy)	1,340
Utilities	1,019
Food and supplies	4,370
Interest and miscellaneous	3,642
Total paid out	$23,491

*Includes payroll taxes.

The center received $16,880 student fees in cash. In addition, parents owed the center $600 for student fees. As of December 31, 1982, Mrs. Nissen estimated that $320 of supplies were still on hand. The center owed food suppliers $520.

In thinking about the future, Mrs. Nissen estimated that for the next six months, ending June 30, student fees received (in addition to the $600 student fees that applied to the first six months) would be $25,600. This was higher than the amount for the first six months because enrollments were higher.

She estimated that the center would pay $13,120 for salaries; $1,280 cash for utilities (which was higher than the first six months because of expected colder weather); $5,600 for additional food and supplies (higher because of the higher enrollment); and $2,720 for interest and miscellaneous (lower than the first six months because certain start-up costs were paid for during the first six months). She also expected to pay back the government loan.

She estimated that supplies on hand as of June 30 would be $320 and that nothing would be owed suppliers. She did not include any additional amounts for insurance or taxes because the amounts paid in the first six months covered these costs for the whole year.

She knew that many companies recorded depreciation on buildings, furniture, and equipment; however, she had a firm offer of $56,000 cash for these assets from someone who wanted to buy the center, so she thought that under these circumstances depreciation was inappropriate.

Questions

1. Prepare a balance sheet for Early Years Day Care Center as of December 31. (In order to minimize errors, it is suggested that you treat each event separately; show the items that are affected and the amount of increase or decrease in each item. For events that affect shareholders' equity, other than the initial investment, increase or decrease the item "Retained earnings."

This item will have a minus amount, which should be indicated by enclosing it in parentheses. Show noncurrent assets at their original cost.)

2. Prepare another balance sheet as of the following June 30.

3. Should the noncurrent assets be reported on the December 31 balance sheet at their cost, at $56,000, or at some other amount (the amount need not be calculated)? If at some amount other than cost, how would the balance sheet prepared in Question 1 be changed?

4. Does it appear likely that Early Years Day Care Center will become a viable company; that is, is it likely to be profitable if Mrs. Nissen's estimates are correct?

3

Basic Accounting Concepts:
The Income Statement

This chapter introduces the idea of income as used in financial accounting and describes the income statement, the financial statement that reports income and its determinants.

In the course of this discussion, the last 6 of the 11 basic concepts listed in Chapter 2 are explained, namely:

6.	Time period.	9.	Matching.
7.	Conservatism.	10.	Consistency.
8.	Realization.	11.	Materiality.

As was the case in Chapter 2, the discussion of topics in this chapter is introductory. Each will be explained in more depth in later chapters.

THE NATURE OF INCOME

Chapter 2 described the balance sheet, which reports the financial condition of an entity as of one moment in time. Chapter 3 describes a second financial statement, the income statement, which summarizes the results of operations for a period of time. It is therefore a *flow* report, as contrasted with the balance sheet, which is a *status* report. These two financial statements illustrate the only two ways in which any entity can be described, whether it be a business, a human body, or the universe: (1) in terms of flows through time and (2) in terms of its status or state as of one moment of time.

55

Flows in a business are continuous. Their essential nature, in many businesses, is indicated by the simplified diagram in Illustration 3–1. The business has a pool of cash that it has obtained from investors or from past profitable operations. It uses these funds to acquire inventories, either by purchasing goods from others or by producing them itself. It also incurs other costs. (Accounts payable and various other assets and liability accounts may intervene between the incurrence of these costs and the cash outflow to pay for them.) It sells the goods to customers. The customers either pay cash or, in many businesses, agree to pay later, thus creating accounts receivable. When the customer pays, the pool of cash is replenished.

ILLUSTRATION 3–1
BASIC BUSINESS FINANCIAL FLOWS

For most types of businesses, the income statement focuses on the section of the flow diagram that is labeled *selling activities*. It reports the nature and magnitude of these activities for a specified period of time. Essentially, this report consists of two elements. One reports the inflows that result from the sale of goods and services to customers; these amounts are called *revenues*. The other reports the outflows that were made in order to generate these revenues; these are called *expenses*. *Income* is the amount by which revenues exceed expenses. Since the word *income* is often used with various qualifying adjectives, the term *net income* is used to refer to the net excess of all the revenues over all the expenses. Some companies use the term *net earnings* rather than net income. If total expenses exceed total revenues, the difference is a *net loss*.

THE TIME PERIOD CONCEPT

It is relatively easy to measure net income for the whole life of an organization. This is simply the difference between the money that comes in and the money that goes out (excluding, of course, money invested by the owners or paid to the owners).

Example. Mr. and Mrs. John Wainwright operated a boys' camp for one summer, renting all the necessary facilities and equipment. Before the camp opened, they invested $8,000 for food, the initial rental payment, and certain other costs. At the end of the summer, after all affairs were wound up, they had the $8,000 back and $5,079 additional. This $5,079 was the net income of the camp business. It was the difference between the revenues they received from parents and the expenses incurred for food, wages, and other costs. The income statement for the business looked like this:

Revenues		$40,800
Less expenses:		
Food	$14,252	
Wages	15,645	
Rental	4,000	
Other costs	1,824	
Total expenses		35,721
Net income		$ 5,079

Relatively few business ventures have a life of only a few months, as was the case with the Wainwright summer camp. Most of them operate for many years. Indeed, in accordance with the going-concern concept, it is usually assumed that the life of a business is indefinitely long. Management and other interested parties are unwilling to wait until the business has terminated before obtaining information on how much income has been earned. They need to know at frequent intervals "how things are going."

This need leads to the *time period concept:* accounting measures activities for a specified interval of time, called the *accounting period.* For the purpose of reporting to outsiders, one year is the usual accounting period. Pacioli, the first author of an accounting text, wrote in 1494: "Books should be closed each year, especially in a partnership, because frequent accounting makes for long friendship."[1] Most corporate bylaws require an annual report to the shareholders, and income tax reporting is also on an annual basis.

In the majority of businesses, the accounting year, or *fiscal year,* corresponds to the calendar year; but many businesses use the *natural business year* instead of the calendar year. For example, nearly all department stores end their fiscal year on January 31, which is after the Christmas rush and its repercussions in the form of returns and clearance sales.

---

[1]Lucas Pacioli, *Summa de Arithmetica Geometria Proportioni et Proportionalita,* from the translation by John B. Geijsbeck.

Interim Reports. Management invariably needs information more often than once a year. Income statements for management are therefore prepared more frequently. The most common period is a month, but the period may be as short as a week or even a day. The Securities and Exchange Commission requires quarterly income statements from companies over which it has jurisdiction. These reports are called *interim* reports to distinguish them from the annual reports.

Businesses are living, ongoing organisms. The act of chopping the continuous stream of business events into time periods is therefore somewhat arbitrary, since business activities do not stop or change measurably as one accounting period ends and another begins. It is this fact that makes the problem of measuring income for an accounting period the most difficult problem in accounting.

> **Example.** If instead of a summer camp the Wainwrights operated a year-round hotel, their income for a year could not be measured simply as the difference between the money taken in and the money paid out. As of the end of the year, some of the guests would not have paid their bills. Yet these unpaid bills are an asset, accounts receivable, that surely increases the "well-offness" of the business even though the cash has not yet been received. Conversely, some of the cash paid out may have been for the purchase of an asset, such as the hotel itself, that will benefit the business beyond the end of this accounting period. It would be incorrect to conclude that the hotel's income has been decreased by the amount of such payments.

Relation between Income and Owners' Equity

As explained in Chapter 2, the net income of an accounting period increases owners' equity. In order to understand the implication of this relationship, let us refer back to the January 4 transaction of Music Mart (page 45). On that day, merchandise costing $500 was sold for $750 cash. Looking first at the effect of this transaction on assets, we note that although inventory decreased by $500, cash increased by $750, so that the total assets increased by the difference, $250. From the dual-aspect concept, which states that the total of the assets must always equal the total of the equities, we know that the equities side of the balance sheet must also have increased by $250. Since no liabilities were affected, the increase must have occurred in owner's equity. In summary, because assets were sold for more than was paid for them, the owner's equity increased. Such net increases in owner's equity are called *income*.

In understanding how this income came about, it is useful to consider two aspects of this event separately: the $750 received from the sale and the $500 decrease in inventory. If we look only at the $750, we see that it is an increase in cash and a corresponding *increase* in owner's equity. The $500, taken by itself, is a decrease in the asset, inventory, and a corresponding *decrease* in owner's equity. These two aspects illustrate the only two ways in which business operations can affect owner's equity: they can increase it or they can decrease it.

Revenues and Expenses.   It follows that revenues and expenses can also be defined in terms of their effect on owners' equity: a *revenue* is an increase in owners' equity resulting from the operations of the entity, and an *expense* is a decrease. Restating the transactions described above in these terms, there was revenue of $750, expense of $500, and income of $250.

The basic equation is:

$$\text{REVENUES} - \text{EXPENSES} = \text{NET INCOME}$$

This equation clearly indicates that income is a *difference*. Sometimes the word *income* is used improperly as a synonym for *revenue*. This is because the approved definitions as given above are of relatively recent origin and some companies have not kept up with the latest developments. For example, Federal-Mogul Corporation reported total "income" in 1981 of $837,367,000; the term should have been "revenues." (Federal-Mogul also used the caption "deductions from income," instead of "expenses.")

On an income statement, no misunderstanding is caused by such an error because revenues, however labeled, appear at the top and income at the bottom. But in other contexts, confusion can be created. For example, if one reads that Company X had an income of a million dollars, a completely false impression of the size of the company is given if the intended meaning was that Company X had *revenues* of a million dollars.[2]

Income Not the Same as Cash Receipts

It is extremely important to understand that the income of a period is associated with changes in owners' equity, and that it has no necessary relation to changes in cash during that period. Income connotes "well-offness." Roughly speaking, the bigger the income, the better off are the owners. An increase in cash, however, does not necessarily mean that the owners are any better off—that their equity has increased. The increase in cash may merely be offset by a decrease in some other asset or by an increase in a liability, with no effect on owners' equity at all.

Again, reference to the transactions of Music Mart may help to clarify this point. When Music Mart borrowed $12,500 from the bank on January 2 (page 45), its cash was increased; but this was exactly matched by an increase in liability to the bank. There was no change in owner's equity. No income resulted from this transaction. The $12,500 was not revenue. Similarly, the purchase of inventory for $5,000 cash on January

---

[2]The income tax Form 1040 still contains the phrases *dividend income* and *interest income* for items that actually are revenues.

3 resulted in a decrease in cash; but there was an exactly corresponding increase in another asset, inventory. Owner's equity was not changed.

As we have already seen, the sale for $750 of inventory costing $500 *did* result in income. But it should be noted that the income was $250, whereas cash increased by $750; so even here the income is different from the amount by which the cash increased. In short, although individuals typically measure their personal income by the amount of money they receive, this concept of income is not correct when applied to a business entity.

THE CONSERVATISM CONCEPT

Managers are human beings, and like most humans they would like to give a favorable report on how well the entity for which they are responsible has performed. Accounting principles have safeguards designed to offset this natural tendency to be optimistic. The idea behind these principles is that recognition of increases in an entity's equity (that is, revenues) require better evidence than recognition of decreases (that is, expenses). This is the *conservatism concept*.

Let us consider the revenue aspect first. If in December 1982, Lynn Jones agrees to buy an automobile from Ace Auto Company for delivery in February 1983, this is good news to Ace Auto Company. It is possible, however, that something will go wrong and the sale will not be consummated. Accounting principles require better evidence than the agreement to buy the automobile. Accounting requires that the revenue not be recorded, that is, *recognized*, until the period in which the automobile is actually delivered. Thus, Ace Auto Company does not recognize revenue from this transaction in 1982. Rather, if the automobile is actually delivered in 1983, revenue is recognized in 1983.

Expenses, however, are viewed differently. Suppose an uninsured automobile disappears from the Ace Auto Company premises in December 1982. Possibly, it will be recovered; possibly, it has been stolen and is gone forever. In the latter case, Ace Auto's equity has decreased; it has incurred an expense. Suppose that Ace Auto is not reasonably certain that the auto is gone forever until early 1983. Nevertheless, the conservatism concept requires that the expense be recognized in 1982, the year in which it became reasonably *possible* that there was an expense, rather than in 1983, the year in which the decrease in owners' equity became reasonably *certain*.

As another example, consider the amount reported as inventory. If in 1983 an entity learns that the selling price of certain goods in its inventory has declined to less than the cost of these goods, a loss (i.e., an expense) is recognized in 1983, even though in actual fact prices may rise again and the goods may be sold in 1984 at a profit. This is because it is reasonably possible that owners' equity has been reduced in 1983.

If, however, the entity learns in 1983 that the selling price of other goods in its inventory has *increased*, the expected increase in profit is *not* recognized in 1983. It is not reasonably certain that the goods will eventually be sold at the higher price.

The conservatism concept therefore has two aspects:

1. Recognize *revenues* (that is, increases in owners' equity) only when they are *reasonably certain*.
2. Recognize *expenses* (that is, decreases in owners' equity) as soon as they are *reasonably possible*.

There are obvious problems in deciding what is meant by "reasonably certain" and "reasonably possible" in various situations, and accounting principles give guidance for many specific problems. For example, the principle that revenue is recognized in the period in which goods are delivered applies to most sales transactions because this is the earliest period in which it is reasonably certain that revenue has been earned.

Application to Revenue Recognition

In general, revenue from the sale of goods is recognized in the period in which goods were delivered to customers. Revenue from the performance of services is recognized in the period in which the services were performed. For many events, cash is received at the time of delivery or performance, and this is excellent evidence that the revenue has been earned. This is the case with most supermarkets, and for many transactions in other retail stores and service firms. It can happen, however, that the cash is received in either an earlier period or a later period than that in which the revenue is recognized. Examples of each are given below.

Precollected Revenue. Magazine companies sell subscriptions that the subscriber pays for in advance; that is, the company receives the cash *before* it renders the service of providing the magazine. Referring to Illustration 3–2, if subscription money is received this year for magazines to be delivered next year, the revenue belongs in next year. The money received is therefore recorded not as revenue for this year but rather as a liability on the balance sheet as of the end of this year. The

ILLUSTRATION 3–2

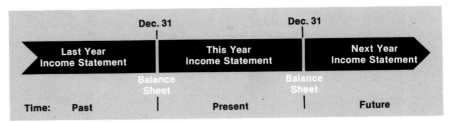

liability, *deferred revenue*, represents the claim that subscribers have to receive the magazine next year. Similarly, rent on property is often paid in advance. When this happens, the revenue is properly recognized in the period in which the services of the rented property are provided, not the period in which the rent payment is received. In sum, precollected revenues have been *paid to* the entity, but have not as yet been *earned by* the entity.

Accounts Receivable. The converse of the above situation is illustrated by sales made on credit; that is, the customer agrees to pay for the goods or services sometime *after* the date on which they are actually received. The revenue is recognized in the period in which the sale is made. If the payment is not due until the following period, an asset, accounts receivable, is shown on the balance sheet as of the end of the current period. When customers pay their bills, the amount received is not revenue. Rather, it reduces the amount of accounts receivable outstanding and increases cash, leaving owners' equity unaffected.

The difference between revenue and receipts is illustrated in the following tabulation, which shows various types of sales transactions and classifies the effect of each on cash receipts and sales revenue for "this year":

			This Year	
	Amount	Cash Receipts	Sales Revenue
1. Cash sales made this year...............	$200	$200	$200
2. Credit sales made last year; cash received this year....................	300	300	0
3. Credit sales made this year; cash received this year....................	400	400	400
4. Credit sales made this year; cash received next year...................	100	0	100
Total		$900	$700

Note that in this illustration total cash receipts do not equal total sales revenue for the year. The totals would be equal in a given accounting period only (1) if the company made all its sales for cash, or (2) if the amount of cash collected from credit customers in the accounting period happened by chance to equal the amount of credit sales made during that period.

Accrued Revenue. When a bank lends money, it is providing a service to the borrower, namely, the use of the money. The bank's charge for this service is called *interest*, and the amount the bank earns is *interest revenue*. The bank earns interest revenue on each day that the borrower is permitted to use the money. For some loan transactions, the borrower does not pay the interest in the year in which the money was used but rather pays it next year. Even if this interest payment is not made until next year, the bank has earned revenue this year for a loan outstanding during the year. The amount earned but unpaid as of the end of this year is an asset on the bank's balance sheet called *accrued interest revenue*. It is similar to an account receivable. In sum, accrued revenue is the reverse of precollected revenue: accrued revenues have been *earned by* the entity but have not as yet been *paid to* the entity.

THE REALIZATION CONCEPT

The conservatism concept suggests the period *when* revenue should be recognized. Another concept, the realization concept, indicates in addition the *amount* of revenue that should be recognized from a given sale.

Realization refers to inflows of cash or claims to cash (e.g., accounts receivable) arising from the sale of services or assets (including, but not limited to, inventories of salable goods). Thus, if a customer buys $50 worth of items at a grocery store, paying cash, the store *realizes* $50 from the sale. If a company sells a 20-year-old machine as scrap metal for $300, the purchaser agreeing to pay within 30 days, the company *realizes* $300 (in receivables) from the sale.

The *realization concept* states that (1) revenues are usually recognized in the period in which goods were delivered to customers or in which services were rendered, and (2) the amount recognized as revenue is the amount that is reasonably certain to be realized. There is room for differences of judgment as to how certain "reasonably certain" is; but the concept does indicate clearly that the amount of revenue recorded may be less than the sales value of the goods and services sold. One obvious situation is the sale of merchandise at a discount, that is, at an amount that is less than its normal price. In such cases, revenue is recorded at the lower amount, not the normal price.

> **Example.** Most stereo receivers have a list price that is quoted in the manufacturer's catalog and set forth in advertisements. Many dealers sell receivers at less than the list price. In these circumstances, revenue is the amount at which the sale is made, rather than the list price. If the list price is $250 and the receiver is actually sold for $210, the revenue is $210.

A less obvious situation arises with the sale of merchandise on credit. When a company makes a credit sale, it expects that the customer will pay the bill. Experience may indicate, however, that not all customers do pay their bills. In measuring the revenue for a period, the amount of sales made on credit should be reduced by the estimated amount of credit sales that will never be realized, that is, by the estimated amount of *bad debts*.

> **Example.** If a store makes credit sales of $100,000 during a period, and if experience indicates that 5 percent of credit sales will eventually become bad debts, the amount of revenue for the period is $95,000, not $100,000.

Although conceptually the estimated amount of bad debts is part of the calculation of revenue, in practice this amount is often treated as an expense. Thus, in the example above, revenue is often reported as $100,000 and there is an expense, bad debt expense, of $5,000. The effect on net income is the same as if the revenue were reported as $95,000.

RECOGNITION OF EXPENSES

Terminology

In discussing the period in which an *expense* is recognized (i.e., recorded), we shall use four terms whose meanings must be kept clear: cost, expenditure, expense, and disbursement.

Cost is the amount of resources used for any purpose. The costs of goods and services acquired in an accounting period are either assets or they are expenses.

An *expenditure* is a decrease in an asset (usually cash) or an increase in a liability (often accounts payable) associated with the incurrence of a cost. The expenditures in an accounting period equal the cost of the goods and services acquired in that period.

An *expense* is an item of cost applicable to the current accounting period. An expense represents resources consumed during the current period. When an expenditure is made, the related cost is either an asset or an expense. If the cost benefits future periods, it is an asset. If not, it is an expense of the current period.

A *disbursement* is the payment of cash.

> **Example.** If an item of inventory costing $1,000 is received in March, if the vendor is paid in April, and if the item is shipped to a customer in May, then there is a cost of $1,000 and an expenditure of $1,000 in March, a disbursement of $1,000 in April, and an expense of $1,000 in May.

The Matching Concept

As noted earlier, the sale of merchandise has two aspects: (1) a revenue aspect, reflecting the increase in owners' equity in the amount realized; and (2) an expense aspect, reflecting the decrease in owners' equity because the merchandise has gone out of the business. Correct measurement of the net effect of this sale on owners' equity in a period requires that both of these aspects be recognized in the same accounting period. This leads to the matching concept: *When a given event affects both revenues and expenses, the effect on each should be recognized in the same accounting period.*

Usually, the matching concept is applied by first determining the items that constitute revenues for the period in accordance with the conservatism concept, and, second, by matching items of cost to these revenues. However, as we shall see in later chapters, in some situations the applicable expenses are identified first, and then revenues are matched to them. Here, we shall assume that applicable revenues of the period have been identified and the problem is to determine what costs match with these revenues and hence are expenses.

Criteria for Expense Recognition

The matching concept provides one criterion for deciding what costs are expenses in an accounting period. There are two others: (1) costs associated with activities of the period are expenses of the period, and (2) costs that cannot be associated with revenues of future periods are expenses. Examples of each criterion are given below.

Direct Matching. The association of cost of sales with revenues for the same goods or services has already been mentioned. Similarly, if salespersons are paid a commission, the commission is reported as expense in the same period in which the revenue arising from these sales is recognized. The period in which the commission is recognized as an expense may be different from the period in which the salespersons receive the commission in cash.

> **Example.** Ms. A was paid $2,000 cash in 1983 as a commission on an order she booked in 1983. But the goods are not to be shipped until 1984. Thus, the $2,000 is an expense of 1984. Mr. B will be paid $1,000 cash in 1984 as a commission on goods that were shipped in 1983. The $1,000 is an expense of 1983.

Period Costs. Some items of expense are associated with a certain accounting period, even though they cannot be traced to any specific revenue transactions occurring in that period. In general, these expenses are the costs of "being in business." In a retail store, they include the costs of operating the store during the period, even though these costs cannot be traced directly to the specific merchandise sold. These expenses are called *period costs*.

> **Example.** If a salesperson is paid a salary rather than a commission as in the previous example, the salary is reported as an expense in the period in which the employee works. Although the amount of the salary is not affected by the volume of sales and hence there is no direct relationship between the cost and the revenue, the salary is one of the costs of operating the business during the period and hence is related in an indirect way to the revenue of the period.

Costs Not Associated with Future Revenue. Even if a cost item is not associated with the operations of a period, it is reported as an expense of that period if it cannot be associated with the revenue of some future period. An item of cost must be either an asset or an expense. For a cost of this period to be an asset, it must, by definition, be expected to provide a benefit in some future period. If it does not qualify as an asset by this test, it must be an expense of the current period. Even if the item of cost benefits the future in some general way but there is no feasible way of associating the benefit with specific future periods, the item is an expense.

> **Example.** Employee training programs are intended to provide benefits to future periods in that the participants are expected to perform better as a result of the training. The future benefits of this training cannot be objectively measured, however. So training costs are charged as an expense of the current period, rather than being treated as an asset.

Under this general principle, many items of cost are charged as expenses in the current period even though they have no connection with the revenues of the period, or even with the ongoing operations of the period. If assets are destroyed by fire or lost by theft, for example, the amount of the loss is an expense of the current period. In general, if a cost is incurred and there is no reasonable basis for classifying the cost as an asset, it is reported as an expense.

If during the period, an item that once was classified as an asset is found to have no value for future periods, the asset amount is removed from the balance sheet and becomes an expense of the period. This can happen, for example, when goods held in inventory are found to have deteriorated, become obsolete, or otherwise become unsalable.

Expenses and Expenditures

Expenditures take place when an entity acquires goods or services. An expenditure may be made by cash, by the exchange of another asset (such as a "trade-in" vehicle), by incurring a liability, or by some combination of these. When expenditures are made, costs are incurred. As already noted, these costs can be either assets or expenses. Over the entire life of an entity, most expenditures become expenses. In any time segment *shorter* than the life of an entity, however, there is no necessary correspondence between expense and expenditure.

> **Example.** Late in 1982, $5,000 of fuel oil was purchased for cash. This was an expenditure of $5,000, which was the exchange of one asset for another. If none of this fuel oil was consumed in 1982, there was no *expense* in 1982. Rather, the fuel oil was an asset as of the end of 1982. If the fuel oil was consumed in 1983, there was an *expense* of $5,000 in 1983.

Four types of transactions need to be considered in distinguishing between amounts that are properly considered as expenses of a given accounting period and the expenditures made in connection with these items. Focusing on "this year" in Illustration 3–2, these are as follows:

1. Expenditures made this year that are also expenses of this year.
2. Expenditures made prior to this year that become expenses during this year. These appeared as assets on the balance sheet at the beginning of this year.
3. Expenditures made this year that will become expenses in future years. These will appear as assets on the balance sheet at the end of this year.
4. Expenses of this year that will be paid for in a future year. On the balance sheet at the end of this year, these appear as liabilities.

Expenditures That Are Also Expenses. This is the simplest and most common type of transaction, and the least troublesome to account for. If an item is acquired during the year, it is an expenditure. If it is consumed during the same year, it is an expense of the year. "Consumed" as used here means, more precisely, "provides its intended benefit." For example, raw materials that are converted into salable goods are not considered to be "consumed" until the goods are sold. At that time, the raw materials cost is a part of the expense, cost of goods sold.

Assets That Become Expenses. On January 1, the balance sheet shows the entity's assets. During this year, some of these assets, which were expenditures made prior to this year, are used up and hence are transformed into expenses. The three principal types of such assets are described below.

First, there are *inventories* of salable goods. These become expenses when the goods are sold.

Second, there are *prepaid expenses* and *deferred charges*. These represent services or other assets purchased prior to this year but not yet used up when the year begins. They become expenses in the year in which the services are used or the assets are consumed. Insurance protection is one such item. The premium on most insurance policies is paid in advance, and the protection bought with this premium is an asset until the accounting period in which the protection is received, at which time it becomes an expense. Prepaid rent follows the same pattern. The rent expense is recognized in the year in which the entity receives the benefit of occupying the rented premises, as opposed to the previous year when the expenditure took place.

> **Example 1.** A company purchased three-year insurance protection on December 31, 1982, for $9,000. The $9,000 appears as an asset on the balance sheet of December 31, 1982. In 1983, $3,000 becomes an expense and $6,000 remains as an asset on the balance sheet of December 31, 1983. In 1984, $3,000 more becomes an expense, and the remaining $3,000 is an expense in 1985.

Example 2. A company paid $120,000 to its landlord on October 1, 1982, representing an advance payment of one year's rent. Of this amount, $30,000 is rent expense of 1982. On the balance sheet of December 31, 1982, $90,000 appears as an asset. This amount becomes rent expense during the first nine months of 1983.

The third category of assets that will become expenses is long-lived assets. With the exception of land, assets have a limited useful life; that is, they do not last forever. They are purchased with the expectation that they will be used in the operation of the entity in future periods, and they will become expenses in these future periods. The principle is exactly the same as that of the insurance policy previously mentioned, which also was purchased for the benefit of future periods. An important practical difference between a long-lived asset, such as a building, and an insurance policy, however, is that the life of a building is usually difficult to estimate, whereas the life of an insurance policy is known precisely. Thus, estimating what portion of a building's cost is an expense of a given accounting period is a more difficult task than that of determining the insurance expense of a period. The mechansim used to convert the cost of fixed assets to expense is called *depreciation* and is described in Chapter 7.

Expenditures That Are Not Yet Expenses. As the preceding examples show, some expenditures made to acquire assets this year are not expenses of this year because the assets have not yet been used up. These include not only the purchase of long-lived assets but also expenditures incurred in connection with the *manufacture* of goods that are to be sold in some future year. Thus, wages and salaries earned by production personnel and all other costs associated with producing goods become part of the cost of the goods produced and remain as an asset, inventory, until the goods are sold. The distinction between production costs (also called *product costs*), which initially are added to inventory amounts, and other operating costs *(period costs)*, which are expenses of the current period, is discussed in more detail in Chapter 6.

Expenses Not Yet Paid. Some expenses that were incurred this year are not paid for by the end of the year. The parties who furnished services during the year have a claim against the entity for the amounts owed them. These amounts are therefore liabilities (called *accrued expenses*) of the entity as of December 31. The liability for wages earned but not yet paid is an example already mentioned. The cost of borrowing money during a period is interest expense of that period. If this interest expense has not been paid, the end-of-period balance sheet will show a liability, accrued interest expense. Several other types of obligations have the same characteristic: although services were rendered prior to the date for which the balance sheet is prepared, these services have not yet been paid for. The *incurrence* of these expenses reduces owners' equity; the subsequent *payment* of the obligation does not affect owners' equity.

For all obligations of this type, the transaction involved is essentially the same: the expense is shown in the period in which the services were used, and the obligation that results from these services is shown in the liability section of the balance sheet as of the end of the period.

> **Example 1.**   In 1982, John Fox earned $80 that was not paid him. This is an expense of $80 in 1982, and there is a corresponding liability of $80 (called accrued wages) on his employer's balance sheet as of December 31, 1982. In 1983, when Fox is paid, the liability is eliminated and there is an $80 decrease in cash. Accrued wages liability will always occur for an entity whose last payday of the year, for example, the fourth Friday in December, does not fall on the last day of the year.

> **Example 2.**   On September 1, 1982, a company borrowed $10,000 for one year at 15 percent interest, the interest and principal to be paid August 31, 1983. The loan itself resulted in an increase of cash, $10,000, and created a liability, loans payable, of $10,000. The total interest cost is $10,000 $\times$ 0.15 = $1,500. One third of this interest, $500, is an expense of 1982. Since is was not paid in 1982, this $500 appears as a liability, accrued interest expense, on the December 31, 1982, balance sheet. The remaining $1,000 interest is an expense of 1983. When the loan is repaid on August 31, 1983, cash is decreased by $11,500. This is balanced by the decrease in loans payable of $10,000, the decrease in accrued interest expense of $500, and the interest expense for 1983 of $1,000.

Note that in these examples, the basic equality, Assets = Equities, is always maintained. The earning of wages resulted in an expense of $80, which was a decrease in owners' equity, and there was an equal increase in the liability, accrued wages; so the total of the equities was unchanged. The payment of the $80 resulted in a decrease in cash and a decrease in the liability, accrued wages; so both assets and equities were reduced by $80. Similar comments apply to the interest expense example.

Dividends

Dividends that a corporation pays to its shareholders are not expenses. Dividends are a distribution of net income, not an item in the calculation of net income. Similarly, in an unincorporated business, owner's or partners' drawings are not treated as expenses.

Summary of Expense Measurement

The proper classification of costs and expenditures as either assets or expenses is one of the most difficult problems in accounting. As an aid in this process, and as a summary of the preceding discussion, Illustration 3–3 gives a decision diagram that should be helpful. It shows that an entity starts an accounting period with certain assets and that during

ILLUSTRATION 3–3
DECISION DIAGRAM: ASSETS AND EXPENSES

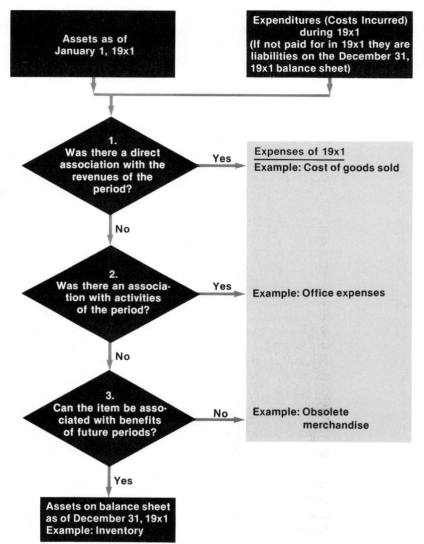

the period it makes expenditures (incurs costs). If these costs are not
paid for in cash or by an exchange of another asset, they result in liabilities on the year-end balance sheet. In preparing the end-of-period balance sheet and the period's income statement, the accountant must classify these assets and expenditures either as expenses, which will appear
on the income statement, or as assets, which will appear on the balance

sheet. In order to do this the three questions shown on the diagram must be addressed.

Gains and Losses   Throughout this chapter, revenue, which increases owners' equity, has been associated with the sale of a company's goods and services. Owners' equity can increase for other reasons. For example, if a company sells marketable securities for more than it paid for them, owners' equity has increased, but this is not sales revenue (unless the company is in the business of selling securities). Technically, such increases in owners' equity are called *gains,* to distinguish them from revenues from the sale of goods and services.

Similarly, decreases in owners' equity for reasons not associated with operations are referred to as *losses,* and these are sometimes distinguished from expenses. Loss of assets by fire or theft has already been mentioned. Sale of securities at an amount less than was paid for them is another example.

As a practical matter, no sharp distinction is made between sales revenues and gains; they both increase owners' equity. Similarly, expenses and losses both decrease owners' equity, so again, in practice no sharp distinction is made between them.

THE CONSISTENCY CONCEPT

The nine concepts that have been described in this and the preceding chapters are so broad that there are in practice several different ways in which a given event may be recorded in the accounts. As mentioned above, for example, bad debts may be recognized either as a reduction in revenue or as an expense. The *consistency concept* requires that once an entity has decided on one method, it will treat all subsequent events of the same character in the same fashion unless it has a sound reason to do otherwise. If an entity made frequent changes in the manner of handling a given class of events in the accounting records, comparison of its accounting figures for one period with those of another period would be difficult.

Because of this concept, changes in the method of keeping accounts are not made lightly. A company's outside auditors include in their opinion (i.e., the letter summarizing the results of their annual examination of accounting records) the statement that the amounts were prepared "in conformity with generally accepted accounting principles *applied on a basis consistent with that of the preceding year*"; or if there were changes in practice, these are spelled out in the opinion.

Note that consistency as used here has a narrow meaning. It refers only to consistency *over time,* not to *logical* consistency at a given moment of time. For example, long-lived assets are recorded at cost, but inventories are recorded at the lower of their cost or market value. Some people argue that this is inconsistent. Whatever the merits of this argument may be, it does not involve the *accounting* concept of consistency. This concept does not mean that the treatment of different categories of transactions must be consistent with one another, but only that transactions in a given category must be treated consistently from one accounting period to the next.

THE MATERIALITY CONCEPT

In law, there is a doctrine called *de minimis non curat lex*, which means that the court will not consider trivial matters. Similarly, the accountant does not attempt to record events so insignificant that the work of recording them is not justified by the usefulness of the results. An example of these trivialities is the accounting treatment of pencils. Conceptually, a brand new pencil is an asset of the entity. Every time someone writes with the pencil, part of this asset is used up, and the owners' equity decreases correspondingly. Theoretically, it would be possible to ascertain the number of partly used pencils that are owned by the entity at the end of the accounting period, and to show this amount as an asset. But the cost of such an effort would obviously be gigantic, and no accountant would attempt to do this. Accountants take the simpler, even though less exact, course of action and consider that the asset was used up either at the time the pencils were purchased or at the time they were issued from supplies inventory to the user.

There is no agreement as to the exact line separating material events from immaterial events. The decision depends on judgment and common sense. It is natural for the beginning student, who does not have an appreciation of the cost of collecting accounting information, to be more meticulous in recording events in the accounts than would the practicing accountant.

> **Example.** When a company buys a three-year insurance policy, it should, strictly speaking, record one year's worth as a current asset and the other two years' worth as a noncurrent asset. This is because current assets include those assets expected to be consumed within one year. In practice, however, the entire three-year policy is recorded as a current asset. The breakdown between current and noncurrent is not material because the amount of prepaid insurance is a trivial fraction of the total current assets.

The materiality concept is important in the process of determining the expenses and revenue for a given accounting period. Many of the expense items are necessarily estimates, and in some cases they are not very close estimates. Beyond a certain point it is not worthwhile to attempt to refine these estimates.

Example. Telephone bills, although rendered monthly, often do not coincide with a calendar month. It would be possible to analyze each bill and classify all the toll calls according to the month in which they were made. This would be following the matching concept precisely. Few companies bother to do this, however. They simply consider the telephone bill as an expense of the month in which the bill is received, on the grounds that a procedure to ascertain the actual expense would not be justified by the accuracy gained. Since in most businesses the amount of the bill is likely to be relatively stable from one month to another, no significant error is involved in this practice.

Materiality is also used in another sense in accounting. The principle of *full disclosure* requires that all material information about the financial condition and activities of an entity must be disclosed in reports prepared for outside parties. In this sense, also, there is no definitive rule that separates material from immaterial information. This topic is discussed further in Chapter 14.

THE INCOME STATEMENT

The accounting report that summarizes the revenues and the expenses of an accounting period is called the *income statement* (or the profit and loss statement, statement of earnings, or statement of operations). In a technical sense the income statement is subordinate to the balance sheet because it shows in some detail the items that together account for the change arising from operations during an accounting period in one balance sheet item, retained earnings. Nevertheless, the information on the income statement is regarded by many to be more important than information on the balance sheet because the income statement reports the results of operations and indicates reasons for the entity's profitability or lack thereof. The importance of the income statement is illustrated by the fact that in situations where accountants in recording an event must choose between a procedure that distorts the balance sheet or one that distorts the income statement (a choice that is unfortunately necessary on occasion), they usually choose the former.

Illustration 3–4 shows an income statement for Garsden Corporation (whose balance sheet was shown in Illustration 2–1). In practice there is considerable variety in the formats and degree of detail used in income statements. Illustration 3–4 is representative of the income statements published in corporations' annual reports to their shareholders (with the exception of a few complex items that are discussed in later chapters). Income statements prepared for use by the managers of an entity usually contain more detailed information than that shown in Illustration 3–4.

The heading of the income statement must show (1) the entity to which it relates (Garsden Corporation), (2) the name of the statement (income statement), and (3) the time period covered (year ended Decem-

ILLUSTRATION 3–4

GARSDEN CORPORATION ← Name of Entity

Income Statement ← Name of Statement

For the Year Ended December 31, 1982 ← Time period

Net sales	$75,478,221
Cost of sales	52,227,004
Gross margin	23,251,217
Research and development expense	2,158,677
Selling, general, and administrative expenses	8,726,696
Operating income	12,365,844
Other revenues (expenses):	
Interest expense	(363,000)
Interest and dividend revenues	43,533
Royalty revenues	420,010
Income before income taxes	12,466,387
Provision for income taxes	6,344,000
Net income	$ 6,122,387
Earnings per share of common stock	$5.58

Statement of Retained Earnings

Retained earnings at beginning of year	$17,384,589
Add: Net income	6,122,387
Deduct: Dividends ($4 per common share)	(4,390,000)
Retained earnings at end of year	$19,116,976

ber 31, 1982). The balance sheet in Illustration 2–1 and the income statement in Illustration 3–4 give information for only one year. To provide a basis for comparison, the SEC requires that corporate annual reports contain income statements for the most recent three years and balance sheets as of the end of the most recent two years.

Comments about the items listed on this income statement and variations often found in practice are given in the following paragraphs.

Revenues

An income statement often reports several separate items in the sales revenue section, the net of which is the *net sales* figure. For example, Garsden's income statement might have shown:

Gross sales		$77,157,525
Less: Returns and allowances	$ 528,348	
Sales discounts	1,150,956	
Net sales		$75,478,221

Gross sales is the total invoice price of the goods shipped or services rendered during the period. It should not include *sales taxes* or *excise taxes* that may be charged the customer. Such taxes are not revenues but rather represent collections that the business makes on behalf of the government. They are a liability to the government until paid. Similarly, postage, freight, or other items billed to the customer at cost are not revenues. These items do not appear in the sales figure but instead are an offset to the costs the company incurs for them. Exceptions are made to these rules when it is not feasible to disentangle the revenue and nonrevenue portions of the items in question.

Sales returns and allowances represent the sales value of goods that were returned by customers or allowances made to customers because the goods were defective or for some other reason. The amount can be subtracted from the sales figure directly, without showing it as a separate item on the income statement; but it is often considered as being important enough information to warrant reporting it.

Sales discounts are the amount of discounts taken by customers for prompt payment. (These are sometimes called *cash discounts*.) For example, assume a business offers a 2 percent discount to customers who pay within 10 days from the date of the invoice and it sells $1,000 of merchandise to a customer who takes advantage of this discount. The business receives only $980 cash and records the other $20 as a sales discount. *Trade discounts*, which are formulas used in figuring the actual selling price from published catalogs or price lists (e.g., "list less 40 percent"), do not appear in the accounting records at all.

Other revenues are revenues earned from activities not associated with the sale of the company's goods and services. Interest or dividends earned on marketable securities owned by the company is an example. Garsden also had revenues from royalties paid by other companies that Garsden has licensed to use its patented manufacturing process. While it is preferable to show such peripheral revenues separately from sales revenues, as in Illustration 3–4, many companies add them to net sales and report a total revenue amount.

Cost of Sales

Because of the matching concept, at the same time that income is increased by the sales value of goods or services sold, it is also decreased by the cost of those goods or services. Indeed, were it not for the fact that the separate amounts for sales revenue and the cost of sales are useful to management, a record could be made only on the net increase in owners' equity that results from a sale. The cost of goods or services sold is called the *cost of sales*. In manufacturing firms and retailing businesses, it is often called the *cost of goods sold*. Procedures for measuring the cost of sales are described in Chapter 6.

Gross Margin

The difference between sales revenue and cost of sales is the *gross margin* or *gross profit*. On many income statements, as in Illustration

3–4, this amount appears as a separate item. It does not appear separately on some companies' income statements but can be calculated as the difference between net sales and cost of sales if the company has disclosed the cost of sales amount.

Some companies do not show cost of sales as one item on the income statement. Instead, they list individual expenses by *object,* such as salaries and wages, usage of goods and services, and interest. In such an income statement, it is impossible to calculate the gross margin. This is because the broad objects (e.g., salaries and wages) intermingle *product* costs (e.g., factory labor) with *period* costs (e.g., administrative salaries). Gross margin is the difference between the revenues generated from selling products (goods or services) and the related product costs.

Expenses

The classifications given in Illustration 3–4 are a minimum. In many income statements, especially those prepared for internal use, the "selling, general, and administrative expense" category is broken down so as to show separately the principal items of which it is composed.

The separate disclosure of *research and development expense* is a relatively recent requirement. Formerly, most companies included this expense as part of general and administrative expenses. Because the amount spent on research and development can provide an important clue as to how energetic the company is in keeping its products and processes up to date, the FASB requires that this amount be reported separately if it is material.

The FASB also requires separate disclosure of the amount of *interest expense* in a period. In some instances, to be discussed in Chapter 7, the interest *expense* of a period is not the same as the interest *cost* incurred during the period.

Many companies' income statements show an amount for *operating income,* as in Illustration 3–4. To operating income are added other revenue items, and other expenses are subtracted (indicated by parentheses in Illustration 3–4); the result is *income before income taxes.* Companies that show an operating income amount want to distinguish between income from the company's primary operating activities and nonoperating revenues and expenses. Other companies reject this distinction. They say, for example, that interest expense reflects the cost of financing assets used in operations and therefore should not be presented in a way that suggests it is a "nonoperating" item. Nearly all companies report a pretax income amount before subtracting the *provision for income taxes* (also called *income tax expense*).

Net Income

Net income is colloquially referred to as "the bottom line" of the income statement for obvious reasons. The bottom line must be labeled *net income* or *net earnings*, with no qualification or modification. Net income is reported not only in total but also per share of stock. The per share amount is obtained by dividing the dollar amount of net income by the number of shares outstanding.

Retained Earnings

Strictly speaking, the income statement ends with the item "Earnings per share." Illustration 3–4 goes beyond this to show other changes in retained earnings that have occurred during the period. This final section links the income statement to the retained earnings item on the balance sheet. It shows that during 1982 retained earnings was increased by the amount of net income (for 1982, $6,122,387) and was decreased by the amount of dividends (for 1982, $4,390,000), so that at the end of 1982 it was $19,116,976. This calculation, whether shown on a separate page or included at the bottom of the income statement, is called a *statement of retained earnings*.

Relation between Balance Sheet and Income Statement

The balance sheet and income statement are said to *articulate*, that is, there is a definite relationship between them. More specifically, the amount of net income reported on the income statement, together with the amount of dividends, explains the change in retained earnings between the two balance sheets prepared as of the beginning and the end of the accounting period. This relationship was shown schematically in Illustration 3–2 and is shown more specifically in Illustration 3–5. Illustration 3–5 uses the Garsden Corporation December 31, 1982, balance sheet that was shown in more detail in Illustration 2–1, and a condensed version of Garsden's income statement from Illustration 3–4. Note how the income statement and related statement of retained earnings, a *flow* report, reconciles the retained earnings amounts from the beginning and ending balance sheets, which are *status* reports.

Income Statement Percentages

In analyzing an income statement, percentage relationships are often calculated. Usually, net sales is taken as 100 percent. Each income statement item can be expressed as a percentage of net sales. The most important are the gross margin percentage and the profit margin.

The *gross margin percentage* in Illustration 3–5 is $23,251,217 ÷ $75,478,221 = 30.8 percent. It indicates the average markup obtained on products (goods or services) sold. The percentage varies widely among industries, but healthy companies in the same industry tend to have similar gross margin percentages.

The *profit margin* is net income divided by net sales: $6,122,387 ÷ $75,478,221 = 8.1 percent. Profit margins also vary widely among industries. A successful supermarket may have a profit margin of about 1.5

ILLUSTRATION 3–5
A "PACKAGE" OF ACCOUNTING REPORTS

GARSDEN CORPORATION

Balance Sheet
As of December 31, 1981

Assets

Current assets	$23,839,904
Plant and equipment	14,255,720
Other assets	180,535
Total assets	$38,276,159

Equities

Current liabilities	$12,891,570
Other liabilities	3,000,000
Common stock	5,000,000
Retained earnings	17,384,589
Total equities	$38,276,159

Income Statement
For the Year 1982

Net sales	$75,478,221
Less: Cost of sales	52,227,004
Gross margin	23,251,217
Less: Expenses	10,784,830
Income before taxes	12,466,387
Provision for income taxes	6,344,000
Net income	6,122,387
Retained earnings, beginning	17,384,589
	23,506,976
Less: Dividends	(4,390,000)
Retained earnings, ending	$19,116,976

Balance Sheet
As of December 31, 1982

Assets

Current assets	$22,651,072
Plant and equipment	13,411,779
Other assets	173,214
Total assets	$36,236,065

Equities

Current liabilities	$ 9,119,089
Other liabilities	3,000,000
Common stock	5,000,000
Retained earnings	19,116,976
Total equities	$36,236,065

percent, while the typical profit margin in healthy manufacturing companies tends to be closer to 8 percent.[3]

OTHER CONCEPTS OF INCOME

We have described how income is measured and reported in accordance with generally accepted accounting principles (GAAP). Not all income statements are prepared in accordance with these principles, however. As noted in Chapter 1, some regulatory bodies prescribe different principles that they require be used by companies within their jurisdiction. Three other variations of the income concept are described below: cash-basis accounting, income tax accounting, and the economic concept of income.

Cash-Basis Accounting

The measurement of income described in this chapter is based on what is called *accrual accounting*. Central to accrual accounting are the realization concept and the matching concept. Accrual accounting measures income for a period as the difference between the revenues recognized in that period and the expenses that are matched with those revenues. As noted previously, the period's revenues are not necessarily the same as the period's cash receipts from customers, and the period's expenses are not necessarily the same as the period's cash disbursements.

An alternative way of measuring income is called *cash-basis accounting*. With this method, sales are not recorded until the period in which they are received in cash. Similarly, costs are subtracted from sales in the period in which they are paid for by cash disbursements. Thus, neither the realization nor matching concept applies in cash-basis accounting.

In practice, there rarely is seen "pure" cash-basis accounting. This is because a pure cash-basis approach would require treating the acquisition of inventories as a reduction in profit when the acquisition costs are paid, rather than when the inventories are sold. Similarly, costs of acquiring items of plant and equipment would be treated as profit reductions when paid in cash, rather than in the later periods when these long-lived items are used. Clearly, such a pure cash-basis approach would result in balance sheets and income statements that would be of limited usefulness. Thus, what is commonly called cash-basis accounting essentially is a mixture of cash basis for some items (especially sales and period costs) and accrual basis for other items (especially product costs and long-lived assets). This mixture is also sometimes called *mod-*

---

[3]Surveys indicate that most Americans believe that corporate profit margins average 25 percent or more. The 1981 average profit margin for the "Fortune 500" industrial firms was only 4.6 percent.

ified cash-basis accounting to distinguish it from a pure cash-basis method.

Cash-basis accounting is seen most often in small firms that provide services and therefore do not have significant amounts of inventories. Examples include restaurants, beauty parlors, and architectural firms. Since many of these establishments do not extend credit to their customers, cash-basis profit may not differ dramatically from accrual-basis income. Nevertheless, cash-basis accounting is *not* permitted by GAAP for any type of business.

Income Tax Accounting

Most business entities must calculate their taxable income and pay a federal tax (and in some cases a state or local tax) based on this income. The amounts of revenues and expenses used to determine federal taxable income are usually similar to, but not identical with, amounts measured in accordance with GAAP. The differences are sufficiently significant so that it is unwise to rely on income tax regulations as a basis for solving business accounting problems, or vice versa. For example, tax regulations permit certain kinds of businesses to report income using the modified cash basis, which, as noted above, is not in accord with GAAP.

Unless tax rates applicable to the business are expected to increase in the future, a business usually reports the minimum possible amount of taxable income in the current year, thus postponing tax payments as much as possible to future years. It does this generally by recognizing expenses as soon as legally possible, but postponing the recognition of revenue for as long as possible. Note that this is a process of shifting revenue and expense from one period to another. Over the long run in most businesses there is little difference between the total expenses and revenues computed for tax purposes and the total expenses and revenues computed for financial accounting. The objective of minimizing current taxes is, as the Supreme Court has pointed out, entirely legal and ethical, provided it is done in accordance with the tax regulations. It is also legal and proper under most circumstances to figure income one way for tax purposes and another way for financial accounting purposes.

> **Example.** Income tax regulations permit the cost of most fixed assets to be charged as expenses (i.e., depreciated) over a shorter time period than the estimated useful life of these assets, and at amounts in the early years that are greater than the cost of the asset services consumed in those years. These practices result in higher tax-deductible expenses, and correspondingly lower taxable income, in the early years of an asset's life, and therefore encourage businesses to invest in new fixed assets. Most businesses use these practices in calculating their taxable income, but they use different practices for financial accounting.

Although tax regulations are not described in detail in this book, references are made to accounting practices that are or are not consistent with them. The manager learns early the importance of becoming thoroughly familiar with the principal tax rules that affect the business and also the importance of consulting tax experts when unusual situations arise.

Economic Income

Economic theory is not constrained by the practical need of reporting an income amount to an entity's owners or other interested parties. Thus, in economic theory, income is defined as the difference between the value of a business at the end of an accounting period and its value at the beginning of the period, after proper adjustments for equity "deposits" (e.g., proceeds from the issuance of additional capital stock) and equity "withdrawals" (i.e., cash dividends). Both economists and accountants recognize that this *economic income* cannot be feasibly measured for a given accounting period. Also, economists regard interest on all equities—both interest-bearing liabilities and owners' equity—as an element of cost. Accountants treat only the interest on borrowings as a cost because the "interest" on the use of owners' capital cannot be objectively measured. Consequently, accounting net income to an economist is a mixture of "true" income and the cost of using shareholders' capital. To an economist, accounting net income is an attempt to measure the income accruing to the entity's *owners;* but it is an overstatement of the income earned by the *entity itself* because the cost of using owners' funds has not been subtracted.

SUMMARY

This chapter described the remaining basic accounting concepts:

6. *Time period.*   Accounting measures activities for a specified interval of time, which is usually one year.
7. *Conservatism.*   Revenues are recognized only when they are reasonably certain, whereas expenses are recognized as soon as they are reasonably possible.
8. *Realization.*   Revenues are usually recognized in the period in which goods were delivered to customers or in which services were rendered. The amount recognized is the amount that customers are reasonably certain to pay.
9. *Matching.*   Costs are reported as expenses in the period (1) when there is a direct association between costs and revenues of the period, (2) when costs are associated with activities of the period itself, or (3) when costs cannot be associated with revenues of any future period.
10. *Consistency.*   Once an entity has decided on a certain accounting method, it will treat all subsequent events of the same character in the same fashion unless it has a sound reason to do otherwise.

11. *Materiality.* Insignificant events may be disregarded, but there must be full disclosure of all important information.

The income statement summarizes the revenues and expenses of an entity for an accounting period. The accounting period is "officially" one year, but interim income statements are usually prepared on a monthly or quarterly basis. The income statement and balance sheet "articulate" in that a period's income statement (and related statement of retained earnings) explains the change in retained earnings between the balance sheets prepared as of the beginning and the end of the period.

Only accrual-basis accounting, which employs the realization and matching concepts, is permitted under GAAP. Income tax accounting regulations differ in some important respects from GAAP, including permitting certain types of businesses to calculate income using cash-basis accounting. Economic income is a theoretical concept, rather than a practical approach to measuring income.

Cases

CASE 3–1   Saunders Company (B)

Helen Saunders was grateful for the balance sheets that her friend prepared (see Saunders Company (A)). In going over the numbers she remarked, "It's sort of surprising that cash increased by $9,279, but net income was only $5,030. Why was that?"

Her friend replied, "A partial answer to that question is to look at an income statement for May. I think I can find the data I need to prepare one for you."

In addition to the data given in the (A) case, her friend found a record of cash receipts and disbursements, which is summarized in Exhibit 1. She also learned that all accounts payable were to vendors for purchase of merchandise inventory and that cost of sales was $11,220 in May.

Questions

1. Prepare an income statement for May in proper form. Explain the derivation of each item on this statement, including cost of sales.

2. Explain why the change in the cash balance was greater than net income.

3. Explain why the following amounts are *incorrect* cost of sales amounts for May: (a) $4,905; and (b) $10,370. Under what circumstances would these amounts be correct cost of sales amounts?

EXHIBIT 1

Cash Receipts and Disbursements
May

Cash Receipts		Cash Disbursements	
Cash sales	$14,773	Equipment purchased	$ 6,000
Credit customers	5,589	Other assets purchased	105
Helen Saunders	3,000	Payments on accounts payable	1,384
Bank loan	5,500	Cash purchases of merchandise	4,905
Total receipts	$28,862	Cash purchase of supplies	900
		Dividends	3,000
		Wages expense	2,327
		Utilities expense	842
		Miscellaneous expenses	120
		Total disbursements	$19,583

Reconciliation:

Cash balance, May 1	$ 7,470
Receipts	28,862
Subtotal	36,332
Disbursements	19,583
Cash balance, May 31	$16,749

CASE 3–2 Homes, Inc.

Homes, Inc., bought and sold houses. During May and June, the following events occurred:

Question

Prepare income statements for May, June, and July.

Date	Event	Effect on Cash
May 2	William Able agreed to buy House A from Homes, Inc., and made an $8,000 down payment.	Increase $8,000
May 15	Homes, Inc., paid $480 commission to the salesperson who sold House A (6% of cash received).	Decrease $480
May	Homes, Inc., general expenses for May were $2,100 (assume for simplicity these were paid in cash in May).	Decrease $2,100
June 2	Helen Baker agreed to buy House B and made a $12,000 down payment.	Increase $12,000
June 5	William Able completed the purchase of House A, paying $70,000 cash. Homes, Inc., delivered the deed to the buyer, thereby delivering ownership of the house to him. (House A cost Homes, Inc., $67,000)	Increase $70,000
June 30	Homes, Inc., paid $720 commission to the salesperson who sold House B.	Decrease $720
June	Homes, Inc., general expenses for June were $2,000.	Decrease $2,000
July 2	Homes, Inc., paid $4,200 additional commission to the salesperson who sold House A.	Decrease $4,200
July 3	Helen Baker completed the purchase of House B, paying $108,000 cash. Homes, Inc., delivered the deed to the buyer, thereby delivering ownership of the house to her (House B cost Homes, Inc., $98,000.)	Increase $108,000
July 30	Homes, Inc., paid $6,480 commission to the salesperson who sold House B.	Decrease $6,480
July	Homes, Inc., general expenses for July were $2,300.	Decrease $2,300

CASE 3–3   Cascade Cafe (B)

In addition to preparing the balance sheet described in Cascade Cafe (A), Mr. Whittaker, the accountant, agreed to prepare an income statement. He said that such a financial statement would show Mrs. Rayburn how profitable operations had been, and thus help her to judge whether it was worthwhile to continue operating the restaurant.

In addition to the information given in the (A) case, Mr. Whittaker learned that cash received from customers through March 30 amounted to $23,651 and that cash payments were as follows:

Monthly payments to partners	$11,300
Wages to part-time employees	2,490
Interest	270
Food and beverage suppliers	4,707
Telephone and electricity	1,617
Miscellaneous	556
Rent payments	5,400

Questions

1. Prepare an income statement.
2. What does this income statement tell Mrs. Rayburn?

CASE 3–4   John Bartlett (A)

John Bartlett was the inventor of a switching device that enabled a video-game or home computer to be connected to the antenna terminals of an ordinary television set. The switch would soon be given a patent whose legal life was 17 years. Having confidence in the switch's commercial value but possessing no excess funds of his own, he sought among his friends and acquaintances for the necessary capital to put the switch on the market. The proposition that he placed before possible associates was that a corporation, Bartlett Manufacturing Company, should be formed with capital stock of $50,000 par value.

The project looked attractive to a number of the individuals to whom the inventor presented it, but the most promising among them—a retired manufacturer—said he would be unwilling to invest his capital without knowing what uses were intended for the cash to be received from the proposed sale of stock. He suggested that the inventor determine the probable costs of experimentation and of special machinery, and prepare for him a statement of the estimated assets and liabilities of the proposed company when ready to begin actual operation. He also asked for a statement of the estimated transactions for the first year of operations, to be based on studies the inventor had made of probable markets and costs of labor and materials. This information Mr. Bartlett consented to supply to the best of his ability.

After consulting the engineer who had aided him in constructing his patent models, Mr. Bartlett drew up the following list of data relating to the transactions of the proposed corporation during its period of organization and development:

1. The retired manufacturer would pay the corporation $20,000 cash for

which he would receive stock with a par value of $20,000. The remaining stock (par value, $30,000) would be given to Mr. Bartlett in exchange for the patent on the switch.

2. Probable cost of incorporation and organization, including estimated officers' salaries during developmental period, $3,300.
3. Probable cost of developing special machinery, $10,000. This sum includes the cost of expert services, materials, rent of a small shop, and the cost of power, light, and miscellaneous expenditures.
4. Probable cost of raw materials: $1,000, of which $600 is to be used in experimental production.

On the basis of the above information, Mr. Bartlett prepared the estimated balance sheet shown in Exhibit 1.

Mr. Bartlett then set down the following estimates as a beginning step in furnishing the rest of the information desired:

1. Expected sales, all to be received in cash by the end of the first year of operation, $168,000.
2. Expected additional purchases of raw materials and supplies during the course of this operating year, all paid for in cash by end of year, $54,000.
3. Expected borrowing from the bank during year but loans to be repaid before close of year, $4,000. Interest on these loans, $300.
4. Expected payroll and other cash expenses and manufacturing costs for the operating year: $66,000 of manufacturing costs (excluding raw materials and supplies) plus $12,000 for selling and administrative expenses, a total of $78,000.
5. New equipment to be purchased for cash, $2,000.
6. Expected inventory of raw materials and supplies at close of period, at cost, $10,000.
7. No inventory of unsold switches expected as of the end of the period. All products to be manufactured on the basis of firm orders received; none to be produced for inventory.
8. All experimental and organization costs, previously capitalized, to be charged against income of the operating year.
9. Estimated depreciation of machinery, $1,200.
10. Dividends paid in cash, $6,000.
11. Estimated tax expense for the year, $8,450. Ten percent of this amount would not be due until early in the following year.

It should be noted that the transactions summarized above would not necessarily

EXHIBIT 1

BARTLETT MANUFACTURING COMPANY
Estimated Balance Sheet
As of Date Company Begins Operations

Assets		*Equities*	
Cash	$ 5,700	Shareholders' equity	$50,000
Inventory	400		
Machinery	10,000		
Organization costs	3,300		
Experimental costs	600		
Parent	30,000		
Total assets	$50,000	Total equities	$50,000

take place in the sequence indicated. In practice, a considerable number of separate events, or transactions, would occur throughout the year, and many of them were dependent on one another. For example, operations were begun with an initial cash balance and inventory of raw materials, products were manufactured, and sales of these products provided funds for financing subsequent operations. Then, in turn, sales of the product subsequently manufactured yielded more funds.

Questions

1. Trace the effect on the balance sheet of each of the projected events appearing in Mr. Bartlett's list. Thus, item 1, taken alone, would mean that cash would be increased by $168,000 and that (subject to reductions for various costs covered in later items) shareholders' equity would be increased by $168,000. Notice that in this question you are asked to consider all items in terms of their effect on the balance sheet.

2. Prepare an income statement covering the first year of planned operations and a balance sheet as of the end of that year.

3. *Assume* that the retired manufacturer received capital stock with a par value of $16,000 for the $20,000 cash he paid to the corporation, John Bartlett still receiving stock with a par value of $30,000 in exchange for his patent. Under these circumstances, how would the balance sheet in Exhibit 1 appear?

4. *Assume* that the management is interested in what the results would be if no products were sold during the first year, even though production continued at the level indicated in the original plans. The following changes would be made in the 11 items listed above: items 1, 6, 7, 10, and 11 are to be disregarded. Instead of item 3, assume that a loan of $156,000 is obtained, that the loan is not repaid, but that interest thereon of $18,700 is paid during the year. Prepare an income statement for the year and a balance sheet as of the end of the year. Contrast these financial statements with those prepared in Question 2.

CASE 3–5   Elmer Kupper

In 1981, Elmer Kupper opened his own retail store. At the end of 1982, his first full year of operation, he thought he had done moderately well, and he was therefore somewhat chagrined when the trade association to which he belonged sent him figures which indicated that he had operated at a loss.

Mr. Kupper had been employed as manager of the local unit of a chain store for several years. In 1981, he had received an inheritance, and this, together with his savings, provided him with enough funds to buy a small store building on the main street of his town for $90,000.

He joined the trade association to which several thousand independent retailers in the same line of business belonged. One of the services furnished by this association was the annual compilation of typical operating figures of member firms. These figures were prepared by Hartje & Mees, a large public accounting firm. Early in 1983, Hartje & Mees sent Mr. Kupper a standard form and requested that he report his revenue and expenses on this form and return it so

EXHIBIT 1
INCOME STATEMENT FOR 1982, AS PREPARED BY MR. KUPPER

Gross sales		$205,782
Less: Returns and allowances to customers		7,278
Net sales		198,504
Cost of merchandise sold		128,258
Gross margin		70,246
Expenses:		
Salaries and wages	$21,696	
Advertising	3,590	
Supplies and postage	2,378	
Taxes, insurance, repairs, and depreciation on building	4,040	
Heat, light, and power	1,434	
Business and social security taxes	2,976	
Insurance	1,536	
Depreciation on equipment	1,124	
Interest expense	720	
Miscellaneous expense	4,960	
Income taxes	3,660	48,114
Net income		$ 22,132

that his figures could be averaged in with those of other member stores. Exhibit 1 shows the figures which, with some difficulty, Mr. Kupper entered on this form.

Subsequently, Mr. Kupper received a request from Hartje & Mees for information on his salary and on the rental value of his building. He answered substantially as follows:

I own my own business, so there is no point in my charging myself a salary. I drew $28,000 from the business in 1982 for my personal use. My annual salary as a manager of a Mogell store in recent years was $24,000, although I don't see what bearing this has on the figures for my own store.

I thought I made it clear in my original submission that I own my own building. It would cost me $10,800 a year to rent a similar building, and you can see from the figures that I save a considerable amount of money by not being forced to rent.

On the basis of the information in this letter, Hartje & Mees revised Mr. Kup-

per's figures and sent him the income statement shown in Exhibit 2. Mr. Kupper was considerably upset by this revised statement.

He showed it to a friend and said:

These fancy accountants have gotten my figures all mixed up. I want to know the profit I have made by operating my own business rather than by working for somebody else. They have turned my profit into a loss by calling part of it salary and part of it rent. This is merely shifting money from one pocket to another. On the other hand, they won't even let me show my income tax as an expense. I realize that the tax is levied on me as an individual rather than on the business as such, but my only source of income is my store, and I therefore think the tax is a legitimate expense of my store.

Questions

1. How much profit did Mr. Kupper's store earn in 1982? How do you explain the difference between the profit shown on Ex-

EXHIBIT 2
INCOME STATEMENT FOR 1982, AS REVISED BY HARTJE & MEES

Gross sales.		$205,782
Less: Returns and allowances to customers.		7,278
Net sales.		198,504
Cost of merchandise sold.		128,258
Gross margin.		70,246
Expenses:		
Salaries and wages	$45,696	
Advertising	3,590	
Supplies and postage	2,378	
Rent	10,800	
Heat, light, and power	1,434	
Business and social security taxes	2,976	
Insurance	1,536	
Depreciation on equipment.	1,124	
Interest expense	720	
Miscellaneous expense	4,960	75,214
Net loss.		$ (4,968)

hibit 1 and the loss shown on Exhibit 2? What, if any, accounting principles are violated in either statement?

2. Should Mr. Kupper continue to operate his own store? Has he been successful?

3. Does the income statement that would be most useful to Mr. Kupper differ from the income statement that would be most useful in compiling average figures for use by the trade association membership?

CASE 3–6   National Helontogical Association

Each December the incoming members of the board of directors of the National Helontogical Association (NHA) met in joint session with the outgoing board as a means of smoothing the transition from one administration to another. At the meeting in December 1982, questions were raised about whether the 1982 board had adhered to the general policy of the association. The ensuing discussion became quite heated.

NHA was a nonprofit professional association whose 3,000 members were experts in helontology,[1] a specialized branch of engineering. The association

[1]Disguised name.

represented the interests of its members before congressional committees and various scientific bodies, published two professional journals, arranged an annual meeting and several regional meetings, and appointed committees that developed positions on various topics of interest to the membership.

The operating activities of the association were managed by George Tremble, its executive secretary. Mr. Tremble reported to the board of directors. The board consisted of four officers and seven other members. Six members of the 1983 board (i.e., the board that assumed responsibility on January 1, 1983) were also on the 1982 board; the other five members were newly elected. The president served a one-year term.

The financial policy of the association was that each year should "stand on its own feet"; that is, expenses of the year should approximately equal the revenues of the year. At the meeting in December 1982, Mr. Tremble presented an estimated income statement for 1982 (Exhibit 1). Although some of the December transactions were necessarily estimated, Mr. Tremble assured the board that the actual totals for the year would closely approximate the numbers shown.

statement, which brought forth the following information from Mr. Tremble:

1. In 1982, NHA received a $30,000 cash grant from the Workwood Foundation for the purpose of financing a symposium to be held in June 1983. During 1982, approximately $1,500 was spent in preliminary planning for this symposium and was included in the item, "Committee meeting expenses." When asked why the $30,000 had been recorded as revenue in 1982 rather than in 1983, Mr. Tremble said that the grant was obtained entirely by the initiative and persuasive-

EXHIBIT 1

Estimated Income Statement
1982

Revenues:	
Membership dues	$159,750
Journal subscriptions	18,060
Publication sales	6,600
Foundation grant	30,000
Annual meeting, 1981 profit	1,892
Total revenues	216,302
Expenses:	
Printing and mailing publications	51,330
Committee meeting expense	27,330
Annual meeting advance	6,000
Word-processing machine	27,000
Administrative salaries and expenses	85,260
Miscellaneous	13,920
Total expenses	210,840
Excess of revenues over expenses	$ 5,462

Wilma Fosdick, one of the newly elected board members, raised a question about the foundation grant of $30,000. She questioned whether this item should be counted as revenue. If it were excluded, there was a deficit; and this showed that the 1982 board had, in effect, eaten into reserves and thus made it more difficult to provide the level of service that the members had a right to expect in 1983. This led to detailed questions about items on the income

ness of the 1982 president, so 1982 should be given credit for it. Further, although the grant was intended to finance the symposium, there was no legal requirement that the symposium be held; if for any reason it was not held, the money would be used for the general operations of the association.

2. In early December 1982, the association took delivery of, and paid for, a new word-processing machine costing $27,000. This machine would greatly

simplify the work of preparing membership lists, correspondence, and manuscripts submitted to the printer for publication. Except for this new machine, the typewriters, desks, and other equipment in the association office were quite old.

3. Ordinarily, members paid their dues during the first few months of the year. Because of the need to raise cash to finance the purchase of the word-processing machine, in September 1982 the association announced that members who paid their 1983 dues before December 15, 1982, would receive a free copy of the book that contained papers presented at the special symposium to be held in June 1983. The approximate per copy cost of publishing this book was expected to be $9, and it was expected to be sold for $15. Consequently, $18,000 of 1983 dues were received by December 15, 1982.

4. In July 1982, the association sent to members a membership directory. Its long-standing practice was to publish such a directory every two years. The cost of preparing and printing this directory was $12,000. Of the 4,000 copies printed, 3,000 were mailed to members in 1982. The remaining 1,000 were held to meet the needs of new members who would join before the next directory came out; they would receive a free copy of the directory when they joined.

5. Members received the association's journals at no extra cost, as a part of the membership privileges. Some libraries and other nonmembers also subscribed to the journals. The $18,060 reported as subscription revenue was the cash received in 1982. Of this amount about $4,500 was for journals that would be delivered in 1983. Offsetting this was $3,000 of subscription revenue received in 1981 for journals delivered in 1982; this $3,000 had been reported as 1981 revenue.

6. The association had advanced $6,000 to the committee responsible for planning the 1982 annual meeting held in late November. This amount was used for preliminary expenses. Registration fees at the annual meeting were set so as to cover all conventional costs, so that it was expected that the $6,000, plus any profit, would be returned to the association after the committee had finished paying the convention bills. The 1981 convention had resulted in a $1,892 profit, but the results of the 1982 convention were not known, although the attendance was about as anticipated.

Question

Did the association have an excess or a deficit in 1982?

4

Accounting Records and Systems

Thus far we have stressed that each individual accounting transaction can be recorded in terms of its effect on the balance sheet. For example, in the Music Mart illustration in Chapter 2, starting with the item "Cash, $25,000" on the balance sheet, a transaction involving an increase of $12,500 in cash was recorded, in effect, by erasing the $25,000 and entering the new number, $37,500. Although this procedure was appropriate as an explanatory device, it is not a practical way of handling the many transactions that occur in the actual operations of an organization.

This chapter describes some of the accounting procedures that are used in practice. It should be emphasized that *no new accounting concepts are introduced*. The procedures described here are no more than the mechanical means of increasing the facility with which transactions can be recorded and summarized. We first describe the procedures used in a manual system, that is, one in which the numbers are recorded by hand. We then show the similarities and the differences between a manual system and a computer-based system.

RECORDKEEPING FUNDAMENTALS

We are not concerned here with recordkeeping procedures for the purpose of training bookkeepers. Some knowledge of these procedures is nevertheless useful for at least two reasons. First, as is the case with many subjects, accounting is something that is best learned by doing—by the actual solution of problems. Although any accounting problem can be solved without the aid of the tools discussed in this chapter, use of these tools will often speed up considerably the problem-solving process. Second, the debit-and-credit mechanism, which is the principal technique discussed here, provides an analytical framework that has much the same purpose and advantages as the symbols and equations of algebra.

The Account

Assume that the item "Cash, $10,000" appears on a balance sheet. Subsequent cash transactions can affect this amount in only one of two ways: they can increase it or they can decrease it. Instead of increasing or decreasing the item by erasing the old amount and entering the new amount for each transaction, considerable effort can be saved by collecting all the increases together and all the decreases together and then periodically calculating the *net* change resulting from all of them. This can be done by adding the sum of the increases to the beginning amount and then subtracting the sum of the decreases. The difference is the new cash *balance*.

In accounting, the device called an *account* is used for just this purpose. The simplest form of account, called a *T-account*, looks like this:

Cash

(Increases)		(Decreases)	
Beginning balance	10,000		2,000
	5,000		600
	4,000		400
	100		1,000
	2,700		
	800		
	22,600		4,000
New balance	18,600		

All increases are listed on one side, and all decreases are listed on the other. Note that the dollar sign ($) is omitted; this is the usual practice in most bookkeeping procedures.

The saving in effort can be seen even from this brief illustration. If the balance were changed for each of the nine items listed, five additions and four subtractions would be required. By using the account device, the new balance is obtained by only two additions (to find the 22,600 and 4,000) and one subtraction (22,600 − 4,000).

In actual accounting systems, the account form is set up so that other useful information, in addition to the amount of each increase or decrease, can be recorded. A common arrangement of the columns is the following:

Cash

January 1983

Date	Explanation	(R)	Amount	Date	Explanation	(R)	Amount
	Balance		10,000	3	Accts. Pay.	2	2,000
2	Sales	1	5,000	4	Supplies	2	600
2	Accts. Rec.	1	4,000				

The essence of this form of the account is the same as that of the T-account; in fact, the T can be observed in the double-ruled lines. Its headings are self-explanatory except that of "R" (standing for "reference"), under which is entered a simple code showing the source of the information recorded. This is useful if one needs to check back to the source of the entry at some future time.

Debit and Credit

The left-hand side of any account is arbitrarily called the *debit* side, and the right-hand side is called the *credit* side. Amounts entered on the left-hand side are called debits, and amounts on the right-hand side, credits. The verb "to debit" means "to make an entry in the left-hand side of an account," and the verb "to credit" means "to make an entry in the right-hand side of an account." *The words debit and credit have no other meaning in accounting.*[1]

In ordinary usage, these words do have other meanings. Credit has a favorable connotation (such as, "she is a credit to her family") and debit has an unfavorable connotation (such as, "chalk up a debit against him"). In accounting, these words do not imply any sort of value judgment; they mean simply "left" and "right." Debit and credit are usually abbreviated as dr. and cr.

If each account were considered by itself without regard to its relationship with other accounts, it would make no difference whether increases were recorded on the debit side or on the credit side. In the 15th century, a Franciscan monk, Lucas Pacioli, described a method of arranging accounts so that the *dual aspect* present in every accounting

---

[1]The noun *debit* is derived from the Latin *debitum*, which means "a debt." *Credit* is derived from the Latin *creditum*, which means "something entrusted to another." Debit and credit do *not* have these meanings in accounting.

transaction would be expressed by a debit amount and an equal and offsetting credit amount. This made possible the following rule, *to which there is absolutely no exception:* for each transaction the debit amount (or the sum of all the debit amounts, if there are more than one) must equal the credit amount (or the sum of all the credit amounts). This is why bookkeeping is called *double-entry* bookkeeping. It follows that the recording of a transaction in which debits do not equal credits is incorrect. It also follows that for all the accounts combined, the sum of the debit balances must equal the sum of the credit balances; otherwise, something has been done incorrectly. Thus, the debit and credit arrangement used in accounting provides a useful means of checking the accuracy with which the transactions have been recorded.

The equality of debits and credits is maintained in the accounts simply by specifying that asset accounts are increased on the debit side while liabilities and owners' equity accounts are increased on the credit side. The account balances, when they are totaled, will then conform to the two equations:

1. Assets = Liabilities + Owners' equity
2. Debits = Credits

This arrangement gives rise to three rules:

1. Increases in *asset* accounts are debits; decreases are credits.
2. Increases in *liability* accounts are credits; decreases are debits.
3. Increases in *owners' equity* accounts are credits; decreases are debits.

From the third rule, we can derive the rule for revenue accounts. Recall that revenues are increases in owners' equity arising from the operations of the entity. Since owners' equity accounts increase on the credit side, then revenues must be credits. Therefore, *deductions* from gross revenues, such as for sales returns and allowances, must be debits. Thus, the fourth rule is:

4. Increases in *revenue* accounts are credits; decreases are debits.

The rule for expenses is derived in the same way. Recall that expenses are decreases in owners' equity; and the third rule above states that owners' equity accounts decrease on the debit side. Thus, expenses must be debits. The greater the expenses recognized in an expense account, the more its debit balance will increase. If for any reason an expense entry must be reversed (such as a reversal in the Cost of Sales account when a customer returns an item in resalable condition for a refund), then the entry that reduces the expense account is a credit. Thus we have the fifth rule:

5. Increases in *expense* accounts are debits; decreases are credits.

These rules are illustrated in the diagram shown in Illustration 4–1. Note that assets, which are colloquially "good" things, and expenses, which are colloquially "bad" things, both increase on the debit side. Similarly, note that liability and revenue accounts both increase on the credit side. This is another illustration of the fact that "debit" and "credit" are neutral terms; they do not connote value judgments.

ILLUSTRATION 4–1
RULES OF DEBIT AND CREDIT

Assets	=	Liabilities	+	Owners' equity
Example:		*Example:*		*Example:*
Cash		**Accounts Payable**		**Retained Earnings**

dr.	cr.		dr.	cr.		dr.	cr.
+	−		−	+		−	+

	Expenses		Revenues
	Example:		*Example:*
	Cost of Sales		**Sales**

dr.	cr.		dr.	cr.
+	−		−	+

Debit balances = Credit balances

The Ledger

A *ledger* is a group of accounts. The reader may have seen a bound book with the title "ledger" or "general ledger" printed on the cover. All the accounts of a small business could be maintained in such a book. The ledger is not necessarily a bound book. It may consist of a set of loose-leaf pages, or, with computers, a set of impulses on a magnetic disk or tape. No matter what its form may be, the essential character of the account and the rules for making entries to it remain exactly as stated above.

The Chart of Accounts

Prior to setting up an accounting system, a list is usually prepared showing each item for which a ledger account is to be maintained. This list is called the *chart of accounts*. Each account on the list is numbered in a way that facilitates arrangement. The beginning of a chart of accounts might appear as follows:

1 – – Current assets
1 1 – Cash

1 1 1   Cash, First National Bank

1 1 2   Cash, Second National Bank

The actual accounts are those numbered 111 and 112, and entries are made only in these accounts. The other items are account categories that are used for summary purposes.

There are at least as many separate accounts as there are items on the balance sheet and income statement. Usually there are many more accounts than this minimum number so that detailed information useful to management can be collected. The number of accounts is governed by management's need for information. For example, although only the single item "Accounts receivable" appears on the balance sheet, a separate account for each customer is maintained in a ledger so as to show how much is owed by each.

There is no limit, other than the cost of recordkeeping, to the proliferation of accounts that may be found in practice. Consider, for example, sales revenue transactions. In the simplest ledger, there would be one account, Sales Revenue. If management wanted information on sales by geographic regions, there would be a separate sales account for each region. The sum of the balances in all these accounts would equal total sales revenue. Going a step further, if management wanted information classified both by sales region and by product class, there would be an account for sales of each product class within each region.

When such multidimensional classifications are desired, the number of separate accounts increases rapidly, for there must be a separate account for the smallest unit of information that is to be aggregated.

> **Example.**   A company divides its sales territory into nine regions. It sells products that it groups into 10 classes. In order to obtain information on sales both by region and by product class, it must have, not 19 (= 9 + 10) accounts but rather 90 (= 9 × 10) accounts.

With a manual system, the sheer bulk of the number of ledger pages constrains the proliferation of accounts that results from the desire for information that is classified in various ways. In a computer-based system, these constraints are much less severe.

The Journal

A *journal* is a chronological record of accounting transactions showing the names of accounts that are to be debited or credited, the amounts of the debits and credits, and any useful supplementary information about the transaction. A simple form of the journal is shown in Illustration 4–2. It helps in understanding these transactions if the reader reasons out the events that gave rise to each of them.

With respect to format, note the following: (1) the debit entry is listed first, (2) the debit amounts appear in the left-hand money column, (3)

ILLUSTRATION 4–2

JOURNAL

1983		Accounts	LF	Debit	Credit
Jan.	2	Cash........................	1	5,047.00	
		Sales....................	41		4,900.00
		Sales Tax Liability.......	21		147.00
	2	Accounts Receivable..........	2	1,711.50	
		Sales....................	41		1,650.00
		Sales Tax Liability.......	21		49.50
		Delivery Fees.............	32		12.00
	2	Cash.......................	1	4,000.00	
		Sales Discounts.............	43	60.00	
		Accounts Receivable.......	2		4,060.00
	3	Sales Returns and Allow— ances...................		47.00	
		Accounts Receivable.......			47.00

the account to be credited appears below the debit entry and is indented, and (4) the credit amounts appear in the right-hand money column. "LF" is an abbreviation for "ledger folio," that is, the page reference to the ledger account where the entry is to be made. This reference is inserted at the time the entry is recorded in the ledger account. Thus, the presence of numbers in the LF column indicates that the entries have been recorded. They also provide an *audit trail*, a way of tracing the amounts in the ledger back to their sources. In the illustration, the first 10 items have been recorded in the accounts, and the remaining two have not yet been recorded. In some bookkeeping systems, a brief explanation is written beneath each journal entry.

The journal contains explicit instructions on the changes to be made to the balances in the accounts. The process of making these changes is called *posting. No account balance is ever changed except on the basis of a journal entry.* (The balance in the account is computed and recorded periodically, but this process does not in any way *change* the balance in the account.)

Thus, the ledger is a device for *reclassifying* and *summarizing*, by accounts, information originally listed in chronological order in the journal. Entries are first made in the journal; they are later posted to ledger accounts.

The Trial Balance

The *trial balance* is simply a list of the account names and the balances in each account as of a given moment of time, with debit balances in one column and credit balances in another column. The preparation of the trial balance serves two principal purposes: (1) it shows whether the equality of debits and credits has been maintained, and (2) it provides a convenient summary transcript of the ledger record as a basis for making the adjusting and closing entires (described in the next section) that precede the preparation of the period's financial statements.

Although the fact that total debits equal total credits does indicate that the integrity of the basic accounting equation has been maintained, it does not prove that errors have not been made. Entries may have been omitted entirely; they may have been posted to the wrong account; offsetting errors may have been made; or a transaction may have been analyzed incorrectly. For example, if the debit for the purchase of a delivery truck is made incorrectly to an expense account rather than correctly to an equipment account, the totals of the trial balance are not affected.

THE ADJUSTING AND CLOSING PROCESS

Need for Adjusting Entries

Most entries to be made in accounts come to the accountant's attention easily and obviously. When checks are drawn against the entity's bank account, it is obvious that an entry must be made crediting Cash and debiting some other account. When invoices are sent out, a credit to Sales and a debit to Accounts Receivable is obviously generated. Entries of this type are called *original entries* or *spot entries*.

Some events that affect the accounts are not evidenced by such obvious documents, however. The effects of these events are recorded at the end of the accounting period by means of *adjusting entries*. The purpose of the adjusting entries is to modify account balances so that they will reflect fairly the situation as of the end of the period.

Continuous Transactions. Most adjusting entries are made in connection with events that are, in effect, continuous transactions. Consider a tankful of fuel oil purchased for $1,000. On the day of delivery, the $1,000 of fuel oil was an asset. But each day thereafter some fuel oil was consumed in the furnace, whereupon part of the $1,000 became an expense. Rather than record this consumption daily, a single adjusting entry is made at the end of the accounting period to show how much of the fuel oil is still an asset at that time and how much has become expense during the period. For example, if $600 has been consumed and hence become an expense, $400 remains as an asset.

There are two ways of handling these events, both of which give the same result. Under one method, the $1,000 expenditure is originally recorded as an asset, Fuel Oil Inventory, as in the following entry:

```
dr.*    Fuel Oil Inventory....................   1,000
    cr.     Accounts Payable .................              1,000
```

---

*As a reminder to the reader, the notations dr. and cr. are used in Chapters 4 and 5 to designate the debit and credit entries for each transaction recorded in the journal. These notations are not used in practice since the accountant distinguishes debits from credits on the basis of the order and indentation of the accounts.

At the end of the accounting period the asset account is adjusted by subtracting the cost of fuel oil consumed, thus:

```
dr.    Fuel Expense.........................    600
   cr.    Fuel Oil Inventory ...............          600
```

Under the other method, the $1,000 expenditure for fuel oil is originally recorded in an expense account (instead of an inventory account). Then the fuel oil remaining at the end of the period is subtracted from expense and shown as an asset, thus:

```
dr.    Fuel Oil Inventory...................    400
   cr.    Fuel Expense .....................          400
```

Although neither method reflects the correct facts *within* the period (with the trivial exception that the first method does reflect the facts on the day the oil was delivered), both reflect a correct statement of the facts as of the *end* of the accounting period. Since accounting focuses on deriving the proper amounts for the statements that are prepared at the end of the accounting period, and since both methods result in the correct final amounts, the choice between these methods depends solely on which is more convenient.

Types of Adjusting Entries

Events that require adjusting entries essentially relate to the differences between expense and expenditure and between revenue and receipts discussed in Chapter 3. Four types of such events, together with examples of each, are given below:

1. *Recorded costs to be apportioned among two or more accounting periods.* The fuel oil transaction given above is one example. Another is:

   For insurance protection, originally recorded as Prepaid Insurance (an asset), $800 of which becomes an expense in the current period:

   ```
   dr.    Insurance Expense.............    800
      cr.    Prepaid Insurance .........          800
   ```

2. *Unrecorded expenses.* These expenses were incurred during the period, but no record of them has yet been made. Example:

   For $50 of wages earned by an employee during the period but not yet paid to the employee:

   ```
   dr.    Wages Expense ................    50
      cr.    Accrued Wages .............          50
   ```

3. *Recorded revenues to be apportioned among two or more accounting periods.* As was the case with recorded costs, these amounts were

initially recorded in one account, and at the end of the accounting period must be properly divided between a revenue account and a liability account. Example: For rent collected during the period and recorded as rent revenue, $600 of which is applicable to the next period and hence is a liability at the end of the current period:

```
dr.     Rent Revenue .....................     600
    cr.     Deferred Rent Revenue .........           600
```

4. *Unrecorded revenues.* These revenues were earned during the period, but no record of them has yet been made. Example: For $20 of interest earned by the business during the period but not yet received:

```
dr.     Accrued Interest Receivable .......     20
    cr.     Interest Revenue ..............           20
```

Depreciation. Most long-lived assets are continuously being converted to an expense, in the same manner as the current assets—fuel oil, prepaid insurance, and supplies—that were discussed above. The item that shows the portion of such long-lived asset costs that have become expense during an accounting period is called *depreciation expense.* Instead of subtracting the depreciation expense for the period directly from the asset amount, however, a separate account, *Accumulated Depreciation,* is used. Such an account is called a *contra* account because it is subtracted from some other account. Accumulated depreciation shows the total of such subtractions to date and is deducted from the cost of the related assets on the balance sheet, thus:

```
Equipment (at cost) ...........................   $10,000
Less: Accumulated depreciation..............     4,000
        Net equipment.........................          $6,000
```

The adjusting entry to record the depreciation expense for a period is therefore in the following form:

```
dr.     Depreciation Expense..................   2,000
    cr.     Accumulated Depreciation ..........         2,000
```

This process is described in more detail in Chapter 7.

Other Adjustments. Accountants make a variety of other adjusting entries in their attempt to make the accounts reflect fairly the results of operations and the status of the entity. An example, discussed in more detail in Chapter 5, is *bad debt expense.* This is an adjustment made in order to recognize the likelihood that not all credit customers will pay their bills, and thus the Accounts Receivable account may overstate the realizable amount of those bills. An adjusting entry that records the estimated amount of bad debts is as follows:

```
dr.     Bad Debt Expense.....................     300
   cr.      Allowance for Doubtful Accounts ...          300
```

On the balance sheet, allowance for doubtful accounts (also a contra account) is subtracted from accounts receivable, thus:

Accounts receivable (gross)......................	$10,000
Less: Allowance for doubtful accounts	400
Net accounts receivable....................	$9,600

A Caution. When the student is given a problem involving the preparation of accounting statements, the precise nature of the original entries must be described, since the student has no other way of finding out about them. Information about the *adjusting* entries will not necessarily be given, however. Students, like accountants, are expected to be on the lookout for situations that require adjustment. For example, if the balance sheet at the beginning of a period shows the asset, prepaid insurance, accountants know that they must make an adjusting entry at the end of the period to show the expired cost, even though no document or explicit instruction tells them to do so.

Closing Entries

Revenue accounts and expense accounts are called *temporary* (or "nominal") accounts, as distinguished from asset, liability, and owners' equity accounts, which are called *permanent* (or "real") accounts. The temporary accounts are actually subdivisions of owners' equity. They are a convenient means of classifying the various revenue and expense transactions that occur during an accounting period so as to provide the information needed to prepare the income statement for the period. The temporary accounts are periodically *closed* to owners' equity in order to determine the net effect of all the revenue and expense transactions, that is, the net income or loss.

Closing procedures differ from entity to entity. Under all closing methods, however, revenue and expense accounts are ultimately closed to an account called *Income Summary* (also called *Profit and Loss* or *Loss and Gain* or *Expense and Revenue Summary*). This account reflects the net income or loss for a given accounting period. Income Summary is a *clearing* account that in turn is closed to an owners' equity account (in a corporation, Retained Earnings) to complete the closing process.

The closing process consists of transferring the balance of each temporary account to the same side of a clearing account. This is done by making a journal entry debiting the account to be closed if it has a credit balance (or crediting it if it has a debit balance) in an amount equal to the balance. This entry has the effect of reducing the balance in the account to zero, thereby closing it. Note that each entry is made on the opposite side from the side with the balance. The other half of this entry is made to Income Summary.

Example 1. If the credit balance in the Sales account at the end of an accounting period if $538,000, the account is closed by the following entry:

```
dr.    Sales.......................... 538,000
    cr.     Income Summary...............           538,000
```

Example 2. If the Salaries and Wages Expense account has a debit balance of $153,000, it is closed by the following entry:

```
dr.    Income Summary.................. 153,000
    cr.     Salaries and Wages Expense....           153,000
```

At the completion of the closing process, all temporary accounts have zero balances; the only accounts remaining open are the permanent accounts—the asset, liability, and owners' equity accounts.

It would be possible to close the revenue and expense accounts simply by drawing lines at the bottom of each account, rather than by making journal entries as described above. This would, however, violate the rule that all changes in account balances must be made by journal entries. The journal entry lessens the chances of errors or omissions and facilitates the task of finding the error if the postclosing trial balance does not balance.

Ruling and Balancing Accounts

At the end of the accounting period, each permanent account is *ruled and balanced* so it is in a convenient form for preparing the end-of-period balance sheet and is ready to begin accumulating entries for the coming period. The procedure is as follows: First, a balancing amount is written in the appropriate column of the account so as to make the totals in the debit and credit columns equal. The totals are then shown and double-ruled to indicate the end of the accounting period sequence. Finally, the new balance is "brought down" on the opposite side from that in which it was first written, as the initial figure for the new period. The account then appears at the top of the next page.[2]

The Worksheet

A worksheet is a preliminary compilation of figures that facilitates recording or analysis. A worksheet is often used preliminary to the formal journalizing and posting of the adjusting and closing entries. Its use permits the accountant to make a "dry run" of the whole process. Since a pencil is ordinarily used, any errors detected on the worksheet can be easily corrected, whereas alterations to the formal records are to be avoided. The worksheet also classifies account balances according to the financial statements in which they are to appear.

----

[2]In introducing the idea of an account on page 94, the line "To Balance 18,600" was omitted. It should be used in the normal bookkeeping process.

	Cash		
Balance	10,000		2,000
	5,000		600
	4,000		400
	100		1,000
	2,700	To Balance	18,600
	800		
	22,600		22,600
Balance	18,600		

A worksheet is often used instead of, rather than preliminary to, the adjusting and closing process. Many entities formally close their books only once a year, but nevertheless prepare monthly financial statements. These interim statements are prepared from a worksheet listing the account balances at the end of the month together with the adjustments necessary to reflect revenue and expense in that month. Statements are prepared from the adjusted account balances developed on this worksheet. The income statement figures on such a worksheet would be cumulative for the year to date. An income statement for the current month can be derived from the cumulative figures simply by subtracting the corresponding figures on the preceding month's worksheet.

Illustration 4–3 shows a sample worksheet for a retail store that sells only on a cash basis and does not own its premises. The five adjustments shown thereon reflect:

a. Cost of merchandise sold, $126,000 (dr. Cost of Goods Sold, cr. Inventory). During the period, all purchases of merchandise had been debited to Inventory, but no entries had been made to show the movement of merchandise out of inventory.

b. Expired insurance of $800 (dr. Insurance Expense, cr. Prepaid Insurance).

c. Accrued interest expense of $100 (dr. Interest Expense, cr. Accrued Interest Payable).

d. Accrued wages of $1,000 (dr. Salaries and Wages, cr. Wages Payable).

e. Accrued employer's tax on wages of $70 (dr. Social Security Tax Expense, cr. Employee Taxes Payable).

f. Estimated income tax for the period of $1,070 (dr. Income Tax Expense, cr. Income Tax Liability).

ILLUSTRATION 4–3
ILLUSTRATIVE WORKSHEET
(in round numbers)

	Trial Balance March 31		Adjustments*		Income Statement		Balance Sheet	
	Dr.	Cr.	Dr.	Cr.	Dr.	Cr.	Dr.	Cr.
Cash	18,600						18,600	
Inventory	213,000			126,000 (a)			87,000	
Prepaid insurance	2,400			800 (b)			1,600	
Accounts payable		45,000						45,000
Employee taxes payable		1,200		70 (e)				1,270
Notes payable		10,000						10,000
Capital stock		20,000						20,000
Retained earnings		22,700						22,700
Sales		174,000				174,000		
Rental and other space costs	9,000				9,000			
Salaries and wages	20,000		1,000 (d)		21,000			
Social security tax expense	1,400		70 (e)		1,470			
Advertising expense	6,600				6,600			
Miscellaneous expenses	1,900				1,900			
Nonoperating revenue		400				400		
Interest expense	400		100 (c)		500			
	273,300	273,300						
Cost of goods sold			126,000 (a)		126,000			
Insurance expense			800 (b)		800			
Accrued interest payable				100 (c)				100
Wages payable				1,000 (d)				1,000
Income tax expense			1,070 (f)		1,070			
Income tax liability				1,070 (f)				1,070
Net income					6,060			6,060
			129,040	129,040	174,400	174,400	107,200	107,200

*Letters in parentheses relate to explanations of these adjustments given in the text.

Note that additional accounts are added as needed at the bottom of the worksheet.

The last item on this worksheet, $6,060, is the net income for the period. It is found by subtracting the sum of the other debits to Income Statement from the sum of the credits to Income Statement. Showing the same amount in the Balance Sheet credit column has the effect of closing the net income to Retained Earnings. After this amount has been entered, each column of a pair should add to the same total; this is a check on the arithmetic accuracy of the whole closing process.

Statement Preparation. So that the connection between the adjusting and closing process and the financial statements will be clear, financial statements prepared from the worksheet in Illustration 4–3 are shown in Illustration 4–4. Since the accounting period was three months, these are examples of interim statements.

Summary of the Accounting Process

1. The first, and most important, part of the accounting process is the *analysis of transactions*. This is the process of deciding which account or accounts should be debited, which should be credited, and in what amounts, in order to reflect events in the accounting records. This requires knowledge of accounting concepts and judgment.

2. Next comes the purely mechanical step of *journalizing original entries*; recording the results of the transaction analysis in the journal.

3. *Posting* is the process of recording changes in the ledger accounts exactly as specified by the journal entries. This is another purely mechanical step.

ILLUSTRATION 4–4
FINANCIAL STATEMENTS

ARCHMONT STORE, INC.
Balance Sheet
As of March 31

Assets		Equities	
Cash	$ 18,600	Accounts payable	$ 45,000
Inventory	87,000	Employee taxes payable	1,270
Prepaid insurance	1,600	Wages payable	1,000
		Notes payable	10,000
		Accrued interest payable	100
		Income tax liability	1,070
		Total liabilities	58,440
		Capital stock	20,000
		Retained earnings	28,760
Total assets	$107,200	Total equities	$107,200

Income Statement
For the First Quarter

Sales		$174,000
Less: Cost of goods sold		126,000
Gross margin		48,000
Expenses:		
Rental and other space costs	$ 9,000	
Salaries and wages	21,000	
Social security tax expense	1,470	
Advertising expense	6,600	
Insurance expense	800	
Miscellaneous expense	1,900	
Interest expense	500	41,270
		6,730
Other revenue		400
Income before income taxes		7,130
Provision for income taxes		1,070
Net income		$ 6,060

4. At the ending of the accounting period, judgment is involved in deciding on the *adjusting entries*. These are journalized and posted in the same way as are original entries.

5. The *closing entries* are journalized and posted. This is a purely mechanical step.

6. *Financial statements* are prepared. This requires judgment as to the best arrangement and terminology, but the numbers that are used result from the judgments made in steps 1 and 4.[3]

These six steps are taken sequentially during an accounting period, and are repeated in each subsequent period. The steps are therefore com-

---

[3]Trial balances may be prepared prior to steps 4 and 5, as another check on accuracy prior to closing the books.

ILLUSTRATION 4–5
THE ACCOUNTING CYCLE

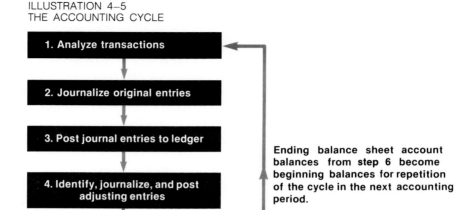

Ending balance sheet account balances from **step 6** become beginning balances for repetition of the cycle in the next accounting period.

monly referred to as the *accounting cycle*. Illustration 4–5 depicts the accounting cycle schematically. Note that the ending balance sheet account balances from step 6 became the beginning balances for the next repetition of the cycle.

ACCOUNTING SYSTEMS

The simple journals, ledgers, and worksheets, together with the rules for using them, described in the preceding pages, constitute an accounting system. But this particular system would not usually be the best system for a given organization. The best system is that one that best achieves the following objectives:

1. To process the information efficiently, that is, at low cost.
2. To obtain reports quickly.
3. To ensure a high degree of accuracy.
4. To minimize the possibility of theft or fraud.

Designing a good accounting system is a specialized job requiring a high degree of skill. Only a few of the principles are noted here.

Special Journals

The journal form shown in Illustration 4–2 is called a *general journal*. This form requires that the title of each account affected by each entry be written down. If many entries are made to a single account, efficiency can be increased by using a *special journal* or *register*. A special journal has several columns, each headed with the name of an account to be debited or credited, plus (usually) a Miscellaneous column in which entries to other accounts may be recorded. Entries to the accounts indicated by column headings are made simply by entering the proper amount in these columns. At the end of the accounting period, all the amounts in each column are added, and the total is posted as one amount to the appropriate account. Entries in the Miscellaneous column are posted individually.

Illustration 4–6 gives an example of a special journal used to record debits to Cash and credits to various accounts. This is called a *cash receipts journal*. Columns are provided for the accounts in which entries are likely to be made frequently (here, Accounts Receivable, for collections, and Sales, for cash sales). A miscellaneous column is also provided for other credits. To illustrate the use of this journal, on May 31, Mary Able made a $300 payment on her account. Fred Black and Henry Cheng also made payments. The check marks in the LF (ledger folio) column indicate that these payments also have been credited to each customer's account in the accounts receivable subsidiary ledger (described in the next section). Also on May 31, $56 interest revenue from a savings account at Peoples Bank was received in cash. The number 561 in the LF column indicates that this transaction has been posted in account 561, Interest Revenue. The total credits in the Accounts Receivable column, $5,360, will be credited as a single entry to Accounts Receivable (account 120). Similarly, $2,430 will be credited to Sales (account 511), and $8,786 will be debited to Cash (account 111).

ILLUSTRATION 4–6

CASH RECEIPTS JOURNAL

Date		Received From	LF	Accounts Receivable Cr.	Sales Cr.	Other Cr.		Cash Dr.
						Account	Amount	
May	31	Brought forward*		4,200.00	2,000.00		940.00	7,140.00
	31	Mary Able	√	300.00				300.00
	31	Fred Black	√	650.00				650.00
	31	Henry Cheng	√	210.00				210.00
	31	Cash Sales			430.00			430.00
	31	Peoples Bank	561			Interest Revenue	56.00	56.00
		Totals		5,360.00	2,430.00		996.00	8,786.00
		(Account No.)		(120)	(511)			(111)

*These are totals from the preceding journal page.

**Control Accounts
and Subsidiary
Ledgers**

Most organizations use one or more *subsidiary ledgers,* which are groups of related accounts taken out of the general ledger. For example, all the separate accounts for individual customers may be kept in an accounts receivable ledger. One advantage of this practice is that several bookkeepers can be working on the ledger accounts simultaneously.

In order to keep the general ledger in balance, a *control account* takes the place of the individual accounts removed to the subsidiary ledger. A control account shows in summary form the debits and credits shown in detail in a subsidiary ledger. When subsidiary ledgers are used, each amount is, in effect, posted twice. It is posted, often daily, to the proper account in the subsidiary ledger. It also becomes a part of the total that is posted at the end of the period to the control account in the general ledger. In a large business, most if not all of the general ledger accounts are control accounts.

Illustration 4–7 shows an accounts receivable ledger and its relation-

ILLUSTRATION 4–7
GENERAL LEDGER AND SUBSIDIARY LEDGER

GENERAL LEDGER			
Cash (111)			
Date	Debit	Credit	Balance
May 1			9,240.00
31	8,786.00		18,026.00
Accounts Receivable (120)			
Date	Debit	Credit	Balance
May 1			6,200.00
31		5,360.00	840.00
Sales (511)			
Date	Debit	Credit	Balance
May 31		2,430.00	2,430.00
Interest Revenue (561)			
Date	Debit	Credit	Balance
May 31		56.00	56.00
(All Other Ledger Accounts)			
Date	Debit	Credit	Balance
May 1			15,440.00 cr.
31		940.00	16,380.00

ILLUSTRATION 4–7 *(concluded)*

ACCOUNTS RECEIVABLE LEDGER			
Mary Able (121)			
Date	Debit	Credit	Balance
May 1 31		 300.00	300.00 –0–
Fred Black (122)			
Date	Debit	Credit	Balance
May 1 31		 650.00	1,000.00 350.00
Henry Cheng (123)			
Date	Debit	Credit	Balance
May 1 31		 210.00	210.00 –0–
(All Other Accounts)			
Date	Debit	Credit	Balance
May 1 (May)		 4,200.00	4,690.00 490.00

ship to the Accounts Receivable account in the general ledger, which is its control account. Each customer's account is posted daily. At the end of the month, the total of all the individual entries (here $5,360.00) is posted to the control account. For simplicity, Illustration 4–7 does not show debits to the customer accounts for sales made on credit. These would be journalized in another special journal, the sales journal, and also posted to the accounts receivable ledger. Note the tie-in between the entries shown in Illustration 4–7 and the cash receipts journal in Illustration 4–6.

Imprest Funds

The imprest fund is another work-saving device. It consists of cash advanced to a responsible person and periodically replenished by additional cash equal to the amount expended by this person.

The operation of an imprest fund is illustrated by its most common version, the *petty cash* fund. The fund is established by drawing a check on the entity's bank account. The person responsible for the fund cashes the check and puts the money in a petty cash box. This transaction is recorded by the following entry:

```
dr.     Petty Cash.........................     50
    cr.     Cash .............................          50
```

The petty cash is used to pay small bills until it is nearly exhausted. At that time, these bills are summarized and a check is drawn for the amount they total. A journal entry is made debiting the various expense or asset accounts represented by the bills; for example:

```
dr.     Office Supplies                      21
        Miscellaneous Expense................ 25
    cr.     Cash .............................          46
```

Note that the credit is to the regular Cash account. Once established, the Petty Cash account in the ledger is not changed unless the size of the fund is changed.

This procedure saves the effort involved in drawing checks and making separate journal entries for small bills. It also provides a safeguard, since the petty cash box should at all times contain cash and receipted bills that together total the amount shown in the Petty Cash account.

The imprest device is by no means limited to petty cash. Many government disbursing agencies operate on the same principle, but in amounts that run into millions of dollars. These agencies are advanced funds by the U.S. Treasury Department, they disburse these funds to pay authorized bills, and they submit these bills to the Treasury Department as a basis for replenishing the fund. The accounting entries are essentially the same as those given above for petty cash.

Internal Accounting Controls

Two objectives of an accounting system stated above—accuracy and protection against theft or fraud—cannot be attained absolutely without conflicting with the other two—speed and economy. A system that "can't be beaten" would be prohibitively expensive and time-consuming. A basic principle of internal accounting control therefore is that the system should make it *as difficult as is practical* for people to be dishonest or careless. Such a principle is based not on a cynical view of people in general but rather on the realistic assumption that a few people will be dishonest or careless if it is easy for them to do so.

Some of the devices used to ensure reasonable accuracy have been touched on already, for example, the idea of verifying one set of figures against another. The idea of divided responsibility is another important one. Whenever feasible, one person should not be responsible for recording all aspects of a transaction, nor should the *custodian* of assets (e.g., the storekeeper or the cashier) be permitted to do the *accounting* for these assets. Thus, one person's work is a check on another's. Although this does not eliminate the possibility that two people will steal through collusion, the likelihood of dishonesty is greatly reduced.

Foreign Corrupt Practices Act. In recent years, the objectives of internal accounting controls have expanded well beyond the traditional focus on protection against theft and fraud. One impetus for this expansion was the Foreign Corrupt Practices Act of 1977 (FCPA). The FCPA makes illegal any direct or indirect payments to foreign officials for the purpose of helping the paying company to obtain or retain sales in foreign countries. In addition, the FCPA requires corporate management to "maintain a system of internal accounting controls sufficient to provide reasonable assurances that: (1) transactions are executed in accordance with management's . . . authorization; and (2) the recorded accountability for assets is compared with the existing assets at reasonable intervals and appropriate action is taken with respect to any differences."

While most executives view control as an integral part of the management process, many resent the implication which they feel underlies the FCPA accounting provisions—that U.S. corporate executives are not adequately attentive to control practices within their companies. Many people feel that the FCPA provisions are vague (e.g., what does the expression "reasonable assurances" mean?), and that these provisions go well beyond the purposes of the act to prevent questionable overseas payments.[4]

These brief comments indicate only the nature of the problem of internal accounting control, which is a big subject. Furthermore, a book that focuses on accounting principles, as this one does, cannot detail the complexities involved in *operating* accounting systems. For example, cash transactions are very easy to analyze, whereas some textbooks on auditing contain a dozen pages of questions that should be considered in connection with the internal accounting control of the single item, cash.

Significant Recordkeeping Ideas

At least two significant ideas should emerge from this description of the recordkeeping process and of accounting systems.

The first is the idea of *debit and credit equality:* "every debit must have an equal credit." This idea is much more than a mechanical bookkeeping requirement. It is a way of thinking that is extremely useful in analyzing what is going on in an organization. There is a natural human tendency to think only about part of the consequences of a decision and to overlook some equally important part. For example, although a growing cash balance superficially looks good, this is only half of the story. It makes considerable difference whether the credits offsetting these debits to cash reflect revenues from profitable operations or whether they reflect emergency bank loans.

---

[4]For an extensive report on the state of the art of internal controls, see *Internal Control in U.S. Corporations* (New York: Financial Executives Research Foundation, 1980).

The second significant idea is that of *balancing*: one total should always equal some other total. Three balancing techniques have been described: (1) the fundamental debit-credit structure; (2) the control-subsidiary relationship, in which the total of the subsidiary items must always equal a control total; and (3) the imprest technique, in which the sum of cash and paid bills must always equal a predetermined total. As noted above, these devices provide a check on arithmetic accuracy, they lessen the risk of loss through dishonesty, and they lessen the chance that some part of a transaction will be overlooked. Numbers derived from a system that does *not* contain such balancing mechanisms should be regarded skeptically; the likelihood of errors or omissions is great.

COMPUTER-BASED ACCOUNTING SYSTEMS

Most large organizations and an increasing number of small ones do their accounting work with an electronic computer, rather than with the manual methods described above. We initially explained the process in terms of manual methods both because the forms and records used in manual systems are visible, whereas the operations that go on inside a computer are invisible, and also because in solving problems of the type encountered in an accounting course, students usually find it more convenient to use manual methods, even if they have access to a computer. In this section we describe the similarities and the differences between a computer-based system and a manual system.

Relationship to Manual Accounting

Any accounting system does the following:

1. It records and stores data.
2. It performs arithmetic operations on data.
3. It sorts and summarizes data.
4. It prepares reports.

The principal differences between manual and computerized accounting systems lie in the means of performance of arithmetic operations and in the storage of data. The diagram in Illustration 4–8 depicts the most significant similarities and differences between the two types of system. Professional accounting judgment in analyzing transactions, and in creating source documents to capture the important information about routine transactions, is required regardless of the degree of computerization in the recordkeeping process. In a computerized system, however, a single human task—entering the data from the source document into a device that transforms the data into computer-readable form—replaces a series of human tasks in a manual system—journalizing entries, posting in general and subsidiary ledgers, taking a trial balance, and report preparation. The computer program, rather than humans, performs these

ILLUSTRATION 4–8
COMPARISON OF MANUAL AND COMPUTERIZED ACCOUNTING SYSTEMS

	Step 1	Step 2	Step 3		Step 4
	Transaction Analysis	Recording Data	Data Storage for Steps 2 and 3	Data Processing	Reports
Computerized	Ⓗ Source data (not necessarily a tangible document)	Ⓗ Entering data into a database in machine-readable format	• Punched cards • Disk • Tape • Other memory	Ⓒ • Update account balances Ⓒ • Trial balance Ⓒ • Worksheets ——— Ⓒ • Adjusting entries Ⓒ • Final trial balance Ⓒ • Reports ———————→	Ⓒ • Financial statements Ⓒ • Numerous specialized management reports
Manual	Ⓗ Source document	Ⓗ Journalizing	• Journals • Subsidiary ledgers	Ⓗ • Summarize journals Ⓗ • Post summaries to ledger(s) Ⓗ • Trial balance Ⓗ • Worksheets Ⓗ • Adjusting entries Ⓗ • Final trial balance Ⓗ • Reports ———————→	Ⓗ • Financial statements Ⓗ • Few general-purpose management reports

Ⓗ = Human operation.
Ⓒ = Computer program operation.

bookkeeping tasks. Of course, accountants still must analyze the trial balance and initiate the proper adjusting entries.

The Matrix Concept   In a manual system the amount of a debit ends up on the debit side of one account and the amount of the corresponding credit ends up on the credit side of another account. In many computerized accounting systems, both the debit and the credit amounts are stored in a single *cell* within the computer. Each such cell has an *address*, which identifies both the debit and the credit portion of a particular transaction. The array of all such cells is called a *matrix*.

Illustration 4–9 shows the portion of a matrix that corresponds to the accounts used to illustrate the ideas of special journals and subsidiary ledgers in Illustrations 4–6 and 4–7. Cell 111:121, for example, records all debits to Cash (account 111) that are also credits to the account, Accounts Receivable, Mary Able (account 121). In the illustration, the amount is $300, representing a cash receipt from Mary Able to settle her account.

The cell numbered 123:511 represents sales revenues (511) from sales on account to Henry Cheng (123). In addition to the dollar amount of the sale, the computer may also store detailed information about the trans-

ILLUSTRATION 4–9
PORTION OF A RECORDKEEPING MATRIX

Account Debits		Account Credits								Total Debits	Begin. Dr. Bal.	New Dr. Bal.
		111	121	122	123	12X	511	561	XXX			
Cash	111		300	650	210	4200	2430	56	940	8786	9240	18026
Accts. Receivable Mary Able	121										300	0
Accts. Receivable Fred Black	122										1000	350
Accts. Receivable Henry Cheng	123										210	0
Accts. Receivable (All other)	12X										4690	490
Sales	511											
Interest Revenue	561											
(Other accounts)	XXX											
Total credits			300	650	210	4200	2430	56	940	8786		
Beginning cr. balance										15440		15440
New credit balance								2430	56	16380			18866

action, such as the name, quantity, and selling price of each item sold to Henry Cheng.

Whenever financial statements are prepared, the computer is instructed to add the numbers in each *row* in the matrix to obtain the debits to each account, to add the numbers in each *column* to obtain the credits, and to adjust the previous account balance for these debits and credits so as to find the new account balance. These computations are illustrated at the bottom (for the credits) and along the right-hand side (for the debits) of Illustration 4–9.

Two Important Differences

Two differences between manual and computerized systems should be noted. The first difference relates to the audit trail. The ability in a manual system to trace every entry in the ledger to its components in journals and eventually to the source document establishes the integrity of the audit trail in a manual system. In computerized systems, because the data storage and arithmetic manipulation are hidden from view, creating an acceptable audit trail becomes more difficult. The integrity of accounting data within computerized databases is an important concern of internal accounting control. Spectacular computer frauds in recent years, while few in number, have made management more aware of the internal control complexities that accompany the computerizing of recordkeeping systems.

The second major difference involves the number of reports generated by computerized systems as compared to manual systems. Since with a manual system the cost of preparing reports other than the basic financial statements is high, most reports are of a broad, general-purpose nature, and identical reports are distributed to many different managers in the organization. On the other hand, the cost of preparing specialized management reports in computerized systems is usually quite low. This often leads to a larger number of different reports oriented toward specific managers and their responsibilities. Such "customized" reports are potentially advantageous if they are carefully designed to meet their recipients' informational needs. However, in some organizations managers suffer from "information overload" as a result of having too many detailed, only partially relevant, reports sent to them every week. In such instances, the managers may cease to use *any* of the reports, making the reports of *no* value, despite the low cost of preparing them.

SUMMARY

The account is a device for collecting information about each item that is to be accounted for. It has two sides: the left-hand, or debit, side; and the right-hand, or credit, side. The rules are such that asset and expense accounts increase on the debit side, whereas liabilities, owners' equity, and revenue accounts increase on the credit side. This maintains both the equation Assets = Liabilities + Owners' equity and the equation Debits = Credits.

A ledger is a group of accounts. Entries are made to ledger accounts on the basis of instructions given in a journal, which is chronological record of transactions.

At the end of an accounting period, adjusting entries are made so that after adjustment, the revenue and expense accounts will show the appropriate amounts for the period. These temporary accounts are then closed to an income summary account, which in turn is closed to Retained Earnings.

In manual accounting systems, special journals, subsidiary ledgers, and other devices facilitate the process of recording accounting data. A computer-based system performs the same functions more rapidly, more accurately, and, if the volume of repetitive transactions is large, at lower cost.

APPENDIX

Locating Errors Revealed by the Trial Balance

Following are four suggested aids in detecting errors revealed by differences between the debit and credit totals of the trial balance:

1. If the difference between the totals is 0.01, 1.00, 100, 1,000, and so forth, the error is probably in addition. Such an error is usually detected by re-adding the columns of the trial balance, or, if necessary, the columns in the ledger accounts.

2. When the discrepancy is an even number, the error may be the result of making a debit entry in a credit column, or vice versa. Divide the difference in totals by 2, and look first through the trial balance and then the ledger accounts for an amount corresponding to this quotient. The difference is divided by 2 because an item placed in the wrong column results in a difference of twice its amount.

3. If the difference is divisible by 9, the error is probably either a transposition or a transplacement, and the search can be narrowed down to numbers where these errors might have been made. A *transposition* occurs when 79 is written for 97, 318 for 813, and so on. A *transplacement* or *slide* occurs when the digits of the number are moved to the left or right, as when $6,328.00 is written as $632.80 or $63.28.

4. When the source of error is not readily discernible, it is advisable to check the trial balance against the ledger to determine whether all the account balances have been copied properly. This check may reveal that certain accounts have been omitted. As a last resort, it may be necessary to check all of the numbers in the ledger with the journal and to check all additions and subtractions in the several accounts.

Care in making the entries, such as writing legibly, doublechecking additions and subtractions as journalizing and posting proceeds, and making sure all entries are entered properly, will save much time otherwise spent in hunting for errors.

SUGGESTIONS FOR FURTHER READING

Cushing, Barry E. *Accounting Information Systems and Business Organizations.* 2d ed. Reading, Mass: Addison-Wesley Publishing, 1978.

Murdick, Robert G. *MIS: Concepts and Design.* Englewood Cliffs, N.J.: Prentice-Hall, 1980.

Pyle, William W., and Kermit D. Larson. *Fundamental Accounting Principles.* 9th ed. Homewood, Ill.: Richard D. Irwin, 1981.

Shelly, Gary B., and Thomas J. Cashman. *Introduction to Computers and Data Processing.* Brea, Cal.: Anaheim Publishing, 1980.

Silver, Gerald A., and Joan B. Silver. *Data Processing for Business.* 3d ed. New York: Harcourt Brace Jovanovich, 1981.

Cases

CASE 4–1 The Computer Room

The Computer Room was a retail store for home computers and hand-held calculators, selling several national brands in each product line. The store was opened in early September by Kay Devlin, a young woman previously employed

EXHIBIT 1

GENERAL JOURNAL

Entry Number	Account	Dr.	Cr.
		Amount	
(1)	Cash	90,000	
	Bank Loan Payable (15%)		60,000
	Proprietor's Capital		30,000
(2)	Rent Expense (September)	800	
	Cash		800
(3)	Merchandise Inventory	75,000	
	Accounts Payable		75,000
(4)	Furniture and Fixtures (10-year life)	3,200	
	Cash		3,200
(5)	Advertising Expense	700	
	Cash		700
(6)	Wages Expense	420	
	Cash		420
(7)	Office Supplies Expense	600	
	Cash		600
(8)	Utilities Expense	97	
	Cash		97

in direct computer sales for a national firm specializing in business computers.

Ms. Devlin knew the importance of adequate records. One of her first acts, therefore, was to hire Fred Cole, a local accountant, to set up her bookkeeping system.

Mr. Cole wrote up the store's preopening financial transactions in journal form to serve as an example (Exhibit 1), and then asked Ms. Devlin to write up the remainder of the store's September financial transactions for his review.

At the end of September, Ms. Devlin had the following items to record:

(9)	Cash sales for September	$22,740
(10)	Credit sales for September	8,220
(11)	Cash received from credit customers	2,050
(12)	Bills paid to merchandise suppliers	50,250
(13)	New merchandise received on credit from supplier	23,200
(14)	Ms. Devlin ascertained the cost of merchandise sold was	21,670
(15)	Wages paid to assistant	300
(16)	Wages earned but unpaid at the end of September	300
(17)	Petty cash fund established	75
(18)	Rent paid for October	800
(19)	Insurance bill paid for one year	1,200
(20)	Bills received, but unpaid, from electric company	85
(21)	Purchased sign, paying $400 cash and agreeing to pay the $800 balance by December 31	1,200

Questions

1. Explain the events that probably gave rise to journal entries 1 through 8 of Exhibit 1.

2. Set up a ledger account (in T-account form) for each account named in the general journal. Post entries 1 through 8 to these accounts, using the entry number as a cross-reference.

3. Analyze the facts listed as 9 through 21, resolving them into their debit and credit elements. Prepare journal entries and post to the ledger accounts. (Do not prepare closing entries.)

4. Consider any other transactions that should be recorded. Why are these adjusting entries required? Prepare journal entries for them and post to ledger accounts.

5. Prepare closing entries and post to ledger accounts. What new ledger accounts are required? Why?

6. Prepare an income statement for September and a balance sheet as of September 30.

CASE 4–2   Picard Company

The account balances in the ledger of the Picard Company on February 28 (the end of its fiscal year), before adjustments, wer s shown at the top of p. 121.

T   data for the adjustments are:

1. Cost of merchandise sold, $229,300.
2. Store equipment had a useful life of 10 years. (All equipment was less than 10 years old.)

3. Supplies inventory, February 28, $1,650. (Purchases of supplies during the year were debited to the Supplies Inventory account.)

4. Expired insurance, $2,500.

Debit Balances

Cash.	$ 29,695
Accounts receivable.	49,200
Merchandise inventory.	348,700
Store equipment	27,400
Supplies inventory.	6,750
Prepaid insurance.	4,800
Selling expense.	4,200
Sales salaries.	18,200
Miscellaneous general expense.	7,310
Sales discounts.	1,290
Interest expense.	4,125
Social security tax expense	690
Total.	$502,360

Credit Balances

Accumulated depreciation on store equipment.	$ 4,410
Notes payable	30,000
Accounts payable.	34,350
Common stock.	40,000
Retained earnings.	11,100
Sales	382,500
Total.	$502,360

5. The note payable was at an interest rate of 15 percent, payable monthly. It had been outstanding throughout the year.

6. Sales salaries earned but not paid to employees, $750.

7. The statement sent by the bank, adjusted for checks outstanding, showed a balance of $29,495. The difference represented bank service charges.

Questions

1. Set up T-accounts with the balances given above.

2. Journalize and post adjusting entries, adding other T-accounts as necessary.

3. Journalize and post closing entries.

4. Prepare an income statement for the year and a balance sheet as of February 28.

CASE 4–3 Olympic Lumber Company*

Jason Cornfield reread the letter that his new boss had given him that morning:

> As your agent, I am indeed happy that you agreed to insure Olympic Lumber's building and inventory with a $1,000,000 fire insurance policy. The policy, which was effective November 1, 1970, will cover the loss from the untimely fire, and will continue to provide coverage through the end of 1974. While I am of course sincerely sorry that you

incurred the loss, I am sure you will agree that the expenditure of $25,000 for the policy was one of Olympic's more prudent decisions. Please call me when you have reconstructed your financial statements.

Jason Cornfield had been hired to replace Olympic's accountant, who had been fired for incompetence in early January 1971. Jason gazed out at the bleak February day and reviewed the events that had led up to his predecessor's dismissal. Until early 1971, Jason had operated a small but successful accounting practice. Shortly after the first of the year he had been offered the job of accountant

*Reprinted from *Stanford Business Cases 1971* with the permission of the publishers, Stanford University Graduate School of Business. © 1971 by the Board of Trustees of the Leland Stanford Junior University.

for Olympic by Bill Woodstock, president of Olympic Lumber Company. Woodstock explained to him that the company had been doing very well, and in fact had had a record sales and profit performance in 1970. To celebrate the success, the company had hosted a party for its suppliers and customers on New Year's Eve. The guests became overly festive in their celebrations and began lighting firecrackers. Unfortunately, a skyrocket landed in the rough two-by-four inventory and burned Olympic's entire inventory and building. Because of the suddenness of the fire, all financial records had been lost.

Woodstock informed Jason that his accountant, Leonard Firebird, had been unable to reconstruct financial statements for the fiscal year that had just ended. He said, "Firebird was OK for the routine stuff, but this assignment, and the challenge of rebuilding Olympic, require real creative talent. That's why I'm counting on you."

Investigating the background of Olympic, Cornfield learned that the company had been formed in early 1966 and that the building, which contained the office and plant, had been purchased and occupied on May 1 of that year. Cornfield next came across a letter to Woodstock from a major supplier, who wrote, "I certainly enjoyed your party and was sorry it ended so abruptly. I appreciated receiving the first installment on the note with which you financed the inventory purchase from us. As we agreed that you will make payments every six months, unless I hear otherwise, I will expect your next payment of $50,000 on June 1 plus the 6 percent interest over the six-month period."

Cornfield next asked Woodstock if he had any records that would help him in his work. The latter searched his briefcase and finally found a balance sheet (Exhibit 1). Woodstock observed that expenditures for salaries and licenses in 1970 had been a third higher than their 1969 levels of $60,000 and $750, respectively. He commented that over the years freight expense had averaged $1,000 per month, that advertising had been 7 percent of sales, and selling expenses had been 20 percent of sales. Utilities had been some 15 percent higher than the previous year's $800 bill.

As Cornfield turned to leave, Woodstock remarked, "One more thing. I found a scrap of paper among the ashes and it said 'Closing entries to be made: Sales, DR 921,000; Supplies, CR 8,210.' The rest was unintelligible. I don't know what that means but maybe it will be helpful to you."

The new accountant then learned that the company had had a physical inventory on December 31, and Cornfield called the auditors who informed him that the lumber inventory on that date had been $414,000. They were also able to supply him with a list of all of Olympic's customers and suppliers. Calling the suppliers, he learned that all of the monies previously owed them had been paid in cash (except for the note referred to above) and that a third of the inventory acquired over the last six months of the year was still owed on account. Cornfield next discovered that total purchases of inventory in the second half of 1970 had been $159,500 more than the amount of the June 30 inventory level. Then he found out that no supplies had been purchased during 1970.

After considerable pencil pushing, Cornfield was still unable to calculate his cash balance. He knew Woodstock was growing impatient for the statements and

EXHIBIT 1

OLYMPIC LUMBER COMPANY
Balance Sheet
June 30, 1970

Assets

Cash		$ 150,000
Accounts receivable		213,172
Supplies		14,427
Inventory—lumber		290,500
Land		90,000
Building	$500,000	
Less accumulated depreciation	75,000	425,000
Total assets		$1,183,099

Liabilities

Accounts payable		$ 72,047
Note payable		200,000
Total liabilities		272,047

Owners' Equity

Capital stock		800,000
Retained earnings		111,052
Total owners' equity		911,052
Total liabilities and owners' equity		$1,183,099

consequently was startled to see the latter charge brusquely into his cluttered cubicle and drop an envelope on the desk. Opening it, Cornfield realized to his relief that it was Olympic's bank statement, dated December 31, with a balance of $200,000.

Cornfield's phone rang and he heard Woodstock's secretary ask him when he would complete the financial statements. He replied, "I realize my answer is due, and I will have the statements ready in a few minutes."

Question

Prepare an income statement for the six months ended December 31, 1970, and a balance sheet as of December 31, 1970. (Ignore income taxes and assume that the sales and supplies figures are for the last six months of 1970 only.)

CASE 4–4 Perrin's Service Station

On March 15, Phil Perrin signed a lease agreement to operate a gasoline service station that was owned by the Octane Oil Company (hereafter, simply "Octane"). Perrin had contacted the regional sales manager of Octane in response to an advertisement that solicited applicants "with $20,000 to invest" to lease and operate a newly erected Octane gasoline service station. Perrin had been able to accumulate approximately $24,000 for investment purposes as a result of an $16,000 inheritance and small savings on the salary of $560 per week that he earned as manager of a service station operated as a separate department of a J. C. Penney store. Most of this $24,000 was held in government bonds.

The regional sales manager for Octane was impressed with Perrin's personal and financial qualifications, and after several interviews, a lease agreement was signed. During one of these meetings, the sales manager informed Perrin that the new station would be ready for occupancy on May 1 at a total investment cost of $480,000. Of this amount, $60,000 had already been paid for land, and a total of $360,000 would be spent for a building that would be "good for about 40 years." In discussing profit potentiality, the sales

signed whereby Octane agreed to sell and Perrin agreed to buy certain minimum quantities of gasoline and other automotive products for the service station operation.

As both an evidence of good faith and as a prepayment on certain obligations that he would shortly incur to Octane, Perrin was required to deposit $16,000 with Octane at the time the lease was signed. Perrin raised the cash for this deposit by liquidating government bonds. Octane used most of this money to defray certain obligations incurred by Perrin to the oil company prior to the opening of the new station. The deductions from the $16,000 deposit were applied as follows:

1.	Opening inventories of gasoline, oil, grease, tires, batteries, and accessories.	$11,800
2.	Rental fee ($800 flat rental for the month of May and $180 figured as $0.04 per gallon on the gasoline delivered in the opening inventory)	980
3.	Down payment (on Perrin's behalf) on equipment costing $5,040	1,040
		$13,820

manager pointed out that Octane's national advertising program and the consumer appeal generated by the attractive station "will be worth at least $24,000 a year to you in consumer goodwill."

The lease agreement stipulated that Perrin pay a rental of $800 per month for the station plus $0.04 for each gallon of gasoline delivered to the station by Octane[1]. A separate agreement was also

The equipment, including floor and hydraulic jacks, a battery charger, tune-up sets, and oil and grease guns, became the property of Perrin. A representative of the oil company stated that this equipment would last about five years. The unpaid, noninterest-bearing balance of $4,000 due for equipment to Octane was to be paid in five semiannual installments of $800 each. The first such payment was due October 30. The $2,180 remaining from the $16,000 originally deposited with Octane was returned to Perrin on April 30. He deposited this money in a special checking account he had set up for his service station venture.

Just before opening for business on May 1, Perrin converted some additional

---

[1]The lease, which covered a period of one year beginning May 1, was automatically renewable unless notice of cancellation was given by either party at least 30 days prior to an anniversary date. The regional sales manager of the Octane Oil Company estimated that approximately 150,000 gallons of gasoline would be delivered to Perrin's Service Station during the first 12 months of operation. Subsequently, Perrin's records revealed that 27,000 gallons were actually delivered during the first two months of operation.

government bonds into $4,000 cash which he also placed in the service station checking account. Prior to May 1, he wrote the following checks: $960 for office furniture that had an expected life of 10 years, and $480 for a fire and casualty insurance policy extending coverage for a 1-year period beginning May 1. On April 30, Perrin transferred $200 from the service station checking account to the cash drawer at the service station. It was Perrin's intention to deposit in the bank all but $200 of the cash on hand at the close of each business day. The balance in the service station checking account at the start of business was, therefore, $4,540. In addition, Perrin had $1,700 in a savings account.

end of June, however, he felt it would be desirable to take a more careful look at how he was making out in his new business venture. Perrin felt that he should record his progress and present position in a form which would be useful not only at the present time but also for comparative purposes in the future, perhaps at six-month intervals ending on June 30 and December 31.

Perris maintained a simple record-keeping system in which cash receipts and cash payments were itemized daily in a loose-leaf notebook. Separate pages were reserved for specific items in this notebook. During the months of May and June, the following cash receipts and payments had been recorded:

Cash receipts (May and June):

Sales of gasoline, motor oils, new and secondhand tires, batteries, and accessories and the revenue from lubrications, washing and polishing, and miscellaneous sales and services	$61,784
Rental from parking area on service station land.......................	480
	$62,264

Cash payments (may and June):

Purchases (includes gasoline, motor oils, lubes, greases, new tires, batteries, and accessories)	$39,728
Rent (does not include $980 deduction from $16,000 deposit)	1,620
Payroll (does not include any payments to Perrin).....................	6,880
Utilities..	456
Advertising	640
Miscellaneous	384
Withdrawals by Perrin (June 1 and June 19)	4,800
	$54,508

On May 1, the service station was opened for business. In his effort to build up a clientele, Perrin worked approximately 60 hours per week compared with 40 in his previous job. In addition, three other people were employed on either a full- or part-time basis. Perrin was reasonably well satisfied with the patronage he was able to build up during the first two months the station was open. At the

The $480 listed in cash receipts as rental from parking area had been received from an adjacent business establishment that used one portion of the service station site as a parking space for certain of its employees. The rental received covered a period extending from May 15 to July 15.

In addition to the record of cash receipts and payments, a detailed listing was kept of the amounts of money that were due from, or owed to, other individuals or companies. An analysis of these records revealed that $144 was due the business for gas, oil, and car servicing from a wealthy widow friend of the Perrin family who preferred to deal on a credit basis. Also, on the evening of June 30, one of the employees completed the waxing of a car for a regular customer who was out of town and would be unable to call for his car until July 3. Perrin had quoted a price of $56 for this job. Perrin recalled that when he was working at the automobile agency, he had heard that setting up a reserve for bad debts equal to 2 percent of all outstanding accounts was a good idea.

Perrin had also jotted down the fact that he and his family had used gas and oil from the service station worth $92 at retail prices, for which no payment had been made. Approximately $72 had been paid to Octane for this merchandise.

A further summary of his records revealed the following unpaid bills resulting from operations in June:

Octane Oil Company for merchandise	$1,604
Rent payable (figured at $0.04 per gallon on most recent delivery of gasoline)	80
Utilities for the month of June	440
	$2,124

The employees had last been paid on Saturday, June 28, for services rendered through Saturday evening. Wages earned on June 29 and 30 would amount to $168 in the following Saturday's payroll.

Perrin took a physical inventory on the evening of June 30, and he found gasoline, motor oils, lubes, greases, tires, batteries, and accessories on hand which had cost $8,904. While Perrin was figuring his inventory position, he compared his recorded gallonage sales of gasoline on hand at the end of the period against the volume of gasoline in the beginning inventory plus deliveries. In this manner, Perrin ascertained that shrinkage due to evaporation, temperature changes, waste, and other causes amounted to 302 gallons of gasoline that he estimated had cost $320.

Late in June, Perrin's married son realized that he would be unable, because of a prolonged illness, to make payment of $192 for interest expense and $800 for principal repayment on a $2,400 bank loan. Perrin, who had acted as cosigner on the note, would be obliged to meet this payment on July 1.

Questions

1. Prepare a May 1 and a June 30 balance sheet for Phil Perrin's service station and an income statement for the intervening period.

2. Has Phil Perrin's investment in the gasoline station been a good one for him? Has his return on his investment been greater or less than he would have received had he invested his funds at 15 percent elsewhere?

CASE 4-5 Pinkham Motel

Mr. and Mrs. George Treml had purchased the Pinkham Motel in 1973 with their life savings, supplemented by a loan from a close personal friend. The motel consisted of 15 units (i.e., rentable rooms) and was located near a vacation area that was popular during both the summer and winter seasons. The Tremls had entered the motel business because Mrs. Treml had long wanted to run a business of her own.

Both Mr. and Mrs. Treml felt that they had been successful. Each year saw a growth in revenue from room rentals. Furthermore, their bank balance had increased. They noted that many of their customers returned year after year. This was attributed to their location and their efforts to provide consistently clean rooms and up-to-date furnishings. Fortunately, no significant competition had arisen along the route on which the Pinkham Motel was situated.

The Tremls had no formal business training but felt their experience since acquiring the motel had alerted them to the management problems involved. Both Mr. and Mrs. Treml devoted their full time to operating the motel. In addition, they hired part-time help for cleaning and chambermaid work. They had no dining facilities but had installed coffee, cigarette, and candy vending machines to supplement room rentals. The vending machines posed no inventory or maintenance problem as the vending machine company provided servicing and maintenance.

A frequent guest at Pinkham Motel was Mr. Fernando Garcia, controller of a large company. Mr. Garcia visited a company branch plant near the motel several times a year. As he stayed at the motel during these trips, he became acquainted with the Tremls.

In August 1978, Mrs. Treml showed Mr. Garcia the July issue of the *Motel/Motor Inn Journal,* a trade journal that contained operating percentages of motels for the calendar year 1977. Data were given for motels with 40 or fewer units. Mrs. Treml commented: "These figures show a profit of 21 percent. Our profit last year was $32,106 on sales of $58,329 or 55 percent. We think 1977 was our best year to date, but we can't make our figures jibe with those in the magazine, and we wonder if we really are 34 percent ahead of the industry average. Can you help us?"

Mr. Garcia was interested and willing to help. He told Mrs. Treml to get the available figures for 1977 so that he could look them over that evening. The principal records the Tremls kept to reflect the motel's financial transactions were a record of receipts taken from the cash register and a checkbook describing cash paid out. In addition, certain rough notations of other expenses incurred were available.

That evening Mrs. Treml showed Mr. Garcia the cash summary for the year 1977, as given in Exhibit 1. Mr. Garcia immediately noted that the difference between receipts and expenditures was $11,371, and asked Mrs. Treml to explain why she had stated the profit was $32,106. Mrs. Treml replied, "Oh, that's easy. Our drawings aren't expenses; after all, we are the owners. My husband and I have consistently taken only about $20,000 a year out because we want the rest of the profits to accumulate in the

EXHIBIT 1

Cash Register and Checkbook Summary during 1977

Receipts

From rooms	$56,371
From vending machines	1,958
Total	$58,329

Checks Drawn

Owners' drawings	$20,735
Salaries and wages	6,263
Paid to laundry	2,095
Replacement of glasses, bed linens, and towels	395
Advertising	556
Payroll taxes and insurance	694
Fuel for heating	2,906
Repairs and maintenance	2,138
Cleaning and other supplies	1,624
Telephone and telegraph	664
Electricity	1,336
Real estate and property taxes	2,269
Insurance	2,758
Interest	2,525
Total	$46,958

EXHIBIT 2

1977 Operating Data for Motels with 40 or Fewer Units*
(expressed as percentages of total revenues)

Revenues:	
Room rentals	98.7
Other revenue	1.3
Total revenues	100.0
Operating expenses:	
Payroll costs	22.5
Administrative and general	4.2
Direct operating expenses	5.9
Fees and commissions	3.3
Advertising and promotion	1.2
Repairs and maintenance	4.8
Utilities	7.5
Total	49.4
Fixed expenses:	
Property taxes, fees	4.4
Insurance	2.5
Depreciation	12.5
Interest	7.7
Rent	2.8
Total	29.9
Profit (pretax)	20.7

*Copyright July 1978 issue of *Motel/Motor Inn Journal,* Temple, Texas. Further reproduction in part or in whole prohibited unless written permission obtained from the copyright owner.

business. As I said, our bank balance has steadily risen. Furthermore, I have a local accountant make out the annual income tax statements so I don't have to worry about them. That income tax business is so complicated that I avoid it."

Mr. Garcia worked with the *Motel/Motor Inn Journal* figures (Exhibit 2) and the cash summary (Exhibit 1) that evening and quickly found he needed more information. He told Mrs. Treml that he was returning to the home office the next morning but would be back in two weeks for another visit to the branch plant. Meanwhile, he wanted Mrs. Treml to get together some additional information. Mr. Garcia suggested to Mrs. Treml that an important noncash expense was depreciation. Mr. Garcia also wanted to know about expenses that had been incurred in 1976 but not paid until 1977. He told Mrs. Treml to check up on wages and salaries, insurance, advertising,

taxes, utilities, and any other items paid in 1977 but applicable to 1976.

In addition, Mr. Garcia instructed Mrs. Treml to try to find items of expense properly chargeable to 1977 but not paid by December 31, 1977. Mrs. Treml told Mr. Garcia the same types of expenses were involved, that is, wages and salaries, insurance, advertising, taxes, and so forth. Also Mr. Garcia inquired about income from room rentals. He asked if any of the cash receipts during 1977 related to rentals during 1976 and if there were any rentals during 1977 that had not been collected.

During the two weeks Mr. Garcia was back at the home office, Mrs. Treml checked the records and compiled the additional information requested by Mr. Garcia. The evening Mr. Garcia returned to the Pinkham Motel, Mrs. Treml gave him a summary of the information she had gathered (Exhibit 3). With all the ad-

EXHIBIT 3

Additional Information about the Business

Chargeable in 1976 but paid in January 1977:

Wages and salaries	$240
Advertising	200
Fuel for heating	303
Telephone and telegraph	33
Electricity	120
Real estate and property taxes	335
Insurance	689
Interest	229
Payroll taxes and insurance	26

Chargeable in 1977 but not paid by December 31, 1977:

Wages and salaries	360
Advertising	332
Fuel for heating	280
Cleaning and other supplies	26
Telephone and telegraph	46
Electricity	164
Real estate and property taxes	373
Interest	193
Payroll taxes and insurance	40

Also, 1977 depreciation charges of $7,365.
Also, 1977 cash receipts included a $395 payment from a company which had rented several units during December 1976 for a convention in the nearby city. There were no such uncollected rentals as of December 31, 1977.

ditional information, Mr. Garcia constructed an operating statement that
matched in form the one appearing in the
Motel /Motor Inn Journal. He calculated
both the dollar amounts and percentage
composition of each expense for more
useful comparison with the *Journal* figures.

Questions

1. Prepare an operating statement such as
   Mr. Garcia prepared.
2. As Mr. Garcia, what comments would you
   make to the Tremls regarding their progress to date?

5

Revenue and Monetary Assets

This and the next four chapters discuss more thoroughly certain balance sheet and income statement items that were treated in an introductory fashion in Chapters 2 and 3. This chapter discusses the two problems in revenue recognition: (1) the timing of revenue recognition and (2) the amount of revenue recognized in a given accounting period. The measurement of monetary assets, a closely related matter, is also discussed.

TIMING OF REVENUE RECOGNITION

Presumably, most activities in a company are intended to contribute to its profit-seeking objective. These activities may include a fairly long chain of events. Illustration 5–1 depicts this sequence, called the *operating cycle*, for a typical manufacturing firm. (The reader should consider how to modify the diagram for other types of businesses.) In accounting, revenue is recognized at a single point in this cycle. The basic reason for choosing a single point, rather than attempting to measure the separate profit contribution of each part of the cycle, stems from the criterion of objectivity. There is no objective way of measuring the amount of profit that is earned in each step of the operating cycle.

ILLUSTRATION 5–1
THE BUSINESS OPERATING CYCLE

Basic Recognition Criteria

The conservatism concept suggests that revenue should be recognized only when there is a reasonable certainty that the entity has earned income. This suggests the following revenue recognition criteria:

Revenue should be recognized in the earliest period in which (1) the entity has performed substantially what is required in order to earn income and (2) the amount of income can be reliably measured.

The criteria are expressed in terms of earning and measuring income, rather than revenue, because both the revenue and expense components of a transaction need to be reliably measurable in order to recognize the revenue. Because of the matching concept, both components are recognized in the same period, and thus income is recognized. Applications of this general idea to certain types of revenues are summarized in Illustration 5–2 and discussed in more detail below.

Delivery Method

The typical business earns revenue by selling goods or services to customers. The business has performed substantially what is required in order to earn income when it delivers these goods to customers or when it provides the services. Thus, the most common basis of revenue recognition is to recognize the revenue in the period in which goods are delivered or services provided.

Revenues for goods are *not* recognized when sales orders are received. Even though in some businesses the amount of income that will be earned can be reliably estimated at that time, there has been no performance until the goods have been shipped.

For services, providing the service is the act of performance. Revenues from renting hotel rooms are recognized each day the room is rented.

ILLUSTRATION 5–2
TIMING OF REVENUE RECOGNITION

Event	Conditions in Which Revenue Is Recognized at This Time	Revenue Recognition Method
1. Sales order received	Never	None
2. Deposit or advance customer payment received	Never	None
3. Goods being produced	Certain long-term contracts	Percentage of completion
4. Production completed; goods stored	Precious metals; certain agricultural products	Production
5. Goods shipped and invoiced to customer	Usually	Delivery
6. Services rendered	Usually	Delivery
7. Customer pays account receivable	Collection is uncertain	Installment

Revenues from maintenance contracts are recognized in each month covered by the contract. Revenue from repairing an automobile is recognized when the repairs have been completed (not when the repairs are only partially completed, because the service is to provide a completed repair job).

In the usual situation, the amount of income that will be earned can be reliably estimated when goods are delivered or services performed. The test of the marketplace, a price agreed to by the customer minus the appropriate cost of sales, is usually excellent evidence of the amount of income earned. Even though some customers may not pay their bills, allowances can be made for this in estimating the amount of revenue.

When goods are delivered, title usually is transferred from the seller to the buyer, but transfer of title is *not* a necessary condition for revenue recognition. When goods are sold on the installment credit basis, for example, the buyer does not have a clear title until the installment payments have been completed. If, however, there is a reasonable certainty that these payments will be made, revenue is recognized at the time of delivery.

Consignment Shipments. In a consignment shipment, the supplier, or *consignor*, ships goods to the *consignee*, who undertakes to sell them. The consignor retains title to the goods until they are sold. The consignee can return any unsold goods to the consignor. In these circumstances, performance has not been substantially completed until the goods are sold by the consignee, so the consignor does not recognize revenue until that time.[1] A consignment shipment therefore represents only the movement of the supplier's asset, inventory, from one place to another. The amount of merchandise out on consignment can be shown by a journal entry, at cost:

```
dr.     Inventory on Consignment.............  1,000
   cr.      Merchandise Inventory ............        1,000
```

In the period in which these goods are sold by the consignee, the effect on the accounts of the consignor would be as in the following entries:

```
dr.     Cost of Goods Sold...................  1,000
   cr.      Inventory on Consignment ..........       1,000
        To record the cost of consigned
        goods sold.

dr.     Accounts Receivable..................  1,400
   cr.      Sales Revenue ....................        1,400
        To record the consignor's sales
        value.
```

Franchises. Some companies (*franchisors*) sell franchises that permit the *franchisee* to use a well-known name (e.g., Kentucky Fried Chicken, Holiday Inn, Avis). The franchisor may also agree to provide advice and other services in return for the franchise fee. A franchisor recognizes revenue during the period in which it provides the services, rather than when the fee is received. In particular, a franchisor often receives a large initial fee for which it agrees to provide site selection, personnel training, advice on equipment selection, and other services. It cannot recognize revenue until these services have been provided; normally, this is after the franchisee commences operations.[2]

Percentage-of-Completion Method

High-rise buildings, bridges, aircraft, ships, space exploration hardware, some types of computer software, and certain other items involve a design/development and construction/production period that extends over several years. Such projects are performed under contracts in which the customer provides the product specifications. The contract also stipulates either (1) predetermined amounts the customer must pay at various points during the project, called a fixed-price contract or (2) some sort of formula that will determine customer payments as a function of

---

[1]FASB, "Revenue Recognition When Right of Return Exists," *Statement of Financial Accounting Standards No. 48* (Stamford, Conn., June 1981). This *Statement* also describes circumstances when revenue may not be recognized even if title to the goods has passed from the consignor to the consignee.

[2]"Accounting for Franchise Fee Revenue," *FASB Statement No. 45*, March 1981.

actual project costs plus a reasonable profit, called a cost-reimbursement contract.

During each accounting period in which the contractor works on the contract, there has been performance. If the income earned by the work done in the period can be reliably estimated, then revenue is appropriately recognized in each such period. This method of revenue recognition is called the *percentage-of-completion method* because the amount of revenue is related to the percentage of the total project work that was performed in the period.

If the amount of income earned in a period cannot be reliably estimated, then the revenue is recognized only when the project has been completed. This is the *completed contract method*. Costs incurred on the project are held as an asset, Contract Work in Progress, until the period in which revenue is recognized.

On a cost-reimbursement contract, the amount of income earned in each period often can be reliably estimated. If the owner agrees to pay cost plus 10 percent, and if the work proceeds as planned, the revenue is 110 percent of the costs incurred in the period. On a fixed-price contract, the amount of income earned in a period is more difficult to estimate. Usually, the contract specifies how the satisfactory completion of each phase of the work is to be measured, and if the contractor completes these phases within the cost estimates that were made for each, the amount of income (and hence revenue) in each period can be reliably measured.

Illustration 5–3 shows the application of these two methods to a

ILLUSTRATION 5–3
LONG-TERM CONTRACT ACCOUNTING METHODS

Year	Customer Payments Received[1]	Project Costs Incurred	Year-End Percent Complete[2]	Completed Contract Method			Percentage-of-Completion Method		
				Revenues	Expenses	Income	Revenues[3]	Expenses[4]	Income
1	$120,000	$160,000	20	$ 0	$ 0	$ 0	$180,000	$160,000	$ 20,000
2	410,000	400,000	70	0	0	0	450,000	400,000	50,000
3	370,000	240,000	100	900,000	800,000	100,000	270,000	240,000	30,000
Total	$900,000	$800,000		$900,000	$800,000	$100,000	$900,000	$800,000	$100,000

Notes:
1. It is common, as in this example, for payments on long-term contracts to lag the incurrence of costs.
2. In this example, as customary in practice, percent complete is measured as *cumulative* costs incurred to date divided by total project costs. It is possible, however, for "real" completion percentages to be less than or greater than the percent of total costs incurred to date, particularly on fixed-price contracts.
3. This amount for a year is the percent of completion *accomplished that year* times total project revenues. In this example, 20 percent, 50 percent, and 30 percent of the work was accomplished in years 1, 2, and 3, respectively.
4. In this example, since the percent-complete calculations are based on project costs incurred, expenses recognized equal costs incurred for each year. These amounts would differ if, as mentioned in note 2, "real" completion percentages differed from percent-of-total-costs-incurred percentages. For example, if in year 1 project costs were $160,000 but percent accomplished was only 15 percent, then year 1 revenues would be $135,000 (= 15 percent × $900,000) and project expenses recognized would be $120,000 (= 15 percent × $800,000).

three-year project. Note that both methods report the same total project income over the entire three-year period; but only the percentage-of-completion method allocates this total to each of the three years. Also note the customer payments (cash inflows) are irrelevant in determining the amount of revenue recognized each year under the percentage-of-completion method.

Until 1981, these two methods were regarded as alternatives for financial reporting purposes. The contractor could choose either method, as long as the same method was applied to all long-term contracts consistently from year to year. Most companies (92 percent in 1981[3]) used the percentage-of-completion method, presumably in order either to "smooth" reported income or to report income to shareholders as soon as possible. In 1981, an AICPA pronouncement set up specific criteria for the use of each method, emphasizing that a method is to be selected on a contract-by-contract basis, rather than applied across the board to all contracts. The percentage-of-completion method is to be used when "estimates of cost to complete and extent of progress toward completion of long-term contracts are reasonably dependable."[4]

For income tax accounting, either method can be used, as long as it is applied to all long-term contracts and is used consistently from year to year. Generally, corporations use the completed contract method for tax purposes because it postpones reporting taxable income, and thus defers tax payments.

Production Method

For certain grains and other crops, the government sets supports prices and assures the farmer that the products can be sold for at least these prices. The minimum amount of income that will be earned can therefore be reliably measured as soon as the crops have been harvested, even though they have not been sold at that time. Furthermore, the farmer's performance has been substantially completed. In these circumstances, a case can be made for recognizing revenue at the time of harvest. This is permitted, but not required, by generally accepted accounting principles (GAAP).[5] These principles also permit revenue recognition when gold, silver, and similar precious metals have been produced from the mine, even though the metals have not yet been sold. In recent years, however, fluctuations in the sales value of these metals have been large, and the rationale for the production method is correspondingly weaker. Relatively few mining companies now use the production method.

---

[3]AICPA, *Accounting Trends & Techniques* (New York, 1981).

[4]AICPA, *Accounting for Performance of Construction-Type and Certain Production-Type Contracts* (New York, 1981); later codified as part of *FASB Statement No. 56* (February 1982).

[5]*APB Statement No. 4*, October 1970, par. 152.

Installment Method   Many retail stores sell merchandise on an installment basis; that is, the customer pays a certain amount per week or per month. If the customers are good credit risks, then the payments are likely to be received and the store can reliably measure its income at the time the sale is made. In other circumstances, a significant number of customers may not complete their payments, and the merchandise is repossessed (if it can be located). In these circumstances, the amount of income that is realized cannot be reliably measured at the time the sale is made, so revenue is not recorded at that time.

Instead, revenue is recognized when the installment payments are received. In the pure *installment method,* the installment payment is counted as revenue, and a proportional part of the cost of sales is counted as a cost in the same period. In a variation, the *cost recovery method,* cost of sales is recorded at an amount equal to the installment payment, so no income is reported until installment payments have recouped the total cost of sales.

The FASB states that sales revenue should "ordinarily" be recognized when the sale is made, and that an installment method is acceptable only when "the circumstances are such that the collection of the sales price is not reasonably assured."[6]

The effect of the installment method is to postpone the recognition of revenue and income to later periods, as compared with the delivery method. If a company wants to report as much income as it legitimately can in the current period, it will therefore prefer to report in its income statement the full amount of the transaction at the time of sale. If it wants to postpone the recognition of taxable income for income tax purposes, it will use the installment method in calculating its taxable income.

Example. A jeweler sells a gold watch in 1982 for $400, and the customer agrees to make payments totaling $200 in 1982 and $200 in 1983. (The customer would ordinarily pay interest in addition to the payments for the watch itself, but this is a separate revenue item that is disregarded here.) The watch cost the jeweler $220. Alternative ways of accounting for this transaction are as follows:

	Effect on Income Statements			
	Delivery Method		Installment Method	
	1982	1983	1982	1983
Sales revenue	$400	$0	$200	$200
Cost of goods sold	220	0	110	110
Gross margin	$180	$0	$ 90	$ 90

---

[6]*APB Opinion No. 10,* December 1966, par. 12.

Although the total gross margin for the transaction is the same under either method, the jeweler can report a lower gross margin, and hence a lower taxable income, for 1982 by using the installment method.

Real Estate Sales.   Some developers sell land to customers who make a small down payment and pay the balance of the purchase price over a number of years. In some cases, the buyer later becomes disenchanted with the deal or becomes unable to continue with the payments. Because of the consequent uncertainty as to the amount of income that will be realized, revenue is not recognized for these transactions until (1) the period of cancellation of the contract with a refund to the buyer has expired; (2) the buyer has made cumulative payments equal to at least 10 percent of the purchase price; *and* (3) the seller has completed improvements (roads, utility connections, and so on), or is making progress on these improvements and is clearly capable of eventually completing them. If the improvements have been completed and the receivable from the buyer is probably collectible, then the full sales price is recognized as revenue, and appropriate costs are matched against the revenue. If the improvements are in progress, the percentage-of-completion method is used to recognize the revenue. If there is doubt as to the collectibility of the receivables, the installment method is used. If all three of the above-mentioned criteria for revenue recognition are not met, the seller records any payments received as a liablity, deposits on land sales.[7]

Similar, but more complex, criteria govern the recognition of revenue on the sale of land for commercial use (office buildings, hotels, and other commercial property) and residential property. The required down payments range from 5 percent to 25 percent, depending on the nature of the property; and certain other requirements must be met.[8]

AMOUNT OF REVENUE RECOGNIZED

In Chapter 3 we stated that the *amount* recorded as revenue is the amount that customers are reasonably certain to pay. This concept requires that certain adjustments be made to the gross sales value of the goods or services sold. These adjustments are discussed in this section.

Bad Debts

The main source of revenue in many businesses is the sale of merchandise to customers on credit, that is, "on account." These sales may involve a single payment, or they may involve a series of payments, as in the installment sales transactions discussed above. They give rise to the sales revenue and also to the asset, accounts receivable. Assume that Essel Company began operations in 1981, and that during the year the

---

[7]"Accounting for Sales of Real Estate," *FASB Statement No. 66*, October 1982.
[8]Ibid.

company made sales of $262,250, all on credit. In the interest of simplicity, further assume that none of these bills had been paid by the end of 1981. The record made of these transactions would show accounts receivable of $262,250 and sales revenue of $262,250. It would be correct to report $262,250 as an asset on the balance sheet as of the end of 1981 and $262,250 as sales on the income statement for 1981 if, *but only if,* it is believed that all customers eventually will pay the full amount of their obligations to Essel Company. The unfortunate fact is, however, that some of these customers may never pay their bills. If they do not, their accounts become *bad debts.*

Consider the extreme case: a person purchases merchandise with no intention of paying for it and in fact does not pay for it. In this case, the company has not actually made a sale at all. No revenue was actually earned; and nothing valuable was added to the asset, accounts receivable, as a result of this transaction. If this event were recorded as an increase in Sales Revenue and as an increase in Accounts Receivable, both of these accounts would be overstated, and income for the period and owners' equity at the end of the period also would be overstated.

In the more usual bad debt situation, the customer fully intends to pay, but for one reason or another never actually does make payment. The effect is the same as that in the extreme case. Such a sale is also recorded initially by debiting Accounts Receivable and crediting Sales Revenue at the sales value of the merchandise. In these situations, another entry must be made to show that the amount debited to Accounts Receivable does not represent a valid asset and that owners' equity has not in fact increased by the amount of the sale.

Accounting Recognition of Bad Debts. When the company made the sale, the fact that the customer would never pay the bill was not known; otherwise the sale would not have been made. Even at the end of the accounting period, the company probably does not know specifically *which* of the amounts carried as accounts receivable will never be collected. An estimate of the amount of bad debts can nevertheless be made, and the accounting records are adjusted at the end of each accounting period to reflect this estimate.

One method of making this adjustment is by a *direct write-off.* Accounts that are believed to be uncollectible are simply eliminated from the records by subtracting the amount of the bad debt from Accounts Receivable and showing the same amount as an expense item on the income statement. The entry to accomplish this would be as follows:

```
dr.    Bad Debt Expense.....................    200
    cr.    Accounts Receivable ..............           200
```

The direct write-off method, however, requires that the specific uncollectible accounts be identified, whereas this usually is not possible.

An alternative procedure, therefore, is to estimate the *total* amount of uncollectible accounts, and to show this estimated amount as a deduction from accounts receivable on the balance sheet and as an expense on the income statement. Instead of reducing the accounts receivable amount directly, the estimate is often shown as a separate number on the balance sheet, so that the reader can observe both the total amount owed by customers and that portion of the amount that the company believes will not be collected.

Accounts Involved.   An account used to record deductions in the amount shown in some other account is called a *contra* account. The balance sheet contra-asset account for Accounts Receivable is labeled *Allowance for Doubtful Accounts* or *Allowance for Uncollectible Accounts.* (In a bank, the title is Allowance for Uncollectible Loans.) At one time it was often labeled Reserve for Bad Debts, but this caused confusion since the word *reserve* connotes to many people that a sum of money has been set aside, and such is not the case. The Allowance for Doubtful Accounts is in the nature of a decrease in Accounts Receivable for specific, but as yet unknown, customers. The corresponding item on the income statement is called *bad debt expense.*

Methods of Making the Estimate.   Any one of several methods may be used to estimate the amount of bad debt expense in an accounting period in those situations where using the direct write-off method is not feasible. Some of the methods commonly used are:

1.   Estimate bad debt expense as a *percentage of total sales* for the period. This method can logically be used only when cash sales are either negligible or a constant proportion of total sales, because bad debt expense is not, of course, related to cash sales.
2.   Estimate bad debt expense as a *percentage of credit sales.*
3.   Adjust the Allowance for Doubtful Accounts contra-asset account so that it equals a prescribed *percentage of accounts receivable* outstanding at the end of the period.

The percentage used in each case depends in part on past experience and in part on management's judgment as to whether past experience reflects the current situation. The allowance for doubtful accounts should be sufficient at all times to absorb the accounts that prove to be uncollectible. Because business conditions fluctuate, the amount may well turn out to be too large in some periods and too small in others. In practice, because of the concept of conservatism, it is common to find that the allowance is too large, rather than too small. On the other hand, there have been some cases where the allowance for doubtful accounts turned out to be woefully inadequate.

Example.   When a new management was installed in W. T. Grant Company in 1974, it decided that the Allowance for Doubtful Accounts was understated by $92 million. It therefore charged this amount as a 1974 expense. This charge, together with other events, resulted in a 1974 net loss of $178 million, compared with a reported net income of $11 million in 1973. The company went bankrupt shortly thereafter.

Aging Accounts Receivable. Sometimes different percentages are applied to accounts outstanding for various lengths of time. This requires the preparation of an *aging schedule*, which is also a useful device for analyzing the quality of the asset, accounts receivable. An example for Essel Company is shown in Illustration 5–4.

ILLUSTRATION 5–4
AGING SCHEDULE FOR ESTIMATING BAD DEBTS

Status as of December 31, 1981	Amount Outstanding	Estimated Percent Uncollectible	Allowance for Doubtful Accounts
Current	$207,605	1	$2,076
Overdue:			
Less than 1 month	26,003	1	260
1 up to 2 months	10,228	5	511
2 up to 3 months	7,685	10	769
3 up to 4 months	3,876	20	775
Over 4 months	6,853	40	2,741
Total	$262,250		$7,132

The Adjusting Entry. Once the amount of the allowance has been determined, it is recorded as one of the adjusting entries made at the end of the accounting period. If Essel Company management estimated the allowance for doubtful accounts on the basis of the above aging schedule, the entry would be:

```
dr.    Bad Debt Expense ....................    7,132
    cr.    Allowance for Doubtful Accounts ...              7,132
```

The accounts receivable section of the December 31, 1981, balance sheet would then appear as follows:

```
Accounts receivable ...........................    $262,250
    Less: Allowance for doubtful accounts .........      7,132
    Accounts receivable, net .................    $255,118
```

The 1981 income statement would show $7,132 of bad debt expense.

For reasons to be described, Allowance for Doubtful Accounts usually will have a balance even before the adjusting entry is made. In these circumstances, the amount reported as bad debt expense on the income statement will be different from the amount reported as allowance for doubtful accounts on the balance sheet. (In the Essel Company example just given, this did not occur because the company was organized in 1981, and the above entry was the first one made to Allowance for Doubtful Accounts.)

When Allowance for Doubtful Accounts has a balance, care must be taken in applying the methods listed above. Methods 1 and 2, which are related to sales revenue, give the amount of bad debt *expense* for the period. This same amount is credited to whatever balance existed in Allowance for Doubtful Accounts prior to the entry. Method 3, which is related to accounts receivable, gives the amount that is to appear as the Allowance for Doubtful Accounts. The journal entry is made in an amount that brings Allowance for Doubtful Accounts *up to* the desired balance.

> **Example.** Assume that at the end of 1982, Essel Company's Allowance for Doubtful Accounts had a credit balance of $500. It was decided that the allowance should be 2.5 percent of accounts receivable, which at that time amounted to $300,000. The allowance balance must be increased to $7,500, which is an increase of $7,000. The journal entry would therefore be the following:

```
dr.     Bad Debt Expense .................     7,000
    cr.     Allowance for Doubtful
                Accounts ...................              7,000
```

The balance sheet as of December 31, 1982, would then show:

```
        Accounts receivable ...........................   $300,000
            Less: Allowance for doubtful accounts ..........      7,500
                Accounts receivable, net .................   $292,500
```

Write-off of an Uncollectible Account. When a company decides that a specific customer is never going to pay a bill, Accounts Receivable is reduced by the amount owed and a corresponding reduction is made in the Allowance for Doubtful Accounts. This entry has *no* effect on Bad Debt Expense, nor on income, of the period in which the account is written off.

> **Example.** If sometime in 1983 the Essel Company decided that John Jones was never going to pay his bill of $200, the following entry would be made:

```
dr.     Allowance for Doubtful Accounts ..     200
    cr.     Accounts Receivable ...........              200
```

A balance sheet prepared immediately after this transaction had been recorded (assuming no other changes since December 31, 1982) would appear as follows:

Accounts receivable............................	$299,800
Less: Allowance for doubtful accounts..........	7,300
Accounts receivable, net..................	$292,500

Note that the *net* amount of accounts receivable is unchanged by this write-off.

Collection of a Bad Debt Written Off. If, by some unexpected stroke of good fortune, John Jones should subsequently pay all or part of the amount he owed, Cash would be increased (i.e., debited) and a corresponding credit would be recorded, usually to add back the amount to Allowance for Doubtful Accounts on the balance sheet.

Summary. Let us summarize the handling of events described above by showing the effect of hypothetical transactions in 1983 on the Essel Company's accounts:

1. *Write-off of $5,000 more of bad debts during the year:*

```
dr.    Allowance for Doubtful Accounts.......    5,000
   cr.     Accounts Receivable ..............             5,000
           (The balance in Allowance for
       Doubtful Accounts becomes $2,300.)
```

2. *Recovery of $500 previously written off:*

```
dr.    Cash..................................      500
   cr.     Allowance for Doubtful
           Accounts......................                 500
           (The balance in Allowance for
       Doubtful Accounts becomes $2,800.)
```

3. *Adjustments at end of 1983,* assuming allowance is to be maintained at 2.5 percent of accounts receivable, which are $400,000 as of December 31, 1983:

```
dr.    Bad Debt Expense......................    7,200
   cr.     Allowance for Doubtful
           Accounts.......................                7,200
           (This brings the allowance up to
       $10,000, which is 2.5 percent of
       accounts receivable.)
```

Sales Discounts   As mentioned in Chapter 2, sales revenue is recorded at not more than the sales value of the actual transaction. Trade discounts and other deductions that may be made from list or catalog prices are disregarded.

Some businesses offer a so-called *cash discount* to induce customers to pay bills quickly. For example, if a business sells merchandise on terms of "2/10, n/30," it permits customers to deduct 2 percent from the invoice amount if they pay within 10 days; otherwise, the full (net) amount is due within 30 days.[9] The cash discount can be recorded in any of three ways:

1. The discount can be recorded as a reduction from gross sales.
2. The discount can be recorded as an expense of the period.
3. Sales revenue can be initially recorded at the *net* amount after deduction of the discount. Amounts received from customers who do *not* take the discount would then be recorded as additional revenue. Thus, a $1,000 sale subject to a 2 percent cash discount would be recorded at the time of sale as:

```
dr.     Accounts Receivable...................    980
    cr.     Sales Revenue ......................            980
```

If the discount were not taken, the entry would be:

```
dr.     Cash.................................  1,000
    cr.     Discounts Not Taken ..............             20
            Accounts Receivable ..............            980
```

Credit Card Sales

Hundreds of thousands of retailers and service establishments who sell on credit have contracted with an outside agency to handle all, or some, of their accounts receivable. There are two types of these credit card plans.

The first type is a bank plan. MasterCard and Visa are examples. In this plan, merchants send their credit slips to the bank along with other bank deposits. The bank arranges to have the charges collected from the customers. If a customer's account is with another bank, the sales slip is sent to that bank for collection. So far as the merchant is concerned, this type of transaction is not a credit sale at all. No accounts receivable appear in the merchant's accounts. The sales slip (assuming it is properly made out) is the same as cash and is credited to the merchant's account by the bank as soon as it is deposited, just like a check or other cash item. The only difference between a credit card sales slip and a check is that in the former case the bank deducts a fee for the service of handling the accounts receivable paperwork and assuming the risk of bad debts.

---

[9]This is a powerful inducement because by foregoing the 2 percent the customer has the use of the money only for an additional 20 days. Since there are about eighteen 20-day periods in a 365-day year, this amounts to an annual interest rate of 18×2 percent $= 36$ percent.

This fee is in the nature of a sales discount and is recorded as such in the merchant's accounts thus:

```
dr.    Cash..................................    960
       Sales Discount (Credit Cards).........     40
    cr.    Sales Revenue .....................         1,000
```

In the other type of plan, the merchant sends the sales slips to a credit card company and receives reimbursement from this company within 30 days, or whatever period is agreed upon. American Express and Diner's Club are examples. Because of the interval that elapses between the submission of sales slips and the receipt of cash, in this plan the merchant does have accounts receivable. These receivables are due the merchant from the credit card company, not from the merchant's customers. There are no bad debts, however, because the credit card company assumes the risk of loss provided the merchant follows instructions in making out and approving the sales slip. When the slips are sent in, the entry is:

```
dr.    Accounts Receivable...................    960
       Sales Discount (Credit Cards).........     40
    cr.    Sales Revenue .....................         1,000
```

When cash is received from the credit card company, Cash is debited and Accounts Receivable is credited.

Sales Returns and Allowances

When customers are dissatisfied with merchandise sold to them, the company may permit them to return the merchandise for credit, or it may refund part or all of the sales price. In these circumstances, the amount originally recorded as revenue turns out to be an overstatement of the true exchange value of the sale. Sales returns and allowances are conceptually similar to bad debts.

Some companies treat sales returns and allowances in the same way that they treat bad debt expense. They estimate the percentage of revenues that will eventually result in returns and allowances, and set up an account for this amount. The offsetting credit is to a liability account, thus:

```
dr.    Sales Returns and Allowances..........   1,000
    cr.    Provision for Returns and
           Allowances.........................         1,000
```

The Sales Returns and Allowances account is analogous to Bad Debt Expense. The Provision for Returns and Allowances account is analogous to Allowance for Doubtful Accounts, except the former is treated as a liability rather than as a contra asset. When goods are returned or allowances made, Provision for Returns and Allowances is debited; the credit is to the customer's account receivable or to Cash (if a refund is made).

Other companies do not attempt to estimate the amount of returns and allowances associated with sales revenue of the current period. Instead, they simply debit Sales Returns and Allowances whenever a sales return or allowance occurs, with an offsetting credit to Accounts Receivable (or to Cash, if the returned goods had already been paid for). When this practice is followed, the sales returns and allowances deducted from revenue of a period do not relate to the actual merchandise included in the sales revenue of that period. The justification for this apparent departure from the matching concept is that the amounts are difficult to estimate in advance, are likely to be relatively constant from one period to the next, and are relatively small. Under these circumstances, the practice is consistent with the materiality concept.

Revenue Adjustment versus Expense

The need for recognizing bad debts, sales discounts, and sales returns and allowances arises because of one aspect of the realization concept— namely, that revenues should be reported at the amount that is reasonably certain to be collected. This concept would seem to require that these amounts be subtracted from gross revenues in order to determine the net revenue of the period. The effect of some of the practices described above, however, is to report the amounts as expenses, rather than as adjustments to revenues.

Whether companies report these amounts as expenses or as adjustments to revenues, the effect on income is exactly the same. The difference between the two methods is in the way they affect revenue and gross margin. The consistency concept requires that a company follow the same method from one year to the next, so comparisons within a company are not affected by these differences in practice. They may have a significant effect when the income statements of companies that use different methods are being compared, however.

> **Example.** Following are income statements for Company A, which treats the items of the type discussed in this section as adjustments to revenue, and Company B, which treats them as expenses. Otherwise, the firms are identical.
>
> Note the differences between the two income statements, not only in the dollar amounts of net sales and gross margin but also, and more importantly, in the percentages. (In reporting percentage relationships on an income statement, *net sales* is customarily taken as 100 percent, and the percentages for other items are calculated by dividing each by the amount of net sales.) Various combinations of these alternatives would produce still different amounts and percentages.

| | Income Statements (000 omitted) | | | |
| | Company A | | Company B | |
	Amount	Percent	Amount	Percent
Gross sales	$1,000	110.0	$1,000	100.0
Less: Sales discounts	20	2.2	0	
Bad debts.	40	4.4	0	
Returns	30	3.3	0	
Net sales.	910	100.0	1,000	100.0
Cost of sales	600	65.9	600	60.0
Gross margin.	310	34.1	400	40.2
Other expenses.	210	23.1	210	21.0
Discounts, bad debts, returns	0		90	9.0
Net income.	$ 100	11.1	$ 100	10.0

Warranty Costs

Companies usually have an obligation to repair or replace defective merchandise. This obligation arises either because it is an explicit part of the sales contract or because there is an implicit legal doctrine that says that customers have a right to receive satisfactory products. In either case, the obligation is called a *warranty.*

If it is likely that a significant amount of costs will be incurred in future periods in replacing or repairing merchandise sold in the current period, both the conservatism and matching concepts require that income in the current period be adjusted accordingly. As is the case with bad debts and sales returns and allowances, the amount of the adjustment is usually estimated as a percentage of sales revenue. This adjustment is recorded as an expense with an entry such as the following:

```
dr.     Estimated Warranty Expense. . . . . . . . . . .    1,000
   cr.     Allowance for Warranties  . . . . . . . . .              1,000
```

When costs are incurred in the future in repairing or replacing the merchandise, Allowance for Warranties, a liability account, is debited, and Cash, Inventory, or some other balance sheet account is credited. Analogous to the write-off of an uncollectible receivable, this warranty repair or replacement transaction affects neither the estimated warranty expense nor the income of the period in which it takes place.

Conceptually, Estimated Warranty Expense is an upward adjustment of Cost of Sales, rather than a downward adjustment of Sales Revenue. We nevertheless have included the topic here because the accounting procedures for warranty costs are so similar to those for bad debts and sales returns and allowances. Also, both types of adjustment reduce the period's reported income.

Interest Revenue

A principal source of revenue to a bank is interest on the money that it lends.[10] Industrial and commercial companies also may earn interest revenue. Under the realization concept, the amount of revenue for a period is the amount the lender earned on the money the borrower had available for use during that period. Accounting for this amount depends on whether interest is paid at *maturity*, that is, when the loan is repaid, or whether it is in effect paid when the money is borrowed. In the latter case, the loan is said to be *discounted*. Examples of each are given below.

Example 1. *Interest Paid at Maturity.* On September 1, 1982, a bank loaned $10,000 for one year at 15 percent interest, the interest and principal to be paid on August 31, 1983. The bank's entry on September 1, 1982, is:

```
dr.     Loans Receivable................ 10,000
   cr.      Cash..........................          10,000
```

On December 31, 1982, an adjusting entry is made to record the fact that interest for one third of a year, $500, was earned in 1982:

```
dr.     Interest Receivable.............     500
   cr.      Interest Revenue.............             500
```

On August 31, 1983, when the loan was repaid, the entry is:

```
dr.     Cash........................... 11,500
   cr.      Loans Receivable.............          10,000
            Interest Receivable..........             500
            Interest Revenue.............           1,000
```

Example 2. *Discounted Loan.* On September 1, 1982, a bank loaned $10,000 for one year at 15 percent discounted. The borrower received $10,000 less the $1,500 prepaid interest, or $8,500.[11] On that day the bank has a liability of $1,500 because it has not yet performed the service of permitting the use of the money. The bank's entry on September 1, 1982, is:

```
dr.     Loans Receivable................ 10,000
   cr.      Cash..........................           8,500
            Unearned Interest Revenue.....           1,500
```

On December 31, 1982, an adjusting entry is made to record the fact that $500 interest (one third of a year) was earned in 1982 and is therefore no longer a liability:

---

[10]In practice, this amount is often called interest *income*, rather than interest *revenue*. Conceptually, it is revenue.

[11]The *effective* interest rate on this loan is more than 15 percent, since the borrower pays $1,500 *interest* for the use of only $8,500 for one year.

```
dr.    Unearned Interest Revenue........    500
   cr.      Interest Revenue.............           500
```

On August 31, 1983, when the loan was repaid, the entry is:

```
dr. '  Cash...........................  10,000
   cr.      Loans Receivable.............          10,000
```

An adjusting entry is also made on December 31, 1983, to record the fact that $1,000 interest (two thirds of a year) was earned in 1983:

```
dr.    Unearned Interest Revenue........  1,000
   cr.      Interest Revenue.............          1,000
```

Corresponding entries are made on the books of the borrower to record interest expense. To illustrate this point, the entries given in the first example above are the counterparts of those described from the viewpoint of the borrower on page 69.

Interest Component of a Sale. When buyers purchase goods on an installment plan, they pay both for the goods themselves and for the interest that the seller charges on the amount of the unpaid balance. Revenue from the sales value of the merchandise should be recorded separately from interest revenue. In most sales to consumers, this separation is easy to recognize since federal regulations require that the amount of interest be specified in the sales contract. Although the merchandise sales value may be recognized at the time of the sale (unless the installment method is used), the interest revenue is recognized in the period or periods in which it is earned; that is, it is spread over the life of the installment contract.

In some sales agreements, the buyer gives a note promising to pay several months, or even years, in the future; but the note does not explicitly indicate that an interest charge is involved. Since any rational merchant expects to receive more money for a sale that is not completed for many months in the future than for a cash sale, it is apparent that the amount of the note includes both the sales value of the goods and an interest charge. In recording the transaction, these two components must be shown separately. If the full amount of the note were recognized as revenue in the period in which the transaction took place, revenue for that period would be overstated by the amount of the interest component. The interest implicit in such a transaction is calculated by applying the going rate of interest for transactions of this general type.[12] The same principle is used for notes that state a rate of interest significantly below the going rate.

---

[12]See "Interest on Receivables and Payables," *APB Opinion No. 21,* August 1971, for details as to how the rate of interest is determined. The interest revenue amount is found by using present value techniques described in Chapter 8, *not* by discounting the face amount of the note.

Example. On September 1, 1982, a customer purchased a piece of equipment and gave in payment a note promising to pay $10,000 one year later, with no interest stated. The going rate of interest was 15 percent. The entry on September 1, 1982, would be:

```
dr.      Notes Receivable................  10,000
   cr.      Sales Revenue................            8,696
            Unearned Interest Revenue.....            1,304
```

The adjusting entry on December 31, 1982, and the entry recording payment of the note on August 31, 1983, would be similar to those given above for a discounted loan.

MONETARY ASSETS

Monetary assets are money or claims to receive fixed sums of money (e.g., accounts or notes receivable). By contrast, most nonmonetary assets are items that will be used in the future in the production and sale of goods and services. No separate classification for monetary assets appears on the balance sheet. The traditional distinction on the balance sheet is between current assets and noncurrent assets. The reason for calling attention to the distinction between monetary and nonmonetary assets is that the concepts governing the amounts at which they appear on the balance sheet differ for these two categories.

Difference in Reporting Monetary and Nonmonetary Assets

In general, and with the notable exception of inventories (discussed in Chapter 6), *nonmonetary* assets appear on the balance sheet at *unexpired cost*. When acquired, they were recorded at cost. The amount shown on the balance sheet at any time thereafter is the amount not yet written off as an expense. If a building was acquired in 1968 at a cost of $1,000,000 and if $375,000 of its cost has been written off as depreciation expense in the intervening 15 years, the balance sheet for December 31, 1983, will report the asset amount of this building at $625,000, *regardless of its market value at that time.*

For *monetary* assets, the idea of "unexpired cost" is not appropriate. As we have seen above, the accounts receivable item is in effect reported at its *estimated realizable value.* This is the effect of the adjustment for the estimated amount of bad debts included in the accounts receivable. Cash, of course, is reported at its face amount, whether on hand or deposited in banks.

Cash

Cash consists of funds that are immediately available for disbursement. Cash is usually held in checking accounts on which no interest is earned. If an entity has a temporary excess of cash, it may loan the excess to a bank and receive interest on it. The evidence of such a loan is called a *certificate of deposit*. A certificate of deposit has a maturity date, and a penalty is involved if the entity cashes it prior to that date. Therefore, these funds are not as liquid as cash in a checking account. Some companies include certificates of deposit in the amount reported for Cash, whereas other companies disclose separately an amount for these certificates.

When a bank loans money to an entity, the bank sometimes requires that a specified minimum amount of cash be kept on deposit. This amount is called a *compensating balance*. No accounting entry is required, since the cash remains in the entity's checking account. However, if the amount is significant, it must be disclosed in a note that accompanies the balance sheet.

Receivables

The accounts receivables discussed in the preceding section were amounts due from customers. These are called *trade* receivables. An entity may advance funds to employees for various reasons, a principal one being to provide for travel expenses. Such receivables are reported separately from trade receivables in an account with a title such as "Due from Employees."

If the amount owed is evidenced by a note or some other written acknowledgement of the obligation, it is recorded in an account called Notes Receivable or Loans Receivable.

Marketable Securities

If an entity has a temporary excess of cash, rather than—or in addition to—investing it in certificates of deposit, the entity may invest it in *marketable securities*. Marketable securities are of several types. *Commercial paper* is a colloquial name for short-term, interest-bearing promissory notes that are issued by large companies with high credit ratings that have a temporary need for more cash. *Treasury bills* are short-term obligations of the U.S. Treasury; that is, the investor in a Treasury bill is making a short-term loan to the federal government. Stocks of companies, and bonds of companies and government entities, are also marketable securities if they are in fact marketable, that is, if they can be readily sold.

Most companies report marketable securities as a separate line item on the balance sheet, some of them preferring the caption "Temporary investments." Some companies include certificates of deposit in the marketable securities or investments total, rather than as a separate item or as a part of Cash. Capital stock of other companies held for the purpose of exercising some control over those companies, or stocks and bonds not traded on a securities market, are reported as *Investments* rather than as marketable securities. (Investments are discussed in Chapter 11.)

Equity Securities.   Because of the short-term nature of most marketable securities, their original cost is approximately equal to their market value as of the balance sheet date. Thus, most companies (78 percent) report the total of these securities at cost and explain parenthetically on the balance sheet or in a note that "cost approximates market."[13] However, *FASB Statement No. 12*[14] sets out explicit rules for the balance sheet valuation of marketable *equity* securities, which are the capital stocks of other companies. The rules differ according to whether the equity securities are classified as current assets or noncurrent assets. This classification depends on whether the company intends, or does not intend, to convert the securities to cash within the next year.

After the company classifies its marketable equity securities into a current portfolio and a noncurrent portfolio, and determines the cost and market value for each portfolio, the balance sheet carrying amount for each portfolio is the lower of its cost or market value. Note that market value here refers to the total market value of *all* the securities in a portfolio, not to individual securities. If a write-down from cost to market value is necessary in the *current* portfolio, Loss on Marketable Securities (an expense account) is debited and Marketable Securities is credited. Thus, a write-down of the current portfolio reduces the net income of the period. Any write-down of the *noncurrent* portfolio is debited directly to Retained Earnings; that is, the write-down does not "flow through" the income statement, as it does in the case of a current portfolio write-down.

These rules do not apply to nonprofit organizations or to enterprises in industries using specialized accounting practices, such as insurance companies and stock brokerage firms. Also, as a practical matter, most corporations' temporary investments are not equity securities but rather are certificates of deposit or negotiable short-term debt instruments such as commercial paper and Treasury bills.[15]

ANALYSIS OF MONETARY ASSETS

Some relationships that are helpful in analyzing a company's monetary assets are described below. They include the current ratio, the acid-test ratio, days' cash, and days' receivables. These ratios will be illustrated using the information given for Bethlehem Steel Corporation in Illustration 5–5.

---

[13]AICPA, *Accounting Trends & Techniques* (1981).

[14]"Accounting for Certain Marketable Securities," *FASB Statement No. 12*, December 1975. Five subsequent *FASB Interpretations, Nos. 10, 11, 12, 13,* and *16,* also deal with the accounting for marketable securities.

[15]Strictly speaking, common stocks, whether classified as Marketable Securities or Investments, are nonmonetary assets because they do not represent a claim to receive a *fixed* sum of money. Nevertheless, in practice, marketable equity securities are thought of as being monetary assets because like other marketable securities and certificates of deposit, they are viewed as highly liquid temporary investments of excess cash.

ILLUSTRATION 5–5
CONDENSED FINANCIAL STATEMENTS

BETHLEHEM STEEL CORPORATION
Balance Sheet
As of December 31, 1981
(millions of dollars)

Assets

Current assets:		
Cash		$ 62.4
Marketable securities (at cost, approximating market)		201.5
Accounts receivable (net of $8.8 allowance)		736.2
Inventories		879.5
Total current assets		1,879.6
All other assets		3,402.5
Total assets		$5,282.1

Liabilities and Shareholders' Equity

Current liabilities		$1,023.2
All other liabilities and shareholders' equity		4,258.9
Total liabilities and shareholders' equity		$5,282.1

Income Statement
Year Ended December 31, 1981
(millions of dollars)

Sales revenues		$7,298.0
Expenses*		7,087.1
Net income		$ 210.9

*Includes depreciation expense of $377.3 million.

Current Ratio

As explained in Chapter 2, the formula for the current ratio is:

$$\text{Current ratio} = \frac{\text{Current assets}}{\text{Current liabilities}} = \frac{\$1,879.6}{\$1,023.2} = 1.84$$

The current ratio is the most commonly used of all balance sheet ratios. It is not only a measure of the company's liquidity but also is a measure of the margin of safety that management maintains in order to allow for the inevitable unevenness in the flow of funds through the current asset and liability accounts. If this flow were absolutely smooth and uniform each day (so that, for example, money coming in from customers exactly equaled maturing obligations), the requirements for such a safety margin would be small. Since a company rarely can count on such an even flow, it needs a supply of liquid funds to be assured of being able to pay its bills when they come due. The current ratio indicates the size of this buffer.

In interpreting the current ratio, consideration of the proportion of various types of current assets is important. A company with a high percentage of its current assets in the form of monetary assets is more liquid than one with a high percentage in inventory, even though the companies have the same current ratio. Also, the nature of the business must be considered. For example, a manufacturer that makes high-fashion clothing needs a relatively high current ratio, since there is high risk involved in both this firm's accounts receivable and its inventory. On the other hand, a metals distributor may safely have a lower current ratio than the clothing manufacturer's, since the distributor's primary current asset would be inventories of steel, copper, and aluminum shapes, which do not become obsolete and whose prices may be increasing because of inflation.

Acid-Test Ratio

Some of the current assets are nonmonetary assets. A ratio that focuses on the relationship of *monetary assets* to current liabilities is called the *acid-test ratio,* or the *quick ratio.* Quick assets are those current assets that are also monetary assets; they therefore exclude inventories and prepaid items. The formula is:

$$\text{Acid-test ratio} = \frac{\text{Monetary current assets}}{\text{Current liabilities}} = \frac{\$1,000.1}{\$1,023.2} = 0.98$$

Days' Cash

Although cash is a necessary asset, it does not earn a return. Thus, although too little cash is an obvious signal of difficulty, too much cash is a sign that management has not taken advantage of opportunities to put cash to work in, say, certificates of deposit or marketable securities.

One way to judge how well the company is managing its cash is to calculate roughly how many days' bills the cash on hand would pay. The first step is to use the income statement to estimate cash expenses: a rough approximation would be to take total expenses and subtract noncash expenses such as depreciation. This total is then divided by 365 (some people use 260, which is 52 weeks of 5 working days) to arrive at daily cash needs:

$$\text{Cash costs per day} = \frac{\$6,246.5}{365} = \$17.11 \text{ per day}$$

This amount can then be divided into the cash balance to determine approximately the "days' cash" on hand:

$$\frac{\text{Cash}}{\text{Cash costs per day}} = \frac{\$51.2}{\$17.11 \text{ per day}} = 3.0 \text{ days}$$

Combining these two steps, the formula is:

$$\text{Days' cash} = \frac{\text{Cash}}{\text{Cash expenses} \div 365}$$

It must be emphasized that this is a rough approximation. The calculation focuses on routine operating expenses; it does not take account of cash needed for major asset purchases or loan repayments. Thus, a firm might appear to have too much cash on hand because it has just issued bonds to finance construction of a new plant. On the other hand, firms with good cash management procedures would not let even that cash sit idle; they would invest it in short-term securities for as long as possible, even if that is only two or three days. The days' cash will usually be one week or less in companies that manage their cash well. (Some analysts calculate this ratio using in the numerator cash plus marketable securities, rather than just "pure" cash. The ratio then indicates short-term liquidity, rather than cash management.)

Days' Receivables

A calculation similar to that used in days' cash can be used to see how many days' worth of sales are represented in accounts receivable. The formula is:

$$\text{Days' receivables} = \frac{\text{Receivables}}{\text{Sales} \div 365} = \frac{\$736.2}{\$7,298.0 \div 365} = 37 \text{ days}$$

The result is also called the average *collection period* for the receivables. If available, the amount of sales in the denominator should be *credit* sales, which is more closely related to receivables than is total sales.

The collection period can be related roughly to the credit terms offered by the company. A rule of thumb is that the collection period should not exceed 1⅓ times the regular payment period; that is, if the company's typical terms call for payment in 30 days, it is said that the average collection period should not exceed 40 days. Like all rules of thumb, this one has a great many exceptions. Changes in the ratio indicate changes in the company's credit policy or changes in its ability to collect its receivables.

As with other ratios, comparisons should be made with the collection period of other firms in the same industry, and also with a firm's own ratio for previous years. For example, in industries with excess capacity, looser credit policies are sometimes used as a competitive marketing tool, thus increasing the days' receivables. What is of concern is a firm's collection period being significantly longer than its competitors', suggesting inadequate collection procedures.

The aging schedule in Illustration 5–4 also provides useful information in analyzing the quality of the accounts receivable. An increase in the proportion of overdue amounts is a serious danger signal. While aging schedules frequently are used within corporations, they are not disclosed in corporate annual reports to shareholders.

SUMMARY

Although a business earns income continuously, accounting recognizes revenue only in the period in which the entity has performed substantially what is required in order to earn income and in which the amount of income can be reliably measured. In the usual case of the sale of goods or services, this is the period in which goods are delivered or services performed. If income cannot be reliably measured at this time, as in certain types of installment sales, revenue recognition is postponed. If the earning process takes place over several accounting periods, the percentage-of-completion method recognizes revenue in each of these periods if reliable measurement is possible.

The realization concept states that the amount of revenue recognized in a period is the amount that is reasonably certain to be collected from customers. Accordingly, the gross sales revenue is reduced by the estimated amount of bad debts that are hidden in credit sales. A corresponding reduction is made in the asset, accounts receivable. Similar reductions may be made for warranty costs and for sales returns and allowances.

Monetary assets are money or claims to receive fixed sums of money. They are reported on the balance sheet in various ways. Cash, certificates of deposit, and accounts receivable are reported at realizable amounts (which in the case of cash and certificates of deposit is the same as the face amount). Marketable equity securities are reported at the lower of cost or current market value.

The current ratio, the acid-test ratio, days' cash, and days' receivables are useful tools in analyzing a company's monetary assets.

SUGGESTION FOR FURTHER READING

Jaenicke, Henry R. *Survey of Present Practices in Recognizing Revenues, Expenses, Gains, and Losses.* Stamford, Conn.: FASB, 1981.

Cases

CASE 5–1 Wyland Corporation (A)

On December 31, 1982, before the yearly financial statements were prepared, the controller of the Wyland Corporation reviewed certain transactions that affected accounts receivable and the allowance for doubtful accounts. The controller first examined the December 31, 1981, balance sheet (Exhibit 1). His subsequent review of the year's transactions applicable to accounts receivable revealed the items listed below:

1. Sales on account during 1982 amounted to $7,898,058.
2. Payment received on accounts receivable during 1982 totaled $7,595,787.
3. During the year, accounts receivable totaling $20,014 were deemed uncollectible and were written off.
4. Two accounts that had been written off as uncollectible in 1981 were collected in 1982. One account for

$1,533 was paid in full. A partial payment of $1,125 was made by the King Company on another account that originally had amounted to $1,807. The controller was reasonably sure this account would be paid in full because reliable reports were circulating that the trustee in bankruptcy for the King Company would pay all obligations 100 cents on the dollar.

5. The allowance for bad debts was adjusted to equal 3 percent of the balance in accounts receivable at the end of the year.

Questions

1. Analyze the effect of each of these transactions in terms of its effect on accounts receivable, allowance for doubtful accounts, and any other account that may be

EXHIBIT 1

WYLAND CORPORATION
Balance Sheet
As of December 31, 1981

Assets

Current assets:

Cash		$ 537,075
Accounts receivable	$ 790,606	
Less: Allowance for doubtful accounts	23,718	766,888
U.S. Treasury securities at cost		219,247
Inventories		1,387,519
Total current assets		2,910,729

Other assets:

Investments		329,835
Land		149,250
Building	1,924,207	
Less: Accumulated depreciation	530,703	1,393,504
Factory machinery	2,740,468	
Less: Accumulated depreciation	1,313,886	1,426,582
Furniture and fixtures	45,187	
Less: Accumulated depreciation	32,319	12,868
Automotive equipment	46,639	
Less: Accumulated depreciation	29,725	16,914
Office machines	34,035	
Less: Accumulated depreciation	22,404	11,631
Tools		49,035
Patent		45,000
Prepaid expenses		80,152
Total assets		$6,425,500

Liabilities and Shareholders' Equity

Current liabilities:

Accounts payable	$ 408,001
Unpaid taxes	567,483
Accrued salaries, wages, and interest	113,182
Long-term debt, due within one year	55,440
Total current liabilities	1,144,106

Noncurrent liabilities:

Long-term debt	997,894

Shareholders' equity:

Common stock	2,002,623
Retained earnings	2,280,877
Total shareholders' equity	4,283,500
Total liabilities and shareholders' equity	$6,425,500

involved, and prepare necessary journal entries.

2. Give the correct totals for accounts receivable and the allowance on doubtful accounts as of December 31, 1982, after the transactions affecting them had been recorded.

3. Calculate the ratios described in the text as of December 31, 1982. Assume that items other than those described in the case are the same as on December 31, 1981.

CASE 5–2   MacDonald's Farm

Early in 1983, Denise Grey was notified by a lawyer that her recently deceased uncle had willed her the ownership of a 2,000-acre wheat farm in Iowa. The lawyer requested information as to whether Grey wanted to keep the farm or sell it.

Grey was an assistant vice president in the consumer credit department of a large New York bank. Despite the distance between New York and Iowa, Grey was interested in retaining ownership of the farm if she could determine its profitability. During the last 10 years of his life, Jeremiah MacDonald had hired professional managers to run his farm while he remained in semiretirement in Florida.

Keeping the farm as an investment was particularly interesting to Grey for the following reasons:

1. Recent grain deals with Communist countries had increased present farm commodity prices substantially; many experts believed these prices would remain high for the next several years.
2. While the number of small farms had decreased markedly in the last 20 years, large farms such as MacDonald's using mechanization and new hybrid seed varieties could be extremely profitable.
3. The value of good farmland in Iowa was appreciating at about 10 percent a year.

Included in the lawyer's letter were data on revenues and expenses for 1982 and certain information on balance sheet items, which are summarized below:

Beginning inventory	0 bushels
1982 wheat production	210,000 bushels
Sold to grain elevator	180,000 bushels
Ending inventory	30,000 bushels

Prices:

The average price per bushel for wheat sold to the grain elevator operator in 1982 was $3.30. The price per bushel at the time of the wheat harvest was $3.15. The closing price per bushel at December 31, 1982, was $3.42.

Accounts receivable:

At year-end, the proceeds from 20,000 bushels had not yet been received from the elevator operator. The average sales price of this wheat had been $3.33 per bushel. There were no uncollected proceeds at December 31, 1981.

Cash:

The farm has a checking account balance of $8,700 and a savings account balance of $22,500.

Land:

The original cost of the land was $375,000. It was appraised for estate tax purposes at $1,050 per acre.

Buildings and machinery:

Buildings and machinery with an original cost of $412,500 and accumulated depreciation of $300,000 are employed on the farm. The equipment was appraised at net book value.

Current liabilities:

The farm has notes payable and accounts payable totaling $33,000.

Owner's equity:

Common stock has a par value of $7,500 plus additional paid-in capital of $450,000. There was no record of retained earnings, although it was known that Jeremiah MacDonald withdrew most of the earnings in the last few years in order to continue the lifestyle to which he had become accustomed in Florida.

1982 Expenses for the MacDonald Farm

A. Variable costs per bushel:

Seed	$ 0.053
Fertilizer and chemicals	0.315
Machinery costs, fuel and repairs	0.097
Part-time labor and other costs	0.038
Variable cost per bushel	$ 0.503

B. Annual costs not related to the volume of production:

Salaries and wages	$ 67,500
Insurance	6,000
Taxes*	22,500
Depreciation	28,500
Other expenses	45,000
Total costs not related to production volume	$169,500

*This figure excludes income taxes since the corporation was taxed as a sole proprietorship.

Looking over the data on revenues and expenses, Grey discovered that there were no monetary numbers for 1982's total revenues or for the ending inventory. The lawyer's letter explained that there was some doubt in his mind about when revenue for the farm should be recognized and about the appropriate way to value the grain inventory. There are at least three alternative stages in the wheat growing cycle at which revenue could be counted.

First, the *production method* could be used. Since wheat has a daily valuation on the Chicago Commodity Exchange, any unsold inventory as of December 31 could be valued at market price very objectively. In this way, revenue can be counted for all wheat produced in a given year, regardless of whether it is sold or not. A decision not to sell this wheat before December 31 is based on speculation about future wheat price increases.

Second, the *sales method* could be used. This would recognize revenue when the grain is purchased from the farm by the grain elevator operator in the neighboring town. In this instance, the owner of the grain elevator had just sold control to a Kansas City company with no previous experience in running such a facility. The manager of the MacDonald Farm had expressed some concern about selling to an unknown operator.

Third, the *collection method* could be used. Under this approach revenue is counted when the cash is actually received by the farm from the grain elevator operator. Full collection often took several months because a grain elevator operator might keep wheat for a considerable time in the hope that prices would rise so he could sell at a greater profit.

Questions

1. Prepare the 1982 income statement and related ending balance sheet for the MacDonald Farm recognizing revenue by the:
    a. Production method.
    b. Sales method.
    c. Collection method.
    Which method would you recommend?

2. Assume that the MacDonald Farm had received a firm offer of $225,000 for 100 acres of the farm that would be used as the site of a new housing development. This development would have no effect on the use of the remaining acreage as a

farm, and Ms. Grey planned to accept it. How would you account in the 1982 financial statements for the economic gain represented by this appreciation in land values?

3. Should Grey retain ownership of the farm?

CASE 5–3 Butler Realty Company

Butler Realty Company was incorporated July 1, 1982, for the purpose of buying eight houses in a bankrupt housing development and then selling these houses. Two persons were involved in the company. Helen Butler was to be responsible for the day-to-day affairs of the company and for selling the houses. Paul Wagner invested $150,000 in cash in return for all the common stock in the company.

The understanding between the two was that Ms. Butler would receive a sales commission of 25 percent of the gross margin on the houses and a bonus at the end of the year. Mr. Wagner would be entitled to a $3,500 cash dividend in 1982, plus one half the income (before income taxes) of the company, after deducting the $3,500. Ms. Butler would receive shares of stock equal in value to the remainder of the pretax income (after the $3,500 and the additional payments to Mr. Wagner).

This arrangement would be continued in succeeding years, except that each stockholder would be entitled to a cash dividend of 5 percent of his or her equity, and the remainder of the income would be divided equally. In this way, Ms. Butler would build up a stock ownership without having to invest cash.

The housing development consisted of 25 houses, of which 17 had been sold before the project went bankrupt. The bank that had taken over the property sold the eight houses to Butler Realty Company for $756,000 on July 1, 1982. Butler Realty paid $100,000 cash and took out a five-year 12 percent loan for $656,000 with the bank; this loan was secured by the inventory of unsold homes that Butler Realty might have at any point in the next five years. Semiannual payments of $65,600 plus interest were to be made on December 31 and June 30.

By the end of 1982, five of the houses had been sold for a total of $546,000; they had cost $472,500. Also, during the year the company had incurred costs of $4,870 for incorporation fees and miscellaneous expenses, about which there were no questions. Questions arose, however, with regard to certain other events that affected the calculation of income; these events are listed below.

1. Because few vacant houses remained, because the neighborhood had acquired a good reputation, and because economic conditions in the area had improved, Ms. Butler judged that the value of the unsold houses had increased by at least 5 percent since July 1. She increased the asking prices accordingly. She recommended that 90 percent of this increase be added to the inventory cost of the houses (the other 10 percent, or 0.5 percent of the original cost, would be recorded as profit when the houses were sold). Mr. Wagner agreed that the value of the houses had increased 5 percent.

2. Ms. Butler disliked the wallpaper in certain rooms in House No. 23, and with Mr. Wagner's concurrence, she had the rooms repapered at a cost of $1,200. She did not increase the asking price of this house to reflect the repapering (the asking price was raised 5 percent, as explained above), although she felt the new paper definitely improved the house's appearance.

3. A maintenance company was hired to mow lawns, rake leaves, and otherwise keep the unsold properties in attractive condition; $4,000 was paid for this work in 1982. No records were kept of the amount attributable to each house, but since this work stopped as soon as a house was sold, it seemed reasonable to Ms. Butler to attribute half to the five sold houses and half to the three unsold houses.

4. For all intents and purposes, House No. 24 was sold. The buyer had executed an agreement to purchase and had made an "earnest" payment of $1,500, which was not returnable so long as Butler Realty acted in good faith. Ms. Butler thought she was entitled to $375 of this amount as commission. The selling price of the house was $111,900, and its cost from the bank was $94,500.

5. During 1982, advertising expense on the three unsold homes amounted to $2,700, which was attributed equally to each house. The other five houses had been sold without the placement of advertisements.

6. During November 1982, a water pipe broke in House No. 25 (an unsold home), causing $2,250 worth of damage. The company's insurance policy covered all but $150 of the damage.

Questions

1. What should Ms. Butler's commission be for the period July 1, 1982, to December 31, 1982?

2. Prepare an income statement for the six months ended December 31, 1982, and a balance sheet as of that date. Be certain that your income statement differentiates between gross margin and income. (Ignore income taxes.) For the balance sheet, assume that the company has no office space or equipment; Ms. Butler runs the business "from her home, phone, and automobile." She has been paid her commission on the five sold houses.

CASE 5–4   Jean Coffin (A)

"Your course unfortunately doesn't give me the answer to a great many real-life problems," said Jean Coffin to an accounting professor. "I've read the text and listened to you attentively, but every once in a while I run across something that doesn't seem to fit the rules."

"Not all of life's complications can be covered in a first course," the professor replied. "As is the case with law, medicine, or indeed any of the professions, many matters are dealt with in advanced courses, and others are not settled in any classroom. Nevertheless, some problems that are not specifically discussed can be solved satisfactorily by relating them to principles that you already have learned. Let's take revenue recognition as a particularly difficult case in point. If you will write down some of the matters about which you are now uncomfortable, I'd be glad to discuss them with you; that is, after you have given some thought as to the most reasonable solution."

A week later, Coffin returned with the list given below.

1. Pay Phones. When a customer deposits coins in a pay phone, the telephone company has earned revenues. It is obviously impossible, however, for the company to count the coins in all the pay phones on the evening of December 31. How does the telephone company know its revenue for a given year?

2. Retainer Fee. A law firm received a "retainer" of $10,000 on July 1, 1983, from a client. In return, it agreed to furnish general legal advice upon request for one year. In addition, the client would be billed for regular legal services such as representation in litigation. There was no way of knowing how often, or when, the client would request advice, and it was quite possible that no such advice would be requested. How much of the $10,000 should be counted as revenue in 1983?

3. Cruise. Raymond's, a travel agency, chartered a cruise ship for two weeks beginning January 23, 1983, for $200,000. In return, the ship's owner agreed to pay all costs of the cruise. In 1982, Raymond's sold all available space on the ship for $260,000. It incurred $40,000 in selling and other costs in doing so. All the $260,000 was received in cash from passengers in 1982. Raymond's paid $50,000 as an advance payment to the ship owner in 1982. How much, if any, of the $260,000 was revenue to Raymond's in 1982? Does the question of whether passengers were entitled to a refund in 1983 if they canceled their reservations make any difference in the answer?

4. Accretion. A nursery owner had one plot of land containing Christmas trees that were four years old on November 1, 1982. The owner had incurred

costs of $3 per tree up to that time. A wholesaler offered to buy the trees for $4 each and to pay in addition all costs of cutting and bundling, and transporting them to market. The nursery owner declined this offer, deciding that it would be more profitable to let the trees grow for one more year. Only a trivial amount of additional cost would be involved. The price of Christmas trees varies with their height. Can the nursery owner recognize any revenue from these trees in 1982?

5. Definition of Revenue. A certain state levies a 5 percent sales tax. A sale was defined as "any transfer of title or possession, or both, of tangible personal property for a consideration. Services which are part of a sale are includable in the sales price." Ms. A. bought a microwave oven and received a bill itemized as follows:

Microwave oven	$500
Delivery charge	30
Installation charge	40

She planned to pay this bill on an installment plan, in which interest costs would amount to $24 in the current year and $33 in the following year.

Mr. B. bought a microwave oven, similar to Ms. A's, from a company that advertised "free delivery and installation." He paid $570 cash.

What should be the sales tax on each purchase?

6. Premium Coupons. A manufacturer of coffee enclosed a premium coupon with each $1.50 (at wholesale) jar of coffee that it sells to retailers. Customers can use this coupon to apply to $0.25 of the price of a new type of instant tea that the manufacturer is introducing and that will also sell for $1.50 wholesale. The manufacturer reimbursed retail stores $0.33 for each such coupon they submitted. Past experience with similar premium offers indicated that approximately 10 percent of such coupons are eventually redeemed. At the end of 1982, however, only about 5 percent of the coupons issued in 1982 will have been redeemed. In recording the revenues for the company for 1982, what allowance, if any, should be made for these coupons? If an allowance should be made, should it apply to the sales revenue of coffee or to the sales revenue of tea?

7. Product Repurchase Agreement. In December 1982, Manufacturer A sold merchandise to Wholesaler B. B used this inventory as collateral for a bank loan of $100,000 and sent the $100,000 to A. Manufacturer A agreed to repurchase the goods on or before July 1, 1983, for $112,000, the difference representing interest on the loan and compensation for B's services. Does Manufacturer A have revenue in 1982?

8. Franchises. A national real estate brokerage firm became highly successful by selling franchises to local real estate brokers. It charges $10,000 for the initial franchise fee and a service fee of 6 percent of the broker's revenue thereafter. For this, it permits use of its well-known name, and provides a one-week initial training course, a nationwide referral system, and various marketing and management aids. Currently, the franchise fee accounts for 25 percent of the national firm's receipts, but it expects that the United States market will be saturated within the next three years, and thereafter the firm will have to depend on the service fee and new sources of revenue that it may develop. Should it recognize the $10,000 as revenue in the year in which the franchise agreement is signed? If it does, what will happen to its profits after the market has become saturated?

9. Government Grants. On July 1, 1983, Linda Cooper, a psychologist with the Institute of Continuing Education, received a National Science Foundation grant to continue her research on learning theory. The grant was for three years with a payment of $5,000 each July 1 from 1983 to 1985. Should this money appear as revenue on the income statement of the Institute? If so, how much is revenue in 1983?

CASE 5–5   Quik-Copy Center

Quik-Copy Center was incorporated on November 20, 1981, and began operating on January 2, 1982. The balance sheet as of the beginning of operations is shown below:

QUIK-COPY CENTER, INC.
Balance Sheet
January 2, 1982

Assets		Equities	
Cash.	$ 1,600	Accounts payable	$ 8,700
Supplies	19,500	Bank loan	19,000
Building and equipment.	240,000	Mortgage.	83,000
Land.	9,600	Capital stock	160,000
Total assets	$270,700	Total equities	$270,700

EXHIBIT 1

Cash Receipts and Disbursements
Record for 1982

Cash Receipts		*Cash Disbursements*	
Cash sales	$141,160	Wages and salaries	$ 63,800
Collection of accounts receivable	51,800	Repairs	6,700
		Property and miscellaneous taxes	5,040
		Heat, light, and power	8,800
		Additional supplies	42,080
		Selling and administration	14,160
		Interest*	3,040
		Insurance†	5,400
		Partial payment of bank loan	
		on December 31	9,500
		Payment of accounts payable	8,700
Total	$192,960	Total	$167,220

Unpaid bills from suppliers (representing purchase of photocopy supplies) .... $ 7,900
Unpaid customer accounts (representing copying services to them).......................... 9,040

*Interest at 16 percent on the bank loan was payable June 30 and December 31. Interest payments for 1982 were made when due.

†Of the total insurance premiums of $5,400 paid in 1982, $1,900 constituted the premium on a two-year policy to expire on December 31, 1983, and the remainder was for 1982 insurance protection.

EXHIBIT 2
OTHER INFORMATION RELATIVE TO
OPERATIONS

1. Wages and salaries were paid monthly on the second of each month for the preceding month. Wages and salaries earned during December but not yet paid totaled $4,800.
2. The yearly depreciation expense on the buildings and equipment was figured at $12,000.
3. Interest on the mortgage at 14 percent was payable annually on January 1. No such interest had yet been paid.
4. An inventory taken of the supplies at the end of the year revealed a supply on hand costing $21,300.
5. Federal income tax for 1982 would be based on current tax rates:
    16 percent for the first $25,000 of taxable income.
    19 percent for taxable income between $25,001 and $50,000.

In preparing financial statements for the first year of operations, the accountant reviewed its cash receipts and disbursements and its file of unpaid bills from suppliers and unpaid customer accounts. This information appears in Exhibit 1.

In addition, the accountant discovered certain other information which had not been recorded. These additional items appear in Exhibit 2.

Questions

1. Prepare an income statement for 1982 and a balance sheet as of December 31, 1982.

2. Be prepared to explain the derivation of each number on these financial statements.

6

Cost of Sales and Inventories

This chapter describes principles and procedures for measuring cost of sales as reported on the income statement, and the related measurement of inventory on the balance sheet. These costs may be accounted for either by the periodic inventory method or the perpetual inventory method; each method is described. The cost of individual units of inventory and of individual goods sold can be measured by any of several methods, including specific identification, average cost, FIFO, and LIFO. Each of these methods is described, and they are compared.

Because the topics discussed in this chapter are interrelated, we start with a brief overview of procedures in three types of companies: merchandising companies, manufacturing companies, and service companies. Next, we describe in detail the procedures in merchandising companies. Since the procedures in manufacturing companies start with the same steps used in merchandising companies and incorporate additional aspects associated with the manufacturing process, we limit the discussion of manufacturing companies to these additional matters.

Types of Companies   A single company may conduct merchandising, service, and/or manufacturing activities. For convenience, we shall assume that each company described here conducts only one type. If a company does conduct more than one type of activity, for each type it will use the appropriate accounting method.

Merchandising Companies. Retail stores, wholesalers, distributors, and similar companies that sell tangible goods are merchandising companies.[1] A merchandising company sells goods in substantially the same physical form as that in which it acquires them. Its cost of sales is therefore the acquisition cost of the goods that are sold. On the balance sheet, a current asset, "Merchandise inventory," shows the cost of goods that have been acquired but not yet sold as of the balance sheet date.

Manufacturing Companies. A manufacturing company converts raw materials and purchased parts into finished goods. Its cost of sales includes the conversion costs, as well as the raw material and parts costs, of the goods that it sells. A manufacturing company has three types of inventory accounts: materials, work in process, and finished goods.

Because both merchandising and manufacturing companies sell tangible goods, their income statements sometimes use the term *cost of goods sold* rather than cost of sales. We shall use the two terms interchangeably for merchandising and manufacturing companies, but use only cost of sales for service organizations.

Service Organizations. Service organizations furnish intangible services rather than tangible goods. They include hotels, beauty parlors and other personal-service organizations, hospitals and other health-care organizations, educational organizations, banks and other financial institutions, and governmental units. In North America, more people are employed in such organizations than are employed in manufacturing organizations.

Service organizations may have materials inventories; for example, the pipe and fittings of a plumbing company. Professional service firms, such as law, consulting, accounting, and architectural firms, may have inventories consisting of costs that have been incurred on behalf of clients but which have not yet been billed to clients. These inventories, often called *Unbilled Costs*, correspond to work in process inventories in a manufacturing company. Service organizations do not have finished goods inventories.

Supplies

In addition to inventory accounts for goods directly involved in the merchandising or manufacturing process, a company may have one or more inventory accounts for supplies. *Supplies* are tangible items, such as office supplies, and lubricants and repair parts for machinery, that will be consumed in the course of normal operations. They are distinguished from merchandise in that they are not sold as such, and they are distinguished from materials in that supplies are not accounted for sep-

---

[1]The word *products* is often used when *goods* is intended. For clarity, throughout this book, we use *goods* for tangible items sold or offered for sale, *services* for intangibles, and *products* for the sum of goods and services. In other words, the outputs of a firm, whether tangible or intangible, are its products.

arately as an element of the cost of goods produced. Paper offered for sale is merchandise inventory in a stationery store; paper is material inventory in a company that manufactures books; and paper intended for use in the office is supplies inventory in any company. Supplies will not be discussed further in this chapter.

MERCHANDISING COMPANIES

We shall now describe in detail the principles and procedures related to accounting for inventories and cost of goods sold in merchandising companies.

Acquisition Cost

Merchandise is added to inventory at its cost, in accordance with the basic cost concept. Cost includes expenditures made to make the goods ready for sale. Thus, merchandise cost includes not only the invoice cost of the goods purchased but also freight and other shipping costs required to bring the goods to the point of sale, and the cost of unpacking and price marking. Since the recordkeeping task of attaching these elements of cost to individual units of merchandise may be considerable, some or all of them may be excluded from merchandise product costs and reported as operating expenses of the period when the amounts are immaterial.

The purchase cost is also adjusted for returns and allowances and for cash discounts given by the suppliers of the merchandise. As was the case with sales discounts (see Chapter 5), purchase discounts can be accounted for either by recording the purchase amount as net of the discount, or by recording the purchase amount at the invoice price and recording the discount when it is taken. If the purchase is originally recorded at the net amount, and if the discount is not subsequently taken, the amount of the lost discount is debited to an account, Purchase Discounts Not Taken. This account provides useful information to management.

Example. If merchandise costing $1,000 is purchased on terms of 2 percent discount if the invoice is paid within 10 days, this acquisition is recorded thus:

```
dr.   Purchases (or Merchandise
         Inventory) .....................   980
   cr.     Accounts Payable..............          980
```

If the company lost the discount by not paying the invoice within 10 days, the entry would be:

```
dr.   Accounts Payable .................   980
      Purchase Discounts Not Taken .....    20
   cr.     Cash...........................        1,000
```

The word *purchases* refers not to the placing of a purchase order but rather to the receipt of merchandise purchased. No accounting entry is made when merchandise is ordered. The entry is made only when the merchandise becomes the property of the buyer. Under commercial law, goods in transit usually belong to the buyer as soon as they are delivered to the transportation company if the terms are "FOB shipping point," that is, if the buyer pays the transportation costs. If the seller pays the transportation costs ("FOB destination"), title does not pass until the goods arrive at the buyer's warehouse.

The Basic Measurement Problem

Think of merchandise inventory as a tank or a reservoir, as in Illustration 6–1. At the beginning of an accounting period, there is a certain amount of goods in the reservoir; this is the beginning inventory. During the period, additional merchandise is purchased and added to the reservoir. Also, during the period, merchandise sold is withdrawn from the reservoir. At the end of the accounting period, the amount of goods remaining in the reservoir is the ending inventory.

ILLUSTRATION 6–1
MERCHANDISE INVENTORY AND FLOWS

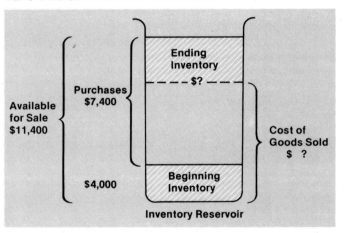

The amount of goods *available for sale* during the period is the sum of the beginning inventory plus the purchases during the period. This sum is $11,400 in Illustration 6–1. The problem to be discussed in this section, and indeed in most of the chapter, is how to divide the amount of goods available for sale between (1) the ending inventory and (2) cost of goods sold. That is, how much of the $11,400 is still on hand at the end of the period and how much has been sold during the period?

There are two approaches to this problem:

1. We can determine the amount of ending inventory (i.e., the amount in the reservoir at the end of the period) and obtain cost of goods sold by subtracting the ending inventory from the goods available for sale. This is the *periodic inventory method*. Or,
2. We can measure the amount actually delivered to customers and obtain the ending inventory by subtracting cost of goods sold from the goods available for sale. This is the *perpetual inventory method*.

Periodic Inventory Method

In the periodic inventory method, a physical count is made of merchandise in the ending inventory. This is called *taking a physical inventory*. Assume that the cost of this remaining merchandise is $2,000. Cost of goods sold is obtained by subtracting the ending inventory from the amount of goods available for sale, thus:

Beginning inventory	$ 4,000
Plus: Purchases	7,400
Equals: Goods available for sale	11,400
Less: Ending inventory	2,000
Cost of goods sold	$ 9,400

The amount of beginning inventory in the above calculation is, of course, the amount found by the physical inventory taken at the end of the *preceding* period.

Some companies show such a calculation in the cost of goods sold section of the income statement itself. Most, although deducing cost of goods sold by the method shown above, do not present the details. Still others report additional detail, particularly on internal reports to management (as opposed to shareholder reports). For example, if there are freight charges and the return of purchased merchandise, the internal income statement might show:

Beginning inventory		$ 4,000
Plus: Purchases, gross	$7,000	
Freight-in	600	
	7,600	
Less: Purchase returns	200	
Net purchases		7,400
Goods available for sale		11,400
Less: Ending inventory		2,000
Cost of goods sold		$ 9,400

Accounts. When the cost of goods sold is deduced by the method described above, a separate account is established for each element in the calculation. Thus, a Purchases account is established, and the invoice cost of merchandise purchased is debited to this account, rather than directly to Merchandise Inventory. Accounts are also established for Freight-In, Purchase Returns, and any other items involved in the calculation.

Rules for debiting and crediting these accounts can be deduced from their relationship to other accounts. Since Purchases shows additions to the asset account, Merchandise Inventory, it increases on the debit side. Purchase Returns is a reduction in Purchases and hence must have the opposite rule; it increases on the credit side. Freight-In adds to the cost of purchases and therefore increases on the debit side. The rules can also be deduced by thinking of the offsetting part of the transaction. Whenever possible, it is simplest to assume that the other account is Cash. Thus, a cash purchase involves a decrease in Cash, which is a credit; therefore, the entry to Purchases must be a debit.

Adjusting and Closing. The accounts described above are temporary accounts that must be closed at the end of each accounting period. Furthermore, when these accounts are used, no entries are made during the accounting period to the Merchandise Inventory account. Therefore, the amount shown in Merchandise Inventory when the adjusting process begins will be the amount of *beginning* inventory. The Merchandise Inventory account must be adjusted to show the proper inventory amount as of the end of the period. These adjusting and closing entries are customarily made in a certain order, which is related to the sequence of steps displayed in the calculation shown above. This order is as follows:

1. Transfer the beginning inventory to Cost of Goods Sold, a temporary clearing account.
2. Close Freight-In, Purchase Returns, and similar accounts to Purchases, thereby showing the amount of net purchases in the Purchases account.
3. Close Purchases to Cost of Goods Sold.
4. Enter the ending inventory by debiting Merchandise Inventory and crediting Cost of Goods Sold.
5. Close Cost of Goods Sold to Income Summary.

Example. Using the numbers given above, these entries would be as follows:

```
                              (1)
dr.   Cost of Goods Sold...................   4,000
   cr.    Merchandise Inventory ............          4,000

                              (2)
dr.   Purchases............................    600
   cr.    Freight—In ......................            600
dr.   Purchase Returns.....................    200
   cr.    Purchases .......................            200
```
Since gross purchases were $7,000, Purchases now has a debit balance of $7,400.

(3)

| dr. | Cost of Goods Sold | 7,400 | |
| cr. | Purchases | | 7,400 |

The Purchases account is now closed.

(4)

| dr. | Merchandise Inventory | 2,000 | |
| cr. | Cost of Goods Sold | | 2,000 |

At this point, Cost of Goods Sold has a debit balance of $9,400. Merchandise Inventory shows the correct beginning balance ($2,000) for the *next* period.

(5)

| dr. | Income Summary | 9,400 | |
| cr. | Cost of Goods Sold | | 9,400 |

Cost of Goods Sold is now closed.

Perpetual Inventory Method

In the perpetual inventory method, a record is maintained of each item carried in the inventory. In a manual system, this record is a card similar to the sample shown in Illustration 6–2. In essence, this record is a subsidiary ledger account, and Merchandise Inventory is its control account. Purchases are entered directly on this record and also debited to Merchandise Inventory; the offsetting credit is to Accounts Payable or Cash. Shipments are entered on this record and are credited to Merchandise Inventory; the offsetting debit is to Cost of Goods Sold. The balance at the end of the period is the amount of that item in the ending inventory. The sum of the balances for all the items is the ending inventory for the company.

Assuming, for simplicity, that the company had only the one item shown in Illustration 6–2, the journal entries for the transactions listed there would be:

For purchases:

(1)

| dr. | Merchandise Inventory | 7,000 | |
| cr. | Accounts Payable | | 7,000 |

For shipments to customers:

(2)

| dr. | Cost of Goods Sold | 8,800 | |
| cr. | Merchandise Inventory | | 8,800 |

For purchase returns:

(3)

| dr. | Accounts Payable | 200 | |
| cr. | Merchandise Inventory | | 200 |

ILLUSTRATION 6–2
PERPETUAL INVENTORY CARD

Item: Cassette Deck, Model S150 Unit: Each								
Date	**Receipts**			**Shipments**			**Balance**	
	Units	Unit Cost	Total	Units	Unit Cost	Total	Units	Unit Cost	Total
Jan. 2							40	100	4,000
12				32	100	3,200	8	100	800
14	70	100	7,000				78	100	7,800
25				56	100	5,600	22	100	2,200
27				2	100	200*	20	100	2,000

*This entry is a purchase return to the manufacturer.

In many perpetual inventory systems, freight-in is not entered on the perpetual inventory cards. Instead, it is accumulated in a separate account. Assuming the same $600 freight-in as in the previous example, the closing entry for this account would be:

(4)

dr.	Cost of Goods Sold....................	600	
cr.	Freight-In		600

Cost of Goods Sold is closed to Income Summary as in the periodic inventory method; that is:

(5)

dr.	Income Summary........................	9,400	
cr.	Cost of Goods Sold		9,400

These entries would be posted to ledger accounts as shown below:

Merchandise Inventory

Balance	4,000	(2) Shipments	8,800
(1) Purchases	7,000	(3) Returns	200
		To balance	2,000
	11,000		11,000
Balance	2,000		

Cost of Goods Sold

(2)	8,800	(5) To Income	
(4) Freight	600	Summary	9,400
	9,400		9,400

Note that in this method, no separate Purchases account is needed; purchases are debited directly to Merchandise Inventory.

Comparison of Periodic and Perpetual Methods

Both inventory methods match the cost of goods sold with the sales revenue *for those same goods.* Thus, either method is in accord with the matching concept. Without this matching, the gross margin amount for a period would not be meaningful.

The perpetual inventory method requires that a record be maintained for each item carried in inventory. It therefore requires additional recordkeeping. This recordkeeping is not likely to be burdensome for a store offering at most a few hundred, relatively high-cost items, such as a jewelry or appliance store. Such recordkeeping may not be worthwhile in stores that stock many low-cost items, such as grocery stores and drugstores. (A large supermarket may stock as many as 10,000 different items.) However, the development of electronic point-of-sale terminals, which have scanners that identify each item sold by reading a bar code on the item's package, has led many such stores to change to the perpetual inventory method.

Advantages of Perpetual Method. The perpetual inventory method has three important advantages. First, the detailed record maintained for each item is useful in deciding when and how much to reorder, and in analyzing customer demand for the item. In many chain stores using point-of-sale terminals with scanners, sales data are used as input to computer models that automatically prepare orders on a central warehouse to replenish the store's inventory. This helps avoid both stockouts and excess inventories of the various items carried by the store.

Second, the perpetual inventory record has a built-in check that is not possible with the periodic method. In the periodic method, the physical inventory at the end of the period is a necessary part of the calculation of cost of goods sold. The difference between the goods available for sale and the goods on hand is *assumed* to be the cost of goods sold. This assumption is not necessarily correct because some of the goods may have been pilfered, lost, thrown away, or overlooked when the physical inventory was taken. Collectively, these goods that are not in inventory but were not sold make up the period's *inventory shrinkage.* In the perpetual inventory system, an actual count of the goods on hand can be used as a check on the accuracy of the inventory records. Shrinkage thus can be identified separately, rather than being "buried" in cost of goods sold.

Third, with a perpetual inventory system, an income statement can be prepared without taking a physical inventory. Thus, an income statement can be prepared every month, with the accuracy of the underlying perpetual inventory records being checked by an annual or semiannual physical inventory.

Retail Method

A store that does not maintain perpetual inventory records can nevertheless prepare reasonably accurate monthly income statements without taking a physical inventory by using the *retail method.* In this method, purchases are recorded at both their cost and their retail selling price. The gross margin percentage of the goods available for sale is calculated from these records. The *complement* of this percentage is applied to sales for the month (obtained from cash register and accounts receivable records) to find the approximate cost of goods sold.

    Example.   Assume the following:

	At Cost	At Retail
Beginning inventory...................	$ 4,000	$ 6,000
Purchases............................	7,000	10,000
Goods available for sale	$11,000	$16,000

    The gross margin percentage is ($16,000 − $11,000) ÷ $16,000 = 31 percent. The complement of this is 100 percent − 31 percent = 69 percent. If sales for the month were $13,000, it is assumed that cost of goods sold was 69 percent of this amount, or $8,970.

In applying the retail method in practice, adjustments must be made for markdowns that are made from initial retail prices, for example, in clearance sales.

    A variation of this method, called the *gross profit method*, simply applies a "normal" gross margin percentage to the amount of sales in order to arrive at an approximation of cost of goods sold. Records are not kept of the retail value of goods available for sale. With this method, a "normal" margin is determined for each department in the store, and the salesperson or checkout clerk records the department number of each item the customer purchases. A department's sales for the month are multiplied by the complement of the department's gross margin percentage to approximate the department's cost of goods sold. Sales and cost of goods sold amounts are then summed across all departments to determine the store's gross margin.

MANUFACTURING COMPANIES

    A manufacturing company has as a major function the conversion of raw materials and purchased parts into finished goods. In any company, cost of sales is the total of the acquisition cost plus conversion costs, if any, of the products that are sold. The manufacturer, therefore, includes in cost of goods sold the cost of materials and parts used, the cost of labor, and other costs incurred in the manufacture of the goods that are sold. The difference between accounting for the cost of sales in a merchandising company and in a manufacturing company arises because the merchandising company usually has no conversion costs. Its cost of goods sold is practically the same as the purchase price of these goods.

The measurement of cost of goods sold is therefore more complicated in a manufacturing company than in a merchandising company. In a merchandising company, this cost is normally obtained directly from suppliers' invoices. In a manufacturing company, it must be obtained by collecting and aggregating the several elements of manufacturing cost.

Inventory Accounts

A manufacturing company has three types of inventory accounts. Their names and the nature of their content are as follows:

1. *Materials Inventory.* Items of material that are to become a part of the ultimately salable goods that result from the manufacturing process. They are costed at acquisition cost, with the same types of adjustments for freight-in and returns as those made in calculating the net purchase cost of merchandise inventory, described above.
2. *Work in Process Inventory.* Goods that have started through the manufacturing process but have not yet been finished. They are costed as the sum of (1) the materials thus far issued for them plus (2) the labor and other manufacturing costs incurred on these items up to the end of the accounting period.
3. *Finished Goods Inventory.* Goods whose manufacture has been completed but which have not been shipped to customers. They are costed at the total cost incurred in manufacturing them. This account is essentially the same as Merchandise Inventory in a merchandising company, except that the items are costed at the cost of manufacturing them rather than at their acquisition cost.

There are wide variations in the relative size of the three types of inventories among companies. Companies with a short production cycle may have so little work in process at the end of the accounting period that they do not have a separate work in process inventory item. Companies that produce items to customer order ship to the customer as soon as the product is completed and thus have little or no finished goods inventory.

A diagram of these accounts and the flow of costs from one to another is shown in Illustration 6–3. We shall trace the flow of costs through these accounts, using the periodic inventory method. Each step is described by giving the relevant journal entries. The effect on ledger accounts is shown in Illustration 6–4.

In describing the procedure in a merchandising company, we established a separate account to show the calculation of Cost of Goods Sold. We could use similar accounts in a manufacturing company to show separately the calculation of Materials Used, Cost of Goods Manufactured, and Cost of Goods Sold. In the following description, however, we have not used these accounts, and instead arrive at the amounts by

ILLUSTRATION 6–3
MANUFACTURING INVENTORIES AND FLOWS

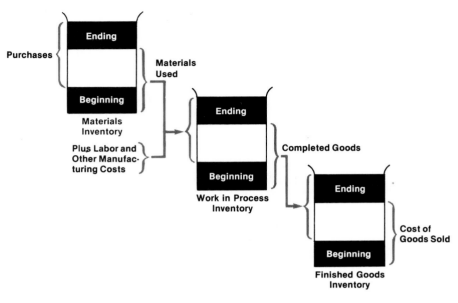

ILLUSTRATION 6–4
FLOW OF COSTS THROUGH INVENTORIES
(000 omitted)

Materials Inventory

Balance, Jan. 1	154	264	
① Purchases	273		Materials used:
			154 + 273 − 163 = 264
Balance, Jan. 31	163	②	

Work in Process Inventory

Balance, Jan. 1	19	570	
Materials used	264		Cost of goods
③ Other manufacturing			manufactured:
costs	330		19 + 264 + 330 − 43 = 570
Balance, Jan. 31	43	④	

Finished Goods Inventory

Balance, Jan. 1	69	573	
Goods manufactured	570		Cost of goods sold:
			69 + 570 − 66 = 573
Balance, Jan. 31	66	⑤	

Cost of Goods Sold

573	573	⟶ Income Summary ⑥

Note: Circled numbers correspond to journal entries explained in the text.

calculations made outside the accounts. There is no substantive difference between the two methods.

Materials Used   During an accounting period, various items of material are issued from a storage area to the production facilities for conversion into goods. The term *materials used* means the sum of all materials issued during the period. Such materials range in their degree of refinement from truly "raw" materials, such as crude oil or iron ore, to sophisticated components, such as motors or miniaturized circuit chips. Traditionally, all such purchased items were referred to as "raw materials." However, there is nothing very "raw" about a motor or circuit chip. We shall use the term *materials inventory* to include the entire range of purchased items that become a part of salable goods as a result of the production process.

In determining the cost of materials used, the assumption may be made that the amount of materials used is the difference between the materials available for use during the period (which is the total of the beginning inventory and the net purchases) and the ending inventory. This assumption does not take into account any waste or spoilage of materials that might have occurred. In practice, waste and spoilage is either disregarded or is collected separately and removed from material costs by crediting Materials Inventory and debiting a separate manufacturing cost account.

We shall make this calculation in the Materials Inventory account. First, the amount of purchases made during the period, which includes $266,000 as the invoice cost of materials received plus $7,000 of freight charges on these materials, is added to Materials Inventory. The temporary accounts in which these amounts were accumulated, Purchases and Freight-In, are closed by the following entry:

(1)

```
Materials Inventory ........................ 273,000
    Purchases ...................................        266,000
    Freight-In ..................................          7,000
```

A physical inventory shows the amount of materials on hand as of the end of the period to be $163,000. Since $154,000 was on hand at the beginning of the period and $273,000 was added by the above entry, the total amount available was $427,000. By subtracting $163,000 from $427,000, the amount of materials used is determined. This is $264,000. It is subtracted from Materials Inventory and added to Work in Process Inventory by the following entry:

(2)

```
Work in Process Inventory ................... 264,000
    Materials Inventory .........................        264,000
```

Cost of Goods Manufactured

The sum of materials used, direct labor, and other manufacturing costs is the total amount of cost added to Work in Process Inventory during the period. Given the amount in Work in Process Inventory at the beginning of the period and the amount remaining at the end of the period, the *cost of goods manufactured*, that is, the goods completed and transferred to Finished Goods Inventory, can be deduced.

The cost of materials used was added by the preceding entry. Other manufacturing costs incurred during the period are added to Work in Process Inventory by the following entry:

(3)

```
Work in Process Inventory .................... 330,000
      Direct Labor .............................          151,000
      Indirect Labor ...........................           24,000
      Factory Heat, Light, and Power ...........           90,000
      Factory Supplies Used ....................           22,000
      Insurance and Taxes ......................            8,000
      Depreciation, Plant and Equipment ........           35,000
```

A physical inventory shows the amount of work in process at the end of the period to be $43,000. Since $19,000 was on hand at the beginning of the period, and $264,000 of materials and $330,000 of other manufacturing costs were added by entries 2 and 3, the total amount available was $613,000. By subtracting $43,000 from $613,000, the cost of goods manufactured during the period is determined. This is $570,000. It is subtracted from Work in Process Inventory and added to Finished Goods Inventory by the following entry:

(4)

```
Finished Goods Inventory ..................... 570,000
      Work in Process Inventory ................          570,000
```

Cost of Goods Sold

Having determined the cost of goods manufactured, the cost of goods sold is found by (1) adding this amount to the beginning Finished Goods Inventory so as to find the total amount available for sale and then (2) subtracting the ending Finished Goods Inventory. As with a merchandising company, the assumption is that if the merchandise is not in inventory, it has been sold.

A physical inventory shows the amount of finished goods at the end of the period to be $66,000. Since $69,000 was on hand at the beginning of the period and $570,000 of manufactured goods were completed during the period and added to finished goods inventory, the total amount available was $639,000. By subtracting $66,000 from $639,000, the cost of goods sold is determined. This is $573,000. It is subtracted from Finished Goods Inventory and recorded as Cost of Goods Sold by the following entry:

(5)

```
Cost of Goods Sold .......................... 573,000
     Finished Goods Inventory .................       573,000
```

The balance in the Cost of Goods Sold account is then closed to Income Summary by the following entry:

(6)

```
Income Summary ............................. 573,000
     Cost of Goods Sold .......................       573,000
```

A detailed income statement derived from these six entries is shown in Illustration 6–5. The format of this statement reinforces the accounting procedures required to determine cost of goods sold in a manufacturing firm. In practice, this amount of detail is seldom seen. At the other extreme, most corporate shareholder report income statements show only a one-line disclosure of cost of sales; Illustration 6–5's gross margin line would be the third line in such income statements. Various levels of detail between these two extremes can be found, particularly in internal income statements prepared for managers of the company.

Cost Accounting Systems

The foregoing entries assumed the use of the periodic inventory method. The same transactions could be accounted for using the perpetual inventory method. In a manufacturing company, the perpetual inventory method is called a *cost accounting system*. In such a system, the cost of each product is accumulated as it flows through the production process. The amounts involved in the journal entries are obtained directly from the cost records, rather than being deduced in the manner described above. The mechanisms used for collecting this information are described in Part 2 of this book.

Product Costs and Period Costs

In the accounting process described above, items of cost included in the cost of producing goods are called *product costs*. Because these product costs "flow through" inventory accounts (see Illustration 6–3), they are also referred to as *inventory costs* or *inventoriable costs*. Product costs are matched with, and subtracted from, the sales revenues in the period in which the goods are sold to arrive at gross margin. Other items of cost that are matched with revenue in a given accounting period are called *period costs*. They are reported on the income statement of the period under a caption such as "Selling, general, and administrative expense."

In accordance with generally accepted accounting principles (GAAP), the cost of each product includes (1) materials cost, (2) labor costs in-

ILLUSTRATION 6–5

ALFMAN MANUFACTURING COMPANY
Income Statement
January

Net Sales			$669,000
Cost of goods sold:			
Raw materials cost:			
Raw materials inventory, Jan. 1		$154,000	
Purchases	$266,000		
Plus: Freight-in	7,000		
Total purchases		273,000	
Material available		427,000	
Less: Raw materials inventory, Jan. 31		163,000	
Cost of materials used		$264,000	
Direct labor cost		151,000	
Production overhead cost:			
Indirect labor	24,000		
Factory heat, light, and power	90,000		
Factory supplies used	22,000		
Insurance and taxes	8,000		
Depreciation—plant and equipment	35,000		
Total production overhead cost		179,000	
Total production costs		594,000	
Add: Work in process inventory, Jan. 1		19,000	
Total		613,000	
Less: Work in process inventory, Jan. 31		43,000	
Cost of goods manufactured		570,000	
Add: Finished goods inventory, Jan. 1		69,000	
Cost of goods available for sale		639,000	
Less: Finished goods inventory, Jan. 31		66,000	
Cost of goods sold			573,000
Gross margin			96,000
Selling and administrative expenses:			
Selling expense		39,000	
Administrative expense		3,000	
Depreciation—nonmanufacturing facilities		32,000	74,000
Operating profit			22,000
Other revenue			15,000
Income before income taxes			37,000
Provision for income taxes			13,000
Net income			$ 24,000

curred directly in producing the product, and (3) a fair share of the other production costs. These other costs are called *indirect production costs* or *production overhead*. Collectively, the materials, labor, and production overhead costs comprise the *full cost* of a product.

Companies differ in their opinions on whether specific items should be treated as product costs or period costs. Some companies include the cost of such functions as production administration, personnel, industrial relations, plant protection, and cost accounting as production overhead and hence as product costs. Other companies include the cost of some or all of these functions as period costs.

The way in which a manufacturing company classifies its costs into period costs and product costs can have an important effect on its reported net income. Period costs are expenses in the accounting period in which they are incurred, whereas product costs add to the inventoriable cost of the product. Product costs do not have an impact on income until the product has been sold, which may be a later accounting period than the period in which the costs were incurred. The larger the inventory in relation to sales, the longer the time interval that elapses between the incurrence of a product cost and its impact on income.[2]

All costs of a merchandising company, except the acquisition cost of the merchandise inventory (and other assets), are period costs. Thus, all labor and other operating costs incurred in a certain period affect the income of that period. In a manufacturing company, on the other hand, those labor and other costs associated with the manufacturing process affect, initially, the value of inventory. They affect income only *in the accounting period in which the products containing these costs are sold.*

> **Example.** Consider a wage increase amounting to $50,000 per year. In a merchandising company, income would be reduced $50,000 in the year in which the increase becomes effective, other things being equal. In a manufacturing company, however, that part of the increase paid to manufacturing employees would first go to increase the inventory value of the products they worked on, and income would not receive the full impact of the increase until these products were sold.

SERVICE COMPANIES

In principle, product costing in service firms is the same as in manufacturing firms. Application of these principles is described below for three types of service organization.

Personal services organizations such as barber shops, beauty parlors, and medical and dental practices have no inventories other than supplies inventory. Thus, in a strict accounting sense, they have no product costs as such. While such organizations may estimate the average cost of a haircut, a wash and set, or a routine office visit to aid them in pricing these services, these costs do not flow through inventory accounts as do product costs in a merchandising or manufacturing firm. A personal services organization may identify the labor costs of the people directly providing the service (e.g., a dental hygienist) and supplies costs (X-ray

---

[2]*FASB Statement No. 34* (October 1979) requires that interest costs related to items produced as "discrete projects" (such as ships) be treated as product costs. (The accounting procedures for this are the same as for capitalized interest on assets produced for an enterprise's own use, described in Chapter 7.) "However, interest cost shall not be capitalized for inventories that are routinely manufactured or otherwise produced in large quantities on a repetitive basis" (*Statement No. 34*, par. 10).

film) as elements of cost of sales, to distinguish them from "office over-head" costs (receptionist, rent, utilities, and so on). While this distinction may be useful for certain purposes, in the accounting sense both types of cost in a personal services organization are period costs.

Another category of service organization includes *building trade firms* (e.g., plumbing and electrical firms) and *repair businesses* that repair or maintain such items as appliances and automobiles. These firms carry inventories of commonly used repair parts and building materials, which are analogous to materials inventories in a manufacturing firm. The accounting for these inventories is conceptually the same as materials inventory accounting in a manufacturing firm. When materials are issued, they are recorded on some sort of cost sheet for the job. The labor costs of tradespersons or repairpersons are also recorded on this sheet, which in effect is a subsidiary work in process inventory record for the job. Since such jobs often are completed in a short time period (perhaps less than an hour for an in-home appliance repair), these job costs may appear to be period costs because the costs are incurred and also recorded as expenses in the same period. However, these job costs are in fact product costs because they flow through a work in process inventory account, however swift the flow might be. This category of service company does not have a finished goods inventory, however.

In the third type of service company, *professional service firms* such as law and accounting firms, there are labor product costs but no materials costs. The accounting procedures are similar to those for building trade and repair businesses. Each project that the firm works on is given a job number and a subsidiary account is set up for the job. Time spent by professionals on a job, and any related travel costs and long-distance telephone charges, are charged to that job's account. Collectively, these job costs constitute the firm's work in process inventory, which is the only inventory (other than supplies) that such firms have. The term *unbilled costs* is frequently used for this inventory because of its intangible nature. When a point is reached in the project where the agreement with the client permits these costs to be billed, a *markup* is added for office overhead and profit, and the client is billed. The related accounting entries record the revenues (often called *billings*) and transfer the costs from the Unbilled Costs account to expense, as in this example:

```
Accounts Receivable ........................ 10,000
    Billings (or Revenues) .................          10,000

Project Expenses ...........................  4,000
    Unbilled Costs (or Work in Process) .......           4,000
```

The project expenses are, in the accounting sense, product costs because they flow through an inventory account. The firm's other expenses, including support personnel, rent, utilities, and the time of the professionals that is not charged to specific projects, are all period costs.

INVENTORY COSTING METHODS

One important topic remains to be discussed, namely, the measurement of inventory amounts and cost of goods sold when there is a change in the unit cost of the goods during the accounting period. The basic problem is that shown in Illustration 6–1: How should the cost of goods available for sale be divided between (1) cost of goods sold and (2) ending inventory? It is important to note that the goods available for sale are assumed to be either sold or still on hand in inventory. It follows that the higher the amount assigned to cost of goods sold, the lower will be the amount of ending inventory, and vice versa. Several acceptable methods of handling this problem exist, and the choice of method can have a significant effect on net income. We shall discuss four widely used methods:

1. Specific identification.
2. Average cost.
3. First-in, first-out (FIFO).
4. Last-in, first-out (LIFO).[3]

We shall illustrate these methods with an example from a merchandising company, but the same principles apply to a manufacturing company. As an illustration we shall assume the following for a year:

	Units	Unit Cost	Total Cost
Inventory, January 1	100	$ 8	800
Purchased June 1	60	9	540
Purchased October 1	80	10	800
Goods available for sale	240	$8.917	$2,140
Goods sold during the year	150	?	?
Ending inventory	90	?	?

Specific Identification Method

When there is a means of keeping track of the purchase cost of each item, such as with a code on the price tag affixed to the item, it is possible to ascertain the actual cost of each item sold. This is common practice with certain "big-ticket" items such as automobiles, and with unique items such as paintings, expensive jewelry, and custom-made furniture. However, for an item of which there is a substantial number sold, all physically similar, this method can be unsatisfactory because the cost of goods sold depends on what items happen to be sold. Indeed, a mer-

---

[3] *Accounting Trends & Techniques* (1981) reports that of the 1,073 mentions of inventory methods in the 600 companies surveyed, 382 used FIFO, 238 used average cost, and 396 used LIFO. (The 600 companies had 1,073 inventories because many companies use different methods for different categories of inventory.) Only 26 companies used LIFO for *all* inventories; another 205 used it for 50 percent or more of their inventories. The number of companies reporting the use of LIFO more than doubled between 1973 and 1974, a period of high inflation, and the number continued to increase (though slowly) during the late 1970s.

chant can deliberately manipulate the cost of goods sold by selecting items that have a relatively high cost or a relatively low cost.

> **Example.** In the illustration, 150 units were sold. If the merchant selected the 100 units with a unit cost of $8 and 50 of the units having a unit cost of $9, the cost of goods sold would be $1,250 (= 100 @ $8 + 50 @ $9). If the 150 units with the highest cost were selected, the cost of goods sold would be $1,420 (= 80 @ $10 + 60 @ $9 + 10 @ $8).

Average Cost Method

With this method, the average cost of the goods available for sale is computed, and the units in both cost of goods sold and ending inventory are costed at this average cost. In the periodic inventory method, this average is computed for the whole period. It is a weighted average in that each unit cost is weighted by the number of units with that cost. In the perpetual inventory method, a new average unit cost is sometimes calculated after each purchase. In either case, the average cost is representative of the cost of all of the items that were available for sale during the period.

> **Example.** Assuming the periodic inventory method, the 240 units available for sale have a total cost of $2,140; hence, the average cost is $8.917. The calculations are as follows:

	Units	Unit Cost	Total*
Cost of goods sold	150	$8.917	$1,338
Ending inventory	90	8.917	802
Total	240		$2,140

*Rounded.

Some companies use a predetermined unit cost for all transactions during the period. This is a *standard cost system* and is discussed in Chapter 19. It is essentially a variation of the average cost method.

The average cost method gives results that are in between the next two methods to be described, FIFO and LIFO. It is therefore a compromise for those who do not find the arguments for one or the other of these methods to be compelling.

First-In, First-Out (FIFO) Method

In the FIFO method, it is assumed that the oldest goods are sold first and that the most recently purchased goods are in the ending inventory. In the illustrative situation, for the 150 units sold it is assumed that the 100 units in beginning inventory were sold first and that the other 50 units sold were from the purchase made on June 1.

Example of FIFO Calculation

	Units	Unit Cost	Total Cost
Cost of goods sold:			
From beginning inventory	100	$ 8	$ 800
From purchase of June 1	50	9	450
Cost of goods sold	150		$1,250
Ending inventory:			
From purchase of June 1	10	$ 9	$ 90
From purchase of October I	80	10	800
Ending inventory	90		$ 890

We shall contrast the LIFO and FIFO methods below. For the moment, it is sufficient to note that with FIFO (1) cost of goods sold is likely to approximate the *physical* flow of the goods because most companies sell their oldest merchandise first and (2) the ending inventory approximates the *current* cost of the goods, since it is costed at the amounts of most recent purchases.

Last-In, First-Out (LIFO) Method

The LIFO method is the opposite of FIFO. Cost of goods sold is based on the most recent purchases, and ending inventory is costed at the cost of the oldest units available.

Example of LIFO Calculation

	Units	Unit Cost	Total Cost
Cost of goods sold:			
From purchase of October 1	80	$10	$ 800
From purchase of June 1	60	9	540
From beginning inventory	10	8	80
Cost of goods sold	150		$1,420
Ending inventory:			
From beginning inventory	90	$ 8	$ 720

At this point, it should be noted that with LIFO (1) cost of goods sold does not reflect the usual physical flow of merchandise and (2) the ending inventory, an asset, may be costed at amounts prevailing several years ago which, in an era of inflation, are far below current costs.

LIFO Dollar Value Method. Originally, LIFO was used only by companies whose inventory consisted of fungible products, such as wheat, each unit of which is physically like every other unit. Other companies, however, argued that this was unfair to them, and LIFO may now be used for almost any kind of inventory. It is applied to an inventory of physically unlike items by the so-called *LIFO dollar value method.* In this method, items whose prices tend to move together are grouped into an *inventory pool.* For example, a pool may consist of all the items in the inventory of a department in a store, such as the housewares department. The calculations required to determine cost of goods sold and inventory amounts with this method are beyond the scope of this book.[4] Compared with the unit-by-unit LIFO method, however, dollar value LIFO saves a considerable amount of recordkeeping effort.

Changes in Inventory.   In a year when the *physical* size of the inventory *increases* above the amount on hand at the beginning of the year, with LIFO the inventory account is increased by the additional quantity valued at the costs existing during that year. During a period of growth, the inventory account will therefore consist of a number of *layers,* a new layer being added each year. If subsequently the physical inventory should *decrease* in size, these layers in effect are stripped off, taking the most recently added layer first, in accordance with the basic LIFO rule. This process can have a peculiar effect on the income statement. If, for example, inventory is decreased below its original size when the LIFO system started, inventory items will be moving into cost of goods sold at costs established several years previously. If there has been constant inflation during the interim, such a decrease in inventory can result in a significant increase in reported income. Some people assert that in a recession some companies deliberately eat into their LIFO inventories in order to increase reported income in a lean year.

LIFO Reserve.   Some companies that use LIFO for determining their balance sheet valuation of inventory nevertheless keep their detailed inventory records on a FIFO or average cost basis. The inventory amounts on these other bases usually will be higher than the LIFO valuation shown on the balance sheet. The difference between the LIFO valuation and the FIFO or average cost valuation is sometimes called the *LIFO Reserve.* This use of this terminology is unfortunate, since "reserve" suggests something set aside or saved for some special future purpose. The LIFO Reserve is nothing more than the mathematical difference between two inventory amounts, one based on LIFO and the other one based on a different method of valuing inventory.

Comparison of Methods

The following table summarizes the illustrative results of three of the four methods described above (the specific identification method depends on the specific items selected):

---

[4]For a description of the procedure, see Welsch, Zlatkovich, and Harrison, *Intermediate Accounting,* 6th ed. (Homewood, Ill.: Richard D. Irwin, 1982).

	Cost of Goods Sold	Ending Inventory	Total
FIFO	$1,250	$890	$2,140
Average cost	1,338	802	2,140
LIFO	1,420	720	2,140

All of the methods described are in accordance with GAAP, and all are acceptable by the Internal Revenue Service for calculating taxable income.

Arguments for FIFO. A primary conceptual argument for using FIFO is that it matches the costs of the goods that are *physically* sold with the revenues generated by selling those goods. Also, many companies set selling prices by adding a gross margin to the cost of the actual goods to be sold. Conceptually, such a price results in the company's recovering the funds it had invested in the particular item to be sold, plus a margin to provide for recovery of selling and administrative costs and a reasonable profit. For example, this pricing philosophy is commonly applied in retailing companies, such as grocery and department stores.

> **Example.** The *Wall Street Journal* printed this brief item that reflects the idea of pricing based on the cost of the goods actually (physically) sold: "Retail coffee prices are being cut by supermarket chains around the nation. The reductions are selective because of lingering high-priced inventories; when these are gone, wholesale-price cuts can be passed on to the public."

Thus, it is argued, if a company's management thinks of gross margin as the difference between selling prices and the cost of the goods physically sold, then it should use FIFO, which will report this same margin in the company's income statement.

The other primary argument for FIFO reflects a balance sheet orientation. Many people feel that to be useful, the amount shown for inventory on the balance sheet should be approximately equal to the current cost of that inventory. The mechanics of FIFO, which assume that the goods in inventory are those most recently acquired, result in an inventory valuation that is closer to current costs than would result if LIFO or average cost were used.

A final argument for FIFO is more practical than conceptual. Many companies select accounting methods with the objective of maximizing in the near term the amount of income that is reported to their shareholders. Since for several decades in this country the costs of the items in most companies' inventories have been increasing, and since FIFO reports a lower cost of goods sold amount than average cost or LIFO does under such inflationary conditions, many companies have preferred FIFO because of its characteristic of maximizing reported income.

Arguments for LIFO.   Proponents of LIFO also base their primary argument on the matching concept. They argue that gross margin should reflect the difference between sales revenues, which are necessarily "current," and the current cost of the goods sold. Although seldom made explicit, this LIFO matching argument assumes that a company's management sets selling prices by adding a margin to current costs, rather than to historical costs. If this is indeed the case, then the gross margin reported using LIFO will reflect management's thinking as to the nature of gross margin.

It should be pointed out that although most conceptual arguments for LIFO involve the concept of the current cost of goods sold, LIFO only approximates these current costs. Generally, "current cost of goods sold" means the cost of acquiring items identical in type and number to those sold to replenish the inventory immediately after a sale. This is also called *replacement cost inventory accounting,* or, more jocularly, "NIFO" (for "next-in, first-out"). LIFO shows as cost of goods sold the cost of the most recent inventory purchase prior to a sale, which in inflationary periods will tend to be somewhat lower than the replacement cost. (How much lower depends on the rate of price increases for a particular item and on how frequently that item is purchased for inventory.) In sum, arguments for LIFO usually in essence are arguments for using replacement costs to determine the cost of goods sold amount.[5]

Another such argument is based on the concept of *maintenance of operating capability,* the ability of an enterprise to maintain a given physical level of operations. According to this concept, a company does not earn a profit unless its revenues exceed the costs of replacing the resources, including inventory, that were used up in generating those revenues. By contrast, FIFO, and all other historical cost accounting methods, are based on the notion that a company earns a profit if its revenues exceed the acquisition costs (i.e., the historical costs) of the resources that were used up in generating those revenues. Focusing on gross margin, LIFO advocates argue that the FIFO method results in a gross margin that includes both "true" margin and "false" inventory profits. LIFO, on the other hand, results in a gross margin that closely approximates the "true" margin, that is, the margin that is the difference between revenues and the replacement cost of the goods sold.

LIFO proponents downplay the impact of LIFO on balance sheet inventory valuation. Because the initial quantity or "base layer" of inventory is valued forever in terms of price levels prevailing when LIFO was adopted, as time goes on the LIFO inventory valuation departs further

---

[5]Replacement costs are not permitted by the IRS for calculating taxable income, nor by GAAP for preparation of "primary" financial statements. However, as discussed in Chapter 12, large corporations are required to disclose as supplementary information certain replacement cost data.

and further from reality, reflecting neither actual purchase costs nor replacement costs. In periods of prolonged inflation, such as the 1970s and early 1980s, this LIFO valuation may be far below current costs, making the inventory figure of dubious usefulness. Thus, while FIFO leads to a cost of goods sold amount of questionable usefulness and thus casts doubt on the usefulness of the income statement, LIFO casts a similar doubt in the usefulness of the balance sheet amount for inventory, and thus on the amounts for current assets, total assets, and owners' equity.

Income Tax Considerations. FIFO, average cost, and LIFO are all permitted for U.S. income tax calculations. However, a company using LIFO for tax purposes must also use LIFO in its published financial statements. This "LIFO conformity" rule is the only significant instance in which the IRS requires use of the same accounting method for income tax and "book" (financial reporting) purposes.

In periods of inflation, LIFO results in lower income than FIFO or average costs, and thus results in lower cash outflows for income tax payments. If the physical size of inventory remains constant or grows, LIFO reduces taxable income indefinitely. Only if LIFO layers are stripped off in future years might taxable income under LIFO exceed taxable income under FIFO; and even in that case, LIFO will have *postponed* some income tax payments. These tax advantages of LIFO, which improve a company's cash flow, lead many companies to select the LIFO method, outweighing any conceptual pros and cons of the various alternatives.

Why Not More LIFO? If LIFO improves a company's cash flow, then why are there not more companies using it for most or all of their inventories? At least three reasons can be given.

First, many large U.S. corporations have operations in countries where LIFO is not permitted. For such a company, the non-LIFO foreign inventories cannot be changed to a LIFO basis when they are added to domestic inventories. Thus, even if all of its domestic inventories are on LIFO, the company is precluded from reporting 100 percent of its inventories on a LIFO basis.

Second, although the economy as a whole may be experiencing inflation, the prices of the *specific items* in a company's inventory are not necessarily increasing. In some instances, particularly in the electronics industry, specific prices fall even while general inflation continues. For example, in 1970, the retail price of a four-function, hand-held calculator with a recharger was $395; today, a similar item retails for about $10. Companies whose inventory replacement costs are trending *downward* will pay lower taxes by using *FIFO* rather than LIFO.

Third, and probably most important, in a company for which LIFO will reduce taxable income, and thus lower income tax payments, because of the IRS LIFO conformity rule, the company also must report the lower LIFO income to its shareholders. This means that the cash flow improvement from LIFO will be accompanied by a decrease in reported earnings per share (relative to cash flows and earnings if FIFO were used). It has been a long-held and widely held view among top managers of U.S. companies that lower reported earnings per share are associated with lower stock prices. Thus, in considering LIFO, these managers saw a dilemma: increasing cash flow is good for the corporation, but decreasing reported earnings is bad for the shareholders. Since top management serves at the pleasure of the Board of Directors, and since the board is supposed to protect shareholders' interests, often the decision was to opt for FIFO and higher reported earnings rather than LIFO and improved cash flows.

LOWER OF COST OR MARKET

All the foregoing had to do with measuring the *cost* of inventory. The LIFO and FIFO methods are alternative ways of measuring cost. The general principle is, however, that inventory is reported on the balance sheet at the *lower* of its cost or its market value.

In the ordinary situation, inventory is reported at its cost. It is reduced below cost (i.e., "written down") only when there is evidence that the value of the items, when sold or otherwise disposed of, will be less than their cost. Such evidence may include physical deterioration, obsolescence, drops in price level, or other causes. When this evidence exists, inventory is stated at "market."

Since the goods in inventory have not in fact been sold, their true market value is not ordinarily known and must therefore be estimated. The FASB states that this estimate should be the current *replacement* cost of the item, that is, what it would cost currently to purchase or manufacture the item. The FASB further sets upper and lower boundaries on "market":

1. It should not be higher than the estimated selling price of the item less the costs associated with selling it. This amount is called the *net realizable value.*
2. It should not be lower than the net realizable value less a normal profit margin.

These principles can be compressed into the following rule: Use historical cost if the cost price is lowest; otherwise use the next-to-lowest of the other three possibilities.

> **Example.** Assume four items with amounts as in the table shown at the top of the next page. The inventory amount to be used for each is starred.

This rule is applied to each item in inventory, unlike the rule for marketable securities, which is applied to the securities portfolio as a whole.

		Item		
	1	*2*	*3*	*4*
a. Historical cost	$ 7*	$9	$9	$10
b. Current replacement cost	8	8*	7	9
c. Net realizable value (ceiling)	10	9	9	8*
d. Net realizable value less profit margin (floor)	9	7	8*	7

ANALYSIS OF INVENTORY

Inventory Turnover

The ratio most commonly used in analyzing the size of the inventory item is inventory turnover:

$$\text{Inventory turnover} = \frac{\text{Cost of goods sold}}{\text{Inventory}}$$

If the cost of goods sold for a period is $1,000,000 and inventory is $250,000, then the inventory turnover is 4.0 times.

Some companies calculate this ratio on the basis of the ending inventory, others on the basis of the average inventory. The average may be simply one half the sum of beginning and ending inventories for the year, or it may be an average of monthly inventory levels. The end-of-period basis is more representative of the current state of the inventory if volume is expected to continue at previous levels. The average basis is a better reflection of events that occurred during the period, since it measures the amount of inventory that supported the sales activity of that period.

Inventory turnover varies greatly with the nature of the business. It should be high for a store that sells fresh produce; otherwise spoilage is likely to be a problem. A supermarket may have an inventory turnover close to 50, and a petroleum refinery, 20. On the other hand, a jewelry store with a wide selection of expensive and unusual items may not turn its inventory as often as once a year, and most art galleries have a turnover much lower than 1.

One must also consider the seasonality of sales. For example, clothing stores have high inventories in the spring and fall when new seasonal merchandise arrives, with lower inventories in between. In such companies, an annual calculation of inventory turnover has little meaning, and inventory measured at various seasonal high and low points is of more significance.

Inventory turnover indicates the velocity with which merchandise moves through a business. Turnover may fall either because of inventory buildup in anticipation of increased sales or because sales volume has declined, leaving excess merchandise on hand. The first is a favorable event; the second is unfavorable. The turnover number itself does not indicate which is the cause.

Days' Inventory. The same relationship can be expressed as the number of days' inventory on hand. This is calculated as follows:

$$\frac{\text{Days'}}{\text{inventory}} = \frac{\text{Inventory}}{\text{Cost of goods sold} \div 365} = \frac{\$250,000}{\$1,000,000 \div 365} = 91 \text{ days}$$

Of course, both the inventory turnover and days' inventory calculations are affected by the company's inventory costing method. Since, relative to FIFO, the LIFO method results in lower reported inventory value on the balance sheet and higher cost of goods sold, a company using LIFO will have a higher indicated inventory turnover ratio and a lower indicated number of days' inventory than if it were using FIFO. Such differences must be taken into account when comparing ratios of companies that use different methods.

SUMMARY

The objectives of inventory accounting are (1) to match the cost of goods sold with the revenue earned from the sale of those goods in an accounting period and (2) to measure the cost of inventory on hand at the end of the period, which is an asset.

A merchandising company has one inventory account. The separation of the cost of the goods available for sale into the amount determined to be cost of goods sold and the amount determined to be ending merchandise inventory can be accomplished either by the periodic inventory method or the perpetual inventory method. In the former, ending inventory is obtained by a physical count, and cost of goods sold is obtained by deduction. In the latter, both amounts are obtained directly from inventory records.

A manufacturing company has three inventory accounts: materials, work in process, and finished goods. In the periodic inventory method, the amount in each account is determined by taking a physical inventory, and then deducing the cost of materials used, the cost of goods manufactured, and the cost of goods sold. In a perpetual inventory system, also called a cost accounting system, these costs are obtained directly from the accounting records.

Inventory is ordinarily measured at its cost. In a merchandising company, cost is essentially the amount expended to acquire the goods. In a manufacturing company, product costs include, in addition to materials costs, the labor cost and other production costs incurred in converting the materials into a finished product. Other operating costs, in either type of company, are called period costs; they are expenses of the current period.

The flow of costs can be measured by any of several methods, including specific identification; average costs; first-in, first-out; and last-in, first-out. Among the factors influencing a company's choice of method are pricing philosophy, perceptions of the relative importance of income statement numbers vis-à-vis balance sheet numbers, specific inventory price trends, and beliefs concerning the importance of reported earnings vis-à-vis cash flows.

If the market value of an inventory item is below cost, the item is reported at its market value.

Two ratios helpful in analyzing inventories are inventory turnover and days' inventory.

Cases

CASE 6–1 Olson Company

Listed below in alphabetical order are certain accounts of the Olson Company with balances for the year ended December 31.

Administrative expense	$ 40,870
Customer returns and allowances	63,050
Depreciation—plant and equipment	41,600
Depreciation—selling	3,780
Direct labor cost	207,320
Dividends	13,000
Factory heat, light, and power	93,540
Factory supplies cost	26,500
Finished goods inventory, 1/1	78,650
Finished goods inventory, 12/31	82,130
Freight-in	9,840
Gain on disposal of machinery	13,600
Goods in process inventory, 1/1	30,970
Goods in process inventory, 12/31	31,920
Income tax expense	4,600
Indirect labor	26,150
Insurance and taxes (factory)	13,860
Interest expenses	10,950
Purchases	302,320
Raw materials inventory, 1/1	185,680
Raw materials inventory, 12/31	162,100
Sales	913,990
Selling expense	41,480

Questions

1. Prepare a detailed income statement for the year ended December 31.
2. Assume that inventories on December 31 were the same amounts as on January 1.

How would an income statement prepared under this assumption differ from that requested in Question 1? Explain the reasons for these changes. (Assume that income tax expense is the same percentage of income before income taxes.)

CASE 6–2   Bedford Manufacturing Company (A)

The management of Bedford Manufacturing Company prepared annually a budget of expected financial operations for the ensuing calendar year. The completed budget provided information on all aspects of the coming year's operations. It included a projected balance sheet as of the end of the year and a projected income statement.

The final preparation of statements was accomplished only after careful integration of detailed computations submitted by each department. This was done to ensure that the operations of all departments were in balance with one another. For example, the finance department needed to base its schedules of loan operations and of collections and disbursements on figures that were dependent upon manufacturing, purchasing, and selling expectations. The level of production would be geared to the forecasts of the sales department, and purchasing would be geared to the proposed manufacturing schedule. In short, it was necessary to integrate the estimates of each department and to revise them in terms of the overall effect on operations to arrive at a well-formulated and profitable plan of operations for the coming year. The budget statements ultimately derived from the adjusted estimated transactions would then serve the company as a reliable guide and measure of the coming year's operations.

At the time the 1983 budget was being prepared, in November of 1982, projected 1982 financial statements were compiled for use as a comparison with the budgeted figures. These 1982 statements were based on nine months' actual and three months' projected transactions. They appear as Exhibits 1, 2, and 3.

Below is the summary of expected operations for the budget year 1983 as finally accepted:

1. *Sales:* All on credit, $2,445,000; sales returns and allowances, $21,000; sales discounts taken by customers, $45,000. (The sales figure is net of expected bad debts.)
2. *Purchases of goods and services:*
   a. New assets:
      Purchased for cash: manufacturing plant and equipment, $99,000; prepaid manufacturing taxes and insurance, $36,000.
      Purchased on accounts payable: materials, $681,000; supplies, $75,000.
   b. Services used to convert materials into work in process,[1] all purchased for cash: direct manufacturing labor, $456,000; in-

---

[1] In a manufacturing company, inventory is assumed to increase in value by the amounts spent to convert materials into salable products. These amounts include the items listed in 2(b) plus the items listed in 3.

EXHIBIT 1

BEDFORD MANUFACTURING COMPANY
Projected Balance Sheet
December 31, 1982

Assets

Current assets:		
Cash and marketable securities.............................		$ 196,600
Accounts receivable (net of allowance for doubtful accounts) ..		369,000
Inventories:		
Materials	$ 177,000	
Work in process.......................................	141,000	
Finished goods..	46,500	
Supplies...	99,000	463,500
Prepaid taxes and insurance		27,000
Total current assets..................................		1,056,100
Other assets:		
Manufacturing plant at cost.............................	1,860,000	
Less: Accumulated depreciation	630,000	1,230,000
Total assets..		$2,286,100

Liabilities and Shareholders' Equity

Current liabilities:		
Notes payable	$ 192,000	
Accounts payable	81,000	
Income taxes payable	15,000	
Total current liabilities.............................		$ 288,000
Shareholders' equity:		
Contributed capital	1,530,000	
Retained earnings......................................	468,100	1,998,100
Total liabilities and shareholders' equity........................		$2,286,100

EXHIBIT 2

BEDFORD MANUFACTURING COMPANY
Projected 1982 Statement of Cost of Goods Sold

Finished goods inventory, 1/1/82................................			$ 501,000
Work in process inventory, 1/1/82..............................		$ 156,000	
Materials used..		543,000	
Plus: Factory expenses:			
Direct manufacturing labor....................................		291,000	
Factory overhead:			
Indirect manufacturing labor	$118,500		
Power, heat, and light	81,000		
Depreciation of plant	87,000		
Social security taxes	16,500		
Taxes and insurance, factory..............................	15,000		
Supplies	47,400	365,400	
		1,355,400	
Less: Work in process inventory, 12/31/82		141,000	
Cost of goods manufactured (i.e., completed)...................			1,214,400
			1,715,400
Less: Finished goods inventory, 12/31/82......................			46,500
Cost of goods sold...			$1,668,900

EXHIBIT 3

BEDFORD MANUFACTURING COMPANY
Projected 1982 Income Statement

Sales		$2,190,000
Less: Sales returns and allowances	$16,800	
Sales discounts allowed	42,000	58,800
Net sales		2,131,200
Less: Cost of goods sold (per schedule)		1,668,900
Gross margin		462,300
Less: Selling and administrative expense		360,600
Operating income		101,700
Less: Interest expense		18,000
Income before federal income tax		83,700
Less: Estimated income tax expense		25,100
Net income		$ 58,600

direct manufacturing labor, $168,000; social security taxes on labor, $28,200; power, heat, and light, $124,800. (Accrued payroll was ignored in these estimates.)

c. Sales and administrative services, purchased for cash: $702,000.

3. *Conversion of assets into work in process:* This appears as an increase in the "value" of work in process and a decrease in the appropriate asset accounts. Depreciation of building and equipment, $78,000; expiration of prepaid taxes and insurance, $24,000; supplies used in manufacturing, $87,000; materials put into process, $777,000.

4. *Transfer of work in process into finished goods:* This appears as an increase in finished goods and a decrease in work in process. Total cost accumulated on goods that have been completed and transferred to finished goods, $1,647,000.

5. *Cost of finished goods sold to customers:* $1,497,000.

6. *Financial transactions:*

a. $180,000, borrowed on notes payable to bank.

b. Notes payable repaid, $210,000.

c. Cash payment to bank of $20,000 for interest on loans.

7. *Cash receipts from customers on accounts receivable:* $2,431,500.

8. *Cash payments of liabilities:*

a. Payment of accounts payable, $747,000.

b. Payment of 1982 income tax, $15,000.

9. *Estimated federal income tax on 1983 income:* $53,350, of which $5,335 is estimated to be unpaid as of December 31, 1983.

10. *Dividends declared for year and paid in cash:* $33,000.

This summary presents the complete cycle of the Bedford Manufacturing Company's budgeted yearly operations from the purchase of goods and services through their various stages of conversion to completion of the finished product to the sale of this product. All costs and cash receipts and disbursements involved in this cycle are presented, including the provision for federal income tax and the payment of dividends.

Questions

1. Journalize each of the projected transactions. Set up T-accounts with balances as shown on the balance sheet for December 31, 1982, and post the journal entries to these accounts.

2. Prepare a projected statement of cost of goods sold for 1983, a projected income statement for 1983, and a projected balance sheet as of December 31, 1983.

3. Describe the principal differences between the 1983 estimates and the 1982 figures as shown in Exhibits 1, 2, and 3. In what respects is 1983 performance expected to be better than 1982 performance, and in what respects is it expected to be poorer?

CASE 6–3   Berkshire Corporation

Berkshire Corporation had traditionally used the FIFO method of inventory valuation. You are given the following information on transactions affecting their inventory account:

	1980
Beginning balance	1,835 cartons @ $18.25
Purchases	600 cartons @ 18.50
	800 cartons @ 19.00
	400 cartons @ 19.25
	200 cartons @ 19.50
Sales	2,815 cartons @ 22.50
	1981
Beginning balance	1,020 cartons
Purchases	700 cartons @ $19.50
	700 cartons @ 19.50
	700 cartons @ 20.00
	1,000 cartons @ 20.25
Sales	3,084 cartons @ 24.00
	1982
Beginning balance	1,036 cartons
Purchases	1,000 cartons @ $20.25
	700 cartons @ 20.50
	700 cartons @ 20.50
	700 cartons @ 20.50
Sales	2,950 cartons @ 24.00

Questions

1. Calculate the cost of goods sold and year-end inventory amounts for 1980, 1981, and 1982 using the (a) FIFO, (b) LIFO, and (c) average cost methods.

2. Berkshire Corporation is considering switching from FIFO to LIFO to reduce its income tax expense. Assuming a tax rate of 30 percent, calculate the tax savings this would make for 1980 to 1982. Would you recommend that Berkshire Corporation make this change?

3. Dollar sales for 1983 are expected to drop by approximately 8 percent, as a recession is forecasted to continue at least through the first three quarters of the year. Total sales are forecasted to be 2,716 cartons.

Berkshire Corporation will be unable to raise its selling price from the 1982 level of $24. However, costs are expected to increase to $20.75 per carton for the whole year. Due to these cost/price pressures, the corporation wished to lower its investment in inventory by holding only the essential inventory of 400 cartons at any time during the year. What are the effects of LIFO and FIFO inventory valuation methods under these circumstances? What method would you recommend now?

4. Despite continuing inflation in the United States in the 1970s and 1980s, many companies continue to use FIFO for all or part of their inventories. Why is this the case?

CASE 6–4 Bradford Press

In the 1930s, Bradford Press had acquired a tract of land on the outskirts of Craneville, with the intention eventually of constructing a branch warehouse thereon. Over the years, however, the company's marketing practices had changed; and by mid-1980, the management concluded that a warehouse would never be needed at Craneville. Consequently, the company sought to dispose of this land.

Bradford Press had paid $3,000 for the land and had made permanent improvements on it at a cost of $1,600, so that it was carried on the accounts of Bradford Press at $4,600. The best cash offer that could be found in 1980 was $400,000. Since an independent appraiser, hired by Bradford Press, had appraised the land at $500,000, the management was unwilling to accept this offer.

As it happened, the Craneville land was located adjacent to a warehouse owned by the Birch Paper Company, one of Bradford's four regular suppliers of paper. Birch expressed an interest in acquiring the property so that it could later expand its own facilities. Birch was unwilling to pay cash but offered instead to exchange 6,000 cwt. (hundredweight) of a high-grade coated paper, to be delivered at the rate of 1,000 cwt. per month for six months. In addition, Bradford was to pay the freight on this paper, in accordance with usual practice. The going market price for this grade of paper was at that time $92 per cwt., plus freight.

Bradford Press typically used more than 1,000 cwt. of this high-grade coated paper per month in the manufacture of booklets, brochures, and similar items; but Bradford Press ordinarily placed orders for delivery not more than two months in the future, unless it had firm contracts from its own customers that required such paper. It had no such contracts in the summer of 1980. After considerable discussion among Bradford executives as to the risk involved in the unusually large commitment for paper, the Bradford management finally decided to accept Birch's offer.

The contract was signed on June 21, 1980, and as of that date the following journal entry was made by Bradford's accountant, recording the paper at its market price, and showing the difference between this amount and the book value of the land as profit:

```
dr.   Inventory Due from Supplier.......... 552,000
    cr.    Craneville Land ...................           4,600
           Profit on Sale of Land ...........         547,400
```

During the next three months of 1980, 3,000 cwt. of the paper was received from Birch as promised, and in the aggregate the entries made to record this receipt had the following effect:

```
dr.     Paper Inventory...................... 277,880
   cr.      Inventory Due from Supplier .......      276,000
            Cash (for freight charges) ........        1,880
```

When he was examining the accounts of Bradford Press for fiscal year 1980, which had ended on September 30, 1980, the company's auditor raised questions about this transaction. He pointed out that the net effect of the above entries was that the entire profit on the transaction was shown in fiscal 1980, despite the fact that only 3,000 cwt. of paper had actually been delivered, and of this only about 2,000 cwt. had actually been used in the manufacture of products. (The physical inventory as of September 30 showed 1,000 cwt. of this paper as still on hand.)

A suggested alternative treatment was to split the profit into two parts. One part, $395,400, was the difference between the book value of the land and the best cash offer; this was to be called "profit on price-level changes" and

shown on the 1980 income statement. The remainder, $152,000, was to be called "profit on sale of land" and divided one third to 1980 and two thirds to 1981, representing the fraction of the total paper consumed in each fiscal year. The auditor stated that such a separation was not usually made, but neither was this an ordinary transaction.

Bradford Press management disliked the implication in the above treatment that they had not made the $547,400 profit in 1980, especially since the price of the high-grade coated paper had risen to $96 per cwt. as of September 30, 1980.

Questions

1. How do you think this transaction should be handled?

2. How would you answer the arguments of those who think it should be handled differently?

3. Would your answer be different if the market price of the paper had decreased to $88 per cwt. as of the end of fiscal 1980?

CASE 6–5   Prentiss Dress Shop

For over 20 years, Muriel Prentiss had owned and operated a women's specialty shop in a suburban town. Early in 1981, Milton Wilcox, a representative of Dynamic Stores, Inc., discussed with Prentiss the possibility of selling her business to Dynamic, which owned 16 specialty shops in the same metropolitan area. Over the past several years, several other chains had approached Prentiss with

similar propositions, but the Dynamic proposal was the first one that she seriously considered.

After a series of conversations, Prentiss told Wilcox that she would consider selling her business provided they could agree on a fair price and provided Dynamic would agree to employ her as store manager. Wilcox assured her that Dynamic would certainly be happy to have

EXHIBIT 1

PRENTISS DRESS SHOP
Balance Sheet
As of December 31, 1979

Assets

Current assets:		$19,379
Cash		3,000
Notes receivable		12,843
Accounts receivable		33,900
Merchandise inventory		69,122
Total current assets		
Other assets:	$10,300	
Furniture and fixtures	5,865	4,435
Less: Accumulated depreciation	2,880	
Office equipment	2,880	0
Less: Accumulated depreciation		$73,557
Total assets		

Equities

Current liabilities:	
Salaries payable	$ 1,230
Notes payable	11,400
Accounts payable	6,280
Total current liabilities	18,910
Owner's equity:	
M. W. Prentiss, prop.	24,750
Retained earnings	29,897
Total equities	$73,557

Prentiss continue as manager of the store, and the discussion then turned to the problem of deciding the selling price.

Wilcox asked what financial information was available, and Prentiss replied:

The only formal statements I have are balance sheets and my income tax returns, which I have a tax expert prepare for me. I expect him to work up the returns for 1980 within the next month. I know what is going on in the business well enough so that I don't need other statements. Of course, I have a checkbook, a file of charge slips showing what customers owe me, and a file of unpaid invoices from suppliers. On New Year's Day, or the preceding afternoon, I take a physical inventory and determine the purchase cost of goods on hand.

I have two salespersons helping me, but I am at the store most of the time, and I try to keep a close tab on everything that takes place. There are two cash registers which everyone uses regardless of the kind of merchandise sold. None of us specializes in the sale of any particular kind of goods.

Wilcox replied that the lack of financial statements for 1980 probably would not prove to be any great obstacle to the conclusion of negotiations. All that was necessary was permission from Prentiss to examine whatever records were available, from which it was highly probable that Dynamic could ascertain all the operating facts about the business that were needed. Prentiss agreed with this arrangement.

EXHIBIT 2
INFORMATION COLLECTED BY MR. WILCOX

Cash Record for 1980

Receipts:		Expenditures:	
Cash sales	$104,643	Payroll	$ 39,733
Collection of accounts receivable	58,677	Rent	6,450
Total receipts	163,320	Advertising	3,648
		Taxes	2,611
		Supplies	5,835
		Travel	1,215
		Telephone	1,368
		Repairs to building	1,065
		Insurance	675
		Miscellaneous expenses	1,467
		Paid on accounts payable for	
		merchandise	111,436
		Total expenditures	175,503
Plus cash balance, December 31,		Plus cash balance, December 31,	
1979	19,379	1980	7,196
Total	$182,699	Total	$182,699

Other Information

The expenditure for payroll includes Ms. Prentiss' salary of $24,000. Social security and withholding taxes may be disregarded since the expense portion was included in the payroll figure and amounts due to the government were immediately deposited in a separate bank account that does not appear on the financial statements.

Wages payable (including taxes thereon) as of December 31, 1980	$ 2,172
Accounts payable represented only invoices for merchandise purchased on credit. As of December 31, 1980, these unpaid invoices amounted to	14,844
Amounts due from customers on December 31, 1980, totaled	25,965
Merchandise inventory, December 31, 1980	56,904

The note receivable carried a 13 percent rate of interest. The note payable carried a 12 percent rate of interest. The note receivable was not collected in 1980, nor was the note payable paid in 1980.

Miscellaneous expenses included $900 paid to Ajax Truck Rental for a three-month lease on a delivery truck. The lease began on December 1, 1980.

Depreciation on furniture and fixtures was computed at 10 percent of cost.

Wilcox was able to gather the data presented in Exhibits 1 and 2. In going over this information with Prentiss, Wilcox commented: "If Dynamic takes over this store, even if you stay on as manager, we will need more figures than you have been gathering for yourself."

Questions

1. From the information given in Exhibits 1 and 2, determine (a) sales, (b) the cost of merchandise sold, and (c) the expenses for the year.

2. Prepare an income statement for 1980 and a balance sheet as of December 31, 1980.

3. Why should more figures apparently be justifiable under chain responsibility than when the store was owned by Ms. Prentiss?

4. How should the parties proceed to decide on a fair selling price for the business?

CASE 6–6   Jean Coffin (B)

Because an earlier visit with the accounting instructor (see Jean Coffin (A)) had cleared up some puzzling matters, Jean Coffin decided to prepare a new list of problems as a basis for a second discussion. As before, Coffin knew that the instructor expected that tentative answers to these questions be worked out prior to the meeting. The list follows.

1. Evidently, there are three ways of handling purchase discounts: they can be deducted from the cost of the purchased goods; they can be reported as other income; or purchase discounts not taken can be reported as an expense of the period. But isn't the effect on net income the same under all these methods? If so, why argue about which is preferable?

2. Calculating cost of goods sold by adjusting total production costs by the *changes* in work in process and finished goods inventories seems to me to be much simpler than the lengthy calculation shown in Illustration 6–5. It would appear to be even simpler to adjust for the change in materials inventory also, so that cost of goods sold would equal total production costs adjusted for the net change in inventories. Would this give the same result as that in Illustration 6–5?

3. It is said that the perpetual inventory method identifies the amount of inventory shrinkage from pilferage, spoilage, and the like, an amount which is not revealed by the periodic inventory method. Having identified this amount, however, how should it be recorded in the accounts?

4. People have said that the LIFO method assumes that the goods pur-chased last are sold first. If this is so, the assumption is clearly unrealistic because companies ordinarily sell their oldest merchandise first. Can a method based on such an unrealistic assumption be supported, other than as a tax gimmick?

5. A certain automobile dealer bases its selling prices on the actual invoice cost of each automobile. In a given model year, the invoice cost for similar automobiles may be increased once or twice to reflect increased manufacturing costs. Would this automobile dealer be wrong if it used the LIFO method? By contrast, a certain hardware dealer changes its selling prices whenever the wholesale prices of its goods change as reported in wholesalers' price lists. Would this hardware dealer be wrong if it used the FIFO method?

6. Are the following generalizations valid?

   a. The difference between LIFO and FIFO is relatively small if inventory turnover is relatively high.

   b. The average cost method will result in net income that is somewhere between that produced by the LIFO method and that produced by the FIFO method.

   c. If prices rise in one year and fall by an equal amount the next year, the total income for the two years is the same under the FIFO method as under the LIFO method.

7. If the LIFO method is used and prices are rising, ending inventory will normally be significantly below prevail-

ing market prices. What justification is there, therefore, for applying the cost-or-market rule to LIFO inventories?

8. For inventories, the cost-or-market rule is applied to each item. For marketable securities, however, the corresponding rule is applied to the whole portfolio of securities. Isn't this inconsistent?

9. A certain distillery manufactured bourbon whiskey which it aged in charred, white oak barrels for four years before bottling and selling it. Whiskey was carried in inventory at approximately $1 per gallon, which was the cost of ingredients, labor, and factory overhead of the manufacturing process. Barrels, which could not be reused, cost $0.70 per gallon. The distillery incurred $0.20 of warehousing costs per gallon per year, including costs involved in moving and testing the barrels. It also incurred $0.10 per gallon of interest costs per year.

If the distillery had consistently earned pretax profit of $600,000 per year on annual production and sale of 1 million gallons, what would happen to profits if it increased production to 1.2 million gallons per year? At what amounts should it carry its whiskey in inventory?

10. A company produced a "made for TV" movie at a total cost of $1 million. It sold the rights to the initial showing to a network for $1 million, and fully expected to sell the rights for a repeat showing the following year for $300,000. It thought that in future years, additional reruns would generate at least another $300,000 of revenue. How much should the company report as cost of sales for the first year? Would the answer be different if in the first year the producing company agreed to pay $100,000 for advertising and promoting the initial showing?

7

Long-Lived Assets and
Their Amortization

Chapters 5 and 6 discussed monetary assets and inventories. This chapter describes other asset categories except investments. (Investments are discussed in Chapter 11.) The common characteristic of these assets is that they have long lives, that is, they provide benefits to the entity for several future years. We describe the accounting principles involved in recording the acquisition of long-lived assets, the conversion of acquisition cost to expenses, and the disposition of such assets when they no longer provide service.

NATURE OF LONG-LIVED ASSETS

When an entity makes an expenditure, the benefits from the goods or services acquired are either obtained in the current period, or they are expected to be obtained in future periods. If the benefits are obtained in the current period, the costs of the goods or services are *expenses*. If benefits are expected in future periods, the costs are *assets* in the current period and the expenditures are said to be *capitalized*. Although inventory and prepaid expenses also are assets because they benefit future periods, the term *capital assets* is usually taken to mean long-lived assets, that is, assets that provide service for several future years.

A capital asset can usefully be thought of as a *bundle of services*. When a company buys a truck that is intended to last for 200,000 miles, it is in effect buying transportation services that will benefit the company over several future years. The cost of these services, that is, the cost of the truck, should be matched with the revenues that are obtained from its use in these future periods. The general name for this matching process is *amortization*, but other names are used for various types of capital assets, as will be described. The portion of the asset's cost that is charged to a given period is an expense of that period. A capital asset is therefore essentially similar to a prepaid insurance policy or other prepaid expense. It is initially recorded as an asset and is converted to an expense in one or more future periods. The difference is that the life of most capital assets is longer than that of most prepaid expenses.

Illustration 7–1 uses T-accounts to depict how expenditures either are

ILLUSTRATION 7–1
EXPENDITURES AND EXPENSES

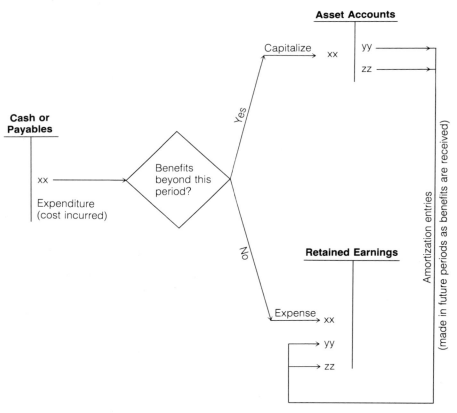

expensed in the current period or are capitalized in an asset account and amortized (expensed) in later periods. The diagram can be applied to expenditures for inventory, as well as for capital assets. The entry "amortizing" capitalized inventory costs is the cost of the goods sold entry.

Types of Long-Lived Assets

Illustration 7–2 lists principal types of long-lived assets and the terms used for the process of amortizing the cost of each type. The principal distrinction is between tangible assets and intangible assets. A *tangible asset* is an asset that has physical substance, such as a building or a machine. An *intangible asset*, such as patent rights or securities, has no physical substance.

ILLUSTRATION 7–2
TYPES OF LONG-LIVED ASSETS AND AMORTIZATION METHODS

Type of Asset	Method of Converting to Expense
Tangible assets:	
Land	Not amortized
Plant and equipment	Depreciation
Natural resources	Depletion
Intangible assets:	
Goodwill	Amortization
Patents, copyrights, etc.	Amortization
Leasehold improvements	Amortization
Deferred charges	Amortization
Research and development costs	Not capitalized
Marketable securities	None (see Chapter 5)
Investments	None (see Chapter 11)

Long-lived tangible assets are usually listed on the balance sheet under the heading "Property, plant, and equipment." The term *fixed assets* is often used in informal discussion and appears in several balance sheets in this book simply because it is shorter. This category includes *land,* which ordinarily is not amortized because its useful life is assumed to be indefinitely long. *Plant and equipment* includes buildings, machinery, office equipment, and other types of long-lived capital assets. The accounting process of converting the cost of these assets to expense is called *depreciation*. Natural resources, such as petroleum and natural gas in the ground (but *not* after they have been taken out of the ground), are usually reported as a separate category. The accounting process of converting the cost of these assets to expense is called *depletion*.

The several categories of intangible assets will be discussed separately in later sections of this chapter. When intangible assets are converted to expenses, the accounting process is called *amortization*. As noted in Illustration 7–2, accounting for marketable securities has been described in Chapter 5, and accounting for investments will be described in Chapter 11.

PLANT AND EQUIPMENT: ACQUISITION

Distinction between Asset and Expense

The distinction between expenditures that are capitalized and expenditures that are charged as expenses of the current period is not entirely clear-cut. Some borderline cases are described in the following paragraphs.

Low-Cost Items. In accordance with the materiality concept, items that have a low unit cost, such as hand tools, are charged immediately as expenses, even though they may have a long life. Each company sets its own criteria for items that are to be capitalized. Generally, the line is drawn in terms of the cost of an item, which may be anywhere from $25 to $500, or even more. Items costing less are expensed.

Nevertheless, the capitalized cost of a new facility may include the cost of the initial outfit of small items that do not individually meet the criteria for capitalization. Examples are the initial outfit of small tools in a factory, the books in a library, and the tableware and kitchen utensils in a restaurant. When these items are replaced, the cost of the replacement items is charged as an expense, not capitalized.

Betterments. Repair and maintenance is work done to keep an asset in good operating condition or to bring it back to good operating condition if it has broken down. Repair and maintenance costs are ordinarily expenses of the accounting period in which the work is done; they are not added to the capitalized cost of the asset. A *betterment* is added to the cost of the asset. The distinction between maintenance expenses and betterments is this: maintenance keeps the asset in good condition, but in no better condition than when it was purchased; a betterment makes the asset better than it was when it was purchased or extends its life beyond the original estimate of life.

In practice, the line between the two is difficult to draw. A new accessory designed to make a machine operate more efficiently or perform new functions is a betterment; an overhaul during which worn-out parts are replaced with new ones in maintenance. In the interest of conservatism, some work that strictly speaking should be considered as a betterment is charged as an expense of the current period.

Replacements. Replacements may be either assets or expenses, depending on how the asset unit is defined. The replacement of an entire asset results in the writing off of the old asset and the recording of the new asset. The replacement of a component part of an asset is maintenance expense. For example, assume that one company treats a complete airplane as a single asset unit and another company treats the airframe as one unit and the engines as another. Then the replacement of an engine results in a maintenance charge in the first company and in a new asset in the second. In general, the broader the definition of the asset unit, the greater will be the amount of costs charged as maintenance and hence expensed in the year the replacement parts are installed.

Capital Leases

In a lease agreement, the owner of property, the *lessor*, conveys to another party, the *lessee*, the right to use plant, property, or equipment for a stated period of time. For many leases, this period of time is short relative to the total life of the asset. Agencies lease (or *rent*, which is another term for lease) automobiles for a few hours or days, and space in an office building may be leased on an annual basis. These leases are called *operating leases*. The lease payments are expenses of the accounting period to which they apply.

Other leases cover a period of time that is substantially equal to the estimated life of the asset or contain other provisions that give the lessee almost as many rights to the use of the asset as if the lessee owned it. Such leases are called *capital leases* (also, *financial leases*). Assets acquired under a capital lease are treated as if they had been purchased.

The FASB has ruled that a lease is a capital lease if one or more of the following criteria are met: (1) ownershp is transferred to the lessee at the end of the term of the lease, (2) the lessee has an option to purchase the asset at a "bargain" price, (3) the term of the lease is 75 percent or more of the economic life of the asset, or (4) the present value of the lease payments is 90 percent or more of the fair market value of the property (subject to certain detailed adjustments).[1]

The lease payments in a capital lease are usually set so that over the life of the lease the lessor will recover (1) the cost of the asset and (2) interest and a profit on the lessor's capital that is tied up in the asset. The amount debited as the cost of the asset acquired with a capital lease, and the offsetting liability for lease payments, is the present value of the stream of minimum lease payments required by the lease agreement. The method of calculating this present value is described in the Appendix to Chapter 8. It should correspond approximately to the value of the asset if it had been sold for cash rather than leased.

The asset amount is amortized just as would be any item of plant or equipment owned by the organization. When lease payments are made to the lessor, part of the payment reduces the liability, and the remainder is interest expense of the period.

> **Example.** A company leases an item of equipment whose useful life is 10 years. Lease payments are $2,000 per year for 10 years. This is a capital

---

[1]"Accounting for Leases," *FASB Statement No. 13*, November 1976.

lease. The present value of the 10 lease payments is $10,000 (derivation of this amount is explained in Chapter 8). When the equipment is acquired, the entry is:

```
Equipment ............................. 10,000
        Capital Lease Obligations ........        10,000
```

Assume that the first annual lease payment consists of $1,500 of interest expense and $500 to reduce the liability. The entry for this payment is as follows:

```
Interest Expense ....................... 1,500
Capital Lease Obligations ..............   500
        Cash ..................................          2,000
```

Also, each year a portion of the asset would be charged as an expense by the depreciation entry to be described in the next section. At the end of the 10 years, all of the $10,000 asset cost will have been charged to expense via the depreciation mechanism. Also, the capital lease obligation will have been reduced to zero, and the annual interest expense will have been recognized in each of the 10 years via entries such as the one shown above.

Most assets of an entity are legally owned by that entity. Assets acquired by a capital lease are an exception to this general rule. They are legally owned by the lessor, but they are accounted for *as if* they were owned by the lessee.

Items Included in Cost

The governing principle is that the cost of an item of property, plant, or equipment includes *all expenditures that are necessary to make the asset ready for its intended use.* In many cases the amount can be determined easily. For example, the cost of a truck purchased for cash is simply the amount of cash paid. In other cases, the problem is more complicated. The cost of a parcel of land includes the purchase price, broker's commission, legal fees, and the cost of grading or of tearing down existing structures so as to make the land ready for its intended use. The cost of machinery includes the purchase price, sales tax, transportation costs to where the machinery is to be used, and installation costs.

Despite the principle stated above, many organizations do not capitalize all the costs incurred to make the asset ready to provide service. Some capitalize only the purchase price. They do this both because it is simpler and also in order to minimize property taxes, which may be calculated on the basis of the capitalized amount.

Self-Constructed Assets. When a company constructs a building or item of equipment for its own use, the amount of capitalized cost includes all the costs incurred in construction. As in the case of product costs, these costs include the materials and labor directly associated with the project, as well as a fair share of the company's indirect costs incurred during the construction period. The FASB now requires that these capitalized costs include interest.[2]

The amount of interest capitalized is the amount related to borrowings made to finance the project (construction loans) if these are identifiable. If not, the company must estimate the interest cost that could have been avoided if the asset in question had not been constructed. The total amount of interest capitalized cannot exceed the company's total interest cost for the period. The interest capitalization period ends when the asset is substantially complete and ready for its intended use. If the company contracts with an outside party to build the asset and makes deposits or progress payments to the contractor, then interest costs associated with these funds are included in the capitalized cost.

As is the case with other items of cost, if interest cost is capitalized rather than expensed, this has the effect of increasing the income of the current period and decreasing income during the years of the asset's useful life. This decrease occurs because each year's depreciation expense for the asset is larger than it would have been had the interest cost not been capitalized.

Noncash Costs. In a great majority of cases, a capital asset is acquired for cash, or for a note or other obligation whose cash equivalent is easily determined. When some other consideration, such as common stock, is given, there may be problems in determining the amount to be capitalized. The general principle is that, first, the fair market value of the consideration given for the asset should be determined; and, second, if it is not feasible to determine this value, then the fair market value of the new capital asset itself is used. (Special rules apply when one capital asset is exchanged in part payment for a new asset, as described in a following section.)

Acquisitions Recorded at Other than Cost

There are a few exceptions to the basic rule that asset acquisitions are recorded in the accounts at cost. If the entity acquires an asset by donation or pays substantially less than the market value of the asset, the asset is recorded at its fair market value. This happens, for example, when a community donates land or a building in order to induce a company to locate there. If property suddenly increases in value shortly after its acquisition because, say, of the discovery of oil or of a mineral deposit, the amount originally recorded for this *fortunate acquisition* may be increased to reflect its current value.

Such exceptions to the general rule are relatively rare, and their rarity emphasizes the importance of the general rule that assets are recorded at cost. Furthermore, as will be seen in the next section, changes in market

---

[2] "Capitalization of Interest Cost," *FASB Statement No. 34*, October 1979.

value do not affect the accounting records for capital assets. Competent investors acquire or build apartment houses or shopping centers with the expectation that part of the profit from this investment will be derived from the appreciation of the property. This appreciation may in fact occur year after year, but it is not recorded in the accounts. The rule is: "property, plant and equipment should not be written up by an entity to reflect appraisal, market or current values which are above cost to the entity."[3]

The reason for the traditional supremacy of the cost concept over a system geared to changes in current value is the importance of the basic criterion of objectivity. We may know in a general way that the value of an apartment house is increasing, but there is no objective way of measuring the amount of increase until a sale takes place. When this happens, a new cost is established, and the asset is recorded at this cost in the accounts of the new owner. Nevertheless, when rapid inflation causes current values to deviate widely from historical costs, many people feel that the estimated current values should be disclosed as supplemental information. Such disclosures will be described in Chapter 12.

Basket Purchases   If an entity acquires in one transaction capital assets that are to appear in more than one balance sheet category, it must divide the cost of the acquisition between the categories on some reasonable basis. Usually this requires an appraisal of the relative value of each asset included in the *basket purchase.*

Such a separation is always required when land and a building are purchased in a single transaction, because the building will subsequently be depreciated whereas the land will remain on the books at its cost. A separation may also be necessary if the capital assets in the "basket" have different useful lives, because they will then be depreciated at different rates.

> **Example.** A parcel of land with a building thereon is purchased for $600,000. An appraiser states that the land is worth $70,000 and the building is worth $630,000, a total of $700,000. Since the appraised value of the land is 10 percent of the total appraised value, the land is entered in the accounts at 10 percent of the total cost, or $60,000. The building is entered at 90 percent of the cost, or $540,000. Note that it would *not* be correct to use the appraised value of one asset as the amount to be capitalized and to capitalize the other asset at the remainder of the purchase price. Thus, it would not be correct to record the land at $70,000 and the building at $530,000.

---

[3] "Status of Accounting Research Bulletins," *APB Opinion No. 6,* October 1965, par. 17.

PLANT AND EQUIPMENT: DEPRECIATION

Unless otherwise indicated, the discussion of depreciation accounting in this section will relate to *financial reporting* (i.e., generally accepted accounting principles), as distinguished from income tax reporting. Depreciation in financial reporting is based on the matching concept. The Economic Recovery Tax Act of 1981 essentially eliminated the matching concept as the basis of income tax depreciation calculations.

With the exception of land, most items of plant and equipment have a limited useful life; that is, they will provide service to the entity over a limited number of future accounting periods. A fraction of the cost of the asset is therefore properly chargeable as an expense in each of the accounting periods in which the asset provides service to the entity. The accounting process for this gradual conversion of plant and equipment capitalized cost into expense is called *depreciation*.[4]

The question is sometimes asked: Why is depreciation an expense? The answer is that the costs of *all* goods and services consumed by an entity during an accounting period are expenses. The cost of insurance protection provided in a year is an expense of that year even though the insurance premium was paid two or three years previously. Depreciation expense is conceptually just like insurance expense. The principal difference is that the fraction of total cost of an item of plant and equipment that is an expense in a given year is difficult to estimate, whereas the fraction of the total cost of an insurance policy that is an expense in a given year can be easily calculated. This difference does not change the fundamental fact that both insurance policies and plant and equipment provide service to the entity over a finite number of accounting periods, and therefore a fraction of their original cost must be charged as an expense of each of these periods.

The useful life of a tangible long-lived asset is limited by either deterioration or obsolescence. *Deterioration* is the physical process of wearing out. *Obsolescence* refers to loss of usefulness because of the development of improved equipment or processes, changes in style, or other causes not related to the physical condition of the asset. We will refer to the time until an asset wears out as its *physical life*, and the time until it becomes obsolete as its *practical life*. Although the word *depreciation* is sometimes used as referring only to physical deterioration, this usage is incorrect. In many cases, a piece of equipment's practical life is shorter than its physical life; computers are a good example.

---

[4] If the asset is used in the production process, a fraction of its cost is properly chargeable as an item of product cost that is initially added to work in process inventory, then flows through finished goods inventory, and becomes an expense (cost of goods sold) in the period in which the product is sold, as described in Chapter 6. In the interests of simplicity, in this chapter we shall not distinguish between the depreciation that is a product cost and the depreciation that is a period expense.

Judgments Required

In order to determine the depreciation expense for an accounting period, three judgments or estimates must be made for each depreciable asset:

1. The *service life* of the asset. That is, over how many accounting periods will it be useful to the *specific entity* that owns its?
2. *Residual value* at the end of its life. The net cost of the asset to the entity is its original cost less any amount eventually recovered through sale, trade-in, or salvage. It is this *net cost* that should be charged as an expense over the asset's life, *not* its original cost. In a great many situations, however, the estimated residual value is so small or uncertain that it is disregarded.
3. *The method of depreciation,* that is, the method that will be used to allocate a fraction of the net cost to each of the accounting periods in which the asset is expected to be used.

Accountants, not being clairvoyant, cannot *know* in advance how long the asset will be used or what its residual value will be, and they often have no scientific or strictly logical way of deciding the best depreciation method. The amount of depreciation expense that results from these judgments is therefore an *estimate.* Because of the arithmetic precision of the calculations that follow *after* these judgments are made, the inexact nature of depreciation expense is sometimes overlooked.

Service Life

The service life of an asset is the period of time over which it is expected to provide service (i.e., benefits) to the entity that controls it. As mentioned above, the service life may be shorter than the physical life because of obsolescence. In addition, an entity may plan to dispose of an asset before either its practical life or physical life ends. For example, although automobiles have an average physical life of about 10 years, many companies trade in their automobiles every 2 years and buy new ones. In these companies, the service life is two years. If the asset's service life to a particular entity is clearly less than the asset's physical life and practical life, then the estimated residual value of the asset should be greater than zero.

Estimating the service life of an asset is a difficult problem. Formerly, the Internal Revenue Service published *guideline lives* for various categories of assets; these lives were allowed for income tax depreciation calculations. Many companies also used these guideline lives for financial reporting purposes, since the guidelines were based on actual corporate asset holding periods. However, the Economic Recovery Tax Act of 1981 eliminated these tax guidelines and substituted "cost recovery periods" that generally are shorter than the assets' useful lives. (For example, buildings have a cost recovery period of only 15 years.) Since

GAAP clearly indicate that depreciation is to be based on realistic service lives, and since the 1981 Tax Act's cost recovery periods are too short to serve as realistic estimates of actual service lives, all companies now must make their own estimates of the useful lives of their various categories of depreciable assets for financial reporting purposes.

Depreciation Methods

Consider a machine purchased for $1,000 with an estimated life of 10 years and estimated residual value of zero. The objective of depreciation accounting is to charge this net cost of $1,000 as an expense over the 10-year period. How much should be charged as an expense each year?

This question cannot be answered directly by observing the amount of asset value physically consumed in a given year. Physically the machine continues to be a machine; usually, there is no observable indication of its decline in usefulness. Nor can the question be answered in terms of changes in the machine's market value during the year, because accounting is concerned with the amortization of cost, not with changes in market values. An indirect approach must therefore be used. Any method that is "systematic and rational" is permitted. Three conceptual ways of looking at the depreciation process are described below, together with the methods that follow from each.

Straight-Line Method. One concept views a fixed asset as providing its services in a level stream. That is, the service provided is equal in each year of the asset's life, just as a three-year insurance policy provides equal insurance protection in each of its three years. This concept leads to the *straight-line method*, which charges as an expense an equal fraction of the net cost of the asset each year. For a machine whose net cost is $1,000 with an estimated service life of 10 years, 1/10 of $1,000 is the depreciation expense of the first year, another 1/10 is the depreciation expense of the second year, and so on. Expressed another way, the machine is said to have a *depreciation rate* of 10 percent per year, the rate being the reciprocal of the estimated useful life.

Accelerated Methods. A second concept recognizes that the stream of services provided by a fixed asset may not be level. Rather, the services may be greatest in the first year, and least in the last year, of the asset's service life. This pattern may occur because the asset's mechanical efficiency tends to decline with age, because maintenance costs tend to increase with age, or because of the increasing likelihood that better equipment will become available and make it obsolete. Often, when a facility is not working at capacity, it is the older equipment that is not used. It is argued, therefore, that when an asset was purchased, the probability that the earlier periods would benefit more than the later periods was taken into account, and that the depreciation method should reflect this. Such a line of reasoning leads to a method which charges a larger fraction of the cost as an expense of the early years than of the later years. This is called an *accelerated method*.[5]

Accelerated methods have been used in financial reporting by some companies since 1954, when their use was first permitted for income tax purposes. The two methods specifically mentioned in the 1954 tax law, the double-declining-balance method and sum-of-the-years'-digits (or simply "years'-digits") method, are described below. The effect of either of these methods is to write off approximately two thirds of the asset's cost in the first half of its estimated life, as contrasted with the straight-line method under which, of course, half the cost is written off in each half of the asset's estimated life. Thus, if an accelerated method is used, depreciation expense is greater in the early years and less in the later years as compared with the straight-line method.

Declining-Balance Method. In a *declining-balance method*, each year's depreciation is found by applying a *rate* to the *net* book value of the asset as of the beginning of that year. (The straight-line method's rate is applied to original cost net of residual value, not to each year's net book value.) *Net book value* at a point in time is the original acquisition cost less total depreciation accumulated up to that time. With a declining-balance method, the asset's estimated residual value, if any, has no effect on the annual depreciation charges because residual value is not part of the calculation of net book value.

The declining-balance rate is a stated percentage of the straight-line rate. Thus, for an asset with a useful life of 10 years (straight-line rate = 10 percent), 200 percent declining balance would use a rate of 20 percent (= 200 percent × 10 percent); 175 percent, a rate of 17.5 percent; and 150 percent, a rate of 15 percent. The 200 percent declining-balance method, permitted for income tax purposes from 1954 to 1981, is called the *double-declining-balance method* because the rate is double the straight-line rate.

Years'-Digits Method. In the *years'-digits method*, the numbers 1, 2, 3, . . . , n are added, where n is the estimated years of useful life. This sum can be found by the equation (using 10 years for the example):

$$\text{SYD} = n\left(\frac{n+1}{2}\right) = 10\left(\frac{10+1}{2}\right) = 55$$

The depreciation rate each year is a fraction in which the denominator is the sum of these digits and the numerator is, for the first year, n; for the second year, n − 1; for the third year, n − 2; and so on.

---

[5]An argument can also be made for an opposite approach, that is, charging a smaller fraction of the cost in the early years and a larger fraction in the later years. This leads to an *annuity method*. It is rarely used in published financial statements.

Comparison of Methods. Illustration 7–3 is an example of the way these three methods work out for a machine costing $1,000 with an estimated life of 10 years and no residual value. Illustration 7–4 shows the same depreciation patterns graphically.

ILLUSTRATION 7–3
COMPARISON OF DEPRECIATION METHODS

Year	Straight Line (10 percent rate)		Double-Declining Balance (20 percent rate)		Years' Digits		
	Annual Depreciation	Net Book Value, 12/31	Annual Depreciation	Net Book Value, 12/31	Rate	Annual Depreciation	Net Book Value, 12/31
0..........		$1,000		$1,000.00			$1,000.00
First........	$ 100	900	$200.00	800.00	10/55	$ 181.82	818.18
Second.....	100	800	160.00	640.00	9/55	163.64	654.54
Third.......	100	700	128.00	512.00	8/55	145.45	509.09
Fourth......	100	600	102.40	409.60	7/55	127.27	381.82
Fifth........	100	500	81.92	327.68	6/55	109.09	272.73
Sixth........	100	400	65.54	262.14	5/55	90.91	181.82
Seventh.....	100	300	52.43	209.71	4/55	72.73	109.09
Eighth......	100	200	41.94	167.77	3/55	54.55	54.54
Ninth.......	100	100	33.55	134.22	2/55	36.36	18.18
Tenth.......	100	0	26.84	107.38	1/55	18.18	0
Eleventh....	—	—	21.48	85.90	—	—	—
Twelfth......	—	—	17.18	68.72*	—	—	—
	$1,000		$931.28*			$1,000.00	

*Under the strict declining-balance method, depreciation continues until the asset is disposed of or until the net book value declines to residual value. Many companies, however, switch from this method to the straight-line method in the later years of life, and thus write off the entire cost in a specified number of years. If this practice were applied to the illustration, the double-declining-balance amount for years 6–10 would be $65.54, leaving the asset fully depreciated at the end of the 10th year.

Units-of-Production Method. A third concept of depreciation also views the asset as consisting of a bundle of service units; but this concept does not assume that these service units will be provided in a mathematical *time-phased* pattern, as is assumed by the straight-line and accelerated methods. The cost of each service unit is the net cost of the asset divided by the total number of such units. The depreciation charge for a period is then related to the number of units consumed in that period. This leads to the *units-of-production method.* For example, if a truck has an estimated net cost of $60,000 and is expected to give service for 300,000 miles, depreciation would be charged at a rate of 20 cents per mile. The depreciation expense in a year in which the truck traveled 50,000 miles would be $10,000.

ILLUSTRATION 7–4
ANNUAL DEPRECIATION CHARGES
For a Machine with Cost of $1,000 and 10-Year Service Life

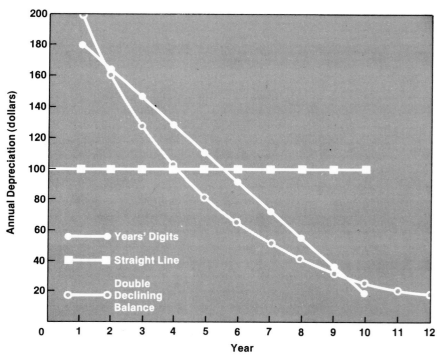

INCOME TAX CONSIDERATIONS

For several decades, the Congress has used the income tax laws as a device to encourage corporations to invest in new productive assets. The two key mechanisms to encourage this capital formation have been depreciation allowances and the investment tax credit.

Income Tax Depreciation

Until 1981, encouragement to invest in capital assets was provided by allowing accelerated depreciation and depreciable lives shorter than the asset's service life, both of which provided higher deductions, and hence less taxable income, in the early years of an asset's life.

Economic Recovery Tax Act of 1981. In this act (hereafter called the "1981 Tax Act") the notion of basing depreciation on the matching concept, and therefore on realistic service lives, was abandoned. In fact, the term *depreciation* was dropped and replaced by the term *accelerated cost recovery system* (ACRS). With ACRS, assets acquired after 1980 were placed into four recovery period classes. Three-year property includes automobiles, light-duty trucks, machinery and equipment used for research and development, and other short-lived tangible personal property. Five-year property generally includes all other tangible personal property, including most machinery and equipment. Most buildings fall in a 15-year class. Certain special types of equipment and buildings in certain industries are in a 10-year class. Residual values, if any, are ignored under ACRS rules.

The ACRS rules also incorporate the *half-year convention;* that is, the first year an asset is owned, half-a-year's cost recovery is allowed, irrespective of when during the year the asset was acquired. Thus, for example, in effect a 5-year class asset is subject to a 4½ -year recovery period. (The half-year convention does not apply to buildings for which first-year cost recovery is based on the number of months the property was owned during that first year.) To simplify cost-recovery calculations, the IRS has published percentage rates for each year to be applied to an asset's original cost. These rates approximate the rates that would be calculated by using the 150 percent declining-balance method, changing to straight line in the latter years of an asset's class life.[6]

> **Example.** A machine in the five-year class, acquired in 1983 at a cost of $100,000, would have the following cost recovery schedule (ignoring the investment tax credit cost recovery adjustment, described below):

Year	Rate	Cost Recovery Deduction
1983	15%	$ 15,000
1984	22	22,000
1985	21	21,000
1986	21	21,000
1987	21	21,000
		$100,000

Investment Tax Credit

In most years since 1962, the tax laws have permitted a reduction in the year's income taxes equal to a percentage of the cost of any business machinery and equipment (but not buildings) acquired during the year. This is called the *investment tax credit* (ITC).[7] The 1981 Tax Act ITC provisions allow a 6 percent credit for property in the three-year class

---

[6]The 1981 act called for rates approximating 150 percent declining balance, changing to straight line, for 1981–84; 175 percent, changing to SYD, for 1985; and 200 percent, changing to SYD, after 1985. However, The Tax Equity and Fiscal Responsibility Act of 1982 repealed the 1985 and 1986 accelerations, retaining the schedule that approximates 150 percent declining balance.

[7]The ITC was suspended in 1966–67 and 1969–71.

and a 10 percent credit for property in the other classes. The credit is a direct reduction in the income tax bill. For example, if a company acquired a $100,000 machine in 1983, it could deduct $10,000 from the income tax it would otherwise pay for 1983. However, in calculating income for tax purposes, cost recovery is based on the cost of the asset less half the ITC (i.e., cost recovery actually is based on $95,000 = $100,000 − ½($10,000), in the previous example).

Either of two methods of accounting for the ITC is permitted for financial reporting purposes. The *flow-through method* reduces reported income tax expense by the amount of the ITC in the year in which the credit is taken. Conceptually, this method treats the ITC as a tax reduction that is "earned" as a result of acquiring assets that qualify for the ITC. The *deferral* or *cost-reduction* method in effect treats the ITC as a reduction in the original cost of the asset that gave rise to the credit. Thus, the depreciation expense for the asset is lower every year of its useful life than if there were no ITC. Conceptually, this method rejects the notion that the act of acquiring as asset (as opposed to using it) should increase net income, which is the effect of the flow-through method. Almost 90 percent of companies use the flow-through method.[8] The accounting entries for the two methods are shown in the following example.

> **Example.**   In late December 1982, a company purchased a $200,000 machine that qualified for a $20,000 investment tax credit. For financial reporting purposes, the machine's useful life is 10 years and straight-line depreciation is used.
>
> With the flow-through method, the ITC would be recorded in 1982 as follows:

```
Income Tax Liability .................... 20,000
     Income Tax Expense ..................         20,000
```

This has the effect of decreasing 1982 income tax expense, and hence increasing 1982 net income by $20,000.

> With the deferral method, the ITC would be recorded as a reduction in the cost of the machine, thus:

```
Income Tax Liability .................... 20,000
     Machinery ...........................         20,000
```

Note that this entry has no effect on the 1982 income statement. In 1983 and subsequent years, depreciation expense would be based on a net cost of $180,000, rather than $200,000, and would therefore be $18,000 per year. This has the effect of increasing net income by $2,000 in each of the next 10 years, as compared with what the net income would have been if

---

[8] *Accounting Trends & Techniques* (1981) reported that only 67 of 600 companies surveyed used the deferral method.

the depreciation expense were $20,000 per year, as it would be with the flow-through method.[9]

Choice of a Method   In deciding on a depreciation method, tax considerations are kept entirely separate from financial accounting considerations. For tax purposes, in most instances corporations will follow the ACRS rules, thereby receiving the tax savings related to depreciation as quickly as possible. The 1981 Tax Act's optional longer class lives and straight-line depreciation would be attractive to a company only if (1) the tax rate applicable to the company is expected to increase[10] or (2) if the company is in the development stage and does not expect to have any taxable income for several years.

With respect to financial reporting, we have previously indicated that each type of method—straight line, accelerated, and units of production—has its own conceptual basis as to the pattern in which an asset provides its bundle of services. In theory, GAAP allows a choice of methods so that a company can match the method to the pattern that obtains for an asset in that particular company. Strictly speaking, this means that different methods would apply to different types of assets in a given company. However, there is little evidence that companies think about service benefit patterns when selecting depreciation methods for their financial accounting. In most cases, a single method is applied to all of a company's depreciable assets. The method usually chosen is straight line.[11]

ACCOUNTING FOR DEPRECIATION

Assume that on January 1, 1971, Trantor Company purchased for $900,000 a building with an estimated service life of 45 years and zero

---

[9]Instead of reducing the cost of the asset and subsequent years' depreciation expense, some companies implement the deferral method by setting up an account called Unamortized Investment Tax Credits, which appears on the equities side of the balance sheet. In the example, this account, rather than Machinery, would be credited for $20,000. In subsequent years, this deferred credit is amortized by debiting Unamortized Investment Tax Credits and crediting Income Tax Expense. In the example, Income Tax Expense would be reduced by $2,000 a year, and depreciation would be $20,000 a year rather than $18,000. Thus, the net effect is the same as shown in the example: net income is increased by $2,000 a year in each of the 10 years of the asset's life, as compared with the flow-through method.

[10]As of 1983, corporate federal income tax rates were 15 percent for the first $25,000 of taxable income, 18 percent for the next $25,000, 30 percent for the third $25,000, 40 percent for the fourth $25,000, and 46 percent for all income in excess of $100,000.

[11]*Accounting Trends & Techniques* (1981) reports the following usage of methods by the 600 companies in its survey (the percentages add to more than 100 percent because some companies used more than one method):

Straight line	94%
Accelerated	27
Units of production	9

residual value. Trantor decided to depreciate this building on a straight-line basis, that is, $20,000 per year. Let us now consider how to record this depreciation in the *financial* accounting records.

It would be possible to reduce the asset value by $20,000 a year and to show on the balance sheet only the remaining amount, which at the end of 1971 would be $880,000. But this is *not* ordinarily done. Instead, a separate contra account is shown on the balance sheet for the accumulated amount of depreciation. This item is usually called *accumulated depreciation,* or it may have some other name such as "allowance for depreciation." Both the original cost and the accumulated depreciation amounts appear on the balance sheet. The figures as of December 31, 1971, would look like this:

Building	$900,000	
Less: Accumulated depreciation	20,000	
Net		$880,000

As of December 31, 1972, another year's depreciation would be added, and the balance sheet would then show:

Building	$900,000	
Less: Accumulated depreciation	40,000	
Net		$860,000

The foregoing amounts can be interpreted as follows:

Original cost of the building	$900,000
That portion of the original cost charged as expense for all periods to date	40,000
That portion of original cost remaining to be charged as expense of future periods	$860,000

The $860,000 is the *book value* of the asset. This is often labeled *net book value* to distinguish it from original cost, which is called the *gross book value.*

On the income statement, the expense item is usually labeled *depreciation expense.* In the income statement for 1971, this item for Trantor Company would be $20,000 (disregarding depreciation on assets other than this building); and $20,000 would also appear in the income statements for 1972, for 1973, and for following years until either the building was disposed of or it was fully depreciated. Usually, the depreciation expense amount in published income statements includes depreciation for all types of depreciable assets. Some companies report a separate accumulated depreciation amount for each category of property, plant, and equipment (buildings, machinery, office equipment, and so forth) except for the category, land, since land is not depreciated. In either case, the underlying asset depreciation records are much more detailed than the summary amounts shown in the financial statements.

The annual journal entry for depreciation, which is one of the adjusting entries, would be as follows:

```
Depreciation Expense ........................ 20,000
    Accumulated Depreciation, Building ........        20,000
```

Change in Depreciation Rates. Suppose that in 1995 Trantor Company decides that the building is likely to last until 2025, which is 10 years longer than the 45 years originally estimated. In theory, Trantor should change the depreciation rate so that the book value remaining in 1995 would be charged off over the newly estimated remaining service life of 30 years. Because of all the uncertainties and estimates inherent in the depreciation process, however, in practice such changes in the depreciation rate usually are not made.

Fully Depreciated Assets. Even if Trantor Company should use its building for more than 45 years, depreciation would cease to be accumulated at the end of the 45th year, since by then the total original cost of the building would have been charged to expense. Until the asset is disposed of, it is customary to continue to show the asset on the balance sheet. Thus, as of December 31, 2015, and for as long thereafter as Trantor owned the building, the balance sheet would show the following:

```
Building....................................... $900,000
    Less: Accumulated depreciation...............  900,000
                      Net.......................            $    0
```

Partial Year Depreciation. Often, half a year's depreciation is recorded in the year of acquisition and half a year's depreciation in the year of disposal, no matter what the actual date of acquisition or disposal is. This practice is justified on the grounds that depreciation is a rough estimate and there is no point in attempting to calculate it to exact fractions of a year. Similarly, if income statements are prepared on a monthly basis, half a month's depreciation expense may be recorded in the month of acquisition.

Disclosure. The amount of the depreciation charged off in the year must be disclosed in the financial statements. In a merchandising company, this can be done by reporting depreciation expense as a separate item on the income statement. In a manufacturing company, a separate income statement item may not be feasible. This is because depreciation of production plant and equipment is part of cost of goods sold, whereas the depreciation of other assets is part of general and administrative expenses, which are period costs. (The distinction between product and period costs was explained in Chapter 6.) In these circumstances, the amount of depreciation expense is reported in a note accompanying the financial statements. If a manufacturing company does not report its cost of goods sold as a separate item, depreciation can be disclosed as a line item on the income statement. The balance sheet, or a note thereto, must disclose the original cost of major classes of depreciable assets, the amount of accumulated depreciation, and the depreciation method or methods used.[12]

Debits to Accumulated Depreciation. If an item of equipment is given an unusual major overhaul that makes it "as good as new," the cost of this overhaul is sometimes debited to Accumulated Depreciation rather than to Maintenance Expense. This practice is justified either on the grounds that the overhaul has actually canceled or offset some of the accumulated depreciation, or on the grounds that the overhaul has extended the useful life of the asset and the depreciation accumulated up to the time of overhaul is therefore excessive. In theory, if the estimated useful life has changed, the depreciation rate should be recalculated and the accounts changed to reflect the new estimate of useful life. In practice, charging the overhaul to Accumulated Depreciation may have approximately the same effect.

PLANT AND EQUIPMENT: DISPOSAL

Suppose that the end of 10 years Trantor Company sells its building. At that time, $^{10}/_{45}$ of the original cost, or $200,000, will have been built up in the Accumulated Depreciation account and the net book value of the building will be $700,000. If the building is sold for $700,000 cash, the accounts are changed as follows:

```
Cash ........................................ 700,000
Accumulated Depreciation .................... 200,000
    Building .................................         900,000
```

This has the effect of eliminating from the accounts both the original cost of the building and the accumulated depreciation thereon.

If the building were sold for less than $700,000, say, $600,000, the $100,000 difference is recorded as a loss, as in the following entry:

```
Cash ........................................ 600,000
Accumulated Depreciation .................... 200,000
Loss on Sale of Building .................... 100,000
    Building .................................         900,000
```

Note that the effect on the Building and Accumulated Depreciation accounts is identical with that in the previous illustration: the amounts relating to this building disappear. The loss is a decrease in Owners' Equity, reflecting the fact that the total depreciation expense recorded for the preceding 10 years was less than what Trantor now knows to

---

[12]"Accounting for Income Taxes," *APB Opinion No. 12*, December 1967.

have been the actual net cost of the building over that period of time. The actual net cost turns out to have been $300,000, whereas the total depreciation expense charged has amounted to only $200,000.

Since the depreciation expense as originally recorded turns out the have been incorrect, the Retained Earnings account that reflects the net of all revenue and expenses to date is also incorrect. There is therefore some logic in closing the Loss on Sale of Building account directly to Retained Earnings, thus correcting the error contained therein. Nevertheless, the matching concept requires that this loss be shown as an expense on the income statement of the current period. An asset amount that no longer benefits future periods in an expense of the current period.

If an asset is sold for *more* than its book value, the entries are analogous to those described above. The account Gain on the Sale of Building (or other category of long-lived asset) is credited for the excess of the selling price over net book value. This account is usually classified as "Other income" on the income statement.

It is important to remember that the *objective* of depreciation accounting is to charge as depreciation expense over the service life of the asset the exact difference between its original cost and its ultimate residual value. This would result in reporting *no* gain or loss when the asset is disposed of, which is consistent with the view that an enterprise earns income by using its fixed assets, not by disposing of them. However, since an asset's ultimate service life and residual value cannot be perfectly forecasted when the asset is acquired, asset disposals usually involve some reported gain or loss.

Market Values. The net book value of an asset usually is not the same as its market value. However, if Trantor's building was sold at the end of 1980 for $600,000, this was, by definition, its market value at that time. Also, the $900,000 original cost was presumably its market value on January 1, 1971, when it was acquired. Thus, the first and the last transactions for the building take account of market values. In the intervening periods, however, changes in market values are disregarded in the financial statements and underlying accounting records.

Exchanges and Trade-Ins

Some items of property and equipment are disposed of by trading them in, or exchanging them, for new assets. When this is done, the value of the old asset is used in calculating the acquisition cost of the new asset. The amount used in this calculation depends on whether or not the asset traded is similar to the new asset. If the trade-in is *similar* (technically, "of like kind"), its value is assumed to be its net book value, that is, its cost less the amount depreciated to date. If the asset traded is *dissimilar*, its value is its estimated fair market value.[13]

---

[13]"Accounting for Nonmonetary Transactions," *APB Opinion No. 29*, May 1973.

Example. Assume a company trades in two automobiles, each of which originally cost $10,000, of which $7,500 has been depreciated; thus, each has a net book value of $2,500. Each has a fair market value as a used car of $3,500.

The first automobile is traded for another automobile with a list price of $15,000, and $10,000 cash is given to the dealer in addition to the trade-in. In this case, the cost of the new automobile is recorded as $12,500; that is, it is the sum of the $10,000 cash and the $2,500 *net book value* of the trade-in.

The second automobile is traded for a machine tool that also has a list price of $15,000; and $10,000 cash is given in addition to the trade-in. In this case, the cost of the new machine tool is recorded as $13,500; that is, it is the sum of the $10,000 cash and the $3,500 *market value* of the trade-in.

The effect of these rules is that no gain or loss is recorded if an old asset is traded in for a new similar asset, but a gain or loss is recognized if the asset traded in is dissimilar to the new asset.

Example. Journal entries for the two transactions described in the preceding example are as follows:

1. *For an exchange "of like kind":*

```
Automobile (new) ......................... 12,500
Accumulated Depreciation (automobile) ...  7,500
    Cash .................................               10,000
    Automobile (old) ....................               10,000
```

2. *For other exchanges:*

```
Machine Tool (new) ...................... 13,500
Accumulated Depreciation (automobile) ...  7,500
    Cash .................................               10,000
    Automobile (old) ....................               10,000
    Gain on Disposal of Automobile .......                1,000
```

Note that in both cases the cost and accumulated depreciation of the old automobile are removed from the accounts. Note also that in both cases the list price of the new asset is disregarded. In the case of an exchange "of like kind," no gain or loss is recognized; in the other case, the gain is recognized. These rules are required both for income tax purposes and for financial accounting purposes.

Reasons for not recognizing a gain or loss on trade-ins "of like kind" are (1) the list price of a new item of equipment, such as an automobile, may not be a fair measure of its real market value, but only a starting point in bargaining between the buyer and seller and (2) there may be no reliable way of measuring the market value of the trade-in. In these circumstances, the assumption that the old asset's value equals its net book value may be the most objective way of arriving at a value for the new asset. When the exchange involves dissimilar assets, this assumption is less likely to be realistic.

Group Depreciation

The procedures described above related to a single fixed asset, such as one building or one automobile. To find the total depreciation expense for a whole category of assets, this procedure could be repeated for each single asset, and the total depreciation for all the assets in the category would then be recorded by one journal entry. This is *item* or *unit depreciation* and is the procedure used in many companies.

An alternative procedure is to treat all similar assets (such as all automobiles) as a group rather than making the calculation for each one separately. The process is called *group depreciation*. Annual depreciation expense under group depreciation is computed in a manner similar to that described above for an individual asset. If the straight-line method is used, for example, the depreciation rate is applied to the total original cost of the whole group of assets.

The accumulation of depreciation does not stop when one item in the group reaches its estimated useful life, however. Rather, depreciation continues indefinitely unless it becomes apparent that the accumulation is too large or too small for the whole group of assets. In this case, the depreciation rate is changed.

If the group method is used, no gain or loss is recognized when an individual asset is sold or otherwise disposed of. Upon disposal, the asset account is credited for the asset's original cost, as in the entries given above; but the difference between cost and the sales proceeds is simply debited or credited to Accumulated Depreciation. This procedure assumes that gains on some sales in the group are offset by losses on others.

Example. A used minicomputer with original cost of $5,000 is disposed of for $600 cash. Assuming group depreciation is used, the journal entry for this transaction is:

```
Cash ......................................    600
Accumulated Depreciation, Computers .....  4,400
    Computers ...........................            5,000
```

SIGNIFICANCE OF DEPRECIATION

The amount shown as accumulated depreciation on the balance sheet does *not* represent the "accumulation" of any *tangible* thing. It is merely that portion of the assets' original cost that already has been matched against revenue.

Occasionally, an entity does set aside money for the specific purpose of purchasing new assets, and this process is sometimes called *funding depreciation.* This is a *financing* transaction, which is completely separate from the *accounting* depreciation mechanism described above. If depreciation is funded, cash or securities are set aside in such a way that they cannot be used in the regular operation of the entity (e.g., a special bank account may be created). *This practice is not common.* It is mentioned here only to emphasize, by contrast, the point that the depreciation process itself is *not* a means of automatically creating a fund for the replacement of assets.

There is a widespread belief that in some mysterious way depreciation does represent money, specifically, money that can be used to purchase new assets. Depreciation is *not* money; the money that the entity has is shown by the balance in its Cash account.

> **Example.** This quotation is from a well-known publication: "Most large companies draw much of the cash flow they employ for expanding and modernizing their operations from their depreciation reserves." This statement is not true in anything remotely approaching a literal sense.

There is also a widespread belief that the net book value of assets is related to their real value, and this is equally erroneous.

> **Example.** An auditor's report included the following statement: "Our inspection of insurance policies in force at the close of the year disclosed that the plant assets on the basis of book values were amply protected against fire." Such a statement has little if any significance. What investors want to know is whether the insurance protection equals the *replacement cost* of the assets, and this is unlikely to correspond to their *book value.*

Concluding Comment

The key to a practical understanding of depreciation is a sentence from *Accounting Research Bulletin No. 43:*[14] *"Depreciation is a process of allocation, not of valuation."* Depreciation expense does *not* represent the shrinkage in market value during an accounting period. Particularly during periods of inflation, a depreciable asset's market value may be even higher at the end of the period than it was at the beginning. Neither does the net book value represent the market value of the depreciable assets. Depreciation expense is a write-off of a portion of the *cost* of the asset. It follows that the net book value of fixed assets reported on the balance sheet represents only that portion of the *original cost* of the fixed asset that has *not yet* been charged to expense.

No one really knows how long an asset will last or what its residual value will be at the end of its life. Without this knowledge, the depreciation number is necessarily an estimate.

---

[14]AICPA, *Accounting Research Bulletin No. 43* (June 1953), chap. 9, sec. C, par. 5.

NATURAL RESOURCES

Natural resources, such as coal, oil, other minerals, and gas, are assets of the company that owns the right to extract them. The general principles for measuring the acquisition cost of these *wasting assets* are the same as those for other tangible assets. If purchased, the cost is the purchase price and related acquisition costs. Many companies acquire these assets as a consequence of exploring for them. There are two strongly held views as to how these exploration costs should be accounted for, particularly for oil and gas companies.

A petroleum company, in a given year, may be exploring in many different locations. It probably will discover oil and gas reserves in only a few of them. Some people argue that all the exploration costs of a year should be capitalized as the asset value of the reserves that are discovered during the year; this is the *full cost* method. Others argue that only the costs incurred at locations in which reserves are discovered should be capitalized as the cost of these reserves, and that the "dry-hole" costs should be immediately expensed; this is the *successful efforts* method.

> **Example.** A petroleum company explores 10 locations, incurring costs of $10 million at each. It discovers oil and gas reserves at only one of these locations. If it uses the full cost method, the asset amount of the newly discovered reserves will be recorded as $100 million. If it uses the successful efforts method, the asset amount will be recorded as $10 million and the other $90 million will be charged to expense.

In its *Statement No. 19* (December 1977), the FASB required the use of the successful efforts method. In August 1978, however, the SEC ruled that either method would continue to be acceptable for SEC filings. This SEC action led the FASB to issue *Statement No. 25* (February 1979), which amended *Statement No. 19* to permit either method.

Depletion

The process of amortizing the cost of natural resources in the accounting periods benefited is called *depletion*. The objective is the same as that for depreciation: to amortize the cost in some systematic manner over the asset's useful life. The units-of-production method is ordinarily used. For example, if an oil property cost $250 million and is estimated to contain 50 million barrels of oil, the depletion rate is $5 per barrel. The total depletion for a year in which 8 million barrels of oil were produced would be $40 million.

For income tax purposes, however, the depletion allowance usually bears no relation to cost; rather, it is a percentage of revenue. The permitted percentage for gas and oil is 16 percent in 1983 and 15 percent for 1984 and thereafter. This is another example of an income tax provision that is inconsistent with GAAP. Advocates of this provision in the tax law claim that it stimulates exploration for an development of new supplies of natural resources and is therefore in the national interest.

Accretion and Appreciation

Accretion is the increase in value of timberland, cattle, and other agricultural products that arises through the natural process of growth. Since accretion does not represent realized revenue, it is ordinarily not recognized in the accounts. However, the *costs* incurred in the growing process are added to the asset value, just as is done in the case of costs incurred in the manufacture of goods.

Appreciation is also an increase in the *value* of an asset. It therefore is *not* the opposite of depreciation, which is a write-off of *cost*. Appreciation of assets is recognized in the accounts only under highly unusual circumstances. For example, if a new owner takes over a business and an appraisal discloses that the current market value of the tangible assets is substantially above their book value, the asset values often are written up to their current value. Generally, however, increases in value are recognized in the accounts only when revenue is realized, whereas expiration of cost is recognized when it occurs.

INTANGIBLE ASSETS

Intangible long-lived assets, such as goodwill, organization cost (i.e., cost incurred to get a company started), trademarks, and patents, are usually converted to expenses over a number of accounting periods. The periodic write-off is specifically called *amortization*, although the word *amortization* is also used in the broad sense of any write-off of a cost over a period of years. The amortization of intangible assets is essentially the same process as the depreciation of tangible assets. Generally, the straight-line method is used for amortization of intangibles.

Goodwill

When one company buys another company and pays more for it than the fair market value of the company's identifiable assets (net of liabilities assumed by the purchaser), the amount of the excess is recorded as an asset of the acquiring company. (Identifiable assets include tangible assets and "identifiable" intangible assets. Patents, licenses, and franchises are examples of identifiable intangibles; customer loyalty and a good sales force are examples of nonidentifiable intangibles.) Although often reported on the balance sheet with a descriptive title such as "Excess of acquisition cost over net assets acquired," the amount is customarily called *goodwill*.

It is important to note that goodwill arises only as part of a *purchase* transaction. In most cases, this is a transaction in which one company acquires all the assets of another company for some consideration other than an exchange of common stock. (More details are given in Chapter 11.) The buying company is willing to pay more than the fair value of the assets because the acquired company has a strong management team, a favorable reputation in the marketplace, superior production methods, or other intangible, unrecorded (nonidentifiable) assets.

The acquisition cost of the identifiable assets acquired is their fair market value at the time of acquisition. Usually, these values are determined by appraisal, but in some cases the net book value of these assets is accepted as being their fair value. If there is evidence that the fair market value differs from net book value, either higher or lower, the market value governs.

> **Example.** Company A acquires all the assets of Company B, giving Company B $1,500,000 cash. Company B has cash of $50,000, accounts receivable that are believed to have a realizable value of $60,000, and other identifiable assets that are estimated to have a current market value of $1,100,000. The amount of goodwill is calculated as follows:

Total purchase price.		$1,500,000
Less:		
Cash acquired.	$ 50,000	
Accounts receivable.	60,000	
Other identifiable assets (estimated).	1,100,000	1,210,000
Goodwill		$ 290,000

Amortization. In most cases, there is no way of estimating the useful life of goodwill, and hence no reliable way of deciding what fraction of the cost should be amortized as an expense in a given year. A company may select whatever period it believes to be reasonable, but in no event can the amortization period exceed 40 years.[15] Amortization must be on a straight-line basis. For income tax purposes, however, goodwill and other intangible assets that do not have a determinable life cannot be amortized at all. For income tax purposes, therefore, the acquiring company wants to value the depreciable assets as high as it legitimately can, leaving the minimum possible amount to be recorded as goodwill.

The amount of annual amortization is ordinarily credited directly to the asset account, rather than being accumulated in a separate contra account as is the case with accumulated depreciation. This is the usual practice for all intangible assets.

Patents, Copyrights, Franchise Rights

Patents, copyrights, franchise rights, and similar intangible assets are initially recorded at their cost. If they are purchased, the cost is the amount paid. If a patented invention is developed within the company, however, the costs involved ordinarily are not capitalized. These are

---

[15]"Intangible Assets," *APB Opinion No. 17*, August 1970, par. 29.

considered to be research and development costs, which are discussed separately in a following section.

The cost of any of these intangible assets is amortized over the useful life of the asset. If the useful life is limited by law or agreement (e.g., 17 years for a patent), the amortization period cannot be longer. It may be shorter if the company believes that because of technological advances or other reasons, the practical life will be shorter than the legal life. In no case may the period exceed 40 years. Amortization is on a straight-line basis.

Leasehold Improvements

Leased property reverts to the owner at the end of the period of the lease. Any improvements made to the property belong to the owner. The lessee loses the use of them when the leased property is returned. There-fore the useful life of such improvements corresponds to the period of the lease. The lease agreement may contain renewal options that effec-tively extend the life beyond the period of the original lease agreement. It follows that although improvements which otherwise meet the criteria for capitalization are capitalized, the useful life of these improvements is not determined by the physical characteristics of the improvements themselves, but rather by the terms of the lease agreement.

> **Example.** A company leases office space and spends $60,000 for re-modeling to suit its needs. The lease is for an original period of three years with an option to renew for another three years. The physical life of the improvements is 10 years. The leasehold improvements are amortized over a period of six years, or $10,000 a year, if the lessee believes it likely that the lease will be renewed. Otherwise, they are amortized over three years, at $20,000 a year. In any event, they are not amortized over 10 years.

Deferred Charges

Deferred charges are conceptually the same as prepaid expenses, a current asset discussed in Chapter 2. They are included as long-lived assets only if they have a relatively long useful life, that is, if they benefit several future accounting periods. Goodwill, patents, copyrights, and in-deed all long-lived assets subject to amortization are deferred charges in the literal sense. However, the term is usually restricted to long-lived intangibles other than those listed in the preceding paragraphs. They may include the cost of organizing a company and the related *preoper-ating* or *start-up* costs of preparing the company or some part thereof, such as a new store, to generate revenue. During the preoperating period, no revenue is being earned, and therefore there is nothing against which to match these costs.

Practice varies greatly with respect to these items. Some companies charge them off as expenses as the costs are incurred, even though there is no offsetting revenue. Other companies capitalize them. If capitalized, they are usually amortized over a relatively short period of time, often in the next year in the case of the preoperating costs of a new store, but rarely more than five years. This reflects the conservatism concept.

Research and Development Costs

Research and development (R&D) costs are costs incurred for the purpose of developing new or improved goods, processes, or services. The fruits of R&D efforts are increased revenues or lower costs. Since these fruits will not be picked until future periods, often five years or more after a research project is started, a good case can be made for capitalizing R&D costs and amortizing them over the periods benefited. This practice was common at one time, but the FASB no longer permits it. Instead, it requires that R&D costs be charged off as an expense of the current period.[16]

The reason given by the FASB for its requirement is that by their very nature, the future benefits to be derived from current R&D efforts are highly uncertain. The efforts that are eventually unsuccessful cannot be identified in advance; otherwise, they would not have been undertaken. Although near the end of the development stage the success of certain projects seems reasonably assured, the FASB has concluded that there is no objective way of distinguishing between these projects and the unsuccessful ones.

The FASB decision in this matter is a particularly interesting example of the inherent conflict between certain concepts. Capitalizing R&D costs and then amortizing them over the future periods likely to benefit is consistent with the matching concept. However, it is inconsistent with the criterion that accounting should be reasonably objective, and it is not in accord with the conservatism concept. The FASB decided that the latter considerations were more important than the matching concept in this instance.

If a company does R&D work for a customer (i.e., another company or a government agency) and is paid for this work, these payments constitute revenue. The related costs are held as an asset in Work in Process Inventory. They are matched against revenue and therefore are charged as expenses in the period in which the revenue is earned.

SUMMARY

Items of property, plant, and equipment are capitalized at their acquisition cost, which includes all elements of cost involved in making them ready to provide service. Except for land, a portion of this cost (less residual value, if any) is charged as depreciation expense to each of the

---

[16]"Accounting for Research and Development Costs," *FASB Statement No. 2*, October 1974.

accounting periods in which the asset is expected to provide service. Any systematic and rational method may be used for this purpose. The straight-line method is ordinarily used for financial accounting purposes, but accelerated methods are the basis for the "cost recovery" deductions allowed for income tax purposes. A corresponding reduction is made each year in the net book value of the asset account.

When an asset is disposed of, its cost and accumulated depreciation are removed from the accounts, and any gain or loss appears on the income statement (unless group depreciation is used).

Natural resources are accounted for in the same way, except that the expense item is called depletion rather than depreciation.

Intangible assets are also recorded at cost. In the case of goodwill, this cost is the difference between the price paid for a company and the fair market value of the identifiable assets acquired (net of any liabilities assumed by the purchaser). If intangible assets have a determinable service life, their cost is amortized over that life, using the straight-line method. For assets with no determinable service life, the amortization period must not exceed 40 years, and is considerably shorter in many cases. R&D costs are expensed as incurred.

Cases

CASE 7–1 Wyland Corporation (B)

After the controller of Wyland Corporation had ascertained the changes in accounts receivable and the allowance for doubtful accounts in 1982, he made a similar analysis of property, plant, and equipment and accumulated depreciation accounts. Again he examined the December 31, 1981, balance sheet (see Exhibit 1 of Wyland Corporation (A), Case 5–1). He also reviewed the following company transactions that he found to be applicable to these accounts:

1. On January 2, 1982, one of the factory machines was sold for its book value, $2,946. This machine was recorded on the books at $23,797 with accumulated depreciation of $20,851.

2. Tools were carried on the books at cost, and at the end of each year a physical inventory was taken to determine what tools still remained. The account was written down to the extent of the decrease in tools as ascertained by the year-end inventory. At the end of 1982, it was determined that there had been a decrease in the tool inventory amounting to $5,982.

3. On March 1, 1982, the company sold for $1,246 cash an automobile that was recorded on the books at a cost of $4,455 and had an accumulated depreciation of $2,763 as of January 1, 1982. In this and other cases of sale of long-lived assets during the year, the accumulated depreciation and depreciation expense items were both increased by an amount that reflected the depreciation chargeable for the months in 1982 in which the asset was held prior to the sale, at rates listed in item 7 below.

237

4. The patent listed on the balance sheet had been purchased by the Wyland Corporation on December 31, 1975, for $75,000. This patent had been granted on December 31, 1973. The cost of the patent was to be written off as an expense over the remainder of its legal life. (The legal life of a patent is 17 years from the date granted.)

5. On July 1, 1982, a typewriter that had cost $685 and had been fully depreciated on December 31, 1981, was sold for $52.

6. On October 1, the company sold a desk for $60. This piece of furniture was recorded on the books at a cost of $358 with an accumulated depreciation of $291 as of January 1, 1982.

7. Depreciation was calculated at the following rates:

Buildings	2%
Factory machinery	10*
Furniture and fixtures	10
Automotive equipment	20
Office machines	10

*Included in the factory machinery cost of $2,740,468 was a machine costing $62,403 that had been fully depreciated on December 31, 1981, and that was still in use.

Questions

1. Analyze the effect of each of these transactions upon the property, plant, and equipment accounts, accumulated depreciation, and any other accounts that may be involved in a manner similar to that used in Wyland Corporation (A), and prepare journal entries.

2. Give the correct totals for property, plant, and equipment, and the amount of accumulated depreciation as of December 31, 1982, after the transactions affecting them had been recorded.

CASE 7–2 Jean Coffin (C)

Jean Coffin said to the accounting instructor, "The general principle for arriving at the amount of a fixed asset that is to be capitalized is reasonably clear, but there certainly are a great many problems in applying this principle to specific situations." Following are some of the problems Ms. Coffin presented:

1. Suppose that the Bruce Manufacturing Company used its own maintenance crew to build an additional wing on its existing factory building. What would be the proper accounting treatment of the following items:

a. Architects' fees.

b. The cost of snow removal during construction.

c. Cash discounts earned for prompt payment on materials purchased for construction.

d. The cost of building a combined construction office and toolshed that would be torn down once the factory wing had been completed.

e. Interest on money borrowed to finance construction.

f. Local real estate taxes for the period of construction on the portion of land to be occupied by the new wing.

g. The cost of mistakes made during construction.

h. The overhead costs of the maintenance department that include supervision; depreciation on buildings and equipment of maintenance department shops; heat, light, and power for these shops; and allocations of cost for such items as the cafeteria, medical office, and personnel department.

i. The cost of insurance during construction and the cost of damages or losses on any injuries or losses not covered by insurance.

2. Assume that the Archer Company bought a large piece of land, including the buildings thereon, with the intent of razing the buildings and constructing a combined hotel and office building in their place. The existing buildings consisted of a theater and several stores and small apartment buildings, all in active use at the time of the purchase.

a. What accounting treatment should be accorded that portion of the purchase price considered to be the amount paid for the buildings that were subsequently razed?

b. How should the costs of demolishing the old buildings be treated?

c. Suppose that a single company had owned this large piece of land, including the buildings thereon, and instead of selling to the Archer Company had decided to have the buildings razed and to have a combined hotel and office building constructed on the site for its own benefit. In what respects, if any, should the accounting treatment of the old buildings and the cost of demolishing them differ from your recommendations with respect to (a) and (b) above?

3. Midland Manufacturing Company purchased a new machine. It is clear that the invoice price of the new machine should be capitalized, and it also seems reasonable to capitalize the transporta-

tion cost to bring the machine to the Midland plant. I'm not so clear, however, on the following items:

a. The new machine is heavier than the old machine it replaced; consequently, the foundation under the machine has had to be strengthened by the installation of additional steel beams. Should this cost be charged to the building, added to the cost of the machine, or be expensed?

b. The installation of the machine took longer and was more costly than anticipated. In addition to time spent by the regular maintenance crew on installation, it became necessary to hire an outside engineer to assist in the installation and in "working out the bugs" to get the machine running properly. His costs included not only his fee but also his transportation, hotel expense, and meals. Moreover, the foreman of the department and the plant superintendent both spent a considerable amount of time assisting in the installation work. Before the new machine was working properly, a large amount of material had been spoiled during trial runs.

c. In addition to the invoice price and transportation, it was necessary to pay a state sales tax on purchasing the machine.

d. In connection with payment for the new machine, the machine manufacturer was willing to accept the Midland Company's old machine as partial payment. The amount allowed as a trade-in was larger than the depreciated value at which the old machine was being carried in the books of the Midland Company. Should the difference have been treated as a reduction in the cost of the new machine or a gain on disposal of the old one?

4. A computer manufacturing company sold outright about 25 percent of its products (in terms of dollar volume) and leased 75 percent. On average, a given computer was leased for four years. The cost of leased computers was initially recorded as an asset and was depreciated over four years. The company assisted new customers in installing the computer and in designing the related systems. The "applications engineering" services were furnished without charge, and the company's cost was reported as part of its marketing expense. Applications engineering costs averaged about 5 percent of the sales value of a computer, but about 20 percent of the first-year rental revenue of a leased computer. Recently, the company's installation of computers grew rapidly. Because the applications engineering cost was such a high percentage of lease revenue, reported income did not increase at all. Research and development costs must be expensed as incurred. Does the same principle apply to applications engineering costs, or could these costs be added to the asset value of leased computers and amortized over the lease period? If so, could other marketing costs related to leased computers be treated in the same way?

5. Using the deferral method of accounting for the investment tax credit in effect reduces the capitalized cost of the asset that gave rise to the credit, whereas the flow-through method reduces reported income tax expense for the period in which the asset was acquired. While I can understand permitting accounting alternatives such as FIFO versus LIFO, and straight line versus accelerated depreciation, I cannot understand the rationale for permitting two different treatments for the investment tax credit. What *is* the latter rationale?

CASE 7–3 Whitmore Trust Company

Whitmore Trust Company conducted a commercial banking business in a city of approximately 100,000. The company did not own its banking quarters but operated under a lease that still had six years to run in 1978. While the lease contained no renewal provisions, the bank had occupied the building since 1925 under successive 10-year leases. Relations with the owner of the building, who was also the operator of a nearby department store, continued to be cordial. The lease provided, however, that the owner could cancel the lease on two years' notice if he required the property for his own business.

In the spring of 1978, the directors of the bank were considering a proposal to remodel the bank quarters. The bank had received firm bids from contractors on the work to be done, and these totaled approximately $125,000.

In the course of the discussion, a debate arose over the way in which the expenditure would be carried in the bank's books. One of the directors favored carrying the improvement as an asset and depreciating it over its physical life, which he estimated at about 25 years.

Several directors objected to this procedure. Under the so-called rule of fixtures, which was a well-established legal principle, permanent improvements to leased property were generally considered to be the property of the owner of the real estate. Since the bank did not own the property, these directors did not think the improvements should be considered as an asset. They favored charging the entire cost of the improvements as an expense in the current year, which had been the procedure with minor renovation expenses in the past.

Other directors felt that capitalizing the expenditure would be acceptable, but they did not think it wise to adopt a depreciation period longer than the life of the lease. They also wondered what con-

sideration should be given to the two-year cancellation provision.

The first director was not convinced by either of these approaches. He said he would not favor the remodeling project were he not convinced that the lease would be renewed as it had been in the past. He was also disturbed about the effect that a rapid write-off might have on the bank's earnings.

Section 178 of the Internal Revenue Code provided that for income tax purposes, as a general rule, improvements made to leased assets should be amortized over either the remaining life of the lease or the life of the improvement, whichever is shorter. If, however, upon completion of the improvement, the remaining life of the lease is less than 60 percent of the useful life of the improvement, it is ordinarily presumed that the lease will be renewed, and this longer life

EXHIBIT 1

WHITMORE TRUST COMPANY
Statement of Condition
December 31, 1977
(thousands of dollars)

Assets

Cash on hand and in banks	$ 4,317
U.S. government securities	10,463
Other securities	825
Loans	20,587
Other assets	570
	$36,762

Liabilities and Equity Capital

Commercial deposits		$26,001
Savings deposits		7,206
Total deposits		33,207
Other liabilities		331
Capital stock	$1,000	
Undivided profits	2,224	
Total equity capital		3,224
		$36,762

(i.e., the remaining life of the lease plus one renewal) will determine the amortization period.

In 1977, Whitmore Trust had gross revenue of $2,647,000, including $2,550,000 revenue from loans and investments in securities. After interest expense and operating expenses, but before income taxes, earnings were approximately $425,000. Federal income taxes amounted to about $95,000. The operating expenses were largely of a fixed nature.

The bank's statement of condition as of December 31, 1977, is given in Exhibit 1. According to the state banking law, trust companies could accept deposits of up to 12 times the amount of their equity capital. The law also required 12 percent of deposits to be maintained as a liquid reserve; the balance could be used for loans and investments in U.S. government and other securities. The bank was not permitted to loan an amount greater than 10 percent of its equity capital to any one individual or firm.

Questions

1. Why should the directors be concerned about this problem?

2. What action do you recommend?

CASE 7–4   Horton Press

Horton Press was founded in 1972 as a one-man job printing firm in a small southwestern town. Shortly after its founding, the owner decided to concentrate on one specialty line of printing. Because of a high degree of technical proficiency, the company experienced a rapid growth.

However, the company suffered from a competitive disadvantage in that the major market for its specialized output was in a metropolitan area over 300 miles away from the company's plant. For this reason, the owner, in 1982, decided to move nearer his primary market. He also decided to expand and modernize his facilities at the time of the move. After some investigation, an attractive site was found in a suburb of his primary market, and the move was made.

A balance sheet prepared prior to the move is shown in Exhibit 1. The transactions that arose from this move are described in the following paragraphs:

1. The land at the old site together with the building thereon was sold for $104,800.

2. Certain equipment was sold for $19,600 cash. This equipment appeared on the books at a cost of $51,500 less accumulated depreciation of $28,600.

3. A new printing press was purchased. The invoice cost of this equipment was $78,400. A 2 percent cash discount was taken by Horton Press so that only $76,832 was actually paid to the seller. Horton Press also paid $314 to a trucker to have this equipment delivered. Installation of this equipment was made by Horton Press employees who worked a total of 60 hours. These workers received $10 per hour in wages, but their time was ordinarily charged to printing jobs at $20 per hour, the difference representing an allowance for overhead ($7.80) and profit ($2.20).

4. The city to which the company moved furnished the land on which the

EXHIBIT 1

HORTON PRESS
Condensed Balance Sheet
As of December, 31, 1982

Assets			*Equities*	
Current assets:			Current liabilities	$112,044
Cash		$ 87,320	Common stock	308,000
Certificates of Deposit		200,000	Retained earnings	233,012
Other current assets		176,076		
Total current assets		463,396		
Property and equipment:				
Land		23,800		
Buildings	$244,800			
Less: Accumulated depreciation	139,200	105,600		
Equipment	185,380			
Less: Accumulated depreciation	125,120	60,260		
Total assets		$653,056	Total equities	$653,056

new plant was built as a gift. The land had an appraised value of $98,000. The appraisal had been made recently by a qualified appraiser. The company would pay property taxes on its assessed value, which was $62,700.

5. Horton Press paid $14,850 to have an old building on the gift plot of land torn down. (The value of this building was not included in the appraised or assessed values named above.) In addition, the company paid $9,500 to have permanent drainage facilities installed on the new land.

6. A new composing machine with an invoice cost of $19,600 was purchased. The company paid $14,600 cash and received a trade-in allowance of $5,000 on a used piece of composing equipment. The used equipment could have been sold outright for not more than $4,200. It had cost $8,400 new, and accumulated depreciation on it was $3,600.

7. The company erected a building at the new site for $392,000. Of this amount, $294,000 was borrowed on a mortgage.

8. After the equipment had been moved to the new plant, but before operations began there, extensive repairs and replacements of parts were made on a large paper cutter. The cost of this work was $3,900. Prior to this time, no more than $280 had been spent in any one year on the maintenance of this paper cutter.

9. Trucking and other costs associated with moving equipment to the new location and installing it were $5,900. In addition, Horton Press employees worked an estimated 125 hours on that part of the move that related to equipment.

10. During the moving operation, a piece of equipment costing $7,000 was dropped and damaged; $1,900 was spent to repair it. The management believed, however, that the salvage value of this equipment had been reduced to $980. Up until that time, the equipment was being depreciated at $560 per year, representing a 10 percent rate after deduction of estimated salvage of $1,400. Accumulated depreciation was $2,240.

11. The $200,000 Certificates of Deposit matured and were cashed.

Questions

1. Analyze the effect of each of these transactions on the items in the balance sheet and income statement. For transactions that affect owners' equity, distinguish between those that affect the net income of the current year and those that do not. In most cases, the results of your analysis can be set forth most clearly in the form of journal entries.

2. Prepare a balance sheet showing the effect of these transactions. (Assume a date as of December 31, 1982, and ignore any usual closing entries.)

CASE 7–5 United States Steel Corporation

United States Steel Corporation (USS) was organized in 1901 as a merger of several independent steel companies. This case discusses aspects of USS accounting for depreciation since that time.

In the first decade of the 20th century, USS continued the practice called *renewal accounting,* which had typically been used by its predecessor companies. It charged as an expense of the current year all expenditures for plant and equipment other than those made to provide additional capacity. (In that period, many industrial companies made no charge against current operations for plant assets, and others charged depreciation as voted by the board of directors, an amount which varied from year to year.)

Influenced by the specific recognition of depreciation in the income tax Revenue Act of 1918, USS shifted to the practice of making a regular annual depreciation charge based on historical cost. In this period, there was no authoritative body that made accounting pronouncements for industrial companies, and "until the early 1930s, depreciation was still a haphazard charge in the accounts of many industrial and commercial companies."[1]

The 1947 Change. For several years prior to 1947, USS management had been concerned with the effects upon the company's asset replacement program of the steady rise in the general price level since the late 1930s. This concern arose chiefly from the realization that expenses for depreciation of plant and equipment were not as large as would be the replacement costs of such facilities when they were worn out or became obsolete.

As a step toward stating depreciation in an amount that would reflect in current dollars of diminished buying power the same purchasing power represented by the original plant expenditure, the company deducted, in arriving at net income for 1947, an amount of $26.3 million over and above its regular depreciation charge (based on the straight-line method). Although the federal tax authorities would not allow the extra depreciation as a deduction in arriving at taxable income, the company's executives considered it essential that they recognize this element of cost in arriving at a measure of income to be used in other matters of company management.

In its 1947 annual report, the management stated that "while awaiting accounting and tax acceptance, U.S. Steel believed that it was prudent for it to give some recognition to increased replacement costs rather than to sit idly by and witness the unwitting liquidation of its

---

[1] Eldon S. Hendriksen, *Accounting Theory,* 3d ed. (Homewood, Ill.: Richard D. Irwin, Inc., 1977), p. 42. The first *Accounting Research Bulletin* of the AICPA Committee on Accounting Procedure was issued in 1939.

business should inadequate recording of costs result in insufficient resources to supply the tools required for sustained production."

In its opinion on the 1947 financial statements, the company's independent auditors stated that the corporation had included in costs additional depreciation of $26.3 million "in excess of the amount determined in accordance with the generally accepted accounting principle heretofore followed of making provision for depreciation on the original cost of facilities."

Carman G. Blough, then director of research of the AICPA, commented on this practice:

> There can be no argument but that a going concern must be able to replace its productive assets as they are used up if it is to continue to do business. It is also important for management to understand that the difference between cost and estimated replacement value may be significant in determining production and pricing policies. It does not follow, however, that the excess of the cost of replacement over the cost of existing assets should be accounted for as current charges to income. All who have dealt with appraisal values know how very difficult it is just to determine current replacement costs, but the most striking difficulty in this respect is the impossibility of predicting what will be the eventual cost of replacing a productive asset. How many men are prepared to state what the price level will be two years from today, to say nothing of trying to guess what it will be five or ten years hence when many of those assets are to be replaced?[2]

Similarly, the AICPA stated in 1947 that it "disapproves immediate write-

downs of plant costs by charges against current income in amounts believed to represent excessive or abnormal costs occasioned by current price levels."[3]

The 1948 Retreat. In its annual report for 1948, USS announced that it was abandoning the policy adopted in 1947 and was substituting in its place a method of charging "accelerated depreciation on cost," which was explained as follows:

> The accelerated depreciation is applicable to the cost of postwar facilities in the first few years of their lives when economic usefulness is greatest. The amount thereof is related to the excess of current operating rates over U.S. Steel's long-term peacetime average rate of 70% of capacity. The annual accelerated amount is 10% of the cost of facilities in the year in which the expenditures are made and 10% in the succeeding year, except that this amount is reduced ratably as the operating rate may drop, no acceleration being made at 70% or lower operations. The accelerated depreciation is an addition to the normal depreciation on such facilities, but the total depreciation over their expected lives will not exceed the cost of the facilities.

This method was made retroactive to January 1, 1947, and there was included in the $55,335,444 deducted for accelerated wear and exhaustion of facilities for 1948 an amount of $2,675,094 to cover a deficiency in the $26,300,000 sum reported in 1947 as "depreciation added to cover replacement cost." In other words, the new method when applied to the 1947 situation resulted in a deduction that exceeded the figure actually reported in 1947. It was again pointed out at this time that the accelerated depreciation

---

[2]"Replacement and Excess Construction Costs," *Journal of Accountancy*, vol. 74 (October 1947), p. 335.

[3]*Accounting Research Bulletin No. 43*, chap. 9, par. 9.

was not "presently deductible for federal income tax purposes." The company's independent auditors stated in their report to the shareholders for 1948 that they "approved" the new policy.

Management's convictions on the change in policy were clearly set forth by the chairman of the board of directors in the following quotation from the company's annual report for 1948:

> U.S. Steel believes that the principle which it adopted in 1947 and continued in 1948 is a proper recording of the wear and exhaustion of its facilities in terms of current dollars as distinguished from the dollars which it originally expended for those facilities. However, in view of the stated position of the American Institute of Certified Public Accountants, which is supported by the Securities and Exchange Commission, that the only accepted accounting principle for determining depreciation is that which is related to the actual number of dollars spent for facilities, regardless of when or what buying power, U.S. Steel has adopted a method of accelerated depreciation based on cost instead of one based on purchasing power recovery.

The 1953 Change. USS continued its policy of charging accelerated depreciation through 1952. Deductions for accelerated depreciation for 1947 through 1952 totaled slightly more than $201 million; none of this sum, however, had been allowed in computing taxable income during that period.

During and after the Korean War, USS was granted Certificates of Necessity that permitted amortization of designated facilities over a 60-month period for tax purposes regardless of the facilities' probable economic life. Management decided to depreciate these facilities in the corporate accounts over the 60-month period.

In 1953, USS changed its accelerated depreciation policy, as explained in this note to the 1953 financial statements:

> Since 1946, U.S. Steel has followed the policy of reflecting accelerated depreciation on the cost of new facilities in the first few years of their lives when the economic usefulness is greatest. The amounts charged to income for accelerated depreciation have been related to U.S. Steel's rate of operations.
>
> Under the Internal Revenue Code, that portion of the cost of facilities certified by the Defense Production Administration as essential to the defense effort is covered by a Certificate of Necessity and can be written off for tax purposes at the rate of 20% per year. The effect of amortization of these facilities is to charge to income a greater portion of their cost in the earlier years of life, and therefore, follows the principle of accelerated depreciation.
>
> U.S. Steel has included in wear and exhaustion in 1953, as a measure of the accelerated depreciation for the year, $105,137,893, representing amortization on its facilities covered by Certificates of Necessity.

In commenting on the effect of accelerated amortization and the tax laws, management pointed out that it had to be regarded as a temporary expedient, since "for many companies the addition of amortization on new facilities to so-called regular depreciation on old facilities may approximate, temporarily, a truer total of wear and exhaustion on all facilities based on current dollar value. But it automatically guarantees something of a future crisis." As an example of this, management cited the recently constructed Fairless Works. A portion of this plant's cost was amortized over five years, thus partially offsetting "inadequate" depreciation charges for other facilities. It was stated that this situation would naturally change when the five-year amortization was completed.

Management noted in 1954 that the new methods of accelerated depreciation, first allowed for tax purposes in 1954, would ease the future crisis, but even these provisions, applicable to new assets only, would fall far short of providing adequate depreciation on the relatively more numerous and older existing facilities.

The 1959 Strike. In 1959, management noted the approaching exhaustion of emergency amortization:

> This [depreciation] deficiency has been aggravated by the running out of 5-year amortization permitted on varying percentages of the total costs of certain defense and defense-supporting facilities covered by Certificates of Necessity. The need for revision of the tax laws as they relate to depreciation . . . continues to be most vital to the maintenance of existing and the addition of new productive capacity.

In the spring of 1959, representatives of the United Steelworkers of America and the major steel companies met to negotiate a new wage contract. The union requested sizable increases in wages and fringe benefits, contending that large steel profits would permit these increases without affecting the prices of finished steel. The steel industry spokesmen argued this was not possible; any *sizable* wage increase would have to be passed along in the form of higher prices. There was considerable government pressure for a settlement without the need for a price increase in order to avoid the threat of further inflation.

A full-page newspaper advertisement in May 1959, paid for by the union, stated that although labor costs were 42.8 percent of sales in 1958 compared with 42.1 percent in 1952, net profits had increased from $144 million to $302 million during the same period.

A nationwide steel strike lasted from July until mid-November.

On December 8, 1959, J. S. Seidman, president of the AICPA, released to the press a statement explaining the issues in the steel strike:

> The industry's contention was that under conventional accounting, depreciation is calculated based on the original dollar cost, and that this is inadequate because it fails to give effect to the tremendous change that has taken place in the purchasing power of the dollar, as a result of which it would cost many more dollars today to replace the plant than were originally spent. The industry maintains that realistic profits should be figured by reference to replacement figures. On that basis, the industry's profits are one half of what the financial statements show.
>
> The labor officials contend that original cost is all that should be recovered, and that anything in excess of that is profit. Furthermore, they say that the original cost should be spread over the expected period in which the plant will be used. However, the companies have been following the tax laws in the way they write off depreciation, and the tax laws have allowed a higher write-off to be bunched in early years and counterbalanced by a lower write-off in later years. The figures presented by the steel industry cover the earlier years where there is the higher write-off. The labor people say that the depreciation amounts should be reduced by this excess write-off in the early years. Reducing the depreciation would result in an increase in profits.
>
> . . . All of this raises a question as to whether the conventional accounting

use of historical dollars is meaningful in an inflationary period.

Investment Credit. By 1962, the inflationary pressures on the economy had diminished. Also in 1962, USS benefited from two changes in the system of federal income taxation: adoption of the new guideline lives for depreciation added $44 million to the wear and exhaustion amounts previously determined, and the use of the investment tax credit resulted in an $8.2 million reduction in federal income taxes.

The investment tax credit provided by the Revenue Act of 1962 was intended to stimulate capital investment. It allowed a credit directly against the company's federal income tax liability of 7 percent of the cost of "qualified" depreciable property. However, rather than treating this in its published financial statements as a reduction in 1962 income tax expense ("flow-through" method), USS spread the reduced taxes over the lives of the assets which qualified for the 7 percent credit ("deferral" method).

1968 Changes. During 1968, economic pressure increased on companies within the steel industry. Foreign imports of steel increased substantially. To meet the stiff price competition, many domestic producers engaged in price discounting. As a result, earnings were sharply reduced. USS 1968 third-quarter profits fell 70 percent below those of the corresponding quarter of 1967, and most other steel companies had a similar decrease.

The effect of the profit decline would have been more severe, except that many of the companies switched from accelerated to straight-line depreciation in the third quarter. Some companies applied the change only to equipment purchased after 1967; others applied it to all depreciable property on hand. Several companies also switched from deferring to flowing through their investment tax credits.

Despite these changes, USS continued to follow its policies of accelerated depreciation and deferral of the investment tax credit through the first three quarters of 1968. However, when the 1968 annual report was issued, it contained this statement:

During 1968, a number of [steel] companies announced a change in their method of determining depreciation for financial reporting purposes whereby depreciation for the year is reported on a straight-line basis rather than on the accelerated basis previously used. . . . [In 1962] U.S. Steel adopted the accounting method by which it deferred this [investment tax] credit over the lives of the properties acquired. All other major steel companies now flow the full investment credit to income as realized.

U.S. Steel considered the procedures it previously followed in connection with depreciation and the investment credit to be preferable to other methods in the reporting of results of operations. However, to enhance the comparability of financial statements in the steel industry and to bring depreciation and investment credit accounting policies more in line with methods followed by U.S. businesses in general, U.S. Steel, for financial reporting purposes, revised the lives of certain properties and changed its methods of recording depreciation and investment credit for the year 1968 to a straight-line basis and a flow-through basis, respectively. The effect of these changes was to increase reported income for the year 1968 by $94.0 million or $1.74 per share of common stock.

Accounting Series Release 190. In subsequent years, USS continued to call attention in its annual report to the inadequacies of depreciation. The following is from the 1977 annual report:

> Engineering estimates by U.S. Steel and others indicate that to replace worn-out facilities requires about three dollars for each dollar that has been allowed as a cost by taxing authorities. The allowances for the cost of depreciation have been inadequate because of the persistent inflation which has prevailed throughout this period. This erosion of capital places an extra penalty on taxpayers who have invested in long-lived facilities. This loss in purchasing power of the dollar must be made up by new borrowing and by diverting after-tax income, which should be available for dividends and for growth, to cover necessary replacements.

The 1977 report also included the chart shown in Exhibit 1.

Effective in 1976, the SEC in its *Accounting Series Release 190* required large companies to include in their 10-K report an estimate of what depreciation expense would have been if it had been calculated on the basis of the replacement cost of assets. USS reported in its 10-K report (but not in its annual report) $0.6 billion of replacement cost depreciation in 1976 and $0.8 billion in 1977 for items subject to ASR 190, compared with the $0.2 billion and $0.4 billion reported for the same items on its income statements. (The amounts were stated in tenths of billions.)

In its 1977 annual report, the following comment was made about these amounts:

> U.S. Steel's annual report on Form 10-K filed with the Securities and Exchange Commission contains quantitative replacement cost information at December 31, 1977, in accordance with SEC Accounting Series Release 190; however, these data do not provide a basis for adjusting reported net income or

EXHIBIT 1
SINCE 1955 U.S. STEEL'S CAPITAL SPENDING HAS SUBSTANTIALLY EXCEEDED WEAR AND EXHAUSTION

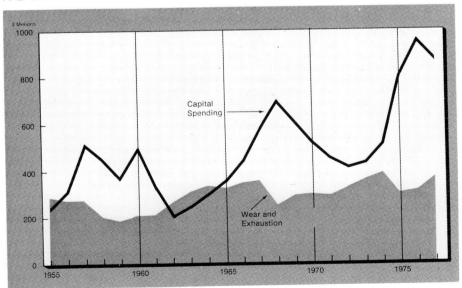

balance sheet values. The replacement costs required do not measure either the erosion in value of the dollar from inflation or the current value of the facilities presently in place. They represent only the estimated current costs of a hypothetical total replacement of productive capabilities at December 31, 1977, which could be substantially offset over the years by the lower operating costs of the more efficient replacement facilities. The required assumptions ignore the fact that the normal process of replacements necessarily takes place over a period of many years with continuing technological advance and changing economic conditions.

FASB-33. In September 1979, the FASB issued *Statement No. 33*, "Financial Reporting and Changing Prices." FASB-33 required large companies to include in their annual reports supplemental income statements employing infla-

EXHIBIT 2
SELECTED FINANCIAL STATISTICS 1946–1981
(millions of dollars)

Year	Net Income	Depreciation	Capital Expenditures	Amortization of Emergency Facilities
1981	$1,077.2	$571.0	$908.0	—
1980	504.5	523.8	752.9	—
1979	(293.0)	531.5	979.0	—
1978	242.0	435.6	667.8	—
1977	137.9	372.0	864.7	—
1976	410.3	308.6	957.3	—
1975	559.6	297.2	787.4	—
1974	630.3	385.7	508.3	—
1973	313.0	358.0	435.8	—
1972	157.0	326.6	412.8	—
1971	154.5	290.1	452.0	—
1970	147.5	296.5	514.5	—
1969	217.2	289.6	601.8	—
1968	253.7	253.1	697.4	—
1967	172.5	354.7	574.7	—
1966	249.2	344.3	440.7	—
1965	275.5	324.5	353.6	—
1964	236.8	335.8	292.6	—
1963	203.5	307.8	244.7	—
1962	163.7	265.9	200.6	—
1961	190.2	210.5	326.8	—
1960	304.2	208.4	492.4	$ 13.7
1959	254.5	189.9	366.1	22.2
1958	301.5	204.9	448.1	57.2
1957	419.4	276.0	514.9	115.8
1956	348.1	277.6	311.8	140.2
1955	370.1	285.2	239.8	147.7
1954	195.4	261.8	227.4	142.8
1953	222.1	236.6	361.4	105.1
1952	143.6	176.9	469.2	46.2
1951	184.3	162.1	352.4	12.8
1950	215.5	143.9	179.3	—
1949	165.9	119.7	179.1	—
1948	129.6	146.0	275.2	—
1947	127.1	114.0	206.6	—
1946	88.6	68.7	201.0	—

tion-adjusted amounts for cost of sales and depreciation expense. The required statements incorporated two inflation-adjusted depreciation amounts: (1) historical-cost depreciation expense restated in dollars of constant purchasing power, and (2) depreciation expense based on the current cost of the depreciable plant and equipment. (The SEC's ASR-190 requirement was suspended.) For 1979, USS reported constant-dollar and current-cost depreciation, respectively, of $859.7 million and $938.9 million; for 1980, these amounts were $910.9 million and $998.7 million; and for 1981, $1,061.6 million and $1,072.3 million. The 1979 annual report commented:

> Supplementary information of this type should be viewed with caution. . . . However, for profitable businesses having plant, equipment or inventory acquired in prior years, [income] statements of this type [using inflation-adjusted amounts for cost of sales and depreciation expense] clearly demonstrate that reported profits, and hence reported taxes, are overstated.

Also in 1979, USS changed its treatment of engineering costs associated with capital (i.e., plant and equipment) projects. Whereas USS formerly had expensed such costs as incurred, starting in 1979 it capitalized these costs as part of the total cost of the capital assets. The FASB requires that the cumulative effect on prior years' earnings of such a change be reported as an element of income in the year in which the change is made;

this cumulative effect increased 1979 reported net income by $90.4 million.

The 1980 annual report contained this comment in the section reporting FASB-33 inflation-adjusted data:

> Confiscation of private property was never contemplated by Congress. Yet, confiscation is occurring—at an accelerated pace. Inflation, when combined with our existing tax laws, is the cause.

Selected financial statistics for the company from 1946–1981 are shown in Exhibit 2.

Questions

1. Do you agree with USS's handling of depreciation in its 1947 report? Should a company be prohibited from using such a method if in its own best judgment this is the best method?

2. Do you agree with the nature and timing of the subsequent changes in depreciation method?

3. Do you agree that in 1968 USS should have changed from depreciation and investment tax credit accounting methods that it considered "preferable to other methods" in order to be comparable with their competitors' methods? Were any of the steel companies justified in making these changes in 1968?

4. Discuss the appropriateness and the timing of USS's 1979 change in the accounting for capital project engineering costs.

5. Does depreciation based on either constant-dollar costs or current costs provide more useful information to users of financial statements than depreciation based on historical costs?

CASE 7–6   Digitrex Company

Digitrex Company had developed and successfully tested a small computer that the company believed had significant ad-

vantages over other computers in its price range. Digitrex was considering marketing the computer under any of three financial arrangements, at the customer's option: (1) outright sale at $30,000, (2) a capital lease at $7,200 per year for five years, and (3) an operating lease at $7,500 per year.

Before making a final decision on the terms for each option, John Ames, financial vice president, decided to estimate the options' relative attractiveness to typical potential customers. For this purpose he devised a hypothetical company, Gamma Company, with financial statements as summarized in Exhibit 1. He assumed that except for the acquisition of a Digitrex computer, the income statements would continue unchanged for the next five years. He asked an assistant to calculate the effect on Gamma of each of the three proposed financing methods, using the following assumptions:

2. Gamma Company's effective income tax rate was 50 percent. (For simplicity, it was assumed that income taxes were paid in cash in the year in which the income tax expense was applicable.)

3. If Gamma purchased the computer, it could take an investment tax credit in 19x2 of $2,000; Gamma used the flow-through method to report such credits. Gamma would depreciate the $30,000 cost on the sum-of-the-years'-digits basis over five years, both for income tax purposes and for its financial statements. It would pay the $30,000 in cash on January 2, 19x2. (Mr. Ames decided not to complicate the calculations by including the possibility that Gamma would borrow part of the purchase price.)

EXHIBIT 1
GAMMA CORPORATION FINANCIAL STATEMENTS
(thousands of dollars)

Balance Sheet
As of December 31, 19x1

Assets			Equities		
Current assets.............		$200	Current liabilities..................		$100
Plant and equipment.......	$600		Long-term debt...................		100
Accumulated depreciation..	300		Shareholders' equity..............		300
Plant and equip., net.....		300			
Total assets..............		$500	Total equities....................		$500

Income Statement for 19x1

Sales revenue	$1,000
Expenses unrelated to computer.....................	900
Pretax margin unrelated to computer.................	100
Computer depreciation	0
Computer interest and lease expense.................	0
Income before income taxes	100
Provision for income taxes	50
Net income.......................................	$ 50

1. The computer would be acquired on January 2, 19x2 (i.e., at the start of the year; January 1 is a legal holiday).

4. If Gamma leased the computer on a capital lease, it would make five annual payments, each of $7,200, with

the first on January 2, 19x2. These payments were assumed to be treated in the same way for both income tax purposes and financial reporting purposes. Digitrex would retain rights to the investment tax credit on all leased computers. For income tax and financial reporting purposes, the interest component of the five annual payments was as follows: 19x2, $2,291; 19x3, $1,797; 19x4, $1,255; 19x5, $657; and 19x6, $0.[1]

5. If Gamma leased the machine on an operating lease, it would make an-

nual payments of $7,500 starting on January 2, 19x2. Gamma could return the computer to Digitrex without further obligation at the end of any year.

Questions

1. For each of the three alternatives, estimate Gamma Company's balance sheet as of January 2, 19x2 (immediately after the acquisition of the computer), and its income statement for each of the years 19x2 through 19x6. Round all numbers to the nearest $100.

2. Are either or both of the lease alternatives so unattractive, as compared with outright purchase, that it would be a waste of effort for Digitrex to attempt to lease the computers?

---

[1]These amounts were determined by using techniques that are described in the Appendix to Chapter 8.

8

Liabilities and Interest Expense

This chapter begins a more detailed description of the equities side of the balance sheet. In this chapter we discuss liabilities and the related interest expense. Chapter 9 includes a discussion of owners' equity. As mentioned in Chapter 2, liabilities and owners' equity represent the sources of the funds that have been used in acquiring the entity's assets. The process of identifying the needs for new funds and acquiring these funds is part of the function known as *financial management*. The treasurer and other executives who are responsible for financial affairs in a company need much technical knowledge about the various means of raising money, the legal and tax rules relating to financing, and so on. Other members of management should have a general understanding of these matters, even though they scarcely can be expected to be conversant with all the details.

This chapter discusses the accounting aspects of liabilities at a level that is intended to provide a general understanding to the nonfinancial manager. In the typical company, arranging new sources of long-term liabilities is an event that occurs infrequently; but when it does occur, it is likely to have a major impact on the financial statements.

The Appendix to the chapter introduces the concept of present value, which is a fundamental concept in the balance sheet valuation of liabilities.

NATURE OF LIABILITIES

In Chapter 2, a liability was defined as an obligation to an outside party. This definition is approximately correct. However, some legal obligations to outside parties are not liabilities in the accounting meaning of this word; and some accounting liabilities are not legally enforceable obligations.

As an example of an obligation that is not a liability, consider the case of an employee who has a written contract guaranteeing employment at a stated salary for the next two years (e.g., professional athletes, coaches, executives). Such a contract is called an *executory contract*; the services specified in the contract will be performed, or executed, at some future time. An executory contract is a legally enforceable claim against the entity as soon as it has been signed, but is is *not* a liability in the accounting sense at that time. The transaction is recorded in the accounts only when the person actually performs the work.

What distinguishes such a contract from those that do give rise to liabilities? Essentially, the distinction is determined by whether or not there is an asset or expense debit to offset the liability credit. When an employee works, the credit to the liability Accrued Wages Payable is offset by the debit to Wages Expense. But when a contract is signed covering *future* employment, no expense account in the current period is affected, nor is an asset created. A liability is not created until the services have been performed.

An estimated allowance for future costs under a warranty agreement is an example of a liability that is not a definite obligation at the time it is set up. When a warranty agreement applies, the liability account is set up in the period in which the revenue is recognized, the offsetting debit being to an expense account such as Estimated Warranty Expense. Later on, when repairs or replacements under warranty are made, the liability account will be debited and other balance sheet accounts such as Parts Inventory will be credited.

Contingencies

A contingency is an occurrence that might arise in the future. Under some circumstances, events that happen in the current period create contingencies that are liabilities; under other circumstances, no liability is recognized. Although the line is by no means clear-cut, the general rule is that a liability is recognized (with an offsetting debit to an expense account) when:

> (a) Information available prior to issuance of the financial statements indicates that it is probable that an asset had been impaired or a liability had been incurred . . . and
>
> (b) The amount of loss can be reasonably estimated.[1]

---

[1]"Accounting for Contingencies," *FASB Statement No. 5*, March 1975, par. 8. See also "Reasonable Estimation of the Amount of a Loss," *FASB Interpretation No. 14*, September 1976.

For example, assume that during the period a lawsuit claiming damages has been filed against a company, or that the Internal Revenue Service has claimed additional income taxes. If the company concludes that there is a reasonable possibility of losing the lawsuit or of having to pay more taxes, *and* if the amount can reasonably be estimated, a liability is recognized. Even if a lawsuit has not been actually filed but the company believes it probable that one will be filed, there is a liability. If the amount of the probable loss can be estimated only within a range, the lower end of this range is the amount of the liability. The possible loss above this lower limit is disclosed in notes to the financial statements, but it is not recorded in the accounts.

> **Example.** A company's internal auditor discovered that an employee had made errors in calculating the amount of customs duties due on imported merchandise, with resulting underpayments totaling $100,000. The company immediately paid the $100,000 to the government. The penalty would be at the discretion of the court, with a maximum of 10 times the value of the merchandise. In this instance, the maximum penalty could be $30 million. On the other hand, there would be no penalty if the court decided that the error was not willful. Based on the experience of other companies with similar customs violations, the company decided that the lower limit of the probable range of penalties was $300,000 and recorded this amount as a liability and an expense. It disclosed the possibility of paying up to $30 million in a note accompanying its balance sheet.

A company is said to be "contingently liable" if it has guaranteed payment of a loan made to a third party. But this is not a liability, in the accounting sense, unless available information indicates that the borrower has defaulted or will probably default. The possibility of loss from future earthquakes or other natural catastrophes is not a liability because the events have not yet happened.

Liabilities as a Source of Funds

As described in Chapter 2, current liabilities are those that are to be satisfied in the near future. One noteworthy aspect of current liabilities is that they often provide funds to the company at no cost. For example, if suppliers permit a company to pay for materials or supplies within 30 days, this credit policy results in an interest-free 30-day loan to the company. Similarly, prepaid rental revenue to a property owner is, in effect, an interest-free loan from the renter. Also, the deferred income tax liability (see Chapter 9) is, in effect, an interest-free loan from the government.

With these exceptions, a company pays for the use of the capital that others furnish. Capital obtained from borrowing is called *debt capital*. Capital obtained from shareholders, either as a direct contribution or indirectly as retained earnings, is called *equity capital*.

DEBT CAPITAL

The debt instruments that a firm uses to obtain capital can be classified generally as either term loans or bonds.

Term Loans

A term loan is a business loan repayable according to a specified schedule, usually with equal installments of principal and interest. The lender is usually a bank or an insurance company. Ordinarily, a company's obligation to repay a term loan extends over a period of several years, making the loan a noncurrent liability. For major corporations, bonds (described below) are a more important source of debt capital than are term loans.

Bonds

A *bond* is a certificate promising to pay its holder a specified sum of money plus interest at a stated rate. Although bonds are usually issued in units of $1,000, the *price* of a bond is usually quoted as a percentage of this face value; thus, a price of 100 means $1,000. Bonds may be issued to the general public through the intermediary of an investment banker, or they may be privately placed with an insurance company or other financial institution.

Long-term creditors usually require the borrowing corporation to maintain certain minimum financial ratios and to refrain from taking actions that might endanger the safety of the money loaned. These requirements, called *covenants*, are spelled out in the loan or bond *indenture*, usually a lengthy document. If any of these covenants is not lived up to, the loan or bond is technically in *default*, and the creditors can require repayment immediately. In the event of default, however, creditors are more likely to require changes in the management or take other corrective action, rather than demand immediate repayment.

A *mortgage bond* (or simply "mortgage") is a bond secured by designated "pledged" assets of the corporation, usually property, plant, and equipment assets. Should the firm default on the mortgage, the pledged assets are sold to repay the mortgage. If the proceeds from the sale of the pledged assets are less than the amount of the mortgage, then the mortgage holder becomes a general creditor for the shortfall. If the bond is not secured by specific assets of the issuing corporation, it is referred to as a *debenture*.

Bond Redemption.   In an ordinary bond issue, the principal amount is paid in one lump sum at the maturity date. In order to accumulate cash for this purpose, the company may be required to deposit money regularly in a sinking fund. Bonds that have such a requirement are *sinking fund bonds*. Sinking funds may be used to redeem outstanding bonds at regular intervals, either by buying them in the open market or by redeeming certain bonds that are randomly selected. Bond sinking funds may be controlled by the originating corporation, but they are usually controlled by a trustee, such as a bank. Prior to maturity, sinking funds are invested by the trustee so as to earn interest on the funds thus tied up. Sinking funds usually appear in the investment section of the assets side of the balance sheet.

Serial bonds are also redeemed in installments. The redemption date for each bond in the bond issue is specified on the bond itself. Often there are slight differences in the interest rate of the various maturities in an issue of serial bonds. The principal difference between a sinking fund bond and a serial bond is that holders of serial bonds know the date when their bonds will be redeemed, whereas holders of sinking fund bonds do not. The latter may end up holding their bonds to maturity, or their bonds may be randomly selected for redemption by the sinking fund at some earlier time.

A bond may also be *callable*; that is, the issuing corporation may, at its option, call the bonds for redemption before the maturity date. If this is done, the corporation usually must pay a premium for the privilege.

Other Features of Bonds. Some bonds are *convertible*; that is, they may be exchanged for a specified number of shares of the corporation's stock if the bondholder elects to do so. Sinking fund bonds and serial bonds may also be callable, convertible, or both.

Finally, some bonds (and also some term loans) are *subordinated*. In the event a company goes bankrupt and is liquidated, the claims of the subordinated debtholders are subordinate (inferior) to the claims of any general or secured creditors. However, subordinated creditors' claims take precedence over those of the company's shareholders (equity investors).

Recording a Bond Issue

To illustrate the entries typically made to record the proceeds from an issue of bonds, assume Mason Corporation issues 100 bonds, each with a *par value* (also called *principal* or *face value*) of $1,000, with a stated interest rate (also called *nominal* or *coupon rate*) of 12 percent ($120 per year), payable in 20 years, and not secured by any specific Mason Corporation assets. Such a bond would be called a "12 percent, 20-year debenture." If the corporation receives $1,000 for each of these bonds, the following entry would be made:

```
Cash ..........................................  100,000
     Bonds Payable ............................           100,000
```

(The account title in practice describes the essential characteristics of the bond. It is abbreviated here for simplicity.)

Discount and Premium. Frequently bonds are issued for less than their par value, that is, at a *discount*, or for more than their par value, at a *premium*. This happens when the prevailing interest rate or "yield" at the time of issuance is different from the *coupon* rate, that is, the rate printed on the bond.

> **Example.** If the prevailing rate of interest in the bond market is more than 12 percent for bonds with a risk similar to those issued by Mason Corporation, potential investors will be unwilling to give $1,000 for a Mason Corporation 12 percent bond.[2] They would be willing to give an amount such that the $120 annual interest on this bond would yield the market rate of interest. Assume that this rate is 14 percent. The bond would therefore be sold at a price of $868, or at a discount of $132.[3]

The words *discount* and *premium* carry no connotation of "bad" or "good." They reflect simply a difference between the coupon interest rate for the issue and the going market rate of interest at the time of issuance. The stated rate may be made intentionally different from the going rate in the belief that this makes the bonds more attractive. The coupon rate also may differ from the going rate because of changed market conditions between the time the coupon rate is established and the time the bond becomes available to investors. Usually, the coupon rate is quite close to the market rate as of the date of issue. In recent years, however, some companies have issued bonds at a coupon rate of zero. These are called *deep discount* bonds.

The discount or premium is a function only of the interest rates prevailing at the time of issuance of the bonds. Subsequent changes in the level of interest rates (and hence in bond prices) do not affect the amount recorded in the accounts.

Issuance Costs. The offering of a bond issue to the public is usually undertaken by an investment banking firm that charges the corporation a fee for this service. In addition to this fee, the corporation also incurs printing, legal, and accounting costs in connection with the bond issue. These bond issuance costs are set up as a deferred charge, which is an asset, and the asset is amortized over the life of the issue.[4] The premium or discount does not include the issue costs; rather it is based on the difference between the amount given for the bond by the investor and the face value of the bond.

---

[2]Although one speaks of investors "paying" for a newly issued bond and of corporations "selling" their bonds, it should be made clear that a bond is *not* an asset of the corporation that is sold, as are goods. Rather bonds are evidence of a contribution of funds to the firm by investors. To the investor, the bond *is* an asset, and it can be sold to another investor. Such a sale has no impact on the flow of funds into or out of the firm, however. (Similar comments apply to new issues of stock.)

[3]The method of making this calculation is described in the Appendix to this chapter.

[4]"Interest on Receivables and Payables," *APB Opinion No. 21*, August 1971, par. 16.

Example. Mason Corporation's bonds, which brought $868 each from investors, also had issue costs to Mason averaging $28 per bond, resulting in a net cash inflow to Mason of $840 per bond. The discount is $132 per bond, not $160.

Accounting Entries. If the conditions of the preceding examples are assumed, and Mason Corporation received $84,000 from the issuance of $100,000 face amount of bonds, the following entry would be made:

```
Cash ........................................  84,000
Bond Discount ..............................  13,200
Deferred Charges ...........................   2,800
    Bonds Payable ...........................          100,000
```

If the corporation received more than the face amount, say $110,000, the corresponding entry would be:

```
Cash ........................................ 110,000
Deferred Charges ...........................   2,800
    Bond Premium ............................           12,800
    Bond Payable ............................          100,000
```

Balance Sheet Presentation

Bonds payable are shown in the long-term liabilities section of the balance sheet until one year before they mature, when ordinarily they become current liabilities. The description should give the principal facts about the issue, for example, "12 percent debentures due 2003." When a bond issue is to be refunded with a new long-term liability, however, it is not shown as a current liability in the year of maturity since it will not require the use of current assets. If the bonds are to be retired in installments (as with serial bonds), that portion to be retired within a year is shown in the current liabilities section.

Bond discount or premium is shown on the balance sheet as a direct deduction from or addition to the face amount of the bond, as illustrated:[5]

If a Discount		*If a Premium*	
Bonds payable:		Bonds payable:	
Principal..................	$100,000	Principal..................	$100,000
Less: Unamortized		Add: Unamortized	
discount................	13,200	premium................	12,800
	$86,800		$112,800

The principal amount less unamortized discount or plus unamortized premium is sometimes referred to as the *book value* of the bond.

---

[5]Ibid. *APB Opinion No. 21* also requires disclosure of the "effective" rate of interest on the bond (determined using techniques described in the Appendix to this chapter).

Bond Interest　　　　An accounting entry is made to record the periodic (usually semiannual) interest payments to bondholders and at the same time to amortize a portion of the bond premium or discount. The effect of this entry is that the *net* debit to Interest Expense reflects not the stated amount of interest actually paid to bondholders (unless the holders paid par for the issue) but rather the *effective* rate of interest, which is larger or smaller than the stated rate, according to whether the bonds were sold at a discount or at a premium. The existence of bond discount in effect increases the interest expense above the stated rate, while the existence of bond premium decreases it.

Bond discount or premium normally is amortized using the compound interest method (described in this chapter's Appendix). With this method, the discount or premium is written off in such a way that the *net* interest expense bears a constant ratio to the book value of the bonds over the whole life of the issue. This ratio is the effective interest rate on the borrowed funds. In the Mason example, if the bonds were sold for $868 each, this rate (yield) is 14 percent.

The following entry records a semiannual bond interest payment and amortization of discount for the 12 percent Mason Corporation bonds that were assumed to have been issued for $868 each:

```
Bond Interest Expense .......................  6,076
     Bond Discount ............................            76
     Cash .....................................         6,000
```

The cash paid out as stated interest is $6,000, which is 12 percent × $100,000 × ½ year. The $76 credit to Bond Discount is determined using the compound interest method.[6] The net interest expense is the sum of these amounts.

Adjusting Entries. If the interest payment date does not coincide with the closing of the company's books, an adjusting entry is made to record accrued interest expense and the amortization of discount or premium. To illustrate, assume that the Mason Corporation bonds are issued for $868 each on September 30, that the interest dates are September 30 and March 31, and that the fiscal year ends on December 31. The following entries would be made:

1. Adjustment on December 31 to record one-fourth year's interest accrued since September 30:

---

[6]The yield rate is 14 percent. Therefore, the *net* interest expense for six months is: 14 percent × $86,800 × ½ year = $6,076. Since $6,000 of this is the *stated* interest payment, the remaining $76 is discount amortization. After this entry, the bonds' book value will be $86,876. Thus, the next six months' discount amortization will be: 14 percent × $86,876 × ½ year − $6,000 = $81. The following six months' discount amortization will be: 14 percent × $86,957 × ½ year − $6,000 = $87; and so on.

```
Bond Interest Expense ...................   3,038
    Bond Discount .........................           38
    Accrued Interest Payable ..............        3,000
```

2. Payment of semiannual interest on March 31; entry to record one-fourth year's interest expense and one-half year's payment:

```
Bond Interest Expense ..................   3,038
Accrued Interest Payable ...............   3,000
    Bond Discount .........................           38
    Cash ..................................        6,000
```

3. Payment of semiannual interest on the following September 30:

```
Bond Interest Expense ...................   6,081
    Bond Discount .........................           81
    Cash ..................................        6,000
```

Bond issuance costs, which are treated as a deferred charge, are usually amortized on a straight-line basis. For example, for a 20-year bond, ¹⁄₂₀th of the issuance costs would be charged to expense each year.

Retirement of Bonds

Bonds may be retired in total, or they may be retired in installments over a period of years (i.e., as with sinking fund or serial bonds). In either case, the retirement is recorded by a debit to Bonds Payable and a credit to Cash, or to a sinking fund that has been set up for this purpose. The bond discount or premium will have been completely amortized by the maturity date, so no additional entry is required for discount or premium at that time.

Refunding a Bond Issue

Callable bonds can be redeemed before their maturity dates by paying investors more than the bonds' par value. In periods when interest rates have declined, a company may consider it advantageous to *refund* a bond issue, that is, to call the old issue and issue a new one with a lower rate of interest. At that point, the company must account for the *call premium* (the difference between the call price and par value), any other costs of the refunding, and any unamortized issue costs and discount (or premium) on the old bonds.

The bonds' face amount, adjusted for unamortized premium or discount and costs of issuance, is called the *net carrying amount* of the debt to be refunded. The amount paid on refunding, including the call premium and miscellaneous costs of refunding, is called the *reacquisition price*. The difference between these two amounts must be reported as a separate loss or gain on the income statement for the period in which the refunding takes place.[7]

Example.   Suppose that the 100 Mason Corporation bonds are called at the end of five years by paying the call price of the bonds at that time, $1,050 per bond, to each bondholder. Assume that miscellaneous refunding costs are $1,000. Also, much of the bond discount and issuance costs will not have been amortized. The $12,290 of unamortized discount is determined using the compound interest method. Unamortized bond issuance costs after five years (one quarter of the bonds' scheduled life) would be: ¾ × $2,800 = $2,100. The loss is determined as follows:

Reacquisition price = $105,000 + $1,000		$106,000
Net carrying amount:		
Face value	$100,000	
Less: Unamortized discount	(12,290)	
Less: Unamortized issuance costs	(2,100)	85,610
Loss on retirement of bonds		$ 20,390

The accounting entries are:

Bonds Payable	100,000	
Loss on Retirement of Bonds	20,390	
Cash		106,000
Bond Discount		12,290
Deferred Charges (issuance costs)		2,100

OTHER LIABILITIES

This chapter thus far has focused on debt capital—long-term loans and bonds. Current liabilities, which are relatively straightforward, were discussed in Chapter 2. Two other liabilities are of importance to many corporations: leases and deferred taxes. Leases are discussed below. Deferred taxes, which are a controversial and complicated topic, are described in Chapter 9.

Capital Leases: Lessee Accounting

Capital leases were described in Chapter 7 from the standpoint of determining the lessee's balance sheet asset amount for property or equipment that an entity has, in effect, purchased by using a lease as the financing vehicle. This asset amount is the present value of the stream of minimum lease payments that the lessee will make to the lessor.

The lessee's liability to make these lease payments is initially shown on the liability side of its balance sheet at the same present value amount

---

[7]"Early Extinguishment of Debt," *APB Opinion No. 26,* October 1972, par. 20. *FASB Statement No. 4,* "Reporting Gains and Losses from Extinguishment of Debt" (March 1975), requires that such a gain or loss be reported as an *extraordinary* gain or loss, below income from operations, on the income statement. (Extraordinary items are discussed in Chapter 9.)

as is shown for the leased items on the asset side. However, after the inception of the lease, amortization of the asset and liability amounts differs. The asset is amortized using the same depreciation method as the lessee uses for other items of plant and equipment. The lease liability is amortized (reduced) by dividing each payment into an interest expense component and a lease liability or "principal" reduction component, using the techniques described in the Appendix.

> **Example.** Talbot Corporation leased equipment requiring annual payments of $5,966 a year for five years. The lease met the criteria for a capital lease. The appropriate discount rate for Talbot to use to find the present value of this lease was 15 percent. As demonstrated in the Appendix, the present value of these lease payments discounted at 15 percent is $20,000. The initial entry to record the transaction is:

```
Equipment ............................... 20,000
    Capital Lease Obligations ............        20,000
```

> If Talbot uses the straight-line depreciation method, and if the equipment has a five-year useful life, for each of the five years there will be the following entry:

```
Depreciation Expense ....................  4,000
    Accumulated Depreciation ............         4,000
```

> The lease obligation will be reduced using the schedule shown in Illustration 8–1 in the Appendix. The entry for the first year to record interest expense and reduction of the lease liability is:

```
Interest Expense ........................  3,000
Capital Lease Obligations ...............  2,966
    Cash ................................          5,966
```

This makes the amount of the lease obligation at the end of the first year equal to $17,034 (= $20,000 − $2,966).

The 15 percent discount rate used by the lessee (Talbot Corporation) in the example is the lessee's incremental borrowing rate. This is the rate the lessee would have had to incur to borrow over a similar term the funds necessary to purchase the leased asset.[8]

Capital Leases: Lessor Accounting

One might think that lessor accounting for a capital lease uses the same amounts as the lessee uses in accounting for the same lease. However, this is not the case.

Classification as a Capital Lease. Chapter 7 described four criteria, any one of which can require a lease to be treated as a capital lease by the *lessee*. The *lessor* treats the lease as a capital lease also if any of

---

[8]"Accounting for Leases," *FASB Statement No. 13*, November 1976.

those four criteria are met, *and* if *both* of the following conditions are also met: (1) collection of the minimum lease payments is reasonably predictable and (2) no important uncertainties exist for unreimbursable costs yet to be incurred by the lessor under the lease.[9]

From the standpoint of the lessor, capital leases are categorized as being either *sales-type* leases or *direct financing* leases. Sales-type leases give rise to a manufacturer's or dealer's profit to the lessor. They arise when the lessor is a manufacturer or dealer using a lease as a means of marketing its products. If the lessor is primarily involved in financing operations, then normally the lease will be classified as a direct financing lease. The lessor's detailed accounting for both categories of capital leases is complicated and beyond the scope of this introductory text.

Operating Leases   Leases not meeting *FASB Statement No. 13* criteria for capital leases are classified as *operating leases*. A lessee records neither an asset nor a liability on an operating lease. As lease payments (generally called *rental* payments for an operating lease) are made by the lessee, Rental Expense is debited and Cash is credited. The lessor depreciates the leased asset like other productive assets and records the lessee's payments as revenue in the periods in which the payments are received.

ANALYSIS OF CAPITAL RELATIONSHIPS

Debt/Equity Raios   The relative amount of a company's capital that was obtained from various sources is a matter of great importance in analyzing the soundness of the company's financial position. In illustrating the ratios intended for this purpose, the following summary of the equities side of a company's balance sheet will be used:

	Dollars (in millions)	Per-cent
Current liabilities	$ 60	26
Long-term liabilities	40	17
Shareholders' equity	130	57
Total equities	$230	100

Attention is often focused on the sources of *permanent* capital, that is, long-term liabilities and shareholders' equity, which are often referred to respectively as debt capital and equity capital. From the point

[9]*FASB Statement No. 13*, par. 8. Important uncertainties might include extensive warranties or protection of the lessee from obsolescence of the leased property.

of view of the company, debt capital is risky because if bondholders and other creditors are not paid promptly, they can take legal action to obtain payment. Such action can, in extreme cases, force the company into bankruptcy. Equity capital is much less risky to the company because shareholders receive dividends only at the discretion of the directors and the shareholders cannot force bankruptcy.[10] Because the shareholders have less certainty of receiving dividends than the bondholders have of receiving interest, shareholders usually are unwilling to invest in a company unless they see a reasonable expectation of making a higher return (dividends plus stock price appreciation) than they could obtain as bondholders. That is, investors would be unwilling to give up the relatively certain prospect of receiving 11 percent or 12 percent interest on bonds, unless the probable, but less certain, return on an equity investment were considerably higher, say, 15 percent or more.

Leverage. From the company's standpoint, the greater the proportion of its invested capital that is obtained from shareholders, the less worry the company has in meeting its fixed obligations. But in return for this lessened worry, the company must expect to pay a higher overall cost of obtaining its capital. Conversely, the more funds that are obtained from bonds, the more the company can use debt funds obtained at relatively low cost in the hopes of earning more on these funds for the shareholders.

The relatively low cost of debt capital arises not only from the fact that investors typically are willing to accept a lower return on bonds than on stocks but also because bond interest is tax deductible to the corporation, while dividends are not. Assuming a 46 percent tax rate, for every $1 that a company pays out in interest, it receives a tax saving of $0.46. Thus, its net cost is only 54 percent of the stated interest rate. Capital obtained from a bond issue with a yield of 12 percent therefore costs the company only about 6½ percent. By contrast, if equity investors require a return of 15 percent, the cost of obtaining equity capital is the full 15 percent.

A company with a high proportion of long-term debt is said to be highly *leveraged*. The debt/equity ratio shows the balance that the management of a particular company has struck between these forces of risk versus cost.

Calculating the Debt/Equity Ratio. The debt/equity ratio is often called simply the *debt ratio*. Unfortunately, it may be calculated in several ways. Debt may be defined as total liabilities, as interest-bearing current liabilities plus noncurrent liabilities, or as only noncurrent liabilities. The user must always be careful to ascertain which method is

---

[10]Note that "risk" is here viewed from the standpoint of the company. From the standpoint of investors, the opposite situation prevails. Thus bondholders have a relatively low risk of not receiving their payments, and stockholders have a relatively high risk. From this latter standpoint, equity capital is called *risk capital*.

used in a given situation. Including current liabilities, the debt/equity ratio for the illustrative company is:

$$\frac{\text{Total liabilities}}{\text{Shareholders' equity}} = \frac{\$100}{\$130} = 77 \text{ percent}$$

Excluding current liabilities, the ratio is:

$$\frac{\text{Long-term liabilities}}{\text{Shareholders' equity}} = \frac{\$40}{\$130} = 31 \text{ percent}$$

The relationship may also be expressed as the ratio of long-term debt to total capital, that is, debt plus equity. This ratio is called the *debt/capitalization ratio*. For our illustrative company, it is the ratio of $40 to $170, or 24 percent. The ratio varies widely among industries, but in the majority of industrial companies it is considerably below 50 percent.

Times Interest Earned

Another measure of a company's financial soundness is the relationship of a company's income to its interest requirements. The numerator of this ratio is the company's income *before* subtraction of interest expense, and also before income taxes. Assuming that for our illustrative company this amount was $43, and that interest expense was $6, the calculation is:

$$\text{Times interest earned} = \frac{\text{Income before interest}}{\text{Interest expense}} = \frac{\$43}{\$6} = 7.2 \text{ times}$$

In this example, interest requirements are said to be *covered* 7.2 times. This ratio is a measure of the level to which income can decline without impairing the company's ability to meet interest payments on its liabilities. Income is taken before income taxes because if income declined, income taxes would decline correspondingly. The ratio implies that income is equivalent to additional cash, which is not necessarily the case, of course.

A company may have fixed obligations in addition to its interest payments, as, for example, when it has payment commitments on leased assets. In such a case, coverage is properly computed by adding these other obligations to the amount of interest, but excluding them from the earnings figure in the numerator, just as interest expense was not included when interest coverage was calculated. The ratio is then labeled *Times Fixed Charges Earned* or *Fixed Charges Coverage*.

SUMMARY

Equities consist of current liabilities, other liabilities (primarily long-term debt), and owners' equity. Current liabilities are distinguished from other liabilities by their time horizon (one year or less). Liabilities are distinguished from owners' equity by their nature as obligations to outside parties. Collectively the equities represent the sources of the funds that are invested in the firm's assets.

The liability arising from the sale of bonds is shown at its face amount, and the difference between this amount and the amount given by the investors for the bonds is recorded as bond premium or discount. Premium or discount is amortized over the life of the issue. This amortization is combined with the periodic interest payments to give the effective interest expense of each period.

If a company has leased equipment but the lease is, in effect, a vehicle to finance the purchase of the equipment, then this capital lease obligation is reported (at its present value) as a liability. Future payments under operating leases are not reported by the lessee as a liability.

Important debt-related ratios are debt/equity, debt/capitalization, and interest coverage.

SUGGESTIONS FOR FURTHER READING

Hawkins, David F. *Corporate Financial Reporting: Text and Cases.* Rev. ed. Homewood, Ill.: Richard D. Irwin, 1977.

Van Horne, James C. *Financial Management and Policy.* 5th ed. Englewood Cliffs, N.J.: Prentice-Hall, 1980.

Welsch, Glenn A.; Charles T. Zlatkovich; and Walter T. Harrison, Jr. *Intermediate Accounting,* chaps. 5, 10, and 17. 6th ed. Homewood, Ill.; Richard D. Irwin, 1982.

Weston, J. Fred, and Eugene F. Brigham. *Managerial Finance.* 7th ed. Hinsdale, Ill.: Dryden Press, 1981.

Seidler, Lee J., and Carmichael, D. R., eds. *Accountants' Handbook.* 6th ed. New York: Ronald Press, 1981.

APPENDIX: PRESENT VALUE

The concept of present value underlies the balance sheet amounts shown for many liabilities. The concept is also applied in valuing certain assets (particularly those of banks) and in analyzing proposals to acquire new long-lived assets. These asset acquisition proposals are called *capital investment decisions* and are described in detail in Chapter 22.

The Concept of Present Value

Many people have difficulty understanding the present value concept because it differs from a notion they are taught as children. Our parents teach us that is a good thing to put money into a piggy bank. We are congratulated when the bank is finally opened and the accumulated coins are counted. Thus, parents teach their children that it is better to have a given amount of money in the future than to use that money today. Stated more formally, parents teach that a dollar received at some future time is more valuable than a dollar received today.

Business managers think differently, however. They expect a dollar invested today to *increase in amount* as time passes because they expect to earn a profit on that investment. It follows that an amount of money available for investment today is more valuable to the manager than an equal amount that will not be available until some future time. This is because money available today can be invested to earn still more money, whereas money not yet received obviously cannot be invested today. To the manager, therefore, the value of a given amount of money today is more than the value of the same amount received at some future time.

Compound Interest. To make the idea of present value more concrete, consider first the idea of *compound interest.* Suppose we invest $1,000 in a savings account that pays interest of 10 percent compounded annually. (Interest is invariably stated at an annual rate; thus, "10 percent" means 10 percent per year.) "Compounded annually" means that interest we earn the first year is retained in the account and earns interest along with the initial $1,000 in the second year; and so on for future years. If we make no withdrawals from this account, over time the account balance will grow as shown below:

Year	Beginning-of-Year Balance	Interest Earned	End-of-Year Balance
1	$1,000.00	$100.00	$1,100.00
2	1,100.00	110.00	1,210.00
3	1,210.00	121.00	1,331.00
4	1,331.00	133.10	1,464.10
5	1,464.10	146.41	1,610.51
⋮	⋮	⋮	⋮
10	2,357.95	235.79	2,593.74

Based on this table, one can make such a statement as: "One thousand dollars invested today at 10 percent interest, compounded annually, will accumulate to $2,593.74 after 10 years." An equivalent statement is that the *future value* of $1,000 invested for 10 years at 10 percent interest is $2,593.74.

Rather than obtaining a future value *(FV)* from a table, it can be calculated using the compound interest formula:

$$FV = p(1 + i)^n$$

where

$$p = \text{"principal" (initial investment)}$$
$$i = \text{interest rate}$$
$$n = \text{number of periods}$$

Thus, the future value of $1,000 invested at 10 percent for 10 years is given by:[11]

$$FV = \$1,000\ (1.10)^{10} = \$2,593.74$$

Discounting. To arrive at *present values*, we "reverse" the future value concept. Reversing interest compounding is called *discounting*. For example, if the future value of $1,000 at 10 percent interest for 10 years is $2,593.74, then we can also say that the *present value* of $2,593.74 discounted at 10 percent for 10 years is $1,000. The interest rate (10 percent in the example) in present value problems is commonly referred to as the *discount rate* or the *rate of return*.

This illustration leads to a more formal definition of present value:

The present value of an amount that is expected to be received at a specified time in the future is the amount which if invested today at a designated rate of return would cumulate to the specified amount.

Thus, assuming a 10 percent rate of return, the present value of $2,593.74 to be received 10 years hence is $1,000, because (as we have illustrated) if $1,000 were invested today at 10 percent, it would cumulate to $2,593.74 after 10 years.

Finding Present Values

The present value (*PV*) of an amount *p* to be received *n* years hence, discounted at a rate of *i*, is given by the formula:

$$PV = \frac{p}{(1 + i)^n}$$

Table A (p. 961) is a table of present values that were derived from this formula. The amounts in such a table are expressed as the present value of *one* dollar to be received some number of years hence, discounted at some rate. Thus, reading from Table A, we can see that the present value of $1 to be received 10 years hence, discounted at 10 percent, is $0.386. We can use our previous illustration to verify this: since the present value of $2,593.74 discounted at 10 percent for 10 years is $1,000, then

---

[11]Interest may be compounded more frequently than once a year. Interest on bonds, for example, is usually compounded semiannually because interest payments are made twice a year. In such a case, both the number of periods and the rate per period must be converted to the period used in compounding. For example, with quarterly compounding, the number of periods is 40 (i.e., 40 quarters in 10 years), and the interest rate *per quarter* is 2.5 percent (= 10% ÷ 4). Thus, the future value is $1,000(1.025)^{40} = \$2,685.06$.

The results of the formulas given in this chapter are available in published tables. Also, the formulas are programmed into many models of hand-held calculators. Readers who work the examples on their calculators (as you are encouraged to do) may find that the results differ slightly from those in the examples. This is because the examples use rates that are rounded, whereas a calculator makes more exact calculations.

the present value of *one* dollar discounted at 10 percent for 10 years should be $1,000 ÷ $2,593.74 = $0.385544, which rounds to $0.386.

To find the present value of an amount other than one dollar, one multiplies the amount by the appropriate present value factor from Table A.

> **Example.** To find the *PV* of $400 to be received 12 years hence, discounted at a rate of 15 percent, we first find the 12 year/15 percent factor from Table A: 0.187. Hence the *PV* of $400 is $400 × 0.187 = $74.80. This means that $74.80 invested today at a return of 15 percent will cumulate to $400 by the end of 12 years.

Inspection of Table A reveals two basic points about present value:

1. Present value decreases as the number of years in the future in which the payment is to be received increases.
2. Present value decreases as the discount rate increases.

Present Value of a Series of Payments

In many business situations, the entity expects to receive a series of payments over a period of several years, rather than simply receiving a single amount at some future point. The present value of a series of payments is found by summing the present values of the individual payments. Computational procedures generally assume that each payment in the series is to be received at the *end* of its respective period, rather than in a continuous flow during the period.

> **Example.** Using an 18 percent discount rate, what is the present value of the following series of payments: year 1, $1,000; year 2, $1,500; year 3, $2,000; and year 4, $2,500?
>
> Solution:

Year	Payment	Discount Factor (Table A)	Present Value
1	$1,000	0.847	$ 847
2	1,500	0.718	1,077
3	2,000	0.609	1,218
4	2,500	0.516	1,290
		Present value of the series:	$4,432

Equal Payments. In many situations, such as the repayment of loans, the series of payments are equal amounts each period. (Technically, such a series of equal payments is called an *annuity*.) If the payments are $1,750 per year for four years, then the present value of the series would be ($1,750 × 0.847) + ($1,750 × 0.718) + ($1,750 × 0.609) + ($1,750 × 0.516) = $1,750 × 2.690 = $4,707.50.

Rather than look up discount factors for each year in such a problem, one can use a table such as Table B on page 962. In that table, the factor for four years at 18 percent is 2.690, the same number as in the previous paragraph when 0.847, 0.718, 0.609, and 0.516 were factored out and added. This example illustrates that each factor in Table B was obtained by cumulating the factors for the corresponding year and all preceding years in the same interest rate column of Table A. Thus, the present value of a level series can be found in one step using Table B.

The values in Table B can also be used to find the present value of a series of equal payments between any two points in time. The procedure is to subtract the Table B factor for the year *preceding* the year of the first payment from the factor for the last year of payment.

Example. What is the present value of $1,000 a year to be received in years 6 through 10, assuming a 14 percent discount rate?

Solution:

Time Period	PV Factor (Table B)
Years 1–10..............	5.216
Years 1–5..............	3.433
Difference (years 6–10)...	1.783
PV = $1,000 × 1.783 =	$1,783

Present Values and Liabilities

The amount shown on the balance sheet for a liability such as a loan often is thought of as being the amount the borrower must repay to satisfy the obligation. This is only partly true. Certainly the borrowing entity must repay the amount borrowed, called the *principal* in the case of a term loan or bond; and the amount shown on the balance sheet of the borrower *is* the amount of unpaid principal. However, the borrower's future payments to satisfy the obligation far exceed the amount of unpaid principal because interest must be paid on the amount of outstanding principal over the life of the loan.

In many cases, the balance sheet liability is properly interpreted as meaning not the dollar amount of the principal obligation but rather the *present value* of the series of future interest payments plus the *present value* of the future principal payments.

Example. Kinnear Company borrowed $20,000, with interest at 15 percent (i.e., $3,000) to be paid annually, and the principal to be repaid in one lump sum at the end of five years. The balance sheet liability would be reported as $20,000. This can be interpreted as the sum of the present values, as follows:

	Present Value
Interest, $3,000 × 3.352 (Table B)	$10,056
Principal, $20,000 × 0.497 (Table A)....	9,940
Total present value	$19,996*

*Does not total exactly $20,000 because of rounding.

If the repayments are a level series that include *both* principal and interest, Table B can be used to find the amount of these payments.

Example.   Kinnear Company borrowed $20,000 with interest at 15 percent to be repaid in equal annual amounts at the end of each of the next five years. The present value of this obligation is $20,000. The amount of the annual installments is $5,966. It is found by dividing $20,000 by the 5 year/15 percent factor in Table B, which is 3.352.

Each payment of $5,966 in the above example consists of two components: (1) interest on the amount of principal outstanding during the year and (2) reduction of that principal. These two amounts can be calculated as shown in Illustration 8–1, which is called an *amortization* or *repayment* schedule.

ILLUSTRATION 8–1
LOAN AMORTIZATION SCHEDULE

Year	(a) Principal Owed at the Beginning of the Year	(b) Annual Payment	(c) Interest Portion of the Payment (a) × 15 percent	(d) Reduction of Principal (b) − (c)	(e) Ending Principal Balance (a) − (d)
1	$20,000	$ 5,966	$3,000	$ 2,966	$17,034
2	17,034	5,966	2,555	3,411	13,623
3	13,623	5,966	2,043	3,923	9,700
4	9,700	5,966	1,454	4,512	5,188
5	5,188	5,966	778	5,188	0
Totals		$29,830	$9,830	$20,000	

Column *c* of the schedule shows how much interest expense on this loan Kinnear Company should recognize each year. Column *e* shows the proper balance sheet valuation of the loan liability as of the end of each year (or, equivalently, as of the beginning of the next year, as shown in column *a*). The amounts in columns *c* and *d* represent the only conceptually correct way to divide each year's payment between interest expense and principal reduction. This approach is called the *compound interest method* of debt amortization.

Note how the amounts in column *c* decrease over time, while the amounts in column *d* increase. Someone not familiar with the compound interest method might assume that each year's $5,966 payment reflects a principal reduction of $4,000 (= $20,000 ÷ 5 years) and interest expense of $1,966. Such an assumption is incorrect.

Note also that the compound interest method amounts are calculated such that the interest expense is always a constant *percentage* of the principal outstanding during the year (15 percent in the illustration). This means that Kinnear Company's interest expense on this loan is a true 15 percent in *every* year the loan is outstanding, and that the true interest rate on the loan over its entire life is 15 percent. This is the same principle mentioned in the chapter text in the illustration of amortization of bond discount. The net or effective interest expense, which is the sum of the cash interest costs and the discount amortization on Mason Corporation's 12 percent bonds issued for $868, will be a constant rate (14 percent) of the book value of the bonds for each of the 20 years they are outstanding, provided that the initial discount is amortized using the compound interest method.

The amounts in column *a* of Illustration 8–1 are also the *present values* of the future payments as of the beginning of each year. For example, at the start of year 1, Kinnear Company faces the prospect of making five annual payments of $5,966. As was calculated in an earlier example, at the time the loan was made the present value of this level series discounted at 15 percent is $5,966 × 3.352 = $20,000. Similarly, we can calculate:

			Annual Payment		*Table B Factor*		
Start of year 2:	PV	=	$5,966	×	2.855	=	$17,034
Start of year 3:	PV	=	5,966	×	2.283	=	13,623
Start of year 4:	PV	=	5,966	×	1.626	=	9,700
Start of year 5:	PV	=	5,966	×	0.870	=	5,188

Present Values and Assets

Accounting for interest-bearing receivables and similar monetary assets is the "mirror image" of accounting for monetary liabilities. For example, in the Kinnear Company loan illustration above, column *c* in Illustration 8–1 shows how much interest *revenue* Kinnear's *lender* should report each year on this loan. Similarly, column *e* shows the proper year-end valuation of the loan *receivable* asset on the lender's balance sheet. We can therefore conclude that the amount shown for a loan receivable or similar monetary asset is the present value of the future payments the asset holder will receive in satisfaction of the credit the asset holder has extended (to Kinnear Company, in the illustration).

Calculating Bond Yields

The *yield* on a bond is the *rate* of return the bondholder earns as a result of investing in the bond. The investor's return is made up of two parts: (1) the bond's interest payments and (2) any difference between what the investor paid for the bond and the proceeds he or she receives upon selling the bond. (This difference is referred to as the investor's *capital gain* or *loss* on the bond.) Both the interest stream and future proceeds must be adjusted to present values to be comparable with the current market price.

Current Yield. The yield to maturity on a bond (described below) should not be confused with the *current yield*, which is the annual interest payment divided by the current price.

Example. If at a given point in time Mason Corporation's 12 percent bonds were selling on a bond market at a price of 96 (= $960), then the current yield at that time would be $120 ÷ $960 = 12.5 percent.

Yield to Maturity. The yield on a bond actually is investor-specific because the capital gain (or loss) portion of the yield depends on what a specific investor paid for the bond and how much he or she sells it for. Thus, in calculating a bond's *yield to maturity*, it is assumed that (1) the bond will be purchased at the current market price and (2) the bond will then be held until maturity. Also, income tax effects are ignored in calculating bond yields.

Example. Exactly 10 years before their maturity, Mason Corporation 12 percent bonds have a market price of $849. For simplicity, assume that Mason makes the $120 per year interest payments in a lump sum at year-end. *The yield of the bond is that discount rate that will make the present value of the series of future interest payments ($120 a year for 10 years) plus the present value of the bond redemption proceeds ($1,000 ten years hence) equal to the current market price of the bond ($849).* This rate is 15 percent, which can be demonstrated as follows:

PV of interest stream: $120 × 5.019*	=	$602
PV of redemption proceeds: $1,000 × 0.247**	=	247
Sum of *PV*s (= market price).................		$849

*From Table B: 10 year, 15 percent factor.
**From Table A: 10 year, 15 percent factor.

This 15 percent yield to maturity is also called the *effective rate of interest* on the bond.

Bond Prices. A similar calculation can be used to determine the "rational" market price of a bond, given current yields on bonds of similar quality.

Example. Assume that when Mason's 20-year, 12 percent bonds *were issued* the prevailing market interest rate (yield) of similar bonds was 14 percent. Then the market price of Mason's bonds should be that price that would result in a yield of 14 percent to a Mason bondholder. This price will be the present value of the 20-year interest stream and the proceeds at maturity (20 years hence):

PV of interest stream: $120 × 6.623*	=	$795
PV of redemption proceeds: $1,000 × 0.073*	=	73
Market price for 14% yield...................		$868

*Twenty year, 14 percent factors from Tables B and A, respectively.

This $868 is the amount that was given in the text in the Mason Corporation example of bonds issued at a discount.

Cases

CASE 8–1   Farrow Corporation (A)

Until 1982, Farrow Corporation, a young manufacturer of specialty consumer products, had not had its financial statements audited. It had, however, relied on the auditing firm of Brakeman & Cleary to prepare its income tax returns. Because it was considering borrowing on a long-term note, and the lender surely would require audited statements, Farrow decided to have its 1982 financial statements attested by Brakeman & Cleary.

Brakeman & Cleary assigned Joan Fuller to do preliminary work on the engagement, under the direction of Mr. Cleary. Farrow's financial vice president had prepared the preliminary financial statements shown in Exhibit 1. In examining the information on which these financial statements were based, Ms. Fuller discovered the facts listed below. She referred these to Mr. Cleary.

1. In 1982, a group of women employees sued the company asserting that their salaries were unjustifiably lower than salaries of men doing comparable work. They asked back pay of $200,000. A large number of similar suits had been filed in other companies, but only a few of them had been settled. Farrow's outside counsel thought that the company probably would win the suit, but pointed out that this type of litigation was relatively new, the decisions thus far were divided, and it was difficult to forecast the outcome. In any event, it was unlikely that the suit would come to trial in 1983. No provision for this loss had been made on the financial statements.

2. The company had a second lawsuit outstanding. It involved a customer who was injured by one of the company's products. The customer asked for $400,000 damages. Based on discussions

EXHIBIT 1

FARROW CORPORATION
Proposed Income Statement (condensed)
For the Year 1982

Net sales	$1,105,420
Cost of sales.	714,460
Gross margin	390,960
Operating expenses	219,400
Operating income	171,560
Nonoperating income and expense (net).	6,240
Pretax income.	165,320
Provision for income taxes.	66,200
Net income	$ 99,120

Proposed Balance Sheet (condensed)
As of December 31, 1982

Assets

Current assets:

Cash and short-term investments.		$ 71,350
Accounts receivable, gross.	$175,270	
Less: Allowance for doubtful accounts	3,500	171,770
Inventories.		250,670
Prepaid expenses		7,210
Total current assets.		501,000
Plant and equipment, at cost	207,330	
Less: Accumulated depreciation	93,220	114,110
Goodwill.		67,390
Development costs		82,710
Other deferred charges		111,640
Total assets.		$876,850

Liabilities and Shareholders' Equity

Current liabilities	$281,180
Noncurrent liabilities	152,470
Total liabilities.	433,650
Common stock (200,000 shares)	22,400
Capital surplus	123,600
Retained earnings	277,200
Reserve for contingencies	20,000
Total liabilities and shareholders' equity	$876,850

with the customer's attorney, Farrow's attorney believed that the suit probably could be settled for $20,000. There was no guarantee of this, of course. On the other hand, if the suit went to trial, Farrow might win it. Farrow did not carry product liability insurance. Farrow reported $20,000 as a Reserve for Contingencies, with a corresponding debit to Retained Earnings.

3. In 1982, plant maintenance expenditures were $26,000. Normally, plant maintenance expense was about $40,000 a year, and $40,000 had indeed been budgeted for 1982. Management decided, however, to economize in 1982, even

though it was recognized that the amount would probably have to be made up in future years. In view of this, the estimated income statement included an item of $40,000 for plant maintenance expense, with an offsetting credit of $14,000 to a reserve account included as a noncurrent liability.

4. In early January 1982, the company issued a 12 percent $50,000 bond to one of its stockholders in return for $40,000 cash. The discount of $10,000 arose because the 12 percent interest rate was below the going interest rate at the time; the stockholder thought that this arrangement gave him an income tax advantage as compared with a $40,000 bond at the market rate of interest. The company included the $10,000 discount as one of the components of "Other deferred charges" on the balance sheet and included the $50,000 as a noncurrent liability. When questioned about this treatment, the financial vice president said, "I know that other companies may record such a transaction differently, but after all we do owe $50,000. And anyway, what does it matter where the discount appears?"

5. The $10,000 bond discount was reduced by $200 in 1982, and Ms. Fuller calculated that this was the correct amount of amortization. However, the $200 was included as an item of "Other expense" on the income statement, rather than being charged to Retained Earnings.

6. In connection with the issuance of the $50,000 bond, the company had incurred legal fees amounting to $300.

These costs were included in nonoperating expenses in the income statement because, according to the financial vice president, "issuing bonds is an unusual financial transaction for us, not a routine operating transaction."

7. On January 2, 1982, the company had leased a new Cadillac sedan, valued at $20,000, to be used for various official company purposes. After three years of $9,200 annual year-end lease payments, title to the car would pass to Farrow, which expected to use the car through at least year-end 1986. The $9,200 lease payment for 1982 was included in operating expenses in the income statement.

Although Mr. Cleary recognized that some of these transactions might affect the "Provision for income taxes," he decided not to consider the possible tax implications until after he had thought through the appropriate financial accounting treatment.

Questions

1. How should each of the above six items be reported on the 1982 income statement and balance sheet?

2. (Optional—requires knowledge of Appendix material.) The bond described in item 4 above has a 15-year maturity date. What is the yield rate to the investor who paid $40,000 for this bond? Is the $200 discount amortization cited in item 5 indeed the correct first-year amount? (Assume that the $6,000 annual interest payment is made in a lump sum at year-end.)

CASE 8–2 Peabody Industries Inc.

Maryanne Peabody sat at her desk, feeling less than content. This was a direct result of Peabody Industries' poor results for the third quarter of 1978 and the even gloomier outlook for the final quarter.

Picking up *The Wall Street Journal,* Maryanne turned to the stock exchange listings, "Oh no!" she groaned, "we've slipped yet another 50 cents; that's $2 in the last month." Despondently she picked up her telephone and was just about to make a call when the name Peabody caught her eye. This time it was in the bond listings:

Bonds	Curr Yield	Vol	Hi	Low	Close	Net Chg
Pbdy 5s95	10.25	7	60	60	60	− ½

"That has lost us money as well," thought Maryanne, "This one is only worth $600 now, and we sold them at $1,000."

For the rest of the morning Maryanne worried about the bond value. The more she thought about it the less she felt it was Peabody Industries that had lost. Suddenly Maryanne hit on a brilliant idea to generate additional income for Peabody Industries. She hurriedly called in her assistant, Keith Edwards, and described her idea, which was to buy back all the bonds at $600 thus making $400 on each bond.

Keith returned to his desk and began to calculate the expected cash availability of Peabody Industries by late December, the date Maryanne wanted to repurchase the bonds. Very quickly it became obvious that $2,400,000 was not available for the repurchase; in fact, $400,000 would have been difficult.

Walking into Maryanne's office, Keith informed her of the cash position and waited for the explosion. Instead, Maryanne smiled at her assistant and said, "I wondered how long it would take you to realize that; but I've already decided we

can achieve my objective by selling some new bonds to buy back the old ones. In fact, we're going to sell $4,000,000 worth so we can make that plant expansion I've been planning for the last two years."

Keith felt obliged to point out that the new issue would sell at the same price as the old issue. "No, no," said Maryanne. "I've already talked to a pension fund that has expressed interest in our bonds. Fortunately, if they undertake the refunding, there will be no underwriting costs and only minimal legal fees. If we issue a 10 percent per annum bond in late December, it will net us $4,000,000 exactly—funny thing is that if we made them 12 percent per annum bonds[1], we would get $4,498,000. That would mean an additional $498,000 profit, so, all in all, we could make $2,098,000 on that issue. That's not bad for one morning's work is it?"

"Sounds OK to me," said Keith. "The only thing that's bothering me is that the figure on the balance sheet for the current debt is not $4,000,000 but about $3,668,000. There is a footnote, but that didn't help me understand the balance sheet number at all." (See Exhibit 1.)

"Let me have a look," said Maryanne. "Yes, you are right; I know these accountants have funny ways of doing things, but this really seems way out to me. I guess I'll have to call my accountant." On completion of the call, Maryanne said to Keith, "Well, that didn't help much at all. I now know we issued a 30-year 5 percent bond on January 1, 1966, and that we pay interest semiannually on June 30 and December 31. I also know that we received $3,446,000 for those bonds; and

---

[1]Semiannual payments of interest. Full payment of capital after 10 years.

EXHIBIT 1
PEABODY INDUSTRIES, INC.
Liabilities and Stockholders' Equity
As of December 31
(thousands of dollars)

	1977	1976
Current liabilities:		
Notes payable—banks	$ 0	$ 2,037
Accounts payable—trade	6,762	5,665
Interest payable on long-term debt (Note 2)	100	100
Accrued and other liabilities	1,811	1,894
Federal income and other taxes	2,122	2,010
Total current liabilities	10,795	11,706
Long-term debt (Note 2)	3,668	3,649
Shareholders' equity:		
Capital stock—par value $7.50 per share (2,000,000 shares authorized; 1,251,321 shares issued)	9,385	9,385
Capital in excess of par value	7,337	7,337
Retained earnings	26,005	25,063
	42,727	41,785
Less: Treasury stock:	1,416	1,417
Total shareholders' equity	41,311	40,368
Total liabilities and shareholders' equity	$55,774	$55,723

Note 2: Long-term debt. On January 1, 1966, the company issued 4,000 five percent bonds payable on December 31, 1995, $1,000 principal per bond. The effective interest rate at issuance was 6.09 percent. As of December 31, 1977, and 1976, respectively, $332,000 and $351,000 of discount remained unamortized. These bonds are reflected on the accompanying balance sheets as follows:

	1977	1976
Bonds payable	$4,000	$4,000
Less: Unamortized discount	332	351
Bonds payable, net	$3,668	$3,649

the discount, whatever that is, is being amortized using the straight-line method. What I don't know is how we can show $3,668,000 when we owe $4 million."

"I don't understand it either," said Keith, "but I think it is going to cut our profit down to $1,268,000 on the repurchase."

"Oh well, I guess we have to go with the 12 percent issue and make do with nearly $2.1 million in profit," chuckled Maryanne.

"Yes, I reckon we can get by on that," laughingly agreed Keith.

Questions

1. *a.* How would you explain to Maryanne and Keith the $3,668,000 on the balance sheet?

   b. How would you explain the $4,000,000 issue price of the 10 percent bond and the $4,498,000 issue price of the 12 percent bond? (No detailed calculations are necessary.)

2. *a.* What amount would you treat as gain on the repurchase? Why?

   b. If they choose to sell the 12 percent bonds, what amount will you treat as gain? Why?

   c. How would you account for these

bonds? Give the long-term debt portion of the balance sheets for Peabody Industries as of December 31, 1978, and 1979.

3. Assuming Peabody Industries only wanted to refinance the $4,000,000 of 5 percent bonds, that is, they only issued bonds to a cash value of $2,400,000, calculate:

   a. For the years 1979, 1980, and 1981, the effect on the income statement due to:

      (1) Refinancing using 10 percent bonds.
      (2) Refinancing using 12 percent bonds.

   b. For the years 1979, 1980, and 1981, the effect on the cash account due to:

      (1) Refinancing using 10 percent bonds.
      (2) Refinancing using 12 percent bonds.

CASE 8–3   Tendex Engineering Company

Tendex Engineering Company was founded by two partners, Meredith Gale and Shelley Yeaton, shortly after they had graduated from engineering school. Within five years the partners had built a thriving business, primarily through the development of a product line of measuring instruments based on the laser principle. Success brought with it the need for new permanent capital. After careful calculation, the partners placed the amount of this need at $1.2 million. This would replace a term loan that was about to mature and provide for plant expansion and related working capital.

At first, they sought a wealthy investor, or group of investors, who would provide the $1.2 million in return for an interest in the partnership. They soon discovered, however, that although some investors were interested in participating in new ventures, none of them was willing to participate as partner in an industrial company because of the risks to their personal fortunes that were inherent in such an arrangement. Gale and Yeaton therefore incorporated the Tendex Engineering Company, in which they owned all the stock.

After further investigation, they learned that Providence Capital Corporation, a venture capital firm, might be interested in providing permanent financing. In thinking about what they should propose to Providence, their first idea was that Providence would be asked to provide $1.2 million, of which $1.1 million would be a long-term loan. For the other $100,000, Providence would receive 10 percent of the Tendex common stock as a "sweetener." If Providence would pay $100,000 for 10 percent of the stock, this would mean that the 90 percent that would be owned by Gale and Yeaton would have a value of $900,000. Although this was considerably higher than Tendex's net assets, they thought that this amount was appropriate in view of the profitability of the product line that they had successfully developed.

A little calculation convinced them, however, that this idea (hereafter, proposal A) was too risky. The resulting ratio of debt to equity would be greater than 59 percent, which was considered unsound for an industrial company.

Their next idea was to change the debt/equity ratio by using preferred stock in lieu of most of the debt. Specifically, they thought of a package consisting of $200,000 debt, $900,000 preferred stock, and $100,000 common stock (proposal B).

They learned, however, that Providence Capital Corporation was not interested in accepting preferred stock, even at a dividend that exceeded the interest rate on debt. Thereupon, they approached Providence with a proposal of $600,000 debt and $600,000 equity (proposal C). For the $600,000 equity, Providence would receive 6/15 (i.e., 40 percent) of the common stock.

The Providence representative was considerably interested in the company and its prospects but explained that Providence ordinarily did not participate in a major financing of a relatively new company unless it obtained at least 50 percent equity as part of the deal. In other words, they were interested only in a proposal for $300,000 debt and $900,000 equity (proposal D). The debt/equity ratio in this proposal was attractive, but Gale and Yeaton were not happy about sharing control of the company equally with an outside party.

Before proceeding further, they decided to see if they could locate another venture capital investor who might be interested in one of the other proposals.

In making calculations of the implications of these proposals, Gale and Yeaton assumed an interest cost of debt of 14 percent, which seemed to be the rate for companies similar to Tendex, and a dividend rate for preferred stock of 16 percent. They assumed, as a best guess, that Tendex would earn $300,000 a year, after income taxes on operating income, but before interest costs and the tax savings thereon. They included their own common stock equity at $900,000.

They also made pessimistic calculations based on income of $100,000 per year and optimistic calculations based on income of $500,000 a year. They realized, of course, that the $100,000 pessimistic calculations were not necessarily the minimum amount of income; it was possible that the company would lose money. On the other hand, $500,000 was about the maximum amount of income that could be expected with the plant that could be financed with the $1.2 million. Applicable income tax rates were 26 percent on $100,000 income, 40 percent on $300,000 income, and 42 percent on $500,000 income.

Questions

1. For each of the four proposals, calculate the return on common shareholders' equity that would be earned under each of the three income assumptions.

2. Calculate the pretax earnings to Providence Capital Corporation under each of the four proposals.

3. Were the parters correct in rejecting proposals A and B?

4. Comment on the likelihood that Tendex Engineering Company could find a more attractive financing proposal than proposal D.

5. Assume that proposal D is accepted, that the net assets (total assets minus liabilities) of the partnership are $700,000, and that 180,000 shares of $1 par value stock are issued, 90,000 to the partners and 90,000 to Providence. Give journal entries for *two* ways of recording these transactions, one recognizing goodwill and the other not recognizing goodwill. Which way is preferable?

CASE 8–4   Julie Banning

Julie Banning was graduating from business school in the spring of 1982. She had accepted a fine job offer, and planning for her future was much on her mind. She had recently noticed several bank and savings and loan association advertisements for Individual Retirement Accounts (IRAs). The ads stressed the extremely large values regular deposits in an IRA would amount to at retirement. An often-heard promise was that IRA accounts would grow to over $1 million at retirement. Ms. Banning wondered if this promise was really true. She began to gather more information on IRAs.

She found that as of January 1, 1982, every income earner became eligible to start an IRA. Annual deposits were tax deductible from current income up to certain limits. These limits were $2,000 a year for individuals, $2,250 a year for couples with one working spouse, and $4,000 a year for two-income couples. Earnings from IRA accounts were not taxable until withdrawals began after age 59½. At this point, upon retirement, it was expected the wage earner(s) would be in a lower tax bracket. Early withdrawals were taxable and also subject to a 10 percent penalty.

In the first quarter of 1982, banks were offering fixed 2½-year rates of approximately 14 percent and 18-month rates of approximately 15 percent on IRAs.

Questions

1. Assuming current rates (14 percent and 15 percent) continue, deposits are made once a year at the beginning of the year for the maximum $2,000 tax-deductible amount, and interest is compounded annually, should Ms. Banning open her IRA at age 30 in order to be a millionnaire at age 60 when she retires? What happens to this goal if she waits until she is 35? Or 40?

2. Under the same assumptions as Question 1, if Ms. Banning marries, at what age must she and her husband, both working, open their IRA account to assure themselves joint membership in this "Millionnaire's Club"? At age 30, 35, or 40? When should the account be opened if Ms. Banning's family is a one-income family and the maximum deposit becomes $2,250?

3. One bank's advertisement based its calculations on a continuing 12 percent interest rate. What requirements does this change put on the number of years of deposits and family circumstances required to achieve $1 million in an IRA at a retirement age of 60?

4. What would be the lowest interest rate that would fulfill the banks' "millionaire" promise, assuming age 20 is the youngest one would be to start an IRA? For how long would the saver(s) have to maintain his or her (their) IRA deposits?

5. In early 1982, inflation was approximately 10 percent and a loaf of bread cost $0.65. If this inflationary trend continues, how much will a loaf of bread cost by the year 2002? 2012? 2022?

CASE 8–5   Jean Coffin (D)

Having recently studied liabilities and the concept of present value, Jean Coffin was interested in discussing with the accounting professor several matters that had recently come to Jean's attention in the newspaper and on television. Each of these matters is described below.

1. One night on the "Johnny Carson Show" a guest described having found a bond in the attic of his home in a small Missouri town. The bond had been issued in 1871 by the town, apparently to finance a municipal water system. The bond was payable to the bearer (whoever happened to have the bond in his or her possession), rather than to a specifically named individual. The face amount of the bond was $100, and the stated interest rate was 10 percent. According to the terms of the bond, it could be redeemed at any future time of the bearer's choosing for its face value plus accumulated *compound* interest. Jean was anxious to use the professor's calculator to determine what this bond was worth because only the amount "several million dollars" was mentioned during the show.

2. Jean also had read about "zero-coupon" bonds, which are bonds that pay no interest. Therefore, they are offered at a substantial discount from par value, since the investor's entire return is the difference between the discounted offering price and the par value. In particular, Jean had read that one company had issued eight-year zero-coupon bonds at a price of $327 per $1,000 par value. Jean wanted to discuss the following with the accounting professor: (a) Was the yield on these bonds 15 percent, as Jean had calculated? (b) Assuming that bond discount amortization is tax deductible by the issuing corporation, that the issuer has a 46 percent income tax rate, and that for tax purposes a straight-line amortization of original discount is permissible, what is the effective or "true" aftertax interest rate to the issuer of this bond? And (c), if instead of issuing these zero-cou-

pon bonds, the company had issued 15 percent coupon bonds with issue proceeds of $1,000 per bond (i.e., par value), what would the issuer's effective aftertax interest rate have been on these alternative bonds?

3. Jean had also read about a new financing gimmick called a "debt-for-equity swap." The technique works as follows: A company's bonds are currently trading on the New York Bond Exchange at a sizable discount because their coupon rate is well below current market interest rates. The company arranges with an investment banking firm to buy up these bonds on the open market. The company then issues new shares of common stock to the investment banker in exchange for the bonds (which are then retired). The shares issued have a value about 4 percent higher than the amount the investment banker has spent acquiring the bonds. Finally, the investment banker sells these shares on the open market, realizing its 4 percent profit. According to the article Jean had read, Exxon Corporation had swapped 1.4 million common shares valued at $43 million for bonds with a face value of $72 million, thereby realizing a tax-free gain of $29 million. Jean wondered two things about such a transaction: (a) Why doesn't the company issue the shares directly and use the proceeds to buy back the bonds on the open market, instead of using an investment banker as an intermediary? And (b), should the gain on such a swap be treated as income for financial reporting purposes since, in a sense, the company has done nothing of substance to earn it?

4. Jean Coffin had thought debt-for-equity swaps were quite sophisticated until she had later read about a technique called *defeasance*. This works as follows:

A company buys a portfolio of government bonds and turns them over to a trustee. The trust agreement provides for the trustee to use the bond portfolio income and any bond redemption proceeds to make interest payments on the company's outstanding bonds, and also to retire those company bonds at maturity. Since the trustee now pays the company's bond obligations, the company eliminates its bond liability (at face value) from its books. Also, if current interest rates are higher than the coupon rate on the company's bonds, the cost of the portfolio of government bonds needed to meet future obligations on the company's bonds is less than the face value of the company's bonds. The difference is reported by the company as a gain in the period in which the arrangement is undertaken. According to the article Jean had read, in one quarter, Exxon Corporation had reduced its balance sheet debt by $515 million and had added $130 million to its reported earnings using this technique; and Kellogg Company had increased its reported earnings for one quarter by 8 cents a share by using the same technique. To Jean, there was a question as to whether a company has "really" earned anything by making such a defeasance arrangement.

9

Other Expenses, Net Income, and Owners' Equity

The preceding chapters discussed the accounting treatment of many of the items that affect net income. This chapter discusses additional items: personnel costs, income taxes, extraordinary items, discontinued operations, and accounting changes. This chapter also describes in more detail the owners' equity section of the balance sheet, thus completing the more detailed discussion of income statement and balance sheet items that began with Chapter 5.

PERSONNEL COSTS

Personnel costs include wages and salaries earned by employees and other costs related to their services. (Customarily, the word *wages* refers to the compensation of employees who are paid on a piece-rate, hourly, daily, or weekly basis, while the word *salaries* refers to compensation expressed in longer terms.) The effect on the accounting records of earning and paying wages and salaries is more complicated than merely debiting expenses and crediting cash. This is because when wages and salaries are earned or paid, certain other transactions occur almost automatically.

Employees are rarely paid the gross amount of wages or salary they earn, since from their gross earnings the following must be deducted:

1. An amount representing the employee's contribution under the Federal Insurance Contribution Act (FICA), which in 1983 was 6.7 percent of the first $35,700 of wages or salary earned each year.
2. The withholding deduction, which is an amount withheld from gross earnings to apply toward the employee's income taxes.
3. Deductions for charitable contributions, savings plans, union dues, and a variety of other items.

None of these deductions represents a cost *to the employer.* In the case of the tax deductions, the employer is acting as a collection agent for the government. The withholding of these amounts and their subsequent transfer to the government does not affect net income or owners' equity. Rather, the withholding creates a liability, and the subsequent transfer to the government pays off this liability. Similarly, the employer is acting as a collection agent in the case of the other deductions. The employee is paid the net amount after these deductions have been taken.

When wages and salaries are earned, other costs are automatically created. The employer must pay a tax equal in amount to the employee's FICA tax, and the employer must also pay an additional percentage of the employee's pay (the rate varies in different states) for the *unemployment insurance tax.* Collectively, FICA and unemployment insurance are called *social security taxes.* The *employer's* share of these taxes is an element of cost.

Thus, if an employee with three dependents earned $300 for work in a certain week in 1983, $20.10 for FICA tax contribution and $29.56 for withholding tax would be deducted from this $300, and the employee's "take-home pay" would be $250.34. (Other possible deductions are omitted in order to simplify.) The *employer* would incur an expense of $20.10 for FICA and an additional expense of, say, $9 for the federal and state unemployment insurance taxes, or a total of $29.10 for the two social security taxes.

The journal entries for these transactions are as follows:

1. When wages are earned:

```
Wages Cost ...................................... 300.00
    Wages Payable.............................          300.00

Social Security Tax Cost ....................  29.10
    FICA Taxes Payable........................           20.10
    Unemployment Taxes Payable................            9.00
```

2. When the employee is paid:

```
Wages Payable ................................. 300.00
    Cash......................................          250.34
    FICA Taxes Payable........................           20.10
    Withholding Taxes Payable.................           29.56
```

3. When the government is paid:

```
FICA Taxes Payable (20.10 + 20.10) .........    40.20
Unemployment Taxes Payable .................     9.00
Withholding Taxes Payable ..................    29.56
    Cash....................................             78.76
```

In practice, the above entries would be made for all employees as a group. The government does require, however, that a record be kept of the amount of FICA tax and withholding tax accumulated for each employee.

Fringe Benefits

In addition to cash wages or salaries, most organizations provide *fringe benefits* to their employees. Among these are pensions, life insurance, health care, and vacations. These amounts are costs of the period in which the employee worked, just as are the cash earnings.

Pensions.   In most organizations, the largest fringe benefit is the pension, that is, payments that employees will receive after they retire. In many companies, pension costs are 10 percent or more of payroll. In some organizations, employees contribute part of their pension cost, and this cost is a payroll deduction, treated just like the other deductions mentioned above. It does not involve a cost to the organization. The employer's contribution for pension benefits *is* a cost to the employer, just as are other fringe benefits.

Pension plans are regulated under the Employee Retirement Income Security Act of 1974 (ERISA). The provisions of this act, and also those of the Internal Revenue Code, are such that in almost all companies, pension plans must be *funded*. This means that the company pays its contribution in cash to a bank, insurance company, or other trustee for the pension fund. The trustee invests the money and pays pension benefits directly to employees after they retire. The pension fund is therefore a separate entity, with its own set of accounts. The company's accounting for pensions ends when it turns over cash to the pension fund. The assets in the fund do not appear on the company's balance sheet. The only accounting entry that the company makes is to record its contribution to the pension fund. The amount contributed is a cost of the current period. The entry is:

```
Pension Cost ..............................   100,000
    Cash ..................................             100,000
```

Types of Pension Plans.   There are two general types of pension plans: (1) defined contribution plans and (2) defined benefit plans.

In a *defined contribution plan*, the employer contributes to the pension fund an agreed amount each year for each employee, and the employee's pension depends on how much has been accumulated for him or her as of the date of retirement. In such plans, which are common in educational institutions but less common in other organizations, the company's pension cost for a year is simply this agreed-upon contribution.

Defined Benefit Plans.   In a *defined benefit plan,* the employer agrees to contribute to the pension fund an amount large enough so that employees will receive a specified amount of monthly benefits after retirement. This amount depends upon the employee's years of service before retirement, the employee's average earnings during some period immediately preceding retirement, and possibly upon other factors also.

In order to calculate its pension contribution in a given year, the company must estimate how many years employees will work before retirement, average earnings on which the pension benefits are calculated, employee turnover, how many years the employee will live after retirement, the probable increases in benefit payments, and the amount that the pension fund will earn on funds invested in it. The calculations are complicated, and there are at least five approved methods of making them. Many companies engage an *actuary,* a professional who specializes in such matters, to make these estimates. The resulting amount is called the *normal cost* for the year.

Whenever a pension plan is "sweetened," that is, when the schedule of benefits is increased to keep up with the cost of living or for other reasons, the amounts originally contributed for work done by employees in the past becomes inadequate to pay the increased benefits. Then additional contributions must be made to the pension fund. This amount is called the *total past service cost.* Past service costs also arise in the year in which a company first adopts a pension plan.

In the year in which a pension plan is changed, the past service cost can be such a large amount that it would distort income if charged off as an expense in that year. The FASB requires companies to spread this cost over a period of not less than 10 years nor more than 40 years in the future.[1]

The annual contribution to the pension fund, and hence the pension cost, in therefore the sum of (1) normal costs and (2) a fraction of the past service cost.

Unfunded Cost.   The amount of past service cost that has not yet been contributed to the pension fund is the company's *unfunded past service cost.* This amount does not appear in the accounts because, even though it is an obligation, it has not yet formally been recognized as a liability. The Securities and Exchange Commission requires that the amount be disclosed.

---

[1]"Accounting for the Costs of Pension Plans," *APB Opinion No. 8,* November 1966; and *FASB Interpretation No. 3,* December 1974.

Disclosure. In addition to reporting the period's pension cost, for its defined benefit plans a company must disclose: (1) the present value of both vested and nonvested accumulated plan benefits, (2) the pension plan asset rate of return assumed in calculating these present values, and (3) the plan's net assets available for benefits.[2] ("Vested" benefits are those to which the employee is already entitled.) Also, the plan itself must make certain disclosures as an entity.[3] Illustrative of the complexity of these pension disclosures and the underlying calculations, *FASB Statement No. 35* is 145 pages long. Despite all of the previous APB and FASB consideration of pension accounting, the topic continues to be controversial and subject to further FASB study. A major issue is whether any of an employer's obligation to provide future benefits should be recognized as a liability in the employer's balance sheet.

Compensated Absences. In some organizations, any vacation and sick leave days that were *earned* this year but *not used* this year can be carried forward and used at some future time. If the amount can be reasonably estimated, the cost of these *future compensated absences* is treated as an expense of the period in which the future absence time is *earned*. The offsetting credit is to an accrued liability account. When the employee is later compensated, the liability account is debited and Cash is credited.[4]

INCOME TAXES

For most revenue and expense transactions, the amount used in calculating taxable income for income tax purposes is the same as the amount reported on the income statement in accordance with generally accepted accounting principles (GAAP). Thus, there is a likelihood that if a company reports an income of $1 million before taxes, and if the tax rate is 46 percent, the Provision for Income Taxes (an expense) should be approximately $460,000. (Although *Provision for Income Taxes* is the preferred term for this item, some companies use *Income Tax Expense* or some similar term.)

Permanent Differences and Timing Differences

There are two important classes of exceptions, however. First, the income tax regulations permit certain credits or deductions from taxable income that will never be counted as expenses, and they permit that certain revenue items be excluded from taxable income. The investment tax credit (Chapter 7) is an example of such a credit, and interest revenue on state and municipal bonds is an example of an item that is ex-

---

[2] "Disclosure of Pension Information," *FASB Statement No. 36*, May 1980.

[3] "Accounting and Reporting by Defined Benefit Pension Plans," *FASB Statement No. 35*, March 1980.

[4] "Accounting for Compensated Absences," *FASB Statement No. 43*, November 1980.

cluded from taxable income. These exceptions create a *permanent* tax difference. In other situations, the income tax regulations permit or require revenues or expenses to be recognized in a different period than the recognition method used in financial accounting. The installment method and completed contract method (Chapter 5) are examples. These create a timing tax difference.

No special accounting arises in the case of permanent tax differences. The amount reported as Provision for Income Taxes of the current period is simply lower than it would be if the preferential treatment did not exist.

Accounting for Timing Differences

In the case of timing differences, an adjustment in Provision for Income Taxes in the current period is required. This adjustment makes the period's Provision for Income Taxes match the amount of income reported on the period's *income statement* (as opposed to the period's income tax return), and is therefore consistent with the matching concept.[5]

We shall illustrate this principle by assuming a company that uses the ACRS cost recovery deductions (described in Chapter 7) in calculating its taxable income, and the straight-line method of depreciation for calculating its net income for financial accounting purposes. This is the most common cause of timing differences in income taxes. For simplicity, we shall assume that the company acquired a single asset in 1983 at a cost of $1,000,000, that the asset has negligible residual value, and that its actual useful life is eight years, but its ACRS class life is five years. (The investment tax credit is ignored, for simplicity.)

Part A of Illustration 9–1 shows how the company would calculate its *income taxes* in each of these five years, assuming income before depreciation and taxes was $925,000 in each year. For income tax purposes, the depreciation expense (recovery allowance) in 1983 is $150,000; so taxable income is $775,000 and the assumed income tax is 40 percent of $775,000, or $310,000. Similar explanations apply to the 1984–90 amounts. Note that by the end of 1987, the asset is fully depreciated for *tax* purposes, even though it has three remaining years of actual service life.

Part B shows the calculations for *financial accounting* purposes, if income taxes were not allocated so as to match with pretax income. Assuming that in its financial accounting the company uses the straight-line method, depreciation expense is one eighth of $1,000,000, or $125,000 each year, and its income before tax is $800,000 each year. Because the income tax *paid*, as calculated in Part A, is not constant for every year, reported net income would also fluctuate if net income were calculated simply by subtracting each year's income tax paid from the

---

[5]"Accounting for Income Taxes," *APB Opinion No. 11*, December 1967.

ILLUSTRATION 9–1
CALCULATION OF TAX ALLOCATION, SINGLE ASSET
(thousands of dollars)

Part A.   Calculation on Income Tax Basis

Year	Income before Depreciation and Taxes	ACRS Recovery Allowance	Taxable Income	Income Tax (at 40 percent)*	Income after Tax
1983	$ 925	$ 150	$ 775	$ 310	$ 465
1984	925	220	705	282	423
1985	925	210	715	286	429
1986	925	210	715	286	429
1987	925	210	715	286	429
1988	925	—	925	370	555
1989	925	—	925	370	555
1990	925	—	925	370	555
	$7,400	$1,000	$6,400	$2,560	$3,840

Part B.   Accounting Income, without Allocation

Year	Income before Depreciation and Taxes	Straight-Line Depreciation	Pretax Income	Income Tax Paid (as in A)	Net Income
1983	$ 925	$ 125	$ 800	310	$ 490
1984	925	125	800	282	518
1985	925	125	800	286	514
1986	925	125	800	286	514
1987	925	125	800	286	514
1988	925	125	800	370	430
1989	925	125	800	370	430
1990	925	125	800	370	430
	$7,400	$1,000	$6,400	$2,560	$3,840

Part C.   Accounting Income, with Allocation

		Provision for Income Taxes				
Year	Pretax Income	Paid (as in A)	Allo-cated	Net	Net Income	Deferred Income Taxes
1983	$ 800	$ 310	+ $10 =	$ 320	$ 480	$ 10
1984	800	282	+ 38 =	320	480	48
1985	800	286	+ 34 =	320	480	82
1986	800	286	+ 34 =	320	480	116
1987	800	286	+ 34 =	320	480	150
1988	800	370	− 50 =	320	480	100
1989	800	370	− 50 =	320	480	50
1990	800	370	− 50 =	320	480	0
	$6,400	$2,560	$30	$2,560	$3,840	

*A 40 percent rate (rather than 46 percent) is used in this illustration so as to eliminate rounding errors.

financial accounting pretax income for that year. This result occurs because the income tax was calculated on a different amount than the financial accounting income before tax; that is, the income tax was *not* *matched* to the financial accounting pretax income.

Part C shows how the Provision for Income Taxes can be made to match the financial accounting reported income. The income tax actually payable for each year is adjusted so that it equals what the tax amount *would have been* if it had been calculated on the same basis as the income reported for financial accounting purposes. Each year, the income before tax is $800,000; and at a tax rate of 40 percent, the income tax on this amount would be $320,000. Provision for Income Taxes is adjusted from the amount actually paid so that it equals $320,000 in each year. In 1983, this requires an addition of $10,000 to the tax actually paid; and by 1988, it requires a subtraction from actual taxes of $50,000.

Note that these adjustments affect only the *timing* of the recognition of income tax expense. As shown by the totals in Parts A, B, and C, over the whole eight-year period the total amount of tax ($2,560,000) and the total amount of net income ($3,840,000) are exactly the same, whether or not the adjustment is made. The matching of tax expense with pretax income simply allocates the $2,560,000 total tax in a pattern that is different from the pattern of actual tax payments.

Accounting Entries

The actual income tax due for a year is calculated as in Part A and is recorded in the following journal entry (for 1983):

```
Provision for Income Taxes ..................  310,000
      Income Tax Liability ......................            310,000
```

The Provision for Income Taxes amount is then adjusted to reflect the income tax that should be matched with accounting income. For 1983, this requires an addition of $10,000 to Provision for Income Taxes, so the entry is:

```
Provision for Income Taxes ..................   10,000
      Deferred Income Taxes ......................            10,000
```

After this entry, Provision for Income Taxes totals $320,000, which is the amount reported on the income statement for 1983.

In 1988, the adjusting entry will have the opposite effect. It will reduce actual income taxes (=$370,000) by $50,000 to arrive at the proper amount for Provision for Income Taxes (=$320,000):

```
Deferred Income Taxes ........................   50,000
      Provision for Income Taxes ................            50,000
```

Nature of Deferred Income Taxes Liability

Deferred Income Taxes, which is the account credited or debited in these adjusting entries, is a liability account. It is shown separately from Income Tax Liability or Taxes Payable, which is the amount actually owed the government at the time. Deferred Income Taxes is not a liability in the sense that the amount is owed to the government as of the date of the balance sheet. It is a liability only in the sense of a deferred credit to income. That is, it is an amount that will reduce income tax expense in the years in which income tax actually paid exceeds the amount of financial accounting income tax expense (1988–90 in the example).

In the example, the $150,000 by which income tax was reduced in the later years (1988–90) exactly equaled the $150,000 by which it was increased in the early years (1983–87). Thus, at the end of the life of the asset, the balance in the Deferred Income Tax account was zero. This is always the case with respect to a *single* asset. If, however, we drop the assumption that the company operates with only a single asset and make instead the more realistic assumption that a company acquires additional assets each year, a strange situation develops in the Deferred Income Taxes liability account. This is shown in Illustration 9–2.

ILLUSTRATION 9–2
BEHAVIOR OF DEFERRED TAX ACCOUNT
(thousands of dollars)

	Changes in Deferred Tax Account								
	1983	1984	1985	1986	1987	1988	1989	1990	1991
Beginning balance	0	10	58	140	256	406	506	556	556
For asset added in:									
1983	10	38	34	34	34	−50	−50	−50	
1984		10	38	34	34	34	−50	−50	−50
1985			10	38	34	34	34	−50	−50
1986				10	38	34	34	34	−50
1987					10	38	34	34	34
1988						10	38	34	34
1989							10	38	34
1990								10	38
1991 (replaces 1983 asset)									10
Ending balance	10	58	140	256	406	506	556	556	556

In Illustration 9–2, it is assumed that the situation described for Illustration 9–1 is repeated each year. That is, each year the company acquires an identical $1,000,000 asset, using the ACRS cost recovery deductions for tax purposes, while depreciating the asset on a straight-line basis over eight years for calculating reported income. For the first eight years (1983–90), these acquisitions make the company grow in size. Thereafter, each year's acquisition only replaces the asset acquired eight years previously, whose service life has just ended.

In 1983, Deferred Income Taxes increases by the $10,000 allocation shown in Part C of Illustration 9–1. In 1984, it increases another $38,000 for the asset acquired in 1983, plus $10,000 for the asset acquired in 1984. From 1985 to 1987, it increases still further. In 1988, the timing differences from the 1983 asset start to "reverse"; this reversal is $50,000 in 1988. But this 1988 reversal is more than offset by the 1988 credits for the 1984–88 assets, so the balance in Deferred Income Taxes continues to increase. By year-end 1989, the balance stabilizes at $556,000 because from 1990 on each year's total $150,000 reversals (debits) equal each year's $150,000 credits. Under the assumed conditions, then, from year-end 1989 on there would be a "permanent" deferred tax liability of $556,000.

"Permanent" Deferrals. Note, however, that as long as the company grows in size, the credit balance in Deferred Income Taxes continues to increase. Even if the company stops growing in size, as is assumed in 1991, a sizable credit balance remains in the account. This balance remains permanently; there will always be a credit balance in the Deferred Income Taxes account unless the company stops acquiring assets. Furthermore, since replacement costs of assets increase in periods of inflation, the credit balance will continue to grow even if the physical size of the company remains constant. For these reasons, many companies report a large deferred income taxes liability on their balance sheet. This is not an obligation owed to some outside party, and it is unlikely that the balance in the account ever will be eliminated, or even that it will decrease. The effective permanency of this increasing credit balance has led many companies to argue against deferred tax accounting since it became a requirement for GAAP in 1967. Since the 1981 Tax Act causes this balance to increase even more rapidly, these arguments have recently intensified.

Deferred Income Taxes Asset

A Deferred Income Taxes account may also appear on the asset side of balance sheet. For example, prepaid rental revenue is taxable income in the year received, even though accounting principles treat it as deferred revenue. A firm owning rental properties could therefore have greater taxes payable than its reported income tax expense, giving rise to a Deferred Income Taxes asset account, for the same reason that accelerated depreciation gives rise to a liability account. If a company has both an asset account and a liability account for deferred taxes, each must be reported separately; they cannot be netted together.

NONOPERATING ITEMS

To the extent feasible, the income statement should show the results of the year's normal operations separately from special and presumably nonrecurring events that affected net income and retained earnings. This permits the reader to see more clearly the profitability of normal activities. This section describes four types of transactions that are reported separately from the revenues and expenses of recurring operations: extraordinary items, discontinued operations, change in accounting principles, and correction of errors. The first three of these affect net income for the period; the fourth is an adjustment to retained earnings. The method of reporting these four types of transactions on the income statement is shown in Illustration 9–3.

ILLUSTRATION 9–3
SEPARATION OF OPERATING INCOME FROM OTHER ITEMS

BASEL CORPORATION
Condensed Statement of Income and Retained Earnings
Year Ended December 31, 1982
(thousands of dollars)

Net sales and other revenue		$60,281
Expenses		46,157
Income from continuing operations before income taxes		14,124
Provision for income taxes		6,780
Income from continuing operations		7,344
Extraordinary loss (less applicable income taxes of $460)		(540)
Discontinued operations (Note A):		
Loss from operations of Division X (less applicable income taxes of $460)	$540	
Loss on disposal of Division X (less applicable income taxes of $828)	972	(1,512)
Cumulative effect of change in accounting principle (Note B)		(400)
Net income		$ 4,892
Retained earnings at beginning of year:		
As previously reported		$41,400
Adjustments (Note C)		(1,200)
As restated		40,200
Add net income		4,892
Deduct dividends		(2,000)
Retained earnings at end of year		$43,092

Extraordinary Items   At one time, companies had considerable latitude in deciding on the types of transactions that should be classified as nonrecurring. The publication of *APB Opinion No. 30* in 1973 greatly reduced this discretion.[6] The basic reason for this change was to correct abuses that sometimes occurred under the former practice. For example, formerly a company might charge certain nonrecurring costs directly to Retained Earnings, so that these costs would not appear on any income statement. In a few companies, the direct debits to Retained Earnings over a period of years almost equaled the sum of the net income amounts reported for these years. Other companies reported a variety of losses as "extraordinary,"

---

[6]"Reporting the Results of Operations," *APB Opinion No. 30*, June 1973, See also, "Reporting the Results of Operations," *APB Opinion No. 9*, December 1966.

in the hope that readers would regard them as abnormal and not likely to recur in the future.

APB Opinion No. 30 requires that in order to qualify as an extraordinary item, an event must satisfy two criteria:

1. The event must be *unusual;* that is, it should be highly abnormal and unrelated to, or only incidentally related to, the ordinary activities of the entity.
2. The event must occur *infrequently;* that is, it should be of a type that would not reasonably be expected to recur in the foreseeable future.

The words of these criteria do not convey their narrowness as clearly as do the illustrations that are used to explain it. The following gains and losses are specifically *not* extraordinary:[7]

1. Write-down or write-off of accounts receivable, inventory, or intangible assets.
2. Gains or losses from changes in the value of foreign currency.
3. Gains or losses on disposal of a segment of a business (discussed in the next section).
4. Gains or losses from the disposal of fixed assets.
5. Effects of a strike.
6. Adjustments of accruals on long-term contracts.

The only items that are mentioned as possible examples of extraordinary items are major casualties (such as earthquakes), the loss when a foreign government expropriates assets, and a major loss resulting from the enactment of a new law, such as a pollution-control law. Subsequently, gains and losses from refunding a bond issue were also classified as extraordinary items.[8]

Accounting Treatment. In those rare cases in which extraordinary gains or losses can be identified, they are reported separately on the income statement below "Income from continuing operations," as shown in Illustration 9–3. The amount reported is the net amount after the income tax effect of the item has been taken into account.

> **Example.** If a company had an extraordinary loss of $1,000,000, its taxable income presumably would be reduced by $1,000,000. At an income tax rate of 46 percent, its income tax would be reduced by $460,000, and the ultimate effect on net income would therefore be only $540,000.

Discontinued Operations

Another type of transaction which, if material, is reported separately on the income statement is the gain or loss from the discontinuance of a division or other identifiable segment of the company.[9] The transaction must involve a whole business unit as contrasted with the disposition of

---

[7]*APB Opinion No. 30*, par. 23.

[8]"Reporting Gains and Losses from Extinguishment of Debt," *FASB Statement No. 4*, March 1975.

[9]*APB Opinion No. 30*, pars. 8, 9, 13–18.

an individual asset or discontinuance of one product in a product line. Discontinuance may occur by abandoning the segment and selling off the remaining assets, or it may occur by selling the whole segment as a unit to some other company. In the former case, a loss is likely, whereas in the latter case, there may be either a gain or a loss, depending on how attractive the segment is to another company.

The effect of the decision to dispose of the segment is recorded on the income statement in the period in which the *decision* is made, which may well be earlier than the period in which the actual sales transaction is consummated. Unless a specific agreement has been implemented in the current period, the amount of gain or loss must be estimated. This estimate may be quite complicated, for it must take into account (1) the estimated revenues and expenses of the discontinued segment during the period in which it continues to be operated by the company, that is, until another company takes it over; (2) the estimated proceeds of the sale; and (3) the book value of the assets that will be written off when the segment is disposed of.

Accounting Treatment. As is the case with extraordinary items, the amounts related to discontinued operations are reported after their income tax effect has been taken into account. As shown on Illustration 9–3, two amounts are reported:

1. The net income or loss attributable to the operations of the segment during the current year.
2. The estimated net gain or loss after taking account of all aspects of the sale, including the amount received and the write-off of assets that are not sold.

Change in Accounting Principles

The third type of nonrecurring item reported on the income statement is the effect of a change in accounting principles. In most circumstances, the consistency concept requires that companies use the same accounting principles from one year to the next. But if a company has a sound reason for doing so, it may occasionally shift from one generally accepted principle to another principle that is also generally accepted. As pointed out in Chapter 7, for example, several methods of depreciation are acceptable; if a company has a sound reason for doing so, it may shift from one method to another.

If the company had used the new method in earlier years, its net income in those years would have been different, and this would have affected the balance in Retained Earnings. Retained Earnings therefore needs to be adjusted to reflect the *cumulative* effect of the change in all prior periods' net income. (For a change in depreciation methods, this would involve all prior years in which the depreciable assets currently on hand were in use.) The cumulative effect of the change is *not* recorded by changing Retained Earnings directly, however. Instead, it is reported as one of the nonrecurring items on the income statement of the year in which the change is made, as shown in Illustration 9–3.[10]

Correction of Errors   Until 1977, companies were permitted to adjust Retained Earnings to take account of the effect of events that had occurred in earlier years but that had been inadvertently omitted from the income statements of those years or had been included in these statements at amounts that turned out to be incorrect. Many of these *prior period adjustments* recorded the effect of settlement of lawsuits or the amount of income taxes finally paid. In its *Statement No. 16*, the FASB severely limited adjustments to Retained Earnings.[11] Only two types are now permitted. One is a technical aspect of income taxes, and the other is the correction of errors.

Errors are defined as "mathematical mistakes, mistakes in the application of accounting principles, or oversight or misuse of facts that existed at the time the financial statements were prepared." Also, "a change from an accounting principle that is not generally accepted to one that is generally accepted is a correction of an error."[12]

In addition, as noted in Chapter 5, a permanent decline in the market value of noncurrent marketable securities can also result in a charge to Retained Earnings. Also, starting in 1983, a period's foreign currency translation adjustments (described in Chapter 12) are charged directly to a special owners' equity account, rather than being flowed through the income statement.[13]

With these exceptions, *Statement No. 16* requires that "all items of profit and loss recognized during a period, including accruals of estimated losses from loss contingencies, shall be included in the determination of net income for that period." The sharp restriction of adjustments to Retained Earnings imposed by *Statement No. 16* is controversial, as indicated by the fact that it was adopted by a 4 to 3 vote of the FASB members.

NET INCOME

The "bottom line" on the income statement is labeled *net income* or *net earnings* (or *net loss*) without any qualifying phrase. The term *net income* never appears as a label for any other item on the income statement. Note that in Illustration 9–3, the label is "Income from continuing operations," not "Net income from continuing operations."

"Net income" therefore means, unambiguously, the net addition to Re-

---

[10]"Accounting Changes," *APB Opinion No. 20*, July 1971.
[11]"Prior Period Adjustments," *FASB Statement No. 16*, June 1977.
[12]*APB Opinion No. 20*, par. 13.
[13]"Foreign Currency Translation," *FASB Statement No. 52*, December 1981.

tained Earnings during the accounting period, regardless of whether it arises from ordinary operations or from other events and regardless of whether the transactions entering into its determination are recurring or are highly unusual.

FORMS OF BUSINESS ORGANIZATION

Before discussing the owners' equity section of the balance sheet, the three principal legal forms of business ownership will be briefly described. These are the single proprietorship, the partnership, and the corporation.

Single Proprietorship

A *single proprietorship* is a business entity owned by an individual. Proprietorship is a simple form for the organization of a business. Essentially all that one does to form a proprietorship is to begin selling goods or one's services. There are no incorporation fees to pay; no special reports to file (except an additional schedule on the proprietor's personal income tax return); and no co-owners with whom to disagree, to share liability for their actions, or to share the profits of the business. A proprietorship's profits (whether withdrawn by the proprietor or retained in the firm) are taxed at the proprietor's personal income tax rate, which may be lower than the corporate tax rate.

On the other hand, sole proprietorships cannot issue stock or bonds, so it is difficult for them to raise capital. They can borrow money from banks or individuals, but they cannot obtain outside equity capital because, by definition, investors who provide equity capital have an ownership interest. Moreover, the proprietor is personally responsible for the entity's debts. In the event of the firm's failure, creditors have claims not only against the assets of the proprietorship but also against the *personal* assets of the proprietor.

Partnership

A *partnership* is a business with essentially the same features as a proprietorship, except that it is owned jointly by two or more persons, called the partners. A partnership also is a relatively simple and inexpensive kind of organization to form. In a partnership each partner is personally liable for all debts incurred by the business, so in the event of the firm's failure, each partner's personal assets are jeopardized. Also, each partner is responsible for the business actions of the other partners. For example, in an architectural firm if one partner makes a mistake in designing a building that ultimately results in a lawsuit, the potential liability extends to *all* the partners. Each partner pays a personal income tax on his or her share of the partnership's taxable income, whether or not the profits are actually distributed to the partners in cash.

Corporations

The *corporation* is a legal entity with essentially perpetual existence. It comes into being under the aegis of the state, which grants it a *charter* to operate. The corporation is an "artificial person" in the sense that it is taxed on its net income as an *entity,* and legal liability accrues to the corporation itself rather than to its owners.

Compared with a proprietorship or a partnership, the corporate form of organization has these disadvantages: there may be significant legal and other fees involved in its formation; the corporation is limited in its activities to those specifically granted in its charter; it is subject ot numerous regulations and requirements; and it must secure permission from each state in which it wishes to operate. Moreover, its income is subject to *double taxation:* the corporation's income is taxed, and distributions of any net income to shareholders in the form of dividends is taxed again, this time at the shareholder's personal income taxe rate.[14]

On the other hand, in addition to its limited liability and indefinite existence, a corporation has the advantage of being able to raise capital from a large number of investors through issuing bonds and stock. Moreover, corporate shareholders can usually liquidate their ownership by selling their shares to others, and organized securities exchanges exist to facilitate such sales. A corporation whose shares are traded is called a *public corporation,* in contrast with a private corporation, whose shares are owned by an individual, or by a relatively few individuals and their families. The financial reports and certain other activities of about 10,000 public corporations are regulated by the SEC.

As of 1977, of the 14.7 million U.S. business firms, 77 percent were proprietorships, 8 percent were partnerships, and 15 percent were corporations. However, the great bulk of *business activity* in the United States is performed by corporations. Using net sales figures as a measure of activity, in 1977 corporations accounted for 87 percent of total $4.4 trillion U.S. business sales, whereas proprietorships accounted for 9 percent and partnerships for only 4 percent.[15]

ACCOUNTING FOR OWNERS' EQUITY

Proprietorship Equity

Not much more need be said about the owner's equity accounts in a single proprietorship than the comments made in Chapter 2. There may be one capital account in which all entries affecting the owner's equity are recorded, or a separate *drawing account* may be set up for recording periodic withdrawals made by the owner. If a drawing account is used, it may either be closed into the capital account at the end of the account-

---

[14]An exception is a "Subchapter S" corporation. These are corporations with 35 or fewer stockholders which, if certain conditions are met, pay no corporate income tax. Instead, as in a partnership, the owners are taxed on their respective shares of taxable income at their personal tax rates.

[15]U.S. Bureau of the Census, *Statistical Abstract of the United States: 1981,* 102d ed. (Washington, D.C., 1981).

ing period, or it may be kept separate so as to show the onwer's original contribution of capital separate from the effect on owner's equity of subsequent events. As far as the ultimate effect is concerned, it is immaterial whether the owner regards withdrawals as salary or as a return of profit; but if the owner wishes to compare the proprietorship income statement with that of a corporation, a certain part of owner withdrawals must be viewed as being salary and only the remainder as equivalent to corporate dividends.

Partnership Equity   A partnership has an owner's equity account for each partner. The amounts credited to each account depend on the terms of the partnership agreement. In the absence of a specific agreement, the law assumes that net income is to be divided equally among the partners. This is also common in written partnership agreements. If such is the case, in a three-person partnership the capital account, or the drawing account, of each partner is credited with one third of net income. It is debited with the actual amount of the partner's withdrawals.

If the agreement is that profits are to be divided in proportion to the capital originally contributed by each partner, then the capital account is maintained to show the amount of that contribution, and other transactions affecting the partners' equity are debited or credited to separate drawings or personal accounts. If one of the partners made a temporary loan to the partnership, it would be shown in a liability account rather than in that partner's equity account.

Partnership agreements may also provide that the partners receive stated salaries and a stated share of residual profits after salaries, or a stated percentage of interest on the capital they have invested and a stated share of residual profits, or a combination of salary and interest. The accounting required in connection with such arrangements depends on the specific terms of the agreement.

> **Example.** The partnership agreement of Jackson and Curtin provided that Jackson (who worked half time) would receive a salary of $15,000 and Curtin a salary of $30,000; that each would receive 10 percent interest on the capital they contributed; and that they would share equally in the remainder of net income. In 1983, the average balance in Jackson's capital account was $20,000 and in Curtin's was $50,000. The partnership net income was $65,000.
>
> The amount to be credited to each partner's equity account would be computed as follows:

	Total	Jackson	Curtin
Salary	$45,000	$15,000	$30,000
Interest on capital	7,000	2,000	5,000
Remainder	13,000	6,500	6,500
Total	$65,000	$23,500	$41,500

Whatever the partnership arrangement, the law does not regard salaries or interest payments to the partners as being different from any other type of withdrawal, since the partnership is not an entity legally separate from the individual partners.

Ownership in a Corporation

Ownership in a corporation is evidenced by a *stock certificate*. This capital stock may be either *common* or *preferred*. Each corporation is authorized in its charter to issue a maximum number of *shares* of each class of stock. Each stock certificate shows how many shares of ownership it represents. Because a corporation's owners hold stock certificates that indicate their shares of ownership, owners' equity in a corporation is called *shareholders' equity* or *stockholders' equity*.

Preferred Stock

Preferred stock pays a stated dividend, much like the interest payment on bonds, except that the dividend is not a legal liability until it has been declared by the directors, nor is it a tax-deductible expense to the corporation. Preferred stock has preference, or priority, over common as to the receipt of dividends, as to assets in the event of liquidation, or as to other specified matters. Preferred stock may be *cumulative* or *noncumulative*. With cumulative preferred, if the corporation is unable to pay the regular dividend, the unpaid dividends add up or cumulate and are paid when the firm resumes payment of preferred dividends. The undeclared dividends are *not* recorded as a liability, however.

> **Example.** In 1982, Cotting Corporation did not pay the $9 dividend on each share of its $9 cumulative preferred stock. Hence, no dividend can be paid on the common stock in 1982. In 1983, holders of Cotting's common stock cannot be paid any dividend unless $18 is paid on the $9 cumulative preferred (the $9 1983 dividend plus the $9 from 1982).

Preferred stock is usually issued with a face or par value of $100 per share. The dividend rate (9 percent in the above example) is analogous to the coupon rate on a bond, although in practice the dividend is stated at its dollar amount rather than as a percentage of par value. Also like bonds, some preferred stock is convertible into a specified number of shares of common stock; this is called a *convertible preferred*. Unlike bonds, however, preferred stock usually does not have a maturity date; that is, there is no provision for redemption of the preferred on a given date at its par value.

Some issues of preferred stock, however, are redeemable on a specified date or at the holder's option. In substance, these *redeemable preferreds* are therefore almost like bonds; but in law, they are still equity securities. Reflecting this duality, on the balance sheet they are reported neither in the liabilities section nor the owner's equity section, but rather in a special section between liabilities and owners' equity.

If a corporation is liquidated, provided assets exist after all liabilities have been settled, preferred stockholders are entitled to receive par for their shares. Also, whereas bondholders can force the firm into bankruptcy if an interest payment on the bonds is missed, preferred stockholders have no such recourse. Interest on bonds is an expense, both for financial accounting purposes and for income tax purposes, whereas a dividend on stock, including preferred stock, is *not* an expense. Accounting treatment of preferred stock is substantially the same as for common stock, described below.

Compared with both common stock and bonds, preferred stock is a relatively small source of corporate funds. In 1980, corporations raised over $78 billion using one of these three instruments: of this amount, 71 percent was raised by issuing bonds, 24 percent by common stock, and only 5 percent by preferred stock.[16] The principal reason for the unpopularity of preferred stock is that its dividends are not a deductible expense for income tax purposes, as is the case with interest on bonds.

Common Stock

Every corporation has common stock. Common shareholders have a residual interest in profits and assets, below that of all other creditors and preferred stockholders. Common stock may be either par value or no-par value. *Par value stock*[17] appears in the accounts at a fixed amount per share that is specified in the corporation's charter or bylaws. Whereas par value on a bond or on preferred stock has meaning, for common stock this amount is arbitrary, essentially meaningless, and hence potentially misleading. Except by coincidence, the par value of the stock in a going concern has no relation either to the stock's market value or to its book value.

No-par-value stock has a *stated value*, which is fixed by the board of directors. The stated value governs the amounts to be entered in the capital stock account just as if it were a par value. The distinction between par value and no-par-value stock is therefore of little practical significance.

Book value of common stock is the total common shareholders' equity as reported on the balance sheet. This section of the balance sheet consists of two parts: (1) the amount invested in the firm by its shareholders, called *contributed capital* and (2) retained earnings. The amount of contributed capital, in turn, is the sum of two accounts: the par or stated value of the outstanding shares of capital stock, and the amount the shareholders have invested in the firm by paying more for their shares than this par or stated value.

----

[16]Ibid.

[17]Henceforth, the word *stock* unmodified by *common* or *preferred* will mean common stock.

**Recording a
Common Stock
Issue**

To illustrate the issuance of stock, let us consider Carroll Corporation, which received a charter from the state authorizing the issuance of 20,000 shares of $1 par value common stock. If 1,000 shares of this stock were issued at par ($1) and the proceeds were received by Carroll immediately, the following entry would be made:

```
Cash ........................................  1,000
     Common Stock .............................         1,000
```

Paid-In Capital.   Common stock is rarely issued at a discount (i.e., at an amount below par) because in most states this is illegal. Even where sale at a discount is permitted, individual shareholders would be required to contribute the amount of the discount in cash if the company should go bankrupt, and such a possibility makes discount stock unattractive to investors. Corporations therefore set the par value or stated value low enough (usually $10, $1, or $0.10) so that in practice stock is almost always sold at a premium. In such situations, the Common Stock account reflects the par or stated value, and the premium is shown separately, in an account variously called *Paid-In Capital, Paid-In Surplus* or *Capital Surplus.* (The FASB suggests the more descriptive but cumbersome title, "Capital contributed in excess of the par or stated value of shares.") If 1,000 shares of Carroll Corporation $1 common stock were issued at $12 a share, the following entry would be made:

```
Cash .........................................  12,000
     Common Stock .............................          1,000
     Paid—In Capital ..........................         11,000
```

Issue Costs.   The offering of an issue of stock is often handled by an investment banking firm that receives a fee or "spread" for this service. Usually the corporation records only the net amount received from the investment banker, that is, the amount remitted by shareholders less the banker's spread.

In connection with the issuance of stock, the corporation itself incurs issue costs over and above the banker's spread. These amounts usually also are deducted from the amount received from the issue. Note that because of the spread and issue costs, the amount actually remitted by the shareholders is greater than the amount by which contributed capital (par value plus paid-in capital) increases on the balance sheet. Note also that these initial issue transactions are between the company and its shareholders. When one shareholder sells stock to another shareholder, the amounts in the company's accounts are not affected in any way; the only change is in the company's detailed record of the identity of shareholders.

Treasury Stock

Treasury stock is a corporation's own stock that has been issued and subsequently reacquired by purchase. The firm may reacquire its shares for a number of reasons: to obtain shares that can be used in the future for acquisitions, bonus plans, exercise of warrants, and conversion of convertible bonds or preferred stocks; to increase the earnings per share; or to improve the market price of the stock. Treasury stock has no voting, dividend, or other shareholder rights.

Treasury stock is clearly not an "economic resource" of an entity. A corporation cannot have a claim against itself. Therefore, treasury stock is not an asset. Rather, it is reported on the balance sheet as a reduction in shareholders' equity, that is, as a reduction in the number and value of the shares outstanding.

Two methods of accounting for treasury stock are permitted. For a given situation, either method has the same effect on *total* owners' equity. With the simpler method, called the *cost method,* when treasury stock is purchased, the amount debited to the Treasury Stock account is its reacquisition cost, regardless of its par or stated value. It continues to be shown at this reacquisition cost until it is canceled or reissued, at which time adjustments are made in shareholders' equity to dispose of any differences between this cost, the paid-in value (i.e., the net proceeds at the time the stock was originally issued), and, in the event of reissuance, the amount then received.

If reissued, any excess of selling price above cost is credited to a contributed capital account (such as Contributed Capital from Treasury Stock Transactions). If treasury stock is sold at a price below its reacquisition cost, the loss may be deducted from the related contributed capital account if such an account already exists from prior transactions; otherwise the loss is debited to Retained Earnings. In no event is a gain or loss on the resale of treasury stock shown on the income statement or recognized for income tax purposes.[18]

Reserves

In an attempt to explain to shareholders why they do not receive dividends equal to the amount shown as Retained Earnings, a corporation may show on its balance sheet an appropriation, or *reserve,* as a separate item that is subtracted from Retained Earnings. For example, a *reserve for future expansion* signals to shareholders the corporation's intention to use internally generated funds (rather than a new bond or stock issue) to finance the acquisition of new assets. Also, if some contingency does not meet the criteria described in Chapter 8 for recording it as a liability, then a *reserve for contingencies* may be shown.

None of these reserves represents money, or anything tangible; the

---

[18]The more complicated *par value method* is described in advanced texts.

assets of a business are reported on the assets side of the balance sheet, not in the shareholders' equity section. The accounting entry creating the reserve involves a debit to Retained Earnings and a credit to the reserve. This entry simply moves an amount from one owners' equity account to another. It does not affect any asset account, nor does the reserve represent anything more than a segregated portion of Retained Earnings. Because the use of the word *reserve* tends to be misleading to unsophisticated readers of financial statements, it is fortunate that such usage is on the decline.

Retained Earnings

The remaining item of owners' equity is Retained Earnings. As pointed out in previous chapters, the amount of retained earnings represents the *cumulative* net income of the firm since its beginning, less the total dividends that have been paid to shareholders (or "drawings," in the case of unincorporated businesses). Stated slightly differently, retained earnings shows the amount of assets that have been financed by "plowing profits back into the business," rather than paying all of the company's net income out as dividends. The importance to owners (and others) of understanding in some detail *why* retained earnings have changed between two balance sheet dates is the essential underlying reason that the income statement is prepared.

Dividends

Dividends are ordinarily paid to shareholders in cash, but they occasionally are paid in other assets—the whiskey once distributed by a distillery corporation to its shareholders being a noteworthy example.

Dividends are debited to Retained Earnings on the date they are declared (i.e., voted) by the board of directors, even though payment is made at a later date. On the date of declaration, the dividends are a legal liability. For example, if Carroll Corporation declared a $5,000 dividend on December 15 to be paid on January 15 to holders of record as of January 1, the entries would be as follows:

1. Declaration of dividend on December 15:

   ```
   Retained Earnings...........................  5,000
       Dividends Payable (a liability account) ..         5,000
   ```

2. Payment of dividend on January 15:

   ```
   Dividends Payable...........................  5,000
       Cash ...................................         5,000
   ```

Stock Dividends.   Sometimes a company wants to retain funds in the business to finance expansion, and this precludes paying a cash dividend; yet the company still wants its shareholders to receive a dividend of some kind. Such a company may declare a *stock dividend*, which increases every shareholder's number of shares by the same percentage. Since each shareholder's holdings are increased by the same proportion, every shareholder's equity in the corporation remains unchanged.

Although a stock dividend does not change either the corporation's earnings, its assets, or its shareholders' proportionate equity, it does increase the number of outstanding shares. In theory, therefore, such a dividend should reduce the per share market price of the stock. However, in practice stock dividends are so small—usually 5 to 10 percent of the number of issued shares—that the market price of the shares occasionally remains unchanged. Hence, the stock dividend may have some value to the shareholder. To record a stock dividend, Retained Earnings is debited with the *fair* value of the additional shares issued, with the credit being to the Capital Stock account.

> **Example.** Bruce Corporation has 100,000 shares of common stock outstanding. Suppose that the directors voted a 5 percent stock dividend. Bruce Corporation would issue 5,000 new shares. Each shareholder would receive ½₀ of a share of new stock for every share then held. If the stock currently had a market value of $12 a share, the Common Stock item on the balance sheet would increase by $60,000 (5,000 shares at $12 per share), and Retained Earnings would decrease by $60,000. But the *total* shareholders' equity would remain exactly as before, as would the *relative* holdings of each shareholder.

An advantage of a stock dividend is that a shareholder may realize cash by selling the dividend stock while keeping the number of owned shares intact. But shareholders should recognize that doing this is actually selling a fraction of their equity in the business.

Stock Splits. A *stock split* (or *stock split-up*) also merely increases the number of shares of stock outstanding, with no change in the total par or stated value of the stock and no change in contributed capital. It has no effect on shareholders' equity; its effect is solely to repackage the evidence of ownership in smaller units. Hence, no transfer is made from Retained Earnings to Capital Stock when a stock split is effected.

A stock split automatically reduces the market price of a share of stock, thus allegedly making the stock appealing to a wider range of investors. In some cases, however, the price reduction is not quite proportional to the split since stock with a fairly low market price per share tends to be more attractive than stock with a high market price per share. Hence, if a stock selling at $150 is split "3-for-1," the new shares occasionally will sell for slightly more than $50 each, resulting in a gain in market value of each shareowner's total holdings of the stock.

The difference between a stock dividend and a stock split is a matter of intent. The intent of a stock dividend is to give shareholders "ostensibly separate evidence" of their interests in the firm without having to distribute cash. The intent of a stock split is to reduce the market price of the shares so as to improve their marketability. The presumption is that any increase in shares smaller than 20 to 25 percent is not a stock split.

Spin-Offs. The stock referred to in the preceding paragraphs is the company's own stock. If the company distributes to its shareholders the shares of some other corporation's stock that it owns, this distribution is similar to a regular cash dividend. It is recorded in the same manner except that the credit is to the Investments asset account rather than to Cash. Such a transaction is called a *spin-off.*

Warrants and Stock Options

Warrants. A *warrant* is the right to purchase shares of common stock at a stated price within a given time period. For example, a warrant could give its holder the right to buy 100 shares of Sterling Company common stock for $25 per share anytime between January 1, 1985, and December 31, 1989. If during this period the market price of Sterling's common stock rises to, say, $31, the holder of the option can *exercise* it by paying Sterling $25. The share of stock received can be sold for $31, so the warrant holder gains $6. Warrants are negotiable, that is, they can be bought and sold. Some companies have enough warrants outstanding that they are traded on stock exchanges, just as are other corporate securities. In this case, the warrant holder can sell the warrant and realize its value without actually exercising it.

Some corporations issue warrants in conjunction with the issuance of bonds, putting an exercise price on the warrants of about 15 to 20 percent above the current market price of the common stock. If the investor expects the firm to prosper, and expects this prosperity to be reflected in the market price of the common stock, then the warrant has value. The investor will then accept a correspondingly lower interest rate on the bond, thus reducing the interest cost of the bond to the issuer. Also, some small firms that investors regard as being very risky would not be able to attract investors to their bonds without using warrants as a "sweetener."

The value of a warrant at the time it is issued is a matter of opinion. It often can be approximated by estimating the higher interest rate that would have been required for the bonds if there were no warrants. Whatever the value is judged to be, the warrants are recorded separately from the bond liability by an entry such as:

```
Cash ........................................ 210,000
    Bonds Payable ............................          200,000
    Bond Premium .............................            6,000
    Warrants Outstanding .....................            4,000
```

Warrants Outstanding is a shareholders' equity account.

Stock Options. A stock option is essentially the same as a warrant except that it is not negotiable. Many corporations grant options to certain officers and employees, either to obtain widespread ownership among employees or as a form of compensation. Sometimes the number of shares purchasable by the option or the option's exercise price (or both) depend upon future events, such as the future market price of the stock or future earnings of the firm. If the options are intended as compensation, then their value should be debited to Wages or Salaries Expense; otherwise the firm would be understating its personnel expense and overstating profits. The procedures for accounting for options issued to employees are complicated and are beyond the scope of this text.[19]

**Balance Sheet
Presentation**

In the shareholders' equity section of the balance sheet (or in a separate statement or note if presentation of all the detail would make the balance sheet itself too long), the following detail is presented:

1. For *each* class of stock, the par or stated value, the number of shares authorized and issued and outstanding, rights and preferences as to dividends and as to amounts received in liquidation, amount of treasury stock, and number of outstanding options. The dollar amounts shown for each class of stock relate to the shares issued; no dollar amounts are shown for shares authorized but unissued.
2. The amount of paid-in capital.
3. The amount of retained earnings, in total, and a note as to any portion of this amount that cannot be distributed as dividends (such as a restriction arising under the terms of a bank loan).

Thus, the basic distinction is maintained between (1) the capital contributed by shareholders and (2) the equity resulting from net income that has been retained in the business.

Illustration 9–4 shows the owners' equity section of an actual corporation's balance sheet.

EARNINGS PER SHARE

In analyzing the financial statements of a corporation, investors pay particular attention to the ratio called *earnings per share*. This is computed by dividing net income applicable to the common stock by the number of shares of common stock outstanding. The FASB requires that

---

[19]For these procedures, see "Accounting for Stock Issued to Employees," *APB Opinion No. 25*, October 1972.

ILLUSTRATION 9–4

Associated Dry Goods Corporation and Consolidated Subsidiaries **Consolidated Balance Sheet** (in thousands)		
	Jan. 30, 1982	Jan. 31, 1981
Shareholders' Equity		
Convertible preferred stock, $4.75	**$140,707**	—
Common stock, $0.50 par value	**6,792**	$ 6,792
Capital in excess of par value		
of common stock	**60,430**	61,619
Retained earnings	**510,710**	474,840
Less treasury shares at cost	**(687)**	(2,008)
Total Shareholders' Equity	**$717,952**	$541,243

earnings per share be reported on the income statement, and has provided detailed guidelines for making the calculation.[20]

If the corporation has a simple capital structure, with only one class of stock, the net income used in this ratio is the same as the net income shown on the income statement.

> **Example.** The 1982 income statement of McLean Corporation showed net income of $7 million. The corporation had one million shares of common stock outstanding in 1982. It therefore earned $7 per share.

The various classes of stock that a corporation might issue can be divided into one of two categories: (1) *senior securities* and (2) *common stock* and its equivalent. Senior securities, usually preferred stock, are those that have a claim on net income ahead of the claim of the common shareholders. The income figure used in the calculation of earnings per share is the amount that remains *after* the claims of the senior securities have been deducted from net income.

> **Example.** Nugent Corporation in 1982 had net income of $7 million. It had outstanding 100,000 shares of $8 preferred stock and one million shares of common stock. Its earnings per share were therefore ($7,000,000 − $800,000) ÷ 1,000,000 shares = $6.20 per share.

---

[20]"Earnings per Share," *APB Opinion No. 15,* May 1969; and "Reporting the Results of Operations," *APB Opinion No. 30,* June 1973.

If the number of shares of common stock outstanding fluctuates within a year, then a weighted-average number of shares is computed.

> **Example.** Optel Corporation in 1982 had net income of $7 million. It had outstanding on January 1 one million shares of common stock, and on July 1 it issued an additional 500,000 shares, which were therefore outstanding for half of the year. Its weighted-average number of common shares outstanding was 1,000,000 + (500,000 × ½) = 1,250,000. Its earnings per share were $7,000,000 ÷ 1,250,000 = $5.60.

A *common stock equivalent* is a security that, although not in form a common stock, contains provisions that enable its holder to become a common shareholder and that, because of its terms and the circumstances under which it was issued, is in substance equivalent to a common stock. The value of a common stock equivalent is derived in large part from the value of the common stock to which it is related. Examples are convertible bonds, convertible preferreds, stock options, and warrants.

When a corporation has securities that are common stock equivalents, the FASB requires that the amount of such securities be taken into account in calculating earnings per share. The detailed criteria for deciding whether a security is a common stock equivalent and, if so, how the equivalent number of shares should be calculated are much too lengthy to be given here.[21] *APB Opinion No. 15* was the longest of the 31 Opinions of the Accounting Principles Board, and it was so complex that the American Institute of CPAs issued an "interpretation" that was over twice as long as the Opinion itself.

APB Opinion No. 15 also states that if a corporation has securities that *may* under certain circumstances have a claim on common earnings—even though these securities are not equivalent common shares—then the corporation should report two numbers for earnings per share: (1) *primary earnings per share*, which is net income divided by the number of common and common equivalent shares, as above and (2) *fully diluted earnings per share*, in which it is assumed that the maximum amount of potential conversion, exercise of warrants, and the like has taken place.

As pointed out earlier in this chapter, gains or losses (net of applicable taxes) related to discontinued operations and extraordinary items must be shown separately in the income statement. This separate treatment also applies to earnings-per-share figures, as shown in Illustration 9–5.

---

[21] "Earnings per Share," *APB Opinion No. 15*, May 1969. This *Opinion* subsequently was amended by *FASB Statements No. 21*, April 1978, and *No. 55*, February 1982.

ILLUSTRATION 9–5
EXAMPLE OF REPORTING EARNINGS-PER-SHARE DATA

	Primary	Fully Diluted
Income from continuing operations	$4.08	$2.91
Income (loss) from discontinued operations	(0.58)	(0.41)
Income before extraordinary items	3.50	2.50
Extraordinary items	1.66	1.18
Net income	$5.16	$3.68

SUMMARY

In analyzing transactions regarding wage and salary costs, a careful distinction must be made between the amount earned by the employee, the additional cost that the employer incurs for payroll taxes, and the amount collected from employees that is to be transmitted to the government. Pension costs are a cost associated with work done in the current period, although the actual pension payments may not begin until many years later.

The Provision for Income taxes is calculated as if the income tax were computed on the amount of financial accounting income reported for the period. The entry required to adjust actual income tax payments liability to this basis creates another liability account, Deferred Income Taxes. This account does not represent an amount due the government.

A few unusual items are reported on the income statement separately from revenues and expenses of recurring operations. These include extraordinary losses or gains, gain or loss from discontinued operations, and the adjustment that results from changing accounting principles.

In a corporation, shareholders' equity consists of two parts that should always be reported separately: (1) the contributed capital, which is the amount paid to the corporation by each class of shareholders, and which is further divided into (a) the par or stated value of stock, and (b) paid-in capital and (2) retained earnings, representing the cumulative amount of net income that has not been paid out as dividends.

Cases

CASE 9–1 Farrow Corporation (B)

In addition to the transactions listed in Farrow Corporation (A), Case 8–1, several other matters were referred to Mr. Cleary for his opinion as to how they should be reported on the 1982 income statement and balance sheet.

1. Farrow had purchased advertising brochures costing $100,000 in 1982. At the end of 1982, one fifth of these brochures were on hand; they would be mailed in 1983 to prospective customers who sent in a coupon request for them. As of March 1, 1983, almost all the brochures had been mailed. Farrow had charged $80,000 of the cost of these brochures as an expense in 1982, and showed $20,000 as a deferred charge as of December 31, 1982.

2. In 1982, the company had placed magazine advertisements, costing $50,000, offering these brochures. The advertisements had appeared in 1982. Because the sales generated by the brochures would not occur until after prospective customers had received the brochures and placed orders, which would primarily be in 1983, Farrow had recorded the full $50,000 as a deferred charge on its December 31, 1982, balance sheet.

3. Farrow's long-standing practice was to capitalize the costs of development projects that were likely to result in successful new products. These amounts were written off as Cost of Sales over a five-year period. During 1982, $37,000 had been added to the asset account and $24,000 had been charged off as an expense. Preliminary research efforts were charged to expense, so the amount capitalized was an amount that related to products added to Farrow's line. In the majority of instances, these products at least produced some gross profit, and some of them were highly successful.

4. In 1982, the financial vice president

315

decided to capitalize, as a deferred charge, the costs of the company's employee training program, which amounted to $23,000. He had read several books and articles on "human resource accounting" which advocated such treatment because the value of these training programs would certainly benefit operations in future years.

5. For many years, Farrow's practice had been to set its Allowance for Doubtful Accounts at 2 percent of Accounts Receivable. This amount had been satisfactory. In 1982, however, a customer who owed $15,230 went bankrupt. From inquiries made at local banks, Farrow Company could obtain no reliable estimate of the amount that eventually could be recovered. The loss might be negligible, and it might be the entire $15,230. The $15,230 was included as an account receivable on the proposed balance sheet.

6. Farrow did not carry fire or theft insurance on its automobiles and trucks. Instead, it followed the practice of self-insurance. It charged as an expense in 1982, $4,000, which was the approximate cost of fire and theft insurance policies, and credited this amount to an insurance reserve, a noncurrent liability. During 1982, only one charge, for $3,000, was made to this reserve account, representing the cost of repairing a truck that had been stolen and later recovered. The balance in the reserve account as of January 1, 1982, was $16,700.

7. Goodwill resulted from an acquisition made in the 1960s. Although *APB Opinion No. 17* required the amortization of goodwill only if it was acquired after October 31, 1970, a question arose as to whether it was a valid asset. Farrow management maintained that the acquisition was profitable and was likely to remain profitable.

8. In 1982, the board of directors voted to sell a hotel that the company had operated for several years. Another company had expressed an interest in buying the hotel for approximately $100,000. In 1982, the pretax income generated by this hotel was $15,000. The book value of the assets that would be sold was $40,000 as of the end of 1982. Farrow did not reflect this transaction in its financial statements because no final agreement had been reached with the proposed buyer, and because the sale would not take place until well into 1983, even if a final agreement were reached in the near future.

9. During 1982, the president of Farrow exercised a stock option and the corporation used treasury stock for this purpose. The treasury stock had been acquired several years earlier at a cost of $8,000 and was carried in the shareholders' equity section of the balance sheet at this amount. In accordance with the terms of the option agreement, the president paid $10,000 for it. He immediately sold this stock, however, for $20,000. Farrow disregarded the fact that the stock was clearly worth $20,000 and recorded the transaction as:

```
Cash ...................  10,000
    Gain on Treasury
        Stock ............          2,000
    Treasury Stock .......          8,000
```

The $2,000 gain was included as a nonoperating income item on the income statement.

10. Farrow's long-standing practice was to declare an annual cash dividend of $50,000 in December and to pay it in January. When the dividend was paid, the following entry was made:

```
Retained Earnings .......  50,000
    Cash .................          50,000
```

(see Farrow Corporation (A))

Questions

1. What changes in the financial statements (see Farrow Corporation (A)) is Farrow required to make in accordance with generally accepted accounting principles? Ignore income taxes and assume that all the transactions are material.

2. As Mr. Cleary, what additional changes, if any, would you recommend to be made in the proposed income statement in order to present the results more fairly?

CASE 9–2   Frink Appliance Company

Frink Appliance Company operated a large retail appliance store in San Diego. The store sold all sorts of household appliances, plus auto and home sound equipment. The company's owner, George Frink (known by his customers as "Big George" because of his rather ample proportions), had for many years been an extremely productive salesman in a San Diego store of the regional Highland Appliance chain. Having built up a large personal clientele during those years, Mr. Frink felt he could easily shift customers to a new store, were he to open one. In 1975, he did just that, and the store had rapidly achieved an annual sales volume of over $1 million.

In 1978, Mr. Frink decided he could increase the store's volume, plus earn interest revenue, if he established an installment credit program to assist buyers in financing their major purchases. The program was a success, with the amount of installment receivables growing in each successive year (except for 1982).

In early 1983, Mr. Frink decided the firm had "outgrown" its sole-practitioner accounting firm; and Mr. Frink retained a national public accounting firm to provide Frink Appliance with various auditing, tax, and consulting services. The accounting firm's partner assigned to the Frink account was Carolyn Sasaki. After reviewing Frink's accounting practices,

Ms. Sasaki met with Mr. Frink to review these practices. Of particular interest to Ms. Sasaki was the fact that Frink used the typical accrual method (formally, the "delivery method") to recognize sales—and hence cost of sales and gross margin—on all sales, irrespective of whether the sales were for cash, were charged to a Visa or MasterCard account, or were financed on Frink's installment credit plan. While she felt this made good sense for preparing income statements for Mr. Frink's use, Ms. Sasaki pointed out that the federal income tax laws (Sec. 453 of the Internal Revenue Code) permit the use of the installment method of revenue and gross margin recognition on installment plan sales.

With the installment method, the retailer recognizes revenues as installment payments are made, and then applies the store's normal gross margin percentage to these payments to determine the gross margin for tax purposes. For example, suppose a customer bought a $700 refrigerator having a cost of $490; then the gross margin percentage is 30 percent (= $210/$700). If the customer's first installment payment were $50 (ignoring interest), the store would at that time recognize $15 (= 30% × $50) gross margin for tax purposes. The effect of using this method for calculating taxable income is that it delays, relative to the delivery basis, the reporting of gross margin, and hence defers the taxes on that margin until the margin is realized through the customer's cash installment payments.

After Ms. Sasaki's explanation of the installment method, Mr. Frink expressed a definite interest in changing to this method for tax purposes. "However," he said, "I want to keep using the regular basis for our monthly and annual income statements because I really feel we earn the margin when the customer signs the installment agreement and we deliver the appliances. But before we change, I'd like to see how much we've been overpaying in taxes the past few years by not using the installment method." To address this question, Ms. Sasaki gathered the data shown in Exhibit 1.

bases for shareholder and income tax reporting. Would we have such an account if we make this change? If so, you will have to explain to me how I should interpret the balance in that account.

"Also, I have a friend who owns an architectural firm that reports on the cash basis for tax purposes. She was telling me the other day that her billings have really dropped this year because of the sad state of the construction industry, and yet she is still having to make tax payments as big as last year's. Could this happen to us if we change our method for reporting installment sales for tax purposes?

"Finally, it occurs to me that we have already paid taxes on the installment sales profits we recognized in 1982, even though many of those sales have not yet

EXHIBIT 1
INSTALLMENT SALES DATA
(thousands of dollars)

	1978	1979	1980	1981	1982
Installment receivables as of December 31	$38.4	$71.1	$106.3	$113.0	$98.8
Pretax profit as reported	67.2	83.9	96.6	99.5	93.2
Gross margin percentage	30.6%	31.1%	30.2%	29.4%	28.2%

Notes:
1. All installment sales contracts were for periods of one year or less.
2. The company's effective federal income tax rate in each year was approximately 25%.

Mr. Frink raised several other questions with Ms. Sasaki. "I understand in general the impact that this method would have on our tax payments; but it's not clear to me what the impact would be on our balance sheet, given that I don't want to change methods on our income statement. I've seen an item called 'deferred taxes' in balance sheets of the annual reports of some companies that I own stock in. I know this is somehow related to reporting income on different

been collected. If we change methods for 1983, are we going to end up paying taxes twice on those uncollected 1982 installment sales—once in 1982 and again in 1983?"

Questions

1. If Frink Appliance Company had used the installment method for tax purposes in the years 1978–82, how different would its tax payments have been in each of those years? What would the year-end

balance in deferred taxes have been in each of those years? (Round calculations to the nearest $100.)

2. How would you respond to Mr. Frink's questions concerning (a) interpretation of the amount of deferred taxes, (b) tax payments in a period of declining sales, and (c) double taxation of installment sales made in 1982?

CASE 9–3 Trelease Industries, Inc.*

Trelease Industries, Inc., was a diversified firm whose stock was traded on a regional stock exchange. Information related to the firm's capital structure and income is given below.

Market Price of Common Stock. The following table reflects the average market price of Trelease's common stock over a three-year period:

	Average Price		
	1982	1981	1980
First quarter	50	45	40
Second quarter	60	52	41
Third quarter	70	50	40
Fourth quarter	70	50	45
December 31 closing price . .	72	51	44

Cash Dividends. Cash dividends of $0.375 per common share were declared and paid for each quarter of 1980 and 1981. Cash dividends of $0.75 per common share were declared and paid for each quarter of 1982.

Convertible Debentures. Ten percent convertible debentures with a principal amount of $10,000,000 due 2000 were issued for cash at a price of 100 in the last quarter of 1980. Each $100 debenture was convertible into two shares of common stock. No debentures were converted during 1980 or 1981. The entire issue was converted at the beginning of the third quarter of 1982 because the issue was called by the company. These convertible debentures were *not* common stock equivalents under the terms of *Opinion No. 15*. The Aa bond[1] rate at the time the debentures were issued was 14 percent. The debentures carried a coupon interest rate of 10 percent and had a market value of $100 at issuance. The cash yield of 10 percent was not less than 66⅔ percent of the Aa bond rate. Cash yield is the same as the coupon interest rate in this case only because the market value at issuance was $100.

Convertible Preferred Stock. At the beginning of the second quarter of 1981, 600,000 shares of convertible preferred stock were issued for assets in a purchase transaction. The annual dividend on each share of this convertible preferred stock is $0.70. Each share is convertible into one share of common stock. This convertible stock had a market value of $53 at the time of issuance and *was* therefore a common stock equivalent under the terms of *Opinion No. 15* at the time of its issuance because the cash yield on market value was only 1.3 percent and the Aa bond rate was 17 percent. Holders of 500,000 shares of this convertible preferred stock converted their preferred

---

*This case is based on the illustrative example given in APB *Opinion No. 15* (May 1969), as amended by *FASB Statement No. 55* (February 1982).

[1]"Aa" is the next-to-highest quality rating given bonds by the two major rating services, Moody's and Standard & Poor's. ("Aaa" is the highest rating.)

stock into common stock during 1982 because the cash dividend on the common stock exceeded the cash dividend on the preferred stock.

Warrants. Warrants to buy 500,000 shares of common stock at $60 per share for a period of five years were issued along with the convertible preferred stock mentioned above. No warrants have been exercised.

The number of common shares represented by the warrants was 71,428 for each of the third and fourth quarters of 1982 ($60 exercise price × 500,000 warrants = $30,000,000; $30,000,000 ÷ $70 per share market price = 428,572 shares; 500,000 shares − 428,572 shares = 71,428 shares). No shares were deemed to be represented by the warrants for the second quarter of 1982 or for any preceding quarter because the market price of the stock did not exceed the exercise price for substantially all of three consecutive months until the third quarter of 1982.

Common Stock. The number of shares of common stock outstanding was as follows:

	1982	1981
Beginning of year	3,300,000	3,300,000
Conversion of preferred stock	500,000	—
Conversion of debentures	200,000	—
End of year	4,000,000	3,300,000

Weighted-Average Number of Shares. The weighted-average number of shares of common stock and common stock equivalents was determined as follows:

	1982	1981
Common stock:		
Shares outstanding from beginning of period	3,300,000	3,300,000
500,000 shares issued on conversion of preferred stock; assume issuance evenly during year	250,000	—
200,000 shares issued on conversion of convertible debentures at beginning of third quarter of 1982	100,000	—
	3,650,000	3,300,000
Common stock equivalents:		
600,000 shares convertible preferred stock issued at the beginning of the second quarter of 1981, excluding 250,000 shares included under common stock in 1982	350,000	450,000
Warrants: 71,428 common share equivalents outstanding for third and fourth quarters of 1982, i.e., one-half year	35,714	—
	385,714	450,000
Weighted-average number of shares	4,035,714	3,750,000

The weighted-average number of shares would be adjusted to calculate fully diluted earnings per share as follows on the next page.

	1982	1981
Weighted-average number of shares........................	4,035,714	3,750,000
Shares applicable to convertible debentures converted at the beginning of the third quarter of 1982, excluding 100,000 shares included under common stock for 1982..	100,000	200,000
Shares applicable to warrants included above...............	(35,714)	—
Shares applicable to warrants based on year-end price of $72..	83,333	—
	4,183,333	3,950,000

Net Income. Income before extraordinary item and net income would be adjusted for interest expense on the debentures in calculating fully diluted earnings per share. Taxes in 1981 and 1982 were 46 percent. Trelease's net income (before preferred stock dividends) was as follows:

1982:	Income before extraordinary item	$12,900,000
	Net income..	13,800,000
1981:	Net income..	10,300,000

Questions

1. Be prepared to explain the calculations shown above for arriving at the weighted-average number of common shares, common stock equivalents, and fully diluted shares.

2. Starting with the item "Income before extraordinary item," complete the remainder of the 1982 and 1981 income statements.

3. Compute Trelease's primary and fully diluted earnings per share for 1982 and 1981.

CASE 9–4 Macomb Lens Company (A)

When John Macomb graduated from technical school, he started making plans for a small business to grind special lenses and to make certain high-quality optical items for the scientific and military market. At the time there was keen demand for a high-quality product, and Macomb thought he could build a substantial business by stressing this quality element. He started his business January 1. After a year of some very disturbing and revealing difficulties in meeting customers' high standards, Macomb thought

he had things going well. By working hard and personally satisfying all complaints, he knew he had created much goodwill for the firm.

Macomb began his business with $30,000 of savings, including some money he had inherited. On April 1, he borrowed $12,000 on a one-year note (13 percent) from his uncle, who had intimated he would renew the note every year so long as Macomb needed the money. He had had large bills for materials, but had been able to keep from falling too far behind in his payments. Except for the accounts indicated below as unpaid, all bills had been paid in cash, including the interest on the note. On April 1, he had paid in advance the first 12 months' interest on the loan.

Macomb purchased some standard equipment on the first of April, agreeing to make a down payment of $6,000 and to pay $1,500 every three months for four years, plus interest at 15 percent on the amount unpaid. During the current year, he made two principal payments of $1.500 each, and interest totaling $1,744. The next payment was due on January 1.

When the equipment was bought, the company insisted on Macomb's taking out four years' insurance that had cost a total of $1,200 cash. The equipment presumably would be useful for at least 10 years; however, Macomb contemplated that if all went according to his plans, he would trade in the equipment in 5 years and buy some with a greater operating capacity. He estimated that the equipment could probably be sold for $3,000 at that time.

By the end of the first year, Macomb had three people working for him. One was a young woman who took care of his office work as well as spending about one third of her time packing the delicate products as they were completed in the shop. The other two workers spent all of their time in the shop. About 20 percent of Macomb's time was spent in office work and on selling trips, but the rest of the time he was to be found in the shop working with the other workers. These four persons' earnings were as follows:

Mary Schultz	$ 7,200
John Bardell	17,700
Jean Nutchell	21,000
John Macomb	36,000
Total	$81,900

Of this total, $54,300 had been paid to the employees, $19,050 had been paid to the U.S. Treasury for FICA and withholding taxes, $7,200 was due the employees, and $1,350 was due the U.S. Treasury.

At the end of the year, Macomb's records included the following:

Rent	$ 12,000
Unpaid bills from suppliers*	30,780
Paid bills from suppliers for materials (excludes payments on loans)	36,360
Cash received from customers	117,750
Uncollected accounts:	
U.S. Navy	30,900
Universities Scientific Supply Company	24,780
Payment due Macomb for subcontract work, completed and shipped,	
December 17—Pegasus Aircraft Company	5,820
Spent on office supplies	1,500
Inventory on hand, at estimated cost, materials	19,200
Office supplies	300
Administrative and selling expenses (including travel, advertising)	16,380
Miscellaneous production costs	2,580
Cash on hand†	4,076

*Does not include the balance due for the equipment.
†Does not include a check for $12,240 from Universities Scientific Supply Company believed to be in the mail as their regular settlement of accounts as of the close the previous month. December billings to Universities Scientific Supply Company were $12,540.

Most of Macomb's sales were to two buyers, the U. S. Navy and the Universities Scientific Supply Company. Macomb had sold some $2,250 worth of goods to one buyer earlier in the year when business was slow; and when the firm became bankrupt with no assets whatever and without having paid its bill, Macomb promised himself, "Never again." Other firms, he was told, protected themselves against such losses by use of a charge of 1 percent of year-ending accounts receivables as an allowance for bad debts.

In October, the Pegasus Aircraft Company had asked Macomb to do some work for them, altering special equipment that they sent on to Macomb's shop. The first lot had been completed before the year-end, but the payment for the work, $5,820 had not been received. A second shipment, apparently valued at $18,000, had just come in (afternoon of December 31) from the Pegasus plant, but the alteration work (which would come to about $6,000) had not yet been started. Mr. Macomb ascertained that the $18,000 value of this incoming material had not been included in the totals for inventory listed above.

The inventory included 200 special items costing $4,800, which had been made for a government order but had not

as yet been shipped. Frankly, Mr. Macomb had wanted the situation to settle a little before making delivery, for a previous shipment of the same size (one half the original order) had not met the specifications of the government inspectors and 20 percent of the shipment was being returned as unsatisfactory. Fortunately the items carried a 30 percent markup over Macomb's cost, so he was not too badly off. Still, Macomb was disturbed about the matter because he thought his inspection standards when the first batch had been made had been no different than those in force at any other time, and besides he was advertising high-quality products. He certainly had no idea as to why the 20 percent had been rejected. He intended to file an appeal to try to collect the full amount that he had billed the government (included in the $30,900 in the year-end listing given above), particularly since the rejected items could not be reworked and were not worth much to any other possible buyer.

Question

Prepare the company's income statement for the year and its ending balance sheet. You should show clearly how any figure not taken directly from the case has been determined.

CASE 9–5   Union Carbide Corporation

The front page of *The Wall Street Journal* on June 20, 1980, carried an article with the headline, "Slick Accounting Ploys Help Many Companies Improve Their Income," and the subhead, "By Proper or Improper Means, They 'Manage' Earnings for the Desired Effect."

Highlighted in the article were certain accounting principle changes that Union Carbide Corporation had adopted starting with the first quarter of 1980. The article quoted a prominent securities analyst as saying, "Carbide's changes . . . are merely an accounting mirage that greatly exaggerates reported earnings," and a well-known accounting professor who said, "It appears to me that Carbide is merely polishing its 1980 profits to make them look a lot better." The rest of this case consists of excerpts from Union Carbide's 1979 and 1980 annual reports related to the company's 1980 accounting changes.

The changes were announced in a special section of the chairman's and president's letter to stockholders at the front of the 1979 annual report:

> In order to improve its financial reporting, Union Carbide is making several accounting changes effective in 1980 . . . [that] will lead to an increase in reported net income and earnings per share in 1980 and subsequent years.
>
> To depreciate the cost of machinery and equipment, Union Carbide will be using revised estimated useful lives rather than the shorter Internal Revenue

Following a new requirement of the Financial Accounting Standards Board, the corporation will capitalize, rather than charge as expense, interest costs attributable to major capital projects in progress. The capitalized interest will be amortized over the average useful life of the assets.

Beginning in 1980, Union Carbide will include investment tax credits in income in the year earned (the flow-through method), rather than deferring them and taking them into income over the average life of the assets earning the credit (the deferral method). The flow-through method will alleviate the decreasing impact of the investment tax credit which results from use of the deferral method during periods of continuing inflation. The large majority of industry utilizes the flow-through method.

We estimate that changes in accounting for the items described above will have the following effects on the results we report for 1980:

	Net Income ($ million)	Earnings per Share ($)
Depreciation......................	+ $ 92	+ $ 1.37
Capitalization of Interest	+ 20	+ 0.30
Investment Tax Credit (ITC).......	+ 17	+ 0.26
	+ 129	+ 1.93
Cumulative Prior ITC Effect.......	+ 217	+ 3.27
	+ $ 346	+ $ 5.20

Service guideline lives. . . . [This change] will result in more realistic historical depreciation costs. . . . On the whole, asset lives will be extended by about 35% over those used before the change. That extension will provide management and others with a better matching of depreciation cost with the revenue-producing capabilities of assets; and it will bring our asset depreciation lives more in line with those used by competitors.

The 1980 annual report included as part of a summary of 1976–80 financial data the information shown in Exhibit 1. The data in Exhibit 1 relating to the years 1978–80 were also included in the income statement. The disclosures shown in Exhibit 1 were required by *APB Opinion No. 20*, "Accounting Changes" (July 1971). The adjustments shown in Exhibit 1 relate only to the change in accounting for the investment tax credit (ITC). A footnote to the 1980 statements disclosed that the effect of the ITC change on 1980 net income (before the cumulative retroactive effect through 1979 of $217 million, or $3.28 per share) was to increase 1980 net income by $24 million, or $0.36 per share.

The change in depreciation useful lives estimates did not require retroactive income statement disclosures because it

closed in a footnote to its 1980 statements that the effect of capitalizing interest costs attributable to major capital projects in process was to increase 1980 net income by $24 million, or $0.36 per share.

In the 1980 report's "Financial Review" section, the effect of the retroactive application of the 1980 change in depreciation lives on 1979 results was dis-

EXHIBIT 1

UNION CARBIDE CORPORATION
Selected Financial Data
For the Years Ending December 31, 1976–1980
(amounts in millions, except per-share figures)

	1980	1979	1978	1977	1976
Income before cumulative effect of change in accounting principle	$ 673	$ 556	$ 394	$ 385	$ 441
Cumulative effect of change in accounting for the ITC	$ 217	—	—	—	—
Net income...........................	$ 890	$ 556	$ 394	$ 385	$ 441
Income per share before cumulative effect of change in accounting principle	$10.08	$8.47	$6.09	$6.05	$7.15
Cumulative effect per share of change in accounting for the ITC.............................	$ 3.28	—	—	—	—
Net income per share	$13.36	$8.47	$6.09	$6.05	$7.15
Pro forma net income with 1980 change in accounting for the ITC applied retroactively..............	$ 673	$ 573	$ 448	$ 431	$ 487
Pro forma net income per share.........	$10.08	$8.73	$6.92	$6.78	$7.89

was a change in accounting *estimates* rather than in an accounting *principle* (APB-20, par. 31). The change involving capitalization of interest costs did not result in any retroactive restatements of income because *FASB Statement No. 34*, "Capitalization of Interest Cost" (October 1979), expressly prohibited such retroactive restatements (par. 23). However, as

required by FASB-34, Union Carbide disclosed as follows:[1]

1979 Data (millions, except per-share figures)

	As Reported	As Restated
Depreciation..........	$470	$315
Net income..........	556	671
Net income per share .	$8.47	$10.23

[1]The report contained these data by quarter of 1979, as well as the total 1979 amounts shown here.

A footnote to the 1980 statements disclosed that the revision of estimated useful lives increased 1980 net income by $94 million, or $1.41 per share.

Also in 1980, Union Carbide increased the estimated future return on pension plan assets used in calculating the actuarial present value of accumulated plan benefits from 7 percent to 8 percent. This revised estimate was not mentioned in the footnote on accounting changes or elsewhere in the annual report, but rather was disclosed in the footnote entitled "Retirement Program." That footnote also included the following table:

Millions of dollars as of January 1*	**1980**	1979
Actuarial present value of accumulated plan benefits:		
Vested	**$1,233**	$1,241
Non-Vested	**121**	133
	$1,354	$1,374
Net Assets Available for Benefits.......	**$1,385**	$1,156

Casewriter's note: FASB-36 requires that these disclosures be made as of the pension plan's "most recent benefit information date for which the data are available." It is not unusual for this date to be earlier than the fiscal year ending date, as is the case here.

As a postscript to the above 1980 accounting change information, the reader may be interested to know that for 1981, Union Carbide reported net income of $649 million (comparable with $673 million for 1980) or $9.56 per share (comparable with $10.08 for 1980). Also, in 1981, the company further increased the estimated rate of return used to determine the actuarial present value of accumulated pension plan benefits from 8 percent to 9 percent. The 1981 retirement plan footnote table comparable with the table shown above was as follows:

Millions of dollars as of January 1	**1981**	1980
Actuarial present value of accumulated plan benefits:		
Vested	**$1,239**	$1,233
Non-Vested	**108**	121
	$1,347	$1,354
Net Assets Available for Benefits.......	**$1,683**	$1,385

Questions

1. Compare the estimated earnings impacts of the 1980 accounting changes that were given in the 1979 annual report with the actual impacts on 1980 earnings as reported in the 1980 annual report. Why are there differences between the estimated and actual amounts? Why are the estimated and actual cumulative prior ITC *total* amounts identical ($217 million)? Why, then, aren't the cumulative prior ITC *per share* amounts identical ($3.27 estimated versus $3.28 actual)?

2. What was the impact on 1980 and 1981

reported earnings of the increases in the estimated rate of return used in pension plan calculations? (Give a general answer; far more data than are given are necessary to develop a precise numerical answer.) What other impacts did these increases have?

3. Evaluate the company's stated reasons for making the various accounting changes in 1980. Also evaluate the adequacy of the company's disclosures concerning the impacts on reported earnings of these changes.

4. Do you feel *The Wall Street Journal's* headline and subhead were appropriate, as concerns Union Carbide's 1980 changes? Do you agree with the quoted comments of the securities analyst and the accounting professor?

10

Funds Flow Statements

Thus far our attention has been focused on the analysis of transactions in terms of their effect on the balance sheet and the income statement. In this chapter we describe the third accounting report that a company must prepare. Although officially called a *statement of changes in financial position*, it is more commonly known by the shorter name, *funds flow statement*.

The discussion of the funds flow statement was deferred to this point because this statement does not affect the way in which transactions are recorded in the accounts. The accounts provide information that is summarized in the balance sheet and the income statement. Information used in preparing the funds flow statement is derived from data reported in the other financial statements, and is therefore only a rearrangement of balance sheet and income statement data.

THE CONCEPT OF FLOW STATEMENTS

A balance sheet is a "snapshot" view of the status of a firm's funds at one instant of time. The equities side of the balance sheet shows the *sources* from which the funds that the firm is currently using were obtained—so much from accounts payable, from long-term creditors, from common shareholders, from retained earnings, and so on. The assets side shows the *uses* that the firm currently is making of these funds—so much is tied up in cash, in inventories, in plant and equipment, and so on.

A flow statement explains the *changes* that took place in a balance sheet account or group of accounts during the period *between* the dates of two balance sheet "snapshots." The income statement (and related statement of retained earnings) is a flow statement: it explains changes that occurred in the Retained Earnings account by summarizing the increases (revenues) and decreases (expenses and dividends) in Retained Earnings during the accounting period.

Purpose of the Funds Flow Statement

The income statement focuses on the economic results of the entity's *operating* activities. The purpose of the funds flow statement is to provide information about the entity's *investing and financing* activities.

The activities that the funds flow statement describes can be classified in two categories: (1) activities that generate funds, called *sources* and (2) activities that involve spending funds, called *uses*. Of course, an entity's operations routinely generate funds (especially from sales revenues) and use funds (for most operating expenses). In order to focus on investing and financing activities, the funds flow statement reports a *net* source of funds generated by operations (or a net use, if operations used more funds than they generated). That is, funds generated by and used for operations are not reported in detail but rather as a single net lump sum.

Including this condensation of operating sources and uses into a single number, there are the following major types of funds sources and uses:

Sources	*Uses*
1. Operations.	1. Cash dividends.
2. New borrowings.	2. Repayment of borrowings.
3. New stock issues.	3. Repurchase of stock.
4. Sale of property, plant, and equipment.	4. Purchase of property, plant, and equipment.
5. Sale of other noncurrent assets.	5. Purchase of other noncurrent assets.

Inspection of the above lists suggests why funds statements are felt to be useful. They help the user answer questions such as the following: Is the company investing enough in new plant and equipment to maintain or increase capacity and to replace old facilities with more efficient ones? To what extent are these investments being financed by internally generated funds, and to what extent by borrowing or other external sources? For the funds obtained externally, what proportion was from debt and what from equity? Is the company in effect having to borrow funds in order to maintain its cash dividend payments? While the funds flow statement cannot provide complete answers to all of these questions, it can at least suggest answers and highlight areas where it would be desirable to gather more information before deciding, for example, whether to buy, sell, or hold one's investment in the company's common stock.

Concepts of Funds   Perhaps the most confusing aspect of funds flow statements is understanding what is meant by "funds." Unfortunately, there is no general agreement as to precisely how "funds" should be defined.

Cash as Funds. To the layperson, the most intuitively understandable concept of funds is that they are cash; that is, each of the activities listed above under "Sources" generates cash, and each activity under "Uses" uses up cash. Thus, defining funds to be cash suggests that funds are very *liquid* resources.

However, defining funds to be cash is a narrow concept of funds. Consider the following example: On January 1 of last year, you personally had cash on hand plus in a checking account totaling $500; by December 31 of last year, the total had risen to $600. If funds are defined to be cash, this means your net cash flow for the year was $100, and your "funds position" at year-end was $100 better than on January 1. Now consider the following additional information: On January 1, you had no unpaid bills, but a friend owed you $50 that was to be repaid by February 1. But on December 31, you owed credit card companies a total of $200, while nobody owed you any money. Thus, if we look not just at cash on hand but also at near-term cash inflows and outflows, a different picture results: On January 1, your near-term "funds position" was $550 ($500 cash plus the $50 owed you); while on December 31, it was $400 ($600 cash minus $200 in short-term debts). Now it appears your year-end "funds position" was $150 *worse* than it was 12 months earlier, that is, your funds flow for the year was −$150.

Net Current Monetary Assets as Funds. The preceding example leads to a new concept of funds, called *net current monetary assets* (also sometimes called *net liquid assets*). This is current monetary assets (cash plus marketable securities and short-term receivables) minus short-term monetary liabilities (accounts payable, taxes payable, and so on). While this is a less liquid concept of funds than was the cash concept, many argue that it is a more meaningful concept. They point out that an entity could easily manipulate its reported net cash flow at year-end by selling off marketable securities or taking out a short-term loan (to increase reported cash flow), or by paying off short-term debts or investing in marketable securities (to decrease reported cash flow). Yet none of these transactions would affect the reported flow of net current monetary assets. In recent years, some companies, including General Electric Company, have adopted the net monetary current asset funds concept, or a variation of it, for their funds flow statements.

Working Capital as Funds.   At present, most companies define funds to be *working capital*, that is, current assets minus current liabilities. The principal difference between this concept and the net current monetary assets concept is that the working capital concept treats inventories as part of funds. This means that, in effect, inventories are treated as being as liquid as the monetary current assets. It also means that an increase in inventories is not regarded as being an explicit investment decision, as it is with the other two funds concepts. Detractors of the working capital funds concept argue that inventories are not sufficiently liquid to be regarded as funds and that well-managed entities use inventory control techniques that explicitly treat the amount of inventories to be carried as an investment decision. Proponents of the working capital concept argue that changes in inventory amounts are just as "automatically" determined by operations as are changes in receivables and payables. They feel the concept of "investments" should be restricted to *long-term* investments, such as for plant and equipment.

FUNDS CONCEPTS ILLUSTRATIONS

To make the above discussion more concrete, we will illustrate the cash and working capital funds concepts. These represent the two extremes of the range of liquidity embodied in various concepts of funds found in actual funds flow statements.

Illustration 10–1 shows a summary of cash receipts and disbursements. It is based on the following situation:

William Snelson started Campus Pizzeria, Inc., on January 1, 1983. During the first year of operation, Campus had cash sales of $96,000. Cash expenses included $46,000 for pizza ingredients, $24,000 for wages, $1,200 for equipment rentals, $9,600 for store rental, $4,000 for utilities, $2,000 for miscellaneous supplies, and $1,300 in payment of estimated taxes. In early January, $6,000 of equipment was acquired, for which Campus paid $2,000 cash down payment and signed a $4,000 mortgage note with the supplier, payable in full (plus interest at 12 percent) in January 1985. Snelson's intent was to depreciate this equipment on a straight-line basis over five years. As of December 31, there was an unpaid December utilities bill of $400 and Campus owed $1,600 to its ingredients vendor. Because the vendor delivered frequently, Campus had only $1,200 of inventory on hand at the end of December. (There was no inventory on January 1, 1983, because operations did not formally commence until the first ingredients delivery arrived on January 3.) Also, Campus had loaned an employee $1,000, which she was to repay in early 1984. Finally, a customer had paid Campus a $200 advance for a pizza party Campus was to cater on New Year's Day 1984, and another customer owed Campus $300 for a Christmas Eve party.

Some, but not all, of these transactions involved cash, and these are shown in Illustration 10–1. The Receipts section shows the sources from which cash was received, and the Disbursements section shows the uses made of cash. A funds flow statement with funds defined to be cash (hereafter called a *cash flow statement*) gives similar information, but it differs from the summary of cash receipts and disbursements in some respects, as will be described below.

ILLUSTRATION 10–1

CAMPUS PIZZERIA, INC.
Summary of Cash Receipts and Disbursements
For the Year 1983

Receipts:	
Sales	$96,000
Advance on party	200
Total receipts	96,200
Disbursements:	
Ingredients	46,000
Wages	24,000
Rentals	10,800
Utilities	4,000
Miscellaneous supplies	2,000
Tax estimate payments	1,300
Equipment down payment	2,000
Loan to employee	1,000
Total disbursements	91,100
Increase in cash balance	$ 5,100

Cash Flow Statement

The cash flow statement differs from a summary of cash receipts and disbursements in three ways. First, it is prepared by a rearrangement of items taken from the income statement and balance sheets, rather than from entries made to the Cash account. Second, it highlights the amount of cash generated by the firm's operations; this amount can be calculated from Illustration 10–1, but it does not appear there explicitly. Third, the cash flow statement shows some items that do not go directly through the Cash account. Because of these differences, the cash flow statement is more informative than the simple summary of cash receipts and disbursements.

The construction of a cash flow statement for Campus Pizzeria, Inc., is described below. The basic data used to construct it are taken from the income statement and balance sheets shown in Illustration 10–2, and the cash flow statement itself is shown in Illustration 10–3. The objective of this cash flow statement is to explain in some detail *why* Campus Pizzeria's Cash balance increased by $5,100, from $2,400 on January 1 to $7,500 on December 31.

The first two steps are to determine the amount of cash that was generated by the operations of the business. This is done by adjusting the

ILLUSTRATION 10–2

CAMPUS PIZZERIA, INC.
Income Statement
For the Year 1983

Revenues*		$96,300
Expenses:		
Ingredients†	$46,400	
Wages	24,000	
Rentals	10,800	
Depreciation ($6,000 cost ÷ 5 years)	1,200	
Utilities ($4,000 cash + $400 payable)	4,400	
Miscellaneous supplies	2,000	
Interest ($4,000 for 1 year at 12%)	480	
Income tax expense	1,300	
Total expenses		90,580
Net income		$ 5,720

*The revenues include the $96,000 cash sales plus the $300 owed Campus for the party it catered on Christmas Eve. The $200 advance payment for the New Year's party is not revenue of this period; it appears as $200 deferred revenue on the balance sheet.

†$0 beginning inventory + $47,600 purchases − $1,200 ending inventory = $46,400 used.

Balance Sheets
As of January 1 and December 31, 1983

	January 1	December 31
Assets		
Cash	$2,400	$7,500
Accounts receivable	0	300
Notes receivable	0	1,000
Inventories	0	1,200
Equipment at cost	$0	$6,000
Accumulated depreciation	0	1,200
Equipment, net	0	4,800
Total assets	$2,400	$14,800
Equities		
Accounts payable	$ 0	$ 2,000
Deferred revenue	0	200
Accrued interest	0	480
Mortgage note payable	0	4,000
Contributed capital	2,400	2,400
Retained earnings	0	5,720
Total equities	$2,400	$14,800

revenue and expense items on the income statement so as to show the cash receipts and cash disbursements associated with these items.

1. Revenues Converted to Cash Inflows. The income statement revenue amount is adjusted to the amount of sales-related cash inflows. First, the $300 accounts receivable increase must be deducted, since an increase in accounts receivable during the year means that the year's revenues exceeded collections (cash inflows from sales). This first ad-

ILLUSTRATION 10-3

CAMPUS PIZZERIA, INC.
Cash Flow Statement
For the Year 1983

Sources of cash:			
From operations:			
Revenues..	$96,300		
Adjustments to convert to cash basis:			
Increase in accounts receivable....................	(300)		
Increase in deferred revenue	200		
Cash generated from revenues			$96,200
Expenses..	90,580		
Adjustments to convert to cash basis:			
Increase in inventories	1,200		
Depreciation expense............................	(1,200)		
Increase in accounts payable.....................	(2,000)		
Increase in accrued interest	(480)		
Cash disbursed for expenses......................		88,100	
Net cash generated by operations		8,100	
From other sources:			
Mortgage note		4,000	
Total sources of cash			12,100
Uses of cash:			
Loan to employee	1,000		
Acquisition of equipment	6,000		
Total uses of cash..............................		7,000	
Net increase in cash.............................			$ 5,100

justment, then, gives us the $96,000 cash collected for 1983 sales. (If accounts receivable had *decreased* during the year, this would mean that the amount of cash collected had exceeded the sales revenue for the period, and the amount of the decrease should therefore be *added* to sales revenue.)

Second, an adjustment is made to reflect the 1983 cash inflow of $200 from the advance payment, which is not included in 1983 revenues because the service (catering the New Year's Day party) will be performed in 1984. Together, these two adjustments to the revenue amount convert it to the amount of cash inflows from selling pizzas, $96,200. The reader can confirm the correctness of these adjustments by noting the $96,200 cash receipts (all from operations) in Illustration 10-1.

2. Expenses Converted to Cash Outflows. Expenses total $90,580. This amount as shown on the income statement must be adjusted to convert it to cash outflows for expenses:

a.   Total expenses include $46,400 for ingredients. Also, inventory increased during the year by $1,200. Thus, ingredients purchases must have been $47,600. (We already knew this, because Illustration 10-1 shows $46,000 disbursements and $1,600 was owed the vendor at year-end. But the user of a cash flow statement would not be privy to the detailed data shown in Illustration 10–1.) *If* all of these purchases had been paid for, then cash outflows for ingredients would have been $1,200 greater than the $46,400 recorded as ingredients expense. Thus, the $1,200 inventory increase is treated as an additional $1,200 cash outflow. (The fact that all $47,600 has not actually been paid is taken care of in adjustment *c*, below.)

b.   The $90,580 total expenses *overstates* cash outflows because the $1,200 depreciation expense did not require a cash outflow (note that there is no $1,200 disbursement for depreciation in Illustration 10–1). Hence, a $1,200 deduction is made to reflect this overstatement.

c.   Expenses included $1,600 of ingredients and $400 of utilities that have not yet been paid out of cash. Thus, again there is an overstatement of cash outflows, and this $2,000 overstatement, the increase in accounts payable, is deducted.

d.   The interest expense of $480 has not been paid. This $480 must also be deducted so as not to overstate cash outflows.

3. Cash Generated by Operations.   The cash inflows and outflows associated with revenues and expenses are then combined into a net amount of cash generated by operations, $8,100. The reader can verify this amount by neting the cash receipts and the cash outflows for operations (all the outflows except the equipment down payment and loan) in Illustration 10–1. Note that the receipts and disbursements statement did not highlight the net amount of cash generated by Campus' ongoing operations of making and selling pizzas. To most users of financial statements, it is highly informative to show clearly how much cash the company's operations have generated (or required).

4. Other Sources of Cash.   The sources of cash other than operations are identified next. In the example, this was the amount of the mortgage note, $4,000.

All Financial Resources Principle.   The treatment of this mortgage note illustrates an important feature of funds flow statements, namely, that they are prepared on what is called the *all financial resources* principle. This means that each significant change in financial resources is set forth separately on the statement, even though a given transaction may not have had a corresponding effect on funds. In the case of the mortgage note, the $4,000 is shown as a source of cash, even though Campus did not actually receive the $4,000 in cash. In effect, the cash flow statement treats the mortgage note and the acquisition of equipment as if they were two separate transactions, one a source of cash (from the mortgage note holder), and the other a use of cash (the purchase of the equipment). The use of cash for the equipment is $6,000, of which $4,000 came from the mortgage note, and the other $2,000 from the Cash account directly. The reason for this treatment is simply to make the statement more informative than it would be if only the net effect of the transaction were shown.

5. Total Sources of Cash. The sources of cash are then totaled. Note that this amount ($12,100) is much smaller than the cash receipts in Illustration 10–1 ($96,200) because cash outflows for expenses are subtracted from inflows from revenues to arrive at a *net* source of cash from operations.

6. Other Uses of Cash. Other uses of cash are identified. Because operating outflows and inflows have already been identified, these uses of cash reflect *nonoperations* outflows. In this case, they are the loan to an employee and the purchase of equipment. Note how the all financial resources principle reflects the economic fact that $6,000 worth of equipment was purchased, whereas in Illustration 10–1 one cannot tell what the cost of the equipment was, since only the $2,000 down payment actually flowed through the Cash account.

7. Net Cash Flow. Finally, the sources and uses of cash are netted to arrive at the $5,100 increase in the Cash account, which was the objective in preparing this cash flow statement. Note how much more useful the cash flow statement is in understanding *why* Campus Pizzeria's cash balance changed than was the statement of receipts and disbursements.

Summary of Cash Flow Statement. The approved title for the cash flow statement described above is *Statement of Changes in Financial Position—Cash Basis.* Its format and method of preparation are not prescribed; in particular, some companies show the "cash generated by operations" in a different manner than that illustrated. The method described here was selected primarily because it highlights and explains the differences between a cash flow statement and a statement of cash receipts and disbursements. In summary, this method is:

1. Find cash generated by sales by adjusting the revenue amount on the income statement:
    a. Add the increase in Deferred Revenues (or subtract a decrease); and
    b. Add the change in the Accounts Receivable balance if it decreased during the period, or subtract if the change was an increase.
2. Find cash disbursed for expenses by adjusting the total expenses on the income statement:
    a. Add to expenses the amount of a buildup in inventories, or subtract the decrease in inventories.
    b. Subtract from expenses the depreciation expense; similarly subtract amortization of patents or goodwill, which are expenses but are not cash outflows.

    c. Subtract from expenses the change in Accounts Payable if it was an increase, or add the change if it was a decrease. Do the same with accrued wages or any other liability that is related to current operations. (Do *not* adjust for changes in Notes Payable, which are usually caused by financial transactions rather than by operations.)

3. Combine the adjusted amounts from steps 1 and 2 to arrive at "net cash generated by operations."

4. Identify any nonoperations sources of cash, for example, loans and issuance of bonds, preferred stock, or common stock. Employ the all financial resources principle for transactions that did not literally flow through the Cash account, but did so in essence.

5. Combine the amounts from steps 3 and 4 to arrive at "total sources of cash."

6. Identify any uses of cash *other than* cash used for expense items. This will include purchase of fixed assets, repayment of loans, refunding bond issues, purchase of treasury stock, and payment of cash dividends.

7. Net the sources and uses to determine the increase or decrease in Cash. This amount can be verified by subtracting the beginning Cash balance from the ending Cash balance.

Working Capital Flow Statements

    In practice, most firms do not prepare a cash flow statement. Instead they prepare a *working capital flow statement.*[1] The offical name for this statement is *Statement of Changes in Financial Position—Working Capital Basis.* By using working capital as the definition of funds, in essence transactions are "put through a coarser sieve" for reporting them in the funds flow statement. For example, paying an account payable affects cash, so this transaction would be reflected in a cash flow statement. However, the transaction has no effect on working capital, since a current asset (Cash) and a current liability (Accounts Payable) decrease by the same amount. Hence, the transaction would not be reported as either a source or a use of funds in a working capital flow statement.

    Working Capital Flows. The central idea behind the working capital flow statement is that it should describe the flows of *permanent capital.* Permanent capital is the capital that is committed to the entity for a fairly long period of time (not literally permanently, because its amount does change); this is noncurrent liabilities plus shareholders' equity. The assets side shows how much of this permanent capital is used for, or

---

[1]According to *Accounting Trends & Techniques* (1981), 541 out of 600 companies (90 percent) used the working capital funds concept. The authors' search of the National Automated Accounting Research System (NAARS) showed that 2,872 out of 3,582 funds flow statements for 1981 (80 percent) referred to working capital.

tied up in, various categories of noncurrent assets. In addition, working capital (current assets minus current liabilities) is regarded as a use of permanent capital.

Thus, the working capital flow statement explains changes in working capital, noncurrent assets, and permanent capital. It disregards the details of the continuous movement of resources between current liabilities and current assets that results from the production and sale of goods and services and the collection of receivables. Because of the recurring nature of these flows, working capital is often called *circulating capital*.

Except for this difference in focus, the working capital flow statement is prepared in exactly the same manner as the cash flow statement. Detailed procedures are described later in this chapter.

Illustration 10–4 depicts resource flows and gives examples of flows between various accounts. Any transaction that changes one account above the dashed line and another account below the dashed line will change working capital, and hence represents a working capital flow that is reflected in the working capital flow statement. Any transaction that

ILLUSTRATION 10–4
RESOURCE FLOWS

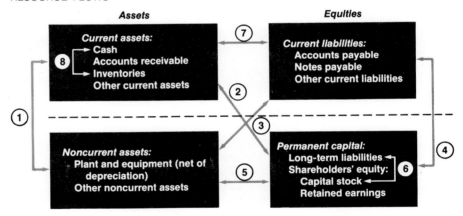

Examples of working capital flows shown on the working capital flow statement:
1. A noncurrent asset is purchased for cash; a noncurrent asset is sold for cash.
2. A bond is redeemed; new common stock is issued.
3. A noncurrent asset is purchased using a one-year note.
4. A long-term note's maturity date becomes less than one year hence; a six-month note is refinanced so as not to be due for two years.

Resource flows not *affecting working capital directly but shown on the working capital flow statement:*
5. A noncurrent asset is purchased using a long-term mortgage note.
6. A convertible bond is converted to common stock.

Resource flows not *affecting working capital and* not *shown on the working capital flow statement:*
7. Materials are purchased on vendor 30-day credit; a 90-day note is repaid.
8. Goods for inventory are purchased for cash; an account receivable is collected.

changes two current asset accounts, two current liability accounts, or one current liability and one current asset account by equal amounts has *no* effect on working capital, and is therefore not reported in the working capital flow statement. On the other hand, transactions such as those represented by arrows 5 and 6 that *do not* affect working capital but *do* constitute significant investment and/or financing activities of the firm are reported on a working capital flow statement, consistent with the all financial resources principle.

A working capital flow statement for Campus Pizzeria, Inc., is given in Illustration 10–5. The top part shows the causes of the increases and decreases in the firm's working capital, that is, the net effect of the firm's financing and investing activities. The lower portion of the statement explains the internal content of the working capital change, that is, how much the various current asset and current liability accounts changed during the period. Although these changes could be calculated from the firm's beginning and ending balance sheets, they are shown in the working capital flow statement to provide a complete picture of the changes in working capital.

ILLUSTRATION 10–5

CAMPUS PIZZERIA, INC.
Working Capital Flow Statement
For the Year 1983

Sources of working capital:		
From operations:		
Net income	$5,720	
Add expenses not using working capital:		
Depreciation	1,200	
Total working capital generated by operations		$ 6,920
From other sources:		
Mortgage note		4,000
Total sources of working capital		10,920
Uses of working capital:		
Acquisition of equipment		6,000
Net increase in working capital		$ 4,920

Changes in Working Capital Accounts

Account	Increase (Decrease) in Working Capital
Cash	$5,100
Accounts receivable	300
Notes receivable	1,000
Inventories	1,200
Accounts payable	(2,000)
Deferred revenue	(200)
Accrued interest	(480)
Net increase in working capital	$4,920

Comparison of Cash and Working Capital Flow Statements

In comparing the funds flow statement in Illustration 10–5 with the one in Illustration 10–3, one notes five differences that arise from focusing on working capital rather than on cash:

1. There is no adjustment for accounts receivable. Revenues increased working capital whether or not they were received in cash.
2. The $200 prepaid revenue was a source of cash in 1983, but was *not* a source of working capital, since it increased both a current asset, Cash, and a current liability, Deferred Revenue, by $200, leaving working capital unchanged. Since the 1983 income statement did not include this $200 as revenue, no adjustment to the net income figure is necessary in arriving at working capital from operations.
3. No working capital flow resulted from the $1,000 short-term loan to an employee, so this was not a use of working capital even though it did use cash.
4. On the other hand, the $400 utilities and $1,600 ingredients expenses, which have not yet used cash (because the bills are unpaid) *have* used working capital; Accounts Payable has been credited, thus reducing working capital by $2,000. As can be seen in Illustration 10–2, the net income amount reflects this use of working capital, and no adjustment is necessary.
5. The $480 accrued interest has not used cash but has decreased working capital during 1983.
6. The $1,200 increase in inventory has not used working capital because the increase in this current asset was offset by a decrease in the current asset Cash or an increase in the current liability Accounts Payable. The previously described cash flow statement expense adjustment of $1,200 assumes the inventory buildup used Cash.

These six differences explain why working capital increased by $4,920, while cash went up by $5,100.

MISCONCEPTIONS ABOUT DEPRECIATION

The way in which working capital generated by operations was determined in Illustration 10–5 often leads to confusion about the nature of depreciation. Hence, this calculation warrants further discussion. Instead of calculating funds generated by operations by showing revenues (a source of funds) and then subtracting the operating expenses that used funds, the starting point in Illustration 10–5 was the net income figure, to which depreciation was added.[2] This add-back of depreciation was done because depreciation was the only expense in Campus' accrual-

---

[2]*Adding* depreciation to net income, as in Illustration 10–5, and *subtracting* depreciation from expenses, as in Illustration 10–3, are completely equivalent, since reducing an expense increases net income.

basis income statement that did not represent a use of working capital. All of Campus' other expenses either reduced Cash or increased Accounts Payable, both of which reduced working capital. By contrast, as is shown by the journal entry to record depreciation expense, neither current assets nor current liabilities was affected, and hence depreciation was neither a source nor a use of working capital:

```
Depreciation Expense .......................  1,200
     Accumulated Depreciation .................       1,200
```

(Note that this entry does not affect Cash, either; depreciation is not a source of cash, nor of any other liquid asset.)

Another way of calculating the funds (either working capital or liquid assets) generated by Campus' operations would be to recast the income statement in a way that segregates expenses using funds from those that do not:

Revenues	$96,300	
Expenses using funds	89,380	
Funds generated by operations	6,920	(1)
Expenses not using funds	1,200	(2)
Net income	$ 5,720	(3)

Funds generated by operations could then be read directly from line (1). However, because an income statement does not use this format, what is usually done is to deduce line (1) by starting with line (3) and adding line (2); the numbers for these lines (2) and (3) can be found in the income statement (or sometimes in a footnote, for depreciation). Either approach results in the same $6,920 amount.

Depreciation Fallacies

Unfortunately, many people misunderstand the nature of this calculation. They have the misconception that depreciation is a source of funds or of cash. Their misunderstanding is compounded by the failure of many corporations to label the add-back of depreciation as an adjustment needed to convert net income to funds generated by operations. Instead, these corporations simply list both net income and depreciation under the heading, "Sources of funds." This confusion about depreciation is exemplified by these quotations:[3]

---

[3]The first is cited by William J. Vatter in "Operating Confusion in Accounting," *Journal of Business*, University of Chicago, July 1963. The second is a comment by the Chairman of Chrysler Corporation, *Business Week*, October 24, 1977, p. 83. The third is from a Robert Morris Associates study, *The Bank Commercial Loan Officer's Credit Decision*, April 1978, pp. 29 and 50.

"Depreciation money is cash. In your bank account, depreciation dollars and profit dollars look alike."

"This kind of [capital] expenditure we write off fairly quickly . . . so that it becomes part of the financing. It's the cash flow."

"The loan may be repaid . . . through cash generated from the gradual liquidation of a fixed asset (represented by depreciation) or the earnings of the borrower. . . . These two items—depreciation and earnings—constitute cash flow."

These statements are fallacious. *Depreciation is not a source of funds.*

Some people argue that depreciation is a source of funds because depreciation expense reduces taxable income and hence reduces the cash outflow in payment of taxes. For example, if Campus Pizzeria used ACRS allowances instead of straight-line depreciation in preparing its tax return, it could reduce taxable income and hence reduce the cash outflow associated with its tax payments. This does not mean, however, that *depreciation* was a source of funds. The funds transaction was the income tax payment, and depreciation merely entered into the calculation of taxable income and hence reduced the tax payment. By the same token, Campus could reduce its taxes this year by increasing *any* expense, such as by throwing a handful of mozzarella cheese on the floor for every one thrown on a pizza. Would one then say that wasted cheese is a source of funds?

Cash Flow Earnings. Since in most companies depreciation is the principal expense item that does not involve the use of cash, the sum of net income plus depreciation is often a good *approximation* of the cash generated by operations. (This is presumably what the author of the third quotation cited above had in mind.) This total is often called *cash flow earnings.* Although depreciation enters into the calculation of this amount, depreciation is not itself a source of funds. The funds are generated by earnings activities, not by an adjusting entry for depreciation.

PREPARATION OF THE FUNDS FLOW STATEMENT

Unlike the balance sheet and income statement, which are prepared directly from the firm's accounts, the funds flow statement is derived *analytically* from those accounts. This statement explains changes in assets and equities between the beginning and ending balance sheets of the period. Therefore, a logical way to prepare a funds flow statement is to use a worksheet that contains the beginning and ending balances in these accounts. We then can analyze the funds flows by reconstructing in summary form the transactions that caused the balance sheet changes.

Illustration 10–6 contains beginning and ending balance sheets for the Fairway Corporation, recast in a format that identifies working capital.

ILLUSTRATION 10–6

FAIRWAY CORPORATION
Balance Sheets
As of December 31, 1982, and 1983

	1982	*1983*
Assets		
Current assets:		
Cash	$ 230,000	$ 122,000
Accounts receivable	586,000	675,000
Inventories	610,000	655,000
Total current assets	1,426,000	1,452,000
Current liabilities:		
Accounts payable	332,000	388,000
Notes payable	142,000	133,000
Long-term debt due within one year	0	35,000
Taxes payable	144,000	108,000
Total current liabilities	618,000	664,000
Working capital	808,000	788,000
Plant and equipment (at cost)	2,000,000	2,337,000
Accumulated depreciation	(1,000,000)	(1,120,000)
Total working capital and noncurrent assets	$1,808,000	$2,005,000
Equities		
Long-term liabilities:		
Bank loans	$ 322,000	$ 370,000
Bonds payable	243,000	233,000
Total long-term liabilities	565,000	603,000
Shareholders' equity:		
Common stock ($1 par)	50,000	60,000
Other paid-in capital	133,000	167,000
Retained earnings	1,060,000	1,175,000
Total shareholders' equity	1,243,000	1,402,000
Total long-term liabilities and shareholders' equity	$1,808,000	$2,005,000

Data in these balance sheets will be used to develop a working capital flow statement.

Funds Flow Worksheet

Illustration 10–7 is the worksheet for preparation of Fairway's 1983 funds flow statement. On it have been entered the balances of working capital and of the noncurrent accounts from Illustration 10–6, and in the final column changes in these account balances have been calculated. The $20,000 decrease in working capital is the amount we must explain. For each of the other accounts, we will "reconstruct" the journal entries that caused the changes. Entries that affect the amount of working capital will be classified as one of three types: Funds from Operations, Funds from Other Sources, or Uses of Funds. (These classifications correspond

ILLUSTRATION 10–7

FAIRWAY CORPORATION
Worksheet to Develop the Funds Flow Statement
For the Year Ended December 31, 1983

	Beginning Balances	Analytical Entries		Ending Balances	Net Change
		Debit	Credit		
Debit-balance accounts:					
Working capital	808,000			788,000	20,000 cr.
Plant and equipment (at cost)	2,000,000			2,337,000	337,000 dr.
Accumulated depreciation	(1,000,000)			(1,120,000)	120,000 cr.
	1,808,000			2,005,000	197,000 dr.
Credit-balance accounts:					
Bank loans	322,000			370,000	48,000 cr.
Bonds payable	243,000			233,000	10,000 dr.
Common stock ($1 par)	50,000			60,000	10,000 cr.
Other paid-in capital	133,000			167,000	34,000 cr.
Retained earnings	1,060,000			1,175,000	115,000 cr.
	1,808,000			2,005,000	197,000 cr.
Funds from operations					
Funds from other sources					
Uses of funds					

to the format of the funds flow statement, and will facilitate its final preparation.) The numbers in the entries that follow correspond to those on the completed worksheet in Illustration 10–9. The reader may wish to refer back to Illustration 10–4 to recall the types of transactions that affect working capital.

Worksheet Entries

Retained Earnings. A good starting point for the analysis is the $115,000 change in Retained Earnings. Illustration 10–8 shows a condensed version of Fairway's income statement and a reconciliation of the beginning and ending balances of Retained Earnings. From these statements we can see that two things affected the level of retained earnings: net income, which is a source of funds; and payment of cash dividends, which is a use of funds. We thus can record these two entries on the worksheet:

(1)

```
Funds from Operations ...................... 170,000
    Retained Earnings ........................         170,000
    (This reflects net income as a source.)
```

(2)

```
Retained Earnings .......................... 55,000
    Uses of Funds ............................          55,000
    (This reflects the dividend payment as a
    use.)
```

ILLUSTRATION 10–8

FAIRWAY CORPORATION
Condensed Income Statement and Statement of Retained Earnings
For the Year Ended December 31, 1983

Sales		$3,190,000
Cost of goods sold		2,290,000
Gross margin		900,000
Less expenses:		
Depreciation	$120,000	
Other expenses	453,000	
Income taxes	157,000	730,000
Net income		$ 170,000
Retained earnings, December 31, 1982		$1,060,000
Add: 1983 net income		170,000
		1,230,000
Less: Cash dividends declared		55,000
Retained earnings, December 31, 1983		$1,175,000

At this point, note that the above two entries result in a net credit to Retained Earnings of $115,000. The last column of the worksheet shows that a change of $115,000 cr. was the amount we needed to explain. Thus, the analysis of the change in Retained Earnings is complete.

Plant and Equipment. The changes in these accounts can be caused by acquisition or disposal of fixed assets, and by changes in accumulated depreciation. As explained above, depreciation is an expense that is quite properly subtracted in arriving at net income, but which, unlike most expenses, does not affect funds. Hence, we must add back the depreciation expense to net income; otherwise, Funds from Operations would be understated. The $120,000 depreciation expense for the period is shown in the income statement in Illustration 10–8. The entry for the worksheet is:

(3)

```
Funds from Operations .......................  120,000
    Accumulated Depreciation .................             120,000
(This adds back to net income an expense
that did not use funds.)
```

Other company records indicate that $337,000 of new equipment was purchased during the year. Thus, as another entry we have:

(4)

```
Plant and Equipment .........................  337,000
    Uses of Funds ............................             337,000
(To reflect the acquisition of new
equipment.)
```

Entries 3 and 4 explain the net increase of $217,000 in Plant and Equipment, so we can move on.

Bank Loans. From internal records, we learn that Fairway did not pay off any of its long-term bank loans but did borrow $83,000 more from one bank. This is clearly a source of funds other than from operations, giving this entry:

(5)

```
Funds from Other Sources ....................   83,000
    Bank Loans ...............................              83,000
(This reflects the additional borrowing.)
```

Since the net change in Bank Loans during the year was only $48,000 cr., there must be one or more other entries with a net effect of $35,000 dr. (because $83,000 cr. + $35,000 dr. = $48,000 cr.). The records indicate that Fairway did *not* repay any bank loans in 1983, so we temporarily have a mystery. Investigation shows that of the $322,000 loans outstanding as of December 31, 1982, one has a payment of $35,000 due on March 1, 1984. Thus, as of December 31, 1983, this $35,000 was a *current* liability—Long-Term Debt Due within One Year. On March 1, 1983, when this amount was reclassified as a current liability, a use of working capital occurred. (Note that on March 1, 1984, when the payment will be made, working capital will *not* be affected by the payment since cash and this current liability will decrease by the same amount.) The entry is:

(6)

```
Bank Loans ..................................   35,000
    Uses of Funds ............................              35,000
(This reflects that a portion of a loan
payable became a current liability.)
```

Now the net change in Bank Loans of $48,000 cr. has been explained.

Bonds Payable. During the year, Fairway Corporation called $10,000 face value worth of its bonds. This payment required cash, so working capital decreased:

(7)

```
Bonds Payable .............................  10,000
    Uses of Funds ...........................            10,000
    (This reflects calling of a portion of
    the bonds.)
```

No other explanation of the Bonds Payable worksheet line is necessary.

Contributed Capital. The remaining two account changes to be analyzed are those in Common Stock at par, and Other Paid-In Capital; that is, contributed capital. The records of Fairway reveal that during the year 10,000 shares of $1 par common stock were issued, for which the firm received $44,000. This nonoperating source of funds leads to this worksheet entry:

(8)

```
Funds from Other Sources ....................  44,000
    Common Stock ($1 par) ....................            10,000
    Other Paid-In Capital ....................            34,000
    (This reflects the issuance of 10,000
    shares of common stock.)
```

This entry completes the analysis of changes on the worksheet (Illustration 10–9). The change of every noncurrent account has been explained, and the offsetting entries have been classified as sources or uses of funds. As a check, the debits (sources) and credits (uses) below the double line are added and the net change compared with the top line of the worksheet. Both changes are $20,000 cr., showing the accuracy of the amounts of the analytical entries.

Disposal of Plant and Equipment. One common type of transaction has been omitted from the above analysis in the interest of simplicity. If plant or equipment is sold, the amount of cash received is a source of funds. The balance sheet and income statement do not show this amount directly, however, and it must be obtained from other records. The transaction itself was recorded by debiting Cash, removing the equipment and its accumulated depreciation from the accounts, and debiting (or crediting) Loss (or Gain) on the Disposal of Equipment, an income statement item. If the changes in Plant and Equipment and Accumulated Depreciation are not fully explained by entries 3 and 4 above, the difference is probably explained by a disposal of plant and equipment.

   Example. Marfax Company sold for $10,000 cash an item of equipment that had cost $100,000 and on which depreciation of $70,000 had been accumulated. Since the net book value of this equipment was $30,000, there was a loss of $20,000 on the transaction. The entry would be recorded on a funds flow statement worksheet as follows:

```
Funds from Other Sources ................  10,000
Accumulated Depreciation ................  70,000
Funds from Operations ...................  20,000
    Plant and Equipment .................          100,000
```

In the above example, the $20,000 debit to Funds from Operations is a particularly difficult item to understand. The income statement included this $20,000 loss as an expense; however, the item, taken by itself, did not use funds. Therefore, it must be added back to net income to "correct" for the fact that net income understates the amount of funds generated by operations. This "correction" is analogous to the adjustment made for depreciation expense. The effect on funds of the asset disposal was solely the $10,000 cash that was received.

T-Account Method

Some people find it easier to work with T-accounts than with the worksheet shown in Illustration 10–9. Illustration 10–10 shows how the T-account method works. A T-account is set up for each noncurrent item on the balance sheet, and the net change in each of these accounts (as shown in the last column of Illustration 10–9) is entered and so labeled. An additional account is set up to accumulate transactions involving Funds from Operations. Entries are made to these accounts until the net of the amounts entered equals the net change in each account. Finally, Funds from Operations is closed into Working Capital by the following entry:

```
                            (9)
Working Capital .............................  290,000
    Funds from Operations ...................          290,000
```

The analytical process is exactly the same under either method.

Preparing the Funds Flow Statement

The actual preparation of the funds flow statement is now straightforward; it is shown in Illustration 10–11. The upper portion of the statement was prepared directly from the lower part of the worksheet. Again, this reflects Fairway's major financing and investing activities during 1983. The lower portion explains the internal content of the $20,000 decrease in working capital; these changes are calculated directly from the balance sheet current asset and current liability accounts.

ILLUSTRATION 10–9

FAIRWAY CORPORATION
Completed Funds Flow Statement Worksheet
For the Year Ended December 31, 1983

	Beginning Balances	Analytical Entries Debit	Analytical Entries Credit	Ending Balances	Net Change
Debit-balance accounts:					
Working capital	808,000	(see below)		788,000	20,000 cr.
Plant and equipment (at cost)	2,000,000	(4)* 337,000		2,337,000	337,000 dr.
Accumulated depreciation	(1,000,000)		(3) 120,000	(1,120,000)	120,000 cr.
	1,808,000			2,005,000	197,000 dr.
Credit-balance accounts:					
Bank loans	322,000	(6) 35,000	(5) 83,000	370,000	48,000 cr.
Bonds payable	243,000	(7) 10,000		233,000	10,000 dr.
Common stock ($1 par)	50,000		(8) 10,000	60,000	10,000 cr.
Other paid-in capital	133,000		(8) 34,000	167,000	34,000 cr.
Retained earnings	1,060,000	(2) 55,000	(1) 170,000	1,175,000	115,000 cr.
	1,808,000			2,005,000	197,000 cr.
Funds from operations:					
Net income		(1) 170,000			
Add: Depreciation expense		(3) 120,000			
Funds from other sources:					
Additional bank loans		(5) 83,000			
Issuance of common stock		(8) 44,000			
Uses of funds:					
Payment of dividend			(2) 55,000		
Purchase of machinery			(4) 337,000		
Bank loan payment currently due			(6) 35,000		
Redemption of bonds			(7) 10,000		
Check:		417,000	437,000		20,000 cr.

*Entry numbers here correspond to those used in the text.

Summary of Preparation Procedures

To prepare a funds flow statement on the working capital basis, the following steps are taken:

1. From the company's balance sheets, calculate the beginning and ending balances of working capital. Enter these amounts, and also the balances of the noncurrent accounts, on a worksheet such as in Illustration 10–9. Calculate the difference between the beginning and ending

ILLUSTRATION 10–10
T-ACCOUNT METHOD OF DEVELOPING THE FUNDS FLOW STATEMENT

Plant and Equipment			Common Stock	
Net change 337,000				Net change 10,000
(4) 337,000				(8) 10,000

Accumulated Depreciation			Other Paid-In Capital	
	Net change 120,000			Net change 34,000
	(3) 120,000			(8) 34,000

Bank Loans			Retained Earnings	
	Net change 48,000			Net change 115,000
(6) 35,000	(5) 83,000		(2) 55,000	

Bonds Payable	
Net change 10,000	
(7) 10,000	

Working Capital

		Net change	20,000
(sources)		(uses)	
(5) Bank loan	83,000	(2) Dividends	55,000
(8) Common stock	44,000	(4) Equipment purchased	337,000
(9) Net from operations	290,000	(6) Bank loan became current	35,000
		(7) Bonds repaid	10,000

Funds from Operations

(1) Net income	170,000	(9) Net from operations	290,000
(3) Depreciation	120,000		

ILLUSTRATION 10–11

FAIRWAY CORPORATION
Statement of Changes in Financial Position
Working Capital Basis
For the Year Ended December 31, 1983

Sources of funds:
From operations:
Net income $170,000
Add: Depreciation expense 120,000

Total funds generated by operations $290,000
From other sources:
Bank loans 83,000
Issuance of common stock 44,000

Total funds generated from other sources 127,000

Total sources of funds 417,000

Uses of funds:
Payment of cash dividend 55,000
Purchase of equipment 337,000
Portion of bank loan currently due 35,000
Redemption of bonds 10,000

Total uses of funds 437,000

Net increase (decrease) in working capital . . . . $(20,000)

Changes in Working Capital Accounts

Account	Working Capital Increase (Decrease)
Cash	$(108,000)
Accounts receivable	89,000
Inventories	45,000
Accounts payable	(56,000)
Notes payable	9,000
Long-term debt due within one year	(35,000)
Taxes payable	36,000
Increase (decrease) in working capital	$ (20,000)

balance for working capital and for each noncurrent account (last column of Illustration 10–9).

2. For each noncurrent account, analyze the nature of the transactions causing the amount of net change, and classify the change from each such transaction as either funds from operations, funds from other sources, or uses of funds. This analysis will require reference to the income statement (e.g., to explain the change in Retained Earnings), and to other financial records of the company. Illustration 10–12 summarizes the nature of such transactions and the place where information about them is likely to be found.

3. After the noncurrent account changes have been analyzed and classified, the debits and credits are totaled, and then combined as a check to see that their net amount is equal to the amount of change in working capital.

ILLUSTRATION 10–12
LOCATING AMOUNTS FOR A WORKING CAPITAL FLOW STATEMENT

Item	Location on Financial Statements
1. *Funds from operations*	
a. Net income...............................	Income statement
b. Plus: Depreciation expense	Income statement (or note thereto)
c. Plus: Depletion	Income statement *or* change in balance sheet item
d. Plus: Amortization of goodwill and other intangibles	Income statement *or* change in balance sheet item
e. Plus: Deferred income taxes (Note 1)................................	Increase in noncurrent tax liability
f. Plus: Loss (or less: gain) on sale of noncurrent assets (Note 2)...............	Income statement
2. *Other sources of funds*	
a. Sale of noncurrent assets	Decrease in net book value less loss (or plus gain) from income statement (Note 2)
b. Issuance of debt........................	Increase in noncurrent liability
c. Issuance of stock	Increase in contributed capital (*not only* par value of stock)
d. Conversion of bonds and stock (Note 3)................................	Balance sheet changes
3. *Uses of funds*	
a. Purchase of noncurrent assets	Increase in asset account (Note 2)
b. Dividends declared	Retained earnings statement
c. Retirement of noncurrent debt (includes shift from noncurrent to current section) ...	Decrease in noncurrent liability
d. Purchase of treasury stock...............	Increase in treasury stock account
e. Conversion of bonds and stock (Note 3)...	Balance sheet changes
4. *Neither a source nor a use*	
a. Change of individual items of current assets and current liabilities.	
b. Stock dividends.	

Notes:
1. A decrease in deferred tax liability is subtracted.
2. The change in the asset account is affected by depreciation, sale of assets, and purchase of assets. The amount of each is reported in a note accompanying the balance sheet and in company records.
3. Although the conversion of bonds to stock and of preferred stock to common stock do not affect the total amount of funds, these are reported separately in accordance with the all financial resources principle.

4. The top portion of the funds flow statement is prepared directly from the worksheet.

5. To complete the funds flow statement, the change in each current asset and current liability account is calculated from the balance sheet. These current account changes are listed in the bottom portion of the funds flow statement so as to explain the change in the internal content of the working capital (i.e., current) accounts. This step also serves as a double check on the correctness of the working capital change calcula-

tion in the upper portion of the statement. When prepared in finished form, the statement is given its official title, "Statement of Changes in Financial Position."

ANALYSIS OF THE FUNDS FLOW STATEMENT

At the outset of this chapter, several questions were mentioned that analysis of the funds flow statement can help answer. Some specific techniques to aid in this analysis will now be suggested.

Ratios

Coverage Ratios. Two "coverage" ratios, *times interest earned* and *fixed charges coverage,* were described in Chapter 8. Both of these ratios would be conceptually sounder if the numerator were based on funds generated by operations rather than on income, because interest, lease payments, and similar "fixed" charges must be paid by using cash. Funds generated by operations should be adjusted to a pretax, pre-fixed-charges basis (as was the case when these ratios were based on income in Chapter 8). These coverage ratios will be higher when based on operating funds rather than on income.

Source and Use Percentages. The amount of total sources of funds can be treated as 100 percent; then each funds flow statement item can be expressed as a percentage of total sources. For example, using Illustration 10–11, one can calculate that internally generated funds provided 70 percent (= $290,000 ÷ $417,000) of the total sources; or that equipment purchases used 81 percent (= $337,000 ÷ $417,000) of the total sources, and that dividends used another 13 percent.

In evaluating corporations' creditworthiness for long-term debt, credit officers consider the *ratio of funds generated by operations to total debt* (both short and long term). For a corporate bond to qualify for a AAA rating from Standard & Poor's, this ratio must be at least 100 percent.

Alternative Format. The format used in Illustration 10–11 is commonly used in published funds flow statements. Some financial analysts have suggested that a rearrangement of the funds flow data would make the statement more useful in understanding a firm's financing and investing activities. One suggested alternative format is shown in Illustration 10–13.[4] This format highlights the fact that Fairway Corporation was unable to finance its investments without raising external funds from borrowing and issuing additional common stock. In recent years, for some companies in depressed industries, this format would reveal that the firm had to raise external funds to maintain its dividend pay-

---

[4]Variations of this format can be found in "Financial Statements for Security Analysts" by John R. Page and Paul Hooper, *Financial Analysts Journal,* September–October 1979, and in the *FASB Discussion Memorandum,* "Reporting Funds Flows, Liquidity, and Financial Flexibility," December 15, 1980, p. 44.

ILLUSTRATION 10–13
ALTERNATIVE FUNDS FLOW STATEMENT FORMAT

FAIRWAY CORPORATION
Working Capital Flow Statement
For the Year Ended December 31, 1983

Funds generated by operations, before interest and taxes..		$522,000
Income taxes......................................		157,000
Funds available to capital suppliers.....................		365,000
Distributions to suppliers of debt capital:		
Interest..	$75,000	
Portion of bank loan currently due..................	35,000	
Retirement of bonds..............................	10,000	120,000
Funds available to suppliers of equity capital............		245,000
Distributions to owners (dividends).....................		55,000
Funds available for investment........................		190,000
Investments (equipment).............................		337,000
Deficit of internally generated funds....................		(147,000)
Financing transactions:		
Long-term loans.................................	83,000	
Issuance of common stock.........................	44,000	127,000
Increase (decrease) in working capital..................		$(20,000)

ments. This would be reflected by a negative amount appearing on the "Funds available for investment" line.

Undoubtedly, as users gain more experience with the funds flow statement, more ratios will be developed, as is the case with the many ratios associated with the "more mature" income statement and balance sheet.

Funds Flow Projections

The purpose of analyzing funds flow statements is not solely to understand what has happened in the past. In addition, this analysis serves as a means of projecting what funds flows may look like in the future.

A projected funds flow statement is an essential device for planning the amount, timing, and character of new financing. These projections are important both to management, in anticipating future funds needs, and to prospective lenders, for appraising a company's ability to repay debt on the proposed terms. Estimated uses of funds for new plant and equipment, for working capital, for dividends, and for the repayment of debt are made for each of the next several years. Estimates are also made of the funds to be provided by operations. The difference, if it is positive, represents the funds that must be obtained by borrowing or the issuance of new equity securities. If the indicated amount of new funds required is greater than management thinks it is feasible to raise, then the plans for new plant and equipment acquisitions and dividend policies are reexamined so that the uses of funds can be brought into balance with anticipated sources of financing them.

For shorter-term financial planning, a projected *cash* flow statement is essential. Projections are made for each of the next several months or several quarters. One way to prepare such a cash flow budget is to list all the estimated uses of cash and all the sources other than from additional financing. The difference between these totals is the amount of cash that must be obtained by borrowing or by issuing additional stock if the planned program is to be carried out. If it is believed that this amount cannot be raised, the indication is that the estimated uses of cash must be cut back.

SUMMARY

A funds flow statement, officially called a statement of changes in financial position, provides information about an entity's investing and financing activities during the accounting period. The concept of funds embodied in this statement can range from very liquid resources (cash) to only moderately liquid (working capital).

A working capital flow statement focuses attention on the major funds flows in the firm, in contrast with the recurring flows among current asset and current liability accounts. A cash flow statement reveals the same major funds flows, but intermixes them with the shorter-term flows among the current accounts.

The net amount of funds generated by operations is not the same as net income. Some expenses (notably, depreciation) that were subtracted in arriving at net income for the period do not use funds. In practice, the amount of funds generated by operations is derived from the net income figure by adding back depreciation and other expenses which did not use funds. However, one must not infer from this calculation that depreciation is itself a source of funds, for it definitely is not.

The funds flow statement reports certain financing and investing activities that do not cause a change in funds, such as the purchase of fixed assets with a long-term mortgage note. These activities are reported in accordance with the all financial resources principle, so that the statement gives a complete picture of the financing and investing activities.

Cases

CASE 10–1 The Great Games Company

The Great Games Company, owned by Terry Bentley, produced a hand-held electronic pinball game marketed under the name "Whiz-Kid." Each "Whiz-Kid" cost Great Games a total of $11.25 to produce.[1] The company sold its product for $15 each.

As of December 31, Bentley had been producing "Whiz-Kid" for three months using rented facilities. The balance sheet on that date was as follows:

THE GREAT GAMES COMPANY
Balance Sheet
As of December 31

Assets

Cash.	$22,700
Accounts receivable.	11,250
Inventory.	11,250
	$45,200

Equities

Common stock.	$42,000
Retained earnings.	3,200
	$45,200

---

[1]For simplicity, the reader can assume that this $11.25 per unit cost includes all company costs, not just production costs.

Bentley was very pleased to be operating at a profit in such a short time. December sales had been 750 units, up from 500 in November. Sales were expected to be 1,000 units in January, and Bentley's projection showed sales increases of 500 units per month after that. Thus, by May, monthly sales were expected to be 3,000 units. By September, that figure would be 5,000 units.

Bentley was very conscious of developing good sales channel relationships in order to increase sales, so "Whiz-Kid" deliveries were always prompt. This required production schedules 30 days in advance of predicted sales. For example, Great Games had produced 1,000 "Whiz-Kids" in December for January sales, and would produce 1,500 in January for February's demand. The company billed its customers 30 days net. Receivables were always collected on time, that is, in the month following the billings.

Bentley's predictions came true. By April, sales had reached 2,500 "Whiz-Kids," and 3,000 units were produced in April for May sale. Customers were all paying on time. Total profit for the year by April 30 had reached $26,250. In order to get a respite from the increasingly hectic activities of running the business, on May 1 Bentley went on a family vacation.

Within the week, the company's bookkeeper called. Great Games' bank balance was zero, so necessary production components could not be purchased. Unless Bentley returned immediately, the entire plant would shut down in two days.

Questions

1. Prepare monthly income statements, balance sheets, cash budgets, and cash flow statements based on sales increases of 500 units per month and 30-day advance production for January through September. When will the company need extra funds? How much will be needed?

2. How is it possible that a company starts with $42,000 in capital and has profitable sales for a period of seven months, and still ends up with a zero bank balance? Why did Great Games need money in May?

CASE 10–2   John Bartlett (B)

Referring to Case 3–4, John Bartlett (A), prepare the following for the accounting period beginning when Bartlett first began to organize his firm (the $20,000 investment by the retired manufacturer) and ending with the last event (No. 11) of the case:

a. A statement of cash receipts and cash expenditures.

b. A cash flow statement.

c. A working capital flow statement.

Compare and contrast (a) with (b) and (b) with (c). Which of the three would you find most useful as a shareholder? As a bank being asked by Bartlett for a 90-day loan? As a manager of Bartlett Manufacturing?

CASE 10–3   Bedford Manufacturing Company (B)

Refer to the situation in Bedford Manufacturing Company (A) (Case 6–2). Prepare a cash flow statement and a working capital flow statement.

CASE 10–4   Macomb Lens Company (B)

Referring to Case 9–4, Macomb Lens Company (A), prepare a cash flow statement and a working capital flow statement for the year ending December 31.

(Optional: Also prepare a funds flow statement using net current monetary assets as the concept of funds.)

CASE 10–5 Anderson State Bank*

Gardencare Company manufactures and sells lawn and garden tools. The company has experienced continued growth over the past three years and has forecast sales of $3 million for 1983. Gardencare applied to Anderson State Bank for a short-term loan of $50,000 to cover expanding working capital needs. This is the first loan application Anderson State Bank has ever received from Gardencare, and the bank is anxious to develop a lasting relationship.

Financial statements supplied by Gardencare at the bank's request are shown in Exhibits 1 and 2.

Other data:

1. Accounts Receivable. Sales are highly seasonal, with most sales occurring in the spring and summer. Gardencare allows many customers to wait until September or October to settle their accounts (a common practice in the industry).

The allowance for uncollectible accounts had a balance of $30,000 on December 31, 1981, and 40,000 on December 31, 1982.

EXHIBIT 1

GARDENCARE COMPANY
Statement of Financial Position
December 31
(unaudited, thousands of dollars)

	1981	1982
Assets		
Current assets:		
Cash	$ 85	$ 60
Marketable securities (cost)	20	20
Accounts receivable (net)	520	600
Inventories	365	475
Prepaid items	40	45
Total current assets	1,030	1,200
Investments (cost)	80	80
Property, plant and equipment (net)	590	520
Total assets	$1,700	$1,800
Liabilities and Stockholders' Equity		
Current liabilities:		
Accounts payable	$ 280	$ 360
Notes payable—officers	100	100
Accrued expenses and taxes	50	40
Total current liabilities	430	500
Long-term debt, 11%	420	400
Total liabilities	850	900
Stockholders' equity	850	900
Total liabilities and stockholders' equity	$1,700	$1,800

*Adapted from a CMA examination.

EXHIBIT 2

GARDENCARE COMPANY
Income Statement
For the Year Ended December 31
(unaudited, thousands of dollars)

	1981	1982
Net sales.	$2,500	$2,800
Cost of sales	1,750	2,100
Gross margin	750	700
Operating expenses:		
Advertising	130	140
Bad debts estimate	25	28
Depreciation	70	70
Insurance	35	36
Lease payment	—	9
Salaries	185	190
Supplies	13	8
Taxes (nonincome)	25	25
Interest	57	54
Total operating expenses	540	560
Earnings before income taxes	210	140
Income taxes	105	70
Net income	$ 105	$ 70

The aged accounts receivable balance on December 31, 1982, is shown below:

Days Past Due	Amount	Industry Collection Experience
Not past due	$340,000	99% collected
1–60	120,000	97% collected
61–120	40,000	90% collected
121–180	70,000	80% collected
Over 181	70,000	50% collected
	$640,000	

2. Inventory.

	1981	1982
Raw materials (LIFO)	$100,000	$100,000
Work in process (FIFO)	50,000	300,000
Finished goods (FIFO)	215,000	75,000

The raw materials consist primarily of plastic. Plastic prices rose approximately 10 percent in 1981 and by the same amount in 1982. Gardencare began its LIFO program on January 1, 1981.

3. Employment Contract. The company president has a five-year contract at $45,000 per year with three years remaining.

4. Insurance. The company has purchased ordinary life insurance on its key officers. The policies have accrued a total of $5,000 cash surrender value.

5. Marketable Securities. The marketable securities were worth $21,000 at December 31, 1982.

6. Investments. The investments of $80,000 consist of 800 shares of Fisher Company, which is owned in part by several of Gardencare's board of directors. Fisher Company discontinued one of its major products as a result of a legal suit concerning product safety standards. The stock declined to $60 per share following this action.

7. Property, Plant, and Equipment. The company uses the same depreciation methods for book and tax purposes. The straight-line method is used on the plant and the double-declining-balance method is used on all equipment.

a. A purchase agreement for a parcel of land was signed in September of 1982. Payment was to be made on January 10, 1983. The check for $10,000 was written on December 27, 1982, and delivered to the seller. The transaction was not recorded in December.

b. In January 1982, a noncancelable lease for equipment was signed by Gardencare. The lease calls for Gardencare to make annual payments of $9,000 for five years. The equipment can be purchased at the end of the lease for $10,000. The purchase price of the equipment was $40,000. The present value of the least payments and the option price at the date the lease was signed was $40,000 (using a 15 percent rate), and the present value of the remaining lease payments and option price on December 31, 1982, is $35,700.

8. Notes Payable—Officers. The officers loaned the company $100,000 early in 1980. The notes have been renewed each year, and it is expected they will be renewed annually for the next three years. The notes are subordinated to other notes outstanding.

9. Dividends. The company paid dividends of $20,000 to its stockholders during 1982.

Questions

1. Calculate the following ratios for 1982 using the financial statements as presented:
   a. Return on average total assets, with aftertax interest added back (see Chapter 13 for the formula).
   b. Acid-test ratio (based on year-end amounts).
   c. Days' receivables (based on year-end receivables).
   d. Inventory turnover (based on average inventories).
   e. Times interest earned.
2. Revise the statement of financial position for December 31, 1982, to make it more useful for the bank's needs.
3. Prepare an estimated cash flow statement for the year ending December 31, 1982.

CASE 10–6 W. T. Grant Company*

In 1976, Sandy Johnson was a business school student enrolled in an accounting course. Johnson had grown up in a neighborhood close to a Grant's store. Johnson had become intrigued by the story of

*The casewriter wishes to acknowledge the cooperation of Professor Clyde P. Stickney in the preparation of this case.

W. T. Grant when that local store closed in late 1975, and had followed the coverage in the popular business press very closely. The firm's bankruptcy proceedings and eventual store closings seemed to take many in the financial world by surprise. Johnson wanted to know if a study of the firm's financial statements would have shown the growing problems the company faced. With this in mind, Johnson went to the business school library and found the W. T. Grant Company income statement and balance sheet data for the period from 1968 to 1975 that are shown in Exhibit 1.

Sandy Johnson used these data to calculate nine ratios. The profitability picture of W. T. Grant was seen by calculating (1) the return on shareholders' equity and (2) the return on assets for each year. Turnover information was derived from the (3) accounts receivable turnover, (4) inventory turnover, and (5) total assets turnover ratios. Insight into Grant's liquidity came from a look at the firm's (6) current ratio and (7) quick ratio. Johnson also calculated solvency ratios such as (8) total liabilities/total equities and (9) long-term debt/total equities.

The company's annual reports also provided other data that drew Johnson's curiosity. These were the W. T. Grant statements of changes in financial position, summarized in Exhibit 2. Johnson noted that these statements were actually what the textbook called funds flow statements prepared on the working capital basis. The statements showed that funds provided by current operations remained fairly stable until 1974. Johnson questioned how this could be in light of the rapid increases in long-term debt the company had experienced after 1971. If funds flow was stable, why the need for so much new debt? Could it be the company was desperately short of cash and had to borrow just to stay afloat? Johnson decided to look into an analysis of cash flows.

Johson's accounting professor was happy to provide a diagram that showed how to convert certain working capital flow data to cash flow data (see Exhibit 3).

EXHIBIT 1
SELECTED DATA FROM W. T. GRANT COMPANY FINANCIAL STATEMENTS
FOR THE YEARS ENDED JANUARY 31, 1968–1975
(thousands of dollars)

	1968	1969	1970	1971	1972	1973	1974	1975
Income Statement Data								
Sales..................	979,458	1,096,152	1,210,918	1,254,131	1,374,812	1,644,747	1,849,802	1,770,484
Cost of merchandise sold.................	669,560	739,459	817,671	843,192	931,237	1,125,261	1,282,945	1,303,267
Net income	32,993	38,183	41,809	39,577	35,212	37,787	8,430	(168,808)
Balance Sheet Data								
Cash and marketable securities...........	25,141	25,639	32,977	34,008	49,851	30,943	45,951	79,642
Accounts receivable....	272,450	312,776	368,267	419,731	477,324	542,751	598,798	468,724
Inventories............	183,721	208,623	222,128	260,492	298,676	399,533	450,637	407,356
Current assets	485,295	551,440	628,409	719,478	831,229	979,876	1,102,686	962,303
Total assets...........	551,607	622,109	706,795	807,628	944,670	1,110,698	1,252,983	1,119,789
Current liabilities	235,448	285,278	366,719	459,000	475,577	633,067	690,064	749,906
Long-term debt	62,622	43,251	35,402	32,301	128,432	126,672	220,336	216,341
Total liabilities..........	310,909	341,988	416,107	505,592	618,925	776,359	929,245	968,430
Shareholders' equity....	240,698	280,121	290,688	302,036	325,745	334,339	323,738	151,359
Total equities	551,607	622,109	706,795	807,628	944,670	1,110,698	1,252,983	1,119,789

EXHIBIT 2

W. T. GRANT COMPANY AND CONSOLIDATED SUBSIDIARIES
STATEMENTS OF CHANGES IN FINANCIAL POSITION
FOR THE YEARS ENDED JANUARY 31, 1968–1975
(thousands of dollars)

	1968	1969	1970	1971	1972	1973	1974	1975
Sources of funds:								
Net income..................	32,993	38,183	41,809	39,577	35,212	37,787	8,430	(168,808)
Depreciation and amortization.................	8,203	8,388	8,972	9,619	10,577	12,004	13,579	14,587
Deferred income taxes	517	390	345	232	1,146	2,262	2,723	(14,649)
Undistributed earnings of unconsolidated subsidiaries	(1,503)	(1,761)	(2,083)	(2,777)	(2,383)	(3,403)	(3,570)	(331)
Net increase (decrease) in other liabilities............	130	231	180	74	(521)	(558)	(499)	(2,013)
Total funds provided by current operations........	40,340	45,431	49,223	46,725	44,031	48,092	20,663	(171,214)
Proceeds from issuance of debt....................	—	—	—	—	100,000	—	100,000	—
Proceeds from sale of common stock..............	4,113	5,432	5,278	6,762	9,944	3,665	2,844	886
Proceeds from disposal of property	59	523	—	—	—	2,229	(600)	—
Total sources of funds......	44,512	51,386	54,501	53,487	153,975	53,986	122,907	(170,328)
Applications of funds:								
Expenditures for plant and equipment	7,887	11,084	14,410	16,465	25,964	26,172	23,184	16,262
Dividends paid to stockholders................	14,367	17,686	19,737	20,821	21,139	21,141	21,122	4,457
Investments in non-consolidated subsidiaries	418	35	—	436	5,951	2,040	5,700	5,182
Retirements of long-term debt.......................	1,971	2,601	2,947	4,049	5,451	2,011	6,954	3,995
Purchase of treasury stock......	—	3,665	21,879	13,224	—	11,466	133	—
Total applications of funds	24,643	35,071	58,973	54,995	58,505	62,830	57,093	29,896
Increase (decrease) in working capital	19,869	16,315	(4,472)	(1,508)	95,470	(8,844)	65,814	(200,224)
Working capital at beginning of the year............	229,978	249,847	266,162	261,690	260,182	355,652	346,808	412,622
Working capital at end of the year	249,847	266,162	261,690	260,182	355,652	346,808	412,622	212,398
Increase (decrease) in working capital by element:								
Cash and securities	(13,899)	498	7,338	1,032	15,842	(18,908)	15,008	33,691
Accounts receivable............	42,023	40,326	55,491	51,464	57,593	65,427	56,047	(130,075)
Inventories	9,090	24,902	13,505	38,364	38,184	100,856	51,104	(43,280)
Prepaid expenses..............	(96)	419	635	(87)	428	1,271	651	(718)
Accounts payable..............	(6,966)	(16,794)	(9,485)	(9,940)	(13,995)	15,888	2,782	(43,301)
Notes payable—short-term......	(1,583)	(18,895)	(64,007)	(64,288)	8,679	(152,293)	(63,063)	(147,598)
Accrued liabilities	(8,700)	(14,141)	(7,949)	(18,053)	(11,261)	(21,085)	3,285	131,057
Increase (decrease) in working capital	19,869	16,315	(4,472)	(1,508)	95,470	(8,844)	65,814	(200,224)

EXHIBIT 3
COMPUTING CASH FLOW PROVIDED BY OPERATIONS FROM PUBLISHED FINANCIAL STATEMENTS

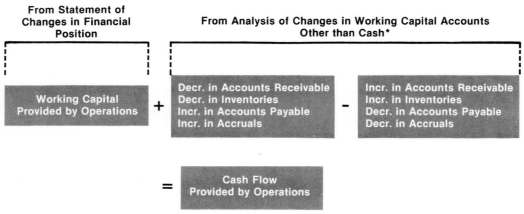

*Accounts such as "Bank Loans" and "Current Portion of Long-Term Debt" must be excluded from the analysis. Even though treated as current liabilities, they represent neither cash provided nor cash used by operations.

Questions:

1. Calculate for yourself the nine ratios mentioned in the case. Some needed formulas to which you have not yet been exposed are:

$$\text{Return on shareholders' equity} = \frac{\text{Net income}}{\text{Shareholders' equity}}$$

$$\text{Return on assets} = \frac{\text{Net income}}{\text{Total assets}}$$

$$\text{Accounts receivable turnover} = \frac{\text{Sales}}{\text{Accounts receivable}}$$

$$\text{Total assets turnover} = \frac{\text{Sales}}{\text{Total assets}}$$

For simplicity, use year-end amounts (rather than averages) for balance sheet items in your calculations. What patterns do the ratios show? In what year does the seriousness of Grant's problems become apparent?

2. Following the method given in Exhibit 3, calculate the cash flow provided by operations for W. T. Grant for each year from 1968 to 1975. Does the depth of Grant's problems show itself sooner with this analysis? Could careful analysis have predicted Grant's failure well in advance?

11

Acquisitions and Consolidated Statements

Many corporations acquire an ownership interest in other corporations. Depending primarily on the percentage of ownership acquired, these acquisitions can be accounted for (1) at their cost, (2) on an equity basis, or (3) on a consolidated basis. This chapter describes these three bases of accounting.

Since the most difficult problems arise in accounting for consolidated entities, most of the chapter deals with such entities. The chapter describes the two possible methods of recording the acquisition itself, which are called the purchase method and the pooling method, and the subsequent preparation of consolidated financial statements for these entities.

COST AND EQUITY METHODS

Cost Method
If one company owns securities of another company, these securities are reported on its balance sheet as an asset, Investments. If the securities constitute only a small fraction of the common stock of the investee company, the *cost method* is used to account for the investment. In the cost method, the investment is initially recorded at its cost, and remains at this cost unless the market value of the whole portfolio of securities declines below cost (as explained in Chapter 5). Dividends received on

these securities are reported as dividend revenue on the income statement.

Equity Method

If the securities constitute a large enough fraction of the ownership interest in the investee company so that the investing company can influence the actions of the investee, the investment is accounted for by the *equity method*. Unless the investing company can demonstrate that it does *not* "exercise significant influence" on the investee company, ownership of 20 percent or more of the investee company's common stock requires the use of the equity method.[1]

In the equity method, the investment is initially recorded at its cost. Thereafter the balance sheet amount is increased to reflect the investing company's share in the investee's net income, and decreased when dividends are received. The offsetting credit to the increase in Investments is an item of revenue on the income statement. Thus, in the cost method the income statement reports dividends, while in the equity method the income statement reports the investing company's share of the investee's net income.

Recording the Acquisition. To illustrate the entries made under the equity method, assume that Merkle Company acquired 25 percent of the common stock of Pentel Company on January 2, 1983, for $150,000 cash. Merkle Company's entry for this transaction would be:

```
Investments ............................... 150,000
    Cash ......................................        150,000
```

Recording Earnings. If Pentel Company's net income for 1983 was $60,000, Merkle Company would increase the amount of its investment by 25 percent of this amount, or $15,000, by the following entry on December 31, 1983:

```
Investments ...............................  15,000
    Investment Revenue .......................         15,000
```

Dividends. If Merkle Company received $5,000 in dividends from Pentel Company during 1983, Merkle would make the following entry:

```
Cash ......................................   5,000
    Investments ...............................          5,000
```

Note that this entry reduces the amount of investments on the balance sheet but does not affect the income statement.

---

[1]"Equity Method for Investments in Common Stock," *APB Opinion No. 18*, March 1971, and "Criteria for Applying the Equity Method of Accounting for Investments in Common Stock," *FASB Interpretation No. 35*, May 1981.

Consolidated Basis. If an investing company owns more than 50 percent of the stock of another company, it usually reports on a consolidated basis, as described below. Such an acquisition is carried on the accounts of the investing company in accordance with the equity method. Consolidated financial statements are prepared by adjusting these accounts.

In summary, three methods of reporting investment are possible depending, with some qualifications, on the amount of stock that a company owns, as follows:

Amount of Ownership	Method of Reporting
Over 50%	Consolidated statements
20–50%	Equity method
Less than 20%	Cost method

BUSINESS COMBINATIONS

A business combination occurs when two companies are brought together in a single accounting entity. In some cases, an acquiring company dissolves the acquired corporation and incorporates its assets and liabilities with its own assets and liabilities. In other cases, the acquired company continues to exist as a separate corporation. It then becomes a *subsidiary* of the acquiring company. The acquiring company is its *parent*.

There are three types of business combinations: horizontal, vertical, and conglomerate. A *horizontal* combination occurs when the combining firms are in the same line of business, for example, the merger of two airlines. A *vertical* combination occurs when the two companies are involved in different stages of the production and marketing of the same end-use product, for example, the acquisition of an oil company by a producer of petrochemicals. A *conglomerate* combination occurs when the combining firms are in essentially unrelated lines of business, for example, the acquisition of a meat-packing firm by an electronics firm.

Purchase versus Pooling

If the acquiring corporation pays cash for the acquired firm, the accounting method used to record the acquisition is called the *purchase* method. However, if the acquiring corporation issues its stock in exchange for the stock of the other firm, the acquisition may be accounted for by use of either the purchase method or the *pooling of interests* method. Prior to 1971, companies usually favored the pooling method because, as will be shown later, this method resulted in more attractive looking financial statements.

Effective November 1, 1970, however, the use of the pooling of interests method was severely restricted by *APB Opinion No. 16.*[2] That opinion set up specific criteria, which are complicated, detailed, and subject to various interpretations. Only a summary of their general thrust is appropriate here. In general, to qualify for pooling treatment, *all* of the following conditions must be met:

- Each combining company is autonomous and independent and has not been a subsidiary or division of another corporation within the previous two years.
- The combination is effected in a single transaction or is completed according to a specific plan within one year.
- The acquiring corporation issues only common stock with rights identical to the majority of its outstanding voting common stock in exchange for substantially all of the voting common stock of the acquired company.
- Neither of the combining companies has recently (usually, within two years) reacquired shares of voting common stock for purposes of using these shares for business combinations.
- The ratio of the interest of an individual common stockholder to those of other common stockholders in a combining company remains unchanged as a result of the exchange of stock.
- No provisions relating to the issue of securities or other consideration are pending.
- The combined corporation does not agree to retire or reacquire any of the common stock issued to effect the combination.
- The combined corporation does not enter into other financial arrangements for the benefit of the former stockholders of one of the combining companies.
- The combined corporation does not intend to dispose of a significant part of the assets of the combining companies within two years after the combination, other than disposals in the ordinary course of business and to eliminate duplicate facilities or excess capacity.

To illustrate accounting for the pooling and purchase methods, we will use the balance sheets for two hypothetical corporations shown in Illustration 11–1. We assume that Corporation A plans to acquire all of the stock of Corporation B, and that it will pay for this stock with 100,000 shares of its own stock that has a market value of $60 per share, a total of $6 million. We assume also that Corporation A can arrange the transaction in such a way that it can qualify either as a pooling or as a purchase, at its discretion. One of the factors A's management will consider in deciding which way to arrange the combination is the impact

---

[2]"Business Combinations," *APB Opinion No. 16*, August 1970.

ILLUSTRATION 11–1

Preacquisition Balance Sheets
(thousands of dollars)

	Corporation A	Corporation B
Assets		
Cash and marketable securities.	$ 6,000	$1,000
Accounts receivable.	5,000	1,400
Inventories.	6,400	1,800
Total current assets.	17,400	4,200
Plant and equipment (net of accumulated depreciation)	10,600	2,800
Total assets.	$28,000	$7,000
Liabilities and Shareholders' Equity		
Accounts payable	$ 6,000	$1,700
Other current liabilities	1,500	300
Total current liabilities.	7,500	2,000
Long-term debt	8,200	1,600
Total liabilities.	15,700	3,600
Common stock (par plus paid-in capital)*	2,500	700
Retained earnings	9,800	2,700
Total shareholders' equity	12,300	3,400
Total liabilities and shareholders' equity.	$28,000	$7,000
*Number of shares outstanding	1,000,000	100,000

on its financial statements of the pooling and purchase accounting treatments, respectively.

Accounting as a Pooling

The underlying premise of pooling accounting is that there is a "marriage" of the two entities, with the two shareholder groups agreeing to a simple merging of the two firms' resources, talents, risks, and earnings streams. Accordingly, under pooling treatment, the balance sheets of A and B simply would be added together to arrive at the new consolidated balance sheet for A, which is the surviving entity. If there were any intercorporate obligations involved, for example, a receivable on A's balance sheet that was due from B, these would be eliminated. With this exception, the new enterprise (the A–B combination) is accounted for as the sum of its parts, as shown in the first column of Illustration 11–2. In particular, it should be noted that the assets and liabilities of the combined firm are carried at the sum of their previous *book* values. Similarly, the Common Stock and Retained Earnings accounts of the combining firms are simply added to determine the combined firm's shareholders' equity. Notice also that when one compares A's preacquisition balance sheet in Illustration 11–1 with the pro forma pooling balance sheet in Illustration 11–2, there is no evidence of the fact that A paid $6 million for B's net assets, which had a book value of only $3.4

ILLUSTRATION 11–2

CORPORATION A
Pro Forma Consolidated Balance Sheets
(thousands of dollars)

	"Pooling" Accounting	"Purchase" Accounting
Assets		
Cash and marketable securities	$ 7,000	$ 7,000
Accounts receivable	6,400	6,400
Inventories	8,200	8,200
Total current assets	21,600	21,600
Goodwill	—	1,500
Plant and equipment (net of accumulated depreciation)	13,400	14,500
Total assets	$35,000	$37,600
Liabilities and Shareholders' Equity		
Accounts payable	$ 7,700	$ 7,700
Other current liabilities	1,800	1,800
Total current liabilities	9,500	9,500
Long-term debt	9,800	9,800
Total liabilities	19,300	19,300
Common stock (par plus paid-in capital)*	3,200	8,500
Retained earnings	12,500	9,800
Total shareholders' equity	15,700	18,300
Total liabilities and shareholders' equity	$35,000	$37,600
*Number of shares outstanding	1,100,000	1,100,000

million. This $2.6 million difference appears nowhere on the balance sheet.

Accounting as a Purchase

The underlying premise of purchase accounting is that instead of a "marriage" of A and B, A is buying the net assets of B. In accordance with the cost concept, the net assets of B go onto A's balance sheet at the amount paid for them, that is, $6 million.

This treatment involves two steps. First, B's tangible assets are revalued to their *fair* value. In Illustration 11–2 it is assumed that all of the assets on B's preacquisition balance sheet were reported at amounts approximately equal to their current values, except for plant and equipment. Plant and equipment had a book value of $2.8 million, but a fair value of $3.9 million, an increase of $1.1 million. Hence, with purchase accounting the consolidated plant and equipment account shows $14.5 million ($10.6 million for A's preacquisition plant and equipment plus the acquired fixed assets of B, newly valued at $3.9 million).

Second, after the revaluation of B's tangible assets, any excess of the purchase price over the total amount of B's revalued tangible net assets is shown on the consolidated balance sheet as an asset called *goodwill*.[3] This amount is $1.5 million, as shown in the second column of Illustration 11–2. It is calculated as follows:

Purchase price	$6,000,000
Less: Book value of net assets acquired	3,400,000
	2,600,000
Less: Write-up of tangible assets to fair value	1,100,000
Goodwill	$1,500,000

Hence, of the $2.6 million excess of the $6 million purchase price over the $3.4 million book value of Corporation B (which excess appeared nowhere under pooling accounting), $1.1 million has been assigned to tangible assets, and the remainder, $1.5 million, is shown on the balance sheet as goodwill. As explained in Chapter 7, goodwill is amortized over a period not to exceed 40 years.

Negative Goodwill. If the purchase price is *less* than the book value of the assets purchased, the presumption is that the book values overstate the fair value of these assets. Otherwise, the acquired company would have been better off to sell the assets piecemeal, rather than to sell the company as a unit. It follows that these assets should be written down so that their total value equals the purchase price. With this line of reasoning, there is rarely a converse of goodwill, that is, there is no "negative goodwill.[4]

Balance Sheet Impact

Comparing the two balance sheets in Illustration 11–2, it can be seen that the pooling transaction will result in a more "attractive" balance sheet than will a purchase, in the sense that the asset costs that will be charged against income in future periods are lower. With pooling accounting, the amount shown for plant and equipment is lower (though physically these assets are identical regardless of accounting method), so future depreciation charges will be lower. Also, no goodwill appears under pooling, so there will be no future goodwill amortization expense.

Earnings Impact

To understand fully the financial reporting impacts of the alternatives, the effect on reported earnings must also be considered. Assume that in the first year after the acquisition there are no benefits from "synergism," and hence the projected combined A–B earnings are the same as the sum of what the projected earnings of the two firms would have been if they

---

[3] As noted in Chapter 7, the preferred caption for this account is "excess of cost over net assets of acquired companies."

[4] These rare exceptions are described in *APB Opinion No. 16*, par. 91.

had remained independent. Assume also, for simplicity, that there are no intercorporate transactions between A and B.

Illustration 11–3 shows that under *pooling* treatment of the combined firm's results, the net incomes of A and B are simply added to arrive at the consolidated figure. A's preacquisition stockholders would benefit from the combination, since net income per share would be $2.58 as compared with $2.27.

ILLUSTRATION 11–3
PRO FORMA CONSOLIDATED INCOME RESULTS
(thousands of dollars, except per share amounts)

	Corporation A	Corporation B
If independent corporations:		
Income before taxes	$4,200	$1,050
Income tax expense (46%)	1,932	483
Net income	$2,268	$ 567
Number of outstanding shares	1,000,000	100,000
Earnings per share	$2.27	$5.67
Combined A–B, pooling treatment:		
Income before taxes	$5,250	
Income tax expense (46%)	2,415	
Net income	$2,835	
Number of outstanding shares	1,100,000	
Earnings per share	$2.58	
Combined A–B, purchase treatment:		
Unadjusted income before taxes (as above)	$5,250	
Less: Additional depreciation expense	110	
Taxable income	5,140	
Income tax expense (46%)	2,364	
Income after tax	2,776	
Less: Amortization of goodwill	50	
Net income	$2,726	
Number of outstanding shares	1,100,000	
Earnings per share	$2.48	

Under *purchase* accounting, in order to arrive at a consolidated income figure, two adjustments must be made to the sum of the two firms' pretax incomes. First, after the acquisition, the consolidated depreciation expense would be greater than the sum of the independent firms' depreciation because Corporation B's plant and equipment amount was written up from $2.8 million to $3.9 million. Illustration 11–3 assumes that this will result in an additional $110,000 depreciation expense for each of the next 10 years. Second, the $1.5 million goodwill must be amortized. Illustration 11–3 assumes an amortization period of 30 years is being used, or $50,000 per year. Furthermore, the amortization of goodwill is not a tax-deductible expense, so net income is decreased by the full amount of the amortization. Thus, under the purchase treatment, net income is lower than with the pooling treatment.

Illustration 11–3 shows why pooling would likely to be preferred to purchase by Corporation A's management. If the combination were accounted for as a purchase, net income would be lower ($2,726,000 versus $2,835,000), but the number of outstanding shares would be the same (1,100,000). Hence, purchase-treatment net income would be $2.48 per share compared to $2.58 with pooling.

The accounting treatment when stock is exchanged in a combination is no longer a matter of management discretion. It is, however, a continuing matter of discussion among accountants, some of whom feel *APB Opinion No. 16* is too restrictive, and others of whom feel pooling treatment should not be permitted under any circumstances.

CONSOLIDATED STATEMENTS

A "company," as it is thought of by its management, its employees, its competitors, and the general public, may actually consist of a number of different corporations, created for various legal, tax, and financial reasons. The existence of a family of corporations is by no means peculiar to "big business." A fairly small enterprise may consist of one corporation that owns its real estate and buildings, another that primarily handles production, another for marketing activities, and over them all a *parent* corporation that is the locus of management and control. Each of these corporations is a legal entity, and each therefore has its own financial statements. The "company" itself may not be a separate legal entity, but it is an important economic entity, and a set of financial statements for the whole business enterprise may be more useful than the statements of the separate corporations of which it consists.

Such statements are called *consolidated financial statements.* They are prepared by first adjusting and then combining the financial statements of the separate corporations. No separate journals or ledgers are kept for the consolidated entity. The adjustments are made on worksheets using data from the accounts of the separate corporations. Also, only legal entities are involved in the consolidation process. If an acquired corporation has been dissolved and its assets consequently have come under the legal ownership of the acquiring company, its assets and liabilities are already reflected in the acquiring company's accounts.

Basis for Consolidation

The legal tie that binds the other corporations, or *subsidiaries,* to the parent is the ownership of their stock. A subsidiary is not consolidated unless more than 50 percent of its voting common stock is owned by the parent. Even though it is 100 percent owned by the parent, a subsidiary may not be consolidated if its business is so different from that of the other companies in the family that including it in the consolidation would result in financial statements that do not well describe the family as a whole. General Motors Corporation does not consolidate the statements of General Motors Acceptance Corporation because GMAC is a huge financial corporation dealing principally in installment payments on automobiles, so its assets and liabilities are quite unlike those of an industrial company. Some companies do not consolidate their foreign subsidiaries.

Consolidation Procedure

Illustration 11–4 shows the consolidation process in the simplest possible situation, consisting of the parent company and one subsidiary company, named "Parent" and "Subsidiary," respectively. Parent owns 100 percent of Subsidiary's stock; this stock is an asset shown on its balance sheet as Investment in Subsidiary. The investment is recorded at cost. It is assumed here that the $55,000 purchase price was equal to Subsidiary's book value (capital stock plus retained earnings) as of the time of acquisition.

ILLUSTRATION 11–4
CONSOLIDATION WORKSHEET

	Separate Statements		Intercompany Eliminations		Consolidated Balance Sheet
	Parent	Subsidiary	Dr.	Cr.	
Assets					
Cash	45,000	12,000			57,000
Accounts receivable	40,000	11,000		(1)* 5,000	46,000
Inventory	30,000	15,000		(4) 2,000	43,000
Fixed assets, net	245,000	45,000			290,000
Investment in subsidiary	55,000	—		(2) 55,000	—
	415,000	83,000			436,000
Liabilities and Shareholders' Equity					
Accounts payable	20,000	13,000	(1) 5,000		28,000
Other current liabilities	25,000	9,000			34,000
Long-term liabilities	100,000	—			100,000
Capital stock	100,000	40,000	(2) 40,000		100,000
Retained earnings	170,000	21,000	(2) 15,000		
			(4) 2,000		174,000
	415,000	83,000			436,000

*Parenthetical numbers correspond with text description.

The two companies have been operating for a year, and at the end of that year their separate balance sheets are as summarized in the first two columns of Illustration 11–4. If the two columns were simply added together, the sum of the balance sheet amounts would contain some items that, so far as the consolidated entity is concerned, would be counted twice. To preclude this double counting, adjustments are made in the next two columns; these are explained below. Essentially, these adjustments eliminate the effect of transactions that have occurred between the two corporations as separate legal entities. Since the consolidated financial statements should report only assets owned by the consolidated entity and the equities of parties *outside* the consolidated entity, these internal transactions must be eliminated. The consolidated balance sheet that results from these adjustments appears in the last column. The adjustments are as follows:

1. **Intercompany Financial Transactions.** The consolidated balance sheet must show as accounts receivable and accounts payable only amounts owed by and owed to parties outside the consolidated business. Therefore, amounts that the companies owe to one another must be eliminated. Assuming that Parent owes Subsidiary $5,000, this amount is eliminated from their respective Accounts Payable and Accounts Receivable accounts. The effect is as in the following journal entry (although it should be remembered that no journal entries actually are made in the books of either corporation):

```
Accounts Payable (Parent) ...................   5,000
    Accounts Receivable (Subsidiary) ..........          5,000
```

The payment of dividends by the subsidiary to the parent is a financial transaction that has no effect on the consolidated entity. In the separate statements, this was recorded on Parent's books as a credit to Revenue from Investments (which was closed to Parent's Retained Earnings), and on Subsidiary's books as a debit to Dividends (which was closed to Subsidiary's Retained Earnings). Since this transaction ultimately affected only the two retained earnings accounts, adding to one the same amount that was subtracted from the other, the act of combining the two of them automatically eliminated its effect. Therefore, no further adjustment is necessary.

2. **Elimination of the Investment.** Parent company's investment in Subsidiary's stock is strictly an intrafamily matter and must therefore be eliminated from the consolidated balance sheet. Since it is assumed that the stock was purchased at book value, the $55,000 cost shown on Parent's books must have equaled Subsidiary's Capital Stock plus Retained Earnings at the time of purchase. We know that Capital Stock is $40,000; the difference, $15,000, must therefore equal the balance of Retained Earnings at that time. The additional $6,000 of retained earnings now shown on Subsidiary's books has been created subsequent to the acquisition by Parent. To eliminate the investment, therefore, the entry in effect is as follows:

```
Capital Stock (Subsidiary) ...................  40,000
Retained Earnings (Subsidiary) ..............  15,000
    Investment in Subsidiary (Parent) ........          55,000
```

3.   Intercompany Sales.   In accordance with the realization concept, the consolidated company does not earn revenue until sales are made to the outside world. The revenue, the related costs, and the resulting profit for sales made between companies in the consolidated entity must therefore be eliminated from the consolidated accounts.

The sales and cost of sales on intercompany transactions are subtracted from the total sales and cost of sales figures on the consolidated income statement. If this were not done, the figures would overstate the volume of business done by the consolidated entity with the outside world. In order to do this, records must be kept that show both the sales revenue and the cost of sales of any sales made within the family.

> **Example.** Subsidiary sold goods costing it $52,000 to Parent for $60,000. Parent then sold these goods to outside customers for $75,000. The total gross margin on these sales was $23,000 ($75,000 minus $52,000). Of this amount, $8,000 appeared on Subsidiary's income statement and $15,000 on Parent's; hence, the consolidated income figure would not be overstated. However, the correct consolidated sales figure is $75,000, not $135,000 ($60,000 plus $75,000). Similarly, the correct consolidated cost of sales amount is $52,000, not $112,000. Thus Subsidiary's sales and Parent's cost of sales must be reduced by the $60,000 intercompany transfer to avoid double counting:

```
Sales (Subsidiary) .....................  60,000
    Cost of Sales (Parent) ..............          60,000
```

These adjustments would be made on the worksheet for the consolidated income statement. (This worksheet is not illustrated here, but it is similar in nature to that for the consolidated balance sheet.)

4.   Intercompany Profit.   If goods sold within the consolidated entity have not been sold to the outside world, these intercompany sales transactions will affect the Inventory account of the company buying the goods and the Retained Earnings account of the company selling them, and adjustments to these accounts are required. Assume that in the preceding example, Parent sold to outside customers only three fourths of the products it acquired from Subsidiary, and the other one fourth remains in Parent's inventory at the end of the year at its cost to Parent of $15,000. The products sold to the outside world present no problem, since they have disappeared from inventory and the revenue has been realized. The $15,000 remaining in Parent's inventory, however, is regarded by Subsidiary as a sale, the $2,000 profit on which (one fourth of Subsidiary gross margin of $8,000) appears in Subsidiary's Retained Earnings. This portion of the profit must be eliminated from the consolidated balance sheet. This is done by reducing Subsidiary's Retained Earnings and Parent's Inventory by the amount of the profit, as in the following entry:

```
Retained Earnings (Subsidiary) ...............   2,000
     Inventory (Parent) .......................            2,000
```

The necessary eliminations having been recorded, the amounts for the consolidated balance sheet can now be obtained by carrying each line across the worksheet.

In the preceding example, two of the most difficult problems in preparing consolidated statements did not arise because of simplifying assumptions that were made. These problems are described below.

Asset Valuation

In the example, it was assumed that Parent purchased Subsidiary's stock at its book value. Often a subsidiary's stock is purchased at an amount different from its book value. As explained earlier in this chapter, purchase accounting for an acquisition requires that the book value of the acquired assets be adjusted to show their fair value, and that any remaining excess of purchase price over the revalued net assets be shown as an asset called Goodwill. In the above illustration, if Parent had paid $65,000, rather than $55,000, for Subsidiary's stock, and if Subsidiary's assets were found to be recorded at their fair value, there would be goodwill of $10,000, and the adjustment marked (2) above would have been:

```
Goodwill ......................................   10,000
Capital Stock (Subsidiary) ...................   40,000
Retained Earnings (Subsidiary) ...............   15,000
     Investment in Subsidiary (Parent) .........           65,000
```

Furthermore, an adjustment to the consolidated financial statement is necessary to write off at least $\frac{1}{40}$ of the goodwill as an expense of the consolidated company for the year. Assuming a 40-year write-off period, the effect of this entry on the balance sheet would be:

```
Retained Earnings ............................    250
     Goodwill ..................................            250
```

This $250 also would be added to expenses on the consolidated income statement.

Minority Interest

If Parent had purchased less than 100 percent of Subsidiary's stock, then there would exist a *minority interest,* that is, the equity of Subsidiary's other owners. On the consolidated balance sheet, this minority interest appears as a separate equity item, just above shareholders' equity. For example, if Parent owned 80 percent of Subsidiary's stock, for which it had paid 80 percent of Subsidiary's book value, or $44,000, adjustment (2) above to eliminate the investment would have been as follows:

```
Capital Stock (Subsidiary) .................... 32,000
Retained Earnings (Subsidiary) ............... 12,000
     Investment in Subsidiary (Parent) ........          44,000
```

As this elimination suggests, at the time Parent acquired 80 percent of Subsidiary's stock, the minority interest amount was $11,000, the sum of the remaining 20 percent of Subsidiary's Capital Stock and Retained Earnings.

After the acquisition, this minority interest would increase by 20 percent of the increase in Subsidiary's Retained Earnings, *after* elimination of Subsidiary's profit on sales to Parent. This intercompany profit adjustment is in effect prorated between Parent and the minority shareholders in proportion to their respective ownership. Hence, if Parent owned 80 percent of Subsidiary, on the consolidated balance sheet the following amounts would appear:

Minority interest	$ 11,800
Shareholders' equity:	
Capital stock	100,000
Retained earnings	173,200

The amount for minority interest is the net of four items:

20% of Subsidiary capital stock	$ 8,000
20% of Subsidiary retained earnings at time of acquisition	3,000
20% of the $6,000 increase in Subsidiary retained earnings since acquisition	1,200
Less 20% of the $2,000 intercompany profit	(400)
Total minority interest	$11,800

Similarly, the consolidated Retained Earnings amount, which was $174,000 when we assumed Parent owned 100 percent of Subsidiary, is now $800 less, reflecting the $1,200 minority interest in the $6,000 postacquisition increase in Subsidiary's Retained Earnings, adjusted downward for the $400 minority interest share of the $2,000 intercompany profit elimination.

Consolidation of Foreign Subsidiaries

If a subsidiary is located in a foreign country, its accounts are kept in the currency of that country. In preparing consolidated statements, these amounts must be translated into U.S. dollars. Complications arise in consolidation because the "price" of the foreign currency vis-à-vis the dollar, that is, the exchange rate, fluctuates. These complications are discussed in Chapter 12.

SUMMARY

Depending on the fraction of stock owned, a corporation reports an investment in other companies (1) on the cost basis, (2) on the equity basis, or (3) by the preparation of consolidated financial statements.

Acquisitions of other companies are reported on the basis of their purchase cost, unless certain stringent criteria are met, in which case they are reported on a pooling-of-interests basis. If treated as a purchase, the acquisitions often give rise to an asset called goodwill, which is the excess of the acquisition cost over the fair value of the net assets acquired. Goodwill must be amortized over a period not to exceed 40 years.

Consolidated balance sheets and income statements are prepared by combining the accounts of the separate corporations in a corporate family. In combining these accounts the effects of transactions occurring within the family are eliminated so that the consolidated statements reflect only transactions between members of the family and the outside world.

Cases

CASE 11–1 Hardin Tool Company

The management of Pratt Engineering Company had agreed in principle to a proposal from Hardin Tool Company to acquire all its stock in exchange for Hardin securities. The two managements were in general agreement that Hardin would issue 100,000 shares of its authorized but unissued stock in exchange for the 40,000 shares of Pratt common stock. Hardin's investment banking firm had given an opinion that a new public offering of 100,000 shares of Hardin common stock could be made successfully at $8 per share.

Depending on how the details of the acquisition were structured, it could be accounted for either as a purchase or as a pooling of interests.

Condensed balance sheets for the two companies, projected to the date of the proposed acquisition, and condensed income statements estimated for the separate organizations are given in Exhibit 1.

EXHIBIT 1

Condensed Balance Sheets
As of the Proposed Acquisition Date
(thousands of dollars)

	Hardin	Pratt
Assets		
Current assets..................	$ 432	$ 246
Plant and equipment	690	312
Total assets	$1,122	$558
Equities		
Current liabilities	$ 263	$ 107
Long-term debt.................	195	10
Common stock ($1 par).........	100	40
Other contributed capital	218	94
Retained earnings..............	346	307
Total equities	$1,122	$ 558

Condensed Income Statements
For the First Year after Combination
(thousands of dollars)

Sales	$2,100	$1,500
Expenses	1,620	1,120
Income	480	380
Income tax expense.............	240	190
Net income.....................	$ 240	$ 190

The income statements reflect the best estimate of results of operations if the two firms were not to merge but were to continue to operate as separate companies. There were no intercompany receivables or payables, and no intercompany sales or other transactions were contemplated.

An appraiser had been retained by the two firms and had appraised Pratt's net assets (assets less liabilities) at $600,000. The difference between this amount and Pratt's book value was wholly attributable to the appraiser's valuation of Pratt's plant and equipment.

Although an exchange of common stock was the most frequently talked about way of consummating the merger, one Pratt shareholder inquired about the possibility of a package consisting of 50,000 shares of Hardin common stock, and $400,000 of either cumulative preferred stock with a 10 percent dividend or debentures with a 10 percent interest rate. Under either of these possibilities, the transaction would be accounted for as a purchase.

Questions

1. Prepare consolidated balance sheets as of the proposed acquisition date, assuming the exchange of 100,000 shares of Hardin common stock (a) on a pooling of interests basis and (b) on a purchase basis.

2. Assuming that in its first year of operations the combined company would achieve the same results of operations as the sum of the two firms' independent operations, what would be the combined company's net income and earnings per share on a pooling basis? On a purchase basis? (Assume a goodwill amortization period of 40 years, an average plant and equipment life of 10 years, straight-line depreciation, and an income tax rate of 50 percent.)

3. As an advisor to Hardin, would you recommend that the transaction be consummated on a purchase basis or on a pooling basis?

4. What would be the combined net income and earnings per share under (a) the preferred stock package and (b) the debenture package? Is one of these proposals preferable to the all common stock proposal?

CASE 11–2 Craver Corporation

Early in 1982, Craver Corporation acquired Tardiff Corporation. Tardiff continued to operate as a Craver subsidiary. At the end of 1982, the president of Craver asked the company's public accounting firm to prepare consolidated financial statements. Data from the separate financial statements of the two corporations are given in Exhibit 1. (For the purpose of this case, these data have been condensed and rounded.)

The following additional information was provided:

1. During 1982, Tardiff delivered and billed to Craver goods amounting to $20,000. Tardiff's cost for these goods was $15,000. Craver had paid Tardiff invoices billed through November 30 that totaled $17,000. All of the Tardiff goods were sold to outside customers in 1982.

2. Late in December 1982, Craver caused Tardiff to loan Craver $19,000 cash. The loan was evidently a five-year note. (No interest on this loan was recorded in the accounts of either company because the transaction occurred so near the end of the year.)

The accountant proceeded to prepare

EXHIBIT 1
FINANCIAL STATEMENT INFORMATION

Balance Sheet Data as of December 31, 1982

	Craver	Tardiff
Assets		
Cash	$ 34,000	$ 12,000
Accounts receivable	65,000	21,000
Inventory	71,000	32,000
Investment in subsidiary	84,000	—
Plant (net)	281,000	79,000
Loans receivable	—	19,000
Total assets	$535,000	$163,000
Equities		
Current liabilities	$ 52,000	$ 37,000
Noncurrent liabilities	100,000	32,000
Capital stock	150,000	60,000
Retained earnings	233,000	34,000
Total equities	$535,000	$163,000

Income Statement Data, 1982

	Craver	Tardiff
Sales	$612,000	$240,000
Cost of sales	480,000	176,000
Gross margin	132,000	64,000
Expenses (including income taxes)	138,000	36,000
Operating income (loss)	(6,000)	28,000
Other income	22,000	—
Net income	16,000	28,000
Dividends	—	18,000
Added to retained earnings	$ 16,000	$ 10,000

consolidated financial statements. In discussing them with the president, however, the accountant discovered that he had made two assumptions:

1. He had assumed that Craver had acquired 100 percent of Tardiff's stock, whereas in fact Craver had acquired only 75 percent.

2. He had assumed that Tardiff's dividend was included in Craver's $22,000 of other income, whereas in fact Craver had not received the dividend in 1982 and had made no entry to record the fact that the dividend had been declared and was owed to Craver as of December 31, 1982.

The accountant thereupon prepared revised consolidated statements.

After these revised statements had been mailed, the accountant received a telephone call from Craver's president: "Sorry, but I was wrong about our sales of Tardiff merchandise," he said. "Craver's sales were indeed $612,000 but only $12,000 was from sales of Tardiff products. We discovered that $8,000 of Tardiff products were in Craver's inventory as of December 31, 1982. Don't bother to prepare new statements, however. Tell me the changes, and I'll make them on the statements you sent me."

Questions

1. Reconstruct the consolidated financial statements that the accountant originally prepared.

2. Prepare revised consolidated financial statements based on the information that the accountant learned in his first conversation with the president.

3. What changes should be made in the financial statements as a result of the president's telephone conversation?

4. Contrast the financial performance and status of the company as reported in the original consolidated statements and as finally revised.

CASE 11–3 United States Steel and Marathon Oil

On March 11, 1982, a special meeting of the shareholders of Marathon Oil Company was held. The meeting had been called to vote on the Agreement of Merger between Marathon and United States Steel Corporation (USS). When consummated, the merger would be accounted for using the purchase method.

During the previous month, Marathon's shareholders had been sent extensive information, including the 1981 financial statements of both companies. Exhibit 1 shows income statements for USS and Marathon Oil for the year ended December 31,1981. Exhibit 2 shows condensed balance sheets for the two firms as of December 31, 1981.

Several adjustments to these individ-

EXHIBIT 1

UNITED STATES STEEL CORPORATION
AND MARATHON OIL COMPANY
Income Statement
For the Year Ended December 31, 1981
(millions of dollars, except per share amounts)

	U.S. Steel	Marathon
Sales	$13,941	$9,733
Cost of sales and other operating costs (excludes items shown below)	12,439	6,816
Wear and exhaustion	571	283
Taxes other than income taxes	227	1,341
Total operating costs	13,237	8,440
Operating income	704	1,293
Nonoperating income	1,224	81
Interest and other financing costs	(225)	(159)
Unusual items	40	—
Income before taxes on income	1,743	1,215
Provision for estimated U.S. and foreign income taxes	666	872
Net income	$ 1,077	$ 343
Net income per common share:		
Primary	$12.07	$5.82
Fully diluted	11.47	—

EXHIBIT 2

UNITED STATES STEEL CORPORATION
AND MARATHON OIL COMPANY
Condensed Balance Sheets
As of December 31, 1981
(millions of dollars)

	U.S. Steel	Marathon
Assets		
Current assets (excluding inventories)	$ 4,214	$ 907
Inventories	1,198	576
Property, plant, and equipment—net	6,676	4,233
Other assets	1,228	278
Total assets	$13,316	$5,994
Liabilities		
Current liabilities	$ 2,823	$1,475
Long-term debt	2,340	1,368
Deferred income taxes	732	588
Redeemable preferred stock of consolidated		
subsidiary	500	—
Other noncurrent liabilities	661	501
Total liabilities	7,056	3,932
Shareholders' Equity		
Common stock*	1,812	198
Additional capital	96	—
Retained earnings	4,352	1,864
Total shareholders' equity	6,260	2,062
Total liabilities and shareholders' equity	$13,316	$5,994
*Number of shares outstanding	90,578,885	58,689,306

ual company statements were necessary to provide the stockholders with pro forma consolidated statements as of December 31, 1981, assuming the purchase had been consummated as of January 1, 1981. These changes relating to a hypothetical January 1, 1981, purchase were as follows:

a. USS's offer was to purchase Marathon Oil for $5.805 billion. The funds for the purchase were to be provided by bank loans and long-term notes for $4.135 billion, plus cash and liquidated marketable securities of $1.670 billion. The large USS debt increase would have caused 1981 consolidated interest and other financing costs to increase by $696 million. The use of cash and marketable se-

curities for the purchase would have cost the consolidated operations $217 million in lost 1981 interest income, which affects the nonoperating income item.

b. Marathon Oil's 1981 year-end inventories were estimated to have a current value $1.244 billion greater than their LIFO book value.

c. Marathon's 1981 year-end oil and gas property reserves were estimated to have a current value of $7.703 billion. In addition, Marathon owned plant and equipment having a 1981 year-end net book value of approximately $1.643 billion.

d. The revaluation caused by the findings in (c) above meant that Marathon Oil's property, plant, and equipment had been amortized too quickly. Adjustment for this would have caused an estimated $392 million postmerger increase in year-end 1981 taxes payable, a current liability, and a $154 million increase in 1981 wear and exhaustion (i.e., amortization) expense.

e. As a result of (d) above, 1981 consolidated year-end deferred income taxes would have been reduced by $392 million, since these taxes would have become currently payable. An additional $196 million of deferred income taxes would have been eliminated as a result of the purchase. Thus, all $588 million of Marathon's 1981 year-end deferred taxes would have been eliminated had the purchase taken place on January 1, 1981.

f. The 1981 net tax expense savings from the adjustments mentioned above would have been $491 million.

g. The net effect on 1981 unadjusted consolidated net income from all of the above pro forma adjustments was to reduce it by $576 million.

Questions

1. Using the information given, prepare adjusting entries to the individual company 1981 financial statements and use these entries to prepare a pro forma consolidated balance sheet as of December 31, 1981, and a pro forma consolidated income statement for the year ended December 31, 1981, assuming the purchase had been consummated on January 1, 1981.

2. Be prepared to describe how you determined the amount of goodwill for the pro forma 1981 year-end consolidated balance sheet.

3. If one divides each company's 1981 net income, as shown in Exhibit 1, by its respective number of outstanding shares, shown in Exhibit 2, the results are not the $12.07 and $5.82 shown in Exhibit 1. What could account for the apparent discrepancy?

4. Approximately what would have been the consolidated 1981 primary earnings per share had the purchase been consummated on January 1, 1981?

5. Calculate the following ratios for USS (without Marathon consolidated) for 1981: profit margin, current ratio, acid-test ratio, long-term debt/equity, times interest earned, and return on equity (= net income/owners' equity). Repeat the ratio calculations, based on your pro forma 1981 consolidated statements. What does a comparison of these two sets of ratios suggest about the short-run benefits to USS's shareholders arising from the purchase of Marathon?

12

Accounting and Changing Prices

The cost concept requires that assets be recorded upon acquisition at their historical cost. Thus, both asset amounts and the related expense items, such as cost of sales and depreciation, reflect the purchasing power of the dollar as of the time the asset costs were incurred. In this chapter we discuss methods that attempt to adjust historical cost data to take account of the phenomenon of changing prices. The adjusted data supplement, rather than replace, historical cost financial statements. A related matter, the changing price of foreign currencies vis-à-vis the dollar, is also discussed.

NATURE OF THE PROBLEM

Suppose that in 1975 you purchased a parcel of land for $20,000. In 1980, an identical parcel adjoining the first one became available, and you purchased it for $28,000. In June 1983, you received an offer to sell either parcel or both for $32,000 each, but decided to continue holding the land. At that point, a balance sheet including your two identical assets would show a total land cost of $48,000; yet you did not pay half of this amount ($24,000) for *either* parcel, and their total *value* in June 1983 was $64,000.

Suppose further that a farmer paid you $1,000 per parcel for the right to grow crops on your land during 1983. Ignoring costs such as property taxes, historical cost accounting indicates a return of 5.0 percent ($1,000 ÷ $20,000) on the first parcel, 3.6 percent on the second, and 4.2 percent on the combined parcels. Yet, in terms of their physical characteristics and market values, the parcels are identical. Moreover, if you had sold them both for $32,000 each, and the *new* owner had been paid $1,000 per parcel by the farmer, the new owner's return on either parcel (or the combined parcels) would have been only 3.1 percent (= $1,000 ÷ $32,000 or $2,000 ÷ $64,000).

Conventional Accounting and Comparisons

Conventional (i.e., historical cost) accounting is useful for many purposes, and it is highly objective and feasible. It also is not totally lacking in relevance. In the above example, you *did* invest $48,000 in the two parcels of land, as conventional accounting reports. The problem with conventional accounting, as the example above suggests, comes when one is making comparisons. These comparison problems can be of two types: (1) when identical assets were acquired by an entity at different points in time ($20,000 versus $28,000 for the land parcels) and (2) when different entities hold identical assets, purchased at different prices ($48,000 you paid for the land, versus $64,000 paid by the new owner if you had sold the land). Since separate entities' different asset prices also relate to purchases made at different points in time, either type of comparison problem boils down to the phenomenon of *changing prices*. As Professor William Paton noted *in 1922*, "the value of the dollar—its general purchasing power—is subject to serious change over a period of years . . . . Accountants . . . deal with an unstable, variable unit; and *comparisons* of unadjusted accounting statements prepared at intervals are accordingly always more or less unsatisfactory and are often positively misleading."[1]

Two Types of Price Changes

Price changes can be described in two ways. One is to track the cost of a specified "market basket" of goods and services over time, and to develop a *price index* that describes the price changes for the market basket. Because there is a diversity of items in the market basket, this is called a *general* price index.

> **Example.** Several U.S. daily newspapers specify a standard weekly grocery market basket of food items—two pounds of hamburger, a dozen eggs, three gallons of milk, and so on. Periodically, they see how much it would cost to buy the standard basket of goods in their respective areas.

---

[1] William A. Paton, *Accounting Theory* (Houston: Reprinted by Scholars Book Company, 1973), p. 427 (emphasis added).

Suppose that when this procedure was started in a given city, the goods cost $40. Some time later in that city the same goods cost $60. Thus, at the starting point, the grocery price index in that city was 100, and at the later point the index was 150 (because $60 ÷ $40 = 150 percent). Of course, *any* point in time can be the base point for the index. It can therefore also be said that if the price index was 100 when the groceries cost $60, then it was 66.7 when they cost $40. In either case, there was 50 percent inflation in the cost of the groceries between the two points in time.

The two most common general price indexes in the United States are the *Consumer Price Index—All Urban Consumers* (CPI or CPI-U) and the *Gross National Product Implicit Deflator* (GNP Deflator). The "market basket" for the CPI includes food and beverages, housing, apparel, transportation, medical care, entertainment, and the other goods and services people buy for day-to-day living. The GNP "market basket" includes *all* goods and services that are the collective outputs of all U.S. enterprises, and thus is as "general" as a U.S. price index can be. The base year (index = 100) is 1967 for the CPI and 1972 for the GNP Deflator.

Rather than measuring broad market-basket price changes, the second approach looks at the price movements of specific items, called *specific prices*. In the land example, the specific price of a parcel was $20,000 at the time the first parcel was purchased, $28,000 when the second was purchased, and $32,000 in June 1983. These prices can also be expressed as a specific price index, whose values respectively would be 100, 140, and 160 for the land example. Specific price indexes in practice are less homogeneous than the one for our two *very* specific parcels of land. For example, a price index for the construction cost per squre foot of new office buildings built anywhere in the United States is considered to be a specific price index, despite the fact that construction costs vary among regions of the country, and also among different types of structures (one story versus high rise).

In the next section, we discuss how both the general price level and specific prices approaches are used to adjust conventional accounting data.

FASB STATEMENT NO. 33

Inflation in the United States was rapid in the 1920s and late 1940s. Nevertheless, because the objectivity and feasibility of inflation-adjusted accounting data were open to question, for decades Professor Paton's 1922 observation had no concrete impact on accounting practice. In 1947, 1948, 1953, and 1965, AICPA committees studied the issue of inflation; these studies focused on the question of whether inflation caused depreciation expense to be understated. In 1969, the APB stated that price-level-adjusted data were useful, but did not require their disclosure.[2] In 1974, the FASB issued a Discussion Memorandum on the subject, but took no immediate action.[3] Growing impatient with the FASB, in March 1976 the SEC issued *Accounting Series Release No. 190,* which required various replacement cost disclosures by large corporations as supplemental information in their financial statements filed with the SEC. However, ASR-190 did not require disclosure of these data in the companies' shareholder annual reports. In September 1979, the FASB issued *Statement No. 33,* "Financial Reporting and Changing Prices" (hereafter abbreviated as FASB-33), and shortly thereafter the SEC suspended its ASR-190 requirements.

The accounting procedures proposed by the FASB to report the effects of inflation on business enterprises are described in the sections that follow. It should be emphasized that the inflation-adjusted data required by FASB-33 are *supplemental* data; that is, they do not replace conventional accounting statement information, but instead augment it. These supplemental disclosures are required only of large publicly owned companies, which are defined to be those with total assets over $1 billion, *or* those with inventories and *gross* (pre-depreciation) property, plant, and equipment amounting in aggregate to more than $125 million.[4]

It should also be emphasized that the FASB regards the requirements of FASB-33 as experimental. The *Statement* itself calls for a comprehensive review of its requirements after no more than five years of experience with them.

Constant Dollar Accounting

The amounts reported in conventional financial statements are on a "units-of-money" basis. The effect of price-level changes can be reported by restating these amounts on a "units of general purchasing power" (GPP) basis. Each such unit of purchasing power presumably represents an ability to purchase the same physical *quantity* of goods and services. The technique for converting statement data to a GPP basis is called (in the United States) *constant dollar accounting* (also, *general purchasing power accounting* or *general price-level-adjusted accounting*). Since, as we shall see, constant dollar accounting involves adjusting historical cost amounts, the FASB refers to the adjusted amounts as *historical cost/*

---

[2]"Financial Statements Restated for General Price-Level Changes," *APB Statement No. 3,* June 1969.

[3]FASB, *Reporting the Effects of General Price-Level Changes in Financial Statements,* January 1974.

[4]Special inflation-adjustment procedures for certain industries with "specialized assets," such as oil and gas properties and motion picture films, are treated in various *FASB Statements* that supplement FASB-33. (See *FASB Statements Nos. 39, 40, 41, 46,* and *54.*)

constant dollar data, whereas the FASB calls the conventional data *historical cost/nominal dollar* amounts. (Unless otherwise indicated, we shall use the shorter term *constant dollar* to mean "historical cost/constant dollar.") Although FASB-33 does not require presentation of complete balance sheets and income statements on a constant dollar basis, the procedures we shall show for developing complete statements are helpful in understanding the amounts that FASB-33 does require to be disclosed.

Monetary Items.   A monetary asset is money or a claim to receive a fixed amount of money. A monetary liability is an obligation to pay a fixed sum of money. Cash, debt securities, accounts receivable, and notes receivable are monetary assets. Essentially all liabilities are monetary, except for deferred revenue (where the obligation is to provide goods or services, rather than pay money) and deferred costs, such as future warranty costs. As of the date of the balance sheet, monetary items are already expressed in units of current purchasing power. For example, $1,000 cash on hand as of December 31, 1983, will buy $1,000 worth of goods and services as of that date. Thus, no restatement of year-end amounts for monetary items is necessary *if the unit of purchasing power to be used for restated amounts is the year-end dollar.*

However, if the amount for a monetary item as of a given point in time is to be restated to units of purchasing power as of *some other* point in time, an adjustment *is* necessary. The adjustment is made by multiplying the nominal dollar amount by a ratio. This ratio is the general price index as of the date to which amounts are being restated, divided by the general price index as of the balance sheet date for the monetary item to be restated.

> **Example 1.**   Bethlehem Steel Corporation had $62.4 million cash as of December 31, 1981. If historical cost amounts for Bethlehem Steel are to be restated to December 1981 units of purchasing power, then no adjustment is needed.

> **Example 2.**   On December 31, 1980, Bethlehem Steel had $51.2 million cash. To make this amount comparable *in terms of purchasing power* with the $62.4 million cash on December 31, 1981, an adjustment is necessary. The CPI in December 1981 was 281.5, and in December 1980 it was 258.4. The December 1980 cash restated in December 1981 units of purchasing power is (in millions):

$$\underset{\substack{\text{(as of}\\ \text{Dec. 80)}}}{\$51.2} \times \frac{281.5 \text{ (Dec. 81 index)}}{258.4 \text{ (Dec. 80 index)}} = \text{C\$55.8}$$

The C$ sign stands for constant dollars, to remind us this amount is expressed in units of purchasing power, not nominal dollars. A more complete, but too clumsy, sign in this case would be CDec.81$.

Example 3. The *average* value for the CPI *during* 1981 was 272.4.[5] If Bethlehem Steel were to prepare comparative 1980 and 1981 balance sheets, restated to average 1981 units of purchasing power, both of the previously mentioned cash amounts would have to be restated as follows (in millions):

$$\underset{\substack{\text{(as of} \\ \text{Dec. 80)}}}{\$51.2} \times \frac{272.4 \text{ (avg. 81 index)}}{258.4 \text{ (Dec. 80 index)}} = \text{C}\$54.0$$

$$\underset{\substack{\text{(as of} \\ \text{Dec. 81)}}}{\$62.4} \times \frac{272.4 \text{ (avg. 81 index)}}{281.5 \text{ (Dec. 81 index)}} = \text{C}\$60.4$$

Interpretation.   Before proceeding, it is important to understand how to interpret the constant dollar amounts in the above three examples. In Example 1, we are saying simply that Bethlehem Steel's December 31, 1981, cash was equivalent to 62.4 million units of December 31, 1981, purchasing power. In Example 2, we are saying that the $51.2 million cash on December 31, 1980, would buy the same quantity of goods and services that $55.8 million would buy on December 31, 1981. In Example 3, we are saying that the amount of cash as of December 31, 1980, was equivalent to 54.0 million units of *average* 1981 purchasing power, whereas the December 31, 1981, cash was equivalent to 60.4 million units of average 1981 purchasing power. Thus, during 1981, the company increased the amount of purchasing power committed to cash by 6.4 million units. (One can minimize confusion in discussing constant dollar amounts if the sign "C$" is read as "units of purchasing power as of _____," rather than as "constant dollars.")

Nonmonetary Items.   These are all assets and liabilities that are not monetary items. Historical amounts for these items must be restated to reflect the purchasing power equivalents of the original cost investments.

Example 4. Assume that Bethlehem Steel acquired a machine for $1 million in March 1969. The CPI for March 1969 is 108.0. If the amount is to be adjusted to restate it in units of average 1981 purchasing power, the calculation is:

$$\underset{\text{(as of Mar. 69)}}{\$1.000 \text{ million}} \times \frac{272.4 \text{ (avg. 81 index)}}{108.0 \text{ (Mar. 69 index)}} = \text{C}\$2.522 \text{ million}$$

This result means that the $1 million spent for this machine in March 1969 would have bought at that time the same quantity of goods and services that would have required $2.522 million to buy during 1981. Accumulated depreciation on depreciable assets is adjusted in the same manner as the assets' original cost.

---

[5]This is not the simple average of 258.4 and 281.5 (=270.0) because inflation did not occur at a *uniform* rate during 1981.

From the illustrative calculations, the reader should see (and remember) that the index value in the numerator of the adjustment ratio always relates to purchasing power as of the period whose purchasing power is being used as the basis of the restatements (price index "now"). The index in the denominator is always matched with the historical cost date of the dollar amount to be adjusted (price index "then").

Income Statement Items. All income statement items are nonmonetary and therefore subject to adjustment. However, *except for cost of sales and depreciation expense,* the FASB permits companies to assume that the flow of revenue and expense items was uniform during the year. This assumption precludes having to adjust these items if they are to be restated in terms of the current year's *average* purchasing power.[6] However, revenue and expense items from prior years must be adjusted if they are to be presented side by side with the current year's items; otherwise the amounts would not be comparable.

> **Example 5.** Bethlehem Steel's 1981 total revenues were $7,419 million. Although it is an approximation, FASB-33 permits Bethlehem Steel to report its 1981 sales also as being 7,419 million units of average 1981 purchasing power (i.e., C$7,419 million).

> **Example 6.** Bethlehem Steel's 1980 total revenues were $7,524 million. To make this amount comparable in terms of 1981 purchasing power with the C$7,419 million figure for 1981 revenues, an adjustment is necessary. The average CPI for 1980 was 246.8, so the calculation is (in millions):

$$\underset{\text{(80 revenues)}}{\$7,524} \times \frac{272.4 \text{ (avg. 81 index)}}{246.8 \text{ (avg. 80 index)}} = \text{C\$8,304}$$

> The average 1980 index rather than the year-end 1980 index is used because 1980 revenues also were a flow throughout the year, not a year-end lump sum.

Note that while the historical cost data indicate that from 1980 to 1981 Bethlehem Steel's sales decreased by 1.4 percent (= $7,419 ÷ $7,524 − 100 percent), the constant dollar data indicate a more substantial decrease of 10.7 percent (= C$7,419 ÷ C$8,304 − 100 percent).

Cost of Sales and Depreciation. The adjustments for cost of sales and depreciation expense must take account of the dates on which the related nonmonetary assets, inventory and plant and equipment, were acquired. These adjustments also will be illustrated with examples.

---

[6]Unless a company prepares complete constant dollar financial statements, which is not required by FASB-33, the company must make its constant dollar disclosures in terms of *average* purchasing power during the company's latest fiscal year. Companies presenting complete constant dollar statements may use either average-for-the-year or end-of-year constant dollars.

Example 7. Assume that the $1 million machine described above in Example 4 is being depreciated on a straight-line basis over 20 years. Then Bethlehem Steel's 1981 total reported depreciation expense would have included $50,000 for this machine. This amount is based on the March 1969 acquisition cost, and therefore must be adjusted using the March 1969 index as follows:

$$\underset{\substack{\text{(write-off of} \\ \text{Mar. 69 cost)}}}{\$50,000} \times \frac{272.4 \text{ (avg. 81 index)}}{108.0 \text{ (Mar. 69 index)}} = \text{C}\$126,111$$

Example 8. For 1981, Bethlehem Steel's year-end inventories totaled $879.5 million, and beginning-of-year inventories were $758.5 million. Analysis of inventory turnover indicates that, *on average*, items remain in inventory 1½ months (i.e., turnover = 8 times). As an approximation, then, we can assume that December 31, 1981, inventories were acquired in mid-November 1981, and that beginning 1981 inventories were acquired in mid-November 1980. Inventory acquisitions during 1981, which are assumed to have occurred as a level flow, totaled $6,445.0 million.

Constant dollar cost of sales is calculated using the periodic inventory method (described in Chapter 6), applied to *constant dollar* amounts (again, restated to average 1981 dollars). All amounts below are millions:

Beginning inventory (restated):

$$\underset{\substack{\text{(mid-Nov.} \\ \text{80 cost)}}}{\$758.5} \times \frac{272.4 \text{ (avg. 81 index)}}{255.1 \text{ (mid-Nov. 80 index)}} = \text{C}\$\ \ 809.9$$

Add purchases (no adjustment needed)   =   6,445.0

Available for sale   =   7,254.9

Subtract ending inventory (restated):

$$\underset{\substack{\text{(mid-Nov.} \\ \text{81 cost)}}}{\$879.5} \times \frac{272.4 \text{ (avg. 81 index)}}{280.3 \text{ (mid-Nov. 81 index)}} = \underline{\qquad 854.7}$$

Constant dollar cost of sales   = C$6,400.2

In practice, a company would use its more detailed cost records to make these cost of sales calculations, rather than the approximations used in the example.

Holding Gains and Losses. By holding monetary assets during a period of inflation, a company incurs a purchasing power loss on these assets. While a conventional income statement reports a return on these assets in the form of interest revenue, it does not report the purchasing power loss that offsets some of this revenue. For example, if a certificate of deposit earns a nominal return of 12 percent in a year in which inflation was 10 percent, the "true" return is said to be only 2 percent. Conversely, reported interest expense is said to overstate the "true" cost of a liability because the liability will be paid off using dollars of lower purchasing power than the dollars that the creditor furnished the company when the liability was incurred.

A purchasing power gain on monetary liabilities, and a loss on monetary assets, could be computed separately. In practice, however, monetary liabilities are subtracted from monetary assets. If the amount is positive, then a holding *loss* on these *net monetary assets* is calculated. If the amount is negative, then a holding *gain* on these *net monetary liabilities* is calculated.

> **Example 9.** At the beginning of 1981, Bethlehem Steel's net monetary liabilities totaled $1,188.1 million. At the end of 1981, the amount was $1,206.2 million. The $18.1 million of net monetary liabilities *added* during 1981 are assumed to have been added in a level flow during the year, and hence do not require adjustment.
>
> The purchasing power gain calculation is as follows (in millions):
>
> Purchasing power of beginning net monetary liabilities:
>
> $1,188.1 $\times \dfrac{272.4 \text{ (avg. 81 index)}}{258.4 \text{ (Dec. 80 index)}}$ $\qquad = \qquad$ C$1,252.5
>
> Increase in net monetary liabilities $\qquad = \qquad$ 18.1
>
> $\qquad\qquad\qquad\qquad\qquad\qquad\qquad\qquad\qquad\qquad$ 1,270.6
>
> Purchasing power of ending net monetary liabilities:
>
> $1,206.2 $\times \dfrac{272.4 \text{ (avg. 81 index)}}{281.5 \text{ (Dec. 81 index)}}$ $\qquad = \qquad$ 1,167.2
>
> Purchasing power gain .... C$ 103.4

In the example, the result is a *gain* to Bethlehem Steel because during 1981 its creditors suffered a decline in the purchasing power of the amounts owed to them by Bethlehem.

Owners' Equity. We have now described the constant dollar calculation procedures for all items except owners' equity. Although detailed procedures exist for separately adjusting each item in owners' equity, all that is of real interest is the total constant dollar owners' equity amount. This is simply the difference between constant dollar assets and constant dollar liabilities. FASB-33 refers to this amount as constant dollar *net assets*, rather than owners' equity.

Summary of Constant Dollar Procedures. In summary, to prepare supplemental constant dollar statements, the steps are:

1. Choose the unit of purchasing power to which historical cost data are to be adjusted. This is normally units of *average* purchasing power for the fiscal year just completed.
2. Adjust monetary items on the beginning and ending balance sheets by multiplying each item by the ratio of the CPI "now" (i.e., average CPI for the most recent year) to the CPI as of the *balance sheet date*.
3. Adjust nonmonetary balance sheet assets and liabilities by multiplying each such item by the ratio of the CPI "now" to the CPI as of the time the nonmonetary item *was acquired*.
4. Having now adjusted all assets and liabilities, find constant dollar

owners' equity simply by subtracting constant dollar liabilities from constant dollar assets.

5. Determine constant dollar cost of sales by applying the periodic inventory method to *constant dollar* amounts for beginning inventory, purchases (no adjustment needed), and ending inventory. The constant dollar inventory amounts are determined in the same manner as other adjusted nonmonetary amounts (step 3). An approximation, basing inventory age on a turnover ratio (as in Example 8), is permissible.

6. Determine constant dollar depreciation expense by adjusting each asset's depreciation charge in the same manner that the asset's original cost and accumulated depreciation are adjusted, that is, by multiplying the historical cost amount by the ratio of the CPI "now" to the CPI as of the asset's acquisition date.

7. If the *average* CPI for the year is being used, no other income statement item requires restatement. These other items, when combined with the adjusted cost of sales and depreciation expense amounts from steps 5 and 6, determine constant dollar net income.

8. Calculate the holding loss on net monetary assets, or the holding gain on net monetary liabilities. FASB-33 requires disclosure of this amount, but does *not* treat it as an element of the calculation of constant dollar net income.

Current Cost Accounting

Because there is ongoing controversy as to whether constant dollar or current cost data are more useful, FASB-33 requires that companies disclose *both* kinds of supplementary information until this issue can be resolved.

Nature of Current Costs. The term *current cost* is somewhat ambiguous. Essentially, by *current cost* the FASB means the cost of replacing specific assets, called *replacement costs* or *specific prices*. For inventories, current cost is the cost as of the balance sheet date for purchasing the goods concerned, or for acquiring the resources needed to produce the goods concerned.

For property, plant, and equipment, current cost means the cost of acquiring the same *service potential* as embodied in the assets owned. FASB-33 permits any of three approaches for estimating the current cost of a used asset: (1) the cost of a new asset with equivalent capabilities, reduced by an allowance for depreciation; (2) the cost of a used asset of the same age and in the same condition; or (3) the cost of a new asset with *different* service potential, adjusted for the difference. The third approach might be necessary, for example, if a beer company owned several small breweries, but current technology and production economies were such that only much larger breweries were now being built. In such a case, asset-specific price indexes can be used to aid in making the current cost estimates.

Recoverable Amounts. FASB-33 requires that inventories, property, plant, and equipment be reported at current cost or *lower recoverable amount*. This is analogous to conventional accounting's "lower-of-cost-or-market" rule for inventories. The recoverable amount is the current worth (i.e., present value) of the *net* amount of cash expected to be recoverable from the use or sale of the asset.

Other Balance Sheet Items. Only inventories and fixed assets are subject to adjustments to a current cost basis. The historical cost amounts for other assets and all liabilities are presumed to reflect adequately their current costs. Current cost owners' equity ("net assets") is found by subtracting liabilities from adjusted total assets; FASB-33 requires disclosure of this amount.

Income Statement Adjustments. Since only inventories and fixed assets are restated on the balance sheet, the only income statement adjustments needed are for the related cost of sales and depreciation expenses. Revenues, other expenses, and income taxes are not adjusted.

Example A. Bolgos Company produces only one product. On January 1, the current cost of this item was $20 per unit. By the end of the year, the current cost had risen to $23 per unit. On January 1, there were 10,000 units on hand. During the year, 60,000 units were produced and 58,000 were sold, leaving 12,000 units on hand at year-end. The relevant balance sheet and income statement current cost amounts are as follows:

January 1 inventory: 10,000 units @ $20	=	$200,000
December 31 inventory: 12,000 units @ $23	=	$276,000
Average unit current cost for the year: ½ ($20 + $23)	=	$21.50
Current cost of sales: 58,000 units @ $21.50	=	$1,247,000

Example B. As of December 31, Bolgos owned a machine acquired three years previously at a cost of $1.0 million. The machine is being depreciated on a straight-line basis over 10 years. Thus, as of the start of the year, the machine was 20 percent depreciated, and was 30 percent depreciated by December 31. The machine's manufacturer has continued to offer for sale an identical model, but the price has been increasing. As of January 1 (when Bolgos' machine was two years old), the price of a new machine was $1.2 million; by the end of the year, it had increased to $1.3 million. The relevant current cost data are as follows:

Machine, as of January 1:	
Current cost	$1,200,000
Accumulated depreciation (20%)	240,000
Net current cost	$ 960,000
Machine, as of December 31:	
Current cost	$1,300,000
Accumulated depreciation (30%)	390,000
Net current cost	$ 910,000
Year's average current cost: ½ ($1,200,000 + $1,300,000) =	$1,250,000
Current cost depreciation expense: $1,250,000 × 10% =	$ 125,000

The reader may find these machine cost calculations troublesome conceptually, even though they are simple computationally. While the balance in current cost accumulated depreciation increased by $150,000 (from $240,000 to $390,000), the current cost depreciation expense was only $125,000. This discrepancy occurs because the year-end current cost *accumulated* depreciation amount includes "catch-up" depreciation for each of the three years' increases in the asset's price. For example, the $390,000 year-end current cost *accumulated* depreciation includes $10,000 depreciation on this year's $100,000 asset price increase [$10,000 = 10 percent × ($1,300,000 − $1,200,000)]. But the calculation of current cost depreciation *expense* is based on the *average* current cost during the year of $1,250,000 and thus includes only $5,000 [= 10 percent × ($1,250,000 − $1,200,000)] as depreciation on this year's asset price increase.[7]

Constant Dollar versus Current Cost Procedures.   Clearly the arithmetic calculations for current cost adjustments are much simpler than for constant dollar adjustments. However, the current cost calculations actually take longer because of the significant time involved in making reliable estimates of current costs. In Example B, it was assumed that identical new machines were still available. But suppose the machine had been custom-built for Bolgos Company 10 years ago; then estimating current cost would involve far more than calling up a dealer to get the current price. Or imagine the effort required to estimate the current cost of inventory if the company stocked 10,000 different items!

It is these estimating problems that cause some people to question the objectivity of current cost data. Constant dollar data, on the other hand, are objective: one multiplies an objective historical cost amount by a ratio of objective price index values. The question with constant dollar data instead is one of relevance. Does someone prefer to know that a five-year-old machine is currently worth about $100,000, or to know that the amount originally spent for the machine is exactly equivalent to $94,535 worth of "general" goods and services at the current year's average prices? If there were a consensus answer to that question, the FASB would not require both types of disclosures.

Inflation-Adjusted Current Costs

A change in the price of a specific item can be thought of as having two causes: (1) a general change in the dollar's purchasing power and (2) factors specific to the item itself. It is possible to use a general price index to isolate these two components of a specific price (current cost) change.

---

[7]A complete reconciliation of the discrepancy between the $150,000 increase in accumulated depreciation and the $125,000 depreciation expense is as follows: The asset's *cumulative* price increases total $300,000; so "catch-up" depreciation (at 10 percent) of $30,000 is needed. $5,000 of this was included in the $125,000 calculated current year's depreciation expense. The remaining $25,000 is the "discrepancy."

Example. In January 1981, a certain automobile repair part cost $100. By January 1982, its price had risen to $112. The CPI was 260.5 in January 1981 and 282.5 in January 1982. *If* the item's January 1981 price had risen at the 1981 rate of inflation, in January 1982 the price would have been:

$$\underset{\substack{\text{(Jan. 81} \\ \text{price)}}}{\$100} \times \frac{282.5 \text{ (Jan. 82 index)}}{260.5 \text{ (Jan. 81 index)}} = \$108.45$$

The two components of the price increase therefore are:

Change due to inflation: $108.45 − $100	=	$ 8.45
Change due to other factors: $112 − $108.45	=	3.55
Total change in price: $112 − $100	=	$12.00

Some people would say that the $3.55 was the "real" price increase.

Since current costs are measured at various points in time (e.g., January 1981 and January 1982 in the preceding two examples), they are expressed in units of money ("nominal dollars") as of those times. When these nominal current costs are adjusted to units of purchasing power as of some point in time (January 1982 in the examples), the resulting amounts are called *current cost/constant dollar* amounts. FASB-33 requires companies to perform current cost/constant dollar calculations such as those in the preceding example to isolate the general price-level component of changes in the current costs of inventories, property, plant, and equipment. This price change analysis must be disclosed, along with any purchasing power gain or loss on monetary items; but neither enters into the calculation of current cost net income.

Summary of Inflation Accounting

Considering all of the techniques described above, we see that FASB-33 describes four different methods of reporting financial accounting information: (1) historical cost/nominal dollar (conventional accounting), (2) historical cost/constant dollar (constant dollar accounting), (3) current cost/nominal dollar (replacement cost accounting), and (4) current cost/constant dollar. Each method reflects a different concept of how asset amounts should be reported, and of what it means for a company to earn a profit. The four profit concepts can be stated as follows.

A company earns a profit when its revenues exceed:

1. The *historical costs* of the resources consumed in generating the revenues (conventional view).
2. The *purchasing power equivalent* of the historical costs of the resources consumed (financial capital maintenance view—constant dollar accounting).
3. The *replacement costs* of the resources consumed (operating capability maintenance view—current cost accounting).

4. The *purchasing power equivalent of the replacement costs* of the resources consumed (inflation-adjusted current costs).

Methods 2, 3, and 4 also view gains or losses on holding monetary liabilities or monetary assets as relevant information, although there is no consensus as to whether these gains or losses are "real" or whether they should be included in the calculation of net income.

Disclosures. Illustration 12–1 shows the FASB-33 required disclosures in 1981 for Levi Strauss & Co. In addition to items previously described, these disclosures include common stock cash dividends and market price per share information for the last five years on both a historical cost and constant dollar basis. While FASB-33 permits disclosure of complete financial statements on both adjusted bases, most companies are limiting their disclosures to the minimum requirements reflected in Illustration 12–1.

Note that Levi Strauss itself points out (at the bottom of its five-year summary table) that it has enjoyed "real growth" in sales and dividends per share. The company similarly could have pointed to the fact that in 1981 it reported growth in net assets on both a constant dollar and current cost basis. Many companies were unable to make these kinds of "real growth" statements in their 1980 and 1981 disclosures. Also note that Levi Strauss' specific prices (current costs) increased less rapidly than the rate of inflation in 1981. This can be seen in two ways: cost of goods sold and depreciation expense are both higher on the GPP basis than on the current cost basis; and current costs of inventories and fixed assets increased only $9.7 million, while on a GPP basis these assets increased $86.4 million. In sum, the disclosures suggest that Levi Strauss coped well with inflation in 1981.

FOREIGN CURRENCY ACCOUNTING PROBLEMS

As mentioned in Chapter 11, changes in the price of a foreign currency vis-à-vis the dollar, that is, fluctuating *exchange rates,* cause problems in preparing consolidated statements involving a foreign subsidiary. These consolidation problems are foreign currency *translation* accounting problems. Also, whether or not a company has a foreign subsidiary, the company may engage in transactions with foreign entities; these transactions lead to foreign currency *transaction* accounting problems. Both types of problems are discussed below.

Foreign Currency Transactions

If an American firm buys or sells goods abroad, or borrows from or grants credit to a foreign entity, the firm may experience a *transaction gain or loss* as a result of exchange rate fluctuations between the date the transaction was entered into and the date cash is transmitted.

ILLUSTRATION 12–1
TYPICAL INFLATION ACCOUNTING DISCLOSURES
LEVI STRAUSS & CO. AND SUBSIDIARIES

Statement of Income Adjusted for Changing Prices (Unaudited)

Year Ended November 29, 1981 (In Millions)	As Reported in the Primary Statements	Adjusted for General Inflation	Adjusted for Current Costs
Net sales	$2,851.2	$2,851.2	$2,851.2
Operating expenses excluding depreciation expense			
Cost of goods sold	1,817.4	1,870.2	1,828.7
Marketing, general and administrative expenses	643.7	643.7	643.7
Depreciation expense	33.7	50.2	40.5
Interest expense	50.2	50.2	50.2
Interest and other income, net	(31.5)	(31.5)	(31.5)
Income before taxes	337.7	268.4	319.6
Provision for taxes on income	165.4	165.4	165.4
Net income	$ 172.3	$ 103.0	$ 154.2
Purchasing power gain on net monetary items held during the year		$ 0.9	$ 0.9
Effect of increase in the general price level on inventories and property, plant and equipment held during the year			$ 86.4
Increase in specific prices (current costs)[1]			9.7
Excess of increase in the general price level over increase in specific prices			$ 76.7

[1]At November 29, 1981, current cost of inventory was $518.2 and current cost of property, plant and equipment, net of accumulated depreciation was $450.0.

Selected Supplementary Financial Data Adjusted for Effects of Changing Prices (Unaudited)

(In Millions, Except Per Share Amounts, Using Average 1981 Dollars)	1981	1980	1979	1978	1977
Net sales:					
At historical costs	$2,851.2	$2,840.8	$2,103.1	$1,682.0	$1,559.3
In constant dollars	2,851.2	3,143.1	2,642.6	2,344.4	2,334.7
Cash dividends per share:					
At historical costs	1.575	1.30	1.00	.80	.50
In constant dollars	1.569	1.43	1.25	1.11	.75
Market price per share at year end:					
At historical costs	28⅞	42¼	31	17⅜	15⅛
In constant dollars	27⅞	44⅝	36⅞	23¼	22⅛
Historical cost information adjusted for general inflation:					
Net income	103.0	172.1		(Pre-1980	
Net income per share	2.48	4.12		Data not	
Net assets	1,098.0	1,015.9		Required	
Current cost information:				by FASB)	
Net income	154.2	195.2			
Net income per share	3.71	4.67			
Net assets	1,012.2	994.0			
Excess of increase in the general price level over increase in specific prices	76.7	18.3			
Purchasing power gain	0.9	1.7			
Average Consumer Price Index (CPI-U) (1967 = 100)	270.4	244.4	215.2	194.0	180.6

The Company has been able to steadily increase its productivity and its dividend rate, in spite of inflation. Net sales, even after adjustment for inflation, have risen 22% during the period 1977-1981. Cash dividends per share in constant dollars doubled from $.75 per share in 1977 to $1.569 in 1981.

Author's Note: Levi Strauss' fiscal year ends the last Sunday in November. Thus, CPI values shown above are different from the calendar year values used in text examples.

Example. Shipley Shoe Store received a shipment of shoes from an Italian manufacturer with an invoice for 1,000,000 lire. On the date the invoice was received and the transaction journalized, the exchange rate was $0.000779 per lira, giving a $779 account payable for the shoes received. Thirty days later, when Shipley paid its bill in lire, the exchange rate had increased to $0.000787 per lira. Thus, Shipley had to pay $787 to buy the required lire, and a currency exchange loss of $8 was realized. This would be accounted for as follows:

```
Accounts Payable. ............................   779
Loss on Foreign Exchange. ....................     8
    Cash. ....................................          787
```

Note that this transaction loss occurred because the transaction was *denominated* in a currency other than the dollar. If Shipley had originally agreed to pay $787, rather than 1,000,000 lire, for the shipment, no transaction loss would have occurred.

Transaction gains and losses are included in the calculation of net income for the period in which the exchange rate changes. This is true whether or not the gain or loss has been *realized*. For example, if Shipley had still owed the 1,000,000 lire as of December 31, 1982, and if at that time the exchange rate was anything other than $0.000779 per lira, then Shipley would have recognized a transaction gain or loss in its 1982 income statement. If the payment were then made on January 12, 1983, another gain or loss would have been recognized if the exchange rate were different on January 12, 1983, than it was on December 31, 1982.[8] The *sum* of these two recognized transaction gains or losses would equal whatever gain or loss was ultimately realized.

Foreign Currency Translation

Usually the accounts of a foreign subsidiary are kept in the currency of the country in which the subsidiary operates, that is, the *functional currency* of the subsidiary. In preparing consolidated statements, the parent must translate these foreign currency amounts into dollars (called more generally the *reporting currency*). Because exchange rates fluctuate, the question arises as to the date or dates that should be used to determine the exchange rates used in this translation process.

FASB-8. There are various possible answers to this question, and at one time GAAP were sufficiently broad that a company could use any of several different methods to make these translations. In 1975, *FASB Statement No. 8* limited the choices to one—the *monetary/nonmonetary method.*[9] With this method, monetary assets and liabilities are translated at the *current rate*, that is, the rate prevailing as of the balance sheet

---

[8]"Foreign Currency Translation," *FASB Statement No. 52,* December 1981, par. 15.

[9]"Accounting for the Translation of Foreign Currency Transactions and Foreign Currency Financial Statements," *FASB Statement No. 8,* October 1975.

date; and nonmonetary items are translated at the rates existing when the transactions occurred, called *historical rates*. Income statement items are translated at the *average rate* prevailing during the accounting period, except for those expenses related to asset costs that are translated at historical rates—e.g., depreciation expense. (This method is analogous to the constant dollar adjustment procedures described earlier in this chapter.)

FASB-8 failed to achieve wide acceptance among business people, primarily because its requirements caused the parent company's reported net income to fluctuate within wide limits as a result of changes in exchange rates. Thus in 1981, the FASB issued a new standard, *Statement No. 52*.

FASB-52. The new statement embodied the *net investment* or *current rate* method. With this method, the parent's investment in a foreign subsidiary is considered to be an investment in the subsidiary's net assets. Accordingly, *all* of the foreign entity's assets and liabilities are translated at the *current exchange rate* as of the balance sheet date. All revenue and expense items are translated at the *average rate* for the period.

To illustrate this method, assume that the Franco Company, a French subsidiary of its U.S. parent, Americo, Inc., was formed on January 1, 19x1. Americo's initial investment in Franco was $850,000, which at the time was equivalent to 5,000,000 francs because the January 1, 19x1, exchange rate was $0.170 per franc. Franco's 19x1 financial statements are shown in Illustration 12–2. All year-end assets and liabilities are translated at the $0.160 per franc exchange rate as of December 31, 19x1. All income statement items are translated at the average 19x1 exchange rate, which was $0.165. Franco's capital stock is translated at the rate in effect when it was issued to Americo, $0.170. The dollar amount for retained earnings is simply the beginning balance (zero) plus net income ($165,000) less dividends (zero).

All of these translation calculations leave the dollar balance sheet's sum of liabilities and owners' equity $55,000 greater than the total assets. The negative $55,000 translation adjustment restores the dollar balance sheet's equality. But this $55,000 downward adjustment can be viewed as more than just a "plug" figure. Since Americo held French franc net assets while the value of the franc fell relative to the dollar, Americo sustained a holding loss in the dollar value of this net assets investment. The calculation of this loss is shown at the bottom of Illustration 12–2. (It is analogous to the GPP calculation of the holding loss on net monetary assets expressed in end-of-year units of purchasing power.) FASB-52 requires that the amount of such a translation loss (or gain) be disclosed and accumulated in a separate translation adjustment account in the owners' equity portion of the translated balance sheet. However, such translation gains or losses do *not* flow through the trans-

ILLUSTRATION 12–2
FOREIGN STATEMENT TRANSLATIONS

FRANCO COMPANY
Balance Sheet
As of December 31, 19x1
(000 omitted)

Assets	Francs	Exchange Rate	Dollars
Cash	Fr 1,000	$0.160	$ 160
Receivables	5,000	0.160	800
Inventories	3,000	0.160	480
Equipment (net)	4,000	0.160	640
	Fr 13,000		$2,080

Liabilities and Owners' Equity			
Liabilities	Fr 7,000	0.160	$1,120
Capital stock	5,000	0.170*	850
Retained earnings	1,000		165
Accumulated translation adjustment	—	†	(55)
	Fr 13,000		$2,080

Income Statement
For the Year Ended December 31, 19x1
(000 omitted)

	Francs		Dollars
Revenues	Fr 20,000	$0.165	$3,300
Cost of sales	12,000	0.165	1,980
Other expenses	7,000	0.165	1,155
Net income	Fr 1,000		$ 165

*Exchange rate as of the date the capital stock was issued.
†Calculation of translation loss:

Jan. 1, 19x1, net assets = Fr 5,000

Translated at Dec. 31, 19x1, rate = 5,000 × $0.160	=	$800
Translated at Jan. 1, 19x1, rate = 5,000 × $0.170	=	850
Loss on beginning-of-year net assets		$(50)

Increment in net assets during 19x1 = Fr 1,000

Translated at Dec. 31, 19x1, rate = 1,000 × $0.160	=	$160
Translated at average 19x1 rate = 1,000 × $0.165	=	165
Loss on increment in net assets		$ (5)

Total loss in dollar value of net assets		$(55)

lated income statement, which pleases most of the critics of FASB-8. The translated foreign subsidiary's statements are then consolidated with the parent's statements, as described in Chapter 11.

SUMMARY

Many people feel that the phenomenon of changing prices makes it problematical to use historical cost data for comparing an entity's performance on a period-to-period basis, or for comparing two or more different entities in the same period. Constant dollar accounting tries to facilitate such comparisons by adjusting historical cost data to a units of purchasing power basis. This information is objective, but not necessarily relevant. Replacement cost accounting uses current costs of inventories and fixed assets. This information is relevant, but not necessarily objective. The FASB currently requires large companies to disclose supplemental information on both bases, in the belief that this will provide insight into whether inflation has caused an erosion of a company's purchasing power or operating capability.

Foreign currency *transaction* gains or losses arise from transactions between a domestic company and a foreign entity, where the transaction is denominated in the foreign entity's currency. Transaction gains and losses are included in net income. Foreign currency *translation* gains or losses arise from a domestic parent's holding an investment in the net assets of a foreign subsidiary. Translation gains and losses are accumulated in the owners' equity section of the parent's consolidated balance sheet, but they are not part of the calculation of consolidated net income.

Many inflation accounting and foreign exchange accounting procedures are analogous. This is because inflation accounting measures one currency at two points in time, whereas foreign exchange accounting measures two currencies at one point in time.

Cases

CASE 12–1   The $2.5 Million Lathe*

For the 18th year, Thompson Products has continued its custom of furnishing its employees with a simple concise report of its financial operations, showing how much money the company took in and what happened to it. Revenues for 1976 totaled $306,508,120. Expenses, not including wages, salaries, or dividends, were $175,535,061, leaving $130,973,059 to be divided among employees and shareholders. Of this, $117,960,454 went for payrolls, $4,183,904 was paid out in dividends, and $8,828,701 was plowed back into the business.

Why was it necessary to plow that much back into the business? The tale of the $2.5 million turret lathe, included in the report, explains that. It seems that in 1962 the company bought a lathe for

*This case consists of a quotation adapted from a report prepared by the management of a company for the information of its employees.

$24,000. Under federal tax laws, it was permitted to depreciate the cost of the lathe over a 14-year period. So, last year, when the lathe became obsolete, the company had $24,000 to buy a new one, plus $2,000, which was the resale value of the old one. But the replacement cost in 1976 was $70,000 for a lathe that would perform the same functions as the old model, or $134,000 for a new one with attachments to meet today's more exacting needs.

The company had only $26,000 to do a $134,000 job. The difference of $108,000 had to come out of profits; and in order to get that amount in 1976, the company had to earn a profit of $225,000 before taxes because $108,000 was all there was left after paying corporate income taxes of 52 percent. And to earn that amount of profit, the company had to sell more than $2.5 million worth of products to customers. It took more than $2.5 million of sales to buy just one machine!

Thus, while $225,000 sounds like a lot of profit, in this case, the shareholders got none of it. The government took more than half, and the rest went to replace a machine. This story is duplicated hundreds of times each year throughout the company in the case of machines, large and small. This is why only a relatively small amount of profit is paid to shareholders in dividends, and why a large portion must be retained to finance expansion and replacement so the company can continue to operate and employees can continue working.

Question

Comment on this statement. Is it the truth, the whole truth, and nothing but the truth?

CASE 12–2 Westchester Manufacturing Company

Westchester Manufacturing Company was too small a firm to fall under the requirements of *FASB Statement No. 33*. However, Mr. Bitterman, the chief financial officer, was curious as to how the company's financial results might look on a constant-dollar basis and on a current-cost basis. Historical cost balance sheets as of December 31, 1980, and 1981, and the historical cost income statement for the year ended December 31, 1981, appear in Exhibit 1.

Mr. Bitterman wrote down the following assumptions to use in converting historical-cost "nominal" amounts to constant-dollar amounts:

a. The company wants to restate its financial statements in *average* 1981 dollars.

b. Inventory turnover is four times per year; i.e., the end-of-year inventories can be thought of as having been acquired on October 1. Production volume was steady during 1981, and production costs totaled $2,375,000, excluding depreciation on production facilities.

c. The average age of plant and equipment can be approximated by dividing the year's depreciation expense into the year-end's accumulated depreciation. In both years, this results in an average age (to the nearest quarter year) of 5½ years. Depreciation is straight line over 10 years.

d. All liabilities are monetary items.

e. Selected values of the Consumer Price Index are as follows (1967 = 100):

July 1975	162.3
July 1976	171.1
October 1980	253.9
December 1980	258.4
Average 1980	246.8
October 1981	279.9
December 1981	281.5
Average 1981	272.4

Mr. Bitterman also assembled the following replacement cost data:

a. At December 31, 1980, and 1981, inventory consisted of 10,000 units and 9,000 units, respectively. Estimated replacement costs (in nominal dollars) were $58 per unit at December 31, 1980, and $70 per unit at December 31, 1981. During 1981, 38,000 units were sold.

b. Current cost of plant and equip-

EXHIBIT 1

WESTCHESTER MANUFACTURING COMPANY
Balance Sheets
As of December 31

	1980	1981
Assets		
Cash and receivables	$ 320,000	$ 385,000
Inventories (FIFO basis)	560,000	605,000
Total current assets	880,000	990,000
Plant and equipment, at cost.	850,000	1,000,000
Accumulated depreciation	(460,000)	(560,000)
Net plant and equipment	390,000	440,000
Total assets	$1,270,000	$1,430,000
Liabilities and Owners' Equity		
Current liabilities.	$ 430,000	$ 580,000
Noncurrent liabilities.	440,000	400,000
Total liabilities	870,000	980,000
Owners' equity.	400,000	450,000
Total liabilities and owners' equity.	$1,270,000	$1,430,000

Income Statement
For the Year Ended December 31, 1981

Sales revenues		$2,810,000
Cost of sales	$2,330,000	
Selling and administrative expenses	220,000	
Depreciation expense	100,000	
Total expenses		2,650,000
Income before taxes		160,000
Income tax expense		80,000
Net income.		$ 80,000

Per Share Data (150,000 shares outstanding):

Net income.	$0.53⅓
Dividends	0.20

ment, measured in nominal dollars as of December 31, 1980, and 1981, was $1,700,000 and $2,200,000, respectively. Accumulated depreciation based on current cost was $959,000 and $1,349,000, giving net current cost of $741,000 and $851,000.

Questions

1. Prepare 1981 income statements and year-end 1980 and 1981 balance sheets (a) expressed in units of average 1981 purchasing power and (b) on a current-cost basis.

2. Using the historical-cost statements given in Exhibit 1 and the two sets of statements you prepared for Question 1, calculate the following ratios on all three bases: current ratio, acid-test ratio, inventory turnover, days' inventory, debt/equity, profit margin, income taxes as a percent of pretax income, net income/assets, and net income/equity. (To simplify your calculations, in ratios involving balance sheet amounts use year-end amounts, even

though using an average of beginning and ending amounts may be conceptually superior in some cases.) Compare your three sets of ratios and comment both on similarities and on differences.

CASE 12–3 Liberty Electronics Company

Liberty Electronics Company produced various types of household electronic equipment, which it sold primarily through two large retail store chains in the United States. On October 1, 1981, Liberty established a wholly owned subsidiary in South Korea, called Liberty-Korea, for the purpose of assembling a small home version of a video arcade game that Liberty had been licensed to produce. The Korean subsidiary sold its output directly to the U.S. retailers that carried the game (as opposed to selling its output to its U.S. parent for resale to U.S. retailers).

Exhibit 1 shows the subsidiary's condensed balance sheet as of September 30, 1982 (fiscal year-end), and an income statement for its first year of operations.

Liberty's controller, Marion Rosenblum, asked a member of the accounting staff to translate these statements into dollars, following the standards of *FASB Statement No. 52*. The controller also was interested in how the statements translated in accord with FASB-52 might differ from those prepared using the method formerly required by FASB-8.

The accounting staff person assembled the following information to assist in preparing the two sets of translated statements:

1. The South Korean unit of currency is the won (abbreviated W). As of October 1, 1981, the exchange rate was one won = $0.00146; as of September 30, 1982, the rate was one won = $0.00130.

EXHIBIT 1

LIBERTY–KOREA
Balance Sheet
As of September 30, 1982
(millions of won)

Assets		*Liabilities and Owners' Equity*	
Cash	W 591	Current liabilities	W 624
Receivables	1,182		
Inventories	552	Capital stock	1,000
Fixed assets	575	Retained earnings	1,276
	W2,900		W2,900

Income Statement
For the Year Ended September 30, 1982
(millions of won)

Revenues	W7,090
Cost of sales	4,415
Other expenses	1,399
Net income	W1,276

2. As of October 1, 1981, Liberty-Korea's assets were W400 million cash and W600 million fixed assets. No additional fixed assets were acquired during the first year of operations. On average, the year-end inventories had been on hand 1½ months; the exchange rate on August 15, 1982, was one won = $0.00132.

3. The capital stock of Liberty-Korea had been issued to Liberty Electronics on October 1, 1981; no additional capital stock transactions had taken place during the fiscal year.

Questions

1. Prepare translated year-end statements for Liberty-Korea using the net investment method, as required by FASB-52.

2. Prepare translated statemements using FASB-8's monetary/nonmonetary method. (Note: Under FASB-8, any translation gain or loss was included as an item in the translated income statement. You may treat any such gain or loss as a "plug" figure; i.e., you are not expected to calculate it in detail.)

3. Compare your two sets of translated statements and comment on any differences between them. If the company were permitted a choice as to which method to use, which method do you think they would prefer?

13

Financial Statement Analysis

In previous chapters the principal focus has been on conveying an understanding of the information contained in the three basic financial statements—the balance sheet, the income statement, and the funds flow statement. This chapter describes how this information is analyzed, both by parties outside the firm and by the company's own management.

BUSINESS OBJECTIVES

All analyses of accounting data involve comparisons. An absolute statement, such as "Company X earned $1 million profit" is, by itself, not useful. It becomes useful only when the $1 million is compared with something else. The comparison may be quite imprecise and intuitive. For example, if we know that Company X is an industrial giant with tens of thousands of employees, we know intuitively that $1 million profit is a poor showing because we have built up in our minds the impression that such companies should earn much more than that. Or, the comparison may be much more formal, explicit, and precise, as is the case when the $1 million profit this year is compared with last year's profit. In either case, it is the process of comparison that makes the figure meaningful.

In order to decide the types of comparisons that are useful, we need first to consider what a business is all about—what its objectives are—

411

for the comparisons are essentially intended to shed light on how well a company is achieving its objectives. As a generalization, it may be said that *insofar as it can be measured quantitatively, the overall objective of a business is to earn a satisfactory return on the funds invested in it, consistent with maintaining a sound financial position.*[1] Note that this statement is limited to facts that can be expressed numerically. Personal satisfaction, social responsibility, ethical considerations, and other non-measurable objectives are also important and must be taken into account whenever possible in appraising the overall success of an enterprise.

The foregoing statement of objectives has two aspects: (1) earning a satisfactory return on investment and (2) maintaining a sound financial position. Each aspect is discussed briefly below.

Return on Investment

Return on investment (ROI) is defined as net income divided by investment. The term *investment* is used in three different senses in financial analysis, thus giving three different ROI ratios: return on assets (ROA), return on owners' equity (ROE), and return on invested capital (ROIC).

Return on assets (net income divided by total assets) reflects how much the firm has earned on the investment of *all* the financial resources committed to the firm. Thus, this ROA measure is appropriate if one considers the "investment" in the firm to include current liabilities, long-term liabilities, and owners' equity, which are the total sources of funds invested in the assets. It is a useful measure if one wants to evaluate how well an enterprise has *used* its funds, without regard to the relative magnitudes of the sources of those funds (short-term creditors, long-term creditors, bondholders, and shareholders). In particular, the ROA ratio often is used by top management to evaluate individual operations *within* a multidivisional firm (e.g., the computer division of an electronics firm). The division manager has significant influence over the assets used in the division but has little control over the financing of those assets because the division does not arrange its own loans, issue its own bonds or capital stock, and in many cases does not pay its own bills (current liabilities).

Return on owners' equity (net income divided by owners' equity) reflects how much the firm has earned on the funds invested by the shareholders (either directly or through retained earnings). This ROE ratio is obviously of interest to present or prospective shareholders, and is also of concern to management, which is responsible for operating the busi-

---

[1]This statement is not consistent with the *profit maximization* assumption often made in economics. The techniques in this chapter are equally applicable under a profit maximization assumption, however, so there is no point in arguing here whether the profit maximization assumption is valid and useful. Discussion of this point is deferred until Chapter 22.

ness in the owners' best interests. The ratio is not generally of interest to division managers, however, because they are primarily concerned with the efficient use of assets, rather than with the relative roles of creditors and shareholders in financing those assets. Illustration 13–1 shows average ROE for various industries. Note that the 1981 range is from −5.9 percent to 24.8 percent.

The third ratio is *return on invested capital* (net income divided by invested capital). Invested capital (also called *permanent capital*) is equal to noncurrent liabilities plus shareholders' equity, and hence rep-

ILLUSTRATION 13–1
RATIOS FOR SELECTED INDUSTRIES, 1981

	Percent Return on Equity	Percent Return on Sales	Price/ Earnings Ratio
Aerospace	15.9	3.4	8
Airlines	−5.9	−0.1	NM
Appliances	10.8	2.7	8
Automotive	−4.0	−0.9	NM
Banks and bank holding companies	13.6	4.4	6
Beverages	15.4	4.6	8
Building materials	7.0	2.9	13
Chemicals	13.1	5.5	8
Conglomerates	15.4	4.6	6
Containers	10.7	3.3	6
Drugs	18.7	9.4	12
Electrical and electronics	15.9	5.2	14
Food processing	14.9	3.4	8
Food and lodging	17.1	6.1	9
General machinery	14.1	5.1	8
Leisure time industries	15.2	7.9	12
Metals and metals mining	9.0	5.0	12
Office equipment and computers	15.2	7.9	12
Oil and coal	18.6	5.1	9
Oil service and supply	24.8	11.7	7
Paper and forest products	11.0	5.3	9
Personal care products	17.7	6.2	9
Publishing, radio, and television	17.2	6.8	11
Railroads	12.5	7.3	6
Retailing, food	15.1	1.1	6
Retailing, nonfood	12.5	2.5	10
Service industries	14.9	2.8	10
Steel	9.4	3.6	6
Textiles and apparel	11.4	3.4	8
Tire and rubber	9.2	2.8	6
Tobacco	19.9	6.3	8
Trucking	13.9	3.5	7
Utilities	13.0	9.0	7
All industry composite	14.0	4.8	9

NM: not meaningful.
Return on equity: Net income ÷ Ending shareholders' equity.
Return on Sales: Net income (before extraordinary items) ÷ Sales.
Price/earnings ratio: Closing price ÷ Primary earnings per share (before extraordinary items).
Source: Calculated from COMPUSTAT data.

resents the funds entrusted to the firm for relatively long periods of time. ROIC focuses on the use of this permanent capital. It is presumed that the current liabilities will fluctuate more or less automatically with changes in current assets, and that both vary with the level of current operations.

Invested capital is also equal to working capital plus noncurrent assets. This equivalency points out that the owners and long-term creditors of the firm in effect must finance the plant and equipment and other long-term assets of the firm, and also the portion of current assets not financed by current liabilities.

Some firms use ROIC to measure divisional performance. This measure is appropriate for those divisions whose managers have a significant influence on all asset acquisition decisions, including purchasing and production scheduling (which determine inventory levels), credit policy (accounts receivable), cash management, and also on the level of their current liabilities.

Sound Financial Position

In addition to desiring a satisfactory return, investors expect their capital to be protected from more than a normal amount of risk. The return on the *shareholders'* investment could be increased if incremental investments in the assets for new projects were financed solely by liabilities, provided the return on these incremental investments exceeds the interest cost of the added debt. This "financial leverage" policy, however, would increase the shareholders' risk of losing their investment. This is because interest charges and principal repayments on the liabilities are fixed obligations, and failure to make these payments could throw the company into bankruptcy. The degree of risk in a situation can be measured in part by the relative amounts of liabilities and owners' equity, and of the funds available to discharge the liabilities. This analysis also involves the use of ratios.

Structure of the Analysis

Many ratios have been described in previous chapters. In this section, these ratios and others are discussed in a sequence that is intended to facilitate an understanding of the total business. Thus, we shall assume here that one first looks at the firm's performance in the broadest terms, and then works down through various levels of detail in order to identify the significant factors which accounted for the overall results. If the values of the ratios used in this analysis are compared with their values for other time periods, this comparison is called a *longitudinal* or *trend analysis*. Dozens of ratios can be computed from a single set of financial statements, but usually only a few are helpful in a given situation. Although many frequently used ratios are described below, the best analytical procedure is not to compute all of them mechanically but rather to decide first which ratios might be relevant in the particular type of investigation being made.

Illustration 13–2 shows some of the important ratios and other relationships that aid in the analysis of how satisfactory a company's performance was.[2] These ratios can be grouped into four categories: overall measures, profitability measures, tests of investment utilization, and tests of financial condition. The ratios calculated below are based on the

ILLUSTRATION 13–2
FACTORS AFFECTING RETURN ON INVESTMENT

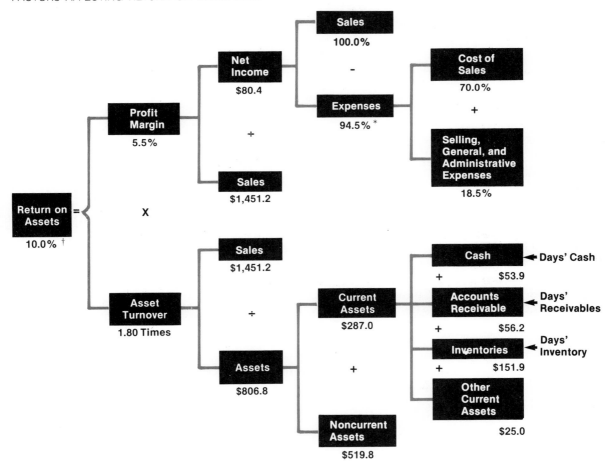

*Percentage includes interest expense and income taxes, in addition to cost of sales and S,G&A.
†Unadjusted for interest expense. (Outside analysts frequently disregard the adjustment described in the text.)

---

[2]Illustration 13–2 can easily be modified to show return on invested capital or return on equity, as alternative ROI measures.

ILLUSTRATION 13–3

❌ Hershey Foods Corporation

Consolidated Balance Sheets
(in millions of dollars)

	December 31 1981	1980
Assets		
Current Assets:		
Cash and short-term investments.	$ 53.9	$ 48.9
Accounts receivable	56.2	46.0
Inventories.	151.9	113.7
Other current assets	25.0	12.8
Total current assets.	287.0	221.4
Property, Plant and Equipment:		
At cost.	598.0	515.0
Less: accumulated depreciation	157.8	135.6
Net property, plant and equipment	440.2	379.4
Goodwill.	53.9	55.2
Investments and Other Assets	25.7	28.5
Total Assets	$806.8	$684.5
LIABILITIES AND STOCKHOLDERS' EQUITY		
Current Liabilities:		
Accounts payable.	$ 48.1	$ 52.5
Accrued liabilities	67.0	57.5
Current portion of long-term debt.	2.1	1.6
Total current liabilities.	117.2	111.6
Long-Term Debt.	158.2	158.8
Deferred Income Taxes	61.7	52.5
Total liabilities.	337.1	322.9
Stockholders' Equity:		
Common stock ($1 stated value)	15.7	14.2
Additional paid-in capital.	54.0	2.3
Retained earnings	400.0	345.1
Total stockholders' equity	469.7	361.6
Total Liabilities and Stockholders' Equity	$806.8	$684.5

Hershey Foods Corporation financial statements shown in Illustration 13–3.

OVERALL MEASURES

Price/Earnings Ratio

$$\frac{\text{Market price per share}}{\text{Net income per share}} = \frac{\$36}{\$5.61} = 6.4 \text{ times}$$

The broadest and most widely used overall measure of performance is the price/earnings, or "P/E," ratio. This measure involves an amount not directly controlled by the company, the market price of its common

ILLUSTRATION 13–3 *(concluded)*

Consolidated Statements of
Income and Retained Earnings[1]
(in millions of dollars except per share amounts)

For the Year Ended December 31, 1981

	Dollars	Percentage
Net Sales	$1,451.2	100.0
Cost of Sales	1,015.8	70.0
Gross Margin	435.4	30.0
Selling, administrative and general	267.9[2]	18.5
Income from Operations	167.5	11.5
Interest expense (net)	12.5[3]	0.9
Income before Taxes	155.0	10.7
Provision for income taxes	74.6	5.1
Net Income	80.4	5.5
Retained Earnings at January 1	345.1	
Less: Cash Dividends	25.5	
Retained Earnings at December 31	$ 400.0	
Net Income per Common Share	$ 5.61[4]	
Cash Dividends per Common Share	$ 1.75	

Notes:
1. Hershey Foods' annual report also included 1980 and 1979 income statements, as required by GAAP. The authors have added the percentage column to the income statement.
2. Includes $29.2 million depreciation and amortization expense.
3. This is $15.3 million interest expense, net of $2.8 million interest revenue.
4. Based on weighted-average number of shares outstanding during 1981, which was 14,321,716. The market price of Hershey's stock on December 31, 1981, was $36 per share.

stock. Thus, the P/E ratio is the best indicator of how *investors* judge the firm's performance.[3] Management, of course, is interested in this market appraisal, and a decline in the company's P/E ratio not explainable by a general decline in stock market prices is cause for concern. Also, management compares its P/E ratio with those of similar companies to determine the marketplace's relative rankings of the firms.

Basically the P/E ratio reflects investors' expectations about the company's performance. As Illustration 13–1 indicates, P/E ratios for industries vary, reflecting differing expectations about the relative rate of *growth in earnings* in those industries. At times the P/E ratios for virtually all companies decline because predictions of general economic conditions suggest that corporate profits will decrease.

Return on Investment

As explained above, return on investment can be calculated in three different ways, depending on whether one views "investment" as being total assets, invested capital, or shareholders' equity. These ratios are calculated as follows:

---
[3] Major newspapers such as *The Wall Street Journal* print firms' P/E ratios along with the daily stock quotations.

$$\frac{\text{Return on}}{\text{assets}} = \frac{\text{Net income} + \text{Interest } (1 - \text{Tax rate})}{\text{Total assets}}$$

$$= \frac{\$80.4 + \$15.3(.52)}{\$806.8} = 11.0 \text{ percent}$$

$$\frac{\text{Return on}}{\text{invested capital}} = \frac{\text{Net income} + \text{Interest } (1 - \text{Tax rate})}{\text{Long-term liabilities} + \text{Shareholders' equity}}$$

$$= \frac{\$80.4 + \$15.3(.52)}{\$158.2 + \$469.7} = 14.1 \text{ percent}$$

$$\frac{\text{Return on share-}}{\text{holders' equity}} = \frac{\text{Net income}}{\text{Shareholders' equity}} = \frac{\$80.4}{\$469.7} = 17.1 \text{ percent}$$

Treatment of Interest. These formulas immediately raise the question, Why is aftertax interest expense added back to net income when figuring ROA or ROIC, but not when calculating ROE? The reason is that in calculating these returns the analyst is attempting to determine how well management has *used* a "pool" of capital, whether that pool is thought of as being all equities, invested capital, or just shareholders' equity. The analyst can then compare these returns with the *cost* of using the pools of funds. However, in arriving at the net income amount, *part* of the cost of capital—the interest on the debt portion—was subtracted as an expense. The resulting net income therefore understates the earnings that have been generated by using either the total equities pool or the invested capital pool.

Note that the amount of the adjustment is the *aftertax* interest cost of the firm. Because interest expense is tax deductible, the aftertax interest cost is the interest expense multipled by the complement of the tax rate. Hershey's tax rate in 1981 was 48 percent (= $74.6 ÷ $155.0). Although the federal tax rate was 46 percent, state and local taxes often bring the total up to about 50 percent, and this percentage is often used in calculations.

On the other hand, in determining the return on the shareholders' investment, interest expense *should* be included in the earnings calculation, since the earnings accruing to the shareholders (i.e., net income) must reflect the fact that payments (in the form of interest) have been made to the creditors for the use of their funds.

Thus, the returns calculated using the above equations reflect the earnings generated by using a pool of funds, *excluding* the cost of those funds. In practice, many analysts ignore the interest addback.

Average Investment. In many situations, a more representative return percentage is arrived at by using the *average* investment during the period, rather than the year-end investment. Ordinarily, the average investment is found by taking one half the sum of the beginning and ending investment. If, however, a significant amount of new debt or equity funds was obtained near the end of the year, using the beginning-of-year amounts rather than the simple average would be more meaningful. Ending balance sheet amounts have been used in the examples so that they can be easily traced back to Illustration 13–3.

Tangible Assets. Percentage returns are sometimes calculated on the basis of tangible assets, rather than total assets; that is, the goodwill of $53.9 million on Hershey Foods' balance sheet would be excluded. When so calculated, the return should be clearly labeled *return on tangible assets*. A similar approach can be used for the return on invested capital or the return on equity by subtracting the amount of intangible assets from the invested capital or the shareholders' equity.

Interest-Bearing Debt. The above calculations did not count deferred income taxes as a liability nor minority interest as a component of owners' equity. This is common practice among the great majority of financial analysts.[4] Some analysts include in invested capital short-term notes and long-term debt maturing in one year, even though these are classified as current liabilities. These people maintain that debt capital includes all funds supplied by investors who expect a return in the form of interest. In any event, the description of the ratio should make clear which approach is used.

Investment Turnover and Profit Margin

As Illustration 13–2 suggests, return on investment (ROI) can be looked at as the combined effect of two factors. Algebraically, it is clear that the following is in fact an equality:

$$\frac{\text{Net income}}{\text{Investment}} = \frac{\text{Net income}}{\text{Sales}} \times \frac{\text{Sales}}{\text{Investment}}$$

Each of the two terms on the right-hand side of the equation has meaning of its own. Net income divided by sales is called *profit margin* or *return on sales*, and sales divided by investment is called *investment turnover*. (If investment is defined as total assets, then the latter ratio is called *asset turnover*.)

These relationships suggest the two fundamental ways that the ROI can be improved. First, it can be improved by improving the profit margin, that is, by earning more profit per dollar of sales. Second, it can be improved by increasing the investment turnover. In turn, the investment turnover can be increased in either of two ways: (1) by generating more sales volume with the same amount of investment or (2) by reducing the amount of investment required for a given level of sales volume.

As one can see from Illustration 13–2, these two factors can be further decomposed into elements that can be looked at individually. The point of this decomposition is that no one manager can significantly influence

---

[4]Backer and Gosman, "The Use of Financial Ratios in Credit Downgrade Decisions," *Financial Management*, Spring 1980, p. 55.

the overall ROI measure, simply because it *is* an overall measure reflecting the combined effects of a number of factors. However, the items on the right-hand side of Illustration 13–2 do correspond with the responsibilities of individual managers. For example, the manager who is responsible for the firm's credit policies and procedures influences the level of accounts receivable. Thus, the outside analyst, as well as the firm's management, can use the ROI chart to identify potential problem areas in the business. Some techniques are described below.

TESTS OF PROFITABILITY

Illustration 13–3 shows each of the items on the income statement expressed as a percentage of sales. Examining relationships within a statement in this way is called a *vertical analysis*. As noted in Chapter 3, net sales is usually taken as 100 percent, as in the illustration. Of the percentages shown, gross margin (30 percent), the operating profit (11.5 percent), income before taxes (10.7 percent), and net income (5.5 percent) are perhaps the most important.

Profit Margin

The profit margin is a measure of overall profitability. This measure is also referred to as the *net income percentage* or the *return on sales* (ROS). Some people treat this measure as if it were the most important single measure of performance. Critics of the social performance of a company or an industry, for example, may base their criticism on its relatively high profit margin. This is erroneous. Net income, considered by itself, does not take into account the investment employed to produce that income. As Illustration 13–1 indicates, electric utilities have a relatively high ROS, but their ROE is below average, reflecting the very large investment base that a utility must finance. On the other hand, supermarkets (food retailers) have only a 1.1 percent ROS, but their ROE is above average. This reflects the facts that (1) supermarkets do not have any accounts receivable to finance, (2) their inventory turnover is very rapid, and (3) many of their premises are rented and do not appear as balance sheet assets.

Illustration 13–2 suggests the things top management needs to examine if the profit margin is unsatisfactory. Perhaps dollar sales volume has declined, either because fewer items are being sold, or they are being sold at lower prices, or both. Perhaps expenses have gotten out of control: perhaps there is a growing inefficiency in production operations, or perhaps management has gotten lax about administrative expenses. Part 2 of this book (particularly Chapters 20 and 26) deals with gaining visibility and control over expenses.

TESTS OF INVESTMENT UTILIZATION

Ratios that deal with the lower "branch" of Illustration 13–2 represent tests of *investment utilization*. Whereas profitability measures focus on income statement figures, utilization tests involve both balance sheet and income statement amounts. We have already looked at the all-encompassing utilization ratio—return on investment (ROI). In this section less broad measures will be examined.

Investment Turnover

As with other ratios involving investment, three turnover ratios can be calculated:

$$\text{Asset turnover} = \frac{\text{Sales revenues}}{\text{Total assets}} = \frac{\$1,451}{\$806.8} = 1.8 \text{ times}$$

$$\text{Invested capital turnover} = \frac{\text{Sales revenues}}{\text{Invested capital}} = \frac{\$1,451}{\$627.9} = 2.3 \text{ times}$$

$$\text{Equity turnover} = \frac{\text{Sales revenues}}{\text{Shareholders' equity}} = \frac{\$1,451}{\$469.7} = 3.1 \text{ times}$$

Because of industry disparities in investment turnover, one must be careful in making judgments about the adequacy of a firm's turnover. ROI is profit margin multiplied by investment turnover. Thus, if two firms have different turnover ratios, to achieve a given level of ROI the firm with the lower turnover will need to earn a higher profit margin, as is the case with utilities. Comparing the turnover ratios of two similar companies in the *same* industry is valid, of course, and may help explain why one achieves a higher ROI than the other. Similarly, comparing profit margins of companies in the same industry is valid.

Capital Intensity

$$\text{Capital intensity} = \frac{\text{Sales revenues}}{\text{Property, plant, and equipment}} = \frac{\$1,451}{\$440.2} = 3.3 \text{ times}$$

The capital intensity ratio (sometimes called *fixed asset turnover*) focuses only on the property, plant, and equipment item. Companies that have a high ratio of plant to sales revenue, such as steel companies, are particularly vulnerable to cyclical fluctuations in business activity. The costs associated with this plant are relatively fixed, so that when their sales revenue drops in a recession they are unable to cover these costs. Conversely, a company that is not capital intensive, as is the case with service businesses, can reduce its costs as its revenues decline, and therefore has less difficulty in a recession.

**Working Capital
Measures**

Management is interested in the velocity with which funds move through the various current accounts. Ratios for days' cash, days' receivables, days' inventory, and inventory turnover, described in earlier chapters, provide the information on these flows.

Days' Payables.   An analogous ratio can be calculated for days' payables:

$$\text{Days' payables} = \frac{\text{Operating payables}}{\text{Pretax cash expenses} \div 365}$$

Pretax cash expenses can be approximated by adding all expenses except taxes, and then subtracting noncash expenses such as depreciation. (This is the same procedure as for the days' cash ratio, except that taxes usually are included there.) Operating payables include accounts payable, accrued wages and payroll taxes, and other items that represent deferred payments for operating expenses. A note payable would be included if its proceeds financed accounts receivable or inventories; otherwise, short-term debt is excluded. For Hershey Foods, the ratio is:

$$\text{Days' payables} = \frac{\$48.1 + \$67.0}{\$1,270 \div 365} = 33 \text{ days}$$

Cash Conversion Cycle.   Days' receivables, days' inventory, and days' payables can be combined to determine the *cash conversion cycle.*[5] This is the length of time for cash to complete the operating cycle shown in Illustration 5–1, after incorporating payment deferrals. It is calculated as follows (using numbers for Hershey Foods):

	Days
Receivables conversion period (days' receivables)	14
Inventory conversion period (days' inventory)	55
Operating cycle	69
Payment deferral period (days' payables)	33
Cash conversion cycle	36

This calculation indicates liquidity (discussed in the next section), and also indicates the time interval for which additional short-term financing might be needed to support a spurt in sales.

Working Capital Turnover.   In addition to the ratios that focus on specific working capital items, it is often useful to look at the turnover of working capital as a whole:

$$\text{Working capital turnover} = \frac{\text{Sales revenues}}{\text{Working capital}} = \frac{\$1,451}{\$169.8} = 8.5 \text{ times}$$

---

[5]Verlyn D. Richards and Eugene J. Laughlin, "A Cash Conversion Cycle Approach to Liquidity Analysis," *Financial Management,* Spring 1980.

Each of these measures of turnover gives an indication of how well the firm is managing its assets. The investment turnover figures permit a comparison of similar firms' investment bases vis-à-vis the sales generated by the firms. The days' cash, receivables, and inventory ratios help identify whether a firm is tieing up excessive amounts of funds in current assets. Excess levels of assets hurt performance because they require additional capital, and there is a cost associated with this capital. To the extent that debt could be reduced by cutting the level of assets, interest costs would fall, increasing net income, and the investment base would decrease, thus having a doubly favorable impact on ROI.

TESTS OF FINANCIAL CONDITION

Whereas the previously discussed ratios deal with the firm's operations and asset management, tests of financial condition look at the company's liquidity and solvency. *Liquidity* refers to the company's ability to meet its current obligations. Thus, liquidity tests focus on the size and relationships of current liabilities and of current assets, which presumably will be converted into cash in order to pay the current liabilities. *Solvency*, on the other hand, pertains to the company's ability to meet the interest costs and repayment schedules associated with its long-term obligations.

Most of the ratios used for this purpose have been discussed in previous chapters: current ratio, acid-test (or quick) ratio, debt/equity ratio, debt/capitalization ratio, times interest earned, and internally generated funds/total debt. Also, the cash conversion cycle, described above, is related to liquidity.

Dividend Policy

$$\text{Dividend yield} = \frac{\text{Dividends per share}}{\text{Market price per share}} = \frac{\$1.75}{\$36} = 4.9 \text{ percent}$$

$$\text{Dividend payout} = \frac{\text{Dividends}}{\text{Net income}} = \frac{\$25.5}{\$80.4} = 32 \text{ percent}$$

These ratios are not, strictly speaking, tests of financial condition. Rather, they reflect one of the company's financial *policies*, that is, its decision as to how its growth should be financed. Each company has a target debt/equity ratio it attempts to maintain. In order to do so, it must raise a certain fraction of additional capital from debt sources, and the remainder from equity sources. Equity capital can be raised either by issuing new stock, or by retaining earnings. If a company finds it expensive to raise new equity capital directly from investors, it can obtain its additional equity capital by retaining earnings. The more of the net income it retains in this fashion, the less it can pay out to shareholders as dividends.

ILLUSTRATION 13—4
SUMMARY OF RATIOS

Name of Ratio	Formula	State Results as	Discussed in Chapter
Overall performance Measures:			
1. Price/earnings ratio	$\dfrac{\text{Market price per share}}{\text{Net income per share}}$	Times	13
2. Return on assets	$\dfrac{[\text{Net income} + \text{Interest} \,(1 - \text{Tax rate})]}{\text{Total assets}}$	%	13
3. Return on invested capital	$\dfrac{[\text{Net income} + \text{Interest} \,(1 - \text{Tax rate})]}{\text{Long-term liabilities} + \text{Shareholders' equity}}$	%	13
4. Return on shareholders' equity	$\dfrac{\text{Net income}}{\text{Shareholders' equity}}$	%	13
Profitability measures:			
5. Gross margin percentage	$\dfrac{\text{Gross margin}}{\text{Net sales revenues}}$	%	3,13
6. Profit margin	$\dfrac{\text{Net income}}{\text{Net sales Revenues}}$	%	3,13
7. Earnings per share	$\dfrac{\text{Net income}}{\text{No. shares outstanding}}$	$	9
Tests of investment utilization:			
8. Asset turnover	$\dfrac{\text{Sales revenues}}{\text{Total assets}}$	Times	13
9 Invested capital turnover	$\dfrac{\text{Sales revenues}}{(\text{Long-term liabilities} + \text{Shareholders' equity})}$	Times	13
10. Equity turnover	$\dfrac{\text{Sales revenues}}{\text{Shareholders' equity}}$	Times	13
11. Capital intensity	$\dfrac{\text{Sales revenues}}{\text{Property, plant, and equipment}}$	Times	13
12. Days' cash	$\dfrac{\text{Cash}}{\text{Cash expenses} \div 365}$	Days	5
13. Days' receivables (or collection period)	$\dfrac{\text{Accounts receivable}}{\text{Sales} \div 365}$	Days	5
14. Days' inventory	$\dfrac{\text{Inventory}}{\text{Cost of sales} \div 365}$	Days	6
15. Inventory turnover	$\dfrac{\text{Cost of sales}}{\text{Inventory}}$	Days	6
16. Working capital turnover	$\dfrac{\text{Sales revenues}}{\text{Working capital}}$	Times	13

ILLUSTRATION 13–4 *(concluded)*

Tests of financial condition:

17. Current ratio	$\dfrac{\text{Current Assets}}{\text{Current liabilities}}$	Ratio	5
18. Acid-test ratio (or quick ratio)	$\dfrac{\text{Monetary current assets}}{\text{Current liabilities}}$	Ratio	5
19. Debt/equity ratio	$\dfrac{\text{Noncurrent liabilities}}{\text{Shareholders' equity}}$	%	8
or	$\dfrac{\text{Total liabilities}}{\text{Shareholders' equity}}$	%	8
20. Debt/capitalization	$\dfrac{\text{Noncurrent liabilities}}{(\text{Noncurrent liabilities} + \text{Shareholders' equity})}$	%	8
21. Times interest earned	$\dfrac{\text{Pretax operating profit} + \text{Interest}}{\text{Interest}}$	Times	8
22. Cash flow/debt	$\dfrac{\text{Funds generated by Operations}}{\text{Total debt}}$	%	10
23. Dividend yield	$\dfrac{\text{Dividends per share}}{\text{Market price per share}}$	%	13
24. Dividend payout	$\dfrac{\text{Dividends per share}}{\text{Net income per share}}$	%	13

Notes:

1. *Averaging.* When one term of a formula is an income statement item and the other term is a balance sheet item, it is often preferable to use the average of the beginning and ending balance sheet amounts, rather than the ending balance sheet amounts.
2. *Tangible assets.* Ratios involving noncurrent assets or total assets often exclude intangible assets such as goodwill and trademarks. When this is done, the word *tangible* is usually used in identifying the ratio.
3. *Debt.* Debt ratios may exclude accounts payable, accrued liabilities, deferred income taxes and other noninterest bearing liabilities. The reader often has no way of knowing whether this has been done, however. Conceptually, *debt* means interest-bearing liabilities.
4. *Coverage ratios.* Times interest earned and other coverage ratios can be calculated using pretax funds generated by operations instead of pretax operating profit.

Of course, the foregoing discussion applies only to a growing company. If a company is in financial difficulty, it simply may not be able to pay dividends.

The dividend yield on stocks is often compared with the yield, or interest, on bonds, but such a comparison is not valid. This is because the earnings of bondholders consist entirely of their interest (adjusted for amortization of discounts and premiums), whereas the earnings of shareholders consist not only of their dividends but also of retained earnings. Although shareholders do not receive retained earnings, the fact that part of the net income has been retained in the business and presumably invested in income-producing assets should enhance future earnings per share. This, in turn, should increase the market value of the shareholders' investment.

The ratios described in this book are summarized in Illustration 13–4 for the convenience of the reader.

GROWTH MEASURES

Analysts are also interested in the growth rate of certain key items such as sales, net income, and earnings per share. These rates are often compared with the rate of inflation to see if the company is keeping pace with inflation or experiencing "true" growth. Common growth-rate calculations include average growth rate and compound growth rate. Both involve looking at information over a period of several years, typically 5 or 10. The calculations will be illustrated using Hershey Food Corporation's 1976–81 sales data (expressed in millions):

	1981	1980	1979	1978	1977	1976
Net sales	$1,451	$1,335	$1,161	$768	$671	$602

To calculate *average growth rate*, first growth is calculated on a year-to-year basis. From 1976 to 1977, this was 11.5 percent (= $671 ÷ $602 − 100 percent); from 1977 to 1978, 14.5 percent; and so on. These five year-to-year rates are then averaged; the result is an average growth rate in sales of 20.2 percent.

The *compound growth rate* calculation uses the compound interest/present value concepts described in the Appendix to Chapter 8. In this instance the question is: At what rate would $602 have to grow to reach the amount of $1,451 after five years? (More formally: What rate of return gives a present value of $602 to a future value of $1,451 five years hence?) This rate can be approximated as being 19 percent using Table A (since $602 ÷ $1,451 = 0.415, which falls between the 18 and 20 percent columns on the five-year line), or calculated using a preprogrammed calculator to be 19.2 percent.

In some cases, the compound growth rate method can give misleading results because either the base year number (here, for 1976) or the final year number (for 1981) is abnormally high or low. In such a case, the average growth rate method is preferable.

MAKING COMPARISONS

Difficulties

An approximately accurate report of actual performance often can be obtained from a company's financial statements. Finding an adequate standard with which these actual amounts can be compared, however, is often a difficult matter. Some of the problems are described below. Financial statement analysis is used as an example, but the same problems arise in analyzing other types of quantitative data.

Deciding on the Proper Basis for Comparison. Subject only to minor qualifications, a youth who can high jump 6 feet is a better high jumper than a youth who can only jump 5 feet. In business, however, there are many situations in which one cannot tell whether a higher number represents better performance than a lower number.

A high current ratio is by no means necessarily better than a low current ratio. For example, the current ratio for the Hershey Foods Corporation on December 31, 1981, was 2.4 to 1. Suppose that $50 million of the current liabilities came due the very next day and that the company in fact paid these liabilities, using almost all of its available cash and short-term liquid investments. A balance sheet prepared subsequent to this transaction would show $237 million of current assets and $67 million of current liabilities, and the current ratio would accordingly be 3.5 to 1, which is almost 1½ times the ratio of the previous day. Yet one could scarcely say that a company that had used up most of its highly liquid assets was in an improved financial condition.

In some comparisons, the direction of change that represents "good" or "better" is reasonably apparent. Generally, a high profit margin is better than a low one, and a high ROI is better than a low one. Even these statements have many qualifications, however. A high return may indicate that the company is only "skimming the cream" off the market; a more intensive marketing effort now could lead to a more sustained growth in the future.

Many standards can usefully be thought of as a *quality range* rather than as a single number. When actual performance goes outside the range, *in either direction*, there is an indication of an unsatisfactory situation. For a certain company, the current ratio may be considered satisfactory it it is within the range 2:1 to 3:1. Below 2:1, there is the danger of being unable to meet maturing obligations. Above 3:1, there is an indication that funds are being left idle rather than being efficiently employed.

Differences in the Situations Being Compared. No reasonable person would expect a 12-year-old youth to run as fast as a 19-year-old athlete. In judging the youth's performance, his or her speed should be compared with that of others of the same age and sex and with similar training. Differences in the factors that affect a company's performance this year as compared with last year are complex. Nevertheless, some attempt must be made to allow for these differences. The task is more difficult when attempting to compare one company with another, even if they are both of the same size and in the same industry. It becomes exceedingly difficult if the two companies are in different industries or if they are of substantially different size.

Changes in the Dollar Measuring Stick. Accounting amounts are expressed in historical dollars. A change in price levels may therefore seriously lessen the validity of comparisons of ratios computed for different time periods. Also, a ratio whose numerator and denominator are expressed in different kinds of dollars may have no useful meaning.

The fact that plant and equipment amounts are stated as unexpired historical dollar costs causes particular difficulty in making comparisons of ratios. Two companies, for example, might have facilities that are physically identical in all respects except age, and they might operate exactly the same way and earn exactly the same net income. If, however, the facilities of one company had been purchased at a time when prices were low or if they had been almost fully depreciated, and if the facilities of the other company had been purchased at a time of higher prices or if they were relatively new, then the ROI of the company that carried its assets at a low book value would be much higher than the ROI of the other company. It is this sort of comparison difficulty that the inflation-adjusted accounting information described in Chapter 12 attempts to address.

Differences in Definition. The term *six feet* used to measure the high jumper is precisely defined and easily measured. But the individual elements making up such terms as *current assets* and *current liabilities* are by no means precisely defined, and there is considerable diversity in practice as to how they should be measured. Similarly, "profit" may mean: net income as determined by using GAAP (which in turn can be a range of values, depending on the particular methods used for depreciation, inventory valuation, and so forth); income after taxes based on the firm's income tax return; profit as determined by procedures required by a regulatory agency; or profit as shown on a report intended only for the use of management.

Hidden Short-Run Changes. A balance sheet may not reflect the typical situation. A balance sheet is prepared as of one moment of time, and it tells nothing about short-term fluctuations in assets and equities that have occurred within the period between the two balance sheet dates. Many department stores, for example, publish annual balance sheets as of January 31. By that date, Christmas inventories have been sold out and many of the Christmas receivables have been paid, but Easter merchandise has not started to arrive and payables for this merchandise have not yet been generated. Current assets (other than cash) and current liabilities as reported on the January 31 balance sheet are therefore likely to be lower than at other times of the year. As a result, ratios such as inventory turnover and the average collection period may not be representative of the situation at other seasons. A company that is analyzing its own data can study these seasonal movements by using monthly, rather than annual, balance sheets; but these are ordinarily not available to the outsider.

Moreover, companies have been known to take deliberate steps to "clean up" their balance sheets. They may, for example, reduce inventories just before the end of the year, which increases the inventory turnover ratio; they then build up inventories again early in the next year. Such *window dressing* of the balance sheet may not be discernible to an outsider.

The Past as an Indication of the Future. Financial statements are historical documents, and financial ratios show relationships that have existed in the past. The manager or analyst is, of course, interested in what is happening now and what is likely to happen in the future, rather than what did happen in the past. Often outside analysts have no choice but to rely on past data as an indication of the current situation. But they should not be misled into believing that the historical ratios necessarily reflect current conditions, and much less that they reflect future conditions.

Possible Bases for Comparison

There are four types of standards against which an actual financial statement amount or ratio can be compared: (1) experience; (2) a goal; (3) a historical amount; and (4) an external amount.

Experience. Managers and analysts gradually build up their own idea as to what constitutes "good" or "poor" performance. One of the important advantages that experienced people have is that they possess a feeling for what are "right" relationships in a given situation. These subjective standards of a competent analyst or manager are more important than standards based on mechanical comparisons.

Goals. Almost all companies prepare *budgets* that show *what performance is expected to be under the circumstances prevailing.* If actual performance corresponds with budgeted performance, there is a reasonable inference that performance was good. There are two important qualifications that affect this inference, however. First, the budgeted amounts may not have been set very carefully in the first instance. The comparison can of course be no more valid than the validity of the standards. Second, the budgeted amounts were necessarily arrived at on the basis of certain assumptions as to the conditions that would be prevailing during the period. If these assumptions turn out to be incorrect, the amounts are also incorrect as a measure of results "under the circumstances prevailing." If, because of a recession or other economic phenomenon outside the control of management, net income is lower than the amount budgeted, it cannot fairly be said that the difference indicates "poor" management performance. Nevertheless, the budget is a type of standard that has fewer inherent difficulties than either historical standards or external standards. Of course, outside analysts frequently do not have access to a company's budget.

Historical Standards. A comparison of current performance with past performance for the same company usually does not run into the problem of differences in accounting practice. If practices have changed, the change must be reported in the financial statements. Moreover, the analyst can also recollect, or find out from supplementary data, some of the circumstances that have changed between the two periods and thus allow for these changes in making the comparison. At best, however, a comparison between a current amount and a historical amount in the same company can show only that the current period is "better" or "worse" than the past. In many cases, this does not provide a sound basis for judgment, for the historical amount may not have represented an acceptable standard. If a company increases its ROI from 1 percent to 2 percent, it has improved, but it nevertheless is not doing very well.

External Standards.   When one company is compared with another, environmental and accounting differences may raise serious problems of comparability. If, however, the analyst is able to allow for these differences, then the outside data provide a check on performance that has the advantage of being arrived at independently. Moreover, the two companies may well have been affected by the same set of economic conditions, so this important cause of noncomparability may not be operating.

Several organizations publish average ratios for groups of companies in the same industry. One of the best known is Dun & Bradstreet, Inc., which publishes ratios for about 125 retailing, wholesaling, and manufacturing lines of business in the magazine, *Dun's Review.* Robert Morris Associates, an organization of analysts in banks, publishes *Annual Statement Studies,* reporting financial and operating ratios for about 300 lines of business, based on information obtained from member banks. The U.S. Federal Trade Commission publishes a *Quarterly Financial Report for Manufacturing, Mining and Trading Corporations.* In addition, many trade associations compile ratios for the industries they represent.

Standard & Poor's Corporation has available a COMPUSTAT service that consists of magnetic tapes containing financial and statistical information for several thousand industrial companies and utilities in the United States and Canada. The information is available on an annual basis for the past 20 years. The financial information consists of typical balance sheet and income statement items, additional statistical items including stock prices, dividends, and a variety of ratios computed from the above. All companies are grouped and coded by industry classifications.

The National Automated Accounting Research System (NAARS) is a computer service in which is stored the actual financial statements of approximately 6,500 companies, with a retrieval system that permits any item to be recalled upon request. NAARS does not contain ratios but provides raw material from which ratios can be calculated.

Use of industrywide ratios involves all the difficulties of using ratios derived from one other company plus the special problems that arise when the data for several companies are thrown together into a single average. Nevertheless, they may give some useful impressions about the average situation in an industry.

Use of Comparisons

The principal value of analyzing financial statement information is that it suggests questions that need to be answered. Such an analysis rarely provides the answers. An unfavorable difference between actual performance and whatever standard is used, if it is large, indicates that something *may be* wrong, and this leads to an investigation. Even when the analysis indicates strongly that something *is* wrong (as when one company's income has declined while incomes of comparable companies have increased), the analysis rarely shows what the *cause* of the difficulty is. Nevertheless, the ability to pick from thousands of *potential* questions those few that are really worth asking is an important one.

It is well to keep in mind the basic relationships shown in Illustration 13–2, or some variation of these that is applicable to the situation being analyzed. The only number that encompasses all these relationships is a ROI ratio. A change in any less inclusive ratio may be misleading as an indication of better or worse performance, because it may have been offset by compensating changes in other ratios. An increase in dollars of net income indicates improved performance only if there was no offsetting increase in the investment required. An increase in the net profit margin indicates improved performance only if there was no offsetting decrease in sales volume or increase in investment. An increase in the gross margin percentage indicates improved performance only if there was no offsetting decrease in sales volume, increase in investment, or increase in expenses.

In short, the use of any ratio other than ROI taken by itself, implies that all other things are equal. This *ceteris paribus* condition ordinarily does not prevail, and the validity of comparisons is lessened to the extent that it does not. Yet the ROI ratio is so broad that it does not give a clue as to which of the underlying factors may be responsible for changes in it. It is to find these factors, which if unfavorable indicate possible trouble areas, that the subsidiary ratios of profitability are used. Furthermore, the ROI ratio tells nothing about the financial condition of the company; liquidity and solvency ratios are necessary for this purpose.

SUMMARY

The numbers on financial statements are usually most useful for analytical purposes when they are expressed in relative terms in the form of ratios. Although a great many ratios can be calculated, only a few are ordinarily necessary in connection with a given problem.

The essential task is to find a standard or norm with which actual performance can be compared. In general, there are four types of standards: (1) subjective standards derived from the analyst's experience; (2) budgets, set in advance of the period under review; (3) historical data, showing performance of the same company in the past; and (4) the performance of other companies, as shown by their financial statements or by industry averages. None of these is perfect, but a rough allowance for the factors that cause noncomparability often can be made.

The comparison may then suggest important questions that need to be investigated; it rarely indicates answers to the questions.

SUGGESTIONS FOR FURTHER READING

Bernstein, Leopold A. *Financial Statement Analysis: Theory, Application, and Interpretation.* Rev. ed. Homewood, Ill.: Richard D. Irwin, 1978.

Foulke, Roy A. *Practical Financial Statement Analysis.* 6th ed. New York: McGraw-Hill, 1968.

McMullen, Stewart Yardwood. *Financial Statements: Form, Analysis, and Interpretation.* 7th ed. Homewood, Ill.: Richard D. Irwin, 1979.

Cases

CASE 13–1   Genmo Corporation

On the night of February 27, 1982, certain records of the Genmo Corporation were destroyed by fire. Two days after that, the president and principal owner had an appointment with an investor to discuss the possible sale of the company. He needed as much information as he could gather for this purpose, recognizing that over a longer period of time a more complete reconstruction would be possible.

On the morning of February 28, the following were available: (1) A balance sheet as of December 31, 1980, and an income statement for 1980 (Exhibit 1). (2) Certain fragmentary data and ratios that had been calculated from the current financial statements (Exhibit 2). The statements themselves had been destroyed in the fire. (In ratios involving balance sheet amounts, Genmo used year-end amounts rather than an average.) And (3) the following data:

1981 revenues $6,341
Current liabilities, December 31, 1981   1,256

EXHIBIT 1
GENMO CORPORATION FINANCIAL STATEMENTS
(thousands of dollars)

Balance Sheet
As of December 31, 1980

Assets

Current assets:

Cash	$ 16
Marketable securities	356
Accounts receivable	377
Inventories	729
Prepaid expenses	70
Total current assets	1,548
Investments	417
Real estate, plant, and equipment	$2,920
Less: Accumulated depreciation	1,521
	1,399
Special tools	94
Total assets	$3,458

Liabilities and Shareholders' Equity

Current liabilities:

Accounts payable	$ 397
Loans payable	167
Accrued liabilities	663
Total current liabilities	1,227
Long-term debt	188
Other noncurrent liabilities	261
Total liabilities	1,676

Shareholders' equity:

Preferred stock	28
Common stock	50
Additional paid-in capital	130
Retained earnings	1,574
Total shareholders' equity	1,782
Total liabilities and shareholders' equity	$3,458

Income Statement, 1980

Total revenues		$5,830
Cost of sales (excluding depreciation and amortization)	$5,210	
Depreciation	146	
Amortization of special tools	272	
	5,628	
Selling, general, and administrative expenses	317	
Provision for income taxes (credit)	(39)	
Total costs and expenses		5,906
Net income (loss)		$ (76)

EXHIBIT 2
SELECTED RATIOS

	1981	1980
Acid-test ratio....................	0.396	0.610
Current ratio.....................	1.092	1.262
Inventory turnover (times).........	7.643	7.147
Days' receivables.................	21.01	23.60
Gross margin percentage..........	12.98	10.64
Profit margin percentage..........	0.52	(1.30)
Invested capital turnover (times)....	2.399	2.613
Debt/equity ratio (percentage)......	49.15	25.20
Return on shareholders' equity......	?	(4.26)

Questions

1. Prepare a balance sheet as of December 31, 1981, and the 1981 income statement.

2. What was the return on shareholders' equity for 1981?

CASE 13–2 Bedford Manufacturing Company (C)

Using the actual 1982 and projected 1983 financial statements based on Bedford Manufacturing Company (A) (Case 6–2), calculate the following ratios for 1982 and 1983. (Use *year-end* balance sheet account amounts throughout.)

1. Return on assets.
2. Return on equity.
3. Gross margin percentage.
4. Return on sales.
5. Asset turnover.
6. Days' cash.

7. Days' receivables.
8. Days' inventories (finished goods only).
9. Inventory turnover (all inventories).
10. Current ratio.
11. Acid-test ratio.
12. Times interest earned.

Question

As an outside analyst, what questions would you want to ask Bedford's management, based on these ratios?

CASE 13–3 Kresge versus May

An article in *Financial Executive* compared the financial statements of S. S. Kresge (corporate name subsequently changed to K mart) and May Department Stores to illustrate the effect of capitalizing leases.[1] At the time these data were

[1]John J. Kalata, Dennis G. Campbell, and Ian K. Shumaker, "Lease Financial Reporting," *Financial Executive*, March 1977, p. 34. Copyright © by Financial Executives Institute. Used by Permission.

prepared, FASB *Statement No. 13*, "Accounting for Leases," had not become effective. Excerpts from this article follow.

Comparison—without Leases. Some interesting results follow from showing leases as assets and liabilities on the balance sheet. For comparison, we selected S. S. Kresge and May Department Stores. We compared these two companies' balance sheets in detail, showing the difference in the financial strengths of the two companies. The following numerical data has been extracted from the fiscal 1974 annual reports of the May Department Stores and S. S. Kresge companies. (See Exhibits 1 and 2.)

Kresge is a company that leases approximately 40 percent of its "available assets" ($3.2 billion), while May, on the other hand, leases 8.7 percent of its "available assets" ($1.3 billion). Kresge's sales in 1974 were $5.6 billion (5th in terms of retailers' sales), and May's were $1.7 billion (18th in sales). Kresge's average annual growth rate (earnings per share) over the last five years was 10.84 percent, while May's was 10.38 percent per annum.

The analysis is based strictly upon the financial ratios that analysts use to judge the profitability, stability, and financial strength of corporations. While the

EXHIBIT 1
FINANCIAL DATA
(millions of dollars)

Balance Sheets

Kresge (1/29/75)			May (2/1/75)	
Leases Capitalized	As Reported	**Assets**	As Reported	Leases Capitalized
$1,105	$1,105	Inventories	$ 211	$ 211
313	313	Other current	420	420
1,418	1,418	Total current	631	631
60	60	Investments and other	54	54
418	418	Fixed assets (net)	521	521
1,283	—	Rights to leased property*	—	115
$3,179	$1,896	Total assets	$1,206	$1,321
		Equities		
$ 779	$ 613	Current liabilities	$ 287	$ 298
212	212	Long-term debt	356	356
1,117	—	Rental obligations*	—	104
50	50	Deferred liabilities	61	61
2,158	875	Total liabilities	704	819
1,021	1,021	Owners' equity	502	502
$3,179	$1,896	Total equities	$1,206	$1,321
$1,283		*Present value of leases		$ 115
166		Current portion (due 1975)		11
1,117		Noncurrent portion		104

*Present value is found by discounting Kresge's obligations at 7.7 percent and May's at 5.7 percent.

Income Statement Data

Kresge (ended 1/29/75)		May (ended 2/1/75)
$5,536	Revenues	$1,697
4,248	Cost of sales	1,432
193	Pretax income	94
105	Net income	47
26	Dividends	24

EXHIBIT 2
KEY FINANCIAL RATIOS

Kresge			May	
Leases Capitalized	As Reported		As Reported	Leases Capitalized
		Working Capital		
—	2.31	Current ratio	2.20	—
—	0.51	Acid-test ratio	1.46	—
—	3.8x	Inventory turnover	6.8x	—
—	6.9x	Working capital turnover	4.9x	—
		Financial Ratios		
—	53.9%	Owners' equity to total assets	41.6%	—
—	162.1%	Current assets/total liabilities	89.6%	—
—	50.7%	Long-term debt/fixed assets	68.3%	—
—	20.8%	Long-term debt/owners' equity	70.9	—
—	17.2%	Debt/invested capital	41.5%	—
—	82.8%	Owners' equity/invested capital	58.5%	—
2.1x	10.7x	Fixed charges coverage	6.8x	4.8x
		Profitability		
—	2.9x	Asset turnover	1.4x	—
—	3.5%	Pretax margin	5.5%	—
—	10.2%	Pretax return on assets	7.8%	—
—	10.3%	Return on equity	9.4%	—
—	75.2%	Earnings retention rate	48.9%	—

growth rate and past profits are the most widely used gauges for determining the soundness of an investment, they are used only in a limited fashion when comparing similar companies. As was previously mentioned, Kresge's growth rate over the past five years has been only 0.46 percent better than May Department Stores. Kresge's pretax margin is over 2 percentage points less than May's. Given that the growth rates of the two companies are roughly equal, the balance sheet is the only other deciding factor to show why Kresge has an AA rating and sold for 29 times earnings, while May has a split rating—AA (S&P) and A (Moody's)—and only sold for 11 times earnings. (Based on uncompiled 1976 data, Kresge, presently, sells for 20 times earnings and May 10 times earnings.)

Liquidity. The *current ratio* is employed by Dun & Bradstreet as the most important single ratio for setting their numerical rating. Their alphabetic rating is more heavily influenced by the company's net worth. Kresge's current ratio is 2.31, which is very good; May's is 2.20, which is also good. This is why Dun & Bradstreet has rated both these companies as 5A1 (its highest rating).

The *acid-test* ratio reduces the current ratio by the inventory value since inventory is not all that liquid and measures the company's immediate solvency. Kresge's ratio is 0.51, while May's is 1.46.

Long-Term Financing. The *equity to total assets ratio* shows Kresge at 0.539 and May at only 0.416; therefore, Kresge is "more satisfactory" than May (0.50 is the satisfactory threshold).

The *liquidity ratio* measures the company's ability to pay off its total liabilities. Kresge's is 1.62, which is very high; and May's is only 0.90, which means that

May would have to try to sell some of its fixed property in order to pay off its creditors.

The *long-term debt to equity ratio* measures the amount of assets after current liabilities are taken care of, which would not be at the disposal of the stockholders. Kresge's ratio is a conservative 20.8 percent, while May's is much worse at 70.9 percent.

Fixed charges times earned indicates the margin of safety of the long-term creditors and stockholders. A coverage range of 3–6x is the standard range indicative of good quality, while 2–3x is low. In this case, both Kresge and May are in the higher bracket, but Kresge is still higher than May.

Profitability. *Asset turnover* measures the efficient use of the operating assets. In this case, Kresge generates $2.90 of sales for every one dollar of assets. May generates only $1.40 per dollar of assets.

The *pretax margin* measures the pretax profit earned on every dollar of sales. We can see that Kresge is a volume-oriented company. May makes fewer sales but makes more money on them.

The *pretax return on assets ratio* gauges how well management has employed the total resources at its command before consideration of taxes. Kresge's management ability can be shown by their 10.2 percent return versus 7.8 percent for May.

The *net return on equity ratio* measures the return on ownership capital after all taxes and interest payments. It is perhaps the most common return on investment figure quoted by recognized financial services. Both companies are relatively high; however, Kresge again maintains a superior return.

The *earnings retention* measures the percentage of net income retained for future expansion. Kresge exhibits a relatively high retention rate (approximately 75 percent) while May retains a lesser percentage of earnings.

As can be inferred from the above analysis, the balance sheet, in its present form, makes Kresge appear to be a good, stable company to invest in. It exhibits a superior financial base and operating record. This, in large part, explains the premium multiple of 29x earnings assigned Kresge. What this means, in essence, is that investors are willing to pay a much higher price for Kresge's financial stability and earnings growth potential. In addition, the company's relatively low leverage and its ability to more than adequately cover its fixed charges have significantly influenced its AA credit rating assigned by both major rating services.

On the other hand, May Department Stores' multiple of 11x earnings and its A rating by Moody's reflect its more extensive use of debt financing (higher leverage), less favorable growth potential, and generally higher risks characteristics.

Comparison—with Leases. Now the balance sheets of the two companies are redone and two accounts inserted—rights to leased property on the asset side and lease obligations on the liability side. The ratios were recalculated to show where the differences actually lie. By returning these "assets" to the balance sheet and setting up the corresponding liabilities, the ratios of course change.

Question

1. Calculate the ratios in Exhibit 2 for the data in Exhibit 1 with leases capitalized.
2. What effect does the capitalization of

leases have on the relative financial position and profitability of the two companies?

3. Which set of financial statements provides more useful information to investors?

CASE 13–4 Springfield National Bank

John Dawson, Jr., president of Dawson Stores, Inc., had a discussion with Stefanie Anderson, a loan officer at Springfield National Bank. Both John and Dawson Stores, Inc., were deposit customers of the bank and had been for several years. Dawson's comments were directly to the point:

> It appears that we are going to have some working capital needs during the next year at Dawson Stores, Inc. I would like to obtain a $100,000 line of credit, on an unsecured basis, to cover these short-term needs. Could you set up the line of credit for a year to be reviewed when next year's statements are available?
>
> I know from my friends that you need information about the company in order to grant this request, so I have brought a copy of the company's statements for the last four years for you. Could you let me know about the line of credit in a few days? We are having a board meeting in two weeks, and I would like to get the appropriate paperwork for you at that time.

In reviewing the reports of previous contacts by bank personnel with Dawson Stores, Inc., Ms. Anderson found the information summarized below:

> Dawson Stores, Inc., had been incorporated in 1881. The stock had been widely dispersed upon the death of John Dawson, Sr., who had divided his shares among his 5 children and 14 grandchildren.

Dawson Stores, Inc., had maintained its deposit accounts with Springfield for many years, even during the years John Dawson, Sr. had managed the company. The accounts had varied over the past few years. Average balances of the accounts were $35,000 for the past year. The company had occasionally purchased certificates of deposit for short periods.

Dawson Stores, Inc. had not used bank credit in the last 10 years. A recent Dun & Bradstreet report requested by a business development officer reported all trade accounts satisfactory and contained only satisfactory information. The D&B report showed the officers were John as president and his brother Bill as vice president and treasurer. The directors were the officers, their two sisters and two cousins, the latter four residing in other states. Credit terms included both revolving (30-day) accounts and installment sales.

Dawson Stores, Inc., has operated seven stores for the past six years. All store locations have been modernized frequently. One store location was moved during the past year to a new location two blocks from the previous location.

The call report from the business development officer reported the premises orderly and well located for this chain of small retail softgoods and hardgoods stores (based upon a visit of three of seven locations), all located in the Springfield trade area. The president was happy with his present bank services, but in the opinion of the business

EXHIBIT 1

DAWSON STORES, INC.
Comparative Balance Sheets
As of January 31

	1980	1981	1982	1983
Assets				
Current assets:				
Cash	$ 8,212	$ 10,808	$ 54,526	$ 70,496
Accounts receivable (net)	220,154	231,315	259,878	289,774
Inventories	200,026	183,309	217,029	237,722
Supplies and prepaid expenses	5,420	7,698	7,033	5,773
Total current assets	433,812	433,130	538,466	603,765
Investments and other assets	22,103	24,453	12,436	15,496
Property, plant, and equipment (net)	378,234	398,888	414,236	439,015
Total assets	$834,149	$856,471	$965,138	$1,058,276
Equities				
Current liabilities:				
Accounts payable	$ 88,711	$ 89,666	$135,922	$ 174,807
Taxes other than income taxes	29,148	29,949	31,883	32,138
Accrued liabilities	31,560	34,930	52,010	60,944
Income taxes, currently payable	17,033	17,606	37,778	36,961
Deferred income taxes, installment sales	28,785	30,882	37,203	45,298
Current portion of long-term debt	9,124	11,019	13,959	10,820
Total current liabilities	204,361	214,052	308,755	360,968
Long-term debt	268,771	263,822	241,211	226,329
Deferred credits	20,470	22,486	18,776	23,268
Shareholders' equity:				
Capital stock	10,000	10,000	10,000	10,000
Retained earnings	330,547	346,111	386,396	437,711
Total equities	$834,149	$856,471	$965,138	$1,058,276

development officer there was little possibility for further business.

The audited financial statements left with Ms. Anderson by John Dawson are summarized in Exhibits 1, 2, and 3. Notes accompanying these financial statements gave the following additional information.

Accounts Receivable. Retail customer accounts receivable are written off in full when any portion of the unpaid balance is past due 12 months. The allowance for losses arising from uncollectible customer accounts receivable is based on historical bad debt experience and current aging of the accounts.

	1980	1981	1982	1983
Accounts receivable:				
Thirty-day accounts	$ 5,203	$ 5,788	$ 3,087	$ 2,465
Deferred payment accounts	200,496	208,377	238,646	276,540
Other accounts	18,841	23,882	26,796	19,309
Less: Allowance for losses	(4,386)	(6,732)	(8,651)	(8,540)
	$220,154	$231,315	$259,878	$289,774

EXHIBIT 2

DAWSON STORES, INC.
Comparative Statements of Income and Retained Earnings
For the Periods Ending January 31

	1980	1981	1982	1983
Revenues	$1,407,476	$1,504,469	$1,690,480	$1,856,013
Cost of sales	985,845	1,067,983	1,166,363	1,271,304
	421,631	436,486	524,117	584,704
Operating expenses	368,349	386,411	417,099	448,448
Earnings before income taxes	53,282	50,075	107,018	136,261
Income taxes:				
Current	18,951	21,181	53,116	62,568
Deferred	7,031	3,711	2,585	8,030
	25,982	24,892	55,701	70,598
Net earnings	27,300	25,183	51,317	65,663
Retained earnings, beginning of the year	312,164	330,547	346,111	386,396
Less: Dividends	8,917	9,619	11,032	14,348
Retained earnings, end of year	$ 330,547	$ 346,111	$ 386,396	$ 437,711
Earnings per share (10,000 shares issued and outstanding)	$2.73	$2.52	$5.13	$6.57

Thirty-day accounts are revolving charge accounts that are billed every 30 days. Deferred payment accounts are monthly payment accounts requiring at least 10 percent of the outstanding balance principal payments with interest rates of 15 percent. Other accounts are for sales contracts from three to five years from the sales of office properties. The following is an aging schedule of accounts receivable as of January 31, 1983:

	30 Days or Less	30 to 60 Days	Over 60 Days
Thirty-day	$ 2,195	$ 221	$ 49
Deferred payment	246,121	22,123	8,296
Other	17,571	1,738	–0–

Inventories. Substantially all inventories are recorded at cost on the last-in, first-out (LIFO) method. Inventories at January 31 are stated less the following amounts that would have been determined under the retail method without regard to last-in, first-out principles.

1980	1981	1982	1983
$21,800	$39,900	$43,064	$50,749

Plant. Property, Plant, and Equipment is carried at cost less accumulated depreciation. Depreciation is computed using the straight-line method for financial reporting purposes and accelerated methods for tax purposes.

	1980	1981	1982	1983
Land	$ 86,776	$ 98,846	$ 72,915	$ 78,696
Building and improvements	357,152	388,481	443,100	459,164
Fixtures and equipment	100,880	109,659	109,797	123,237
Construction in progress	25,274	23,361	20,438	26,986
Accumulated depreciation	(191,848)	(221,459)	(232,014)	(249,068)
	$378,234	$398,888	$414,236	$439,015

EXHIBIT 3

Comparative Statements of Changes in Financial Position
For the Periods Ending January 31

	1980	1981	1982	1983
Funds provided by:				
Operations:				
Net earnings	$27,300	$ 25,183	$ 51,317	$ 65,663
Items not affecting working capital:				
Depreciation and amortization	25,279	27,559	29,861	32,603
Equity in loss of joint ventures			2,840	2,929
Increase (decrease) in noncurrent				
deferred income taxes	2,337	1,614	(3,736)	(65)
Other	910	789	1,504	126
Funds provided by operations	55,826	55,145	81,786	101,256
Increase in long-term debt	17,639	8,000	7,437	16,755
Disposals of property and equipment	9,681	10,589	2,268	22,101
Increase (decrease) in deferred income	(*)	(*)	(52)	4,460
	$83,146	$ 73,734	$ 91,439	$144,572
Funds used for:				
Addition to property, plant, and				
equipment	$55,775	$ 58,160	$ 39,786	$ 79,483
Mortgages assumed by purchasers				
of office properties and prepayment				
on long-term debt	7,907	12,949	16,098	7,812
Scheduled reductions of long-term debt	9,124	11,019	13,950	23,825
Cash dividends	8,917	9,619	11,032	14,348
Investments	1,328	2,113	28	3,543
Other (net)	(3,067)	(9,753)	(87)	2,475
Increase in working capital	3,162	(10,373)	10,632	13,086
	$83,146	$ 73,734	$ 91,439	$144,572
Increases (decreases) in components				
of working capital:				
Cash	$ (9,645)	$ 2,596	$ 43,717	$ 15,970
Accounts receivable	29,121	11,161	28,563	29,896
Merchandise inventories	2,190	(16,717)	33,720	20,693
Supplies and prepaid expenses	530	2,278	(665)	(1,260)
Increase in current assets	22,196	(682)	105,335	65,299
Accounts payable	6,861	955	46,256	38,885
Accrued expenses and others	12,077	6,268	25,335	17,284
Income taxes, currently payable	(741)	573	20,172	(817)
Current portion of long-term debt	837	1,895	2,940	(3,139)
Increase in current liabilities	19,034	9,691	94,703	52,213
Net increase	$ 3,162	$(10,373)	$ 10,632	$ 13,086

*Included in other (net) under "Funds used for."

Annual minimum rentals on long-term noncancellable leases are as follows:

1983	$ 18,862
1984	18,322
1985	17,389
1986	17,050
1987	16,815
Beyond 1987	142,172

Contingent rentals are based upon a percentage of sales. Most leases require additional payments for real estate taxes, insurance, and other expenses that are included in operating costs in the accompanying statement of income and retained earnings.

Income Taxes. Deferred income taxes are provided for income and expenses that are recognized in different accounting periods for financial reporting than for income tax purposes. The timing differences and the related deferred taxes are as follows:

	1980	1981	1982	1983
Excess of tax over book depreciation	$2,155	$1,704	$1,930	$ 357
Deferred income on installment sales	5,048	1,796	5,958	8,019
Other	(172)	211	(5,303)	(346)
Total	$7,031	$3,711	$2,585	$8,030

Long-Term Debt. The long-term debt of Dawson Stores, Inc., is composed of mortgage loans from three savings institutions on the store properties that the company occupies. There is no debt agreement that places restrictions on the company's operations or financing.

Questions

1. Appraise the recent performance and financial position of Dawson Stores, Inc., using selected financial ratios as appropriate.

2. As Stefanie Anderson, would you conclude that the company is a good credit risk?

14

Understanding Financial Statements

The first section of this chapter describes certain information contained in annual reports that was not discussed in preceding chapters. The next section reviews the criteria and concepts introduced in Chapters 1, 2, and 3, bringing together amplifications and qualifications to the concepts that have been developed in later chapters. Alternative treatments of accounting transactions that are possible within the framework of these concepts are described. Finally, the chapter discusses the meaning of information contained in financial reports in view of all the above.

ADDITIONAL INFORMATION IN ANNUAL REPORTS

The annual report that a company prepares for the use of shareholders, financial analysts, and other outside parties contains important information in addition to the three financial statements. At its option, a company may include information about products, personnel, facilities, or any other topics. Often this information is accompanied with colored photographs and diagrams of various kinds. A company is *required* to provide certain other types of information, including the auditors' opinion, notes to the financial statements, business segment information, and comparative data.

**The Auditors'
Opinion**

All companies whose securities are listed on an organized stock exchange, most other corporations, and a great many unincorporated businesses have their financial statements and the underlying accounting records examined by independent, outside public accountants called *auditors*. Usually, these are certified public accountants (CPAs) who meet prescribed professional standards and who are licensed to practice by the state in which they do business. The auditors' examination relates only to the financial statements, including notes, and not to other material that may appear in a company's annual report. The results of the auditors' examination are presented in a report, which is commonly called the *auditors' opinion*. This report consists of two paragraphs, a scope paragraph and an opinion paragraph.[1]

Scope Paragraph. The paragraph describing the scope of the auditors' examination reads as follows:

> We have examined the accompanying balance sheets of _____ Company as of December 31, 19x1, and 19x0, and the related statements of income and changes in financial position for each of the three years in the period ended December 31, 19x1. Our examination was made in accordance with generally accepted auditing standards and, accordingly, included such tests of the accounting records and such other auditing procedures as we considered necessary in the circumstances.

The key words in this paragraph are: *such tests . . . as we considered necessary.* They signify that the auditors, not management, are responsible for deciding on how thorough an audit is required. Management cannot ask the auditors, for example, to "make as much of an audit as you can for $20,000."

In making their examination, auditors no longer rely primarily on a detailed rechecking of the analysis, journalizing, and posting of each transaction. Rather, they satisfy themselves that the accounting *system* is designed to ensure that the data are processed properly. This reliance on the system is relatively new. For example, up until 1949, the U.S. General Accounting Office received a copy of every one of the millions of accounting documents generated annually in the federal government and, theoretically at least, checked each of them for propriety and accuracy. When the GAO changed its emphasis to a reliance on properly designed accounting systems, it was able to release several *thousand* employees.

In addition to the examination of the adequacy of the accounting system, the auditors (1) make test checks of how well it is working; (2) verify the existence of assets [for example, they must observe the taking of physical inventory]; (3) ask a sample of customers to *confirm* or verify

---

[1]"Reports on Audited Financial Statements," *AICPA Statement on Auditing Standards No. 2,* 1973.

the accuracy of the accounts receivable; (4) check bank balances and investment securities; and (5) make sure that especially important or nonroutine transactions are recorded in conformity with generally accepted accounting principles (GAAP). The observation of inventories and the confirmation of accounts receivable are regarded as being so important that the omission of either of these tests must be specifically mentioned in the auditors' report.

These checks provide reasonable assurance that errors have not been committed through oversight or carelessness and that there has been no fraudulent activity. They do not provide absolute assurance, however, for almost any system can be beaten. Although spectacular frauds receive much publicity, they occur in only a tiny fraction of companies.

Opinion Paragraph. The other paragraph in the auditors' report ordinarily reads as follows:

> In our opinion, the accompanying financial statements present fairly the financial position of _____ Company as of December 31, 19x1, and 19x0, and the results of its operations and changes in its financial position for each of the three years in the period ended December 31, 19x1, in conformity with generally accepted accounting principles applied on a consistent basis.

The three significant points in this paragraph are indicated by the words: (1) *present fairly,* (2) *in conformity with generally accepted accounting principles,* and (3) *applied on a consistent basis.*

Fairness. The word *fairly* should be contrasted with the word *accurately.* The auditors do not say that the reported net income is the only, or even the most accurate, number that could have been reported. Rather, they say that of the many alternative principles that could have been used, those actually selected by management do give a fair picture in the circumstances relevant to the particular company. This contrast between "fairness" and "accuracy" is further emphasized by the fact that the auditors' report is called an *opinion.* Auditors do not certify the accuracy of the statements; instead, they give their professional opinion that the presentation is fair. (Of course, a fair presentation requires *arithmetic* accuracy.)

Many people have the impression that the auditors are responsible for *preparing* the financial statements. This is not so. The letter says that the auditors "have examined" the financial statements. Management, not the auditor, is responsible for the *preparation* of the statements.

When two or more alternative practices are permitted by GAAP, and either is "fair" (which is of course an ambiguous criterion), management, not the auditors, decides which one is to be used. In the opinion letter the auditors do not state that management has necessarily made the *best* choice among alternative principles, but only that the choice made by management was an acceptable one.

Principles.   The second phrase means that each of the accounting principles used in preparing the statements is "generally accepted." For many transactions there are several generally accepted alternative treatments, and the auditors' opinion merely states that management has selected one of these. If the FASB (or its predecessor bodies) has issued a pronouncement on a certain point, this constitutes a "generally accepted accounting principle." Rule 203 of the AICPA Code of Professional Ethics states that no departures from such pronouncements can be regarded as a generally accepted accounting principle "unless the member can demonstrate that due to unusual circumstances the financial statements would otherwise have been misleading." Such circumstances are exceedingly rare. If they do exist, the report must describe the departure, give the reasons for making it, and show its approximate effect on the reported results. Thus, for all practical purposes, generally accepted accounting principles are what the FASB says they are.

Consistency.   The third point, *consistency,* refers specifically to consistency with practices followed in *the preceding years*. It does not mean *internal* consistency; that is, it does not mean that the principle used to measure plant and equipment is consistent with that used to measure inventory, or even that each corporation in a consolidated enterprise follows practices that are consistent with those of other corporations in the same enterprise. The consistency doctrine is nevertheless of great significance because it does mean that the amounts for one year are comparable with those of the preceding years. Assurance of such comparability is essential if meaningful comparisons are to be made.

Other-than-Clean Opinions.   An auditors' report containing only the words in the two paragraphs quoted above is called a *clean opinion.* Other opinions are said to be *qualified.* If the company has changed an accounting method (e.g., from FIFO to LIFO), the auditors must give a *consistency qualification.* If the accounting method change was required by an FASB pronouncement, the typical wording of the consistency sentence will be ". . . applied on a consistent basis, *except for* the change in accounting for interest cost, *with which we concur.*"[2]

Sometimes a major uncertainty, such as a pending lawsuit, may ultimately have a material effect on the company's financial position. Auditors are required to call attention to such uncertainties (without predicting the eventual outcome) in the opinion paragraph. This is called a *subject-to* opinion, because the auditors' report says that their opinion is subject to the ultimate resolution of the uncertain matter.

In rare cases, the auditors' opinion may be a *disclaimer;* that is, they report that they are unable to express an opinion. This may happen either because limitations were placed on the scope of the audit, or

---

[2]Emphasis added. *FASB Statement No. 34* requires that some interest costs, formerly expensed, be capitalized (see Chapter 7).

because the company is in such shaky financial condition that there are doubts as to whether it is a going concern. (Recall that one of the basic accounting concepts is that the company *is* a going concern.) If the auditors conclude that the financial statements do *not* "present fairly" the situation, they write an *adverse* opinion. This may occur if the company has departed from GAAP, or if it clearly is no longer a going concern. Adverse opinions and disclaimers are extremely serious matters. Usually, they result in a suspension of trading in the company's stocks.

Notes to Financial Statements

We have discussed three required financial statements: the balance sheet, the income statement, and the statement of changes in financial condition (funds flow statement). A fourth type of required information is also important. This consists of the notes that accompany, and are deemed to be an integral part of, the financial statements themselves. The requirements for these notes are becoming increasingly elaborate and detailed.

One of these notes, usually the first, summarizes the accounting policies the company has followed in preparing the statements. Among other topics, this note usually describes the basis of consolidation if the statements are consolidated statements, depreciation methods, policies with respect to the amortization of intangible assets, inventory methods, and policies regarding the recognition of revenues.

Other notes give details on long-term debt, including the maturity date and interest rate of each bond issue; a description of stock option plans and other management incentive plans; a description of pension plans; and the total rental expense and the minimum amount of rent that must be paid in the future under current lease commitments.[3] Additional detail on the composition of inventories and of depreciable assets is given. A note on income taxes explains the difference between the reported provision for income taxes and the amount that would result if the statutory rate (46 percent in 1983) were applied to reported pretax income. (State and local income taxes and the investment tax credit are two common causes of this difference.) Many annual reports have several pages of these notes.

As described in Chapter 12, large corporations must make the supplementary constant dollar and replacement cost disclosures required by *FASB Statement No. 33*. Most companies include these disclosures near the end of the notes to the financial statements.

Segment Reporting

Current economic and political forces affect different industries in different ways. Moreover, typical margins, return on assets, and other financial ratios vary widely among industries. Analysts therefore find it

---

[3]This is required by "Accounting for Leases," *FASB Statement No. 13*, November 1976.

difficult to estimate the effect of these forces and to use typical ratios if the financial statements report only the aggregate results.

For this reason, corporations (except small, privately owned corporations) are required to supplement the overall financial statements with additional information about the principal *industry segments* in which they operate. Each company can decide for itself the most useful way of dividing its operations into segments. In some cases, the nature of the product lines provides a natural basis for classification; in other cases, it is the nature of the production process or the marketing methods. No company is required to report on more than 10 segments.

For each segment, the company reports (1) revenues; (2) operating profit or loss; and (3) identifiable assets, including usually depreciation expense on these assets. Which expense items to include in the calculation of "operating profit" is open to some differences in interpretation. In general, they include all the expenses that can be identified with the segment, but not expenses of corporate headquarters, interest expense, or income tax expense.

In addition to this report on industry segments, corporations are also required to provide other information, including amounts of sales and profit in each major geographical area of the world, and sales to government agencies or to single customers if these sales constitute a significant fraction of the total.[4]

Full Disclosure

A fundamental accounting principle is that the financial statements and the accompanying notes must contain a full disclosure of material financial information. This includes not only information known as of the balance sheet date but also information coming to light after the end of the accounting period that may affect the information contained in the financial statements. For example, if in January 1984 one of the company's plants was destroyed by fire, this fact should be disclosed in the company's 1983 annual report, even though the amount of plant on the December 31, 1983, balance sheet was correct as of that time.

There is disagreement as to what constitutes full disclosure. In general, if an item of economic information would cause informed investors to appraise the company differently than would be the case without that item of information, it should be disclosed. Clearly, there is room for differences of opinion as to what such items are, but in recent court decisions an increasingly broad view has been taken of disclosure re-

---

[4]"Financial Reporting for Segments of a Business Enterprise" and "Disclosure of Information about Major Customers," *FASB Statement No. 14* and *No. 30*, December 1976 and August 1979, respectively.

quirements. These decisions have resulted in a corresponding increase in the amount of information disclosed in annual reports.

Comparative Statements

In addition to the financial statements for the current year, the annual report must also contain the previous year's balance sheet, and the preceding two years' income and funds flow statements. Many companies also include summaries of important financial statement items for a period of 5 or 10 years.

The information from prior years that is published in the current annual report is usually the same information as that originally published. There are some circumstances, however, in which information for prior years is restated. If the accounting entity is changed, either by the acquisition of other companies or by the disposition of segments of the business, the amounts for prior years are restated so as to show data for the entity as it currently exists.

> **Example.** If the Cameron Company in 1983 acquired Subsidiary A and disposed of one of its own subsidiaries, B, the financial statements of 1983 and earlier years would be restated by adding the financial data for Subsidiary A and subtracting those of Subsidiary B.

The financial statements for prior years must also be restated to reflect certain changes in accounting principles.[5] These include the following: (1) a change from the LIFO method of inventory to another method; (2) a change in the method of accounting for long-term contracts from the completed contract method to the percentage of completion method, or vice versa; and (3) a change in certain accounting practices of extractive industries.

With these few exceptions, however, prior year statements are not restated. Instead, when a company makes a change in its accounting practices that affects the net income reported in prior periods, the *cumulative* effect of this change on the net income of all prior periods is calculated, and this amount is reported on the *current* year's income statement. When a company has reason to believe that estimates that influenced the reported net income in prior years were incorrect (such as when subsequent events show that the estimated service life of depreciable assets was too long or too short), it does not go back and correct the financial statements for the prior years. These rather strict restrictions on recasting the data in prior year financial statements exist because of the belief that public confidence in the financial statements would be lessened if they were subject to frequent restatement as time went on.

---

[5]"Accounting Changes," *APB Opinion No. 20*, July 1971.

Securities and Exchange Commission Reports

In addition to the annual report to its shareholders, every company that is under the jurisdiction of the Securities and Exchange Commission must file an annual report with the SEC. This report is filed on SEC Form 10-K, and is therefore known as the 10-K report. In general, the financial data in this report are consistent with, but in somewhat more detail than, the data in the annual report. Rules governing the preparation of Form 10-K are contained in SEC *Regulation S-X*. These rules are, with few exceptions, consistent with the standards of the FASB.

The SEC also requires that certain financial data be included in the notice of annual meeting sent to all shareholders. These include the compensation of each top executive, the compensation of officers and directors as a group, a description of proposed changes in incentive compensation plans, and a description of any of the company's financial transactions that involved officers and directors as individuals (such as loans made by a bank whose president was a director of the company).

Interim Statements. Companies under the jurisdiction of the SEC also file quarterly reports on Form 10-Q. These interim statements contain a summary of financial statements for the current quarter and for the year to date. Although they are not audited, in the strict sense, the auditors go over them to ensure that they appear to be reasonable. If significant events occur at any time, such as a major investment by one company in the stock of another, or a decision to dispose of a division, the company must report these events to the SEC on Form 8-K, usually within a month of their occurrence.

All SEC reports are widely available. Because they often contain more detailed information than the company's annual report and because the data are set forth in a standard format, financial analysts use these reports as well as those published by the company.

REVIEW OF CRITERIA AND CONCEPTS

In Chapter 1 we listed three criteria that governed financial accounting concepts and principles, and in Chapters 2 and 3 we described 11 basic concepts. It is appropriate here that we consider these criteria and concepts again with the benefit of the additional material that has been discussed in the intervening chapters.

Criteria

There are three basic accounting criteria:

1. Accounting information should be *relevant*. Accounting reports should provide information that describes as accurately and completely as possible the status of assets and equities, the results of operations, and changes in financial position.
2. Accounting information should be *objective*. The amounts reported

should not be biased, particularly by the subjective judgments of management.

3. The reporting of accounting information should be *feasible.* Its value should exceed the cost of collecting and reporting it.

There is an inevitable conflict between the criterion of *relevance,* on the one hand, and the criteria of *objectivity* and *feasibility,* on the other. Accounting concepts and principles reflect a workable compromise between these opposing forces. Failure to appreciate this fact is behind the feeling of many of the uninitiated that "accounting doesn't make sense."

Of the many examples of this conflict, perhaps the most clear-cut is that relating to the measurement of property, plant, and equipment. In general, the most relevant rule for stating the amounts of these items— the rule that would provide readers of financial statements with what they really want to know—would be to state these assets at their current value, what they are really worth. But such a rule would be neither objective nor feasible in most situations.

Conceptually, the worth of an asset is measured by the present value of the future cash flows it will generate. But it is infeasible to make this calculation. In the first place, the subjective opinions of management as to future cash flows and the appropriate discount rate would have to be used. Second, for many assets, such as administrative offices, it is not really meaningful to think of the asset as generating cash flows (or at least not *positive* cash flows). Although more feasible, even replacement cost numbers can have a high degree of subjectivity, especially if the asset is a specialized piece of equipment and is not, in fact, likely to be replaced at the end of its service life. Furthermore, an entity is more than the sum of its individual assets, and the financial statements cannot possibly report what the *total resources,* both physical *and* human, are actually worth.

At the other extreme, the most objective and feasible rules for measuring property, plant, and equipment would be either (1) state these assets at acquisition cost and report them as an asset at cost until they are disposed of or (2) write them off the books immediately. In most cases, either rule would be perfectly simple to apply and would involve little, if any, subjective judgment. But with either rule, accounting could not report the depreciation expense that is properly charged to the operations of each accounting period. A net income figure that includes such an estimate of asset cost expiration is much more relevant for most purposes than one that omits depreciation altogether.

So accounting takes a middle ground. Assets are originally booked at cost, which is an objectively determined amount in most cases, and this cost is charged as an expense in each accounting period over the useful life of the asset. The annual depreciation charge is an estimate, and any of several ways of making this estimate is permitted; but the number of permitted alternatives is small, and freedom to tamper with the estimates is further restricted by the concept of consistency.

Concepts

Eleven basic financial accounting concepts were stated in Chapters 2 and 3. Other persons would classify and describe the basic concepts somewhat differently than we have. (The FASB concepts statements total over 200 pages, but contain no succinct list of basic concepts.) The 11 concepts are repeated below, and amplifications and qualifications are given for certain of them.

1. Money Measurement. *Accounting records only those facts that can be expressed in monetary terms.*

In the accounts, there are no exceptions to this concept, although nonmonetary information is often provided as supplementary data. Assets are recorded at the number of dollars (or dollar equivalents) paid to acquire them. Although the purchasing power of the monetary unit changes because of inflation, accounting does not reflect these changes in purchasing power, except in supplementary financial information that only some firms publish. Thus, the monetary unit used in accounting is *not* a unit of constant purchasing power.

2. Entity. *Accounts are kept for entities as distinguished from the person(s) associated with those entities.*

In small businesses, particularly unincorporated businesses, some problems arise in distinguishing between transactions affecting the entity and transactions affecting the owners. In parent companies that have subsidiaries, there may be important problems involved in defining the entity for which consolidated financial statements are prepared. In general, a subsidiary is considered to be part of the consolidated entity if the parent owns more than 50 percent of its common stock, but there are some exceptions, as described in Chapter 11. With these exceptions, there are few problems in applying the entity concept in a corporation. Since governments and other nonprofit organizations do not control subunits by stock ownership, there are great difficulties in defining the entity in many such organizations.

3. Going Concern. *Accounting assumes that an entity will continue to exist indefinitely and that it is not about to be liquidated.*

The going-concern concept does not assume that the entity will exist forever. Rather, it assumes that the entity will continue to operate long enough to use up its long-lived assets and to pay off its long-lived liabilities as they mature, that is, for the foreseeable future. This concept explains why generally accounting does not attempt to keep track of the liquidation value or current market value of individual long-lived assets.

There is one important qualification to this statement. If there is strong evidence that the entity will *not* continue in existence, asset amounts *are* recorded at their estimated liquidation value.

4. Cost. *An asset is ordinarily entered in the accounts at the amount paid to acquire it; and this cost, rather than current market value, is the basis for subsequent accounting for the asset.*

There are important qualifications to this concept. If the amount paid is obviously less than the fair market value of the asset, as in the case of donated assets, the asset is recorded at fair market value. There are differences of opinion as to how the cost of products manufactured by a company should be measured, as noted in Chapter 6.

Also, market value does affect the subsequent accounting for certain types of assets. Inventory and marketable equity securities are reported at the lower of their cost or their current market value. Certain investments are reported at the book value of the company whose stock is owned (i.e., the equity method), rather than at cost. These are all exceptions to the general rule, however.

Depreciation, depletion, and amortization are write-offs of the assets' cost; they do not reflect changes in market value.

5. Dual Aspect. *The total amount of assets equals the total amount of equities.*

There are absolutely no exceptions to this concept. It is important not only because mechanically it lessens the possibility of making errors in recording transactions but also because conceptually it aids in understanding the effect of transactions on an accounting entity. The fact that "for every debit there must be a credit" helps one to recognize both aspects of a transaction.

6. Time Period. *Accounting measures activities for a specified interval of time, which is usually one year.*

Reporting on results at frequent intervals is obviously necessary, both to management and to outside parties. The necessity for doing this, however, causes most of the difficult problems in accounting. These are the problems associated with accrual accounting. In measuring the net income of an accounting period, the revenues and expenses that properly belong to that period must be estimated. These estimates depend in part on what is going to happen in future periods, which is unknown.

7. Conservatism. *Revenues are recognized only when they are reasonably certain, whereas expenses are recognized as soon as they are reasonably possible.*

This concept explains why bad debt expense is recognized in the period in which the related sales revenues are recorded, rather than later when some customers actually default on their payments. Similarly, the concept is the basis for recognizing future warranty costs as an expense in the period in which the warranted goods are sold, rather than later when the warranty costs are paid. The conservatism cost also explains why certain assets are recorded at the lower of cost or market value. It is also a reason behind the FASB's decision that most research and development costs should be expensed as incurred, rather than capitalized.

Although it is possible these costs will benefit future periods, it is also reasonably possible they will not.

8. Realization. *Revenues are usually recognized in the period in which goods were delivered to customers or in which services were rendered. The amount recognized is the amount that customers are reasonably certain to pay.*

Many problems arise in deciding on both the period in which the revenue for a given transaction should be recognized and the amount of such revenue. In unusual circumstances, the amount of revenue recognized may reflect a considerable amount of optimism as to future earnings, but the auditors will ordinarily detect and call attention to revenues whose realization is not reasonably certain. Chapter 5 is suggested as a refresher for exceptions and clarifications of this concept.

9. Matching. *When a given event affects both revenues and expenses, the effect on each should be recognized in the same accounting period.*

Costs are reported as expenses in the period (1) when there is a direct association between costs and revenues of the period, (2) when costs are associated with activities of the period itself, or (3) when costs cannot be associated with revenues of any future period.

Differences of opinion about the application of this concept and of the realization concept are at the heart of most accounting controversies. We shall discuss these further in connection with our discussion of the income statement.

10. Consistency. *Once an entity has decided on a certain accounting method, it will treat all subsequent events of the same character in the same fashion unless it has a sound reason to do otherwise.*

This concept is always adhered to in theory, but the practical problem is to decide when a "sound reason" for a change exists. Although the desire to increase the amount of net income reported in the current period is at the root of some changes in method, this is definitely not an acceptable reason for making a change. Nevertheless, some companies make a change for this purpose and devise other reasons to justify it.

11. Materiality. *Insignificant events may be disregarded, but there must be full disclosure of all important information.*

This concept is probably the least precise of any. Although books have been written on the meaning of materiality, although elaborate surveys have been conducted on what informed persons think the term should mean, and although many attempts have been made to define specifically what the concept means, there is (in 1983) no authoritative, explicit statement in existence. In the absence of specific guidelines, accountants rely on their own judgment. The general notion is that an item is material if its disclosure is likely to lead the user of accounting information to act differently. Recent court cases have tended to lead to an increasingly strict interpretation of materiality.

The materiality concept can also be invoked as a reason to depart from the other concepts in the interest of simplicity, when the effect of such a departure is not material. For example, FASB *Statements* include as the last sentence of every standard: "The provisions of this Statement need not be applied to immaterial items."

These concepts govern the accounting in all business organizations. Somewhat different accounting practices are followed by governments and by other nonprofit organizations, and these are not consistent with the conservatism, realization, and matching concepts. A discussion of these differences is outside the scope of this book.[6]

Importance of the Concepts. The many practices and procedures described in earlier chapters were amplifications and applications of these basic concepts, rather than additions to them. As a matter of practice, for example, accumulated depreciation is shown in a separate account rather than being credited directly to the asset account. But the basic idea of depreciation accounting is nevertheless in accordance with the concepts that assets are recorded at cost, and costs are matched with revenues.

Any conceivable transaction, provided it is clearly described, can be analyzed in terms of its effect on the assets and equities of the entity in accordance with the basic accounting concepts. For an extremely large fraction of the transactions in a typical business, the analysis is simple: for a cash sale, debit Cash and credit Sales; for receipts from a credit customer, credit Accounts Receivable and debit Cash.

In a relatively small number of transactions, the analysis is difficult. For example, a number of transactions involve a credit to Cash or Accounts Payable for the purchase of something. The question is whether the offsetting debit is to an asset account or to an expense account. The answer to this question depends on whether the entity has, or has not, acquired something that has beneficial value beyond the end of the accounting period, which is sometimes a matter of judgment.

In still other cases, the FASB has prescribed a certain procedure. Also, there are transactions that have no unique "right" answer: accounting principles permit any of several treatments. In these cases, accountants simply use their best judgment.

Many of these situations require judgment because of inevitable uncertainties about the future. How long will the building really last? Is a decline in the market value of inventory only temporary, or should the inventory be written down? There are no unequivocal answers to such questions, and hence no way of arriving at a result with which everyone would agree.

Misconceptions about Concepts. Some of the basic concepts are intuitively sensible, for example, the idea that account data are ex-

---

[6]For a discussion, see Robert N. Anthony, *Financial Accounting in Nonbusiness Organizations* (Stamford, Conn.: Financial Accounting Standards Board, 1978).

pressed in monetary terms. Certain concepts, however, are rather different from the impression that typical laypersons have about accounting information.

Undoubtedly the greatest misconception relates to the cost concept. To those who do not understand accounting, it seems only reasonable that the accountant should report the *value* of assets—what they are really worth—rather than merely the flow of costs. They find it difficult to believe that the balance sheet is not, even approximately, a statement showing what the entity is worth, especially when they see on some balance sheets an item labeled *net worth*. Even if they eventually recognize that the balance sheet does not in fact report current values, they criticize accounting and accountants for not doing this.

A related misconception results from a failure to appreciate the significance of the going-concern concept. Only after a person has accepted the idea that productive assets are held not for sale but rather for their future usefulness, can there be an appreciation of the fact that the market value of these assets is not of enough significance to warrant displacing the more objective historical cost data.

The matching concept is also a difficult one to comprehend. When people make a personal expenditure to the grocer, to the service station, and so on, they know that they are that much "out of pocket." They have difficulty in understanding the fact that many business expenditures are merely the exchange of one asset for another, with the business getting as much as it gives up. Expenses occur in the time period when costs expire—when they are used up—and this time period is not necessarily the same as the time period in which the expenditure is made.

Those who do understand the basic concepts do not necessarily agree with all of them. The accounting profession is constantly involved in debates over one or another of the currently accepted principles. Since they are not laws of nature, they are subject to change, and in recent years they have been changing with increasing frequency. At the same time, the users of accounting information must do the best they can with the situation as it exists. Users may wish that the principles were different, but as they read an accounting report they need to know how it *was* prepared, not how it *might have been* prepared.

ACCOUNTING ALTERNATIVES

Notwithstanding the basic concepts and generally accepted accounting principles (GAAP), there are considerable differences in the way a given transaction may be recorded. In part, these differences result from requirements imposed by regulatory agencies in certain industries, but more importantly, they result from (1) the latitude that exists within GAAP and (2) judgments that must be made in applying a given principle.

Regulatory Requirements

Certain groups of companies are required to adhere to accounting principles that are not necessarily consistent with those required by the FASB. Railroads and other common carriers follow rules prescribed by the Interstate Commerce Commission; public utilities, by the Federal Energy Regulatory Commission and by state regulatory agencies. In approving the financial statements of such bodies, if the statements are not prepared in accordance with GAAP, the auditors' opinion says the statements are "consistent with practice followed in the industry," or words to that effect.

> **Example.** Prior to 1982, railroads did not depreciate the cost of their tracks. The asset account showed original cost for as long as the track was used, except that original cost was increased if track of a better quality was installed. Replacements were charged as an expense in the year in which the replacement was made. ConRail installed approximately 700 miles of track and 4 million ties in 1976. According to the Railway Association, ConRail's 1976 operating loss would have been $200 million smaller if these betterments were capitalized instead of being expensed.

When regulatory requirements differ from GAAP, most organizations prepare *two* sets of financial statements, one consistent with GAAP, and the other consistent with the requirements of the regulatory agency.

Income Tax Principles

Principles governing the calculation of income for federal income tax purposes are basically the same as the principles of financial accounting. There are, however, important differences, some of which are described below.

Under certain conditions, taxpayers may elect to disregard the accrual concept and to be taxed on the difference between cash receipts and cash expenditures. Many small business do this.

The depletion allowance computed for tax purposes bears no relation to the depletion principle of financial accounting.

In taxation, a distinction is made between ordinary income and capital gains, with the latter being taxed less heavily than the former. In financial accounting, the distinction, although present, is not so important since both ordinary income and capital gains usually enter into the measurement of net income.

The accrual basis of accounting is not completely followed in income tax accounting. For example, in income tax accounting, prepaid rent is counted as revenue when the cash is received; but this is a deferred revenue liability in financial accounting.

Finally, as already pointed out, although the principles are basically the same, a company usually applies them differently in its tax accounting and its financial accounting. It does this primarily by changing the timing, rather than the *amount*, of revenues and expenses. Thus, for tax purposes, a company usually reports costs as early as it legitimately can and defers revenue until as late as it legitimately can. For financial accounting purposes, it tends to report costs in later time periods and revenues in earlier time periods.

Latitude in Methods

In his *Inventory*, Grady listed some 35 topics on which alternative treatments are permitted within GAAP, and gave from two to eight alternatives for each.[7] These topics range in importance from cash discounts on sales, which may be accounted for either at the time the sale is made or the time the receivable is collected, to the basic question of whether an acquisition is to be recorded as a purchase or a pooling of interests.

Examples that have been mentioned in earlier chapters are as follows: inventory can be recorded at LIFO, at FIFO, or at average cost, or some parts of inventory may be handled one way and some another; inventory cost may or may not include inward transportation, storage costs, handling costs, or cash discounts on purchases. Assets may be depreciated by any systematic and rational method. Revenue on long-term contracts may be recognized either by the percentage of completion method or the completed contract method. Revenue on installment sales may be recognized either on the installment basis or on the delivery basis.

In recent years, standards promulgated by the FASB have reduced the amount of latitude that is permitted. In some cases, such as the treatment of R&D costs, the FASB eliminated all but one of the alternatives. In other cases, such as the treatment of an acquisition as a purchase or a pooling of interests, the FASB has carefully spelled out the circumstances under which each alternative practice can be used. Nevertheless, many of the alternatives on Grady's list are still permitted as generally accepted accounting principles.

CIFO — inventory value low
FIFO — inventory value high

in food services — we're forced to use LIFO

Controversies over Principles

In many cases, an accounting requirement described matter-of-factly in this text has evolved only after years of controversy; in some instances, the requirement has not quelled the controversy. For example, many people feel there is no justification for permitting both the deferral and flow-through methods of accounting for the investment tax credit. In its *Opinion No. 2*, the APB required that only the deferral method be used.[8] However, because of great business opposition to *Opinion No. 2*, the APB backed down less than two years later, and again permitted either method, saying "The Board has determined that its conclusions [as expressed in *Opinion No. 2*] have not attained the degree of accept-

---

[7] Paul Grady, *Inventory of Generally Accepted Accounting Principles* (AICPA Accounting Research Study No. 7, 1965), pp. 373–79.

[8] "Accounting for the 'Investment Credit'," *APB Opinion No. 2*, December 1962.

ability which it believes is necessary to make the Opinion effective."[9] Similar lack of support from the business community eventually caused the FASB to change the accounting standards for foreign currency translation from those described in *Statement No. 8* to those in *Statement No. 52.*[10]

The usefulness of reporting supplemental inflation-adjusted financial data was mentioned over 50 years ago by some academics, and the APB formally affirmed this usefulness in 1969 in its *Statement No. 3.*[11] However, it was not until 1979 that the FASB required supplemental inflation-adjusted disclosures, and then only of large companies.[12] Controversy continues on whether the required constant dollar amounts are very relevant, and whether the replacement cost amounts are sufficiently objective.

In this matter, as in the others cited (and still others that we have not mentioned), a clear consensus on what is "right" does not exist. In some instances, the business community is unable to reach such a consensus. In others, businesspeople may be in general agreement, but security analysts, accounting academics, or even the chief accountant of the SEC may have differing views.

Efficient Markets Hypothesis. Many accounting academics, and a few issuers and users of financial statements, have been influenced in their views on accounting principles by research studies dealing with the *efficient markets hypothesis* (EMH). One aspect of EMH research deals with the effect that changes in a company's accounting methods have on its stock price. EMH proponents say, for example, that it does not really matter whether a company uses straight-line or accelerated depreciation in its statements prepared for shareholders. As long as the company is using the ACRS deductions on its *income tax* return, it is minimizing its current cash outflows to pay income taxes. A change in its shareholder reporting depreciation method has no impact on stock price, therefore, because the price reflects "real" cash flows, not "artificial" accounting numbers, and these cash flows are unaffected by the financial accounting method change.

Other academics feel these studies whose results are used to support the EMH are inconclusive. They argue that the inability of the EMH research tools to *detect* an effect on stock prices is not the same as *proving* there has been no effect. Certainly, most nonacademics remain dubious about the EMH point of view. Otherwise, how does one explain the great management uproar over the effect that *FASB Statement No. 8* (foreign currency translations) had on reported earnings, when corporate cash

---

[9]"Accounting for the 'Investment Credit'," *APB Opinion No. 4*, March 1964.

[10]"Accounting for the Translation of Foreign Currency Transactions and Foreign Currency Financial Statements," and "Foreign Currency Translation," *FASB Statement No. 8* and *No. 52*, October 1975 and December 1981, respectively.

[11]'Financial Statements Restated for General Price-Level Changes," *APB Statement No. 3*, June 1969.

[12]"Financial Reporting and Changing Prices," *FASB Statement No. 33*, September 1979.

flows are not affected by the accounting method used for these translations? Or why do many companies that could save taxes, and thus improve cash flows, by changing to LIFO continue to use FIFO? In sum, EMH research has added a new dimension to the ongoing controversies over accounting principles.

Judgment in the Application of Principles

Within GAAP, there is much room for judgment in analyzing specific transactions. In part, these matters reflect differences in personal opinion as to what is or is not *material* and as to the importance that should be attached to the *conservatism* concept. In attempting to describe a complex situation, such differences are inevitable. In part, the differences reflect customs that have grown up in particular companies or industries.

Implications of These Differences

The existence of diversity in accounting practice should not be considered as a reason for criticizing accountants or accounting. The fundamental fact is that a business is a complex organism. There is no conceivable way of prescribing a uniform set of rules for reducing the significant facts about that organism to a few pages of numbers, any more than there is any way of formulating a standard set of rules for biographers. Standard procedures for listing physical cahracteristics, birth dates, marital status, and certain other information about a person can easily be specified, but these details do not really describe the person completely. The accuracy and usefulness of the "picture" of a person that emerges from a biography depends on the author's skill and judgment in the collection, analysis, and presentation of information about the subject. So it is with financial statements.

Nor should the existence of diversity lead to frustration on the part of the user. The *consistency* concept prevents diversity from becoming chaos. Although Company A may follow practices that differ from those of other companies, Company A ordinarily follows the same practices year after year, or if it changes, the concept of consistency requires that it disclose the change. Thus, its statements are likely to be comparable with one another from year to year. Also, companies in a given industry tend to use the same methods in order to facilitate intercompany comparisons within the industry.

Inherent Limitations

In addition to the points noted above, it is important to remember that accounting has inherent limitations. The two most important limitations—limitations that no foreseeable improvement in accounting practice can overcome—are (1) accounting reports are necessarily monetary and (2) they are necessarily influenced by estimates of future events.

Accounting reports are limited to information that can be expressed in monetary terms. Nothing in the accounts explicitly describes the ability of the entity's personnel, the effectiveness of its organization, the impact of outside forces, or other nonmonetary information that is vital to the complete understanding of an entity.

Some accounting numbers are influenced by future events that cannot conceivably be foreseen; these numbers are necessarily estimates. The depreciation expense of the current period, for example, depends partly on how long the assets will be used in the future. The real significance of accounts receivable and the related item of sales revenue cannot be assessed until the number of credit customers who will not pay their bills is known. The actual value of inventory depends on what the goods can be sold for in the future. The possible impacts of contingent future events, such as the results of pending litigation, retroactive agreements on wage rates, and redetermination of profits on contracts, are not shown in the financial statements, although if material they should appear in a footnote.

In accounting, one refers to the *measurement* of income rather than to the *determination* of income. To determine is "to fix conclusively and authoritatively"; accounting cannot do this. A measurement, on the other hand, is an approximation, according to some agreed-upon measuring stick, and this is what accounting sets out to do.

MEANING OF THE FINANCIAL STATEMENTS

Preceding chapters have discussed in detail the treatment of specific items that are reported on the financial statements. With this discussion as background, we shall now attempt to summarize the meaning of each statement as a whole.

The Income Statement

The income statement is the dominant financial statement in the sense that when it comes to a choice between a fair income statement presentation and a fair balance sheet presentation, the decision is usually made in favor of the former. For example, those who advocate the LIFO inventory method do so in the belief that it provides a better measure of income than does FIFO, although they know that it can result in unrealistically low inventory amounts on the balance sheet. Many balance sheet items are simply the offsetting debits or credits for entries that were designed to measure revenues or expenses properly on the income statement. The deferred income tax item is the most notable example; although recorded as a liability, it does not in fact represent an obligation.

The income statement measures the changes in retained earnings that have occurred during the accounting period for whatever reason, except for the payment of dividends and infrequent other transactions. It does not necessarily reflect only the results of normal operations, since it also includes extraordinary transactions, the effect of accounting changes, the loss or gain on the disposal of assets, and even the loss or gain on the disposal of a major division.

In the majority of companies, the amount of revenues realized from the sale of goods and services can be measured within fairly close limits. Adjustments to gross revenue are necessary to provide for uncollectible accounts, warranty costs, and similar items; but the proper amount of such adjustments often can be estimated within a narrow range. In some companies, such as those that sell on an installment basis, the amount of revenue that should be recognized is more difficult to estimate.

Usually, the appropriate amounts of expenses that should be deducted from revenues are more difficult to measure than are the revenue items. Judgments about these matters can have an important influence on net income.

Capitalization. One important source of difficulty is the distinction between capital costs, product costs, and expenses. The effect on current income of expenditures made during the current period depends significantly on how these expenditures are classified. The difference is diagrammed in Illustration 14–1. Consider, for example, the expenditure of $1,000 for labor services. If the labor cost is incurred for selling, general, or administrative activities, it is an expense, and the entire $1,000 affects income of the current period. If the labor cost is incurred in manufacturing a product, it is a product cost, and the $1,000 affects income only in the period in which the product is sold. (The diagram assumes that 40 percent of the products are sold in the current year.) If the labor cost is incurred in building a depreciable asset, it is capitalized as part of the cost of the asset, and it affects net income over a succession of future

ILLUSTRATION 14–1
EFFECT ON INCOME OF ALTERNATIVE COST PRACTICES

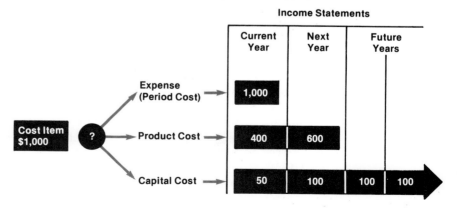

periods, as the cost is depreciated. Wide latitude exists as to which expenditures are to be capitalized and which are to be expensed. For those items that *are* capitalized, the amount to be charged as expense in a given period can vary widely depending on the estimate of service life and the method of depreciation, depletion, or amortization that is used.

Effect of Inflation. The expenses reported on the income statement are measured in terms of the acquisition cost of the resources used. In a period of inflation, acquisition cost is less than the current cost of the same resources. The amount of net income reported may therefore overstate the success of the business as measured in terms of current costs. This is particularly so in the case of depreciation expense, which may greatly understate the current cost of fixed assets used during the period. For this reason, net income is not an amount that is available for distribution to the shareholders. Part of the reported net income must be thought of as an amount necessary to replace existing assets with higher-cost assets.

> **Example.** Assume a company owns a single item of equipment, acquired at a cost of $1 million. Its service life is 10 years, and straight-line depreciation is used. For simplicity, ignore all other costs (including taxes). If the business earns revenues of $150,000 a year, its annual income will be $50,000 after the $100,000 annual depreciation expense. Over the 10-period, its income will total $500,000, and its operations will generate cash equal to the total revenues of $1.5 million (since the annual depreciation expense does not use cash). Suppose that instead of accumulating this much cash, the company only accumulates $1 million because each year it pays a dividend equal to reported income, that is, $50,000. If at the end of 10 years a replacement piece of equipment costs $1.3 million, the business will be $300,000 short of having enough cash to buy the replacement. By paying dividends over the 10-year period totaling $500,000, the business has reduced its operating capability and will have to raise $300,000 additional capital to restore this capability. With hindsight, it should have paid only $200,000 in dividends, not $500,000, if it wished to maintain is operating capability. Alternatively, one can say the comany's *distributable income* over this period was $200,000, which is much less than the reported net income of $500,000.[13]

Quality of Earnings. The reliability of the income statement as a report of the company's performance differs widely among various types of companies. Analysts make judgments about the impact of these differences and refer to the *quality of earnings* as reported on a given income statement as contrasted with the reported *amount* of earnings. The net income of a retail store that sells only for cash, has a high inventory turnover, and leases its building and equipment, is of high quality be-

---

[13]This example fully holds only if the company has no debt capital. If its debt/equity ratio is not zero, then its distributable income was more than $200,000 (but still less than $500,000).

cause the reported amount is relatively uninfluenced by estimates. By contrast, an income statement is of lower quality if it contains large items that require estimates of future events (such as depreciation expense), significant nonrecurring gains or losses, or changes in accounting principles.

Statement of Changes in Financial Position

The statement of changes in financial position, or funds flow statement, is a derived statement in the sense that it is prepared from data originally collected for the balance sheet or income statement. It shows the sources of additional funds that the business obtained during the period, and the purposes for which these funds were used. The information on this statement is not nearly so much affected by judgments about the capitalization of assets and the write-off of expenses as is the income statement. For example, the choices of depreciation method and service life can have a significant effect on net income, but they have no effect on the funds flow statement, because the amount of depreciation charged is neither a source nor a use of funds. This is the principal reason that financial analysts like the funds flow statement. It is much more definite, much less subject to judgmental decisions and to manipulation. It does not, however, show how net income was earned, and since net income is the best overall measure of how well the business has performed during the period, a funds flow statement is not a substitute for the income statement.

The Balance Sheet

In a very broad sense, the balance sheet can be viewed as a statement of resources controlled by an entity and of the sources of the funds used to acquire these resources. There is no single overall characterization that fits the individual balance sheet items, however. Rather, the balance sheet must be viewed as a collection of several types of items, with the amounts for each type being reported according to different concepts and the whole being tied together only in the mechanical sense that the sum of the debit balances equals the sum of the credit balances. The balance sheet is, therefore, literally a "sheet of balances." In terms of the method of measurement used, the principal types of balance sheet items are (1) monetary assets and liabilities, (2) unexpired costs, (3) inventories, (4) investments, and (5) other equities.

Monetary Items.   These items include cash and other assets that represent a specific monetary claim against some external party, and liabilities that represent a specific monetary obligation to some external party. Accounts receivable is a monetary asset. The amount that each customer owes is definite, and it is usually possible to estimate the amount of uncollectible accounts within fairly close limits. Marketable securities are usually considered to be monetary assets. Monetary assets are reported at essentially their current cash equivalent, and monetary liabilities (which include most liabilities) are reported at the current cash equivalent of the obligation.

Unexpired Costs. Property, plant and equipment, intangible assets, prepaid expenses, and deferred charges are initially recorded at acquisition cost, and (except for land) are charged off as expenses in a succession of future accounting periods. Amounts reported on a given balance sheet, therefore, are amounts that have not yet been charged off. The balance sheet is the "temporary home" of these costs until the time comes for them to appear as expenses on an income statement.

Inventories. These assets are reported at the lower of cost or market value. Except for the recognition of market value when it is below cost, inventories are reported in the same way as other unexpired costs.

Investments. Investments in other-than-marketable securities are usually owned in order to exercise control over another company. Special rules govern the way in which they are reported, as described in Chapter 11.

Other Equities. These include deferred income taxes, which is an item that arises as a consequence of the procedure that matches income tax expense with reported net income, and which definitely is not a claim by the government against the business. They also include redeemable preferred stock and the owners' equity section of the balance sheet. The amount shown in the owners' equity section is strictly a residual. It arises from the net effect of the methods of measurement used for the other items. In particular, for reasons indicated above, the retained earnings amount does not indicate the amount that is available for payment of dividends.

Omissions. The balance sheet does not show all the valuable things that a business controls, nor all its obligations. It does not show the value of an entity's human resources, the value of new products or processes that result from research and development activities, or the value of future revenues that will result from current expenditures for advertising and sales promotion. The liabilities side obviously cannot report contingencies that the accountant does not know about, such as the costs involved in recalling a product that is subsequently found to be defective, or the cost of complying with pollution control regulations that were not in existence when a plant was built. In extreme cases, these unknowns can bankrupt a company when they come to light.

SUMMARY

In addition to the financial statements, the annual report contains the auditors' opinion, which states that the underlying records have been examined and that the information is fair, consistent, and conforms to generally accepted accounting principles. The annual report contains explanatory notes, and may contain additional information about the company.

Although accounting principles are developed in accordance with three criteria and 11 basic concepts, these principles permit considerable latitude in the treatment of transactions. Also, accounting reports are necessarily influenced by judgments. A business is a complicated organism, and no set of numbers can convey an accurate picture of its activities or its status.

The income statement reports revenues and expenses measured in accordance with accounting principles. It does not report the economic "well-offness" of the business, primarily because expenses are measured in terms of historical cost rather than current cost. The statement of changes in financial position is less affected by estimates and a company's practices with respect to the matching concept than is the income statement. Balance sheet items are reported under a variety of measurement concepts.

SUGGESTIONS FOR FURTHER READING

Bernstein, Leopold A. *Financial Statement Analysis. Theory, Application, and Interpretation.* Rev. ed. Homewood, Ill.: Richard D. Irwin, 1978.

Hendricksen, Eldon S. *Accounting Theory.* 4th ed. Homewood, Ill.: Richard D. Irwin, 1982.

Meyer, Philip E. *Applied Accounting Theory.* Homewood, Ill.: Richard D. Irwin, 1980.

Most, Kenneth S. *Accounting Theory.* 2d ed. Columbus, Ohio: Grid Publishing, 1982.

Staubus, George J. *Making Accounting Decisions.* Houston: Scholars Book Company, 1977.

Cases

CASE 14–1   Evans Corporation

Professor Harold Evans was preparing an examination for his financial accounting course. He has put together a problem that covers the essential topics studied thus far in the course. As his student grader and assistant, he has asked you to work through the problem and prepare the solution to be used in grading. The problem starts with the beginning-of-year balance sheet for Evans Corporation:

EVANS CORPORATION
Balance Sheet
As of January 1

Assets

Cash.	$ 7,500
Inventory	15,000
Total current assets	22,500
Property, plant, and equipment	22,500
Less: Accum. depreciation	7,500
Net fixed assets.	15,000
Total assets	$37,500

Equities

Accounts payable.	$15,000
Total current liabilities.	15,000
Capital stock	15,000
Retained earnings.	7,500
Total owners' equity	22,500
Total equities	$37,500

Following this balance sheet, Professor Evans has listed 11 items that summarize the events of the year. These are:

1. Net sales for the year amounted to $37,500. Of this amount, $22,500 was collected in cash and $15,000 was outstanding at year-end. The inventory sold had a book value of $19,500.

2. A customer deposit of $3,000—on merchandise not yet shipped—was received by the company in the fourth quarter.

3. Accounts payable in the amount of $12,000 were paid during the year.

4. $15,000 worth of additional inventory was purchased on account during the year.

5. The firm borrowed $15,000 on July 1. The debt was represented by renewable, 14 percent, 90-day notes. The entire amount was outstanding at year-end while interest of $525 was paid during the first week of October.

6. During the course of the year, the following cash costs were incurred and paid:

469

a. Selling and administrative—$4,500.

b. Cost of preparing inventory for sale—$7,500.

7. A three-year insurance policy was purchased on January 1 for cash at a cost of $450.

8. The company received an out-of-court settlement of $4,500 (net of legal costs) as a result of legal action instituted four years earlier. This related to an antitrust suit against one of the suppliers to the company. The auditor's opinion on the financial statements of the company four years earlier had been qualified as a result of this lawsuit.

9. An uninsured loss of $4,500 in inventory resulted from an early-morning fire.

10. Depreciation in the amount of $1,500 for book purposes and $3,000 for tax purposes was to be taken for the year.

11. The tax rate to be used in the problem is 50 percent on all taxable income.

Questions

1. Prepare journal entries for the year.

2. Set up, and post, a set of T-accounts for use in collecting, summarizing, and rearranging the year's transactions.

3. Prepare a balance sheet for Evans Corporation as of December 31.

4. Prepare an income statement for the year ending December 31. How will this differ from the income statement submitted with the firm's tax return?

5. Prepare a cash flow statement for the year ending December 31.

CASE 14–2 Clover Lunch

In mid-1982, Mr. and Mrs. Robert Matthews decided to go into the restaurant business. Mr. Matthews was dissatisfied with his job as cook in a restaurant where he earned $5.75 an hour. During July 1982, the Matthews found a business that seemed to be what they wanted. This was the Clover Lunch, a lunch counter located in Fisher's Department Store in a working-class section of town. The Clover Lunch was operated under a lease with the department store; only the equipment was actually the property of the operator of the lunchroom. The equipment was old, but Mr. Matthews thought that it was in fairly good condition.

The couple opened negotiations with the current lunchroom operator and quickly reached an agreement to take over the lease and equipment on September 1, and to pay the operator a price of $5,800. Of this price, Mr. Matthews estimated that $2,600 represented the fair value of the equipment. The lease expired on August 31, 1983, and was renewable for three years if Fisher's consented. Under the terms of the lease, Fisher's furnished space, heat, light, and water, and the operators (i.e., the Matthews) paid Fisher's 15 percent of gross receipts as rent.

The Matthews paid the $5,800 from their personal savings account and also transferred $2,900 to a checking account that they opened in the name of Clover Lunch.

Shortly after they started operations,

the cooking range broke down. The Matthews thereupon sold the range for $231 (which was approximately its estimated value as a part of the $2,600) and purchased a new range for $2,300. It was installed immediately, and they paid $347 for its installation. The coffee urn also broke down, but Mr. Matthews was able to repair it himself by working 16 hours one Sunday.

Early in 1983, the Matthews called in a firm that specialized in making out reports for small businesses and requested financial statements for Clover Lunch for the period ended December 31, 1982. From their cash register and checkbook, they had the following figures:

The Matthews also explained to the accountant that the cash receipts of $18,554 included $2,100 received from the sale of 140 "coupon books" at $15 each. Each book contained coupons with a face value of $17, which could be used to pay for meals. As of December 31, coupons with a face value of $1,500 had been used to pay for meals; therefore, coupons with a face value of $880 were still outstanding.

Questions

1. Prepare a balance sheet as of December 31, 1982, and an income statement and cash flow statement for the four-month

Cash receipts:	
Cash receipts from customers	$18,554
Sale of cooking range	231
Total cash receipts	$18,785
Cash disbursements:	
Food and supplies	$ 7,985
City restaurant license, valid September 1, 1982, to August 31, 1983	125
15 percent rent paid to Fisher's for September, October, and November	1,936
New cooking range	2,300
Installation of cooking range	347
Other operating expenses	50
Withdrawals for personal use	2,167
Total cash disbursements	$14,910

Before going home on December 31, the Matthews had estimated the value of food and supplies then on hand to be about $422 at cost.

Early in January, they paid two bills, the December meat bill of $499 and the December rent of $847.

period ending December 31, 1982. Explain briefly your treatment of the coupon books and of anything else you believe needs comment.

2. Comment briefly on the significant information revealed by your financial statements.

CASE 14–3   Limited Editions, Inc.

If you haven't learned to love it by 1987, we'll buy it back at the original price.

The above statement appeared as the prominent headline in a Limited Editions, Inc., advertisement placed in a monthly magazine catering to a select, high-income readership. Its intent was to announce the company's new porcelain figurine, "Foxes in Spring," which would be offered in limited quantities at a price of $2,000. Limited Editions' idea was to offer literally "a beautiful investment opportunity" with capital gains potential to a wealthy investor. By guaranteeing that production would be limited, the figurines could immediately attain status similar to an antique.

The guarantee offered by Limited was quite simple:

> Subject to being in its original condition, we guarantee to repurchase any of our "Foxes in Spring" figurines at the original price of $2,000 at any time after five years from the date of purchase.

The guarantee was not restricted to the original purchaser and hence was transferable from one party to another. The only other return provision allowed a purchaser to recieve an 80 percent refund of the purchase price if the figurine was returned within three months from the date of purchase.

The figurines were offered for sale in only one extremely reputable store in each of 10 large American cities. These stores were individually identified in the advertisement. Each of the 10 was provided with one "Foxes in Spring" figurine to be used for display. It was informally understood that Limited Editions would not ask for the return of the figurine. The stores otherwise had no inventory. When a customer signed a "subscription request," the store forwarded it to Limited Editions. The "subscription" was an indication of interest but carried no contractual obligation on the part of the buyer. Limited would fill the subscription by shipping directly to the cus-

tomer. Upon notification of shipment, the retail store would then bill the customer. Upon collection, the store deducted its 10 percent commission and forwarded the net amount of $1,800 to Limited Editions. If a figurine was returned in the first three months, Limited Editions simply sent an 80 percent refund ($1,600) to the customer. Limited Editions did not request a refund of the 10 percent sales commission from the retail store.

Production of "Foxes in Spring" was strictly limited to 500 pieces. The design of the figurine and the mold from which it would be produced were created by an artist for a fee of $50,000. This fee was paid in 1982. Production was contracted out to a reputable company, which agreed to run batches of 100 pieces upon instructions from Limited Editions. When a batch was produced, each figurine was then hand painted and finished by skilled workers. Because of the extremely high-quality standards demanded by Limited Editions, the early batches cost substantially more to produce, paint, and finish than did the latter batches. Figurine statistics for 1982 are shown in Exhibit 1. Production cost data are summarized in Exhibit 2.

Limited Editions, Inc., was incorporated in June 1982. The stock was sold

EXHIBIT 1
STATISTICS FOR 1982

	Number
Figurines produced.	400
Figurine subscriptions received	320
Figurines shipped to customers	290
Figurines sent to retailers for display	10
Figurines returned	0
Figurines in inventory	100
Figurines for which cash was collected by December 31, 1982	240
Figurines shipped but not paid for by December 31, 1982	50

EXHIBIT 2
BATCH PRODUCTION DATA

Batch	Date	Units	Cost	Average Cost per Unit
1	July 1982	100	$100,000	$1,000
2	September 1982	100	80,000	800
3	October 1982	100	60,000	600
4	December 1982*	100	40,000	400
5	March 1983†	100	20,000	200

*The manufacturer was paid for the December shipment in January 1983.
†As of December 31, 1982, Limited Editions was not really sure what the last batch of 100 figurines would cost. The $20,000 ultimately paid would have been a reasonable estimate as of December 31, 1982.

for $10,000. One half of the stock was owned by a small, diversified, over-the-counter company engaged in a variety of businesses, and the other half was owned by a small number of venture capitalists who played on active role in managing the company. The venture capitalists' interest in Limited Editions, Inc., was in part nurtured by the widely publicized success stories of companies like The Franklin Mint[1] that capitalized on the public's recent interest in "collector items" as an investment hedge against inflation. Both the management and the owners of Limited Editions hoped to build the company into a leader in this new, unexploited figurine market. Encouraged by the apparent success of the company's first figurine, management was already making plans for a number of future offerings.

Design and production began in July 1982; promotion in September; and sales in October. The bulk of 1982 sales appeared to be related to the year-end Christmas season. Of the 290 figurines shipped to customers in 1982, 100 were to shareholders (or members of their families). Since these sales were not made through a retail dealer, the full $2,000 purchase price was received in cash by Limited Editions. Of the 190 pieces shipped to nonrelated parties, cash had been received by year-end from the retailers for 140 pieces. None of the 190 pieces was returned in 1982, but 20 of them were returned early in 1983, some after the three-month period had expired. Each of the 20 customers was promptly paid the $1,600 refund.

Promotional and advertising costs of $25,000 were paid in 1982. Limited Editions planned to do no further advertising of "Foxes in Spring" in 1983. General and administrative expenses for 1982 were $50,000, and all these expenses were paid in cash before year-end. It was expected that these costs would continue at roughly the same level in future years.

_____
[1]The Franklin Mint, traded on the New York Stock Exchange, was recognized as one of the leading producers of limited edition collectibles. Its issues included commemorative and art medals in silver and gold, sculptures in pewter and bronze, deluxe leather bound books, and works of art in fine crystal.

Question

Prepare an income statement and cash flow statement for 1982, and a balance sheet as of December 31, 1982. You may ignore income taxes.

CASE 14–4   Royal Crest, Inc.

The Houston office of Ogilby, Mc-Kinnon & Co., a large national accounting firm, had been engaged to review the 1976 financial statements of Royal Crest, Inc., for purposes of rendering an opinion on the Form 10-K report to the SEC and the Annual Report to Shareholders. The accounting firm had been the auditors for Royal Crest, a leading manufacturer and distributor of citizens' band radios and other communications equipment, since January 1972. There had been very good relations between the auditors and Royal Crest management in prior audits. However, near the completion of the 1976 audit, a question was raised as to the proper valuation of the citizens' band radio inventory which produced opposing views. The financial statements in question are shown in Exhibits 1 and 2.

The Citizens' Band.   In 1958, the U.S. Federal Communications Commission (FCC) allocated part of the AM shortwave radio band as a "citizens' band" (CB) to be used for local, personal, and business communication. This part of the AM band had been previously unusable by radio amateurs for long-distance communication because of heavy natural interference. The FCC assured that the CB band would not be used for long-distance transmission by limiting the maximum transmitter power to four watts, far less than the 250-watt signal used by the smallest commercial AM radio stations. To offset its stringent technical limitations, the FCC removed almost all legal barriers to access the CB airwaves. The only application requirements were a $4 license application fee and that the applicant be at least 18 years of age.

Until 1974, the CB radio was used primarily by businesses that needed a method of communication between a home office and a vehicle. Also, many long-haul truckers used CBs to share in-

EXHIBIT 1

ROYAL CREST, INC.
Income Statement

	Year Ended August 31	
	1976 (unaudited)	1975
Net sales.	$72,143,451	$26,123,929
Cost of sales	43,411,164	16,198,173
Gross profit	28,732,287	9,925,756
Expenses:		
Selling and advertising	10,921,566	2,212,009
General and administrative	4,442,103	2,247,801
Interest	522,722	565,712
	15,886,391	5,025,522
Earnings before income taxes	12,845,896	4,900,234
Income taxes	1,764,360	2,047,713
Net earnings	$11,081,536	$ 2,852,521
Earnings per share	$8.76	$2.57
Average common shares outstanding	1,265,367	1,110,386

EXHIBIT 2

ROYAL CREST, INC.
Balance Sheet

	August 31	
	1976 (unaudited)	1975
Assets		
Current assets:		
Cash and temporary investments	$ 1,972,496	$ 313,861
Marketable equity securities (market value $771,500)	762,450	
Accounts receivable (net)	12,434,941	6,072,787
Inventories (see Note A below)	18,411,680	6,283,383
Other	61,678	22,874
Total current assets	33,643,245	12,692,905
Property, plant, and equipment (at cost)	6,073,765	3,385,946
Less: Accumulated depreciation and amortization	(1,551,784)	(1,161,888)
	4,521,981	2,224,058
Other assets and deferred charges	262,661	262,610
Total assets	$38,427,887	$15,179,573
Liabilities and Stockholders' Equity		
Current liabilities:		
Notes payable to bank	$ 7,398,619	$ 3,281,373
Current maturities on long-term debt	85,797	167,346
Accounts payable	7,009,786	3,175,270
Accrued expenses	1,300,231	763,766
Income taxes payable	182,634	2,001,420
Total current liabilities	15,977,067	9,389,175
Long-term portion of long-term debt	1,000,291	1,640,901
Deferred income taxes	136,206	58,905
Total liabilities	17,113,564	11,088,981
Stockholders' equity:		
Capital stock	7,615,254	825,572
Retained earnings	13,699,069	3,265,020
Total liabilities and stockholders' equity	$38,427,887	$15,179,573

Note A:	Antennas and Accessories	CB Radios	
Inventories:			
Finished goods	$ 369,218	$ 8,025,641	
Work in process	966,596	2,701,010	
Raw materials	857,386	5,134,181	
	$2,193,200	$15,860,832	$18,054,032
Supplies			357,648
Total			$18,411,680

formation with each other. The oil embargo and resultant fuel shortage of 1974, however, changed the usage of the CB radio. During the fuel shortage, truckers informed each other via CB of the availability of diesel fuel. Some motorists, noticing that truckers always seemed to know where to find fuel, learned about the truckers' secret weapon and began to use it themselves. The general public soon realized the usefulness of the CB in obtaining highway information in emergencies, or simply for companionship.

The surge in consumer demand was evident in the number of CB applications received by the FCC, which in the first 8 months of 1974 equaled the total number filed in the previous 15 years. Requests for CB licenses hit an all-time high in January 1976, following the unprecedented Christmas sales the month before. As of November 1, 1976, approximately seven million CB licenses had been granted by the FCC since 1958. Industry experts felt that this number understated the actual number of CB radios in use, because not all CB operators complied with the license requirement.

The Product. A CB radio is a transceiver, that is, it is equipped to both send and receive messages. Various solid-state circuits and a speaker are required to receive the signal and make it audible to the user. A microphone, additional circuits, and a transformer are needed to convert the human voice to a radio signal and transmit it. Finally, a tuner and several quartz crystals are necessary to allow selection of a desired channel. All of these parts were available from a number of suppliers. Also, the assembly of the CB radio was quite simple and required no elaborate equipment or skilled labor. Firms with small amounts of capital and a sufficient supply of semiskilled labor therefore could easily establish themselves in the CB business. Because of this ease of entry, from 1958 to 1974 several foreign firms entered the industry and soon dominated it, producing some 80 percent of the U.S. demand. Few U.S. firms remained in the production end of the CB industry, and those that did catered to a small group of hobbyists.

When the demand for CBs spurted in 1974, many U.S. firms did not have adequate production facilities and thus had to rely heavily on Japanese manufacturing firms for radios built to the U.S. companies' design specifications. It was impossible, though, for any CB manufacturer, foreign or domestic, to keep pace with the skyrocketing demand. Inventories of component parts—particularly the 12 to 14 high-precision quartz crystals necessary to tune the radio to the correct frequencies—were insufficient. Also, production facilities, which had been geared to a much lower demand level, fell far short of total capacity required to meet demand. Thus, throughout 1974–75, there was a major shortage of CBs.

By 1976, new production facilities for both CB radios and components had started operations. More importantly, a technological break through called "phase-locked-loop" design used semiconductors to replace all but three of the quartz crystals. These events eased the shortage. Also, since the United States was a leader in semiconductor technology, more CB production plants opened in the United States to capitalize on this new technology that significantly reduced the domestic manufacturing cost of CB radios.

Marketing. The marketing of CBs was probably least affected by the changes wrought in 1974. Most producers sold their products through some 20 manufacturers' representatives to hundreds of small dealers, many of whom carried several competing CB lines. All sales to dealers were made with the right to return goods to the manufacturer.

During the 1974–75 shortage, some CB manufacturers began to allocate their monthly production to the representatives and let them assume the responsibility to distribute the radios to their dealers as they saw fit. The allocation formulas used by both manufacturers and representatives were complicated by the fact that many astute dealers had deliberately overordered and/or placed duplicate orders with different companies in anticipation of insufficient deliveries of radios to keep their inventories well stocked.

Sales to the ultimate consumer were almost always handled by the dealer. Most radios sold in the $100–$250 price range, with the price of a typical CB averaging $150. Installation and accessories, especially antennas, were extra. It was common practice for manufacturers to provide a 90-day warranty against malfunction of the radio, but some gave warranties of up to one year's duration. Repairs under the warranty agreement were usually performed by local "factory-authorized" shops.

The Industry. The growth in the number of companies involved in the manufacture or sales of CBs paralleled the increased popularity of the CB itself. The number of manufacturers or importers of CB radios stood at 15 by 1974, at 30 by 1975, and at anywhere from 45 to 60 by the end of 1976. Most of these companies were dependent on Japanese products, but a growing number, for technological, promotional, or logistical reasons, were increasing their domestic manufacturing capability. Competition was keen, and products were differentiated on the bases of quality, price, service, technical features, "gadgets" (such as digital channel number readout), and duration of warranties.

Until 1975, most U.S. firms involved in CB production and/or distribution lacked substantial financial or technological resources. With the exception of Radio Shack, most companies were small, undercapitalized, and obviously beneficiaries of being "in the right place at the right time."

A number of the small firms took advantage of the soaring demand by making large stock offerings to an eager Wall Street—some "going public" for the first time—to obtain needed capital for growth and expansion. By 1975, however, large established companies with strong financial resources began to enter the CB industry, attracted by the smaller companies' soaring profits and the vast potential market. Some industry observers felt that the smaller firms might actually benefit because of the infusion of advertising and development money the larger companies would make. Although this would increase competition, it would also improve the quality of the product and further heighten public awareness of CBs. However, a number of financial analysts who followed the industry felt that several of the smaller companies would be unable to take the financial strain of this competition and that a "shakeout" of the industry would occur—particularly when supply caught up with demand.

Royal Crest, Inc. Royal Crest, Inc. was founded in Corpus Christi, Texas, in 1967, by two brothers, William and Robert Hopkins, who previously owned an electronic parts distributorship. Initially, the firm manufactured principally radio and television antennas in a plant located in Mexico. This manufacturing strategy provided advantages of lower duties than those imposed on Japanese goods, and lower transportation costs. Sales blossomed from $300,000 in the first year to $2.5 million by 1970, and profit rose to $500,000 before taxes by the latter date.

At that time, William Hopkins proposed that Royal Crest expand its product line to include two-way communications equipment, principally CB radios. Not only would their Mexican production strategy be equally applicable to this endeavor, but because of the popularity of Royal Crest antennas, distributors and retailers would readily provide shelf space to other products carrying the Royal Crest brand name. After negotiation of a $1 million loan with Houston banks and some 18 months' work expanding the Mexican facility, Royal Crest CBs were on the shelves of U.S. dealers. Through 1972 and 1973, sales were somewhat lower than expected but were still encouraging. By 1974, however, the "boom" had begun and a second production shift had to be added to the Mexican plant in September to keep up with demand. In 1975, though, two production shifts could no longer meet demand, and the Hopkins brothers were forced to contract with a major Japanese firm for part of their needs, at least until a major expansion could be made to the Mexican plant. They realized that this temporary strategy eliminated their cost advantage, but, given the "seller's market," they felt that this deviation was advisable.

These conditions prevailed until early 1976, when supply and demand began to equilibrate. At the same time the major expansion of the Mexican plant, which was partially financed by the firm's first public stock offering in August 1975, was completed. Soon, dealers finding themselves receiving full shipments of CB radios from several companies at once began returning all or portions of the shipments to the manufacturers.

The FCC Decision. From the beginning of the CB craze, the entire industry had been petitioning the FCC for an increase in the number of channels available for CB traffic. The industry feared that the 23 existing CB channels would become so congested that they would become virtually unusable, which could eventually lead to the industry's demise. On July 27, 1976, the FCC ruled that:

1. The number of CB radio channels would be increased from 23 to 40, effective January 1, 1977.
2. The new 40-channel CB radios could not be sold until January 1, 1977, and the FCC would not approve any 40-channel radio designs until November 1, 1976. Therefore, manufacturers who entered the models into production before that date ran the risk that the product would be unmarketable.
3. Current inventories of 23-channel CBs could be "retrofitted" to conform to the new 40-channel standards, but radios already sold to final users could not be remanufactured. After intense pressure by CB manufacturers, the FCC withdrew its decision prohibiting the remanufacture of previously sold radios. As a result, several manufacturers, including Royal Crest, offered CB purchasers the option of sending their radios back to the company for remanufacture at a cost of $25 to $30.

The FCC's decision sent shock waves through the industry because it had only four months to design and build workable prototypes of new 40-channel models. But public reaction to the announcement created an even bigger shock. Since new radios with expanded channel capacities were authorized by the FCC, there was a great deal of uncertainty among customers as to the purchase of 23-channel radios. Sales to consumers began to fall noticeably. Distributors, already canceling duplicate purchase orders because of oversupply, further canceled orders and returned merchandise to manufacturers due to the drop in demand. Also, panicking, some dealers and manufacturers slashed prices. In early October 1976, the following was reported in a well-known publication:

> Prices on the once costly CB units have now come down well below the $100 mark, and some mass merchandisers have shocked old CBers with prices below $60. Profit margins for retailers that were once in the 35% area are now dissolving rapidly.[1]

The FCC decision and its aftermath could not have caught Royal Crest at a worse time. Like others in the industry, they were finishing production of 23-channel CB radios for the peak Christmas season ahead. Also, they had recently entered into an agreement with their Japanese supplier for an additional 2,000 CB radios. Technically, they could still cancel the shipment, but the Japanese manufacturers had made it clear to the entire CB industry that cancellation (which forced the supplier to take the loss) could result in the permanent severance of relations between that supplier and the U.S. buyer. The Hopkins brothers felt this risk was too great because a secondary source of supply might be necessary for 40-channel CB radios, especially if demand for them was equal to the 1975 demand for 23-channel CBs. Thus, a shipment of now-unwanted CBs came in from Japan to Royal Crest's central warehouse.

It was this situation that Royal Crest's auditors had to assess as they reviewed the annual financial statements for the fiscal year ending August 31, 1976.

---

[1]"Some CB Marketers Buck the Trend," *Advertising Age,* October 4, 1976.

The 1976 Audit. On October 10, Ogilby, McKinnon & Co., began the final steps in their annual audit. Within a few days, Mary Lynch, one of the senior accountants on the audit engagement, was alerted by one of the junior staff auditors of a potential trouble spot, namely, Royal Crest's inventory of 23-channel CB radios. On August 31, the company had accumulated some $8 million worth of radios in their warehouse and factory. This amount exceeded the cost of the radios they had sold in the entire fourth quarter (see Exhibit 3 for the fiscal 1976 quarterly results). Furthermore, unit sales had been dropping steadily since that date, even though Royal Crest had marked down their selling price some 30 percent. After performing some rough computations, Lynch determined that at current prices, a minor write-down of the ending inventory valuation might be necessary. (Approximate sales price and production cost breakdowns are provided in Exhibit 4.) However, given the tremendous competition in the market and the apparent glut of 23-channel CBs within the industry's distribution channels, she doubted whether current prices were a realistic yardstick by which to measure the inventory's net realizable value.

In considering the problem, Lynch soon realized that it would be quite difficult to convince Royal Crest management to go along with any write-down proposal. Not only would a write-down be based on subjective estimates of future events—which had often proved wrong in this flourishing industry—but management had two strong incentives to fight the proposal. First, because the capital needs for the planned 40-channel radio operations were made more critical by the slumping 23-channel radio sales, Royal Crest was currently negotiating a

EXHIBIT 3

ROYAL CREST, INC.
Fiscal 1976 Quarterly Results (Unaudited)

	11/30/75	2/28/76	5/31/76	8/31/76
Net sales	$13,991,415	$19,974,501	$26,474,981	$11,702,554
Cost of sales	7,731,410	11,580,922	15,555,017	8,543,815
Gross profit	6,260,005	8,393,579	10,919,964	3,158,739
Operating expenses	2,244,285	3,410,236	4,829,304	5,402,566
Earnings (loss) before income taxes	4,015,720	4,983,343	6,090,660	(2,243,827)
Income taxes	515,531	252,698	762,668	233,463
Net earnings (loss)	$ 3,500,189	$ 4,730,645	$ 5,327,992	$ (2,477,290)
Earnings (loss) per share	$2.96	$4.01	$3.95	($1.81)

EXHIBIT 4
SALES PRICE AND COST BREAKDOWNS

Retail selling price, average CB radio	$150–$160
Average dealer cost (manufacturer's selling price)	$100
Gross margin (of manufacturer)	38%
Average manufacturing cost/unit	$62
Materials and overhead	$45.50
Labor...................5 hours @ $3.30 =	16.50
	$62.00

large increase in its unsecured line of credit with its Houston banks. In addition to the requirement that the company have an unqualified auditors' report, the current bank agreement also required that Royal Crest maintain a current ratio of two to one. Second, the company was exploring, on a preliminary basis, the possibility of acquiring a small manufacturer of two-way office intercom systems through a swap of its common stock.

Lynch attempted to resolve the inventory write-down issue by investigating common industry practice. However, most other firms in the industry had December 31 year-ends, well beyond the date by which Royal Crest's statements had to be prepared.

After discussions with her audit manager, Lynch decided that a write-down of the 23-channel CB radio inventory should be brought to the attention of manage-

ment. Thus, on November 8, she approached Will Hopkins to gain his views on a write-down and the following exchange occurred:

Lynch: We're tremendously concerned about your inventory of 23-channel CBs. By current valuation, on August 31 you had over $8 million in finished CBs in stock, and your margins on them had declined to about 15 percent above your cost. And the price deterioration has continued, as you well know. Even that $10 gross margin has just about evaporated. Frankly, with the intense competition in the industry and all those radios on the verge of becoming obsolete, I can see only one direction for the gross margin—down! We are beginning to think that a substantial write-down to realizable value may be necessary—on the order of $1 to $2 million—to state the inventory value fairly.

Hopkins: A write-down? Well, Mary, I think you've forgotten some important details.

First, even though we've had some cancellations of Christmas orders, we don't think the holiday sales period will be all that bad at current price levels. The worst of the price deterioration is behind us.

Lynch: But what if one of the shakier companies dumps its inventory on the market to raise cash?

Hopkins: It's possible, but I doubt it. By now, any company with serious intentions of staying in the CB business has arranged credit to finance production of the 40s. Those companies that were strapped for cash would have dumped long ago, as some did. Besides, have you seen the sales figures we've put together on those 40s?

Lynch: Yes.

Hopkins: Well, then, you know we expect to sell the 40-channel rigs at about 25 percent more than the suggested retail on our current line—some $40 more than the 23-channel rigs were selling for before they were discounted! I have a feeling a lot of people will think twice before paying those higher prices. A lot of 23-channel rigs will sell, at current prices, on that basis. Besides, its not like the 40-channel CBs are going to materialize magically on store shelves on January 1. We haven't begun building sets yet, and we're not going to until we get our design tested and accepted by the FCC. By the time we get the 40-channel rigs off the assembly line, catalogs printed for our sales reps, and the CBs into the stores, it probably won't be earlier than February or maybe March. So there are going to be three additional months where the 23-channel rigs won't have competition from the 40s.

Also, we can remanufacture the 23s we have in stock to accommodate 40 channels for about $25. And, come to think of it, a lot of them aren't even going to need to be remanufactured. The only places where the 23 channels are congested are in the metropolitan areas which have high population densities. But in rural areas, folks don't need 40 channels! In fact, a lot of them in rural areas don't even need 23. And we sell a lot of sets in those areas. Why, the Midwest and South are our best sales territories! So, we fully expect to sell them off, either by remanufacture or as-is, quickly and without further price reductions.

Lynch: I doubt that you can sell remanufactured sets for the same price you could sell new 40-channel sets.

Hopkins: True, but we won't have to give them away, either. Don't forget that technology is on our side; that new phase-locked-loop design has lowered our material costs 40 percent.

Lynch: I understand what you're saying, but I still have a few problems. The 23-channel radios are the only CBs on the market now. Everyone knows the 40s can't be sold for another two months or so, and I'm sure some customers have been told by dealers, who are as anxious as you are to be rid of the 23s, that it'll be even longer than that. Nevertheless, the 23s don't seem to be selling.

Also, why are customers going to buy 23s in January or February when the delivery date on the 40s is even closer? They're probably waiting for the higher-priced product if they haven't bought a CB by December 31.

I just can't see margins on the 23s staying where they are, bad though they may be. I really believe that there has been a material economic loss on these sets and they should be written down.

Hopkins: Look, I'll grant you I'm speculating a little, but so are you. Neither of us can say with precision what the public's going to do. I just can't see that profit margins will decline so much further that we need to write the inventory down now.

Lynch: Well, you know my position. Let me look into this situation some more and discuss it with members of my firm and I'll get back to you.

Hopkins: Well that's fine so long as you communicate my position to them. Time is running short. In fact, I'm on my way over to Houston now to meet with the banks. They are really anxious to see the audited 1976 statements.

Two other brief discussions were held in the next few days, but neither position changed significantly. On November 15, Mary Lynch received a call from William Hopkins.

Hopkins: I thought I'd let you know about a couple of items that came to my attention in the last few days, Mary. First, I received a November 8 press release from Electronic Industries Association, our trade association, predicting that sales of 23s will rise in the next couple of months after our minidepression last summer.

Also, there was a piece in the November 15 *Electronic News* about inventory write-downs in the CB industry. I'll admit I'm a bit surprised, because a few major companies are taking write-downs; but there's a pretty substantial amount of evidence that backs up my position too. In fact, there was something in the article I forgot to mention before. We have been looking into sales of our radios in Canada. Canada's staying with the 23-channel rigs, and we expect to work off a lot of our inventory there. So there's even less need for a write-down in my opinion.

Lynch: I've seen the EIA piece, but I haven't seen that article. Could you send me a copy?

Hopkins: Sure, I'll put it in the mail today!

As promised, the next day the article arrived in the mail. What Will Hopkins had told Lynch over the phone was true. There was backing in the article for his position. But there was an equal amount of support for her own stand on the matter, as evidenced by several companies' substantial inventory write-downs. Also, the article raised a question as to whether even those were sufficient. Though the trade association had indeed predicted increased sales, there was little, if any, backing for their claims contained in the article. Neither article, in effect, settled anything, and Lynch was placed in even more of a quandary as to the proper course of action in the situation.

Questions

1. What additional steps should Mary Lynch take in completing the Royal Crest audit?
2. If you were William Hopkins, what additional steps would you take if the auditors insist on a write-down?
3. Should the value of the inventory be written down? How would you prepare the adjustment?
4. How would you phrase your auditors' opinion if the inventory were not written down?

CASE 14–5 SafeCard Services, Inc.

In 1981, SafeCard Services, Inc., had as its primary business a credit card loss notification service called Hot-Line. For an annual fee of $12, SafeCard would immediately notify the customer's credit card issuers (i.e., American Express, Visa, oil companies, department stores, and so on) if the customer's credit cards were stolen or otherwise lost. This Hot-Line service was marketed through direct-mail advertising campaigns in conjunction with the credit card services of major oil companies (e.g., Gulf and ARCO), department stores (including Sears and J. C. Penney), banks, and others—about 75 credit card issuers in total.

SafeCard's marketing approach was as follows. First, the customer of a credit card issuer was sent a description of the Hot-Line service. This description explained that the Hot-Line customer would keep on file with SafeCard a list of all of his or her credit cards. SafeCard provided a toll-free number through which a customer could inform SafeCard if some or all of the customer's credit cards became lost. SafeCard would then immediately notify the issuers of the lost cards to cease honoring them and would assist the customer in obtaining replacement cards. Second, the prospective Hot-Line customer was offered six months of free Hot-Line service. If this offer were accepted, at the end of the six months the credit card issuer (e.g., Gulf Oil) through which SafeCard had reached the prospect would bill the customer $12 to continue the service for another year. At this point, the customer could either cancel the service or could pay the $12 to continue it. About 50 percent paid to continue the service after their six-month free trial. Those who did subscribe in this way were automatically billed by the credit card issuer every 12 months to renew the service for another year. According to SafeCard, about 80 percent of a year's paid subscribers renewed the service for the following year.

SafeCard incurred substantial costs in obtaining new customers, primarily for direct-mail descriptive materials and postage. Until fiscal 1980, SafeCard capitalized these costs of obtaining *new* subscribers and amortized them over three years. Beginning in fiscal 1980, SafeCard extended the amortization period to 10 years, using an accelerated amortization pattern that was essentially the same as 250 percent declining balance. Thus, after five years, each $100 of initially capitalized marketing cost would have been written down to about $24.

When a new subscriber signed up for a year's *paid* Hot-Line service, or when a subscriber renewed for another year, SafeCard debited Accounts Receivable for $12, credited about 80 percent of this amount to Customers' Advance Payments, and credited the remainder to Allowance for Cancellations.

SafeCard also paid an annual commission to the credit card issuing company through which SafeCard had secured the subscription. This commission compensated the issuing company for its services in billing and collecting the $12 annual fee. The commission was deducted by the credit card company from the subscription revenues it remitted to Safe-Card. When SafeCard received a payment from a credit card company, it debited Cash for the actual cash proceeds and debited Prepaid Direct Marketing Costs for the commission (i.e., the two debits totaled $12 for each new or renewal subscription). The $12 credit was to Accounts Receivable. These commissions were amortized on a straight-line basis over 12 months, as were the prepaid revenues that had been credited to Customers' Advance Payments.

SafeCard's accounting practices were the subject of an article in *Barron's* on July 6, 1981, written by Professor Abraham J. Briloff, a well-known critic of certain corporate accounting practices. Briloff was critical of SafeCard's capitalization of marketing costs, particularly those related to generating new subscriptions. He pointed out that SafeCard expensed these costs as incurred for tax purposes, with the result that the company in fiscal 1980 reported a $4.3 million loss to the IRS while reporting pretax earnings of $5.8 million to its shareholders. Briloff noted that SafeCard had never had to pay income taxes and would not have to do so in the near future because of its $5.9 million operating loss tax carryforwards as of October 31, 1980. Briloff concluded that SafeCard's accounting practices left "room for serious doubt" as to whether the company was "as profitable as its reported results would seem to suggest."

SafeCard's financial statements related to its 1979 and 1980 fiscal years, and the first half of fiscal 1981, are shown in Exhibits 1 and 2. Exhibit 3 shows the company's marketing costs and the division of these costs between expense and assets (deferrals) for the same time frame. Professor Briloff felt that the costs incurred in getting new subscribers should be capitalized for 6 months (the free trial period), then written off evenly over the ensuing 12 months. Thus, for example, the $2.8 million incurred in the fourth quarter of fiscal 1978 (i.e., August 1–October 31, 1978) would be written off as $700,000 expense in each of the quarters starting with the second quarter of fiscal 1979 (i.e., February 1–April 30, 1979) and ending with the first quarter of fiscal 1980 (i.e., November 1, 1979–January 31, 1980).

EXHIBIT 1

SAFECARD SERVICES, INC.
Consolidated Statements of Earnings
(millions of dollars)

	Year Ended October 31		Six Months Ended April 30,
	1979	1980	1981
Revenues:			
Direct-mail marketing revenues:			
Sales of service programs	$10.0	$15.3	$11.4
Sales of merchandise	1.9	*	—
Interest and other income	0.6	0.8	0.8
Net revenues	12.5	16.1	12.2
Operating costs and expenses:			
Cost of service programs	5.1	7.8	6.3
Cost of merchandise	2.0	*	—
General and administrative expenses	1.5	2.3	1.4
Other expenses	0.2	0.2	—
	8.8	10.3	7.7
Earnings before income taxes	3.7	5.8	4.5
Income taxes:			
Currently payable	—	—	—
Deferred	1.7	2.7	2.2
Net earnings	$ 2.0	$ 3.1	$ 2.3

*Less than $0.1 ($100,000).

EXHIBIT 2

SAFECARD SERVICES, INC.
Consolidated Balance Sheets
(millions of dollars)

	October 31			April 30, 1981
	1978	*1979*	*1980*	
Assets				
Current assets:				
Cash	$ 3.9	$ 7.2	$ 7.1	$10.1
Accounts receivable (net)	2.5	2.3	6.6	1.6
Prepaid direct marketing costs	3.4	4.8	9.0	9.8
Total current assets	9.8	14.3	22.7	21.5
Property, equipment, and leasehold improvements (net)	0.4	0.4	0.6	0.7
Deferred direct marketing costs	3.9	4.9	11.4	15.2
	$14.1	$19.6	$34.7	$37.4
Liabilities and Stockholders' Equity				
Current liabilities:				
Accounts payable	$ 0.3	$ 0.6	$ 1.8	$ 0.6
Accrued expenses	0.1	*	0.1	*
Allowance for cancellations	1.1	1.6	4.7	3.6
Customers' advance payments	4.2	5.3	10.1	10.7
Deferred income taxes	0.3	1.6	1.2	1.5
Total current liabilities	6.0	9.1	17.9	16.4
Deferred income taxes	1.9	2.3	5.5	7.4
Shareholders' equity:				
Common stock†	3.9	3.9	3.9	3.9
Retained earnings	2.3	4.3	7.4	9.7
	$14.1	$19.6	$34.7	$37.4

*Less than $0.1 ($100,000).
†Approximately 5.2 million shares were outstanding in each period.

EXHIBIT 3

SAFECARD SERVICES, INC.
Marketing Costs
(millions of dollars)

Quarter*	Costs Incurred	Costs Expensed	Increase in Deferrals
1978—4	$ 2.8	$0.8	$ 2.0
1979—1	1.4	1.1	0.3
1979—2	1.4	1.2	0.2
1979—3	1.3	1.2	0.1
1979—4	3.4	1.6	1.8
Total 1979	7.5	5.1	2.4
1980—1	4.5	1.5	3.0
1980—2	3.9	1.7	2.2
1980—4	4.3	1.9	2.4
1980—4	5.8	2.7	3.1
Total 1980	18.5	7.8	10.7
1981—1	5.2	2.9	2.3
1981—2	5.7	3.4	2.3
First half, 1981	10.9	6.3	4.6

*These are quarters of SafeCard's *fiscal* years. Thus, for example, 1978—4 is the period from August 1–October 31, 1978.

Questions

1. What would SafeCard's pretax income have been in fiscal 1979 and 1980 and the first half of fiscal 1981 if marketing costs were (a) expensed immediately as incurred? (b) expensed as proposed by Professor Briloff? (Not enough data are given in Exhibit 3 to calculate fiscal 1979 income using Briloff's approach.)

2. One of the FASB's objectives for financial reporting is to provide information that helps financial statement users assess an enterprise's prospective cash flows. From the information given in Exhibits 1, 2, and 3, prepare cash flow statements for fiscal 1979 and 1980 and the first half of fiscal 1981. (Note: Because the information in the exhibits is somewhat condensed and has been rounded to the nearest $0.1 million, you may need an "other" or "unexplained" item in your cash flow statements to make them reconcile with SafeCard's reported cash balances.)

3. Do you feel that SafeCard's accounting practices were misleading? If so, what alternative practices would you recommend?

4. Shortly after the *Barron's* article appeared, SafeCard's common stock (traded over the counter) dropped from $25 to $10 per share. Was this warranted? How does this price decrease relate to the efficient markets hypothesis?

PART 2

MANAGEMENT ACCOUNTING

15

Basic Management Accounting Concepts

Part 1 focused on information reported in financial statements prepared primarily for shareholders, creditors, and other interested outside parties. The remainder of the book discusses accounting information intended for the use of management.

This chapter distinguishes management accounting information from other types of information. It describes the three types of management accounting information and their uses. The chapter also compares and contrasts management accounting information with information used for financial reporting, and makes some general observations regarding the use of accounting information by management.

MANAGEMENT ACCOUNTING AS ONE TYPE OF INFORMATION

As explained in Chapter 1, *management accounting* is the process within an organization that provides information used by an organization's managers in planning, coordinating, and controlling the organization's activities. Management accounting is applicable to all organizations. It is used by profit-oriented manufacturing, merchandising, financial, and service businesses, and also by nonprofit organizations of all types. The term *management accounting* is also used to describe the *information* that is collected, summarized, reported, and analyzed in the management accounting process.

Whereas financial accounting has been written about for over 400 years, little was written about management accounting until the 20th century. The actual practice of management accounting goes back much further, however. The need for a type of accounting not aimed primarily at the preparation of financial statements was set forth in this 1875 memorandum by Thomas Sutherland, a British business executive:[1]

> The present system of bookkeeping . . . is admirably suited for . . . ascertaining once a year or oftener the profits upon the company's transactions; but it is evident that in a business of this kind much detailed information is necessary regarding the working of the Company, and this information should be obtainable in such a practical form as to enable the [managers] to see readily and clearly the causes at work in favor of or against the success of the Company's operations.

Information

Information is a fact, datum, observation, perception, or any other thing that adds to knowledge. The number 1,000 taken by itself is not information; the statement that 1,000 students are enrolled in a certain school *is* information. Management accounting is one type of information. Its place in the whole picture was shown in Illustration 1–1. Because 13 chapters have intervened since we first introduced organizations' information requirements, at this point the reader should again read "The Need for Information" section starting on page 3, as well as the subsection titled "Operating Information."

It should be emphasized that managers want whatever type of information that will help them do their jobs, whether the information be accounting or nonaccounting, quantitative or nonquantitative. A rumor that an important customer is dissatisfied with a company's product and is about to change suppliers is neither accounting nor quantitative information, but it is certainly important information.[2]

Management Accounting

Part 1 focused on the three required financial statements: the balance sheet, income statement, and statement of changes in financial position (funds flow statement). Most of the information used in preparing these statements is obtained by classifying and summarizing the various streams of detailed operating information.

The financial statements, though prepared for use by shareholders, creditors, and other interested "outsiders," obviously are also useful to

---

[1] This memorandum was called to our attention by Professor Lyle E. Jacobsen, who saw it reprinted in the London *Economist* in 1960.

[2] Books on organizational behavior discuss in depth this nonquantitative information. For example, in *The Nature of Managerial Work* (New York: Harper & Row, 1973), p. 36, Henry Mintzberg reports that "gossip, speculation, and hearsay form a most important part of the manager's information diet."

management. They provide an overall picture of an entity's financial condition and the results of its activities. Management uses of this information were described in Part 1. Management needs much more detailed financial information than that contained in the financial statements, however. In this Part 2, we focus on this additional information.

As suggested by Illustration 1–1, operating information provides many of the raw data for management accounting. Much of this information is not of direct interest to managers, however. In the normal course of events, a manager does not care about the amount of money that an individual customer owes, the amount that an individual employee earned last week, or the amount that was deposited in the bank yesterday. Records must be kept of these facts, but ordinarily these records are used by operating personnel rather than by managers. The manager is interested in summaries drawn from these records rather than in the underlying details.

In general, therefore, management accounting information is *summary* information. In order to understand it, one needs to know something about the source of raw data used for these summaries, but only enough to be able to understand the resulting summaries.

TYPES OF MANAGEMENT ACCOUNTING INFORMATION AND THEIR USES

Financial accounting is essentially a single process, governed by a single set of generally accepted accounting principles (GAAP), and unified by the basic equation, Assets = Liabilities + Owners' equity. By contrast, in management accounting there are *three* sets of principles that govern the compilation of data; there is no single unifying equation. Information prepared according to each set of principles is used for certain purposes but is not helpful—and may even be misleading—if used for a purpose for which it is not applicable.

The three types of management accounting constructions and their uses are summarized in Illustration 15–1. Each construction applies to revenues, costs, and assets; but for convenience, this brief introduction to them will discuss them primarily in terms of cost. The three are (1) full costs, (2) differential costs, and (3) responsibility costs. The remaining chapters of this book are arranged so that each type of accounting construction is discussed separately. Chapters 17–20 focus on full costs, Chapters 21 and 22 on differential costs, and Chapters 23–26 on responsibility costs.

These accounting constructions apply to two types of data: historical data and future estimates. The former is a record of what has happened, and the latter is an estimate of what is going to happen in the future. In the useful characterization of Simon, historical data tend to be *attention-directing* information, whereas future estimates tend to be *problem-solv-*

ILLUSTRATION 15–1
TYPES OF ACCOUNTING INFORMATION AND THEIR USES

Cost, Revenue, or Asset Construction	Uses	
	Historical Data	Future Estimates
1. Full	External financial reporting (especially inventory and cost of sales) Analyzing economic performance Cost-type contracts	Programming Normal pricing decisions
2. Differential	NONE	Alternative choice decisions (including contribution pricing)
3. Responsibility	Analyzing managers' performance Motivating managers	Budgeting

ing information.[3] The former alerts management to the existence of a problem; the latter helps management decide the best way of solving it. We shall describe briefly below the uses of both the historical and the estimating types of these accounting constructions. Examples of the use of each type of cost will be given, drawn from the experience of Morgan Ford Company, the automobile dealership introduced in Chapter 1.

Full Cost Accounting

The full cost of producing goods is the sum of (1) the costs directly traceable to the goods, called *direct costs,* plus (2) a fair share of costs incurred jointly in producing these and other goods, called *indirect costs.* Full cost accounting also measures the direct and indirect costs of providing services, or of any other activity of interest to management. Thus, full cost accounting is *not* restricted solely to measuring the costs of manufactured goods, as some people assume.

> **Example.** In Morgan Ford Company, the direct costs of an automobile repair job include the cost of the parts used in the job and the cost of the time of the mechanic who performed the job. The full cost of the job includes these direct costs plus a fair share of the indirect costs such as heating and lighting the repair shop, the shop supervisor's salary, property taxes, insurance, and even Lee Carroll's (the president's) salary.

Historical full costs are used in financial reporting. We have already discussed this use, particularly in Chapter 6, which gave the journal entries that accumulated materials costs, direct labor costs, and other pro-

---

[3]Herbert A. Simon, *Administrative Behavior,* 2d ed. (New York: Macmillan, 1957), p. 20.

duction costs for goods as these goods moved through the production process. Historical full costs are also used in many reports of performance prepared for the use of management, and for the analysis of performance as revealed by these reports. This type of analysis was described in Chapter 13. In many contractual arrangements, the buyer agrees to pay the seller the cost of the goods produced or of the services rendered plus a profit margin; "cost" in this context usually means full cost.

Estimates of *future* full costs are used in some types of planning activities, particularly in the type of long-range planning that is called programming. In deciding what price to charge for its goods or services, a company often uses estimates of full costs plus a profit margin as a guide in arriving at the final selling price. Nonprofit organizations whose operations are financed by fees charged to clients (such as college students or hospital patients) base these fees on the full cost of the services rendered.

Differential Accounting

Differential accounting estimates how costs, revenues, and/or assets would be different if one course of action were adopted as compared with an alternative course of action.

> **Example.** Ford Motor Company has offered Morgan Ford the opportunity to sell and service Ford trucks, in addition to Ford automobiles. In considering this offer, Lee Carroll and the dealership's accountant estimated the additional annual revenues truck sales and service might provide, as well as the additional cost of sales and costs of a truck salesperson and truck mechanics, and additional asset costs for truck parts inventory and an expansion of the repair shop. These revenue, operating cost, and asset items are all differential to Morgan Ford's present mode of operations. Carroll decided to reject the offer because the differential return on investment was unsatisfactory.

By definition, differential costs are always estimates of future costs. As with estimates of all types, they are sometimes *derived* from historical cost records. But there is no such thing as an historical record of differential costs as such because these costs are always specific to the particular alternatives being considered.

As the above description suggests, differential costs are used in decision problems that involve a choice among alternative courses of action. These problems are therefore called *alternative choice problems.* Many such decisions involve short-run problems and involve a specific segment of the business. In these decisions, it is primarily direct costs that are differential. For longer-range decisions, estimates of full costs are appropriate. Indeed, in the long run, all costs are differential, as we shall discuss in Chapter 21. Deciding which costs are differential in a specific situation is one of the more difficult tasks of the management accountant.

Responsibility Accounting

Responsibility accounting traces costs (and also revenues and/or assets) to individual organization units, each of which is headed by a manager. These units are called *responsibility centers*.

Estimates of future responsibility costs are used in the planning process, particularly in the annual planning process called budgeting. A historical record of actual costs incurred in a responsibility center is used in reporting and analyzing the performance of that responsibility center. Such reports are useful for many management purposes because they identify the manager who is responsible for performance. Corrective action can be taken only by individuals, so if performance is unsatisfactory, the person responsible must be identified before corrective action can be taken.

> **Example.** Morgan Ford Company's June service department income statement indicated that the cost of repair parts was higher than it usually was for a similar dollar volume of service department activity. In investigating this matter, Lee Carroll realized that the service department's statement did not distinguish between parts used for service department repair jobs and those sold by the parts counter to service stations and to people who repair their cars themselves. After careful consideration, Lee Carroll decided to divide the service department into two responsibility centers, one responsible for repair work, and the other responsible for parts sales (whether sold to outsiders or "sold" to the repair work department). In the future, separate reports would be prepared for each of these responsibility centers.

Relation to Planning and Control

In Chapter 1 the management functions of planning, coordinating, and control were described. It should be emphasized that there is *not a one-to-one correspondence* between the three types of management accounting construction and these three management functions. The task of understanding management accounting would be much simpler if such a correspondence existed, but it does not. Overall planning uses primarily responsibility accounting, but to a certain extent it also uses full cost accounting and differential accounting. Some operating decisions use full cost information, while others use differential accounting information.

Thus, the central scheme of this second part of the book is to discuss each of the three types of management accounting separately, explaining what it is and discussing its use for various management purposes.

CONTRAST BETWEEN MANAGEMENT ACCOUNTING AND FINANCIAL REPORTING

Management accounting differs from the financial reporting process that was the focus of Part 1 in several ways. In order to facilitate the transition from the study of financial accounting to management accounting, it seems desirable to state these differences, and also point out similarities. The principal differences are described below.

Differences

1. **Necessity.** Financial accounting *must* be done. Enough effort must be expended to collect data in acceptable form and with an acceptable degree of accuracy to meet the requirements of the FASB, the SEC, the IRS, and other outside parties, whether or not the management regards this information as useful. Management accounting, by contrast, is entirely optional. No outside agencies specify what must be done, or indeed that *anything* need be done. Being optional, there is no point in collecting a piece of management accounting information unless its value, as an aid to management, is believed to exceed the cost of collecting it.

2. **Purpose.** The purpose of financial accounting is to produce financial statements for outside users. When the statements have been produced, this purpose has been accomplished. Management accounting information, on the other hand, is only a means to an end, the end being the planning, coordinating, and controlling functions of management. Management accountants assist management in using accounting data; they do not regard preparing the numbers as an end in itself.

3. **Users.** The users of financial accounting information (other than management itself) are essentially a "faceless" group. The managements of most companies do not know personally many of the shareholders, creditors, or others who use the information in the financial statements. Moreover, the information needs of most of these external users must be presumed; most external users do not individually request the information they would like to receive. By contrast, the users of management accounting information are known managers plus the people who help these managers analyze the information. The number of such internal users generally is small relative to the number of external users. Internal users' information needs are relatively well known because the controller's office solicits these needs in designing or revising the management accounting system.

4. **Underlying Structure.** As already noted, financial accounting is built around one fundamental equation, Assets = Liabilities + Owners' equity. In management accounting, there are three types of accounting, each with its own set of principles.

5. **Source of Principles.** Financial accounting information must be reported in accordance with generally accepted accounting principles (GAAP), primarily those promulgated by the FASB. Outside users usually have no choice but to accept information just as the company provides it. They need assurance that the financial statements are prepared in accordance with a mutually understood set of ground rules; otherwise, they could not understand what the numbers mean. GAAP provide

these common ground rules. An organization's management, by contrast, can employ whatever accounting rules it finds most useful for its own purposes, without worrying about whether these conform to some outside standard. Thus, in management accounting there may well be information on unfilled sales orders (i.e., "backlog"), even though these are not financial accounting transactions; fixed assets may be stated at current values rather than historical cost; certain production overhead costs may be omitted from inventories; or revenues may be recorded before they are realized—even though each of these concepts is inconsistent with GAAP. The basic question in management accounting is the pragmatic one: "Is the information useful?" rather than, "Does it conform to GAAP?"

6. Time Orientation. Financial accounting records and reports the financial *history* of an organization. Entries are made in the accounts only after transactions have occurred. Although financial accounting information is used as a basis for making future plans, the information itself is historical. Management accounting includes, in its *formal* structure, numbers that represent estimates and plans for the future, as well as information about the past. (Some financial accounting entries, such as those for depreciation, require that estimates of future conditions be made; the basic thrust of financial accounting is nevertheless historical.)

7. Information Content. The financial statements that are the end product of financial accounting include primarily monetary information. Management accounting deals with nonmonetary as well as monetary information. Although the accounts themselves primarily contain money amounts, much of the information in management accounting reports is nonmonetary. These reports show quantities of material, as well as its monetary cost; number of employees and hours worked, as well as labor costs; units of products sold, as well as dollar amounts of revenue; and so on.

8. Information Precision. Management needs information rapidly, and is often willing to sacrifice some precision in order to gain speed in reporting. Thus, in management accounting, approximations are often as useful as, or even more useful than, numbers that are worked out to the last dollar. While financial accounting cannot be absolutely precise either, the approximations used in management accounting are greater than those in financial accounting.

9. Report Frequency. Corporations issue detailed financial statements only annually, and less detailed interim reports quarterly. By contrast, fairly detailed management accounting reports are issued monthly in most larger companies; and reports on certain activities may be prepared weekly, daily, or in a few instances, even hourly.

10. Report Timeliness. Because of the needs for precision and a review by outside auditors, plus the time requirements of typesetting, financial accounting reports are distributed several weeks after the close of the accounting period. Larger corporations' annual reports for a fiscal year ending December 31 generally are not received by shareholders until March or April. By contrast, because of the attention-getting role of management accounting reports, they are usually issued within a few days of the end of a month (or the next morning, for a daily report). Some companies even estimate revenues and expenses for the last week of the month so that top management can have a preliminary statement of that month's income in its hands by the last day of the month. Also, timeliness is enhanced by the fact that many management accounting reports do not have to be typed because they are prepared by the computer system that processes the raw operating information that is summarized in the report.

11. Report Entity. The financial statements describe the organization as a whole. Although companies that do business in several industries are required to report revenues and income for each industry, these are large segments of the whole enterprise. In management accounting, by contrast, the main focus is on relatively small parts of the entity; that is, on individual products, on individual activities, or on individual divisions, departments, and other responsibility centers. As we shall see, the necessity for dividing the total costs of an organization among these individual parts creates important problems in management accounting that do not exist in financial accounting.

12. Liability. Although it happens infrequently, a company may be sued by its shareholders or creditors for allegedly reporting misleading financial information in its annual report or in SEC filings. For example, in June 1982, over a dozen suits had been filed against Datapoint Corporation and its auditors, alleging that the company misleadingly recognized more revenues than permitted by GAAP in order to maintain its record of 39 quarter-to-quarter income increases. (The company publicly admitted making a shipment to an imaginary "Joe Blow" to boost one quarter's revenues.)[4] By contrast, as previously stated, management accounting reports need not be in accord with GAAP, and are not public documents. While a manager may be held liable for some inappropriate action, and management accounting information conceivably may have played some role in his or her taking that action, it is the action itself, not the management accounting documents, that gives rise to the liability.

These 12 contrasts between management accounting and financial reporting are summarized in Illustration 15–2.

---

[4]"Datapoint Kept Trying to Set Profit Records until the Bubble Burst," *The Wall Street Journal*, May 27, 1982, p. 1.

ILLUSTRATION 15-2
MANAGEMENT ACCOUNTING CONTRASTED WITH FINANCIAL REPORTING

Dimension	Management Accounting	Financial Reporting
1. Necessity	Optional	Required
2. Purpose	A means to the end of assisting management	Produce statements for outside users
3. Users	Relatively small group; known identity	Relatively large group; mostly unknown
4. Structure	Varies according to use of the information	One fundamental equation: Assets = Equities
5. Principles	Whatever is useful to management	GAAP
6. Time orientation	Historical and estimates of the future	Historical
7. Information content	Monetary and nonmonetary	Primarily monetary
8. Precision	Many approximations	Fewer approximations
9. Frequency	Varies with purpose; monthly and weekly common	Quarterly and annually
10. Timeliness	Reports issued promptly after period covered ends	Delay of weeks, or even months
11. Liability potential	Virtually none	Few lawsuits, but threat is always present

Similarities

Although differences do exist, most elements of financial accounting are also found in management accounting. There are two reasons for this. First, the same considerations that make GAAP sensible for purposes of financial accounting are likely to be relevant for purposes of management accounting. For example, management cannot base its reporting system on unverifiable, subjective estimates of profits submitted by lower echelons, which is the same reason that financial accounting adheres to the cost and realization concepts.

Second, operating information is used both in preparing the financial statements and in management accounting. There is a presumption, therefore, that the basic data will be collected in accordance with generally accepted financial accounting principles, for to do otherwise would require duplication of data collection activities.

Source Disciplines

Accounting is an applied subject. All applied subjects are based on foundations and concepts developed in a basic science or discipline. Whereas financial accounting has a single source discipline, management accounting has two such source disciplines. Financial accounting and part of management accounting are related to *economics*, which deals with the principles governing decisions on the use of scarce resources. Another part of management accounting is related to *social psychology,* which deals with the principles governing human behavior in organizations.[5] These two disciplines are quite different from one another, and this fact causes problems in understanding the management accounting principles that are derived from them. For example, for the purpose of deciding whether to purchase a new long-lived asset, the relevant accounting information is that developed according to principles that the economist specifies; but for the purpose of preparing a budget for the responsibility center in which that same asset is used, the principles of social psychology are at least equally important. The latter principles may lead to quite different accounting constructions.

Some economists and some social psychologists criticize management accounting. Much of this criticism arises because each group has the mistaken belief that management accounting relates solely to their discipline. One of the significant problems in the real world is to give the appropriate weight to each of these disciplines.

SOME GENERAL OBSERVATIONS

Before getting into the details, we here make some general observations about the nature and use of management accounting information. These usefully can be kept in mind throughout the rest of the book.

Different Numbers for Different Purposes

In mathematics, there are definitions that are valid under a wide variety of circumstances. Such is not the case with most accounting definitions. Each of the several purposes described in the preceding section requires a different accounting approach. Since these different numbers may superficially resemble one another, a person not familiar with them may easily become confused or frustrated.

The most common source of confusion is the word *cost.* In management accounting, there are historical costs, standard costs, overhead costs, variable costs, differential costs, marginal costs, opportunity costs, direct costs, estimated costs, full costs, and other kinds of costs. Some of these terms are synonyms; others are almost but not quite synonyms; still others, although not synonyms at all, are used by some people as if they were.

Accounting numbers should always be discussed in terms of the particular problem that they are intended to help solve, rather than in any abstract sense. A statement that "the cost of such-and-such is $100" lit-

---

[5]The boundaries of social psychology are not entirely clear. We mean to include those principles of psychology and of sociology that are intended to explain how individuals behave in situations ranging from two-person interactions to large groups.

erally has no meaning unless those who hear this statement understand clearly which of the several possible concepts of cost was intended.

Accounting Numbers Are Approximations

As is the case with any measurement, an accounting number is an approximation rather than a precisely accurate amount. Most of the data used in the physical sciences are also measurements. Like scientists and engineers, users of accounting information must acquire an understanding of the degree of approximation that is present in the data. Consider, for example, the concept of temperature. With the proper instruments, the human body's temperature is easily measured to a tenth of a degree, but the sun's temperature is measurable only with an accuracy of a hundred degrees or so. Although these measurements differ widely in their precision, each is useful for a particular purpose.

Similarly, some accounting numbers, such as the amount of cash on hand, may be accurate within very narrow limits, while others are only rough approximations. The degree of approximation is especially high in the case of numbers used for planning purposes because these are always estimates of what will happen in the future.

Working with Incomplete Data

No one could reasonably ask students to solve a mathematics problem without furnishing them all the needed information. In a management problem, on the other hand, one almost never has exactly the information one would like to have. The person struggling with the problem usually can think of additional information that would be helpful if it were available. Conversely, there are many decision-making situations in which page after page of numbers are available, but only a small fraction of them is truly relevant to the problem at hand, and perhaps none of them is quite what one needs to solve it.

It is a fact of life, however, that problems must be solved. Management decisions must be made, and often the decision cannot be delayed until all the pertinent information is available. We do the best we can with what we have, and then move on to the next problem. As John W. Gardner writes:

> Anyone who accomplishes anything of significance has more confidence than the facts would justify. It is something that outstanding executives have in common with gifted military commanders, brilliant political leaders, and great artists. It is true of societies as well as of individuals. Every great civilization has been characterized by confidence in itself.[6]

On the other hand, a decision should not be made if a vital, obtainable piece of evidence is missing. Deciding whether or not to act on the available evidence is one of the most difficult parts of the whole decision

---

[6]*Annual Report 1965*, Carnegie Corporation.

process. As the late Wallace B. Donham put it: "The art of business is the art of making irrevocable decisions on the basis of inadequate information."

Accounting Evidence Is Only Partial Evidence

Few, if any, management problems can be solved solely by the collection and analysis of numbers. Usually, there are important factors that cannot be, or have not been, reduced to quantitative terms. For example, consider how the performance of a baseball player is judged. Detailed records are kept on each player's times at bat, walks, hits, strikeouts, putouts, stolen bases, and so on. Nevertheless, when the manager of the team must decide whether player A is better than B, the manager knows better than to rely completely on this numerical information. Such factors as how well a player gets along with teammates, ability to hit in crucial situations, and other unmeasurable characteristics must also be taken into account.

Most organizations are much more complicated than baseball teams; the "game" of business goes on all day, every day, rather than a discrete number of times a year, and business results are not expressed by the number of games won and lost. Business measurements are therefore much more difficult and less precise than baseball measurements.

Some people act as if most problems can be completely solved by numerical analysis. At the other extreme, there are those who believe that intuition is the sure guide to a sound decision; they therefore pay no attention to numbers. Although the correct attitude is clearly somewhere between these extremes, there is no way to describing precisely where it is. The essential difficulty has been well summed up by G. K. Chesterton:

> The real trouble with this world of ours is not that it is an unreasonable world, nor even that it is a reasonable one. The commonest kind of trouble is that it is nearly reasonable, but not quite. Life is not an illogicality; yet it is a trap for logicians. It looks just a little more mathematical and regular than it is; its exactitude is obvious, but its inexactitude is hidden; its wildness lies in wait.[7]

People, Not Numbers, Get Things Done

An obvious fact about organizations is that they consist of human beings. Anything that an organization accomplishes is the result of these persons' actions. Numbers can assist the people in an organization in various ways, but the numbers by themselves accomplish nothing. But numbers don't talk back; they give the appearance of being definite and precise, and it is a comforting illusion to imagine that the construction of a set of numbers is synonymous with acting on a real problem.

---

[7]*Orthodoxy* (London: Bodley Head, 1949 reprint), p. 131.

An accounting system may be well designed and carefully operated, but the system is of no use to management unless it results in *action* by human beings. For instance, three companies may use exactly the same system with entirely different results. In one company, the system may be *useless* because management never acts on the information collected, and the organization has become aware of this fact. In the second company, the system may be *helpful* because management uses the information as a general guide for planning, coordinating, and control, and has educated the organization to use it in the same spirit. In the third company, the system may be *worse than useless* because management overemphasizes the importance of the numbers and therefore takes unwise actions.

SUMMARY

Accounting is one type of information. The total amount of information available to a manager includes nonquantitative as well as quantitative elements. The quantitative elements include both monetary and nonmonetary amounts. Accounting is primarily monetary, but includes related nonmonetary data.

Most accounting information, in terms of quantity of data, is operating information. The mass of operating data flowing through an organization consists of streams of information about production, purchasing and materials, payroll, plant and equipment, sales and accounts receivable, and finance. Data in these streams provide the raw materials for financial statements. These statements are essentially summaries to meet the needs of investors and other outside parties. They are also used by managers inside the organization.

There is no single, unified management accounting system. Rather, there are three different types of information, each used for different purposes. These are called (1) full cost accounting, (2) differential accounting, and (3) responsibility accounting. The remainder of this book will deal in turn with each of these three types.

As contrasted with financial reporting, management accounting is optional rather than required; is a means to an end rather than an end in itself; is used by a relatively small group of known individuals with known information needs rather than by a "faceless" large group of outsiders whose needs must be presumed; has several sets of principles rather than one; is not governed by GAAP; has more emphasis on the future; includes more nonmonetary information; has less emphasis on precision; involves more frequently issued reports, which are issued on a more timely basis; and does not expose the company to lawsuits by users of the reports. Nevertheless, the two types of accounting have much in common.

In solving management accounting problems it is well to keep in mind that terms, principally *cost*, are defined differently depending on the purpose; that accounting numbers are approximations; that they rarely provide exactly the information needed; that much more than accounting information is needed in the solution of a problem; and that people, not numbers, get things done.

SUGGESTIONS FOR FURTHER READING

Caplan, Edwin H. *Management Accounting and Behavioral Science.* 2d ed. Reading, Mass.: Addison-Wesley Publishing, 1981.

Cyert, Richard M., and James G. March. *A Behavioral Theory of the Firm.* Englewood Cliffs, N.J.: Prentice-Hall, 1963.

Homans, George C. *Social Behavior: Its Elementary Forms.* Rev. ed. New York: Harcourt Brace Jovanovich, 1974.

Lawler, Edward E., and John G. Rhode. *Information and Control in Organizations.* Santa Monica, Calif.: Goodyear Publishing, 1976.

Lawrence, Paul R., and Jay W. Lorsch. *Organization and Environment: Managing Differentiation and Integration.* Homewood, Ill.: Richard D. Irwin, 1969.

McClelland, David C. *The Achieving Society.* New York: Halsted Press, 1976.

Steers, Richard M., and Lyman W. Porter, eds. *Motivation and Work Behavior.* 2d ed. New York: McGraw-Hill, 1979.

Case

CASE 15–1 Bates Boatyard

Upon returning to civilian life after several years in the Navy, Sarah Bates sought a small business that she might buy. Being a thrifty person with no dependents, she had built up a fair amount of savings, the accumulation of which had been aided by the fact that she had seen considerable duty in areas where there had been nothing to buy.

Bates finally located a small boatyard for sale in a town on the coast of Maine where she had spent many summers. The proprietor was getting along in years and wished to retire. He was offering the yard for sale at what Bates believed to be a fair starting price that could probably be worked down to a very reasonable figure through negotiation.

It is not necessary here to go into the details of investigation and negotiation. Bates bought the yard. The business being somewhat larger than she could finance alone, she had borrowed the additional funds required from a friend, giving a mortgage on the property as security.

Bates realized the need for adequate accounting records if she was to manage the business successfully. The records on hand were for cash receipts and disbursements only. Actual balance sheets and profit and loss statements that had been prepared for the former owner for tax purposes were also available. A person who was a reasonably capable bookkeeper and general office factotum had been inherited with the business.

Having had a course in accounting in college, Bates felt capable of using cost and financial information with some intelligence, but did not feel capable of initiating a suitable accounting system. Knowing that you, an old friend of hers, have been studying such matters, she has asked your advice as to what kind of accounting records should be kept and what kind of financial and cost information should be developed to control operations and to make proper charges to customers for service rendered. In addition to the information above, she has told you the following facts about the business.

One of the properties of the business was a large shed for the winter storage of boats. Being the most suitable building in the locality for such storage, there was great demand for space in it on the part of owners of expensive boats among the summer people.

There was plenty of empty land on the shorefront for outdoor storage. In most cases where space was rented for this purpose, the yard was also hired to haul the boats in on equipment that it had for the purpose.

In the spring, and from time to time during other seasons, there was a goodly amount of business available in painting and repair work on boats.

There was a large-sized work shed containing woodworking tools and space in which to construct at one time about six boats up to 40 feet in length. Larger boats could be built outside when the weather was suitable, but Bates did not expect to get many, if any, orders for such craft. She did, however, expect to have from one to six boats up to 40 feet in length in construction at all times, some for local fishermen and some for summer people.

The property included a good-sized wharf and float, a store for the sale of marine hardware and supplies, and gasoline pumps. There being no yacht club in the town, the summer people who were boating-minded tended to gather around this wharf and store. Bates intended to encourage this and to add fishing tackle, sporting goods, and refreshments to the items handled by the store.

Question

What would you tell Bates concerning her accounting needs?

16

The Behavior of Costs

An understanding of how costs behave as the level of activity changes, or cost-volume relationships, is a prerequisite for the further discussion of the three types of management accounting in Chapters 17–26. Accordingly, this chapter presents the concepts of fixed and variable costs. Cost behavior information can be combined with revenue information to develop a profitgraph; this is also described in the chapter, along with the related concept of contribution.

RELATION OF COSTS TO VOLUME

If an entity significantly increases the amount of goods or services it produces, that is, its volume of outputs, then the amount of resources required to produce this higher volume, that is, its costs, should also increase. In many instances, however, the percentage increase in costs is *less than* the percentage increase in volume. To understand how this could be the case, it is necessary to understand the concept of variable and fixed costs.

Variable and Fixed Costs

Variable costs are items of cost that vary directly and proportionately with volume. If volume increases 10 percent, the *total* amount of variable cost also increases by 10 percent. Direct labor, direct material, lubricants, power costs, and supplies often are examples of variable costs.

In general usage, the word *variable* means simply *changeable;* but in accounting, *variable* has a more restricted meaning. Variable refers not to changes in cost that take place over time, nor to changes associated with the seasons, but only to changes associated with the level of activity, that is, with the volume of output. If the *total* amount of a cost item increases proportionately with a volume increase, the item is a variable cost; otherwise, it is not.

Fixed costs do not vary at all with volume. Building depreciation, property taxes, supervisory and other management salaries, and occupancy costs (heat and light, and rent, if the building is not owned) often behave in this fashion. These costs increase because of the passage of time, rather than because of the level of activity within a specified period of time. The amount of a supervisor's salary for two months is double the amount for one month, but it is unaffected by changes in the level of activity within a month.

Although the term *fixed cost* may imply that the amount of cost cannot be changed, such an implication is incorrect. The term refers only to items of cost that do not "automatically" change with changes in volume. Fixed costs can be changed for other reasons, such as a deliberate management decision to change them. The term *nonvariable* is therefore more appropriate than *fixed;* but since *fixed cost* is in widespread use, we use it here.

> **Example.** Property protection costs, such as the wages of guards, are ordinarily fixed costs, since these costs do not vary with changes in volume. Property protection costs will increase, however, if management decides that the current level of protection is inadequate. Alternatively, they will decrease if management decides that reductions in the current level are prudent.

Semivariable costs vary in the same direction as, but *less* than proportionately with, changes in volume. If volume increases by 10 percent, the *total* amount of a semivariable cost will increase, but by less than 10 percent. Semivariable costs are also called *semifixed* or *partly variable* costs. Examples may be indirect labor, maintenance, and clerical costs.

Cost-Volume Diagrams

The relationship between costs and volume can be displayed in a *cost-volume* or *C-V diagram*. Illustration 16–1 shows diagrams of total costs versus volume for the three patterns of cost behavior described above. Each line in the illustration can be described by the equation $y = mx + b$, where y is the cost at a volume of x; m is the rate of cost change per unit of volume change, or the "slope;" and b is the "vertical intercept," which represents the fixed cost component.

ILLUSTRATION 16–1
RELATION OF TOTAL COST TO VOLUME

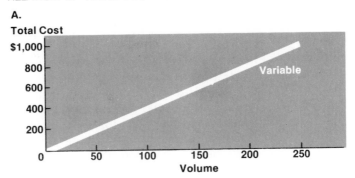

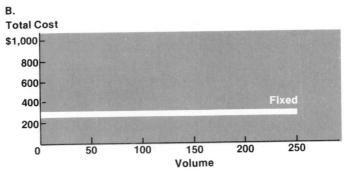

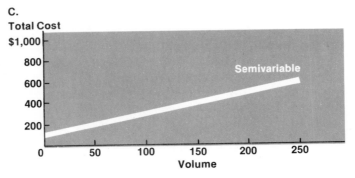

In a C-V diagram, the following notation is easier to remember:

$$TC = \text{total cost}$$
$$TFC = \text{total fixed cost (per time period)}$$
$$UVC = \text{unit variable cost (per unit of volume)}$$
$$X = \text{volume}$$

Thus:

$$TC = TFC + UVC \cdot X$$

The equations for the three cost lines in Illustration 16–1 are:

    A.   Variable cost line: $TC = \$4 \cdot X$

    B.   Fixed cost line: $TC = \$300$

    C.   Semivariable cost line: $TC = \$100 + \$2 \cdot X$

Illustration 16–2 gives a generalized picture of cost behavior. This illustration was constructed simply by combining (i.e., graphically adding) the three separate elements shown in Illustration 16–1. Thus, the fixed cost is $300 *for a period* of time regardless of the volume in that period. The variable cost is $4 *per unit of volume,* which means that the *total* variable cost in a period varies proportionately with volume. The semivariable cost has a fixed element of $100 per period of time and a variable element of $2 per unit of volume.

Since a semivariable cost can be split into fixed and variable components, the behavior of *total costs* can be described in terms of only *two* components—a *fixed* component, which is a total amount *per period,*

ILLUSTRATION 16–2
RELATION OF TOTAL COSTS TO VOLUME

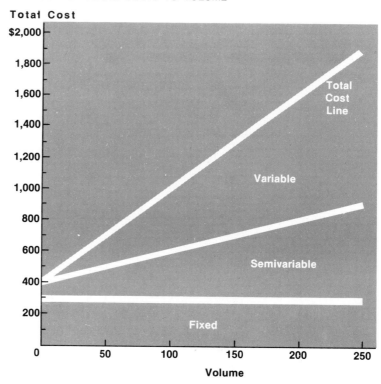

and a *variable* component, which is an amount *per unit of volume*. In Illustration 16–2, the fixed amount is $400 per period (= $300 + $100) and the variable amount is $6 per unit of volume (= $4 + $2). Thus, the equation of the total cost line is $TC = \$400 + \$6 \cdot X$. For example, if $X = 200$ units, $TC = \$400 + \$6(200) = \$400 + \$1,200 = \$1,600$. Note in this equation that the semivariable cost has disappeared as a separate entity, part of it being combined with the variable cost and the remainder being combined with the fixed cost. This combination can be made for any semivariable cost item that is expressed as a fixed dollar amount per period plus a rate per unit of volume, that is, any item for which there is a linear relationship between cost and volume. From this point on, we usually shall consider only the fixed and variable components of cost.

Relation to Unit Costs

The foregoing description of variable, fixed, and semivariable costs was expressed in terms of *total* costs for a period. In terms of *unit* costs, the description of these types of cost is quite different. Variable cost per unit of volume is a *constant*; that is, it does not change as volume changes. Fixed cost per unit *does* change with changes in volume: as volume increases, fixed cost per unit decreases. Semivariable cost per unit also changes with changes in volume, but the amount of change is smaller than that for fixed costs.

To demonstrate the behavior of *per unit* costs, let UC stand for unit cost. Then at a volume of X, since unit cost is total cost divided by volume, we have symbolically:

$$UC = \frac{TC}{X} = \frac{TFC + UVC \cdot X}{X} = \frac{TFC}{X} + UVC$$

Since *UC* is the total cost at a volume of X divided by X, *UC* is the *average* cost per unit at *that* volume. As the equation indicates, average unit cost changes with changes in volume (X) because the fixed costs (TFC) are "spread" over different volumes. Using the equations for the lines in Illustration 16–1 we have the following cost-per-unit equations:

A. Per unit variable cost: $UVC = \dfrac{TVC}{X} = \dfrac{\$4 \cdot X}{X} = \$4$

B. Per unit fixed cost: $UFC = \dfrac{TFC}{X} = \dfrac{\$300}{X}$

C. Per unit semivariable cost: $USC = \dfrac{TSC}{X} = \dfrac{\$100 + \$2 \cdot X}{X} = \dfrac{\$100}{X} + \$2$

These three equations are graphed in Illustration 16–3.

ILLUSTRATION 16–3
RELATION OF UNIT COST TO VOLUME

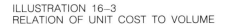

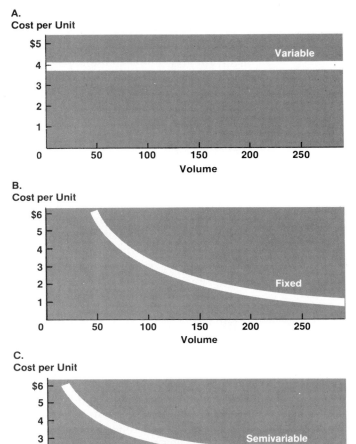

A.
Cost per Unit

Variable

B.
Cost per Unit

Fixed

C.
Cost per Unit

Semivariable

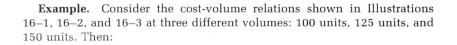

Example.   Consider the cost-volume relations shown in Illustrations 16–1, 16–2, and 16–3 at three different volumes: 100 units, 125 units, and 150 units. Then:

		Volume (X) =		
		100	125	150
Total cost:				
Variable:				
$TVC =$	$\$4 \cdot X$	$ 400	$ 500	$ 600
Fixed				
$TFC = \$300$		300	300	300
Semivariable:				
$TSC = \$100 + \$2 \cdot X$		300	350	400
Sum:				
$TC = \$400 + \$6 \cdot X$		$1,000	$1,150	$1,300
Cost per unit:				
Variable:				
$UVC =$	$\$4$	$ 4.00	$4.00	$4.00
Fixed:				
$UFC = \dfrac{\$300}{X}$		3.00	2.40	2.00
Semivariable:				
$USC = \dfrac{\$100}{X} + \$2$		3.00	2.80	2.67
Sum:				
$UC = \dfrac{\$400}{X} + \$6$		$10.00	$9.20	$8.67

Observe in the table above that as volume increases by 50 percent (i.e., from 100 to 150 units):

- Total variable cost increases by 50 percent.
- Total fixed cost remains unchanged.
- Total semivariable cost increases, but by less than 50 percent.
- Variable cost per unit remains unchanged.
- Fixed cost per unit decreases.
- Semivariable cost per unit decreases, but not as much as fixed cost per unit.

Cost Assumptions   Illustrations 16–1 and 16–2 were based on several implicit assumptions as to the behavior of costs, two of which we shall now make explicit. The first is usually a reasonable one, but the second is quite unrealistic.

The Linear Assumption. One cost behavior assumption is that all costs behave according to one of the three patterns depicted in Illustration 16–1—variable, fixed, or semivariable—each of which is expressed by a straight line; that is, each relationship of total cost to volume is *linear.* Actually, some items of costs may vary in *steps,* as in Illustration 16–4. This happens when the cost occurs in discrete "chunks," as when

ILLUSTRATION 16–4
A COST ELEMENT WITH A STEP FUNCTION

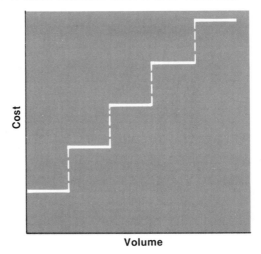

one supervisor is added for every 1,200 additional hours of labor per month. Other items of cost may vary along a curve rather than a straight line; and in rare circumstances still others, such as the maintenance cost of idle machines, may actually decrease as volume increases.

In most situations, however, the effect of these discontinuities and nonlinear cost functions on total costs is minor, and the assumption that total costs vary linearly with volume is a satisfactory working approximation. This is most fortunate. Many theoretical treatises discuss cost functions with various types of complicated curves. Such curves are seldom used in practice, for it is usually found that the straight-line assumption, although perhaps not a perfect representation of C-V relationships, is close enough for practical purposes. In this book, therefore, we primarily describe linear relationships. If a real-life problem does involve nonlinear relationships, the general approach is similar to that described here; the only difference is that the arithmetic is more complex.

Relevant Range. A second cost behavior assumption implicit in Illustrations 16–1 and 16–2 is that costs move along a straight line throughout the *whole range* of volume, from zero to whatever number is at the far right of the diagram. This assumption is unrealistic. For example, at zero volume (i.e., when the production facilities are not operating at all), management decisions may cause costs to be considerably lower than the $400 of fixed costs shown in Illustration 16–2. Also, when production gets so high that a second shift is required, costs may behave quite differently from how they behave under one-shift operations. Even within the limits of a single shift, costs usually will behave differently when the production facilities are very busy from the way they do when the facilities are operating at a significantly lower volume. In short, a single straight line gives a good approximation of the behavior of costs *only within a certain range of volume*. This range is referred to as the *relevant range* because it is the range that is relevant for the situation being analyzed.

Illustration 16–5 shows the same cost pattern as Illustration 16–2, and the relevant range is indicated by the dashed lines at 100 units and 200 units. Although the cost line extends back to zero, it does not imply that costs actually will behave in this fashion at volumes lower than 100 units. Rather, the cost line is drawn on the diagram solely as a means of identifying the fixed component of total costs within the relevant range. The fixed component (i.e., $400 per period) is the amount of costs indicated by the point where the total cost line touches the vertical axis.

ILLUSTRATION 16–5
DESIGNATION OF RELEVANT RANGE

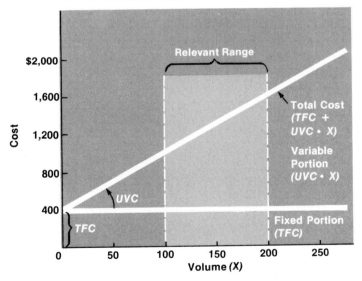

Assumed Set of Conditions.   It is also important to note that the diagram shows the estimated relationship between costs and volume under a *certain set of conditions*. This is not an assumption; it is a fact. If any of these conditions should change—for example, if there is an increase in wage rates—the diagram is obsolete, and a new one must be drawn.

**Estimating the
Cost-Volume
Relationship**

In order to construct a C-V diagram, estimates must be made of what the amounts of costs are expected to be at various volumes. These estimates often are made as part of the budgeting process, which is described in Chapter 25. In this process, estimates are made of all significant items of revenue and cost. These estimates show what revenues and costs are expected to be at various volume levels in the following year.

Any of the following methods can be used to derive the TFC and UVC terms for the cost-volume formula, $TC = TFC + UVC \cdot X$:

1. Estimate total costs at each of two volume levels; this establishes two points on the line. (This is often called the *high-low method* because one of the volumes selected is likely to be quite high and the other quite low. The upper and lower limits of the relevant range often are selected for this purpose.) Then proceed as follows:
   a. Subtract total cost at the lower volume from total cost at the higher volume, and subtract the number of units for the lower volume from the number of units for the higher volume.
   b. Divide the difference in cost by the difference in volume, which gives UVC, the amount by which total cost changes with a change of one unit of volume (i.e., the "slope" of the C-V line).
   c. Multiply either of the volumes by UVC and subtract the result from the total cost at that volume, thus removing the variable component and leaving the fixed component, TFC (i.e., the "vertical intercept").
2. Estimate total costs at one volume, and estimate how costs will change with a given change in volume. This gives UVC directly, and TFC can be found by subtraction, as described above.
3. Build up separate estimates of the behavior of each of the items that make up total costs, identifying each item's fixed and variable components. From these estimates, derive the total TFC component by adding the individual items' fixed components, and similarly add to get the total UVC.
4. Make a *scatter diagram* in which actual costs recorded in past periods are plotted (on the vertical axis) against the volume levels in those periods (on the horizontal axis). Data on costs and volumes for each of the preceding several months might be used for this purpose. Draw a line that best fits these observations. Such a diagram is shown in Illustration 16–6. The line of best fit is drawn by visual inspection of the plotted points. The TFC and UVC values are then determined by reading the values for any two points on the line and using the high-low method described above.
5. Fit a line to the observations by the statistical technique called the *method of least squares* or *linear regression*. The procedure gives the TFC and UVC values directly. (Many hand-held calculators are programmed to perform linear regression calculations.) In many cases, a

ILLUSTRATION 16–6
SCATTER DIAGRAM

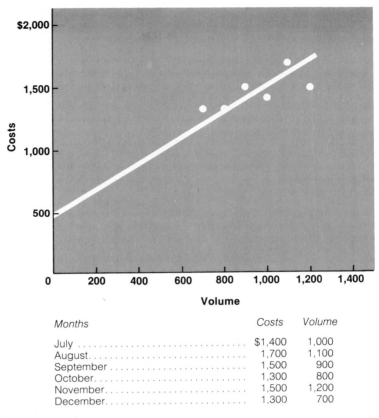

Months	Costs	Volume
July	$1,400	1,000
August	1,700	1,100
September	1,500	900
October	1,300	800
November	1,500	1,200
December	1,300	700

line drawn by visual inspection is better than a mathematically fitted line because judgment can be used to adjust for unusual observations.[1]

Problems with Statistical Estimates. Estimating C-V relationships by means of a scatter diagram or linear regression is a common practice, but the results can be misleading. In the first place, this technique shows, at best, what the relationship between costs and volumes *was in the past,* whereas we are interested in what the relationship *will be in the future.* The future is not necessarily a mirror of the past. Also, the relationship we seek is that prevailing under a *single set of operating conditions,*

---

[1]In one study of companies' use of C-V diagrams, only 13 percent of the respondents preferred linear regression over judgment in analyzing cost behavior (Roy A. Anderson and Harry R. Biederman, "Using Cost-Volume-Profit Charts," *The Controller's Handbook* [Homewood, Ill.: Dow Jones-Irwin, 1978], chap. 6.)

whereas each point on a scatter diagram may represent changes in factors other than the two being studied, namely, cost and volume.

Illustration 16–7 shows a common source of difficulty. In this scatter diagram, volume is represented by sales revenue, as is often the case. Each dot is located by plotting the costs for one year on the y axis and the sales revenue for that year on the x axis. The dots lie along a well-defined path, which is indicated by the straight line; but this line may *not* indicate a relationship between costs and volume. It may, instead, indicate nothing more than the tendency for both revenues *and* costs to increase over the past six years because of inflationary factors. If this is the case, then the line shows the trend, or *drift*, of costs *through time*, not the relationship between cost and volume *at a given time*. Any scatter diagram in which volume is measured in *revenue* dollars (rather than in units, as in our previous diagrams), covering a period of years in which revenues were generally increasing each year, is likely to have this characteristic. The longer the period covered, the more unreliable the diagram becomes.

ILLUSTRATION 16–7
SCATTER DIAGRAM ILLUSTRATING DRIFT

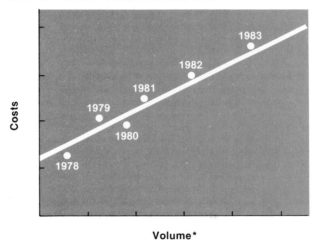

Volume*

*As measured by sales revenue.

Even if the volume is measured in "constant" dollars (i.e., dollars of a given purchasing power) or physical units, regression analysis can lead to misleading inferences. Consider a cost element that behaves as a step function, and assume that the company's volume (expressed in physical units of output) has been increasing each year from 1979 to 1983, as in Illustration 16–8. *Within* a given year, the cost may have been fixed; that

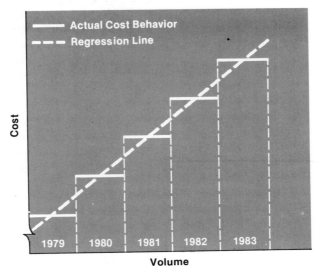

ILLUSTRATION 16–8
MISLEADING INFERENCE FROM REGRESSION ANALYSIS

is, actual cost was on one of the "stair steps" of the diagram. But if regression analysis were applied to the five annual cost amounts, the resulting C-V line would make the cost *appear* to be almost entirely variable. Thus, great care must be taken not to draw *short-run* cost behavior inferences from a regression analysis of *long-run* data. (In fact, Illustration 16–8 illustrates the notion that costs that are fixed in the short run may not be fixed from a long-run perspective.)

Measures of Volume

So far we have been describing a single-product company in which volume can be measured by the number of units produced. In the more common case of a company that makes several different products, the number of units produced is unlikely to be a reliable measure of activity for the obvious reason that some products cost more per unit than others. In these companies, therefore, other measures of volume must be used. Among the "common denominator" volume measures used in practice are labor-hours, labor dollars, homogeneous quantity units such as tons or barrels, or sales value (i.e., the revenues that eventually will be generated by the items produced). Presumably, a certain measure is selected because it most closely reflects the conditions that *cause* costs to change.

In selecting a volume measure, two basic questions must be answered: (1) should the measure be based on *inputs*, or should it be based on *outputs?* and (2) should the measure be expressed in terms of *money amounts*, or should it be expressed in terms of *physical quantities?* Each of these questions is discussed below.

Input versus Output Measures. *Input measures* relate to the resources used in a responsibility center. Examples for a production center are direct labor-hours worked, direct labor cost, machine-hours operated, or pounds of raw material used. *Output measures* relate to the goods and services that flow out of the center.

For C-V diagrams that show the relationship between indirect production costs and volume, an input measure such as direct labor-hours may be a good measure of volume since many elements of indirect product costs tend to vary more closely with other input factors than with output. Other indirect costs, such as inspection costs, might vary more closely with the quantity of products produced, that is, with output.

If the C-V diagram represents total costs for a production center, and if volume is measured in terms of direct labor, which is itself one element of cost, it can be argued that the same numbers affect both costs and volume. This is true, but the diagram nevertheless reflects changes in costs other than direct labor and is therefore useful.

Monetary versus Nonmonetary Measures. A volume measure expressed in physical quantities, such as direct labor-hours, is often better than one expressed in dollars, such as direct labor cost, because the former is unaffected by changes in prices. A wage increase would cause direct labor costs to increase, even if there were no actual increase in the volume of activity. If volume is measured in terms of direct labor dollars, such a measure could be misleading. On the other hand, if price changes are likely to affect both direct labor costs and indirect production costs to the same degree, the use of direct labor cost as the measure of volume in a C-V diagram for total indirect production costs may be a means of allowing implicitly for the effect of these price changes.

Choice of a Measure. These considerations must be tempered by practicality. Total direct labor costs are often available in the cost accounting system without extra calculation, whereas the computation of total direct labor-hours, or machine-hours, may require additional work. Also, since the volume measure for analytical purposes is often (but not always) the same as that used in allocating indirect production costs to products for the purpose of valuing inventories in financial accounting, the appropriateness of the measure for the latter purpose must also be taken into account.

THE PROFITGRAPH

The C-V diagram in Illustration 16–5 can be expanded into a useful device called the *profitgraph* (or *cost-volume-profit graph* or *C-V-P graph*) simply by the addition of a revenue line to it. A profitgraph shows the expected relationship between total costs and revenue at various volumes.[2] A profitgraph can be constructed either for the business as a whole, or for some segment of the business such as a product, a product line, or a division.

On a profitgraph, the measure of volume may be the number of units produced and sold, or it may be dollars of sales revenue. We have already stated the formula for the cost line: $TC = TFC + UVC \cdot X$. Revenue is plotted on the profitgraph on the assumption of a constant selling price per unit. Assuming that volume is to be measured as units of product sold and designating the unit selling price as UR (unit revenue), the number of units of volume as X, and the total revenue as TR, the total revenue (TR) equals the unit selling price (UR) times the number of units of volume (X); or $TR = UR \cdot X$. For example, if the unit selling price is $8.50, the total revenue from the sale of 200 units will be $1,700.

A profitgraph showing these relationships is shown in Illustration 16–9. Although not shown explicitly on the diagram, it should be understood that the relationships are expected to hold only within the relevant volume range. Sometimes, several revenue lines are drawn on a profitgraph, each one showing what revenue would be at a specified unit sell-

ILLUSTRATION 16–9
PROFITGRAPH

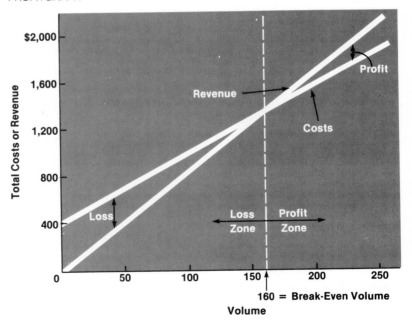

2This graph is also called a "break-even chart," but such a label has the unfortunate implication that the objective of a business is merely to break even.

ing price. This procedure helps to show how a change in selling price affects the profit at any given volume.

The profitgraph is a useful device for analyzing the overall profit characteristics of a business. To illustrate such an analysis, assume the following situation, which is the same as that shown in previous diagrams:

Fixed costs *(TFC)*	$400 per period
Variable costs *(UVC)*	$6 per unit
Selling price *(UR)*	$8.50 per unit

For simplicity, we shall assume that the company makes only one product.

Break-Even Volume

At the *break-even volume*, total costs equal total revenue. This is simply a geometric fact. The break-even point is of little practical interest in a profitable company because attention is focused on the profit region, which should be considerably above the break-even volume. At lower than break-even volumes, a loss is expected; and at higher volumes, a profit is expected. The amount of loss or profit expected at any volume is the vertical distance between the points on the total cost and revenue lines at that volume. The break-even volume is computed as follows:

Since revenue *(TR)* at any volume *(X)* is $TR = UR \cdot X$

And cost *(TC)* at any volume *(X)* is $TC = TFC + UVC \cdot X$

And since at the break-even volume,
  costs = revenue, or $TR = TC$

Then the break-even volume is the
  volume at which $UR \cdot X = TFC + UVC \cdot X$

If we let X equal the break-even volume, then for the above situation, we have:

$$\$8.50 \cdot X = \$400 + \$6 \cdot X$$
$$X = 160 \text{ units}$$

At the break-even volume of 160 units, revenue equals 160 units at $8.50 per unit, which is $1,360; and total costs equal $400 + 160 units at $6 per unit, which is also $1,360.

The equation for the break-even volume, X, can also be stated in the following form:

$$X = \frac{TFC}{UR - UVC}$$

In words, this equation says that the *break-even volume can be found by dividing the fixed costs (TFC) by the difference between selling price per unit (UR) and variable cost per unit (UVC).*[3]

Contribution

Using the same relationships as in Illustration 16–9, we can demonstrate that the *average* profit per unit changes with volume. For example, at 200 units, revenue is $1,700, costs are $1,600 (=$400 + $6 × 200), and profit is $100; for the 200 units, this is an average profit of $0.50 per unit. But at 250 units, revenue is $2,125, costs are $1,900, and profit is $225, for an average profit of $0.90 per unit. This increase in per unit profit occurs because as volume increases, average per unit cost decreases since the average *fixed* cost of each unit decreases. This phenomenon is referred to loosely as "spreading the fixed costs over a higher volume," or more formally as *operating leverage.*[4]

Although profit per unit is different at each volume, there is another number that is constant for all volumes within the relevant range. This number is called the *unit contribution, unit contribution margin,* or *marginal income.* It is the difference between selling price and *variable* cost per unit.

In our example, the unit contribution is $2.50 (= $8.50 − $6.00) per unit. Because this number is a constant, it is an extremely useful way of expressing the relationship between revenue and cost at any volume. For each change of one unit of volume, profit will change by $2.50. Starting at the lower end of the relevant range, each additional unit of volume increases profit by the amount of unit contribution.

We can use the above notation to express these relationships, adding the symbol I for total income or profit:

$$I = (UR - UVC) \cdot X - TFC$$

In words, *total income at any volume is unit contribution (UR − UVC) times volume, minus fixed cost.* In the above example, at a volume of 250 units,

$$(UR - UVC) \cdot X \quad - TFC = I$$
$$(\$8.50 - \$6.00) \cdot 250 - \$400 = \$225$$

---

[3]In an economic sense, a company does not truly break even unless its revenues cover both operating costs *and* the cost of funds employed to finance its assets—that is, the *cost of capital.* Frequently, analysts exclude interest costs on debt from break-even calculations; this understatement of costs results in a lower indicated break-even volume than the "true" break-even volume. Also, as discussed in financial management texts, owners' equity capital is not cost-free; but because its cost cannot be measured objectively or accurately, this cost is often ignored. Omission of owners' equity cost from break-even calculations causes a further understatement of the true break-even volume.

[4]Note in the example that volume went up 25 percent (from 200 to 250 units), but total profit increased 125 percent (from $100 to $225); that profit increased relatively more than volume is the "leverage" phenomenon.

In words, the contribution of $2.50 per unit, times 250 units, minus the fixed cost of $400 gives total income of $225. Stated another way, if the unit contribution is $2.50 per unit and fixed costs are $400, then 160 units must be sold before enough contribution will be earned to cover fixed costs. After that, a profit of $2.50 per unit will be earned. The break-even formula can now be expressed as:

$$\text{Break-even volume} = \frac{\text{Fixed costs}}{\text{Unit contribution}}$$

Break-even volume can also be stated in terms of *revenues*, rather than physical units. In words the formula is:

$$\text{Break-even volume} = \frac{\text{Fixed costs}}{\text{Contribution percent}}$$

The denominator is contribution as a *percent* of revenues. In the example, this is $2.50 ÷ $8.50 = 29.4 percent (0.294). Thus, the break-even volume is $400 ÷ 0.294 = $1,360, which is equivalent to the earlier break-even volume of 160 units at $8.50 per unit.

Contribution Profitgraphs

Using the unit contribution concept, another useful form of profit-graph can be constructed, as shown in Illustration 16–10. In this profit-graph, the vertical axis shows *income*. Note that the income line (1) has a value of zero at 160 units, the break-even volume; (2) has a slope of $2.50 per unit of volume, the unit contribution;[5] and (3) shows a loss of $400 at zero volume (because $400 is the amount of fixed cost, which will have no contribution to offset it at zero volume).

Cash versus Accrual Profitgraphs

The revenue and cost numbers used in profitgraphs and break-even calculations may be either cash-basis or accrual-basis amounts. The choice in a break-even analysis depends on whether the analyst is interested in determining (1) the volume at which cash inflows from sales equal related cash outlays for operating costs or (2) the volume at which reported revenue equals the related expenses. While in a given time period, revenue and cash inflows from sales (i.e., collections) tend to be about equal, the noncash nature of *depreciation* will cause the period's reported fixed expenses to be larger than the related cash outflows. Thus, when using a profitgraph, it is important to know whether the underlying figures are cash flows or accrual-basis amounts.

For the profitgraphs in the illustrations to be meaningful on a *cash* basis, one must assume that the period's sales volume and production

---

[5]For example, as volume goes from 160 to 200 units, income goes from $0 to $100; slope = $\Delta y / \Delta x$ = $100/40 units = $2.50 per unit.

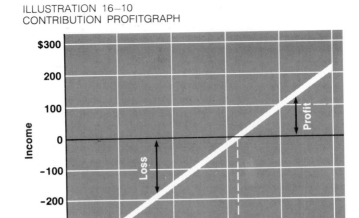

ILLUSTRATION 16–10
CONTRIBUTION PROFITGRAPH

volume (both expressed in physical units) are *equal*. For example, suppose that May sales were 200 units but that May production output was 250 units. It is not meaningful to call May's profit the difference between (1) the cash revenues from 200 units and (2) the cash costs of producing 250 units plus May's cash selling and administrative costs. Hence, the profitgraph implicitly assumes sales volume and production volume equality for cash-basis numbers. However, with accrual accounting's matching concept, if 200 units are sold, then only 200 units' costs are charged as the related expense (i.e., costs of goods sold is based on 200 units), and the costs of the other 50 units are capitalized in the asset account, Finished Goods Inventory. Thus, one need not assume production and sales volume equality for an accrual-basis profitgraph to be meaningful, *provided* one remembers to interpret total "cost" as the period's *cost of goods sold* plus selling and administrative costs, rather than the period's *production* costs plus selling and administrative costs.

Improving Profit Performance

These C-V-P relationships suggest that a useful way of studying the basic profit characteristics of a business is to focus not on the profit per unit (which is different at every volume) but rather on the total fixed costs and the contribution per unit. In these terms, there are four basic ways in which the profit of a business that makes a single product can be increased:

1. Increase selling price per unit (UR).
2. Decrease variable cost per unit (UVC).
3. Decrease fixed costs (TFC).
4. Increase volume (X).

The separate effects of each of these possibilities are shown in the following calculations and in the contribution profitgraphs displayed in Illustration 16–11. Each starts from the present situation that is assumed to be: selling price, $8.50 per unit; variable cost, $6 per unit; fixed costs, $400 per period; volume, 200 units; and hence profit, $100 (= $2.50 · 200 − $400). The effect of a 10 percent change in each profit-determining factor would be:

| | | Effect on— | | New | Income |
Factor		Revenue	Costs	Income	Increase*
A.	Increase selling price by 10%.......	$+170	$ 0	$270	170%
B.	Decrease variable cost by 10%	0	− 120	220	120
C.	Decrease fixed cost by 10%........	0	− 40	140	40
D.	Increase volume by 10%	+170	+ 120	150	50

*Increase over present income of $100.

If instead of varying each factor separately we look at some of the interrelationships among them, we can calculate, for example, that a 34 percent (i.e., $136) increase in fixed costs could be offset either by an 8 percent increase in selling price, a 27 percent increase in volume, or an 11 percent decrease in variable costs.

The foregoing calculations assume that each of the factors is independent of the others, a situation that is rarely the case in the real world. An increase in selling price often is accompanied by a decrease in volume, for example. Changes in the factors must therefore usually be studied simultaneously rather than separately.

Margin of Safety.   Another calculation made from a profitgraph is the *margin of safety*. This is the amount or ratio by which the current volume exceeds the break-even volume. Assuming current volume is 200 units, the margin of safety in our illustrative situation is 40 units (200 − 160 break-even volume), or 20 percent of current volume. Sales volume can decrease by 20 percent before a loss is incurred, other factors remaining equal.

Several Products

The C-V-P relationships described above apply in the situation in which the company makes only a single product. The C-V-P relationships also hold in a company that mkes several products if each

ILLUSTRATION 16–11
EFFECT OF 10 PERCENT CHANGE IN PROFIT FACTORS

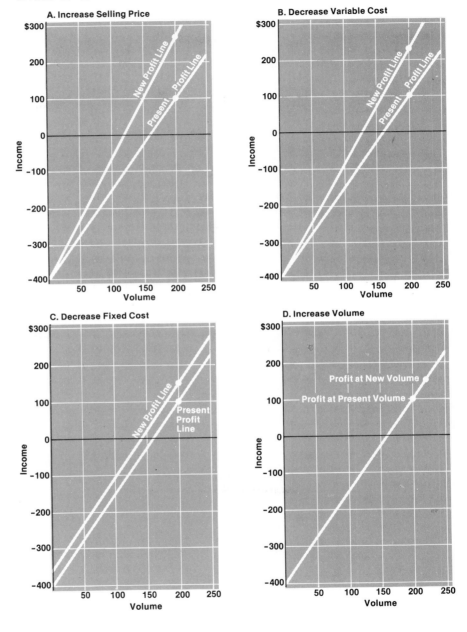

product has approximately the same unit contribution as a *percentage of sales*. A profitgraph could be constructed for such a company by using sales *revenue*, rather than units, as the measure of volume. In such a company, each dollar of sales revenue produces approximately the same marginal income (i.e., contribution) as every other dollar of sales revenue.

If, however, the company makes several products and they have *different* unit contributions, the depiction of a valid C-V-P relationship is more complicated. If the *product mix* remains relatively constant, then a single profitgraph is still valid. It shows the *average* unit contribution for all products, rather than the individual unit contribution of any product.

Changes in the product mix affect profits in a way that is not revealed by the type of profitgraph described above. For example, even if sales revenue does not change from one period to the next, profits will increase if in the latter period the proportion of products that have a high unit contribution is greater than it was in the first period.

When products have different unit contributions and when the product mix changes, one approach to C-V-P analysis is to treat each product as a separate entity, and to construct a profitgraph for that entity, just as we did for the business as a whole. This method requires that all costs of the business be allocated to individual products, using the approaches to be described in Chapter 19. The break-even point on such a profitgraph is the volume at which the unit contribution of that product covers that product's equitable share of the company's fixed costs.

Other Influences on Costs

C-V diagrams and profitgraphs show only what total costs are expected to be at various *levels* of volume. For example, such diagrams will show that the total variable cost of 200 units is double the variable cost of 100 units. There are many reasons, other than the level of volume, why the costs in one period are different from those in another period. Some of these are listed below.

1. *Changes in input prices.* One of the most important causes of changes in a C-V diagram is that the prices of input factors change. Inflation is a persistent, and probably permanent, phenomenon. Wage rates, salaries, material costs, and costs of services all go up. A C-V diagram can get seriously out of date, and hence be misleading, if it is not adjusted for the effect of these changes.

2. *The rate at which volume changes.* Rapid changes in volume are more difficult for personnel to adjust to than are moderate changes in volume. Therefore, the more rapid the change in volume, the

more likely it is that costs will depart from the straight-line cost-volume pattern.

3. *The direction of change in volume.* When volume is increasing, costs tend to lag behind the straight-line relationship either because the organization is unable to hire the additional workers that are assumed in the cost line or because supervisors try to "get by" without adding more costs. Similarly, when volume is decreasing, there is a reluctance to lay off workers and to shrink other elements of cost, and this also causes a lag.

4. *The duration of change in volume.* A temporary change of volume, in either direction, tends to affect costs less than a change that lasts a long time, for much the same reasons as were given in the preceding paragraph.

5. *Prior knowledge of the change.* If production managers have adequate advance notice of a change in volume, they can plan for it. Actual costs therefore are more likely to remain close to the C-V line than is the case when the change in volume is unexpected.

6. *Productivity.* The C-V diagram assumes a certain level of productivity in the use of resources. As the level of productivity changes, the cost changes. Overall productivity in the United States has fluctuated in recent years (after increasing at a rate of 3 percent per year in the 1950s and 1960s); labor costs have fluctuated correspondingly (in constant dollar terms).

7. *Management discretion.* Some cost items change because management has decided that they *should* change. Some companies, for example, have relatively large headquarters staffs, while others have small ones. The size of these staffs, and hence the costs associated with them, can be varied within fairly wide limits, depending on management's judgment as to what the optimum size is. Such types of cost are called *discretionary costs.* They are discussed in more detail in Chapter 24.

For these and other reasons, it is not possible to predict the total costs of an organization in a certain period simply by predicting the volume for that period and then determining the costs at that volume by reading a C-V diagram. Nevertheless, the effect of volume on costs and profits is so important that the C-V diagram and the profitgraph are extremely useful tools in analysis. In using them, interpretation of relationships they depict must be tempered by estimates of the influence of other factors.

Learning Curves. Studies have shown that the reduction in unit production cost associated with increased productivity has, in many situations, a characteristic pattern that can be estimated with reasonable accuracy. This pattern is called the *learning curve,* or the *experience curve.* It is described in the Appendix to this chapter.

SUMMARY

An understanding of cost behavior is basic to the further study of full cost accounting, differential accounting, and responsibility accounting. Total variable costs vary in direct proportion with volume, whereas unit variable cost is a constant. Total fixed costs do not vary with volume, but unit fixed cost decreases as volume increases. Semivariable costs can be decomposed into a variable cost and a fixed cost component.

The level of volume has an important effect on costs. The effect can be depicted in a C-V diagram, or, if the relationship is approximately linear, by the equation $TC = TFC + UVC \cdot X$. The diagram and the equation state that the total costs (TC) at any volume are the sum of the fixed costs (TFC) plus the unit variable costs (UVC) times the number of units (X). These relationships hold only within a certain range of volume, the relevant range.

When a revenue line is superimposed on a C-V diagram, the diagram becomes a profitgraph. The profitgraph shows the relationship between revenue and costs (and hence the profit or loss) at any volume within the relevant range. A special case shown on the profitgraph is the break-even volume, which can be calculated by dividing fixed costs by the unit contribution (unit price minus unit variable costs). The profitgraph can also be used to analyze the probable consequences of various proposals to change the basic relationships depicted therein. Since profit is affected by factors other than volume, however, the profitgraph does not tell the whole story.

APPENDIX: LEARNING CURVES

In many situations, productivity increases as a function of the *cumulative* volume of output of a product. The phenomenon was first observed in the aircraft industry, where it was found that certain costs tend to decrease, per unit, in a predictable pattern as the workers and their supervisors become more familiar with the work; as the work flow, tooling, and methods improve; as less materials waste and rework result; as fewer skilled workers need to be used; and so on. The decreasing costs are a function of the learning process, which results (in part) in fewer labor-hours being necessary to produce a unit of product as more units of the same product are completed. It should be noted, however, that every cost element does not necessarily decrease. For instance, material costs often are not subject to the learning process, except to the extent that they may decrease because waste is eliminated, or less expensive substitute materials are discovered.

Research in a number of industries has shown that there is a regular pattern to this cost reduction, and that this is likely to be a constant percentage reduction in average unit cost when *cumulative* production doubles. For example, an 80 percent learning curve means that if the average unit cost is $50 when production has reached 10,000 units, cumulative average unit cost will decline to $40 per unit when production cumulates to 20,000 units. (Cumulative average cost is the total cost to date divided by the total number of units produced to date.) Such a relationship is a straight line when plotted on log-log graph paper.[6]

> **Example.** Assume a company introduced product A in 1973, makes 10,000 units a year, that the costs of product A were subject to an 80 percent learning curve, and that the total cost for the 10,000 units made in 1973 was $500,000. The average unit cost in 1973 therefore was $50.
>
> In 1974, an additional 10,000 units were made. If the 80 percent learning curve held, cumulative average unit cost of the 20,000 total units would be 80 percent of $50, or $40. The total cost of the 20,000 units would be $800,000 (=20,000 × $40), the costs for 1974 would be $300,000 (=$800,000 − $500,000 costs of 1973), and the unit cost for 1974's production would be $30 (=$300,000 ÷ 10,000), a $20 decrease from 1973.
>
> Carrying the example into later years gives a much less dramatic decline. For example, by the end of 1982, 100,000 units would have been produced. Thus, 10,000 units produced in 1983 would represent only a 10 percent increase in the cumulative quantity, and the unit cost in that year would decrease by only about $0.50. In more detail:

Years since Introduction	Cumulative Quantity	Cumulative Average Unit Cost	Unit Cost for Increment	Average Annual Decrease
1	10,000	$50.00	$50.00	—
2	20,000	40.00	30.00	$20.00
4	40,000	32.00	24.00	3.00
8	80,000	25.60	19.20	1.20
16	160,000	20.48	15.36	0.48

Illustration 16–12 shows two examples of these cost-cumulative production relationships. Note the persistence of the approximately straight-line relationship over a number of years.

Because of this phenomenon, historical unit costs tend to be higher than future costs, in terms of *constant dollars*. This is especially the case with new products, for the learning phenomenon has relatively little effect on the costs of products that have been manufactured for many years. Such products are said to be "near the bottom of the learning curve."

This characteristic decline in average unit cost does not happen

---

[6] The learning-curve formula is $Y_i = ai^k$, where i = cumulative units produced, Y_i = cumulative average unit cost of i units, $a = Y_1$ (cost of the first unit), and k is a parameter determined by the rate of learning (e.g., for an 80 percent learning curve, $k = -0.3219$). Expressed in logarithms, the formula becomes $\log Y_i = \log a + k \log i$; hence, the linearity when graphed on log-log paper.

ILLUSTRATION 16–12
EXAMPLES OF LEARNING CURVES

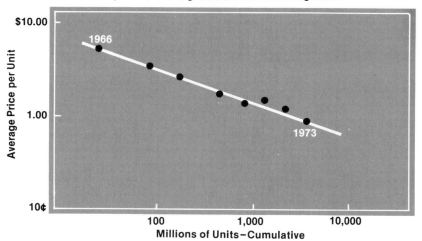

A. World Shipments of Integrated Circuits Learning Curve

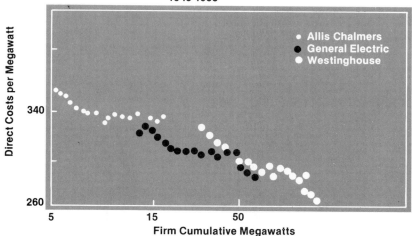

B. Direct Cost per Megawatt—Steam Turbine Generators
1946-1963

Source: From the publication *Perspectives,* by the Boston Consulting Group. The integrated circuits curve appeared originally in the First Quarter Report of Texas Instruments, Incorporated, April 18, 1973. The steam turbine generator curve was compiled from information furnished by General Electric, Westinghouse, and Allis Chalmers in connection with antitrust litigation.

automatically. Rather, it depends on *management efforts* to increase efficiency. It is important, therefore, that the learning potential be exploited, and that management realize that costs as depicted on a C-V diagram are probably too high if cumulative volume has increased significantly since the diagram was prepared.

SUGGESTIONS FOR FURTHER READING

Abernathy, William J., and Kenneth Wayne. "Limits of the Learning Curve." *Harvard Business Review,* September–October 1974, p. 109.

Anderson, Lane K. "Expanded Breakeven Analysis for a Multi-Product Company." *Management Accounting,* July 1975, p. 30.

Anderson, Roy A., and Harry R. Biederman. "Using Cost-Volume-Profit Charts." *The Controller's Handbook,* chap. 6. Homewood, Ill.: Dow Jones-Irwin, 1978.

Jaedicke, Robert K., and Alexander A. Robichek. "Cost-Volume-Profit Analysis under Conditions of Uncertainty." *The Accounting Review,* October 1964, p. 917.

Raun, Donald L. "The Limitations of Profit Graphs, Breakeven Analysis, and Budgets." *The Accounting Review,* October 1964, p. 930.

Cases

CASE 16–1   Chris Collins

Chris Collins was supervisor of an assembly department in Dexter Electronics Company. In recent weeks, Collins had become convinced that a certain component, number S-36, could be produced more efficiently if certain assembly methods changes were made. Collins had described this proposal to the company's industrial engineer, but the engineer had quickly dismissed Collins' ideas—mainly, Collins thought, because the engineer had not thought of them first.

Collins had frequently thought of starting a business, and felt that the ability to produce the S-36 component at a lower cost might provide this opportunity. Dexter's purchasing agent assured Collins that Dexter would be willing to buy S-36s from Collins if the price were 10–15 percent below Dexter's current cost of $1.65 per unit. Working at home, Collins experimented with the new methods, which

were based on the use of a new fixture to aid in assembling each S-36. This experimentation seemed successful, so Collins proceeded to prepare some estimates for large-scale S-36 production. Collins determined the following:

1. A local toolmaker would make the new fixtures for a price of $500 each. One fixture would be needed for each assembly worker.

2. Assembly workers were readily available, on either a full-time or part-time basis, at a wage of $3.75 per hour. Collins felt that another 20 percent of wages would be necessary for fringe benefits. Collins estimated that on the average (including restbreaks), a worker could assemble, test, and pack 15 units of the S-36 per hour.

3. Purchased components for the S-36 should cost about $0.85 per unit over

534

the next year. Shipping supplies and delivery costs would amount to approximately $0.05 per unit.

4. Suitable space was available for assembly operations at a rental of $600 per month. A 12-month lease was required.

5. Assembly tables, stools, and other necessary equipment would cost about $300 per assembly worker.

6. Collins, as general manager, would receive a salary of $2,000 per month.

7. A combination office manager-bookkeeper was available for a salary of $900 per month.

8. Miscellaneous costs, including maintenance, supplies, and utilities, were expected to average about $325 per month.

9. Dexter Electronics would purchase between 400,000 and 525,000 units of S-36 a year, with 450,000 being Dexter's purchasing agent's "best guess." However, Collins would have to commit to a price of $1.40 per unit for the next 12 months.

Collins showed these estimates to a friend who was a cost analyst in another electronics firm. This friend said that all of the estimates appeared reasonable, but told Collins that in addition to the required investment in fixtures and equipment, about $70,000 would be needed to finance accounts receivable and inventories. The friend also advised buying enough fixtures and other equipment to enable producing the maximum estimated volume (525,000 units per year) on a one-shift basis (assuming 2,000 labor-hours per assembler per year). Collins thought this was good advice.

Questions

1. What are Collins' expected variable costs per unit? Fixed costs per month? What would the *total* costs per year of Collins' business be if volume was 400,000 units? 450,000 units? 525,000 units? (Limit yourself to *cash* costs; ignore depreciation of fixtures and equipment. Also, disregard any interest costs Collins might incur on borrowed funds.)

2. What is the average cost *per unit* of S-36 at each of these three volumes?

3. Reanswer Questions 1 and 2 assuming that (1) Collins wanted to guarantee assembly workers 2,000 hours of pay per year; (2) enough workers would be hired to assemble 450,000 units a year; (3) these workers could work overtime at a cost (including fringes) of $6.75 per hour; and (4) no additional fixed costs would be incurred if overtime were needed. (Do not use these assumptions for Question 4.)

4. Reanswer Questions 1 and 2, now including depreciation as an expense. Assume the fixtures and other equipment have a useful life of six years, and that straight-line depreciation will be used.

5. Do you think Chris Collins should resign from Dexter Electronics and form the proposed enterprise?

CASE 16–2 Hospital Supply, Inc.

Hospital Supply, Inc., produced hydraulic hoists that were used by hospitals to move bedridden patients. The costs of manufacturing and marketing hydraulic hoists at the company's normal volume of 3,000 units per month are shown in Exhibit 1.

EXHIBIT 1
COSTS PER UNIT FOR HYDRAULIC HOISTS

Unit manufacturing costs:

Variable materials	$100	
Variable labor	150	
Variable overhead	50	
Fixed overhead	120	
Total unit manufacturing costs		$420

Unit marketing costs:

Variable	50	
Fixed	140	
Total unit marketing costs		190
Total unit costs		$610

Questions

The following questions refer only to the data given above. Unless otherwise stated, assume there is *no connection* between the situations described in the questions; each is to be treated independently. Unless otherwise stated, a regular selling price of $740 per unit should be assumed. Ignore income taxes and other costs that are not mentioned in Exhibit 1 or in a question itself.

1. What is the break-even volume in units? In sales dollars?

2. Market research estimates that volume could be increased to 3,500 units, which is well within hoist production capacity limitations, if the price were cut from $740 to $650 per unit. Assuming the cost behavior patterns implied by the data in Exhibit 1 are correct, would you recommend that this action be taken? What would be the impact on monthly sales, costs, and income?

3. On March 1, a contract offer is made to Hospital Supply by the federal government to supply 500 units to Veterans Administration hospitals for delivery by March 31. Because of an unusually large number of rush orders from their regular customers, Hospital Supply plans to produce 4,000 units during March, which will use all available capacity. If the government order is accepted, 500 units normally sold to regular customers would be lost to a competitor. The contract given by the government would reimburse the government's share of March production costs, plus pay a fixed fee (profit) of $50,000. (There would be no variable marketing costs incurred on the government's units.) What impact would accepting the government contract have on March income?

4. Hospital Supply has an opportunity to enter a foreign market in which price competition is keen. An attraction of the foreign market is that demand there is greatest when demand in the domestic market is quite low; thus, idle production facilities could be used without affecting domestic business.

    An order for 1,000 units is being sought at a below-normal price in order to enter this market. Shipping costs for this order will amount to $75 per unit, while total costs of obtaining the contract (marketing costs) will be $4,000. Domestic business would be unaffected by this order. What is the minimum unit price Hospital Supply should consider for this order of 1,000 units?

5. An inventory of 230 units of an obsolete model of the hoist remains in the stockroom. These must be sold through regular channels at reduced prices, or the inventory will soon be valueless. What is the minimum price that would be acceptable in selling these units?

6. A proposal is received from an outside contractor who will make and ship 1,000 hydraulic hoist units per month directly to Hospital Supply's customers as orders are received from Hospital Supply's sales force. Hospital Supply's fixed marketing costs would be unaffected, but its variable marketing costs would be cut by 20 percent (to $40 per unit) for these 1,000 units produced by the contractor. Hospital Supply's plant would operate at two thirds of its normal level, and total fixed manufacturing costs would be cut by 30 percent (to $252,000). What in-house unit cost should be used to compare with the quotation received from the supplier? Should the proposal be accepted for a price (i.e., payment to the contractor) of $425 per unit?

7. Assume the same facts as above in Question 6 *except* that the idle facilities would be used to produce 800 modified hydraulic hoists per month for use in hospital operating rooms. These modified hoists could be sold for $900 each, while the costs of production would be $550 per unit variable manufacturing expense. Variable marketing costs would be $100 per unit. Fixed marketing and manufacturing costs would be unchanged whether the original 3,000 regular hoists were manufactured or the mix of 2,000 regular hoists plus 800 modified hoists was produced. What is the maximum purchase price per unit that Hospital Supply should be willing to pay the outside contractor? Should the proposal be accepted for a price of $425 per unit to the contractor?

CASE 16–3 Bill French

Bill French picked up the phone and called his boss, Wes Davidson, controller of Duo-Products Corporation. "Say, Wes, I'm all set for the meeting this afternoon. I've put together a set of break-even statements that should really make people sit up and take notice—and I think they'll be able to understand them, too." After a brief conversation about other matters, the call was concluded and French turned to his charts for one last checkout before the meeting.

French had been hired six months earlier as a staff accountant. He was directly responsible to Davidson and up to the time of this case had been doing routine types of analysis work. French was an alumnus of a graduate business school and was considered by his associates to be quite capable and unusually conscientious. It was this latter characteristic that had apparently caused him to "rub some of the working folks the wrong way," as one of his co-workers put it. French was well aware of his capabilities and took advantage of every opportunity that arose to try to educate those around him. Wes Davidson's invitation for French to attend an informal manager's meeting had come as some surprise to others in the accounting group. However, when French requested permission to make a presentation of some break-even data, Davidson acquiesced. The Duo-Products Corporation had not been making use of this type of analysis in its planning or review procedures.

Basically, what French had done was to determine the level at which the company must operate in order to break even. As he phrased it,

The company must be able at least to sell a sufficient volume of goods so that it will cover all the variable costs of producing and selling the goods; further, it will not make a profit unless it covers the fixed, or nonvariable, costs as well. The level of operation at which total costs (that is, variable plus nonvariable) are just covered is the break-even volume. This should be the lower limit in all our planning.

The accounting records had provided the following information that French used in constructing his chart:

Plant capacity—2 million units.
Past year's level of operations—1.5 million units.
Average unit selling price—$1.20
Total fixed costs—$520,000
Average variable unit cost—$0.75.

From this information, French observed that each unit contributed $0.45 to fixed costs after covering the variable costs. Given total fixed costs of $520,000, he calculated that 1,155,556 units must be

sold in order to break even. He verified this conclusion by calculating the dollar sales volume that was required to break even. Since the variable costs per unit were 62.5 percent of the selling price, French reasoned that 37.5 percent of every sales dollar was left available to cover fixed costs. Thus, fixed costs of $520,000 require sales of $1,386,667 in order to break even.

When he constructed a break-even chart to present the information graphically, his conclusions were further verified. The chart also made it clear that the firm was operating at a fair margin over the break-even requirements, and that the pretax profits accruing (at the rate of 37.5 percent of every sales dollar over break even) increased rapidly as volume increased (see Exhibit 1).

Shortly after lunch, French and Dav-

EXHIBIT 1
BREAK-EVEN CHART—TOTAL BUSINESS

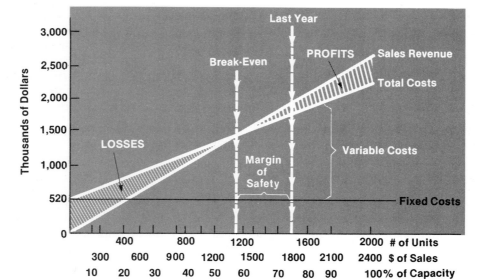

Sales Performance in Thousands
Break-Even Volume = 1,156,000 Units, or $1,387,000

idson left for the meeting. Several representatives of the manufacturing departments were present, as well as the general sales manager, two assistant sales managers, the purchasing officer, and two people from the product engineering office. Davidson introduced French to the few people whom he had not already met, and then the meeting got under way. French's presentation was the last item on Davidson's agenda, and in due time the controller introduced French, explaining his interest in cost control and analysis.

French had prepared enough copies of his chart and supporting calculations for everyone at the meeting. He described carefully what he had done and explained how the chart pointed to a profitable year, dependent on meeting the volume of sales activity that had been maintained in the past. It soon became apparent that some of the participants had known in advance what French planned to discuss; they had come prepared to challenge him and soon had taken control of the meeting. The following exchange ensued (see Exhibit 2 for a checklist of participants with their titles):

EXHIBIT 2
LIST OF PARTICIPANTS IN THE MEETING

Bill French.	Staff accountant
Wes Davidson	Controller
John Cooper.	Production control
Fred Williams	Manufacturing
Ray Bradshaw	Assistant sales manager
Arnie Winetki	General sales manager
Anne Fraser	Administrative assistant to president

Cooper [production control]: You know, Bill, I'm really concerned that you haven't allowed for our planned changes in volume next year. It seems to me that you should have allowed for the sales department's guess that we'll boost sales by 20 percent,

unit-wise. We'll be pushing 90 percent of what we call capacity then. It sure seems that this would make quite a difference in your figuring.

French: That might be true, but as you can see, all you have to do is read the cost and profit relationship right off the chart for the new volume. Let's see—at a million-eight units we'd . . . .

Williams [manufacturing]: Wait a minute, now!!! If you're going to talk in terms of 90 percent of capacity, and it looks like that's what it will be, you had better note that we'll be shelling out some more for the plant. We've already got okays on investment money that will boost your fixed costs by $10,000 a month, easy. And that may not be all. We may call it 90 percent of plant capacity, but there are a lot of places where we're just full up and we can't pull things up any tighter.

Cooper: See, Bill? Fred is right, but I'm not finished on this bit about volume changes. According to the information that I've got here—and it came from your office—I'm not sure that your break-even chart can really be used even if there were to be no changes next year. It looks to me like you've got average figures that don't allow for the fact that we're dealing with three basic products. Your report here on costs (see Exhibit 3), according to product lines, for last year makes it pretty clear that the "average" is way out of line. How would the break-even point look if we took this on an individual product basis?

French: Well, I'm not sure. It seems to me that there is only one break-even point for the firm. Whether we take it product by product or in total, we've got to hit that point. I'll be glad to check for you if you want, but. . . .

Bradshaw [assistant sales manager]: Guess I may as well get in on this one, Bill. If you're going to do anything with individual products, you ought to know that we're looking for a big swing in our prod-

EXHIBIT 3
PRODUCT CLASS COST ANALYSIS
Normal Year

	Aggregate	"A"	"B"	"C"
Sales at full capacity (units)	2,000,000			
Actual sales volume (units)	1,500,000	600,000	400,000	500,000
Unit sales price	$ 1.20	$ 1.67	$ 1.50	$ 0.40
Total sales revenue	1,800,000	1,000,000	600,000	200,000
Variable cost per unit	0.75	1.25	0.625	0.25
Total variable cost	1,125,000	750,000	250,000	125,000
Fixed costs	520,000	170,000	275,000	75,000
Profit	155,000	80,000	75,000	—0—
Ratios:				
Variable cost to sales	0.63	0.75	0.42	0.63
Marginal income to sales	0.37	0.25	0.58	0.37
Utilization of capacity	75.0%	30.0%	20.0%	25.0%

uct mix. It might even start before we get into the new season. The "A" line is really losing out, and I imagine that we'll be lucky to hold two thirds of the volume there next year. Wouldn't you buy that Arnie? [Agreement from the general sales manager.] That's not too bad, though, because we expect that we should pick up the 200,000 that we lose, and about a quarter million units more, over in "C" production. We don't see anything that shows much of a change in "B". That's been solid for years and shouldn't change much now.

Winetki [general sales manager]: Bradshaw's called it about as we figure it, but there's something else here too. We've talked about our pricing on "C" enough, and now I'm really going to push our side of it. Ray's estimate of maybe half a million—450,000 I guess it was—increase on "C" for next year is on the basis of doubling the price with no change in cost. We've been priced so low on this item that it's been a crime—we've got to raise, but good, for two reasons. First, for our reputation; the price is out of line classwise and is completely inconsistent with our quality reputation. Second, if we don't raise the price, we'll be swamped and we can't handle it. You heard what Williams said about capacity. The way

the whole "C" field is exploding, we'll have to answer to another half million units in unsatisfied orders if we don't jack the price up. We can't afford to expand that much for this product.

At this point, Anne Fraser (administrative assistant to the president) walked up toward the front of the room from where she had been standing near the rear door. The discussion broke for a minute, and she took advantage of the lull to interject a few comments.

Fraser: This has certainly been enlightening. You clearly have a valuable familiarity with our operations. As long as you're going to try to get all the things together that you ought to pin down for next year, let's see what I can add to help you:

Number One: Let's remember that everything that shows in the profit area here on Bill's chart is divided just about evenly between the government and us. Now, for last year we can read a profit of about $150,000. Well, that's right. But we were left with half of that, and then paid our dividends of $50,000 to the stockholders. Since we've got an anniversary year coming up, we'd like to put out a special dividend of about 50 percent extra. We ought to retain $25,000 in the business, too. This means that we'd like to hit $100,000 profit *after* taxes.

Number Two: From where I sit, it looks as if we're going to have negotiations with the union again, and this time it's liable to cost us. All the indications are—and this isn't public—that we may have to meet demands that will boost our production costs—what do you call them here, Bill—variable costs—by 10 percent across the board. This may kill the bonus-dividend plans, but we've got to hold the line on past profits. This means that we can give that much to the union only if we can make it in added revenues. I guess you'd say that that raises your break-even point, Bill—and for that one I'd consider the company's profit to be a fixed cost.

Number Three: Maybe this is the time to think about switching our product emphasis. Arnie may know better than I which of the products is more profitable. You check me out on this Arnie—and it might be a good idea for you and Bill to get together on this one, too. These figures that I have (Exhibit 3) make it look like the percentage contribution on line "A" is the lowest of the bunch. If we're losing volume there as rapidly as you sales folks say, and if we're as hard pressed for space as Fred has indicated, maybe we'd be better off grabbing some of that big demand for "C" by shifting some of the facilities over there from "A".

Davidson: Thanks, Anne. I sort of figured that we'd wind up here as soon as Bill brought out his charts. This is an approach that we've barely touched upon, but, as you can see, you've all got ideas that have got to be made to fit here somewhere. Let me suggest this: Bill, you rework your chart and try to bring into it some of the points that were made here today. I'll see if I can summarize what everyone seems to be looking for.

First of all, I have the idea that your presentation is based on a rather important series of assumptions. Most of the questions that were raised were really about those assumptions. It might help us all if you try to set the assumptions down in black and white so that we can see just how they influence the analysis.

Then, I think that John would like to see the unit sales increase taken up, and he'd also like to see whether there's any difference if you base the calculations on an analysis of individual product lines. Also, as Ray suggested, since the product mix is bound to change, why not see how things look if the shift materializes as he has forecast? Arnie would like to see the influence of a price increase in the "C" line; Fred looks toward an increase in fixed manufacturing costs of $10,000 a month, and Anne has suggested that we should consider taxes, dividends, expected union demands, and the question of product emphasis.

I think that ties it all together. Let's hold off on our next meeting until Bill has time to work this all into shape.

With that, the participants broke off into small groups and the meeting disbanded. French and Davidson headed back to their offices and French, in a tone of concern asked Davidson, "Why didn't you warn me about the hornet's nest I was walking into?"

"Bill, you didn't ask!"

Questions

1. What are the assumptions implicit in Bill French's determination of his company's break-even point?

2. On the basis of French's revised information, what does next year look like:

    a. What is the break-even point?

    b. What level of operations must be achieved to pay the extra dividend, ignoring union demands?

    c. What level of operations must be achieved to meet the union demands, ignoring bonus dividends?

    d. What level of operations must be

achieved to meet both dividends and expected union requirements?

3. Can the break-even analysis help the company decide whether to alter the existing product emphasis? What can the company afford to invest for additional "C" capacity?

4. Calculate *each* of the three product's break-even points using the data in Exhibit 3. Why is the *sum* of these three volumes not equal to the 1,155,556 units aggregate break-even volume?

5. Is this type of analysis of any value? For what can it be used?

CASE 16–4   Azienda Vinicola Italiana

Azienda Vinicola Italiana produced and bottled wines. A large percentage of its sales were of special table wine. Most of its customers, located in the principal Italian cities, were served through local representatives. Its prices were in line with those of competitors.

In 1982, the firm sold 704,000 liters[1] of wine, in 871,850 bottles. In recent years, demand had been increasing, and the firm had approached the limit of its productive capacity, which was estimated to be 900,000 bottles a year.

The production process was not complicated, since the firm did not buy grapes but rather bought either mosto[2] or bulk wine. This policy had the disadvantage that the firm could not assure itself of a consistently high-quality product. Moreover, it was estimated that if grapes were purchased, the price of raw material would be reduced by about Lit.[3] 110 per bottle. On the other hand, the purchase and installation of equipment needed for pressing grapes would require an addi-

tional investment of about Lit. 550 million. No significant increase in labor costs was anticipated under such a practice.

In the production department there were 40 employees who worked a total of about 90,000 hours in 1982, and whose average wage per hour, including fringe benefits, was Lit. 4,000. The administrative manager was of the opinion that 40 percent of this labor expense should be considered as being fixed, while the remainder could be considered as varying proportionally with production volume.

In 1982, production had required 700,000 liters of mosto and bulk wine, purchased at a total cost of Lit. 602,272,000. The average cost incurred for auxiliary materials (bottles, stoppers, neckbands, labels, and so forth) was about Lit. 450 per bottle.

The income statement for 1982 is shown in Exhibit 1.

The administrative manager wished to reorganize the firm in order to exploit its productive capability to the utmost and, above all, to increase the net profit, which the owners did not consider satisfactory. They were of the opinion that a net profit of 8 or 9 percent of sales could be realized.

As a basis upon which to make decisions, the administrative manager intended to use charts of costs and reve-

---

[1] One liter is slightly more than one United States liquid quart.

[2] Mosto is the juice of grapes before the fermentation process takes place. The fermentation process takes about one month. During this process, carbon dioxide develops and the sugar is converted into alcohol. Therefore, mosto is an unstable product, and wine is a stable product.

[3] In 1982, 100 Italian lire (abbreviated "Lit.") equaled approximately U.S. $0.077.

EXHIBIT 1

Income Statement
For 1982 in Lire
(000 omitted)

Sales		1,921,370
Costs		
Labor	357,136	
Raw materials	602,272	
Auxiliary materials	393,514	
General manufacturing expenses (including pay		
of two cellar foremen)	52,744	1,405,666
Gross margin		515,704
General administrative expenses (including the		
salary of a person skilled in the art of making		
and preserving wine)	184,196	
Depreciation	115,940	
Interest	82,500	
Advertising	86,900	469,536
Net income		46,168

nues that he had seen other firms use and that he considered helpful. The first step in this graphic analysis was a study of costs, separating fixed costs from variable costs. For that purpose, he examined the income statements of preceding years and came to the conclusion that the figures for 1982 were representative. He also noticed that the different types of wine had been sold in more or less the same relative proportions each year, despite large fluctuations in the total volume of business, and this fact confirmed his belief that the figures for 1982 were representative. He therefore prepared the following analysis (in thousands of lire):

Fixed costs:

40% of labor cost	142,854
Staff salaries	118,196
General manufacturing expenses	52,744
General administrative expenses	66,000
Advertising expenses	86,900
Interest	82,500
Depreciation	115,940
	665,134

Variable costs:

60% of labor cost	214,282
Raw materials	602,272
Auxiliary materials	393,514
	1,210,068

The administrative manager assumed a maximum capacity of 900,000 bottles a year. At current prices he estimated this would produce sales revenue of Lit. 1,980 million.

With the present structure of costs and revenue, the profits resulting from an annual production of 900,000 bottles would be small. The administrative manager decided, therefore, to try to discover a way to change costs and revenue so as to obtain a profit of Lit. 176 million a year, which would be almost 9 percent of sales of Lit. 1,980 million.

Questions

1. Accepting the distribution between fixed and variable elements as estimated by the administrative manager, prepare a chart of costs and revenues. Determine the volume of production at which the firm reaches its break-even point and the profit at capacity operation.

2. Draw three other charts, each constructed so that a production of 900,000 bottles will produce a profit of Lit. 176 million, one in which selling price is assumed to increase, another in which fixed costs are

assumed to decrease, and a third in which variable costs are assumed to decrease. What are the break-even points in each of these situations?

3. What are the most likely alternatives to consider so as to achieve a profit of Lit. 176 million?

CASE 16–5 Morrin Aircraft Company

On several occasions since late 1980, Morrin Aircraft Company had received contracts from airlines for MA-900 passenger aircraft. In March 1983, Tom Scott, one of the buyers for Morrin, was trying to decide upon a fair price to offer the Pierce Company, a subcontractor, for the manufacture of metal containers used for passenger luggage and other cargo. These enclosed containers were loaded and unloaded in an airline's luggage or cargo area at an airport. They essentially eliminated manual handling of goods at the point where the airplane was parked. In addition to permitting quicker loading/unloading of the plane itself, the containers eliminated damage to goods caused by inclement weather and resulted in more efficient usage of a plane's cargo hold.

The containers, made of a special lightweight alloy, required some difficult machining operations. Because the containers were put on or taken off aircraft by using special equipment, and since each airplane's cargo hold was equipped with special tracks to accommodate the containers, it was crucial that they be made exactly to Morrin's dimensions and other specifications.

Pierce had been manufacturing these containers for Morrin since December 1980, at which time its bid of $1,518[1] per

container for the 120 containers then required was the lowest of the several bids considered. With each new order for the MA-900 that Morrin received, Scott had successfully negotiated new contracts for the manufacture of the containers with Ken White, a Pierce salesperson. During this period, Pierce continued to meet all quality standards and delivery schedules.

On each successive contract after the original one signed in December 1980, Scott had applied an 80 percent learning curve to the price of the previous order, excluding the cost of raw material and also excluding profit. Scott assumed that the tooling cost incurred by Pierce Company in manufacturing the containers was amortized over the cost of the original contract, and therefore he made no allowance for tooling cost in estimating the price of subsequent contracts. Although it appeared to Scott that White was not familiar with the use of learning curves in purchase contracting, White agreed to manufacture the containers at the prices quoted by Scott. As a result, the price paid per unit for the containers was lowered on each successive contract. Pierce's production of containers was essentially continuous over this time period. (Application of the learning curve would not be valid if production was not reasonably continuous.)

In making his calculations of the price to offer Pierce after the first contract had been fulfilled, Scott had to rely on his

---

[1] All monetary amounts in this case are stated in constant dollars, i.e., dollars of equivalent purchasing power.

own estimates of raw material price, tooling cost, and Pierce's profit. Scott knew from his previous experiences with Pierce that this company would refuse to reveal its cost and profit figures. Because of his past experience in purchasing and the use of the learning curve, however, Scott was confident that his estimates were fairly accurate. Morrin's own labor-hour records showed that an 80 percent curve was appropriate for the production of similar containers for another airplane made in the 1970s, and this led Scott to conclude that the same 80 percent curve was applicable to the Pierce Company.

Breaking down the original bid of $1,518 per container, Scott estimated the profit was around $138, which was 10 percent of total cost, and the raw material was about $480 per unit. He estimated that Pierce's tooling cost was about $21,600 and that this had probably been amortized over the 120 containers ordered under the first contract.

In order to set up his 80 percent curve to find the cumulative average price on which he could base his future price offers, Scott made these calculations:

Original price per container...........................		$1,518
Less: Profit at 10% of cost...........................	$138	
Tooling cost on first order: $21,600 ÷ 120 units	180	
Raw material cost per unit...........................	480	
Items not subject to learning curve...................		798
Costs subject to learning curve		$ 720

The adjusted cost of $720 per container for 120 units was plotted on log-log graph paper (see Exhibit 1). Scott then took double the quantity of the original order (or 240 units) and 80 percent of the unit cost ($576) and plotted his second point on the log-log graph paper. Through these two points he drew a straight line.

When Morrin required 40 more con-

EXHIBIT 1
EIGHTY PERCENT LEARNING CURVE
MA-900 Cargo Containers

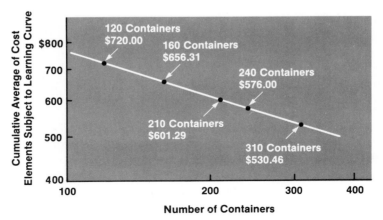

tainers, Scott looked at his graph to find the new cumulative average of cost elements subject to learning for the total quantity of the old and new orders, 160 containers. The new cumulative average cost was $656.31 per container (see Exhibit 1). Using this information, Scott calculated:

160 units at $656.31 per unit average for cost elements subject to learning curve......................................	$105,010
Less: 120 units purchased at $720 per unit average for cost elements subject to learning curve............................	86,400
Total price to be paid on new order for cost elements subject to learning curve...............................	$ 18,610

The new average price per container to be paid on the new order for cost elements subject to learning was $18,610 ÷ 40 containers, or $465.25. To this $465.25, Scott added back the cost items not subject to the curve that previously had been subtracted:

Cost elements subject to learning curve	$ 465.25
Plus: Raw material...	480.00
Average price per unit before profit	945.25
Plus: Profit at 10% of cost	94.52
Total price per unit on the new order	$1,039.77

Scott believed this figure of $1,039.77 per container was appropriate to use in his negotiations with White, who finally, but grudgingly, accepted this figure.

In subsequent negotiations, the prices Scott offered Pierce Company on successive contracts for the containers became lower and lower. White became more emphatic in his objections and warned Scott that "this learning curve business is going too far." However, each time Scott asked to see Pierce's cost data to justify some other price, White would give the same answer: "Our cost data are none of your business!"

On February 2, 1983, about one month

before the final delivery of the latest order, which had been contracted for in November 1982, White complained that Pierce had experienced an unusually large increase in material cost that added $24 to the cost per container. Furthermore, While stated that modifications in the design of the containers since the original contract had increased the raw material cost per unit by another $36. White stated that because of these increased costs and the low $996 per unit price paid by Morrin for the currently produced containers, he was quite skeptical as to whether his company would take on any further contracts for containers, especially since at that time it could get all the business it wanted. He went on to say that his company was "sick and tired of producing containers at a loss for Morrin and having to make up these losses out of contracts with other companies." While Scott believed that the raw material cost increases mentioned by White were correct, he did not have any way of appraising the validity of White's statements about Pierce's losing money on this contract with Morrin.

Two weeks after this conference between Scott and White, Morrin received aircraft orders that would require 100 more containers. Again Scott was confronted with the task of securing more containers. From December 1980 to March 1983, Pierce would have produced 210 containers. Over this period, the price paid for the containers had decreased from $1,518 per unit on the first order to $996 per unit on the current order contracted for in November 1982 and scheduled for completion within the next two weeks. The total price of the 210 units *for the cost elements subject to the learning curve* was $126,270. This sum compared to $151,200 that would have been paid on 210 containers for these same cost elements if the learning curve had not been applied. A further saving to Morrin was realized because the profit that Pierce received per unit was a fixed percentage of cost. Thus, with the lower calculated cost per unit based on the learning curve, the profit to Pierce was cut correspondingly.

Scott realized that it was important to continue dealing with Pierce for the additional 100 containers. He recalled that in 1980 the Pierce Company's first bid of $1,518 per unit was the lowest of the several bids submitted; the next lowest bid at that time was $1,632. If Pierce refused to accept any more orders, dealing with a new subcontractor would probably result in a substantial increase in price. Scott estimated that the lowest price for which he could currently purchase containers from another subcontractor would be in the neighborhood of $1,680 per unit (including the amortized cost, over 100

units, of new tooling). Furthermore, Scott considered Pierce an excellent source of supply because it produced a satisfactory product and always met its delivery schedule.

On the other hand, Scott knew that the validity of the learning curve had been widely accepted in the aircraft industry and that it was especially applicable to the manufacture of items such as the containers, for which direct labor was a major cost component. Furthermore, it was his job as a purchasing agent for Morrin to get as low a price as possible commensurate with a satisfactory product.

Scott had an appointment with White the next day, at which time they would open negotiations for the 100 additional containers. Scott knew that White would suggest a substantial upward revision in the price.

Questions

1. If he used the 80 percent learning curve, what price would Mr. Scott calculate for the new order of 100 containers?

2. What price should Mr. Scott use as a basis for his negotiations?

3. What is the highest price that the Morrin Aircraft Company should pay to the Pierce Company for the containers?

4. What are the implications of the use of learning curves in purchase contracting to both the prime contractor and the subcontractor?

5. In what situations would the use of the learning curve in purchase contracting not be appropriate?

17

Full Costs and Their Uses

This is the first of four chapters describing the measurement and use of full cost information, which is one of the three types of management accounting information. This chapter introduces full cost concepts and describes in a general way how costs are recorded in a cost accounting system. The uses of full cost information are also discussed. Subsequent chapters will describe in more detail how direct and indirect costs are measured for the costing of products, and how this information can be analyzed to aid in controlling production costs.

COST CONCEPTS

Cost is the most slippery word in accounting. It is used for many different notions. If someone says, without elaboration, "The cost of a widget is $1.80," it is practically impossible to understand exactly what is meant. The word *cost* becomes more meaningful when it is preceded by a modifier, making phrases such as *direct cost, full cost, opportunity cost, differential cost,* and so on. But even these phrases do not convey a clear meaning unless the context in which they are used is clearly understood.

General Definition

A broad definition of cost is: *Cost is a measurement, in monetary terms, of the amount of resources used for some purpose.*

Three important ideas are included in the definition. First and most

549

basic is the notion that cost measures the use of resources. The cost elements of producing a tangible good or an intangible service are physical quantities of material, hours of labor service, and quantities of other resources. Cost measures how many of these resources were used. The second idea is that cost measurements are expressed in monetary terms. Money provides a common denominator that permits the amounts of individual resources, each measured according to its own scale, to be combined so that the total amount of all resources used can be determined. Third, cost measurement always relates to a purpose. These purposes include products, departments, projects, or any other thing or activity for which a measurement of costs is desired.

Cost Objective

Cost objective is the technical name for the purpose for which costs are measured. (Some people prefer *cost object*.) In each instance, the cost objective must be carefully stated and clearly understood. In a blue jeans factory, for example, the manufacture of a batch comprised of four dozen pairs of Style 607 jeans may be one cost objective, the manufacture of one batch of Style 608 jeans may be another cost objective, and the manufacture *and sale* of a batch of Style 607 jeans may be still another cost objective.

A cost objective can be defined as broadly or as narrowly as one wishes. At one extreme, all the jeans manufactured in a jeans factory could be considered as a single cost objective. But if such a broad definition were used, differences in the resources used for the various styles of jeans would not be measured. At the other extreme, each pair of jeans manufactured could be considered as a single cost objective. But if such a narrow definition were used, the amount of recordkeeping involved in measuring costs would be tremendous. As it happens, many jeans factories use a batch of a single style and material as the unit of costing. Although different sizes of jeans use slightly different amounts of materials, usually the cost objective definition does not differentiate among sizes of the same material. For example, one batch of Style 703 corduroy jeans W 32″ - L 31″ would not be a different cost objective from one batch of Style 703 corduroy W 34″ - L 32″.

Similarly, a variety of cost objective definitions is possible in a service organization. For example, in a hospital, any of the following could be cost objectives: the hospital as a whole, the nursing staff, the X-ray department, the emergency room, the personnel office, the cardiovascular ward, an individual patient, the performance of a certain type of blood test, and so on.

Full Cost

Full cost means all the resources used for a cost objective. In some circumstances, full cost is easily measured. If Ms. X pays $30 for a pair of jeans at a store, the full cost of the pair of jeans to Ms. X is $30; that is, she used $30 of her resources to acquire the pair of jeans.

But suppose we ask: What was the full cost of *manufacturing* the pair of jeans? This is a much more difficult question. A jeans factory may make thousands of pairs of jeans a month. Some are plain while others have intricate pocket stitching, some are made of denim while others are made of other material, and some are large while some are small. Clearly, different amounts of resources are used for these different styles and sizes of jeans; that is, they have different costs.

Direct and Indirect Costs

The various items of cost can be divided into two categories, one called direct costs and the other, indirect costs. *The full cost of a cost objective is the sum of its direct costs plus a fair share of applicable indirect costs.*

The *direct costs* of a cost objective are items of costs that are specifically *traced to* or *caused by* that cost objective. Denim used in manufacturing a batch of jeans is a direct cost of that batch of jeans, and so are the earnings of the employees who worked directly in making that batch of jeans.

Indirect costs are elements of costs that are associated with or caused by two or more objectives *jointly*, but that are not directly traced to each of them individually. The nature of an indirect cost is such that it is not possible, or at least not feasible, to measure directly how much of the cost is attributable to a single cost objective. Examples of indirect costs of a batch of jeans include the factory manager's salary and insurance on the factory building and equipment. (Note here that the cost objective, that is, a batch of jeans, was explicitly stated. The factory manager's salary and the insurance are *direct* costs of the factory as a whole—a different and broader cost objective than one batch of jeans.)

Although it is intuitively obvious that the cost elements directly traced to a cost objective are a part of its cost, it is by no means obvious that some fraction of the elements of indirect cost are part of the cost. One can actually see the denim in a pair of jeans, and it is obvious that labor services were involved in fashioning this denim into jeans. Thus, there is no doubt about the appropriateness of counting such material and labor as part of the cost of the jeans. But what is the connection between, say, the salary of the purchasing agent (who buys denim and other materials) and the cost of the jeans? The purchasing agent did not work on the jeans; the purchasing office may not even be in the same building where the jeans were made.

The basic rationale is that indirect costs are caused jointly by the several cost objectives; to argue otherwise would be to assert that indirect costs are sheer waste. For example, although the purchasing agent's salary is not traceable to specific batches of jeans, if there were no purchasing agent there would be no materials on hand from which to make the jeans. Thus, some fraction of the purchasing agent's salary—along with other indirect costs—must be part of the total cost of each batch of jeans.

These comments also apply to cost objectives other than the manufacture of goods. The full cost of occupancy of a hotel room includes a fair share of the costs of the hotel lobby and registration desk. The full cost of a university accounting course includes a fair share of the school's administrative, secretarial, maintenance, and utilities costs. We shall defer until later the question of how the fraction, or fair share, of indirect costs applicable to each cost objective is measured.

Applicable Accounting Principles

The measurement of the costs applicable to an accounting period and to the products manufactured in that period is in general governed by the cost concept and the matching concept (discussed in Chapters 6, 7, and 9). These concepts and the principles related to them do not give much guidance as to how total product costs are to be assigned to individual products or groups of products, however. They permit any "systematic and rational" method of doing this.

In 1971, the Congress created the Cost Accounting Standards Board (CASB), and many cost accounting standards (which is a term synonymous with "principles") have been published by that Board. Although the CASB's authority explicitly includes only the measurement of full costs on *defense contracts*, its pronouncements have been adopted by many government agencies.[1] CASB standards also have a considerable influence on other types of full cost measurement. This is because in most respects the problems of measuring the full cost of government contracts are the same as the problems of measuring full costs in other situations.

Elements of Product Cost

The most common cost objective of interest in a business is a product. A "product" can be either a tangible good, such as a batch of jeans, or a service, such as a repair job on an automobile. Elements of product cost are either material, labor, or services. In a full cost accounting system, these elements are customarily recorded in certain categories. These categories are shown in Illustration 17–1 and described below.

Direct Material Cost. Direct materials (often called *raw materials* or just *materials*) are those materials that actually become part of the finished product. They are to be distinguished from *supplies* or *indirect materials*, which are materials used in the production process but not directly in the product itself. Examples of supplies include lubricating oil for machinery or cooking oil used in a restaurant's kitchen.

Direct Labor Cost. The direct labor costs of a product are those that are specifically traced to or identified with the product. The earnings of workers who assemble parts into a finished product, or who operate

---

[1]Although the CASB was disbanded in 1980, its standards continue in effect.

ILLUSTRATION 17–1
ELEMENTS OF PRODUCT COST

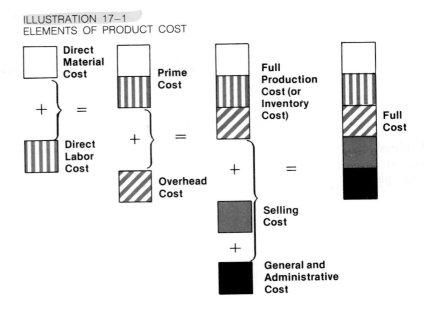

machines in the process of production, are direct labor costs of the product. The cost of a repairperson's time spent fixing a television set is a direct cost of the repair job.

   Prime Cost.   Conventionally, prime cost is defined as the sum of direct labor cost and direct material cost. In view of the increased importance of energy, some companies treat energy costs as a third element of prime cost and accumulate product energy costs in the way that we shall describe for direct labor and direct material costs.

   Overhead Cost.   Overhead cost includes all indirect production costs, that is, all production costs *other than* direct material and direct labor.[2] One element of overhead is indirect labor, which represents the earnings of employees who do not work directly on a single product or similar cost objective but whose efforts are related to the overall process of production. Examples include supervisors, janitors, materials handlers, stockroom personnel, inspectors, and timekeepers. Another element of overhead is indirect material costs, described above. Overhead also includes such services as heat, light, power, maintenance, depreciation, taxes, and insurance related to assets used in the production process.

   Full Production Cost.   Full production cost is the sum of direct material, direct labor, and overhead costs. In a manufacturing firm, full pro-

---

[2]*Indirect production cost* is a more precise term than *overhead*, but the latter is more commonly used. Other terms meaning the same thing include *factory overhead* and *burden* (which is gradually falling into disuse).

duction cost often is called *inventory cost* because this is the cost at which completed goods are carried as inventory and the amount that is shown as cost of sales when the goods are sold. Note that the cost at which goods are carried in inventory does not include distribution costs, or those general and administrative costs that are unrelated to production operations. In a manufacturing firm, it includes only the costs that are incurred "up to the factory exit door."

Selling Cost.   Selling costs can be classified as either marketing costs or logistics costs. *Marketing* or *order-getting costs*, such as marketing management, advertising, sales promotion, and salespersons' compensation and travel expenses, are those incurred in the efforts to generate sales. *Logistics costs*—also called *order-filling* or *physical distribution costs*—are those costs incurred "beyond the factory exit door" in storing the completed product, in transferring it to the customer, and in doing the associated recordkeeping. They include warehousing costs, billing costs, and transportation costs.

General and Administrative Cost.   This is a catchall classification to cover items not included in the above categories. Examples of such "G&A" items are costs incurred in the general and executive offices; research, development, and engineering costs; public relations costs; donations; and miscellaneous items. General and administrative costs may include the cost of interest on borrowed funds, but in most companies interest is not counted as a cost at all for the purpose of measuring the full cost of cost objectives. Instead, it is counted as an overall financial cost of the company.[3]

Full Cost.   The full cost of a product is simply the sum of all the cost elements described above. However, in practice accountants often use the term *full cost* to mean only *full production cost*. This is another example of the lack of precision inherent in persons' use of cost-related terms, and another reason why one must "look beyond the label" to be certain what the user of a term really has in mind.

SYSTEMS FOR COST ACCUMULATION

A *cost accounting system* is a particular method of collecting costs and assigning them to cost objectives. There are many types of such systems. At this point we shall describe the essentials of a common type of product costing system that is used to measure full production costs and to assign them to goods in a manufacturing company. In Chapter 6 we described this measurement process in overall terms. The description that follows is not for a *different* process; it merely describes in more detail the flows discussed in Chapter 6.

---

[3]In their income statements, many companies include all expenses except cost of sales and interest in an item called Selling, General, and Administrative Costs, commonly referred to as S, G&A.

**The Account
Flowchart**

An account flowchart is helpful in understanding the flow of costs through a cost accounting system. Such a flowchart depicts the accounts used in a system, shown in T-account form, with lines indicating the flow of amounts from one account to another.

Most of the accounts on a cost accounting flowchart are either asset accounts or expense accounts. A characteristic of both asset and expense accounts is that increases are shown on the debit (left-hand) side and decreases are shown on the credit (right-hand) side. A line on a flowchart indicates a transfer "from" one account "to" another account, signifying that the first account is being decreased and the second is being increased. It follows that the typical line on a flowchart leads from the credit side of one account to the debit side of another. These flows represent events that happen during the production process. In addition to the lines designating "flow," other lines indicate entries for certain external transactions that are associated with the production process; for example, the transaction for the acquisition of raw material from an outside vendor, which is a debit to Materials Inventory and a credit to Accounts Payable or Cash.

Although the essentials of a product costing system are the same whether the product is a tangible good or an intangible service, we will illustrate these concepts and techniques in a manufacturing setting where the products are tangible and thus easily visualized. Illustration 17–2 shows the flowchart concept and the essential cost flows in a manufacturing company. This flowchart contains a hypothetical set of figures for a month's operation in a small company, Marker Pen Company, which manufactures and sells felt-tip pens. The flowchart is divided into three sections: (1) *acquisition*, containing the accounts related to the acquisition of resources, which are asset and liability accounts; (2) *production*, containing the accounts related to the production process; and (3) *sale*, the accounts related to the sale of products.

The cycle of operations depicted on the flowchart may be explained as follows (the reader should trace each journal entry described to Illustration 17–2):

1. During the month, $52,000 of materials were purchased on open account, $20,000 of various other assets were purchased for cash, and $60,000 of accounts payable were paid. The journal entries recording these transactions are as follows:

   a. Materials Inventory 52,000
         Accounts Payable   52,000

   b. (Other asset and liability accounts) 20,000
         Cash   20,000

   c. Accounts Payable 60,000
         Cash   60,000

ILLUSTRATION 17–2
ACCOUNT FLOWCHART OF MARKER PEN COMPANY ($000 omitted)

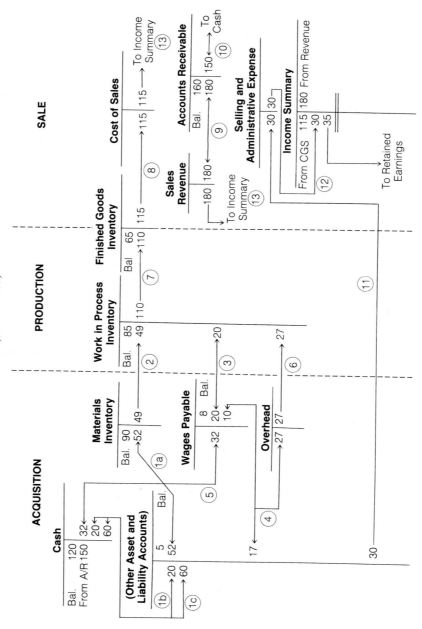

Note: Circled numbers refer to events and journal entries described in the text.

2. During the month, materials costing $49,000 (principally felt tips, plastic, ink, and wicks) were withdrawn from inventory and sent to the factory to be worked on. This decrease in Materials Inventory and increase in Work in Process Inventory is recorded in the following journal entry:

```
Work in Process Inventory ...............   49,000
    Materials Inventory ..................              49,000
```

3. During the month, employees converted this material into pens. The $20,000 that they earned adds to the amount of Work in Process Inventory, and the resulting liability increases Wages Payable, as recorded in the following journal entry:

```
Work in Process Inventory ...............   20,000
    Wages Payable ........................              20,000
```

4. Overhead costs amounting to $27,000 were incurred during the month. Of the total, $12,000 was ascertained from current invoices for such things as electricity and telephone bills, so the offsetting credits were to Accounts Payable. Indirect labor costs were $10,000, with the offsetting credit to Wages Payable. The remaining $5,000 represented depreciation, the charge-off of prepaid expenses, and other credits to asset accounts. All of these items are here summed up in the general account, Overhead, but in practice they are usually recorded in separate indirect cost accounts, one for each type of cost. The journal entry follows:

```
Overhead .................................   27,000
    Wages Payable ........................              10,000
    (Other asset and liability accounts) .              17,000
```

5. Employees were paid $32,000 cash. This decreased the liability account, Wages Payable, and also decreased Cash. (The payment of wages also involves FICA taxes, withholding taxes, and other complications, which have been omitted from this introductory diagram.) The journal entry follows:

```
Wages Payable ...........................   32,000
    Cash .................................              32,000
```

6. Since the overhead cost is a part of the cost of the pens that were worked on during the month, the total cost incurred is transferred to Work in Process Inventory, as in the following journal entry:

```
Work in Process Inventory ...............   27,000
    Overhead .............................              27,000
```

7. Pens whose total cost was $110,000 were completed during the month and were transferred to Finished Goods Inventory. This resulted in a decrease in Work in Process Inventory, as recorded in the following journal entry:

```
Finished Goods Inventory ...............  110,000
    Work in Process Inventory ...........           110,000
```

8. Pens with a cost of $115,000 were sold during the month. Physically, these pens were removed from inventory and shipped to customers. On the accounting records, this is reflected by a credit to Finished Goods Inventory and a debit to Cost of Sales,[4] as in the following journal entry:

```
Cost of Sales ..........................  115,000
    Finished Goods Inventory ............           115,000
```

9. For the same pens, sales revenue of $180,000 was earned, and this is recorded in the accounts as a credit to Sales Revenue and a debit to Accounts Receivable. Note that the Sales Revenue credit described here and the Cost of Sales debit described in entry 8 related to the same physical pens. The difference between the balances in the Sales Revenue and Cost of Sales accounts, which is $65,000, therefore represents the gross margin earned on pens sold during the month. The journal entry for the sales transaction is as follows:

```
Accounts Receivable ....................  180,000
    Sales Revenue .......................           180,000
```

10. Accounts receivable collected during the month amounted to $150,000. Some of these collections were for sales made in the current month, but most were for sales made in previous months. The journal entry follows:

```
Cash ...................................  150,000
    Accounts Receivable .................           150,000
```

11. During the month, $30,000 of selling and administrative expenses were incurred, $17,000 of which represented credits to Accounts Payable and $13,000 credits to various asset and liability accounts. These are recorded in the following journal entry:

```
Selling and Administrative Expense ......  30,000
    (Other asset and liability accounts) .           30,000
```

---

[4] As noted in Chapter 6, some manufacturing companies use the term *Cost of Goods Sold* rather than *Cost of Sales*.

12. Since these expenses were applicable to the current period, the Selling and Administrative Expense account is closed to the Income Summary account, as in the following journal entry:

```
Income Summary ........................   30,000
     Selling and Administrative Expense ...            30,000
```

13. The balances in the Sales Revenue and Cost of Sales accounts are also closed to Income Summary. The $35,000 balance in Income Summary then reflects the pretax income for the period. (To simplify the example, income taxes and certain nonoperating and financial items normally appearing on income statements have been excluded.) These closing journal entries follow:

```
Sales Revenue ..........................  180,000
     Income Summary .....................           180,000

Income Summary .........................  115,000
     Cost of Sales ......................           115,000
```

Strictly speaking, the cost accounting system as such ends with entry 8. The other entries are given in order to show the complete set of transactions for the company.

The income statement for the Marker Pen Company is shown in Illustration 17–3.

ILLUSTRATION 17–3

MARKER PEN COMPANY
Income Statement
For the Month of _____

Sales...	$180,000
Cost of sales....................................	115,000
Gross margin	65,000
Selling and administrative expense.................	30,000
Income (before income taxes)	$ 35,000

Chapter 18 will further describe product costing systems, including the details of measuring the direct costs of products and of assigning products their fair share of indirect costs. Before becoming familiar with those additional aspects of product costing, however, it is worthwhile to consider full cost information for cost objectives other than tangible goods.

NONMANUFACTURING COSTS

Until the last two or three decades, most cost accounting systems dealt solely with measuring the costs of manufacturing goods. This was probably because these costs must be measured in order to obtain the amounts for Work in Process Inventory and Finished Goods Inventory on the balance sheet and the amount for Cost of Sales on the income statement. Other costs are reported as expenses on the income statement in aggregate amounts, and hence there was no need to assign them to specific cost objectives for external financial reporting purposes.

In more recent years, cost accounting systems have been expanded to include other types of cost. For industrial firms, these include the selling, general, and administrative costs mentioned earlier in this chapter. Instead of treating such costs as broad categories, cost systems can treat them as a series of more specific cost objectives. For example, each marketing function—advertising, personal selling, market research, and so on—can be a cost objective. Some of these can be subdivided into still smaller cost objectives. For example, personal selling costs can be categorized by customer, industry, geographical region, or even individual field salesperson; each such category is a cost objective.

In whatever manner these cost objectives are defined by a company, the guiding principle remains the same: the full cost of a cost objective is the sum of its direct costs plus an equitable share of indirect costs. For example, if the cost objective is an individual field salesperson, the direct costs include the person's salary (or commissions), travel expenses, and costs of entertaining clients. The indirect costs, a fair share of which are assigned to this salesperson, include the salary of the district sales manager and the various costs of operating the district sales office that provides support services to the field salesperson. The principles for making the indirect cost assignment are the same as those for assigning indirect costs to products (described in Chapters 18 and 19).

Merchandising Companies

In drugstores, department stores, supermarkets, and other merchandising companies, cost of sales is essentially the merchant's invoice cost of the goods sold. These companies therefore need only a very simple cost accounting system in order to find the cost of sales. They do, however, use full cost information for other purposes, a principal one being to measure the profitability of various selling departments within the company. Each selling department is a cost objective.

Service Organizations

The same general approach used in measuring the cost of tangible goods is also applicable to measuring the cost of services. In the United States, more people are employed by service organizations (including government agencies) than by manufacturing firms.

In some service organizations, it is appropriate to treat providing services to a specific client as a "job" and establish a cost objective for each job. For example, automobile repair shops accumulate on a "job-cost record" the costs incurred for each car that they service. This cost record includes direct costs, such as for mechanics' labor and repair parts, and a share of the indirect costs of the repair shop, such as the shop supervisor's salary, occupancy costs (heat, light, rent, and so on), and depreciation of shop equipment. This cost record is, in effect, a work in process inventory account for that particular job, which is a cost objective. Accounting in firms providing legal, architectural, engineering, and consulting services similarly uses a job-cost record for each job or project worked on by the firm. Similarly, hospital and medical clinic accounting systems treat each patient as a cost objective, establishing a job-cost record for the services the patient is provided. Chapter 18 discusses in more detail the principles of *job costing;* these apply either to manufacturing or service organizations.

In other cases, it is not appropriate for a service organization to establish a cost record for each "job." For example, in a hospital laboratory, a separate cost record is not established for each individual blood analysis performed. To determine the cost of such a blood test, an averaging process must be used. First, the direct costs of performing these tests are identified; these are primarily the costs of the lab technicians' time and of the specialized supplies they use to perform the blood tests. Second, since the lab performs other tests in addition to blood tests, the cost of the laboratory supervisor, lab occupancy costs, and similar general costs are joint costs of the various types of tests performed. Thus, a share of these indirect (joint) costs must be assigned to the blood test cost objective. Finally, a count is kept of the number of blood tests performed. For a given time period, the full cost of the blood test cost objective divided by the number of tests performed gives the average per unit cost of a blood test. This approach is called *process costing,* and is described further in Chapter 18.

Nonprofit Organizations

A *nonprofit organization* is an organization whose primary objective is something other than earning a profit. Most nonprofit organizations provide services rather than manufacture tangible goods. Health care, educational, and membership organizations are predominantly nonprofit organizations. Government organizations are nonprofit organizations. The cost accounting practices of nonprofit organizations are in many respects similar to those of profit-oriented organizations. Both nonprofit and profit-oriented organizations use resources; and in both cases, the problem of cost measurement is to identify the amount of resources used for each of the various cost objectives that the organization has. For various reasons, however, accounting systems in some nonprofit organizations, particularly government organizations, differ from those in profit-oriented companies. A description of these differences is beyond the scope of this book. In general, they do not affect the way in which cost information is accumulated.

For certain parts of their operations, some nonprofit organizations use cost systems that we have already described. For example, a hospital gift shop is, in effect, a merchandising company; and accounting for client-specific services such as hospital care or blood tests, described above, is conceptually the same whether the hospital is a profit-seeking or nonprofit organization.

Many nonprofit organizations' activities, however, do not involve client-specific transactions such as those just described. Rather, the activities are in the form of "programs" that make available services to the organization's membership or to the general public. For example, a public library lends books through its circulation department, has a periodicals reading room, provides a reference service, and has a special children's division that (among other things) has special reading appreciation presentations on Saturday mornings. Each of these sets of related activities constitutes a *program* of the library, and can be treated as a cost objective. The full cost of each program is the sum of its direct costs and a fair share of the library's indirect costs, such as heat, lighting, and general maintenance and upkeep.

Despite significant improvements over the last decade in many nonprofit organizations' cost accounting systems, many other nonprofit organizations still do not have well-developed systems. Some omit depreciation from their costing procedures, and some still use cash-basis rather than accrual accounting. Both of these latter weaknesses preclude arriving at an accurate picture of the costs of using resources.

USES OF FULL COST

Some of the uses that management makes of information on full costs are in (1) financial reporting; (2) analysis of profitability; (3) answering the question, "What did it cost?"; (4) arriving at prices in regulated industries; and (5) normal pricing.

Financial Reporting

We have already described how full production cost is the basis for reporting work in process inventory and finished goods inventory on the balance sheet, and cost of sales on the income statement. When a company constructs a building, a machine, or some other fixed asset for its own use, the amount at which this asset is recorded in the accounts and reported on the balance sheet is its full cost.

Cost accounting information is also used to measure the income of the principal segments of the business. As pointed out in Chapter 14, the FASB requires that shareholder annual reports of large companies include revenues, operating profit, and identifiable asset amounts for each significant business segment.

Analysis of Profitability

Chapter 13 discussed ratios and other techniques that are useful in analyzing the profitability of an *entire* business. Cost accounting makes it possible to make similar analyses of individual *parts* of a business, such as an individual product, product line (a family of related products), plant, division, sales territory, or any other subdivision of the company that is of interest. Using the principles of cost accounting, the direct costs and an appropriate share of the indirect costs of a part can be determined. If the part does not earn a reasonable profit, that is, if the revenue generated by this part does not exceed these costs by an amount representing a reasonable return on assets employed, there is an indication that something is wrong.

What Did it Cost?

The problem of measuring the cost of something arises in a great many contexts: What was the cost of eliminating pollution in a certain river? What did the last presidential election cost? What was the cost of police protection in city X? What did it cost the U.S. Postal Service to send a letter from Chicago to San Francisco? What was the cost of operating a school cafeteria? What was the cost of a certain research project? These questions are usually answered by measuring the full cost of the cost objective.

Cost-Type Contracts. Full costs are used in contracts in which one party has agreed to buy goods or services from another party at a price that is based on cost. There are tens of billions of dollars of such contracts annually. Because of the variations in methods of measuring cost, it is necessary that the method to be used in the particular contract be spelled out in some detail so as to avoid misunderstanding.

Setting Regulated Prices

Many prices are set not by the forces of the marketplace but rather by regulatory agencies. These include prices for electricity, gas and water, telephone and telegraph, insurance premiums, and many others. In each of these cases, the regulatory agency (Federal Communications Commission, Federal Energy Regulatory Commission, state public utility and insurance commissions, and so on) allows a price equal to full cost plus an allowance for profit. In most cases, the regulatory agency provides a manual, which may contain several hundred pages, spelling out in great detail how costs are to be measured.

Normal Pricing

As was discussed in Chapter 13, a principal economic objective of a business is to earn a satisfactory return on its investment, that is, on the assets that it uses. In order to earn a satisfactory return, revenues from the sale of goods and services must be large enough both to (1) recover all costs and (2) earn a profit that provides a satisfactory return on investment. The business will prosper if *for all its products combined,* total sales revenues exceed total costs by a sufficiently large amount. But selling prices must be set separately for *each product.* How can this be done for *each* product so that a satisfactory profit is earned for *all* products?

The general answer to this question is that each product should bear a *fair share* of the total costs of the business. We can expand this statement to say that in general the selling price of a product should be high enough (1) to recover its direct costs, (2) to recover a fair share of all applicable indirect costs, and (3) to yield a satisfactory profit. Such a price is a *normal price.*

The foregoing is a statement of general tendency rather than a prescription for setting the selling price for each and every product. For a number of reasons, the selling price of a given product usually is not set simply by ascertaining each of the cost and profit components and then adding them up. Often, for example, prices are set by estimating the perceived value of a product from the buyer's standpoint. Sometimes there is a dominant company in the industry that is a *price leader,* and smaller competitors feel it necessary to match this leader's price. Nevertheless, the measurement of the cost of a product provides a starting point in an analysis of what the actual selling price *should* be.

The Profit Component of Price. The fact that an economic objective of a profit-oriented business is to earn a satisfactory return on assets employed suggests that the profit component of a product's price should be related to assets employed in making the product. Nevertheless, it is common pricing practice to relate the profit component to costs rather than to the amount of assets employed.

In some situations, it is easy to establish a profit margin expressed as a percentage of cost in such a way that the resulting selling price will give a satisfactory return on assets employed. In general, this is the case when all products have approximately the same unit cost and/or when the assets employed by products vary proportionately with their cost.

> **Example.** A retail shoe store decides that a satisfactory profit is a 15 percent return (before income taxes) on its investment. If its total investment in inventory, accounts receivable, and other assets is estimated to be $600,000, then its profit must be $600,000 × 15 percent = $90,000 for the year. If its total operating costs, excluding the cost of the shoes, are estimated to be $210,000, then its selling prices must be such that the gross margin above the costs of the shoes comes out to $210,000 + $90,000 = $300,000. If the store expects to sell shoes that cost in total $900,000, then total sales revenue must be $1,200,000 in order to obtain this $300,000. The store can obtain the desired $300,000 by setting a selling price that is 33⅓ percent above the cost of the shoes ($1,200,000 ÷ $900,000 = 133⅓ percent). This pricing policy would generate revenue of $1,200,000 for the

year if the expected sales volume were realized, of which $900,000 would go for the cost of the shoes, $210,000 for operating costs, and $90,000 for profit. Shoe store owners customarily describe such a set of numbers as demonstrating that they make a profit of 7.5 percent on sales (= $90,000 ÷ $1,200,000); but what is more important is that it is a return of 15 percent on assets employed (= $90,000 ÷ $600,000).

Although setting the profit margin as a percentage of costs or of selling price works satisfactorily if the assets employed for each product are proportionate to the costs of each product, it breaks down if this condition does not exist. As described in Chapter 13, companies, or products, with a relatively low asset turnover require a relatively high profit margin, as a percentage of costs or of selling price, in order to earn a satisfactory return on assets employed.

Assigning assets employed to products involves essentially the same techniques as assigning costs to products. These techniques are not described here. Until fairly recently, it was widely believed that the accounting effort required to assign assets employed to products was so great and the results so unreliable that the effort was not worthwhile. Now, however, it is recognized that practical ways of doing this are not so difficult as had been thought.

Time and Material Pricing. In this method one pricing rate is established for direct labor and a separate pricing rate for direct material. Each of these rates is constructed so that it includes allowances for indirect costs and for profit. This method of pricing is used in automobile garages, job printing shops, television repair shops, and similar types of service establishments. It is also used by many professional persons and organizations, including physicians, lawyers, engineers, ski instructors, consultants of various types, and public accounting firms.

In time and material pricing the *time* component is expressed as a labor rate per hour, which is calculated as the sum of (1) direct salary and fringe benefit costs of the employee; (2) an equitable share of all indirect costs, except those related to material; and (3) an allowance for profit. In professional service firms, this rate is usually called a *billing rate.* The material component includes a *material loading* that is added to the invoice cost of materials used on the job. This loading consists of an allowance for material handling costs and storage costs plus an allowance for profit.

Nonprofit Organizations. In nonprofit organizations, the same pricing practices as those described above are appropriate, with one exception. Since a nonprofit organization has no shareholders' equity, it does not need to earn a profit as a return on this investment. The profit component is therefore omitted from the price calculation.

Adjusting Costs to Prices. Pricing, quite naturally, is usually thought of as the process of arriving at selling prices. However, there are some situations in which the process works in reverse: the selling price that must be charged in order to meet competition is taken as a given; the problem then is to determine how much cost the company can afford to incur if it is to earn a satisfactory profit at the given price. In the apparel business, for example, it is customary to use discrete retail "price points"—$19.95, $29.95, $39.95, and so on. The manufacturer designs individual garments to "fit" one of these price points. In order to ensure that the manufacturer makes a satisfactory profit on a garment, the retail selling price is taken as a given, the retailer's normal gross margin is deducted to arrive at the manufacturer's selling price, and then the manufacturer's normal gross margin is subtracted. The remainder is how much the manufacturer can afford to spend on cloth, labor, and other elements of production cost.

Contribution Pricing. In the situations described above, the company makes pricing decisions using information on full costs as a first approximation. There are other situations in which individual products may be sold at a loss, that is, at a price below full costs. Even though these products are sold at a loss, under certain conditions they may increase the company's total profit. These are special situations, and they require special cost constructions. The approach is called *contribution pricing,* and it is described in Chapter 21.

Importance of Timely Cost Data. Whatever the basis of pricing—including following a price leader—the relevant cost data are current costs and estimates of near-term future costs. However, the cost system data may not report current costs. This is especially true in inflationary times. This is not to say that companies are always willing or able to pass these increases on to their customers in the form of higher prices. It is important, though, for management to know that costs have increased so that price increases can at least be considered. Every year hundreds of businesses (most of them small) go bankrupt because their managers did not know the current costs of producing the firms' goods or services, and hence set inadequate prices.

SUMMARY

Cost measures the monetary amount of resources used for some purpose, called a cost objective. In a manufacturing company, its products are cost objectives, and organization units, projects, or any activity for which cost information is desired also are cost objectives.

Full cost means all the resources used for a cost objective. Full cost is the sum of (1) the cost objective's direct costs, that is, the costs that are directly traceable to it and (2) a fair share of the indirect costs, that is, those costs incurred jointly for several cost objectives. Cost accounting systems routinely collect costs and assign them to cost objectives. A T-account flowchart of a cost accounting system is helpful in understanding how the system works.

Cost accounting systems are well developed for tangible goods. In recent years, the same principles have increasingly been applied to services and to selling and administrative activities, both in profit-seeking and nonprofit organizations. Full cost information for goods and services is used in financial reporting; in analyzing the profitability of parts of a business; in answering the question, "What did X cost?"; as a basis for setting regulated prices; and as a first approximation in deciding on selling prices under normal circumstances.

SUGGESTIONS FOR FURTHER READING (For Chapters 17–26)

Horngren, Charles T. *Cost Accounting: A Managerial Emphasis.* 5th ed. Englewood Cliffs, N.J.: Prentice Hall, 1982.

Kaplan, Robert S. *Advanced Management Accounting.* Englewood Cliffs, N.J.: Prentice-Hall, 1982.

Matz, Adolph, and Milton F. Usry. *Cost Accounting: Planning and Control.* 7th ed. Cincinnati: South-Western Publishing, 1980.

Rappaport, Alfred. *Information for Decision Making: Readings in Cost and Managerial Accounting.* 3d ed. Englewood Cliffs N.J.: Prentice-Hall, 1982.

Rayburn, L. Gayle. *Principles of Cost Accounting: Managerial Applications.* Rev. ed. Homewood, Ill.: Richard D. Irwin, 1983.

Shillinglaw, Gordon. *Managerial Cost Accounting.* 5th ed. Homewood, Ill.: Richard D. Irwin, 1982.

Cases

CASE 17–1 Delaney Motors*

Frank Delaney owned and operated Delaney Motors, a General Motors automobile dealership in Ohio. Its operations consisted of new-car sales, used-car sales, parts sales, vehicle lease and rentals, vehicle service, and automobile body repairing and repainting. The dealership was profitable, earning almost 5 percent on sales, but the reported profit on the body shop operation seemed low to Mr. Delaney. Consequently, he engaged a consultant to study the body shop operation and make recommendations.

As background for his study, the consultant took Mr. Delaney's data for the most recent year and made certain adjustments, as set forth in Exhibit 1. He ex-

plained them in the following paragraphs taken from his report:

> Most semivariable costs contain a significant portion of common costs. For example, the accountant performs many common services in order to maintain the corporate structure (e.g., preparing and filing the dealer's tax returns). The attorneys and the owner also spend much of their time providing general services.
>
> Although many of the expenses would not be significantly reduced if the owner sold certain departments, each department benefits from these expenses, and thus should be allocated a portion of these costs. The body shop, for example, should pay its proportionate share of accountant's fees relating to the preparation and filing of the dealership's income tax returns.
>
> Telephone expenses and the fixed costs could properly be allocated to the

*This case is based on material in Alan Reinstein, "Improving Cost Allocation for Auto Dealers," *Management Accounting*, June 1982, pp. 52–57. Used by permission.

EXHIBIT 1

DELANEY MOTORS
Analysis of Body Shop Profitability

Line

1	Sales: body shop.	$306,652
2	Gross profit: body shop.	91,107
3	Gross profit percentage (line 2 ÷ line 1).	29.7%
	Analysis of semivariable costs	
4	Legal and auditing (body shop).	0
5	Owner's salary (body shop)	0
6	Telephone and telegraph (body shop)	839
7	Total body shop semivariable costs	839
8	Legal and auditing (company)	2,113
9	Owner's salary (company).	21,600
10	Telephone and telegraph (company)	21,676
11	Total company semivariable costs.	45,389
12	Body shop percentage (line 7 ÷ line 11)	1.85%
13	Body shop employees as percent of total (5/23)	21.7%
14	Revised body shop semivariable costs	
	(line 11 × line 13).	9,867
15	Increase in body shop semivariable costs	
	(line 14 − line 7).	9,028
	Analysis of fixed costs	
16	Body shop fixed costs, as now allocated.	6,106
17	Total company fixed costs.	25,815
18	Body shop percentage (line 16 ÷ line 17)	23.65%
19	Revised body shop fixed costs (20% of line 17)	5,163
20	Decrease in body shop fixed costs (line 19 − line 16)	(943)
	Summary of findings	
21	Net increase in costs (line 15 − line 20).	8,085
22	Unrevised body shop profit.	9,009
23	Revised body shop profit (line 22 − line 21)	924
24	Unrevised profit to sales (line 22 ÷ line 1)	2.94%
25	Revised profit to sales (line 23 ÷ line 1)	0.30%

Other Dealers

		No. 9	*No. 6*	*No. 3*
1	Sales, body shop	$363,662	$505,025	$681,201
3	Gross profit percent	32.9%	30.0%	30.6%
14	Body shop, semivariable*	9,547	13,913	18,177
19	Body shop, fixed*	12,767	11,134	12,233
22	Body shop profit, unrevised	4,453	26,338	56,401
23	Body shop profit (loss)*.	(8,190)	19,386	36,650
24	Unrevised percent profit to sales.	1.22%	5.22%	8.28%
25	Revised percent profit to sales*.	(2.25)%	3.84%	5.38%

*Revised, as described in text.

departments if the necessary documentation were available. Since they are not, other cost allocation methods must be considered.

A potentially controversial issue involves the owner's salary. The body shop manager could claim that because he exercises no control over the owner's salary, this cost should not be charged to his department. The owner puts his time and name in all aspects of the business, however, and his salary should be allocated accordingly. Furthermore, industry data show that owners' salaries tend to vary with sales volume.

Semivariable costs can be allocated to operating departments in several ways, thereby better appraising departmental and managerial performance. These bases include units of production, machine-hours, material costs, sales dollars, direct labor costs, and direct labor-hours. Valid cost allocation bases reliably relate semivariable costs to the basis used for the allocation. Because the operating departments produce heterogeneous products which require dissimilar materials and machines (the new-car and used-car departments probably use no machines), the first three allocation bases—units of production, machine-hours, and material costs—clearly are inappropriate.

Sales dollars also is an invalid cost allocation basis. For example, the cost of sales ratio from a $9,000 new automobile usually exceeds the cost of sales ratio from a $1,000 body shop repair, thereby implying an unequal allocation basis.

Direct labor costs do constitute a valid cost allocation basis in companies in which semivariable costs are labor related (i.e., the operations are predominantly manual), and hourly rates among and within departments are fairly uniform. But because the dealership's semivariable costs are not labor related, and the hourly rates are usually not uniform, direct labor costs do not constitute a competent activity basis for your company.

Direct labor-hours will provide an acceptable cost allocation base. Although some semivariable costs do not vary directly with direct labor-hours, such as legal and audit fees, in the interest of practicality, and because the other methods clearly are not acceptable, allocating semivariable costs based on direct labor-hours appears to be the most viable alternative.

Your financial statements list the number of direct and indirect employees in each department, but fail to disclose the number of departmental hours worked. It is assumed that all direct employees work approximately the same number of hours per week. The number of direct laborers consequently becomes the cost allocation base for semivariable costs. As discussed later, fixed costs are allocated based on the ratio of departmental square footage to total dealer square footage, adjusted by a weighting factor.

Calculations

A summary of selected data extracted from your financial statements is shown in Exhibit 1.

The body shop's and dealership's semivariable costs are shown in lines 7 and 11, respectively. Semivariable cost allocations are based upon direct labor-hours, assuming that each employee works the same number of hours per week. In line 13, the number of body shop employees performing the direct labor work is divided by the total number of employees for the entire dealership. Based on this method, the increase in semivariable costs, as seen in line 15, shows that you have underallocated overhead to the body shop manager, whose bonus includes a portion of his department's profit. The cost accounting system therefore should be changed to more accurately reflect each department's use of dealership resources.

Fixed costs for the body shop and the dealership are summarized in lines 16 and 17. The quotient of these two amounts appears in line 18. In line 19, the revised allocation of fixed costs is shown. Many GM dealers allocate fixed costs to the body shop based on the ratio of body shop square footage to dealer's total square footage. This allocation base accurately allocates fixed building costs but fails to account for the various machinery, equipment, furniture, and fixtures located throughout the dealership.

To allocate these fixed costs more properly, "weights," similar to those developed by Volkswagen, should be used.[1] Volkswagen dealers multiply the square footage of each dealership segment by a value factor to weight the proper distribution of fixed costs. For example, used vehicles and body shop weights are 2.4 and 1.0, respectively. Assuming that these weights also apply to you, you should reduce your allocation to the body shop to 20 percent. Line 19 thus represents this 20 percent balance of the dealership's fixed costs.

Lines 21 through 25 summarize the findings. The revised cost allocations decrease the body shop's profits from 2.94 percent of sales to 0.30 percent of sales.

The consultant had collected data similar to that shown in Exhibit 1 for 11 other dealerships. Summary data for three of these are shown at the bottom of Exhibit 1. They are arranged in order of the body shop profit percentage (line 25),

that is, Dealer No. 3 had the third highest percentage, Dealer No. 6 was in the middle, and Dealer No. 9 was third from the bottom.

The consultant pointed out that the body shop was even less profitable than Mr. Delaney had thought, and he suggested that Mr. Delaney consider selling it, leasing it to another party, increasing prices, or, if the body shop demand was thought to be elastic, lowering prices. He pointed out that selling or leasing the body shop would permit Mr. Delaney to devote more time to other areas of the dealership.

Mr. Delaney considered this recommendation, but he was by no means sure that profitability should be the major consideration. He felt that the dealership had an obligation to provide high-quality body shop work to its customers, and that a lessee might provide below-standard service. He was not sure that prices could be raised, but asked the consultant to find out more about the prices charged by competitive dealers before making a judgment on this.

Questions

1. Comment on the consultant's adjustments made in Exhibit 1. Do you agree with each of them? If not, can you suggest better methods of making the adjustments for the stated purpose?

2. Assuming Mr. Delaney decides to keep the body shop and the consultant reports that it is feasible to raise prices, should Mr. Delaney do so? If he does, what general guide can you suggest as to how much prices should be increased?

3. What action should Mr. Delaney take?

---

[1]Volkswagen Dealers' Accounting and Management Procedures Manual, *Distribution of Occupancy Expenses*, pp. K80-K81.

CASE 17–2   Lipman Bottle Company

In November 1982, Robert Lipman, vice president of Lipman Bottle Company, was wondering what pricing strategy he should recommend to his father. Located in Albany, New York, Lipman Bottle began operations as a bottle distributor in 1909. Distributors maintain a close working relationship with several major bottle manufacturers (e.g. Owens-Illinois). In return for acting as a sales representative, distributors receive a discount of 5–8 percent off regular prices. This permits distributors to charge users of bottles the same price as if a purchase were made directly from the manufacturer.

Typically, distributors maintain a warehouse with an inventory of commonly used bottles and closures. For special orders or large orders, distributors arrange for an order to be shipped directly from the manufacturer to the distributor's customer. The manufacturer bills the distributor at factory price less 5–8 percent, and the distributor bills the user at factory price. The advantages for the manufacturer are that a smaller sales force is required and that the distributor will service accounts too small to be served by one manufacturer. The advantages to the user are that the distributor can provide immediate delivery of many items, can offer the advantage of greater buying power, and can serve as an expert who is familiar with bottles and closures from many manufacturers.

In the past 20 years, the growing use of plastics had increased business for bottle distributors for at least two reasons. First, the choice of bottles had expanded greatly, making expert advice more valuable. The growing variey of caps, lids, and spray pumps handled by distributors had had a similar effect. A second reason was that distributors began specializing in printing labels directly on to plastic bottles. For many users it was convenient to have both purchasing and printing of plastic bottles handled by one vendor.

The Firm. In 1981, Lipman had total sales of $6.2 million, with $500,000 from printing operations. Although the printing operation was only marginally profitable, that service was considered essential for obtaining the more profitable bottle sales. While he realized that printing should not be viewed solely in terms of its profits, Mr. Lipman felt that the firm was offering a valuable service and should price that service to earn a reasonable return:

Last year printing sales were $500,000, and we made $30,000. This year, with the economy worse, we'll sell $450,000 and about break even (Exhibit 1). We have capacity for $1.0 million. I'm not sure what to do. We're the leading firm in Albany; there is another firm here, about half our size. There's also a new small firm causing trouble with price cutting. Our main competitor has begun to cut prices as well. I hate to, but I have to do the same thing. What worries me is that I don't really know what my prices should be, or which prices to cut. We can charge a little more than the large bottle manufacturers, but not much.

Albany is still a good market even with the competition. There is some price cutting, but I know we can keep our market share. The market here, though, is primarily to industrial users.

EXHIBIT 1

LIPMAN BOTTLE COMPANY
Income Statement—Printing Operations
10 Months Ended October 31, 1982

		Variable with Machine-Hours	Variable with No. of Passes	Fixed
Sales revenues	$379,880			
Expenses:				
Payroll	216,258	$161,258		$ 55,000
Supplies	12,458		$12,458	
Factory expense	20,389	10,389	5,000	5,000
Machine parts	4,457		4,457	
Depreciation	22,505	17,505		5,000
Rent	23,770			23,770
Heat, light, and power	20,897		18,897	2,000
Health insurance	19,176	14,000		5,176
Miscellaneous	7,933	7,933		
Insurance	14,541	10,000		4,541
Payroll tax	17,793	13,000		4,793
Advertising	1,664			1,664
Total expenses	381,841*	$234,085	$40,812	$106,944
Profit (loss)	$ (1,961)			
Total machine-hours (including setup)		16,000		
Variable cost per machine-hour		$14.63		
Total passes			15,500,000	
Cost per thousand passes			$2.63	

*Scrap costs are not included in the printing department expenses.

The real market is New York–New Jersey. That's where the cosmetics and pharmaceutical manufacturers are located. If we could get a couple of shampoo bottles, we'd really grow.

Pricing. The bottle printing industry consists of two primary types of printers aside from distributors. Bottle manufacturers provide printing as a service to customers who purchase their plastic bottles. Price lists are published for printing, with the cost of scrap bottles included in the price. Discounts from list prices are unusual.

The second class of printers is custom decorating houses. Price lists are rarely published, although custom pricing is similar to price lists published by bottle manufacturers, adjusted for difficulty of design. Small discounts, however, are widespread. Since printing is normally done on bottles supplied by the customer, the printer is not responsible for scrap costs, but does not receive a commission on sale of bottles.

Lipman had far more printing capacity than needed to print bottles that the firm sold. Thus, Lipman both published a price list for simple designs and acted as a custom decorating house with special pricing. As shown in Exhibit 2, the price list of a major bottle manufacturer, prices are influenced by three factors:

A. *Bottle size* (capacity in fluid ounces). Bottles are loaded onto a chuck, then rotated while a silk screen moves horizontally to print directly onto the plastic bottle. Since

EXHIBIT 2
PRINTING PRICES CHARGED BY INDUSTRY LEADERS
Price per thousand (M) Bottles
At Various Order Quantities

Bottle Size (oz.)	Order Quantity					
	Under 10M	10M	25M	50M	100M	250M
One Separation						
0– 4.9	40.45	31.80	24.40	21.20	20.25	18.20
5– 9.9	47.00	36.60	27.90	24.10	23.40	20.80
10–14.9	59.00	46.00	35.30	30.80	29.00	26.10
15–23.9	68.80	53.20	41.00	35.60	34.10	30.50
24–32.9	72.40	56.80	43.10	37.90	36.10	32.20
Two Separations						
0– 4.9	94.00	72.10	55.70	48.60	46.50	42.40
5– 9.9	106.00	82.60	63.40	55.40	52.50	47.30
10–14.9	132.00	103.00	78.90	69.00	66.10	59.15
15–23.9	158.60	122.80	94.60	82.80	79.00	70.50
24–32.9	162.20	125.60	96.10	84.10	80.40	71.40

larger bottles take longer to print and require more warehouse space, prices increase as bottle size increases.

B. *Quantity.* Each run requires setup time to load ink and a silk screen onto a machine and to set the machine to accept a bottle. In addition, there may be a slight learning effect with each bottle. Thus, cost per bottle decreases as quantity increases.

C. *Separations.* "Separations" means the number of individual impressions required to print a single bottle. When round bottles are printed, they are rotated horizontally in place in the printing machine. A silk screen with the image to be printed is positioned above the bottle and slides horizontally, synchronized to move at the same speed as the surface of the bottle. Because it rotates 360°, a round bottle can be printed front and back in a single machine cycle, i.e., this is a one-separation or single "pass" operation. However, two-sided bottles (commonly called ovals) cannot rotate and thus, generally, only one side can be printed per pass. Printing both front and back of an oval usually requires the entire lot of bottles to be loaded and unloaded twice—one pass per side, or a total of two separations.

When decorating a bottle in multiple colors, the artwork must be *separated* into its color components and a separate screen prepared for each color. To decorate a round bottle in three colors, for example, requires three separate screens and three passes, whereas oval bottles require one screen and one pass per color, per side (a total of six separations, for a three-colored oval).

Operations. The Lipman graphics department included a camera and a developing lab for producing silk screens for printing. Since customers were charged separately for these services, that department was close to a break-even operation.

Production operations consisted of 10 printing machines and 8 drying ovens. Bottles were loaded onto a machine for printing, then placed on a conveyor that carried those bottles through a drying oven. Two extra printing machines were available so that they could be rolled to the setup area and prepared for a new job. This permitted greater utilization of costly ovens and the space which they occupied.

Eight of the machines were semiautomatic. Each bottle had to be loaded into the machine and unloaded onto the dryer belt by hand. Ovals, as described above, had to be printed on one side, allowed to dry, then reloaded for printing on the reverse side. However, one machine had an automatic feature for oval bottles. An operator still had to load and unload that machine manually, but ovals could be printed on both sides before being unloaded into the drying oven. The remaining machine was fully automatic. One operator loaded bottles into a feed hopper, while a second operator observed the printing operations for quality. Oval bottles could be printed on both sides in a single machine cycle and were automatically unloaded into the drying oven.

The Problem. Mr. Lipman asked Thomas Shull, a consultant, to review the firm's pricing policy:

> We publish a price list for simple jobs printed on our bottles. Since we earn a commission on the bottles, prices aren't all that important for printing. However, I'm not sure that the industry pricing is correct. Prices decrease with order size and increase with bottle size. I think that the decrease in price with order size is reasonable, since we don't have to search for more business to keep our shop full if we have large orders.

> Bottle size pricing doesn't seem quite right, however, It does take longer to print a large bottle than a small one, but the difference isn't all that great. Maybe the price differential shouldn't be as large as it is.

> A second factor is the new automatic machines that print both sides of an oval without reloading. Most of our competitors use semiautomatic machines. Maybe we shouldn't be charging as much for ovals with the new machines.

> The final problem is our custom decorating. We are trying to expand in the New York–New Jersey area, and almost all of the business we might get would be custom decorating. We would have no commissions on bottles, so our profit would be entirely from printing. We would also have to pay freight.

> I would like to see our published price list revised to reflect our costs. However, I don't want it to vary greatly from the ones published by major manufacturers. I would also like to know variable cost for bidding on custom decorating. That won't be published, since I have to adjust each price for difficulty of the order; but I'll use the cost list as a guide. Finally, I'd like costs adjusted for transportation to New York–New Jersey. My goal is to earn 30 percent on sales before tax when we're at capacity.

Before preparing price lists, Mr. Shull, Mr. Lipman, and the operations manager agreed that the scrap and shipping costs in Exhibit 3, and the operating information in Exhibit 4, would be used in pricing calculations.

Questions

1. Calculate the variable costs per thousand bottles for one-separation rounds, two-separation rounds, and two-separation ovals, assuming that all ovals are printed on the machine with the auto-

EXHIBIT 3
SCRAP AND SHIPPING COSTS

		Cost of Scrap			
		One Separation	Two Separations		
Size	Cost of 1,000 Bottles	Cost of 2 Percent Lost Bottles (scrap)	Cost of 4 Percent Lost Bottles (scrap)	Loss of 2 Percent of Printing*	Total Cost of Scrap
0–1 oz....	$ 70	1.40	$2.80	$0.50	$3.30
1¼–4.......	84	1.68	3.36	0.50	3.86
5–6.......	94	1.88	3.76	0.50	4.26
7–10......	116	2.32	4.64	0.50	5.14
11–12......	125	2.50	5.00	0.50	5.50
13–16......	130	2.60	5.20	0.50	5.70
17–32......	145	2.90	5.80	0.50	6.30

Cost of Shipping to New York–New Jersey Area

Size	Bottles per Truckload	Cost per 1,000 Bottles†
0–1 oz.	1,040,000	$ 1.06
1¼–4.................	280,000	3.93
5–6.................	190,000	5.79
7–10................	145,000	7.59
11–12................	120,000	9.17
13–16................	86,000	12.79
17–32	42,000	26.19

*Preliminary estimate of printing costs is $25 per thousand.
†Estimated cost per truckload is $1,100.

EXHIBIT 4
OPERATING INFORMATION

1. Cost per hour of setup time and of operating time are approximately equal.
2. Setup time for a job is approximately two hours per separation.
3. Average operating time for one-separation jobs on semiautomatic machines is approximately 0.95 hour per 1,000 bottles, regardless of quantity. Sizes 0–1 ounce and 17–32 ounces are approximately 5 percent slower than average (1.0 hour per 1,000), while all other sizes are approximately 5 percent faster than average (0.9 hour per 1,000).
4. Average operating time for two-separation jobs on semiautomatic machines is approximately 1.1 hours per 1,000 passes (2.2 hours per 1,000 bottles), regardless of quantity. Sizes 0–1 ounce and 17–32 ounces are approximately 10 percent slower than average (1.2 hours per 1,000 passes, 2.4 hours per 1,000 bottles), and other sizes 10 percent faster (1.0 hour per 1,000 passes, 2.0 hours per 1,000 bottles).
5. Average operating times for ovals on the semiautomatic machine with automatic feature for ovals is approximately 0.80 hour per 1,000 passes (1.6 hours per 1,000 bottles), regardless of quantity. Sizes 0–1 ounce and 17–32 ounces are approximately 10 percent slower than average (0.88 hour per 1,000 passes, 1.76 hours per 1,000 bottles), while all other sizes are approximately 10 percent faster than average (0.72 hour per 1,000 passes, 1.44 hours per 1,000 bottles).
6. The fully automatic machine is approximately twice as fast on rounds as the semiautomatic machines and approximately twice as fast on ovals as the semiautomatic machine with automatic feature for ovals. However, two people are required to operate the machine and it is approximately twice as costly to operate. Thus, this machine can be ignored for costing purposes.

matic feature for ovals. Do one set of calculations for the Albany area (scrap included) and another for New York–New Jersey (freight included, but not scrap). To keep the number of calculations you need to do within reason, consider only two bottle size ranges—0–1 ounce and 17–32 ounces, and only two order·quantity ranges—5,000–9,999 and 100,000–249,999. (Together with the two sales areas, this results in 24 combinations for which to calculate variable costs.)

2. Prepare a suggested price list for the Albany area. Consider only one-separation rounds and two-separation rounds or ovals, and only the two sizes and order quantities described in Question 1. How did Mr. Lipman's goal of a 30 percent margin (at capacity) affect your price recommendations?

3. Which products should the company attempt to sell in New York–New Jersey? Explain.

18

Additional Aspects of
Product Costing Systems

This chapter describes the two general types of product cost accounting system, job-order costing and process costing. The measurement of direct material and direct labor costs is discussed in some detail, as are the techniques for arriving at a product's fair share of indirect costs. This discussion describes, in effect, how the numbers that flow through a cost accounting system, such as the one diagrammed in Illustration 17–2, are determined. As in the preceding chapter, these systems and techniques will be illustrated in a manufacturing setting, since tangible products are easily visualized. However, the concepts and techniques apply also to nonmanufacturing settings.

JOB-ORDER COSTING AND PROCESS COSTING

**Production
Processes**

The various types of production processes employed by companies can be thought of in terms of four classifications: unit production, batch production, assembly-line production, and process production. In *unit production*, the focus of activity is a physically identifiable job, such as producing a large steam turbine generator, building a custom-designed house, or performing a consulting job for a client. In *batch* (or *lot*) production, a batch of identical items (for example, 100 carburetors) are worked on in one factory work station before being moved on as a batch to the next work station. In *assembly-line production,* the jobs are separately identifiable, but they tend to be similar (or identical) to one another, such as assembling Pontiac "Firebirds," Atari videogame consoles, and Whirlpool refrigerators. In *process production,* outputs are not identifiable as individual units of product until late in the production process; examples are found in the petroleum, chemical, milling, steel, distillery, forest products, and glass container industries.

As with many classification schemes, the lines between these categories are not clear-cut. Rather, any production process falls somewhere on a continuum or spectrum, with "pure" unit production operations—called *job shops*—at one end, "pure" process operations at the other end, and batch and assembly-line operations falling somewhere in between. (See Illustration 18–1.)

ILLUSTRATION 18–1
SPECTRUM OF PRODUCTION PROCESSES

| Unit Production | Batch Production | Assembly-Line Production | Process Production |

In accounting, there are two basic types of cost accumulation systems: job-order cost systems and process cost systems. Job-order cost systems are usually used in unit production and batch operations, and process cost systems in assembly-line and process production. Although the general characteristics of each cost system will be described separately below, it should be understood that in practice a given system may have some characteristics of a job-order system and other characteristics of a process system, especially if production operations fall somewhere near the center of the spectrum.

Essentially, a *job-order* cost system collects cost for *each* physically identifiable job or unit of product as it moves through the production process, regardless of the accounting period in which the work is done. A *process* cost system collects costs for *all* the products worked on during an accounting period and determines unit costs by dividing the total costs by the total number of units worked on.

Job-Order Costing

The "job" in a job-order cost system may consist of a single unit (e.g., a turbine or a house), or it may consist of a batch of identical or similar products covered by a single job or production order (e.g., 10,000 copies of a book or 12 dozen Style 885 jeans). Each job is given an identification number, and its costs are collected on a *job-cost record* that is set up for that number. Costs are recorded as the job moves through the various steps in the production process; these steps usually correspond to separate departments. Anyone who has had an automobile repaired at a garage has seen such a record, except that the amounts that the customer sees have been converted from costs to retail prices.

The sum of all the costs charged to job-cost records during an accounting period is the basis for the entries debiting Work in Process (WIP) Inventory and crediting Materials Inventory, Wages Payable, and Overhead accounts (i.e., entries 2, 3, and 6 in Illustration 17–2). When each job is completed, the total cost recorded on the job-cost record is the basis for the entry transferring the product from WIP Inventory to Finished Goods Inventory (i.e., entry 7), and this same cost is the basis for the entry transferring the product from Finished Goods Inventory to Cost of Sales when the product is sold (entry 8). The total cost recorded on all job-cost records for jobs that are still in process as of the end of an accounting period therefore equals the total of the WIP Inventory account at that time.

In some companies, such as professional service firms and repair shops, there is no inventory of finished goods. When a job is completed and billed to the client, Cost of Sales is debited and WIP Inventory is credited. (In professional service firms, the name Cost of Services is sometimes used, rather than Cost of Sales.)

Process Costing   In a process cost system, all production costs for an accounting period, such as a month, are collected in WIP Inventory. These costs are *not* identified with *specific units* of product. A record of the number of units worked on is also maintained. By dividing total costs by the number of units produced, one derives an average cost per unit. This cost per unit is used as the basis for calculating the dollar amount of the entries that record the transfer from WIP Inventory to Finished Goods Inventory and the subsequent transfer from Finished Goods Inventory to Cost of Sales.

Equivalent Production. A special problem in process costing is taking into account the products that are only partially completed at the end of an accounting period. The units that were *worked on* in, say, September include (1) units that were both started and completed during September, (2) units that were started in August (or earlier) and completed in September, and (3) units that were worked on but not completed by the end of September.

Since the units of the first type were produced in their entirety in September, but the units of the second and third types were—or will be—partially completed in some period other than September, the production activity for September cannot be determined simply by adding up the number of units worked on during September. The three types of units must be converted to a common base, called the *equivalent unit of production*, that is, the equivalent of one completed unit.

In order to convert the number of uncompleted products into their equivalence in terms of completed units, the assumption is often made that units in process at the beginning and the end of the period are 50 percent complete. Thus, in order to calculate the number of equivalent units, each unit completed would be given a weight of one, and each unit in process at the beginning or end of the period would be given a weight of one half.[1]

Although the cost accounting system does not record the equivalent units worked on during a month, this amount can be deduced. The number of equivalent units in the beginning and ending WIP inventories is known, and the number of units completed and transferred to finished goods inventory is also known. Thus, the missing term, equivalent units worked on (or "equivalent production"), can be deduced.

Having found the equivalent units of production, the cost per unit is found by dividing the sum of the cost of beginning WIP inventory plus the production costs of the period by the sum of the equivalent units in beginning WIP inventory and the equivalent units of production.

> **Example.** Illustration 18–2 shows how this calculation is made. In a certain factory, production costs incurred in May amounted to $60,600. On May 1, 500 equivalent units (1,000 half-completed units) were in WIP Inventory. During May, 2,450 completed units were transferred from WIP Inventory to Finished Goods Inventory. On May 31, 550 equivalent units (1,100 half-completed units) were in WIP Inventory. Thus, during May, 2,500 equivalent units were produced, as is deduced in Part B of Illustration 18–2.
>
> Note how the procedures (Part C) assign the $72,600 sum of beginning WIP Inventory and May production costs to Finished Goods Inventory and ending WIP Inventory. It can also be noted that the company's unit production costs increased in May, since beginning WIP Inventory, valued based on April's costs, was $24 per unit (= $12,000 ÷ 500), whereas the per unit cost in May was $24.20.

Direct Material Costs.   The foregoing applies to direct labor costs and overhead. Direct material costs may be treated differently, depending on when material enters the production process. If material is added evenly throughout the process, it could reasonably be costed along with direct labor and overhead by use of the 50 percent assumption described above. If, as is more common, all the materials for a unit are issued at

---

[1] A more precise procedure would be to estimate the actual stage of completion, but this involves more effort. At the other extreme, some companies disregard the units in process and show no WIP Inventory account. If the work in process inventory is small, or if it remains relatively constant in size, no serious error is introduced. Another variation is to apply the 50 percent assumption separately to each department through which the product passes rather than to the factory as a whole.

ILLUSTRATION 18–2
EQUIVALENT PRODUCTION CALCULATIONS

A. Assumed Situation

	Equivalent Units	Cost
Beginning WIP Inventory (1,000 × ½)	500	$12,000
Production	?	60,600
Transferred to Finished Goods Inventory	2,450	?
Ending WIP Inventory (1,100 × ½)	550	?

B. Calculation of Equivalent Units of Production (= X)

Units in Beginning Inventory	+	Units Produced	=	Units Transferred	+	Units in Ending Inventory
500	+	X	=	2,450	+	550
		X	=	2,500		

C. Calculation of Cost

	Equivalent Units	Cost
Beginning WIP Inventory	500	$12,000
Production	2,500	60,600
Total	3,000	$72,600

Unit cost: $72,600 ÷ 3,000 = $24.20

	Equivalent Units		Cost
To Finished Goods Inventory	2,450 @ $24.20 =	$59,290
Ending WIP Inventory	550 @ $24.20 =	13,310
Total	3,000		$72,600

Work In Process Inventory

Balance, May 1	12,000	To Finished Goods Inventory (2,450 units @ $24.20)	59,290
May production costs	60,600	Balance, May 31 (550 units @ $24.20)	13,310
	72,600		72,600
Balance, May 31	13,310		

the *beginning* of the production process, the calculations for materials are done first, treating *all* units as 100 percent complete as regards their materials content. (In the example, for purposes of *materials* calculations, there were 1,000 units on hand May 1, 2,450 units transferred out during May, and 1,100 units on hand May 31, so materials were issued for 2,550 units.) The results of these materials calculations are combined with those for direct labor and overhead (as in Illustration 18–2) to arrive at the total amounts for transfers to Finished Goods Inventory and month-end WIP Inventory.

Choice of a System

In most situations, the nature of the production process indicates whether a job-order system or process system is more appropriate. Nevertheless, since a process cost system requires less recordkeeping than a job-order system, there is a tendency to use it even though the products manufactured are not entirely alike. Thus, a manufacturer of children's shoes may use a process cost system, even though there are some differences in cost among the various sizes, styles, and colors of shoes manufactured. By contrast, manufacturers of men's or women's shoes usually employ a job-order system because the differences among the costs of the various styles are so significant that a process cost system would not provide adequate product cost information.

In a process cost system, the unit costs are *averages* derived from the total costs of the period. Differences in the costs of individual products are not revealed. Thus, if there are important reasons for keeping track of the cost differences between one product and another, or between one production lot of the same type of product and another, then a job-order system is more appropriate. For example, a job-order system would invariably be used if the customer paid for the specific item, production order, or services on the basis of its cost (as is often the case in repair shops, printing shops, consulting firms, hospitals, and other job-shop operations). Also, use of a job-order system makes it possible to examine actual costs on specific jobs; this may help one to locate trouble spots and can serve as an aid in pricing similar jobs in the future. In a process cost system, costs cannot be traced to specific units or batches.

For our purposes, there is no need to study differences in the detailed records required for the two types of systems. Both systems are essentially devices for collecting full production costs. Either furnishes the information required for the accounting entries shown in Illustration 17–2.

Variations in Practice

The accounting system outlined in Illustration 17–2 will probably never be precisely duplicated in actual practice since it is a schematic representation of underlying structures. Organizations build on the basic structure by adding accounts that collect the data in more detail so as to meet their particular needs for information. A company may, for example, set up several materials inventory accounts, each one covering a different type of material, instead of a single account as shown in Illustration 17–2. Alternatively, the Materials Inventory account may be a controlling account, controlling dozens of individual subsidiary accounts. Another common variation is to have several work in process accounts, one for each main department or "cost center" in the organization. Such a system is essentially like that shown in Illustration 17–2 except that work is transferred from one department to another. The finished goods of one department become, in effect, the raw material of the next department.

MEASUREMENT OF DIRECT COSTS

As defined in Chapter 17, an item of cost is *direct* with respect to a specified cost objective if it is *traceable* to that cost objective or if only that cost objective *caused* incurrence of the cost. Also, to treat a cost item as direct it must be *feasible* to measure the amount of resource that was used for the specified cost objective.[2] If the causal relationship for a single item of cost applies to two or more cost objectives, the cost item is indirect with respect to these cost objectives.

In this chapter the cost objectives we are interested in are products, that is, goods and services. For these cost objectives, direct costs are those that are directly caused by the production of the specified products. For other types of cost objectives, the word *direct* could refer to quite different items of cost. Thus, the salary of a department supervisor is a direct cost of the department that this person manages, but it is an indirect cost of the products produced in that department because no exclusive causal relationship exists between any single product and the supervisor's salary.

We shall now discuss in more detail the two principal types of direct product costs: direct labor cost and direct material cost. The discussion is in the context of a job-order system, but similar considerations are relevant in a process cost system.

Direct Labor Cost

There are two aspects of the measurement of direct labor cost: (1) measuring the *quantity* of labor time expended and (2) ascertaining the *price* per unit of labor time.

Measuring the quantity of labor time is relatively easy. A daily timecard, or comparable record, is usually kept for each direct worker, and on it a record is made of the time the worker spends on each job. Or, if direct workers are paid a piece rate, the record shows the number of pieces completed. These timecards are used both to measure labor costs and also as a basis for payroll computations. Problems arise concerning the treatment of idle time, personal time, overtime, and so on; but these problems are beyond the scope of this introductory treatment.

Deciding on the best way to price these labor times is conceptually more difficult than measuring the quantity of time. Many companies have a simple solution: they price direct labor at the amounts actually earned by the employees concerned (so much an hour if employees are paid on a day-rate or hourly rate basis; so much a piece if they are paid on a piece-rate basis). There may be either a separate labor rate for each employee or an average labor rate for all the direct labor employees in a

---

[2]Cost Accounting Standards Board, *Restatement of Operating Policies, Procedures, and Objectives,* May 1977, p. 6. This source also uses a "benefit" criterion, but this is unnecessary.

department of a given skill classification. For example, public accounting firms typically use an average labor rate for each of several job categories—staff assistant, senior, supervisor, and so on—when charging labor costs to jobs, even though there is variation in the actual rates paid employees in any given category.

Example.   Assume that a certain job is worked on in four departments and that the time worked in each department (as shown by the timecards) and the labor rates are as indicated below. The direct labor cost of the job would be computed as follows:

Department	Direct Labor-Hours on Job	Departmental Hourly Rate	Total Amount
A	20	$7.00	$140.00
B	3	9.50	28.50
C	6	8.80	52.80
D	40	8.00	320.00
Total direct labor cost of job			$541.30

Some companies add *labor-related costs* to the basic wage rate. They reason that each hour of labor effort costs the company not only the wages paid to the employee but also the FICA taxes, pension contributions, and other fringe benefits paid by the employer.[3] The company must pay these labor-related benefits; they are caused by the fact that the employee works, and they are therefore part of the real cost of using the employee's services. A few companies even include a share of the costs of the personnel department and employee welfare programs as a part of direct labor cost. Using such a higher labor price gives a more accurate picture of direct labor costs. It also involves additional recordkeeping, however. Many companies do not believe the gain in accuracy is worthwhile, and thus treat labor-related costs as part of overhead.[4]

Direct Material Cost

The measurement of direct material cost also has the two aspects of the *quantity* of material used and the *price* per unit of quantity. The quantity is usually determined from requisitions that are used to order material out of the storeroom and into production. The problem of pricing this material is similar to that for pricing direct labor. Material may be priced at solely its purchase or invoice cost, or there may be added some or all of the following *material-related costs:* inward freight, inspection costs, moving costs, purchasing department costs, and interest and space charges associated with holding material in inventory.

---

[3]But *not* the *employee's* FICA contribution. This is a deduction from the employee's earnings; it is therefore not a cost to the company. (See Chapter 9.)

[4]For example, a 1977 study made by the Cost Accounting Standards Board reported that 84 percent of the respondents treated health insurance and pension costs applicable to direct labor as overhead costs (CASB, *Progress Report to the Congress,* 1977, p. 38).

As was the case with labor costs, it is conceptually desirable to include these material-related items as part of material cost. To do so, however, may involve more recordkeeping than a company believes worthwhile. Many companies therefore treat material-related costs as part of overhead.[5]

The measurement of direct material costs is also affected by the assumption made about the flow of inventory costs, that is, LIFO, FIFO, or average cost. The effect of these alternative flow assumptions was discussed in Chapter 6.

Direct Cost versus Variable Cost

Much confusion between direct and variable costs exists in practice. This confusion occurs because if the cost objective is a product (as in the above discussion), many costs that are direct to the product are also variable with the production volume of the product. Since, for example, raw materials costs and the costs of production employees (as opposed to the costs of these employees' supervisors) usually are both direct costs of a product and also variable with the volume of that product, people tend to use the words *direct* and *variable* interchangeably. (*Indirect* and *fixed* also are often used as though they were synonyms.)

It is important to recognize that the two sets of terms are based on very different concepts. The direct/indirect dichotomy relates to the *traceability* of costs to cost objectives; the variable/fixed dichotomy relates to the *behavior* of costs as volume fluctuates. In a sense, cost traceability is an accountant's concept, whereas cost behavior is an economist's concept—although both concepts are important in management accounting. The point is that common *usage* of these terms does not always coincide correctly with the underlying concepts, so one must be careful not to infer that the user of the terms necessarily is using them as precisely as we do throughout this book.

ALLOCATION OF INDIRECT COSTS

Distinction between Direct and Indirect Costs

For a given cost objective, it is conceptually desirable that a given item of cost be classified as a direct cost rather than as an indirect cost. This is because an item of direct cost is assigned directly to the cost objective, whereas the assignment of indirect costs to cost objectives is a more roundabout and usually less accurate process. Nevertheless, the category of indirect costs does, and must, exist.

Costs are not traced directly to a product (the cost objective for a prod-

---

[5]The CASB study cited in the preceding footnote reported that whereas 52 percent of the respondents treated inward freight as part of direct material cost, only 36 percent accounted for incoming material inspection costs as direct. Only 43 percent treated cash discounts as a reduction in direct material cost; the others treated these discounts as a reduction in overhead.

uct costing system) for one of three reasons: (1) it is *impossible* to do so, as in the case of a factory superintendent's salary. (2) It is *not feasible* to do so; that is, the recordkeeping required for such a direct tracing would cost too much. (For example, the thread and copper rivets that are used on a pair of jeans cost only a few pennies, and it is not worthwhile to trace them to each batch of jeans; they are therefore classified as indirect materials.) (3) Management *chooses* not to do so; that is, many companies classify certain items of costs as indirect simply because it has become customary in the industry to do so.

Problems of Drawing Distinctions. Problems arise in attempting to define the precise line between items of cost that are directly caused by a product, and other costs. For example, a cost may not be *caused* by a product even though it is incurred at the same time as the product is being made.

> **Example.** In a certain week, Sara Clark, a draftsperson in an architectural firm, was originally scheduled to spend 25 hours on project A and 15 hours on project B. As it happened, project A, which had to be done first, required 35 hours of her time. Consequently, Ms. Clark worked 50 hours during the week: 35 regular hours on A, 5 regular hours on B, and 10 weekend hours (at 50 percent premium) on B. The overtime premium should be charged to project A because it was A, not B, that caused Ms. Clark to work on the weekend.

Moreover, there are differences of opinion as to how close the causal relationship between the cost and cost objective must be in order to classify a cost item as direct. In many production operations, such as assembly lines, refineries, and other continuous process operations, a basic work force is required no matter what output is produced. Some would argue that the labor cost of this work force constitutes a cost that is required to operate the plant in general, much like heat and light, and that it is therefore an indirect cost. Nevertheless, most companies consider such costs as direct labor.

Nature of Allocation

The cost of a cost objective includes, in addition to its direct costs, a *fair share* of the indirect costs that were incurred for several cost objectives, of which the cost objective in question is one. Thus, the cost of an automobile repair job includes a fair share of all the indirect costs (i.e., the overhead costs) in the repair shop. The idea of "fair share" sounds vague, and it is vague; but it is the only way of approaching the problem of measuring the indirect costs of a cost objective.

What is a fair share? Probably the best way to think about this is in terms of what proportions of the indirect costs are *caused by* each of the various cost objectives. For example, a job that requires the use of relatively expensive equipment (with attendant relatively high costs for depreciation, maintenance, insurance, and property taxes) causes more overhead costs than a job requiring the same number of direct labor-hours, but which can be performed using only hand tools. Thus, in an automobile garage, three hours of labor spent performing an engine tune-up and wheel balancing and alignment causes more overhead than three hours spent waxing the car. Similarly, a job requiring three hours of a worker's time causes more overhead than a job requiring only half as much of that worker's time. It is also apparent that for a given time period (such as a month), all of the jobs performed collectively caused in some sense all of the period's costs, whether those costs are ultimately classified as direct or indirect with respect to each job cost objective.

From the above line of reasoning, it follows that (1) all items of production cost should be assigned to cost objectives, and (2) the amount assigned to an individual cost objective should depend on the causal incurrence, to the extent that a causal relationship exists.

The process of assigning indirect costs to individual cost objectives is called *allocation*. The verb *to allocate* means "to assign indirect costs to individual cost objectives." Indirect costs are allocated to products by means of an overhead rate (also sometimes called an absorption rate or a burden rate). Usually this rate is established annually, prior to the beginning of the accounting year. The method of calculating overhead rates will be described below. Before describing these calculations, we need first to explain the term *cost center*.

Cost Centers

A *cost center* is a cost objective for which costs of one or more related functions or activities are accumulated. Marker Pen Company, for example, has a department that manufactures wicks. The wick department is an example of a cost center; the costs incurred in that department are for the function or activity of manufacturing wicks for pens.

In a cost accounting system, items of cost are first accumulated in cost centers, and then they are assigned to products. For this reason a cost center is often called an *intermediate cost objective* to distinguish it from a product, which is a *final cost objective*.

Recall from Chapter 15 that a responsibility center is an organization unit headed by a manager. The wick department in the pen factory is a responsibility center. The wick department is also a cost center. Indeed, most responsibility centers are also cost centers.

Not all cost centers are responsibility centers, however. The printing department in a company may operate a number of printing presses of different sizes and capabilities. Each printing press may be a cost center, even though only the whole printing department is a responsibility center. Conversely, when the goods flowing through a factory are essentially similar, an entire factory may be treated as a single cost center, even though the factory consists of several responsibility centers each headed by a supervisor.

Production and Service Cost Centers. There are two types of cost centers: production cost centers and service cost centers. A *production cost center* is a cost center that produces a product or a component of a product. The barrel, wick, and assembly departments in the pen factory are production cost centers. The individual printing presses mentioned above are also production cost centers. Each selling department in a store is, in essence, a production cost center.

All other cost centers are *service cost centers*. They provide services to production cost centers and to other service cost centers, or they perform work for the benefit of the organization as a whole. The maintenance department and the general factory office are examples. Not all service cost centers are identifiable organization units, however. For example, in many organizations there is an "occupancy" cost center, in which are accumulated all the costs associated with the physical premises, including rent or depreciation, property taxes, insurance, and utilities costs.

Service cost centers are often called *indirect cost pools* or *overhead pools*. The term conveys the idea that they are repositories in which indirect costs are accumulated. The costs subsequently flow out of these pools to other cost centers.

Calculating Overhead Rates

The calculation of an overhead rate for a cost center is accomplished only after a series of steps in which total overhead costs are assigned to the production cost centers. Illustration 18–3 is a diagram of the procedure involved in allocating overhead costs to products. The situation illustrated is that of the pen factory. The factory consists of three production cost centers and two service cost centers. The production cost centers are the barrel, wick, and assembly departments. One of the service cost centers is the occupancy center. The other is the general cost center, in which other overhead costs are accumulated. These include the costs of operating storerooms, the maintenance department, and the factory office. (In many factories, there would be separate service cost centers for each of these activities.)

Direct material and direct labor costs are assigned directly to product cost objectives by the techniques described earlier in this chapter. The allocation of overhead cost to product (final) cost objectives involves three steps:

1. All overhead costs for an accounting period are assigned to the service and production cost centers, which are intermediate cost objectives. This flow is shown in Section A of Illustration 18–3.
2. The total cost accumulated in each service cost center is reassigned to production cost centers (Illustration 18–3, Section B.).
3. The total overhead costs accumulated in each production cost cen-

ILLUSTRATION 18–3
ALLOCATING OVERHEAD COSTS TO PRODUCTS

A. Initial Assignment to Cost Centers

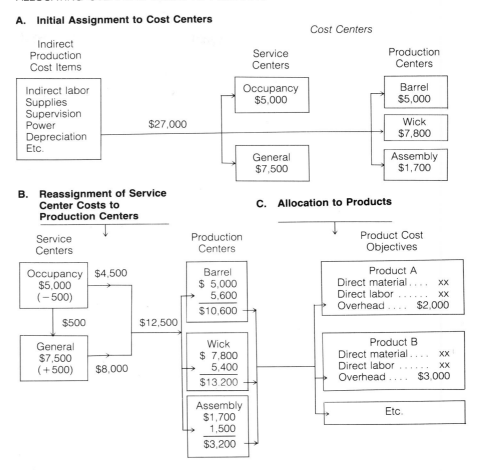

**B.   Reassignment of Service
Center Costs to
Production Centers**

C.   Allocation to Products

ter, including the reassigned service center costs, are allocated to products that pass through the production cost center (Illustration 18–3, Section C).

We shall now describe these three steps in more detail.

1.   Initial Assignment to Cost Centers.   The first step in the allocation of overhead costs is to assign all items of indirect production cost for the period to the cost centers. Indirect labor costs are assigned to the specific cost centers in which the indirect employees work.[6] The costs

---

[6]Recall that these labor costs are usually *direct* with respect to the intermediate cost objectives, the specific cost centers. They are called *indirect* labor costs because they are indirect with respect to products, the final cost objectives.

of supplies and other indirect materials are also assigned to the specific cost centers in which the materials are used. Depreciation on machinery and power costs associated with the machines are assigned to the cost centers in which the machines are located. The costs of electricity for general lighting, steam for heating the production facilities, and rent or depreciation on these facilities are assigned to the occupancy cost center.

These indirect cost items are charged to the cost centers one cost item at a time; that is, the total overhead costs are *not* added and then this *total* distributed to the centers. When this item-by-item assignment process is completed, the sum of the overhead costs assigned to all the cost centers equals the total overhead cost for the period.

Section A of Illustration 18–4 shows how the $27,000 of overhead costs were assigned initially to cost centers. For example, of the $10,000 of indirect labor cost, zero was assigned to the occupancy cost center (because no personnel were charged to this cost center), $5,000 to the general cost center, $1,700 to the barrel department, $3,300 to the wick department, and zero to the assembly department (because its supervisor worked directly on products and it had no other indirect employees).

ILLUSTRATION 18–4
ALLOCATING OVERHEAD COSTS

		Service Centers		Production Centers		
	Total	Occupancy	General	Barrel	Wick	Assembly
Cost Item		**A. Initial Assignment to Cost Centers**				
Indirect labor	$10,000	$ 0	$ 5,000	$ 1,700	$ 3,300	$ 0
Supplies	5,000	600	1,500	500	1,500	900
Other	12,000	4,400	1,000	2,800	3,000	800
Subtotals	27,000	5,000	7,500	5,000	7,800	1,700
		B. Reassignment of Service Center Costs				
Occupancy		(5,000)	500	1,500	2,000	1,000
General			(8,000)	4,100	3,400	500
Indirect cost	$27,000	$ 0	$ 0	$10,600	$13,200	$3,200
		C. Calculation of Overhead Rates				
Direct labor-hours	7,000			2,100	3,500	1,400
Overhead rate per direct labor-hour				$5.05	$3.77	$2.29

(   ) indicates subtraction.

2. Reassignment of Service Center Costs. The second step in the allocation of overhead costs is to reassign the total cost accumulated in each *service* cost center so that eventually all overhead costs are assigned to the *production* cost centers. Some service center costs are assigned directly to the cost centers that receive the service.[7] Maintenance department costs may be assigned directly to production cost centers on the basis of the maintenance service actually performed, for example. The costs of a power-generating plant may be assigned according to the metered usage of electricity in each cost center, just as if the electricity had been purchased from an outside company.

Allocation Bases. Some overhead cost items cannot be directly assigned to cost centers, and some service center costs cannot be directly reassigned to other cost centers. These costs must be allocated—that is, assigned to other cost centers on some reasonable basis. The basis of allocation should correspond as closely as feasible to the basic criterion given above: it should express a causal relationship between the cost centers and the costs. The dozens of alternative *allocation bases* that are used in practice can be grouped into the following principal categories:

1. *Payroll related.* Social security taxes paid by the employer, health insurance, and other fringe benefits may be allocated on the basis of the total labor costs. Alternatively, as mentioned above, fringe benefit costs for direct workers may enter into the calculation of direct labor costs; if so they will not appear as overhead costs at all.

2. *Personnel related.* Personnel department costs, and other costs associated with the number of employees rather than with the amount that they are paid, may be allocated on the basis of number of employees.

3. *Material related.* This category of cost may be allocated on the basis of either the quantity or the cost of direct material used in production cost centers, or, alternatively, it may be excluded from overhead costs and charged to products as part of direct material cost, as already mentioned.

4. *Space related.* Some items of cost are associated with the space that the cost center occupies, and they are allocated to cost centers on the basis of the relative area or cubic content of the cost centers. Occupancy cost in Illustration 18–4 is an example.

5. *Activity related.* Some costs are roughly related to the overall level of activity in the cost center; or at least there is a presumption that the more work a cost center does, the greater the costs that are properly allocated to it. Electrical power costs and steam costs, if not directly assigned, fall into this category. So do the costs of a variety of other service cost centers which, although not demonstrably a function of activity, are more realistically allocated in this way than in any other. The measure of activity may be an overall indicator of the amount of work done by the cost center, such as its total labor cost, its total direct costs, or the total cost of its output. Alternatively, the measure of activity may

---

[7]Again, note that a cost item that is indirect with respect to a final product may be direct with respect to a cost center.

be more closely related to the function of the service cost center whose costs are being allocated. For example, electricity costs may be allocated on the basis of the total horsepower of motors installed in each cost center.

Example. The middle section of Illustration 18–4 shows the reassignment of service center costs to production cost centers.

Occupancy costs are space related, so the $5,000 of occupancy cost is allocated on the basis of the relative floor space in each cost center, as follows:

Cost Center	Percent of Floor Space	Occupancy Cost
General	10	$ 500
Barrel	30	1,500
Wick	40	2,000
Assembly	20	1,000
	100	$5,000

The costs of the general cost center are allocated on the basis of the total prime costs (i.e., direct material + direct labor) charged to the three production cost centers. The total general cost is, after the addition of the allocated share of occupancy cost, $8,000. This amount is allocated as follows:

Cost Center	Percent of Prime Costs	General Costs
Barrel	51	$4,100
Wick	43	3,400
Assembly	6	500
Total	100	$8,000

Step-Down Order. Note that in Illustration 18–4 part of the cost of the occupancy service cost center is charged to the general service cost center. Conceivably, part of the cost of the general cost center should be charged to the occupancy cost center, and this creates a problem. Whenever there are a number of service cost centers, the interrelationships among them could theoretically lead to a long series of distributions, redistributions, and re-redistributions.[8] In practice, however, these redistributions usually are avoided by allocating the service center costs in a prescribed order, which is called the *step-down order*.

There are no hard-and-fast rules for determining this step-down order. In general, organizations allocate first either (1) the costs of the service

---

[8]Techniques of matrix algebra are sometimes used to perform this series of distributions and redistributions. These techniques are described in advanced cost accounting texts.

center that *provides the most* services to other cost centers or (2) the costs of the service center that *receives the fewest* services from other service centers. In the illustration, the prescribed order is occupancy first, and general second; this is because occupancy provides services to all of the other cost centers, and receives no services from the general service center. No additional cost is allocated to a service cost center after its costs have been allocated. Since the step-down order is adhered to in all calculations, the results are always consistent.

3. Allocation of Overhead Costs to Products. Having collected all the overhead costs in production cost centers, the final step is to allocate these costs to the products worked on in these cost centers. In a process cost system, this is easy. The total equivalent units of production for the month is determined by the method described previously, and the total overhead cost is divided by the number of equivalent units. This gives the unit overhead cost for each product.

In a job-cost system, however, the procedure is more complicated. The various jobs worked on in the production center are of different sizes and complexities, and therefore they should bear different amounts of overhead cost. To the extent feasible, we want to allocate overhead costs to jobs such that each job bears its fair share of the total overhead cost of the cost center. In order to do this, an overhead rate is calculated.

The function of the *overhead rate* is to allocate an equitable amount of overhead cost to each product. In thinking about how this rate should be constructed, therefore, we need to address the question, Why, in all fairness, should one product have a higher overhead cost than another product? Depending on the circumstances, the following are among the plausible answers to this question:

1. Because more labor effort was expended on one product than on another, and indirect costs are presumed to vary with the amount of labor effort.
2. Because one product used more machine time than another, and indirect costs are presumed to vary with the amount of machine time.
3. Because one product had higher direct costs than another and therefore, in fairness, should bear a higher amount of indirect costs.

Each of these answers respectively suggests a quantitative basis of activity that can be used to allocate indirect costs to products:

1. The number of labor-hours or labor dollars required for the product.
2. The number of machine-hours.
3. The total prime costs (i.e., direct material plus direct labor).

The machine-hours basis is common for production cost centers that consist primarily of one machine (such as a papermaking machine) or a group of related machines. The direct labor-hours basis is frequently used in other situations. Different production centers in a given plant may use different bases, reflecting the fact that some are relatively labor-intensive while others are more capital-intensive. The decision as to the best measure of activity is judgmental. By definition, there is no precisely accurate way of measuring how much overhead cost actually should attach to each product. If there were such a way, the item would be a direct cost.

Having selected what appears to be the most appropriate measure in a given production cost center, the overhead rate for that production cost center is calculated by dividing its total overhead cost by its total amount of activity for the period.

> **Example.** Continuing with the example in Illustration 18–4, let us assume that the number of direct labor-hours (DLH) is the appropriate activity measure for the allocation of overhead costs to products in all three production cost centers. In the barrel department, the DLH for the month totaled 2,100. Dividing the 2,100 DLH into the total overhead cost of $10,600, gives an overhead rate of $5.05 per DLH for the barrel department.

Usually, there is only one overhead rate for each production cost center. Thus, although overhead and service center costs are assigned to production cost centers by a variety of methods, with each method reflecting the causal relationship for a particular cost item, the total amount of indirect cost for a production cost center is allocated to products by one overhead rate.

The overhead cost for each product that passes through the production cost center is calculated by multiplying the cost center overhead rate by the number of activity units accumulated for that product.

> **Example.** Referring to the situation in Illustration 18–4, if in this factory a certain batch of pens, Job No. 307, required 30 DLH in barrel, 20 DLH in wick, and 5 DLH in assembly, its total overhead cost would be calculated as follows:

Production Cost Center	DLH	Overhead Rate	Overhead Cost
Barrel	30	$5.05	$151.50
Wick	20	3.77	75.40
Assembly	5	2.29	11.45
Total overhead cost of Job No. 307			$238.35

Thus, Job No. 307 had $238.35 of overhead costs *allocated* to it (also *applied* to it, or *absorbed* by it).

Predetermined Overhead Rates

The preceding description of the accumulation of overhead costs in cost centers and their eventual allocation to products followed the same chronological order as that used for the accounting for direct material and direct labor. That is, the amount of cost for the month was first ascertained, and subsequently this amount was allocated to products. This approach was used for pedagogical reasons: it is the easiest way of relating the flow of overhead costs to the physical activities of the production process.

A better way of allocating overhead costs in most situations is to establish an overhead rate for each production cost center *in advance*, usually once a year, and then to use these *predetermined* overhead rates throughout the year. We shall limit the discussion of predetermined overhead rates to a job-cost system, but similar considerations apply to a process cost system.

Why Overhead Rates Are Predetermined.   There are three reasons why calculating an estimated annual overhead rate in advance is preferable to computing an actual rate at the end of each month:

1. If overhead rates were computed monthly, they would be unduly affected by conditions peculiar to that month. Heating costs in the winter, for example, are higher than in the summer. But no useful purpose would be served by reporting that pens manufactured in the summer cost less than pens manufactured in the winter. As will be explained below, fluctuations in the volume of activity also can cause gyrations in the overhead rates. Misleading information on overhead costs would be presented if the overhead costs assigned to products were affected by these fluctuations.
2. The use of a predetermined overhead rate permits product costs to be calculated more promptly. Direct material and direct labor costs can be assigned to products as soon as the time records and material requisitions are available. If, however, overhead rates were calculated only at the end of each month, overhead costs could not be assigned to products until after all the information on overhead costs for the month had been assembled. With the use of a predetermined overhead rate, overhead costs can be allocated to products at the same time that direct costs are assigned to them.
3. Calculation of an overhead rate once a year requires less effort than going through the same calculation every month.

Procedure for Establishing Predetermined Rates

In order to establish predetermined overhead rates, a calculation is made that follows exactly the same steps described above, except that the numbers represent what the activity levels and costs are *estimated to be* during the coming year, rather than what they *actually were*.

Flexible Overhead Budget.   In many companies this estimate is made in the form of a *flexible overhead budget* (or *variable overhead budget*) that is prepared for each production cost center. Such a budget shows what overhead costs are expected to be at various volume levels (i.e., activity levels). Since some cost elements are fixed and others are variable or semivariable, total overhead costs will be different at each ume level. As will be explained in later chapters, the flexible overhead budget is an important tool for cost control.

Illustration 18–5 is a flexible budget for total monthly overhead costs in the wick department of the pen company, using direct labor-hours (DLH) as the volume measure. As suggested by this illustration, the budget can be presented either in tabular form or in graphic (C-V diagram) form. The column headed 3,500 DLH is similar to the column for the wick department in Illustration 18–4, except the Illustration 18–4 column showed *actual* overhead costs of $13,200 for a volume of 3,500 DLH, whereas Illustration 18–5 shows *budgeted* amounts for this volume. The other columns show budgeted amounts for several different DLH levels. The procedures for developing *each column* of Illustration 18–5 are the same as those described for Illustration 18–4, except that

ILLUSTRATION 18–5
FLEXIBLE OVERHEAD BUDGET

MARKER PEN COMPANY
Wick Department

Costs	Volume (DLH)			
	2,500	*3,000*	*3,500*	*4,000*
Indirect labor	$ 3,300	$ 3,300	$ 3,300	$ 3,300
Supplies	1,050	1,260	1,470	1,680
Other	2,500	2,750	3,000	3,250
Subtotals	6,850	7,310	7,770	8,230
Occupancy allocation	2,000	2,000	2,000	2,000
General allocation	3,400	3,400	3,400	3,400
Total indirect cost	$12,250	$12,710	$13,170	$13,630

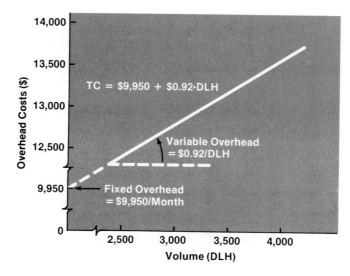

the costs here are estimates rather than actuals. Analysis of the estimates in Illustration 18–5 will reveal that (1) indirect labor is a fixed cost (at $3,300 per month), as are the allocations of occupancy costs ($2,000 per month) and general costs ($3,400 per month); (2) supplies is a variable cost (at $0.42 per DLH); and (3) other costs are semivariable (at $1,250 per month plus $0.50 per DLH). Thus, total budgeted overhead costs are expected within this range of volume to vary according to the equation, $TC = \$9,950 + \$0.92 \cdot DLH$.

Estimating Volume. The second step in establishing the predetermined overhead rate is to estimate what the average level of activity in each production cost center is going to be during the coming year. This involves first estimating the volume of the factory as a whole for the coming year, and then converting this estimate into a volume estimate for each production cost center. In Marker Pen Company, it is estimated that in the coming year the factory will operate at 75 percent of capacity. When the factory operates at this level, the wick department's volume is 3,000 DLH per month. This is called the standard volume, and is discussed further below.

Overhead Rate. The final step is to calculate each production cost center's overhead rate. This is simply the center's budgeted overhead costs at standard volume, divided by that standard volume. For the wick department, this is $12,710 ÷ 3,000 DLH or $4.24 per DLH. Note that because of the presence of fixed costs in the flexible budget, the higher the standard volume, the lower will be the overhead rate. For example, if standard volume were only 2,500 DLH, the rate would be $4.90 per DLH; at a standard volume of 4,000 DLH, the rate would be $3.41 per DLH.

Also note that once standard volume is estimated, all the budgeted cost data for volumes other than the standard volume are irrelevant *for purposes of calculating the overhead rate.* The rate remains the same for the entire year, even if volume fluctuates from month to month. If the rate were changed every month to correspond precisely to that month's volume, then a primary reason for using predetermined rates—to avoid misleading month-to-month product cost fluctuations—would be lost. (The other columns in the table are useful, however, for monthly overhead *cost control* purposes.) Once the annual rate is determined, it is used to charge overhead costs to products passing through the cost center in exactly the same manner as was previously illustrated for actual overhead rates.

Standard Volume. The most uncertain part of the process of establishing predetermined overhead rates is estimating what the level of activity will be. This amount is called the *standard volume* or the *normal volume.* In most companies, standard volume is the volume anticipated for the next year. Some companies use instead the *average volume* expected over a *number of years* in the future.

As noted above, the estimate of volume has a significant influence on overhead rates. Many items of overhead cost are fixed costs. To take the extreme case, if *all* overhead costs were fixed, the overhead rate would vary inversely with the level of volume estimated for the forthcoming year. To the extent that not all overhead costs are fixed, changes in overhead rates associated with changes in the estimate of volume are not as severe, but they are nevertheless significant in most situations. It is therefore important that careful attention be given to making the best possible estimate of volume as part of the procedure of calculating predetermined overhead rates.

Example. A papermaking machine is a large, expensive machine that either runs at capacity or doesn't run at all. Its depreciation, the costs associated with the building in which it is housed, and most other items of overhead cost are unaffected by how many hours a year the machine operates. Assume that these overhead costs are estimated to be $1,000,000 a year, and that they are entirely fixed, that is, they are estimated to be $1,000,000 regardless of how many hours the machine operates during the year. If the measure of activity used in establishing the overhead rate is machine-hours, overhead rates will vary as shown below for various estimates of machine-hours to be operated during the year:

Cost	No. of Machine-Hours	Overhead Rate (per machine-hour)
$1,000,000	8,000	$125
1,000,000	6,000	167
1,000,000	4,000	250

The effect of the volume estimate on the amount of overhead cost assigned to products during the year is therefore great. Indeed, in a situation like this, in which fixed overhead costs are large relative to total costs, including direct labor and direct material, the accounted cost of the product may be affected more by the estimate of annual volume than by any other single factor.

The important point to remember is that the predetermined overhead rate will be relatively low if the estimated volume of activity is relatively high because the same amount of fixed cost will be spread over a larger number of units.

Unabsorbed and Overabsorbed Overhead

When a predetermined overhead rate is used, the amount of overhead costs allocated to (or "applied to" or "absorbed by") products in a given month is likely to differ from the amount of overhead costs actually incurred in that month. This is because the actual overhead costs assigned to the cost center in the month, and/or the actual activity level for the month, are likely to be different from the estimates that were used when the predetermined overhead rate was calculated. If the amount of overhead cost absorbed by products exceeds the amount actually incurred, overhead is said to be *overabsorbed;* and if the amount is less, overhead costs are *underabsorbed* (or *unabsorbed*). For management purposes, the amount of unabsorbed or overabsorbed overhead can be analyzed, as will be discussed in Chapter 20.

For simplicity, no account for overabsorbed or unabsorbed overhead was shown in the cost accounting flowchart given in Illustration 17–2. Such an account is often labeled an *Overhead Variance* account. In effect, the journal entry debits Work in Process Inventory for the amount of costs absorbed, credits indirect production cost accounts for the amount of overhead costs actually incurred, and debits or credits Overhead Variance for the difference.

> **Example.** If actual indirect production costs were $28,000 and if only $27,000 was applied to products on the basis of the overhead rates, the entry would be:

```
Work in Process Inventory .................. 27,000
Overhead Variance ........................  1,000
   Overhead ...............................          28,000
```

Note that the overhead variance occurs solely because a *predetermined* overhead rate is used. (The details underlying the preceding entry will be described in Chapter 19.)

SUMMARY

There are two main types of product costing systems. With job-order costing, costs are accumulated separately for each individual item or for a batch of similar items. With process costing, costs are accumulated for all units together, and then are divided between completed units (in Finished Goods Inventory) and partially completed units (in ending Work in Process Inventory) according to some reasonable assumption as to their stage of completion at the end of the period.

Measurement of both direct material costs and direct labor costs involves measuring both a resource quantity and a price per unit of resource. The unit price measurement aspect is more difficult because of the question of how to handle material-related costs such as inventory holding cost and labor-related costs such as fringe benefits.

Items of cost are indirect because it is not possible to assign them directly, because it is not worthwhile to do so, or because the management chooses not to do so. Overhead costs are allocated to products by means of an overhead rate. This rate is usually calculated prior to the beginning of the accounting year. The overhead rate is used to allocate overhead costs to the products that pass through the production cost center. The number of units of activity required for each product multiplied by the overhead rate gives the total amount of overhead cost absorbed by that product.

Cases

CASE 18–1 Problems in Full Cost Accounting

A. Maxfield Company

Maxfield Company makes two products, A and B. At the beginning of October, account balances were:

Raw Material X.............	$10,000 (1,000 lbs.)
Raw Material Y.............	6,000 (2,000 lbs.)
Work in Process, A..........	0
Work in Process, B..........	0
Finished Goods, A	0
Finished Goods, B	0
Wages Payable	0

Overhead is allocated to products at a rate of $7 per direct labor-hour. During October, the following transactions took place:

1. 800 pounds of raw material X were issued for the manufacture of 1,000 units of product A.
2. 400 direct labor-hours at an average hourly rate of $10 were used in manufacture of product A.
3. 1,000 pounds of raw material Y were issued for manufacture of product A.
4. 1,000 pounds of raw material Y were issued for the manufacture of 2,000 units of product B.
5. 300 direct labor-hours at an average hourly rate of $10 were incurred in manufacturing product B.
6. 2,000 pounds of raw material X were purchased at a cost of $12 per pound.
7. 1,000 pounds of raw material Y were purchased at a cost of $3.25 per pound.
8. 500 pounds of raw material X were issued for the manufacture of product B.
9. 800 units of product A and 1,500 units of product B were completed. The incomplete units of product A had required 75 hours of direct labor; the incomplete units of product B had required 50 hours.
10. Actual overhead expenses totaled $4,900.

Maxfield used the FIFO inventory accounting method.

Questions

1. Prepare T-accounts and indicate how each of the above transactions flows through the accounting system.

2. If 1,000 units of product B were sold during October, what are the amounts for product B October Cost of Sales and month-end product B Finished Goods?

B. Northwoods Outfitters Company

Northwoods Outfitters Company produces backpacks, tents, and sleeping bags. Each is produced in a separate production center. The company also has a purchasing department, which buys nylon, goosedown, aluminum tubing and other items, and a small engineering department, which also does R&D and quality control work. Major items of production overhead expense are rent, heating, electricity, indirect labor, and supplies. Rent costs are allocated to cost centers on the basis of square footage; heating costs, on the basis of cubic feet. Electricity is charged to cost centers on the basis of metered usage; indirect labor and supplies are also charged on the basis of actual usage. The costs of purchasing and engineering are allocated to the three production departments on the basis of direct labor-hours.

For April, preliminary figures showed the following:

Rent expense was $1,200; heating costs were $300.

Question

Calculate the overhead rate per direct labor-hour for each production cost center in April.

C. Sullivan Company

Sullivan Company does custom information retrieval and report preparation for a variety of clients. There are two production cost centers: Information Retrieval and Report Writing. Supporting service cost centers are Data Processing and Library Services. Sullivan Company does not attempt to charge costs for Data Processing and Library Services to projects according to actual use of these services, but rather at month-end allocates these costs to Information Retrieval and Report Writing according to the number of direct labor hours spent on projects in those two production centers. Then each project is charged an amount per direct labor-hour for each production cost center's overhead.

Indirect costs are primarily rent, utilities, and labor. Rent and utilities are allocated to the four cost centers according to square footage of office space; indirect labor is assigned to each department as incurred. Information Retrieval and Re-

			Cost Centers		
	Backpacks	Tents	Sleeping Bags	Purchasing	Engineering
Square feet..............	700	1,000	1,000	400	500
Cubic feet...............	8,400	1,500	12,000	4,800	6,000
Electricity...............	$300	$100	$100	$50	$100
Indirect labor	$600	$600	$650	$1,500	$3,000
Supplies	$100	$50	$75	$200	$500
Direct labor-hours.........	640	800	960		

port Writing each occupy 5,000 square feet. Data Processing occupies 1,250 square feet, and Library Services occupies 10,000 square feet.

The following transactions took place in November:

1. $720 (80 hours) of direct information retrieval labor were incurred for project A.
2. $225 (25 hours) of direct information retrieval labor were incurred for project B.
3. $1,440 (160 hours) of direct information retrieval labor were incurred for project C.
4. $180 (20 hours) of direct report preparation labor were incurred for project A.
5. $90 (10 hours) of direct report preparation labor were incurred for project B.
6. $450 (50 hours) of direct report preparation labor were incurred for project C.
7. $2,500 rent expense.
8. $4,000 indirect Data Processing labor expense.
9. $1,725 indirect Library Services labor expense.
10. $450 indirect Information Retrieval labor expense.
11. $500 utilities expense.
12. $1,250 other Data Processing expense.
13. $130 other Library Services expense.

Questions

1. Determine the amount of direct costs for each project during November.
2. Calculate indirect costs for each of the production and service departments for November.

3. Calculate the rates at which indirect costs should be allocated to each project for each of the two production departments.
4. Determine the full costs of each of the three projects carried out in November.

D. Repromat Company

Repromat Company is a small copying company that specializes in electrostatic copying. It is located in a small college town, so the amount of work varies considerably with the seasons. On the last Sunday afternoon in June, the company made 1,200 copies. Only one person worked Sunday afternoons; this person was paid $5 an hour for the four hours Repromat was open on Sunday. The cost of paper averages 1½ cents per copy; other supplies and electricity cost about ½ cent per copy. Other monthly operating costs are:

Rent	$1,000
Equipment rental	500
Manager's salary	1,200
Advertising	500
Other	600

Volume over the year totals three million copies. There are an average of 7,280 direct labor-hours worked per year at an average rate of $5 an hour.

Questions

1. Calculate the total variable cost of the copying jobs done on the last Sunday in June.
2. Calculate the total labor cost of these jobs.
3. Suggest a way to assign labor and indirect costs to the cost of a copy, and defend your suggestion.
4. Determine the full cost of one copy on the last Sunday in June, using the costing method you suggested for the preceding question.

5. Determine the average *annual* full cost of one copy.

6. Repromat is paid 5 cents per copy. Should they stay open on Sunday afternoons if the above situation is typical? (Assume the copy center is open 50 Sunday afternoons per year.)

CASE 18–2 Huron Automotive Company

Sandy Bond, a recent business school graduate who had recently been employed by Huron Automotive Company, was asked by Huron's president to review the company's present cost accounting procedures. In outlining this project to Bond, the president had expressed three concerns about the present system: (1) its adequacy for purposes of cost control, (2) its accuracy in arriving at the true cost of products, and (3) its usefulness in providing data to judge supervisors' performance.

Huron Automotive was a relatively small supplier of selected automobile parts to the large automobile companies. Huron competed on a price basis with larger suppliers that were long-established in the market. Huron had competed successfully in the past by focusing on parts that, relative to the auto industry, were of small volume and hence did not permit Huron's competitors to take advantage of economies of scale. For example, Huron produced certain parts required only by four-wheel-drive vehicles.

Bond began the cost accounting study in Huron's carburetor division, which accounted for about 40 percent of Huron's sales. This division contained five production departments: casting and stamping, grinding, machining, custom work, and assembly. The casting and stamping department produced carburetor cases, butterfly valves, and certain other carburetor parts. The grinding department prepared these parts for further machining, and precision ground those parts requiring close tolerances. The machining department performed all necessary machining operations on standard carburetors; whereas the custom work department performed part of the machining and certain other operations on custom carburetors, which usually were replacement carburetors for antique cars or other highly specialized applications. The assembly department assembled and tested all carburetors, both standard and custom.

Thus, custom carburetors passed through all five departments and standard carburetors passed through all departments except custom work. Carburetor spare parts produced for inventory went through only the first three departments. Both standard and custom carburetors were produced to order; there were no inventories of completed carburetors.

Bond's investigation showed that with the exception of materials costs, all carburetor costing was done based on a single, plantwide direct labor hourly rate. This rate included both direct labor and factory overhead costs. Each batch of carburetors was assigned its labor and overhead cost by having workers charge their time to the job number assigned the batch, and then multiplying the total

EXHIBIT 1
CALCULATION OF PLANTWIDE LABOR AND
OVERHEAD HOURLY RATE
Month of July

	Dollars	Hours
Labor:		
Casting/stamping	$ 27,302	2,528
Grinding	19,260	2,140
Machining	95,938	7,675
Custom work	40,832	3,712
Assembly	145,892	15,357
Total labor	329,224	31,412
Overhead	551,336	
Total labor and overhead	$880,560	

$$\text{Hourly rate} = \frac{\$880,560}{31,412} = \$28.03 \text{ per hour}$$

$$(= \$10.48 \text{ labor} + \$17.55 \text{ overhead})$$

hours charged to the job number by the hourly rate. Exhibit 1 shows how the July hourly rate of $28.03 was calculated.

It seemed to Bond that because the average skill level varied from department to department, each department should have its own hourly costing rate. With this approach, time would be charged to each batch *by department*; then the hours charged by a department would be multiplied by that department's costing rate to arrive at a departmental labor and overhead cost for the batch; and finally these departmental costs would be added (along with materials cost) to obtain the cost of a batch.

Bond decided to see what impact this approach would have on product costs. The division's accountant pointed out to Bond that labor hours and payroll costs were already traceable to departments. Also, some overhead items, such as departmental supervisors' salaries and equipment depreciation, could be charged directly to the relevant department. However, many other overhead items, including heat, electricity, property taxes, and insurance, would need to be allocated to each department if the new approach were implemented. Accordingly, Bond determined a reasonable allocation basis for each of these joint costs (e.g., cubic feet of space occupied as the basis of allocating heating costs), and then used these bases to recast July's costs on a departmental basis. Bond then calculated hourly rates for each department, as shown in Exhibit 2.

In order to have some concrete numbers to show the president, Bond decided to apply the proposed approach to three carburetor division activities: production of model CS-29 carburetors (Huron's best-selling carburetor), production of spare parts for inventory, and work done by the division for departments in other Huron divisions. Exhibit 3 summarizes the hourly requirements of these activities by department. Bond then costed these three activities using both the July plantwide rate and the pro forma July departmental rates.

EXHIBIT 2
PROPOSED DEPARTMENTAL LABOR AND OVERHEAD
HOURLY RATES

Department	Labor Rate per Hour	Overhead per Hour	Total Cost per Hour
Casting/stamping	$10.80	$15.73	$26.53
Grinding	9.00	15.07	24.07
Machining	12.50	31.33	43.83
Custom work	11.00	20.33	31.33
Assembly	9.50	10.64	20.14

EXHIBIT 3
DIRECT LABOR-HOUR DISTRIBUTION FOR THREE CARBURETOR
DIVISION ACTIVITIES

Department	CS-29 Carburetors (per batch of 100)	Spare Parts for Inventory (per typical month)	Work for other Divisions (per typical month)
Casting/stamping	21 hrs.	304 hrs.	674 hrs.
Grinding	12	270	540
Machining	58	1,115	2,158
Custom work	—	—	—
Assembly	35	—	—
Total	126 hrs.	1,689 hrs.	3,372 hrs.

Upon seeing Bond's numbers, the president noted that there was a large difference in the indicated cost of CS-29 carburetors as calculated under the present and proposed methods. The present method was therefore probably leading to incorrect inferences about the profitability of each product, the president surmised. The impact of the proposed method on spare parts inventory valuation was similarly noted. The president therefore was leaning toward adopting the new method, but told Bond that the supervisors should be consulted before any change was made.

Bond's explanation of the proposal to the supervisors prompted strong opposition from some of them. The supervisors of the outside departments for which the carburetor division did work each month felt it would be unfair to increase their costs by increasing charges from the carburetor division. One of them stated:

> The carburetor division handles our department's overflow machining work when we're at capacity. I can't control costs in the carburetor division, but if they increase their charges, I'll never be able to meet my department's cost budget. They're already charging us more than we can do the work for in our own department, if we had enough capacity, and you're proposing to charge us still more!

Also opposed was the production manager of the carburetor division:

> I've got enough to do getting good quality output to our customers on time, without getting involved in more paperwork! What's more, my department su-

pervisors haven't got time to become bookkeepers, either. We're already charging all of the division's production costs to products and work for other departments; why do we need this extra complication?

The company's sales manager also did not favor the proposal, telling Bond:

We already have trouble being competitive with the big companies in our industry. If we start playing games with our costing system, then we'll have to start changing our prices. You're new here, so perhaps you don't realize that we have to carry some low-profit—or even loss—items in order to sell the more profitable ones. As far as I'm concerned, if a product *line* is showing an adequate profit, I'm not hung up about cost variations among items *within* the line.

The strongest criticism of Bond's proposed new system came from Huron's director of financial planning:

Departmentalizing the costing rate may be a good idea, but I'm not sure you're attacking the main problem. How can we do anything with these cost estimates when you change the rates every month? When volume is rising, all of our products make money, no matter which system you use. But when overall volume is falling, some products begin

to show losses even though their own sales continue to hold up. I don't know whether they're really losing money or whether they just can't carry a full share of the costs of idle capacity. I don't see how your system is going to help me answer that question.

Faced with all these arguments, Bond decided to make some more calculations before going back to the president. First, Bond asked the industrial engineering department to estimate the monthly volume at which each of the five production departments typically operated over the course of a year (normal volume). Then Bond assembled a new set of overhead cost estimates and recalculated the proposed overhead rates, as shown in Exhibit 4. Finally, Bond recalculated the labor and overhead costs of a 100-unit lot of model CS-29 carburetors and of a typical month's spare parts production and work for other divisions, based on the "normalized" departmental rates.

When Bond circulated these new calculations, the production manager of the carburetor division was even more perturbed than before:

That's even worse! Now you're piling paperwork on paperwork! And on top of everything, we won't be able to charge out all of our costs. What am I supposed

EXHIBIT 4
DEPARTMENTAL OVERHEAD RATES BASED ON NORMAL VOLUME

	Normal Volume (DLH)	Normal Overhead Cost	Overhead per Direct Labor-Hour
Casting/stamping	2,500	$ 39,690	$15.88
Grinding	2,400	32,840	13.68
Machining	8,000	242,470	30.31
Custom work	3,600	75,260	20.91
Assembly	17,500	167,790	9.59
Total	34,000	$558,050	$16.41

to do with the costs in machining and assembly if I can't charge them to products or spare parts or the work we do for other divisions?

When Bond reported the various managers' opposition to the president, the president replied:

> You're not telling me anything that I haven't already heard from unsolicited phone calls from several supervisors the last few days. I don't want to cram anything down their throats—but I'm still not satisfied our current system is adequate. Sandy, what do you think we should do?

Questions

1. Using the data in the exhibits, determine the cost of a 100-unit batch of CS-29 carburetors, a month's spare parts, and a month's work done for other divisions under the present method, Bond's first proposal, and Bond's revised proposal.

2. Are the cost differences among the methods significant? What causes these differences?

3. Suppose that Huron purchased a new machine costing $400,000 for the custom work department. Its expected useful life is five years. This machine would reduce machining time and result in higher quality custom carburetors. As a result, the department's direct labor-hours would be reduced by 30 percent, and this extra labor would be transferred to departments outside the carburetor division. About 10 percent of the custom work department's overhead is variable with respect to direct labor-hours. Using July's data:
   a. Calculate the plantwide hourly rate (present method) if the new machine were acquired. Then calculate indicated costs for the custom work department in July, using both this new plantwide rate and the former $28.03 rate.
   b. Calculate the hourly rate for the custom work department only (first proposed method), assuming the machine were acquired and the first proposed costing procedure were adopted. Then calculate indicated costs for the custom work department in July, using both this new rate and the former $31.33 rate.
   c. Under the *present* costing procedures, what is the impact on indicated custom carburetor costs if the new machine is acquired? What is this impact if the first *proposed* costing procedure is used? What inference do you then draw concerning the usefulness of the present and proposed methods?

4. Assume that producing a batch of 100 model CS-29 carburetors requires 126 hours, distributed by department as shown in Exhibit 3, and $1,400 worth of materials. Huron sells these carburetors for $51 each. Should the price of a CS-29 carburetor be increased? Should the CS-29 be dropped from the product line? (Answer using both the present and the first proposed costing methods).

5. Assume that Huron also offers a model CS-30 carburetor that is identical to a CS-29 in all important aspects, including price, but is preferred for some applications because of certain design features. Because of the CS-30's relatively low sales volume, Huron buys certain major components for the CS-30 rather than making them in-house. The total cost of purchased parts for 100 units of model CS-30 is $2,800; the labor required per 100 units is 12, 7, 17, and 35 hours, respectively, in the casting/stamping, grinding, machining, and assembly departments. If a customer ordered 100 carburetors and said that either model CS-29 or CS-30 would be acceptable, which model should Huron ship? Why? (Answer using only the first proposed costing method.)

6. What benefits, if any, do you see to Huron if either proposed costing method is

adopted? Consider this question from the standpoint of (a) product pricing, (b) cost control, (c) inventory valuation, (d) charges to outside departments, (e) judging departmental performance, and (f) diagnostic uses of cost data. What do you conclude Huron should do regarding their costing procedures?

CASE 18–3 Rosemont Hill Health Center

In March, 1983, Florence Mitchell, administrator of the Rosemont Hill Health Center (RHHC), expressed concern about RHHC's cost accounting system. The extensive funding RHHC had received during its early years was decreasing, and Ms. Mitchell wanted to prepare the center to be self-sufficient; yet it lacked critical cost information.

At a meeting with Robert Simi, RHHC's new accountant, Ms. Mitchell outlined the principal issues:

> First of all, our deficit is increasing. We obviously have to reverse this trend if we're going to become solvent. But to do that, we have to know where our costs are incurred. That leads to the second problem: we don't know the cost of each of the services we offer. Although our patients receive a variety of services, we charge everyone the same per visit fee.

Ms. Mitchell provided a further motivation for analyzing RHHC's costs, in that federal and local funding was available for family planning and mental health programs; but to qualify, RHHC would need a precise calculation of cost per visit in these departments. Likewise, to receive third-party reimbursement for patient visits, RHHC's fee schedule had to be reasonably related to costs.

Background. RHHC was established in 1975 by a consortium of community groups. Situated in Roxbury, an inner-city residential neighborhood of Boston, the center was intended to provide comprehensive health care to residents of Roxbury and neighboring communities. Eight years after its inception, RHHC maintained strong ties with the community groups responsible for its development and for its subsequent acceptance in Roxbury.

Funding for RHHC was initially provided by the federal government as part of the Department of Health and Human Services' attempt to equalize health care in the United States. When these operating funds were depleted in 1981, the city of Boston supplemented RHHC's income with a small three-year grant. Because Ms. Mitchell realized that government support could not continue indefinitely, she intended to make the center self-sufficient as soon as possible. RHHC's 1982 income statement is shown in Exhibit 1.

RHHC was composed of eight departments: pediatrics, adult medicine, family planning, nursing, mental health, social services, dental, and community health. In addition, the center had a laboratory and medical records department. Community health, which had been designed by RHHC's clients, was a multidisciplinary department providing a link between the health and social services at RHHC and the schools and city services of the community. The department was staffed by a part-time speech pathologist, a part-time learning specialist, and a full-time nutritionist. In total, RHHC had 22

EXHIBIT 1

ROSEMONT HILL HEALTH CENTER
Income Statement
For the Year Ended December 31, 1982

Revenue from patient fees		$690,900
Other revenue		10,000
Total revenues.		700,900
Expenses:		
Program services	$470,000	
Utilities.	20,000	
Laboratory	50,000	
General and administrative.	184,000	
Total expenses		724,000
Surplus (deficit).		$ (23,100)

paid employees, and a volunteer staff of 6–10 students who were acquiring clinical and managerial experience.

The Existing Information System. RHHC's previous accountant had established a cost system to determine the fee charged to patients. According to this method, shown in Exhibit 2, the fee was derived from the average yearly cost of one patient visit. The accountant would first determine the direct cost of each department. He would then add overhead

EXHIBIT 2
EXPENSES AND PATIENT VISITS* FOR 1982, BY DEPARTMENT

Department	Number of Patient Visits	Expenses		
		Salaries†	Other‡	Total
Pediatrics	5,000	$ 40,000	$ 16,000	$ 56,000
Family planning	10,000	10,000	30,000	40,000
Adult medicine.	2,100	60,000	32,000	92,000
Nursing	4,000	54,000	12,000	66,000
Mental health	1,400	30,000	16,000	46,000
Social services.	1,500	64,000	16,000	80,000
Community health	2,500	10,000	20,000	30,000
Dental	6,400	40,000	20,000	60,000
Subtotal.	32,900	308,000	162,000	470,000
Administration		76,000	4,000	80,000
Rent.			72,000	72,000
Utilities.			20,000	20,000
Laboratory work.		32,000	18,000	50,000
Cleaning			12,000	12,000
Recordkeeping		14,000	6,000	20,000
Total.		$430,000	$294,000	$724,000

Number of patient visits.		32,900
Average cost per visit ($724,000 ÷ 32,900)		$22.00

*Patient visits rounded to nearest 100; expenses rounded to nearest $1,000.
†Includes fringe benefits.
‡Materials, supplies, contracted services, depreciation, and other nonpersonnel expenses.

costs, such as administration or rent and utilities, to the total cost of all the departments to determine the center's total costs. Finally, he would divide that total by the year's number of patient visits. Increased by an anticipated inflation figure for the following year (approximately 8 to 10 percent), this number became the charge per patient visit for the subsequent year.

In reviewing this method with Mr. Simi, Ms. Mitchell explained the problems she perceived. She said that although she realized this was not a precise method of determining charges for patients, the center's charge had to be held at a reasonable level to keep the health services accessible to as many community residents as possible. Additionally, she anticipated complications in determining the cost per patient visit for each of RHHC's departments:

> You have to consider that our overhead costs, such as administration and rent, have to be included in the cost per patient visit. That's easy to do when we have a single overall cost, but I'm not certain how to go about it when determining costs on a departmental basis. Furthermore, it's important to point out that some of our departments provide services to others—nursing, for example. There are three nurses in that department, all earning the same salary. But one works exclusively for adult medicine, and another divides her time evenly between family planning and pediatrics. Only the third spends his entire time in the nursing department seeing patients who don't need a physician, although he occasionally refers patients to physicians. In the social service department, the situation is more complicated. We have two MSW's [Masters in Social Work], each earning $24,000 a year, and one bachelor's degree social worker

earning $16,000. The two MSW's yearly see about 1,500 patients who need general social work counseling, but they also spend about 50 percent of their time in other departments. The BA social worker cuts pretty evenly across all departments except dental, of course, where we don't need social work assistance.

Mr. Simi added further dimensions to the problems:

> I've spent most of my time so far trying to get a handle on allocating these overhead costs to the departments. It's not an easy job, you know. Administration, for example, seems to help everyone about equally, yet I suppose we might say more administrative time is spent on the departments where we pay more salaries. Rent, on the other hand, is pretty easy: that can be done on a square-foot basis. We could classify utilities according to usage if we had meters to measure electricity, phone usage, and so forth; but because we don't, we have to do that on a square-foot basis as well. This applies to cleaning too, I guess. It seems to me that recordkeeping can be allocated on the basis of the number of records, and each department generates one record per patient visit.
>
> Laboratory work is the most confusing. Some departments don't use the laboratory at all, while others use the laboratory regularly. I guess the fairest would be to charge for laboratory work on an hourly basis. Since there are two people in the laboratory, each working about 2,000 hours a year, the charge per hour would be about $8.00. But this is a bit unfair, since the laboratory also uses supplies, space, and administrative time. So we should include those other costs in the laboratory hourly rate. Thus, the process is confusing and I haven't really decided how to sort it out. However, I have prepared totals for floor space and laboratory usage (Exhibit 3).

EXHIBIT 3
FLOOR SPACE AND LABORATORY USAGE, BY DEPARTMENT*

Department	Floor Space (sq. ft.)	Laboratory Usage (hrs./yr.)
Pediatrics	1,000	1,000
Family planning	1,300	200
Adult medicine.	1,800	2,400
Nursing	300	100
Mental health	1,000	—
Social services.	500	—
Community health	1,100	100
Dental	1,000	200
Administration	500	—
Recordkeeping	300	—
Laboratory.	1,200	—
Total	10,000	4,000

*All amounts are rounded to the nearest 100.

The Future. As Ms. Mitchell looked toward the remainder of 1983, she decided to calculate a precise cost figure for each department. RHHC was growing, and she estimated that total patient volume would increase by about 10 percent during 1983, spread evenly over each department. She anticipated that costs would also increase by about 10 percent. She asked Mr. Simi to prepare a step-down analysis for 1982 so that they would know RHHC's costs for each department. She planned to use this information to assist her in determing patient fees for the remainder of 1983.

Questions

1. Using an appropriate step-down procedure to allocate service center costs to production centers, determine the total 1982 costs and cost per visit for each production center.

2. What does your analysis suggest about how the center should charge its patients for services?

CASE 18–4 Aurora Printing Company

Aurora Printing Company provided various printing services to businesses and the general public. Among the items it printed were personal and business stationery, sales slips and other business forms, wedding invitations, promotional brochures, and advertising circulars. Several other local printing firms, most of them larger than Aurora, provided these same services.

Although Aurora was open for business Monday through Saturday, normally the actual printing work was done on a one-shift basis Monday through Friday. August tended to be a slow month; accordingly, employees were encouraged to take at least part of their paid vacation time in August, and any major routine maintenance or overhaul work on the presses was performed that month. On the other hand, at certain times during the year, overtime work (at premium pay) was required to complete jobs by their promised dates. Specifically, May tended to be an unusually busy month because of a great influx of wedding invitation orders, and December was hectic because of jobs requiring imprinting of names on Christmas cards and because many businesses ordered stocks of business forms for use in the upcoming year. During the course of a year, overtime hours worked amounted to about 5 percent of regular-time hours.

In recent months, Fran Baranek, owner and general manager of Aurora Printing Company, had become increasingly concerned about the firm's low profit margin. In early November, when Aurora's bookkeeper had prepared the third quarter (July–September) income statement, the results showed that Aurora had just barely broken even. This had prompted Baranek to ask a nephew, who was taking some management courses at the state college, to spend part of his Christmas vacation studying Aurora's business procedures, with special emphasis on the cost accounting system.

Aurora's present job accounting procedures were as follows. The form on which the services to be performed for a customer were described contained a serial number; this number became the job number for costing purposes. This same form also showed the price estimate that had been given the customer for the described services. This estimate usually was the same as the amount ultimately charged the customer; ordinarily it was not changed unless the customer subsequently changed his or her requested services. The original copy of this form followed each job through the printing shop; a carbon copy was given to the customer to serve as a claim check.

When paper stock for a job was withdrawn from the stockroom, the employee withdrawing the stock wrote on the back of the job form the quantity and type of stock (e.g., 2 reams of 16-pound 8½″ × 11″ 25% cotton bond). On jobs calling for a nonstandard quantity (e.g., 400 sheets instead of the standard 500-sheet ream), the employee wrote down the required quantity but "eyeballed" the amount removed from the stockroom rather than counting it out. (Each press had a counter on it, so the customer received exactly the quantity ordered.) Any excess amounts withdrawn were supposed to be returned to the stockroom, although sometimes an employee simply threw the excess away if it was a small quantity. When completed job order forms reached the bookkeeper, these entries for stock were extended at actual costs on a first-in, first-out basis.

Pressroom employees also recorded on the back of the job form the time they had spent on that job. Each entry, rounded to the nearest 10th of an hour, included the employee's name. There was no indication in these entries whether the time had been worked during regular hours or on overtime basis. After a job was completed, the bookkeeper converted these times to actual labor costs using each employee's regular time hourly wage rate. Because there were only four pressroom employees, the bookkeeper had each one's wage rate memorized and did not have to look it up.

Overhead was assigned to jobs after the completion of each quarter year. The quarterly overhead rate was determined by adding all of Aurora's operating costs for the quarter other than paper stock costs and pressroom wages (excluding overtime premium), and dividing this total by the total number of hours that had been assigned to that quarter's jobs. This rate was then applied to the labor-hours charged to each job to determine the job's overhead costs.

Finally, for each job the three job-cost components—paper stock, pressroom labor at regular-time rates, and overhead—were added to determine the total cost of that job. Fran Baranek, who for most jobs had figured the price estimate given the customer, looked at each fully costed job form so as to keep abreast of the costs of various types of jobs and thereby avoid underpricing future jobs.

In preparing quarterly income statements, the bookkeeper charged to the quarter all of the expenses actually incurred during the quarter. The completed job order forms' cost data were used in income statement preparation only to determine a quarter's paper stock expenses; all other expense data came directly from the ledger. Although a physical inventory was taken each January 2, none was taken for purposes of preparing these quarterly interim income statements.

Revenues were recorded as customers paid for their jobs. This procedure was used, rather than recording revenue as a job was completed, because it tended to minimize each year's income taxes. Although most of Aurora's nonbusiness customers (e.g., prospective brides buying wedding invitations) paid cash when they picked up their orders, Aurora had had to grant liberal credit terms to its larger business customers in order to be competitive with other local printers. These terms included no interest charges; collection period for credit sales averaged about 45 days.

On December 26, when Baranek's nephew came to the shop to begin his review of Aurora's business procedures, Baranek described two specific problems to him.

Apart from our overall low profitability, I am concerned about the erratic behavior of our profits on a job-by-job basis. Part of this seems to result from the fact that when I am unavailable to estimate a customer's job, the pressroom superintendent estimates it. Although I've explained to him my rule of thumb for making these estimates—estimate paper stock costs and labor, add an amount for overhead, and add 10 percent of costs for profit—he seems to come up with a different estimate for a job than I would. His estimates are not always higher or always lower than mine would be, but they are frequently quite different.

Also, although I know our paper stock costs are constantly increasing, and we try to give our employees wage increases that at least keep up with inflation, the profits on similar jobs that I myself have estimated during the year jump all over the place. As things stand now, I can estimate a job in April, and—after allowing for paper stock price increases—estimate an identical job in July, and have one job end up showing a good profit and the other one a loss. Maybe you can suggest something that will help me estimate jobs so that each one ends up making a reasonable profit.

Finally, with regard to overall profits, I've only owned this business a couple of years, but I'm bothered by the pattern of profits from quarter to quarter. For example, the last two months of the year are very busy ones for us, and our people put in a lot of overtime, especially the two weeks before Christmas. Then things slow down considerably in January and February. Yet our quarterly income statements show the January–

March quarter to be as profitable as the October–December one. You know, I've never studied accounting, and when I ask the bookkeeper anything when she's here on Saturday mornings, the answer I get usually sounds to me like a combination of English and some foreign language. Maybe you can explain things to me more clearly than she can.

Before returning to college, Baranek's nephew presented Baranek with a report of his study. Included in his report was a proposal on how to systematize the process of estimating prices for customers' jobs. This proposal is shown in Exhibit 1.

EXHIBIT 1
PROPOSAL FOR PRICE ESTIMATING METHODOLOGY
Written by Fran Baranek's nephew

In my study of your estimating procedure, I determined that the paper stock portion of the estimates has been quite accurate, independent of whether you or the pressroom superintendent prepared the estimate. It is on the labor, overhead, and profit parts of the estimate where there are discrepancies between him and you. The superintendent tends to think in terms of the specific pressroom operator who will probably run a given job, and what the labor cost—hours times wage rate—will be for that operator on that job. He then multiplies this by a factor to cover overhead, adds the materials cost to get the total cost, and then adds 10 percent of this total cost for profit. He says the factor he uses for overhead is the most recent quarter's overhead rate.

On the other hand, since you naturally take a broader view of the business than the superintendent does, you mentally estimate the total hours that *everyone* will spend on a job—not just the pressroom hours that get charged to the back of each job order form but also the time you will spend copy editing and proofreading the galley proof before the press run is made. You then multiply this by the average hourly wage rate of *everyone* in the company, including your own wages as manager; then you apply a factor for overhead and add 10 percent of total costs for profit. The bookkeeper gives you a lower overhead rate to use for price estimating, based on the last quarter, than she uses to cost completed jobs, because you are explicitly accounting for copy editing and proofreading, whereas those costs are part of the job costing overhead rate. Finally, because you look over the previous quarter's actual job cost data, job by job, and because you are more aware of competitors' prices than is the pressroom superintendent, you often make judgmental adjustments to your "formula" estimate, whereas the superintendent does not.

In my opinion, both of you are approaching this pricing matter incorrectly. A business like yours is not really selling wedding invitations or brochures—you are actually selling paper stock and *press time*. Accordingly, I have worked with the bookkeeper and superintendent to develop a standard price per hour of press time. This price includes labor, overhead, and profit. Thus, all you need to do to estimate a job is estimate the press time, multiply it by the standard price per press-hour, and add paper stock cost. Since each of your presses is quite different in the type of work that can be done on it, and since the cost of a press and its operator differ from press to press (e.g., Multilith versus three-color), I have developed a standard price for each of your presses.

My derivation of these prices per press-hour is attached [Exhibit 2]. The "press-hours per quarter" numbers are based on an analysis of the July–September quarter, the most recent quarter for which there are complete data. Since the job order forms show who worked on a job in the pressroom, and since a given person usually operates the same press every day, these should be fairly accurate estimates of how many hours each press was used last quarter. Unless the "press mix" required by a quarter's jobs shifts significantly from quarter to quarter—and the superintendent didn't feel this was the case—there is no need to recalculate these press-hour totals every quarter. You can simply inflate each press-hour price each quarter to account for the inflationary trend in all of your labor and overhead costs.

Following these procedures should eliminate most of the inconsistencies between your estimates and the superintendent's, and ensure that your prices are adequate to cover all costs plus your target 10 percent profit margin.

EXHIBIT 2
DERIVATION OF STANDARD PRICE PER PRESS-HOUR
Cost data are for July–September quarter

	Press A	Press B	Press C	Press D
Direct pressroom expenses:*				
Direct labor	$2,583	$ 3,215	$ 3,127	$2,864
Ink and other supplies	479	624	531	490
Power	85	117	102	91
Repairs and maintenance	754	460	318	205
Depreciation	360	546	489	627
Direct labor fringes	517	643	625	573
Total direct expenses	4,778	5,605	5,192	4,850
Pressroom overhead†	1,213	2,021	1,887	1,617
General and administrative‡	1,633	1,757	2,163	2,343
Total costs	7,624	9,383	9,242	8,810
Profit @ 10% of costs	762	938	924	881
Revenues needed per press	$8,386	$10,321	$10,166	$9,691
Press-hours per quarter	290	312	384	416
Price per press-hour	$28.92	$33.08	$26.47	$23.30

*All of these costs except direct labor are treated as part of overhead under the present system.

†All pressroom costs other than those directly assignable, allocated to presses based on square feet of shop space occupied by a press and the working area around it. Includes overtime premium.

‡All costs not included in one of the two pressroom categories; allocated to presses based on press-hours.

Questions

1. What changes, if any, would you make in Aurora's present accounting procedures?

2. Should Baranek's nephew's price estimating proposal be implemented?

19

Standard Costs, Joint Costs,
and Variable Costing Systems

This chapter continues the discussion of product costing systems. Most of
the chapter deals with standard cost systems, which are product costing
systems based on estimates of what costs should have been incurred,
rather than an actual costs. Also described are two complicated problems in full costing, those involved in costing joint products and by-
products. The chapter concludes with the description of an alternative
to full cost product costing systems, called variable costing systems.

STANDARD COSTS

The basic objective of the system described in Chapters 17 and 18 was
to charge units of product with the *actual* costs incurred in making these
products, that is, with actual direct costs plus a fair share of indirect
costs. Some cost accounting systems, in contrast, are based wholly or in
part on the principle that the costs charged to individual products are
the costs that *should have been incurred* on those products rather than
the costs that *actually were incurred*. Such a system is called a *standard
cost system*. Standard costs can be used either with a job-order cost system or a process cost system.

In a standard cost system, each unit of product has for each production cost center a standard direct material cost, a standard direct labor
cost, and a standard overhead cost. The cost center's total standard cost

for the month is obtained by multiplying these standard unit costs by the number of units flowing through the cost center in that month.

For direct material, the standard represents the quantity of material that should be required to produce a unit of product priced at what the price of this material should be. The same principle applies to direct labor. Each job is charged at a standard direct labor cost for a unit of the product, which is calculated by multiplying the standard number of hours that should be required to produce one unit by the standard labor cost per hour. (If employees are paid on a piece-rate basis, the piece rate is the standard direct labor cost per unit.)

For reasons given in Chapter 18, in most actual cost systems, overhead is assigned to products by means of predetermined overhead rates. In a standard cost system, there also are predetermined overhead rates, but the overhead cost of a product is calculated by multiplying these rates by *standard* quantities for each production cost center, such as the standard direct labor-hours for the product in each center. With this exception, the treatment of overhead costs is usually the same under the two systems.

Variance Accounts

Illustration 19–1 shows the system for the pen factory described in Chapter 17, shifted to a standard cost basis. It is basically the same as the actual cost system shown in Illustration 17–2 except that four *variance accounts* have been added. The standard costs for a period are usually different from the costs actually incurred in that period, and variance accounts are a repository for these differences. For example, if the standard direct labor costs of all the operations performed during a month totaled $17,000, Work in Process (WIP) Inventory would be debited for $17,000. If actual direct labor costs for the month were $20,000, the credit to the liability account Wages Payable must be $20,000. The $3,000 difference between these two amounts would be debited to the Labor Variance account. Entries to variance accounts are debits if actual costs are greater than standard costs, and they are credits if actual costs are less than standard costs. For this reason, debit variances are often called *unfavorable* variances, and credit variances are called *favorable*.

Entries in Illustration 19–1 are for the same transactions, and are numbered the same, as the entries on Illustration 17–2. The entries in which standard costs are introduced are as follows:

Purchase of materials (entry 1). A credit material price variance of $2,000 is created because the actual cost of the materials received was $52,000, whereas the standard cost of this quantity of materials was $54,000. The actual cost was the actual quantity received times the *actual* unit price paid, whereas Materials Inventory was debited for the actual quantity received times the *standard* unit price.

Usage of materials (entry 2). The standard materials cost of pens

ILLUSTRATION 19–1
A STANDARD COST SYSTEM FOR MARKER PEN COMPANY
($000 omitted)

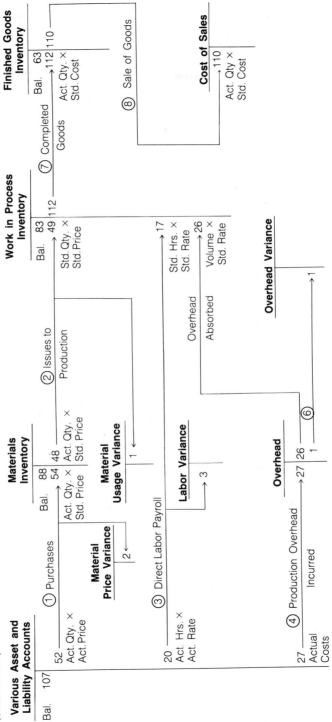

Note: Circled numbers refer to events described in Chapter 17 (Illustration 17-2 and related text).

processed was $49,000 (standard quantity times standard unit price); but the materials actually used during the month had a standard cost of only $48,000 (actual quantity issued multiplied by standard price). Therefore there was a credit material usage variance of $1,000.

Direct labor (entry 3), explained above. Note that the actual labor cost was, of course, the actual hours times actual rates, whereas Work in Process Inventory was debited for standard hours—the number of hours that *should* have been worked—times standard labor rates.

Overhead (entry 6). Indirect production costs applied to products by means of standard overhead rates were $26,000; that is, $26,000 was "absorbed." Actual factory overhead costs incurred were $27,000. There was, therefore, a debit overhead variance of $1,000.

Finished goods (entries 7 and 8). The sum of the *per unit* standard costs for materials, labor, and overhead is the total per unit standard cost. When goods are completed, the actual quantity transferred from work in process to finished goods is multipied by the standard unit cost to arrive at the amount for the respective credit and debit entries. For example, if the standard unit cost for a pen is $0.20 and 560,000 pens are completed, then Work in Process Inventory is credited for $112,000 and Finished Goods Inventory is debited for $112,000, as in entry 7. Similarly, if 550,000 pens are sold, Finished Goods Inventory is credited for $110,000 and Cost of Sales is debited for $110,000, as in entry 8.

Overhead Clearing Account. The Overhead T-account and entry 6 in Illustration 19–1 warrant further explanation. This T-account is called a *clearing* account because it contains costs that are to be "cleared," that is, transferred, to other accounts. Each time an actual overhead cost is incurred, the appropriate asset or liability account is credited and the Overhead account is debited. For example, the factory manager's monthly salary would be recorded as follows:

```
Overhead (clearing) ............................. 3,000
    Wages Payable ...................................        3,000
```

Thus, the debit side of the Overhead account can be thought of as an adding machine tape that is accumulating the month's *actual* overhead costs.

The credit side of the Overhead account shows the amount of overhead *absorbed* by (that is, charged to) products during the month. For example, if the wick department's annual predetermined overhead rate is $4.24 per DLH (as developed in Chapter 18), and in a given month the labor content of the wick department's production was 2,000 *standard* DLH, then $8,480 (= 2,000 × $4.24) of overhead would be absorbed by this entry:

```
Work in Process Inventory ...................... 8,480
     Overhead (clearing) ..........................        8,480
```

Similar entries would be made to absorb overhead for the barrel and assembly departments. In Illustration 19–1, the sum of these three overhead absorption entries is $26,000.

Except in rare circumstances, the month's actual overhead costs (Overhead debits) will not exactly equal the amount of overhead absorbed (Overhead credits). Any balance remaining in Overhead is closed periodically (usually monthly) to Overhead Variance. In the illustration, this is a debit variance of $1,000. This occurred because actual overhead was $27,000, whereas only $26,000 was absorbed into Work in Process Inventory. It can thus be seen that a debit entry to Overhead Variance means that the period's actual overhead costs were underabsorbed (actual greater than absorbed), whereas a credit to Overhead Variance occurs when actual overhead costs are overabsorbed (absorbed greater than actual).

In summary, the only mechanical difference between the accounts in a standard cost system and those in an actual cost system is that the former has variance accounts. Variance accounts are necessarily introduced whenever one part of a transaction is at standard cost and the other part is at actual cost.

Variations in the Standard Cost Idea

In the system shown in Illustration 19–1, standard costs were introduced when materials entered Materials Inventory and when material, labor, and overhead were debited to WIP Inventory. This is common practice; but standard costs can also be introduced at other points. For example, instead of debiting Materials Inventory at actual quantity received times standard unit prices, some companies carry materials at actual cost (i.e., actual quantity times actual unit price), and make the conversion to standard cost when the materials are issued for use in the production process. In such a system, there would be no material price variance account, and the material variance account would combine both the price and the usage components of the variance.

Some companies do not use standard costs for all elements of cost. They may, for example, use standard direct labor costs, but actual direct material costs; or they may do the reverse. The choice depends on the advantages that are obtainable in the particular situation. Regardless of these variations, the essential points are (1) in a standard cost system, some or all of the elements of cost are recorded in at least one of the inventory accounts at standard rather than at actual and (2) at whatever point a shift from actual to standard is made, a variance account is generated.

**Terminology
Ambiguities**

As explained above, a total cost for material, labor, or overhead is obtained by multiplying a quantity (or volume) times a unit price (or rate). Either the quantity or the price or both can be an actual amount or a standard amount. Thus, there are four possible multiplications involved in determining a total cost:

1. Actual quantity × Actual unit price.
2. Actual quantity × Standard unit price.
3. Standard quantity × Actual unit price.
4. Standard quantity × Standard unit price.

Clearly the first total is an "actual" amount, and the fourth is a "standard" amount. But what about the second and third totals? In practice, they also are usually referred to as "standard" amounts, even though they are not standard in the same sense as the fourth total. Thus, when one hears, for example, that "material costs are debited to Work in Process at standard," one must check further to determine whether "standard" is being used in the second, third, or fourth sense described above.

**Uses of Standard
Costs**

A standard cost system may be used for any or all of these reasons: (1) it provides a basis for controlling performance, (2) it provides cost information that is useful for certain types of decisions, (3) it may provide a more rational measurement of inventory amounts and of cost of sales, and (4) it may reduce the cost of recordkeeping.

Use in Control. A good starting point in the control of managers' performance is to compare what the managers' departments actually did with what they should have done. Standard costs provide a basis for such comparisons, as will be discussed in detail in Chapter 20.

> **Example.** If the standard direct material cost for all the jeans manufactured in a month was $243,107, and if the actual cost of the direct material used on those jeans was $268,539, there is an indication that direct material costs were $25,432 higher than they should have been. Without some standard, there is no starting point for examining the appropriateness of the $268,539 actual direct material cost.

Use in Decision Making. Standard costs are often used as a basis for arriving at normal selling prices or price bids, as described in Chapter 17. In some alternative choice decisions, as discussed in Chapters 21 and 22, standard direct costs are often the best available approximation of the differential costs that are relevant in making such decisions.

More Rational Costs. A standard cost system eliminates what otherwise might be an undesirable quirk in the accounting system. A standard cost system records the *same* costs for *physically identical* units of products, whereas an actual cost system may record different costs for physically identical units. For example, the actual direct labor cost of each batch of a given style of jeans could be different, depending on such factors as whether the employees who worked on the jeans had a relatively high wage rate because of long seniority. The jeans themselves, however, are physically the same. Realistically, there is no good reason for carrying one pair of physically similar jeans in inventory at one cost and another pair at a different amount, or for charging cost of sales at different amounts. In a standard cost system, all jeans of the same style would be carried in inventory and charged to cost of sales at the same unit cost.

Saving in Recordkeeping. Because of the addition of standard costs to the system, it might appear that a standard cost system requires more recordkeeping than an actual cost system. In fact, when standard costs are used instead of actual costs, there may be a *reduction* in the effort required to operate the system. All the individual material requisitions for a month can be totaled and posted as a single credit to Materials Inventory. Instead of making separate entries for direct material cost on each job-cost sheet, one amount, the standard unit material cost, is all that is needed. Neither is there any need for workers to keep track of the time they spend on individual batches. One amount, the predetermined standard direct labor cost, is all that is needed.

There is also a considerable reduction in the amount of recordkeeping required for finished goods inventory and cost of sales. Since all units of the same product have the same cost, the complications involved in keeping track of costs according to a LIFO, FIFO, or average cost assumption (as described in Chapter 6) disappear. For example, if 12,000 pairs of jeans are sold by a blue jean manufacturer in May, to determine the cost of sales entry the cost accountant using a standard costing system does not need to be concerned about what the actual cost was of the various batches of inventoried jeans from which the shipments were made. The cost of sales total is simply the sum of the amounts obtained by multiplying the number of pairs shipped of each style of jeans times that style's standard unit cost.

One aspect of a standard cost system, determining the individual standards, does involve additional effort. In many situations, the effort required to do this is not great, but there can be no doubt that some effort is involved. The determination of standard unit *quantities* is done only occasionally, however. Once a standard quantity has been determined, it is used for months, or even years, without change. Only a change in production methods or significant "learning effects" (described in Chapter 16) require changing unit quantities. However, the *price* component of a standard cost usually is updated annually or more often to reflect the impact of inflation. Updating prices requires much less effort than redetermining standard quantities.

An illustration of some of the procedural details of a standard cost system is shown in Appendix A to this chapter.

JOINT PRODUCTS AND BY-PRODUCTS

Joint Products   *Joint products* are two or more dissimilar end products that are produced from a single batch of raw material or from a single production process. The classic example is the variety of end products made from a steer. These include hides, many different cuts of meat, frozen meat dishes, pet food, fertilizers, and a variety of chemicals.

Up to a certain point in the production process, the raw material is treated as a single unit. That point is called the *split-off point*. Beyond the split-off point, separate end products are identified and costs are accumulated for each of these end products during subsequent stages of the production process. For example, up to the point at which the steer is slaughtered and dressed, the costs of feed, grazing, transportation, and other items are accumulated for the steer as a whole. At that point, these costs must be divided among the many end products that are made from the steer. The problem of joint costing is to find some reasonable basis for allocating to each of the joint products the costs that were incurred up to the split-off point.

This problem is essentially the same as that of allocating indirect costs to cost centers. In both cases, the objective is to assign a fair share of the joint or common costs to the separate end products, and in neither case can the results be an entirely accurate measure of the actual costs.

Sales-Value Method.   One common basis of allocating joint costs is in proportion to the *sales value* of the end products, minus the separate processing and marketing costs that are estimated to be incurred for each end product beyond the split-off point. If the selling price depends on cost, this method involves a certain amount of circular reasoning, but there may be no better alternative. If gasoline sells for twice the price of kerosene, it is reasonable that gasoline should bear twice as much of the joint costs.

Example.   In June, Kruse Company produced 200 units of product A and 300 units of product B, having sales values respectively of $2,000 ($10 per unit of A) and $6,000 ($20 per unit of B). Joint production costs up to the split-off point were $3,000. Beyond the split-off point, $600 of additional production and marketing costs is incurred for A and $1,500 is incurred for B. With the sales-value method, the $3,000 joint costs are allocated as follows:

Joint Products	(1) Sales Value	(2) Costs beyond Split-Off	(1) − (2)	Proportion of Joint Costs Allocated to Each Product
A	$2,000	$ 600	$1,400	14/59 × $3,000 = $ 712
B	6,000	1,500	4,500	45/59 × 3,000 = 2,288
			$5,900	$3,000

Unit costs would then be as follows:

	Product A	Product B
Joint costs.........	$712 ÷ 200 = $3.56	$2,288 ÷ 300 = $ 7.63
Other costs........	600 ÷ 200 = 3.00	1,500 ÷ 300 = 5.00
Unit cost..........	$6.56	$12.63

Weight Method. Another basis of apportionment is *weight;* that is, the joint costs are divided in proportion to the weight of the joint material in the several end products. In the case of the steer, this method implicitly assumes that the hamburger is as valuable as the sirloin steak, which is unrealistic. But in other situations, the assumption that costs are related to weight might be reasonable. In any event, the amount of cost charged to each end product must be recognized as resulting from a judgmental decision, and hence as not entirely accurate.

Having allocated joint costs to products up to the split-off point, the measurement of costs *beyond* this point is done in the usual manner. Beyond the split-off point each product is a separate cost objective, and the additional material, labor, and overhead costs of completing the finished product are assigned to it.

By-Products

By-products are a special kind of joint product. If management wishes to manufacture products A and B in some predetermined proportion, or if it wishes to make as much of each end product as possible from a given quantity of raw material, then these products are ordinary joint products. By contrast, if management's objective is to make product A but in so doing some quantity of product B inevitably emerges from the process, then product A is a main product and product B is a by-product. The intention is to make from a given amount of raw material as much of the main product and as little of the by-product as possible.

As management's intention changes, the classification changes. For example, early in the 20th century kerosene was the main product made from crude oil. Subsequently, with the growth in consumption of gasoline, kerosene became a by-product. Currently, kerosene has become a main product again because it is an important component of jet engine fuel.

A by-product is usually costed so that zero profit is reported for it. That is, it is charged with joint costs equal to its sales revenue less any costs incurred beyond the split-off point. Consequently, all profits are attributed to the main product. In the preceding example, if A were regarded as a by-product rather than a joint product, it would be charged with $1,400 of the $3,000 joint costs, thus reducing A's profit to zero.

VALIDITY OF FULL COSTS

From the description given in this and the preceding two chapters, it should be apparent that the full costs of a cost objective cannot be measured with complete precision if some items of cost are indirect, as is usually the case. Two equally well-informed and competent accountants can arrive at different costs for the same product or other cost objective. These differences arise from differences in judgment on the following matters, among others:

1. *Capital, product, and period costs.* In Chapter 14 it was shown how the judgment as to whether a given item of cost should be classified as a capital cost, a product cost, or a period cost affects both the measurement of costs and the measurement of net income for a period.

2. *Measurement of direct costs.* If Company A classifies only the wages of direct workers as direct labor, but Company B includes labor-related costs, Company A's direct labor costs will be less than those of Company B. Since labor-related costs may amount to 25 percent or more of wages, this difference can be substantial.

3. *Distinction between direct and indirect costs.* In the above example, the labor-related costs that Company A excluded from direct costs were part of its indirect (overhead) costs. Although a share of these overhead costs is allocated to products, the method of allocation is such that a different amount may be allocated to a given product than would be the case if the item were treated as a direct cost.

4. *Alternative allocation methods.* Many judgments must be made in deciding how overhead cost items and the costs of service cost centers are assigned to production cost centers.

5. *Choice of an activity measure.* The amount of overhead allocated to a product is affected by the measure of activity (volume) used in the overhead rate. Measuring volume in terms of direct labor-hours gives different results than measuring it in terms of direct labor dollars, for example.

6. *Estimate of volume.* As illustrated in Chapter 18, the estimate of standard volume used in arriving at the predetermined overhead rate can have a significant influence on the unit overhead charge.

7. *Definition of cost center.* The amount of overhead allocated to a product can be significantly influenced by judgment as to how a cost center is defined. In some manufacturing companies, each important machine is a cost center. At the other extreme, the entire plant may be a single cost center, giving rise to a *plantwide overhead rate.* There are a number of choices between these two extremes. In general, the more narrow the definition of a cost center, the more equitable is the resulting amount of indirect cost allocated to the product. On the other hand, it is also true that the more narrow the definition of the cost centers, the more cost centers there will be, and

therefore more work will be required to compute and apply separate overhead rates.

Tendencies toward Uniformity

Because of these and other factors, no one can measure precisely the "actual" amount of resources used in producing a good or service when indirect costs are involved. Nevertheless, there are forces tending toward uniformity of method. Most importantly, a given company usually uses the same practices for measuring full costs throughout the company. Consequently, comparisons of the costs of various products can validly be made. Furthermore, within an industry, there tends to be a similarity of costing practices, and this facilitates cost comparisons within the industry.

VARIABLE COSTING SYSTEMS

The cost accounting systems described above are called *full cost* or *absorption cost* systems because the full costs of producing goods or services are "absorbed by" (i.e., charged to) those products. Generally accepted accounting principles (GAAP) and tax regulations both require that work in process and finished goods inventories be stated at approximately full production cost. This is in accord with the financial accounting concept that assets are measured at cost.

Nevertheless, some companies find it useful for management accounting purposes to state inventories only at *variable* production costs—material, direct labor, and variable overhead—and to treat fixed overhead costs as expenses of the *period* in which these costs were incurred. Conceptually, these fixed costs are regarded as the costs of maintaining *capacity* during the period, rather than as *product* (i.e., inventoriable) costs.

A system that treats only variable production costs as inventoriable *product* costs and treats fixed production costs as *period* costs is called a *variable costing system*. It is also commonly—but incorrectly—called a *direct costing system.*[1]

Those who advocate variable costing assert that it has the following advantages over absorption costing systems:

1. Because in variable costing, fixed overhead costs are not charged to individual units of product, no overhead rate for the fixed component of overhead costs need be used in the cost accounting system.

---

[1]If the cost objective is a unit of a product, then direct costs generally include only material and direct labor; variable costs include both of these *plus* variable overhead. Therefore, the correct name for the system we are discussing is *variable* costing. However, the first article on this subject—by Jonathan Harris in the January 15, 1936, issue of the *N.A.C.A. Bulletin*—repeatedly referred to these variable costs as "direct costs," and thus the misnomer, "direct costing system," was established in practice.

As shown earlier, this calculation can be complicated; in particular it requires an estimate of standard volume. (Although such a rate is needed for financial accounting and income tax calculations, a rough approximation, calculated only at the end of the year, usually suffices.)

2. Overhead variances in variable costing occur solely because of over- or underspending overhead budgets. In absorption costing, if actual volume is different from the standard volume used in setting an overhead rate, this volume difference will cause part of the overhead variance. (This point will be explained in detail in Chapter 20.)

3. Variable costing systems separate variable and fixed production costs. This separation is useful for control purposes, since variable cost items tend to be controlled on a *cost-per-unit* basis, while fixed cost items are controlled on a *total cost per period* basis. This separation is also useful for the differential analyses discussed in detail in Chapters 21 and 22, and for doing the break-even calculations described in Chapter 16. (It is possible to make this same separation in an absorption system by having a variable overhead rate and a separate fixed overhead rate.)

4. With variable costing, reported income is related directly to sales volume. With absorption costing, reported income is affected *both* by the period's sales volume *and also* by its production volume. That is, a change in the physical size of finished goods inventory, which always occurs when there is an imbalance between production and sales volumes, also affects the period's reported income. For example, under absorption costing it is possible for sales to increase from one period to the next but for reported income to decrease because inventory was reduced during the period. Since it is reasonable to expect that income should fluctuate with sales volume—the higher the volume, the higher the profit—this advantage of variable costing is an important one.

Comparison of Absorption and Variable Costing

Illustration 19–2 compares absorption costing and variable costing systems. The illustration is based on these assumptions:

Beginning inventory, period 1	0 units
Production volume	100 units per period
Sales volume, period 1	80 units @ $50
Sales volume, period 2	120 units @ $50
Standard variable costs ($15 prime costs + $5 variable overhead)	$20 per unit
Budgeted fixed production overhead	$1,000 per period
Standard full production cost:	

$$\underbrace{\$20}_{\text{Variable}} + \underbrace{\frac{\$1,000}{100 \text{ units}}}_{\text{Allocated Fixed}} \quad\quad \$30 \text{ per unit}$$

Selling and administrative costs (all fixed)	$1,400 per period

Note that in period 1, when there was an inventory buildup because production volume exceeded sales volume by 20 units, absorption costing reported a *higher* income than did variable costing. On the other hand, when sales volume exceeded production volume in period 2, absorption costing reported a *lower* income than did variable costing. Taking the two periods *combined*, sales and production volumes were *equal* (at 200 units for the combined periods), and both systems reported the *same* income ($1,200 for the combined periods).

As illustrated by the example, the following relationships always hold (as is proved in Appendix B at the end of this chapter):

1. If the period's sales volume (in physical units) is *equal* to production volume, both systems report the same income.
2. If the period's sales volume *exceeds* production volume—that is, there is a decrease in the physical size of finished goods inventory—then absorption costing reports a *lower* income than does variable costing.
3. If the period's sales volume is *less than* production volume—that is, there is an increase in the physical size of finished goods inventory—then absorption costing reports a *higher* income than does variable costing.

As is demonstrated in the income reconciliations of Illustration 19–2, these differences in reported income between the two approaches are explained by the fact that absorption accounting *capitalizes* (defers) fixed production overhead costs in the inventory asset accounts until the period in which the products are sold, whereas variable costing expenses these fixed costs as they are incurred. This can be illustrated by an extreme example.

> **Example.** Using the data for Illustration 19–2, assume the plant was operated during period 3, but there were *zero* units *sold* during the period. Before taking account of selling and administrative costs, absorption costing will report zero income, while variable costing will report a $1,000 loss. All of the period 3 fixed overhead cost will be deferred under absorption costing until such time as the goods produced in period 3 are sold—at which time these fixed costs will be "released" from inventory and charged to cost of goods sold at the rate of $10 per unit sold (along with the variable costs of $20 per unit). With variable costing, only the variable costs are held in inventory; the $1,000 period 3 fixed overhead costs are an expense of that period, and only the $20 per unit variable cost will be "released" from inventory in later periods when the goods produced in period 3 are actually sold.

Overhead Rates in the Two Systems. As the previous illustration indicates, in a standard variable costing system, the accounting for overhead costs is essentially the same as the accounting for direct material and direct labor costs, because all three costs are variable. However, the overhead rate in an absorption costing system is, in effect, the sum of

ILLUSTRATION 19–2
COMPARISON OF ABSORPTION AND VARIABLE COSTING

Income Statement
Period 1

	Absorption Costing (Unit cost = $30)		Variable Costing (Unit cost = $20)	
Sales (80 units @ $50)		$4,000		$4,000
Cost of goods sold:				
Beginning inventory	$ 0		$ 0	
Cost of goods produced (100 units)	3,000		2,000	
Available for sale	3,000		2,000	
Less: Ending inventory (20 units)	600		400	
Cost of goods sold (80 units)		2,400		1,600
Gross margin		1,600		2,400
Less: Period costs:				
Production overhead	—		1,000	
Selling and administrative	1,400		1,400	
Total period costs		1,400		2,400
Income before taxes		$ 200		$ 0

Income reconciliation between two methods: 20 units increased inventory × $10 per unit absorbed fixed overhead costs = $200 greater income with absorption costing because $200 of fixed overhead costs were capitalized in inventory.

Income Statement
Period 2

	Absorption Costing (Unit cost = $30)		Variable Costing (Unit cost = $20)	
Sales (120 units @ $50)		$6,000		$6,000
Cost of goods sold:				
Beginning inventory (20 units)	$ 600		$ 400	
Cost of goods produced (100 units)	3,000		2,000	
Available for sale (120 units)	3,600		2,400	
Less: Ending inventory	0		0	
Cost of goods sold (120 units)		3,600		2,400
Gross margin		2,400		3,600
Less: Period costs:				
Production overhead	—		1,000	
Selling and administrative	1,400		1,400	
Total period costs		1,400		2,400
Income before taxes		$1,000		$1,200

Income reconciliation between two methods: 20 units decrease in inventory × $10 per unit absorbed fixed overhead costs = $200 lower income with absorption costing. This results from the "release" from inventory of $200 of fixed overhead costs actually incurred in period 1 but deferred until the goods were sold in period 2.

two rates, one to absorb the variable overhead costs, and the other to charge each unit of activity with its fair share of fixed overhead costs. The variable overhead rate is relatively easy to determine: in Illustration 18–5, it is simply the slope of the flexible overhead budget line ($0.92 per DLH in that example). The fixed overhead absorption rate cannot be determined, however, without first estimating the standard volume over which the fixed overhead costs are to be spread; in Illustration 18–5, this is $9,950 fixed costs ÷ 3,000 DLH standard volume, or $3.32 per DLH. Note that the sum of these two pieces of the absorption rate, $0.92 + $3.32 = $4.24, is indeed the full cost overhead rate we calculated from Illustration 18–5.

For some purposes, it is useful to think of the full cost overhead absorption rate as the sum of these two individual components, one related to budgeted variable overhead costs, the other to the per unit allocation of budgeted fixed overhead costs. In particular, it is important to remember that (again using Illustration 18–5 figures) one more DLH is expected to *cause* the company to incur $0.92 more actual overhead costs. But one more DLH is *not* expected to increase *actual* fixed overhead costs by $3.32; it will only cause $3.32 more overhead to be *absorbed* into WIP Inventory. Avoiding the potential confusion between a volume change's effect on actual overhead costs versus its effect on absorbed overhead costs is one of the advantages mentioned by variable costing advocates.

Why Use Full Costing?

Surveys indicate that despite its purported advantages, variable costing is used by only a small minority of companies in their management accounting systems.[2] One reason for this is that while it is conceptually easy to distinguish between fixed and variable costs, in practice it may be difficult to identify separately variable costs as products flow from one department to another. Decomposition of semivariable costs into their fixed and variable components may be particularly difficult. Moreover, most companies need full costs for at least some of the various purposes described in Chapter 17, and they are required to use full costs for financial reporting and tax accounting. Many companies prefer not to use for management accounting purposes a system that is inconsistent with that required for financial reporting. In particular, with variable costing, management accounting balance sheets show inventories at amounts significantly below what is reported to the shareholders and other outside parties. Finally, some people reject the conceptual basis underlying variable costing; they maintain that income *should* reflect the effect of an imbalance between production volume and sales volume.

---

[2]For example, in their survey of the *Fortune* 1,000 industrial companies, Reece and Cool found that only 5 percent of the companies used variable costing in their internal reports. ("Measuring Investment Center Performance," *Harvard Business Review*, May–June 1978.) Several other surveys report similar results.

In any event, the "either-or" tone of most discussions about variable *versus* absorption costing is somewhat misleading. *If* a company feasibly can maintain its accounts so as to keep variable overhead costs segregated from fixed overhead costs, it can quite readily prepare management reports on *both* a variable costing basis and an absorption costing basis. Management then can use the type of report it feels gives the more useful information in the context of some specific analysis or decision.

COST SYSTEM DESIGN CHOICES

Pulling together the various aspects of costing systems described in this and the preceding two chapters, it becomes clear that an organization faces many choices in designing a costing system. Should it be a job-order or a process system? Should it be an actual cost or standard cost system? Should absorption costing, variable costing, or both be used? How many cost centers should be defined? How should volume be measured in each of them? What is the appropriate step-down order for allocating the costs of service centers to other cost centers? Should labor-related and material-related costs be treated as direct costs or as a part of overhead costs? If standard costing is to be used, at what point in the system should the shift from actual costs to standard costs be made?

Clearly, designing an appropriate cost system requires that all of these questions (and more) be answered. Moreover, with the increasing diversity of organizations' activities, the questions must be answered several times, once for each segment of an organization's operations. This is true not only of diversified corporations but also of many other organizations. For example, a cost system for a hospital's gift shop differs from that for its cafeteria, and both of these differ from the system upon which patient billing is based. Thus, one of the jobs of today's management accountant, designing these systems in conjunction with top management, is a far more complex task than was the case when cost accounting was in its infancy.

SUMMARY

The essential idea of a standard cost accounting system is that costs and inventory amounts are recorded as what costs *should* have been rather than what they actually were. At some point in the flow of costs through the system there is a shift from actual costs to standard costs. Wherever this shift occurs, a variance develops. This can be as early in the process as the receipt of raw materials (in which case the variance is a material price variance), or it can be as late as the movement of finished products from the production facilities to finished goods inventory.

When joint product costs or by-product costs are involved, costs up to the split-off point must be divided among the several cost objectives in some equitable fashion.

Although it is impossible to measure full costs precisely whenever indirect costs are involved, such measures are useful if the costing practices are comparable within a company or an industry.

Variable costing systems treat only variable production costs as product (inventoriable) costs, and treat fixed indirect production costs as an expense of the period in which these costs are incurred. Variable costing may have certain advantages for internal (management) accounting in some companies, but it is not widely used in practice.

APPENDIX A

Standard Costing Illustration: Black Meter Company

As an illustration of some of the procedural details of a standard cost system, the system of the Black Meter Company (which is the disguised name of an actual company) is described below.

Black Meter Company manufactures water meters in one standard design but in a wide range of sizes. The water meters installed in most homes are an example of its product. The meters consist basically of a hard rubber piston that is put in motion by the flow of water past it, a gear train that reduces this motion and registers it on a dial, and two heavy bronze castings that are bolted together around the measuring device.

The company has several production departments. The castings and many interior parts of meters are cast in the foundry and then are sent to one of the three machining departments, depending upon their size. Some of the mechanical parts are sent to a subassembly department where they are assembled into gear trains. Other parts go directly to the meter assembly department. There are also several departments that provide service to the production departments.

Overview of System. Since the company ships meters to customers as soon as the meters are completed, its Finished Goods Inventory account reflects primarily repair parts, not complete meters. It also has Materials Inventory and WIP Inventory accounts. It uses a standard full cost system. Standard costs are established for each element of direct labor, direct material, and manufacturing overhead.

During the month, actual costs are accumulated: material is purchased, the earnings of workers are recorded, and manufacturing overhead items, such as water or electricity, are purchased and paid for. These entries are made at actual cost. Elements of cost are debited into WIP Inventory at predetermined *standard* costs, however. Since actual costs are different from standard costs, variance accounts are necessary.

Establishing Standard Costs. A standard unit cost is established for every type of material that is purchased. This is done annually by adjusting the current market price for any changes that are expected for the following year. For example, if the current price of a certain grade of phospher bronze is $1.65 a pound, and no change is predicted, the standard cost for that bronze for the next year will be $1.65 per pound.

Standard hourly rates for direct labor and overhead are also determined annually. These rates are used to assign costs to products according to the number of standard direct labor hours incurred in the manufacture of each product. This is done on a departmental basis. For each production department, the accountants start with data on the actual direct labor payroll, including fringe benefits, and the number of direct labor-hours worked in each of the past few years. The departmental supervisors give their opinions as to adjustments that should be made to take account of future conditions. An amount for total labor cost and an amount for hours worked under normal conditions of activity is thus derived. By dividing the payroll amount by the normal number of hours, a standard direct labor rate per standard direct labor-hour for each department is found.

Overhead costs for a production department include both the overhead costs incurred in that department plus an allocated portion of the costs of service departments. Estimates are made of these amounts for each production department under conditions of normal volume. These estimated total overhead costs are divided by the standard number of direct labor-hours for each producing department (the same number that had been used in calculating the standard labor rate) to arrive at an overhead rate per standard direct labor-hour. Those rates relevant to later illustrations in this example are given in Illustration 19-3.

Developing Standard Product Costs. These standard hourly rates (which include both direct labor and overhead) are used to develop a standard cost for each type of meter. Examples of these calculations are

ILLUSTRATION 19–3

	STANDARD LABOR AND OVERHEAD RATES (partial listing)			
Department Number	Department Name	Rate per hour		
		Labor	Overhead	Total Rate
120A	Foundry—molding	$6.75	$8.67	$15.42
120B	Foundry—grinding and snagging	5.25	4.35	9.60
122	Small parts manufacture	5.58	5.07	10.65
123	Interior parts manufacture	5.52	5.60	11.12
130	Train, register, and interior assembly	5.55	5.96	11.51
131	Small meter assembly	5.25	6.02	11.27

given in Illustrations 19–4, 19–5, and 19–6. The examples show the development of the standard cost of a 100-unit batch of ⅝-inch HF meters.

Illustration 19–4 shows the calculation for a ⅝-inch chamber ring that is manufactured in the foundry, and which is one component of the ⅝-inch HF meter. As in the case with most parts, costs are calculated for a lot size of 100 units. The standard material cost is entered in the upper right-hand box. These parts are cast from bronze that has a standard cost of $1.65 a pound. Since the standard quantity of bronze required for 100 pieces is 91 pounds, the standard material cost is $1.65 × 91 = $150.15, as shown in the "Material Cost" box. The 91 pounds standard quantity was determined by Black Meter's industrial engineering department. The standard cost of the pattern used in the casting, $14.20, is also entered.

ILLUSTRATION 19–4

FOUNDRY STANDARD COST							
Drawing No. D–2408	*Part* 5/8″ HF Chamber Rings				*Material Cost*		150.15
					Pattern Cost		14.20
Material Phosphor Bronze #806 100 pcs. 91.0# at $1.65							
Std. Hrs. per 100 Pcs.	*Prod. Center*	*Oper. No.*	*Operations and Tools*	*Machine*	*Std. Rate per Hr.*	*Total Cost*	*Total*
1.76	120 A	1	Mold	Match Plate	15.42	27.14	
0.45	120 B	2	Grind	Wheel	9.60	4.32	
0.68	120 B	3	Snag	Bench	9.60	6.53	
			Total				202.34

In order to apply the standard direct labor and manufacturing overhead rates to any part, it is necessary to have the standard direct labor-hours for the operations involved in making that part. These are obtained from time studies performed by the industrial engineering department, and are entered in the first column of the foundry form. The standard time to mold 100 chamber rings is 1.76 direct labor-hours; to grind them, 0.45 hours; and to snag them, 0.68 hours. In the first column of numbers on the right-hand side of the foundry form, the combined standard direct labor and manufacturing overhead rate per standard direct labor-hour for the operation is recorded. For example, Illustration 19–3 shows the labor and overhead rate for molding in Department 120A as $15.42 per standard direct labor-hour, and this amount appears on Illustration 19–4 as the standard rate per hour for the molding operation. It is multiplied by the standard direct labor time of 1.76 hours to give a standard cost of labor and overhead of $27.14. The same procedure is followed for the other two foundry operations. The total standard foundry cost of 100 chamber rings is $202.34.

Illustration 19–5 accumulates additional standard costs for these 100 chamber rings as they pass through the parts manufacture department. They enter the parts department at the standard cost of $202.34, the same cost at which they left the foundry. After the operations listed on Illustration 19–5 have been performed on them, they become finished chamber rings. These operations have increased the standard cost to $370.36.

ILLUSTRATION 19–5

PARTS DEPARTMENT STANDARD COST						
Drawing No. X–2408			*Part* 5/8" HF Chamber Ring		*Material Cost*	
Plating H.T. & E.T.			*Material* Bronze 100 pcs. 89#		202.34	
Std. Hours per 100 Pcs.	*Prod. Center*	*Oper. No.*	*Operations and Tools*	*Machine*	*Std. Rate per Hr.*	*Total*
0.75	122	1	Broach outlet #734	P.P.	10.65	7.99
0.55	123	2	Finish tap–plate bore and face	Heald	11.12	6.12
0.93	123		Drill 6 holes	Drill	11.12	10.34
0.47	123	3	C–sink 3 holes tap–plate side	Drill	11.12	5.23
0.17	123		Tap 3 holes tap–plate side	Heskins	11.12	1.89
5.00	123	4	Rough & Finish inside & outside	Heald	11.12	55.60
0.20	123		C–sink 3 holes on bottom	Drill	11.12	2.22
0.30	123	5	Tap 3 holes on bottom	Drill	11.12	3.34
0.47	123		Spline inside	Spliner	11.12	5.23
0.50	123	6	Spline outside	Miller	11.12	5.56
5.80	123		Dress	Bench	11.12	64.50
			Total			370.36

Similar standard cost sheets are prepared for each of the other components of the ⅝-inch meter. As shown in Illustration 19–6, these parts are assembled into complete meters. In each of these assembly operations, standard costs are added; the total standard cost of 100 meters is $3,470.33.

ILLUSTRATION 19–6

ASSEMBLY DEPARTMENT STANDARD COST								
Drawing No. 2735				*Assembly* 5/8″ HF ET FB				
Parts of Assembly				*Cost*	*Parts of Assembly*			*Cost*
X–2408	Chamber Ring			370.36	K–5030 5/8″ HF Dur. Bolt (6)			125.68
K–2414	Chamber Top Plate			146.55	K–4630 5/8″ HF ac Nut (6)			70.84
K–2418	Chamber Bot. Plate			140.12	K–5068 5/8″ HF Washers (6)			40.23
K–2465	Disc Piston Assem.			302.70	2782 Chamber Pin			8.02
2761	Top Case			540.60	6172 Misc. Train Conn.			34.12
X–2770	Bottom Case			200.28	K–2776 Casting Gasket			26.50
3209	5/8″ Closed Train			1,200.02	2779 Casting Strainer			33.04
					2412 5/8″ HF Sand Plate			30.00

Std. Hrs. per 100 Pcs.	Prod. Center	Oper. No.	Operations and Tools	Machine	Std. Rate per Hr.	Total Cost	Total
7.5	130	1	Assem. Disc Interior	Bench	11.51	86.32	
4.6	131	2	Assem. Train and Strainer to Case	Bench	11.27	51.84	
5.6	131	3	Assem. Int. & Bottom to Meter	Bench	11.27	63.11	
			Total				3,470.33

In the same manner, standard costs are calculated for all the meters that Black Meter manufactures.

Accounting Entries. All direct material, direct labor, and overhead costs are debited to WIP Inventory at standard costs. Actual costs are collected in total for the period, by department, but no actual costs are collected for individual batches of meters.

Material. As soon as any material is received, the standard cost of that material is penciled on the vendor's invoice. Each purchase is journalized in an invoice and check register. This register contains columns in which to credit the actual cost of the material to Accounts Payable, to debit Materials Inventory for the standard cost, and to debit or credit the difference to a Material Price Variance account. When material is issued for use in production, the quantity is the standard amount (e.g., 91 pounds in the example shown in Illustration 19–4), and the entry crediting Materials Inventory and debiting WIP Inventory is made at the standard cost (e.g., $150.15 in the example shown in Illustration 19–4).

A physical inventory is taken every six months and is valued at standard cost. Any difference between this amount and the balance as shown in the Materials Inventory account is debited or credited to a Material Usage Variance account.

Labor.   The basic document for recording direct labor costs is the job timecard. Each production employee fills out such a card for each order on which he or she works during a week. The timecard reproduced as Illustration 19–7 shows that B. Harris worked all week on one order. On the timecard Harris records the quantity finished, the actual hours worked, and the standard hours. A payroll clerk enters each employee's daywork rate, the standard direct labor rate for that department, and extends the acual and standard direct labor cost of the work completed.

ILLUSTRATION 19–7

Mach. No.	Prod. Center		Quantity Ordered		Order Number		
	130		*3,000*		*2I-86572*		*337* Clock No.
	Part Name						
		⅝" Cl. Trains					
Prev. Quan. Fin.	Oper. No.		Operation Name				
0	*9*		*Finish Assem.*				
Quan. Finished	Std. Hours Per 100		Std. Hours	Std. Rate	Standard Labor		
2,300	*1.75*		*40. 25*	*5 55*	*223.39*		
Quan. Finished							*J. HARRIS* Name
2,300				TIME CARD			
	Stop		Actual Hours	D.W. Rate	Earnings		
Sept. 20	*40. 0*		*40. 0*	*5. 50*	*220. 00*		
	Start		*R.H.L.* Foreman		Gain or (Loss)		
Sept. 16	*00. 0*				*3 39*		

By totaling all the job timecards, the payroll clerk obtains the actual wages earned by each employee in each department, and also the total standard labor cost of the work done in each department. These amounts are the basis for an entry that credits Wages Payable for the actual amount and debits WIP Inventory for the standard amount of direct labor. The variance is recorded in a Direct Labor Variance account.

Overhead. For each department, a cost clerk multiplies the standard direct labor-hours worked by the overhead rate for that department (as obtained from Illustration 19–3). This gives the amount of absorbed overhead cost for each department for that month. These amounts are credited to the Overhead clearing account and debited to WIP Inventory. During the month, actual manufacturing overhead costs have been accumulated and debited to the Overhead clearing account. The month-end balance in this account, which is the difference between the actual overhead costs and the absorbed overhead cost, is the overhead variance. This is debited or credited to the Overhead Variance account.

When these transactions have been recorded, all material, direct labor, and overhead have been charged into the WIP Inventory account at standard cost, and the variance accounts have been debited or credited for the difference between actual and standard. These variance accounts are closed to the income statement each month.

Sales and Cost of Sales. A duplicate copy of each sales invoice is sent to the office where a clerk enters in pencil the standard cost of the items sold (see Illustration 19–8). At the end of the month, the cost clerk totals the figures on these duplicate invoices to get amounts for sales revenue and for the standard cost of goods sold. The standard cost is a credit to Inventory and a debit to Cost of Sales. The total sales amount is a credit to Sales and a debit to Accounts Receivable. When this work is completed, the accounting department is in a position to obtain the monthly income statement (see Illustration 19–9). Note, incidentally, that although the net amount of the variance on this income statement is relatively small, there are sizable detailed variances that tend to offset one another. Management investigates these variances and takes action when warranted.

ILLUSTRATION 19–8
CARBON COPY OF SALES INVOICE

```
┌─────────────────────────────────────────────────────────────────────────┐
│ Village of Vernon, Water Dept.                                            │
│ Attn: E. J. Blackburn, Mayor                                              │
│ Vernon, N.Y. 13476                                                        │
│                                                                           │
│                     Prepaid                                               │
│                                                                           │
│  10     5/8" × 3/4" Model HF Meters                                       │
│           SG SH ET FB & 3/4"              49.58      495.80               │
│                                                                           │
│   1     Change Gear #46X--shipped 8-10     5.20        5.20     501.00    │
│                                                                           │
│         Ship gear by UPS                                                  │
│                                              Meters 347.03                │
│                                              Parts    2.60                │
│                                                                           │
└─────────────────────────────────────────────────────────────────────────┘
```

ILLUSTRATION 19–9

BLACK METER COMPANY
Income Statement
For the Month of June

Net sales.		$2,396,468
Less: Cost of sales at standard cost	$1,663,736	
Variances (detailed below)	(10,714)	1,653,022
Gross manufacturing margin		743,446
Selling expense.	184,214	
General and administrative expense	354,724	538,938
Income before income taxes		204,508
Income taxes.		98,640
Net income.		$ 105,868

Variances

	Debit	Credit
Favorable variances:		
Material price.		$ 125,216
Unfavorable variances:		
Material usage.	$ 44,914	
Direct labor	32,468	
Overhead	37,120	(114,502)
Net variance.		$ 10,714

APPENDIX B

Absorption versus Variable Costing: Income Impact

This Appendix proves the three statements about the effects of absorption costing and variable costing on reported income that were made on page 631. Note in Illustration 19–2 that both systems treat revenues, variable costs, and selling and administrative costs in the same way. Hence, our proof can focus on the different treatment in the two systems of *fixed production overhead costs*.

Let:

S = sales volume (in units)
P = production volume (in units)
F = fixed production overhead costs per period

With absorption costing, the amount of fixed overhead charged to the income statement is $\frac{F}{P} \cdot S$. (F/P is the *fixed* cost absorption rate.) Variable costing charges F. The difference in these amounts is:

$$\underbrace{\frac{F}{P} \cdot S}_{\text{Absorption}} - \underbrace{F}_{\text{Variable}} = \underbrace{\frac{F}{P}(S - P)}_{\text{Difference}}$$

Case 1: S = P (*no change* in finished goods inventory). In this case, $S - P = 0$, so the difference in fixed overhead cost charged to the income statement is *zero*. Thus, income is the *same* under both methods.

Case 2: S > P (*decrease* in finished goods inventory). Now $S - P > 0$, so the difference in fixed overhead charges is positive. That is, absorption costing charges *more* fixed overhead cost to income than does variable costing. Thus, absorption costing reports *lower* income than does variable costing.

Case 3: S < P (*increase* in finished goods inventory). In this case, $S - P < 0$, so the difference is negative. That is, absorption costing charges *less* fixed overhead cost to income, and therefore results in *higher* reported income, than does variable costing.

Note also that these calculations demonstrate the fourth feature of variable costing that was stated in the text: Variable costing income is *not* a function of period's production volum *(P)*. This is true because with variable costing the income statement is charged with F dollars of fixed overhead, regardless of P; whereas absorption costing income is affected by P because the period's income statement is charged with $\frac{F}{P} \cdot S$ fixed overhead costs. In particular, for a given sales volume, S, absorption costing income can be *increased* by increasing *production* volume, P, since the fixed overhead expense term, $\frac{F}{P} \cdot S$, gets smaller as P increases.

In other words, a company (or responsibility center within a company) can increase reported income under absorption costing by building up finished goods inventory. This is called "increasing profits by selling overhead to inventory."[3]

---

[3]The above proof assumes a constant level of production, as in Illustration 19–2. Without this assumption, but presuming that predetermined overhead rates are used, the proof becomes more complex, owing to overhead volume variances, which are not explained until Chapter 20. If the period's overhead volume variance is closed to the income statement (as is common practice for *management* accounting monthly or quarterly income statements), the conclusions still hold. For the reader wanting to prove this after studying Chapter 20, let r = the predetermined *fixed* overhead rate. Then the overhead volume variance is $F - Pr$, and absorption costing charges the period's income with $Sr + F - Pr$ fixed overhead costs. Variable costing still charges F. The difference becomes $(Sr + F - Pr) - F = r(S - P)$, and the arguments in Cases 1, 2 and 3 above still hold.

Cases

CASE 19–1 Bennett Body Company

Ralph Kern, controller of Bennett Body Company, received a memorandum from Paul Bennett, the company's president, suggesting that Kern review an attached magazine article and comment on it at the next executive committee meeting. The article described the Conley Corporation's cost accounting system. Bennett Body was a custom manufacturer of truck bodies. Occasionally, a customer would reorder an exact duplicate of an earlier body, but most of the time some modifications caused changes in design and hence in cost.

The Conley System. Kern learned from the article that Conley also manufactured truck bodies but that these were of standard design. Conley had 12 models that it produced in quantities based upon management's estimates of demand. In December of each year, a plan, or budget, for the following year's operations was agreed upon, which included estimates of costs and profits as well as of sales volume.

Included in this budget were estimated costs for each of the 12 models of truck bodies. These costs were determined by totaling estimated labor at an expected wage rate, estimated materials at an expected cost per unit, and an allocation for overhead that was based on the proportion of estimated total overhead costs to estimated total direct labor dollars. This

644

estimate for each model became the standard cost of the model.

No attempt was made in Conley's accounts to record the actual costs of each model. Costs were accumulated for each of the four direct production departments and for several service departments. Labor costs were easily obtainable from payroll records, since all employees assigned to a production department were classified as direct labor for that department. Material sent to the department was charged to it on the basis of signed issue slips. Overhead costs were charged to the department on the basis of the same percentage of direct labor as that used in determining the standard cost.

Since Conley's management also knew how many truck bodies of each model were worked on by each department monthly, the total standard costs for each department could easily be calculated by multiplying the quantity of that model produced by its standard cost. Management watched closely the difference between the actual cost and the standard cost as the year progressed.

As each truck body was completed, its cost was added to Finished Goods Inventory at the standard cost figure. When the truck body was sold, the standard cost became the Cost of Sales figure. This system of cost recording avoided the necessity of accumulating detailed actual costs on each specific body that was built; yet the company could estimate, reasonably well, the costs of its products. Moreover, management believed that the differences between actual and standard cost provided a revealing insight into cost fluctuations that eventually should lead to better cost control. An illustrative tabulation of the costs for Department 4 is shown in Exhibit 1. No incomplete work remained in this department either at the beginning or at the end of the month.

The Bennett System. Because almost every truck body that Bennett built was in some respect unique, costs were accumulated by individual jobs. When a job was started, it received a code number, and costs for the job were collected weekly under that code number. When materials used for a particular job were issued to the workers, a record of the quantities issued was obtained on a requisition form. The quantity of a given material—so many units, board feet, linear feet, pounds, and so on—was multiplied by its purchase cost per unit to ar-

EXHIBIT 1
SUMMARY OF COSTS, DEPARTMENT 4, NOVEMBER

Standard	Number of Bodies	Material		Labor		Overhead	
		Per Unit	Total	Per Unit	Total	Per Unit	Total
Model 101	10	$ 945	$ 9,450	$1,386	$ 13,860	$1,386	$ 13,860
109	8	1,260	10,080	1,104	8,832	1,104	8,832
113	11	1,923	21,153	1,323	14,553	1,323	14,553
154	20	597	11,940	1,221	24,420	1,221	24,420
Total	49		$ 52,623		$ 61,665		$ 61,665
Actual costs.			57,456		63,189		63,189
Variances.			$ −4,833		$ −1,524		$ −1,524

rive at the actual cost of material used. Maintenance of cumulative records of these withdrawals by code number made the total material cost of each job easy to determine.

Likewise, all labor costs of making a particular truck body were recorded. If a worker moved from job to job, a record was made of the worker's time spent on each job, and the worker's weekly wages were divided among these jobs in proportion to the amount of time spent on each. Throughout the shop, the time of any person working on anything directly related to an order—Job No. 1375J, for example—was ultimately converted to a dollar cost and charged to that job.

Finally, Bennett's overhead costs that could not be directly associated with a particular job were allocated among all jobs on the proportional basis of direct labor-hours involved. Thus, if in some month 135 direct labor-hours were spent on Job No. 1375J, and this was 5 percent of the 2,700 direct labor-hours spent on all jobs at Bennett that month, then Job No. 1375J received 5 percent of all the overhead cost—supplies, salaries, depreciation, and so forth—for that month.

Under this system, Bennett's management knew at the end of each month what each body job in process cost to date. They could also determine total factory cost and therefore gross profit at the completion of each job.

The note that Mr. Bennett attached to the magazine article read:

Ralph:

Please review the system of cost accounting described in this article with the view of possible applications to our company. Aside from the overall comparison, I am interested particularly in your opinion on—

1. Costs of paperwork and recordkeeping, as compared with our system.
2. Possible reasons for cost differences between the actual and standard costs under Conley's system.
3. How you think Conley develops the standard cost of factory overhead for a particular model for the purpose of preparing the budget.
4. Whether you think that we should change our period for determining the overhead allocation rate from monthly to annually. If so, why?
5. Which system is better from the standpoint of controlling costs?

These are just a few questions which might be helpful in your overall analysis. I would like to discuss this question at the next executive committee meeting.

Thank you.

Paul Bennett

Questions

1. As Mr. Kern, what would you be prepared to say in response to Mr. Bennett's memorandum?
2. How, if at all, should Bennett modify its present system?

CASE 19–2   Black Meter Company

Refer to the description of Black Meter's cost accounting system in the Appendix and consider the following:

1. Trace through the cost accounting procedures described so that you are able to show how the numbers in each illustration are derived from, and/or help derive, the other illustrations.

2. Try to imagine what an actual cost system for Black Meter would look like. How would it compare with the standard cost system in terms of:
   a. Recordkeeping effort required?
   b. Usefulness of cost information to Black Meter's management?

3. Develop a flowchart for Black Meter's system similar to the one in Illustration 19–1. Do not use dollar amounts, but indicate flows between accounts and show whether entries are at standard or actual costs. In what respects, if any, do these two flowcharts differ?

4. Suppose that the direct labor rate for Department 120A was increased to $7.75 per hour, and that for Department 131 was increased to $6.25 per hour. What effect would these changes have on the succeeding illustrations and on the total standard cost of 100 ⅝-inch HF meters?

5. As a consultant to Black Meter Company's controller, what would be your evaluation of the present system?

CASE 19–3 Omicron Company

Omicron Company produced one item, product Y, which was produced from raw materials A and B. Omicron used a standard cost system. In Omicron's system, all debits to Work in Process were made at standard amounts, that is, standard quantities at standard prices. As of January 1, all inventory accounts had zero balances. The following transactions occurred in January:

1. 1,000 pounds of raw material A were purchased for $10.50 per pound and put into inventory at the standard price of $10 per pound.

2. 600 pounds of raw material B were purchased for $19.70 per pound and put into inventory at the standard price of $20 per pound.

3. 700 pounds of raw material A were issued to production. The standard quantity of material for the units begun was 675 pounds.

4. 275 pounds of raw material B were issued to production. The standard quantity for the units begun was 300 pounds.

5. 500 pounds of raw material A were purchased for $9.80 per pound.

6. 620 pounds of raw material A were issued to production to begin units that at standard required 600 pounds.

7. 250 pounds of raw material B were issued to production to begin units for which the standard amount was 235 pounds.

8. 1,200 hours of direct labor at $9.80 were used in the manufacture of product Y. The work that was accomplished called for a standard 1,100 hours at $10.

9. Overhead costs of $8,400 were incurred. Overhead was charged to Work in Process at a rate of $8 per standard direct labor-hour.

10. 900 units of product Y at a standard full cost of $36 each were completed in January.

11. 800 units of product Y were sold for $40,000.

Questions

1. Set up T-accounts and post all of the above transactions.

2. What was Omicron Company's gross margin for January? In answering this question, please state and defend your treatment of the variances that were generated by January production operations.

CASE 19–4   Nemad Company

Nemad Company decided to adopt a standard cost system. The production manager wanted to set standards to use during the next year for the production of selector lever assemblies. Each assembly contained eight slotted levers made of steel. Due to the high tolerances required, an average of 10 percent of the levers cut do not meet specifications and must be discarded. The steel lever stock cost was $0.30 per piece at the end of this year, each lever required one piece of stock.

The workweek for production workers at Nemad Company was 40 hours. Included in this time were two daily 15-minute breaks. Management estimated that over the course of a year, an average worker would spend 15 percent of his or her nominal working time waiting for tools, for machine setups, and for necessary interruptions of work. Time-study observations indicated that a worker could make a selector lever assembly in 12 minutes. Management estimated that workers under observation for time-study produce at about 90 percent of their normal rate. The average pay for production workers was $12 per hour.

Inflation was expected to increase production costs at a rate of about 8 percent for the next year. Production volume was level throughout the year.

Question

What should be the direct material and direct labor standards for the manufacture of one selector lever assembly for next year?

CASE 19–5   Pilbeam Company

Pilbeam Company made radio antennas, which were sold through retail stores and mail-order catalogs. These antennas were used by vehicle owners to replace antennas that had been vandalized or had otherwise become ineffective. Pilbeam made two models: the F-100 was used for fender mounting, and the S-100 was used for side mounting (e.g., on truck cabs).

Pilbeam used a standard cost system, which included these standards *per dozen* antennas:

	F-100	S-100
Materials:		
Chrome-plated tubing	$ 8.25	$ 7.50
Cable and plug	7.20	7.20
Mounting device	4.42	5.62
	19.87	20.32
Direct labor (@ $6 per hour)	9.00	9.00
Overhead (@ 125% of direct labor)	11.25	11.25
Total cost per dozen	$40.12	$40.57

Materials were debited to Materials Inventory at standard cost upon receipt, any difference between the standard amount and actual invoice price being entered in the Material Price Variance account. Credits to Materials Inventory reflected the actual quantities issued, costed at standard cost per unit. All debits to Work in Process Inventory were based on standard quantities and standard prices or rates. Credits to Work in Process Inventory, debits to Finished Goods Inventory, and credits to Cost of Sales were all based on the $40.12 and $40.57 full standard production costs shown above. Variance accounts were closed to the Income Summary account at the end of the month.

The following descriptions relate to April operations:

1. On April 1, balance sheet account balances were as follows:

	Dr.	Cr.
Materials Inventory	$ 50,250	
Work in Process Inventory	75,600	
Finished Goods Inventory	155,400	
All other assets	325,500	
Accounts Payable		$104,700
Wages Payable		6,150
All other liabilities		47,250
Shareholders' Equity		448,650
Total	$606,750	$606,750

2. During April, Pilbeam received materials for 2,500 dozen F-100 antennas and 1,000 dozen S-100 antennas. The invoice amounts totaled $68,550.

3. During April, Pilbeam paid $102,300 worth of accounts payable. It collected $192,000 due from its customers. (Both Cash and Accounts Receivable are included in "All other assets" in the above account list.)

4. The stockroom issued materials during April for 3,200 dozen F-100 antennas and 700 dozen S-100 antennas, consistent with the planned production for the month. Stockroom requisitions also included issues of materials in excess of quantities needed to produce these 3,900 dozen antennas. These issues were to replace parts that had been bent or broken during the production process, and were as follows: 100 dozen F-100 tubes; 20 dozen S-100 tubes; 45 dozen cables and plugs; 20 dozen F-100 mounting devices; and 4 dozen S-100 mounting devices. The original parts issued that these extra issues replaced were all thrown into the trash bin, because they had no significant scrap value.

5. Direct labor expense incurred in April was $36,150. Indirect labor expense was $20,250. Wages paid were $58,350. (Ignore social security taxes and fringe benefits.)

6. Actual production overhead costs (excluding indirect labor) in April totaled $27,900. Of this amount, $18,750 was credited to Accounts Payable and the rest to various asset accounts (included above in "All other assets").

7. Selling and administrative expenses in April were $39,375; this same

amount was credited to various asset accounts.

8. April's standard cost sheets showed the following standard costs for antennas worked on during the month: direct labor, $39,600; and overhead, $49,500.

9. During April, 3,000 dozen F-100 antennas and 800 dozen S-100 antennas were delivered to the finished goods storage area; work on some of these goods had been started during March.

10. April sales were $154,800 for 2,400 dozen F-100 antennas and $59,400 for 900 dozen S-100 antennas. The offsetting entries were to Accounts Receivable (included in "All other assets").

Questions

1. Set up T-accounts, post beginning balances, and then record the above transactions. Adjust and close the accounts, determine April's income (ignore income taxes), and close this income to Shareholders' Equity. Do not create any balance sheet T-accounts not listed above.

2. Prepare the April income statement (again, disregarding income taxes). Why is your number for April income only an approximation?

3. Prepare a balance sheet as of April 30.

CASE 19–6   Craik Veneer Company

The sales manager of Craik Veneer Company received from Groton Company an offer to buy one million feet per month of sound "backs" of ¼-inch birch veneer[1] at $16 per thousand surface feet. The sales manager wanted to accept the offer, but the production manager argued that it should not be accepted because the cost of production was at least $20 per thousand feet and probably more.

Craik manufactured rotary-cut birch veneer from high-grade logs bought in Vermont. Selected sections called *blocks* were cut out of those logs, the length of the block varying from 84 inches to 98 inches. These blocks, as cut for the lathe, cost an average of $400 per thousand board feet. A thousand board feet, log measure, was an amount of logs which, being sawed, would produce a thousand board feet of lumber. (A board foot is 1 square foot 1 inch thick.) After being cut, the blocks were put in vats filled with hot water and left there for 24 to 48 hours until the entire log was heated through.

Manufacturing Process.   In the rotary veneer process, a block was put in a lathe in which a knife longer than the block, with a heavy frame, guide bars, and pressure bars, was brought against the side of the block so that it cut off a thin slice of wood the entire length of the block. The process was similar to unrolling a large roll of paper held on a horizontal shaft. The process could be controlled with skillful operation so it would produce veneer of uniform thickness. Craik produced principally ¼-inch veneer, and for the purposes of this case it may be assumed that all of its product was ¼-inch.

The sheet of veneer from the lathe, for instance from a 98-inch block, was brought onto a clipping table approximately 60 feet long. This table had rubber

[1] Veneer is a term applied to thin leaves or layers of wood. Generally, veneer is made of valuable wood and is laid over a core of inferior wood.

belts on its upper surface which moved the veneer along to the clipper. At this point the veneer was like a long sheet of paper moving along the table, the veneer being 98 inches along the grain. The clipper was a long knife extending entirely across the table. The clipper operator was one of the most highly skilled workers in the plant. Constantly inspecting the sheet of veneer, the operator first took one cut to get a straight edge. If the next section of the sheet was of high quality, the operator advanced the sheet not over 3 feet 8 inches, depending on customers' requirements. If the sheet showed a defect within 3 feet 8 inches, the operator made the cut just short of the defect. A worker called the "off bearer" piled these sheets on a hand truck reserved for high-grade or "face" veneer. If the defect was a knot, the clipper operator then advanced the sheet enough to clear the knot and took another cut, making a piece of waste possibly 3 inches wide. If the operator decided that a section of the sheet was not of face quality, it was cut off for "backs," either 3 feet 8 inches or in lesser widths. Backs were put on another hand truck.

The clipper operator thus separated the whole sheet of veneer into faces, backs, and waste. The faces consisted of pieces of veneer 98 inches long along the grain and anywhere from 6 inches to 3 feet 8 inches wide. The sound backs were of the same size. The waste went to a chipper and was then burned. The term *faces* came from the fact that these veneer sheets were substantially perfect and could be used on the exposed parts of furniture or on the best face of plywood.[2] The backs had minor defects and were so called because they were used on the

back of plywood panels. The quality required for faces was established by specifications of the industry. The dividing line between sound backs and waste was similarly established. Craik had a reputation for using high-grade logs and for producing a high grade of veneer both on faces and backs.

Groton Company's Offer. Groton Company's product design department had developed two new lines of furniture, one in blond modern and one in colonial, in which the table tops, dresser tops and panels, drawer fronts, and other exposed parts were of birch veneer over lower-grade birch or poplar cores, with table legs, dresser frames, and so on, of solid birch. Groton's people knew that while all sheets of backs contained defects, 50 to 60 percent of the area of backs as produced by Craik were of face quality. They had discovered that by buying backs 84 inches to 98 inches long they could cut clear face-quality veneer into lengths that would match their use requirements: enough 54 inches for their longest dresser tops and enough of other lengths down to 14-inch drawer fronts. The remainder of the veneer that was not of face quality could be used for such purposes as making plywood for drawer bottoms. The methods developed in the product design department had been tested by cutting up several carloads of backs bought from Craik and by the manufacture and sale of the furniture.

On the basis of this experience, Groton Company offered Craik $16 per thousand feet for 1 million feet per month of sound backs in 1/24-inch birch veneer for the next 12 months.

Cost Information. Craik cut an average of 12,000 board feet of logs a day in one eight-hour shift. With the high quality of logs it bought, it got a yield of 18,000 surface feet of 1/24-inch veneer per

---

[2] Veneer is a single thin sheet of wood. Plywood consists of several sheets (three, five, or nine) glued together with the grain of alternate courses at right angles to add to the strength.

1,000 board feet cut; this graded on the average 50 percent faces and 50 percent backs.

Labor and factory overhead costs together averaged $16 per thousand surface feet of veneer; selling costs averaged $3. Both the cost of the blocks and operating costs for the heating, lathe turning, and clipping operations were joint costs; backs had to be produced in order to get the faces. The remaining operations in drying, a slight amount of reclipping, storing, and shipping were in a sense separate costs as the operations were done on backs separately, although with the same equipment. The labor and factory overhead costs through clipping averaged $13.50 per 1,000 surface feet of veneer; those for drying and later operations, $2.50.

The selling price for $\frac{1}{24}$-inch birch faces 84 inches to 98 inches long was $80 per thousand surface feet. Face veneer 84 inches to 98 inches had a high price because it could be used on large surfaces, such as flush birch doors that require lengths up to 8 feet. The veneer shorter in length along the grain, made from recutting backs, had a somewhat lower price because it could not be used for these purposes. Unlike faces, the price of backs fluctuated widely. Sometimes Craik could get $20 per thousand feet, but the insistence of the production manager on $20 had led to the accumulation of a heavy inventory of backs. Faces were easy to sell and were shipped essentially as fast as they were produced.

More effort was required to sell backs than to sell faces, although both were sold to the same customers by the same sales force. Sometimes buyers of faces were required to take a percentage of backs in order to get a carload of faces. For these reasons Groton's offer was attractive to the sales manager.

Discussion of Offer. When the production manager was first informed by the sales manager of the offer of $16 per thousand surface feet, the production manager contended that "Your salespersons are so lazy, they would give veneer away if nobody watched them." The production manager went on to say:

> If a birch block cost $400 per thousand and we get 18,000 feet of $\frac{1}{24}$-inch-thick veneer from every thousand board feet of the block, the cost of the block to be allocated to a thousand feet of veneer, whether backs or faces, is $400 divided by 18,000 feet, or about $22.22 per thousand feet. Simple arithmetic proves that selling backs at $16 per thousand doesn't even pay for the material, let alone labor and overhead.

The sales manager countered that this argument was fallacious:

> Allocating the cost of the block to the veneer in this manner implies that backs are as valuable as faces, which is not the case. The $22.22 material figure for a thousand feet of veneer that you get is merely an average of the value of faces and backs. The material for faces is worth considerably more per thousand feet than this figure; the material for backs is worth considerably less.

The sales manager suggested that the proper procedure was to allocate the cost of the block to faces and backs in proportion to the amounts for which the products were sold. Using this method, the ratio that the revenue of one of the two grades of veneer bore to the revenue received from both grades of veneer would be applied to the total cost of the block, the result representing the cost to be allocated to that particular grade. To illustrate this method, assume a block of a thousand board feet cost $400, and the selling prices and quantities of faces and backs are as shown in the following table:

Grade	1/24-Inch Veneer in Feet	Sales Revenue per 1,000 Feet	Net Value	Percent of Total	Cost Applicable to Each
Faces.............	9,000	$80	$720	83.3	$333.33
Back..............	9,000	16	144	16.7	66.67
	18,000		$864	100.0	$400.00

The material cost applicable to each product, then, per thousand feet of 1/24-inch veneer would be $333.33/9,000 feet × 1,000 feet, or $37.04, for faces; and $66.67/9,000 feet × 1,000 feet, or $7.41, for backs.

The production manager again argued that this did not represent the true material cost, which was the same for both products, and added:

> Under your method the material cost allocated to either faces or backs would be a function of their relative selling prices. If the selling price of faces fell from $80 per thousand to $40 per thousand and the price of backs remained the same, you would then charge much more material cost to backs, and much less to faces. Your method of allocating cost doesn't make sense.

The sales manager at this point said:

> OK, if you don't think that method is justified, then let's treat backs as a by-product. I think you'll agree that we would prefer to be making faces all the time, yet we can't. As long as we manufacture faces, we're going to produce backs as an undesirable consequence. Now if we consider backs as a by-product, we can charge all block costs to faces. The net proceeds from the sale of backs, after allowing for all conversion, selling and administrative expenses, can be credited to the raw material cost of faces. All profits and losses of the business would be borne by the main product.

The production manager, however, pointed out again that the cost of material allocated to faces would still be a function of the selling price of backs and, furthermore, there would be some difficulty in trying to value inventories at the end of an accounting period; and that any profits arising from the sale of backs would be hidden, since it would be included in the credit to faces. "It is important to determine the profit or loss being realized on the sale of backs so we can establish a firm sales policy," the production manager asserted.

Because of their inability to resolve this question, the production manager and the sales manager consulted Craik's president, who in turn, asked the controller to examine the cost situation to determine whether the $16 per thousand surface feet of 1/24-inch backs would, or not, result in a profit.

Questions

1. As controller, what method of allocating raw material costs would you recommend? What similarities and differences would be encountered in allocating labor and overhead costs as compared to material costs?

2. Should the sales manager accept Groton's $16 per thousand feet offer for the 1/24-inch backs?

3. If a group of blocks containing 1,000 board feet costs $410, what would be the cost applicable to faces and backs under each of the methods of allocating costs de-

scribed in the case, and other methods that you may devise, if the following conditions existed:

a. The current market price of ¹⁄₂₄-inch faces is $80 per thousand feet; ¹⁄₂₄-inch backs are currently selling at $18 per thousand.

b. 10,000 feet of ¹⁄₂₄-inch faces and 8,000 feet of ¹⁄₂₄-inch backs were produced from a group of blocks.

c. Factory labor and overhead cost averaged $16 per thousand feet of veneer ($13.50 for operations through clipping and $2.50 for drying and later operations). Selling costs averaged $3 per thousand feet of veneer. If backs were not manufactured (i.e., if they were treated the same as waste), labor, overhead, and selling costs amounting to roughly $4 per thousand feet of backs might be saved.

CASE 19–7 Landau Company

In early August, Terry Silver, the new marketing vice president of Landau Company, was studying the July income statement. Silver found the statement puzzling: July's sales had increased significantly over June's, yet income was lower in July than in June. Silver was certain that margins on Landau's products had not narrowed in July, and therefore felt that there must be some mistake in the July statement.

When Silver asked the company's chief accountant, Meredith Wilcox, for an explanation, Wilcox stated that production in July was well below standard volume because of employee vacations. This had caused overhead to be underabsorbed, and a large unfavorable volume variance had been generated, which more than offset the added gross margin from the sales increase. It was company policy to charge all variances to the monthly income statement, and these production volume variances would all wash out by year's end, Wilcox had said.

Silver, who admittedly knew little about accounting, found this explanation to be "incomprehensible. With all the people in your department, I don't understand why you can't produce an income statement that reflects the economics of our business. In the company that I left to come here, if sales went up, profits went up. I don't see why that shouldn't be the case here, too."

As Wilcox left Silver's office, a presentation at a recent National Association of Accountants meeting came to Wilcox's mind. At that meeting, the controller of Winjum Company had described that firm's variable costing system, which charged fixed overhead to income as a period expense and treated only variable production costs as inventoriable product costs. Winjum's controller had stressed that, other things being equal, variable costing caused income to move with sales only, rather than being affected by both sales and production volume as was the case with full absorption costing systems.

Wilcox decided to recast the June and July income statements and balance sheets using variable costing. (The income statements as recast and as originally prepared, and the related balance sheet impacts, are shown in Exhibit 1.) Wilcox then showed these statements to Terry Silver, who responded, "Now that's more like it! I *knew* July was a better

EXHIBIT 1
EFFECTS OF VARIABLE COSTING

Income Statements
June and July

	June		July	
	Full Costing	*Variable Costing*	*Full Costing*	*Variable Costing*
Sales revenues.....................	$865,428	865,428	$931,710	$931,710
Cost of sales @ standard	484,640	337,517	521,758	363,367
Standard gross margin..............	380,788	527,911	409,952	568,343
Production cost variances:*				
Labor	(16,259)	(16,259)	(11,814)	(11,814)
Material	12,416	12,416	8,972	8,972
Overhead volume	1,730	—	(63,779)	—
Overhead spending	3,604	3,604	2,832	2,832
Actual gross margin	382,279	527,672	346,163	568,333
Fixed production overhead	—	192,883	—	192,883
Selling and administrative	301,250	301,250	310,351	310,351
Income before taxes...............	81,029	33,539	35,812	65,099
Provision for income taxes...........	38,894	16,099	17,190	31,248
Net income	$ 42,135	$ 17,440	$ 18,622	$ 33,851

*Parentheses denote unfavorable (debit) variances.

Impact on Balance Sheets
The only asset account affected by the difference in accounting method was Inventories; on the liabilities and owners' equity side, only Accrued Taxes and Retained Earnings were affected.

	As of June 30		As of July 31	
	Full Costing	*Variable Costing*	*Full Costing*	*Variable Costing*
Inventories	$1,680,291	$1,170,203	$1,583,817	$1,103,016
Accrued taxes...............	450,673	205,831	467,863	237,079
Retained earnings.............	3,112,980	2,847,734	3,131,602	2,881,585

month for us than June, and your new 'variable costing' statements reflect that. Tell your boss [Landau's controller] that at the next meeting of the executive committee I'm going to suggest we change to this new method."

At the next executive committee meeting, Silver proposed adoption of variable costing for Landau's monthly internal income statements. The controller also supported this change, saying that it would eliminate the time-consuming efforts of allocating fixed overhead to individual products. These allocations had only led to arguments between operating managers and the accounting staff. The controller added that since variable costing segregated the costs of materials, direct labor, and variable overhead from fixed overhead costs, management's cost control efforts would be enhanced.

Silver also felt that the margin figures provided by the new approach would be more useful than the present ones for comparing the profitability of individual products. To illustrate the point, Silver had worked out an example. With full costing, two products in Landau's line, numbers 129 and 243, would appear as follows:

Product	Standard Production Cost	Selling Price	Unit Margin	Margin Percent
129	$2.54	$4.34	$1.80	41.5
243	3.05	5.89	2.84	48.2

Thus Product 243 would appear to be the more desirable one to sell. But on the proposed basis, the numbers were as follows:

Product	Standard Production Cost	Selling Price	Unit Margin	Margin Percent
129	$1.38	$4.34	$2.96	68.2
243	2.37	5.89	3.52	59.8

According to Silver, these numbers made it clear that product 129 was the more profitable of the two.

At this point, the treasurer spoke up. "If we use this new approach, the next thing we know you marketing types will be selling at your usual markup over *variable* costs. How are we going to pay the fixed costs *then*? Besides, in my 38 years of experience, it's the lack of control over long-run costs that can bankrupt a company. I'm opposed to any proposal that causes us to take a myopic view of costs."

The president also had some concerns, having further considered the proposal. "In the first place, if I add together the June and July profit under each of these methods, I get almost $61,000 with the present method, but only $51,000 under the proposed method. While I'd be happy to lower our reported profits from the standpoints of relations with our employe union and income taxes, I don't think it's a good idea as far as our owners and bankers are concerned. And I share Sam's [the treasurer's] concern about controlling long-run costs. I think we should defer a decision on this matter until we fully understand all of the implications."

Questions

1. Critique the various pros and cons of the variable costing proposal that were presented in the meeting. What arguments would you add?

2. Should Landau adopt variable costing for its monthly income statements?

20

Production Cost
Variances

A standard cost system generates variances, which are differences between actual costs and standard costs. These variances provide important information for management. This chapter describes techniques for analyzing production cost variances in a way that provides managers with insights into the performance of the production function.

This managerial use of variance information is part of the responsibility accounting process, to be discussed in later chapters. Nevertheless, we discuss production cost variances at this point in the text because the topic is most easily understood immediately following the study of standard cost systems. Variances in gross margin and nonproduction costs are described in Chapter 26 as part of the discussion of the performance evaluation aspects of responsibility accounting.

For production variances, there are two general analytical approaches. One applies to direct material costs and direct labor costs; the other, somewhat different, approach applies to overhead costs.

DIRECT MATERIAL AND LABOR VARIANCES

**Nature of Direct
Material Variances**

A standard cost represents what the cost should be. The standard direct material cost of *one unit* of product is found by multiplying the quantity of material that should be used in producing one unit by the price that should be paid per unit of material (e.g., 9 pounds per unit at $4 per pound = $36 per unit). The *total* standard direct material cost for as *accounting period* is the standard material cost per unit multiplied by the number of units produced in that period (e.g., if 100 units are produced, the total standard material cost is $3,600). The total standard material cost is also the total standard quantity (100 units at 9 pounds per unit = 900 pounds) times the standard cost per unit of material (900 pounds × $4 per pound = $3,600).

Similarly, the *actual* direct material cost of one unit is the actual quantity of material used in producing that unit multiplied by the actual price paid per unit of material. The total actual direct material cost for a period is the sum of these actual costs for all the units produced in the period.

The direct material cost variance is the difference between the total standard and total actual material cost of the goods *produced*. Since each of these totals was computed by multiplying a physical quantity (e.g., 900 pounds) by a unit price (e.g., $4 per pound), it is possible to decompose the total variance into a quantity component and a price component. More specifically, these components are:

1. The variance caused by the fact that the actual quantity of material used for the goods produced differed from the standard quantity. This is called the *material usage variance* (also the *yield* variance or simply the *quantity* variance).
2. The variance caused by the fact that the actual unit price of the material differed from the standard unit price. This is called the *material price variance.*

The algebraic sum of these two variances is the total material variance, that is, the difference between total actual direct material costs for the period and total standard direct material costs. This is the amount that often would appear in a Material Variance account in a standard cost system. (As noted in Chapter 19, in some systems the two components are already separately identified in the accounts.)

Favorable and Unfavorable Variances. If actual cost is lower than standard cost, the variance is said to be *favorable;* if the reverse, the variance is said to be *unfavorable.* As explained in Chapter 19, favorable variances appear as credits in variance accounts, whereas unfavorable variances are debits in variance accounts. We shall use these adjectives in the description that follows. However, it should be recognized that "favorable" does not necessarily mean that performance was "good"; it means only that actual costs were lower than standard costs. The interpretation of these variances, once they have been identified, is discussed later in the chapter.

Formulas for Direct Material Variances

The commonly used rules for finding the two direct material variances are as follows:

1. The *material usage variance* is the difference between total standard quantity and total actual quantity of material, with each total quantity priced at the *standard* price per unit of material. Both total quantities are based on the number of units of product actually produced.
2. The *material price variance* is the difference between the standard price per unit of material and the actual price per unit of material, multiplied by the *actual* quantity of material used.[1]

Using the symbol Δ (delta) to stand for the difference between an actual amount and a standard amount, these rules can be stated as:

$$\text{Usage variance} = \Delta\,\text{Quantity} \times \text{Standard price}$$

$$\text{Price variance} = \Delta\,\text{Price} \times \text{Actual quantity}$$

Example. Each unit of product X is supposed to require 9 pounds of direct material costing $4 per pound. In March, 100 units of X were made, and their production consumed 825 pounds of material costing $5 per pound. The total amounts for materials are calculated as follows:

	Unit Price	×	Physical Quantity	=	Total Cost
Standard............................	$ 4	×	900*	=	$3,600
Actual..............................	5	×	825	=	4,125
Difference (Δ)......................	$(1)		75		$ 525 U†

*100 units produced × 9 pounds per unit.
†U = Unfavorable; F = Favorable.

Applying the above rules, the $525 U total material variance can be decomposed as follows:

$$
\begin{array}{ccccc}
\Delta\,\text{Quantity} & \times & \text{Standard price} & = & \text{Usage variance} \\
75 & \times & \$4 & = & \$300\ \text{F}
\end{array}
$$

$$
\begin{array}{ccccc}
\Delta\,\text{Price} & \times & \text{Actual quantity} & = & \text{Price variance} \\
\$(1) & \times & 825 & = & \$825\ \text{U}
\end{array}
$$

Note that the algebraic sum of the price and usage variances is the net or total variance ($300 F + $825 U = $525 U).

---

[1] As pointed out in Chapter 19, some companies identify the material price variance when the material is received into materials inventory. When this is done, the material in inventory is automatically valued at its standard price, so no material price variance is developed during the production process. In these companies, the material usage variance usually is developed when materials are issued to production, as shown in Illustration 19–1.

Graphic Aids

Many people find their first exposure to variance formulas to be somewhat perplexing. We therefore present two graphic aids that many have found helpful in understanding the formulas.

Illustration 20–1 is one such graphic aid. The three columns in the illustration reflect (1) how much cost should have been incurred for materials, based on a *standard* physical amount of material per unit of product, a standard price for each unit of material, and the actual number of units produced (the column labeled *SQSP*); (2) how much cost should have been incurred for the quantity of material that was *actually* used (AQSP); and (3) how much cost was actually incurred for the material actually used.

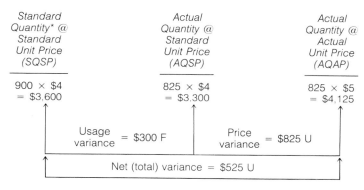

ILLUSTRATION 20–1
DIAGRAM OF DIRECT MATERIAL VARIANCES

*Standard quantity for the actual volume; that is, the quantity that should have been used to produce the actual output.

Illustration 20–2 depicts the material variance components geometrically. The variance components are the areas where the total standard cost rectangle and total actual cost rectangle do *not* coincide.

In both illustrations, the usage variance is favorable because a lesser quantity of material was used than was allowed by the standard. The price variance is unfavorable because the actual price per unit of material was higher than was allowed by the standard.

Uses of the Variances

The separation of the direct material net variance into its price and usage components facilitates analysis and control of material costs. The price variance often is the responsibility of the purchasing department, whereas the usage variance is the responsibility of the department that uses the material.

The fact that these two material variances can be separated does not

ILLUSTRATION 20–2
GEOMETRIC DEPICTION OF DIRECT MATERIAL VARIANCES

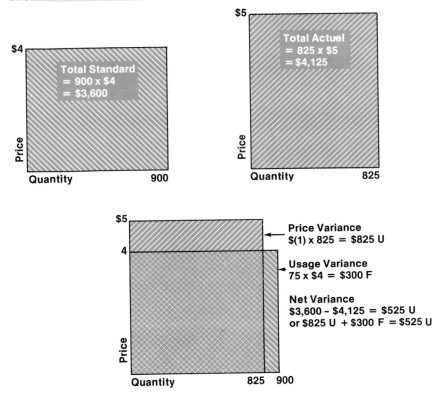

mean that they are necessarily independent, however. For example, investigation of a favorable price variance may reveal that material of substandard quality was bought at a discount price; and the substandard quality caused abnormal spoilage in production operations, as reflected in an unfavorable usage variance. In this case, the price variance is not "favorable" in any literal sense, and the purchasing department, not a production department, has caused the usage variance.

Joint Variance

Illustration 20–2 shows clearly the nature of the two direct material variances when one of them is favorable and the other is unfavorable. The situation is less clear, however, when *both* variances are favorable or when *both* are unfavorable. Illustration 20–3 shows the nature of the difficulty. It is based on the same assumptions as the earlier example, except that 1,000 pounds of material were actually consumed (instead of 825 pounds).

ILLUSTRATION 20–3
DIAGRAM OF A JOINT VARIANCE

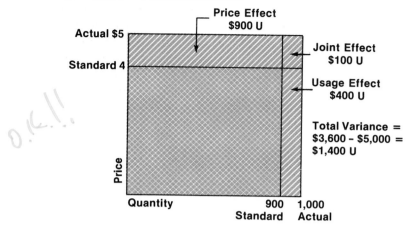

In this situation, the $1,400 U variance arose partly because the actual per unit material price exceeded standard by $1, and partly because the quantity actually used was 100 pounds in excess of standard. *At least* $900 U is a price variance because $1 per pound over the standard price was paid for the 900 pounds that should have been used; and *at least* $400 U is a usage variance because 100 extra pounds at the standard $4 price would have cost $400. There remains $100 U variance to be explained, however ($1,400 U − $900 U − $400 U = $100 U). As shown in the upper-right corner of Illustration 20–3, this $100 results from the *combination* of off-standard per unit price and off-standard usage.

This *joint variance* is not usually reported separately. The rules stated above (which are the ones commonly used in practice) assign this $100 as part of the price variance. The rationale for this treatment is that it is the purchasing agent's job to buy materials at the standard price, even though the quantity required may exceed standard.

Direct Labor Variances

Direct labor variances are analyzed in the same way as direct material variances. The standard direct labor cost of *one unit* of product is the standard labor time (usually expressed in hours) that should be spent producing that unit multiplied by a standard rate per unit of time (e.g., standard earnings per hour). If workers are paid on a piece-rate basis, the standard labor cost per unit of product is simply the piece rate or rates for producing that unit. Total standard direct labor cost of *an accounting period* is the standard labor cost per unit multiplied by the number of units produced in that period. Actual labor costs per unit or per period are calculated similarly.

The variance between total actual and total standard direct labor costs can be decomposed into two components: (1) an *efficiency variance* (also called *labor quantity* or *usage* variance), caused by the fact that actual time differed from standard time and (2) a *rate variance* (or *labor price variance*), caused by the fact that actual hourly rates or actual piece rates differed from standard rates.

The formulas for decomposing the net labor variance into these two components are parallel to the formulas for direct material variances:

$$\text{Efficiency variance} = \Delta \text{ Time} \times \text{Standard rate}$$

$$\text{Rate variance} = \Delta \text{ Rate} \times \text{Actual time}$$

Example. Product Y has a standard time of 9 hours per unit at a standard rate of $4 per hour. In April, 100 units of Y were produced, with an expenditure of 825 labor-hours costing $5 per hour. Thus, total actual direct labor was $4,125 (= 825 hours @ $5), while the standard was $3,600 (= 100 units × 9 hours per unit @ $4 per hour). The net variance is $525 U, which is decomposed as follows:

$$\Delta \text{ Rate} \times \text{ Actual time} = \text{Rate variance}$$
$$\$(1) \times 825 = \$825 \text{ U}$$

$$\Delta \text{ Time} \times \text{ Standard rate} = \text{Efficiency variance}$$
$$75 \times \$4 = \$300 \text{ F}$$

Illustrations 20–1 and 20–2 also apply to this example: just change the word *material* to *labor*, *quantity* to *time*, *price* to *rate*, and *usage* to *efficiency*.

Interpretation of the Direct Labor Variance. The reason for decomposing the total direct labor variance is that the labor rate variance is evaluated differently from the labor efficiency variance. The rate variance may arise because of a change in wage rates for which the supervisors in charge of the production responsibility centers cannot be held responsible. On the other hand, the supervisors may be held entirely responsible for the efficiency variance because they should control the number of hours that direct workers spent on the production for the period.

A valid distinction between the rate variance and the efficiency variance cannot be made in all cases, for there are many situations in which the two factors are interdependent. For example, a supervisor may find it possible to complete the work in less than the standard time by using workers who earn a higher than standard rate, and be perfectly justified in doing so. Even so, the use of the technique described above may lead to a better understanding of what actually happened.

OVERHEAD VARIANCES

Recall from Chapter 18 that most cost systems assign overhead costs to products by a predetermined overhead rate, which is calculated by dividing the estimated production volume into the total overhead costs estimated to be incurred at that volume. The estimated amount of cost at any volume is shown on a flexible overhead budget[2] as was described in Chapter 18. Such a flexible budget usually can be plotted graphically as a straight line, as in Part A of Illustration 20–4. The equation for this line is $TC = TFC + UVC \cdot X$; in the context of overhead budgeting, the symbols in this equation have the following meanings:

$$TC = \text{total overhead cost}$$
$$TFC = \text{total fixed overhead cost per period}$$
$$UVC = \text{variable overhead cost per unit}$$
$$X = \text{volume, in units}$$

ILLUSTRATION 20–4
BEHAVIOR AND ABSORPTION OF OVERHEAD COST

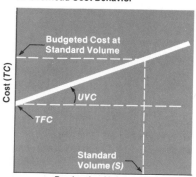

A. Overhead Cost Behavior

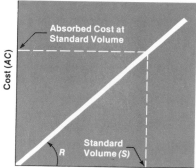

B. Overhead Cost Absorption

The overhead rate, R, is the average overhead cost per unit at the *standard* volume. It therefore is found by dividing the total costs at the standard volume by the number of units (S) represented by that volume; that is:

$$R = \frac{TFC + UVC \cdot S}{S}$$

---

[2]The words *standard* and *budget* both connote estimates of what costs *should* be. In practice, "standard" is used with *per unit* cost amounts, while "budget" is used with *total* amounts; for example, "The standard labor cost of product Z is $10 per unit," or "The labor cost budget for 50 units of Z is $500."

Example. Assuming budgeted fixed overhead costs are $500, budgeted variable overhead costs are $1 per unit, and standard volume is 1,000 units, the overhead rate is $1.50 per unit, calculated as follows:

$$R = \frac{\$500 + \$1 \cdot 1,000}{1,000} = \$1.50$$

The *overhead variance* (also called the *net overhead variance*) is the difference between the overhead costs actually incurred and the overhead costs absorbed by (charged to) production in the WIP Inventory account. As was diagrammed in Illustration 19–1 and explained in the related text, actual overhead costs are debited to the Overhead clearing account, and absorbed overhead costs are credited to that account. The overhead variance is developed by closing the balance in the Overhead clearing account to the Overhead Variance account (entry 6 in Illustration 19–1). The resulting amount that appears in the Overhead Variance account is the net overhead variance.

This variance can be decomposed into two elements: (1) a production volume variance and (2) a spending variance. The production volume variance is caused by the way in which the overhead rate is calculated, as explained in the next section. The overhead spending variance is caused by actual overhead costs being different from the amount allowed by the flexible overhead budget, as explained in a later section.

Production Volume Variance

Each unit produced will be charged overhead at the overhead rate. The amount of overhead *absorbed* by the units produced is therefore the overhead rate times the number of units actually produced. Algebraically, $AC = R \cdot X$, in which AC means absorbed cost and X equals the actual production volume. Graphically, the amount absorbed at any volume is a straight line, starting at zero and with the slope R, as shown in Part B of Illustration 20–4. However, since the *budgeted* costs at any volume behave in the fashion indicated in Part A of Illustration 20–4, budgeted costs and absorbed costs will be equal *only* at the standard volume.

Example. Using the relationships assumed above, the budgeted and absorbed costs at various volumes will be:

Actual Volume (X)	Budgeted $500 + $1 · X	Absorbed $1.50 · X	Difference
800	$1,300	$1,200	$−100
900	1,400	1,350	−50
1,000	1,500	1,500	0
1,100	1,600	1,650	+50
1,200	1,700	1,800	+100

At any volume below the standard volume, the amount of overhead costs absorbed will be less than the budgeted cost at that volume. At these volumes, budgeted costs are said to be unabsorbed (or underabsorbed). Conversely, at any volume higher than the standard volume, budgeted overhead costs will be overabsorbed. This difference between budgeted and absorbed costs is caused solely by the fact that actual volume is different from the standard volume, that is, the volume used in arriving at the predetermined overhead rate. It is therefore called a production volume variance. Note that the production volume variance is in no way related to the amount of actual costs incurred.[3]

In particular, if the overhead rate was based on the average volume expected during the year (as is usually the case), when results for a given month are being analyzed, one should expect to see a volume variance for that month unless the month's volume was exactly $\frac{1}{12}$ of the volume assumed for the year as a whole. Because of seasonal and other short-term influences, such an exact correspondence is unlikely. Also, even if the actual total volume for the year turns out to equal the year's standard volume exactly, volume variances for certain months are likely. In this case, the variances for the high-volume months will exactly offset those for the low-volume months, so the net volume variance for the year will be zero.

Spending Variance

Illustration 20–5 shows graphically the relationship between budgeted and absorbed overhead costs at various volumes. It was constructed by merging the two diagrams in Illustration 20–4. The dot labeled "actual" is to the left of the standard volume, indicating that volume in the month illustrated is lower than the standard volume. Consequently, there was an unfavorable production volume variance in that month. Its amount is the difference between the budgeted amount for the actual volume and the amount absorbed. The remaining difference is the spending variance. It is the difference between the actual overhead costs incurred in the period and the budgeted overhead costs for the period's actual level of production volume. In the diagram, the spending variance is favorable because actual costs are below the budgeted amount.

The spending variance for overhead costs has the same significance as the sum of the usage and price variances (i.e., the net variance) for direct material cost and direct labor cost. Indeed, it is possible to decompose the spending variance, item by item (electricity, supervision, property taxes, etc.), into usage and price components in the same manner as was described for these direct costs. Companies do this for overhead costs, however, only if they find this additional breakdown worthwhile. For

---

[3]The production volume variance would not arise if all overhead costs were variable with respect to production volume. The reader wishing to pursue this point is referred to Appendix A at the end of this chapter.

ILLUSTRATION 20–5
BUDGETED, ABSORBED, AND ACTUAL OVERHEAD COSTS

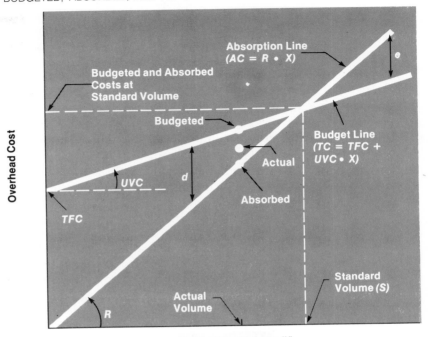

Production Volume (X)

example, because of the importance of energy costs, a variance in electricity spending may be decomposed into a variance caused by a difference between budgeted and actual prices per kilowatt-hour and a variance caused by the difference between actual and budgeted kilowatt-hour usage. The price component is noncontrollable, while the usage component is controllable.

A Caution. To master the overhead variance calculations described in the next section, it is important to understand fully the different meanings of the two lines in Illustration 20–5. The flexible budget line shows the *expected* relationship between volume and actual overhead costs. Amounts determined by the formula for this budget line are *not* the basis of entries of the Overhead clearing account; hence, the "outside-the-accounts" decomposition of the net overhead variance that is determined when this account is closed. The overhead costs that actually are incurred will be debited to the Overhead clearing account. The absorption line shows the relationship between production volume and the total amount of credits to the Overhead clearing account (and accompanying debits to WIP Inventory). Note that the absorption line *looks*

ImPoRtANt

just like a graph of variable costs; but, as the flexible budget line indicates, actual overhead costs are *not* expected to be entirely variable.

Also note that both the flexible budget and overhead absorption lines are based on *production* volume. The period's *sales* volume plays *no role* in the accounting for production overhead costs. (While this statement may seem obvious, some students always seem to forget it when applying the overhead variance formulas in practice.)

Calculation of Overhead Variances

The net overhead variance is the algebraic sum of the volume variance and the spending variance. In order to understand how each variance is calculated, refer again to Illustration 20–5. The situation illustrated in that diagram is one in which actual volume is below standard volume, and actual costs are below the budgeted costs for the actual volume, but they are higher than absorbed costs. Note that budgeted costs are the amount of costs budgeted for the production volume level *actually attained* in the period. That is, they are the amount that *would have been* budgeted had it been known *ahead of time* what the actual volume would be. The following relationships hold:

The *net overhead variance is the difference between absorbed costs and actual costs.* In Illustration 20–5, the variance is unfavorable. As stated above, the net overhead variance is also the algebraic sum of the volume variance and the spending variance.

The *production volume variance is the difference between absorbed costs and budgeted costs.* In Illustration 20–5, this variance is unfavorable.

The *spending variance is the difference between budgeted costs and actual costs.* In Illustration 20–5, this variance is favorable.

Example. Assume that—

Actual volume in an accounting period is 900 units of product.

Actual overhead costs are $1,380.

The flexible budget formula is $500 fixed overhead per period plus $1 variable overhead per unit of product.

The standard volume is 1,000 units; hence, the absorption rate is $1.50 per unit of product.

Then:

Budgeted cost at the actual volume	= $500 + $1(900)	= $1,400
Absorbed cost at the actual volume	= $1.50 × 900	= $1,350
Net variance = Absorbed − Actual	= $1,350 − $1,380	= $30 U
Volume variance = Absorbed − Budgeted	= $1,350 − $1,400	= $50 U
Spending variance = Budgeted − Actual	= $1,400 − $1,380	= $20 F

This analysis is shown in diagram form in Illustration 20–6.

attributable to a low volume but your controlled (?) your spending

Review

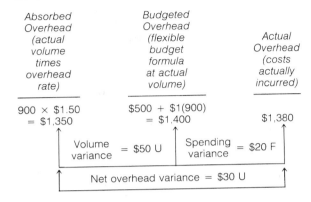

ILLUSTRATION 20–6
DIAGRAM OF OVERHEAD VARIANCES

Absorbed Overhead (actual volume times overhead rate)	Budgeted Overhead (flexible budget formula at actual volume)	Actual Overhead (costs actually incurred)
$900 \times \$1.50$ $= \$1,350$	$\$500 + \$1(900)$ $= \$1,400$	$\$1,380$

$$\underset{\text{variance}}{\text{Volume}} = \$50\ U \qquad \underset{\text{variance}}{\text{Spending}} = \$20\ F$$

Net overhead variance $= \$30\ U$

Use of the Overhead Variances. Presumably, managers are responsible for the spending variance in their responsibility centers. Because the flexible budget cannot take account of all the *noncontrollable* factors that affect costs, however, there may be a reasonable explanation for the spending variance. The existence of an unfavorable variance is therefore not, by itself, grounds for criticizing performance. Rather, it is a signal that investigation and explanation are required.

In appraising spending performance, the analyst should look behind the total spending variance and examine the individual overhead items of which it consists. The total budgeted cost is the sum of the budgeted amounts for each of the separate items of cost. A spending variance can and should be developed for each important item; it is the difference between actual cost incurred and the budget allowance for that item. Attention should be focused on significant spending variances for individual elements of overhead costs.

In some situations, the manager may also be responsible for the volume variance. For example, the failure to obtain the standard volume of output may result from an inability to keep products moving through the department at the proper speed, or production quality problems may have hurt sales volume. The volume variance is more likely to be someone else's responsibility, however. It may result because the sales department was unable to obtain the planned volume of orders; because some earlier department in the manufacturing process failed to deliver materials, components, or subassemblies as they were needed; or because vendors did not deliver items when needed.

Overhead "Efficiency" Variance. In some instances, the net overhead variance can be decomposed into three (rather than two) elements, one of which is usually called an overhead "efficiency" variance. Such a variance arises only in one, fairly unusual, type of cost accounting system. It is described in Appendix B at the end of this chapter.

DISPOSITION OF PRODUCTION COST VARIANCES

In a standard cost system, production costs variances represent the amount by which the goods produced in an accounting period have been "mis-costed" by the standard costs. Conceptually, to correct these costs and convert them back to actual costs, first the output of the period's production efforts should be "traced" to partially completed goods (Work in Process), completed but unsold goods (Finished Goods Inventory), and to goods both made and sold during the period (Cost of Sales); and then the production variances should be allocated proportionately among these accounts. This procedure is consistent with the matching concept, which states that production costs should appear as expenses on the income statement in the period when an item is *sold*, rather than when it was produced.

As a practical matter, however, this disposition of production cost variances is difficult to accomplish, since the "tracing" of output is a nontrivial exercise. More importantly, management wants variances reported as promptly as practicable so as to minimize the time lag between a variance's occurrence and the subsequent managerial investigation. Therefore, for *management accounting* purposes, variances are usually treated as expenses of the period in which they were incurred, even though the matching principle is violated by this treatment.

For external financial statements and for income tax returns, however, the conceptually correct treatment governs. Nevertheless, the expedient method of treating these production variances as period costs is acceptable *if* this method does not result in materially different inventory and cost of sales amounts than the conceptually correct method.

SUMMARY

A variance is the difference between a standard cost and an actual cost. A standard cost system generates production cost variances related to direct material cost, direct labor cost, and overhead cost. The direct material variance can be decomposed into usage and price components; the direct labor variance can be divided into efficiency and rate components; and the overhead variance can be separated into production volume and spending components.

The purpose of decomposing variances into these components is to facilitate managers' analysis of actual results. Responsibility for a variance component is assigned to a specific responsibility center. However, variance components may be interdependent. Also, the terms *favorable* and *unfavorable* should be used with care; they denote the algebraic sign of a variance, not value judgments of managers' performance.

APPENDIX A: FIXED COSTS AND THE OVERHEAD VOLUME VARIANCE

The volume variance arises solely because of the presence of *fixed* production costs. We shall explain this fact in this Appendix.

As a simple intuitive "proof," consider line segment p in Illustration 20–7. By definition, the length of this segment is the volume variance (difference between absorbed and budgeted overhead at actual volume). Now imagine a gradual change in the overhead cost structure, such that budgeted costs at standard volume remain the same (point n), but the fixed cost portion (TFC) gradually diminishes. Note what happens to p as TFC approaches zero: p also approaches zero. In the limit (TFC = 0), the absorption and budget lines coincide, and there is no volume variance. (This is why there is no volume variance with a variable costing system: fixed costs are ignored for absorption purposes, so the budget and absorption lines are the same, both representing solely variable costs.) Thus, were there no fixed overhead costs, there would be no volume variance.

ILLUSTRATION 20–7
OVERHEAD VOLUME VARIANCE

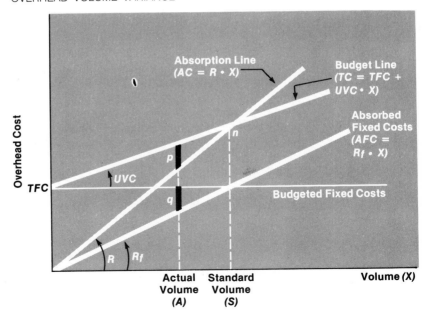

A more rigorous proof first involves realizing that the overhead rate (R in Illustration 20–7, the slope of the absorption line) is the sum of the variable overhead cost per unit of volume (UVC) and a rate which absorbs the fixed costs. This second rate is fixed costs, TFC, divided by standard volume, S; geometrically it is the slope, R_f, of the line labeled "absorbed fixed costs." It is easily demonstrated that, in fact, $R = R_f + UVC$:

$$R = \frac{\text{Budgeted cost at S}}{\text{Standard volume (S)}} = \frac{TFC + UVC \cdot S}{S} = \frac{TFC}{S} + UVC$$
$$= R_f + UVC$$

Now by definition, if actual volume is A, then:

$$
\begin{aligned}
\text{Volume variance} &= \text{Absorbed cost at } A - \text{Budgeted cost at } A \\
p &= R \cdot A - (TFC + UVC \cdot A)
\end{aligned}
$$

We want to prove that q, which is the difference between budgeted and absorbed *fixed* costs, is equal to p.

$$
\begin{aligned}
q &= \text{Absorbed fixed cost at } A - \text{Budgeted fixed cost at } A \\
&= R_f \cdot A - TFC \\
&= (R - UVC) \cdot A - TFC \\
&= R \cdot A - UVC \cdot A - TFC \\
&= R \cdot A - (TFC + UVC \cdot A) \\
&= p = \text{Volume variance}
\end{aligned}
$$

Thus volume variance arises solely from the underabsorption or overabsorption of budgeted *fixed* costs.

The above also suggest a quick way to calculate the overhead volume variance. Note that at standard volume (S), absorbed fixed costs, $R_f \cdot S$, exactly equals budgeted fixed costs, TFC. Then:

$$
\begin{aligned}
q &= R_f \cdot A - TFC = R_f \cdot A - R_f \cdot S \\
&= R_f (A - S)
\end{aligned}
$$

In words, volume variance equals the *fixed* cost absorption rate times the difference between actual and standard volumes. Volume variance is unfavorable if $A < S$, and favorable if $A > S$.

APPENDIX B: THREE-PART OVERHEAD VARIANCE ANALYSIS

In some companies, a production department's overhead is absorbed into WIP Inventory on the basis of a measure of *output* (e.g., *standard* direct labor-hours "allowed" or "earned" for the goods actually produced), but the overhead budget used for evaluating the department manager's overhead spending performance is based on *input* (e.g., *actual* direct labor-hours worked). The rationale for this budgeting procedure is that many overhead costs are caused by the actual level of input factors, not by some "theoretical" level representing what inputs *should* have been for the output produced.

> **Example.** In the welding department of the Staton Company, each direct labor-hour worked costs the firm $3 for fringe benefits. In May, 500 direct labor-hours were worked by the welders, although the welding work *accomplished* should (at standard times) have required only 460 hours. Although the budget for fringes *would* have been $1,380 (= 460 × $3) *if* the welding work had been performed in the standard time, in fact 500 hours were worked, so the appropriate fringe benefit budget is $1,500; that is, 500 labor-hours would be expected to cause $1,500 fringe benefit costs.

In companies where overhead is absorbed into WIP Inventory based on outputs produced but input volume is used for overhead budgeting, the usual overhead spending variance described in the text can be decomposed into two pieces:

$$\begin{array}{ccccc} \text{Spending} \\ \text{variance} \end{array} = \begin{array}{c} \text{Budgeted overhead} \\ \text{at input volume} \end{array} - \begin{array}{c} \text{Actual} \\ \text{overhead} \end{array}$$

$$\begin{array}{ccccc} \text{Efficiency} \\ \text{variance} \end{array} = \begin{array}{c} \text{Budgeted overhead} \\ \text{at output volume} \end{array} - \begin{array}{c} \text{Budgeted overhead} \\ \text{at input volume} \end{array}$$

To illustrate, assume all the same facts as were used in Illustration 20–6, and add these assumptions:

- Volume is measured in direct labor-hours (rather than units of product).
- Each unit has a standard direct labor time of 1.0 hour.
- Only 860 direct labor-hours were actually worked in producing the 900 units of product.

Then the three-part overhead variance analysis becomes that shown in Illustration 20–8.

ILLUSTRATION 20–8
THREE-PART OVERHEAD VARIANCE ANALYSIS

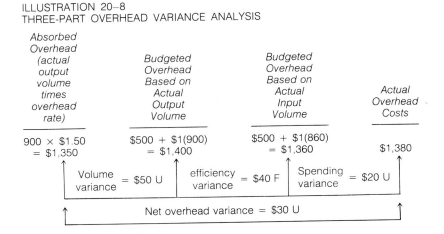

It is important to note from the illustration that the so-called overhead efficiency variance has nothing to do with *overhead* efficiency; rather, it is ths result of *labor* efficiency. It shows how much the flexible overhead budget changed because actual and budgeted labor costs were not the same.

It should also be remembered that this three-part analysis is applicable only if overhead is absorbed into WIP Inventory on the basis of *output.* If, instead, overhead is absorbed (debited) into WIP Inventory based on actual *input* volume (e.g., actual direct labor dollars), but goods are transferred from WIP Inventory to Finished Goods Inventory at standard unit costs (including standard overhead per unit), then the overhead efficiency variance is "buried" in WIP Inventory. It will remain "buried" there until a physical inventory is taken and costed at standard to establish a new beginning balance for WIP Inventory. This physical inventory results in an adjustment to WIP Inventory, and the overhead efficiency variance is part of this adjustment (along with pilferage, accounting errors, and—if labor and material were debited to WIP Inventory at actual but credited at standard—material and labor variances.)

Cases

Case 20–1 **Problems in Variance Analysis**

Alpha Company

Alpha Company calculates prime cost variances monthly. For May, the following data apply to its two products:

(Relates to Alpha Company)

	Standard Material per Unit	Standard Labor per Unit	Units Produced in May
Product 1	9 lbs.	7.5 hrs.	500
Product 2	11	9.0	800

Actual usage in May was 14,000 pounds of materials and 10,000 labor-hours.

Questions

1. Calculate the material usage variance in pounds and the labor efficiency variance in hours.

2. If the standard materials price is $24 per pound and the standard labor rate is $7.50 per hour, restate the variances in monetary terms.

Beta Company

Beta Company produces two products, A and B, each of which uses materials X and Y. The following unit standard costs apply:

(Relates to Beta Company)

	Material X	Material Y	Direct Labor
Product A	2 lbs. @ $10	1 lb. @ $8	⅕ hr. @ $12
Product B	3 lbs. @ $10	2 lbs. @ $8	⅓ hr. @ $12

During November, 4,200 units of A and 3,600 units of B were produced. Also, 19,000 pounds of X were purchased at $9.80, and 11,500 pounds of Y were purchased at $8.10; all of these materials (but no other materials) were used for the month's production. This production required 2,050 direct labor-hours at $11.60.

Questions

1. Calculate the material price and usage variances for the month.
2. Calculate the labor rate and efficiency variances for the month.
3. How would your answers to Questions 1 and 2 change if you had been told that November's *planned* production activity was 4,000 units of A and 4,000 units of B?
4. How would your answers to Questions 1 and 2 change if you had been told that November's sales were 4,000 units of A and 3,500 units of B?

Gamma Company

Gamma Company makes one product, which passes through two production operations. Under normal conditions, 150 pounds of raw material are required to make 100 units of product; all of the materials for a unit are issued to and used in operation 1. In operation 1, standard output is eight partially completed units per direct labor-hour, with a standard wage rate of $9 per hour. In operation 2, standard labor time is 12.5 hours per 100 units, at a standard wage rate of $9.90. Normal volume is 550,000 units per month. In March, output was 479,000 units and 732,864 pounds of raw material were consumed. No spoilage occurred in operation 2. Since the production cycle is very short, there was no beginning or ending work in process inventory. March

direct labor-hours and costs were as follows:

	Direct Labor	
	Hours	Costs
Operation 1	60,354	$547,713
Operation 2	58,438	575,907

Questions

1. Prepare an analysis of direct labor in March for Gamma's two operations.
2. Suppose that in operation 1, standard labor performance was expressed as 12 pounds of raw material processed per direct labor-hour (rather than eight partially completed units per direct labor-hour). Assume that the off-standard raw material yield in March was caused by the purchasing agent's buying raw materials of an off-standard quality. How, if at all, would this change your analysis of direct labor costs for March?

Delta Company

Delta Company's flexible budget formula for overhead costs is $50,000 per month fixed costs plus $12 per unit variable costs. Standard volume is 5,000 units a month. Actual overhead costs for May were $135,000, and output was 6,000 units.

Questions

Determine the following:
1. Budgeted overhead at standard volume.
2. Overhead absorption rate.
3. Overhead costs absorbed in May.
4. May's overhead production volume variance.
5. May's overhead spending variance.
6. May's net overhead variance.

Epsilon Company

Epsilon Company's expected volume for the year was 360,000 units. At this volume, planned annual overhead costs were $216,000 variable overhead and $72,000 nonvariable overhead. In March, output was 25,000 units and actual overhead expense was $19,200. Determine for March (a) the overhead flexible budget formula, (b) standard overhead per unit of output, and (c) the overhead variances.

Zeta Company

Zeta Company absorbed overhead at the rate of 75 cents per direct labor dollar. According to Zeta's flexible budget for overhead, for a direct labor payroll of $8,000, overhead should be $5,600; and overhead should be $6,800 for a payroll of $10,000. What is the budget formula? If actual overhead costs turned out to be $6,000 and $7,000, respectively, at these two volumes, what would be the overhead volume, spending, and net variances? What is Zeta's standard volume?

Eta Company

In June, Eta Company's overhead volume variance was $0 and its spending variance was a debit of $600; actual overhead expense was $7,000 for an output of 800 tons. In July, overhead expense was $5,600 and output was 600 tons; spending variance was $0. In August, output was 900 tons and actual overhead expense was $7,100. What was July's volume variance? What was the budget amount for August? How much overhead was absorbed in August? What were the August overhead variances?

Theta Company

Department 12 of the Theta Company manufactured rivets and no other products. All rivets were identical. The company used a standard cost system plus a variable budget for overhead expense. Standard unit overhead cost was determined by dividing budgeted costs at an expected average volume by the number of rivets (in thousands) which that volume level represented.

Certain cost information is shown in the following table, and you are requested to fill in the blank spaces. The clue to determining the expected average volume can be found by a close analysis of the relationships among the figures given for allocated service and general overhead.

	Actual Cost, August	Standard Charge per 1,000 Rivets	Total Standard Cost, August	Overhead Budget, August	Overhead Budget Formula
Direct labor	$10,500	$3.00	$ ___	Not used	
Direct material	22,000	5.00	20,000	Not used	
Department direct overhead expense	9,500	___	___	$ 9,200	$6,000 per month plus $0.80 per thous. rivets
Allocated service and general overhead	5,000	1.00	4,000	5,000	$5,000 per month
Total	$47,000	$ ___	$ ___	$14,200	

Questions

1. How many rivets were produced in August?
2. What was the expected average volume (in terms of rivet output) at which the standard unit overhead charge was determined?
3. Fill in the blanks.
4. Explain as much of the difference between total actual costs and total standard costs as you can on the basis of the information given.

Iota Company

Iota Company uses a standard cost system. One month's data for one of the company's products are given below:

1. Standard pounds of material in finished product: 3 pounds per unit.
2. Standard direct material cost: $4.80 per pound.
3. Standard hours of direct labor time: 1 hour per unit.
4. Standard direct labor cost: $8 per hour.
5. Materials purchased and received (12,000 pounds): $56,640.
6. Materials used: 11,000 pounds.
7. Direct labor cost incurred (3,475 hours): $28,355.
8. Actual production: 3,500 units.
9. Overhead budget formula: $22,400 per month plus $4 per direct labor-hour.
10. Overhead incurred: $34,216.
11. Standard volume: 4,000 units.

Questions

1. Compute the material usage and price variances.
2. Compute the labor efficiency and rate variances.
3. Compute the overhead volume and spending variances.

CASE 20–2   SunAir Boat Builders, Inc.

Located in New Hampshire, SunAir Boat Builders served boaters with a small, lightweight fiberglass sailboat capable of being carried on a car roof. While the firm could hardly be considered as one of the nation's industrial giants, its burgeoning business had required it to institute a formal system of cost control. Jan Larson, SunAir's president, explained, "Our seasonal demand, as opposed to a need for regular, level production, means that we must keep a good line of credit at the bank. Modern cost control and inventory valuation procedures enhance our credibility with the bankers and, more importantly, have enabled us to improve our operations. Our supervisors have realized the value of good cost accounting, and the main office has, in turn, become much more aware of problems in the barn."

SunAir's manufacturing and warehouse facilities consisted of three historic barns converted to make 11-foot "Silver Streak" sailboats. The company's plans included the addition of 15- and 18-foot sailboats to its present line. Longer-term plans called for adding additional sizes and styles in the hope of becoming a major factor in the regional boat market.

The "Silver Streak" was an open-cockpit, day sailer sporting a mainsail and small jib on a 17-foot, telescoping, aluminum mast. It was ideally suited to the many small lakes and ponds of the region, and after three years it had become quite popular. It was priced at $1,012 complete.

Manufacturing consisted basically of three processes: molding, finishing, and assembly. The molding department mixed all ingredients to make the fiberglass hull, performed the actual molding, and removed the hull from the mold. Finishing included hand additions to the hull for running and standing rigging, reinforcement of the mast and tiller steps, and general sanding of rough spots. Assembly consisted of the attachment of cleats, turnbuckles, drain plugs, tiller, and so forth, and the inspection of the boat with mast, halyards, and sails in place. The assembly department also prepared the boat for storage or shipment.

Mixing and molding fiberglass hulls, while manually simple, required a great deal of expertise, or "eyeball," as it was known in the trade. Addition of too much or too little catalyst, use of too much or too little heat, or failure to allow proper time for curing could each cause a hull to be discarded. Conversely, spending too much time on adjustments to mixing or molding equipment or on "personalized" supervision of each hull could cause severe underproduction problems. Once a batch of fiberglass was mixed there was no time to waste being overcautious or it was likely to "freeze" in its kettle.

With such a situation, and the company's announced intent of expanding its product line, it became obvious that a standard cost system would be necessary to help control costs and to provide some reference for supervisors' performance.

Randy Kern, the molding department supervisor, and Bill Schmidt, SunAir's accountant, agreed after lengthy discussion to the following standard costs:

```
Materials—Glass cloth—120 sq. ft. @ $ .90 = $108.00
         —Glass mix  —  40 lbs.   @ $1.65 =   66.00
Direct labor—Mixing  —  0.5 hrs.  @ $9.00 =    4.50
           —Molding     1.0 hrs.  @ $9.00 =    9.00
Indirect costs—Absorb at $10.80 per hull*  =   10.80
Total cost to mold hull                    = $198.30
```

*The normal volume of operations for overhead derivation purposes was assumed to be 450 hulls per month. The estimated monthly indirect cost equation was: Budget = $4.32 × hulls + $2,916.

Analysis of Operations. After several additional months of operations, Schmidt expressed disappointment about the apparent lack of attention being paid to the standard costs. Molders tended to have a cautious outlook toward mixing too little or "cooking" too long. No one wanted to end up throwing away a partial hull because of too little glass mix.

In reviewing the most recent month's production results, Schmidt noted the following actual costs for production of 430 hulls:

Materials:
- Purchased: 60,000 sq. ft. glass cloth @ $.825/sq. ft. 20,000 lbs. glass mix @ $1.785/lb.
- Used: 54,000 sq. ft. glass cloth 19,000 lbs. glass mix

Direct labor: Mixing 210 hrs. @ $9.375/hr. Molding 480 hrs. @ $9.00/hr.

Overhead: Incurred $4,950

Before proceeding with further analysis, Schmidt called Kern to arrange a discussion of variances. He also told Jan Larson, "Maybe we should look into an automated molding operation. Although I haven't finished my analysis, it looks like there will be unfavorable variances again. Kern insists that the standards are reasonable, then never meets them!''

Larson seemed disturbed and answered, "Well, some variances are inevitable. Why don't you analyze them in some meaningful manner and discuss your ideas with Kern, who is an expert in molding whose opinion I respect. Then the two of you meet with me to discuss the whole matter.''

Questions

1. Determine the molding department's direct cost variances and overhead variances. Why do you think they occurred?

2. Do you think SunAir's standards are meaningful? How would you improve them?

3. Assume that the month's actual and standard production costs for items *other than* molding hulls amounted to $409.20 per boat, and that 430 boats were sold. Prepare a statement of budgeted and actual gross margin for the month, assuming planned sales of 450 boats.

CASE 20–3   Medi-Exam Health Services, Inc.

Medi-Exam Health Services, Inc. (MEHS), located in a major metropolitan area, provides annual physical screening examinations, including a routine physical, EKG, and blood and urine tests. MEHS's clients are companies offering

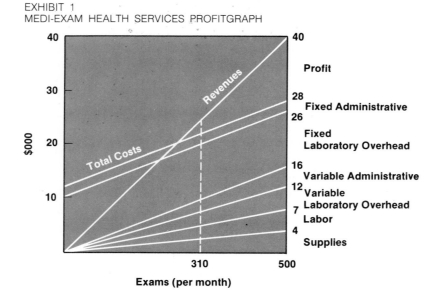

EXHIBIT 1
MEDI-EXAM HEALTH SERVICES PROFITGRAPH

EXHIBIT 2

MEDI-EXAM HEALTH SERVICES, INC.
Income Statement
For August

Revenues (310 examinations billed)...............		$24,600
Expenses:		
Standard cost of services billed	$13,640	
Variances:		
Volume (debit)..............................	800	
All other (debit).............................	560	
Administrative expenses........................	4,600	19,600
Net profit (before income taxes)		$ 5,000

annual physicals for their employees, but which are too small to warrant having a full-time medical staff of their own to provide this service. MEHS has its own portable equipment, which it moves from client to client so that examinations can be done at the customer's facilities. MEHS also has its own central laboratory for obtaining test results. A standard examination is priced at $80 per patient.

While conducting examinations for Peterson Electronics Company, Dr. James Molloy, one of the owners of MEHS, began talking with Peterson's head of financial planning. The patient told Dr. Molloy how Peterson used a profitgraph to help indicate the approximate profit the firm could expect to earn at various levels of output.

At the next meeting with MEHS's accountant, Jane Mattick, Dr. Molloy asked if such a technique would be useful for MEHS. Ms. Mattick said she would draw up a profitgraph for 500 physicals, a normal month's number of examinations. Her chart appears in Exhibit 1.

On September 1, Dr. Molloy learned that 310 physical examinations had been billed in August. Using the chart, he determined that profit should be approximately $3,000 for August. On September 8, Dr. Molloy received a copy of the income statement for August, showing a book profit of $5,000 (Exhibit 2).

Although he was pleasantly surprised by these results, Dr. Molloy was curious as to why the pretax profit was approximately 70 percent higher than he had expected, based on the profitgraph.

Questions

1. Compute the monthly break-even volume for Medi-Exam Health Services.

2. Compute the exact profit indicated by the profitgraph for a volume of 310 examinations.

3. Determine the number of examinations *performed* (as opposed to billed) in August.

4. Reconcile the profit just computed with the August book profit of $5,000.

CASE 20–4   Cotter Company, Inc.

In preparing its annual profit plan, the management of Cotter Company, Inc., realized that its sales were subject to monthly seasonal variations, but expected that for the year as a whole the profit before taxes would total $240,000, as shown below:

tal production overhead budgeted for the year consisted of $240,000 of variable costs (25 percent of $960,000) and $600,000 of fixed costs. All of the selling and general expenses were fixed, except for commissions on sales equal to 5 percent of the selling price.

	Annual Budget	
	Amount	Percent of Sales
Sales	$2,400,000	100
Standard cost of sales:		
Prime costs............................	960,000	40
Production overhead	840,000	35
Total standard cost..................	1,800,000	75
Gross margin............................	600,000	25
Selling and general expenses	360,000	15
Income before taxes.....................	$ 240,000	10

Management defined *prime costs* as those costs for labor and materials that were strictly variable with the quantity of production. The production overhead included both fixed and variable costs; management's estimate was that within a range around planned sales volume of plus or minus $1,000,000 per year, variable production overhead would be equal to 25 percent of prime costs. Thus, the to-

Sal Cotter, the president of the company, approved the budget, stating that, "A profit of $20,000 a month isn't bad for a little company in this business." During January, however, sales suffered the normal seasonal dips, and production was also cut back. The result, which came as some surprise to the president, was that January showed a loss of $7,000.

Operating Statement
January

Sales		$140,000
Standard cost of sales.................		105,000
Standard gross margin		35,000
Manufacturing variances...............	Favorable or (Unfavorable)	
Prime cost variances	$ (3,500)	
Production overhead:		
Spending variance	1,000	
Volume variance	(12,500)	(15,000)
Actual gross margin....................		20,000
Selling and general expenses		27,000
Loss before taxes		$ (7,000)

Questions

1. Explain, as best you can with the data available, why the January profit was $27,000 less than the average monthly profit expected by the president.

2. At what level of monthly volume does Cotter expect to earn exactly zero profit? (Hint: For simplicity, assume that Cotter makes only one product, which has a selling price of $1 per unit.)

3. What was Cotter's January production volume? (Use the hint from Question 2.)

4. How much did finished goods inventory change in January?

5. What were actual production overhead costs in January?

6. Continuing to use the assumption in Question 2's hint, assume further that Cotter's standard prime production costs per unit are as follows: materials, 2.5 pounds at 10 cents; labor, 1.0 minute at $9 per hour. In January, 390,000 pounds of materials were used, at a cost of 9 cents per pound. Total direct labor costs were $28,400 for 2,500 hours. Calculate the four detailed prime cost variances.

Case 20–5   Lupton Company

Lupton Company manufactured two products, for simplicity called here A and B. Lupton used a standard cost system; were a flowchart of this system prepared, it would be identical to the flowchart shown in Illustration 19–1. Thus, the price and usage components of the raw materials variance were captured in the accounts. However, decomposing the labor and production overhead variances required "outside-the-accounts" calculations, which Lupton's management performed on an ad hoc basis rather than routinely. Standards were used without change for the entire calendar year. All monthly variances were closed to the monthly income statement.

The company had hired as a summer employee a student majoring in business administration. In early June, when the May income statement became available, the production manager asked this student to make a detailed analysis of the April and May results (see Exhibit 1). As guidance to the student, as well as to calibrate the student's accounting expertise,

the production manager had prepared a list of questions to answer:

1. In April and May, did we spend more for our production operations than would be expected, assuming our standard costs represent reasonable expectations? (Answer without considering the supplementary data in Exhibit 1.)

2. If actual production overhead costs were the same both months, what could have caused the decrease in unfavorable overhead variance for May?

3. Was April's production level above or below standard volume (which is $123,000 direct labor dollars per month for every month)? (Answer without considering the supplementary data in Exhibit 1.)

4. Was May's production level higher or lower in April's? Was it above or below standard volume? (Answer without considering the supplementary data in Exhibit 1.)

EXHIBIT 1

LUPTON COMPANY
Gross Margin Statements
For April and May

	April		May	
Sales revenues....................		$738,000		$553,500
Cost of sales at standard:				
Materials	$196,800		$147,600	
Direct labor.....................	184,500		123,000	
Overhead.......................	147,600	528,900	98,400	369,000
Gross margin at standard		209,100		184,500
Production variances:				
Materials price	(2,460)		(7,380)	
Materials usage	(1,230)		(3,690)	
Labor	(1,230)		(4,920)	
Overhead.......................	(55,360)	(60,280)	(18,460)	(34,450)
Actual gross margin		$148,820		$150,000

Supplementary Data

1. Debits to Work in Process for materials related to product A totaled $35,055 and $31,365 in April and May, respectively. For product B materials, these debits totaled $1,845 and $79,335, respectively.
2. The direct labor debited to Work in Process in *March* was $135,300. Budgeted production overhead for *March* was $102,090.
3. April's and May's actual production overhead costs were equal.
4. May's actual production overhead costs were equal to the budgeted overhead at standard volume.
5. Product A's standard material cost per unit was $12.30; its full standard cost was $45.51.

5. The percentage decrease in total standard gross margin from April to May was less than the percentage decrease in total sales revenues. What could account for this?

6. In May, the actual purchase price per pound of one of our raw materials decreased. In view of this, how could there have been an increase in the unfavorable materials price variance?

7. Some of this lower priced raw material was put into production in May. What items on the May gross margin statement were affected by this?

8. Some of this lower-priced raw material was included in products that were *sold* in May. How did this af-

fect amounts on the May gross margin statement?

9. Although our standard volume is expressed in terms of direct labor dollars per month, I can't remember whether we absorb overhead on the basis of direct labor dollars or material dollars. Can you figure out which basis we use?

10. What is the standard direct labor cost per unit of product A?

11. Given the information in supplementary data item 1, could performance with respect to total material usage actually have improved from April to May?

12. Was the *combined* dollar balance in

Work in Process and Finished Goods higher or lower at the end of May than it was at the end of April?

13. Did the proportion of product A sold increase from April to May?

14. Given the information in the supplementary data items, what was May's overhead spending variance?

15. What was the overhead production volume variance in May?

16. What was the overhead production volume variance in April?

17. What was the overhead spending variance in April?

Question

Answer, with complete yet concise responses, the production manager's 17 questions.

CASE 20–6 C. F. Church Manufacturing Company

C. F. Church Manufacturing Company was established in 1898 for the purpose of manufacturing toilet seats. The manufacturing process was quite simple. First, the seats were shaped out of wood at a branch plant. They were then shipped to the main plant, where they underwent the particular finishing processes required. Some units were sprayed with paint, but the best seats were coated with cellulose nitrate sheeting. After the seats were coated, the rough edges were filled and the seats were sanded, buffed, and polished. Finally, hinges and rubber bumpers were added, and the seats were packed for shipment. Most operations were performed by hand with the aid of small machines, such as paint spray guns and buffing wheels.

1. Accounting

Collection of Material and Labor Cost. A major part of the work required in the cost system was the accumulation of data on actual and standard costs. The procedure used for materials was as follows. When an order for a particular style was started through the factory, the supervisor of the department that performed the first operation received a manufacturing order. On the basis of this order, the supervisor filled out a stores requisition slip for the necessary materials. Items listed on this requisition subsequently were priced by entering their purchase cost on the requisition on a LIFO basis. (Since raw material was purchased infrequently in large contract lots, this procedure was not difficult.) When seats were ready to be assembled and packed, the assembly department supervisor made out an assembly order (Exhibit 1). This included a requisition for hinges, screws, bumpers, cartons, and fillers, which were also costed at LIFO. The totals of the requisition slips for the month served as the basis for credits to the respective materials inventory accounts and a debit to Work in Process for the cost of material put into process.

The direct labor debit to Work in Process was equally straightforward. Daily, each productive employee made out a time and production report (Exhibit 2) on which he or she recorded the factory order number, the operation, the time spent on each operation, and the number of pieces that he or she had finished. A clerk in the payroll department entered

EXHIBIT 1

ASSEMBLY ORDER №. 6291 Coated		
Date __August__	Plate No. __2000__	
Shipping Order No.		
Work Order No.	Quantity __100__	
Seats 2,000 – 917		
Covers 2,000 – 917		
Hinges 2,000		
Special Instructions		

FOR COST DEPT. ONLY	UNIT COST†		AMOUNT		✓
Material	5	51	551	00	
Labor		92	92	00	
Burden	1	90	190	00	
Total Cost	8	33	833	00	

REQUISITION №. 6291 Hinges – Screws – Bumpers		
Date __August__		

DESCRIPTION		QUANTITY
Hinges 2,000		100
Screws 3/4 x 7		
Screws 5/8 x 7		
1 1/4 x 8		400
Brass Ferrules		200
Bar Bumpers		200
Tack Bumpers		200
Delivered by		

	UNIT COST *	AMOUNT	✓
Hinges			
Screws			
Screws			
Ferrules			
Bar Bumpers			
Tack Bumpers			

REQUISITION №. 6291 Cartons – Fillers		
Date __August__		

DESCRIPTION		QUANTITY
Cartons 25		100
Fillers		200
	800	
	214	100
	105	
Blocks		
Delivered by		

	UNIT COST *	AMOUNT	✓
Cartons			
Filler No. 1			
No. 105			
No. 800			
No. 214			
Blocks			

*These were actual amounts on a LIFO basis.
†These were standard amounts (see Exhibit 4).

EXHIBIT 2

FORM C-
STR 7918

C. F. CHURCH MFG. CO.
Time and Production
Date __August__ —

Employee No. __313__   Name

Order No.	Oper. No.	TIME			Labor or Piece Rate	No. Pieces	Cost		✓
		Started	Finished	Elapsed					
2068	31	7:20	12:00	4.7	3.40	550	18	70	
2068	31	1:00	4:20	3.3	3.40	400	13	60	
								32	30	

the correct piece rate or hourly rate and made the proper extension. The total of the direct labor thus computed provided the credit to the Accrued Wages account and the debit (for direct labor) to Work in Process.

Flexible Overhead Budget (Annual). The debit to Work in Process for production overhead was based on estimates made annually of the relation of monthly overhead expenses to direct labor costs for each department. These estimates were made so that for each department there was available a schedule of standard overhead expenses at varying possible rates of capacity utilization, i.e., a flexible budget. Exhibit 3 illustrates such a budget for the coating department, Department No. 3.

The process used to prepare these departmental flexible overhead budgets was as follows:

1. Determine 100 percent capacity of each department in terms of direct labor-hours and direct labor dollars by theoretically loading each unit of productive machinery and equipment with the number of workers required to operate it, together with the necessary productive employees on floor or benchwork. Consider, however, the normal sales volume of different types of products and limitations as to type of equipment in any one department that affect the capacity of the plant as a whole. For example, output might be limited to the capacity of the coating and spraying departments.

2. Establish monthly overhead expense allowances for each department, considering four general classifications: indirect labor, indirect supplies, fixed charges, and charges from nonproductive (i.e., service) departments.

3. Base allowance for indirect labor and indirect supplies on the past year's experience, making adjustments if necessary for changes in wage rates and the prices of supplies. Compute these projections first for the 100 percent capacity determined above, and from this point use a sliding or graduated scale for the lower percentages of capacity. Give due recognition to the fact that some of these costs do not vary at all with production, that others vary in the same ratio as production, and that others, although not fixed, do not move proportionately with the rate of actual plant activity.

4. Prorate power expense according to the number of horsepower hours used and metered in the respective departments; water expense (after consideration is given to any special demands for water in particular departments) according to the number of employees; insurance, taxes, and depreciation with reference to the net book value of buildings and equipment. Charge directly to the department involved specific insurance that definitely can be assigned to an individual department, such as insurance on trucks in the shipping department or boiler indemnity for the steam department.

5. Distribute the total expense of nonproductive departments such as steam, general plant, shipping, and plant administration to the productive departments on the most logical basis: steam according to floor area, general plant and plant administration according to direct labor-hours, and shipping according to direct labor dollars. The estimated cost of defective work for the whole plant was distributed to operating departments on the basis of the expected distribution of direct labor dollars. This item of expense was included in the total of "Charges from other departments," shown at the bottom of Exhibit 3.

6. Revise the flexible overhead budgets

during the year only for unexpected increases or decreases in wage rates or indirect material costs or an important change in the manufacturing processes.

Standard Overhead Rate. After a department's flexible overhead budget was prepared, executives estimated the average monthly percentage of capacity utilization expected in that department during the coming year. The standard overhead rate was the rate shown on Exhibit 3 for the estimated percentage of capacity. For example, it was estimated that during the year the coating department would operate at an average of 80 percent of capacity. The standard overhead rate for the coating department was therefore 200 percent of direct labor, as shown at the bottom of the 80 percent column in Exhibit 3. The other columns in Exhibit 3 were used for control purposes, as described below.

Actual Overhead Costs (Monthly). Actual overhead costs incurred during the month were debited to the Overhead clearing account in the general ledger and to an appropriate detail account in an overhead subsidiary ledger. There was a detail account for each item listed in Exhibit 3 (supervision, general labor, and so forth) in each department. Service department and other overhead costs were allocated to the producing departments. At the end of the month, the amount of absorbed overhead was calculated by multiplying the overhead rate for each department by the actual direct labor cost of the department for the month. In the coating department, for example, the actual direct labor for August was $5,915.60, and this multiplied by 200 percent gave $11,831.20, the absorbed overhead. (Note that the rate used was the overhead rate determined annually, *not* the overhead rate under the column

in Exhibit 3 that relates to the actual volume of the current month.)

The absorbed overhead for all departments was debited to Work in Process and credited to the Overhead clearing account. Any balance remaining in the Overhead account (i.e., the net overhead variance) was then closed to Cost of Goods Sold. In August, for example, actual overhead was $45,914.98, absorbed overhead was $45,904.44, so $10.54 was debited to Cost of Goods Sold.

Standard Product Costs. Deliveries from work in process to finished goods were recorded by completion in the factory of the assembly order (Exhibit 1). On the lower left corner of that form there was space for the cost department to fill in the standard cost per unit and the total amount of standard cost for the order, and the total of these standard costs entries for a month was credited to Work in Process and debited to Finished Goods Inventory.

The standard costs per unit mentioned in the previous paragraph were prepared for each product in the form illustrated in Exhibit 4. Because the lines on the standard cost sheets were arranged by successive operations, they showed the cumulative cost of a product at the completion of every operation as well as the final cost at which the product was delivered to finished goods inventory. For each operation and for the total cost there was a breakdown that showed separately the standard costs of materials, labor, and overhead. The method of arriving at these costs is described below.

Standard materials costs consisted of a predetermined physical amount per unit priced at the expected purchase price for each classification of raw stock or of finished parts stock. Standard labor costs for the various piece-rate operations were

EXHIBIT 3
FLEXIBLE OVERHEAD BUDGET, DEPARTMENT NO. 3 (COATING)

	100%	95%	90%	85%	80%	75%	70%	65%	60%	50%	40%
Indirect labor:											
01 Supervision	775.00	775.00	775.00	775.00	775.00	775.00	775.00	775.00	775.00	775.00	775.00
08 General labor	625.00	595.00	565.00	535.00	505.00	470.00	440.00	405.00	375.00	315.00	250.00
10 Idle and lost time											
11 Guaranteed rate cost	375.00	356.00	338.00	319.00	300.00	281.00	263.00	244.00	225.00	188.00	150.00
16 Overtime bonus	100.00	100.00	95.00	95.00	90.00	85.00	80.00	75.00	50.00	25.00	25.00
19 Repairs and maint.	175.00	175.00	165.00	165.00	160.00	160.00	160.00	150.00	150.00	100.00	100.00
Total indirect labor	2,050.00	2,001.00	1,938.00	1,889.00	1,830.00	1,771.00	1,718.00	1,649.00	1,575.00	1,403.00	1,300.00
Indirect supplies:											
31 Repairs and maint.	25.00	25.00	25.00	25.00	25.00	20.00	20.00	20.00	15.00	15.00	10.00
35 Acetone and isotone	1,625.00	1,545.00	1,465.00	1,385.00	1,305.00	1,220.00	1,140.00	1,055.00	975.00	815.00	650.00
37 Sandpaper and sandbelts	11.00	10.00	10.00	9.00	9.00	8.00	8.00	7.00	7.00	5.00	4.00
38 Glue and cement	775.00	736.00	700.00	660.00	620.00	580.00	540.00	500.00	465.00	385.00	310.00
41 Consumable supplies	125.00	120.00	112.00	106.00	100.00	94.00	88.00	81.00	75.00	63.00	50.00
42 Loose and hand tools	50.00	48.00	45.00	43.00	40.00	38.00	35.00	33.00	30.00	25.00	20.00
46 Miscellaneous	15.00	14.00	14.00	13.00	12.00	11.00	10.00	9.00	9.00	7.00	6.00
Total indirect supplies	2,626.00	2,498.00	2,371.00	2,241.00	2,111.00	1,971.00	1,841.00	1,705.00	1,576.00	1,315.00	1,050.00
Fixed charges:											
65 Insurance— bldgs. and equip.	21.58	21.58	21.58	21.58	21.58	21.58	21.58	21.58	21.58	21.58	21.58
66 Insurance—L. and C.	161.00	153.00	145.00	137.00	129.00	121.00	113.00	105.00	97.00	80.00	64.00
68 Power	27.00	26.00	24.00	23.00	22.00	21.00	19.00	18.00	16.00	14.00	11.00
69 Water	17.25	17.25	17.25	17.25	17.25	17.25	17.25	17.25	17.25	17.25	17.25
70 Taxes—city and town	28.68	28.68	28.68	28.68	28.68	28.68	28.68	28.68	28.68	28.68	28.68
71 Taxes—social security	530.00	504.00	477.00	450.00	424.00	398.00	371.00	345.00	318.00	265.00	212.00
72 Depreciation	81.25	81.25	81.25	81.25	81.25	81.25	81.25	81.25	81.25	81.25	81.25
73 Provision for vacations	725.40	725.40	725.40	725.40	725.40	725.40	725.40	725.40	725.40	725.40	725.40
78 Group insurance	112.70	112.70	112.70	112.70	112.70	112.70	112.70	112.70	112.70	112.70	112.70
80 Pensions	420.36	420.36	420.36	420.36	420.36	420.36	420.36	420.36	420.36	420.36	420.36
Total fixed charges	2,125.22	2,090.22	2,053.22	2,017.22	1,982.22	1,947.22	1,910.22	1,875.22	1,838.22	1,766.22	1,694.22
Total dept. expense	6,801.22	6,589.22	6,362.22	6,147.22	5,923.22	5,689.22	5,469.22	5,229.22	4,989.22	4,484.22	4,044.22
Charges from other depts.	9,435.37	9,333.33	9,240.12	9,140.56	9,040.03	8,945.27	8,826.90	8,751.83	8,630.42	8,440.11	8,235.38
Total overhead expense	16,236.59	15,922.55	15,602.34	15,287.78	14,963.25	14,634.49	14,296.12	13,981.05	13,619.64	12,924.33	12,279.60
Direct labor dollars	9,375.00	8,906.00	8,437.00	7,969.00	7,500.00	7,031.00	6,562.00	6,094.00	5,625.00	4,687.00	3,750.00
Overhead rate	173%	179%	185%	192%	200%	208%	218%	229%	242%	276%	327%

EXHIBIT 4

Standard Cost				
Date January 1			Plate No. 2000	
Description	Material	Labor	Overhead	Total
Receive woodwork	1.17	0.004	0.008	1.182
Insp. and hand sand		0.012	0.024	1.218
Bottom coat	0.542	0.038	0.076	1.874
Trim T.B. and O.F. seats		0.011	0.022	1.907
Sand edges T.B.C.F. out		0.003	0.008	1.918
Sand edges T.B.C.F. in		0.003	0.008	1.929
Inspect		0.012	0.024	1.965
Top coat	0.543	0.079	0.158	2.745
Shave		0.010	0.020	2.775
Sand edges—upright belt		0.005	0.014	2.794
Sand seats and covers		0.039	0.107	2.940
Inspect and file		0.015	0.030	2.985
Dope		0.004	0.008	2.997
Buff seats and covers		0.108	0.208	3.313
Inspect		0.012	0.024	3.349
Buff repairs		0.044	0.085	3.478
Trademark		0.007	0.014	3.499
Drilling		0.004	0.008	3.511
Total seat	2.255	0.410	0.846	3.511
Total cover no.	1.983	0.399	0.826	3.208
Total seat and cover	4.238	0.809	1.672	6.719
Assemble		0.032	0.064	6.815
Cleanup polish		0.033	0.066	6.914
Seal end of carton		0.006	0.012	6.932
Inspect and wrap		0.034	0.068	7.034
Seat, label, and pack		0.010	0.020	7.064
Bar bumpers	0.043			7.107
Tack bumpers	0.019			7.126
Screws 1¼-8	0.047			7.173
Hinge	1.04			8.213
Carton and filler 2—No. 1	0.125			8.338
Total cost	5.512	0.924	1.902	8.338

simply the current piece rates; in the case of daywork operations, they were the quotients obtained by dividing the daywork rate by an estimated attainable average ouuput. Standard overhead costs were found by multiplying the departmental overhead rates selected for the year by the standard labor costs for the operations concerned. For example, the standard cost sheet for a style calling for a coated finish might show for an operation in the coating department a standard labor charge of $0.079. As indicated above, operations in the coating department for the year were estimated to be at 80 percent of capacity, which for the coating department meant an overhead rate of 200 percent of direct labor. Thus, the standard overhead cost for the coating operation with a labor charge of $0.079 was set at 200 percent of this amount, or $0.158.

These standard product costs were used to price deliveries into finished goods, to cost work in process physical inventories, and to transfer production between accounts. Once the standard costs were prepared, it was expected that they would remain constant for the year, unless there was a significant and unanticipated change in material costs, labor rates, or the departmental overhead rates.

Variances. At the end of each month a physical inventory of raw materials, supplies, work in process, and finished goods was taken. For this inventory, raw materials and supplies were priced on the basis of LIFO purchase cost, and work in process and finished goods were priced according to the standard cost sheets described above. The difference between the inventory thus determined and the book balance of each inventory account was closed into Cost of Goods Sold. The most important of these differences was for work in process inventory.

A work in process statement (Exhibit 5) was prepared each month. This report showed the beginning inventory at standard cost plus actual direct materials, actual labor, and actual absorbed overhead added during the period in each department. From this total cost figure, there were subtracted the actual deliveries to finished goods as indicated on the completed assembly orders, plus defects and less products transferred from Finished Goods back to Work in Process for reworking, all costed at standard cost. The resulting book value of work in process was compared with the figure obtained by valuing, at standard, the results of the physical inventory ($80,959.69). Any difference indicated by this comparison constituted the variance of actual cost from standard and was closed to Cost of Goods Sold. The physical inventory balance at standard constituted the debit to Work in Process at the beginning of the next month. If this Work in Process variance was large, its causes were investigated and action was taken accordingly.

A descriptive summary of the inventory accounts is given in Exhibit 6.

2. Control of Overhead Expenses

Budgeted Overhead Expenses. The company used the departmental flexible overhead budgets to set targets for the supervisors who were responsible for incurring expenses. A knowledge of the actual amount of direct labor for each productive department made it a simple matter to determine which column of figures to use as the benchmark for evaluating the spending performance of each supervisor. For example, the coating department (Exhibit 3) might be expected to operate, on the *average*, at 80 percent of capacity; but in any one month the actual operations might vary considerably from this average. Thus, if direct labor dropped to $7,031, the supervisor would be expected to spend only $580 for glue and cement rather than the $620 allowable at the average operating level. For nonproductive departments, the budget column selected was the one that listed the expenses expected for the percentage of capacity nearest the average operating level of all productive departments.

Comparison of Actual and Budget. The departmental comparisons of the actual overhead expenses, by accounts, with the appropriate budgeted allowance for that volume, are illustrated in the departmental budget sheet, Exhibit 7. The August budgeted expense figures for the coating department are based upon an output level of 65 percent of capacity. This figure was arrived at by comparing

EXHIBIT 5

Work in Process

Period Ending August   Order No. GENERAL

Detail	Amount					
Balance from Last Period				158	597	19
DIRECT MATERIALS				76	338	21
DIRECT LABOR						
1 Varnish						
2 Spray	2	990	25			
3 Coating	5	915	60			
4 Filing		998	83			
5 Sanding	1	637	53			
6 Buffing & Polishing	6	175	78			
8 Assembling and Packing	4	788	60			
Total Direct Labor				22	506	59
OVERHEAD						
1 Varnish						
2 Spray	6	180	50			
3 Coating	11	831	20			
4 Filing	1	937	73			
5 Sanding	4	489	05			
6 Buffing & Polishing	11	888	76			
8 Assembling and Packing	9	577	20			
10 Shipping						
Total Overhead				45	904	44
TOTAL COST				303	346	43
Less Deliveries				222	386	74
BALANCE IN PROCESS at Std. Cost				80	959	69

DELIVERIES AT Std. Cost

Date		Amount		Date		Amount		Date		Amount	
8/31	Del.	220	876	63							
	Var.	1	259	07							
	Defect.		251	04							
	Net	222	386	74							

the actual direct labor expense for the month, amounting to $5,915.60, to the closest corresponding direct labor expense, $6,094, which is under the 65 percent column shown on Exhibit 3. (Exhibit 7 is a standard form, and only those lines that are pertinent to the operations of the coating department are filled in on the example shown.)

Exhibit 7 also showed two items over

EXHIBIT 6
SUMMARY OF ENTRIES TO INVENTORY ACCOUNTS
August

Raw Materials

(Several accounts according to nature of material)

$151,204 Balance

$343,640.19 Purchases at invoice cost (credit to Accounts Payable).

$1,101.67 Materials salvaged from returned goods (credit to Cost of Goods Sold).

$76,318.21 Requisitions, priced at last-in, first-out cost (debit to Work in Process).

$138.32 Adjustment to physical inventory (Dr. or Cr.).

A physical inventory of all raw materials was taken each month and the difference between inventory and book balance written off to Cost of Goods Sold.

Work in Process

$158,597.19 Balance

$76,318.21 Direct materials from requisitions priced at last-in, first-out cost (credit to Raw Materials).

$22,506.59 Direct labor from payroll summary (credit to Accrued Wages).

$20.00 Materials purchased not usually carried in inventory (credit to Accounts Payable).

$17.61 Transfers from finished goods for re-working or alteration, at standard cost (credit to Finished Goods).

$45,904.44 Absorbed overhead from overhead summary sheet (credit to Overhead).

$220,894.24 Deliveries to finished goods at standard costs (debit to Finished Goods).

$251.04 Defective work, from defective work order (debit to Overhead).

$1,259.07 Adjustment to physical inventory (Dr. or Cr.)

A physical inventory was taken of all work in process every month. This was priced and totaled according to standard costs at last operation performed; the difference between the inventory and balance in the Work in Process account, representing the cost variation, was written off to Cost of Goods Sold.

Finished Goods

$429,682.73 Balance

$220,894.24 Deliveries to finished goods at standard costs (credit to Work in Process).

$400,954.09 Shipment at standard costs (debit to Cost of Goods Sold).

$17.61 Transfers to work in process for re-working or alteration at standard cost (debit to Work in Process).

EXHIBIT 7

C. F. CHURCH MFG. CO.

HOLYOKE

Analysis of Overhead Expenses

DEPARTMENT #3 Coating   Month August

		Budget	Actual Expense	Over or Under Actual	
1	INDIRECT LABOR				1
2	01 Supervision	7 7 5 00	7 5 6 00	1 9 00	2
3	04 Truck Drivers & Helpers				3
4	06 Shipping				4
5	08 General Labor	4 0 5 00	1 7 1 22	2 3 3 78	5
6	09 Repair and Rework				6
7	10 Idle and Lost Time		1 77	(1 77)	7
8	11 Guaranteed Rate Cost	2 4 4 00	2 8 14	2 1 5 86	8
9	16 Overtime Bonus	7 5 00	3 2 98	4 2 02	9
10	19 Repairs & Maint.	1 5 0 00	3 8 26	1 1 1 74	10
11	17 Vacations		4 6 00	(4 6 00)	11
12	21 Paid Holidays				12
13	Total	1 6 4 9 00	1 0 7 4 37	5 7 4 63	13
14	INDIRECT SUPPLIES				14
15	31 Repairs & Maint.	2 0 00	3 6 0 18	(3 4 0 18)	15
16	33 Repairs & Maint. Trucks				16
17	35 Acetone & Isotone	1 0 5 5 00	7 3 9 48	3 1 5 52	17
18	36 Buffing Compounds & Buffs				18
19	37 Sandpaper & Sandbelts	7 00	9 60	(2 60)	19
20	39 Labels, Tape, etc., Glue & Cement	5 0 0 00	7 3 4 71	(2 3 4 71)	20
21	40 Shipping Cartons				21
22	41 Consumable Supplies	8 1 00	5 5 54	2 5 46	22
23	42 Loose & Hand Tools	3 3 00	1 3 55	1 9 45	23
24	46 Miscellaneous	9 00	7 51	1 49	24
25	Total	1 7 0 5 00	1 9 2 0 57	(2 1 5 57)	25
26	OTHER OVERHEAD expenses:				26
27	Insurance, power, taxes, social				27
28	security, depreciation, group				28
29	insurance & pension	1 8 7 5 22	1 4 7 2 46	4 0 2 76	29
30					30
31	DEFECTIVE WORK (memo)	6 0 0 00	2 5 1 04	3 4 8 96	31
32					32
33	DIRECT LABOR	6 0 9 4 00	5 9 1 5 60	1 7 8 40	33
34					34
35					35
36					36
37					37
38					38
39					39
40					40

which the supervisor had no control. Other Overhead expenses was the total amount of fixed charges allocated to the department on the basis of the percentage distributions described earlier. Defective Work was the total amount of defective work budgeted ($600) and actual ($251.04) for the *entire plant*, and it bore no direct relation to the work done in the coating department. The amount allocated to each department for defective work was not shown on Exhibit 7 because the basis of allocation was considered too arbitrary. The amounts for both Other Overhead expenses and for Defective Work were shown in the Analysis of Overhead Expenses principally as a matter of information for the supervisor. They were not considered as being controllable by the supervisor.

Each month the accounting department prepared Exhibit 8, summarizing the actual, budgeted, and absorbed overhead costs for each operating department. The amount shown as Actual Expense was obtained by adding the Charges from Other Departments to the other overhead items shown in Exhibit 7 (excluding defective work). The Budgeted Expense was the total overhead for each department as shown on the flexible overhead budget (Exhibit 3 for the coating department) at the applicable level of operations (65 percent for the coating department in August).

The amount of Absorbed Expense was computed by applying the *annual* overhead rate to the direct labor in each productive department, as explained in the preceding section.

In the opinion of the management the entries in the column headed (Loss) or Gain on Budget could be considered a measure of the effectiveness of departmental supervision, whereas the amount Over- or (Under-) absorbed was influenced both by efficiency and by the volume of production.

The departmental overhead budget constituted the point of real control over expenditures. At the end of each month, the factory manager met with the cost accountant and the supervisors to discuss spending. At these meetings the supervisors were encouraged to discuss their performance as indicated by the budget report. When the system was first installed, the cost accountant did most of the talking, but with increasing familiarity with the costs for which they were responsible, each supervisor gradually became "cost conscious," and after a short time each supervisor knew approximately what the monthly performance would be, even before seeing the budget comparison report.

The supervisor in charge of the coating department was particularly interested in

EXHIBIT 8
OVERHEAD SUMMARY AND STATISTICS

Plant—Holyoke   Period Ending—August 31

Dept. No.	Description	Direct Labor	Actual Expense	Budgeted Expense	(Loss) or Gain on Budget	Absorbed Expense	Over- or (Under-) absorbed
1							
2	Spray	2,990.25	6,464.64	7,103.64	639.00	6,180.50	(284.14)
3	Coating	5,915.60	12,829.53	13,981.05	1,151.52	11,831.20	(998.33)
4	Filing	998.83	2,590.83	2,190.20	(400.63)	1,937.73	(653.10)
5	Sanding	1,637.53	3,907.74	5,243.47	1,335.73	4,489.05	581.31
6	Buffing	6,175.78	11,275.76	10,750.25	(525.51)	11,888.76	613.00
7							
8	Assemble and pack	4,788.60	8,846.48	8,998.58	152.10	9,577.20	730.73
	Total plant	22,506.59	45,914.98	48,267.19	2,352.21	45,904.44	(10.54)

EXHIBIT 9
SUMMARY OF PERFORMANCE IN THE COATING DEPARTMENT

	April		May		June		August	
	Actual	(Over) or Under	Actual	(Over) or Under	Actual	(Over) or Under	Actual	(Over) or Under
01 Supervision	811	(36)	782	(7)	756	19	756	19
08 General labor	654	(119)	558	(23)	418	22	171	234
10 Idle and lost time	—	—	—	—	—	—	2	(2)
11 Guaranteed rate cost	313	6	154	165	50	213	28	216
16 Overtime bonus	63	32	45	50	37	43	33	42
19 Repairs and maint	89	76	30	135	35	125	38	112
17 Vacations	—	—	—	—	—	—	46	(46)
Total	1,930	(41)	1,569	320	1,296	422	1,074	575
Indirect supplies:								
31 Repairs and maint	5	20	85	(60)	176	(156)	360	(340)
35 Acetone and isotone	1,300	85	1,134	251	1,031	109	739	316
37 Sandpaper and sandbelts	10	(1)	14	(5)	5	3	10	(3)
39 Labels, tape, glue, and cement	575	85	462	199	182	358	735	(235)
41 Consumable supplies	66	40	116	(10)	48	40	56	25
42 Loose and hand tools	37	6	14	29	10	25	14	19
46 Miscellaneous	27	(14)	9	3	9	1	8	1
Total	2,020	221	1,834	407	1,461	380	1,922	(217)
Other overhead: Insurance, power, taxes, social security, deprec., group insur., pension	1,456	561	2,014	3	1,836	74	1,472	403
Defective work (memo)	391	209	656	(56)	594	6	251	349
Direct labor	7,812	157	8,024	(55)	6,599	(36)	5,916	178

controlling the overhead costs under his jurisdiction. During the first week of September, he received the analysis of overhead expenses for August (Exhibit 7), and he checked all the items carefully to learn if there were any costs out of line with his expectations for that month. He copied the August figures onto a sheet (Exhibit 9) on which he had previously summarized the figures for recent months (except for July, which included a vacation shutdown). After he felt that he had a good idea of his cost position, he arranged for a meeting with the factory manager and the cost accountant to review the situation with them.

Questions

1. What are the major purposes of the standards developed by the company?

2. How does the company develop standard overhead rates? How often do you think they should be changed?

3. What steps are involved in the development of the standard cost sheet (Exhibit 4)? How accurate do you judge the figures to be?

4. Try to explain fully the basis of each entry in Exhibit 6. In particular, what are the possible causes of the $138.32 credit to Raw Materials and the $1,259.07 credit to Work in Process labeled "Adjustment to physical inventory" in Exhibit 6?

5. Reconcile the amounts in Exhibit 5 with the entries shown in Exhibit 6.

6. Explain so as to distinguish them clearly from one another, the figures $12,829.53, $13,981.05, and $11,831.20 shown for the coating department on Exhibit 8.

7. If you were the plant manager, what evaluation would you make of the performance of the coating department supervisor in controlling his overhead costs? About which items in Exhibits 7 and 9 would you be likely to question him?

8. How many dollars of the coating department variances reported in Exhibit 8 are attributable to "Charges from Other Departments"? Of what significance are these variances to (a) the coating department and (b) the service departments that created these charges? Should they be included in the overhead summary and statistics report?

21

Differential Accounting:
Short-Run Decisions

This chapter begins a discussion of the second management accounting information construct, differential accounting. The concept of differential costs (and also differential revenues) is introduced and contrasted with the full cost concept. The use of differential accounting in the analysis of several types of problems, each having a relatively short time horizon, is described. These problems are called alternative choice problems because in each instance the manager seeks to choose the best one of several alternative courses of action. Alternative choice problems involving longer time horizons will be discussed in Chapter 22.

THE DIFFERENTIAL CONCEPT

Cost Constructions for Various Purposes

Chapters 17–19 discussed the measurement of full costs, which is one type of cost construction. In this chapter we introduce a second main type of cost construction, called *differential costs*. Some people have difficulty in accepting the idea that there is more than one type of cost construction. They say, "When I pay a company $180 for a desk, the desk surely cost me $180. How could the cost be anything else?" It is appropriate therefore that we establish the points that (1) "cost" does have more than one meaning; (2) differences in cost constructions relate to the purpose for which the cost information is to be used; and (3) unless these differences are understood, serious mistakes can be made.

To explain these points, consider a company that manufactures and sells desks. According to its cost accounting records, the full cost of making and marketing a certain desk is $200. Suppose that a customer offered to buy such a desk for $180. If the company considered that the only relevant cost for this desk was the $200 full cost, it would of course refuse the order. Its revenue would be only $180 and its costs would be $200; therefore, the management would conclude that it would incur a loss of $20 on the order. But it might well be that the additional *out-of-pocket* costs of making and selling this one desk—the lumber and other material, the earnings of the cabinetmaker who worked on the desk, and the commission to the salesperson—would be only $125. The other items making up the $200 *full* cost were items of cost that would not be affected by this one order. The management might therefore decide to accept this order at $180. If it did, the company's costs would increase by $125, its revenue would increase by $180, and its income would increase by the difference, $55. Thus, the company would be $55 better off by accepting this order than by refusing it. Evidently, in this problem the wrong decision could be made if the company relied on the full cost information.

In this example, we used both $200 and $125 as measures of the "cost" of the desk. These numbers represent two types of cost constructions, each of which is used for a different purpose. The $200 measures the full cost of the desk, which is the cost used for the purposes described in Chapter 17. The $125 is another type of cost construction, and it is used for other pruposes, one of which is to decide, under certain circumstances, whether an order for the desk should be accepted. We shall label this latter type of cost construction *differential cost*.

Differential Costs and Revenues

Differential costs are costs that are different under one set of conditions than they would be under another set of conditions.[1] Differential costs always relate to a specific situation. In the previous example, the differential cost of the desk was $125. Under another set of circumstances—for example, if a similar problem arose several days later—the differential costs might be something other than $125. The differential cost to the *buyer* of the desk was $180; the buyer incurred a cost of $180 that would not have been incurred if the desk had not been purchased.

The differential concept also applies to revenues. *Differential revenues* are those that are different under one set of conditions than they would be under another set of conditions. In the desk example, the differential revenue of the desk manufacturer was $180; its revenue would

---

[1]Differential costs are also called *relevant* costs, but this term is not descriptive. All types of cost constructions are relevant for certain types of problems.

differ by $180 if it accepted the order for the desk from what revenue would be if it did not accept the order.

Contrasts with Full Costs

There are three important differences between full costs and differential costs.

1. Nature of the Cost. The full cost of a product or other cost objective is the sum of its direct costs plus an equitable share of applicable indirect costs. Differential costs include only those elements of cost that are different under a certain set of conditions. This is the most important distinction between full costs and differential costs.

In the example of the desk given above, the volume, or output, of the desk manufacturer would be higher, by one desk, if it accepted the order compared with what volume would have been if it did not accept the order. The proposal under consideration therefore had an effect on volume as well as on costs. This is the case with a great many problems involving differential costs. A thorough understanding of the cost behavior concepts discussed in Chapter 16 is therefore a prerequisite for the analysis of many differential accounting problems.

2. Source of Data. Information of full costs is taken directly from a company's cost accounting system. That system is designed to measure full costs on a regular basis, and to report these costs routinely. There is no comparable system for collecting differential costs. The appropriate items that constitute differential costs are assembled to meet the analytical requirements of a specific problem.

Since the cost items that are differential in a given problem depend on the nature of that specific problem, it is not possible to identify items of differential cost in the accounting system and to collect these costs on a regular basis. Instead, the accounting system is designed so that it can furnish the raw data that are useful in *estimating* the differential costs for a specific problem. If feasible, an accounting system should be designed so that—

a. It identifies items of *variable costs* separately from items of fixed cost.

b. It identifies the *direct costs* of various cost objectives.

In many companies, this can be done by the proper classification of accounts. Direct material costs and direct labor costs are variable costs, so no special identification is needed for them. For indirect production costs and for selling, general, and administrative costs, items of cost that are variable may be identified as such in the account structure. Similarly, items of cost that are direct with respect to the principal cost objectives may be separately identified in the accounts. This is done, of course, only to the extent that such separate identification is believed to be worthwhile.

3. Time Perspective. The full cost accounting system collects historical costs; that is, it measures what the costs *were*. For some purposes, such as setting prices, these historical costs are adjusted to reflect the estimated impact of future conditions. But for other purposes, such as financial reporting, the historical costs are used without change. *Differential costs always relate to the future;* they are intended to show what the costs *would be* if a certain course of action were adopted, rather than what the costs *were.*

CONTRIBUTION ANALYSIS

In calculating break-even volume (Chapter 16), the notion of unit contribution was introduced. In this section, this notion is extended to a technique called *contribution analysis.* We do so both because contribution analysis is an important tool in analyzing differential costs, and also because in explaining the technique we can clarify the relationships among, and differences between, variable costs, fixed costs, direct costs, indirect costs, full costs, and differential costs. Contribution analysis focuses on what is called the contribution margin.

The *contribution margin* for a company, or for a product line, division, or other segment of a company, is the difference between its total revenues and its total variable costs.[2] Illustration 21–1 contrasts the conventional income statement for a laundry and dry cleaning company with the same data rearranged so as to measure the contribution margin for each of its two services. Analysis of the underlying records shows that of the $21,000 total revenues in June, $16,200 was earned on dry cleaning work and $4,800 on laundry. The expense items[3] on the income statement were analyzed to determine which amounts were variable, and of these, how much was attributable to dry cleaning and how much to laundry. Of the total amount of $9,900 for salaries and wages, $3,900 of wages was a variable expense of dry cleaning and $2,100 was a variable expense of laundry. The remaining $3,900 of salaries was a fixed expense applicable to the business as a whole. The other variable expenses were found to be supplies and power. The total amount of variable expense was $9,150 for dry cleaning and $3,150 for laundry.

The contribution margin, which is the difference between revenues and total variable expenses, was therefore $7,050 for dry cleaning and $1,650 for laundry.

In addition to variable expenses, dry cleaning had $1,800 of direct

---

[2] We use *contribution margin* for the difference between *total* revenues and *total* variable costs, and we use *marginal income* or *unit contribution* for the difference *per unit.* The term *unit contribution margin* is often used in practice instead of marginal income.

[3] Since this is an income statement, amounts deducted from revenues are called expenses. As pointed out in Chapter 3, expenses are one type of cost. Thus, although the description in this chapter uses the broader term *costs,* it applies equally well to that type of cost that is labeled *expense.*

ILLUSTRATION 21–1
CONTRAST BETWEEN CONVENTIONAL AND CONTRIBUTION MARGIN INCOME
STATEMENTS

A. Income Statement—Conventional Basis
Month of June

Revenues		$21,000
Expenses:		
Salaries and wages	$9,900	
Supplies	5,400	
Heat, light, and power	1,200	
Advertising	600	
Rent	2,100	
Depreciation on equipment	2,400	
Other (telephone, insurance, etc.)	900	
Total expense		22,500
Income (loss)		$(1,500)

B. Income Statement—Contribution Margin Basis
Month of June

	Dry Cleaning	Laundry
Revenues	$16,200	$4,800
Variable expenses:		
Wages	$3,900	$2,100
Supplies	4,500	900
Power	750	150
Total variable expenses	9,150	3,150
Contribution margin	7,050	1,650
Direct fixed expenses:		
Depreciation on equipment	1,800	600
Contribution to indirect expenses	5,250	1,050
Total contribution	$6,300	
Indirect fixed expenses:		
Salaries	$3,900	
Heat and light	300	
Advertising	600	
Rent	2,100	
Other	900	
Total indirect fixed expenses	7,800	
Income (loss)	$(1,500)	

fixed expense; this was the depreciation on the dry cleaning equipment. Laundry had $600 of direct fixed expenses. Subtracting these direct, but fixed, expenses from the contribution margin shows how much each service contributed to the indirect fixed costs of the business. These amounts were $5,250 for dry cleaning and $1,050 for laundry, a total of $6,300. Since the total of the indirect fixed costs was $7,800, this contribution was not large enough to produce income for the month. The difference was the loss of $1,500.

Types of Cost

We shall use these numbers to review the types of costs previously discussed:

- *Variable costs* (here expenses) are $9,150 for dry cleaning and $3,150 for laundry. They are variable because they vary proportionately with the volume of dry cleaning and laundry done.
- *Fixed costs* are the $2,400 of depreciation on equipment plus the $7,800 of indirect fixed expenses, a total of $10,200.
- *Direct costs* of the two services (cost objectives) include not only the variable costs ($12,300) but also the depreciation of the dry cleaning equipment ($1,800) and of the laundry equipment ($600), a total of $14,700. These are direct because they are *traced* directly to the separate services, but they are not all variable costs because the amount of depreciation does not change with the volume of work done.
- *Indirect costs* are those amounts (totaling $7,800) that are not traced directly either to dry cleaning or to laundry.
- *Full costs* are not shown in the analysis. In order to obtain full costs, it would be necessary to allocate the $7,800 of indirect costs to dry cleaning and to laundry on some equitable basis.

In the above list, we omitted mention of *differential* costs. This is because differential costs cannot be identified in general. Rather, they must always be related to a specific alternative choice problem.

> **Example.** Suppose the management is considering certain actions that are intended to increase the volume of dry cleaning work and it asks how increased volume will affect income. In this situation, the differential costs are the variable costs (and the revenue is, of course, differential revenue). Each additional dollar of dry cleaning business is expected to add 44 cents to profit, the percentage of contribution margin to sales revenues (i.e., $7,050 \div $16,200 = 44$ percent).

The message conveyed by the contribution analysis statement differs from the message conveyed by the conventional income statement. The income statement indicates that the business operated at a loss. Moreover, if the indirect expenses were allocated to the two services in proportion, say, to their variable expenses, each of the two services would also show a loss, viz:

	Total	Dry Cleaning	Laundry
Contribution to indirect expenses..........	$ 6,300	$5,250	$1,050
Allocated indirect expenses	7,800	5,802	1,998
Income (loss)	$(1,500)	$ (552)	$ (948)

From these numbers, someone might conclude that one or the other of these services should be discontinued in order to reduce losses. By contrast, the contribution analysis shows that each of the services made a contribution to indirect costs and that the total loss of the business would therefore not be reduced by discontinuing either of them. This type of analysis will be discussed further in a later section of this chapter.

ALTERNATIVE CHOICE PROBLEMS

In an *alternative choice problem,* two or more alternative courses of action are specified and the manager chooses the one that he or she believes to be the best.[4] In many alternative choice problems, the choice is made on a strictly judgmental basis. That is, there is no systematic attempt to define, measure, and assess the advantages and disadvantages of each alternative. Persons who make judgmental decisions may do so simply because they are not aware of any other way of making up their minds, or they may do so because the problem is one in which a systematic attempt to assess alternatives is too difficult, too expensive, or simply not possible. No mathematical formula will help solve a problem in which the attitudes of the individuals involved are dominant factors. Nor is there any point in trying to make calculations if the available information is so sketchy or inaccurate that the results would be completely unreliable.

In many other situations, however, it is useful to reduce at least some of the potential consequences of each alternative to a quantitative basis and to weigh these consequences in a systematic manner. In this and the next chapter, we discuss techniques for making such an analysis.

Business Objectives In an alternative choice problem, the manager seeks the alternative most likely to accomplish the objectives of the organization. When investors furnish funds to a business, they do so in the expectation of earning a return, that is, a profit, on these investments. Presumably the more profit that is earned on a given investment, the greater the satisfaction of the investors. This idea leads to the economists' statement that the objective of a company is to *maximize the return on investment* (ROI).

The maximization idea, however, is too difficult to apply in most practical situations. The manager does not know, out of all the alternative courses of action available, which one will produce the absolute maximum ROI. Furthermore, many actions that could increase ROI are ethically unacceptable. For these reasons, the idea that an important objective of a business is to earn a *satisfactory* return on its investment is more realistic and more ethically sound.

Satisfactory ROI is important, but it is by no means the only objective of a business. In many practical problems, personal satisfaction, friendship, community responsibilities, or other considerations may be much

---

[4]In a broad sense, *all* business problems involve a choice among alternatives. The problems discussed here are those in which the alternatives are clearly specified.

more important than ROI. The company may have other measurable objectives, such as maintenance of its market position, stabilization of employment, or increasing its reported net income. When these considerations are dominant, the solution to the problem cannot be reached by the techniques discussed here. The most these techniques can do is show the effect on ROI of seeking some other objective.

Thus, the decision maker seeks *a* course of action which will produce a satisfactory ROI. If there are two alternative solutions to a problem, the manager will choose the one which is likely to yield the *greater* ROI, provided this is consistent with other objectives. If the amount of investment is unaffected by the decision, then the preferred alternative is the one resulting in the higher profit.

Steps in the Analysis

The analysis of most alternative choice problems involves the following steps:

1. Define the problem.
2. Select possible alternative solutions.
3. Measure those consequences of each selected alternative that can be expressed in quantitative terms.
4. Identify those consequences that cannot be expressed in quantitative terms and weigh them against each other and against the measured consequences.
5. Reach a decision.

We shall focus primarily on information that can be expressed in quantitative terms. Thus, we are here interested primarily in step 3 of the above list. Brief mention will be made of the other steps.

Steps 1 and 2: Define the Problem and Alternative Solutions. Unless the problem is clearly and precisely defined, quantitative amounts that are relevant to its solution cannot be determined. In many situations, the definition of the problem may be the most difficult part of the whole process. Moreover, even after the problem has been identified, the possible alternative solutions to it may not be obvious.

> **Example.** A factory manager is considering a proposal to buy a certain machine to produce a part that is now being produced manually. At first glance, there appear to be two alternatives: (*a*) continue to make the part by manual methods or (*b*) buy the new machine. Actually, however, several additional alternatives should be considered: (*c*) buy a machine other than the one proposed, (*d*) improve the present manual method, or even (*e*) eliminate the manufacturing operation altogether, and buy the part from an outside source. Some thought should be given to these other possibilities before attention is focused too closely on the original proposal.

On the other hand, the more alternatives that are considered, the more complex the analysis becomes. For this reason, having identified all the possible alternatives, the analyst should eliminate on a judgmental basis those that are clearly unattractive, leaving only a few for detailed analysis.

In most problems, one alternative is to continue what is now being done, that is, to reject a proposed change. This status quo alternative is called the *base case.* It is used as a benchmark against which other alternatives are compared.

Step 3: Measure the Quantitative Factors. Usually, many advantages and disadvantages are associated with each alternative. The decision maker's task is to evaluate each relevant factor and to decide, on balance, which alternative has the largest net advantage. If the factors, or variables, are expressed solely in words, such an evaluation is an exceedingly difficult task.

> **Example.** Consider the statement: "A proposed production process will save labor, but it will result in increased power consumption and require additional insurance protection." Such a statement provides no way of weighing the relative importance of the saving in labor against the increased power and insurance costs. If, by contrast, the statement is: "The proposed process will save $1,000 in labor, but power costs will increase by $200 and insurance costs will increase by $100," the net effect of these three factors can easily be determined; that is, $1,000 - ($200 + $100) indicates a net advantage of $700 for the proposed process.

The reason for expressing as many factors as possible in quantitative terms is demonstrated in the above example: once this is done, one can find the net effect of these factors simply by addition and subtraction.

Step 4: Evaluate the Unmeasured Factors. For most problems, there are important factors that are not measurable. Yet the final decision must take into account both measurable and unmeasurable differences between the alternatives. The process of weighing the relative importance of these unmeasured factors, both as compared with one another and as compared with the net advantage or disadvantage of the measured factors, is a judgmental process.

It is easy to overlook the importance of these unmeasured factors. The numerical calculations for the measured factors often require hard work and result in a number that appears to be definite and precise. Yet all the factors that influence the final number may be collectively less important than a single factor that cannot be measured. For example, many persons could meet their transportation needs less expensively by using public conveyances rather than by operating an automobile; but they nevertheless own a car for reasons of prestige, convenience, or other factors that cannot be measured quantitatively.

To the extent that calculations can be made, it is possible to express as a single number the net effect of many factors that bear on the decision. The calculations therefore reduce the number of factors that must be considered separately in the final judgment process that leads to the decision. That is, they narrow the area within which judgment must be exercised. Rarely, if ever, do they eliminate the necessity for this crucial judgment process.

Step 5: Reach a Decision. After the first attempt to identify, evaluate, and weigh the factors, the decision maker has two choices: (1) seek additional information or (2) make a decision and act on it. Many decisions could be improved by obtaining additional information, and it is usually obtainable. However, obtaining the additional information always involves effort (which means cost), and more importantly, it involves time. There comes a point, therefore, when the manager concludes that it is better to act than to defer a decision until more data have been collected.

DIFFERENTIAL COSTS

Earlier in this chapter we introduced the type of cost construction called differential costs. Since differential costs are normally used in analyzing alternative choice problems, we now discuss them in more depth.

If some alternative to the base case or status quo is proposed, differential costs are those that will be different under the proposed alternative than they are in the base case. Items of cost that will be unaffected by the proposal are not differential and can be disregarded. The term *out-of-pocket costs* is used generally to mean the same thing as differential cost. There is no general category of costs that can be labeled *differential;* that is, differential costs always relate to the specific alternatives being analyzed.

Example. A company is considering buying Part No. 101 from an outside supplier instead of manufacturing the part. The base case (case 1) is to continue manufacturing Part No. 101, and the alternative (or case 2) is to purchase it from the outside supplier. All revenue items, selling and administrative expenses, and production costs other than those directly associated with the manufacture of Part No. 101 will probably be unaffected by the decision. If so, there is no need to consider them. Items of differential cost could be as follows:

	If Part No. 101 Is Manufactured (base case)	If Part No. 101 Is Purchased (Case 2)	Difference −	+
Direct material	$ 570	$ 0	$ 570	
Purchased parts	0	1,700		$1,700
Direct labor	600	0	600	
Power	70	0	70	
Other costs	150	0	150	
Total	$1,390	$1,700	$1,390	$1,700
				−1,390
Net differential cost				$ 310

Since costs would be increased by $310 if Part No. 101 were purchased, the indication is that the proposal to purchase Part No. 101 should be rejected.

Mechanics of the Calculation

There is no prescribed format for comparing the differential costs of several alternatives. The arrangement should be that which is most convenient and which most clearly sets forth the facts to the decision maker.

> **Example.** For the problem described in the preceding example, the same result can be obtained, with somewhat less effort, by finding the net differences between the alternatives, viz:

Purchase price of Part No. 101		$1,700
Costs saved by not manufacturing Part No. 101:		
Direct material	$570	
Direct labor	600	
Power	70	
Other costs	150	
Total costs saved		− 1,390
Net disadvantage in purchasing		$ 310

Costs that Are Unaffected. Although cost items unaffected by the decision are not differential and may be disregarded, a listing of some or all of these unaffected costs nevertheless may be useful. If this is done, it is essential that the unaffected costs be treated in exactly the same way under each of the alternatives. The net difference between the costs of the two alternatives, which is the result sought, is not changed by adding equal amounts to the cost of each alternative.

> **Example.** Part No. 101 is a component of product A. It may be convenient to list each of the items of cost and the revenue of product A for each of the alternatives, as in Illustration 21–2. The difference in profit is the same $310 arrived at in the earlier examples, because the proposal to purchase Part No. 101 had no effect on product A revenue, nor on product A costs, other than those already listed.

The calculation in Illustration 21–2 requires somewhat more effort than those in the preceding examples, but it may be easier to understand. Also, the practice of listing each item of cost and revenue may help to ensure that no items of differential cost are overlooked.

Danger of Using Full Cost. The full costs that are measured in a full cost accounting system may be misleading in alternative choice problems. In particular, when estimating differential costs, items of cost that are *allocated* to products should be viewed with skepticism. For example, a company may allocate production overhead costs to products as 100 percent of direct labor costs. But this does *not* mean that if direct labor costs are decreased by $600 there will be a corresponding decrease

ILLUSTRATION 21–2
CALCULATION OF DIFFERENTIAL PROFIT

	Profit on Product A	
	Base Case	Purchase of Part No. 101
Revenue...............................	$10,000	$10,000
Costs:		
Direct material......................	$1,570	$1,000
Purchased parts	0	1,700
Direct labor........................	3,000	2,400
Power..............................	200	130
Other costs........................	1,450	1,300
Occupancy costs	800	800
General and administrative	2,000	2,000
Total costs	9,020	9,330
Profit...............................	980	$ 670
	−670 ←	
Differential profit of base case.........	$ 310	

of $600 in overhead costs. Overhead costs may not decrease at all; they may decrease, but by an amount less than $600; or they may even increase, as a result of an increased procurement and inspection work load resulting from the purchase of Part No. 101. In order to estimate what will actually happen to overhead costs, one must go behind the overhead rate and analyze what will happen to the various elements of overhead cost.

Example. The full costs of product A shown in Illustration 21–2 included $800 for occupancy costs and $2,000 for general and administrative costs. Occupancy cost is the cost of the building in which product A is manufactured, and the $800 represents the share of total occupancy cost allocated to product A. If Part No. 101, one part in product A, is purchased, the floor space in which Part No. 101 is now manufactured no longer would be required. It does not necessarily follow, however, that occupancy costs would thereby be reduced. The costs of rent, heat, light, and other items of occupancy cost might not be changed at all by the decision to purchase Part No. 101. Unless the actual amount of occupancy cost were changed, this item of cost is not differential.

Similarly, general and administrative costs of the whole company probably would be unaffected by a decision to purchase Part No. 101. Unless these costs would be affected, they are not differential.

Fringe Benefits. Labor costs are an important item of cost in many decisions. The real cost of labor is significantly higher than the actual amount of wages earned. It includes such items as the employer's share of social security taxes; insurance, medical, and pension plans; vacation and holiday pay; and other fringe benefits. In general, these benefits average about 35 percent of wages earned. In estimating differential labor costs, fringe benefits usually should be taken into account.

Opportunity Costs. *Opportunity cost* measures the value of the opportunity that is lost or sacrificed when the choice of one course of action requires that an alternative course of action be given up. Opportunity costs are not measured in accounting records, and they are not relevant in many alternative choice problems. They are significant, however, in situations where resources are *constrained* (i.e., limited). In such situations, a decision to undertake a certain activity precludes performing some other activity. In general, if accepting an alternative requires that facilities or other resources must be devoted to that alternative that otherwise could be used for some other purpose, there is an opportunity cost. This cost is measured by the income that would have been earned had the resources been devoted to the other purpose.

> **Example.** If the floor space required to make Part No. 101 can be used for some other profit-producing purpose, then the sacrifice involved in using it for Part No. 101 is an opportunity cost of making that part. This cost is measured by the *income* that would be sacrificed if the floor space is used for Part No. 101; this is not likely the same as the *allocated* occupancy cost. If the floor space used for Part No. 101 could be used to manufacture another item that could be sold for a profit of $400, the $400 then becomes a cost of continuing to manufacture Part No. 101.

Opportunity costs are by their very nature "iffy." In most situations, it is extremely difficult to estimate what, if any, additional profit could be earned if the resources in question were devoted to some other use.

Other Terminology   The term *differential costs* does not necessarily have the same meaning as the term *variable costs*. Variable costs are those that vary proportionately with changes in the volume of output. By contrast, differential costs are always related to specific alternatives that are being analyzed. If, in a specific problem, the alternatives involve operating at different volumes, then differential costs may well be the same as variable costs. Depending on the problem, however, the differential costs may include nonvariable items. A proposal to change the number of plant guards and their duties, for example, involves no elements of variable cost. A proposal to discontinue a product may involve some differential fixed costs, as well as the differential variable costs.

Marginal cost is a term used in economics for what accountants call variable costs. The marginal cost of a product is the cost of producing one additional unit of that product. Thus, marginal costs may be the same as differential costs in those problems in which an alternative under consideration involves changing the volume of output. *Incremental cost* and *relevant cost* are terms that usually mean the same thing as differential cost.

Estimates of Future Costs

Because the alternatives being analyzed always relate to the future, differential costs are always estimates of future costs. Nevertheless, in many instances the best information about future costs is derived from an analysis of historical costs. One can easily lose sight of the fact that historical costs, as such, are irrelevant. Historical costs may be a useful guide as to what costs are likely to be in the future, but using them as a guide is basically different from using them as if they were factual statements of what the future costs are going to be.

Except where future costs are determined by long-term contractual arrangements, differential costs are necessarily estimates. Usually they cannot be close estimates. An estimated labor saving of $50,000 a year for five years, for example, implies assumptions as to future wage rates, future fringe benefits, future labor efficiency, future production volume, and other factors that cannot be known with certainty. Consequently, there is ordinarily no point in carrying computations of cost estimates to several decimal places. In fact, there is a danger of being misled by the illusion of precision that such calculations give.

Sunk Costs

An element of historical cost that causes considerable difficulty is the book value of plant and equipment assets and the related depreciation expense. The book value of depreciable assets is a *sunk cost*. A sunk cost exists because of actions taken in the past, not because of a decision made currently. Therefore, a sunk cost is *not* a differential cost. No decision made today can change what has already happened. Decisions made now can affect only what *will* happen in the future.

It is sometimes suggested that when a proposed alternative involves disposal of an existing machine, the depreciation on that machine will no longer be a cost, and that this saving in depreciation expense should therefore be taken into account as an advantage of the proposed alternative. This is not so. This argument overlooks the fact that the book value of the machine will, sooner or later, be recorded as an expense, regardless of whether the proposed alternative is adopted. If the alternative is *not* adopted, depreciation on the machine will continue. If the alternative *is* adopted, the remaining book value will be written off when the machine is disposed of. In either case, the total amount of cost is the same, so the book value is not a differential cost.

> **Example.** Assume that Part No. 101 from the previous examples is now manufactured on a certain machine, and that depreciation of $1,000 on this machine is one of the items of "other costs" in Illustration 21–2. The machine was purchased six years ago for $10,000, and since depreciation has been recorded at $1,000 a year, a total of $6,000 has been recorded to date. The machine therefore has a net book value of $4,000. The machine has zero scrap value.
>
> It is sometimes argued that the calculation in Illustration 21–2 neglects the $1,000 annual saving in depreciation costs that will occur if the machine is disposed of, and that purchasing Part No. 101 is therefore the

preferable alternative. (If the cost of purchasing Part No. 101 is reduced by $1,000, then the profit of this alternative becomes $1,670, which is $690 greater than the $980 profit for the base case.) This is a fallacious argument. The fact is that if the machine is scrapped, its book value must be written off, and this amount exactly equals the total depreciation charge over the machine's remaining life. Thus, there is no differential cost associated with the book value of the existing machine.

The irrelevance of sunk costs is demonstrated in Illustration 21–3 by comparison of two income statements for the complete time periods of the remaining life of the machine. One shows the results of operations if Part No. 101 is purchased and the machine is scrapped. The other shows the results if Part No. 101 continues to be made on the machine. Illustration 21–3 shows that over the four-year period the differential profit favoring the base case is $1,240. This is $310 per year, the same amount shown in Illustration 21–2.

ILLUSTRATION 21–3
IRRELEVANCE OF SUNK COSTS

	Profit on Product A (total for four years)	
	Base Case	Purchase of Part No. 101
Revenue.	$40,000	$40,000
Costs, other than machine.	$32,080*	$33,320†
Depreciation	4,000	0
Loss on disposal of machine	0	4,000
Total costs.	36,080	37,320
Profit.	3,920	$ 2,680
	− 2,680 ←	
Differential profit of base case, four years	$ 1,240	
Annual differential profit ($1,240 ÷ 4).	$310‡	

*($9,020 − $1,000) × 4 years.
†($9,330 − $1,000) × 4 years.
‡Same amount as in Illustration 21–2.

The cost of an asset is supposed to be written off over its useful life. If a machine is scrapped, its useful life obviously has come to an end. If its total cost has not been written off by that time, one knows by hindsight that an error has been made, because if depreciation had been charged correctly, the net book value of the machine would be zero when it is scrapped. Although this was an error, it was an error made in the past, and no current decision can change it.[5]

If the machine had a market value, this fact *would* be a relevant con-

___
[5]Note that the error was an incorrect judgmental *estimate* of the machine's useful life at the time it was acquired, not an arithmetic mistake.

sideration, since its sale would then bring in additional cash. If the income tax effect of writing off the loss on disposal were different from the tax effect of writing off depreciation over the four-year period, the effect of taxes is relevant. (The method of allowing for this tax effect will be discussed in Chapter 22.) The book value of the machine itself however, is not relevant.

Importance of the Time Span

The question of what costs are differential depends to a considerable extent on the time span of the problem. If the proposal is to make only one additional unit of an item, only the direct material costs may be differential. The work could conceivably be done without any differential labor costs if workers were paid on a daily basis and had some idle time. At the other extreme, if the proposal involves a commitment to produce the item over the foreseeable future, practically all items of production costs would be differential.

In general, the longer the time span of the proposal, the more items of cost that are differential. In the very long run, *all* costs are differential. Thus, in very long-run problems, differential costs include the same elements as full costs, because in the long run one must consider even the replacement of buildings and equipment, which are sunk costs in the short run. In many short-run problems, relatively few cost items are subject to change by a management decision.

Example: Operating an Automobile

As an example of the fact that the cost elements that are differential in an alternative choice problem vary with the nature of the problem, consider the costs that are relevant for various decisions that may be made about owning and operating an automobile. A study made by Runzheimer and Co. and published by the American Automobile Association gives the national average cost in early 1982 of operating a 1982 six-cylinder Citation four-door hatchback (equipped with standard accessories—radio, automatic transmission, and power brakes and steering, but no air conditioning) as follows:

	Average per Mile
Variable costs:	
Gasoline and oil	6.74¢
Maintenance	1.00
Tires	0.63
Total variable costs	8.37¢

	Amount per Year
Fixed costs:	
Insurance	$ 449
License, registration, taxes	54
Depreciation	1,356
Total fixed costs	$1,859

Assume that these costs are valid estimates of future costs (which actually is not the case because of inflation). What are the differential costs in each of these circumstances?

1. You own a car like the one described above and have it registered. You are thinking about making a trip of 1,000 miles. What is the differential cost?

   Answer: The differential costs are 8.37 cents a mile times the estimated mileage of the trip. A trip of 1,000 miles therefore has a differential cost of $83.70. The fixed costs are not relevant since they will continue whether or not the trip is made. (Note that although no *cash* outlays may be made for maintenance or tires on this trip, these costs are nevertheless differential since the trip will cause these costs to be incurred sooner than if the trip were not made.)

2. You own a car but have not registered it. You are considering whether to register it for next year or to use alternative forms of transportation that you estimate will cost $2,000. If you register the car, you expect to drive it 10,000 miles during the year. Should you register it?

   Answer: The differential costs are the insurance and fees of $503 plus 8.37 cents a mile times the 10,000 miles you expect to travel by car, a total of $1,340. The $503 has become a cost because it is affected by the decision as to registration. If alternative transportation costs $2,000, you are well advised to register the car.

3. You do not own a car but are considering the purchase of the car described above. If your estimate is that you will drive 10,000 miles per year for five years and that alternative transportation will cost $2,000 per year, should you do so?

   Answer: The differential costs are $1,859 a year plus 8.37 cents a mile times the 10,000 miles you expect to travel per year, or $1,859 + $837 = $2,696. If alternative transportation costs $2,000 a year, you are well advised to use alternative transportation (disregarding noneconomic considerations).

Each of the above answers is, of course, an oversimplification because it omits nonquantitative factors and relies on averages. In an actual problem, the person would have data that more closely approximated the costs of his or her own automobile.

TYPES OF ALTERNATIVE CHOICE PROBLEMS

As noted earlier, a dominant objective of a business is to earn a satisfactory return on investment (ROI). Three basic elements are involved in a company's ROI: (1) costs, (2) revenue, and (3) investment, because:

$$ROI = \frac{Revenues - Costs}{Investment}$$

Although the general approach to all alternative choice problems is similar, it is useful to discuss three subcategories separately. First, there are problems that involve only the cost element. Problems of this type are discussed in the next section. Second, there are problems in which both the revenue and cost elements are involved. Problems of this type are discussed in the latter part of this chapter. Third, there are problems that involve investment as well as revenues and costs. These are discussed in Chapter 22.

Problems Involving Costs

Alternative choice problems involving only costs have these general characteristics: The base case is the status quo, and an alternative to the base case is proposed. If the alternative is estimated to have lower differential costs than the base case, it is accepted (assuming nonquantitative factors do not offset this cost advantage). If there are several alternatives, the one with the lowest differential cost is accepted. Problems of this type are often called *trade-off problems* because one type of cost is traded off for another. Some examples are mentioned below.

Methods Change. The alternative being proposed is the adoption of some new method of performing an activity. If the differential costs of the proposed method are significantly lower than those of the present method, the method should be adopted (unless offsetting nonquantitative considerations are present).

Operations Planning. In a factory that has a variety of machines, or in a chemical processing plant, several routes for scheduling products through the plant are possible. The route with the lowest differential costs is preferred. Similar planning problems exist in nonmanufacturing settings: deciding which of several warehouses should ship appliances to each of the retailers selling these appliances; or deciding which group of architects should be assigned to work on a new project.

Other production decisions can be analyzed in terms of differential costs. One example is deciding whether to use one-shift plus overtime, or to add a second shift. Another is deciding, when demand is low, whether to operate temporarily at a very low volume or to shut down until operations at normal volume are again economical.

Make or Buy. Make-or-buy problems are among the most common type of alternative choice problems. At any given time, an organization performs certain activities with its own resources, and it pays outside firms to perform certain other activities. It constantly seeks to improve the balance between these two types of activities by asking: Should we contract with some outside party to perform some function that we are now performing ourselves? Or, should we ourselves perform some activity that we now pay someone else to do?

As the example given in Illustration 21–2 shows, the cost of the outside service (the "buy" alternative) usually is easy to estimate. The more difficult problem is to find the differential costs of the "make" alternative because of the short-run nondifferential nature of many of the cost items.

Order Quantity. When the production of an item involves setup costs that are incurred only once for each lot produced, the question arises of how many units should be made in one lot. If the demand is predictable and if sales are reasonably steady throughout the year, the optimum quantity to produce at one time, called the economic lot size or *economic order quantity*, is arrived at by considering two offsetting influences—setup costs (or ordering costs) and inventory carrying costs. The relevant costs are differential costs. A similar problem arises in deciding on the quantity of an item that should be purchased. A technique for analyzing this problem is given in the Appendix at the end of this chapter.

Problems Involving Both Revenues and Costs

In the second class of alternative choice problems, both costs and revenues are affected by the proposal being studied. Insofar as the quantitative factors are concerned, the best alternative is the one with the largest difference between differential revenue and differential cost, that is, the alternative with the most *differential income* or *differential profit*. Some problems of this type are described briefly below.

Supply/Demand/Price Analysis. In general, the lower the selling price of a product, the greater the quantity that will be sold. This relationship between a product's selling price and the quantity sold is called its *demand schedule,* or demand curve. As the quantity sold increases by one unit, the *total* cost of making the product increases by the variable cost of that additional unit. Since fixed costs do not change, total costs increase less than proportionately with increases in demand. This semivariable relationship between total production costs and volume is called the product's *supply schedule,* or supply curve; it looks like the C-V diagram in Illustration 16–5.

The supply schedule usually can be estimated with a reasonable degree of accuracy. If the demand schedule also can be estimated, then the optimum selling price can be determined. This optimum price is found by estimating the total revenues and total variable costs for various quantities sold, and selecting the selling price that yields the greatest total contribution.

Example.   Assume that fixed costs for a product are $20,000 per month, and that variable costs are $100 per unit. The supply/demand analysis is given in the following table:

Unit Selling Price	Unit Variable Cost	Unit Contri- bution	Estimated Quantity Sold	Total Contri- bution	Fixed Costs	Profit
$300	$100	$200	125	$25,000	$20,000	$ 5,000
250	100	150	200	30,000	20,000	10,000
200*	100	100	310	31,000	20,000	11,000
150	100	50	450	22,500	20,000	2,500
125	100	25	550	13,750	20,000	(6,250)

*Preferred alternative.

Clearly, $200 is the best selling price, for at that price profit is $11,000, which is higher than the profit at either a higher or lower price. Since the fixed costs are a constant, they could be eliminated from the calculation; that is, the same decision can be reached by choosing the price that yields the greatest total contribution.

This type of analysis is feasible only if the demand schedule can be estimated. In many situations there is no reliable way of estimating how many units will be sold at various selling prices; this type of analysis cannot be used in such circumstances. Instead, the selling price is arrived at by adding a profit margin to ths full cost of the product, as described in Chapter 17, or is set by competitive market forces.

Contribution Pricing. Although, as described in Chapter 17, full cost is the normal basis for setting selling prices, and although a company must recover its full costs or eventually go out of business, there are some pricing situations where differential costs and revenues are appropriately used. In normal times, a company may refuse to take orders at prices that are not high enough to yield a satisfactory profit. But if times are bad, such orders may be accepted if the differential revenue obtained from them exceeds the differential costs that will be incurred if the order is accepted but will not be incurred if it is not accepted. The company is better off to receive some revenue above its differential costs than to receive nothing at all. These discount-price orders make some contribution to fixed costs and profit. Such a selling price is therefore called a *contribution price,* to distinguish it from a normal price.

Dumping, the practice of selling surplus quantities of a product in a selected marketing area at a price below full costs, is another version of the contribution idea. However, dumping may violate the Robinson-Patman Amendment in domestic markets, and is in general prohibited by trade agreements in foreign markets.

It is difficult to generalize on the circumstances that determine whether full costs or differential costs are the appropriate approach to setting prices. Even in normal times, an opportunity may be accepted to make some contribution to profit by using temporarily idle facilities. Conversely, even when current sales volume is low, the contribution concept may be rejected on the grounds that the low price may "spoil the market," or that orders can in fact be obtained at normal profit margins if the sales organization works hard enough.

Discontinuing a Product. If the selling price of a product is below its full cost, then conventional accounting reports will indicate that the product is being sold at a loss. This fact may lead some people to recommend that the product be discontinued. Actually, such an action may make the company worse off rather than better off. If there is excess production capacity, it is better to retain a product that makes some contribution to fixed overhead and profit than not to have the product at all. Only if the product's total contribution is less than the *differential* fixed costs that could be saved were the product dropped will the company be better off by dropping the product.[6] An analysis of differential revenues and differential costs is the proper approach to problems of this type.

Adding Services. A company can add to its income if it can find additional ways of using its facilities such that the differential revenue from these uses exceeds the differential costs of providing them. For this reason, a chain of hamburger restaurants may add breakfast items to its menu and open four hours earlier each day; a grocery store may decide to remain open on Sundays; and a hotel may offer special package deals on weekends when volume is low. In all these situations, differential costs, rather than full costs, are relevant. In analyzing such problems, care must be taken to ensure that the differential revenue is truly differential and that it does not represent a diversion from normal revenue. For example, a grocery store will not earn additional income by staying open Sundays if the revenue earned on Sunday comes from customers who would otherwise have shopped at that store on some other day of the week.

Sale versus Further Processing. Many companies, particularly those that manufacture a variety of finished products from basic raw materials, must address the problem of whether to sell a product that has reached a certain stage in the production process or whether to do additional work on it. Meat packers, for example, can sell an entire carcass of beef, or they can continue to process the carcass into hamburger and various cuts, or they can go even further and make frozen dinners out of some of the cuts. The decision requires an analysis of the differential revenues and differential costs.

Let us designate the alternative of selling the product at a certain stage as case 1 and that of processing it further as case 2. The case 2 product, having received more processing than the case 1 product, presumably can be sold at a higher revenue. But the case 2 product also involves incurring additional processing costs (and possibly marketing costs) not

---

[6]Recall that if the alternatives involve producing the product at various volumes, only the variable costs are differential. But if one alternative is to discontinue the product, *all* of its variable costs will be saved, and *some* of its fixed costs may be saved.

incurred in case 1. If the differential revenue in case 2 (i.e., the difference between the case 2 revenue and the case 1 revenue) exceeds the additional processing and marketing costs, then case 2 is preferred. The important point to note about this analysis is that all costs up to the point in the production process where this decision is made may be disregarded. These costs are incurred whether or not additional processing takes place, and they are therefore not differential.

Other Marketing Tactics. The same analytical approach can be used for a number of other marketing problems. Examples include deciding which customers are worth soliciting by sales personnel and how often the salesperson should call on each customer; deciding whether to open additional warehouses or, conversely, whether to consolidate existing warehouses; deciding whether to improve the durability of a product in order to reduce the number of maintenance calls; deciding on the minimum size of order that will be accepted; and deciding whether to put more meat in each hamburger and increase its price.

SOME PRACTICAL POINTERS

The following points may be helpful in attacking specific problems:

1. Use imagination in choosing the alternatives to be considered, but don't select so many that you bog down before you begin. There is only a fine line between the alternative that is a "stroke of genius" and the alternative that is a "harebrained idea," but it is a crucial one.

2. Don't yield to the natural temptation to give too much weight to the factors that can be reduced to numbers, even though the numbers have the appearance of being definite and precise.

3. On the other hand, don't slight the numbers because they are "merely" approximations. A reasonable approximation is much better than nothing at all.

4. Often, it is easier to work with total costs rather than with unit costs. Unit cost is a fraction:

$$\frac{\text{Total cost}}{\text{Number of units}} = \text{Unit cost}$$

Changes in either the numerator or the denominator result in changes in unit costs. An error is made if one of these changes is taken into account and the other is overlooked.

5. There is a tendency to underestimate the cost of doing something new because all the consequences may not be foreseen.

6. The *number* of arguments is irrelevant in an alternative choice problem. A dozen reasons may be, and often are, advanced against trying out something new, but all these reasons put together may not be so strong as a single argument in favor of the proposal.

7. Be realistic about the margin of error in any calculation involving

the future. Precise conclusions cannot be drawn from rough estimates, nor is an answer necessarily valid just because you spent a
long time calculating it.

8. Despite uncertainties, a decision should be made if as much information is available as you can obtain at reasonable cost and within
a reasonable time. Postponing action is the same as deciding to per-
petuate the existing situation, which may be the worst possible decision.

9. Show clearly the assumptions you made and the effect on these on
your estimates so that others going over your analysis can substitute
their own judgments if they wish.

10. Do not expect that everyone will agree with your conclusion simply
because it is supported with carefully worked-out numbers. Think
about how you can sell your conclusion to those who must act
on it.

SUMMARY

Differential costs (or revenues) are those that are different under one
set of conditions than they would be under another set. Differential costs
are always constructed for a specified set of future conditions. Variable
costs are an important category of differential costs in situations where
changes in volume are involved. But fixed costs also are differential in
many alternative choice problems.

When an alternative choice problem involves changes in costs but not
changes in revenue or investment, the best solution is the one with the
lowest differential costs, insofar as cost information bears on the
solution. Although historical costs may provide a useful guide to what
costs will be in the future, we are always interested in future costs, and
never in historical costs for their own sake. In particular, sunk costs are
irrelevant. Also, allocated costs must be analyzed with care to see if they
are differential. The longer the time span involved, the more costs that
are differential.

When the problem involves both cost and revenue considerations,
differential revenues, as well as differential costs, must be estimated.
The best alternative is the one having the largest differential profit.

Differential costs and revenues rarely provide the answer to any
business problem, but they facilitate comparisons and narrow the area
within which judgment must be applied in order to reach a sound decision.

APPENDIX: USEFUL DECISION MODELS

A model is a statement, usually in mathematical terms, of the relationships among variables in a specified set of circumstances. The contribu-
tion-basis income statement for the laundry and dry cleaning business

illustrated in this chapter is a model. The relationships shown therein were (Laundry revenues − Laundry direct costs) + (Dry cleaning revenues − Dry cleaning direct costs) − Indirect costs = Income. More complicated models are useful in certain types of alternative choice problems. Some of these and related mathematical techniques are described below.

Economic Order Quantity

   As already noted, under certain circumstances the economic order quantity to purchase, or the economic lot size to produce in a manufacturing process, can be estimated by considering the relationship between ordering costs (or setup costs) and inventory carrying costs. The nature of the problem is indicated in Illustration 21–4. This shows how two alternative policies for an item with annual sales of 1,200 units, occurring at an even rate of 100 per month, affect inventory levels and the number of setups. Part A shows that if the whole 1,200 units were manufactured in one lot, only one setup a year would be necessary; but inventory carrying costs would be high since the inventory would start with 1,200 units and would average 600 units over the year.[7] By contrast, as shown in Part B, the manufacture of four lots of 300 units each (i.e., one lot each quarter) would involve four times as much setup cost, but a relatively low inventory carrying cost since there would be an average of only 150 units in inventory at any one time.

   Thus, there is a trade-off between setup costs and inventory carrying cost. The objective is to minimize the sum of these two costs. This sum can be expressed algebraically as

$$T = \left(S \cdot \frac{R}{Q} \right) + \left(\frac{Q}{2} \cdot C \cdot K \right)$$

where

   R = annual requirements (in units)
   C = production cost per unit (or the price per unit if purchasing from an outside vendor)
   S = cost of one setup (or, if bought outside, cost of preparing an order and processing the vendor's invoice)
   Q = order quantity (number of units in one lot)
   K = cost of carrying one unit in inventory for one year (expressed as a percentage of C)

The first term in the equation represents total setup costs: $R \div Q$ setups will be required per year at a cost of $S each. The second term is the

---

[7] Inventory is 1,200 units immediately after the lot has been manufactured and declines to zero a year later. Assuming that the decline is at a roughly even rate throughout the year, the average inventory for the year is one half the sum of the beginning plus ending inventories; thus: ½ (1,200 + 0) = 600.

ILLUSTRATION 21–4
DIFFERENT PRACTICES REGARDING SIZE OF ORDERS

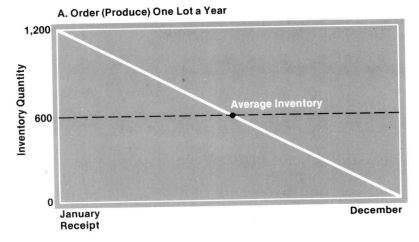

A. Order (Produce) One Lot a Year

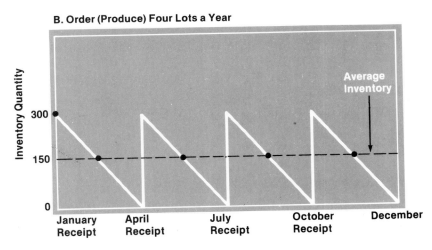

B. Order (Produce) Four Lots a Year

carrying cost. The *average* number of units in inventory will be $Q \div 2$. Each unit represents an investment of $C. The annual carrying cost of *one* unit is K percent of C, so the *total* carrying cost is CK times the average inventory. Using calculus, it can be proven that T is minimized at one value of Q, called the *economic order quantity* or *EOQ*:

$$EOQ = \sqrt{\frac{2SR}{CK}}$$

Example. Estimates for a certain item are:

S (setup cost). $300
R (annual requirements). . . . . 1,200 units
C (production cost). . . . . $10 per unit
K (carrying charge). 20%

$$EOQ = \sqrt{\frac{2 \times \$300 \times 1,200}{\$10 \times 0.2}}$$
$$= \sqrt{360,000}$$
$$= 600 \text{ units}$$

Since 1,200 units are required per year, there must be $1,200 \div 600 = 2$ lots manufactured per year. If the item were purchased rather than produced in-house, only a few words change: setup cost (S) becomes ordering cost, and production cost (C) becomes the purchase price per unit.

The costs used in this equation are differential costs. The differential setup costs include the extra labor costs involved in making the setup, including fringe benefits, plus any differential overhead costs associated with making a setup. The differential inventory carrying charge includes financing costs, inventory insurance, the costs associated with warehouse occupancy, inventory handling, shrinkage, and obsolescence—that is, all costs that are expected to be variable with the amount of inventory on hand. Making these cost estimates is quite difficult in practice.[8]

Expected Value

All the numbers used in alternative choice problems are estimates of what will happen in the future. In the text examples we used *single value* estimates; that is, each estimate was a single number representing someone's best estimate as to what differential costs or revenues would be. Some companies use estimates made in the form of probability distributions rather than as single numbers. Instead of stating, "I think sales of item X will be $100,000 if the proposed alternative is adopted," the estimator develops a range of possibilities, together with his or her estimate of the probability that each will occur. These separate possibilities

---

[8]Conceptually, fixed production costs should be excluded from the equation for T; that is, C should be variable production cost, not full production cost. This is because fixed costs for the year are independent of the lot size. Although these fixed costs are capitalized in inventory with a full (absorption) costing system, and therefore accounting inventory valuation at full cost is dependent on Q, the *actual pattern of cash flows* for fixed production costs is not altered by the lot size decision. On the other hand, the *pattern* of cash outflows for materials, labor, and variable overhead is affected by Q.

Nevertheless, in practice companies tend to use full production cost for C. First, this number is readily available from the usual full cost accounting system. Second, inventory carrying cost per unit of product is $K \cdot C$. If C is variable production cost for items manufactured in-house, but full cost plus a manufacturer's profit for similar items purchased from outside manufacturers, then the carrying cost on a purchased item appears to be much higher than for a similar item made in-house. This discrepancy is rejected as counterintuitive by many managers.

are weighted by the probabilities. The sum of these weighted amounts is called the *expected value* of the probability distribution. It is computed as in the following example:

Possibilities: Sales Volume (a)	Estimated Probability (b)		Weighted Amount (a × b)
$ 60,000	0.1		$ 6,000
80,000	0.1		8,000
100,000	0.4		40,000
120,000	0.2		24,000
140,000	0.2		28,000
	1.0	Expected value	$106,000

The probability 0.1 opposite $60,000 means that there is estimated to be 1 chance in 10 that sales will be $60,000. The sum of the probabilities must always add to 1.0 because the estimates must include all possible outcomes. Although sales conceivably could be any amount between zero and an extremely high number, estimators clearly cannot assign probabilities to each of a long list of possibilities. Therefore, they work only with a few numbers that are intended to be representative of the complete distribution. Five, as in the example above, is common, and the use of only three possibilities is also common.

The expected value of $106,000 would be used as the "best" estimate of differential revenue. If a single-value estimate rather than an expected value were used, it would be $100,000 because this is the outcome with the highest probability. The $106,000 expected value is a better estimate of sales because it incorporates the whole probability distribution.

People in business do not find it easy to develop estimates in the form of probability distributions. But if they can do so, the validity of the estimates can be greatly increased.

Sensitivity Analysis   In a calculation of differential costs or differential income, some items have a greater influence on the final result than others. In some problems, the most significant item is obvious. For example, the estimate of sales volume is often a major factor in a problem in which the quantity sold varies among the alternatives. In other problems, it is useful to locate the items that have an important influence on the final results so that they can be subjected to special scrutiny. Techniques for doing this are called *sensitivity analysis.*

One such technique is to vary each of the estimates, in turn, by a given percentage, say, 10 percent, and determine what effect the variation in that item has on the final results. If the effect is large, the result is *sensitive* to that item.

Another technique is to calculate a number of possible results, varying each of the elements according to an amount that is selected by chance from a probability distribution. A computer can calculate 1,000 such possible outcomes in a few seconds. Because the numbers are selected by chance, as in a gambling situation, this approach has come to be called the *Monte Carlo method*.[9] The results of these 1,000 "trials" are arrayed from "best" to "worst" outcome. If all the results fall within a narrow range, that is, if the "best" and "worst" outcomes are quite close together, it can safely be assumed that the outcomes are relatively insensitive to the estimates of individual items. If the range is wide, the indication is that a calculation based on single-value estimates is quite uncertain, and the numerical results must therefore be used cautiously.

Decision Tree Analysis

A characteristic of the problems described in this chapter was that a single decision had to be made, and as a consequence of that decision estimated revenues would be earned and estimated costs would be incurred. There is another class of problems in which a series of decisions has to be made, at various time intervals, with each decision influenced by the information that is available at the time it is made. An analytical tool that is useful for such problems is the *decision tree*.

In its simplest form, a decision tree is a diagram that shows the several decisions or *acts* and the possible consequences of each act; these consequences are called *events*. In a more elaborate form, the probabilities and the revenues or costs of each event's outcomes are estimated, and these are combined to give an *expected value* for the event.

Since a decision tree is particularly useful in depicting a complicated series of decisions, any brief illustration is somewhat artificial. Nevertheless, the decision tree shown in Illustration 21–5 will suffice to show how the technique works.

The assumed situation is this. A company is considering whether to develop and market a new product. Development costs are estimated to be $100,000. There is a 0.7 probability that the development effort will be successful, that is, that the product developed will work (perform its intended function). If the product works, it will be produced and marketed. There are two production processes available. An old process costs $50,000 differential fixed costs plus $2 variable cost per unit. A new process, employing more equipment and less labor, costs $100,000 differential fixed costs and $1 per unit. The process must be chosen *before* any sales are known. It is estimated that—

a. If the product is a big success (probability 0.4), 100,000 units will be sold at $6 each. Production costs using the old process will be

---

[9]For an excellent nontechnical description of this technique, see David Hertz, "Risk Analysis in Capital Investment," *Harvard Business Review*, September–October 1979.

ILLUSTRATION 21–5
DECISION TREE ANALYSIS

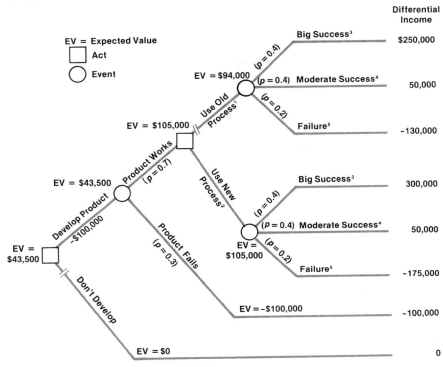

Notes:
[1] Old process costs $50,000 plus $2 per unit.
[2] New process costs $100,000 plus $1 per unit.
[3] Big success is 100,00 units @ $6 = $600,000 revenues.
[4] Moderate success is 50,000 units @ $6 = $300,000 revenues.
[5] Failure is 5,000 units @ $6 = $30,000 revenues.

$250,000 (= $50,000 + 100,000 × $2), giving income (after subtracting the $100,000 development cost) of $250,000. If the new process is used, production costs will be $200,000 (= $100,000 + 100,000 × $1), and income will be $300,000.

b. If the product is a moderate success (probability 0.4), 50,000 units will be sold at the $6 price. Either old or new process production costs will be $150,000, giving income (net of development costs) of $50,000.

c. If the product is a failure (probability 0.2), only 5,000 units will be sold at $6 each. Production will cost $60,000 using the old process, or $105,000 using the new process, giving losses of $130,000 and $175,000 respectively.

To decide (1) whether or not to develop the product and (2) *if the* product works, whether to use the old or new process, the decision tree must be "collapsed" or "folded back," using these rules:

1.   Replace each *event* "node" with the expected value of that event's outcomes.
2.   At each *act* "node," choose the act with the highest expected value.

These expected values (EVs) are shown in Illustration 21–5. For example, *if* the product is developed, *if* it works, and *if* management chooses to use the old process, then the EV of the three possible sales outcomes is $94,000 (=0.4 × $250,000 + 0.4 × $50,000 + 0.2 × $–130,000). Similarly, if the developed product works, using the new process has an EV of $105,000. Therefore, *if* the product is successfully developed, management should use the new process; this is shown by "chopping off" (with the double "hash mark") the branch labeled Use Old Process. Now, if the development is undertaken, either the product will work, with an EV of $105,000, or it will fail, with a loss of $100,000. (Following a product failure, the probability of this loss is 1.0, so the EV is $–100,000.) Thus, the expected value of the decision to undertake development is $43,500 (=0.7 × $105,000 + 0.3 × $–100,000); but the EV of not developing the product (which is the base case), is $0. Therefore, the development effort should be undertaken, as indicated by "chopping off" the Don't Develop branch. In sum, the *optimal strategy*— that is, that sequence of decisions having the highest EV—is to develop the product and, if development succeeds, to use the new production process. That strategy has an EV of $43,500.

This does not mean, however, that the ultimate outcome is "guaranteed" to be differential income of $43,500. In fact, *none* of the possible outcomes results in $43,500 income, as can be seen by looking at the decision tree endpoint values. Rather it means that based on the estimates that have been made in considering this decision, management should "gamble" and go ahead with the development because the *expected* payoff from this gamble is positive whereas if the gamble is not taken there will be zero payoff.

Linear Programming

In the situations described thus far, it has been assumed implicitly that the available resources are adequate to carry out whichever alternative is selected. However, in some situations this assumption is not valid. For example, a machine has only a certain amount of capacity, and if that capacity is used by one product it cannot be used for another. Similarly, a factory building has room for only so many machines. In these situations, there are *constraints* on the uses of resources. *Linear programming* is a model for solving problems with several constraints.

In linear programming, a series of mathematical statements is developed. The first, called the *objective function*, is the quantity to be optimized. This is usually a formula for differential costs which the model will minimize, or one for differential income, which is to be maximized. The other statements express the constraints of the situation.

Example. A company makes two products, each of which is worked on in two departments. Department 1 has a capacity of 500 labor-hours per week; Department 2, 600 labor-hours. The labor requirements of each product in each department are as follows:

	Labor-Hours per Unit Product A	Product B
Department 1	5.0	2.5
Department 2	3.0	5.0

As many units of B as can be made can also be sold, but a maximum of 90 units of A can be sold per week. The unit contribution (i.e., unit price minus unit variable costs) is $2 for A, and $2.50 for B. How many units of each should be made in order to maximize total contribution?

The problem can be expressed mathematically as follows:

Maximize: $C = 2A + 2.5B$ (maximize contribution, the objective function)

Subject to:
$$5A + 2.5B \leq 500 \quad \text{(Department 1 capacity constraint)}$$
$$3A + 5B \leq 600 \quad \text{(Department 2 capacity constraint)}$$
$$A \leq 90 \quad \text{(Product A sales constraint)}$$
$$A \geq 0, B \geq 0 \quad \text{(A negative number of units cannot be made)}$$

In words, the above says: find the number of units of A and B that should be made each week so as to maximize total contribution margin, where contribution is $2 per unit for A and $2.50 per unit for B, subject to the constraint that a unit of A requires 5 hours in Department 1 and a unit of B requires 2.5 hours there, and only 500 hours per week are available in Department 1; and so forth.

This situation can be illustrated graphically as in Illustration 21–6. One can see from the table above that Department 2 could make 200 units of A if it worked only on A, or 120 units of B if it worked only on B. In Illustration 21–6 the line between these two extremes, labeled Dept. 2 Capacity Constraint, shows all of the possible A-B product combinations that would utilize all of Department 2's available capacity of 600 hours. The other lines are drawn in the same manner.

The shaded area in Illustration 21–6, bounded by the axes and the three constraint lines, is called the *feasible set* because any A-B product-mix combination in that area can be produced and sold, whereas combinations outside that area are infeasible. The optimum A-B combination must lie on the "northeast" boundary of the feasible set. This is true because any point inside that boundary does not use up all the available

ILLUSTRATION 21-6
LINEAR PROGRAMMING GRAPHICAL SOLUTION

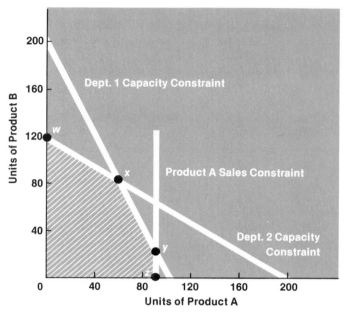

manufacturing capacity and/or A sales "capacity," and hence does not maximize contribution since more units could be made and sold. It is also true, but not intuitively obvious, that the optimum A-B combination lies at a *vertex* of that boundary; that is, at either point w, x, y, or z.

What a linear programming computer program does, in effect, is calculate the contribution, C, at each vertex of the feasible set boundary and identify that point which gives the highest contribution. Of course, for more realistic problems, such as determining the least costly delivery routes for a fleet of trucks or determining the most profitable mix of petroleum products to be refined from a quantity of crude oil, tens or even hundreds of mathematical statements are involved, and the problem cannot be solved manually. Computers can, and do, solve such problems rapidly.

Shadow Prices. As part of the solution to a linear programming problem, ths computer program also calculates a *shadow price* (also called *opportunity cost*) for each constrained resource, that is, for each resource that is completely utilized at the optimum solution. For example, if the optimum solution involves using all of Department 2's capacity, the shadow price for this capacity would indicate the amount by which contribution would increase if the capacity could be increased by

1 hour (to 601 hours). This shadow price would be the maximum amount the company should be willing to spend to add a unit of capacity (i.e., 1 labor-hour per week) in Department 2.

SUGGESTIONS FOR FURTHER READING

Bierman, Harold; Charles P. Bonini; and Warren H. Hausman. *Quantitative-Analysis for Business Decisions.* 6th ed. Homewood, Ill.: Richard D. Irwin, 1981.

Raiffa, Howard. *Decision Analysis.* Reading, Mass.: Addison-Wesley Publishing, 1968.

Vatter, Paul A., et al. *Quantitative Methods in Management:* Text and Cases. Homewood, Ill.: Richard D. Irwin, 1978.

Cases

CASE 21–1   Import Distributors, Inc.

Import Distributors, Inc. (IDI), imported appliances and distributed them to retail appliance stores in the Rocky Mountain states. IDI carried three broad lines of merchandise: audio equipment (tuners, turntables, CB radios, etc.), television equipment (including videotape recorders), and kitchen appliances (refrigerators, freezers, and stoves that were more compact than U.S. models). Each line accounted for about one third of total IDI sales revenues. Although each line was referred to by IDI managers as a "department," until 1983, the company did not prepare departmental income statements.

In late 1982, departmental accounts were set up in anticipation of preparing quarterly income statements by department starting in 1983. In early April of 1983, the first such statements were distributed to the management group. Although in the first quarter of 1983 IDI had earned net income amounting to 4.3 percent of sales, the television department had shown a gross margin that was much too small to cover the department's operating expenses (see Exhibit 1).

The television department's poor showing prompted the company's accountant to suggest that perhaps the department should be discontinued. "This is exactly why I proposed that we parpare departmental statements—to see if each department is carrying its fair share of the load," the accountant explained. This suggestion led to much discussion amoung the management group, particularly concerning two issues: First, was the first quarter of the year representative enough of longer-term results to consider discontinuing the television department? And second, would discontinuing television equipment cause a drop in sales in the other two departments? One manager, however, stated that "even if the quarter

732

EXHIBIT 1

Television Department Income Statement
For the First 3 months of 1983

		Percent
Net sales revenues	$930,233	100.0
Cost of sales	820,658	88.2
Gross margin	109,575	11.8
Operating expenses:		
Personnel expenses (Note 1)	5,850	
Department manager's office	7,078	
Rent (Note 2)	28,908	
Inventory taxes and insurance	21,094	
Utilities (Note 3)	1,734	
Delivery costs (Note 4)	19,272	
Sales commissions (Note 5)	37,209	
Administrative costs (Note 6)	19,403	
Inventory financing charge (Note 7)	13,678	
Total operating expenses	154,226	16.6
Income taxes (credit)	(21,395)	(2.3)
Net income (loss)	$ (23,256)	(2.5)

Notes:
1. These were warehouse personnel. Although merchandise in the warehouse was arranged by department, these personnel performed tasks for all three departments on any given day.
2. Allocated to departments on the basis of square footage utilized. IDI had a five-year noncancelable lease for the facilities.
3. Allocated to departments on the basis of square footage utilized.
4. Allocated on the basis of sales dollars. A delivery from IDI to a retail store typically included merchandise from all three departments.
5. Salespersons were paid on a straight commission basis; each one sold all three lines.
6. Allocated on the basis of sales dollars.
7. An accounting entry that was not directly related to the cost of financing inventory; assessed on average inventory, in order to motivate department managers not to carry excessive stocks. This charge tended to be about three times the company's actual out-of-pocket interest costs.

was typical and other sales wouldn't be hurt, I'm still not convinced we'd be better off dropping our television line."

Question

What action should be taken with regard to the television department?

CASE 21–2 Sheridan Carpet Company

Sheridan Carpet Company produced high-grade carpeting materials for use in automobiles and recreational vans. Sher- idan's products were sold to finishers, who cut and bound the material so as to fit perfectly in the passenger compartment or cargo area (e.g., automobile trunk) of a specific model automobile or van. Some of these finishers were captive operations of major automobile assembly divisions, particularly those that assembled the "top of the line" cars that included high-grade carpeting; other finishers concentrated on the replacement and van customizing markets.

Late in 1982, the marketing manager and the chief accountant of Sheridan met to decide on the list price for carpet number 104. It was industry practice to announce prices just prior to the January–June and July–December "seasons." Over the years, companies in the industry had adhered to their announced prices throughout a six-month season unless significant unexpected changes in costs occurred. Sales of carpet 104 were not affected by seasonal factors during the two six-month seasons.

Sheridan was the largest company in its segment of the automobile carpet industry; its 1981 sales had been over $40 million. Sheridan's salespersons were on a salary basis, and each one sold the entire product line. Most of Sheridan's competitors were smaller than Sheridan; accordingly, they usually awaited Sheridan's price announcement before setting their own selling prices.

Carpet 104 had an especially dense nap; as a result, making it required a special machine, and it was produced in a department whose equipment could not be used to produce Sheridan's other carpets. Effective January 1, 1982, Sheridan had raised its price on this carpet from $3.90 to $5.20 per square yard. This had been done in order to bring 104's margin up to that of the other carpets in the line. Although Sheridan was financially sound, it expected a large funds need in the next few years for equipment replacement and plant expansion. The 1982 price increase was one of several decisions made in order to provide funds for these plans.

Sheridan's competitors, however, had held their 1982 prices at $3.90 on carpets competitive with 104. As shown in Exhibit 1, which includes estimates of industry volume on these carpets, Sheridan's price increase had apparently resulted in a loss of market share. The marketing manager, Mel Walters, estimated that the industry would sell about 630,000 square yards of these carpets in the first half of 1983. Walters was sure

EXHIBIT 1
CARPET 104: PRICES AND PRODUCTION, 1980–1982

Selling Season*	Production Volume (square yards)		Price (per square yard)	
	Industry Total	Sheridan Carpet	Most Competitors	Sheridan Carpet
1980–1	549,000	192,000	$5.20	$5.20
1980–2	517,500	181,000	5.20	5.20
1981–1	387,000	135,500	3.90	3.90
1981–2	427,500	149,500	3.90	3.90
1982–1	450,000	135,000	3.90	5.20
1982–2	562,500	112,500	3.90	5.20

*198x–1 means the first 6 months of 198x; 198x–2 means the second-six months of 198x.

Sheridan could sell 150,000 yards if it dropped the price of 104 back to $3.90. But if Sheridan held its price at $5.20, Walters feared a further erosion in Sheridan's share. However, because some customers felt that 104 was superior to competitive products, Walters felt that Sheridan could sell at least 65,000 yards at the $5.20 price.

During their discussion, Walters and the chief accountant, Terry Rosen, identified two other aspects of the pricing decision. Rosen wondered whether competitors would announce a further price decrease if Sheridan dropped back to $3.90. Walters felt it was unlikely that competitors would price below $3.90, be-

cause none of them was more efficient than Sheridan, and there were rumors that several of them were in poor financial condition. Rosen's other concern was whether a decision relating to carpet 104 would have any impact on the sales of Sheridan's other carpets. Walters was convinced that since 104 was a specialized item, there was no interdependence between its sales and those of other carpets in the line.

Exhibit 2 contains cost estimates that Rosen had prepared for various volumes of 104. These estimates represented Rosen's best guesses as to costs during the first six months of 1983, based on past cost experience and anticipated inflation.

EXHIBIT 2
ESTIMATED COST OF CARPET 104 AT VARIOUS PRODUCTION VOLUMES
First Six Months of 1983

	Volume (square yards)					
	65,000	87,500	110,000	150,000	185,000	220,000
Raw materials	$0.520	$0.520	$0.520	$0.520	$0.520	$0.520
Materials spoilage	0.052	0.051	0.049	0.049	0.051	0.052
Direct labor	1.026	0.989	0.979	0.962	0.975	0.997
Department overhead:						
Direct*	0.142	0.136	0.131	0.130	0.130	0.130
Indirect† . ⎰ℛℛ	1.200	0.891	0.709	0.520	0.422	0.355
General overhead‡	0.308	0.297	0.294	0.289	0.293	0.299
Factory cost	3.248	2.884	2.682	2.470	2.391	2.353
Selling and administrative§	2.111	1.875	1.743	1.606	1.554	1.529
Total cost	$5.359	$4.759	$4.425	$4.076	$3.945	$3.882

*Materials handlers, supplies, repairs, power, fringe benefits.
†Supervision, equipment depreciation, heat, and light.
‡30 percent of direct labor.
§65 percent of factory cost.

Questions

1. What was the relationship (if any) between the 104 pricing decision and the company's future need for capital funds?

2. Assuming no intermediate prices are to be considered, should Sheridan price 104 at $3.90 or $5.20?

3. If Sheridan's competitors hold their prices at $3.90, how many square yards of 104 would Sheridan need to sell at a price of $5.20 in order to earn the same profit as selling 150,000 square yards at a price of $3.90?

4. What additional information would you wish to have before making this pricing decision? (Despite the absence of this information, still answer Question 2!)

5. With hindsight, was the decision to raise the price in 1982 a good one?

CASE 21–3   Hanson Manufacturing Company

In February 1982, Herbert Wessling was appointed general manager by Paul Hanson, president of Hanson Manufacturing Company. Wessling, age 56, had wide executive experience in manufacturing products similar to those of the Hanson Company. The appointment of Wessling resulted from management problems arising from the death of Richard Hanson, founder and, until his death in early 1981, president of the company. Paul Hanson had only four years' experience with the company, and in early 1982 was 34 years old. His father had hoped to train Paul over a 10-year period, but the father's untimely death had cut this seasoning period short. The younger Hanson became president after his father's death, and had exercised full control until he hired Mr. Wessling.

Paul Hanson knew that during 1981 he had made several poor decisions and that the morale of the organization had suffered, apparently through lack of confidence in him. When he received the income statement for 1981 (Exhibit 1), the loss of almost $200,000 during a good year for the industry convinced him that he needed help. He attracted Mr. Wessling from a competitor by offering a stock option incentive in addition to salary, knowing that Wessling wanted to acquire financial security for his retirement. The two men came to a clear understanding that Wessling, as general manager, had full authority to execute any changes he desired. In addition, Wessling would explain the reasons for his decisions to Mr. Hanson and thereby train him for successful leadership upon Wessling's retirement.

Hanson Manufacturing Company made

EXHIBIT 1

HANSON MANUFACTURING COMPANY
Income Statement
For Year Ending December 31, 1981

Gross sales		$40,690,234
Cash discounts		622,482
Net sales		40,067,752
Cost of sales		25,002,386
Gross margin		15,065,366
Less: Selling expense	$7,058,834	
General administration	2,504,597	
Depreciation	5,216,410	14,779,841
Operating income		285,525
Other income		78,113
Income before interest		363,638
Less: Interest expense		555,719
Income (loss)		$ (192,081)

in its single plant only three industrial products, 101, 102, and 103. These were sold by the company sales force for use in the processes of other manufacturers. All of the sales force, on a salary basis, sold the three products but in varying proportions. Hanson sold throughout New England and was one of eight companies with similar products. Several of its competitors were larger and manufactured a larger variety of products. The dominant company was Samra Company, which operated a plant in Hanson's market area. Customarily, Samra announced

prices, and the other producers followed suit.

Price cutting was rare; the only variance from quoted selling prices took the form of cash discounts. In the past, attempts at price cutting had followed a consistent pattern: all competitors met the price reduction, and the industry as a whole sold about the same quantity but at the lower prices. This continued until Samra, with its strong financial position, again stabilized the situation following a general recognition of the failure of price cutting. Furthermore, because sales were

EXHIBIT 2
ANALYSIS OF PROFIT AND LOSS BY PRODUCT
Year Ended December 31, 1981

| | Product 101 | | Product 102 | | Product 103 | | Total |
	Thou-sands	$ per Cwt.	Thou-sands	$ per Cwt.	Thou-sands	$ per Cwt	Thou-sands
Rent	721	0.3383	603	0.5856	718	0.7273	2,042
Property taxes	240	0.1125	192	0.1862	153	0.1555	585
Property insurance	201	0.0941	153	0.1486	202	0.2047	556
Compensation insurance	317	0.1486	167	0.1620	172	0.1747	656
Direct labor	4,964	2.3282	2,341	2.2740	2,640	2.6746	9,945
Indirect labor	1,693	0.7941	814	0.7903	883	0.8947	3,390
Power	86	0.0403	96	0.0929	116	0.1171	298
Light and heat	57	0.0269	49	0.0472	39	0.0392	145
Building service	38	0.0180	30	0.0288	28	0.0288	96
Materials	2,935	1.3766	1,809	1.7572	1,862	1.8862	6,606
Supplies	201	0.0941	183	0.1774	135	0.1363	519
Repairs	68	0.0319	57	0.0557	39	0.0396	164
Total	11,522	5.4036	6,493	6.3059	6,986	7.0787	25,002
Selling expense	3,496	1.6397	1,758	1.7069	1,805	1.8286	7,059
General administration	1,324	0.6209	499	0.4850	681	0.6904	2,505
Depreciation	2,169	1.0172	1,643	1.5955	1,404	1.4223	5,216
Interest	201	0.0941	153	0.1490	202	0.2043	556
Total cost	18,711	8.7755	10,546	10.2423	11,078	11.2243	40,338
Less other income	39	0.0184	20	0.0192	19	0.0192	78
	18,672	8.7571	10,526	10.2231	11,059	11.2051	40,260
Sales (net)	19,847	9.3084	9,977	9.6900	10,243	10.3784	40,068
Profit (loss)	1,175	0.5513	(549)	(0.5331)	(816)	(0.8267)	(192)
Unit sales (cwt.)	2,132,191		$1,029.654		986,974		
Quoted selling price	$9.41		$9.91		$10.56		
Cash discounts taken, percent of selling price	1.08%		2.22%		1.72%		

Note: Figures may not add exactly because of rounding.

to industrial buyers and the products of different manufacturers were similar, Hanson was convinced it could not unilaterally raise prices without suffering volume declines.

During 1981, Hanson's share of industry sales was 12 percent for type 101, 8 percent for 102, and 10 percent for 103. The industrywide quoted selling prices were $9.41, $9.91, and $10.56, respectively.

Wessling, upon taking office in February 1982, decided against immediate major changes. Rather, he chose to analyze 1981 operations and to wait for results of the first half of 1982. He instructed the accounting department to provide detailed expenses and earnings statements by products for 1981 (see Exhibit 2). In addition, he requested an explanation of the nature of the costs including their expected future behavior (see Exhibit 3).

To familiarize Paul Hanson with his methods, Wessling sent copies of these exhibits to Hanson, and they discussed them. Hanson stated that he thought product 103 should be dropped immediately as it would be impossible to lower expenses on product 103 as much as 83 cents per hundredweight (cwt.). In addition, he stressed the need for economies on product 102.

Wessling relied on the authority arrangement Mr. Hanson had agreed to earlier and continued production of the three products. For control purposes, he had the accounting department prepare monthly statements using as standard costs the costs per cwt. from the analytical profit and loss statement for 1981 (Exhibit 2). These monthly statements were his basis for making minor marketing and production changes during the spring of 1982. Late in July 1982, Wessling received from the accounting department

EXHIBIT 3
ACCOUNTING DEPARTMENT'S COMMENTARY ON COSTS

Direct labor: Variable. Nonunion shop at going community rates. No abnormal demands foreseen. It may be assumed that direct labor dollars is an adequate measure of capacity utilization.

Compensation insurance: Variable. Five percent of direct and indirect labor is an adequate estimate.

Materials: Variable. Exhibit 2 figures are accurate. Includes waste allowances.

Supplies: Variable. Exhibit 2 figures are accurate.

Repairs: Variable. Varies as volume changes within normal operating range. Lower and upper limits are fixed.

General administrative, selling expense, indirect labor, interest, and other income: These items are almost nonvariable. They can be changed, of course, by management decision.

Cash discount: Almost nonvariable. Average cash discounts taken are consistent from year to year. Percentages in Exhibit 2 are accurate.

Light and heat: Almost nonvariable. Heat varies only with fuel cost changes. Light is a fixed item regardless of level of production.

Property taxes: Almost nonvariable. Under the lease terms, Hanson Company pays the taxes; assessed valuation has been constant; the rate has risen slowly. Any change in the near future will be small and independent of production volume.

Rent: Nonvariable. Lease has 12 years to run.

Building service: Nonvariable. At normal business level variances are small.

Property insurance: Nonvariable. Three-year policy with fixed premium.

Depreciation: Nonvariable. Fixed-dollar total.

the six months' statement of cumulative standard costs including variances of actual costs from standard (see Exhibit 4). They showed that the first half of 1982 was a successful period.

During the latter half of 1982, the sales of the entire industry weakened. Even though Hanson retained its share of the market, its profit for the last six months was small. In January 1983, Samra announced a price reduction on product 101 from $9.41 to $8.64 per cwt. This cre-

EXHIBIT 4
PROFIT AND LOSS BY PRODUCT, AT STANDARD
Showing Variations from January 1 to June 30, 1982

Item	Product 101 Standard per Cwt	Product 101 Total at Standard	Product 102 Standard per Cwt.	Product 102 Total at Standard	Product 103 Standard per Cwt.	Product 103 Total at Standard	Total Standard (thousands)	Total Actual (thousands)	Variances
Rent	0.3383	337	0.5856	417	0.7273	365	1,119	1,021	+ 98
Property taxes	0.1125	112	0.1862	133	0.1555	78	323	307	+ 16
Property insurance	0.0941	94	0.1486	106	0.2047	103	302	278	+ 24
Compensation insurance	0.1486	148	0.1620	115	0.1747	88	351	348	+ 3
Direct labor	2.3282	2,321	2.2740	1,619	2.6746	1,341	5,281	5,308	− 27
Indirect labor	0.7941	792	0.7903	563	0.8947	448	1,803	1,721	+ 82
Power	0.0403	40	0.0929	66	0.1171	59	165	170	− 5
Light and heat	0.0269	27	0.0472	34	0.0392	20	80	83	− 3
Building service	0.0180	18	0.0288	21	0.0288	14	53	50	+ 3
Materials	1.3766	1,372	1.7572	1,251	1.8862	946	3,569	3,544	+ 25
Supplies	0.0941	94	0.1774	126	0.1363	68	288	288	—
Repairs	0.0319	32	0.0557	40	0.0396	20	91	88	+ 3
Total	5.4036	5,387	6,3059	4,490	7.0787	3,548	13,425	13,206	+219
Selling expense	1.6397	1,635	1.7069	1,215	1.8286	917	3,767	3,706	+ 62
General administration	0.6209	619	0.4850	345	0.6904	346	1,310	1,378	− 68
Depreciation	1.0172	1,014	1.5955	1,136	1.4223	713	2,863	2,686	+177
Interest	0.0941	94	0.1490	106	0.2043	102	302	290	+ 12
Total cost	8.7755	8,748	10.2423	7,294	11.2243	5,626	21,668	21,266	+402
Less other income	0.0184	18	0.0192	14	0.0192	10	42	42	—
	8.7571	8,730	10.2231	7,280	11,2051	5,617	21,626	21,224	+402
Actual sales (net)	9.3084	9,279	9.6900	6,900	10.3784	5,202	21,382	21,382	—
Profit or loss	0.5513	550	(0.5331)	(380)	(0.8267)	(414)	(244)	158	+402
Unit sales (cwt.)	996,859		712,102		501,276				

Note: Figures may not add exactly because of rounding.

ated an immediate pricing problem for its competitors. Wessling forecast that if Hanson Company held to the $9.41 price during the first six months of 1983, their unit sales would be 750,000 cwt. He felt that if they dropped their price to $8.64 per cwt., the six months' volume would be 1,000,000 cwt. Wessling knew that competing managements anticipated a further decline in activity. He thought a general decline in prices was quite probable.

The accounting department reported that the standard costs in use would probably apply during the first half of 1983, with two exceptions: materials and supplies would be about 5 percent above standard; and light and heat would increase about 7 percent.

Wessling and Hanson discussed the pricing problem. Hanson observed that especially with the anticipated increase in materials and supplies costs, a sales price of $8.64 would be below cost. He therefore wanted the $9.41 to be continued since he felt the company could not be profitable while selling a key product below cost.

Questions

1. If the company had dropped product 103 as of January 1, 1982, what effect would that action have had on the $158,000 profit for the first six months of 1982?

2. In January 1983, should the company reduce the price of product 101 from $9.41 to $8.64?

3. What is Hanson's most profitable product?

4. What appears to have caused the return to profitable operations in the first six months of 1982?

CASE 21–4   Liquid Chemical Company

Liquid Chemical Company manufactured and sold a range of high-grade products throughout Great Britain. Many of these products required careful packing, and the company had always made a feature of the special properties of the containers used. They had a special patented lining, made from a material known as GHL, and the firm operated a department especially to maintain its containers in good condition and to make new ones to replace those that were past repair.

Dale Walsh, the general manager, had for some time suspected that the firm might save money, and get equally good service, by buying its containers from an outside source. After careful inquiries, he approached a firm specializing in container production, Packages, Ltd., and asked for a quotation from it. At the same time he asked Paul Dyer, his chief accountant, to let him have an up-to-date statement of the cost of operating the container department.

Within a few days, the quotation from Packages, Ltd., came in. The firm was prepared to supply all the new containers required—at that time running at the rate of 3,000 a year—for £87,500[1] a year, the contract to run for a guaranteed term of five years and thereafter to be renewable from year to year. If the required number of containers increased, the contract price would be increased proportionally. Additionally, and irrespective of whether the above contract was concluded or not, Packages, Ltd., would undertake to carry out purely maintenance work on containers, short of replacement, for a sum of £26,250 a year, on the same contract terms.

Walsh compared these figures with the cost figures prepared by Dyer, covering a year's operations of the container department, as shown at the top of page 741.

Walsh's conclusion was that no time should be lost in closing the department and in entering into the contracts offered by Packages, Ltd. However, he felt bound to give the manager of the department, Sean Duffy, an opportunity to question this conclusion before he acted on it. He therefore called him in and put the facts before him, at the same time making it clear that Duffy's own position was not in jeopardy; for even if his department were closed, there was another managerial position shortly becoming vacant to which he could be moved without loss of pay or prospects.

Duffy asked for time to think the matter over. The next morning, he asked to speak to Walsh again, and said he thought there were a number of considerations that ought to be borne in mind before his department was closed. "For

---

[1] At the time of this case, one British pound (£) was worth about $2.

	£	£
Materials		49,000
Labor		35,000
Department overhead:		
Manager's salary	5,600	
Rent	3,150	
Depreciation of machinery	10,500	
Maintenance of machinery	2,520	
Other expenses	11,025	
		32,795
		116,795
Proportion of general administrative overhead		15,750
Total cost of department for year		132,545

instance," he said, "what will you do with the machinery? It cost £84,000 four years ago, but you'd be lucky if you got £14,000 for it now, even though it's good for another five years or so. And then there's the stock of GHL we bought a year ago. That cost us £70,000, and at the rate we're using it now, it'll last us another four years or so. We used up about one fifth of it last year. Dyer's figure of £49,000 for materials probably includes about £14,000 for GHL. But it'll be tricky stuff to handle if we don't use it up. We bought it for £350 a ton, and you couldn't buy it today for less than £420. But you wouldn't have more than £280 a ton left if you sold it, after you'd covered all the handling expenses."

Walsh thought that Dyer ought to be present during this discussion. He called him in and put Duffy's points to him. "I don't much like all this conjecture," Dyer said. "I think my figures are pretty conclusive. Besides, if we are going to have all this talk about 'what will happen if,' don't forget the problem of space we're faced with. We're paying £5,950 a year in rent for a small warehouse a couple of miles away. If we closed Duffy's department, we'd have all the warehouse space we need without renting."

"That's a good point," said Walsh.

"But I'm a bit worried about the workers if we close the department. I don't think we can find room for any of them elsewhere in the firm. I could see whether Packages can take any of them. But some of them are getting on. There are Walters and Hines, for example. They've been with us since they left school 40 years ago. I'd feel bound to give them a small pension—£1,050 a year each, say."

Duffy showed some relief at this. "But I still don't like Dyer's figures," he said. "What about this £15,750 for general administrative overhead? You surely don't expect to sack anyone in the general office if I'm closed, do you?" "Probably not," said Dyer, "but someone has to pay for these costs. We can't ignore them when we look at an individual department, because if we do that with each department in turn, we shall finish up by convincing ourselves that directors, accountants, typists, stationery, and the like don't have to be paid for. And they do, believe me."

"Well, I think we've thrashed this out pretty fully," said Walsh, "but I've been turning over in my mind the possibility of perhaps keeping on the maintenance work ourselves. What are your views on that, Duffy?"

"I don't know," said Duffy, "but it's

worth looking into. We shouldn't need any machinery for that, and I could hand the supervision over to a foreman. You'd save £2,100 a year there, say. You'd only need about one fifth of the workers, but you could keep on the oldest. You wouldn't save any space here or at the rented warehouse, so I suppose the rent would be the same. I shouldn't think the other expenses would be more than £4,550 a year." "What about materials?" asked Walsh. "We use about 10 percent of the total on maintenance," Duffy replied.

"Well, I've told Packages, Ltd., that I'd let them know my decision within a week," said Walsh. "I'll let you know what I decide to do before I write to them."

Questions

1. Identify the four alternatives implicit in the case.

2. Using cash flow as the criterion, which alternative is the most attractive?

3. What, if any, additional information do you think is necessary in order to make a sound decision?

CASE 21–5   Baldwin Bicycle Company

In May 1983, Suzanne Leister, marketing vice president of Baldwin Bicycle Company, was mulling over the discussion she had had the previous day with Karl Knott, a buyer from Hi-Valu Stores, Inc. Hi-Valu operated a chain of discount department stores in the Northwest. Hi-Valu's sales volume had grown to the extent that it was beginning to add "house-brand" (also called "private-label") merchandise to the product lines of several of its departments. Mr. Knott, Hi-Valu's buyer for sporting goods, had approached Ms. Leister about the possibility of Baldwin's producing bicycles for Hi-Valu. The bicycles would bear the name "Challenger," which Hi-Valu planned to use for all of its house-brand sporting goods.

Baldwin had been making bicycles for almost 40 years. In 1983, the company's line included 10 models, ranging from a small beginner's model with training wheels to a deluxe 12-speed adult's model. Sales were currently at an annual rate of about $10 million. (The company's 1982 financial statements appear in Exhibit 1.) Most of Baldwin's sales were through independently owned toy stores and bicycle shops. Baldwin had never before distributed its products through department store chains of any type. Ms. Leister felt that Baldwin bicycles had the image of being above average in quality and price, but not a "top of the line" product.

Hi-Valu's proposal to Baldwin had features that made it quite different from Baldwin's normal way of doing business. First, it was very important to Hi-Valu to have ready access to a large inventory of bicycles, because Hi-Valu had had great difficulty in predicting bicycle sales, both by store and by month. Hi-Valu wanted to carry these inventories in its regional warehouses, but did not want title on a bicycle to pass from Baldwin to Hi-Valu until the bicycle was shipped from one of its regional warehouses to a specific Hi-Valu store. At that point, Hi-Valu would regard the bicycle as having been purchased from Baldwin, and would pay for it within 30 days. However, Hi-Valu

EXHIBIT 1
FINANCIAL STATEMENTS
(thousand of dollars)

BALDWIN BICYCLE COMPANY
Balance Sheet
As of December 31, 1982

Assets		*Liabilities and Owners' Equity*	
Cash	$ 342	Current liabilities	$3,478
Accounts receivable	1,359	Noncurrent liabilities	1,512
Inventories	2,756		4,990
Plant and equipment (net)	3,635	Owners' equity	3,102
	$8,092		$8,092

Income Statement
For the Year Ended December 31, 1982

Sales revenues	$10,872
Cost of sales	8,045
Gross margin	2,827
Other expenses	2,354
Income before taxes	473
Income tax expense	218
Net income	$ 255

would agree to take title to any bicycle that had been in one of its warehouses for four months, again paying for it within 30 days. Mr. Knott estimated that on average, a bike would remain in a Hi-Valu regional warehouse for two months.

Second, Hi-Valu wanted to sell its Challenger bicycles at lower prices than the name-brand bicycles it carried, and yet still earn approximately the same dollar gross margin on each bicycle sold—the rationale being that Challenger bike sales would take away from the sales of the name-brand bikes. Thus, Hi-Valu wanted to purchase bikes from Baldwin at lower prices than the wholesale prices of comparable bikes sold through Baldwin's usual channels.

Finally, Hi-Valu wanted the Challenger bike to be somewhat different in appearance from Baldwin's other bikes. While the frame and mechanical components could be the same as used on current Baldwin models, the fenders, seats, and handlebars would need to be some-

what different, and the tires would have to have the name "Challenger" molded into their sidewalls. Also, the bicycles would have to be packed in boxes printed with the Hi-Valu and Challenger names. These requirements were expected by Ms. Leister to increase Baldwin's purchasing, inventorying, and production costs over and above the added costs that would be incurred for a comparable increase in volume for Baldwin's regular products.

On the positive side, Ms. Leister was acutely aware that the "bicycle boom" had flattened out, and this plus a poor economy had caused Baldwin's sales volume to fall the past two years. As a result, Baldwin currently was operating its plant at about 75 percent of one-shift capacity. Thus, the added volume from Hi-Valu's purchases could possibly be very attractive. If agreement could be reached on prices, Hi-Valu would sign a contract guaranteeing to Baldwin that Hi-Valu would buy its house-brand bicycles only from Baldwin for a three-year period. The contract would then be automatically extended on a year-to-year basis, unless one party gave the other at least three-months' notice that it did not wish to extend the contract.

Suzanne Leister realized she needed to do some preliminary financial analysis of this proposal before having any further discussions with Karl Knott. She had written on a pad the information she had gathered to use in her initial analysis; this information is shown in Exhibit 2.

Question

Does Hi-Valu's proposal appear to be financially attractive to Baldwin Bicycle Company?

EXHIBIT 2
DATA PERTINENT TO HI-VALU PROPOSAL
(Notes taken by Suzanne Leister)

---

1. *Estimated first-year costs of producing Challenger bicycles* (average unit costs, assuming a constant mix of models):

Materials	$39.80*
Labor	19.60
Overhead (@ 125% of labor)	24.50†
	$83.90

    *Includes items specific to models for Hi-Valu, not used in our standard models.
    †Accountant says about 40 percent of total production overhead cost is variable; 125 percent of DL$ rate is based on volume of 100,000 bicycles per year.

2. *One-time added costs* of preparing drawings and/or arranging sources for fenders, seats, handlebars, tires, and shipping boxes that differ from those used in our standard models: approximately $5,000 (based on estimated two man-months of effort at $2,500 per month).

3. *Unit price and annual volume:* Hi-Valu estimates it will need 25,000 bikes a year and proposes to pay us (based on the assumed mix of models) an average of $92.29 per bike for the first year. Contract to contain an inflation escalation clause such that price will increase in proportion to inflation-caused increases in costs shown in item 1, above; thus, the $92.29 and $83.90 figures are, in effect, "constant-dollar" amounts. Knott intimated that there was very little, if any, negotiating leeway in the $92.29 proposed initial price.

4. *Asset-related costs* (annual variable costs, as percent of dollar value of assets):

Pretax cost of funds (to finance receivables or inventories)	18.0%
Recordkeeping costs (for receivables or inventories)	1.0
Inventory insurance	0.3
State property tax on inventory	0.7
Inventory-handling labor and equipment	3.0
Pilferage, obsolescence, breakage, etc.	0.5

5. *Assumptions for Challenger-related added inventories* (average over the year):

    Materials: two months' supply.
    Work in process: 1,000 bikes, half completed (but all materials for them issued).
    Finished goods: 500 bikes (awaiting next carload lot shipment to a Hi-Valu warehouse).

6. *Impact on our regular sales:* Some customers comparison shop for bikes, and many of them are likely to recognize a Challenger bike as a good value when compared with a similar bike (either ours or a competitor's) at a higher price in a nonchain toy or bicycle store. In 1982, we sold 98,791 bikes. My best guess is that our sales over the next three years will be about 100,000 bikes a year if we forego the Hi-Valu deal. If we accept it, I think we'll lose about 3,000 units of our regular sales volume a year, since our retail distribution is quite strong in Hi-Valu's market regions. These estimates do not include the possibility that a few of our current dealers might drop our line if they find out we're making bikes for Hi-Valu.

CASE 21–6 Lindholm Snowmobile Company*

Lindholm Snowmobile Company produced two models of snowmobiles, which are small, open vehicles with powered drive tracks that will operate on snow-covered terrain. The company had four departments: body fabrication, engine production, model S assembly, and model V assembly. Monthly production capacity in these departments was as follows:

	Model S	Model V
Body fabrication.............	25,000	35,000
Engine production...........	33,333	16,667
Model S assembly...........	22,500	—
Model V assembly...........	—	15,000

For example, if only model S snowmobiles were to be produced, the body department could make 25,000 bodies a month and the engine department could produce 33,333 engines a month. Equivalently, if the body department capacity is expressed as being 25,000 body units, then each model S body requires one unit of capacity, and each model V body requires only five sevenths of a unit of capacity. Similarly, it can be said that each model S engine uses up one of the 33,333 units of capacity in the engine department, whereas a model V engine requires 2 units of engine department capacity. These capacity relationships are shown in Exhibit 1.

*This case is adapted from an example used by Robert Dorfman in "Mathematical or 'Linear' Programming: A Nonmathematical Exposition," *American Economic Review*, December 1953.

EXHIBIT 1
DIAGRAM OF FEASIBLE PRODUCT MIXES

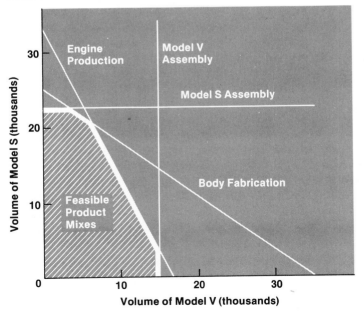

Exhibit 2 shows prices and cost data for each model. At present, Lindholm was able to sell as many snowmobiles as it could produce. In recent months, production (and, therefore, sales) had been 3,333 model S and 15,000 model V. This product mix used up all of the capacity in the engine department and the model V assembly department, but did not require the other two departments to operate at capacity.

It was not clear to Lindholm's management group that the current product mix was the best one. This was a matter of concern because of the company's poor profit showing in recent months. In an executive committee meeting called to discuss the matter, the sales manager offered the opinion that company profits would increase if the model S were dropped and resources were devoted exclusively to the model V. "When you sub-tract our selling costs, which average about 4 percent of sales, model S doesn't even show a profit. You can't lose money on each model S and then make it up on volume!"

The controller, on the other hand, said that the present product mix appeared to be the best one. "No matter how you look at it, we should make as many model V as we can: it has the larger gross margin per unit, the larger per unit excess of revenues over out-of-pocket costs, and the larger per unit absorption of overhead costs. But we would have excess capacity in the engine department if we didn't make *any* model S; so we should make all the units of V we can, plus enough units of S to get the engine department up to capacity too."

The production manager added another possibility: "I know that the Devon Engine Company is hungry for work—

EXHIBIT 2
PER UNIT GROSS MARGIN DATA

	Model S		Model V	
Selling price...................		$1,250		$1,600
Production costs:				
Materials:				
Body	191		238	
Engine...................	329		299	
Assembly	52	572	84	621
Direct labor:				
Body	63		45	
Engine...................	102		204	
Assembly	45	210	45	294
Overhead:*				
Body	126		90	
Engine...................	204		408	
Assembly	90	420	90	588
Total..................		1,202		1,503
Gross margin.................		$ 48		$ 97

*Approximately 40 percent of these per unit overhead amounts were costs that varied with volume. Thus, at the present production mix (3,333 model S and 15,000 model V), total overhead costs were about $10,220,000, of which about $4,088,000 was variable.

one of my friends who works there just got laid off. If we could provide them with our list of engine components suppliers, and a set of drawings, they could produce engines for model S snowmobiles; then we could use up more of our body and model S assembly capacities." The sales manager responded, "I don't see the merit in that idea. Devon will surely charge us more than our own costs of making an engine, and that will just give us a bigger loss on each model S, after subtracting selling costs from its gross margin."

Questions

1. Given the present capacity constraints, what is the most profitable product mix for Lindholm? (Assume nonproduction costs are the same for any mix that causes the plant to operate at full capacity.)

2. What is the most that Lindholm could pay Devon for a model S engine without reducing Lindholm's profits?

3. Should Lindholm consider purchasing from an outside supplier completed model V engines? If so, what is the most Lindholm could pay for such engines without reducing its profits?

4. Subsequent to the events described in the case, Lindholm's management was contacted by a consulting industrial engineer, who claimed that she could advise the company on how to increase the effective capacity in its two assembly departments without having to make any significant additional investment in the departments. Her fee for this advice was very high, so Lindholm's management wanted to know how much this added capacity would be worth before buying her services. How much would Lindholm's optimal monthly profit increase if it had one more unit of model S assembly capacity? One more unit of model V assembly capacity? How, if at all, do your answers change if Lindholm can buy engines from an outside supplier at an attractive price?

CASE 21–7 Gentle Electric Company

Robert Edison, general manager of Gentle Electric Company (GEC), was contemplating several recent developments in the power transformer market. Mr. Edison was concerned because in its production of control units for passenger and freight elevators, GEC used five large transformers each working day of the month. (GEC operated on a 20-day per month schedule.) For several years, the transformers had been produced in only two locations in the United States, one in New England and the other on the West Coast. Luckily for GEC, the New England producer was located several miles away and offered free delivery to GEC within hours.

Several months earlier, Mr. Edison had compiled the following information about the transformers:

Information		Source of Information
Total annual usage	1,200 units	Purchasing
Requisitions per year	48 times (weekly)	Purchasing
Units per requisition	25 units	Purchasing
Inventory carrying cost	20%	Controller
Weight per unit	500 lbs.	Shipping and receiving
Cost of unloading	$0.10 per cwt.	Warehouse manager
Clerical cost per requisition	$10	Purchasing
Expediting cost per requisition	$15	Shipping and receiving
Warehouse capacity	200 units	Warehouse manager
Outside warehouse costs	$12 per unit per year*	Warehouse manager

*There is existing space in the warehouse for 200 units. Additional space must be leased for a year. As a result, if an order of more than 200 units arrives, part of the order must be stored in leased space.

Several months after compiling this information, Mr. Edison was informed by his purchasing agent that GEC's local supplier had followed its West Coast competitor in announcing a new price structure:

Units per Order	Unit Price*
First 100	$500
Next 100	490
Each unit over 200	475

*For example, an order of 210 units would cost
100($500) + 100($490) + 10($475) = $103,750.

Just recently, GEC's local supplier announced that it was discontinuing production of transformers, forcing GEC to deal with the West Coast supplier whose prices are the same as the local supplier except that they are FOB, California. The traffic department informed Mr. Edison that the transportation cost per hundredweight is $6 for carload lots of 50,000 pounds. The LCL (less than carload) rate is $10 per hundredweight. The replenishment cycle will normally take one week.

Mr. Edison wonders what effects these new developments will have on its cost structure for transformer purchases.

Questions

1. The optimal value of Q shown in the text minimizes the function:

$$T = RC + S \cdot \frac{R}{Q} + \frac{Q}{2} \cdot C \cdot K$$

The first term in this function is annual acquisition costs; the second is annual ordering (or setup) costs; and the third is annual inventory holding costs.

   a. Be sure you understand what each term represents and how it was derived. Try to make explicit the assumptions that are built into the model (i.e., formula).

   b. If you remember calculus, prove that the Q given on page 000 in fact minimizes T.

2. Assume the original transformer price was $500 per unit. Was Gentle Electric initially replenishing its inventory in the most economical way? (Assume all requisitions are subject to both clerical and expediting costs.)

3. When Gentle Electric was offered a volume discount, which costs were affected? What happened to EOQ?

4. What should be Gentle Electric's ordering rule when it begins to deal with the West Coast firm?

Hint: For 3 and 4, there are discontinuities in the total annual cost function, T (acquisition costs plus ordering costs plus holding costs). You will need to develop a "customized" formula for Gentle Electric's annual costs for each smooth segment of the total cost curve.

CASE 21–8   Warren Agency

Thaddeus Warren operated a real estate agency that specialized in finding buyers for commercial properties. Warren was approached one day by a prospective client who had three properties that she wished to sell. The client indicated the prices she wished to receive for these properties as follows:

Property	Price
A	$ 25,000
B	50,000
C	100,000

Warren would receive a commission of 4 percent on any of the properties he was able to sell.

The client laid down the following conditions: "Mr. Warren, you have to sell A first. If you can't sell it within a month, the entire deal is off—no commission and no chance to sell B or C. If you sell A within a month, then I'll give you the commission on A and the option of (a) stopping at this point, or (b) selling either B or C next under the same conditions (i.e., sell within a month or no commission on the second property and no chance to sell the third property). If you succeed in selling the first two properties, you will also have the option of selling the third."

After the client had left, Warren proceeded to analyze the proposal that had been made to him to determine whether or not to accept it. He figured his selling costs and his chances of selling each property at the prices set by the client to be:

Property	Selling Costs	Warren's Assessment of Probability of Sale
A	$800	0.7
B	200	0.6
C	400	0.5

He believed that sale of a particular property would not make it any more or less likely that the two remaining properties could be sold. Selling costs would have to be incurred whether or not a particular property was sold but could be avoided by deciding not to attempt to sell the property.

Since property A would have to be sold before any further action could be taken, Warren prepared the following table in an attempt to determine whether or not to accept property A:

Outcome	Probability	Accept A	Refuse A
		Act	
A sold	0.7	$ 200	$0
A not sold	0.3	−800	0
Expected value		$ −100	$0

Thus, accepting A would be unprofitable looked at by itself. Warren was not very happy with this conclusion, however, because he reasoned that success in selling A would entitle him to offer either B or C, and it looked as if either of these properties would result in an expected profit. He felt that somehow or other the value of this opportunity should be taken into consideration.

Questions

1. Develop a decision tree for Warren's problem. (Hint: The tree will have 11 endpoints.)

2. Based on the decision tree analysis, what should Warren do?

3. Suppose that before any of the properties is listed, another realtor approaches Warren and offers to buy from Warren the rights to this deal (i.e., with all of the conditions that were stipulated by the client). For what amount should Warren be willing to sell these rights?

22

Longer-Run Decisions:
Capital Budgeting

Chapter 21 discussed those types of alternative choice problems that tend to have a relatively short time horizon. That is, those decisions do not commit or "lock in" the organization to a certain course of action over a considerable period in the future. Similarly, those short-run decisions usually do not significantly affect the amount of funds that must be invested in the organization. In this chapter, we extend the discussion of differential accounting problems to those that do involve relatively long-term differential investments of capital. Such problems are called *capital investment problems*. They are also commonly called *capital budgeting problems* because a capital budget is a list of the capital investment projects that an organization has decided to carry out.

In these problems, differential costs and revenues are treated in the same manner as in Chapter 21. The only difference is that the longer time horizon of capital budgeting problems magnifies the problems of estimating these cost and revenue items. However, the long-term investment aspect of capital budgeting problems leads to a more complicated analytical approach. It is important that these complications be mastered because capital budgeting decisions *do* lock in the organization to a course of action for several, if not many, future years.

NATURE OF THE PROBLEM

When an organization purchases a fixed asset, it makes an *investment*. The organization commits funds today in the expectation of earning a return on those funds over some future period. Such an investment is similar to that made by a bank when it lends money. The essential characteristic of both types of transactions is that funds are committed today in the expectation of earning a return in the future. In the case of the bank loan, the future return is in the form of interest plus repayment of the principal. In the case of the fixed asset, the future return is in the form of earnings generated by profitable use of the asset. We shall designate such earnings as the cash inflows. *An investment is thus the purchase of a future stream of expected cash inflows.*

When an organization is considering whether or not to purchase a new fixed asset, the essential question is whether the future cash inflows are likely to be large enough to warrant making the investment. The problems discussed in this chapter all have this general form: It is proposed that a certain amount be invested now in the expectation that a return will be earned on the investment in future years. Is the amount of anticipated future cash inflows large enough to justify investing these funds in the proposal? Illustrative problems are the following:

1. *Replacement.* Shall we replace existing equipment with more efficient equipment? The future expected cash inflows on this investment are the cost savings resulting from lower operating costs, or the profits from additional volume produced by the new equipment, or both.

2. *Expansion.* Shall we build or otherwise acquire a new facility? The future expected cash inflows on this investment are the profits from the goods and services produced in the new facility.

3. *Cost reduction.* Shall we buy equipment to perform an operation now done manually; that is, shall we spend money in order to save money? The expected future cash inflows on this investment are savings resulting from lower operating costs.

4. *Choice of equipment.* Which of several proposed items of equipment shall we purchase for a given purpose? The choice often turns on which item is expected to give the largest return on the investment made in it.

5. *Lease or buy.* Having decided that we need a building or a piece of equipment, should we lease it or buy it? The choice turns on whether the investment required to purchase the asset will earn an adequate return because of the cash inflows that will result from avoiding the lease payments. (Avoiding a cash outflow is equivalent to receiving a cash inflow.)

6. *New product.* Should a new product be added to the line? The choice turns on whether the expected cash inflows from the sale of the new product are large enough to warrant the investment in equipment, working capital, and the costs required to make and introduce the product.

General Approach

Note that all these problems involve two quite dissimilar types of amounts. First, there is the investment, which is usually made in a lump sum at the beginning of the project. Although not literally made "today," it is made at a specific point in time that for analytical purposes is called *today*, or *Time Zero*. Second, there is a stream of cash inflows that are expected to result fcom this investment over a period of future years.

These two types of amounts cannot be compared directly with one another because they occur at different points in time. In order to make a valid comparison, we must bring the amounts involved to equivalent values at the same point in time.

The most convenient point to calculate the values is at Time Zero. In order to do this, we need not adjust the amount of the investment since it is already stated at its Time Zero or present value. We need only to convert the stream of future cash inflows to their present value equivalents, and we can then compare them directly with the amount of the investment.[1] To do this, we multiply the cash inflow for each year by the present value of $1 for that year at the appropriate rate of return (Table A on page 961). This process is called *discounting* the cash inflows. The rate at which the cash inflows are discounted is called the *required rate of return, discount rate,* or *hurdle rate.*

Net Present Value. The difference between the present value of the cash inflows and the amount of investment is called the *net present value* (NPV). If the NPV is a nonnegative amount, the proposal is acceptable.

Example. A proposed investment of $1,000 is expected to produce cash inflows of $625 per year for each of the next two years. The required rate of return is 14 percent. The present value of the cash inflows can be compared with the present value of the investment as follows:

	Year	Amount	Discount Factor (Table A)	Total Present Value
Cash inflow	1	$ 625	0.877	$ 548
Cash inflow	2	625	0.769	481
Present values of cash inflows				1,029
Less: Investment	0	1,000	1.000	1,000
Net present value				$ 29

The proposed investment is acceptable.

The decision rule given above is a general rule, and some qualifications to it will be discussed later. To apply it, the approach is as follows:

---

[1] If the reader is not familiar with the concept of present value, the Appendix to Chapter 8 up to the section titled "Calculating Bond Yields" should be read before continuing with this chapter.

1. Estimate the amount of investment.
2. Estimate the amount of cash inflow in each future year.
3. Find the present value of these cash inflows. This is done by discounting the cash inflow amounts at the required rate of return.
4. Subtract the amount of investment from the total present value of the inflows to determine the net present value.

Return on Investment

So far, we have shown how the net present value can be calculated if the investment, cash inflows, and the required rate of return are given. It is useful to look at the situation from another viewpoint: How can the rate of return be calculated when the investment and the cash inflows are given?

Consider a bank loan. If a bank lends $20,000 and receives interest payments of $3,000 at the end of each year for five years, with the $20,000 loan principal being repaid at the end of the fifth year, the bank correctly is said to earn a return of 15 percent on its investment of $20,000. Note that the return percentage is found by dividing the annual return by the amount of investment outstanding during the year. In this case, the amount of loan outstanding each year was $20,000 and the return was $3,000 in each year, so the rate of return was $3,000 ÷ $20,000, or 15 percent.

If, however, a bank lends $20,000 and is repaid $5,966 at the end of each year for five years, the problem of finding the return is more complicated. In this case, only part of the $5,966 annual cash inflow represents the return, and the remainder is a repayment of the principal. This is the same loan that was used in the Kinnear Company example in the Appendix to Chapter 8. As was demonstrated there, this loan also has a return of 15 percent, in the same sense as the loan described in the preceding paragraph: the $5,966 annual payments will repay the loan itself and in addition will provide a return of 15 percent of the *amount of principal still outstanding each year*. The fact that the return is 15 percent is demonstrated in Illustration 8–1. Of the $5,966 repaid in the first year, $3,000, or 15 percent of the $20,000 then outstanding, is the return; the remainder, or $2,966, reduces the principal down to $17,034. In the second year, $2,555 is a return of 15 percent on the $17,034 of principal then outstanding, and the remainder, $3,411, reduces the principal to $13,623; and so on.

As seen in the above examples, when an investment involves annual interest payments with the full amount of investment being repaid at its termination date, the computation of the return is simple. But when the annual payments combine both principal and interest, the computation is more complicated. Some investment problems are of the simple type. For example, if a business buys land for $20,000, rents it for $3,000 a year for five years, and then sells it for $20,000 at the end of five years, the return is 15 percent. Many capital investment decisions, on the other hand, relate to depreciable assets, which characteristically have little or no resale value at the end of their useful life. The cash inflows from these investments must therefore be large enough for the investor both to recoup the investment itself during its life and also to earn a satisfactory return on the amount not yet recouped, just as in the situation shown in Illustration 8–1.

Stream of Cash Inflows. The cash inflows on most capital investments are a series of amounts received over several future years. Calculating the present value of a series or stream of cash inflows was explained in the Appendix to Chapter 8. Recall that for a *level* stream, the factors in Table B (page 962) can be used.

Table A and Table B are often used in combination, as shown in the next example. This example also demonstrates that the return on investment for the business renting its land, mentioned above, is indeed 15 percent.

> **Example.** Is a proposed investment of $20,000 acceptable if it is expected that annual cash inflows will be $3,000 a year for the next five years with the $20,000 to be repaid at the end of five years, and if the required rate of return is 15 percent?
>
> *Solution:* As shown by the following calculation, the cash inflows discounted at 15 percent have a present value of $20,000, which is equal to the original investment. Thus, the investment's return is 15 percent, and it is therefore acceptable.

Year	Inflow	15 Percent Discount Factor	Present Value
1–5	$3,000/year	3.352 (Table B)	$10,056
End of 5	$20,000	0.497 (Table A)	9,940
Total present value			$19,996*

*Would be $20,000 if discount factors included more decimal places.

Other Compounding Assumptions. Tables A and B are constructed on the assumption that cash inflows are received once a year and on the last day of the year. For many problems this is not a realistic assumption because cash in the form of increased revenues or lower costs is likely to flow in throughout the year. Nevertheless, annual tables are customarily used in capital investment problems, on the grounds that (1) they are easier to understand than tables constructed on other assumptions, such as monthly or continuous compounding and (2) they are good enough considering the inevitable margin of error in the basic estimates.

Annual tables *understate* the present value of cash inflows if these inflows are in fact received throughout the year rather than entirely on the last day of the year. Tables are available showing the present values of earnings flows that occur quarterly, monthly, or even continuously.

> **Example.** The table below illustrates the degree to which annual tables understate the present value of inflows received during the year. The numbers in the table show the ratio of the present value of periodic, within-the-year receipts to the present value of an equal annual total received at the end of one year.

Frequency of Inflow	Discount Rates			
	6 Percent	10 Percent	15 Percent	25 Percent
Semiannually...............	1.014	1.023	1.032	1.049
Monthly...................	1.026	1.043	1.062	1.096
Continuously	1.029	1.047	1.068	1.106

ESTIMATING THE VARIABLES

We now discuss how to estimate each of the four elements involved in capital investment calculations. These are:

1. The required rate of return.
2. The economic life, which is the number of years for which cash inflows are anticipated.
3. The amount of cash inflow in each year.
4. The amount of investment.

Required Rate of Return

Two alternative ways of arriving at the required rate of return will be described: (1) trial and error and (2) cost of capital.

Trial and Error. Recall that the higher the required rate of return, the lower the present value of the cash inflows. It follows that the higher the required rate of return, the fewer the investment proposals that will have cash inflows whose present value exceeds the amount of the investment. Thus, if a given rate results in the rejection of many proposed investments that management intuitively feels are acceptable, there is an indication that this rate is too high. Conversely, if a given rate results in the acceptance of a flood of projects, there is an indication that it is too low. As a starting point in this trial-and-error process, a company may select a rate that other companies in the same industry use.

Cost of Capital. In economic theory, the required rate of return should be equal to the company's *cost of capital*. This is the cost of debt capital plus the cost of equity capital, weighted by the relative amount of each in the company's capital structure.

Example. Assume a company in which the cost of debt capital (e.g., bonds) is 7 percent and the cost of equity capital (e.g., common stock) is 18 percent, and in which 40 percent of the total capital is debt and 60 percent is equity. The cost of capital is calculated as follows:

Type	Capital Cost	Weight	Weighted Cost
Debt (bonds)	7%	0.4	2.8%
Equity (stock)	18	0.6	10.8
Total		1.0	13.6%

Thus, the cost of capital is 13.6 percent or, rounded, 14 percent.

In the above example, the 7 percent used as the cost of debt capital may appear to be low. It is low because it has been adjusted for the income tax effect of debt financing. Since interest on debt is a tax-deductible expense, each additional dollar of interest expense ultimately costs the company only $0.54 (assuming a tax rate of 46 percent) because income taxes are reduced by $0.46 for each additional interest dollar. For reasons to be explained, capital investment calculations should be made on an aftertax basis, so the rate of return should be an aftertax rate.[2]

The difficulty with the cost-of-capital approach is that, although the cost of debt is usually known within narrow limits, the cost of equity is difficult to estimate. Presumably, the rate of return that investors expect, which is the cost of equity capital, is reflected in the market price of the company's stock. But the market price is also influenced by such factors as general economic conditions, investors' estimates of the company's future earnings, and dividend policy. Techniques for estimating the cost of equity capital are described in finance texts.

Selection of a Rate. Most companies use a judgmental approach in establishing the required rate of return. Either they experiment with various rates by the trial-and-error method described above, or they judgmentally settle upon a rate because they feel elaborate calculations are likely to be fruitless.

Nonprofit organizations do not obtain equity capital from investors, so they have a difficult problem in arriving at the rate to be used in their capital investment decisions. Some use the interest rate on debt (which for them is the pretax rate because they do not pay income taxes). If the

---

[2]Note that in the example, the cost of capital is approximately the same as the *pretax* interest cost of debt. This approximate equality holds for many corporate financial structures. Nevertheless, companies usually use a required earnings rate that is somewhat above the pretax interest cost of debt capital.

organization has endowment funds, it may use the rate earned on these funds.

The required rate of return selected by the techniques described above applies to investment proposals of *average* risk. In general, the return demanded for an investment varies with the investment's risk. Thus, the required return for an *individual* investment project of greater-than-average risk should be higher than the average rate of return on all projects.

Effect of Nondiscretionary Projects.   Some investments are made out of necessity, rather than based on an analysis of their profitability. Examples include employee recreational facilities, pollution control equipment, and installation of safety devices. These investments use capital, but provide no demonstrable cash inflows. Thus, if the other, discretionary investments had a net present value of zero when discounted at the cost of capital, the company would not recover all of its capital costs. In effect, the discretionary projects must not only stand on their own feet but *also* must carry the capital-cost burden of the nondiscretionary (i.e., necessity) projects. For this reason, many companies use a required rate of return that is higher than the cost of capital.

> **Example.**   Zeta Company typically has $10 million invested in capital projects, of which 20 percent represents necessity projects. If Zeta's cost of capital is 15 percent, its capital projects must earn $1.5 million per year in addition to recovering the amount invested. The $8 million of discretionary projects must therefore earn 18.75 percent, not 15 percent (because $8 million $\times$ 0.1875 = $1.5 million). Even the 18.75 percent is an understatement, for the $2 million capital invested in the necessity projects must also be recovered.

Economic Life

The economic life of an investment is the number of years over which cash inflows are expected as a consequence of making the investment. Even though cash inflows may be expected for an indefinitely long period, the economic life is usually set at a specified maximum number of years, such as 10, 15, or 20. This maximum is often shorter than the life actually anticipated both because of the uncertainty of cash inflow estimates for distant years and because the present value of cash inflows for distant years is so low that the amount of these cash inflows has no significant effect on the calculation. For example, at a discount rate of 14 percent, a $1 cash inflow in year 21 has a present value of only 6.4 cents.

The end of the period selected for the economic life is called the *investment horizon*. The term suggests that beyond this time cash inflows are not visible. Economic life can rarely be estimated exactly. Nevertheless, it is important that the best possible estimate be made, for the economic life has a significant effect on the calculations.

When a proposed project involves the purchase of equipment, the economic life of the investment corresponds to the estimated service life of the equipment *to the user*. There is a tendency when thinking about the life of equipment to consider primarily its *physical life*, that is, the number of years until the equipment wears out. Although the physical life is an upper limit, in most cases the economic life of the equipment is considerably shorter than its physical life. One reason is that technological progress makes equipment obsolete, and the investment in the equipment will cease to earn a return when it is replaced by even better equipment.

The economic life also ends when the entity ceases to make profitable use of the equipment. This can happen because the operation performed by the equipment is made unnecessary by a change in style or process; because the market for the product made with the equipment has vanished; or because the entity decides, for whatever reason, to discontinue the product.

The key question is: Over what period of time is the investment likely to generate cash inflows for *this* entity? For whatever reason, when the investment no longer produces cash inflows, its economic life has ended. In view of the uncertainties associated with the operation of an organization, most managers are conservative in estimating what the economic life of a proposed investment will be.

Uneven Lives. For many types of equipment, it is reasonable to assume that the present equipment could be used for a period of time that is at least as long as the economic life of the proposed equipment. In situations in which this assumption is not valid, however, differential cash flows on a proposed asset purchased now will not in fact occur each year of the period being considered, because a new asset must be purchased anyway when the physical life of the present one ends. Thereafter, there may be no difference in the annual cost of the two alternatives (purchase the asset now versus don't purchase it now).

If the expected physical life of the present equipment is significantly shorter than the expected economic life of the proposed equipment, some way must be found of making an equivalence between the time periods covered by the two alternatives. For example, if the proposed equipment has an economic life of 10 years but the present equipment has a remaining physical life of only 6 years, the differential cash flows will occur for only 6 years. One approach is to estimate the remaining value of the new equipment at the end of the sixth year of its life. The analysis would then cover only the six-year period, with this remaining value being treated as a residual value, or implicit cash inflow, at the end of the sixth year.

Cash Inflows

The earnings from an investment are essentially the additional *cash* that is estimated to flow in as a consequence of making the investment as compared with what the cash inflows would be if the investment were not made. The *differential* concept emphasized in Chapter 21 is therefore equally applicable here, and the discussion in that chapter should carefully be kept in mind in estimating cash inflows for the type of problem now being considered. In particular, recall that the focus is on *cash* inflows. Accounting numbers based on the accrual concept are not necessarily relevant.

Consider, for example, a proposal to replace existing equipment with better equipment. What are the cash inflows associated with this proposal? We note first that the existing equipment must still be usable, for if it no longer works, there is no alternative and hence no analytical problem; it *must* be replaced. The comparison, therefore, is between (1) continuing to use the existing equipment (the base case) and (2) investing in the proposed equipment. The existing equipment has certain labor, material, power, repair, and other costs associated with its future operation. If the new equipment is proposed as a means of reducing costs, there will be different, lower costs associated with its use. The difference between these two amounts of cost is the cash inflow anticipated if the new equipment is acquired. (Note that in this example, the differential cash inflow is really a reduction in cash outflows.)

If the proposed equipment is not a replacement but instead increases productive capacity, the differential income from the higher sales volume is a cash inflow anticipated from the use of the proposed equipment. This differential income is the difference between the added sales revenue and the additional costs required to produce that sales revenue. These differential costs include any material, labor, selling costs, or other costs that would not be incurred if the increased volume were not produced and sold.

Inflation. If inflation is expected to continue in future years, the *purchasing power* of a $1 cash inflow decreases as the length of time until the inflow will be received increases. The question arises as to whether future inflows should therefore be restated in terms of current (Time Zero) purchasing power before discounting them. In general, the answer is no. This is because the discount rate in effect includes an inflation component; that is, the discount rate is higher if inflation is expected than the rate would be if there were no expectations of future inflation. The rate is higher either because (1) management intentionally increases the rate to account for future inflation or (2) because the company's cost of capital reflects the financial markets' inflation expectations (e.g., bond interest rates are higher in inflationary periods than in periods of stable prices).

Depreciation

Depreciation on the proposed equipment is not an item of differential cost. Depreciation is omitted from the calculation of net present value because the calculation procedure itself allows for the recovery of the investment, and to include depreciation as a cost would be double counting. When we say an investment of $1,000 that produces a cash inflow of $400 a year for five years has a net present value of $341 at a required rate of return of 15 percent, we mean that the cash inflow is large enough to (1) recover the investment of $1,000, (2) earn 15 percent on the amount of investment outstanding, and (3) earn $341 in addition. This recovery of investment is equivalent to the sum of the annual depreciation charges that are made in the accounting records. Therefore, it would be incorrect to include a separate item for depreciation in calculating cash inflow.

Depreciation on the existing equipment is likewise not relevant because the book value of existing equipment represents a sunk cost. For the reason explained in Chapter 21, sunk costs should be disregarded.

Income Tax Impact. For alternative choice problems in which no investment is involved, aftertax income is 54 percent of pretax income, assuming a tax rate of 46 percent.[3] Thus, if a proposed cost reduction method is estimated to save $10,000 a year pretax, it will save $5,400 a year after tax. Although $5,400 is obviously not as welcome as $10,000 would be, the proposed cost reduction method would increase income, and in the absence of arguments to the contrary, the decision should be made to adopt it. This is the case with *all* the alternative choice problems discussed in Chapter 21; that is, if the proposal is acceptable on a pretax basis, it is also acceptable on an aftertax basis.

When depreciable assets are involved in a proposal, however, the situation is quite different. In proposals of this type, *there is no simple relationship between pretax cash inflows and aftertax cash inflows.* This is primarily because depreciation is not a factor in estimates of operating cash flows, whereas depreciation *is* an expense taken into account in calculating taxable income. Depreciation offsets part of what would otherwise be additional taxable income. It is therefore called a *tax shield* in investment calculations because it shields the pretax cash inflows from the full impact of income taxes.

In order to calculate the *aftertax* cash inflows, we must take account of this depreciation tax shield. At the same time, we must be careful not to permit the amount of depreciation itself to enter into the calculation of *cash* flows for the reasons referred to above. Illustration 22–1 shows a net present value calculation including the tax shield.

Accelerated Depreciation. The example in Illustration 22–1 for simplicity assumed straight-line depreciation. In fact, most companies use accelerated depreciation[4] in calculating taxable income because it

---

[3] In examples in this book, we use a 46 percent tax rate. Actual corporate income tax rates may be different because (a) Congress changes the rate from time to time and (b) many corporations pay state and/or local taxes on income. In discussions and in certain calculations, many people use a rate of 50 percent as an adequate approximation.

[4] The 1981 Tax Act uses the term *accelerated cost recovery* rather than *accelerated depreciation.*

ILLUSTRATION 22–1
CALCULATION OF NET PRESENT VALUE WITH TAX SHIELD

Assumed situation: A proposed machine costs $10,000 and will provide estimated pretax cash inflows of $3,500 per year for five years. The required rate of return is 14 percent, the tax rate is 46 percent, and straight-line depreciation is used.

	Taxable Income Calculation	Present Value Calculation
Annual pretax cash inflow..............................	$3,500	$ 3,500
Less: Additional depreciation.........................	2,000	
Differential taxable income.............................	1,500	
Differential income tax (@ 46%).......................		−690
Aftertax annual cash inflow............................		2,810
Present value of $2,810 over 5 years (factor = 3.433)....		9,647
Less: Investment.....................................		10,000
Net present value.....................................		$ (353)

The proposal is unacceptable.

increases the present value of the depreciation tax shield. Since accelerated depreciation results in nonlevel amounts of taxable income, Table B cannot be used in calculating present values because it assumes a level flow each year. Instead, one must compute the aftertax income each year and find the present value of each annual amount by using Table A.

Differential Depreciation. If the proposed asset is to replace an asset that has not been fully depreciated for tax purposes, then the tax shield is based on only the *differential* depreciation, that is, the difference between depreciation on the present asset and that on the new one. If the new asset is purchased, the old one will presumably be disposed of, so its depreciation will no longer provide a tax shield to the operating cash flows. In this case, the present value of the tax shield of the remaining depreciation on the old asset must be calculated (usually year by year), and this amount must be subtracted from the present value of the depreciation tax shield on the proposed asset.

Tax Effect of Interest. Interest actually paid (as distinguished from imputed interest) is an allowable expense for income tax pruposes. Therefore, if interest costs will be increased as a result of the investment, it can be argued that interest provides a tax shield similar to depreciation and that its impact should be estimated by the same method as for depreciation. Customarily, however, interest is *not* included anywhere in the calculations either of cash inflows or of taxes. This is because the calculation of the required rate of return includes an allowance for the tax effect of interest; that is, the estimate of the cost of debt is the aftertax cost of debt.

In problems where the method of financing is an important part of the proposal, the tax shield provided by interest may appropriately be considered. In these problems, the rate of return that results from the calculation is a return on that part of the investment which was financed by the shareholders' equity, not a return on the total funds committed to the investment.

> **Example.** A company is considering an investment in a parcel of real estate and intends to finance 70 percent of the investment by a mortgage loan on the property. It may wish to focus attention on the return on its own funds, the remaining 30 percent. In this case, it is appropriate to include in the calculation both the interest on the mortgage loan and the effect of this interest on taxable income. The rationale is that these debt funds—that is, the mortgage—would not have been available to the company were it not investing in the real estate.

Investment

The investment is the amount of funds an entity risks if it accepts an investment proposal. The relevant investment costs are the differential costs, that is, the outlays that will be made if the project is undertaken but that will not be made if it is not undertaken. The cost of the asset itself, any shipping and installation costs, and costs of training employees in the use of the new asset are examples of differential investment costs. These outlays are part of the investment, even though some of them may not be capitalized (treated as assets) in the accounting records.

Existing Assets. If the purchase of a new asset results in the sale of an existing asset, the net proceeds from the sale reduce the amount of the differential investment. In other words, the differential investment represents the total amount of *additional* funds that must be committed to the investment project. The net proceeds from the existing asset are its selling price less any costs incurred in selling it and in dismantling and removing it.

Residual Value. A proposed asset may have a *residual value* (i.e., salvage or resale value) at the end of its economic life. In a great many cases, the estimated residual value is so small and occurs so far in the future that it has no significant effect on the decision. Moreover, any salvage or resale value that is realized may be approximately offset by removal and dismantling costs. In situations where the estimated residual value is significant, the net residual value (after removal costs) is viewed as a cash inflow at the time of disposal and is discounted along with the other cash inflows.

Investments in Working Capital. An investment is the commitment, or locking up, of funds in any type of asset. Although up to this point depreciable assets have been used as examples, investments also include commitments of funds to additional inventory, repair parts, and to other current assets. In particular, if new equipment is acquired to produce a new product, additional funds will probably be required for inventories, accounts receivable, and increased cash needs. Part of this increase in current assets may be supplied from increased accounts payable; the remainder must come from permanent capital. This additional working capital is as much a part of the Time Zero differential investment as is the equipment itself.

Often it is reasonable to assume that the *terminal value* of investments in working capital is approximately the same as the amount of the initial working capital investment; that is, that at the end of the project, these items can be liquidated at their cost. The amount of terminal working capital is treated as a cash inflow in the last year of the project, and its present value is found by discounting that amount at the required rate of return.

Deferred Investments. Many projects involve a single committment of funds at one moment of time, which we have called Time Zero. For some projects, on the other hand, the commitments are spread over a considerable period of time. The construction of a new facility may require disbursements over several years, or a proposal may involve the construction of one unit of a facility now and a second unit five years later. In order to make the present value calculations, these investments must be brought to a common point in time. This is done by the application of discount rates to the amounts of cash outflow involved. In general, the appropriate rate depends on the uncertainty that the investment will be made; the lower the uncertainty, the lower the rate. Thus, if the commitment is an extremely definite one, the discount rate may be equivalent to the interest rate on high-grade bonds (which also represent a definite commitment). If, however, the future investments will be made only if earnings materialize, then the rate can be the required rate of return.

Investment Tax Credit. Income tax regulations permit a company under specified conditions to take an *investment tax credit* when it purchases new machinery, equipment, and certain other types of depreciable assets. As explained in Chapter 7, if a company buys a new machine for $100,000 it can subtract up to 10 percent of that amount, or $10,000, from its current tax obligation. This is a direct reduction of $10,000 in the net investment; that is, the effective cash cost of the machine is only 90 percent of the invoice amount.[5]

Capital Gains and Losses. When existing equipment is replaced by new equipment, the transaction may give rise to either a gain or loss, depending on whether the amount realized from the sale of the existing equipment is greater or less than its net book value, and depending on whether the new equipment is or is not of "like kind." The income tax treatment of this gain or loss may well differ from the financial account-

---

[5]Note that the treatment of the tax credit for our purposes here is independent of whether the company intends to use the flow-through method or the deferral method of accounting for the credit in its financial statements (Chapter 7). Congress changes the rate, or suspends the credit entirely, from time to time. As of 1983, depreciation for tax purposes, and hence the depreciation tax shield, is based on the asset's cost minus *one half* of the amount of the investment tax credit; i.e., $95,000 for the example given.

ing treatment. Depending on the circumstances, (1) the gain or loss may be included in the calculation of taxable income and thus subject to the regular income tax rate of, say, 46 percent or (2) it may be subject to a lower percent tax rate that is applicable to capital gains. Expert tax advice is therefore needed on problems involving gains and losses on the sale of depreciable assets. In any event, when existing assets are disposed of, the relevant amount by which the new investment is reduced is the proceeds of the sale, adjusted for taxes.

Nonmonetary Considerations

We have described the quantitative analysis involved in a capital investment proposal. This analysis does not provide the complete solution to the problem because it encompasses only those elements that can be reduced to numbers. A full consideration of the problem involves nonmonetary factors. Many investments are undertaken without a calculation of net present value. They may be undertaken for the convenience or comfort of employees, to enhance community relations, because they are required in order to meet pollution control or other legal requirements, or because they increase safety. For some proposals of this type, no economic analysis is necessary; if an unsafe condition is found, it must be corrected regardless of the cost. For other proposals, these nonmonetary factors must be considered along with the numbers that are included in the economic analysis. For all proposals, the decision maker must take into account the fact that all the numbers are estimates, and must apply judgment as to the validity of these estimates in arriving at a decision.

Based on a survey of 177 industrial companies, Fremgen reports that only 27 percent believed that the economic analysis was the most critical part of the capital investment decision process and only 12 percent believed it was the most difficult.[6] The others said that proper definition of the proposal, estimation of cash inflows, and implementation of a decision after it has been made were more important. Thus, the techniques described in this chapter are by no means the whole story. They are, however, the only part of the story that can be described as a definite procedure; the remainder must be learned through experience.

Summary of the Overall Analytical Process

Following is a summary of the previous presentation of the steps involved in using the *net present value method* in analyzing a proposed investment:

1. Select a required rate of return. This rate applies to projects deemed

---

[6]James M. Fremgen, "Capital Budgeting Practices; A Survey," *Management Accounting,* May 1973, p. 19. A 1976 study by Gitman and Forrester produced similar results ("A Survey of Capital Budgeting Techniques Used by Major U.S. Firms," *Financial Management,* Fall 1977, p.66).

ILLUSTRATION 22-2
CASH FLOW DIAGRAM

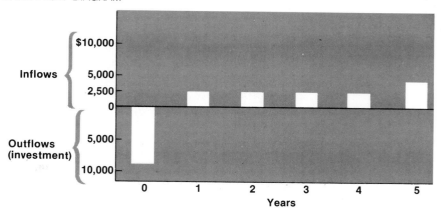

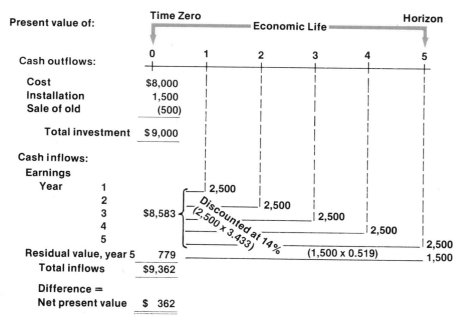

to be of average risk, and may be adjusted for a specific proposal whose risk is felt to be well above or below average.
2.   Estimate the economic life of the proposed project.
3.   Estimate the differential cash inflows for each year or series of years during the economic life.
4.   Find the net investment, which includes the additional outlays

made at Time Zero, less the proceeds from disposal of existing equipment and the investment tax credit, if any.

5. Estimate the residual values at the end of the economic life, which consist of the disposal value of equipment plus working capital that is to be released.

6. Find the present value of all the inflows identified in steps 3 and 5 by discounting them at the required rate of return, using Table A (for single annual amounts) or Table B (for a series of equal annual flows).

7. Find the net present value by subtracting the net investment from the present value of the inflows. If the net present value is zero or positive, decide that the proposal is acceptable, insofar as the monetary factors are concerned.

8. Taking into account the nonmonetary factors, reach a final decision. (This part of the process is at least as important as all the other parts put together, but there is no way of generalizing about it.)

As an aid to visualizing the relationships in a proposed investment, it is often useful to use a diagram of the flows similar to that shown in Illustration 22–2.

OTHER METHODS OF ANALYSIS

So far, we have limited the discussion of techniques for analyzing capital investment proposals to the net present value (NPV) method. We shall now describe three alternative ways of analyzing a proposed capital investment: (1) the internal rate of return method, (2) the payback method, and (3) the unadjusted return on investment method.

Internal Rate of Return Method

When the NPV method is used, the required rate of return must be selected in advance of making the calculations, because this rate is used to discount the cash inflows in each year. As already pointed out, the choice of an appropriate rate of return is a difficult matter. The *internal rate of return (IRR) method* avoids this difficulty. It computes the rate of return which equates the present value of the cash inflows with the amount of the investment, that is, that rate which makes the NPV equal zero. This rate is called the *internal rate of return,* or the *project rate of return.* The IRR method is variously called the discounted cash flow (DCF) method, time-adjusted-return method, or the investor's method.

If the management is satisfied with the internal rate of return, then the project is acceptable. If the IRR is not high enough, then the project is unacceptable. In deciding what rate of return is "high enough," the same considerations as those involved in selecting a required rate of return apply.

Level Inflows.   If the cash inflows are level, that is, the same amount each year, the computation is simple. It will be illustrated by a proposed $1,200 investment with estimated cash inflow of $400 a year for four years. The procedure is as follows:

1. Divide the investment, $1,200, by the annual inflow, $400. The result, 3.0, is called the *investment/inflow ratio.*
2. Look across the four-year row of Table B. The column in which the figure closest to 3.0 appears shows the approximate rate of return. Since the closest figure is 3.037 in the 12 percent column, the return is approximately 12 percent.
3. If management is satisfied with a return of approximately 12 percent, then it should accept this project (aside from qualitative considerations). If it requires a higher return, it should reject the project.

The number 3.0 in the above example is simply the ratio of the investment to the annual cash inflows. Each number in Table B shows the ratio of the present value of a stream of cash inflows to an investment of $1 made today, for various combinations of rates of return and numbers of years. The number 3.0 opposite any combination of year and rate of return means that the present value of a stream of inflows of $1 a year for that number of years discounted at that rate is $3. The present value of a stream of inflows of $400 a year is in the same ratio; therefore, it is $400 times 3, or $1,200. If the number is more than 3.0, as is the case with 3.037 in the example above, then the return is correspondingly more than 12 percent.

In using Table B in this method, it is usually necessary to interpolate, that is, to estimate the location of a number that lies between two numbers in the table. There is no need to be precise about these interpolations because the final result can be no better than the basic data, which are ordinarily only rough estimates. A quick interpolation made visually is usually as good as the accuracy of the data warrants.

Uneven Inflows.   If cash inflows are not the same in each year, the IRR must be found by trial and error. The cash inflows for each year are listed, and various discount rates are applied to these amounts until a rate is found that makes their total present value equal to the amount of the investment. This rate is the internal rate of return. This trial-and-error process can be quite tedious if the computations are made manually. However, computer programs and calculators are available that perform the calculations automatically.

Payback Method

The number referred to above as the investment/inflow ratio is also called the *payback period* because it is the number of years over which the investment outlay will be recovered or paid back from the cash inflows *if* the estimates turn out to be correct. That is, the project will "pay for itself" in this number of years. If a machine costs $1,200 and generates cash inflows of $400 a year, it has a payback of three years.

Payback is often used as a quick, but crude, method for appraising proposed investments. If the payback period is equal to or only slightly less than the economic life of the project, then the proposal is clearly unacceptable. If the payback period is considerably less than the economic life, then the project begins to look attractive.

If several investment proposals have the same general characteristics, then the payback period can be used as a valid way of screening out the acceptable proposals. For example, if a company finds that equipment ordinarily has a life of 10 years and if it requires a return of at least 15 percent, then the company may specify that new equipment will be considered for purchase only if it has a payback period of five years or less. This is because Table B shows that a payback period of five years is equivalent to a return of approximately 15 percent if the life is 10 years.

The danger of using payback as a criterion is that it gives no consideration to differences in the length of the estimated economic lives of various projects. There may be a tendency to conclude that the shorter the payback period, the better the project. However, a project with a long payback may actually be better than a project with a short payback if it will produce cash inflows for a much longer period of time.

Discounted Payback Method. A more useful and more valid form of the payback method is the *discounted payback method*. In this method the present value of each year's cash inflows is found, and these are cumulated year by year until they equal or exceed the amount of investment. The year in which this happens is the discounted payback period. A discounted payback of five years means that over a five-year period, the total cash inflows will be large enough to recoup the investment *and* *also* to provide the required return on investment.

Unadjusted Return on Investment Method

The *unadjusted return* method computes the net income expected to be earned from the project each year, in accordance with the principles of financial accounting, including a provision for depreciation expense. The unadjusted return on investment is found by dividing the annual net income by either the amount of the investment or by one half the amount of investment. (The use of one half the investment is on the premise that over the whole life of the project, an average of one half the initial investment is outstanding because the investment is at its full amount at Time Zero and shrinks gradually to nothing, or substantially nothing, by its terminal year.) This method is also referred to as the *accounting rate of return* or *average return* method.

Since normal depreciation accounting provides, in a sense, for the recovery of the cost of a depreciable asset, one might suppose that the return on an investment could be found by relating the investment to its accrual accounting income after depreciation; but such is *not* the case. Earlier we showed that an investment of $1,200 with cash inflows of $400 a year for four years has a return of 12 percent. In the unadjusted return method, the calculation would be as follows (ignoring taxes):

Gross earnings	$400
Less depreciation (¼ of $1,200)	300
Net income	$100

Dividing net income by the investment ($100 ÷ $1,200) gives an indicated return of 8⅓ percent. But we know this result is incorrect; the true return is 12 percent. If we divide the $100 net income by one half the investment, that is, $600, the result is 16⅔ percent, which is also incorrect.

This error arises because the unadjusted return method makes no adjustment for the differences in present values of the inflows of the various years. That is, it treats each year's inflows as if they were as valuable as those of every other year, whereas actually the prospect of an inflow of $400 next year is more attractive than the prospect of an inflow of $400 two years from now, and that $400 is more attractive than the prospect of an inflow of $400 three years from now, and so on.

The unadjusted return method, based on the *gross* amount of the investment, will always *understate* the true return. The shorter the time period involved, the more serious is the understatement. For investments involving very long time periods, the understatement is insignificant. If the return is computed by using *one half* the investment, the result is always an *overstatement* of the true return. No method which does not consider the time value of money can produce an accurate result.

Multiple Decision Criteria

Despite the conceptual superiority of the methods that involve discounting, surveys show that the payback and unadjusted return methods are also widely used in practice. Surveys also show that most companies use two or more methods in their investment proposal analyses—and the larger the company's annual capital budget, the greater the variety of techniques used.

Several factors explain the use of decision criteria that do not involve discounting. First, corporate managers tend to be concerned about the short-run impact a proposed project would have on corporate profitability as reported in the published financial statements. Thus, a project that is acceptable according to the NPV criterion may be rejected because it will reduce the company's reported net income and accounting return on investment (ROI) in the first year or two of the project. If management believes that the accounting ROI is used by securities analysts in evaluating a company's securities, management may use the unadjusted return method as one of its decision criteria.

In companies having a number of quasi-independent businesses called *profit centers*, a profit center manager may have similar concerns. If the profit center manager feels that his or her superiors are closely watching near-term profitability of the profit center, then a proposal that would have an adverse short-run impact on those profits may never be submitted to corporate headquarters. In this regard, it is important to remember that *people* generate capital budgeting proposals; these proposals do not magically materialize on their own.

Risk Aversion. Another factor explaining why projects that have an acceptable NPV or IRR are sometimes rejected (or not even proposed) is managers' *risk aversion*. Although a given proposal may constitute an acceptable "gamble" from an overall company point of view, a manager may feel that he or she will be penalized if the project does not work out as anticipated.

> **Example.** A profit center manager is considering a project that has an estimated IRR of 20 percent. If the company's required rate of return is 15 percent, the project would be acceptable on this criterion. However, there is a remote possibility, to which the manager has assessed a probability of 0.1 (1 chance in 10), that the project will be an economic failure. Although the company would be willing to take this risk, the manager decides not to prepare the formal request. This manager expects to be eligible for a major promotion about the time this project could "go sour," and doesn't want to run even a 10 percent chance of losing out on that promotion.

Risk aversion probably explains the widespread use of the payback criterion. If project A has an estimated IRR of 20 percent and a payback of eight years, while project B's estimated IRR is 15 percent and its payback is three years, the profit center manager may well prefer project B. Project A's time horizon is long, increasing the uncertainty of the estimates made in calculating its IRR. Moreover, it will be a number of years until it is known for sure whether A was a good investment. By eight years from now the manager hopes to have been promoted at least once, and some unknown successor will reap most of project A's benefits. But project B can make the manager look good in the near term, and help him or her to be promoted.

In sum, factors other than the true economic return (i.e., IRR) of a project greatly—and legitimately—influence whether a project is approved, and even whether the project is formally proposed to top management.

PREFERENCE PROBLEMS

There are two classes of investment problems: screening problems and preference problems. In a *screening problem* the question is whether or not to accept a proposed investment. The discussion so far has been limited to this class of problem. Many individual proposals come to management's attention, and by the techniques described above, those that are worthwhile can be screened out from the others.

In *preference problems* (also called ranking or capital rationing problems), a more difficult question is asked: Of a number of proposals, each of which has an adequate return, how do they rank in terms of preference? If not all the proposals can be accepted, which ones do we prefer? The decision may merely involve a choice between two competing proposals, or it may require that a series of proposals be ranked in order of their attractiveness. Such a ranking of projects is necessary when there are more worthwhile proposals than there are funds available to finance them, which is often the case.

Criteria for Preference Problems

Both the IRR and NPV methods are used for preference problems. If the *internal rate of return method* is used, the preference rule is as follows: the higher the IRR, the better the project. A project with a return of 20 percent is said to be preferable to a project with a return of 19 percent.

If the *net present value method* is used, the present value of the cash inflows of one project cannot be compared directly with the present value of the cash inflows of another unless the investments are of the same size. Most people would agree that a $1,000 investment that produced cash inflows with a present value of $2,000 is better than a $1,000,000 investment that produces cash inflows with a present value of $1,001,000, even though they each have an NPV of $1,000. In order to compare two proposals under the NPV method, therefore, we must relate the size of the discounted cash inflows to the amount of money risked. This is done simply by dividing the present value of the cash inflows by the amount of investment, to give a ratio that is called the *profitability index*. Thus, a project with an NPV of zero has a profitability index of 1.0. The preference rule is: the higher the profitability index, the better the project.

Comparison of Preference Rules. Conceptually, the profitability index is superior to the internal rate of return as a device for deciding on preference. This is because the IRR method will not always give the correct preference as between two projects with different lives or with different patterns of earnings.

> **Example.** Proposal A involves an investment of $1,000 and a cash inflow of $1,200 received at the end of one year; its IRR is 20 percent. Proposal B involves an investment of $1,000 and cash inflows of $305 a year for five years; its IRR is only 16 percent. But proposal A is *not necessarily* preferable to proposal B. Proposal A is preferable only if the company can expect to earn a high return during the following four years on some other

project in which the funds released from A at the end of the first year are reinvested. Otherwise, proposal B, which earns 16 percent over the whole five-year period, is preferable.

The incorrect signal illustrated in this example is not present in the profitability index method. Assuming a discount rate of 12 percent, the two proposals described above would be analyzed as follows:

Proposal	Cash Inflow (a)	Discount Factor (b)	Present Value (c) = (a) × (b)	Investment (d)	Index (c) ÷ (d)
A	$1,200 − 1 yr.	0.893	$1,072	$1,000	1.07
B	305 − 5 yrs.	3.605	1,100	1,000	1.10

The profitability index signals that proposal B is better than proposal A. This is in fact the case if the company can expect to reinvest the money released from proposal A so as to earn only 12 percent on it.[7]

Although the profitability index method is conceptually superior to the IRR method, and although the former is also easier to calculate since there is no trial-and-error computation, the IRR method is widely used in practice. There seem to be two reasons for this. First, the profitability index method requires that the required rate of return be established before the calculations are made; but many analysts prefer to work from the other direction, that is, to find the IRR and then see how it compares with their idea of the rate of return that is appropriate in view of the risks involved. Second, the profitability index, like any index, is an abstract number that is difficult to explain, whereas the IRR is similar to interest rates and earnings rates with which every manager is familiar.

SUMMARY

A capital investment problem is essentially one of determining whether the anticipated cash inflows from a proposed project are sufficiently attractive to warrant risking the investment of funds in the project.

In the net present value method, the basic decision rule is that a proposal is acceptable if the present value of the cash inflows expected to be derived from it equals or exceeds the present value of the investment. In order to use this rule, one must estimate: (1) the required rate of return, (2) the economic life, (3) the amount of cash inflow in each year, and (4) the amount of investment.

The internal rate of return method finds the rate of return that equates the present value of cash inflows to the present value of the investment.

---

[7]Proof of this statement appears in advanced texts on financial management. In most comparisons, IRR and the profitability index give the same relative ranking.

The simple payback method finds the number of years of cash inflows that are required to equal the amount of investment. The unadjusted return on investment method computes a project's net income according to the principles of financial accounting and expresses this as a percentage of either the initial investment or the average investment. The simple payback and unadjusted return methods have conceptual weaknesses.

Preference problems are those in which the task is to rank two or more investment proposals in order of their desirability. The profitability index, which is the ratio of the present value of cash inflows to the investment, is the most valid way of making such a ranking.

The foregoing are monetary considerations. Nonmonetary considerations are often as important as the monetary considerations and in some cases are so important that no economic analysis is worthwhile. In some instances, a manager's aversion to risk may cause a project with an acceptable return to the rejected, or not even proposed.

SUGGESTIONS FOR FURTHER READING

Bierman, Harold, and Seymour Smidt. *The Capital Budgeting Decision,* 5th ed. New York: Macmillan, 1980.

Grant, Eugene L., et al. *Principles of Engineering Economy.* New York: John Wiley & Sons, 1982.

Joy, O. Maurice. *Introduction to Financial Management.* Rev. ed. Homewood, Ill.: Richard D. Irwin, 1980.

Van Horne, James C. *Financial Management and Policy.* 5th ed. Englewood Cliffs, N.J.: Prentice-Hall, 1980.

Weston, J. Fred, and Eugene F. Brigham. *Managerial Finance,* 7th ed. Hinsdale, Ill.: Dryden Press, 1981.

Cases

CASE 22–1 Gallup Company

A. Equipment Replacement

Gallup Company is considering the purchase of new equipment to perform operations currently being performed on different, less efficient equipment. The purchase price is $150,000, delivered and installed.

A Gallup producton engineer estimates that the new equipment will produce savings of $30,000 in labor and other direct costs annually, as compared with the present equipment. He estimates the proposed equipment's economic life at 10 years, with zero salvage value. The present equipment is in good working order and will last, physically, for at least 20 more years.

The company can borrow money at 12 percent, although it would not plan to negotiate a loan specifically for the purchase of this equipment. The company requires a return of at least 20 percent before taxes on an investment of this type. Taxes are to be disregarded.

Questions

1. Assuming the present equipment has zero book value and zero salvage value, should the company buy the proposed equipment?

2. Assuming the present equipment is being depreciated at a straight-line rate of 10 percent, that it has a book value of $72,000 (cost, $120,000; accumulated depreciation, $48,000), and has zero net salvage value today, should the company buy the proposed equipment?

3. Assuming the present equipment has a book value of $72,000 and a salvage value today of $45,000, and that if retained for 10 more years its salvage value will be zero, should the company buy the proposed equipment?

4. Assume the new equipment will save only $15,000 a year, but that its economic life is expected to be 20 years. If other conditions are as described in (1) above, should the company buy the proposed equipment?

B. Replacement Following Earlier Replacement

Gallup Company decided to purchase the equipment described in Part A (hereafter called "model A" equipment). Two years later, even better equipment (called "model B") comes on the market and makes the other equipment completely obsolete, with no resale value. The model B equipment costs $300,000 delivered and installed, but it is expected to result in annual savings of $75,000 over the cost of operating the model A equipment. The economic life of model B is estimated to be 10 years. Taxes are to be disregarded.

Questions

1. What action should the company take?
2. If the company decides to purchase the model B equipment, a mistake has been made somewhere, because good equipment, bought only two years previously, is being scrapped. How did this mistake come about?

C. Effect of Income Taxes

Assume that Gallup Company expects to pay income taxes of 46 percent and that a loss on the sale or disposal of equipment is treated as a capital loss resulting in a tax saving of 28 percent. Gal-

lup uses a 10 percent discount rate for analyses performed on an aftertax basis. Depreciation of the new equipment for tax purposes is computed on the sum-of-years'-digits basis. (*Note:* The present value of the sum-of-years'-digits depreciation stream per $1 of depreciable investment, using a 10-year life and 10 percent discount rate, is 0.701.) The new equipment qualifies for an 8 percent investment tax credit, which will *not* reduce the cost basis of the asset for calculating depreciation for tax purposes.

Questions

1. Should the company buy the equipment if the facts are otherwise as described in Part A (1)?
2. If the facts are otherwise as described in Part A (2)?
3. If the facts are otherwise as described in Part B?

D. Change in Earnings Pattern

Assume that the savings are expected to be $37,500 in each of the first five years and $22,500 in each of the next five years, other conditions remaining as described in Part A (1).

Questions

1. What action should the company take?
2. Why is the result here different from that in Part A (1)?
3. What effect would the inclusion of income taxes, as in Part C, have on your recommendation?

CASE 22–2   Rock Creek Golf Club*

Rock Creek Golf Club (RCGC) was a public golf course, owned by a private corporation. In January, the club's manager, Lee Jeffries, was faced with a decision involving replacement of the club's fleet of 40 battery-powered golf carts. The old carts had been purchased five years ago, and had to be replaced. They were fully depreciated; RCGC had been offered $150 cash for each of them.

Jeffries had been approached by two salespersons, each of whom could supply RCGC with 40 new gasoline-powered carts. The first salesperson, called here simply A, would sell RCGC the carts for $1,600 each. Their expected salvage value at the end of five years was $200 each.

Salesperson B proposed to lease the same model carts to RCGC for $400 per cart per year, payable at the end of the year for five years. At the end of five years, the carts would have to be returned to B's company. The lease could be canceled at the end of any year, provided 90 days' notice was given.

In either case, out-of-pocket operating costs were expected to be $300 per cart per year, and annual revenue from renting the carts to golfers was expected to be $60,000 for the fleet.

Although untrained in accounting, Jeffries calculated the number of years until the carts would "pay for themselves" if purchased outright, and found this to be less than two years, even ignoring the salvage value. Jeffries also noted that if the

*Adapted from an example used by Gordon B. Harwood and Roger H. Hermanson in "Lease-or-Buy Decisions," *Journal of Accountancy*, September 1976, pp. 83–87, © American Institute of Certified Public Accountants.

carts were leased, the five-year lease payments would total $2,000 per cart, which was more than the $1,600 purchase price; and if the carts were leased, RCGC would not receive the salvage proceeds at the end of five years. Therefore, it seemed clear to Jeffries that the carts should be purchased rather than leased.

When Jeffries proposed this purchase at the next board of directors meeting, one of the directors objected to the simplicity of Jeffries' analysis. The director had said, "Even ignoring inflation, spending $1,600 now may not be a better deal than spending five chunks of $400 over the next five years. If we buy the carts, we'll probably have to borrow the funds at 12 percent interest cost. Of course, our effective interest cost is less than this, since for every dollar of interest expense we report to the IRS we save 22 cents in taxes. And it's also true that we could get a 10 percent investment tax credit if we buy the carts; as I understand it, this 10 percent is allowed on two thirds of the cost of the carts, provided we use them at least five years, but no more than seven years. This would save us taxes a year from now. But the lease payments would also be tax deductible, so it's still not clear to me which is the better alternative. There's a sharp new person in my company's accounting department; let's not make a decision until I can ask her to do some further analysis for us."

Questions

1. Assume that in order to purchase the carts, RCGC would have to borrow $64,000 at 12 percent interest for five years, repayable in five equal year-end in-

stallments. Prepare an amortization schedule for this loan, showing how much of each year's payment is for interest and how much is applied to repay principal. (Round the amounts for each year to the nearest dollar.)

2. Assume that salesperson B's company also would be willing to sell the carts outright at $1,600 per cart. Given the proposed lease terms, and assuming the lease is outstanding for five years, what interest rate is implicit in the lease? (Ignore tax impacts to the leasing company when calculating this implicit rate.) Why is this implicit rate lower than the 12 percent that RCGC may have to pay to borrow the funds needed to purchase the carts?

3. Should RCGC buy the carts from A, or lease them from B? (Assume that if the carts are purchased, RCGC will use the years'-digits depreciation method for income tax purposes, based on an estimated life of five years and an estimated residual value of $200 per cart.)

4. Assume arbitrarily that purchasing the carts has an NPV that is $3,000 higher than the NPV of leasing them. (This is an arbitrary difference for purposes of this question and is not to be used as a "check figure" for your earlier calculations.) How much would B have to reduce the proposed annual lease payment to make leasing as attractive as purchasing the cart?

CASE 22–3   KLS Steel Company

Headquartered in Milwaukee, KLS Steel Company is one of the larger regional steel service centers in the Midwest. KLS maintains warehouses in 15 medium-size cities in the Midwest. Local firms purchase steel from these warehouses, rather than directly from steel producers, for a variety of reasons. Since service centers are able to buy in carload quantities, freight costs are often lower for a service center. Also, by purchasing for a large number of customers, a service center is able to obtain quantity discounts. Thus, the price to the user may be no higher than if the user were to purchase directly from a steel producer. At the same time, the user is able to reduce its steel inventories, since delivery time is often far shorter from a service center than from a steel producer.

As an additional incentive for their customers, steel service centers often provide special services, such as heat treating, cutting to length, and light assembly. A special service that KLS provides is cold-drawn steel (CDS). That service is performed in the Milwaukee warehouse for all 15 KLS warehouses. To cold-draw steel, one end of a steel bar is tapered, or pointed. The pointed end is then passed through a die (a block of hardened steel with a tapered hole through the center). On the other side of the die, a set of steel jaws grasps the pointed end of the bar and a heavy steel chain attached to the jaws pulls (or draws) the remainder of the steel bar through the die. That process compresses the steel slightly to provide more uniform qualities and to provide a smoother surface on the bar. Bars are then processed on a straightener, since the drawing process often puts a slight twist or bend in a bar. Finally, bars are cut to length on a saw. Although KLS owns other saws, one saw is required for the CDS department. In addition, an overhead crane is required specifically for that department. Several additional pieces of equipment are also used primarily by the CDS department.

The CDS department is of some concern to KLS's president:

> The previous president bought most of the drawing equipment from a bankrupt firm in 1950. We could just as easily purchase cold-drawn steel from firms who specialize in that process. There is no real reason for us to provide the service, other than that we own the equipment. Since we have the equipment, we may as well stay in the business. We process about 17,000 tons a year. Although the CDS charge is based on a number of factors, on average we charge about $180 a ton for the service. If we eliminated our CDS department, we would buy CDS from a specialty producer and then resell it. We would make about $5 a ton, after tax, if we used an outside supplier. That is reasonably close to what we do in-house (see Exhibit 1). If we tried to sell our equipment, I know that we wouldn't get much more than $100,000 (after tax), so the

department is performing reasonably well.

The problem is that some of the equipment is getting old. The crane, which was purchased in 1951, is still in pretty good shape. However, the draw bench and the straightener were originally purchased in the 1920s. The draw bench uses too much electricity, and scrap cost is too high. Both the draw bench and the straightener are often broken, and repair costs keep increasing. Even though the saw is only 15 years old and is still in good shape, newer ones are faster. The draw bench may be a good investment since a new one would save quite a bit on repairs and would also save on scrap and electricity. We can analyze the other equipment later.

We use discounted cash flow analysis to evaluate all corporate investments and expect to earn 10 percent, after tax, on the investment. I've had our accountants and engineers put together an estimate of operating costs for both the new and the old draw bench (Exhibit 2). I expect no real changes in our operations. Sales, adjusted for inflation, will probably stay at the 1980 level. I would expect our costs to go up at about the same rate as inflation, except for repair costs on the equipment. Exhibit 2 shows all amounts in 1980 dollars, since the 10 percent goal is in addition to inflation.

I'm concerned about one other thing. I have a friend at a consulting firm in Boston. She claims that you shouldn't invest in businesses where you have a low market share and low growth. That is clearly the case with our CDS department, but if an investment in that department has a greater discounted cash flow than an investment in other departments, it seems to me we have to invest in the CDS department. I asked her about that, but she seemed to think that discounted cash flow didn't work for such businesses.

EXHIBIT 1

KLS STEEL COMPANY
CDS Department Income Statement
Year Ended December 31, 1980

Service revenues*	$3,083,000
Cost of sales†	2,665,000
Selling, general and administrative	238,000
Income before taxes	180,000
Income taxes	90,000
Net income	$ 90,000

*Does not include revenues from the price of the "raw" steel that undergoes the cold-drawing process.

†Includes straight-line depreciation of $4,000 per year. All equipment will be fully depreciated in five years. The draw bench is already fully depreciated. Does not include "raw" steel cost, except for scrap losses.

EXHIBIT 2
DRAW BENCH PROPOSAL
(all amounts in 1980 dollars)

	1980	1/1/81	1981	1982	1983
Operating expense:					
1. Current equipment	288,000		290,000	350,000*	288,000
2. New draw bench......................			202,000	204,000	206,000
3. Savings (1 − 2).......................			88,000†	146,000	82,000
4. Less: Depreciation (DDB)†...........			100,000	80,000	64,000
5. Net savings before tax (3 − 4).......			(12,000)	66,000	18,000
6. State and federal tax (50%)			6,000	(33,000)	(9,000)
7. Investment tax credit			50,000	—	—
8. Net change in income (5 + 6 + 7).....			44,000	33,000	9,000
9. Add: Depreciation....................			100,000	80,000	64,000
10. Add: Increase in salvage value‡......			—	—	—
11. Cash flow (8 + 9 + 10)...............			144,000	113,000	73,000
Investment, net of trade-in.............		500,000			
NPV (10%)............................		59,203.28			
IRR		12.99%			

Cost of operating equipment

Questions

1. Should KLS purchase the new draw bench?

2. Evaluate the consultant's comment.

economic life = 10 years

CASE 22–4 Pressco, Inc.

In June 1979, John Smythe, a marketing representative for Pressco, Inc., was attempting to put together a financial presentation designed to help close the sale of some mechanical drying equipment to Paperco, Inc. The equipment Mr. Smythe hoped to sell Paperco would replace less efficient facilities that Paperco had placed in service only 2½ years previously. The cost savings (exclusive of depreciation charges) that Mr. Smythe felt certain Paperco would realize from the proposed new equipment installation amounted to $700,000 per year. Of this amount, $450,000 in savings was expected to come from more efficient fuel utilization, a factor that Mr. Smythe be-

lieved would qualify the full $2.9 million investment for a tax credit of 20 percent.[1] Capital expenditures without such energy saving features normally qualified for only a 10 percent investment tax

---

[1] The actual amount of the energy tax credit was subject to some uncertainty. As noted in the *New York Times* financial pages in early 1979:

At this point, the business energy tax credit, too, lacks quality and performance standards.

The IRS has not yet drawn up any regulations implementing the Energy Tax Act of 1978, and none are expected before year-end.

The Revenue Service's slow pace has drawn criticism from many quarters. Senator John H. Chaffee, Republican of Rhode Island, has said that because many energy-saving projects take years to engineer and construct, they may be

EXHIBIT 2 *(continued)*

1984	1985	1986	1987	1988	1989	1990
300,000	355,000*	290,000	304,000	360,000*	292,000	308,000
208,000	210,000	212,000	250,000*	210,000	212,000	214,000
92,000	145,000	78,000	54,000	150,000	80,000	94,000
51,200	40,960	32,770	32,770	32,770	32,770	32,760
40,800	104,040	45,230	21,230	117,230	47,230	61,240
(20,400)	(52,020)	(22,615)	(10,615)	(58,615)	(23,615)	(30,620)
—	—	—	—	—	—	—
20,400	52,020	22,615	10,615	58,615	23,615	30,620
51,200	40,960	32,770	32,770	32,770	32,770	32,760
						75,000
—	—	—	—	—	—	
71,600	92,980	55,385	43,385	91,385	56,385	138,380

every three years

*Includes equipment overhaul and additional production overtime needed because of overhaul. All overhaul costs are expensed in the year in which they are incurred.

†Zero salvage value, double-declining-balance depreciation will be used for both income tax and financial reporting purposes.

‡Salvage value in 1990, aftertax, is estimated to be:

	New Draw Bench	Old Draw Bench
Draw bench	$ 85,000	$10,000
Remaining equipment............	40,000	40,000
Total	$125,000	$50,000

abandoned unless regulations are proposed and issued promptly. On a similar note, the Business Roundtable has sent a memorandum to the Treasury Department complaining that the absence of IRS regulations may defeat the objectives of the act. Many energy-saving projects have lead times of five years or more, the memorandum says, and a termination date for the credit is less than three and a half years away.

The IRS has said that business need not wait until it issues standards before investing in energy property, but many businesses remain skittish about making such commitments.

"It's a Catch-22 situation," says Steven F. Meyer of the Washington office of Peat, Marwick, Mitchell & Co. "In the absence of regulations, the only thing you can do is look for the intent of Congress as evidenced in the House, Senate and Committee reports," he notes.

credit. (See Exhibit 1 for a description of the investment tax credit.)

In its internal management reports and in its reports to shareholders, Paperco used straight-line depreciation. In its tax reports, however (and thus in calculating relevant cash flows on investments), Paperco used double-declining-balance depreciation. (See Exhibit 2 for the relevant depreciation projections.[2])

[2] The IRS permitted taxpayers to switch from the double-declining-balance method to the straight-line method for an asset at whatever point the switch became advantageous. Such a switch at the most advantageous time is incorporated in the data presented in Exhibit 2.

EXHIBIT 1
INVESTMENT TAX CREDIT
(as of 1979)

IRS regulations allow a credit against tax for investment in certain depreciable property. To get the full investment credit available, the investment must have a useful life of seven years or more when acquired. If useful life is five or six years, the full credit is allowed on two thirds of the investment. If life is three or four years, only one third of the investment qualifies. If the useful life is less than three years, there is no credit.

If equipment is retired before seven years, investment credits relating to that equipment are recaptured in accordance with the amount of time the equipment was actually in service.

The current investment credit rate is 10 percent. An additional 10 percent investment credit for the period beginning 10/1/78 and ending 12/31/82 is added to the credit noted above for investment in property that qualifies as energy property under the rules outlined below. The additional 10 percent investment tax credit was part of the Energy Tax Act of 1978.

a. *Alternative energy property* includes certain equipment that uses an alternate substance—a substance other than oil, gas or oil and gas products—as a fuel or that aids in the use of such a substance. Specifically it includes: (1) a boiler, or a burner for a combuster other than a boiler, if its primary fuel is an alternate substance; (2) equipment for converting an alternate substance into a synthetic fuel (other than coke or coke gas); (3) equipment for modifying oil and gas-using equipment to use another fuel or an oil mixture that is 25 percent made up of another substance; (4) equipment using coal as a feedstock for manufacturing products other than coke or coke gas; (5) pollution-control equipment required by government regulations to be installed in connection with equipment in categories (1)–(4), except equipment required to be installed by regulations in effect on 10/1/78, which is installed in connection with property using coal or lignite as of that date; (6) equipment used to handle, store or prepare an alternate substance at the point of use for use in equipment described in categories (1)–(5); and (7) equipment to produce, distribute or use geothermal energy, but only, in the case of electrical generation, equipment up to the electrical transmission stage. [Sec. 48(1) (3)]

b. *Solar or wind energy property* includes equipment that uses solar or wind energy to generate electricity, or to heat or cool (or provide hot water for use in) a structure. [Sec. 48(1) (4)]

c. *Specifically defined energy property* includes certain listed equipment installed in connection with an existing industrial or commercial facility to reduce the amount of energy consumed in an existing industrial or commercial process. The IRS may specify other similar items of energy conservation equipment eligible for the credit. The listed items are: recuperators, heat wheels, regenerators, heat exchangers, waste heat boilers, heat pipes, automatic energy control systems, turbulators, preheaters, combustible gas recovery systems and economizers. [Sec. 48(1) (5)]

d. *Recycling equipment* means equipment used exclusively to recycle solid waste or to sort and prepare it for recycling. It does not include equipment used after the point where a marketable product, such as newsprint, paperboard, metal ingots or textile fibers, has been produced. In the iron and steel industry the credit is limited to equipment used before the reduction of solid waste to a molten state. No more than 10 percent use of virgin materials is permissible. Equipment used to convert solid waste into fuel or useful energy is recycling equipment. [Sec. 48(1) (6)]

e. *Shale oil equipment* is equipment for producing oil from shale. Equipment for hydrogenation, refining or other processes subsequent to retorting is not included. [Sec.48(1) (7)]

f. *Equipment for producing natural gas from geopressured brine* is energy property. Whether a well qualifies as producing natural gas from geopressured brine will be determined by the Federal Energy Regulatory Commission under the definition in the Natural Gas Pricing Act, but the Secretary of the Treasury will determine if equipment used in connection with a well qualifies for the credit. [Sec. 48(1) (8)]

EXHIBIT 2
DOUBLE-DECLINING-BALANCE DEPRECIATION
ON NEW AND REPLACED EQUIPMENT
(thousands of dollars)

Year*	New Equipment and Installation			Replaced Equipment and Installation		
	Equipment	Installation	Total	Equipment	Installation	Total
1.............	370	200	570	88	125	213
2.............	296	150	446	70	94	164
3.............	237	113	350	56	70	126
4.............	189	84	273	45	53	98
5.............	152	64	216	36	40	76
6.............	122	63	185	29	40	69
7.............	121	63	184	29	39	68
8.............	121	63	184	29	39	68
9.............	121	—	121	29	—	29
10.............	121	—	121	29	—	29
	1,850†	800	2,650	440‡	500	940

*Year 1 for the new equipment is 1981; year 1 for the equipment to be replaced is 1977.
†$2,100 thousand original cost less $250 thousand estimated salvage value.
‡$500 thousand original cost less $60 thousand estimated salvage value

The assumptions Mr. Smythe planned to use in his presentation of the investment opportunity to Paperco's management were as follows:

1. Equipment cost.. $2,100,000
    Shipment—12 months following receipt of order.
    Start up of facility—18 months following receipt of order.

2. Equipment payment terms:
    20% ($420,000) with order.
    20% ($420,000) 120 days after order.
    60% ($1,260,000) 30 days after equipment delivery.

3. Installation cost.. 800,000
    $80,000 per month for the last 10 of the 18 months from receipt of order to start up.

4. Paperco cost of capital: 12%.

5. Depreciable life and estimated salvage value:

	Proposed New Facility	Facility to Be Replaced
Equipment depreciation period....................................	10 years	10 years
Installation depreciation period....................................	8 years	8 years
Estimated salvage value at end of life.............................	$250,000	$60,000

6. Facility to be replaced
    Original equipment cost (Jan. 1977)..................................... $500,000
    Original installation cost (Jan. 1977)..................................... 500,000
    Estimated market value of equipment if sold in
        18 months (when displaced).. 150,000
    Estimated remaining physical life as of June 1979.................... 11½ years

7. Paperco paid federal income taxes at the rate of 48 percent.

Questions

1. What is the net present value of the mechanical drying equipment investment opportunity assuming a 12 percent cost of capital for Paperco? (Assume the 48 percent tax rate applies both to ordinary income and capital gains or losses.)

2. What is the internal rate of return on this project?

3. How many years will it take Paperco to recover its full investment on an aftertax cash flow basis?

4. The estimated annual cost saving produced by the mechanical drying equipment is subject to errors in engineering estimates of as much as ± 20 percent. Since this issue would inevitably arise in his presentation to Paperco's management, Mr. Smythe wondered how small the annual cost savings could become before the project would be uneconomic for Paperco.

5. How high could Pressco have priced the mechanical drying equipment and still have it be attractive to Paperco, given Mr. Smythe's other original assumptions?

6. Given Mr. Smythe's original assumptions, what will be the *pretax* profit implications of the proposed investment in the first year and the second year following the completion of the new project according to Paperco's internal management reports? What will be the impact of the project in terms of the year-end net book value of assets utilized in the first and second years following the completion of the new project? How might these facts influence the Paperco division manager responsible for this investment decision, assuming the manager's incentive compensation was based on pretax profits of the division versus the year-end net book value of assets employed in the division (i.e., incentive based on ROI fraction)?

7. Given Mr. Smythe's original assumptions, what will be the *aftertax* profit implications of the proposed investment in the first year and second year following the completion of the new project according to Paperco's internal management reports? How might these facts influence Paperco's chief executive officer's perception of the investment opportunity, assuming the CEO's incentive compensation was given based on earnings per share growth?

CASE 22–5   Orkney Biscuit Company, Ltd.

Percy Jones, managing director of Orkney Biscuit Company, Ltd., was trying to decide whether to expand the company by adding a new product line. The proposal seemed likely to be profitable and adequate funds to finance it could be obtained from outside investors.

Orkney Biscuit had long been regarded as a well-managed company. It had succeeded in keeping its present product lines up to date and had maintained a small but profitable position in a highly competitive industry.

The amount of capital presently employed by the company was approximately £4,000,000, and was expected to remain at this level whether the proposal for the new product line was accepted or rejected. Net income from existing operations amounted to about £400,000 a year, and Jones's best forecast was that this would continue to be the income from present operations.

Introduction of the new product line would require an immediate investment of £400,000 in equipment and £250,000

EXHIBIT 1
INCOME FORECAST FOR NEW PRODUCT LINE

Year	(1) Forecasted Incremental Cash Flow from Operations	(2) Depreciation on New Equipment	(3) Forecasted Incremental Income before Tax (1) − (2)	(4) Income Tax at 40 Percent*	(5) Forecasted Incremental Net Income after Tax (3) − (4)
1...	−£ 350,000	£50,000	−£400,000	−£160,000	−£240,000
2...	− 100,000	50,000	− 150,000	− 60,000	− 90,000
3...	0	50,000	− 50,000	− 20,000	− 30,000
4...	+ 200,000	50,000	+ 150,000	60,000	90,000
5...	+ 500,000	50,000	+ 450,000	180,000	270,000
6...	+ 1,000,000	50,000	+ 950,000	380,000	570,000
7...	+ 900,000	50,000	+ 850,000	340,000	510,000
8...	+ 650,000	50,000	+ 600,000	240,000	360,000

*When income before taxes was negative, the company was entitled to a tax rebate at 40 percent, either from taxes paid in previous years or from taxes currently due on other company operations.

in additional working capital. A further £100,000 in working capital would be required a year later.

Sales of the new product line would be relatively low during the first year, but would increase steadily until the sixth year. After that, changing tastes and increased competition would probably begin to reduce annual sales. After eight years, the product line would probably be withdrawn from the market. At that time, the company would sell the equipment for its scrap value and liquidate the working capital. The cash value of the equipment and working capital at that time would be about £350,000.

The low initial sales volume, combined with heavy promotional outlays, would lead to heavy losses in the first two years, and no net income would be reported until the fourth year. The profit forecasts for the new product line are summarized in Exhibit 1.

Jones was concerned about the effect this project would have on Orkney's overall reported return on investment in the next three years. In response to this concern, his accountant provided him with the following figures (in thousands):

Year	Total Investment Start of Year	Net Income after Tax	Reported Return on Investment
1	£4,000	£160	4.0%
2	4,600	310	6.7
3	4,650	370	8.0
4	4,600	490	10.7
5	4,550	670	14.7
6	4,500	970	21.6
7	4,450	910	20.4
8	4,400	760	17.3

On the other hand, "eyeballing" the figures in Exhibit 1 led Mr. Jones to guess that if the proposal were analyzed using aftertax cash flows discounted at 10 percent, it might well show a positive net present value, and hence would be a worthwhile investment opportunity.

Questions

1. Find the net present value of the proposal, discounting aftertax cash flows at 10 percent.

2. To what extent, if any, would the low anticipated rate of return on investment in the first three years be likely to affect the decision to launch the new product line:
   a. If the Orkney Biscuit Company were a private company, owned entirely by Mr. Jones?
   b. If the Orkney Biscuit Company were a publicly owned company, with shares owned by a large number of small investors, and Mr. Jones purely a salaried administrator?
   c. If the Orkney Biscuit Company were a wholly owned subsidiary of a much larger company and Mr. Jones expected to be a candidate to succeed one of the parent company's top executives who will retire from the company about two years from now?

3. Do you think that your analysis of these figures indicates that accountants should consider making major changes in their approach to income measurement?

CASE 22–6   Climax Shipping Company

The controller of the Climax Shipping Company, located near Pittsburgh, was preparing a report for the executive committee regarding the feasibility of repairing one of the company's steam riverboats or of replacing the steamboat with a new diesel-powered boat.

Climax was engaged mainly in the transportation of coal from nearby mines to steel mills, public utilities, and other industries in the Pittsburgh area. The company's steamboats also, on occasion, carried cargoes to places as far away as New Orleans. The boats owned by Climax were all steam-powered, and were between 15 and 30 years old.

The steamboat the controller was concerned about, the Cynthia, was 23 years old and required immediate rehabilitation or replacement. It was estimated that the Cynthia had a useful life of another 20 years provided that adequate repairs and maintenance were made. Whereas the book value of the Cynthia was $118,500, it was believed that she would bring somewhat less than this amount, possibly around $75,000, if she were to be sold. The total of immediate rehabilitation costs for the Cynthia was estimated to be $345,000. It was estimated that these general rehabilitation expenditures would extend the useful life of the Cynthia for about 20 years.

New spare parts from another boat, which had been retired recently, were available for use in the rehabilitation of the Cynthia. An estimate of their fair value, if used on the Cynthia, was $130,500, which was their book value. Use of these parts would, in effect, decrease the immediate rehabilitation costs from $345,000 to $214,500. It was believed that if these parts were sold on the market, they would bring only around $90,000. They could not be used on any of the other Climax steamboats.

Currently, the Cynthia was operated by a 20-member crew. Annual operating costs for this crew would be approximately as follows:

Wages and fringes	$348,840
Commissary supplies	46,260
Repairs and maintenance	73,200
Fuel and lubricants	105,150
Miscellaneous service and supplies	36,000
Total	$609,450

It was estimated that the cost of dismantling and scrapping the Cynthia at the end of her useful life after the overhaul would be offset by the value of the scrap and used parts taken off the boat.

An alternative to rehabilitating the steamboat was the purchase of a diesel-powered boat. Quapelle Company, a local boat manufacturer, quoted the price of $975,000 for a diesel boat. An additional $225,000 for a basic parts inventory would be necessary to service a diesel boat, and such an inventory would be sufficient to service up to three diesel boats. If four or more diesels were purchased, however, it was estimated that additional spare parts inventory would be necessary.

The useful life of a diesel-powered boat was estimated to be 25 years, at the end of which time the boat either would be scrapped or would be completely rehabilitated at a cost approximating that of a new boat. The possibility of diesel engine replacement during the 25-year life was not contemplated by the controller, since information from other companies having limited experience with diesel-powered riverboats did not indicate that such costs needed to be anticipated. But a general overhaul of the engines, costing at current prices $180,000, would be expected every 10 years.

One of the features Quapelle pointed out was the 12 percent increase in average speed of diesel-powered boats over the steamboats. The controller discounted this feature, however, because the short runs and lock-to-lock operations involved in local river shipping would prohibit the diesel boats from taking advantage of their greater speed since there was little opportunity for passing and they would have to wait in turn at each lock for the slower steamboats. The controller felt it would be many years, if at all, before diesel boats displaced the slower steamboats.

After consulting Quapelle and other companies operating diesel-powered boats, the controller estimated that the annual operating costs of a diesel-powered boat would total $469,920, broken down as follows:

Wages and fringes, 13-member crew	$244,410
Commissary supplies	30,060
Repairs and maintenance*	65,100
Fuel and lubricants	86,400
Extra stern repairs	6,000
Miscellaneous service and supplies	37,950
Total	$469,920

*Excluding possible major overhaul of diesel engines.

Although the controller had not considered the matter, the reader of this case may assume that at the end of the 20th year the diesel boat would have a realizable value of $97,500, and the remaining inventory of parts would have a book and realizable value of $112,500.

The controller was also concerned about a city smoke ordinance that would take effect in two years. To comply with the ordinance, all hand-fired steamboats had to be converted to stoker firing. Several of the Climax steamboats were already stoker-fired; the Cynthia, however, was hand-fired. The additional cost of converting the Cynthia to stoker firing was estimated to be $120,000, provided it was done at the same time as the general rehabilitation. This $120,000 included the cost of stokers and extra hull conversion and was not included in the $345,000 rehabilitation figure. The controller also knew that if $345,000 were spent presently in rehabilitating the Cynthia and it was found out later that no relief, or only temporary relief for one or two years, was to be granted under the smoke ordinance, the cost of converting to stoker firing would no longer be $120,000, but around $210,000. The higher cost would be due to rebuilding, which would not be necessary if the Cynthia was converted to stoker firing at the time of her general rehabilitation.

Conversion would reduce the crew from 20 to 18, with the following details:

were based on a two-shift, 12-hour working day, which was standard on local riverboats. He had been informed, however, that the union representing crew members wanted a change to a three-shift, eight-hour day. If the union insisted on an eight-hour day, accommodations on board the steamers or the diesels would have to be enlarged. The controller was perturbed by this fact because he knew the diesels could readily be converted to accommodate three crews whereas steamers could not. How strongly the union would insist on the change and when it would be put into effect, if ever, were questions for which the controller could get no satisfactory answers. He believed that the union might have a difficult time in getting acceptance of its demands for three eight-hour shifts on steamers, since it would be very difficult, if not impossible, to convert the steamers to hold a larger crew, because of space limitations. The controller thought that the union might succeed in getting its demands accepted, however, in the case of diesel-powered boats. One of the diesel boats currently operating in the Pittsburgh area had accommodations for three crews, although it was still operating on a two-shift basis. The diesel boats that Quapelle offered to build for Climax could be fitted to accommodate three crews at no additional cost.

Another factor the controller was considering was alternative uses of funds.

Wages and fringes	$318,360
Commissary supplies	41,640
Repairs and maintenance*	73,200
Fuel and lubricants*	105,150
Miscellaneous service and supplies*	36,000
Total	$574,350

*These costs would remain the same, whether the crew was 20 or 18.

All operating data the controller had collected pertaining to crew expenses

Climax had sufficient funds to buy four diesel-powered boats; however, there were alternative uses for these funds. The other projects management was considering had an estimated return of at least 10 percent after taxes. The income tax rate at the time was 50 percent.

The company was conservatively managed and had no long-term debt outstanding. Its net worth exceeded $6 million. The company occasionally used unsecured bank loans to provide working capital during seasonal periods of peak need. Presently the company's liability for bank loans amounted to $450,000, which had been borrowed at 14 percent interest. The "prime" loan rate in New York City currently was 12 percent.

As a further inducement to have a contract to build a diesel boat, Quapelle offered to lease a diesel boat to Climax. The lease terms offered called for year-end annual payments of $142,865 for 15 years. (Quapelle would retain the rights to the investment tax credit.) At the end of 15 years, when Quapelle had in effect recovered the value of the boat, it would charge a nominal rental of $8,400 a year. Title to the boat would continue to remain in the hands of Quapelle. Climax would incur all costs of operating and maintaining the boat, including general overhaul every 10 years, and would still need to invest $225,000 in a basic spare parts inventory.

Questions

1. *If* management chooses to rehabilitate the Cynthia, should the stoker conversion be done immediately or delayed for two years? (For simplicity, assume straight-line depreciation in all of your analyses.)

2. *If* Climax acquires the diesel-powered boat, should they buy it or lease it?

3. Which alternative would you recommend?

4. (Optional) What is the effective interest rate on the 15-year Quapelle lease, assuming the investment tax credit is 10 percent ($97,500)?

23

Responsibility Accounting:
The Management Control
Structure

This chapter introduces responsibility accounting, the third type of management accounting information. After discussing general organizational characteristics and their relation to the process of management control, the responsibility center structure that underlies management control is described. This structure involves four types of responsibility centers: expense centers, revenue centers, profit centers, and investment centers. Each of these is discussed in some detail. Transfer pricing, which is a necessary device when profit centers exist, is also discussed.

CHARACTERISTICS OF ORGANIZATIONS

An organization is a group of persons who work together for one or more purposes, called its *goals* or *objectives*. The goals of business organizations were described in Chapter 21, where it was noted that one important goal is earning a satisfactory return on investment.

An organization consists of human beings who work together. A building with its equipment is not an organization. Rather, it is the persons who work in the building that constitute the organization. A crowd walking down a street is not an organization, nor are the spectators at a football game when they are behaving as individual spectators. But the cheering section at a game is an organization; its members work together under the direction of the cheerleaders.

Management

An organization has one or more leaders. Except in rare circumstances, a group of persons can work together to accomplish the organization's goals only if they are led. These leaders are called managers, or, collectively, the management. An organization's managers decide what the organization's goals should be; communicate these goals to members of the organization; decide on the tasks that are to be performed in order to achieve these goals and on the resources that are to be used in carrying out these tasks; ensure that the activities of the various organizational parts are coordinated; match individuals to tasks for which they are suited; motivate these individuals to carry out their tasks; observe how well these individuals are performing their tasks; and take corrective action when the need arises. The leader of a cheering section performs these functions; so does the president of General Motors Corporation.

Organization Hierarchy

A manager can supervise only a limited number of subordinates. (Old Testament writers put this number at 10.) It follows that in an organization of substantial size there must be several layers of managers in the organization structure. Authority runs from the top unit down through the successive layers. Such an arrangement is called an *organization hierarchy.*

The formal relationships among the various managers can be diagrammed in an *organization chart.* A partial organization chart is shown in Illustration 23–1. A number of organization units report to the president, who is the chief executive officer. Some of these are *line* units; that is, their activities are directly associated with achieving the goals of the organization. They produce and market goods or services. Others are *staff* units; that is, they exist to provide various support services to other units and to the president.

The principal line units are here called divisions. Within each division there are a number of departments, and within each department there are a number of sections. Other names are used for these layers of organization units in different companies, and in nonbusiness organizations.

All the units in Illustration 23–1 are *organization units.* Thus, Section A of Department 1 of Division A is an organization unit. Division A itself, including all of its departments and sections, also is an organization unit. Each of these units is headed by a manager who is responsible for the work done by the unit; each unit therefore is called a *responsibility center.* Managers are responsible in the sense that they are held accountable for the activities of their organization units. These activities include not only the work done within the responsibility center but also its relationships with the *environment,* which includes customers, suppliers, competitors, the community, regulatory agencies, and other outside parties.

ILLUSTRATION 23–1
PARTIAL ORGANIZATION CHART

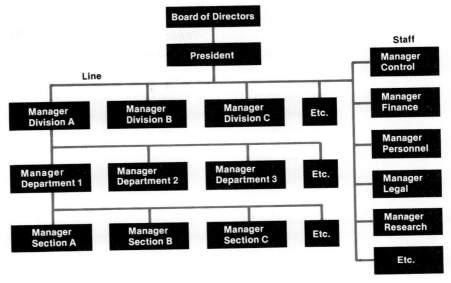

MANAGEMENT CONTROL

As explained in Chapter 1, management control involves three types of activities: planning, coordination, and control. *Planning* is deciding what should be done and how it should be done. *Coordination* is integrating the activities of the various responsbility centers. *Control* is assuring that desired[1] results are attained. Although the words *planning* and *coordination* are not included in the name of the management control process, it should be understood that these activities are fully as important as control activities in this process. Formally, *management control* is defined as the process by which managers influence members of the organization to implement its strategies effectively and efficiently.

Strategic Planning and Task Control

The management control process takes place with a framework of organizational goals and broad strategies for attaining these goals. The process of arriving at these goals and broad strategies is called *strategic planning*.

Management control should be distinguished from another planning, coordination, and control process called *task control*. This is the process of assuring that specific tasks are carried out effectively and efficiently.

---

[1]"Desired" results are not necessarily the same as "planned" results. Changes in circumstances that occur after a plan has been prepared may make it desirable to depart from the plan.

Task control involves little management judgment and relatively little interaction among managers. The control system for inventories based on economic order quantity, described in Chapter 21, is an example of a task control technique.

Thus, there are three management processes: strategic planning, management control, and task control. We focus on the middle one.

Any system can be described in terms of how it works (its process) and what it looks like (its structure). For example, medical students study the human body (a system) in terms of process (physiology) and structure (anatomy). Chapter 24 will describe the management control process. In this chapter we shall discuss the management control structure.

RESPONSIBILITY CENTERS

Illustration 23–2 provides a basis for describing the nature of responsibility centers. The top section depicts an electricity generating plant, which in some important respects is analogous to a responsibility center. Like a responsibility center, the plant (1) uses *inputs*, (2) to do *work*,

ILLUSTRATION 23–2
NATURE OF A RESPONSIBILITY CENTER

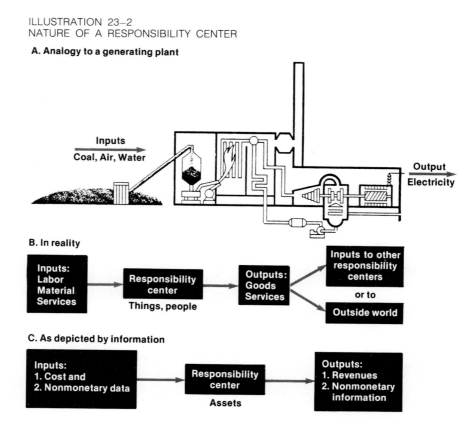

A. Analogy to a generating plant

Inputs
Coal, Air, Water

Output
Electricity

B. In reality

Inputs:
Labor
Material
Services

→

Responsibility
center

Things, people

→

Outputs:
Goods
Services

→

Inputs to other
responsibility
centers

or to

Outside world

C. As depicted by information

Inputs:
1. Cost and
2. Nonmonetary data

→

Responsibility
center

Assets

→

Outputs:
1. Revenues
2. Nonmonetary
information

(3) which results in *outputs*. In the case of the generating plant, the inputs are coal, water, and air, which the plant combines to do the work of turning a turbine connected to a generator rotor. The outputs are kilowatts of electricity.

Inputs and Outputs

As shown in Part B of Illustration 23–2, a responsibility center also has inputs, which are physical quantities of material, hours of various types of labor, and a variety of services. It performs work with these resources. Usually, both current and noncurrent assets are also required. As a result of this work, it produces outputs, which are either goods, if tangible, or services, if intangible. These goods or services go either to other responsibility centers within the organization or to customers in the outside world.

Part C of Illustration 23–2 shows information about these inputs and outputs. Accounting measures inputs in terms of cost. Although the resources themselves are nonmonetary things such as pounds of material and hours of labor, for purposes of management control it is necessary to measure these things with a monetary common denominator so that the physically unlike elements of resources can be combined. The monetary measure of the resources used in a responsibility center is *cost*. In addition to cost information, nonaccounting information on such matters as the physical quantity of material used, its quality, the skill level of the work force, and so on, is also useful.

If the outputs of a responsibility center are sold to an outside customer, accounting measures these outputs in terms of revenue. If, however, goods or services are transferred to other responsibility centers within the organization, an accounting measure of output is more difficult to obtain. In some situations, a monetary measure of output, such as the cost of the goods or services transferred, is feasible. Alternatively, a nonmonetary measure, such as the number of units of output, can be used.

Responsibility Accounting

Responsibility center managers need information about what has taken place in their respective responsibility centers. In addition to historical information about inputs (costs) and outputs, managers also need information about planned *future* inputs and outputs. The management accounting construction that deals with both planned and actual accounting information about the inputs and outputs of a responsibility center is called *responsibility accounting*. Unlike the construction of differential costs and revenues, which is tailor-made for each decision problem, responsibility accounting involves a continuous flow of information, corresponding to the continuous flow of inputs into and outputs from an organization's responsibility centers.

Contrast with Full Cost Accounting. An essential characteristic of responsibility accounting is that it focuses on responsibility centers. Full cost accounting focuses on goods and services, which formally are called *products* or *programs*, rather than focusing on responsibility centers. This difference in focus is what distinguishes responsibility accounting from full cost accounting. In making this distinction, we do not mean to imply that program cost accounting and responsibility accounting are two separate accounting systems. In fact, they are closely related and are more accurately described as two parts of the management accounting system.

Illustration 23–3 shows a useful way of thinking about the distinction between responsibility costs and full program costs. The rows of the matrix represent responsibility centers, while the columns represent programs, which in a profit-oriented business are principally product lines. In many organizations, a given responsibility center performs work related to several programs. (For example, the Plymouth Reliant and Dodge Aries automobiles are assembled in the same plants.) This is de-

ILLUSTRATION 23–3
MATRIX OF PROGRAM COSTS AND RESPONSIBILITY COSTS

	Program 1	Program 2	Program 3	Program 4	Program 5
Responsibility Center A		X	X		
Responsibility Center B	X		X	X	
Responsibility Center C		X		X	X
Responsibility Center D			X		
Responsibility Center E	X	X	X	X	X
Responsibility Center F	X				X

Adding costs by column gives program (usually, product) data, which is full cost data.

Adding costs by row gives responsibility accounting data.

Note: Each X represents the costs incurred in a given responsibility center (see the row name) on behalf of a given program (see the column name).

picted by the Xs in Illustration 23–3, each of which represents the cost incurred on behalf of a given program in a given responsibility center. *Row* totals of these costs are responsibility accounting data, useful especially for cost control purposes. *Column* totals are program accounting data, useful for pricing decisions and program profitability evaluation.

We will now give a specific example of how the framework in Illustration 23–3 is applied.

Example. Company Y makes two products, 1 and 2. It has two production departments, A and B, each of which is a production cost center. It also has two other departments: C is the production support department, and D is the selling and administrative department. (All four departments are responsibility centers.) The full costs of Y's products for a month are assembled and reported as shown in Part A of Illustration 23–4. Note that

ILLUSTRATION 23–4
CONTRAST BETWEEN FULL COSTS AND RESPONSIBILITY COSTS

A. Full Product Costs

Cost element:	Total	Product 1	Product 2
Direct material	$20,000	$14,000	$ 6,000
Direct labor	13,000	8,000	5,000
Indirect production	9,620	6,218	3,402
Selling and administrative	5,500	3,645	1,855
Total costs	$48,120	$31,863	$16,257

B. Responsibility Costs

		Departments (responsibility centers)			
	Total	A	B	C	D
Cost element:					
Direct material	$20,000	$18,000	$ 2,000		
Direct labor	13,000	4,000	9,000		
Supervision	4,240	800	1,200	$ 840	$1,400
Other labor costs	6,970	1,500	170	2,200	3,100
Supplies	1,290	660	330	100	200
Other costs	2,620	880	440	500	800
Total costs	$48,120	$25,840	$13,140	$3,640	$5,500

C. In Matrix Format

	Product 1	Product 2	Responsibility Costs
Department A	17,015	8,825	$25,840
Department B	8,928	4,212	13,140
Department C	2,275	1,365	3,640
Department D	3,645	1,855	5,500
Product Costs	$31,863	$16,257	$48,120

from this information, it is impossible to identify what costs the managers of three departments (A, B, and C) were responsible for. In particular, the costs of Department C have been allocated to the two products, as have overhead costs in Departments A and B, to give the amounts shown as each product's indirect production costs.

By contrast, responsibility accounting does identify the amount of costs that each of the four departmental managers is responsible for, as shown in Part B of the illustration. Note that Part B, however, does not show the costs of the two products. Both types of information are needed. Note also that the total product costs ($48,120) are equal to the total responsibility costs. The two parts are different arrangements of the same underlying data.

That full product costs and responsibility costs are two different ways of "slicing the same pie" is depicted in Part C of the illustration, which shows both product (program) costs and responsibility costs in matrix format.

The separate items of cost in Illustration 23–4 are called *cost elements* (or, less descriptively, *line items*). A carefully designed cost system can identify a direct material or direct labor cost item on all three of these dimensions: *what resource* the cost represents (i.e., the specific cost element); *where* that resource was used (responsibility cost); and for *what purpose* the cost was incurred (program, or product, cost).

Effectiveness and Efficiency

The performance of a responsibility center manager can be measured in terms of the effectiveness and efficiency of the work of the responsibility center. By *effectiveness*, we mean how well the responsibility center does its job, that is, the extent to which it produces the intended or expected results. *Efficiency* is used in its engineering sense, that is, the amount of output per unit of input. An efficient operation is one that produces a given quantity of outputs with a minimum consumption of inputs, or one that produces the largest possible outputs from a given quantity of inputs.

Effectiveness is always related to the organization's *objectives*. Efficiency, per se, is not related to objectives. An efficient responsibility center is one that does whatever it does with the lowest consumption of resources. However, if what it does (i.e., its output) is an inadequate contribution to the accomplishment of the organization's objectives, it is ineffective.

Example. If a department responsible for processing incoming sales orders does so at a low cost per order processed, it is efficient. If, however, the department is slow in answering customer queries about the status of orders, and thus antagonizes customers to the point where they take their business elsewhere, the department is ineffective.

In many responsibility centers, a measure of efficiency can be developed that relates actual costs to a number that expresses what costs *should be incurred* for a given amount of output, that is, to a standard or budget. Such a measure can be a useful indication of efficiency, but it is never a *perfect* measure for at least two reasons: (1) recorded costs are not a precisely accurate measure of resources consumed and (2) standards are, at best, only approximate measures of what resource consumption ideally should have been in the circumstances prevailing.

A responsibility center should be *both* effective *and* efficient; it is not a case of one or the other. In some situations, both effectiveness and efficiency can be encompassed within a single measure. For example, in profit-oriented organizations, profit measures the combined effect of effectiveness and efficiency. When an overall measure does not exist, it is useful to classify the various performance measures used as relating either to effectiveness (e.g., warranty claims per thousand units sold) or efficiency (e.g., labor-hours per unit produced).

TYPES OF RESPONSIBILITY CENTERS

As previously noted, an important business goal is to earn a satisfactory return on investment (ROI). Return on investment is the ratio:

$$ROI = \frac{Revenues - Expenses}{Investment}$$

The three elements of this ratio lead to definitions of four types of responsibility centers that are important in management control systems. These are (1) expense centers, (2) revenue centers, (3) profit centers, and (4) investment centers.

Expense Centers

If the control system measures the expenses (i.e., the costs) incurred by a responsibility center but does *not* measure its outputs in terms of revenues, the responsibility center is called an *expense center*. Every responsibility center has outputs; that is, it does something. In many cases, however, it is neither feasible nor necessary to measure these outputs in terms of revenues. For example, it would be extremely difficult to measure the monetary value of the accounting or legal department's outputs. Although generally it is relatively easy to measure the revenue value of the outputs of an individual production department, there is no reason for doing so if the responsibility of the department manager is to produce a stated *quantity* of outputs at the lowest feasible cost. For these reasons, most individual production departments and most staff units are expense centers.

Expense centers can be further categorized according to the nature of the costs incurred in the center. If the bulk of the responsibility center's costs are of a nature such that accountants and industrial engineers working together can estimate the right or proper amount of cost that should be incurred to accomplish the center's tasks, then it is an *engi-*

neered *expense center*. (The standard costs for direct labor and materials described in Chapter 19 are examples of engineered costs.) Production departments performing repetitive tasks usually are engineered expense centers.

If most of a responsibility center's costs are *discretionary* in nature, that is, if the "right" amount to spend for its activities is a matter of judgment rather than an industrial engineering study, then the center is a *discretionary expense center*. Personnel and legal departments are examples. (Engineered and discretionary costs are described in more detail in Chapter 24.) These subcategories indicate only the nature of *most* of the center's costs. There are elements of discretionary cost in most engineered expense centers, and there are elements of engineered cost in most discretionary expense centers.

Expense centers are not quite the same as cost centers. Recall from Chapter 18 that a *cost center* is a device used in a full cost accounting system to collect costs that are subsequently to be charged to cost objectives. In a given company, most, but not all, cost centers are also expense centers. However, a cost center such as "Occupancy" is not a responsibility center at all, and hence is not an expense center.

Revenue Centers

If a responsibility center manager is held accountable for the outputs of the center as measured in monetary terms (revenues) but is not responsible for the costs of producing the goods or services that the center sells, then the responsibility center is a *revenue center*. Many companies treat regional sales offices as revenue centers. A sales organization treated as a revenue center also usually has responsibility for controlling its selling expenses—for example, travel, advertising, point-of-purchase displays, and so on. Therefore, revenue centers often are *also* expense centers.

Profit Centers

Revenue is a monetary measure of outputs, and expense (or cost) is a monetary measure of inputs, or resources consumed. Profit is the difference between revenue and expense. If performance in a responsibility center is measured in terms of the difference between (1) the revenue it earns and (2) the expense it incurs, the responsibility center is a *profit center.*

Although in financial accounting revenue is recognized only when it is realized by a sale to an outside customer, in responsibility accounting revenue measures the outputs of a responsibility center in a given accounting period, *whether or not the company realizes the revenue in that period.* Thus, a factory is a profit center if it "sells" its output to the sales department and records the revenue and cost of such sales. Likewise, a service department, such as the data processing department, may "sell" its services to the responsibility centers that receive these services. These "sales" generate revenues for the service department. Since the difference between sales revenues and the cost of these sales is profit, the service department is a profit center if both of these elements are measured.

A given responsibility center is a profit center only if management *decides* to measure its outputs in terms of revenues. Revenues for a company as a whole are automatically generated when the company makes sales to the outside world. By contrast, revenues for an internal organization unit are recognized only if management decides that it is a good idea to do so. No accounting principle *requires* that revenues be measured for individual responsibility centers within a company. With some ingenuity, practically any expense center could be turned into a profit center because some way of putting a selling price on the output of most responsibility centers can be found. The question is whether there are sufficient *benefits* in doing so.

Advantages of Profit Centers.   A profit center resembles a business in miniature. Like a separate company, it has an income statement that shows revenue, expense, and profit. Most of the decisions made by the profit center manager affect the numbers on this income statement. The income statement for a profit center therefore is a basic management control document. Because their performance is measured by profit, the managers of profit centers are motivated to make decisions about inputs and outputs that will increase the profit reported for their profit centers. Since they act somewhat as they would act if they were running their own businesses, the profit center is a good training ground for general management responsibility. The use of the profit center idea is one of the important tools that has made possible the decentralization of profit responsibility in large companies.

Criteria for Profit Centers.   In deciding whether to treat a responsibility center as a profit center, the following points are relevant:

1. Extra recordkeeping is involved if the profit center idea is used. In the profit center itself, there is the extra work of measuring output in revenue terms, and in the responsibility centers that receive its outputs there is the work of recording the cost of goods or services received.
2. If the manager of a responsibility center has little authority to decide on the quantity and quality of its outputs or on the relation of output to costs, then a profit center is usually of little use as a control device. This does not imply that the manager of a profit center must have *complete* control over outputs and inputs, for few, if any, managers have such complete authority.
3. When top management *requires* responsibility centers to use a service furnished by another responsibility center, the service probably

should be furnished at no charge, and the service unit therefore should not be a profit center. For example, if top management requires that internal audits be made, the units that are audited probably should not be asked to pay for the cost of the internal auditing service, and the internal auditing unit should therefore not be a profit center.

4. If outputs are fairly homogeneous (e.g., cement), a nonmonetary measure of output (e.g., hundredweight of cement produced) may be adequate, and there may be no substantial advantage to be gained in converting these outputs to a monetary measure of revenue.

5. To the extent that the profit center technique puts managers in business for themselves, it promotes a spirit of competition. In many situations, competition provides a powerful incentive for good management. In other situations, however, organization units should cooperate closely with one another. In these situations, the profit center device may generate excessive friction between profit centers, to the detriment of the company's overall welfare. Also, it may generate too much interest in short-run profits to the detriment of long-run results.

Transfer Prices

A *transfer price* is a price used to measure the value of products (i.e., goods or services) furnished by a profit center to other responsibility centers within a company. It is to be contrasted with a *market price*, which measures exchanges between a company and the outside world. Internal exchanges that are measured by transfer prices result in *revenue* for the responsibility center furnishing (i.e., "selling") the product, and in *cost* for the responsibility center receiving (i.e., "buying") the product. Whenever a company has profit centers, transfer prices usually are required. There are two general types of transfer prices: the market-based price and the cost-based price.

Market-Based Transfer Prices. If a market price for the product exists, a *market-based transfer price* is usually preferable to a cost-based price. The buying responsibility center should ordinarily not be expected to pay more internally than it would have to pay if it purchased from the outside world, nor should the selling center ordinarily be entitled to more revenue than it could obtain by selling to the outside world. If the market price is abnormal, as when an outside vendor sets a low "distress" price in order to use temporarily idle capacity, then such temporary aberrations are ordinarily disregarded in arriving at transfer prices. The market price may be adjusted downward for credit costs and for certain selling costs that are not incurred in an internal exchange.

Market-based prices, where available, are widely used in decentralized companies.[2] They have the benefit of being relatively objective, rather than a function of the relative negotiating skills of the selling and buying profit centers' managers. Also, most decentralized companies almost literally expect their profit centers to deal with one another "at arm's length" as independent businesses, and market-based prices add to the realism of this simulation of arm's-length business relationships. In practice, however, it is sometimes not clear what "the" market price is because different suppliers may set different prices on essentially identical items. A clearly stated policy (e.g., "the lowest available price, after consideration of supplier reliability and other factors such as warranty and delivery terms") or an arbitration mechanism (described below) is needed to deal with these market price ambiguities.

Cost-Based Transfer Prices. In a great many situations, there is no reliable market price that can be used as a basis for the transfer price. In these situations, a *cost-based transfer price* is used. If feasible, the cost should be a *standard cost*. If it is an actual cost, the selling responsibility center has little incentive to control efficiency because any cost increases or decreases will be automatically passed on to the buying center in the transfer price.

The method of computing cost and the amount of profit to be included in the transfer price may be specified by top management in order to lessen arguments that may otherwise arise. To avoid disputes, any policy statement as to how costs and profit are to be computed must be thorough and carefully worded. In particular, short-term per unit costs may be different from longer-term costs. There can also be questions as to whether all of the cost elements normally included in the seller's definition of full cost should be included in the definition of cost used to determine internal prices. Also, disputes—or at least resentment on the part of the buyer—may occur if market conditions have squeezed the seller's outside profit margins to a lower level than that specified in the policy statement.

Negotiation and Arbitration. Because of the potential areas for disagreement in both market-based and cost-based transfer prices, transfer

---

[2]Based on a survey of 239 large companies, Vancil reported the prevalence of various transfer pricing policies as follows:

Basis of Transfer Price	Percent
Market price	31
Negotiation	22
Full cost plus profit	17
Full cost	25
Variable cost	5
	100

(Richard F. Vancil, *Decentralization: Managerial Ambiguity by Design* [New York: Financial Executives Research Foundation, 1979], p. 180.)

prices sometimes are negotiated between buyer and seller, rather than being set by reference to outside prices or by a formula applied to the seller's costs as recorded in the cost accounting system. Also, at times the seller is willing to depart from the normal company transfer price policy. For example, the selling responsibility center may be willing to sell below the normal market price rather than lose the business, which could happen if the buying responsibility center took advantage of a temporarily low outside price. In such circumstances, the two parties negotiate a "deal."

Unless both responsibility center managers have complete freedom to act, these negotiations will not always lead to an equitable result because the parties may have unequal bargaining powers. That is, the prospective buyer may not have the power of threatening to take its business elsewhere, and the prospective seller may not have the power of refusing to do the work. Thus, there usually needs to be an *arbitration* mechanism to settle disputes concerning transfer prices. Such negotiations and arbitration can be very time consuming.

> **Example.** A U.S.-based automobile company decided to market a car in the United States that would be manufactured in one of the company's European plants. It took almost *one year* for the European manufacturing profit center and the U.S. marketing profit center to reach agreement on the transfer price.

Risk of Suboptimization. Profit centers are not, in fact, legally independent business entities. When they engage in transactions among themselves, there is sometimes the risk that a decision that will enhance a given profit center's reported income will *not* enhance the *total* company's income. This is called the *risk of suboptimization*. This risk may exist when the selling profit center's normal transfer price is higher than its short-run costs, which is almost always the case.

> **Example.** Division B buys component X from Division A. Division B uses this component in product Y. The current transfer price for X, which includes full costs plus a profit margin, is $50. Division B's *variable* cost of product Y, including the $50 for component X, is $150 per unit (i.e., $100 of variable cost is added by B's production and selling operations). Both divisions currently have considerable excess capacity. This has led Division B to consider temporarily contribution pricing (described in Chapter 21) product Y. Division B has the opportunity, without spoiling the market, to sell 1,000 units of Y to a new customer on a one-time basis for $145 per unit. Since this is less than B's $150 per unit variable cost, B rejects this opportunity.
>
> However, it happens that A's *variable* cost for X is only $20 per unit, making the *company's* variable cost for Y only $120 per unit ($20 variable cost in A plus $100 in B). Thus, the *company* could earn a contribution of $25 per unit (= $145 price − $120 variable costs) on the deal that B has turned down. Division B has done the right thing from *its* perspective, but the transfer price policy caused this to be the wrong thing from the perspective of the *overall company*.

This example of "suboptimization" may be found more often in texts than in practice. Since it is in the self-interest of both managers that the sale be made to the outside customer at a contribution price, the sensible course of action is for them to get together and negotiate a mutually agreeable transfer price. This price would be higher than the selling division's variable cost but lower than its normal transfer price. In effect, the contribution margin from the transaction would be divided fairly between the two divisions.

In sum, companies seek many things in their transfer pricing policies: objectivity, realism, equitability to all parties involved, a minimum of time spent in negotiating and arbitrating, and minimum risk of suboptimization. They also want the prices eventually to result in measured profits that reflect the "true" economics of each of the profit centers involved. For example, if Division A sells to Division B on an ongoing basis, corporate management does not want Division B to look more profitable than it "really is" solely because unrealistically low transfer prices result in profit arbitrarily being shifted from A to B. These various criteria often conflict, particularly realism versus risk of suboptimization. It is not surprising, therefore, that one frequently hears profit center managers' expressions of dissatisfaction concerning any particular transfer pricing approach used in a decentralized company.

Investment Centers

An *investment center* is a responsibility center in which the manager is held responsible for the use of assets, as well as for profit.[3] It is therefore the ultimate extension of the responsibility idea. In an investment center the manager is expected to earn a satisfactory return on the assets employed in the responsibility center.

Some companies having investment centers measure each center's return on investment (ROI) along the lines described in Chapter 13. Return on assets (Profit ÷ Total assets) and return on "net assets" or invested capital (Profit ÷ Assets − Current liabilities) are commonly used, in part because these ROI measures correspond to ratios calculated by outside analysts. Other companies measure an investment center's *residual income*, which is defined as profit (before interest expense) minus a capital charge rate (analogous to the return rate used in discounted cash flow techniques) levied on the investment in the center's assets or net assets.[4]

> **Example.** Division Z of ABC Corporation is an investment center. In 19x1, the division's profit was $150,000 (net of interest expense of

---

[3]Note that in an investment center *both* profit *and* assets are measured. Many companies refer both to their profit centers and to their investment centers as "profit centers."

[4]James S. Reece and William R. Cool found in a survey of the 1,000 largest U.S. industrial firms that of those companies having investment centers, 65 percent used only an ROI measure, 2 percent used only residual income, 28 percent used both measures, and the remaining 5 percent either used some other method or did not disclose their method ("Measuring Investment Center Performance," *Harvard Business Review*, May–June 1978).

$30,000), and the division employed $1,000,000 of assets. For purposes of calculating residual income, ABC levies a 10 percent capital charge on assets employed. Division Z's ROI and residual income for the year would be calculated as follows:

$$\text{ROI} = \frac{\text{Profit}}{\text{Investment}} = \frac{\$150,000}{\$1,000,000} = 15 \text{ percent}$$

$$\genfrac{}{}{0pt}{}{\text{Residual}}{\text{income}} = \genfrac{}{}{0pt}{}{\text{Profit (pre-}}{\text{interest)}} - \left(\genfrac{}{}{0pt}{}{\text{Capital}}{\text{charge}} \times \text{Investment} \right)$$

$$= \$180,000 - 0.10 \times (\$1,000,000) = \$80,000$$

[handwritten margin note: net of interest expense]

This example can be used to illustrate the conceptual superiority of residual income over ROI as a performance measure. Suppose the Division Z manager could increase profits by $12,000 a year by making an investment of $100,000. Because the 12 percent accounting rate of return (i.e., $12,000 \div $100,000 = 12 percent) on this investment is less than the 15 percent average return the division is already earning, the manager may shy away from making this investment. However, if the incremental capital cost rate is truly 10 percent, the investment would increase corporate "wealth" by the amount of additional annual residual income that the investment would produce, which is $2,000 [= $12,000 − 0.10 ($100,000)]. Despite this conceptual advantage of residual income, many companies do not use it as an investment center measure because (1) ROI percentages are ratios that can be used to compare investment centers of differing sizes, whereas residual income is an absolute dollar amount that is a function of the investment center's size and (2) a company's residual income is an internal figure that is not reported to shareholders and other outsides.[5]

[handwritten margin note: you take here—as we are 3 separate entities]

Whether ROI or residual income is used, the measurement of assets employed, or the *investment base,* poses many difficult problems. For example, consider cash. The cash balance of the company is a safety valve, or buffer, protecting the company against short-run fluctuations in funds requirements. Compared with an independent company, an investment center needs relatively little cash because it can obtain funds from headquarters on short notice. Part of the headquarters cash balance therefore exists for the financial protection of the investment centers, and it can therefore logically be allocated to them as part of their capital employed. There are several ways of allocating this cash to investment centers just as there are several ways of allocating general overhead costs.

[handwritten margin note: I can → I am't allocated; Can't control initial amount]

Similar problems arise with respect to each type of asset that the investment center uses. Valuation of plant and equipment is especially controversial. A discussion of these problems is outside the scope of this

---

[5]General Electric Company generally is credited with developing the residual income measure in the early 1950s. However, the measure gradually fell into disuse in GE for the reasons cited, and today ROI is used instead.

introductory treatment. For our present purpose, we need only state that many problems exist and that there is much disagreement as to the best solution. Despite these difficulties, a growing number of companies find it useful to create investment centers.[6]

The investment center approach is normally used only for a relatively "freestanding" product division, that is, a division that both produces and markets a line of goods or a set of services, and significantly influences its own level of assets. This approach has the effect of "putting managers in business for themselves" to an even greater extent than does the profit center. Reports on performance show not only the amount of profit that the investment center has earned, which is the case with reports for a profit center, but also the amount of assets used in earning that profit. This is obviously a more encompassing report on performance than a report that does not relate profits to assets employed. On the other hand, the possible disadvantages mentioned above for profit centers exist in a magnified form in investment centers.

Two Misconceptions. Some people think that the principal reason for using the investment center approach is to enhance control over *non-current* assets. This is not the case. Most companies exercise this control via the capital investment procedures described in Chapters 22 and 25, which preclude a responsibility center manager from unilaterally making large investments in noncurrent assets. Rather, the investment center approach primarily directs managers' attention to the *current* assets under their day-to-day control, particularly inventories and receivables.

Second, many companies monitor the ROI or residual income of their profit centers to see if the company is continuing to earn a satisfactory return on the capital tied up in those units. This measurement process *does not* make those units investment centers. Such a unit is an investment center only if its *manager* is held accountable for the ROI or residual income of the unit.

Nonmonetary Measures

The fact that each responsibility center is treated as either an expense, revenue, profit, or investment center does not mean that only monetary measures are used in monitoring its performance. Virtually all responsibility centers have important nonfinancial objectives, such as the quality of their goods or services, employee morale, and so on. Particularly in discretionary expense centers, these nonmonetary factors may be more important than monetary measures. Many companies employ, in addition to their monetary control systems, formal systems for establishing and measuring these nonmonetary factors. Such systems are frequently called *management by objectives* or *MBO* systems; they are described in Chapter 25.

---

[6]Reece and Cool, "Measuring Investment Center Performance," found that 74 percent of the 1,000 largest U.S. industrial firms have investment centers and another 22 percent have profit centers. Companies considerably smaller than these 1,000 have also adopted the investment center technique.

SUMMARY

An organization consists of responsibility centers. Management control involves the planning, coordinating, and control of these centers' activities. It is to be distinguished from strategic planning, which sets goals and broad strategies, and from task control, which deals with the performance of specific routine tasks.

Responsibility centers use inputs and assets to produce outputs. Responsibility accounting focuses on planned and actual amounts for responsibility center inputs and outputs. It is to be contrasted with full cost accounting, which focuses on programs, especially goods and services, rather than on responsibility centers.

There are four types of responsibility centers: expense centers, in which inputs are measured in monetary terms; revenue centers, in which outputs are measured in monetary terms; profit centers, in which both inputs and outputs are measured in monetary terms; and investment centers, in which both profits and assets employed are measured and related to each other. In profit centers and investment centers, a transfer price is used to measure products furnished to other responsibility centers. Nonmonetary measures are also important in all types of responsibility centers.

SUGGESTIONS FOR FURTHER READING
FOR CHAPTERS 23 and 24
(also see references at the end of Chapter 15)

Anthony, Robert N. *Planning and Control Systems: A Framework for Analysis.* Boston: Harvard Business School Division of Research, 1965.

Anthony, Robert N., and John Dearden. *Management Control Systems: Text and Cases.* 4th ed. Homewood, Ill.: Richard D. Irwin, 1980.

Anthony, Robert N., and Regina Herzlinger. *Management Control in Nonprofit Organizations.* Rev. ed. Homewood, Ill.: Richard D. Irwin, 1980.

Dalton, Gene W., and Paul R. Lawrence. *Motivation and Control in Organizations.* Homewood, Ill.: Irwin-Dorsey, 1971.

Hopwood, Anthony. *Accounting and Human Behavior.* Englewood Cliffs, N.J.: Prentice-Hall, 1976.

March, James G., and Herbert A. Simon. *Organizations.* New York: John Wiley & Sons, 1958.

Mintzberg, Henry. *The Nature of Managerial Work.* New York: Harper & Row, 1973.

Rappaport, Alfred, ed. *Information for Decision Making.* 3d ed. Englewood Cliffs, N.J.: Prentice-Hall, 1982.

Schiff, Michael, and Arie Y. Lewin, eds. *Behavioral Aspects of Accounting.* Englewood Cliffs, N.J.: Prentice-Hall, 1974.

Solomons, David. *Divisional Performance: Measurement and Control.* Homewood, Ill.: Richard D. Irwin, 1968.

Vancil, Richard F. *Decentralization: Managerial Ambiguity by Design.* New York: Financial Executives Research Foundation, 1979.

Cases

CASE 23–1   Shuman Automobiles, Inc.

Clark Shuman, owner and general manager of an automobile dealership, was nearing retirement and wanted to begin relinquishing his personal control over the business' operations. (See Exhibit 1 for current financial statements.) The reputation he had established in the community led him to believe that the recent growth in his business would continue. His long-standing policy of emphasizing new-car sales as the principal business of the dealership had paid off, in Shuman's opinion. This, combined with close attention to customer relations so that a substantial amount of repeat business was generated, had increased the company's sales to a new high level. Therefore, he wanted to make organizational changes to cope with the new situation, especially given his desire to withdraw from any day-to-day managerial responsibilities.

Accordingly, Shuman divided up the business into three departments: new-car sales, used-car sales, and the service department. He then appointed three of his most trusted employees managers of the new departments: Janet Moyer, new-car sales; Paul Fiedler, used-car sales; and Nate Bianci, service department. All of these people had been with the dealership for several years.

Each manager was told to run his or her department as if it were an independent business. In order to give the new managers an incentive, their remuneration was to be calculated as a straight percentage of their department's gross profit.

Soon after taking over as manager of new-car sales, Janet Moyer had to settle upon the amount to offer a particular customer who wanted to trade his old car as a part of the purchase price of a new one

EXHIBIT 1

SHUMAN AUTOMOBILES, INC.
Income Statement
For the Year Ended December 31

Sales of new cars			$3,821,873
Cost of new-car sales*		$3,456,401	
Sales remuneration		76,372	3,532,773
			289,100
Allowances on trade†			86,112
New-car gross profit			202,988
Sales of used cars		1,695,696	
Cost of used-car sales*	$1,457,277		
Sales remuneration	51,564		
		1,508,841	
		186,855	
Allowances on trade†		31,118	
Used-car gross profit			155,737
			358,725
Service sales to customers		547,511	
Cost of work*		404,884	
		142,627	
Service work on reconditioning:			
Charge		236,580	
Cost*		244,312	(7,732)
Service work gross profit			134,895
			493,620
General and administrative expenses			191,710
Income before taxes			$ 301,910

*These amounts include all costs assignable directly to the department, but exclude allocated general dealership overhead.

†Allowances on trade represent the excess of amounts allowed on cars taken in trade over their appraised value.

with a list price of $9,600. Before closing the sale, Moyer had to decide the amount she would offer the customer for the trade-in value of the old car. She knew that if no trade-in were involved, she would deduct about 8 percent from the list price of this model new car to be competitive with several other dealers in the area. However, she also wanted to make sure that she did not lose out on the sale by offering too low a trade-in allowance.

During her conversation with the customer, it had become apparent that the customer had an inflated view of the worth of his old car, a far from uncommon event. In this case, it probably meant that Moyer had to be prepared to make some sacrifices to close the sale. The new car had been in stock for some time, and the model was not selling very well, so she was rather anxious to make the sale if this could be done profitably.

In order to establish the trade-in value of the car, the used-car manager, Fiedler, accompanied Moyer and the customer out to the parking lot to examine the car. In the course of his appraisal, Fiedler estimated the car would require reconditioning work costing about $525, after which the car would retail for about $3,700. On a wholesale basis, he could either buy or sell such a car, after reconditioning, for about $3,200. The wholesale price of a car was subject to much greater fluctuation than the retail price, depending on color, trim, model, and so forth. Fortunately, the car being traded in was a very popular shade. The retail automobile dealer's handbook of used-car prices, the "Blue Book," gave a cash buying price range of $2,750 to $2,930 for the trade-in model in good condition. This range represented the distribution of cash prices paid by automobile dealers for that model of car in the area in the past week. Fiedler, estimated that he could get about $2,400 for the car "as is" (that is, without any work being done to it) at next week's auction.

The new-car department manager had the right to buy any trade-in at any price she thought appropriate, but then it was her responsibility to dispose of the car. She had the alternative of either trying to persuade the used-car manager to take over the car and accepting the used-car manager's appraisal price, or she herself could sell the car through wholesale channels or at auction. Whatever course Moyer adopted, it was her primary responsibility to make a profit for the dealership on the new cars she sold, without affecting her performance through excessive allowances on trade-ins. This primary goal, Moyer said, had to be "balanced against the need to satisfy the customers and move the new cars out of inventory—and there is only a narrow line between allowing enough on a used car and allowing too much."

After weighing all these factors, with particular emphasis on the personality of the customer, Moyer decided to allow $3,250 for the used car, provided the customer agreed to pay the list price for the new car. After a certain amount of hag-

gling, during which the customer came down from a higher figure and Moyer came up from a lower one, the $3,250 allowance was agreed upon. The necessary papers were signed, and the customer drove off.

Moyer returned to the office and explained the situation to Joanne Brunner, who had recently joined the dealership as accountant. After listening with interest to Moyer's explanation of the sale, Brunner set about recording the sale in the accounting records of the business. As soon as she saw the new car had been purchased from the manufacturer for $8,160, she was uncertain as to the value she should place on the trade-in vehicle. Since the new car's list price was $9,600 and it had cost $8,160, Brunner reasoned the gross margin on the new-car sale was $1,440. Yet Moyer had allowed $3,250 for the old car, which needed $525 repairs and could be sold retail for $3,700 or wholesale for $3,200. Did this mean that the new-car sale involved a loss? Brunner was not at all sure she knew the answer to this question. Also, she was uncertain about the value she should place on the used car for inventory valuation purposes. Brunner decided that she would put down a valuation of $3,250, and then await instructions from her superiors.

When Fiedler, the used-car manager, found out what Brunner had done, he stated forcefully that he would not accept $3,250 as the valuation of the used car. His comment went as follows:

> My used-car department has to get rid of that used car, unless Janet (Moyer) agrees to take it over herself. I would certainly never have allowed the customer $3,250 for that old tub. I would never have given any more than $2,675, which is the wholesale price less the

cost of repairs. My department has to make a profit too, you know. My own income is dependent on the gross profit I show on the sale of used cars, and I will not stand for having my income hurt because Janet is too generous towards her customers.

Brunner replied that she had not meant to cause trouble but had simply recorded the car at what seemed to be its cost of acquisition, because she had been taught that this was the best accounting practice. Whatever response Fiedler was about to make to this comment was cut off by the arrival of Clark Shuman, the general manager, and Nate Bianci, the service department manager. Shuman picked up the phone and called Janet Moyer, asking her to come over right away.

"All right, Nate," said Shuman, "now that we are all here, would you tell them what you just told me?"

Bianci said, "Clark, the trouble is with this trade-in. Janet and Paul were right in thinking that the repairs they thought necessary would cost about $525. Unfortunately, they failed to notice that the rear axle is cracked; it will have to be re-placed before we can retail the car. This will probably use up parts and labor costing about $400.

"Beside this," Bianci continued, "there is another thing that is bothering me a good deal more. Under the accounting system we've been using, I can't charge as much on an internal job as I would for the same job performed for an outside customer. As you can see from my department statement (Exhibit 2), I lost almost 8,000 bucks on internal work last year. On a reconditioning job like this, which costs out at $925, I don't even break even. If I did work costing $925 for an outside customer, I would be able to charge about $1,250 for the job. The Blue Book gives a range of $1,225 to $1,275 for the work this car needs, and I have always aimed for about the middle of the Blue Book range.[1] That would give my department a gross profit of $325, and my own income is based on that gross profit.

---

[1]In addition to the Blue Book for used-car prices, there was a Blue Book that gave the range of charges for various classes of repair work. Like the used-car book, it was issued weekly and was based on the actual charges made and reported by vehicle repair shops in the area.

EXHIBIT 2

Analysis of Service Department Expenses
For the Year Ended December 31

	Customer Jobs	Reconditioning Jobs	Total
Number of jobs	3,780	751	4,531
Direct labor	$168,471	$ 98,820	$267,291
Supplies	58,392	32,755	91,147
Department overhead	49,720	26,067	75,787
	276,583	157,642	434,225
Parts	128,301	86,670	214,971
	404,884	244,312	649,196
Charges made for jobs to customers or other departments	547,511	236,580	784,091
Gross profit (loss)	142,627	(7,732)	134,895
General overhead proportion			77,080
Departmental profit for the year			$ 57,815

Since it looks like a large proportion of the work of my department is going to be the reconditioning of trade-ins for resale, I figure that I should be able to make the same charge for repairing a trade-in as I would get for an outside repair job."

Fielder and Moyer both started to talk at once at this point. Fiedler managed to edge out Moyer: "This axle business is unfortunate, all right; but it is very hard to spot a cracked axle. Nate is likely to be just as lucky the other way next time. He has to take the rough with the smooth. It is up to him to get the cars ready for me to sell."

Moyer, after agreeing that the failure to spot the axle was unfortunate, added: "This error is hardly my fault, however. Anyway, it is ridiculous that the service department should make a profit on jobs it does for the rest of the dealership. The company can't make money when its left hand sells to its right."

At this point, Clark Shuman was getting a little confused about the situation. He thought there was a little truth in everything that had been said, but he was not sure how much. It was evident to him that some action was called for, both to sort out the present problem and to prevent its recurrence. He instructed Ms. Brunner, the accountant, to "work out how much we are really going to make on this whole deal," and then retired to his office to consider how best to get his managers to make a profit for the company.

A week after the events described above, Clark Shuman was still far from sure what action to take to motivate his managers to make a profit for the business. During the week, Bianci had reported to him that the repairs to the used car had cost $996, of which $463 represented the cost of those repairs which

had been spotted at the time of purchase, and the remaining $533 the cost of supplying and fitting a replacement for the cracked axle. To support his own case for a higher allowance on reconditioning jobs, Bianci had looked through the duplicate invoices over the last few months and had found examples of similar (but not identical) work to that which had been done on the trade-in car. The amounts of these invoices averaged $1,276, which the customers had paid without question, and the average of the costs assigned to these jobs was $945. (General overhead was not assigned to individual jobs.) In addition, Bianci had obtained from Ms. Brunner the cost analysis shown in Exhibit 2. Bianci told Shuman that this was a fairly typical distribution of the service department expense.

Questions

1. Suppose the new-car deal is consummated, with the repaired used car being retailed for $3,700, the repairs costing Shuman $996. Assume that all sales personnel are on salary (no commissions) and that general overhead costs are fixed. What is the dealership incremental gross profit on the total transaction (i.e., new and repaired-used cars sold)?

2. Assume each department (new, used, service) is treated as a profit center, as described in the case. Also assume in a–c that it is known with certainty *beforehand* that the repairs will cost $996.
   a. In your opinion, at what value should this trade-in (unrepaired) be transferred from the new-car department to the used-car department? Why?
   b. In your opinion, how much should the service department be able to charge the used-car department for the repairs on this trade-in car? Why?
   c. Given your responses to *a* and *b*,

what will be each department's incremental gross profit on this deal?

3. Is there a strategy in this instance that would give the dealership more profit than the one assumed above (i.e., repairing and retailing this trade-in used car)? Explain. In answering *this* question, assume the service department operates at capacity.

4. Do you feel the three-profit-center approach is appropriate for Shuman? If so, explain why, including an explanation of how this is better than other specific alternatives. If not, propose a better alternative and explain why it is better than three profit centers and any other alternatives you have considered.

CASE 23–2 Birch Paper Company

"If I were to price these boxes any lower than $480 a gross," said James Brunner, manager of Birch Paper Company's Thompson Division, "I'd be countermanding my order of last month for our sales force to stop shaving their bids and to bid full cost quotations. I've been trying for weeks to improve the quality of our business. If I turn around now and accept this job at $430 or anything less than $480, I'll be tearing down this program I've been working so hard to build up. The division can't show a profit by putting in bids that don't even cover a fair share of overhead costs, let alone give us a profit."

Birch Paper Company was a medium-sized, partly integrated paper company, producing white and kraft papers and paperboard. A portion of its paperboard output was converted into corrugated boxes by the Thompson Divison, which also printed and colored the outside surface of the boxes. Including Thompson, the company had four producing divisions and a timberland division, which supplied part of the company's pulp requirements.

For several years each division had been judged on the basis of its profit and return on investment. Top management had been working to gain effective results from a policy of decentralizing responsibility for all decisions except those relating to overall company policy. Top management felt that the concept of decentralization had been successfully applied and that the company's profits and competitive position had definitely improved.

Early in the year, the Northern Division designed a special display box for one of its finished papers in conjunction with the Thompson Division, which was equipped to make the box. Thompson's package design and development staff spent several months perfecting the design, production methods, and materials that were to be used; because of the unusual color and shape, these were far from standard. According to an agreement between the two divisions, Thompson was reimbursed by Northern only for the out-of-pocket cost of its design and development work.

When the specifications were all prepared, the Northern Division asked for bids on the box from the Thompson Division and from two outside companies, West Paper Company and Erie Papers, Inc. Birch's division managers normally were free to buy from whichever supplier they wished; and even on sales within the company, divisions were expected to meet the going market price if they wanted the business.

At this time the profit margins of converters such as the Thompson Division were being squeezed. Thompson, as did many other similar converters, bought its board, liner, or paper; and its function was to print, cut, and shape it into boxes. Though it bought most of its materials from other Birch divisions, most of Thompson's sales were to outside customers. If Thompson got the order from Northern, it probably would buy its linerboard and corrugating medium from the Southern Division of Birch. The walls of a corrugated box consist of outside and inside sheets of linerboard sandwiching the corrugating medium.

About 70 percent of Thompson's out-of-pocket cost of $400 a gross for the order represented the cost of linerboard and corrugating medium. Though Southern had been running below capacity and had excess inventory, it quoted the market price, which had not weakened as a result of the oversupply. Its out-of-pocket costs on liner and corrugating medium were about 60 percent of selling price.

The Northern Division received bids on the boxes of $480 a gross from the Thompson Division, $430 a gross from West Paper, and $432 a gross from Erie Papers. Erie offered to buy from Birch the outside linerboard with the special printing already on it, but would supply its own inside liner and corrugating medium. The outside liner would be supplied by the Southern Division at a price equivalent to $90 per gross of boxes, and would be printed for $30 a gross by the Thompson Division. Of the $30, about $25 would be out-of-pocket costs.

Since this situation appeared to be a little unusual, William Kenton, manager of the Northern Division, discussed the wide discrepancy of bids with Birch's marketing vice president. He told the marketing vice president, "We sell in a very competitive market, where higher costs cannot be passed on. How can we be expected to show a decent profit and return on investment if we have to buy our supplies at more than 10 percent over the going market?"

Knowing that Brunner had on occasion in the past few months been unable to operate the Thompson Division at capacity, the marketing vice president thought it odd that Brunner would add the full 20 percent overhead and profit charge to his out-of-pocket costs. When he asked Brunner about this over the telephone, his answer was the statement that appears at the beginning of the case. Brunner went on to say that having done the design and developmental work on the box at only out-of-pocket cost, he felt entitled to a normal markup on the production of the box itself.

The vice president thought about the cost structures of the various divisions. He remembered a comment the controller had made to the effect that costs that for one division were variable could be largely fixed for the company as a whole. He knew that in the absence of specific orders from top management, Kenton would accept the lowest bid, namely, that of West Paper for $430. However, it would be possible for top management to order the acceptance of another bid if the situation warranted such action. And though the volume represented by the transactions in question was less than 5 percent of the volume of any of the divisions involved, other transactions could conceivably raise similar problems later.

Questions

1. What are the additional costs to Birch Paper Company if Northern buys the boxes from West or Erie, rather than from Thompson?

2. Does the present system motivate Mr. Brunner in such a way that actions he takes in the best interests of the Thompson division are also in the best interests of the Birch Paper Company? If your answer is "no," give some specific instances related as closely as possible to the type of situation described in the case. Would the managers of *other* divisions be correctly motivated?

3. What should the vice president do?

CASE 23–3   Enager Industries, Inc.

I don't get it. I've got a nifty new product proposal that can't help but make money, and top management turns thumbs down. No matter how we price this new item, we expect to make $130,000 on its pretax. That would contribute over 10 cents per share to our earnings after taxes, which is more than the 9-cent earnings-per-share increase in 1982 that the president made such a big thing about in the shareholders' annual report. It just doesn't make sense for the president to be touting e.p.s. while his subordinates are rejecting profitable projects like this one.

The frustrated speaker was Sarah McNeil, product development manager of the Consumer Products Division of Enager Industries, Inc. Enager was a relatively young company, which had grown rapidly to its 1982 sales level of over $74 million. (See Exhibits 1–3 for financial data for 1981 and 1982.)

EXHIBIT 1

ENAGER INDUSTRIES, INC.
Income Statements
For 1981 and 1982
(thousands of dollars, except earnings per share figures)

	Year Ended December 31	
	1981	1982
Sales	$70,731	$74,225
Cost of sales	54,109	56,257
Gross margin	16,622	17,968
Other expenses:		
Development	4,032	4,008
Selling and general	6,507	6,846
Interest	594	976
Total	11,133	11,830
Income before taxes	5,489	6,138
Income tax expense	2,854	3,192
Net income	$ 2,635	$ 2,946
Earnings per share (500,000 and 550,000 shares outstanding in 1981 and 1982, respectively)	$5.27	$5.36

EXHIBIT 2

ENAGER INDUSTRIES, INC.
Balance Sheets
For 1981 and 1982
(thousands of dollars)

	As of December 31	
	1981	1982
Assets		
Current assets:		
Cash and temporary investments	$ 1,404	$ 1,469
Accounts receivable	13,688	15,607
Inventories	22,162	25,467
Total current assets	37,254	42,543
Plant and equipment:		
Original cost	37,326	45,736
Accumulated depreciation	12,691	15,979
Net	24,635	29,757
Investments and other assets	2,143	3,119
Total assets	$64,032	$75,419
Liabilities and Owners' Equity		
Current liabilities:		
Accounts payable	$ 9,720	$12,286
Taxes payable	1,210	1,045
Current portion of long-term debt	—	1,634
Total current liabilities	10,930	14,965
Deferred income taxes	559	985
Long-term debt	12,622	15,448
Total liabilities	24,111	31,398
Common stock	17,368	19,512
Retained earnings	22,553	24,509
Total owners' equity	39,921	44,021
Total liabilities and owners' equity	$64,032	$75,419

Enager had three divisions, Consumer Products, Industrial Products, and Professional Services, each of which accounted for about one third of Enager's total sales. Consumer Products, the oldest of the three divisions, designed, manufactured, and marketed a line of houseware items, primarily for use in the kitchen. The Industrial Products Division built one-of-a-kind machine tools to customer specifications; i.e., it was a large "job shop," with the typical job taking several months to complete. The Professional Services Division, the newest of the three, had been added to Enager by acquiring a large firm that provided land planning, landscape architecture, structural architecture, and consulting engineering services. This division had grown rapidly, in part because of its capability to perform "environmental impact" studies, as required by law on many new land development projects.

Because of the differing nature of their activities, each division was treated as an essentially independent company. There

EXHIBIT 3
RATIO ANALYSIS FOR 1981 AND 1982

	1981	1982
Net income ÷ Sales	3.7%	4.0%
Gross margin ÷ Sales	23.5%	24.2%
Development expenses ÷ Sales	5.7%	5.4%
Selling and general ÷ Sales	9.2%	9.2%
Interest ÷ Sales	0.8%	1.3%
Asset turnover*	1.10x	0.98x
Current ratio	3.41	2.84
Quick ratio	1.38	1.14
Days' cash*	8.1	7.9
Days' receivables*	70.6	76.7
Days' inventories*	149.5	165.2
EBIT ÷ Assets*	9.5%	9.4%
Return on invested capital*,†,‡	5.6%	5.6%
Return on owners' equity*	6.6%	6.7%
Net income ÷ Assets*,§	4.1%	3.9%
Debt/capitalization*	24.0%	28.0%

*Ratio based on year-end balance sheet amount, not annual average amount.

†Invested capital includes current portion of long-term debt, excludes deferred taxes.

‡Adjusted for interest expense add-back.

§Not adjusted for add-back of interest; if adjusted, 1981 and 1982 ROA are 4.6 percent and 4.5 percent.

were only a few corporate-level managers and staff people, whose job was to coordinate the activities of the three divisions. One aspect of this coordination was that all new project proposals requiring investment in excess of $500,000 had to be reviewed by the corporate vice president of finance, Henry Hubbard. It was Hubbard who had recently rejected McNeil's new product proposal, the essentials of which are shown in Exhibit 4.

Performance Evaluation. Prior to 1981, each division had been treated as a profit center, with annual division profit budgets negotiated between the president and the respective division general managers. In 1980, Enager's president, Carl Randall, had become concerned about high interest rates and their impact on the company's profitability. At the urging of Henry Hubbard, Randall had decided to begin treating each division as an investment center so as to be able to relate each division's profit to the assets the division used to generate its profits.

Starting in 1981, each division was measured based on its return on assets, which was defined to be the division's net income divided by its total assets. Net income for a division was calculated by taking the division's "direct income before taxes" and then subtracting the division's share of corporate administrative expenses (allocated on the basis of divisional revenues) and its share of income tax expense (the tax rate applied to the division's "direct income before taxes" after subtraction of the allocated corporate administrative expenses). Although Hubbard realized there were other ways to define a division's income, he and the president preferred this method since "it made the sum of the [divisional] parts equal to the [corporate] whole."

EXHIBIT 4
FINANCIAL DATA FROM NEW PRODUCT PROPOSAL

1. Projected asset investment:*
Cash	$ 50,000
Accounts receivable	150,000
Inventories	300,000
Plant and equipment†	500,000
Total	$1,000,000

2. Cost data:
Variable cost per unit	$3.00
Differential fixed costs (per year)‡	$ 170,000 30 %

3. Price/market estimates (per year):

Unit Price	Unit Sales	Break-even Volume
$6.00	100,000 units	56,667 units
7.00	75,000	42,500
8.00	60,000	34,000

*Assumes 100,000 units' sales.
†Annual capacity of 120,000 units.
‡Includes straight-line depreciation on new plant and equipment.

Similarly, Enager's total assets were subdivided among three divisions. Since each division operated in physically separate facilities, it was easy to attribute most assets, including receivables, to specific divisions. The corporate-office assets, including the centrally controlled cash account, were allocated to the divisions on the basis of divisional revenues. All fixed assets were recorded at their balance sheet values, that is, original cost less accumulated straight-line depreciation. Thus, the sum of the divisional assets was equal to the amount shown on the corporate balance sheet ($75,419,000 as of December 31, 1982).

In 1980, Enager had as its return on year-end assets (net income divided by total assets) a rate of 3.8 percent. According to Hubbard, this corresponded to a "gross return" of 9.3 percent; he defined gross return as equal to earnings *before* interest *and* taxes (EBIT) divided by assets. Hubbard felt that a company like Enager should have a gross (EBIT) return

on assets of at least 12 percent, especially given the interest rates the corporation had had to pay on its recent borrowings. He therefore instructed each division manager that the division was to try to earn a gross return of 12 percent in 1981 and 1982. In order to help pull the return up to this level, Hubbard decided that new investment proposals would have to show a return of at least 15 percent in order to be approved.

1981–1982 Results. Hubbard and Randall were moderately pleased with 1981's results. The year was a particularly difficult one for some of Enager's competitors, yet Enager had managed to increase its return on assets from 3.8 percent to 4.1 percent, and its gross return from 9.3 percent to 9.5 percent. The Professional Services Division easily exceeded the 12 percent gross return target; Consumer Products' gross return on assets was 8 percent; but Industrial Products' return was only 5.5 percent.

At the end of 1981, the president put

pressure on the general manager of the Industrial Products Division to improve its return on investment, suggesting that this division was not "carrying its share of the load." The division manager had bristled at this comment, saying the division could get a higher return "if we had a lot of old machines the way Consumer Products does." The president had responded that he did not understand the relevance of the division manager's remark, adding, "I don't see why the return on an old asset should be higher than that on a new asset, just because the old one cost less."

The 1982 results both disappointed and puzzled Carl Randall. Return on assets fell from 4.1 percent to 3.9 percent, and gross return dropped from 9.5 percent to 9.4 percent. At the same time, return on sales (net income divided by sales) rose from 3.7 percent to 4.0 percent, and return on owners' equity also increased, from 6.6 percent to 6.7 percent. These results prompted Randall to say the following to Hubbard:

> You know, Henry, I've been a marketer most of my career; but, until recently, I thought I understood the notion of return on investment. Now I see in 1982 our profit margin was up and our earnings per share were up; yet two of your return on investment figures were down, one—return on invested capital—held constant, and return on owners' equity went up. I just don't understand these discrepancies.

Moreover, there seems to be a lot more tension among our managers the last two years. The general manager of Professional Services seems to be doing a good job, and she's happy about the praise I've given her. But the general manager of Industrial Products looks daggers at me every time we meet. And last week, when I was eating lunch with the division manager at Consumer Products, the product development manager came over to our table and politely chastised me about a new product proposal of hers you rejected the other day.

I'm wondering if I should follow up on the idea that Karen Kraus in personnel brought back from that two-day organization development workshop she attended over at the university. She thinks we ought to have a one-day off-site "retreat" of all the corporate and divisional managers to talk over this entire return-on-investment matter.

Questions

1. Why was McNeil's new product proposal rejected? Should it have been? Explain.

2. Evaluate the manner in which Randall and Hubbard have implemented their investment center concept. What pitfalls did they apparently not anticipate?

3. What, if anything, should Randall do now with regard to his investment center approach?

24

Responsibility Accounting:
The Management Control
Process

Responsibility centers and the measurement techniques used in them, described in the preceding chapter, constitute the main elements of the management control system structure. In this chapter we begin to address how the management control system works, that is, the management control process. The principal steps in the process will be described, followed by a discussion of management control accounting information and of the behavioral aspects of the control process.

PHASES OF MANAGEMENT CONTROL

Much of the management control process involves informal communication and interactions. Informal communication occurs by means of memoranda, meetings, conversations, and even by such signals as facial expressions. Although these informal activities are of great importance, they are not amenable to a systematic description. In addition to these informal activites, most companies and many nonprofit organizations also have a *formal* management control system. It consists of the following phases, each of which is described briefly below and in more detail in succeeding chapters:

1. Programming.
2. Budgeting.
3. Operating and reporting.
4. Evaluation.

ILLUSTRATION 24–1
PHASES OF MANAGEMENT CONTROL

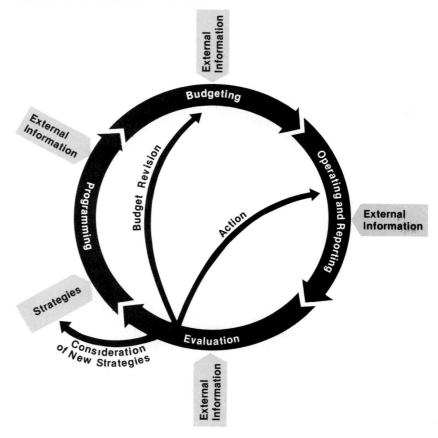

As shown in Illustration 24–1, each of these phases leads to the next. They recur in a regular cycle, constituting a "closed loop."

Programming

    Programming is the process of deciding on the programs the organization will undertake and the approximate amount of resources to be allocated to each program. Programs are the principal activities the organization has decided to follow in order to implement its strategies. In a profit-oriented company, each principal product or product line is a program. There are also various research and development programs (some aimed at improving existing products or processes, others searching for marketable new products), personnel development programs, public relations programs, and so on. Program decisions are made within the context of the goals and strategies that have previously been decided upon. In some organizations, program decisions are made informally, while in others a formal programming or "long-range planning" system is used.

Budget Preparation

Programming is a planning process; so is budgeting. An essential difference between programming and budgeting is that programming looks forward several years into the future, whereas budgeting focuses on the next year. A *budget* is a plan expressed in quantitative, usually monetary, terms that covers a specified period of time, usually one year. Most organizations have a budget.

In preparing a budget, each program is translated into terms that correspond to the responsibility of those managers who have been charged with executing the program or some part of it. Thus, although the plans are originally made in terms of individual *programs*, in the budgeting process the plans are translated into terms of *responsibility centers*. The process of developing a budget is essentially one of negotiation between managers of responsibility centers and their superiors. The end product of these negotiations is an approved statement of the revenues expected during the budget year, and of the resources to be used in each responsibility center for achieving the objectives of the organization. (Chapter 25 describes both programming and budgeting in further detail.)

Operating and Reporting

During the period of actual operations, records are kept of resources actually consumed (i.e., costs) and of revenues actually earned. These records are structured so that cost and revenue data are classified both by programs (i.e., by products, research/development projects, and the like) and also by responsibility centers. Data classified according to programs are used as a basis for future programming, and data classified by responsibility centers are used to measure the performance of responsibility center managers. For the latter purpose, data on actual results are reported in such a way that they can be readily compared with the budget, so that variances can be calculated. (Techniques for calculating production cost variances were described in Chapter 20. Techniques for calculating other variances are described in Chapter 26.)

The management control system communicates both accounting and nonaccounting information to managers throughout the organization. Some of the nonaccounting information is generated within the organization, and some of it describes what is happening in the outside environment. This information keeps managers informed as to what is going on and helps to ensure that the work done by the separate responsibility centers is coordinated. This information is conveyed in the form of reports.

Reports are also used as a basis for control. Essentially, control reports are derived from an analysis that compares actual performance with planned (budgeted) performance and attempts to explain the difference (variance). (Control reports are discussed in Chapter 26.)

Evaluation

Based on these formal control reports, in conjunction with personal observations and other informally communicated information, managers evaluate what, if any, action should be taken. As indicated in Illustration 24–1, four types of response or "feedback loops" are possible. First, current operations may be altered in some way. For example, the purchasing agent may be instructed to locate a new source of supply for a material whose substandard quality is creating large unfavorable material usage variances. Second, operating budgets may be revised. For example, an unexpected, lengthy truckers' strike may have caused plant shutdowns, with the result that both expense and revenue budgets need revision in order to be realistic under the new circumstances. Third, programs may need to be revised or eliminated. For example, a few years ago General Electric Company eliminated its line of vacuum cleaners because it had been consistently unprofitable. Finally, analysis of current results and future prospects may indicate the need for basic changes in strategic plans. For example, NCR Corporation (formerly National Cash Register) no longer makes mechanical cash registers but is essentially a computer systems company today.

ACCOUNTING INFORMATION USED IN MANAGEMENT CONTROL

Both full cost accounting and differential accounting are used in the management control process. Full cost accounting is used to make decisions of the type described in Chapter 17, particularly those relating to pricing products. These data are also used in making certain programming decisions, as in the above example of discontinuing a product line. Differential accounting data are also used in the programming phase. These data assist managers in deciding what capital investments to make, in analyzing make-or-buy decisions, and in making other kinds of alternative choice decisions.

In addition, responsibility accounting is an important aid in the management control process, because its responsibility center focus is relevant in preparing budgets and in comparing actual performance with budgeted performance. Control can be exercised only through the managers of responsibility centers. Responsibility accounting deals both with data relating to plans and also with data relating to actual performance, that is, both with future data and with historical data.

In explaining the nature and use of responsibility accounting information, we need to introduce two new ways of classifying costs: (1) as controllable or noncontrollable and (2) as engineered, discretionary, or committed.

Controllable Costs   An item of cost is *controllable* if the amount of cost assigned to a responsibility center is significantly influenced by the actions of the manager of the responsibility center. Otherwise, it is noncontrollable. There are two important aspects of this definition: (1) it refers to a specific responsibility center, and (2) it suggests that controllability results from a *significant* influence rather than from a *complete* influence. Each of these aspects is discussed below.

The word *controllable* must be used in the context of a specific responsibility center rather than as an innate characteristic of a given cost item. When an organization is viewed as a complete entity, *all costs are controllable*. For any item of cost, there is someone, somewhere in the organization who can take actions that influence it. In the extreme case, costs for any segment of the organization can be reduced to zero by closing down that segment; costs incurred in producing a good or service within the organization can be changed by purchasing that good or service from an outside supplier; and so on. Thus, the important question is not what costs are controllable in general, but rather what costs are controllable in a *specific responsibility center*, because it is these costs on which the management control system must focus.

The definition of "controllable" refers to a *significant* influence rather than to *complete* influence because only in rare cases does one manager have complete control over *all* the factors that influence any item of cost. The influence that the manager of a certain department has over its labor costs may actually be quite limited: wage rates may be established by the personnel department or by union negotiations; the amount of labor required for a unit of activity in the department (e.g., assembling one unit of a product) may have been determined by someone outside the department who specified the detailed steps of the process; and the level of activity (i.e., volume) of the department may be influenced by the actions of other departments, such as the sales group or some earlier department in the production process. Nevertheless, a department manager usually has a significant influence on the amount of labor cost incurred in that department. He or she has some control over the amount of workers' idle time, the speed and efficiency with which work is done, whether laborsaving equipment is acquired, and other factors that to some extent effect labor costs.

Direct material and labor costs in a given production responsibility center are usually controllable. Some elements of overhead cost are controllable by the responsibility center to which the costs are assigned, but others are not. Indirect labor, supplies, and electricity are usually controllable. So are charges from service centers that are based on services actually rendered. However, an *allocated* cost is *not* controllable by the responsibility center to which the allocation is made. The amount of cost allocated depends on the formula used to make the allocation rather than on the actions of the responsibility center manager. This is so unless the cost is actually a direct cost that is allocated only for convenience, as in the case of social security taxes on direct labor.

Contrast with Direct Costs.   The cost items in a responsibility center may be classified as either direct or indirect with respect to that center. Indirect costs are allocated to the responsibility center and are therefore not controllable by it, as explained above. All controllable costs are therefore direct costs. Not all direct costs are controllable, however.

> **Example.**   Depreciation on major departmental equipment is a direct cost of the department; but the depreciation charge is often noncontrollable by the departmental supervisor since he or she may have no authority to acquire or dispose of expensive equipment. The rental charge for rented premises is another example of a direct but noncontrollable cost.

Contrast with Variable Costs.   Neither are controllable costs necessarily the same as variable costs, that is, costs that vary proportionately with the volume of output. Some costs, such as indirect labor, heat, light, and magazine subscriptions, may be unaffected by volume, but they are nevertheless controllable. Conversely, although most variable costs are controllable, that is not always the case. In some situations, the cost of raw material and parts, whose consumption varies directly with volume, may be entirely outside the influence of the departmental manager.

> **Example.**   In an automobile assembly department, one automobile requires an engine, a body, seats, and so on, and there is nothing the supervisor can do about it. The supervisor is responsible for not damaging or wasting these items, but not for the main flow of the items.

Direct labor, which is usually thought of as an obvious example of a controllable cost, may be noncontrollable in certain types of responsibility centers. Situations of this type must be examined very carefully, however, because supervisors tend to argue that more costs are noncontrollable than actually is the case, in order to avoid being held responsible for them.

> **Example.**   If an assembly line has 20 work stations and cannot be operated unless it is staffed by 20 persons of specified skills and hence specified wage rates, direct labor cost on that assembly line may be noncontrollable. Nevertheless, the assumption that such costs are noncontrollable may be open to challenge, for it may be possible to find ways to do the job with 19 persons, or with 20 persons who have a lower average skill classification and hence have lower wage rates.

Cultural norms may also affect controllability. For example, supervisors in most large Japanese companies cannot lay off employees because these companies provide their workers with career employment. However, the supervisor can have the employee *transferred* to another responsibility center, thus saving some labor cost in the *supervisor's* department (but not for the company overall). Labor contract work rules can also affect controllability in unionized departments.

Converting Noncontrollable Costs to Controllable Costs.   A noncontrollable item of cost can be converted to a controllable cost in either of two related ways: (1) by changing the basis of cost assignment from an allocation to a direct assignment or (2) by changing the locus of responsibility for decisions.

As noted above, allocated costs are noncontrollable by the responsibility center to which they are allocated. Many costs that are allocated to responsibility centers could be converted to controllable costs simply by assigning the cost in such a way that the amount of costs assigned is influenced by actions taken by the manager of the responsibility center.

> **Example.**   If all electricity coming into a facility is measured by a single meter, there is no way of measuring the actual electrical consumption of each department in the facility. The electrical cost is therefore necessarily allocated to each department and is noncontrollable. Electricity cost can be changed to a controllable cost for the several departments in the facility simply by installing meters in each department so that each department's actual consumption of electricity is measured.

Services that a responsibility center receives from service units can be converted from allocated to controllable costs by assigning the cost of services to the benefiting responsibility centers on some basis that measures the amount of services actually rendered.

> **Example.**   If maintenance department costs are charged to production responsibility centers as a part of an overhead rate, they are noncontrollable. But if responsibility centers are charged on the basis of an hourly rate for each hour that a maintenance employee works there, and if the head of the responsibility center can influence the requests for maintenance work, then maintenance is a controllable element of the cost of the production responsibility center.

Practically any item of indirect cost could conceivably be converted to a direct and controllable cost. For some (such as charging the president's salary on the basis of his or her time spent on the problems of various parts of the business), however, the effort involved in doing so clearly is not worthwhile. There are nevertheless a great many unexploited opportunities in many organizations to convert noncontrollable costs to controllable costs.

The same principle applies to costs that, although actually incurred in responsibility centers, are not assigned to the responsibility centers at all, even on an allocated basis. Under these circumstances, the materials or services are "free" insofar as the heads of the responsibility centers are concerned. Since these managers do not have to "pay" for these costs (as part of the costs for which they are held responsible), they are unlikely to be concerned about careful use of these materials or services.

> **Example.** For many years, New York City did not charge residents for the amount of water that they used. When water meters were installed and residents were required to pay for their own use of water, the total quantity of water used in the city decreased by a sizable amount.

Decentralization. Changing the locus of responsibility for cost incurrence is another way to convert noncontrollable costs to controllable ones. Although the most important decisions affecting costs are made at or near the top of an organization, the further removed these decisions are from the "firing line" where resources are actually used, the less responsive they can be to conditions currently existing at that place. Although there is no way of making a precise distinction, an organization in which a relatively high proportion of decisions are made at the top is said to be *centralized,* and one in which lower level managers make relatively more decisions is said to be *decentralized.*

In the context of our present discussion, a decentralized organization is one in which a relatively large portion of total costs is controllable in the lower-level responsibility centers. Many organizations have found that if they have a good system for controlling performance, top management can safely delegate responsibility for many decisions, and thus use to advantage the knowledge and judgment of the person who is intimately familiar with current conditions at lower levels.

Reporting Noncontrollable Costs. In responsibility center performance reports, it is essential that controllable costs be clearly separated from noncontrollable costs. Some people argue that the *separation* of controllable from noncontrollable costs is not enough. They insist that noncontrollable costs should not even be reported. Actually, there may be good reasons for reporting the noncontrollable costs assigned to a responsibility center. One reason is that top management may want the manager of the responsibility center to be concerned about such costs, the expectation being that this concern may indirectly lead to better cost control.

> **Example.** The control report of a production department may list an allocated portion of the cost of the personnel department, even though the supervisor of the production department has no direct responsibility for personnel department costs. Such a practice can be justified either on the grounds that the supervisor will refrain from making unnecessary requests of the personnel department if made to feel some responsibility for its costs, or on the grounds that the supervisor may in various ways put pressure on the manager of the personnel department to exercise good cost control.

Another reason for reporting noncontrollable costs in responsibility centers is that if managers are made aware of the total amount of costs that are incurred in operating their responsibility centers, they may have a better understanding of how much other parts of the organization contribute to their operations. This is particularly important for profit and investment centers whose managers have authority to set selling prices because, in the long run, the responsibility center's revenues must recover all of the costs incurred in producing the center's goods and services, including those support costs incurred in other responsibility centers.

Engineered, Discretionary, and Committed Costs

Another classification of costs that is useful in management control is that among (1) engineered, (2) discretionary, and (3) committed costs. Although both engineered and discretionary costs are controllable, the approach to the control of one is quite different from that of the other. Committed costs are not controllable in the short run, but they are controllable in the long run.

Engineered Costs. Items of cost for which the right or proper amount of cost that should be incurred can be estimated are *engineered costs*. Direct material cost is the clearest example. Given the specifications for a product, engineers can determine within reasonably close limits the physical quantities of materials that should be used for each unit of product. The total amount of direct material costs that should be incurred can then be estimated by translation of these quantities into money by means of a standard price for each type of material, to arrive at a standard material cost per unit of product. The standard unit cost multipled by the number of units of product gives what the total amount of direct material cost should be. Since production engineering is not an exact science, and since prices of materials cannot be perfectly forecasted, the standard amount per unit of product is not necessarily the exact amount that should be spent. But the estimates usually can be made close enough so that there is relatively little ground for disagreement. In particular, there can be no reasonable ground for denying that there is a direct relationship between volume (i.e., output) and costs; two units require approximately double the amount of material that one unit requires. Similarly, in most situations, direct labor costs are engineered costs.

Discretionary Costs. Items of costs whose amount can be varied at the discretion of the manager of the responsibility center are *discretionary costs*. They are also called *programmed* or *managed* costs. The amount of a discretionary cost can be whatever management wants it to be, within wide limits. Unlike engineered costs, there is no scientific way of deciding what the "right" amount of a discretionary cost should be. How much should be spent for research and development, advertising, public relations, employees' parties, donations, or for the accounting department is a matter of *judgment*, not engineering studies. In most companies, the discretionary cost category includes all general and administrative activities, most marketing activities, and many items of indirect production cost.

Although there is no "right" total amount for a discretionary cost item, valid standards may be developed for controlling *some* of the detail within it.

> **Example.** Although no one knows the optimum amount that should be spent for the accounting function as a whole, it is nevertheless possible to measure the performance of individual clerks in the accounting department in terms of number of postings or number of invoices typed per hour. Similarly, although we cannot know the "right" amount of total travel expense, we can set standards for the amount that should be spent per day or per mile.

Furthermore, new developments in management accounting result in a gradual shift of items from the discretionary cost category to the engineered cost category. Several companies have recently started to use what they believe to be valid techniques for determining the "right" amount that they should spend on advertising in order to achieve their sales objectives, or the "right" number of sales personnel.

Discretionary Cost Relationships.   One must be aware of *spurious relationships* in the area of discretionary costs. The decision as to how much should be spent for a discretionary cost item may take several forms, such as (1) "spend the same amount as last year," (2) "spend x percent of sales," or (3) "spend y dollars plus x percent of sales." These three decision rules result in historical spending patterns which, when plotted against volume, have the same superficial appearance as the patterns of engineered cost: fixed, variable, or semivariable. These relationships are fundamentally different from those observed for engineered costs, however. For engineered variable costs, the pattern is inevitable: an increase in volume *causes* the amount of cost to increase. For discretionary costs, the relationship exists only because of a management decision, and this relationship can be changed simply by making a different management decision.

> **Example**   A company may have decided that research and development (R&D) costs should be 3 percent of sales revenue. There can be no scientific reason for such a decision, for no one knows the optimum amount that should be spent for R&D. In all probability, such a rule exists because management thinks that this is what the company can afford to spend. In this company, there will be a linear relationship between sales volume and R&D costs. This is not a cause-and-effect relationship, however; and there is no inherent reason why future R&D costs should conform to the historical pattern.

Another example of a potentially misleading cost-volume relationship is *marketing costs*. They include the costs of the selling organization, advertising, sales promotion, and so on. These costs may vary with sales volume, but the relationship is the *reverse* of that for production costs: marketing cost is the independent variable, and sales volume is the dependent variable. Marketing costs vary not in response to sales volume but rather *in anticipation of* sales volume, according to decisions made by management.[1] They are therefore discretionary costs.

If management has a policy of spending more for marketing activities when sales volume is high, then a scatter diagram of the relationship between marketing costs and sales volume will have the same *appearance* as the diagrams for the relationship between production costs and production volume. The two diagrams should be interpreted quite differently, however. The production cost diagram indicates that production cost *necessarily* increases as volume increases, while the selling cost diagram shows either that selling cost has been *permitted* to increase with increases in volume, or that the higher costs have *resulted in* the higher volume. Further, subject to some qualifications, it may be said that for total production costs, the lower they are, the better; whereas low marketing costs may reflect inadequate selling effort. The "right" level of marketing costs is a judgment made by management.

Committed Costs.   Items of cost that are the inevitable consequences of commitments previously made are *committed costs* (also called *sunk costs*). Depreciation is an example. Once a company has purchased a building or a piece of equipment, there is an inevitable depreciation charge so long as the asset continues to be owned. Salaries of managers who have employment contracts also are committed costs.

In the short run, committed costs are noncontrollable. They can be changed only by changing the commitment, for example, by disposing of the building or equipment whose depreciation is being recorded. Committed costs may or may not be direct costs for a given responsibility center.

BEHAVIORAL ASPECTS OF MANAGEMENT CONTROL

The management control process involves human beings, from those in the lowest responsibility center of the organizational hierarchy up to and including each member of top management. The management control process in part consists of inducing these human beings to take those actions that will help attain the organization's goals and to refrain from taking actions that are inconsistent with these goals. Although for some purposes an accumulation of the costs of producing goods or ser-

---

[1]Exceptions are salespersons' commissions and other payments related to sales revenue. These items of course vary directly with sales revenue.

vices is useful, management cannot literally "control" a product or the costs of producing it. What management does—or at least what it attempts to do—is influence the actions of the *people* who are responsible for incurring these costs. The discipline that studies the behavior of people in organizations is called *social psychology*. It is this discipline, rather than economics, that provides the underlying principles that are relevant in the control process. We shall note briefly some aspects of behavior that are essential to an understanding of this process.

Behavior of Participants

Each person in an organization is called a *participant*. People become participants—that is, they join an organization—because they believe that by doing so they can achieve their *personal* goals. Their decision to contribute to the productive work of the organization once they have become members of it is also based on their perception that this will help them achieve their personal goals.

Needs. An individual's behavior in an organization (and elsewhere) is influenced or motivated by his or her *needs*. These needs cause various objects or outcomes to be attractive to a person. One categorization of needs, based on Maslow's work, is the following:

Extrinsic needs:
1. "Existence" needs, including oxygen, food, shelter, and sex.
2. A security need.
3. A social need.
4. A need for esteem and reputation.
5. A need for self-control and independence.

Intrinsic needs:
6. Needs for competence, achievement and self-realization.

The first five kinds of needs can be satisfied by outcomes external to the person, for example, food, money, or praise from a colleague; these are called *extrinsic* needs. The sixth category of needs, however, can be satisfied only by outcomes persons "give" to themselves; these are called *intrinsic* needs.

People seek *both* intrinsic and extrinsic need satisfaction. Research indicates that existence and security needs must be satisfied before higher order needs (i.e., categories 3–6) come into play. Also, once a given need is satisfied, people cease seeking outcomes relevant to that need; thus, a satisfied need is not a motivator. The exception to this is the sixth category—competence, achievement, and self-realization. These needs are never fully satisfied; once self-realization begins to take place, it continues to be a strong motivator.

Some outcomes satisfy several needs. The best example is pay, which for many people satisfies existence, security, and esteem needs. But it is difficult to generalize about how outcomes will motivate or satisfy members of an organization because different persons assign different degrees of importance to the various needs. A job that is dull to one person is satisfying to another.

> **Example.** A number of workers in an automobile plant quit more interesting and challenging jobs in favor of routine work on the assembly line. To these people, the higher pay on the assembly line (an extrinsic reward) was more important than the potentially greater intrinsic rewards in their former jobs.[2]

Also, individuals' needs are influenced by background, culture, education, and type of job (e.g., manager versus nonmanager). Further complicating any generalizations about how various outcomes will motivate a person is the fact that a given person's needs are different at different times.

Motivation

Given this complexity of individuals' needs, how do people behave so as to achieve these needs? In recent years, a number of psychologists have been dealing with this question based on the expectancy theory model of motivation. This theory states that the motivation to engage in a given behavior is determined by (1) a person's beliefs or "expectancies" about what outcomes are likely to result from that behavior and (2) the attractiveness the person attaches to those outcomes as a result of the outcomes' ability to satisfy the person's needs. For example, a person who has a high need for achievement and who is not a good player of card games will probably not join a bridge club whose members are skilled card players. However, another person, no better at playing bridge than the first, might be motivated to join the bridge club because of having a high need for social contacts. The first person has a low expectancy that playing bridge with the club's members will satisfy the need for achievement, while the second person feels there is a good chance that affiliating with the group will help satisfy his or her social need. A third person, who is a superb bridge player and is somewhat introverted, may decline an invitation to join the bridge club because neither winning more bridge games nor socializing with the other players is an important (i.e., attractive) outcome to that person.

At present, expectancy theory seems to be a useful way of trying to understand motivation. However, it is still a theory, and much more research needs to be done in order for us to have better insights into persons' behavior in organizations.

Research indicates that motivation is weakest when a person perceives a goal (i.e., need fulfillment) as being unattainable or too easily attainable. Motivation is strongest when there is roughly a 50-50 chance

---

[2]Cited in Anthony Hopwood, *Accounting and Human Behavior* (Englewood Cliffs, N.J.: Prentice-Hall, 1976), p. 34.

of achieving a goal. This is particularly relevant to the *budgeting* phase of the management control process, as will be discussed in Chapter 25.

Incentives

Individuals are influenced both by positive incentives and by negative incentives. A *positive incentive,* also called a *reward,* is an outcome that results in increased need satisfaction. A *negative incentive,* also called a *punishment,* is an outcome that results in decreased need satisfaction. People join organizations in order to receive rewards that they cannot obtain without joining. Organizations dispense rewards to participants who perform in agreed-upon ways. Research on incentives tends to support the following:

- Top management's attitude toward the management control system can itself be a powerful incentive. If top management signals by its actions relating to the management control system that it regards the system as important, other managers will react positively. If top management pays little attention to the system, other managers also are likely to pay relatively little attention to it.
- Individuals tend to be more strongly motivated by the potential to earn rewards than by the fear of punishment.
- What constitutes a reward is situational. For example, money is not a status factor in some cultures, and promotion to management is not always regarded as a status factor (e.g., in universities).
- Monetary compensation is an important means of satisfying certain needs, but beyond the subsistence level the amount of compensation is not necessarily as important as nonmonetary rewards. Nevertheless, the amount of a person's earnings is often important indirectly as an indication of how his or her achievement and ability are regarded. A person receiving $50,000 a year may be disgruntled if a colleague of perceived equal ability receives $51,000 a year.
- Intrinsic motivation depends on persons' receiving reports (feedback) about their performance. Without such feedback, people are unlikely to obtain a feeling of achievement or self-realization.
- The optimal frequency of feedback is related to the "time span of discretion" of the task. This is the time between performance of the task and when inadequate performance is detectable. At lower levels in the organization, this span may be only hours; for top management, it may be a year or more.
- The effectiveness of incentives diminishes rapidly as the time elapsed between an action and administration of the reward or punishment begins to exceed the time span of discretion.
- A person tends to accept feedback about his or her performance more willingly and to use it more constructively when it is presented in a

manner that he or she regards as objective, that is, without personal bias.

- Beyond a certain point, adding more incentives (which adds more pressure) for improved performance accomplishes nothing. This optimum point is far below the maximum amount of pressure that conceivably could be exerted. When the coach says, "Don't press; don't try too hard," he or she is applying this principle.

Types of Incentives.   Incentives need not be monetary, nor even formal. In some situations, a quite simple signal can be effective.

> **Example.**   In the New York City government there was a project to sort out and discard files on those Medicaid cases that had been closed. These files occupied 1,200 file cabinets. When the job started, each clerk was examining an average of 150 files a day, which was unsatisfactory. The supervisor then made the following change: instead of discarding files in a common container, each clerk was asked to pile them in front of his or her work station. As the piles mounted, it became apparent to everyone how much work each clerk was doing. Production immediately increased to 300 files a day.[3]

A more formal incentive is relating the managers' compensation by formula to their performance; that is, managers are paid a bonus based on a comparison of planned and actual results. In view of the importance that many people attach to monetary compensation, this is a strong incentive indeed. In some cases it is too strong, for unless the standards are very carefully worked out, incessant arguments will go on about the fairness of the reported results. Thus, a bonus plan is most successful when there is general agreement that the basis of measurement is fair.

Negative incentives include not receiving a bonus (where there is a bonus system and the employee is eligible); not receiving a pay increase, or receiving a smaller one than peer employees received; not being promoted (when the person thought he or she was a candidate for promotion); and, in more extreme cases, pay cuts, demotions, suspensions, and being discharged. As this partial list indicates, punishments often take the form of not receiving a reward, rather than explicit penalties such as demotions.

Again, it is important to remember that rewards and punishments are highly personalized. For example, management might feel it is punishing an employee by not promoting this person to an available higher-level job. But if the employee feels undeserving of the promotion, or if this person does not have a high need for achievement, then the employee may not perceive not being promoted as a punishment. Similarly, a person receiving a $25,000 bonus may not be satisfied if this person feels a $35,000 bonus is deserved, even though top management views

---

[3]From *Management Accounting*, December 1972, p. 63.

the $25,000 bonus as a handsome reward. Because individuals differ in their needs and in their reactions to incentives, an important function of any manager is to attempt to adapt application of the management control system to the personalities and attitudes of the individuals whom he or she supervises.

Role of Line Managers. Since subordinates are responsible to their superiors, they should receive praise, criticism, and other forms of incentives from their superiors. Staff people should not be directly involved in these motivation activities (except with respect to control of the staff organizations themselves). Line managers are the focal points in management control. Staff people collect, summarize, and present information that is useful to managers in the management control process. There may be many such staff people; indeed, the controller department is often the largest staff department in an organization. However, the significant decisions and control actions are the responsibility of the line managers, not of the staff.

Goal Congruence

Since an organization does not have a mind of its own, the organization itself cannot literally have goals. The "organizational goals" that we have referred to are actually the goals of top management. Top management wants these organizational goals to be attained, but other participants have their own personal goals that *they* want to achieve. These personal goals are the satisfaction of their needs. In other words, participants act in their own self-interest.

The difference between organizational goals and personal goals suggests the principal criterion for the design of the management control system: *it should be designed such that the actions it leads people to take in accordance with their perceived self-interest are actions that are also in the best interest of the organization.* In the language of social psychology, the system should encourage *goal congruence.* That is, it should be structured so that the goals of participants, so far as feasible, are consistent with the goals of the organization as a whole.

Perfect goal congruence does not exist; but as a minimum the system should not encourage the individual to act *against* the best interests of the organization. For example, if the management control system signals that the emphasis should be only on reducing costs, and if a manager responds by reducing costs at the expense of adequate quality, then the manager has been motivated, but in the wrong direction. It is therefore important to ask two separate questions when evaluating any practice used in a management control system:

1. What action does it motivate people to take in their own perceived self-interest?
2. Is this action in the best interests of the organization?

An Example: The Data Processing Department

As an illustration of how management control practices affect the behavior of individual managers, consider the problem of controlling the costs of processing information in a company that has a central data processing department providing services to other responsibility centers. These services may include producing various reports, or they may involve the use of the computer in analyzing alternative choice problems or in other analyses. There are many ways of charging computer costs to the responsibility centers that use computer services, and each conveys a different message to the operating managers and to the data processing manager. Thus, each method motivates these managers differently.

At one extreme, no charge at all might be made. If the computer is offered as a free service, operating managers are encouraged to explore the possibility of using the computer for work that was formerly done manually or for special analyses that otherwise would not be undertaken. This practice is often used when a company has substantial excess computer capacity and wants to promote its use. This method also signals that the data processing manager is responsible for decisions regarding computer usage. If the demand for computer work becomes greater than the computer capacity, the data processing manager rations the available capacity among the uses that he or she considers to be most important.

Another possibility is to make no charge for recurring reports prepared by the computer but to charge for special analyses. This provides an incentive for shifting recurring data processing to the computer, but motivates the operating manager to consider whether elaborate studies of special problems are worth their cost.

As still another alternative, the total data processing costs might be allocated to all responsibility centers as a part of allocated general overhead costs. The amount allocated to a responsibility center would be based on its relative size. Since the cost is allocated, it is not controllable by the responsibility center managers. This method would, however, make these managers aware of the magnitude of computer costs and could lead them to raise questions about the efficiency of the computer operation.

Another possibility is to charge a transfer price that is either related to prices charged by outside computer service organizations or is built up from full cost plus a profit margin. This motivates responsibility center managers to decide whether each computer application is worth its cost. The manager might also be permitted to use an outside computer service if the outside service charged a lower price. This would motivate the data processing manager to operate the computer center efficiently so that its prices would be equal to or less than outside prices.

As a variation on this method, computer work done at night might be charged for at a lower rate than computer work done in the daytime. (Many time-sharing systems use this approach.) This would motivate users to decide whether the unattractiveness of using the computer after regular working hours is offset by the lower price. It thus tends to spread the work load over the whole 24-hour period.

Each of these methods of handling data processing costs motivates the managers involved—both the managers of operating responsibility centers and the manager of data processing—to act differently. The best method is the one that motivates them to act as top management *wants* them to act. Any of those described, or others, can be best under a certain set of circumstances.

The above example indicates the considerations that are important in structuring responsibility accounting information. These considerations are basically different from those involved in full cost accounting, where the purpose is to measure the amount of resources used for goods or services. They are also different from those involved in differential accounting, where the purpose is to estimate the amounts that are differential for a proposed course of action. Neither full cost accounting nor differential accounting is influenced by behavioral considerations. *In responsibility accounting, behavioral considerations are dominant.*

Cooperation and Conflict

The appearance of an organization chart implies that the way in which organizational goals are attained is that the top manager makes a decision, communicates that decision down through the organizational hierarchy, and managers at lower levels of the organization proceed to implement it. It should now be apparent that this is *not* the way in which an organization actually functions.

What actually happens is that each subordinate reacts to the instructions of top management in accordance with how those instructions affect the subordinate's personal needs. Since usually more than one responsibility center is involved in carrying out a given plan, the interactions between their managers also affect what actually happens. For example, although the manager of the maintenance department is supposed to ensure that the maintenance needs of the operating departments are satisfied, if there is friction between the maintenance manager and an operating manager, the needs of that operating manager's department may, in fact, be slighted. For these and many other reasons, *conflict* exists within organizations.

At the same time, the work of the organization will not get done unless its participants work together with a certain amount of harmony. Thus, there is also *cooperation* in organizations. Participants realize that unless there is a reasonable amount of cooperation, the organization will dissolve, and the participants will then be unable to satisfy *any* of the needs that motivated them to join the organization in the first place.

An organization attempts to maintain an appropriate balance between conflict and cooperation. Some conflict is not only inevitable, it is desirable. Conflict results in part from the competition among participants for promotion or other forms of need satisfaction; and such competition is, within limits, healthy. A certain amount of cooperation is also obviously essential. But if undue emphasis is placed on engendering cooperative attitudes, some participants may be denied the opportunity of satisfying their intrinsic needs for competence, achievement, and self-realization.

Other Types of Control

Responsibility accounting is related primarily to *formal* controls. However, it is important to emphasize that there are two other forms of control that influence the behavior of an organization's participants. *Social controls* are informal in nature, but can be very influential. These controls take the form of "group norms," which relate to such things as appropriate attire (e.g., managers' not wearing jeans at work) or level of personal productivity (e.g., chastising a "rate buster" who makes others in the group appear inefficient by comparison). *Self controls* relate to an individual's motivation and personal values. When an employee takes pride in performing work of a high quality, even though the organization or peer group may be pressuring this person to work faster and not be so concerned about quality, this person is exercising a level of self control that overrides the social and administrative controls.

SUMMARY

The four phases of the management control process cycle are programming, budgeting, operating and reporting, and evaluation. Each of these phases leads to the next. There are also feedback loops from evaluation to the other phases and to strategic planning.

Management control uses responsibility accounting information in addition to full cost accounting and differential accounting. Responsibility accounting reports both planned and actual accounting information in terms of responsibility centers. Responsibility accounting cost concepts include the notions of controllable, engineered, discretionary, and committed costs. Controllable costs are items of cost whose amount can be significantly influenced by actions of the manager of a responsibility center. Engineered costs are those for which the "right" amount to be incurred can be estimated, whereas discretionary cost amounts are a function of managerial judgment. Committed costs are noncontrollable in the short run.

In the management control process, behavioral considerations are as important as economic considerations. In particular, the motivational impact of various practices needs to be considered. This is a difficult matter, for individuals have differing needs, and even a given person's needs change over time.

Cases

CASE 24–1   Tru-Fit Parts, Inc.

Tru-Fit Parts, Inc., manufactured a variety of parts for use in automobiles, trucks, buses, and farm equipment. These parts fell into three major groupings: ignition parts, transmission parts, and engine parts. Tru-Fit's parts were sold both to original-equipment manufacturers (the "OEM" market) and to wholesalers, who constituted the first link in the channel of distribution for replacement parts (the "aftermarket" or "AM").

As shown in Exhibit 1, Tru-Fit had a manufacturing division for each of its three product groupings. Each of these divisions, which were treated as investment centers for management control purposes, was responsible not only for manufacturing parts but also for selling its parts in the OEM market. Also, each manufacturing division sold parts to the fourth division, AM Marketing. This division was solely responsible for market-

ing all Tru-Fit parts to AM wholesalers. It operated several company-owned warehouses in the United States and overseas. AM Marketing was also treated as an investment center.

Before elimination of intracompany sales, the sum of the four divisions' sales was about $500 million a year. Of this, approximately $130 million was attributable to the Ignition Parts Division, $100 million to the Transmission Parts Division, $90 million to the Engine Parts Division, and $180 million to AM Marketing. After elimination of intracompany sales from the manufacturing divisions to AM Marketing, outside sales totaled about $400 million. Thus, intracompany sales constituted almost one third of the manufacturing divisions' volume. Top management's goal was to increase to 50 percent the AM portion of outside sales from the present level of 45 percent.

EXHIBIT 1
PARTIAL ORGANIZATION CHART

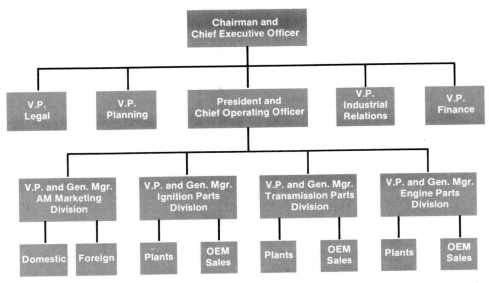

Within each manufacturing division, each plant also was treated as an investment center. OEM sales were credited to the plants, which maintained finished goods inventories; shipments to OEM customers were made directly from the plants. A plant's ROI target was based on budgeted profit (including allocations of division and corporate overhead and an imputed income tax) divided by actual beginning-of-year "net assets" (defined to be total assets less current liabilities). Actual ROI was actual profit divided by actual beginning-of-year net assets. The reason that the profit figure included allocated overheads and taxes was so that the figure would correspond to the manner in which profit was calculated for shareholder reporting purposes. According to top management, this gave a plant manager a clearer perspective of the plant's contribution to the corporate "bottom line." Beginning-of-year net assets

was used because, according to top management, added investment in a given year resulted in little incremental profit in that year, but rather increased later years' profits. Since the investment base for the year was "frozen" at the beginning-of-year level, during the year maximizing profits was equivalent to maximizing ROI. (AM Marketing's ROI was measured in the same manner as was the plants' ROI.)

The OEM sales department in each manufacturing division was responsible for working with OEM company engineers to develop innovative and cost-effective new parts, and for servicing customer accounts for parts already being supplied the OEM by Tru-Fit. Each of these OEM sales departments was treated as a revenue center. Because of the differing nature of OEM and AM marketing, it was not felt desirable by top management to consolidate AM and OEM marketing activities in a single organization. Even OEM marketing was not consolidated, because each division's OEM marketers tended to work with different people within a given customer's organization. Moreover, two of the three manufacturing divisions had been independent companies before being acquired by Tru-Fit, and so there was a tradition of their doing their own OEM marketing.

According to Tru-Fit executives, the factors critical to success in the OEM market were (1) the ability to design innovative and dependable parts that met the customer's performance and weight specifications; (2) meeting OEM delivery requirements so that the OEM company could minimize its own inventories; and (3) controlling costs, since the market was very price competitive. In the AM market, availability was by far the most important factor, followed by quality and price.

Approximately 50 Tru-Fit line managers and staff group heads participated in an incentive bonus plan, which worked as follows. First, the size of the corporate-wide bonus pool was established; its size was related by a formula to corporate earnings per share. Each participant in the bonus plan had a certain number of "standard bonus points;" the higher the participant was in the organizational hierarchy, the more standard points he or she had. The total of these points for all participants was divided into the bonus pool to arrive at a standard dollar award per point. Then this amount was multiplied by the participant's number of standard points to arrive at the participant's "standard bonus." This standard award could be varied upward or downward as much as 25 percent at the discretion of the participant's superiors.

In the case of a plant manager, the standard award was also adjusted by a formula that related percent of standard award to the plant's profit variance. For example, if the plant's actual profit for the year exceeded its budgeted profit by 5 percent, the plant manager's bonus was raised from 100 percent of standard to 110 percent of standard. In making this bonus adjustment, the plant's actual profit was adjusted for any favorable or unfavorable gross margin variance caused by sales volume to the AM Marketing division being higher or lower than budgeted. For example, if all of a plant's favorable profit variance were attributable to a favorable gross margin volume variance on sales to AM Marketing, the plant manager's bonus would not be raised above 100 percent of standard. Similarly, the plant manager would not be penalized if AM Marketing actually purchased less from the plant than the amount that had been estimated by AM Marketing when the plant's annual profit budget had been prepared.

In general, top management was satisfied with the present performance measurement scheme. In discussions with the casewriter, however, they mentioned three areas of concern.

First, there always seemed to be a few disputes over transfer prices from the manufacturing divisions to AM Marketing. Whenever possible, transfers were made at outside OEM market prices. In the case of a part sold as an OEM part several years earlier, the former OEM market price was adjusted upward for inflation to arrive at the AM transfer price; this procedure caused virtually no disputes. The problems occurred when the part being transferred was strictly an AM part, i.e., one that had never been sold by Tru-Fit in the OEM market, and for which there was neither a current OEM outside market price nor a former OEM market price that could be adjusted upward for inflation. Usually, such transfer price issues were resolved by the two divisions involved, but occasionally the corporate controller was asked to arbitrate a dispute.

Second, top management felt that the manufacturing divisions too often tended to treat AM Marketing as a "captive customer." For example, it was felt that when AM Marketing and an outside OEM customer were placing competing demands on a plant, the plant usually favored the OEM customer, because the OEM customer could take its business elsewhere, whereas AM Marketing could not. (Management was not willing to let AM Marketing sell a competitor's product, feeling this would reflect adversely

on the overall image of the company.)

Third, top management felt that both AM Marketing and the three manufacturing divisions carried excessive inventories most of the year. The controller said, "Thank goodness we have a generous Christmas vacation policy here; at least the inventories get down to a reasonable level at year end, when our production volume is low because of employee holiday vacations."

Questions

1. What would you recommend to top management regarding the three problems they have identified?

2. Are there any matters not mentioned by top management that you feel are problematical?

CASE 24–2 Pullen Lumber Company

John Pullen, founder and president of Pullen Lumber Company, was considering an incentive compensation plan for his managers that had been prepared at his request. Currently, the 700 Pullen employees were paid a straight salary (plus overtime when applicable). They were also paid an annual bonus equal to two weeks' salary. The proposed plan would apply only to the 43 managers of lumberyards, the 5 district managers, and the 5 senior managers at headquarters. Instead of the annual bonus, these managers would be eligible for a bonus according to a proposal described later in the case.

The Company. Pullen Lumber Company operated 43 lumberyards located in four midwestern states. Few interdependencies existed among the yards; and

each carried a line of lumber, plywood, roofing materials, doors, windows, tools, paint, flooring, and builders' supplies. Sales were made to contractors, homebuilders, and to individual homeowners and hobbyists. The lumberyards were supervised by five district offices. Each district office also had a sales force that solicited business from large contractors. As a service, the district offices sometimes aided contractors in preparing the material components in bids and gave informal advice on the material best suited to a job. Yard managers also gave this advice to smaller contractors.

There was a fixed budget for each yard and each district showing planned revenues and expenses. Actual revenues and expenses were reported annually. Data on the company's financial condition and performance for the most recent year are provided in Exhibits 1 and 2.

The company had enjoyed profits the past few years that were considerably greater than those of most of its competition, for whom the average aftertax return on investment in total assets was approximately 6 percent. Although the company as a whole had done well in the opinion of the company president, some of its yards and districts had incurred operating losses. Meanwhile, competitive pressures had been growing and the difference in profits between Pullen and its competitors had narrowed significantly. Because of this, the individual differ-

ences in the performances of the yards, and Mr. Pullen's often-expressed desire to gain a larger market share in each of the company's lines of business, the proposed bonus plan assumed added significance.

Background of the Plan. At an executive committee meeting in September, Mr. Pullen introduced the idea of a bonus plan, and it seemed to be favorably received. At the end of this meeting, he appointed a committee to draft a bonus plan. It consisted of the controller, who was to serve as chairperson, the general sales manager, and the director of purchases. The first problem they tackled was identification of the persons to

EXHIBIT 1

PULLEN LUMBER COMPANY
Balance Sheet
As of December 31
(thousands of dollars)

Assets

Current assets:		
Cash and short-term investments		$ 1,346
Accounts receivable (net)		5,330
Inventory		11,260
Total current assets		17,936
Fixed assets:		
Trucks, automobiles, and equipment	$ 3,450	
Less: Accumulated depreciation	1,260	2,190
Land and buildings	10,040	
Less: Accumulated depreciation	4,020	6,020
Total fixed assets		8,210
Other assets		2,900
Total assets		$29,046

Equities

Liabilities:	
Current payables	$ 5,478
Long-term note payable	5,000
Total liabilities	10,478
Owners equity:	
Capital stock (250,000 shares outstanding)	10,000
Retained earnings	8,568
Total owners' equity	18,568
Total equities	$29,046

EXHIBIT 2

PULLEN LUMBER COMPANY
Income Statement
For the Year Ended December 31
(thousands of dollars)

Sales (net)		$56,127
Service revenue		2,148
		58,275
Cost of sales		41,458
Gross margin		16,817
Operating expenses:		
Payroll	$6,705	
Property expense*	1,688	
Advertising	1,312	
Bad debt expense	836	
Equipment expense†	1,127	
Other expenses	1,529	
Total operating expenses		13,197
Operating income		3,620
Interest expense	400	
Loss on sale of equipment	32	432
Income before taxes		3,188
Provision for income taxes		1,476
Net income		$ 1,712

*Property expense includes real estate taxes, rentals, depreciation, and utilities expense.
†Equipment expense includes depreciation, maintenance and repairs, and routine operating expenses.

whom the plan should apply. Three groups were initially considered: (1) district salespersons, (2) buyers, and (3) managers.

The sales manager foresaw great difficulties in identifying improved sales volume with individual salespersons. Many of the company's best customers had dealt with the company for years, and no substantial selling effort was required. Furthermore, personal friendships existed between the top officers of some companies that were good customers and the top officers of Pullen Lumber Company. These conditions made it relatively unimportant which salesperson called upon and serviced the account. The volume of business from these customers would remain virtually unchanged, regardless of the salespersons' efforts.

The director of purchases also foresaw problems in attempting to recognize and reward individual buyers. The discounts obtained on an order related to factors over which the buyer had so little control as not to be a valid basis for a bonus award.

The committee therefore decided that the bonus plan should be limited to managers—the managers of individual lumberyards, the district managers, and the senior management group at headquarters.

In considering the managers' responsibility for profit performance, the committee agreed generally on the following points:

1. The yard manager is the primary factor in influencing customers' loy-

alty toward Pullen by giving good service, by having the goods on hand when the customer wants them, and by proper supervision of yard personnel.

2. Although standard selling prices are set by the central purchasing department, yard managers have latitude in reducing prices to meet competition and in the markdowns they allow for defective or old merchandise.

3. The yard manager is responsible for inventory, both to replenish stocked items and to decide what items should be added to or deleted from inventory within limits specified by headquarters.

4. Yard managers have major responsibility for bad debts, although for large accounts they are expected to ask headquarters for a credit check.

5. An aggressive yard manager will generate new business by calling on prospective customers.

6. The yard manager has considerable discretion in advertising, although the artwork and much of the copy of space advertising is prepared at headquarters. Catalogs and direct-mail pieces are also prepared at headquarters.

7. The yard manager is responsible for expense control.

8. The district manager is generally responsible for the yards in his or her district.

9. The district office also helps profitability by the services it renders to large customers. Orders from these customers are shipped from the yard nearest to the job.

10. Sales volume varies with construction activity in the territory served by the yard.

Most of the yard managers had only a high school education; in the opinion of the controller, they understood very little of the relationship between their performance and the profitability of their yards. It was the controller's view that a concentrated management training program for managers, supplemented by a bonus plan, would make them conscious of the necessity of increasing profits through better management and would furnish them the incentive to put better practices into effect.

When the committee reported back to the president, it was their consensus that the controller should devise a bonus plan along the lines outlined above. Shortly thereafter, the controller submitted the following proposed bonus plan:

General Statement of Plan. This bonus plan is designed to provide company managers with an opportunity to earn additional compensation for improved performance as reflected by an increased return on the company's investment at the yards under their management.

Definition of Terms

A. *Investment* at each location will include the annual average of the following:
   1. Month-end cash balances.
   2. Month-end inventory, at cost, excluding central stocks placed at a given location by the purchasing department.
   3. Month-end accounts receivables associated with bonusable sales.
   4. Investment in automobiles and trucks assigned to the location, at depreciated cost.
   5. Investment in equipment, furniture, and fixtures assigned to the location, at depreciated cost.
   6. Land and buildings, at depre-

ciated cost, assigned to the location (if property is rented, the rent will show up as an expense).

B. *Bonusable sales* are all shipments made from the location except sales orders written by district or headquarters sales personnel. These latter orders will be coded as they are written and deducted from the gross sales of the yard.

C. *Expenses* include:
1. Cost of goods sold on bonusable sales.
2. Operating expenses of the yard, including rental and depreciation.
3. Actual cost of services provided by district offices to the yard and to customers of the yard. (If the customer cannot be identified with a specific yard, these costs will be included in district office cost.)
4. Actual cost of credit investigations and collection efforts for the benefit of the yard.
5. Advertising material, catalogs, and other material supplied to the yard at actual cost. *Note:* Costs of district advertising (space and TV) for items not carried in a given yard will not be charged to that yard.
6. Pro rata share of office expenses for purchasing. This will be determined on the basis of the yard's receipts into inventory as a proportion of total company receipts into inventory.
7. Pro rata share of district office and headquarters expenses not charged directly to a yard. This will be determined on the basis of each yard's gross sales as a proportion of total company sales.
8. The following operating losses will be charged to the yard when the district manager determines that these are the responsibility of the yard manager:
   a. Inventory shortages.
   b. Cost of repairing damaged property.
   c. Loss on sale of fixed assets.
   d. Bad debt losses.

D. *Bonusable profit* is bonusable sales minus expenses.

E. *Return on investment* is bonusable profit divided by investment in total assets.

Calculation of the Bonus

A. The total bonus pool will be $90,000 plus 5 percent of the corporation's pretax income in excess of $2,000,000.

B. The total bonus pool will be divided as follows:

Yard managers.........................	65%
District managers.....................	15
Senior management	20

C. The yard managers' bonus pool will be divided among yard managers on the basis of the number of bonus units that they earn. The manager of a yard whose return on investment is 5 percent will earn one bonus unit. For each full percentage point above 5, the manager will earn an additional bonus unit, up to a maximum of six total bonus units. The monetary value of one bonus unit is found by dividing the total dollar amount in the yard managers' pool by the total number of bonus units earned by all yard managers.

D. The bonus units awarded to any yard manager who has been in that position for less than one year will be decided by the district manager, applying the above principle as closely as is feasible.

E. The district managers' bonus pool will be divided among district managers in relation to the total bonus units earned by the yards in their district as a proportion of the total bonus units earned by all yards.

F. The headquarters' bonus pool will be divided as decided by the president.

G. Bonuses will be paid in cash as soon after the end of the year as they can be calculated.

Mr. Pullen looked over the plan quickly and observed that it was drawn to include only managers. He said, "You can bet your bottom dollar that the district salespersons aren't going to be happy when they hear about a bonus plan for yard managers. What does the sales manager have to say about the proposed plan?"

The sales manager explained that the committee recognized the role of the district sales and sales service personnel, but that there was no practical way of measuring their contribution to profitability because actual sales were booked through the yards that made delivery.

The controller also explained the rationale behind the recommended size of the bonus pool. The elimination of the present annual bonus for the 53 managers in the plan would create $40,000 of available funds. In addition, the usual annual salary increase to these managers of about $50,000 would not be given. Thus, at the current level of profits, a bonus of $90,000 would not affect costs. If the plan resulted in profits greater than $2,000,000 before taxes, the bonus would be correspondingly higher.

Questions

1. Evaluate the proposed bonus plan that Mr. Pullen is considering. Does your evaluation suggest any generalizations for exercising management control through payment schemes?

2. How, if at all, would you modify the proposed plan?

CASE 24–3   Empire Glass Company

Organization.   Empire Glass Company was a container and packaging company organized into several major product divisions. Each division was headed by a vice president who reported to the company's executive vice president, Landon McGregor. The Glass Products Division, the focus of this case, was responsible for manufacturing and selling glass food and beverage bottles.

McGregor's corporate staff included three financial department heads—the controller, chief accountant, and treasurer. The controller's department consisted of only two people—James Walker and his assistant, Ellen Newell. The market research and labor relations departments also reported in a staff capacity to McGregor.

All the product divisions were organized along similar lines. Reporting to each division vice president were staff members in the customer service and product research areas. Reporting in a line capacity to each vice president were general managers of manufacturing and of marketing who were responsible for all the division's manufacturing and marketing activities. Both of these executives were assisted by a small staff of specialists. Exhibit 1 presents an organization chart of top management and of the Glass Products Division's management group. All corporate and divisional managers and staff were located in British City, Canada. Exhibit 2 shows the typical organization structure of a plant within the Glass Products Division.

Products and Technology. Glass Products operated seven plants in Canada. Food jars constituted their largest product group, including jars for products like catsup, mayonnaise, jams, pickles, and instant coffee. Beer and soft-drink bottles were also produced in large quantities. A great variety of containers for wines, liquors, drugs, cosmetics, and chemicals were produced in smaller quantities. Most of the thousands of different products, varying in size, shape, color, and decoration, were produced to order. The typical lead time between a customer's order and shipment from the plant was two to three weeks.

The principal raw materials were sand, soda ash, and lime. The first manufacturing step was to melt batches of these materials. The molten mass was then passed into automatic or semiautomatic machines, which filled molds with the molten glass and blew the glass into the desired shape. The ware then went through

EXHIBIT 1
TOP MANAGEMENT AND GLASS PRODUCTS MANAGEMENT

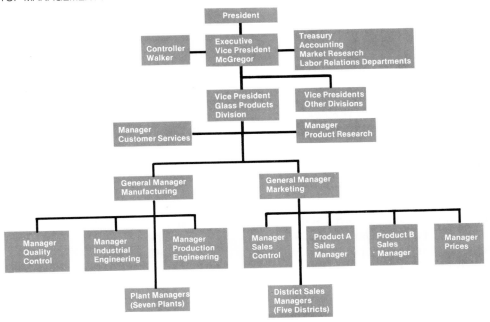

EXHIBIT 2
TYPICAL PLANT ORGANIZATION—GLASS PRODUCTS DIVISION

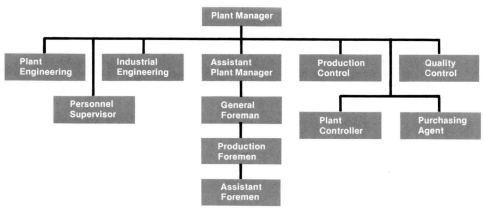

an automatic annealing oven, where it was cooled slowly under carefully controlled conditions. If the glass was to be coated on the exterior to increase its resistance to abrasion and scratches, this coating was applied at the oven. Any decorating (such as a trademark or other design) was then added, the product inspected again, and the finished goods packed in corrugated containers.

Quality inspection was critical. If the melt in the furnace was not completely free from bubbles and stones, or if the fabricating machinery was slightly out of adjustment or molds were worn, the rejection rate was very high. Although a number of machines were used in the inspection process, including electric eyes, much of the inspection was still visual.

Although glass bottles had been machine molded at relatively high speed for over 70 years, Glass Products spent substantial sums each year to modernize its equipment. These improvements had greatly increased the speed of operations and had substantially reduced the visual

inspection and manual handling of glassware.

Most of the jobs were relatively unskilled, highly repetitive, and gave the worker little control over work methods or pace. The moldmakers who made and repaired the molds, the machine repairpersons, and those who made the equipment setup changes between different products were considered to be the highest classes of skilled workers. Wages were relatively high in the industry, in part because the plants were noisy and hot. Production employees belonged to two national unions, and bargaining was conducted on a national basis. Output standards were established for all jobs, but no bonus was paid to hourly workers for exceeding standard.

Marketing. Over the years, Glass Products' sales had grown at a slightly faster rate than had the total glass container market. Until the late 1950s, the division had charged a premium for most of its products, which were of better quality than competitive products. Subsequently, however, the competitive products' quality had improved and it now matched the division's quality level, but competitors had retained their former price structure. Consequently, Glass Products had been forced to lower its prices to meet its competitors' prices. According to one division executive:

> Currently, price competition is not severe, particularly among the two or three larger companies that dominate the glass bottle industry. Most of our competition is with respect to product quality and customer service. . . . In fact, our biggest competitive threat is from containers other than glass. . . .

Transportation costs limited each plant's market primarily to its immediate vicinity. While some of the customers were large and bought in huge quantities, many were relatively small.

Budgetary Control System

James Walker, Empire Glass Company controller for over 15 years, described the company's budgetary control system to a casewriter. Excerpts from that interview are reproduced below.

"To understand the role of the budgetary control system, you must first understand our management philosophy. We have a divisional organization based on broad product categories. Divisional activities are coordinated by the executive vice president, and the head office group provides a policy and review function for him. Within broad policy limits, we operate on a decentralized basis; each of the divisions performs the full management job that normally would be inherent in any independent company. The only exceptions are the head office group's sole responsibilities for sources of funds and labor relations with bargaining units that cross division lines.

"Given this form of organization, the budget is the principal management tool used by head office to coordinate the efforts of the various segments of the company toward a common goal. Certainly, in our case, the budget is much more than a narrow statistical accounting device."

Sales Budget. "As early as May 15 of the year preceding the budget year, top management asks each of the division vice presidents to submit preliminary reports stating what they think the division's capital requirements, sales, and income will be during the next budget year. In addition, top management wants an expression of the division vice president's general feelings toward the trends in these items over the two years following the upcoming budget year. At this stage, head office is not interested in much detail but rather a forecast based on the operating executives' practical feel for the market. Since all divisions plan their capital requirements five years in advance and had made predictions of the forthcoming budget year's market when the budget estimates were prepared last year, these rough estimates of next year's conditions and requirements are far from wild guesses.

"After the opinions of the division vice presidents are in, the market research staff goes to work. They develop a formal statement of the marketing climate in detail for the forthcoming budget year and in general terms for the subsequent two years. Once these general factors have been assessed, a sales forecast is constructed for the company and for each division. Consideration is given to the relationship of the general economic climate to our customers' needs and Empire's share of each market. Explicitly stated are basic assumptions as to price, weather conditions, introduction of new products, gains or losses in particular accounts, forward buying, new manufacturing plants, industry growth trends, packaging trends, inventory carry-overs, and the development of alternative packages. This review of all the relevant factors is followed for each of our product lines, regardless of its size and importance. The completed forecasts of the market research group are then forwarded to the appropriate divisions for review, criticism, and adjustments.

"The primary goal of the head office group in developing these sales forecasts is to assure uniformity among the divisions with respect to the basic assumptions on business conditions, pricing, and the treatment of possible emergencies. Also, we provide a yardstick so as to assure us that the company's overall sales forecast will be reasonable and attainable.

"The division top management then goes back to the district managers and asks them what they expect to do in the way of sales during the budget year. Head office and the divisional staffs will give the district managers as much guidance as they request, but it is the sole responsibility of each district manager to come up with the district's sales budget.

"After the district sales managers' budgets are received by divisional management, they are consolidated and reviewed by the marketing general manager, who may suggest revisions. District managers know little of what's happening outside their territories; but at headquarters we can estimate the size of the whole market for, say, liquor, and each

of our customer's market share. That's where the market research forecasts come in handy. Let me emphasize, however, that nothing is changed in the district manager's budget unless he or she agrees. Then, once the budget is approved, nobody is relieved of responsibility without top-management approval. Also, no arbitrary changes are made in the approved budgets without the concurrence of all the people responsible for the budget.

"Next, we go through the same process at the division and headquarters levels. We continue to repeat the process until everyone agrees that the sales budgets are sound. Then, each level of management takes responsibility for its particular portion of the budget. These sales budgets then become fixed objectives.

"I would say a division has four general objectives in mind in reviewing its sales budget:

1. A review of the division's competitive position, including plans for improving that position.
2. An evaluation of its efforts to gain either a larger share of the market or offset competitors' activities.
3. A consideration of the need to expand facilities to improve the division's products or introduce new products.
4. A review and development of plans to improve product quality, delivery methods, and service."

Manufacturing Budgets. "Once the division vice presidents, executive vice president, and president have given final approval to the sales budget, we make a sales budget for each plant by breaking down the division sales budget according to the plants from which the finished goods will be shipped. These plant sales budgets are then further broken down on a monthly basis by price, volume, and product end use. With this information available, the plants then budget their contribution, fixed expenses, and income before taxes. Contribution is the difference between the fixed sales dollar budget and variable manufacturing costs. Income is the difference between contribution and fixed costs. It is the plant manager's responsibility to meet this budgeted *profit* figure, even if actual dollar sales drop below the budgeted level.

"Given the plant's sales budget, it is up to the plant manager to determine the fixed overhead and variable costs—at standard—that the plant will need to incur so as to meet the demands of the sales budget. In my opinion, requiring the plant managers to make their own plans is one of the most valuable things associated with the budget system. Each plant manager divides the preparation of the overall plant budget among the plant's various departments. First, the departments spell out the program in terms of the physical requirements, such as tons of raw material, and then the plans are priced at standard cost.

"The plant industrial engineering department is responsible for developing engineered cost standards. This phase of the budget also includes budgeted cost reductions, budgeted unfavorable variances from standards, and certain budgeted programmed fixed costs in the manufacturing area, such as service labor. The industrial engineer prepares this phase of the budget in conjunction with departmental line supervision.

"Before each plant sends its budget in to British City, a group of us from head office goes out to visit each plant. In the case of Glass Products, Ellen Newell, as-

sistant controller, and I, along with representatives of the division's manufacturing staffs, visit each of the division's plants. Let me stress this point: We do not go on these trips to pass judgment on the plant's proposed budget. Rather, we go with two purposes in mind. First, we wish to acquaint ourselves with the thinking behind the figures that each plant manager will send in to British City. This is helpful because when we eventually review these budgets with top management—that is, the president and executive vice president—we will have to answer questions about the budgets, and we will know the answers. Second, the review is a way of giving guidance to the plant managers as to whether or not they are in line with what the company needs to make in the way of profits.

"Of course, when we make our field reviews we do not know what each of the other plants is planning. Therefore, we explain to the plant managers that while their budget may look good now, when we put all the plants together in a consolidated budget the plant managers may have to make some changes because the projected profit is not high enough. When this happens, we tell the plant managers that it is not their programs that are unsound. The problem is that the company cannot afford the programs. I think it is very important that the plant managers have a chance to tell their story. Also, it gives them the feeling that we at headquarters are not living in an ivory tower.

"These plant visits are spread over a three-week period, and we spend about half a day at each plant. The plant managers are free to bring to these meetings any of their supervisors they wish. During the visit, we discuss the budget primarily. However, if I have time I like to wander through the plant and see how things are going. Also, I go over in great detail the property replacement and maintenance budget with the plant engineer.

"About September 1, the plant budgets come into British City and the accounting department consolidates them. Then, the division vice presidents review their respective division budgets to see if they are reasonable in terms of what the vice president thinks the corporate management wants. If the vice president is not satisfied with the consolidated plant budgets, the various plants within the division will be asked to trim their budgeted costs.

"When the division vice presidents and the executive vice president are satisfied, they will send their budgets to the president. He may accept the division budgets at this point. If he doesn't, he will specify the areas to be reexamined by division and, if necessary, by plant. The final budget is approved at our December board of directors meeting."

Comparison of Actual and Standard Performance. "At the end of the sixth business day after the close of the month, each plant telexes to the head office certain operating variances, that we put together on what we call the variance analysis sheet. Within a half-hour after the last plant report comes through, variance analysis sheets for the divisions and plants are compiled. On the morning of the seventh business day, these reports are on the desks of top management. The variance analysis sheet highlights the variances in what we consider to be critical areas. Receiving this report as soon as we do helps us at head office to take timely action. Let me emphasize, however, we do not accept the excuse that

plant managers have to go to the end of the month to know what happened during the month. They have to be on top of these particular items daily.

"When the actual results come into the head office, we go over them on the basis of exception; that is, we only look at the unfavorable variances. We believe this has a good effect on morale. The plant managers don't have to explain everything they do. They have to explain only where they go off base. In particular, we pay close attention to the net sales, contribution margin, and the plant's ability to meet its standard manufacturing cost. When analyzing sales, we look closely at price and mix changes, which are the sales group's responsibility.

"All this information is summarized on a form known as the Profit Planning and Control Report No. 1 (see Exhibit 3). This document is backed up by a number of supporting documents (see Exhibit 4). The plant PPCR No. 1 and the month-end trial balance showing both actual and budget figures are received in British City at the close of the eighth business day after the end of the month. These two very important reports, along with the supporting reports (PPCR No. 2–PPCR No. 11) are then consolidated by the accounting department to show the results of operations by division and company. The consolidated reports are distributed the next day.

"In connection with the fixed cost items, we want to know whether the plants carried out their planned programs. If they have not, we want to know why. Also, we want to know if they have carried out these programs at the cost they said they would.

"To me, the three most important items on PPCR No. 1 are the P/V ratio,

EXHIBIT 3
PROFIT PLANNING AND CONTROL REPORT NO. 1

| MONTH | | | | | YEAR TO DATE | | |
| Income Gain (+) or Loss (−) From | | | | | | Income Gain (+) or Loss (−) From | |
Prev. Year	Budget	Actual	Ref.		Actual	Budget	Prev. Year
			1	Gross Sales to Customers			
			2	Discounts & Allowances			
			3	Net Sales to Customers			
%	%		4	% Gain (+)/Loss (−)		%	%
				DOLLAR VOLUME GAIN (+)/ LOSS (−) DUE TO:			
			5	Sales Price			
			6	Sales Volume			
			6(a)	Trade Mix			
			7	Std. Variable Cost of Sales			
			8	Contribution Margin			
				CONTRIB. MARGIN GAIN (+)/ LOSS (−) DUE TO:			
			9	Profit Volume Ratio (P/V)*			
			10	Dollar Volume			
%	%	%	11	Profit Volume Ratio (P/V)*	%	%	%
			12	Budgeted Fixed Mfg. Cost			
			13	Fixed Manufacturing Cost-Transfers			
			14	Plant Income (standard)			
%	%	%	15	% of Net Sales	%	%	%
%	%	%	16	% Mfg. Efficiency	%	%	%
			17	Manufacturing Variances			
			18	Methods Improvements			
			19	Other Revisions of Standards			
			20	Material Price Changes			
			21	Division Special Projects			
			22	Company Special Projects			
			23	New Plant Expense			
			24	Other Plant Expenses			
			25	Income on Seconds			
			26				
			27				
			28	Plant Income (actual)			
%	%		29	% Gain (+)/Loss (−)		%	%
	%	%	30	% of Net Sales	%	%	%
			36A				
				CAPITAL EMPLOYED			
			37	Total Capital Employed			
%	%	%	38	% Return	%	%	%
			39	Turnover Rate			

_____   _____   _____ 19 ____
   Plant   Division   Month

*The P/V ratio was defined to be: $\dfrac{\text{Price} - \text{Variable cost}}{\text{Price}}$.

EXHIBIT 4
BRIEF DESCRIPTION OF PPCR NO. 2–PPCR NO. 11

Individual Plant Reports

Report	*Description*
PPCR No. 2	Manufacturing expense: Plant materials, labor, and variable overhead incurred. Detail of actual figures compared with budget and previous year's figures for year to date and current month.
PPCR No. 3	Plant expense: Plant fixed expenses incurred. Details of actual figures compared with budget and previous year's figures for year to date and current month.
PPCR No. 4	Analysis of sales and income: Plant operating gains and losses due to changes in sales revenue, contribution margins, and other sources of income. Details of actual figures compared with budget and previous year's figures for year to date and current month.
PPCR No. 5	Plant control statement: Analysis of plant raw material gains and losses, spoilage costs, and cost reduction programs. Actual figures compared with budget figures for current month and year to date.
PPCR No. 6	Comparison of sales by principal and product groups: Plant sales dollars, contribution margin, and P/V ratios broken down by end product use (i.e., soft drinks, beer). Compares actual figures with budgeted figures for year to date and current month.

Division Summary Reports

Report	*Description*
PPCR No. 7	Comparative plant performance, sales, and income: Gross sales and income figures by plants. Actual figures compared with budget figures for year to date and current month.
PPCR No. 8	Comparative plant performance, total plant expenses: Contribution margin, total fixed costs, manufacturing efficiency, other plant expenses, and P/V ratios by plants. Actual figures compared with budgeted and previous year's figures for current month and year to date.
PPCR No. 9	Manufacturing efficiency: Analysis of gains and losses by plant in areas of materials, spoilage, supplies, and labor. Current month and year-to-date actuals reported in total dollars and as a percentage of budget.
PPCR No. 10	Inventory: Comparison of actual and budget inventory figures by major inventory accounts and plants.
PPCR No. 11	Status of capital expenditures: Analysis of the status of capital expenditures by plants, months, and relative to budget.

actual plant income, and percent return on capital employed. At the plant level, capital employed includes inventories at standard variable cost plus the replacement value of fixed assets. We use replacement value because it puts plants having disparate fixed asset original acquisition costs on an equal footing. At the division level, accounts receivable also are included in capital employed.

"In addition to these reports, at the beginning of each month, the plant managers prepare current estimates for the upcoming month and quarter on forms similar to the variance analysis sheets. Since our budget is based on known programs, the value of this current estimate is that it gets the plant people to look again at their programs. Hopefully, they will realize that they cannot run their plants just on a day-to-day basis.

"If we see a sore spot coming up, or if the plant manager draws our attention to a potential trouble area, we may ask that daily reports concerning this item be sent to division top management. In addition, the division top management may send a division staff specialist—say, a quality control expert—to the plant concerned. The division staff members can make recommendations, but it is up to the plant manager to accept or reject these recommendations. Of course, it is well known throughout the company that we expect the plant managers to accept gracefully the help of the head office and division staffs."

Sales-Manufacturing Relations. "If a sales decline occurs during the early part of the year, and if the plant managers can convince us that the change is permanent, we may revise the plant profit budgets to reflect these new circumstances. However, if toward the end of the year actual sales suddenly drop below budget, we don't have much time to change the budget plans. What we do is ask the plant managers to go back over their budgets with their staffs and see where reduction of expense programs will do the least harm. Specifically, we ask them to consider what they may be able to eliminate this year or delay until next year.

"I believe it was Confucius who said: 'We make plans so we have plans to discard.' Nevertheless, I think it is wise to make plans, even if you have to discard them. Having plans makes it a lot easier to figure out what to do when sales fall off from the budgeted level. The under-

standing of operations that comes from preparing the budget removes a lot of the potential chaos that might arise if we were under pressure to meet a stated profit goal and sales declined quickly and unexpectedly at year end, just as they did last year. In these circumstances, we don't try to ram anything down the plant managers' throats. We ask them to tell us where they can reasonably expect to cut costs below the budgeted level.

"Whenever a problem arises at a plant between sales and production, the local people are supposed to solve the problem themselves. For example, a customer's purchasing agent may insist on an immediate delivery, which will disrupt the production department's plans. The production group can make recommendations as to alternative ways to take care of the problem, but it's the sales manager's responsibility to get the product to the customer. The sales force are supposed to know their customers well enough to judge whether or not the customer really needs the product. If the sales manager says the customer needs the product, that ends the matter. As far as we are concerned, the customer's wants are primary; our company is a case where sales wags the rest of the dog. Of course, if the change in the sales program involves a major plant expense that is out of line with the budget, then the matter is passed up to division top management for a decision.

"The sales department has responsibility for revenue variances related to product price, sales mix, and volume. They do not have responsibility for plant operations or profit. However, it is understood that the sales group will cooperate with the plant people whenever possible."

Motivation. "There are various ways

in which we motivate the plant managers to meet their profit goals. First of all, we only promote capable people. Also, an incentive program has been established that provides substantial bonuses if they achieve or exceed their profit goals. In addition, each month we put together a bar chart that shows, by division and plant, their ranking with respect to manufacturing efficiency.[1] We feel the plant managers are fully responsible for variable manufacturing costs, since all manufacturing standards have to be approved by plant managers. Most of the plant managers give wide publicity to these bar charts. The efficiency measure itself is perhaps a little unfair in some respects when you are comparing one plant with another. Somewhat different mixes of products are run through different plants. These require different setups, and so forth, that have an important impact on the position of a plant. However, in general, the efficiency rating is a good indication of the quality of the plant managers and their supervisors.

"Also, a number of plants run competitions within the plants that reward department heads based on their relative standing with respect to a certain cost item. The plant managers, their staffs, and employees have great pride in their plants.

"The number one item now stressed at the plant level is quality. The market situation is such that in order to make sales you have to meet the market price and exceed the market quality. By quality I mean not only the physical characteris-

tics of the product but also delivery schedules. The company employee publications' message is that if the company is to be profitable it must produce high-quality items at a reasonable cost. This is necessary so that the plants can meet their obligation to produce the maximum profits for the company in the prevailing circumstances."

The Future. "An essential part of the budgetary control system is planning. We have developed a philosophy that we must begin our plans where the work is done—in the line organization and out in the field. Perhaps, in the future, we can avoid or cut back some of the budget preparation steps and start putting together our sales budget later than May 15. However, I doubt if we will change the basic philosophy. Frankly, I doubt if the line operators would want any major change in the system; they are very jealous of the management prerogatives the system gives them.

"It is very important that we manage the budget. We have to be continually on guard against it managing us. Sometimes, the plants lose sight of this fact. They continually have to be made conscious of the necessity of having the sales volume to make a profit. And when sales fall off and their programs are reduced, they do not always appear to see the justification for budget cuts—although I suspect they see more justification for these cuts than they will admit. It is this human side of the budget to which we have to pay more attention in the future."

---

[1]Manufacturing efficiency percent =
$$\frac{\text{Total standard variable manufacturing costs}}{\text{Total actual variable manufacturing costs}} \times 100.$$

Questions

1. Compare the descriptive material in this case with the diagram in Illustration 24–1. What aspects of the management con-

trol cycle are *not* explicitly described in the case?

2. Trace through Empire's profit budgeting process, beginning on May 15. For each step:
   a. Relate the information flow to Exhibits 1 and 2.
   b. Try to visualize who is involved and what "game playing" may occur.
   c. Speculate as to why Empire includes this step in the process (as opposed to some more expeditious method).

Then evaluate Empire's budgeting process.

3. Comment on the strong points and weak points of Empire's management control system. Be sure to consider the question of whether the plants should be held responsible for profits.

25

Programming and Budgeting

This chapter describes the two principal types of planning activities that are part of the management control process. One, called programming, is the process of making decisions on major programs to be undertaken. Programming involves formulating long-range plans. The other, called budgeting, is the process for planning activites of the entire organization for the next period, usually the next year. We will deal primarily with what managers and others do in the course of preparing and using budgets, which is the *managerial* aspect of budgeting, rather than with how budget numbers are calculated and assembled, which is the *technical* aspect of budgeting.

PROGRAMMING

Successful managers spend a considerable amount of time thinking about the future and making decisions that have an effect on future operations. Some actions, such as constructing a new facility, take a long time to implement. Decisions on such matters therefore must be made years in advance so that the resources will be available when needed. In thinking about these future needs, managers focus on product lines and other programs, and the process is therefore called *programming*. It is also called *long-range planning*. *Programming is the process of deciding on the programs that the organization will undertake and the approximate amount of resources that will be allocated to each major program.*

There are three main parts to the programming process: (1) reviewing ongoing programs, (2) considering proposals for new programs, and (3) coordinating programs by means of a formal programming system.

Ongoing Programs

In the typical organization, most activities in which the organization will engage in the next few years are similar to those it is now carrying on. If a company currently manufactures and sells 20 lines of packaged foods, it probably will handle almost all of those lines next year, and the year after. It is dangerous to be complacent about these ongoing programs, however. People's needs and tastes change, competitive conditions change, production methods change. It is important that the implications of these changes be recognized and that decisions be made to adapt to the changed conditions. Thus, there needs to be a systematic, thorough way of reviewing each of the existing programs to ensure that new conditions are anticipated and the appropriate actions are decided upon.

Zero-Base Review. A systematic way of making an analysis of ongoing programs is called a *zero-base review*. It gets this name because in deciding on the costs that are appropriate for a program, the cost estimates are built up "from scratch," from zero, rather than taking the current level of costs as a starting point as is customary in the annual budgeting process. Such reviews are useful for major programs in order to overcome the natural tendency toward complacency and inertia. They are also useful for *discretionary* expense centers, such as the accounting department, the personnel department, and indeed most staff activities. Because a zero-base review is time consuming and upsetting to the normal functioning of the responsibility center, it probably cannot be conducted *every* year for *every* program and *every* discretionary expense center. About the most that can be expected is that each part of the whole organization will be reviewed thoroughly every three to five years.[1]

In making a zero-base review of a discretionary expense center, basic questions are raised about the activity, such as:

1. Should this activity be performed at all?
2. Is too much being done? Too little?
3. Should it be done internally, or should it be contracted to an outside firm (the familiar make-or-buy question)?

---

[1]There are references in the literature to "zero-base budgeting." This term implies that such reviews should be made *annually* for all programs, as a part of the annual budget process. A *good* zero-base review requires far more time than is normally available during the preparation of the annual budget, however. In 1978, President Carter instituted *annual* "zero-base budgeting" in the federal government, with much attendant fanfare. This practice was abandoned in 1981 (with much less publicity) because the Reagan administration concluded it "had proved cumbersome . . . and hadn't achieved significant results in holding down federal government spending" (*The Wall Street Journal*, August 10, 1981).

4. Is there a more efficient way of obtaining the desired results?
5. How much should it cost?

In making a zero-base review of a product line, basic questions are asked about the demand for the product, the impact of competition, the marketing strategy, the production strategy, and so on.

Zero-base reviews are particularly appropriate in government agencies and other nonprofit organizations, which tend to have high proportions of discretionary costs. Without such reviews, it is possible for an agency to establish a program to address some societal need, and for the program still to be in place years later when the need has subsided, or even disappeared. For this reason, legislatures subject certain programs to "sunset laws," which require that a zero-base review be conducted after a specified number of years.

Proposed New Programs

Management should be on the alert for proposed new programs, either to counter a threat to existing operations or to take advantage of new opportunities. These proposals are analyzed whenever the need or the opportunity comes to management's attention. In business, these proposals usually involve new capital investments, and the appropriate analytical techniques are therefore those described in Chapter 22, which dealt specifically with this topic.

Benefit/Cost Analysis.   Revenue is a measure of the output of a profit-oriented organization. Nonprofit organizations also have outputs, but many of these organizations cannot measure their outputs in monetary terms. Similarly, the outputs of many organization units within a profit-oriented company cannot be expressed as revenue. In these situations, analysis of a new program proposal based on differential profit or return on investment is not possible. Nevertheless, it is sometimes possible to use a similar approach by comparing differential costs with some nonmonetary measure of the benefits that are expected as a consequence of incurring the additional costs. This approach is called a *benefit/cost analysis.*

Benefit/cost analysis is widely used for analyzing programs in nonprofit organizations. It is also used in profit-oriented companies for analyzing such program proposals as spending more money to improve safety conditions, to reduce pollution, to improve the company's reputation with the public, or to provide better information to management. Zero-base reviews also usually require extensive use of this approach.

In a benefit/cost analysis, the cost calculations are usually straightforward. The difficult part of the analysis is the estimate of the value of the benefits. In many situations, no meaningful estimate of the quantitative amount of benefits can be made. In such situations, the anticipated benefits are carefully described in words, and then the decision maker must answer the question: Are the perceived benefits worth *at least* the estimated cost? For example, "If $85,000 is added to the costs of the city park summer recreation program, will the increased output of the program be worth at least $85,000?" The answer to this question is necessarily judgmental, but the judgment can be aided by a careful estimate of the differential costs and a careful assessment of the probable benefits.

Formal Programming Systems

Every organization should review its ongoing programs and make decisions on proposed new programs. Although many organizations do this informally, most large companies have a formal system in which the financial and other consequences of these programs are projected for a number of years in the future. Such a projection is called a *long-range plan*. It shows revenues, costs, and other information for individual programs for a number of years ahead—usually 5 years, but possibly as few as 3, or, in the case of certain public utilities, as many as 20.

Usually the programming process begins several months prior to the start of the budgeting process. Formal programming begins with top-management discussions of and decisions on changes in basic goals and strategies, and dissemination of these to operating managers. These managers prepare tentative programs, following the guidelines set forth by top management. Next, these proposed programs are discussed at length with top management, and out of these discussions emerges a set of programs for the whole company. These approved programs form the basis of the budgeting process.

Although widely used in industrial companies, formal programming systems are relatively new in government and other nonprofit organizations. In the early 1960s, Secretary of Defense Robert S. McNamara installed a formal programming system in the U.S. Department of Defense. (It is noteworthy that Mr. McNamara formerly was president of the Ford Motor Company and had introduced a formal programming system in that organization.) This system was dubbed "PPBS," for "planning, programming, and budgeting system." Most federal agencies, many states and municipalities, and a number of other nonprofit organizations now use a formal programming system.

BUDGETING

A *budget* is a plan expressed in quantitative, usually monetary terms, covering a specified period of time, usually one year. Practically all companies, except some of the smallest, prepare budgets. Many companies refer to their annual budget as a *profit plan*, since it shows the planned activities that the company expects to undertake in its responsibility centers in order to obtain its profit goal. Almost all nonprofit organizations also prepare budgets.

Uses of the Budget   The budget serves several purposes:

1. As an aid in making and coordinating short-range plans.
2. As a device for communicating these plans to the various responsibility center managers.
3. As a way of motivating managers to achieve their responsibility centers' goals.
4. As a benchmark for controlling ongoing activities.
5. As a basis for evaluating the performance of responsibility centers and their managers.
6. As a means of educating managers.

Planning.   Although major planning decisions are usually made in the programming process, the process of formulating the budget leads to a refinement of these plans. In preparing the budget, managers must consider how conditions in the future may change and what steps they should take to get ready for these changed conditions.

Furthermore, each responsibility center affects, and is affected by, the work of other responsibility centers. The budgetary process helps coordinate these separate activities to ensure that all parts of the organization are in balance with one another. Most importantly, production plans must be coordinated with marketing plans to ensure that the production processes are geared up to produce the planned sales volume. Similarly, cash management plans (e.g., plans for short-term borrowing or for short-term investment of excess funds) must be based on projected inflows from sales and outflows for production costs.

Communication.   Management's plans will not be carried out (except by accident) unless the organization understands what the plans are. These plans include such specific things as how many goods and services are to be produced; what methods, people, and equipment are to be used; how much material is to be purchased; and what selling prices are to be. The organization also needs to be aware of policies and constraints to which it is expected to adhere. Examples of these kinds of information include the maximum amounts that may be spent for advertising, maintenance, and administrative costs; wage rates and hours of work; and desired quality levels. A most useful device for communicating quantitative information concerning these plans and limitations is the approved budget.

Motivation.   If the atmosphere is right, the budget process can also be a powerful force in *motivating* managers to work toward the goals of their responsibility centers, and thereby the goals of the overall organization. Such an atmosphere cannot exist unless the managers of responsibility centers have had communicated to them what is expected of their responsibility centers. Motivation will be greatest when these managers have played an active role in the formulation of their budgets, as described later in this chapter.

Control.   As described in Chapter 23, *control* is assuring that desired results are attained. A budget is a statement of results desired as of the time the budget was prepared. A carefully prepared budget is the best possible standard against which to compare actual performance. This is because it incorporates the estimated effect of all variables that were foreseen when the budget was being prepared. Until fairly recently, the general practice was to compare current results with results for last month or for the same period a year ago. This is still the basic means of comparison in some organizations. Such an historical standard has the fundamental weakness that it does not take account of either changes in the underlying forces at work or in the planned programs for the current year.

A comparison of actual performance with budgeted performance provides a "red flag;" that is, it directs attention to areas where action may be needed. An analysis of the variance between actual and budgeted results may (1) help identify a problem area that needs attention; (2) reveal an opportunity, not predicted in the budgeting process, that should be capitalized upon; or (3) reveal that the original budget was unrealistic in some way.

Evaluation.   Monthly variances from budgets are used for control purposes *during* the year. The comparison of actual and budgeted results for the *entire* year is frequently a major factor in the year-end evaluation of each responsibility center and its manager. In some companies, a manager is awarded a bonus that is calculated using some predetermined percentage of the net favorable variance in his or her responsibility center.

Education.   Budgets also serve to educate managers about the detailed workings of their responsibility centers and the interrelationships of their centers with other centers in the organization. This is particularly true for a person who has been newly appointed to the position of responsibility center manager. Any person who has attempted preparing an annual budget for his or her personal financial affairs can appreciate the educational nature of this process.

Multiple-Use Complications.   Because the budget serves multiple purposes, complications can arise in budget preparation. For example, some profit center managers propose budgets that are somewhat more optimistic than top management's "best guess" as to the amount of profit the profit center will actually achieve; but such budgets are accepted for motivational purposes. Nevertheless, the corporate treasurer needs realistic numbers for cash flow planning purposes. This raises difficult questions: Should there be, in effect, two sets of budget figures? Should the manager be evaluated based on the realistic amount or the optimistic amount? There are no pat answers to these questions.[2]

---

[2]For a more thorough discussion of the complications arising from the multiple uses of budgets, see M. Edgar Barrett and LeRoy B. Fraser, III, "Conflicting Roles in Budgeting for Operations," *Harvard Business Review*, July–August 1977.

The Master Budget   Although we have referred to "the" budget, the complete "budget package" in an organization includes several items, each of which is also referred to as a budget. We shall therefore refer to the total package as the *master budget*. Illustration 25–1 shows the components of this package in a typical company. The three principal parts of the master budget are:

1. An *operating budget*, showing planned operations for the coming year, including revenues, expenses, and changes in inventory and other working capital items.
2. A *cash budget*, showing the anticipated sources and uses of cash in that year.
3. A *capital expenditure budget*, showing planned changes in property, plant, and equipment.

We shall first describe the nature of the operating budget and the steps

ILLUSTRATION 25–1
TYPES OF BUDGETS

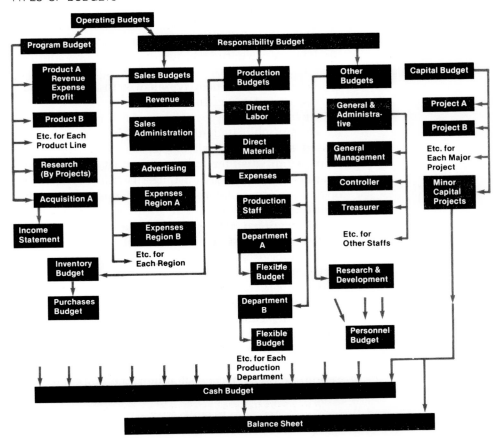

involved in its preparation. We shall then describe the cash budget and the capital expenditure budget. Another document, the *budgeted balance sheet,* is derived directly from the other budgets and is therefore not described separately.

THE OPERATING BUDGET

The operating budget usually consists of two parts, a program budget and a responsibility budget. These represent two ways of depicting the overall operating plan for the organization, as was shown in Illustration 23–3.

Program Budgets and Responsibility Budgets

The *program budget* consists of the estimated revenues and costs of the major programs the organization plans to undertake. Such a budget might be arranged, for example, by product lines and show the anticipated revenue and costs associated with each product line. This type of budget is useful to a manager who is analyzing overall balance among the various programs of a business. It helps to answer such questions as these: Is the return on investment for each product line satisfactory? Is production capacity in balance with the size and capability of the sales organization? Can we afford to spent so much for research? Are adequate funds available? A negative answer to any of these questions indicates the necessity for revising the plan.

The *responsibility budget* sets forth plans in terms of the responsibility centers obligated for carrying them out. It is an excellent control device since it is a statement of the performance expected for each responsibility center manager against which actual performance can later be compared. Each manager is responsible for preparing those parts of the operating budget that correspond to his or her sphere of responsibility.

For the production process, for example, there should be a responsibility budget for each department, showing the costs that are controllable by its supervisor. There may also be a program budget showing planned costs for each program, including both direct costs and allocated costs. The numbers in each set of budgets add up to total production costs. But if several products are made in a facility in which there are several responsibility centers, the program budget will not be useful for control purposes, since the costs shown on it cannot ordinarily be related to the responsibility of specific managers. (Again, refer to Illustration 23–3.)

Responsibility budgets are broken down into *cost elements,* for example, labor, materials, maintenance, supervision, electricity, interest, and taxes. Such a breakdown is useful both as a guide to spending and also as a basis for identifying the areas of inadequate performance if actual spending exceeds the budgeted amounts.

Project Budgets.   Some organizations work on defined projects. The producer of a motion picture or a television "special" has a budget for that particular project, and control is exercised in terms of that budget. This is also the case in the construction of major capital assets: buildings, dams, roads, bridges, ships, and the like. The manager of the project may use personnel and other resources from various functional departments in the organization. If so, the project budget contains amounts that are also reported in the budgets for the functional responsibility centers.

If personnel from functional departments are assigned temporarily to a project, they have two "bosses," the project manager and the manager of their functional department. Such a practice results in a *matrix organization*. Because there are dual lines of authority and responsibility, the control of a matrix organization is complicated. In budget preparation, it is important that the project budgets be consistent with the budgets of the functional departments involved.

Variable or Flexible Budgets

If the total costs in a responsibility center are expected to vary with changes in volume, as is the case with most engineered expense centers, the responsibility budget may be in the form of a *variable budget* or *flexible budget*. Such a budget shows the planned behavior of costs at various volume levels, and is appropriately used in responsibility centers with a high proportion of engineered costs. (One use of flexible budgets for production overhead costs was described in Chapter 18.) The variable budget is usually expressed in terms of a cost-volume equation, that is, a fixed amount for a specified time period plus a variable amount per unit of volume.

When there is a variable budget, the costs at *one* volume level are used as part of the master budget. That volume level is the planned level of operations for the budget period, which is usually the same as the *standard volume* used for setting predetermined overhead rates (as described in Chapter 18). Budgeted costs at other volume levels are used in the evaluation phase of the management control cycle, at which time actual costs are compared with the budgeted costs for the *actual* volume level that was experienced.

Management by Objectives

The foregoing description of budgets emphasized monetary information because such information is incorporated in an accounting system. Accounting information alone cannot provide an adequate benchmark for the performance of a responsibility center, however. At best, it measures profitability; and although profitability is one important goal in a profit-oriented company, it is by no means the only goal. In expense centers in profit-oriented companies, and in nonprofit organizations, profit is not a goal at all. Furthermore, the income reported for a profit center measures only short-run performance. It shows the results of the manager's decisions on *current* profits, but tells nothing about actions the manager may have taken that influence *future* profits.

As a way of overcoming these inadequacies, many organizations supplement the monetary accounting information with other information about the results of the manager's actions. A system that does this is called a *management by objectives* or *MBO* system. It gets this name because the system states specific objectives that the responsibility center manager is expected to achieve during the period covered by the budget. These objectives are analogous to the revenues, expenses, and profit amounts in financial budgets. This approach is especially useful in discretionary expense centers and in nonprofit organizations where actual-versus-budgeted cost comparisons are of limited usefulness in evaluating performance.

For example, a sales manager may be expected to open three new sales offices next year, or a factory superintendent may be expected to have a new training program developed or to take certain steps to improve safety standards. Such actions often cause the incurrence of additional expenses in the current period, which reduces current profits, but they are expected to lead to improved profitability in future periods or to the attainment of other company goals. MBO helps ensure that these actions are not foregone in an attempt to improve short-term cost performance.

Experience with MBO in businesses has shown that it tends to improve performance in those responsibility centers where monetary measures are felt to be relatively unimportant. Without MBO, there is a tendency in such areas not to measure results at all. For MBO to be successful, however, it must be actively supported by top management and carefully integrated with other aspects of the management control system. In some companies, MBO has proven ineffective because it was implemented by the personnel department and was not integrated with the management control system administered by the controller's department. MBO should be an integral part of the management control system, not a separate system.

At the profit or investment center level, MBO seems more appropriate for new endeavors than for mature ones. If a division is formed to enter a business that is new to the company, in the division's early years nonfinancial objectives such as developing channels of distribution and building market share are dominant. But as the division matures, financial objectives such as return on investment or net cash flow generated become more important.

PREPARING THE OPERATING BUDGET

The preparation of a budget can be studied both as an accounting process and also as a management process. From an accounting standpoint, one studies the mechanics of the system, the procedures for assembling data, and budget formats. The procedures are similar to those described in Part 1 for recording actual transactions, and the end result of the calculations and summarizations is a set of financial statements—a balance sheet, income statement, and funds flow statement—identical in format with those resulting from the accounting process that records historical events. The principal difference is that the budget amounts reflect planned future activities rather than data on what has happened in the past. We shall focus here on the preparation of an operating budget as a *management* process.

Organization for Preparation of Budgets

A *budget committee,* consisting of several members of the top-management group, usually guides the work of preparing the budget. This committee recommends to the chief executive officer (CEO) the general guidelines that the organization is to follow, disseminates these guidelines after the CEO's approval, coordinates the separate budgets prepared by the various organizational units, resolves differences among them, and submits the final budget to the CEO and board of directors for approval. (In a small company, this work is done by the CEO, or by the CEO's immediate subordinate.) Instructions go down through the regular chain of command, and the budget comes back up for successive reviews and approvals through the same channels. Decisions about the budget are made by the line organization, and the final approval is given by the CEO, subject to ratification by the board of directors.

The line organization usually is assisted in its budget preparations by a staff unit headed by the *budget director.* As a staff person, the budget director's functions are to disseminate instructions about budget preparation mechanics (the forms and how to fill them out), to provide past performance data that are useful in preparing the budget, to make computations based on decisions reached by the line organization, to assemble the budget numbers, and to ensure that all managers submit their portions of the budget on time.

The budget staff may do a very large share of the budget work. It is not the crucial part, however, for the significant decisions are always made by the line organization. Once the line organization members have reached an agreement on such matters as labor productivity and wage rates, for example, the budget staff can calculate the detailed amounts for labor costs by products and by responsibility centers. This is a considerable job of computation, but it is based entirely on the decisions of the line managers.

The budget staff is usually a unit of the controller's department. The budget staff is like a telephone company. It operates an important communication system; it is responsible for the speed, accuracy, and clarity with which messages flow through the system, but it does not decide on the content of the messages themselves.

Budget Timetable

Most organizations prepare budgets once a year covering the upcoming fiscal year. Separate budget estimates are usually made for each month or each quarter within the year. In some organizations, data are initially estimated by months only for the next three months or the next six months, with the balance of the year being shown by quarters. When this is done, a detailed budget by months is prepared shortly before the beginning of each new quarter.

Some organizations follow the practice of preparing a new budget every quarter, but for a full year ahead. Every three months the budget amounts for the quarter just completed are dropped, the amounts for the succeeding three quarters are revised if necessary, and budget amounts for the fourth succeeding quarter are added. This is called a *rolling budget*.

Most components of a company's operating budget (see Illustration 25–1) are affected by decisions or estimates made in constructing other components. Nearly all components are affected by the planned sales volume; the purchases budget is affected by planned production volume and decisions as to materials inventory levels; and so on. Thus, there has to be a carefully worked out timetable specifying the order in which the several parts of the operating budget are developed and the time when each must be completed. In general, the steps covered by this timetable are as follows:

1. Setting planning guidelines.
2. Preparing the sales budget.
3. Initial preparation of other budget components.
4. Negotiation to agree on final plans for each component.
5. Coordination and review of the components.
6. Final approval.
7. Distribution of the approved budget.

In a typical organization, the elapsed time for the whole budget preparation process is approximately three months, with the most hectic part (steps 4, 5, and 6 above) requiring approximately one month. A small business may go through the whole process in one afternoon, however.

Setting Planning Guidelines

The budget preparation process is *not* the mechanism through which most major program decisions are made, but rather is a means of detailed planning to implement these decisions. When budget preparation begins, a great many decisions affecting the budget year already have been made. The maximum level of operations has been set by the amount and character of available facilities. If an expansion of facilities is to take place during the budget year, the decision would ordinarily have been made a year or more previously because of the time required to build buildings and to acquire and install machinery. If a new product is to be introduced, considerable time would have already been spent prior to the budget year on product development, testing, design, and initial promotional work. Thus, the budget is not a *de novo* creation; it is built within the context of ongoing operations.

If the organization has a formal long-range plan, this plan provides a starting point in preparing the budget. If there is no long-range plan, top management establishes policies and guidelines that are to govern budget preparation. These guidelines vary greatly in content in different organizations. At one extreme, there may be only a brief general statement, such as "Assume that industry volume next year will be 5 percent higher than the current year." More commonly, detailed information and guidance are given on such matters as projected economic conditions, allowance to be made for price increases and wage increases, changes in the product line, changes in the scale of operations, allowable number of personnel promotions, and anticipated productivity gains. In addition, detailed instructions are issued as to what information is required from each responsibility center and how this information is to be recorded on the budget documents.

Preparing the Sales Budget

The amount of sales and the sales mix (i.e., the proportion represented by each product or product line) govern the level and general character of a company's operations. Thus, a sales plan must be made early in the budget process, for it affects most of the other plans. *The sales budget is different from a sales forecast.* A forecast is merely passive, while a budget should reflect the results of positive actions that management plans to take in order to influence future events. For example, this may be the sales *forecast:* "With the present amount of sales effort, we expect sales to run at about the same level as currently." By contrast, the sales *budget* may show a substantial planned increase in sales, reflecting management's intention to add sales personnel, to increase advertising and sales promotion, or to add or redesign products.

At the same time the sales budget is prepared, a selling expense budget should also be prepared because the size and nature of the marketing efforts that are intended to influence sales revenue are given in the selling expense budget. However, in this early stage, it may suffice to show the main elements of selling expense, with such details as the expenses of operating field selling offices left until the next step.

In almost all companies the sales budget is the most difficult plan to make. This is because a company's sales revenue depends on the actions of its customers, which are not subject to the direct control of management. In contrast, the amounts of cost incurred are determined primarily by actions of the company itself (except for the prices of certain input factors), and therefore can be planned with more confidence.

Basically, there are two ways of making estimates as a basis for the sales budget:

1. Make a *statistical forecast* on the basis of a mathematical analysis of general business conditions, market conditions, product growth curves, and the like; or

2. Make a *judgmental estimate* by collecting the opinions of executives and salespersons. In some companies, sales personnel are asked to estimate the sales of each product to each of their customers; in others, regional managers estimate total sales in their regions; in still others, the field organization does not participate in the estimating process.

There are advantages and weaknesses in both the statistical and the judgmental methods. In a study of large corporations' forecasting practices, Cerullo and Avila reported that 60 percent used a combination of methods, while 28 percent relied solely on judgment. Although about one fourth used sophisticated statistical techniques—regression analysis, input-output analysis, and econometric models—these methods generally did not result in more accurate forecasts than did "naive" methods, including judgment and extrapolation of past results.[3]

Another sales budgeting approach is to buy a forecast of industry sales that has been prepared by professional economists using sophisticated mathematical techniques. The company must then forecast its own market share and apply this to the industry forecast to arrive at a sales budget. Other companies use test markets to refine their estimates of sales of new products, but this has the potential problem of giving other firms more time to develop their own competitive new products.

In some companies, revenue budgets are negotiated at various levels in the sales organization. For example, salespersons may negotiate sales targets with their district sales manager. In cases where such negotiations take place, the comments below on negotiating expense budgets also apply.

Initial Preparation of Other Budget Components

The budget guidelines prepared by top management, together with the sales budget, are disseminated down through the successive levels in the organization. Managers at each level may add other, more detailed information for the guidance of their subordinates. When these guidelines

---

[3]Michael J. Cerullo and Alfonso Avila. "Sales Forecasting Practices: A Survey," *Managerial Planning,* September–October 1975, p. 33.

arrive at the lowest responsibility centers, their managers prepare proposed budgets for the items within their sphere of responsibility, working within the constraints specified in the guidelines.

In discretionary expense centers, the budgets prepared reflect the managers' best judgments as to the amounts of resources required to effectively carry out their centers' functions. These amounts may have been tentatively agreed upon in a previous zero-base review. Alternatively (and more commonly), the manager focuses on how the coming year's activities will *differ* from the current year's, and then adjusts the current year's budget amounts for these differences plus increased salaries and other inflationary impacts. This approach is called *incremental budgeting*.

In engineered expense centers, current standards for physical *quantities* (e.g., labor-hours, pounds of material) for the various products are reviewed to determine their ongoing applicability. These standards may be adjusted downward for "learning curve" effects (described in Chapter 16), or for significant anticipated changes in production processes that will increase productivity. Next year's unit material *prices* and labor *rates* are also estimated. Together, the quantity and price/rate standards determine the budgeted direct cost for each unit of product. These per unit amounts are then multiplied by the budgeted production volumes for the various products to arrive at total budgeted costs for direct material and direct labor. The budgeted indirect costs are then added to arrive at the center's total budgeted costs. As previously mentioned, some companies prepare flexible budgets for their engineered expense centers in order to facilitate subsequent analysis of actual-versus-budgeted performance, and also to let managers know in advance how their costs are expected to change with changes in output volume.

Negotiation

Now comes the crucial stage in the process from a control standpoint: negotiations between the managers who prepared the budgets, called the *budgetees,* and their superiors.[4] The value of the budget as a plan of what is to happen, as a motivating device, and as a standard against which actual performance will be measured, depends largely on having this negotiation conducted and on how skillfully it is conducted. Numerous studies have shown that participation in standard setting enhances most budgetees' motivation to achieve the goals. It is important that budgetees feel that their participation is meaningful, and that the negotiation is not a sham.

A number of studies have also shown that the budget is most effective as a motivating device when it represents a "tight," but attainable, goal.

---

[4]In a perceptive study, G. H. Hofstede describes this process as a "game"; see *The Game of Budget Control* (Assen, The Netherlands: Van Gorcum & Co., N.V., 1968). A negotiation is a game, in the formal sense, as the reader who has participated in budget negotiations can appreciate.

If it is too tight, it is rejected as too difficult; if it is too loose, it does not challenge the manager nor satisfy the manager's need for achievement. The budgetee and superior therefore seek to arrive at this desirable middle ground.

The negotiating process applies principally to revenues and to items of discretionary cost. If engineered costs have been properly analyzed, there is little room for differences of opinion about them. Committed costs, by definition, are not subject to negotiation so long as the commitment remains in force.

Slack. Few machines and no organizations operate at 100 percent efficiency. Human beings will not exert maximum effort, hour after hour and day after day, and no reasonable manager expects them to do so. There is a great deal of waste motion, miscommunication, and duplication of effort in any organization. For all these reasons there is *slack* in an organization, that is, a difference between the potential output and actual output. The actual amount of slack cannot be measured. A certain amount of it is desirable; otherwise, the organization would not be an attractive place in which to work. The problem is to keep it within reasonable bounds. This is a main objective of the negotiating process.

Negotiating Tactics. As did the budgetee, the superior usually must take the current level of expense as the starting point in negotiations, modifying this according to his or her perception of how satisfactory the current level is. The superior does not have enough time during the budget review to reexamine each of the elements of expense so as to ensure that the budgetee's estimates are optimum. One way of addressing the problem of slack is to make an arbitrary cut, say, 5 percent, in the budget estimates. But this has the weakness of any arbitrary action— it affects efficient and inefficient managers alike. Furthermore, if budgetees know that an arbitrary cut is going to be made, they can counter it by padding their original estimates by a corresponding amount.

There are more reasonable tactics for keeping costs in line during the negotiating process. The superior should require a full explanation of any proposed cost increases. He or she attempts to find reasons why costs may be expected to decrease, such as a decrease in the work load of the responsibility center or an increase in productivity resulting from the installation of new equipment or a new method, recognizing that these prospective decreases may not be voluntarily disclosed by the budgetee. Questions may be raised as to why certain competitors in the industry appear to be more efficient than the budgetee's responsibility center.

For their part, budgetees defend their estimates. They justify proposed cost increases by explaining the underlying causes, such as additional work they are expected to do, the effect of inflation, the need for better-quality output, and so on.

The Commitment. The end product of the negotiation process is an agreement that represents a *commitment* by each party, the budgetee and the superior. By the act of agreeing to the budget estimates, the budgetee says to the superior, in effect: "I can and will operate my responsibility center in accordance with the plan described in this budget." By approving the budget estimates, the superior says to the budgetee, in effect: "If you operate your responsibility center in accordance with this plan, you will do what we consider to be a good job." Both of these statements contain the implicit qualification of "subject to adjustment for unanticipated changes in circumstances." Both parties recognize that actual events (such as changes in price levels and in general business conditions) may not correspond to those assumed when the budget was prepared and that these changes may affect the budget plans. In judging whether the commitment is in fact being accomplished as the year progresses, management must take these changes into account.

The nature of the commitment, both as to individual objects of expense and as to the total expense of the responsibility center, may be one of three types: (1) it may represent a *ceiling* (e.g., "not more than $X should be spent for books and periodicals"); (2) it may represent a *floor* (e.g., "at least $Y should be spent for employee training"); or (3) it may represent a *guide* (e.g., "approximately $Z should be spent for overtime"). Often, the individual items are not explicitly identified as to which of these three categories they belong in, but it is obviously important that the two parties have a clear understanding as to which item belongs in which category.

Coordination and Review

The negotiation process is repeated at successively higher levels of responsibility centers in the organizational hierarchy, up to the very top. Negotiations at higher levels may, of course, result in changes in the detailed budgets agreed to at lower levels. If these changes are significant, the budget should be recycled back down the organizational hierarchy for revision. However, if the budget process is well understood and well conducted by those who participate in it, such recycling ordinarily is not necessary. In the successive stages of negotiation, the manager who has the role of superior at one level becomes the budgetee at the next higher level. Since managers are well aware of this fact, they are strongly motivated to negotiate budgets with their budgetees that can be defended successfully with their superiors. If a superior demonstrates that a proposed budget is too loose, this reflects adversely on the budgetee's ability as a manager and as a negotiator.

As the individual budgets move up the organizational hierarchy in the negotiation and review process, they are also examined in relationship to one another. This examination may reveal aspects of the plan that are out of balance. If so, some of these budgets may need to be changed. The individual responsibility center budgets may also reveal the need to change planned amounts in the program budgets, and these changes may in turn disclose that parts of the overall program appear to be out of balance. Various summary documents, including the budgeted income statement, the budgeted balance sheet, and the cash flow budget, are also prepared during this step.

Final Approval and Distribution

Just prior to the beginning of the budget year, the proposed budget is submitted to top management for approval. If the guidelines have been properly set and adhered to, and if significant issues that arise during the budgeting process are brought to top management for resolution, the proposed budget should contain no great surprises. Approval is by no means perfunctory, however, for it signifies the official agreement of top management to the proposed plans for the year. The chief executive officer therefore usually spends considerable time discussing the budget with immediate subordinates. After top management approves the budget, it is submitted to the board of directors for final ratification.

The components of the approved budget are then transmitted down through the organization to the appropriate responsibility centers. Each center's approved budget constitutes authority to carry out the plans specified therein.

Revisions

The budget incorporates certain assumptions as to conditions that will prevail during the budget year. Actual conditions will never be exactly the same as those assumed, and the differences may be significant. The question then arises: Should the budget be revised to reflect what is now known about current conditions? There is considerable difference of opinion on this question.

Those who favor budget revision point out that the budget is supposed to reflect the plan in accordance with which the organization is operating, and that when the plan has to be changed because of changing conditions, the budget should reflect these changes. If the budget is not revised, it is no longer realistic and loses its potential to motivate, they maintain.

The opponents of revising the budget argue that the revision process not only is time-consuming but also may obscure the goals that the organization originally intended to achieve and the reasons for departures from these goals. In particular, a revision may reflect the budgetee's skill in negotiating a change, rather than reflecting an actual change in the underlying assumed conditions. Since revisions for spurious reasons stretch the credibility of the budget, critics refer to such a revised budget as a "rubber baseline." Many organizations therefore do not revise their budgets during the year, and take account of changes in conditions when they analyze the difference between actual and budgeted performance. An equitable analysis of variance should preclude motivation problems, these people argue.

Some companies solve this problem by having two budgets—a *baseline budget* set at the beginning of the year, and a *current budget* reflecting the best current estimate of revenue and expenses. A comparison of actual performance with the baseline performance shows the extent of deviation from the original plan. A comparison of the current budget with the baseline budget shows how much of this deviation is attributable to changes in current conditions from those originally assumed.

Variations in Practice

The preceding is a generalized description of the budget process. Some organizations treat the process more casually than is implied in the above description. A few organizations formulate their budgets in a process that is essentially the reverse of that described. Instead of having budget estimates originate at the lowest responsibility centers, the budget is prepared by a high-level staff, approved by top management, and then transmitted down through the organization. This *imposed budget* or "top down" budget is a less effective motivating device because standards set by others are less likely to be understood and more likely to be seen as difficult or unfair.

Merchandising Companies. In retail stores and other merchandising companies, the budgeting process is somewhat simpler than that described above. This is because the complexities of preparing a production budget and coordinating it with a sales budget are not present. Each responsibility center, including selling departments and support functions, does, of course, prepare an expense budget, and the selling departments also prepare sales budgets.

Instead of preparing a monthly budget showing the goods to be purchased for inventory, retail store buyers generally use the *open-to-buy* procedure. Buyers are given a dollar limit for the sum of goods on hand and on order at any time, and they must govern their purchases so that this limit is not exceeded. For example, if the sporting goods buyer has an open-to-buy of $100,000, and $80,000 of sporting goods are on hand or on order, additional orders totaling up to $20,000 may be placed.

Nonprofit Organizations. The budgeting process in most nonprofit organizations is even more important than in a profit-oriented company. This is because the profit measure for a business provides guidance as to what actions not contemplated by the budget should be taken during the year, whereas managers of nonprofit organizations must conform their actions to mandates imposed by their governing bodies. These mandates are set forth in the approved budget. Municipal, state, and federal government bodies are prohibited by law from exceeding the budgeted amounts.

Even more so than businesses, nonprofit organizations tend to prepare program budgets, as well as responsibility center budgets. These program budgets set forth the amount to be spent on each program the organization plans to undertake during the year. For example, the programs for a community health care center might include nutrition, mental health, dental care, pediatrics, pre-natal care, drug abuse, and general medicine.

THE CASH BUDGET

The operating budget is usually prepared in terms of revenues and expenses. For financial planning purposes, it must be translated into terms of cash inflows and cash outflows. This translation results in the *cash budget*. The financial manager uses the cash budget to make plans to ensure that the company has enough, but not too much, cash on hand during the year ahead.

There are two approaches to the preparation of a cash budget:

1. Start with the budgeted balance sheet and income statement, and adjust the amounts thereon to reflect the planned sources and uses of cash. This procedure is substantially the same as that described for the cash flow statement in Chapter 10, except that the data are estimates of the future rather than historical. Its preparation is therefore not described again here.

2. Analyze those plans having cash flow implications to estimate each of the sources and uses of cash. An example of this approach is shown in Illustration 25–2. Some points about this technique are briefly described below.

ILLUSTRATION 25–2
CASH BUDGET (in thousands of dollars)

	January	February	March	April	May	Totals for Year
Gross shipments	1,200	1,987	2,063	1,387	2,363	21,000
Cash balance beginning of month	375	396	152	150	157	375
Add: Cash receipts:						
Collections of accounts receivable	1,380	1,350	1,605	1,635	1,680	19,305
Miscellaneous receipts	66	81	70	105	105	1,050
Total receipts	1,446	1,431	1,675	1,740	1,785	20,355
Total cash available	1,821	1,827	1,827	1,890	1,942	20,730
Less: Cash disbursements:						
Operating expenses	810	915	1,035	885	975	10,730
Materials purchases	503	570	1,050	600	607	7,140
Taxes		60	412	13		1,310
Equipment purchases					100	100
Dividends	112			135		517
Pension contribution		210				247
Total disbursements	1,425	1,755	2,497	1,633	1,682	20,044
Cash balance or (deficiency) end of month before bank loans or (repayments)	396	72	(670)	257	260	686
Bank loans or (repayments)		80	820	(100)	(100)	0
Cash balance end of month	396	152	150	157	160	686

Collection of accounts receivable is estimated by applying a "lag" factor to estimated sales. This factor may be based simply on the assumption that the cash from this month's sales will be collected next month. Or there may be a more elaborate assumption, for example, that 10 percent of this month's sales will be collected this month, 60 percent next month, 20 percent in the second month, 9 percent in the third month, and the remaining 1 percent will never be collected.

The estimated amount and timing of *materials purchases* is obtained from the materials purchases budget, and is translated into cash outlays by applying a lag factor for the time interval that ordinarily elapses between receipt of the material and payment of the invoice.

Other operating expenses are often taken directly from the expense budget since the timing of cash outlays is likely to correspond closely to the incurrence of the expense. Depreciation and other items of expense not requiring cash disbursements are excluded. Capital expenditures are also shown as outlays, with amounts taken from the capital budget.

The bottom section of Illustration 25–2 shows how cash plans are made. The company desires a minimum cash balance of about $150,000 as a cushion against unforeseen needs. From the budgeted cash receipts and cash disbursements, a calculation is made of whether the budgeted cash balance exceeds or falls below this minimum. In January, the budgeted cash balance exceeds the minimum. In this company no action is planned, but in other situations, the company might decide to invest the excess cash in marketable securities. In February, the budget indicates a balance of only $72,000; consequently, plans are made to borrow $80,000 to bring the balance to the desired level. The lower portion of the cash budget therefore shows the company's short-term financing plans.

THE CAPITAL EXPENDITURE BUDGET

The *capital expenditure budget* is essentially a list of what management believes to be worthwhile projects for the acquisition of new facilities and equipment together with the estimated cost of each project and the timing of the related expenditures.

Proposals for capital investment projects may originate anywhere in the organization. The capital expenditure budget is usually prepared separately from the operating budget, and in many companies it is prepared at a different time and cleared through a capital appropriations committee that is separate from the budget committee.

In the capital expenditure budget, individual projects are often classified by purposes, such as the following:

1. Cost reduction and replacement.
2. Expansion and improvement of existing product lines.

3. New products.
4. Health, safety, pollution control.
5. Other.

Proposals in the first two categories usually are susceptible to an economic analysis of the type described in Chapter 22. Some new-product proposals can also be substantiated by an economic analysis, although in a great many situations the estimate of sales of the new product is essentially a guess. Proposals in the other categories usually cannot be quantified sufficiently to make an economic analysis feasible.

As proposals for capital expenditures come up through the organization, they are screened at various levels, and only the sufficiently attractive ones flow up to the top and appear in the final capital expenditure budget. Estimated cash outlays are shown by years, or by quarters, so that the cash required in each time period can be determined. At the final review meeting, which is usually at the board-of-director level, not only are the individual projects discussed but also the total amount requested on the budget is compared with estimated funds available. Many apparently worthwhile projects may not be approved, simply because the funds are not available.

Authorization   Approval of the capital budget usually means approval of the projects *in principle*, but does not constitute final authority to proceed with them. For this authority, a specific *authorization request* is prepared for the project, spelling out the proposal in more detail, perhaps with firm price quotations on the new assets. These authorization requests are approved at various levels in the organization, depending on their size and character. For example, each supervisor may be authorized to buy tools or other equipment items costing not more than $200 each, provided the total for the year does not exceed $3,000. At the other extreme, all projects costing more than $100,000 and all projects for new products, whatever their cost, may require approval of the board of directors. In between, there is a scale of amounts that various echelons in the organization may authorize without the approval of their superiors.

A few companies use *post-completion audits* to follow up on capital expenditures. These include both checks on the spending itself and also an appraisal after the project has been completed as to how well the estimates of cost and revenue actually turned out. In a few companies, there is tight "linkage" between the cost savings estimated in a capital expenditure request and operating budget figures for the periods of projected savings. Such linkage, like post-completion audits, is aimed at motivating mangers to make realistic savings estimates in their capital budgeting requests.

SUMMARY

Organizations make two main types of plans: (1) program plans, which usually cover several future years and are focused on major programs and (2) budgets, which are usually annual plans structured by responsibility centers. Budgets are used as a device for making and coordinating plans, for communicating these plans to those responsible for carrying them out, for motivating managers at all levels, as a benchmark for controlling ongoing activities, as a standard with which actual performance subsequently can be compared, and as a means of educating managers.

The operating budget is prepared within the context of basic policies and plans that have already been decided upon in the programming process. The principal steps are the (1) dissemination of guidelines stating the overall plans and policies and other assumptions and constraints that are to be observed in the preparation of budget estimates; (2) preparation of the sales plan; (3) preparation of other estimates by the managers of responsibility centers, assisted by, but not dominated by, the budget staff; (4) negotiation of an agreed budget between budgetee and superior, which gives rise to a bilateral commitment by these parties; (5) coordination and review as these initial plans move up the organizational chain of command; (6) approval by top management and the board of directors; and (7) dissemination of the approved budget back down through the organization.

The *cash budget* translates revenues and expenses into cash receipts (inflows) and disbursements (outflows), and thus facilitates financial planning.

The *capital expenditure budget* is a list of worthwhile projects for the acquisition of new capital assets. Often it is prepared separately from the operating budget. Approval of the capital expenditure budget constitutes only approval in principle, for a subsequent authorization is usually required before work on the project can begin.

SUGGESTIONS FOR FURTHER READING

Hofstede, G. H. *The Game of Budget Control.* Assen, The Netherlands: Van Gorcum & Co., N.V., 1968.

MacDonald, Charles R. *MBO Can Work!: How to Manage by Contract.* New York: McGraw-Hill, 1982.

Maciariello, Joseph A. *Program-Management Control Systems.* New York: John Wiley & Sons, 1978.

Steiner, George A. *Strategic Planning.* New York: Macmillan, 1979.

Welsch, Glenn A. *Budgeting: Profit Planning and Control.* 4th ed. Englewood Cliffs, NJ.: Prentice-Hall, 1976

Cases

CASE 25–1   Downtown Parking Authority

In January, a meeting was held in the office of the mayor of Oakmont to discuss a proposed municipal parking facility. The participants included the mayor, the traffic commissioner, the administrator of Oakmont's Downtown Parking Authority, the city planner, and the finance director. The purpose of the meeting was to consider a report by Richard Stockton, executive assistant to the Parking Authority's administrator, concerning estimated costs and revenues for the proposed facility.

Mr. Stockton's opening statement was as follows:

"As you know, the mayor proposed two months ago that we construct a multilevel parking garage on Elm Street. At that time, he asked the Parking Authority to assemble pertinent information for consideration at our meeting today. I would like to summarize our findings.

"The Elm Street site is owned by the city. It is presently occupied by the remains of the old Embassy Cinema, which was gutted by fire last June. The proprietors of the Embassy have since used the insurance proceeds to open a new theater in the suburbs; their lease of the city-owned land on which the Embassy was built expired last month.

"We estimate that it would cost approximately $40,000 to demolish the old Embassy. A building contractor has estimated that a multilevel structure, with space for 800 cars, could be built on the site at a cost of about $2 million. The useful life of the garage would be around 40 years.

"The city could finance construction of the garage through the sale of bonds. The finance director has informed me that we could probably float an issue of 20-year tax-exempts at 5 percent interest. Redemption would commence after three

884

years, with one seventeenth of the original number of bonds being called in each succeeding year.

"A parking management firm has already contacted us with a proposal to operate the garage for the city. They would require a management fee of $30,000 per year. Their proposal involves attendant parking, and they estimate that their costs, exclusive of the fee, would amount to $240,000 per year. Of this amount, $175,000 would be personnel costs; the remainder would include utilities, mechanical maintenance, insurance, and so forth. Any gross revenues in excess of $270,000 per year would be shared 90 percent by the city and 10 percent by the management firm. If total annual revenues are less than $270,000, the city would have to pay the difference.

"I suggest we offer a management contract for bid, with renegotiations every three years. The city would derive additional income of around $50,000 per year by renting the ground floor of the structure as retail space. It's rather difficult for the Parking Authority to estimate revenues from the garage for as you know, our operations to date have been confined to fringe-area parking lots. However, we conducted a survey at a private parking garage only three blocks from the Elm Street site; perhaps that information will be helpful.

"This private garage is open every day from 7 A.M. until midnight. Their rate schedule is as follows: 75 cents for the first hour; 50 cents for the second hour; and 25 cents for each subsequent hour, with a maximum rate of $2 per day. Their capacity is 400 spaces. Our survey indicated that during business hours 75 percent of their spaces were occupied by 'all-day parkers'—cars whose drivers and passengers work downtown. In addition,

roughly 400 cars use the garage each weekday with an average stay of three hours. We did not take a survey on Saturday or Sunday, but the proprietor indicated that the garage is usually about 75 percent utilized by short-term parkers on Saturdays until 6 P.M., when the department stores close; the average stay is about two hours. There's a lull until about 7 P.M., when the moviegoers start coming in; he says the garage is almost full from 8 P.M. until closing time at midnight. Sundays are usually very quiet until the evening, when he estimates that his garage is 60 percent utilized from 6 P.M. until midnight.

"In addition to this survey, we studied a report issued by the City College economics department last year. This report estimated that we now have approximately 50,000 cars entering the central business district (CBD) every day from Monday through Saturday. Based on correlations with other cities of comparable size, the economists calculated that we need 30,000 parking spaces in the CBD. This agrees quite well with a block-by-block estimate made by the Traffic Commissioner's office last year, which indicated a total parking need in the CBD of 29,000 spaces. Right now we have 22,000 spaces in the CBD. Of these, 5 percent are curb spaces (half of which are metered, with a two-hour maximum limit of 20 cents), 65 percent are in open lots, and 30 percent are in privately owned and operated garages.

"Another study indicated that 60 percent of all auto passengers entering the CBD on a weekday were on their way to work; 20 percent were shoppers; and 20 percent were businesspersons making calls. The average number of people per car was 1.75. Unfortunately, we have not yet had time to use the data mentioned thus far to work up estimates of the revenues to be expected from the proposed garage.

"The Elm Street site is strategically located in the heart of the CBD, near the major department stores and office buildings. It is five blocks from one of the access ramps to the new crosstown freeway that we expect will be open to traffic next year, and only three blocks from the Music Center that the mayor dedicated last week. As we all know, the parking situation in that section of town has steadily worsened over the last few years, with no immediate prospect of improvement. The demand for parking is clearly there, and the Parking Authority therefore recommends that we go ahead and build the garage."

The mayor thanked Mr. Stockton for his report and asked for comments. The following discussion took place:

Finance director: I'm all in favor of relieving parking congestion downtown, but I think we have to consider alternative uses of the Elm Street site. For example, the city could sell that site to a private developer for at least $1 million. The site could support an office building from which the city would derive property taxes of around $200,000 per year at present rates. The office building would amost certainly incorporate an underground parking garage for the use of the tenants, and therefore we would not only improve our tax base and increase revenues but also increase the availability of parking at no cost to the city. Besides, an office building on that site would serve to improve the amenity of downtown. A multilevel garage built above ground, on the other hand, would reduce the amenity of the area.

Planning director: I'm not sure I agree completely with the finance director. Within a certain range we can increase the value of downtown land by judicious provision of parking. Adequate, efficient parking facilities will encourage more intensive use of downtown traffic generators such as shops, offices, and places of entertainment, thus enhancing land values. A garage contained within an office building might, as the finance director suggests, provide more spaces, but I suspect these would be occupied almost exclusively by workers in the building and thus would not increase the total available supply.

I think long-term parking downtown should be discouraged by the city. We should attempt to encourage short-term parking—particularly among shoppers—in an effort to counteract the growth of business in the suburbs and the consequent stagnation of retail outlets downtown. The rate structure in effect at the privately operated garage quoted by Mr. Stockton clearly favors the long-term parker. I believe that if the city constructs a garage on the Elm Street site, we should devise a rate structure which favors the short-term parker. People who work downtown should be encouraged to use our mass transit system.

Finance director: I'm glad you mentioned mass transit because this raises another issue. As you know, our subways are presently not used to capacity and are running at a substantial annual deficit that is borne by the city. We have just spent millions of dollars on the new subway station under the Music Center. Why build a city garage only three blocks away that will still further increase the subway system's deficit? Each person who drives downtown instead of taking the subway represents a loss of 50 cents (the average round trip fare) to the subway system. I have read a report stating that approximately two thirds of all persons entering the CBD by car would still have made the trip *by subway* if they had *not* been able to use their cars.

Mayor: On the other hand, I think shoppers prefer to drive rather than take the subway, particularly if they intend to make substantial purchases. No one likes to take the subway burdened down by packages and shopping bags. You know, the Downtown Merchants Association has informed me that they estimate that each new parking space in the CBD generates on average an additional $10,000 in annual retail sales. That represents substantial extra profit to retailers; I think retailing aftertax profits average about 3 percent of gross sales. Besides, the city treasury benefits directly from our 3 percent sales tax.

Traffic commissioner: But what about some of the other costs of increasing parking downtown and therefore, presumably, the number of cars entering the CBD? I'm thinking of such costs as the increased wear and tear on city streets, the additional congestion produced with consequent delays and frustration for the drivers, the impeding of the movement of city vehicles, noise, air pollution, and so on.

How do we weigh these costs in coming to a decision?

Parking administrator: I don't think we can make a decision at this meeting. I suggest that Dick Stockton be asked to prepare an analysis of the proposed garage along the lines of the following questions:

1. Using the information presented at this discussion, should the city of Oakton construct the proposed garage?
2. What rates should be charged?
3. What additional information, if any, should be obtained before we make a final decision?

Mayor: I agree. Dick, can you let us have your answers to these questions in time for consideration at our meeting next month?

Question

How should Mr. Stockton respond to the three questions raised by the parking administrator?

CASE 25–2 Società Rigazio

Società Rigazio manufactured a wide variety of metal products for industrial users in Italy and other European countries. Its head office was located in Milan, and its mills in northern Italy provided about 80 percent of the company's production volume. The remaining 20 percent was produced by two subsidiaries, one in Lyon, France, and the other in Linz, Austria, both serving local markets exclusively through their own sales organizations.

Until recently, the methods used by the Milan headquarters to review subsidiary operations were highly informal. The managing director of each subsidiary visited Milan twice a year, in October and

April, to review the subsidiary's performance and discuss its plans for the future. At other times, the managing director would call or visit Milan to report on current developments or to request funds for specified purposes. These latter requests were usually submitted as a group, however, as part of the October meeting in Milan. By and large, if sales showed an increase over those of the previous year and if local profit margins did not decline, the directors in Milan were satisfied and did nothing to interfere with the subsidiary managers' freedom to manage the businesses as they saw fit.

Last year, Società Rigazio found itself for the first time in 12 years with falling sales volume, excess production capacity, rising costs, and a shortage of funds to finance new investments. In analyzing this situation, the Milan top management decided that one thing that was needed was a more detailed system of cost control in its mills, including flexible budgets for the overhead costs of each factory.

The Lyon mill was selected as a "pilot plant" for the development of the new system. Because the Lyon mill produced a wide variety of products in many production departments, it was not possible to prepare a single flexible budget for the entire mill. In fact, Gino Spreafico, the company's controller, found that the work done in most of the production departments was so varied that useful cost/volume relationships could not even be developed on a departmental basis. He began, therefore, by dividing many of the departments into cost centers so that a valid single measure of work performed could be found for each one. Thus, a department with both automatic and hand-fed cutting machines might be divided into two cost centers, each with a group of highly similar machines doing approximately the same kind of work.

The establishment of the cost centers did not change the responsibility pattern in the factory. Each department had a foreman who reported to one of two production supervisors; the latter were responsible directly to Jean Forclas, the plant manager. Each foreman continued to be responsible for the operations of all the cost centers in his or her department. In some cases, a cost center embraced an entire department, but most departments contained between two and five cost centers.

Once he had completed this task, Spreafico turned to the development of flexible budgets. For each cost center he

selected the measure or measures of volume that seemed most closely related to cost (e.g., machine-hours) and decided what volume was normal for that cost center (e.g., 1,000 machine-hours per month). The budget allowance at the normal level of operations was to be used later as an element of standard product costs, but the budget allowance against which the foremen's performance was to be judged each month was to be the allowance for the volume actually achieved during that particular month.

Under the new system, a detailed report of overhead cost variances would be prepared in Lyon for the foreman in charge of a particular cost center and for his or her immediate superior, the production supervisor. A summary report, giving the total overhead variance for each cost center, would be sent to the plant manager and to Jacques Duclos, the managing director of Rigazio France, S. A., Lyon. The Milan top management would not receive copies of any of these reports but would receive a monthly profit and loss summary, with comments explaining major deviations from the subsidiary's planned profit for the period.

The preparation of the budget formulas had progressed far enough by midyear to persuade Spreafico to try them out on the September cost data. A top-management meeting was then scheduled in Milan to discuss the new system on the basis of the September reports. Duclos and Forclas flew to Milan to attend this meeting, accompanied by the controller of Rigazio France and a production supervisor responsible for some 30 cost centers in the Lyon factory.

Enrico Montevani, Società Rigazio's managing director, opened the meeting by asking Spreafico to explain how the budget allowances were prepared. Spreafico began by saying that the new system was just in its trial stages and that many changes would undoubtedly be necessary before everyone was satisfied with it. "We started with the idea that the standard had to be adjusted each month to reflect the actual volume of production," he continued, "even though that might mean that we would tell the factory they were doing all right when in fact they had large amounts of underabsorbed overhead. In that case, the problem would be that we had failed to provide enough volume to keep the plant busy, and you can't blame the foremen for that. When you have fixed costs, you just can't use a single standard cost per hour or per ton or per unit, because that would be too high when we're operating near capacity and too low when we're underutilized. Our problem, then, was to find out how overhead cost varies with volume so that we could get more accurate budget allowances for overhead costs at different production volumes.

"To get answers to this question, we first made some preliminary estimates at headquarters, based on historical data in the accounting records both here and in Lyon. We used data on wage rates and purchase prices from the personnel and purchasing departments to adjust our data to current conditions. Whenever we could, we used a mathematical formula known as 'least squares regression' to get an accurate measure of cost variability in relation to changing volume, but sometimes we just had to use our judgment and decide whether to classify a cost as fixed or variable. I might add that in picking our formulas we tried various measures of volume and generally took the one that seemed to match up most closely with cost. In some cost centers we actually used two different measures of volume, such as direct labor-hours and product tonnage, and based some of our budget allowances on one and some on the other. These estimates were then discussed with Jean Forclas and his people at Lyon, and the revised budget formulas were incorporated in a computer program for use in monthly report preparation.

EXHIBIT 1
OVERHEAD COST SUMMARY—COST CENTER 2122
September (in francs)

	Standard Allowance at Normal Volume (500 DLH,* 25 tons)	Budgeted at Actual Volume (430 DLH, 23 tons)	Actual, Month of September	Over (Under) Budget
Supervision	360	360	291	(69)
Indirect labor	3,000	2,720	3,219	499
Waiting time	210	181	355	174
Hourly wage guarantee	140	120	60	(60)
Payroll taxes, etc.	3,213	2,820	2,997	177
Materials and supplies	300	258	281	23
Tools	1,500	1,290	1,276	(14)
Maintenance	3,200	3,072	3,752	680
Scrap loss	4,220	3,882	4,913	1,031
Allocated costs	10,520	10,520	10,609	89
Total	26,663	25,223	27,753	2,530
Per ton	1066.52	1096.65	1206.65	110.00

*DLH = direct labor-hours.

"Although you have a complete set of the cost center reports, perhaps we might focus on the one for cost center 2122 [Exhibit 1]. You can see that we have used two measures of volume in this cost center, direct labor-hours and product tonnage. During September, we were operating at less than standard volume, which meant that we had to reduce the budget allowance to 25,223 francs, which averaged out at 1,097 francs per ton. Our actual costs were almost exactly 10 percent higher than this, giving us an overall unfavorable performance variance of 2,530 francs, or 110 francs per ton.

"I know that Jacques Duclos and Jean Forclas will want to comment on this, but I'll be glad to answer any questions that any of you may have. Incidentally, I have brought along some extra copies of the formulas I used in figuring the September overhead allowances for cost center 2122, just in case you'd like to look them over" (Exhibit 2).

EXHIBIT 2
FLEXIBLE BUDGET FORMULA—COST CENTER 2122
(in francs)

| | Allowance Factors | | |
	Fixed Amount per Month	Variable Rate	Remarks
Supervision	360	—	Percent of foreman's time spent in cost center
Indirect labor	1,000	4.00/DLH*	
Waiting time	—	0.42/DLH	Wages of direct labor workers for time spent waiting for work
Hourly wage guarantee	—	0.28/DLH	Supplement to wages of workers paid by the piece to give them guaranteed minimum hourly wage.
Payroll taxes, etc.	408	5.61/DLH	Payroll taxes and allowances at 30 percent of total payroll, including direct labor payroll†
Materials and supplies	—	0.60/DLH	—
Tools.	—	3.00/DLH	—
Maintenance.	1,600	64.00/ton	Actual maintenance hours used at predetermined rate per hour, plus maintenance materials used
Scrap loss.	—	168.80/ton	Actual scrap multiplied by difference between materials cost and estimated scrap value per ton
Allocated costs.	10,520	—	Actual cost per month, allocated on basis of floor space occupied

*DLH = direct labor-hours.
†Budgeted direct labor at standard volume, 500 hours at 14.0 francs per hour; actual direct labor cost for September was 6,106 francs.

Questions

1. Do you agree with Spreafico that 1,096.65 francs per ton (see Exhibit 1) is a more meaningful standard for cost control than the "normal" cost of 1,066.52 francs?

2. Comment on the variances in Exhibit 1. Which of these are likely to be controllable by the foreman? What do you think the production supervisor should have done on the basis of this report?

3. What changes, if any, would you make in the format of this report or to the basis on which the budget allowances are computed?

4. In developing the budget allowances, did Spreafico make any mistakes that you think he could have avoided? Does his system contain any features that you particularly like?

CASE 25–3 Whiz Calculator Company

In August, Bernard Riesman was elected president of the Whiz Calculator Company. Riesman had been with the company for five years, and for the preceding two years had been vice president of manufacturing. Shortly after taking over his new position, Riesman held a series of conferences with the controller in which the subject of discussion was budgetary control. The new president thought that the existing method of planning and controlling selling costs was unsatisfactory, and he requested the controller to devise a system that would provide better control over these costs.

Whiz Calculator manufactured a complete line of electronic calculators, which it sold through branch offices to wholesalers and retailers, as well as directly to government and industrial users. Most of the products carried the Whiz brand name, which was nationally advertised. The company was one of the largest in the industry.

Under the procedure then being used, selling expenses were budgeted on a "fixed" or "appropriation" basis. Each October, the accounting department sent to branch managers and to other managers in charge of selling departments a detailed record of the actual expenses of their departments for the preceding year and for the current year to date. Guided by this record, by estimates of the succeeding year's sales and by their own judgment, these department heads drew up and submitted estimates of the expenses of their departments for the succeeding year. The estimates made by the branch managers were then sent to the sales manager, who was in charge of all branch sales. He determined whether or not they were reasonable and cleared up any questionable items by correspondence. Upon approval by the sales manager, the estimates of branch expenses were submitted to the manager of marketing, Paula Melmed, who was in charge of all selling, promotional, and warehousing activities.

Melmed discussed these figures and the expense estimates furnished by the other department heads with the managers concerned, and after differences were reconciled, she combined the estimates of all the selling departments into a selling expense budget. This budget was submitted to the budget committee for final approval. For control purposes, the annual budget was divided into 12 equal amounts, and actual expenses were compared each month with the budgeted figures. Exhibit 1 shows the form in which these monthly comparisons were made.

Riesman believed that there were two important weaknesses in this method of setting the selling expense budget. First, it was impossible for anyone to ascertain with any feeling of certainty the reasonableness of the estimates made by the various department heads. Clearly, the expenses of the preceding year did not constitute adequate standards against which these expense estimates could be judged, since selling conditions were never the same in two different years. One obvious cause of variation in selling expenses was the variation in the "job to be done," as defined in the sales budget.

Second, selling conditions often changed substantially after the budget was adopted, but there was no provision for making the proper corresponding changes in the selling expense budget. Neither was there a logical basis for relating selling expenses to the actual sales volume obtained or to any other measure of sales effort. Riesman believed that it was reasonable to expect that sales expenses would increase, though not proportionately, if actual sales volume were greater than the forecasted volume; but that with the existing method of control it was impossible to determine how large the increase in expenses should be.

As a means of overcoming these weaknesses, the president suggested the possibility of setting selling cost budget stan-

EXHIBIT 1
BUDGET REPORT CURRENTLY USED

Month: October	Branch Sales and Expense Performance Branch A				Mgr: N. L. Darden
	This Month				
	Budget†	Actual	Over* Under	Percent of Sales	Over* Under Year to Date
Net sales	310,000	261,000	49,000		70,040*
Manager's salary	2,500	2,500	—	0.96	—
Office salaries	1,450	1,432	18	0.55	1,517
Sales force compensation	15,500	13,050	2,450	5.00	3,502*
Travel expense	3,420	3,127	293	1.20	1,012*
Stationery, office supplies	1,042	890	152	0.34	360
Postage	230	262	32*	0.10	21
Light and heat	134	87	47	0.03	128
Subscriptions and dues	150	112	38	0.04	26
Donations	125	—	125	0.00	130
Advertising expense (local)	2,900	2,700	200	1.03	1,800*
Social security taxes	1,303	1,138	165	0.44	133*
Rental	975	975	—	0.37	—
Depreciation	762	762	—	0.29	—
Other branch expense	2,551	2,426	125	0.93	247*
Total	33,042	29,461	3,581	11.29	4,512*

†One twelfth of annual budget.

dards on a fixed and variable basis, a method similar to the techniques used in the control of manufacturing expenses. The controller agreed that this manner of approach seemed to offer the most feasible solution, and he therefore undertook a study of selling expenses to devise a method of setting reasonable standards. Over a period of several years, the accounting department had made many analyses of selling costs, the results of which had been used for allocating costs to products, customers, and territories, and in assisting in the solution of certain special problems, such as determining how large an individual order had to be in order to be profitable. Many of the data accumulated for these purposes were helpful in the controller's current study.

The controller was convinced that the fixed portion of selling expenses—the portion independent of any fluctuation in sales volume—could be established by determining the amount of expenses that had to be incurred at the minimum sales volume at which the company was likely to operate. He therefore asked Paula Melmed to suggest a minimum volume figure and the amount of expenses that would have to be incurred at this volume. A staff assistant studied the company's sales records over several business cycles, the long-term outlook for sales, and sales trends of other companies in the industry. From the report prepared by this assistant, Melmed concluded that sales volume would not drop below 65 percent of current factory capacity.

Melmed then attempted to determine the selling expenses that would be incurred at the minimum volume. With the help of her assistant, she worked out a hypothetical selling organization that in her opinion would be required to sell merchandise equivalent to 65 percent of factory capacity, complete as to the number of persons needed to staff each branch office and the other selling departments, including the advertising, merchandising, and sales administration departments. Using current salary and commission figures, the assistant calculated the amount required to pay salaries for such an organization. Melmed also estimated the other expenses, such as advertising, branch office upkeep, supplies, and travel, that would be incurred by each branch and staff department at the minimum sales volume.

The controller decided that the variable portion of the selling expense standard should be expressed as a certain amount per sales dollar. He realized that the use of the sales dollar as a measuring stick had certain disadvantages in that it would not reflect such important influences on costs as order size, selling difficulty of certain territories, changes in buyer psychology, and so on. The sales dollar, however, was the measuring stick most convenient to use, the only figure readily available from the records then being kept, and also a figure that everyone concerned thoroughly understood. The controller believed that a budget that varied with sales would certainly be better than a budget that did not vary at all. He planned to devise a more accurate measure of causes of variation in selling expenses after he had an opportunity to study the nature of these factors over a long period of time.

As a basis for setting the variable expense standards, using linear regression the controller determined a series of equations that correlated actual annual expenditures for the principal groups of expense items for several preceding years with sales volume. Using these equations, which showed to what extent these items had fluctuated with sales volume in the past, and modifying them in accordance with his own judgment as to future conditions, the controller determined a rate of variation (i.e., slope) for the variable portion of each item of selling expense. The controller thought that after the new system had been tested in practice, it would be possible to refine these rates, perhaps by the use of a technique analogous to the time-study technique that was employed to determine certain expense standards in the factory.

At this point the controller had both a rate of variation and one point (i.e., at 65 percent capacity) on a selling expense graph for each expense item. He was therefore able to determine a final equation for each item. Graphically, this was equivalent to drawing a line through the known point with the slope represented by the rate of variation. The height of this line at zero volume represented the fixed portion of the selling expense formula. The diagram in Exhibit 2 illustrates the procedure, although the actual computa-tions were mathematical rather than graphic.

The selling expense budget for the coming year was determined by adding the new standards for the various fixed components and the indicated flexible allowances for the year's estimated sales volume. This budget was submitted to the budget committee, which studied the fixed amounts and the variable rates underlying the final figures, making only minor changes before passing final approval.

The controller planned to issue reports each month showing actual expenses for each department compared with budgeted expenses. The variable portion of the budget allowances would be adjusted to correspond to the actual volume of sales obtained during the month. Exhibit 3 shows the budget report that he planned to send to branch managers.

One sales executive privately belittled the controller's proposal. "Anyone in the selling game knows that sometimes customers fall all over each other in their

EXHIBIT 2
BUDGET FOR "OTHER BRANCH EXPENSE," BRANCH A

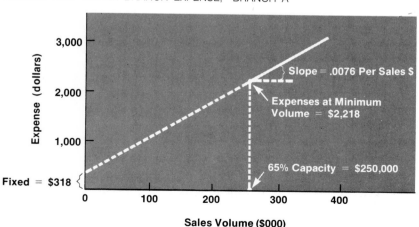

EXHIBIT 3
BUDGET REPORT PROPOSED BY CONTROLLER

Expense Budget Report	Budget Factors		This Month			Year to Date
	Fixed	Variable	Flexible Budget	Actual	Over* Under	Over* Under
Net sales			261,000	261,000		
Manager's salary	2,500	—	2,500	2,500	—	†
Office salaries	139	0.0041	1,209	1,432	223*	
Sales force compensation	—	0.0500	13,050	13,050	—	
Travel expense	568	0.0087	2,839	3,127	288*	
Stationery, office supplies	282	0.0026	961	890	71	
Postage	47	0.0006	204	262	58*	
Light and heat	134	—	134	87	47	
Subscriptions and dues	10	0.0005	141	112	29	
Donations	20	0.0003	98	—	98	
Advertising expense (local)	35	0.0100	2,645	2,700	55*	
Social security taxes	177	0.0036	1,117	1,138	21*	
Rental	975	—	975	975	—	
Depreciation	762	—	762	762	—	
Other branch expense	318	0.0076	2,302	2,426	124*	
Total	5,967	0.0880	28,937	29,461	524*	

†The controller had not recalculated budgets for previous months, and figures were therefore not available for this column.

hurry to buy, and other times, no matter what we do, they won't even nibble. It's a waste of time to make fancy formulas for selling cost budgets under conditions like that."

Questions

1. From the information given in Exhibits 1 and 3, determine insofar as you can, whether each item of expense is (a) nonvariable, (b) partly variable with sales volume, (c) variable with sales volume, or (d) variable with some other factors.

2. What bearing do your conclusions in Question 1 have on the type of budget that is most appropriate?

3. Should the proposed sales expense budget system be adopted?

4. If a variable budget is used, should dollar sales be used as the measure of volume?

5. (Optional—requires calculator with linear regression routine.) Consider the following five-year time series of annual sales and some element of annual branch selling expense:

Year	Sales ($000)	Expense ($)
1	2,686	25,007
2	2,920	27,461
3	3,174	29,813
4	3,450	31,975
5	3,750	35,052

Find the least-squares linear regression equation that relates annual expense to annual sales. Describe how this equation can be used to determine a flexible budget for the expense on a *monthly* basis.

CASE 25–4   Midwest Ice Cream Company (A)

Frank Roberts, marketing vice president of Midwest Ice Cream Company, was pleased when he saw the final earnings statement for the company for 1973. He knew that it had been a good year for Midwest, but he hadn't expected a large, favorable operating income variance. Only the year before, the company had installed a new financial planning and control system; 1973 was the first year for which figures comparing budgeted and actual results were available.

Midwest's Planning and Control System. The following description of the financial planning and control system installed at Midwest in 1972 is taken from an internal company operating manual.

THE PLANNING FUNCTION

The starting point in making a profit plan is separating costs into fixed and variable categories. Some costs are purely variable and will require an additional amount with each increase in volume level. The manager has little control over this type of cost other than to avoid waste. The accountant can determine the variable manufacturing cost per unit for any given product or package by using current prices and yield records. Variable marketing cost is based on the allowable rate, for example 6 cents per gallon for advertising. Costs that are not purely variable are classified as fixed, but they, too, will vary if significant changes in volume occur. There will be varying degrees of sensitivity to volume changes among these costs, ranging from a point just short of purely variable to an extremely fixed type of expense that has no relationship to volume.

The reason for differentiating between fixed and variable costs is because a variable cost requires no decision as to when to add or take off a unit of cost; it is dictated by volume. Fixed costs, on the other hand, require a management decision to increase or decrease the cost. Sugar is an example of a purely variable cost; only the yield can be controlled. Route salespersons' salaries are an example of a fixed cost that is fairly sensitive to volume, but not purely variable. As volume changes, pressure will be felt to increase or decrease this expense, but management must make the decision; the change in cost level is not automatic. Depreciation charges for plant are an example of a relatively fixed cost in that large increases in volume can usually be realized before this type of cost is pressured to change.

We shall now explain and illustrate each of the four steps in the profit planning process. (The numbers in the tables illustrating each step are not intended to be realistic.)

The first step is to develop a unit standard cost for each element of variable cost by product and package size. Examples of four different products and/or packages are shown in Step 1. The accountant can do this by using current prices and yield records for material

STEP 1
ESTABLISH STANDARDS FOR SELLING PRICE, VARIABLE EXPENSES, AND
MARGINAL CONTRIBUTION PER GALLON*

| | Regular | | | Premium |
Item	One-Gallon Paper Container	One-Gallon Plastic Container	Two-Gallon Paper Container	One-Gallon Plastic Container
Dairy ingredients	0.53	0.53	0.53	0.79
Sugar	0.15	0.15	0.15	0.15
Flavorings	0.10	0.10	0.105	0.12
Production	0.10	0.16	0.125	0.16
Warehouse	0.06	0.08	0.07	0.08
Transportation	0.02	0.025	0.02	0.025
Total manufacturing	0.96	1.045	1.00	1.325
Advertising	0.06	0.06	0.06	0.06
Delivery	0.04	0.04	0.04	0.04
Total marketing	0.10	0.10	0.10	0.10
Total variable costs	1.06	1.145	1.10	1.425
Selling price	1.50	1.70	1.45	2.40
Marginal contribution/gallon before packaging	0.44	0.555	0.35	0.975
Packaging	0.10	0.25	0.085	0.25
Marginal contribution/gallon	0.34	0.305	0.265	0.725

*In practice, a standard cost is developed for each flavor in order to recognize differing ingredients costs.

costs and current allowance rates for marketing costs. Advertising is the only cost element not fitting the explanation of a variable cost given in the preceding paragraph. Advertising costs are set by management decision rather than being an "automatic" cost item like sugar. In this sense, advertising is just like route salespersons' expense. However, management has decided that the advertising allowance is equal to 6 cents per gallon for the actual number of gallons sold. This management decision, therefore, has transformed advertising into a variable expense.

After the unit variable cost has been developed, this amount is subtracted from the selling price to arrive at marginal contribution per unit. At any level of volume, it is easy to determine the contribution that should be generated to cover fixed costs and provide profits. This will be illustrated in Step 4.

Step 2 is perhaps the most critical of all because all plans are built around the sales forecast. Much thought should be given to forecasting a realistic sales level and product mix. Consideration should be given to the number of days in a given period, as well as to the number of Fridays and Mondays, as these are two of the heaviest days and will make a difference in the sales forecast. Other factors that should be considered are (1) general economic condition of the marketing area, (2) weather, (3) anticipated promotions, and (4) competition.

Step 3 involves setting fixed cost budgets based on management's judgment as to the need in light of the sales forecast.

STEP 2
ICE CREAM SALES FORECAST IN GALLONS

	January	February		December	Total
One-gallon paper	100,000	100,000	. . .	100,000	1,200,000
One-gallon plastic	50,000	50,000	. . .	50,000	600,000
Two-gallon paper	225,000	225,000	. . .	225,000	2,700,000
One-gallon premium	120,000	120,000	. . .	120,000	1,440,000
Total	495,000	495,000	. . .	495,000	5,940,000

STEP 3
BUDGETED FIXED EXPENSES

	January	February		December	Total
Manufacturing expense:					
Labor	7,333	7,333	. . .	7,333	88,000
Equipment repair	3,333	3,333	. . .	3,333	40,000
Depreciation	6,667	6,667	. . .	6,667	80,000
Taxes	3,333	3,333	. . .	3,333	40,000
Total	20,667	20,667	. . .	20,667	248,000
Delivery expense:					
Salaries—general	10,000	10,000	. . .	10,000	120,000
Salaries—drivers	10,667	10,667	. . .	10,667	128,000
Helpers	10,667	10,667	. . .	10,667	128,000
Supplies	667	667	. . .	667	8,000
Total	32,000	32,000	. . .	32,000	384,000
Administrative expense:					
Salaries	5,167	5,167	. . .	5,167	62,000
Insurance	1,667	1,667	. . .	1,667	20,000
Taxes	1,667	1,667	. . .	1,667	20,000
Depreciation	833	833	. . .	833	10,000
Total	9,333	9,333	. . .	9,333	112,000
Selling expense:					
Repairs	2,667	2,667	. . .	2,667	32,000
Gasoline	5,000	5,000	. . .	5,000	60,000
Salaries	5,000	5,000	. . .	5,000	60,000
Total	12,667	12,667	. . .	12,667	152,000

It is here that good planning makes for a profitable operation. The number of routes needed for both winter and summer volume is planned. The level of manufacturing payroll is set.[1] Insurance and taxes are budgeted, and so on. After Step 4 has been performed, it may be necessary to return to Step 3 and make adjustments to some of the costs that are discretionary in nature.

Step 4 is the profit plan itself. By combining the marginal contributions developed in Step 1 with the Step 2 sales forecast, we arrive at a total marginal contribution by month. Subtracting the

---

[1]Because this system is based on a one-year time frame, manufacturing labor is considered to be a fixed cost. The level of the manufacturing work force is not really variable unless a time frame longer than one year is adopted.

STEP 4
THE PROFIT PLAN

	Marginal Contribution (See Step 1)	Gallons Sold/ Month	Contribution			
			January	February	December	Total
One-gallon paper........	0.34	100,000	$ 34,000	$ 34,000 ...	$ 34,000	$ 408,000
One-gallon plastic	0.305	50,000	15,250	15,250 ...	15,250	183,000
Two-gallon paper	0.265	225,000	59,625	59,625 ...	59,625	715,500
One-gallon premium	0.725	120,000	87,000	87,000 ...	87,000	1,044,000
Total contribution			195,875	195,875 ...	195,875	2,350,500
Fixed costs (see Step 3):						
Manufacturing.........			20,667	20,667 ...	20,667	248,000
Delivery			32,000	32,000 ...	32,000	384,000
Administrative			9,333	9,333 ...	9,333	112,000
Selling...............			12,667	12,667 ...	12,667	152,000
Total fixed costs.....			74,667	74,667 ...	74,667	896,000
Operating profit			121,208	121,208 ...	121,208	1,454,500
Income tax.............			60,604	60,604 ...	60,604	727,250
Net profit			$ 60,604	$ 60,604 ...	$ 60,604	$ 727,250

→ or of the variable in Step 1.

fixed cost budgeted in Step 3, we have operating profit. If this profit figure is not sufficient, then a new evaluation should be made of the fixed costs developed in Step 3.

THE CONTROL FUNCTION

To illustrate the control system, we will take the month of January and assume sales for the month to be 520,000 gallons, as shown in Exhibit A. From Step 2 we see that 495,000 gallons had been forecasted. When we apply our marginal contribution per unit for each product and package, we find that the 520,000 gallons have produced $6,125 less standard contribution than the 495,000 gallons would have produced at the forecasted mix. So even though there has been a nice increase in sales volume, the mix has been unfavorable. The $6,125 represents the difference between standard contribution at forecasted volume

and standard contribution at actual volume. It is thus due to differences in volume and product mix. The impact of each of these two factors is shown on the bottom of Exhibit A.

Exhibit B shows a typical departmental budget sheet comparing actual with budget. A sheet is issued for each department so the person responsible for a particular area of the business can see the items that are in line and those that need attention. In our example, there is an unfavorable operating variance of $22,700. You should note that the budget for variable cost items has been adjusted to reflect *actual* volume, thereby eliminating cost variances that are due strictly to the difference between planned and actual volume.

Since the level of fixed costs is independent of volume anyway, it is not necessary to adjust the budget for these items for volume differences. The original

EXHIBIT A

Contribution Analysis

January

	Actual Gallon Sales	Standard Contribution per Gallon	Total Standard Contribution
One-gallon paper	90,000	0.34	$ 30,600
One-gallon plastic	95,000	0.305	28,975
Two-gallon paper	245,000	0.265	64,925
One-gallon premium	90,000	0.725	65,250
Total	520,000		189,750

Forecast (Step 2) 495,000 gallons
Forecasted contribution (at 495,000 gallons) 195,875
Over (under) forecast .... $ (6,125)

	Planned	Actual
Gallons	495,000	520,000
Contribution	$195,875	$189,750
Average per gallon	$0.3957	$0.3649
Difference		$0.0308 U

Variance due to volume:
  25,000 gallons × $0.3957 = $ 9,892 F
Variance due to mix:
  $0.0308 × 520,000
    gallons   =   16,017 U
      Total variance = $ 6,125 U

(handwritten: where from?)

EXHIBIT B

Manufacturing Cost of Goods Sold

January

Month			Year to Date	
Actual	Budget		Actual	Budget
312,744	299,000	Dairy ingredients		
82,304	78,000	Sugar		
56,290	55,025	Flavorings		
38,770	37,350	Warehouse		
70,300	69,225	Production		
11,514	11,325	Transportation		
571,922	549,925	Subtotal, variable		
7,300	7,329	Labor		
4,065	3,333	Equipment repair		
6,667	6,667	Depreciation		
3,333	3,333	Taxes		
21,365	20,662	Subtotal, fixed		
593,287	570,587	Total		

budget for fixed-cost items is still appropriate. The totals for each department are carried forward to an earnings statement, Exhibit C. We have assumed all other departments' actual and budget are in line, so the only operating variance is the one for manufacturing. This variance added to the sales volume and mix variance of $6,125 results in an overall unfavorable variance from the original plan of

EXHIBIT C

Earnings Statement
January

	Month			Year to Date	
Actual	Budget			Actual	Budget
867,750	867,750	Total ice cream sales			
593,287	570,587	Mfg. cost of goods sold			
52,804	52,804	Delivery expense			
31,200	31,200	Advertising expense			
76,075	76,075	Packaging expense			
12,667	12,667	Selling expense			
9,334	9,334	Administrative expense			
775,367	752,667	Total expense			
92,383	115,083	Profit or (loss)			
46,192	—	Provision for income taxes			
46,191	—	Net profit or (loss)			

Actual profit before taxes 92,383 (1)
Original profit forecast (Step 4) 121,208 (2)
Revised profit forecast based on actual volume . . . 115,083 (3)

Variance due to volume and mix (unfavorable) = (2) − (3) = 121,208 − 115,083 = 6,125 U

Variance due to operations (unfavorable) = (3) − (1) = 115,083 − 92,383 = 22,700 U

Total variance = (2) − (1) = 121,208 − 92,383 = 28,825 U

$28,825, as shown at the bottom of Exhibit C.

The illustration here has been on a monthly basis, but there is no need to wait until the end of the month to see what is happening. Each week, sales can be multiplied by the contribution margins to see how much standard contribution has been generated. This can be compared to one fourth of the monthly forecasted contribution to see if volume and mix are in line with forecast. Neither is it necessary to wait until the end of the month to see if expenses are in line. Weekly reports of such items as production costs or sugar can be made, comparing budget with actual. By combining the variances as shown on weekly reports, and adjusting the forecasted profit figure, an approximate profit figure can be had long before the books are closed and monthly statements issued. More important, action can be taken to correct an undesirable situation much sooner.

Questions

1. Explain in as much detail as possible where *all* the numbers for Steps 1–4 would come from. (You will need to use your imagination; the case does not describe all details of the profit planning process.)

2. Explain the difference between a month's

planned profit as shown in Step 4 and a month's budgeted profit as shown in Exhibit C. Would would Midwest want to have *two* target profit amounts for a *given*

month? (Hint: Study the variance calculations at the bottom of Exhibit C.)

3. Evaluate Midwest's planning and control processes.

CASE 25–5   Reading Manufacturing Company

In July 1983, Richard Berks, treasurer of Reading Manufacturing Company, was reviewing the firm's working capital position. It was his custom to calculate working capital needs for the next six months in January and July of each year, and to formulate plans for meeting such needs.

Reading Manufacturing Company, which had been founded in 1971, operated a machine shop. The company had originally made custom manufacturing tooling for nearby companies. In 1978, a newly designed industrial fastening machine was introduced by the company.

Operating losses and poor financial management had kept the company in financial difficulty during the greater part of its early history. In the spring of 1979, this situation came to the attention of Mr. Berks, a businessman who specialized in rehabilitating financially weak concerns. He analyzed the company and found that it employed a number of skilled machinists and possessed good equipment suitable for precision work. He was also impressed by prospects for the company's fastening machine, which was far superior to competitive products. As a result of his analysis, he concluded that with competent management the company could be operated profitably. The stockholding group was approached and an agreement worked out whereby Berks became, in effect, head of the company. For

his efforts he was to receive a fixed salary plus a percentage of profits.

During the next few years, Berks concentrated on obtaining fixed-price Army contracts for the manufacture of precision equipment. Because of rigid economies he instituted, these contracts proved highly profitable. These profits and Berk's skillful financial management soon rehabilitated the company. By the end of 1981, the deficit accumulated during the years of unprofitable operations had been eliminated. (Financial statements for 1981, 1982, and the first half of 1983, appear in Exhibits 1 and 2.)

When the Army contracts were completed and no follow-on work with the Army could be obtained, Berks took steps to curtail overhead expenses, but he retained the company's skilled machinists. Efforts were concentrated on the industrial fastening machine, demand for which was good. Monthly shipments during the first half of 1983 averaged about 75 units priced at $1,200 each. More units could have been sold and shipped, but Berks did not wish to risk overextending the company while conditions were so unsettled.

Early in May an invitation was received to bid on an Army contract for the manufacture of 301 specialized field trailers. Berks thought that a good profit could be made on the trailers, so he decided to submit a bid. His first bid of

EXHIBIT 1

READING MANUFACTURING COMPANY
Balance Sheets

	Dec. 31, 1981	Dec. 31, 1982	June 30, 1983
Assets			
Current assets:			
Cash....................................	$ 77,892	$ 96,396	$166,518
Accounts receivable, net........................	288,642	177,498	117,558
Inventory...................................	273,084	204,096	
Raw material...............................			78,804
Work in process............................			39,816
Prepaid expenses...........................	4,350	7,074	1,950
Total current assets	643,968	485,064	404,646
Fixed assets:			
Plant and equipment, at cost...................	279,042	282,918	286,656
Less: Accumulated depreciation................	87,204	119,496	126,342
Plant and equipment, net	191,838	163,422	160,314
Total assets	$835,806	$648,486	$564,960
Liabilities and Shareholders' Equity			
Current liabilities:			
Accounts payable...........................	$166,008	$104,028	$ 54,396
Accrued liabilities...........................	57,552	11,016	28,662
Taxes payable..............................	138,024	193,656	110,358*
Total current liabilities......................	361,584	308,700	193,416
Long-term liabilities.............................	214,980		
Shareholders' equity:			
Common stock..............................	228,000	228,000	228,000
Retained earnings...........................	31,242	111,786	143,544
Total liabilities and shareholders' equity..............	$835,806	$648,486	$564,960

*Payable as follows: $41,721 on September 15, 1983, and December 15, 1983; $6,729 on March 15, 1984, June 15, 1984, September 15, 1984, and December 15, 1984.

$4,320 a unit was rejected, but a second bid of $3,690 was accepted. One "proto-type" trailer was to be produced during August for the purpose of testing production methods. It was to be retained at the plant but invoiced on September 1 at $3,690. This unit was to be manufactured from materials on hand. Direct labor for this unit was estimated at $3,000. The lessons learned making the first unit were expected to enable the company to start trailer production at full scale about September 1. Production was expected to be maintained at a fairly constant rate until November 30. Delivery of the trailers was to start the first week in October and was to be made at the rate of 100 units a month during October, November, and December.

Estimated per unit direct costs of producing the trailer were as follows: labor, $1,452; and material, $768. In addition to the estimated direct labor cost of $1,452 per unit, Berks estimated that the buildup of the additional labor force needed for trailer production would re-

EXHIBIT 2

Income Statements

	Twelve Months Ending 12/31/81	Twelve Months Ending 12/31/82	Six Months Ending 6/30/83
Sales, net	$1,697,328	$1,989,450	$521,796
Cost of Sales:			
Material	219,288	582,390	130,080
Direct labor	698,196	514,548	91,674
Depreciation	39,090	32,292	19,452
Factory overhead	317,052	287,640	123,084
Total cost of sales	1,273,626	1,416,870	364,290
Gross margin	423,702	572,580	157,506
Less: Operating expense:			
Shipping expense	57,366	35,316	1,410
Selling expense	62,652	44,880	—
Administrative expense	189,198	259,800	88,650
Total operating expense	309,216	339,996	90,060
Net operating income	114,486	232,584	67,446
Other charges	1,848	3,126	—
Income before taxes	112,638	229,458	67,446
Tax expense	50,700	145,098	26,922
Net income	$ 61,938	$ 84,360	$ 40,524

quire some $15,000 in extra wage expense during August. Similarly, some $18,000 of additional wage expense was budgeted for December so as to permit less abrupt reduction of the work force upon completion of the contract. Virtually all of the $18,000 would be paid out in the first three weeks of December.

To insure against delays in delivery, Berks intended to keep a minimum of one month's supply of raw material on hand at all times during the production period. Work in process inventory for trailer production was expected to average $120,000 during the period of full-scale production. The great majority of the company's purchases were made on terms of amount due in 30 days ("net/30") after the purchased items were received, and invoices were paid promptly

when due. Wages were paid weekly.[1] The production process from raw material to finished product was estimated to take a month. The Army would accept shipments in lots of 25 units, and payment would be received about 60 days after shipment.

Estimated per unit direct costs of producing the fastening machine were as follows: materials, $240; and labor, $216. A minimum inventory of a three months' supply of raw material was currently considered necessary because of unsettled conditions. Work in process inventory for fastening machine production was expected to continue at the present level. All current inventory was usable.

---

[1]There were four paydays in July, five in August, four each in September and October, five in November, and four in December.

The length of the production process was four weeks. Units were shipped as soon as produced, and terms of sale were net/ 30. The company had a backlog of orders for 350 machines. Production and shipments, however, were expected to continue at the rate of about 75 units a month through the first quarter of 1984.

Monthly indirect expenses were currently running as follows: depreciation, $3,240; other factory overhead, $21,000; and administration, $14,100. Tooling for the Army contract started in July. During July and August, tooling expenses and experimental manufacture of the prototype were expected to increase factory overhead by about $7,200 a month. Starting in September, when full-scale production of the trailers was to begin, factory overhead was expected to become about $27,000 a month until the end of November. Administration expense was expected to increase to about $18,000 a month from September 1 to the end of December.

The Army contract had made necessary the purchase of $12,000 of special tools. Delivery of these tools was expected in August; it was to be paid for COD. Upon completion of the contract, these tools would be scrapped. An additional $30,000 would also have to be spent for the replacement of old machinery that appeared to be nearing the end of its useful life. There was no way of knowing, however, when this machinery would finally break down. Berks was confident that he could find replacement equipment within a few days in the event of an emergency.

Berks worked out a tentative purchase schedule for the various material requirements (Exhibit 3). It shows the amounts of purchases in the months that the purchased items were expected to be received by Reading.

The company maintained a small deposit account with a local bank and kept the remainder of its cash in an account with the Fourth National Bank, a medium-sized bank with a legal loan limit of $900,000. Berks had discussed the company's prospects in general terms with the bank's officers on a number of occasions, but he had never requested a loan.

Berks considered the current cash balance of almost $167,000 to be in excess of operating needs. He was willing to reduce cash to a minimum of $30,000. No dividend payments were scheduled for the rest of 1983.

It was Berk's policy not to plan more than six months in advance, since he believed it was impossible to predict with any accuracy what was going to happen for a longer period. The company's plans for the first half of 1984 would be made

EXHIBIT 3

Tentative Schedule of Purchases
July–December, 1983

	July	Aug.	Sept.	Oct.	Nov.	Dec.
Raw material (fasteners)	—	$ 11,964	$18,000	$18,000	$18,000	$18,000
Raw material (trailers)	—	76,800	76,800	76,800	—	—
Special tools (trailers)	—	12,000	—	—	—	—
Total	—	$100,764	$94,800	$94,800	$18,000	$18,000
Replacement machinery	$30,000 (uncertain date)					

in the light of conditions as they developed and of the company's prospective financial condition at the end of 1983.

Questions

1. Set up a worksheet, with columns for each of the next six months (July–December 1983), and develop a schedule of monthly cash inflows and outflows. In preparing this schedule, assume the following:

    a. All accounts receivable as of June 30, 1983, are collected in July, and all June 30, 1983, accounts payable are paid in July.

    b. Work in process inventories, prepaid expenses, and accrued liabilities will remain constant at their June 30, 1983, levels.

    c. The $30,000 machine will be purchased in July 1983.

    Remembering Berk's desire to have a min-imum cash balance of $30,000, what does your schedule reveal about Reading's borrowing needs over the next six months?

2. Use the data from the case and from your cash flow worksheet to prepare a budgeted income statement for the six months ending December 31, 1983; a projected balance sheet as of December 31, 1983; and a budgeted cash flow statement for the six months ending December 31, 1983. Assume a tax rate of 40 percent and ignore interest on any new borrowings that will be needed during these six months. Assume the old machine replaced in July had originally cost $20,000, was fully depreciated, and had no residual value. For preparing these three statements, you will probably find it useful to draw up T-accounts for each balance sheet and income statement account, and post six-month totals from your cash flow worksheet (appropriately adjusted to the accrual basis) to these accounts.

26

Analyzing and Reporting Performance

This chapter describes analytical techniques for identifying the several types of variances between planned and actual results. These techniques decompose the total difference between planned and actual performance into elements that can be assigned to individual responsibility centers. Based on these assigned variances, management is able to ask relevant questions about the causes of the variances and to take appropriate action based on this investigation. Also described in this chapter is the use of control reports for communicating actual results to managers.

OVERVIEW OF THE ANALYTICAL PROCESS

Management wants to know not only *what* the amounts of the differences between actual and planned results were, but also, and more importantly, *why* these variances occurred. In a given company, the techniques used to analyze variances depend on management's judgment as to how useful the results are likely to be. Some companies do not use any formal techniques; others use only a few of those described here; and still others use even more sophisticated techniques. There are no prescribed criteria beyond the general rule that any technique should provide information worth more than the costs involved in developing it.

We shall refer to the data with which actual performance is being compared as the *budgeted* data because, as was emphasized in Chapter

25, a carefully prepared budget is usually the best indication of what performance should be. The same techniques can be used to analyze actual performance in terms of any other basis of comparison, such as performance in some prior period or in some other responsibility center. Although our principal focus is in analyzing the performance of responsibility centers in a business company, the same general approach can be used for analyzing any situation in which inputs are used to produce outputs.

In Chapter 19, we used the term *variance* for the difference between actual and standard production costs. We shall now broaden the meaning of this word to include the difference between the actual amount and the budgeted amount of *any* revenue or cost item, or of margin (contribution margin, gross margin, or operating margin).

An *unfavorable* variance is one whose effect is to make actual net income lower than budgeted net income. Thus, an unfavorable revenue variance occurs when actual revenue is *less* than budgeted revenue, but an unfavorable cost variance occurs when actual cost is *higher* than budgeted cost. Corresponding statements can of course be made about favorable variances.

It should be reemphasized, however, that the words *favorable* and *unfavorable* do *not* necessarily connote value judgments about managerial performance. For example, a purchasing agent might create a "favorable" material price variance by purchasing substandard materials, which probably is not a "good" thing for the company. Similarly, many variances are uncontrollable by a company's managers (e.g., an increase in fuel oil cost per gallon), and so do not connote either good or poor management performance. Thus, "unfavorable" and "favorable" indicate *only the algebraic impact* of a variance on net income. As in Chapter 20, these terms will be abbreviated as "U" and "F," respectively.

In looking at the business as a whole, attention ultimately is directed to the "bottom line," the amount of net income. (In this discussion we exclude nonoperating items, extraordinary items, and income taxes, and hence focus on *operating income*.) If in a certain company budgeted operating income in April was $82,000 and actual operating income was only $78,000, the $4,000 U variance indicates that something went wrong in April. It does not, however, indicate *what* went wrong. In order to take effective action, management needs to identify the variances in specific items that together explain the total unfavorable variance.

Variance items can be grouped into three categories, each of which corresponds roughly to an area of responsibility within a company:

1. Marketing variances, which are the responsibility of the marketing organization.
2. Production cost variances, which are the responsibility of the production organization.

ILLUSTRATION 26–1
OVERVIEW OF VARIANCE ANALYSIS

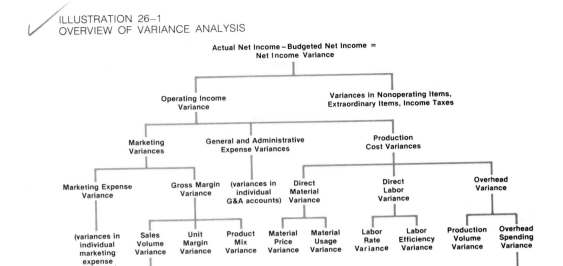

3. Other variances (administrative, nonoperating items, and so on), which are the responsibility of top management and its staff units.

This categorization, together with more detailed subdivisions, is depicted in Illustration 26–1. This variance "tree" serves to remind us that whatever the specific variance we are calculating, the overriding objective is to explain why budgeted and actual *net income* differed.

MARKETING VARIANCES

The objectives of the typical marketing organization include: (1) generating its budgeted gross margin and (2) doing so within the spending limits described in its expense budget.[1] Analysis of its success in meeting these objectives requires the calculation of marketing expense variances and gross margin variances.

Most marketing expense variance components are easy to calculate: for each item of marketing expense, actual costs are subtracted from the budgeted amount. For example, if the year's advertising budget was $750,000, but actual advertising costs were $800,000, then clearly there was a $50,000 unfavorable variance. What is *not* easy is determining

---

[1] Many marketers view their overall goal as generating budgeted *revenues*. This, however, is too narrow a view of marketing's real impact on a company's profitability.

whether there was sufficient justification for overspending the advertising budget. This is because advertising, like most marketing expenses, is a *discretionary* cost.

Gross Margin Variance

Gross margin is the difference between sales revenue and cost of sales. Total sales revenue is the sum of the multiplications of each product's sales volume (in physical units) times its unit selling price. Similarly, total cost of sales is the sum of the multiplications of each product's sales volume times its unit cost. In most instances, the marketing department is responsible for products' sales volumes and unit selling prices, but not for their unit costs. Accordingly, when calculating gross margin variances, *cost* per unit should be a *standard* amount. This procedure is followed so that differences between actual and standard unit costs, which are *production* variances, do not cloud the picture of which variances the marketing organization can reasonably be asked to explain.

The total gross margin variance is the difference between actual and budgeted total gross margin (both based on *standard* unit costs). For example:

	Actual	Budgeted	Difference (Δ)
Unit gross margin	$ 11*	$ 10†	$ 1
Volume, units	900	1,000	(100)
Gross margin	$9,900	$10,000	
Gross margin variance		$100 U	

*Based on $33 actual selling price and $22 standard unit cost.
†Based on $32 budgeted selling price and $22 standard unit cost.

Why Work with Margins?   Before illustrating how this gross margin variance can be decomposed into several elements, we should first explain why it is more useful to work with gross margins, rather than separately with revenues and cost of sales. The reason why this is so can be seen by first considering this table:

	Unit Amount*	Budget		Actual		
		Units	Total	Units	Total	Variance
Sales revenue	$25	1,000	$25,000	800	$20,000	$5,000 U
Cost of sales	15	1,000	15,000	800	12,000	3,000 F
Gross margin	$10	1,000	$10,000	800	$ 8,000	$2,000 U

*Budgeted and actual.

Since budgeted and actual unit margins were the same ($10 per unit), the $2,000 unfavorable gross margin variance clearly was caused by the 200-unit shortfall in sales volume. The $5,000 U revenue variance overstates the *income* impact of this shortfall, however, because this was partially offset by the related $3,000 F cost of sales variance. The *real* impact of the lower volume was the net of these two amounts, which is the $2,000 U variance in gross margin. This $2,000 is the appropriate amount about which to question the marketing group, for it is their job to generate gross margin, the *spread* between sales revenue and cost of sales.

Types of Gross Margin Variances.   The gross margin variance can be decomposed into three components:

1.   The *unit margin variance*, which arises because the actual gross margin per unit was different from the budgeted gross margin.
2.   The *sales volume variance*, which arises because the actual sales volume, in units, was different from the budgeted sales volume.
3.   The *mix variance*, which arises because some products had higher unit margins than others and the actual proportions of products (i.e., product mix) with various unit margins were different from the budgeted proportions.

We shall first describe how to isolate the unit margin and sales volume variances. In order to defer the description of the mix variance, we shall assume in these calculations that the company has a single product.

Unit Margin and Sales Volume Variances.   The $100 U gross margin variance ($9,900–$10,000) calculated in the earlier example is explainable in terms of a $1 variance in unit margin (in this case caused by a change in the unit selling price) and a 100-unit variance in sales volume. One can see almost intuitively that (1) the higher unit margin increased gross margin by $900 ($1 per unit for each of the 900 units sold) and (2) the 100-unit volume shortfall would have decreased gross margin by $1,000 (100 units at $10) *if* the per unit margin had been as planned. Using Δ to denote the difference between an actual and a budgeted amount, this intuitive derivation can be formalized as follows:

Δ Unit margin	×	Actual volume	=	Unit margin variance
$1	×	900	=	$900 F
Δ Volume	×	Budgeted unit margin	=	Sales volume variance
(100)	×	$10	=	$1,000 U
Actual gross margin	−	Budgeted gross margin	=	Net gross margin variance
$9,900	−	$10,000	=	$100 U

Note that these formulas are set up in such a way that favorable variances will be algebraically positive and unfavorable variances will be algebraically negative. However, it is easier—and a better test of understanding—to use common sense rather than formula memorization to determine whether a variance is favorable or unfavorable.

Graphic Aids. The graphic aids that were presented in Illustrations 20–1 and 20–2 can be easily adapted to apply to gross margin variances. Illustration 26–2 (adapted from Illustration 20–1) shows that in decomposing the total margin variance into its volume and unit margin components, in effect we create a hypothetical "after-the-fact" margin budget, based on *actual* volume but *budgeted* unit margin. This is the middle column in Illustration 26–2, labeled AVBM. The sales volume variance is the difference between the original margin budget, BVBM, and this hypothetical budget. The unit margin variance is the difference between total actual gross margin (again, based on actual volume and actual unit price, but on *standard* unit cost), AVAM, and the hypothetical budget, AVBM.

ILLUSTRATION 26–2
DIAGRAM OF GROSS MARGIN VARIANCES

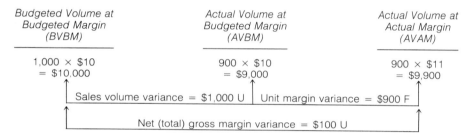

Budgeted Volume at Budgeted Margin (BVBM)	Actual Volume at Budgeted Margin (AVBM)	Actual Volume at Actual Margin (AVAM)
1,000 × $10 = $10,000	900 × $10 = $9,000	900 × $11 = $9,900

Sales volume variance = $1,000 U | Unit margin variance = $900 F

Net (total) gross margin variance = $100 U

If during the period the standard unit cost turns out to be equal to the standard unit cost that was budgeted, then any Δ unit margin will be caused solely by a difference between actual and budgeted selling price per unit. For this reason, the unit margin variance is sometimes called a *selling price* variance. But the importance of the unit margin variance is in monitoring whether the *spread* between selling price and cost of goods sold has been maintained, not whether selling price has been changed. Thus, if during the period *both* the standard unit cost *and* the selling price were increased by equal amounts, the budgeted and actual unit margins would be the same and there would be zero unit margin variance. In periods of rapid inflation, it is not unusual for both standard unit costs and selling prices to be increased one or more times during a year.

Further Decomposition of Variances. It is sometimes possible to break down the margin variances even further, and since these variances are usually the most important causes of changes in net income, further breakdowns are worthwhile. The volume variance can be subdivided if data are available on total sales of a product by all companies. From these data, a company can compute its *market share*, that is, the percentage of its sales to total industry sales. Variances caused by changes in total industry sales reflect general economic conditions, whereas variations caused by changes in market share are the responsibility of the company's own marketing organization. The formulas for this decomposition of sales volume variance are:

$$\frac{\text{Industry}}{\text{volume variance}} = \frac{\Delta\,\text{Industry}}{\text{volume}} \times \frac{\text{Budgeted}}{\text{market share}} \times \frac{\text{Budgeted}}{\text{unit margin}}$$

$$\frac{\text{Market}}{\text{share variance}} = \frac{\Delta\,\text{Market}}{\text{share}} \times \frac{\text{Actual}}{\text{industry volume}} \times \frac{\text{Budgeted}}{\text{unit margin}}$$

Similarly, the unit margin variance can sometimes be decomposed into the portion attributable to general price movements and the portion attributable to the company's own pricing tactics.

In multiproduct companies, margin variance analyses are performed for each product line, and in some instances for individual products within a line. It is also possible to subdivide margin variances by different responsibility centers, such as a firm's district sales offices.

Mix Variance. When a company sells several products having *different* unit gross margins, the total gross margin is influenced by the relative proportions or "mix" of high-margin to low-margin products that are sold. The difference in gross margin caused by the difference between the proportions assumed in the budget and the actual proportions sold is the *mix variance*. This variance did not show up in the preceding examples because we assumed the company had only one product. Neither would it show up in a multiproduct situation if the actual and budgeted unit margins were the *average* of those for all products.

The portion of the mix variance attributable to each product is calculated from the difference between the actual quantity sold and the budgeted *proportion* for that product, that is, the quantity that would have been sold if that product's sales had been the budgeted *percentage* of actual sales volume. The mix variance is the sum of these amounts for all products.

The calculations of all three margin variances are shown in Illustration 26–3. The assumed situation is similar to that in Illustration 26–2, except that we now assume that the company makes three products, each with a different gross margin. In the budget, it was planned that 30 percent of sales would be in product A, which has a relatively low unit margin, and 30 percent would be in product C, which has a relatively high unit margin. In the period, actual sales (in units) of the low-margin product A were only 20 percent of the total, and actual sales of the high-margin product C were 40 percent of the total. The actual mix was thus "richer" than planned; this produced a favorable mix variance of $180.

Note in Illustration 26–3 that the approach is similar to Illustration 26–2, except that in 26–3 we create *two* hypothetical after-the-fact margin budgets. One is based on what the volume of each product *would have been* had the actual total volume been distributed among

ILLUSTRATION 26–3
MARGIN VARIANCES FOR MULTIPLE PRODUCTS

A. Assumed Situation

Product	Budget Volume Per-cent	Budget Volume Units	Budget Unit Margin	Budget Total Margin	Actual Volume Per-cent	Actual Volume Units	Actual Unit Margin	Actual Total Margin
A	30	300	$ 9.00	$ 2,700	20	180	$ 9.50	$1,710
B	40	400	10.00	4,000	40	360	11.00	3,960
C	30	300	11.00	3,300	40	360	11.75	4,230
Total	100	1,000	$10.00*	$10,000	100	900	$11.00*	$9,900

*These are averages derived from total volume and total margin: that is, $10,000 ÷ 1,000 = $10.00; $9,900 ÷ 900 = $11.00.

B. Variance Calculations

Product	Budgeted Volume at Budgeted Mix at Budgeted Margin	Sales volume variance	Actual Volume at Budgeted Mix at Budgeted Margin*	Mix variance	Actual Volume at Actual Mix at Budgeted Margin	Unit margin variance	Actual Volume at Actual Mix at Actual Margin
A	300 @ $9 = $2,700		270 @ $9 = $2,430		180 @ $9 = $1,620		180 @ $9.50 = $1,710
		$ 270 U		$810 U		$ 90 F	
B	400 @ $10 = $4,000		360 @ $10 = $3,600		360 @ $10 = $3,600		360 @ $11 = $3,960
		400 U		0		360 F	
C	300 @ $11 = $3,300		270 @ $11 = $2,970		360 @ $11 = $3,960		360 @ $11.75 = $4,230
		330 U		990 F		270 F	
Total	$10,000	$1,000 U	$9,000	$180 F	$9,180	$720 F	$9,900

*Budgeted volume percentage for each product applied to total actual volume (e.g., 30 percent × 900 = 270 for product A).

the products in the *budgeted* mix proportions. The other is based on *actual* mix. If we work only with the budgeted and actual *average* margins of $10 and $11, respectively (shown in Part A of 26–3), Illustration 26–2 can be applied to this multiproduct situation. But if we look at products individually (as in 26–3), the $900 F unit margin variance in 26–2 is shown to be the sum of a $720 F unit margin variance and a $180 F mix variance.[2]

The mix concept is often used in analyzing gross margin variances. It is important to know to what extent the total variance was caused by changes in the "richness" of the sales mix. The mix concept has wider applicability, however. In general, a mix variance can be developed whenever a cost or revenue item is broken down into components, and the components have different unit prices. When a price variance is computed by use of an average price, we do not know whether the variance is caused by a true difference in prices, or whether it is caused by a change in the proportion of the elements that make up the total, that is, by a change in mix. For example, if instead of using the total number of direct labor-hours and the *average* hourly earnings rate in calculating the labor variances, we use the number of direct labor-hours in each skill category and the hourly earnings rate for that skill category, a labor mix variance can be developed. In general, in situations where there are multiple inputs (e.g., material prices, labor rates) or multiple outputs (e.g., several products), a price or unit margin variance calculated using average prices or margins can be decomposed into a "true" price or unit margin variance and a mix variance.

Some chemical companies and other companies whose manufacturing process consists primarily of combining several raw materials into finished products compute a material mix variance. Most companies do not compute material and labor mix variances, however. They have decided that the additional information is not worth the cost of calculating it.

Other Approaches. In the above analysis, we have assumed the company uses a standard full cost system, and cost of goods sold therefore is stated at full standard production cost. This, in fact, is a common approach, since most companies want to explain the gross margin variance using the same accounting conventions as they use in their shareholder income statements. However, other approaches are possible. If the company uses a variable cost system, cost of goods sold will include

---

[2] A short-cut formula for calculating *total* mix variance is:

$$\left(\begin{array}{c} \text{Average budgeted margin} \\ \text{at actual mix} \end{array} - \begin{array}{c} \text{Average budgeted margin} \\ \text{at budgeted mix} \end{array} \right) \times \begin{array}{c} \text{Actual} \\ \text{volume} \end{array}$$

In the example, the average budgeted margin at actual mix is [(180 × $9) + (360 × $10) + (360 × $11)] ÷ 900 = $10.20. Therefore, mix variance = ($10.20 − $10.00) × 900 = $180 F. However, this short-cut formula does not reveal each product's portion of the mix variance. For this reason also, we have not presented the "one-line" formulas for total unit margin and sales volume variances in a multiproduct situation.

only the variable production costs, and this will lead to some differences in the analysis of variances. At the other extreme, if the company treats the factory as a profit center, goods will be transferred to the marketing department at an amount that includes an element for profit, and this will affect the analysis also. These alternatives are discussed in advanced texts.

PRODUCTION COST VARIANCES

Because of their close relationship with standard costing systems (Chapter 19), production cost variances were described in Chapter 20. At this point we shall review one aspect of production cost variances that many people find especially difficult.

Using the formulas presented in Chapter 20, variances can be calculated for each of the three elements of production cost: direct labor, direct material, and production overhead. When calculating these variances, it is necessary to understand clearly what is meant by the "budgeted" amounts in production cost variance formulas because the concept of a production cost budget differs from that of a gross margin budget.

Correct Volume Measures

The overall goal in variance analysis is to explain the difference between actual and budgeted net income. Actual net income is a function of actual *sales* volume, and budgeted net income is dependent on budgeted *sales* volume. Thus, the formula for gross margin sales volume variance appropriately was based on the difference between these actual and budgeted sales volumes.

The analysis of production variances makes no use of *sales* volumes. The only relevant volume is the *production* volume, and a difference between actual and budgeted production volume generates only one variance, the overhead volume variance that was explained in Chapter 20. No volume variance arises for direct material costs or direct labor costs, however, because net income is *not* affected by a difference between the actual and planned production volume for these items. This is because these production costs are capitalized in inventory accounts as incurred, and these costs do not impact the income statement until the period in which the goods are sold. Thus, for a given level of actual sales volume, if production volume is greater than was planned, the additional direct material and direct labor costs are reflected in an inventory (asset) buildup, not on the income statement. (A similar statement applies when actual production volume is less than was planned.)

For this reason, when calculating material and labor cost variances as part of an analysis of income variance, the *budgeted* production volume is essentially an irrelevant number. Rather, we want to compare what these costs actually were with what these costs should have been for the *actual* volume of goods produced. Thus, in material and labor cost variance formulas, "actual cost" means actual cost at actual volume, and "budgeted cost" or "standard cost" means standard costs for the *actual volume.* In other words, for purposes of material and labor cost variance analysis, the budgeted cost amount is developed *after the fact,* based on the *known actual* production volume, rather than on the production volume that was planned prior to the start of the accounting period.

To illustrate the irrelevance of planned production volume in an analysis of material and labor cost variances, consider this example:

	Month of August	
	Budget	Actual
Production volume, units	500	600
Direct materials cost, per unit...................	$10.00	$10.00
Direct materials cost, total......................	$5,000	$6,000

In an important sense, there is *no* direct materials variance here. The amount that *should* have been spent for direct materials for the 600 units produced in August was $10 per unit, or $6,000 total; and $6,000 *was* the actual direct materials cost. The $1,000 difference between budgeted and actual total direct materials cost only reflects the fact that, for whatever reason, 100 more units were produced than had originally been planned. In particular, this $1,000 difference does *not* suggest poor performance relative to the usage of materials.

Knowing the reasons why production volume was 100 units above plan *is* important. But the fact that it *was* 100 units larger (and $1,000 greater for the direct materials component of these goods) than if the original production plan had been followed gives us no useful insights for explaining net income variance or for raising questions about managerial performance. Specifically, if the company's August net income variance was $12,000 U, *no part* of this $12,000 variance is accounted for by the $1,000 difference between actual direct materials cost and the original materials budget.[3]

In summary:

- The gross margin sales volume variance results from a difference between budgeted and actual *sales* volume.
- The overhead volume variance, which results from a difference between budgeted and actual *production* volume, relates solely to overhead costs.
- There is no volume variance for direct material costs or direct labor costs.

---

[3]This $1,000 difference, caused solely by a difference between planned and actual production volumes, is called by some authors a "production volume variance" or "budget adjustment variance." These labels are misleading, since this difference is not a component of overall net income variance.

OTHER VARIANCES

Conceptually, it would be possible to decompose the total variance in items of general and administrative expenses, and some nonoperating items, into volume and spending components, as was done for production overhead costs. Ordinarily this is not done, however. Instead, the differences between actual and budgeted amounts are simply listed. Most of these items are discretionary costs, and the expectation is that the budgeted amounts will be adhered to regardless of volume fluctuations. Isolation of a volume variance under these circumstances would not be appropriate.

COMPLETE ANALYSIS

As a way of summarizing the techniques described in Chapter 20 and in this chapter, the complete analysis of a simple situation is shown in Illustration 26–4. The income statement (Section A) shows a variance between the month's actual and budgeted income of $59 U. (For simplicity, all amounts except *unit* costs and margins are in thousands; thus, a volume of 200 means 200,000 units, and $59 means $59,000.) The question is: What accounts for this $59 variance? The answer to this question

ILLUSTRATION 26–4
COMPUTATION OF VARIANCES

A. Income Statement
Month of November

	Budget	Actual	Variance
Sales	$540	$551	
Less: Standard cost of sales	440	418	
Gross margin at standard cost	100	133	$33 F
Production variances	0	82	82 U
Gross margin	100	51	49 U
Selling, general, and administrative expense	40	50	10 U
Income before taxes	$ 60	$ 1	$59 U

B. Summary of Variances

Unit margin	$38 F
Sales volume	5 U
Net margin	33 F
Material price	16 U
Material usage	4 F
Labor rate	8 U
Labor efficiency	24 U
Overhead production volume	15 U
Overhead spending	23 U
Net production	82 U
Selling, general, and administrative	10 U
Income variance	$59 U

ILLUSTRATION 26–4 *(concluded)*

C. Gross Margin Variances

	Sales (units)	Unit Margin	Total Margin
Underlying data:			
Budget................................	200	$0.50	$100
Actual................................	190	0.70	133
Net margin variance......................			$ 33 F

Unit margin variance:

$$\Delta \text{ Unit margin } \times \text{ Actual units } = \text{ Unit margin variance}$$
$$\$0.20 \quad \times \quad 190 \quad = \quad \$38 \text{ F}$$

Sales volume variance.

$$\Delta \text{ Volume } \times \text{ Budgeted unit margin } = \text{ Sales volume variance}$$
$$(10) \quad \times \quad \$0.50 \quad = \quad \$5 \text{ U}$$

D. Production Cost Variances

Underlying Data, Costs

Item	Standard	Actual
Production volume	200 units*	170 units
Direct material	2 lbs./unit at $0.20 per lb.	320 lbs. at $0.25 = $80
Direct labor	0.4 hrs./unit at $2.00 per hr.	80 hrs. at $2.10 = $168
Overhead	$100 per mo. + $0.50 per unit	$208

* Based on annual standard volume of 2,400 units.

Computation of Cost Variances

(1) *Material price variance:*

$$\Delta \text{ Price } \times \text{ Actual quantity } = \text{ Material price variance}$$
$$(\$0.05) \quad \times \quad 320 \quad = \quad \$16 \text{ U}$$

(2) *Material usage variance:*

$$\Delta \text{ Quantity } \times \text{ Standard price } = \text{ Material usage variance}$$
$$20^* \quad \times \quad \$0.20 \quad = \quad \$4 \text{ F}$$

*170 units at 2 lbs per unit standard minus 320 lbs. actual.

(3) *Labor rate variance:*

$$\Delta \text{ Rate } \times \text{ Actual hours } = \text{ Labor rate variance}$$
$$(\$0.10) \times \quad 80 \quad = \quad \$8 \text{ U}$$

(4) *Labor efficiency variance:*

$$\Delta \text{ Hours } \times \text{ Standard rate } = \text{ Labor efficiency variance}$$
$$(12^*) \quad \times \quad \$2.00 \quad = \quad \$24 \text{ U}$$

*170 units at 0.4 hours per unit standard minus 80 hours actual.

(5) *Overhead production volume variance:*

Absorbed overhead: 170 units × $1 per unit*......................	$170
Budgeted overhead: $100 + ($0.50 × 170 units).................	185
Overhead production volume variance	$ 15 U

*Annual overhead rate = [$1,200 + ($0.50 × 2,400 units)] ÷ 2,400 units = $1 per unit.

(6) *Overhead spending variance:*

Budgeted overhead (as above).................................	$185
Actual overhead	208
Overhead spending variance.................................	$ 23 U

is given in Section B, which decomposes the total variance into elements. The remainder of the Illustration shows how each of these elements was found.

Marketing Variances

The first step in the computation is to analyze the difference between budgeted and actual gross margins. This part of the analysis is shown in Section C. The unit margin is the difference between *standard* unit cost of sales (which was $2.20) and selling prices. Budgeted selling price was $2.70 per unit, and actual selling price was $2.90 per unit, so the budgeted unit margin was $0.50 and the actual unit margin was $0.70.

The unit margin variance is determined by multiplying the actual sales quantities for each product by the difference between actual and budgeted unit margins. (In the interest of brevity, a mix variance is not shown.) The sales volume variance is the loss or gain in gross margin that results from a difference between actual and budgeted sales volume. The algebraic sum of the unit margin variance ($38 F) and the sales volume variance ($5 U) is the $33 F shown as the variance in gross margin on the income statement. Note that margin variances are favorable when actual is greater than budget, which is of course the opposite situation from cost variances.

Although the separate accounts making up the "Selling, general, and administrative expense" category are not detailed in Illustration 26–4, in practice those accounts related to marketing activities would be isolated, and budgeted versus actual amounts would be calculated. These marketing-related variances would then be added to the gross margin variances to arrive at the total marketing variance.

Production Cost Variances

Next we turn to an analysis of the production cost variances. Note that, as shown in Section D, actual production volume (170 units) is less than actual sales volume (190 units), the difference being made up out of inventory that is carried at standard cost. Note also that the monthly standard volume of 200 units is irrelevant to the calculation of direct material and direct labor variances. It does signal us that there will be an overhead volume variance in November because actual volume differs from 200 units, which is the volume used for setting the predetermined overhead rate. Carrying the inventory at standard cost means that expense variances are treated as period costs (for management accounting purposes) and charged directly to cost of sales during the period in which they occur. The labor, material, and production overhead variances described in Chapter 20 are calculated in Section D. Their algebraic sum equals the $82 U production cost variance noted on the income statement.

An examination of variances in general and administrative expense items completes the analysis of the income variance. This is not shown. It would consist of an analysis of the amount of and reasons for differences between the budgeted amount and the actual amount for each item of general and administrative expense.

Uses of Variances   Analyzing the difference between actual and budgeted income involves many detailed calculations of individual variances. It is easy to get so involved in these details that one loses sight of the purpose of variance analysis, which is to identify the various *causes* of the overall income variance. The decomposition of income variances into many elements enables assigning these elements to specific responsibility centers, and hence to specific managers.

This assignment of variance elements to managers only raises questions about performance, however. Variance calculations themselves do not explain performance,. Although an unfavorable variance means that actual income is lower than planned, that is all that is connoted by the "unfavorable" label. It does *not* necessarily mean that a manager performed poorly. Similarly, favorable variances do not necessarily imply good performance.

> **Example.** For December, the machining department of Apex Valve Company had a $7,000 U spending variance in its maintenance account (one of the production overhead accounts). Investigation revealed that the department's manager had spent $8,000 in December for an unanticipated overhaul of a machine. Without the overhaul, the variance would have been $1,000 F. However, the maintenance department had advised the machining department's manager that the machine would be worn beyond repair in six months without the overhaul, requiring a replacement machine costing $70,000. After understanding the situation, the factory manager praised the machining department manager for exercising good judgment in authorizing the overhaul.

As this example indicates, incorrect and inequitable signals may be given to managers about their performance if their superiors automatically draw performance inferences from variance reports, rather than investigating the causes of the variances.

Another natural—but unwise—tendency is for managers to pay far more attention to unfavorable variances than to favorable ones. The example above illustrates the problems inherent in not investigating favorable variances. The variance would have been $1,000 F without the overhaul, yet the decision not to overhaul the machine would have been a poor one.

It is also important when investigating variances to distinguish between those that are *controllable* by a responsibility center's manager from those that are noncontrollable. While both types of variances are helpful in explaining the responsibility center's *economic* performance, for purposes of evaluating the center's *managerial* performance the focus should be on the controllable variances.

The example also illustrates a possible cause of *any* variance: the budgeted amounts may have been based on assumed conditions that were different from those that actually prevailed. In the example, the overhaul was not anticipated when the budget was prepared. Thus, variances often reflect managers' forecasting fallibilities rather than their operating management weaknesses.

In sum, variances can be very useful in signaling *possible* managerial strengths or shortcomings. But automatically equating "favorable" to "good performance," and "unfavorable" to "poor performance," can sometimes lead to unjustified appraisal judgments by superiors, and can thereby demoralize subordinate managers and create hostility on their part.

CONTROL REPORTS

Types of Management Reports

Three types of reports are prepared for the use of managers: (1) information reports; (2) economic performance reports; and (3) personal performance, or control, reports. We shall discuss primarily the third type, but will mention briefly the nature of the other two types because they are important parts of the total communications that managers receive.

Information reports are designed to tell management what is going on. Each reader studies these reports to detect whether or not something has happened that requires investigation. If nothing of significance is noted, which is often the case, the report is put aside without action. If something does strike the reader's attention, an inquiry or an action is initiated. The information on these reports may come from the accounting system. It may also come from a wide variety of other sources, including such external information as news summaries, stock prices, information from industry trade associations, and economic information published by the government.

Performance Reports. There are two general types of reports about the performance of a responsibility center. One type deals with its performance as an *economic entity*. A conventional income statement prepared for a profit center is an *economic performance report,* and the net income shown is a basic measure of economic performance. Economic performance reports are derived from conventional accounting information, including full cost accounting.

The other type of performance report focuses on the performance of the *manager* of the profit center. This is usually referred to as a *control report*. Control reports are prepared from responsibility accounting information. Essentially they report how well the manager did compared with some standard of what the manager was expected to do.

The control report may show that a profit center manager is doing an excellent job, considering the circumstances. But if the profit center is not producing a satisfactory profit, action may be required regardless of this fact. There are therefore two different ways in which the performance of a responsibility center is judged. The control report focuses on the manager's responsibility for turning in an actual performance that corresponds to the commitment made during the budget preparation process. *Behavioral* considerations are important in the use of this report. The economic performance report focuses on an analysis of the responsibility center as an economic entity. In this analysis, *economic* considerations are dominant. The following discussion is limited to control reports.

Contents of Control Reports

The essential purpose of a control report is to compare actual performance in a responsibility center with what performance should have been under the *circumstances prevailing*, in such a way that reasons for the difference between actual and standard performance are identified and, if feasible, quantified. It follows that three kinds of information are conveyed in such reports: (1) information on what performance *actually was*; (2) information on what performance *should have been*; and (3) *reasons for the difference* between actual and expected performance.

The foregoing suggests three essential characteristics of good control reports:

1. Reports should be related to personal responsibility.
2. Actual performance should be compared with the best available standard.
3. Significant information should be highlighted.

As a basis for discussing these points, we shall use the set of control reports shown in Illustration 26–5.

Focus on Personal Responsibility. In Chapters 23 and 24 we emphasized *responsibility accounting*, the type of accounting that classifies costs and revenues according to the responsibility centers that are responsible for incurring the costs and generating the revenues. Responsibility accounting therefore provides information that meets the criterion that reports should be related to personal responsibility.

Responsibility accounting also classifies the costs assigned to each responsibility center according to whether they are controllable or noncontrollable. Many companies' control reports show only controllable costs. Other companies' reports also contain noncontrollable costs for information purposes. In Illustration 26–5, only controllable costs are reported—direct labor and controllable overhead. Direct material cost is not included on these reports because neither the quantity nor the price of material used is controllable by these department managers. The drill press manager is responsible, however, for repair and rework costs of material or products that are defective, and this item of controllable cost does appear on the report.

Selection of a Standard. A report that contains information *only* on actual performance is virtually useless for control purposes. It becomes useful when actual performance is compared with some standard. Standards used in control reports are of three types: (1) predetermined standards or budgets, (2) historical standards, or (3) external standards.

Predetermined standards or budgets, if carefully prepared, are the

ILLUSTRATION 26–5
PACKAGE OF CONTROL REPORTS

A. First-Level (or, lowest) Report

Drill press department (supervisor)	Actual		(Over) or under Budget	
	June	*Year to Date*	*June*	*Year to Date*
Output:				
Standard direct labor-hours...............	810	4,060	85	401
Direct labor cost:				
Amount...........................	$ 3,860	$ 22,140	$ 360	$ 1,140
Efficiency variance...................			622	1,807
Rate variance			(262)	(667)
Controllable overhead:				
Setup costs........................	1,187	7,224	(265)	90
Repair and rework	520	2,916	180	91
Overtime premium	484	2,748	(75)	(530)
Supplies..........................	215	1,308	(121)	(386)
Small tools........................	260	1,521	160	(82)
Other............................	644	3,888	91	195
Total overhead	$ 3,310	$ 19,605	$ (30)	$ (620)

B. Second-Level Report

Production department cost summary (general superintendent)	Actual		Variance	
	June	*Year to Date*	*June*	*Year to Date*
Direct labor:				
Drill press........................	$ 3,860	$ 22,140	$ 360	$ 1,140
Lathe............................	5,240	31,760	540	1,560
Total	$27,120	$161,970	$3,020	$ 5,130
Controllable overhead:				
Office	$ 1,960	$ 12,300	$ (115)	$ (675)
Drill press........................	3,310	19,605	(30)	(620)
Lathe............................	3,115	18,085	90	(135)
Punch press	5,740	33,635	(65)	(640)
Plating...........................	1,865	9,795	(175)	825
Heat treating	3,195	18,015	210	35
Assembly	5,340	35,845	(625)	(1,380)
Total overhead	$24,525	$147,280	$ (710)	$(2,590)

ILLUSTRATION 26–5 *(concluded)*

C. Third-Level Report				
Factory cost summary (vice president of production)	Actual		(Over) or under Budget	
	June	Year to Date	June	Year to Date
Controllable overhead:				
Vice president's office.	$ 2,110	$ 12,030	$ (315)	$ 35
General superintendent	24,525	147,280	(710)	(2,590)
Production control	1,235	7,570	(125)	(210)
Purchasing.	1,180	7,045	95	75
Maintainance.	3,590	18,960	(235)	245
Tool room.	4,120	25,175	160	(320)
Inspection	2,245	13,680	180	(160)
Receiving, shipping, stores	3,630	22,965	(70)	(730)
Total overhead	$42,635	$254,705	$(1,020)	$(3,655)
Direct labor	$27,120	$161,970	$ 3,020	$ 5,130

best formal standard. The validity of such a standard depends largely on how much care went into its development. If the budget numbers were arrived at in a slipshod manner, they obviously will not provide a reliable basis for comparison.

Historical standards are records of past actual performance. Results for the current month may be compared with results for last month, or with results for the same month a year ago. This type of standard has two serious weaknesses: (1) conditions may have changed between the two periods in a way that invalidates the comparison; and (2) when managers are measured against their own past record, there may be no way of knowing whether the prior period's performance was acceptable to start with.

External standards are standards derived from the performance of other responsibility centers. The performance of one branch sales office may be compared with the performance of other branch sales offices, for example. If conditions in these responsibility centers are similar, such a comparison may provide a useful basis for judging performance. In practice, it is not easy to find two responsibility centers that are sufficiently similar, or whose performance is affected by the same factors, to permit such comparisons on a regular basis.

Highlighting Significant Information. The problem of designing a good set of control reports has changed drastically since the advent of the computer. When data had to be processed manually, care had to be taken to limit the quantity of information in reports because the cost of preparing them was relatively high. By contrast, a computer can print more figures in a minute than a manager can assimilate in a day. Thus, the current problem is to decide on the *right type* of information that should be given to management.

Individual cost and revenue elements therefore should be reported only when they are likely to be significant. The significance of an item is not necessarily proportional to its size. Management may be interested in a cost item of relatively small amount if this item is one which is largely discretionary and therefore warrants close attention (such as travel expense), or if costs incurred for the item may be symptomatic of a larger problem (such as rework costs, which may indicate quality control problems).

A management control system should operate on the *exception principle*. That is, a control report should focus management's attention on the relatively small number of items in which actual performance is significantly different from the standard. Little or no attention need to be given to the relatively large number of situations where performance is satisfactory.

No control system makes a perfect distinction between the situations that warrant management attention and those that do not. For example, although those items for which actual spending significantly *exceeds* the budgeted amount are usually "red flagged" for further investigation, the investigation of these items may reveal that the variance was entirely justified. Conversely, even though actual spending exactly matches the budget allowance, an unsatisfactory situation may exist.

> **Example.** When the general superintendent reads the production department cost summary report (Part B of Illustration 26–5), his or her attention is not called to the overhead performance of the drill press department in June because its actual costs were only $30 in excess of standard, an insignificant amount. We can observe from the details of drill press performance in Part A, however, that setup costs, overtime premium, and supplies are considerably in excess of standard, and these excesses may indicate that problems do exist.

Note that Illustration 26–5 does not show the budgeted amounts, but only the differences between actual and budget. Many control reports have three columns: (1) actual, (2) standard (or budget), and (3) variance. The "standard" column is actually not necessary because one can determine each standard amount by adding the actual and the variance.

Key Variables. In most organizations, and in most responsibility centers within them, there is a limited number of factors that must be watched closely. These are called *key variables* or *key success factors*. They are factors that can shift quickly and in an unpredictable way, and when they do shift they have a significant effect on performance. The number of such variables is small, no more than six or so in a given responsibility center. The reporting system should be designed so that particular attention is paid to them.

> **Example.** A dentist states that she needs to keep track of only three items to know how well she is doing financially: (1) billed hours (the

number of hours spent daily with patients), (2) accounts receivable as a ratio to monthly billings (as an indication of whether patients are paying their bills promptly), and (3) ratio of expenses of revenues.

Timing of Reports	The proper *control period*, that is, the period of time covered by one report, is the shortest period of time in which management can usefully intervene and in which significant changes in performance are likely. The period is different for different responsibility centers and for different items of cost and output within responsibility centers. Spoilage rates in a production operation may be reported hourly, or oftener, because if a machine starts to function improperly the situation must be corrected at once. Reports on sales orders received or sales revenue are often made daily or weekly. Reports on overall performance, particularly those going to top levels of management, usually are on a monthly basis.

The other aspect of report timing is the *interval* that elapses between the end of the period covered by the report and the issuance of the report itself. For monthly reports, the interval desirably should be less than a week. In order to meet this deadline, it may be necessary to make approximations of certain "actual" amounts for which exact information is not available. Such approximations are worthwhile because an approximately accurate report provided promptly is far preferable to a precisely accurate report that is furnished so long after the event that no effective action can be taken.

Use of Control Reports	The first question to be raised about a comparison between actual and expected performance is: Of what use is it? Managers' performance can be measured only *after* they have performed. But at that time the work has already been done, and no subsequent action by anyone can change what has been done. Of what value, therefore, are reports on past performance? There are two valid answers to this question.

First, if people know in advance that their performance is going to be measured, reported, and judged, they tend to act differently from the way they would have acted had they believed that no one was going to check up on them. Second, even though it is impossible to alter an event that has already happened, an analysis of how people have performed in the past may indicate ways of obtaining better performance in the future. Corrective action taken by people themselves is important; the system should "help people to help themselves." Action by the superior is also necessary. Such action ranges in severity from giving verbal criticism or praise, to suggesting specific means of improving future performance, to the extremes of firing or promoting a person.

Feedback. In engineering, the process called *feedback* refers to circuits that are arranged so that information about a device's current performance is fed back in such a way that the future performance of that device may be changed. A thermostat is a feedback device. If the temperature of a room drops below a prescribed level, the thermostat senses that information and activates the furnace. In an engineering diagram, the circuitry and associated control apparatus is called a *feedback loop*.

Control reports are feedback devices, but they are only one part of the feedback loop. Unlike the thermostat, which acts automatically in response to information about temperature, a control report *does not by itself* cause a change in performance. A change results only when managers take actions that lead to change. Thus, in management control, the feedback loop requires both the control report *plus* management action.

Steps in the Control Process

These are three steps in the control process: (1) *identify* areas that require investigation; (2) *investigate* these areas to ascertain whether action is warranted; and (3) *act*, when investigation indicates the need for action.

Identification.   The control report is useful only in the first step in the process. It suggests areas that *appear* to need looking into. The manager interprets the variances in the light of his or her own knowledge about conditions in the responsibility center. This person may have already learned, from conversations or personal observation, that there is an adequate explanation for the variance, or may have observed the need for corrective action before the report itself was issued. Some managers say that an essential characteristic of a good management control system is that reports should contain *no surprises*. By this they mean that managers of responsibility centers should inform their superiors as soon as significant events occur and should institute the necessary action immediately. If this is done, significant information will already have been communicated informally to the superior prior to receipt of the formal report.

In examining the report, the manager attempts to judge both the efficiency and the effectiveness of the responsibility center. In order to do this, information on outputs is needed. Control reports for engineered expense centers usually contain reliable output information. But in many other responsibility centers, output cannot be expressed in quantitative terms. This is the case with most discretionary expense centers of a company and also generally with nonprofit organizations. In these cases, the report shows, at best, whether the manager of the responsibility center spent the amount that was planned to be spent. It does not show what was accomplished, that is, effectiveness. The reader of the report must therefore form a judgment by other means as to how effective the manager was, usually by conversations with those who are familiar with the work done, or by personal observation.

For all types of responsibility centers, the evaluating manager must also distinguish between items of engineered cost and items of discretionary cost. With respect to engineered costs, the general rule is "the lower they are, the better," consistent with quality and safety standards.

With respect to discretionary costs, however, often good performance consists of spending the amount agreed on. Spending too little may be as bad as, or worse than, spending too much. A production manager can easily reduce current costs by skimping on maintenance; a marketing manager can reduce advertising expenditures; top management may eliminate a research project. None of these actions may be in the overall, long-run best interest of the company, although all of them result in lower costs on the current (short-run) reports of performance.

Superiors must also remember that a variance is meaningful only if it is derived from a valid standard. Although it is convenient to refer to "favorable" and "unfavorable" variances, these words imply value judgments that are valid only to the extent that the standard is a valid measure of what performance should have been. Even a standard cost may not be an accurate estimate of what costs should have been under the circumstances for either or both of two reasons: (1) the standard was not set properly or (2) although set properly in the light of conditions existing at the time, those conditions have changed so that the standard has become obsolete. An essential first step in the analysis of a variance, therefore, is an examination of the validity of the standard.

In short, the proper interpretation of a control report involves much more than a look at the size of the variances. In order to determine what, if any, investigation should be made, managers bring to bear all their experience regarding the work of the responsibility centers, all the information they have obtained from informal sources, and their intuitive judgment or "feel" for what needs attention.

Investigation. Usually, an investigation of possible significant areas takes the form of a conversation between the head of a responsibility center and his or her superior. In this conversation, the superior probes to determine whether further action is warranted. More often than not, it is agreed that special circumstances not anticipated in the budget have arisen that account for the variance. If the changed circumstances are noncontrollable, this, rather than inefficiency, may be the explanation for an unfavorable variance, and the responsibility center manager therefore cannot be justifiably criticized. Corrective action may nevertheless be required because the unfavorable variance indicates that the company's overall profit is going to be less than planned.

Another possible explanation of an unfavorable variance is some unexpected, random occurrence, such as a machine breakdown. The supervisor should be less concerned about these random events than about tendencies that are likely to continue in the future unless corrected. Thus, there is particular interest in variances that persist for several months, especially if they increase in magnitude from one month to the next. The supervisor wants to find out what the underlying causes of these trends are, and how they can be corrected.

Action. Based on this investigation, the manager decides whether further action is required. The superior and the manager should agree on the steps that will be taken to remedy unsatisfactory conditions revealed by the investigation. Equally important, if investigation reveals that performance has been good, a "pat on the back" is appropriate.

Of course, in many situations, no action at all is indicated. The superior judges that performance is satisfactory, and that is that. The superior should be particularly careful not to place too much emphasis on short-run performance. An inherent characteristic of management control systems is that they tend to focus on *short-run* rather than long-run performance. Thus, if too much emphasis is placed on results as shown in current control reports, long-run profitability may be hurt.

SUMMARY

The difference between budgeted and actual net income can be decomposed into a number of variances, each of which helps management to understand why the income variance occurred. These variances are grouped into three categories: marketing, production cost, and other. In the marketing area, the components of gross margin variance tend to be the most important, while in the production area the labor and material price and usage variances and the overhead spending variance are the most useful.

In using variances as part of the process of evaluating managerial performance, it is important to distinguish between those variances that are controllable by a manager and those that are not. Also, variances may be caused by inappropriate standards or budgets rather than by managers' operating performance. Finally, inferences about managerial performance should not be automatically based on whether a variance is "favorable" or "unfavorable," for these labels are only algebraic in nature.

The purpose of control reports is to communicate how well the managers of responsibility centers performed. This is done by comparing actual performance with what performance should have been under the circumstances prevailing. In most circumstances, the best standard for expressing what performance should have been is the budget, but historical standards and comparisons with other responsibility centers are sometimes used. Reports should be designed so that they highlight significant information.

The time period covered by a report should be the shortest time period in which management can usefully intervene. Reports should be issued as soon after the close of that period as is feasible. They should communicate clearly. The set of reports should be integrated with one another. The value of reports obviously should be greater than their cost.

In using reports, managers first try to identify areas that require investigation. They then investigate these areas to find out whether action is warranted, and they take action when the investigation indicates that action is needed.

Cases

CASE 26–1   Gotham Industries, Inc.

Gotham Industries, Inc., was a multidivisional firm whose several divisions competed in different industries. This case deals with variance analysis problems in several of the divisions.

Alpha Division

In its annual profit budget, Alpha Division budgeted product A's sales volume at 24,000 units. Product A's budgeted price was $32 per unit; its standard cost was $19 per unit. Actual sales of product A turned out to be $737,000 for a volume of 22,000 units.

Question

Determine Alpha Division's gross margin variances.

Beta Division

Beta Division makes three products. Last month's budgeted and actual sales and margins for these products were as follows:

	Budget		Actual	
	Unit Sales	Unit Margin	Unit Sales	Unit Margin
Product 1	3,200	$6.00	2,850	$6.26
Product 2	1,700	9.00	2,500	8.53
Product 3	5,100	5.00	4,250	4.80
	10,000	$6.00	9,600	$6.20

Question

Determine the gross margin mix, selling price, and sales volume variances. Calculate the net gross margin variance directly, then as a check see if it equals the sum of the three variance components you calculated individually.

Gamma Division

Gamma Division makes a product for which the standard raw materials cost

Note: This problem contains a raw materials mix variance, analogous to the gross margin mix variance described in this chapter.

Delta Division

Delta Division makes two products, A and B. Both products use the same raw material and are produced in the same factory by the same work force. In preparing its annual statement of budgeted gross margin, Delta's management used the following assumptions:

	Products	
	A	B
Sales (units)...........................	1,900	3,100
Unit selling price.....................	$119.50	$74.20
Standard unit costs:		
Raw materials (@ $0.85/lb.)..........	$34.00	$25.50
Direct labor (@ $9.00/hr.)...........	$22.50	$13.50
Overhead (@ 120% of DL$)..........	$27.00	$16.20
Other production standards:		
Production volume (units)............	1,900	3,100
Overhead budget: $0.80 per DL$ plus $33,840 fixed		
Overhead absorption: Based on *actual* DL$		

per 100 pounds of finished product is as follows:

60 lbs. of material X @ $0.60/lb..........	$36.00
40 lbs. of material Y @ 0.90/lb..........	36.00
100 lbs. of materials with total cost........	$72.00

Because materials were not supposed to be spoiled during production, these standards included no waste allowance.

During June, actual raw materials usage and costs were:

Material X: Used 5,500 lbs. @ $0.60/lb. = $3,300	
Material Y: Used 4,500 lbs. @ 0.95/lb. = 4,275	
10,000 lbs.	$7,575
Actual finished product: 9,900 lbs.	

Question

Calculate the raw materials variances for June, referring back to Chapter 20 if necessary.

The year's actual results were as follows:

1. 1,750 units of A were sold for a total of $216,125.
2. 3,250 units of B were sold for a total of $241,150.
3. Production totaled 1,800 units of A and 3,300 units of B.
4. 180,000 pounds of raw materials were purchased and used; their total cost was $156,600.
5. 9,450 hours of direct labor were worked at a total cost of $84,294.
6. Actual overhead costs were $99,880.

Questions

1. Do as detailed an analysis of variances as the data given permit.
2. Prepare a summary statement for presen-

tation to Delta's top management showing the year's budgeted and actual gross margin and an explanation of the difference between them.

CASE 26–2   Woodside Products, Inc.

Phil Brooks, president of Woodside Products, Inc., called Marilyn Mynar into his office one morning in early July 1983. Ms. Mynar was a business major in college and was employed by Woodside during her college summer vacation.

"Marilyn," Brooks began, "I've just received the preliminary financial statements for our 1983 fiscal year, which ended June 30. Both our board of directors and our shareholders will want, and deserve, an explanation of why our pretax income was virtually unchanged even though revenues were up by $175,000. The accountant is tied up working with our outside CPA on the annual audit, so I thought you could do the necessary analysis. What I'd like is as much of a detailed explanation of the $625 profit increase as you can glean from these data [Exhibit 1]. I'd also like you to draft a statement for the next board meeting that explains the same $625 profit increase, but in a fairly intuitive, summary way. Of

EXHIBIT 1

WOODSIDE PRODUCTS, INC.
Operating Results
For Years Ended June 30

1982		1983
$3,613,125	Sales revenues	$3,788,100
2,115,000	Cost of sales	2,313,260
1,498,125	Gross margin	1,474,840
902,400	Selling and administrative	878,490
$ 595,725	Income before taxes	$ 596,350

Other 1982 Data

1. Sales = 88,125 units @ $41.
2. Cost of sales = 88,125 units @ $24.
3. Selling and administrative costs were $1.84 per unit variable selling cost plus $740,250 fixed S&A.
4. Production volume and sales volume were equal.
5. Production costs per unit were:

Materials	$ 9.60 (8 lbs. @ $1.20)
Direct labor	4.80 (0.75 hrs. @ $6.40)
Variable overhead	1.60 (per unit)
Fixed overhead	8.00 (based on long-term std. volume of 88,125 units)
	$24.00

Other 1983 Data

1. Sales = 82,350 units @ $46.
2. Cost of sales includes 1983 production cost variances.
3. Selling and administrative costs were $2 per unit variable selling cost plus $713,790 fixed S&A.
4. Production volume was 81,100 units; standard volume was 88,125 units.
5. 626,200 pounds of material @ $1.40 were consumed by production.
6. 64,860 direct labor-hours were worked @ $6.90.
7. Actual variable overhead costs were $152,000.

course, that doesn't mean 'don't use any numbers'!''

Question

Prepare the detailed analysis of the $625 profit increase from fiscal 1982 to fiscal 1983, and draft an explanation for Woodside's board of directors, as requested by Phil Brooks. For the board's report, you may make any reasonable conjectures you wish as to what caused the variances you have calculated. For both years, assume that inventory was valued at $24 per unit. Assume also that none of the members of the board of directors has expertise in accounting calculations or terminology.

CASE 26–3 Dawkins Manufacturing Company

Early in January 1983, the cost report shown in Exhibit 1 was submitted to Peter Dawkins, president of Dawkins Manufacturing Company. This report was for the frame department, one of the company's primary producing departments. Mr. Dawkins was alarmed by the report because of the increase in cost. He commented that the only area of efficiency seemed to be in the use of indirect labor. Mr. Dawkins requested an investigation of the situation, which produced the following additional information.

The department made two types of metal frames used in the construction industry. The primary difference in the types was their size. The larger size, called the J frame, required more material than the small frame (S frame), but less direct labor time was required because of an automatic assembly process that had not yet been adapted to the small frames. The department supervisor said the J frame required about two units of raw material (primarily metal stripping), whereas the S frame required only one unit. The supervisor indicated that these quantities were based on normal operating efficiency. An investigation of the records showed that 560,000 units of raw materials had been issued during 1982, whereas 535,000 units had been issued during 1981.

The direct labor requirement was the

EXHIBIT 1
COMPARISON OF MANUFACTURING COSTS
Metal Frame Department

	1981	1982	Variance, 1982 over 1981
Raw materials................	$1,926,000	$2,217,600	$291,600
Direct labor..................	468,000	486,000	18,000
Department overhead:			
Indirect labor	180,000	36,000	(144,000)
Supervision.................	36,000	36,000	—
Power......................	14,800	17,100	2,300
Depreciation................	54,000	180,000	126,000
General overhead	417,600	476,100	58,500
Total..................	$3,096,400	$3,448,800	$352,400

opposite of the raw material. A J frame required about one half the amount of labor time as did the S frame. The foreman estimated that under normal working conditions, the department should produce about 10 J frames per labor-hour. The direct labor in the department was about the same insofar as the level of skill required, and the average wage rate per hour was $9. Failure to schedule work properly and failure to provide adequately for absenteeism (primarily the responsibility of the personnel department) sometimes resulted in a night shift which was paid a 10 percent premium. The policy of the company was to avoid night shift work if at all possible.

While the price of raw materials had gone up in 1982 about 10 percent (a unit of raw material cost $3.60 in 1981), the basic direct labor rate stayed about the same. An investigation showed that about 52,000 direct labor-hours were actually paid for during 1982, while about 50,500 hours had been paid in 1981. The actual direct labor rate did vary from the $9 rate because of some night shift work and also because in February 1982, some workers were transferred into the frame department to cover excess absenteeism due to a flu epidemic. These transferred workers received a wage rate somewhat higher than the average for the frame department.

An investigation of the general overhead revealed that this cost was an assigned cost. The company's practice was to assign the general administration overhead (the cost of such departments as accounting, personnel, general factory management, and engineering) to producing departments on the basis of total direct and indirect labor dollars (excluding supervision). The total general overhead for the company was $2,070,000 in 1982 and

$2,088,000 in 1981. The total direct and indirect labor cost for all producing departments was $2,268,000 in 1982 and $3,240,000 in 1981.

During 1982, the company purchased and installed some portable conveyers that made it possible to release several material handlers who made up the largest element of indirect labor. The desirability of the equipment had been assessed by using a 10-year economic life, and this period was chosen for depreciation purposes. A full year's depreciation had been included for 1982.

The power cost was assigned to the frame department by using the unit cost of power as determined by the power service department. In 1981, this cost was 2.9 cents ($0.029) per kilowatt-hour, whereas the rate went up to 3.2 cents in 1982 because of an increase in the cost of fuel used to make the power. The foremen of the power and frame departments agreed that power consumption was highly dependent on direct labor-hours. The frame foreman said that a fairly good rule of thumb used in the past was 10 kilowatt-hours of power for every hour of direct labor. He said that if power were used efficiently, this rate of consumption should be attainable.

A check of the production reports showed that production of completed frames for each of the two years was as follows:

	1981	1982
S frames	150,000	150,000
J frames	180,000	200,000

Questions

1. Explain, insofar as possible, the significance of and reasons for the increase in costs.

2. In general, how would you rate the efficiency of the metal frame department in 1982?

3. Can you suggest a better way of reporting cost for the department in the future?

CASE 26–4 Midwest Ice Cream Company (B)

In 1972, Midwest Ice Cream Company installed a financial planning and control system. (See Case 25–4 for details of this system.) After receiving the 1973 operating results, Jim Peterson, president of Midwest, had asked Frank Roberts, marketing vice president, to make a short presentation at the next board of directors meeting commenting on the major reasons for the favorable operating income variance of $71,700. He asked him to draft his presentation in the next few days so that the two of them could go over it before the board meeting. Peterson wanted to illustrate to the board how an analysis of profit variance could highlight those areas needing management attention as well as those deserving of a pat on the back.

The Profit Plan for 1973. Following the four-step approach outlined in Case 25–4, the management group of Midwest

Ice Cream prepared a profit plan for 1973. The timetable they followed is shown in the accompanying table.

Based on an anticipated overall ice cream market of about 11,440,000 gallons in their marketing area and a market share of 50 percent, Midwest forecasted overall gallon sales of 5,720,329 for 1973. Actually, this forecast was the same as the latest estimate of 1972 actual gallon sales.[1] Rather than trying to get too sophisticated on the first attempt at budgeting, Mr. Peterson had decided just to go with 1972's volume as 1973's forecast. He felt that there was plenty of time in later years to refine the system by bringing in more formal sales forecasting techniques.

---

[1] Since the 1973 budget was being done in October of 1972, final figures for 1972 were not yet available. The latest revised estimate of actual gallon volume for 1972 was thus used.

		October 1972 (weeks)				November 1972 (weeks)			
		1	2	3	4	1	2	3	4
I	Variable cost standards		X						
II-A	Sales forecast		X						
II-B	Approval of sales forecast			X					
III-A	Preliminary payroll budget			X					
III-B	Preliminary budget for other operating expenses			X					
III-C	Approval of payroll budget and other expenses budget				X				
IV-A	Preliminary profit plan					X			
IV-B	Approval of profit plan						X		
IV-C	Board of directors meeting							X	

This same general approach was also followed for standard variable product costs and for fixed costs. Budgeted costs for 1973 were just expected 1972 results, adjusted for inflation, and a few items were clearly out of line in 1972. A summary of the 1973 profit plan is shown in Exhibit 1.

Actual Results for 1973. By the spring of 1973, it had become clear that sales volume for 1973 was going to be higher than forecast. In fact, Midwest's actual sales for the year totaled 5,968,366 gallons, an increase of about 248,000 gallons over budget. Market research data indicated that the total 1973 ice cream market in Midwest's marketing area was 12,180,000 gallons, as opposed to the forecast of about 11,440,000 gallons. The revised profit plan for the year, based on actual volume, is shown in Exhibit 2.

The fixed costs in the revised profit plan are the same as before, $1,945,900. The variable costs, however, have been adjusted to reflect a volume level of 5,968,366 gallons instead of 5,720,329 gallons, thereby eliminating wide cost variances due strictly to the difference between planned volume and actual volume. Assume, for example, that cartons

EXHIBIT 1
PROFIT PLAN FOR 1973

	Standard Contribution Margin/Gallon	Forecasted Gallon Sales	Forecasted Contribution Margin
Vanilla	$0.4329	2,409,854	$1,043,200
Chocolate	0.4535	2,009,061	911,100
Walnut	0.5713	48,883	28,000
Buttercrunch	0.4771	262,185	125,000
Cherry Swirl	0.5153	204,774	105,500
Strawberry	0.4683	628,560	294,400
Pecan Chip	0.5359	1,157,012	84,100
Total	$0.4530	5,720,329	$2,591,300

BREAKDOWN OF BUDGETED TOTAL EXPENSES

	Variable	Fixed	Total
Manufacturing	$5,888,100	$ 612,800	$6,500,900
Delivery	187,300	516,300	703,600
Advertising*	553,200	—	553,200
Selling	—	368,800	368,800
Administrative	—	448,000	448,000
Total	$6,628,600	$1,945,900	$8,574,500

*The 1973 advertising allowance was 6 percent of sales dollars.

Recap:	
Sales	$9,219,900
Variable cost of sales	6,628,600
Contribution margin	2,591,300
Fixed costs	1,945,900
Income from operations	$ 645,400

EXHIBIT 2
REVISED PROFIT PLAN FOR 1973
Budgeted Profit at Actual Volume

	Standard Contribution Margin/Gallon	Actual Gallon Sales	Forecasted Contribution Margin
Vanilla	$0.4329	2,458,212	$1,064,200
Chocolate	0.4535	2,018,525	915,400
Walnut	0.5713	50,124	28,600
Buttercrunch	0.4771	268,839	128,300
Cherry Swirl	0.5153	261,240	134,600
Strawberry	0.4683	747,049	349,800
Pecan Chip	0.5359	164,377	88,100
Total	$0.4539	5,968,366	$2,709,000

BREAKDOWN OF BUDGETED TOTAL EXPENSES

	Variable	Fixed	Total
Manufacturing	$6,113,100	$ 612,800	$6,725,900
Delivery	244,500	516,300	760,800
Advertising	578,700	—	578,700
Selling	—	368,800	368,800
Administrative	—	448,000	448,000
Total	$6,936,300	$1,945,900	$8,882,200

Recap:	
Sales	$9,645,300
Variable cost of sales	6,936,300
Contribution margin	2,709,000
Fixed costs	1,945,900
Income from operations	$ 763,100

are budgeted at 4 cents per gallon. If the forecast volume is 10,000 gallons, the carton budget is $400. If actual sales are only 8,000 gallons but $350 worth of cartons are used, it is misleading to say that there is a favorable variance of $50. The variance is unfavorable by $30, but this only shows up if the budget is adjusted to actual volume:

Carton allowance	= $0.04 per gallon
Forecast volume	= 10,000 gallons
Actual volume	= 8,000 gallons
Variance (based on forecast volume)	= $400 − $350 = $50 Favorable
Variance (based on actual volume)	= $320 − $350 = $30 Unfavorable

For costs that are highly volume dependent, variances therefore should be based on a budget that reflects the volume of

EXHIBIT 3

Earnings Statement
December 31, 1973

| Month | | | Year to Date | |
Actual	Budget		Actual	Budget
		Sales—net	$9,657,300	$9,645,300
		Manufacturing cost of goods sold—Schedule A–2*	6,824,900	6,725,900
		Delivery—Schedule A–3	706,800	760,800
		Advertising—Schedule A–4	607,700	578,700
		Selling—Schedule A–5	362,800	368,800
		Administrative—Schedule A–7	438,000	448,000
		Total expenses	8,940,200	8,882,200
		Income from operations	717,100	763,100
		Other income—Schedule A–B	12,500	12,500
		Other expense—Schedule A–9	6,000	6,000
		Income before taxes	723,600	769,600
		Provision for income taxes	361,800	
		Net earnings	$ 361,800	

Analysis of Variance from Forecasted Operating Income

Month			Year to Date	
		1. Actual income from operations	$717,100	
		2. Budgeted profit at forecasted volume	645,400	
		3. Budgeted profit at actual volume	763,100	
		Variance due to sales volume— [(3) minus (2)]	117,700 F	
		Variance due to operations— [(1) minus (3)]	46,000 U	
		Total variance—[(1) minus (2)]	$ 71,700 F	

*Schedules A–3 through A–9 have not been included in this case. Schedule A–2 is reproduced as Exhibit 4.

operation actually attained. Since the level of fixed costs is independent of volume anyway, it is not necessary to adjust the budget for fixed-cost items.

Exhibit 3 is the 1973 earnings statement. (The monthly figures for December have been excluded for purposes of this case.) Exhibit 4 is the detailed expense breakdown for the manufacturing depart-ment. (The detailed expense breakdowns for the other departments have been excluded for purposes of this case.)

Analysis of the 1973 Profit Variance. Three days after Jim Peterson asked Frank Roberts to pull together a presentation for the board of directors analyzing the profit variance for 1973, Roberts came into Peterson's office to review

EXHIBIT 4

Manufacturing Cost of Goods Sold
December 31, 1973

| | Month | | | Year to Date | |
Actual	Budget	**Variable Costs**	Actual	Budget
		Dairy ingredients	$3,679,900	$3,648,500
		Milk price variance	57,300	—
		Sugar	599,900	596,800
		Sugar price variance	23,400	—
		Flavoring (including fruits and nuts)	946,800	982,100
		Cartons	567,200	566,900
		Plastic wrap	28,700	29,800
		Additives	235,000	251,000
		Supplies	31,000	35,000
		Miscellaneous	3,000	3,000
		Subtotal	6,172,200	6,113,100
		Fixed Costs		
		Labor—cartonizing and freezing	425,200	390,800
		Labor—other	41,800	46,000
		Repairs	32,000	25,000
		Depreciation	81,000	81,000
		Electricity and water	41,500	40,000
		Miscellaneous	1,500	30,000
		Spoilage	29,500	
		Subtotal	652,700	612,800
		Total	$6,824,900	$6,725,900

his first draft. He showed Peterson the following schedule:

schedule and then to comment briefly on each item. Peterson said he thought the

Favorable variance due to sales:		
Volume	$117,700 F	
Price*	12,000 F	$129,700 F
Unfavorable variance due to operations:		
Manufacturing	99,000 U	
Delivery...........................	54,000 F	
Advertising	29,000 U	
Selling	6,000 F	
Administration	10,000 F	58,000 U
Net variance—favorable		$ 71,700 F

*This price variance is the difference between the standard sales value of the gallons actually sold and the actual sales value ($9,657,300 − $9,645,300).

Roberts said that he planned to give each member of the board a copy of this

schedule was okay as far as it went, but that it just didn't highlight things in a manner that indicated what corrective actions should be taken in 1974 or what really had caused the favorable overall variance. He suggested that Roberts try to break down the sales volume variance into the part attributable to sales mix, the part attributable to market share shifts, and the part actually attributable to volume changes. He also suggested breaking down the manufacturing variance to indicate what actions are called for in 1974 to correct the unfavorable variance. How much of the total was due to price differences versus quantity differences, for example? Finally, he suggested that Roberts call on John Vance, the controller, if he needed help in the mechanics of breaking out these different variances.

As Roberts returned to his office he considered Peterson's suggestion of getting Vance involved in revising the schedule to be presented to the board. Roberts did not want to consult Vance unless it was absolutely necessary because Vance always went overboard on the technical aspects of any accounting problem. Roberts couldn't imagine a quicker way to put the board members to sleep than to throw one of Vance's number-filled, six-page memos at them. "Peterson specifically wants a nontechnical presentation for the board," Roberts thought to himself, "and that rules out John Vance. Besides, you don't have to be a CPA to focus in on the key variance areas from a general management viewpoint."

Questions

1. Review the variance analysis in Exhibit 3, being certain you understand it. (This is the same idea as in Exhibit C of Case 25–4.)

2. Calculate the gross margin mix variance for 1973, using the approach shown in the lower portion of Exhibit A of Case 25–4. Then calculate a detailed (i.e., flavor-by-flavor) mix variance, using the approach illustrated in Part B of text Illustration 26–3. For what purposes would the detailed analysis be more useful than the aggregate mix variance calculation?

3. How would you modify Frank Roberts' variance analysis before explaining the $71,700 F profit variance to the board of directors?

4. Considering both this case and Case 25–4, evaluate Midwest's budgetary control system.

CASE 26–5   Crompton, Ltd.

In 10 years, Crompton, Ltd., had achieved noteworthy success in penetrating the highly competitive British abrasive products industry. Located in Sheffield, England, its factory employed more than 300 people, manufacturing grinding wheels for sale to steel converters and cutlery manufacturers in the Sheffield area.

From the time the company started in business, John Lucas, the factory man-ager, had controlled factory operations primarily by direct personal supervision. Because he had been so familiar with operations, he had known which departments were having difficulties and what they were doing to cope with them. He had worked very closely with the departmental supervisors and they, in turn, had never been afraid to call on him for help and advice.

With the growth of the company, this

arrangement became more and more difficult. Lucas had to rely more and more on the individual supervisors to inform him of problems they were having, and he was quite sure that some of them, particularly the newer ones, were not as effective as they should have been. Unfortunately, he had no evidence on which to decide which departments needed attention. With this in mind, he asked Lou Field, a local accountant, to draw up a system of monthly reports that would supplement the knowledge that he would continue to gain by direct observation.

In the production of grinding wheels, abrasive grain was mixed with a bonding material according to the customer's requirements; molded in either a hot or a cold press, depending on the kind of bond; baked in a kiln; fitted with a bushing to take a motor spindle; "trued" to take off rough edges; shaped specially if needed; tested for balance and ability to withstand high speeds; and finally packed and shipped to the customer.

After several weeks of study and discussion with Crompton factory personnel, Field proposed that a report in the form illustrated in Exhibit 1 be prepared for each of the 18 production centers in the factory. One copy of the report would go to the supervisor in charge of that production center; a second copy would go to Lucas.

Field explained that the objective had been to produce a simple report, with as few figures as possible. Accordingly, the report had been limited to the following four items:

1. Gross production.
2. Rejection rate.
3. Net production per labor-hour.
4. Direct labor cost.

Gross production was measured by the total "list price" of the products passing through the department. Field considered using some other indicator of production volume, such as the total number of units or total weight of the output, but rejected all these because the output varied so widely in size and complexity. The "list price" was a stabilized amount for each wheel, established several years earlier and unchanged since that time. Actual customer prices were set each year by

EXHIBIT 1
HOT PRESS DEPARTMENT OPERATION REPORT, NOVEMBER*

	Gross Production (£)†	Rejections (percent)	Net Production per Labor-Hour (£/hr.)	Direct Labor (£)
November (4 weeks)	260,684	6.35	194.3	6,460
October (4 weeks)	166,204	10.48	172.4	4,632
September (5 weeks).................	242,720	10.78	215.3	4,666
August (2 weeks)	62,567	9.10	140.6	1,758
July (4 weeks)	158,915	13.41	168.7	4,477
January–June (26 weeks).............	1,112,202	8.90	155.8	32,183
Last fiscal year (52 weeks).............	1,536,684	11.14	112.1	49,624

*Each "month" consists of either four or five full weeks, except August when the factory is closed for two weeks. A "year" consists of 52 weeks (50 working weeks plus two vacation weeks); approximately one year in every five, a calendar year includes 53 payroll dates, and that "year" consists of 53 weeks.
†£ = pounds, the British monetary unit.

multiplying the list price by a percentage (e.g., 145 percent) which management felt was "right" for the current market.

Rejections occurred in all production departments, although the majority were discovered in the testing department. At a weekly conference, the plant superintendent determined the source of the defect and allocated responsibility accordingly. Rejections were quoted as a percentage of gross production handled.

Net production per labor-hour was gross production, minus rejects, all measured at list prices, divided by the number of direct labor-hours.

Direct labor costs were the actual direct labor-hours for the month multiplied by the actual wage rates paid individual workers during the month, including any premium payments for overtime hours. Departmental supervisors were responsible for scheduling work in their departments and thus were expected to keep overtime premiums to the lowest level consistent with their delivery commitments.

Each report provided three sets of figures with which the most recent month's record could be compared: (1) the four immediately preceding months, separately for each month; (2) the six months prior to that, as semiannual totals; and (3) the most recent complete fiscal year, as annual totals. Thus, the November figures could be compared with those for October, September, August, and July; for January–June; and for the 12 months January–December of the preceding fiscal year.

Finally, Field suggested that the departments could be compared with each other to determine which were the most productive, which were showing the most improvement, and which seemed to need Lucas' attention the most.

Questions

1. In what ways does Exhibit 1 differ from the financial accounting reports you have studied?

2. What did Lucas mean by "control information"? Why did he need it?

3. What suggestions would you make for improving Exhibit 1 so as to be more useful to Lucas?

27

Management Accounting
System Design

When a person looks at a photograph or a painting, the eye takes in the total picture and conveys it to the brain. Even at a first glance, the relationships among the parts of the picture can be perceived. By contrast, a book must be read a page at a time, and it is only when one has finished the book that the total "picture" described in the book can be perceived. In this chapter we will briefly review some of the topics and concepts of management accounting in order to help tie together the various parts of the total picture. This review will serve as the basis for a discussion of some key elements in the design of a management accounting system.

TYPES OF ACCOUNTING INFORMATION

Part 1 of this book emphasized financial accounting information, which is prepared in accordance with GAAP and reported to shareholders and other interested outside parties. Unlike financial accounting, which is built around the single basic equation, Assets = Liabilities + Owners' equity, management accounting has three structures: full cost accounting, differential accounting, and responsibility accounting. The full cost and responsibility accounting structures include both attention-directing historical data and problem-solving and planning-related future estimates. Differential accounting, however, is always future oriented.

Full Cost Accounting. Cost is a measurement, in monetary terms, of the amount of resources used for a cost objective. The most pervasive cost objectives in a company are the goods and services it produces and sells, and companies operate cost accounting systems to collect these product costs on a routine basis. Generally, these systems account for the full costs of a product, that is, the sum of the product's direct costs and a fair share of its applicable indirect costs. This same principle can be used to measure the full cost of any cost objective, not only products. Full costs are used in financial reporting to measure inventories and the related cost of sales. Full costs are used in management accounting to arrive at normal prices and regulated rates, and in analyzing the economic performance of business segments and the profitability of the products these segments produce and sell.

Differential Accounting. This type of accounting considers costs, revenues, and assets that are different under one set of conditions than they would be under another set of conditions, and it measures those differences. Differential accounting's principal use is in the economic analysis portion of alternative choice problems. In shorter-run problems, a contribution analysis often is appropriate, whereas longer-run problems usually involve determining present values of revenue inflows and cost outflows. Differential accounting analyses are not at all routine because, by definition, there is no routine costing system that can capture the differential costs that are relevant to a specific decision. Much judgment must be exercised in these analyses; for example, costs that are not differential in the short run may be differential in the longer run.

Responsibility Accounting. This type of management accounting information focuses on responsibility centers, which are organization units headed by managers who are held accountable for these units' performance. Responsibility accounting deals extensively with planned inputs and outputs, as well as with the measurement of actual inputs and outputs. In the management control process, managers compare these planned and actual amounts, identify the source of the significant variances, investigate their causes, and take appropriate actions. In this process, behavioral considerations are at least as important as accounting considerations.

The reader is asked at this point to refer back to Illustration 15–1 (page 492), which summarizes the distinct uses of the different types of management accounting information—and which should seem far less vague now than when first encountered in Chapter 15.

Relative Importance. It is important to remember that each of these three types of management accounting information is useful for the purposes indicated in Illustration 15–1, but is not helpful for a purpose for which it is not applicable. It is pointless to consider the *relative* importance of the three types: an organization needs all three of them. In particular, in a classroom environment there may be a tendency to overemphasize the importance of differential accounting vis-à-vis full cost accounting. Differential cost problems tend to be intellectually challenging, and they often have important consequences to the organization (particularly the "big-buck" capital investment problems). Nevertheless, in most organizations, these differential cost problems arise far less frequently than decisions involving the use of full cost information. For example, a selling price must be arrived at for every product, and in profit-seeking organizations, the profitability of these products, along with that of the business units that produce and market them, is (or at least, should be) analyzed routinely. Although these full cost calculations are somewhat mechanical once the cost accounting system has been properly set up, it is nevertheless important that they be made correctly. Of course, all organizations also need responsibility accounting as a foundation of their management control process.

COST CATEGORIES

In discussing both financial and management accounting, we have introduced a number of different categories of "cost." While in practice cost terminology is not used with the same degree of precision we have tried to employ, the fact remains that there are different *concepts* underlying the various adjectives used to modify that slippery term called "cost." The following review may help clarify the distinctions among eight of the various ways of categorizing costs.

1. By Accounting Treatment. When a cost is incurred, it is treated either (1) as a reduction in retained earnings (i.e., an expense), in which case we say the cost has been *expensed* or (2) as an asset, in which case the cost is said to have been *capitalized*. An expense is also called a *period cost*. Capitalized costs include not only the cost of plant and equipment but also the cost of work in process or of finished goods inventory. These latter two are *product costs*. Product costs are expensed when the product is sold, in accord with the matching concept.

2. By Traceability to a Cost Objective. Costs that are traced to, or caused by, a single cost objective are *direct costs* of the cost objective. Costs associated with two or more cost objectives jointly are *indirect costs* of those cost objectives. The *full cost* or a cost objective is the sum of its direct costs and its fair share of indirect cots.

The terms *direct cost* and *indirect cost* are meaningless in isolation. To be meaningful, they must be related to a specified cost objective. For example, a plant manager's salary is a direct cost of the plant but is an indirect cost of each product made in the plant (unless the plant makes only *one* product). Indirect *production* costs are frequently called *production overhead* or *factory overhead*, or, less descriptively, simply *overhead*.

3. By Cost Element. The adjective modifying "cost" may indicate the *cost element* for which the cost was incurred. Examples include materials cost, direct labor cost, interest cost, supervision cost, and so on.

4. By Behavior with Respect to Volume. An item of cost whose total amount varies proportionately with volume is called a *variable cost.* The clearest example is materials cost in a production setting. A cost item whose total does not vary at all with volume is called a *nonvariable* or *fixed cost.* Some costs vary in the same direction as, but less than proportionately with, volume; these are *semivariable costs,* and they can be decomposed into their fixed and variable cost components.

It is important to remember that in describing cost behavior with respect to volume, a relevant range is stated (or at least implied). Also, a time period must be stated (or implied); a cost that is fixed with respect to volume over the next week may be variable with respect to volume in the longer run.

5. By Time Perspective. Many cost data are for economic events that have already transpired; these are *historical costs* or *actual costs.* However, for many uses—particularly in management accounting—the relevant data are *future costs.* Estimated future costs may take the form of *standard costs* (usually per unit amounts) or *budgets* (usually amounts per time period).

6. By Degree of Managerial Influence. If a responsibility center manager can significantly influence the amount of an item of cost, that cost is said to be *controllable* by that manager; otherwise it is *noncontrollable.* Note that this cost concept refers to a specific manager. Responsibility center costs not controllable by the center's manager presumably are controllable by someone else in the organization.

7. By Ability to Budget "Right" Amounts. If the "right" or "proper" amount to spend for some activity can be predetermined, then that cost item is an *engineered cost.* Direct materials cost in a production setting is the clearest example. If, on the other hand, the proper amount to spend is a matter of judgment, the item is a *discretionary cost* (sometimes called a *programmed* or *managed* cost). A cost which is the inevitable consequence of some past decision can be budgeted with certainty. This is a *committed cost,* for example, rent that was established in a 10-year lease signed last year.

8. By Changeability with Respect to Specified Conditions. Costs that are different under one set of conditions than they would be under another set are called *differential costs* (or incremental costs). The notion of differential costs is meaningful only for specified problems. That is, two or more alternative situations (one of which may be the status quo) must be specified in order for differential costs to be calculated.

These eight ways of categorizing costs are not all-inclusive. Even though we used 20 different cost terms in describing those eight categories, we did not mention replacement costs, opportunity costs, imputed costs, marginal costs, sunk costs, or several other kinds of costs. However, the person who understands the differences among these eight categorizations—and some of the distinctions are quite subtle—is in a good position to think and communicate clearly about whatever costs may be involved in a particular report or problem analysis. Illustration 27–1 summarizes a number of these cost distinctions.

ILLUSTRATION 27–1
SUMMARY OF TYPES OF COST

Full Cost Accounting	Differential Accounting	Responsibility Accounting
Direct: Costs traced to a single cost objective. **Indirect:** Not traced; an equitable portion is allocated to the cost objective. **Full:** Direct costs + Indirect costs.	Costs that would be different if a proposed alternative were adopted. Construction depends on nature of the specific problem.	Costs incurred in responsibility centers. **Controllable:** Manager can exercise significant (but not necessarily complete) influence. **Noncontrollable:** Other costs, including committed and allocated costs.
Capitalized: Asset to be amortized over several future periods. **Product:** Direct + Indirect production cost of product. **Period:** Expense of current period.	**Variable:** Costs that vary proportionately with volume. **Fixed:** Costs that do not vary with volume. **Semivariable:** Costs that vary with volume, but less than proportionately. Can be decomposed into variable and fixed components.*	**Engineered:** "Right" amount can be estimated. **Discretionary:** Amount subject to manager's discretion; agreed on in budget process. **Committed:** Will not change in the short run (a type of fixed cost).
Full costs are either historical costs or estimated future costs.	Differential costs are always estimated future costs.	Responsibility costs are either historical costs or estimated future costs.

*An understanding of variable, fixed, and semivariable cost behavior is important in *all three* types of management accounting, but is particularly important for performing differential cost analyses.

DESIGNING THE MANAGEMENT ACCOUNTING SYSTEM

To conclude our consideration of management accounting systems, we will highlight some of the desirable characteristics of such systems that we have mentioned in previous chapters. As we have already stressed, the system should fit with other organizational characteristics, including goals and objectives, nature of the goods and services produced, organization structure, and the level of sophistication that managers have in using management accounting information. Thus, all of the considerations we mention below will not necessarily apply to a given organization.

Accounting Data Base

As we have seen in both Parts 1 and 2 of this book, accounting information does not just magically materialize when it is needed. The raw data must be "captured" from various *source documents*. These documents include vendor invoices, employee time cards and other personnel-related records, customer billing and payment records, and so forth. These raw data constitute the organization's *operating information*, which is recorded using double-entry recordkeeping procedures in the organization's *accounts*. The complete set of these accounts, called the *chart of accounts*, determines the structure of the organization's accounting data base.

Level of Detail.   A major design issue in management accounting is how detailed the chart of accounts should be. For financial accounting purposes, not much detail is required. For example, solely for financial accounting purposes, all sales could be credited to a single Sales Revenue account and debited either to Cash or Accounts Receivable. However, this would make it difficult to perform an analysis of sales by product line, profit center, sales district, or individual customer.

The kinds of analysis management wants to perform on a more-or-less *routine* basis determine the amount of detail in the chart of accounts. The chart of accounts design question is, in effect: For each item of cost (or revenue or assets), how many "ID tags" do we want to "tie onto" that item?

> **Example.**   On June 5, a department of the Farnsworth Company used $1,000 worth of materials for a product it was making that day. Any of the following questions might be asked concerning this "event":
>
> 1. What *specific* materials were used?
> 2. What was the *product line* to which the product in question belongs?
> 3. In which *department* were the materials used?
>
> The first question relates to a more detailed *cost element* description; the second, to a *program* description; the third, to a *responsibility center* description. Answering each of these "what?," "why?," and "where?" questions requires "hanging a separate ID tag on the item of cost."
>
> More formally, answering all three implies that the chart of accounts should include as one detailed account, "Material X Used in Product Y in Department Z." If Farnsworth Company uses 100 raw materials for 20 products that are made in 10 responsibility centers, this could require as many as *20,000* (= 100 × 20 × 10) detailed accounts, all relating only to a *single* general category, the materials component of work in process inventory.

In the above example, if the company wants to report program and responsibility center data on a routine basis, then the account structure must incorporate the second and third ID tags. If, in addition, it routinely wants to know how many dollars worth of material X are used *throughout* the company (as opposed to all kinds of materials used collectively), the first ID tag is necessary. Many organizations *do* want detailed information on all three of these dimensions, so the example does not exaggerate how many detailed *account building blocks* larger organizations actually have.

The accounting data base can be further elaborated if an organization wants to segregate fixed and variable cost elements. (Remember that semivariable costs also can be decomposed into fixed and variable components.) This elaboration might be appropriate if the organization performed many short-run differential cost analyses, or if it wanted to prepare internal income statements in a variable costing format. A still further elaboration would occur if the organization wanted the account structure to identify costs as to whether or not they are controllable in the responsibility center in which they are incurred (or to which they are charged).

There are no formulas to determine the "right" level of detail in the account structure. Management must exercise judgement in making the omnipresent benefit/cost trade-off. It does seem to be true, however, that more organizations feel they suffer from having too little detail in the accounting data base than feel they have too much. In many instances, long-standing charts of accounts were not reviewed when the organization computerized its accounting data base. While the need for more detail is recognized today, the costs of rewriting all of the computer programs to accommodate more detail is viewed as prohibitive. On the other hand, there are examples of unnecessarily costly systems whose designers concerned themselves with providing information for *any conceivable* analysis rather than just for more-or-less *routinely* performed analyses.

Cost Accounting Systems

An organization faces many choices when designing its cost accounting system. Those choices include job costing versus process costing, actual costs versus standard costs, volume measures, and several other choices that were listed in the final section of Chapter 19, "Cost System Design Choices." Many organizations' activities are sufficiently diverse that, in effect, several cost accounting systems must be designed for a given organization. However, there should be one integrated accounting data base underlying the several systems, because each different system in essence simply aggregates account building blocks in a different way.

Differential Analyses. The design of a cost accounting system also affects the ease with which certain differential accounting analyses can be performed. But recall that, by definition, the ad hoc nature of these analyses means that there can be no such thing as a differential costing *system*. Moreover, differential costs are *future* costs. Although data in the cost accounting system can aid in estimating the relevant differential costs for a particular problem, strictly speaking, historical costs themselves are not relevant in differential analyses.

Management Control Systems

While the availability of detailed accounting data base information may be crucial to support full cost and differential accounting analyses, in the management control process, behavioral considerations are at least as important as responsibility accounting information. Every existing or proposed practice in the management control system must be held up to the *goal congruence* test by considering these questions:

1.   What action will it motivate managers to take in their own perceived self-interest?
2.   Will this action be in the best interests of the organization?

It is not uncommon for organizations to neglect considering these questions, particularly when establishing policies for such things as how transfer prices will be set or for the specifics of measuring the ROI of various investment centers. This neglect often results in a procedure's having unintended consequences, which, with hindsight, do not really seem all that surprising.

> **Example.** In measuring an investment center's ROI, most companies include fixed assets in the investment base at net book value, that is, original cost less accumulated depreciation. With foresight one can see that, other things being equal, this practice will cause an investment center's ROI "automatically" to increase each year, because the investment base (ROI fraction denominator) becomes smaller due to each year's addition to accumulated depreciation.
>
> Some companies blame their investment center managers' lack of motivation to propose productivity-increasing modernization projects on this ROI measurement scheme. Such a scheme normally causes ROI to decrease if a significant new project is undertaken, and investment center managers may not be convinced that their superiors will later recognize the underlying reason for their investment centers' *apparent* ROI performance deterioration. In fact, a gradually *rising* ROI might indicate that the investment center's productive capability is *deteriorating*. In any case, top management is responsible for deciding on how ROI is to be measured. If there are unintended consequences from a particular approach, it is top management, *not* the investment center managers, who is to blame.

Another common mistake in management control is for superiors to *assume*, without investigation, that unfavorable variances imply poor managerial performance. Managerial morale can suffer tremendously if managers receive edicts "from on high" to correct unfavorable variances, without the managers' having the opportunity to discuss the causes of the variances with their superiors. Managers also resent a tendency in many organizations for superiors to pay a great deal of attention to unfavorable variances, while remaining essentially silent with respect to favorable variances.

It is important to note that these problems are not shortcomings of the control system *design* per se, but rather are matters of *managerial style*. To repeat, in the management control process, *behavioral* considerations are at least as important as accounting considerations. Thus, a conceptually sound management control system design will not be effective if managers feel that their superiors are using responsibility accounting information in an arbitrary or unfair way.

Cases

CASE 27–1 Western Pants, Inc.*

Western Pants, Inc., was founded in the mid-19th century. The firm weathered lean years and the Depression largely as the result of the market durability of its dominant, and at times only, product—blue-denim jeans.

In the early 1960s, Western became the first pants manufacturer to establish itself in the revolutionary "wash-and-wear" field. With the advent of "mod" clothing and the generally casual yet stylish garb that became acceptable attire at semiformal affairs, pants became fashion items rather than the mere clothing staples they had been in years past. Subsequently, Western gained a foothold in the bell-bottom and flare market, and from there grew with the "leg look" to its present

*Adapted from Charles T. Horngren's *Cost Accounting: A Managerial Emphasis*, 5th ed. (Englewood Cliffs, N.J.: Prentice-Hall, 1982). Used by permission.

position as the free world's largest clothing manufacturer. Currently, Western offered a complete line of casual trousers, an extensive array of "dress and fashion jeans" for both men and boys, and a complete line of pants for women. Last year the firm sold approximately 30 million pairs of pants.

Production. In each of the last 20 years, Western Pants sold virtually all its production and often had to begin rationing its goods as early as six months prior to the close of the production year. The firm had 25 plants. They varied somewhat in output capacity, but the average was about 20,000 pairs of trousers per week. With the exception of two or three plants that usually produced only blue-denim jeans during the entire production year, Western's plants produced various pants types for all of Western's marketing departments. The firm augmented its own productive capacity by contractual agreements with independent manufacturers of pants. Currently, there were nearly 20 such contractors producing all lines of Western's pants (including blue jeans). In the most recent year, contractors produced about one third of the total volume in units sold by Western.

Tom Wicks, the vice president for production and operations, commented on the firm's use of contractors. "The majority of these outfits have been with us for some time—five years or more. Several of them have served Western efficiently and reliably for over 30 years. In our eagerness to get the pants made, we understandably hook up with some independents who don't know what they're doing and who are forced to fold their operations after a year or so because their costs are too high. Usually we can tell from an independent's experience and per unit contract price whether or not he's going to be able to make it in pants production.

"Contract agreements with independents are made by me and my staff. The ceiling we are willing to pay for each type of pants is pretty well established by now. If a contractor impresses us as being both reliable and capable of turning out quality pants, we will pay him that ceiling. If we aren't sure, we might bid a little below that ceiling for the first year or two, until he has proved himself. Initial contracts are for two years. The time spans lengthen as our relationship with the independent matures."

Mr. Wicks noted that the start-up time for a new contractor would often be as short as one year. The failure rate in the garment industry was quite high; hence, new entrepreneurs often stepped in and assumed control of existing facilities.

The Control System. "We treat all our plants pretty much as expense centers,"

Mr. Wicks continued. "Of course, we exercise no control whatever over the contractors. We just pay them the agreed price per pair of pants. Our own operations at each plant have been examined thoroughly by industrial engineers. You know, time-and-motion studies and all. We've updated this information consistently for over 10 years. I'm quite proud of the way we've been able to tie our standard hours down. We've even been able over the years to develop learning curves that tell us how long it will take production of a given type of pants to reach the standard allowed hours per unit after initial start-up or a product switchover. We even know the rate at which total production time per unit reaches standard for every basic style of pants that Western makes!

"We use this information for budgeting a plant's costs. The marketing staff figures out how many pants of each type it wants produced each year and passes that information onto us. We divvy the total production up among plants pretty much by eyeballing the total amounts for each type of pants. We like to put one plant to work for a whole year on one type of pants, if that's possible. It saves time losses from start-ups and changeovers. We can sell all we make, you know, so we like to keep plants working at peak efficiency. Unfortunately, marketing always manages to come up with a lot of midyear changes, so this objective winds up like a lot of other good intentions in life.

"The budgeting operation begins with me and my staff determining what a plant's quota for each month should be for one year ahead of time. We do this mostly by looking at what past performance at a plant has been. Of course, we add a little to this. We expect people to improve around here. These yearly budgets are updated at the end of each month in the light of the previous month's production. Budget figures, incidentally, are in units of production (i.e., pairs of pants). If a plant manager beats this budget figure, we feel he's done well. If he can't meet the quota, his people haven't been working at what the engineers feel is a very reasonable level of speed and efficiency. Or possibly absenteeism or turnover, big problems in all our plants, have been excessively high. At any rate, when the quota hasn't been made, we want to know why, and we want to get the problem corrected as quickly as possible.

"Given the number of pants that a plant actually produces in a month, we can determine the number of labor-hours each plant should have accumulated during the month. We measure this figure against the hours we actually paid for to determine how a plant performed as an expense center. I phone every plant manager each month to give prompt feedback on either satisfactory or unsatisfactory performance.

"We also look for other things in evaluating a plant manager. Have his community relations been good? Are his people happy? The family that owns almost all of Western's stock is very concerned about that."

A Christmas bonus constituted the core of Western's reward system. Mr. Wicks and his two chief assistants subjectively rated a plant manager's performance for the year on a one-to-five scale. Western's top management at the close of each year determined a bonus base by evaluating the firm's overall performance and profits for the year. That bonus base had recently been as high as $6,000. The performance rating for each member of Western's management cadre was multiplied by this bonus base to determine a given manager's bonus: for example, a manager with a three-point rating would receive an $18,000 bonus.

Western's management group included many finance and marketing specialists. The casewriter noted that these personnel, who were located at the corporate headquarters, were consistently awarded higher ratings by their supervisors than were plant managers. This difference consistently approached a full point. Last year the average rating for the headquarters staff group was 3.85; the average for plant managers was 2.92.

Evaluation of the System. Mia Packard, a recent business school graduate, gave the casewriter her opinions regarding Western's production operation and its management control procedures.

"Mr. Wicks is one of the nicest men I've ever met, and a very intelligent businessman. But I really don't think that the system he uses to evaluate his plant managers is good for the firm as a whole. I made a plant visit not long ago as part of my company orientation program, and I accidently discovered that the plant manager 'hoarded' some of the pants produced over quota in good months to protect himself against future production deficiencies. That plant manager was really upset that I stumbled onto his storehouse. He insisted that all the other managers did the same thing and begged me not to tell Mr. Wicks. This seems like precisely the wrong kind of behavior in a firm that usually has to turn away orders! Yet I believe the quota system that is one of Western's tools for evaluating plant performance encourages this type of behavior. I don't think I could prove this, but I suspect that most plant managers aren't really pushing for maximum production. If they do increase output, their quotas are going to go up, and yet they won't receive any immediate monetary rewards to compensate for the increase in their responsibilities or requirements. If I were a plant manager, I wouldn't want my production exceeding quota until the end of the year.

"Also, Mr. Wicks came up to the vice presidency through the ranks. He was a very good plant manager himself once. But he has a tendency to feel that everyone should run a plant the way he did. For example, in Mr. Wick's plant there were 11 workers for every supervisor or member of the office and administrative staff. Since then, Mr. Wicks has elevated this supervision ratio of 11:1 to some sort of sacred index of leadership efficiency. All plant managers shoot for it, and as a result, usually understaff their offices. Because of this, we can't get timely and accurate reports from plants. There simply aren't enough people in the offices out there to generate the information we desperately need when we need it!

"Another thing—some of the plants have been built in the last five years or so and have much newer equipment, yet there's no difference between the standard hours determined in these plants and the older ones. This puts the managers of older plants at a terrific disadvantage. Their sewing machines break down more often, require maintenance, and probably aren't as easy to work with."

Soviet System. Ms. Packard thought that Western Pants would do well to study a new management control system used by the Soviet government about which she had read recently. The new management control system was a part of sweeping economy reforms that took effect in January 1966. As stated in Bertrand Horwitz, *Accounting Controls and the Soviet Economic Reforms of 1966* (Sarasota, Fla.: American Accounting Association, 1970), p. 23:

> Prior to January 1966, when the reforms first took effect, the director of a Soviet enterprise was confronted with the requirement of satisfying numerous physical and accounting goals. The enterprise was essentially a cell in a tautly administered system which allowed the director little room for independent action because the number of physical and accounting indexes by which he could be judged highly constrained his economic actions.

The new bonus system was based on the enterprise's increase in profits and the rate of return on assets employed in the enterprise. The exact formula used to compute the total bonuses to be distributed to the enterprise's employees was as follows:

$$X_t = A\left(\frac{P_t - P_{t-1}}{P_{t-1}}\right) + B\left(\frac{P_t}{K_t}\right) \qquad (1)$$

and the total amount of the bonus for the enterprise was:

$$T_t = W_t X_t \qquad (2)$$

where

W_t = wage fund for the current year (i.e., year t), which is centrally determined

P_t = profit in year t, which is net of explicit charges for the use of current and gross fixed assets at original cost

T_t = total amount of enterprise bonus for year t

K_t = average current and gross fixed assets at original cost

A,B = coefficients that are centrally assigned norms; both are less than one and are nonnegative

The first parenthetical term of equation (1) is the rate of increase in earnings over the previous year. The second parenthetical term is the ROI for the enterprise based on its total gross assets. Multiplying these two terms by A and B respectively gives a factor (X) that when multiplied by the enterprise's wage fund (W) determines the total bonus for the enterprise. Thus, the total bonus for the enterprise depends on the enterprise's increase in profit over the previous year and its ROI.

The wage fund (W) for the enterprise in a period is centrally determined and therefore is a given amount for purposes of computation of the bonus. The accounting profit (P) is the enterprise's income before capital charges, minus (a) charges at the rate of 6 percent of gross assets, for the use of property, plant, and equipment and normal or planned current assets; (b) fixed-rent payments; and (c) interest on bank credit. The charge of 6 percent is essentially the enterprise's cost of capital because the enterprise gets its fixed assets from the government. The charge is also based on gross assets (i.e., no depreciation is included). The rent payments are designed to eliminate the differences between different enterprises because of natural operating conditions. Thus, a firm with very favorable conditions would have to make rent payments, while one operating under less favorable conditions would not. The interest is for short-term loans from the central bank.

Average gross assets (K) is used as the investment base in order to motivate managers to replace their older, less efficient assets. The purpose is to get managers to modernize their equipment. The coefficients A and B are centrally assigned and are set so that the resulting bonuses will be reasonable in light of the enterprise's operating conditions. This is essentially another way of equalizing the natural operating conditions of the various enterprises in the economy.

Questions

1. Assume that a Soviet enterprise did not have to make any rent payments and had no short-term loans from the central bank. Suppose the enterprise had the following profit (after deductions), gross assets, and wage fund, in thousands of rubles:

$$P_t = 3,000 \qquad K_t = 20,000$$
$$P_{t-1} = 2,800 \qquad W_t = 4,000$$

Also, suppose that the central planners had assigned the firm an $A = 0.5$ and $B = 0.25$. Compute the total enterprise bonus.

2. What actions would the Soviet approach motivate a plant manager to take?

3. Evaluate the management control system used for Western's plants. What, if any, changes should be given serious consideration?

APPENDIX TABLES

Lump Sums

TABLE A
PRESENT VALUE OF $1

Years Hence	1%	2%	4%	6%	8%	10%	12%	14%	15%	16%	18%	20%	22%	24%	25%	26%	28%	30%	35%	40%	45%	50%
1	0.990	0.980	0.962	0.943	0.926	0.909	0.893	0.877	0.870	0.862	0.847	0.833	0.820	0.806	0.800	0.794	0.781	0.769	0.741	0.714	0.690	0.667
2	0.980	0.961	0.925	0.890	0.857	0.826	0.797	0.769	0.756	0.743	0.718	0.694	0.672	0.650	0.640	0.630	0.610	0.592	0.549	0.510	0.476	0.444
3	0.971	0.942	0.889	0.840	0.794	0.751	0.712	0.675	0.658	0.641	0.609	0.579	0.551	0.524	0.512	0.500	0.477	0.455	0.406	0.364	0.328	0.296
4	0.961	0.924	0.855	0.792	0.735	0.683	0.636	0.592	0.572	0.552	0.516	0.482	0.451	0.423	0.410	0.397	0.373	0.350	0.301	0.260	0.226	0.198
5	0.951	0.906	0.822	0.747	0.681	0.621	0.567	0.519	0.497	0.476	0.437	0.402	0.370	0.341	0.328	0.315	0.291	0.269	0.223	0.186	0.156	0.132
6	0.942	0.888	0.790	0.705	0.630	0.564	0.507	0.456	0.432	0.410	0.370	0.335	0.303	0.275	0.262	0.250	0.227	0.207	0.165	0.133	0.108	0.088
7	0.933	0.871	0.760	0.665	0.583	0.513	0.452	0.400	0.376	0.354	0.314	0.279	0.249	0.222	0.210	0.198	0.178	0.159	0.122	0.095	0.074	0.059
8	0.923	0.853	0.731	0.627	0.540	0.467	0.404	0.351	0.327	0.305	0.266	0.233	0.204	0.179	0.168	0.157	0.139	0.123	0.091	0.068	0.051	0.039
9	0.914	0.837	0.703	0.592	0.500	0.424	0.361	0.308	0.284	0.263	0.225	0.194	0.167	0.144	0.134	0.125	0.108	0.094	0.067	0.048	0.035	0.026
10	0.905	0.820	0.676	0.558	0.463	0.386	0.322	0.270	0.247	0.227	0.191	0.162	0.137	0.116	0.107	0.099	0.085	0.073	0.050	0.035	0.024	0.017
11	0.896	0.804	0.650	0.527	0.429	0.350	0.287	0.237	0.215	0.195	0.162	0.135	0.112	0.094	0.086	0.079	0.066	0.056	0.037	0.025	0.017	0.012
12	0.887	0.788	0.625	0.497	0.397	0.319	0.257	0.208	0.187	0.168	0.137	0.112	0.092	0.076	0.069	0.062	0.052	0.043	0.027	0.018	0.012	0.008
13	0.879	0.773	0.601	0.469	0.368	0.290	0.229	0.182	0.163	0.145	0.116	0.093	0.075	0.061	0.055	0.050	0.040	0.033	0.020	0.013	0.008	0.005
14	0.870	0.758	0.577	0.442	0.340	0.263	0.205	0.160	0.141	0.125	0.099	0.078	0.062	0.049	0.044	0.039	0.032	0.025	0.015	0.009	0.006	0.003
15	0.861	0.743	0.555	0.417	0.315	0.239	0.183	0.140	0.123	0.108	0.084	0.065	0.051	0.040	0.035	0.031	0.025	0.020	0.011	0.006	0.004	0.002
16	0.853	0.728	0.534	0.394	0.292	0.218	0.163	0.123	0.107	0.093	0.071	0.054	0.042	0.032	0.028	0.025	0.019	0.015	0.008	0.005	0.003	0.002
17	0.844	0.714	0.513	0.371	0.270	0.198	0.146	0.108	0.093	0.080	0.060	0.045	0.034	0.026	0.023	0.020	0.015	0.012	0.006	0.003	0.002	0.001
18	0.836	0.700	0.494	0.350	0.250	0.180	0.130	0.095	0.081	0.069	0.051	0.038	0.028	0.021	0.018	0.016	0.012	0.009	0.005	0.002	0.001	0.001
19	0.828	0.686	0.475	0.331	0.232	0.164	0.116	0.083	0.070	0.060	0.043	0.031	0.023	0.017	0.014	0.012	0.009	0.007	0.003	0.002	0.001	
20	0.820	0.673	0.456	0.312	0.215	0.149	0.104	0.073	0.061	0.051	0.037	0.026	0.019	0.014	0.012	0.010	0.007	0.005	0.002	0.001	0.001	
21	0.811	0.660	0.439	0.294	0.199	0.135	0.093	0.064	0.053	0.044	0.031	0.022	0.015	0.011	0.009	0.008	0.006	0.004	0.002	0.001		
22	0.803	0.647	0.422	0.278	0.184	0.123	0.083	0.056	0.046	0.038	0.026	0.018	0.013	0.009	0.007	0.006	0.004	0.003	0.001	0.001		
23	0.795	0.634	0.406	0.262	0.170	0.112	0.074	0.049	0.040	0.033	0.022	0.015	0.010	0.007	0.006	0.005	0.003	0.002	0.001			
24	0.788	0.622	0.390	0.247	0.158	0.102	0.066	0.043	0.035	0.028	0.019	0.013	0.008	0.006	0.005	0.004	0.003	0.002	0.001			
25	0.780	0.610	0.375	0.233	0.146	0.092	0.059	0.038	0.030	0.024	0.016	0.010	0.007	0.005	0.004	0.003	0.002	0.001				
26	0.772	0.598	0.361	0.220	0.135	0.084	0.053	0.033	0.026	0.021	0.014	0.009	0.006	0.004	0.003	0.002	0.002	0.001				
27	0.764	0.586	0.347	0.207	0.125	0.076	0.047	0.029	0.023	0.018	0.011	0.007	0.005	0.003	0.002	0.002	0.001	0.001				
28	0.757	0.574	0.333	0.196	0.116	0.069	0.042	0.026	0.020	0.016	0.010	0.006	0.004	0.002	0.002	0.002	0.001	0.001				
29	0.749	0.563	0.321	0.185	0.107	0.063	0.037	0.022	0.017	0.014	0.008	0.005	0.003	0.002	0.002	0.001	0.001					
30	0.742	0.552	0.308	0.174	0.099	0.057	0.033	0.020	0.015	0.012	0.007	0.004	0.003	0.002	0.001	0.001						
40	0.672	0.453	0.208	0.097	0.046	0.022	0.011	0.005	0.004	0.003	0.001	0.001										
50	0.608	0.372	0.141	0.054	0.021	0.009	0.003	0.001	0.001	0.001												

STREAMS

TABLE B
PRESENT VALUE OF $1 RECEIVED ANNUALLY FOR N YEARS

Years (N)	1%	2%	4%	6%	8%	10%	12%	14%	15%	16%	18%	20%	22%	24%	25%	26%	28%	30%	35%	40%	45%	50%
1	0.990	0.980	0.962	0.943	0.926	0.909	0.893	0.877	0.870	0.862	0.847	0.833	0.820	0.806	0.800	0.794	0.781	0.769	0.741	0.714	0.690	0.667
2	1.970	1.942	1.886	1.833	1.783	1.736	1.690	1.647	1.626	1.605	1.566	1.528	1.492	1.457	1.440	1.424	1.392	1.361	1.289	1.224	1.165	1.111
3	2.941	2.884	2.775	2.673	2.577	2.487	2.402	2.322	2.283	2.246	2.174	2.106	2.042	1.981	1.952	1.923	1.868	1.816	1.696	1.589	1.493	1.407
4	3.902	3.808	3.630	3.465	3.312	3.170	3.037	2.914	2.855	2.798	2.690	2.589	2.494	2.404	2.362	2.320	2.241	2.166	1.997	1.849	1.720	1.605
5	4.853	4.713	4.452	4.212	3.993	3.791	3.605	3.433	3.352	3.274	3.127	2.991	2.864	2.745	2.689	2.635	2.532	2.436	2.220	2.035	1.876	1.737
6	5.795	5.601	5.242	4.917	4.623	4.355	4.111	3.889	3.784	3.685	3.498	3.326	3.167	3.020	2.951	2.885	2.759	2.643	2.385	2.168	1.983	1.824
7	6.728	6.472	6.002	5.582	5.206	4.868	4.564	4.288	4.160	4.039	3.812	3.605	3.416	3.242	3.161	3.083	2.937	2.802	2.508	2.263	2.057	1.883
8	7.652	7.325	6.733	6.210	5.747	5.335	4.968	4.639	4.487	4.344	4.078	3.837	3.619	3.421	3.329	3.241	3.076	2.925	2.598	2.331	2.108	1.922
9	8.566	8.162	7.435	6.802	6.247	5.759	5.328	4.946	4.772	4.607	4.303	4.031	3.786	3.566	3.463	3.366	3.184	3.019	2.665	2.379	2.144	1.948
10	9.471	8.983	8.111	7.360	6.710	6.145	5.650	5.216	5.019	4.833	4.494	4.192	3.923	3.682	3.571	3.465	3.269	3.092	2.715	2.414	2.168	1.965
11	10.368	9.787	8.760	7.887	7.139	6.495	5.937	5.453	5.234	5.029	4.656	4.327	4.035	3.776	3.656	3.544	3.335	3.147	2.752	2.438	2.185	1.977
12	11.255	10.575	9.385	8.384	7.536	6.814	6.194	5.660	5.421	5.197	4.793	4.439	4.127	3.851	3.725	3.606	3.387	3.190	2.779	2.456	2.196	1.985
13	12.134	11.343	9.986	8.853	7.904	7.103	6.424	5.842	5.583	5.342	4.910	4.533	4.203	3.912	3.780	3.656	3.427	3.223	2.799	2.468	2.204	1.990
14	13.004	12.106	10.563	9.295	8.244	7.367	6.628	6.002	5.724	5.468	5.008	4.611	4.265	3.962	3.824	3.695	3.459	3.249	2.814	2.477	2.210	1.993
15	13.865	12.849	11.118	9.712	8.559	7.606	6.811	6.142	5.847	5.575	5.092	4.675	4.315	4.001	3.859	3.726	3.483	3.268	2.825	2.484	2.214	1.995
16	14.718	13.578	11.652	10.106	8.851	7.824	6.974	6.265	5.954	5.669	5.162	4.730	4.357	4.033	3.887	3.751	3.503	3.283	2.834	2.489	2.216	1.997
17	15.562	14.292	12.166	10.477	9.122	8.022	7.120	6.373	6.047	5.749	5.222	4.775	4.391	4.059	3.910	3.771	3.518	3.295	2.840	2.492	2.218	1.998
18	16.398	14.992	12.659	10.828	9.372	8.201	7.250	6.467	6.128	5.818	5.273	4.812	4.419	4.080	3.928	3.786	3.529	3.304	2.844	2.494	2.219	1.999
19	17.226	15.678	13.134	11.158	9.604	8.365	7.366	6.550	6.198	5.877	5.316	4.844	4.442	4.097	3.942	3.799	3.539	3.311	2.848	2.496	2.220	1.999
20	18.046	16.351	13.590	11.470	9.818	8.514	7.469	6.623	6.259	5.929	5.353	4.870	4.460	4.110	3.954	3.808	3.546	3.316	2.850	2.497	2.221	1.999
21	18.857	17.011	14.029	11.764	10.017	8.649	7.562	6.687	6.312	5.973	5.384	4.891	4.476	4.121	3.963	3.816	3.551	3.320	2.852	2.498	2.221	2.000
22	19.660	17.658	14.451	12.042	10.201	8.772	7.645	6.743	6.359	6.011	5.410	4.909	4.488	4.130	3.970	3.822	3.556	3.323	2.853	2.498	2.222	2.000
23	20.456	18.292	14.857	12.303	10.371	8.883	7.718	6.792	6.399	6.044	5.432	4.925	4.499	4.137	3.976	3.827	3.559	3.325	2.854	2.499	2.222	2.000
24	21.243	18.914	15.247	12.550	10.529	8.985	7.784	6.835	6.434	6.073	5.451	4.937	4.507	4.143	3.981	3.831	3.562	3.327	2.855	2.499	2.222	2.000
25	22.023	19.523	15.622	12.783	10.675	9.077	7.843	6.873	6.464	6.097	5.467	4.948	4.514	4.147	3.985	3.834	3.564	3.329	2.856	2.499	2.222	2.000
26	22.795	20.121	15.983	13.003	10.810	9.161	7.896	6.906	6.491	6.118	5.480	4.956	4.520	4.151	3.988	3.837	3.566	3.330	2.856	2.500	2.222	2.000
27	23.560	20.707	16.330	13.211	10.935	9.237	7.943	6.935	6.514	6.136	5.492	4.964	4.524	4.154	3.990	3.839	3.567	3.331	2.856	2.500	2.222	2.000
28	24.316	21.281	16.663	13.406	11.051	9.307	7.984	6.961	6.534	6.152	5.502	4.970	4.528	4.157	3.992	3.840	3.568	3.331	2.857	2.500	2.222	2.000
29	25.066	21.844	16.984	13.591	11.158	9.370	8.022	6.983	6.551	6.166	5.510	4.975	4.531	4.159	3.994	3.841	3.569	3.332	2.857	2.500	2.222	2.000
30	25.808	22.396	17.292	13.765	11.258	9.427	8.055	7.003	6.566	6.177	5.517	4.979	4.534	4.160	3.995	3.842	3.569	3.332	2.857	2.500	2.222	2.000
40	32.835	27.355	19.793	15.046	11.925	9.779	8.244	7.105	6.642	6.234	5.548	4.997	4.544	4.166	3.999	3.846	3.571	3.333	2.857	2.500	2.222	2.000
50	39.196	31.424	21.482	15.762	12.234	9.915	8.304	7.133	6.661	6.246	5.554	4.999	4.545	4.167	4.000	3.846	3.571	3.333	2.857	2.500	2.222	2.000

Index

*This book has been set Linotron 202 in 10 and 9
point Melior, leaded 2 points. Part numbers are 18
point Quadrata, and part titles are 20 point Quadrata. Chapter numbers are 36 point Quadrata, and
chapter titles are 18 point Quadrata. The size of the
type page is 37 by 47 picas.*